AA

THE
HOTEL
GUIDE
2019

Published by AA Publishing, a trading name of AA Media Limited, whose registered office is Fanum House, Basing View, Basingstoke, Hampshire RG21 4EA. Registered number 06112600

First published by the Automobile Association in 1967

© AA Media Limited 2018

52nd edition

The contents of this publication are believed correct at the time of printing. Nevertheless, the publishers cannot be held responsible for any errors or omissions or for any changes in the details given in this guide or for the consequences of any reliance on the information provided by the same. This does not affect your statutory rights.

Assessments of AA inspected establishments are based on the experience of the Hotel and Restaurant inspectors on the occasion(s) of their visit(s) and therefore descriptions given in this guide necessarily contain an element of subjective opinion which may not reflect or dictate a reader's own opinion on another occasion. See 'AA Star Classification' in the preliminary section for a clear explanation of how, based on our inspectors' inspection experiences, establishments are graded. If the meal or meals experienced by an inspector or inspectors during an inspection fall between award levels the restaurant concerned may be awarded the lower of any award levels considered applicable.

AA Media Limited strives to ensure accuracy of the information in this guide at the time of printing. Due to the constantly evolving nature of the subject matter the information is subject to change. AA Media Limited will gratefully receive any advice from our readers of any necessary updated information.

For queries relating to the guide, please contact: lifestyleguides@theAA.com

Website addresses are included in entries and specified by the respective establishment. Such websites are not under the control of AA Media Limited and as such AA Media Limited will not accept any responsibility or liability in respect of any and all matters whatsoever relating to such websites including access, content, material and functionality. By including the addresses of third party websites the AA does not intend to solicit business or offer any security to any person in any country, directly or indirectly.

Image credits:
The Automobile Association wishes to thank the following photographers and organisations for their assistance in the preparation of this book.

Abbreviations for the picture credits are as follows – (t) top; (b) bottom; (l) left; (r) right; (c) centre; (AA) AA World Travel Library.

3 Courtesy of Heacham Manor Hotel; 4 Courtesy of The Grove (Sequoia Spa), Chandler's Cross; 7 Courtesy of Tilney Hall Hotel, Rotherwick; 9 Courtesy of Dormy House Hotel, Broadway; 10 Courtesy of The Northcote Hotel, Blackburn; 12 Courtesy of Stapleford Park, Melton Mowbray; 14 Courtesy of Fawsley Hall Hotel & Spa, Daventry; 15 Courtesy of Best Western Plus The Connaught Hotel, Bournemouth; 16-19 BG AA/C Sawyer; 16 Courtesy of Great Fosters Hotel, Egham; 17 Courtesy of Four Seasons Hotel at Ten Trinity Square, London EC3; Courtesy of Old Course Hotel. Golf Resort and Spa, St Andrews; 18 Courtesy of Trefiddian Hotel, Aberdyfi; Courtesy of Bishops Gate Hotel, Londonderry Derry; 19 All images courtesy of Harbour Hotels; 26-27 AA/A Burton/AA; 195 AA/D Clapp/AA; 196–197 AA/J Tims; 216 AA/J Tims; 411 AA/W Voysey; 422-423 AA/J Smith; 463 AA/J Henderson; 464-465 AA/M Bauer; 492 AA/C Hill; 498-499 AA/C Jones; 524 AA/P Wilson; 530 Courtesy of San Pietro Restaurant Rooms.

Every effort has been made to trace the copyright holders, and we apologise in advance for any unintentional omissions or errors. We would be pleased to apply any corrections in a following edition of this publication.

Photographs in the gazetteer are provided by the establishments.

This guide was compiled by the AA Lifestyle Guides team and Servis Filmsetting Ltd, Stockport.

Cover design by Austin Taylor.

Maps prepared by the Mapping Services Department of AA Publishing.

Maps © AA Media Limited 2018.

Contains Ordnance Survey data © Crown copyright and database right 2018.

Ireland map contains data available from openstreetmap.org © under the Open Database License found at opendatacommons.org

A CIP catalogue record for this book is available from the British Library.

Printed in the UK by Bell & Bain.

ISBN: 978-0-7495-7983-8

A05603

Visit www.theaa.com/hotels

Contents

Welcome to the AA Hotel Guide 2019

From the most opulent and sophisticated of London's elite hotels to personally-run, small hotels in the British countryside; from the practical and convenient budget hotel aimed at business or air travellers, to the luxurious country house hotel catering for leisure and sporting guests, *The AA Hotel Guide* has it all.

Year-round inspections

All year round, our specially-trained team of expert inspectors are visiting, grading and advising the hotels that appear in this guide. Each one is judged on presentation, quality of accommodation, leisure and sporting facilities, food operation, service, hospitality, conference facilities and cleanliness. It is then rated according to our classification system (pages 12–13).

Any hotel applying for AA recognition receives a regular unannounced visit to check standards. If the hotel changes hands, the new owners must reapply for classification, as AA recognition is not transferable.

AA Awards

Our inspectors have also chosen their Hotels of the Year, for England, London, Scotland, Wales, and Northern Ireland, as well as Hotel Group of the Year (see pages 16–19).

Our Hospitality Awards website features details about current and previous awards – visit www.theaa.com/hospitality-awards

Red Stars and Inspector's Choice

All of the hotels in this guide should be of a high standard, but some are a cut above, and these are specially selected by our inspectors. At these establishments you can expect a little more of everything: more comfort, more facilities, more extras and more attention. From two Red Stars to five Red Stars, these are the best of British hotels. Every Red Star hotel is highlighted as an Inspector's Choice, but these are not the only places that are singled out.

Silver Stars and Highly Recommended

Hotels with Silver Stars ★ have been selected for their superior levels of quality, high standards of hotel keeping and for the quality of food within their star rating. These are highlighted as HIGHLY RECOMMENDED.

Rosettes

Most of the hotels in this guide have their own restaurants, and a large proportion of them serve food that has attained an AA Rosette award, including some that have reached the four and five Rosette level, making them among the finest restaurants in the world. These are regularly visited by the AA inspectorate and awarded Rosettes strictly on the basis of the inspector's experience alone.

Dine & Stay: Restaurants with Rooms

At the back of the guide, you'll find a special section (pages 530 onwards) dedicated to Restaurants with Rooms, which are rated under our Guest Accommodation scheme. Most will have been awarded AA Rosettes for their food. So, if you're looking for accommodation with excellent dining options, then this is the section for you.

Anonymous inspection

All hotel and restaurant inspections are made anonymously. After taking a meal or staying overnight at the hotel, the inspector will announce to a member of staff and ask to speak to the manager, or the chef in the case of a Rosette visit.

Tell us what you think

We welcome your feedback about the hotels included in this guide, and about the guide itself. Please write in, or email us at: **lifestyleguides@theaa.com**.

The hotels are visited throughout the year by our team of inspectors. For the very latest updates, you can search for the hotel of your choice at www.theaa.com/hotels

Using the guide

1.

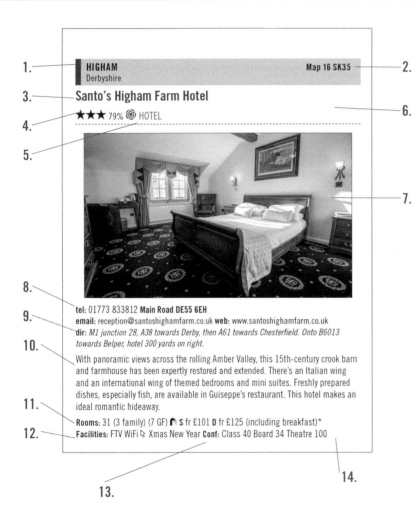

HIGHAM
Derbyshire

Map 16 SK35

2.

6.

3.

Santo's Higham Farm Hotel

4.

★★★ 79% ◉ HOTEL

5.

7.

8.

9.

10.

tel: 01773 833812 **Main Road DE55 6EH**
email: reception@santoshighamfarm.co.uk **web:** www.santoshighamfarm.co.uk
dir: *M1 junction 28, A38 towards Derby, then A61 towards Chesterfield. Onto B6013*
towards Belper, hotel 300 yards on right.

With panoramic views across the rolling Amber Valley, this 15th-century crook barn
and farmhouse has been expertly restored and extended. There's an Italian wing
and an international wing of themed bedrooms and mini suites. Freshly prepared
dishes, especially fish, are available in Guiseppe's restaurant. This hotel makes an
ideal romantic hideaway.

11.

Rooms: 31 (3 family) (7 GF) ☛ **S** fr £101 **D** fr £125 (including breakfast)*

12.

Facilities: FTV WiFi ▷ Xmas New Year **Conf:** Class 40 Board 34 Theatre 100

14.

13.

1. Location
Towns are listed alphabetically within
each country (the county name appears
under the town name).

2. Map reference
Map page number followed by a
National Grid reference (see page 9).

3. Hotel name

4. Grading
Hotels are listed in star rating and merit
score order (see page 8) within each
location (for full explanation of ratings
and awards see pages 12–13).
★ Star rating
% Merit score
◉ Rosette award
≋ Breakfast award

5. Type of hotel
See page 10.

6. Hotel logo
If a symbol appears here it represents
a hotel group or consortium (see pages
20–24).

7. Picture
Optional photograph supplied by
the establishment.

8. Address and contact details

9. Directions
Brief details of how to find the hotel.

10. Description
Written by the AA inspector at the time of the last inspection.

11. Rooms
Number of rooms and prices (see page 8).

12. Facilities
Additional facilities including those for children, and leisure activities

13. Conference
Conference facilities as available (see page 8).

14. Notes
Additional information may be present (see page 8).

Key to symbols and abbreviations

★	Black stars	⊕	Heated indoor swimming pool
★	Red stars – indicate AA Inspector's Choice	⌇	Heated outdoor swimming pool
★	Silver stars – indicate superior level of quality – Highly Recommended	♫	Entertainment
		Child facilities	
◉	AA Rosettes – indicate an AA award for food		Children's facilities (see page 8)
		Xmas/New Year	
	Breakfast Award		Special programme for Christmas/New Year
%	Inspectors' Merit score (see page 8)		Tennis court
A	Associate Hotels (see page 10)		Croquet lawn
○	Hotel due to open during the currency of the guide (see page 10)		Golf course
		Conf	Conference facilities
U	Star rating not confirmed (see page 10)	Theatre	Number of theatre-style seats
		Class	Number of classroom-style seats
GF	Ground floors rooms available	Board	Number of boardroom-style seats
☌	Bedrooms with walk-in showers available	No children	
Smoking	Number of bedrooms allocated for smokers		Children cannot be accommodated (a number followed by 'years' indicate that children below that age are not accommodated)
S	Single room		
D	Double room	RS	Restricted opening time
✳	2018 prices	Civ Wed	Establishment licensed for civil weddings (+ maximum number of guests at ceremony)
fr	From (minimum price)		
FTV	Freeview television		
STV	Satellite television	LB	Special leisure breaks available
WiFi	Wireless network connection	Spa	Hotel has its own spa
⇗	High speed internet connection (bedrooms)		
HL	Hearing loop installed		
Air con	Air conditioning		

How to use the guide *continued*

Merit Score (%)

AA inspectors supplement their reports with an additional quality assessment of everything the hotel provides – including hospitality – based on their findings as a 'mystery guest'. This wider ranging quality assessment results in an overall Merit Score which is shown as a percentage beside the hotel name. When making your selection of hotel accommodation this enables you to see at a glance that a three star hotel with a Merit Score of 79% offers a higher standard overall than one in the same star classification but with a Merit Score of 69%. To gain AA recognition, a hotel must achieve a minimum score of 50%.

AA Awards

Every year the AA presents a range of awards to the finest AA-inspected and rated hotels from England, London, Scotland, Wales, and Northern Ireland. The Hotel of the Year is our ultimate accolade and is awarded to those hotels that are recognised as outstanding examples in their field. Often innovative, the winning hotels always set high standards in hotel keeping. The winners for all the 2018–19 awards are listed on pages 16–19.

Rooms

Where the information has been provided by the hotelier, each entry shows the total number of en suite rooms available (this total will include any annexe rooms). The total number may be followed by a breakdown of the type of rooms available, i.e. the number of annexe rooms; number of family rooms (family); number of ground-floor rooms (GF); and number of rooms available for smokers.

Bedrooms in an annexe or extension are only noted if they are at least equivalent in quality to those in the main building, but facilities and prices may differ. In some hotels all bedrooms are in an annexe or extension.

If the hotel has highspeed or broadband internet access in the bedrooms, this may be chargeable.

Prices

Prices are minimum prices per room per night and are provided by the hoteliers in good faith. These prices are indications and not firm quotations. An asterisk (*) indicates 2018 prices. Many hotels have special rates, so it is worth looking at their websites for the latest information.

Children

Child facilities may include baby intercom, baby-sitting service, playroom, playground, laundry, drying/ironing facilities, cots, high chairs or special meals. In some hotels children can sleep in parents' rooms at no extra cost – check when booking.

If 'No children' is indicated, a minimum age will also given e.g. No children 4 years indicates that no children under 4 years of age would be accepted.

Some hotels, although accepting children, may not have any special facilities for them.

Leisure breaks (LB)

Some hotels offer special leisure breaks. The cost of these may differ from those quoted in this guide and availability may vary through the year.

Parking

We indicate the number of parking spaces available for guests. This may include covered parking. Please note that some hotels make a charge for the use of their car park.

Civil weddings (Civ Wed)

Indicates that the establishment holds a civil wedding licence, and we indicate the number of guests that can be accommodated at the ceremony.

Conference facilities

We include three types of meeting layouts – Theatre, Classroom and Boardroom style – and state the maximum number of delegates for each. We also show if WiFi connectivity is available, but please check with the hotel that this is suitable for your requirements.

Dogs

Although many hotels allow dogs, they may be excluded from some areas of the hotel, and some breeds, particularly those requiring an exceptional licence, may not be acceptable at all. Under the Equality Act 2010 access should be allowed for guide dogs and assistance dogs. Please check the hotel's policy when making your booking.

Entertainment (♫)

This indicates that live entertainment will be available at least once a week all year. Some hotels provide live entertainment only in summer or on special occasions.

Hotel logos

If an establishment belongs to a hotel group or consortium their logo is included in their entry (see pages 20–24).

Map references

Each town is given a map reference – the map page number and a map reference based on the National Grid. For example: **Map 05 SU48**:

05 refers to the page number of the map section at back of the guide.

SU is the National Grid lettered square (representing 100,000sq metres) in which the location will be found.

4 is the figure reading across the top or bottom of the map page.

8 is the figure reading down at each side of the map page.

Hotels in London and the Greater London area can be located on the London Plans 1–9 on pages 202–214. They are listed in the London index on 198–201 and their plan numbers are also located close to their rating in each entry.

Restricted service

Some hotels have restricted service (RS) during quieter months – usually during the winter – and at this time some of the listed facilities will not be available. If your booking is out-of-season, check with the hotel and enquire specifically.

Spa

For the purposes of this guide the word 'Spa' in an entry indicates that the hotel has its own spa which is either managed by themselves or outsourced to an external management company. Facilities will vary but will include a minimum of two treatment rooms. Any specific details are also given, and these are as provided to us by the establishment (i.e. steam room, beauty therapy etc).

Smoking regulations

If a bedroom has been allocated for smokers, the hotel is obliged to clearly indicate that this is the case. If either the freedom to smoke, or to be in a non-smoking environment is important to you, please check with the hotel when you book.

Types of hotel

The majority of establishments in this guide fall under the category of Hotel; other categories are listed below.

Town House Hotel A small, individual city or town centre property, which provides a high degree of personal service and privacy.

Country House Hotel These are quietly located in a rural area.

Small Hotel Has fewer than 20 bedrooms and is owner-managed.

Metro Hotel A hotel in an urban location that does not offer an evening meal.

Budget Hotel These are usually purpose-built modern properties offering inexpensive accommodation. Often located near motorways and in town or city centres.

Restaurant with Rooms This category of accommodation is assessed under the AA's Guest Accommodation Scheme. They appear in a dedicated section starting on page 530. They all have star ratings, but these are Guest Accommodation Scheme ratings, details of which can be found at the start of the section or in the latest edition of *The AA Bed and Breakfast Guide*.

A These are establishments that have not been inspected by the AA, but by one of the national tourist boards in Britain and Northern Ireland. An establishment marked as 'Associate' has paid to belong to the AA Associate Hotel Scheme.

U A small number of hotels in the guide have this symbol because their star classification was not confirmed at the time of going to press. This may be due to a change of ownership or because the hotel has only recently joined the AA rating scheme. If you want to find out more about these places, you should check www.theaa.com/hotels for updates, including their eventual rating.

AA Advertised
These establishments are not rated or inspected by the AA, but are displayed for advertising purposes only.

O These hotels were not open at the time of going to press, but will open in late 2018, or in 2019.

Welcome

TO THE WORLD OF ELITE HOTELS

Gourmet restaurants with a sense of old world charm, our beautifully appointed bedrooms and suites, and the wealth of health, leisure and beauty amenities available are all complemented by unparalleled levels of service.

Ashdown Park Hotel & Country Club
East Sussex, 01342 824988
★★★★ 🏵 🏵

Luton Hoo Hotel, Golf & Spa
Bedfordshire
01582 734437
★★★★★ 🏵 🏵

Tylney Hall Hotel & Gardens
Hampshire
01256 764881
★★★★ 🏵 🏵

The Grand Hotel, Eastbourne
East Sussex
01323 412345
★★★★★ 🏵 🏵

4 Distinctive Hotels, 4 Distinctive Experiences

www.elitehotels.co.uk

AA classifications and awards

AA assessment

Since 2006, Common Quality Standards for inspecting and rating accommodation have been applied throughout the British Isles in association with VisitBritain, VisitScotland and VisitWales.

Any hotel applying for AA recognition receives an unannounced visit from an AA inspector to check standards. Although AA inspectors do not stay overnight at Budget Hotels, they do carry out regular visits to verify standards and procedures.

A guide to some of the general expectations for each star classification is as follows:

★ One Star

Polite, courteous staff providing a relatively informal yet competent style of service, available during the day and evening to receive guests

- At least one designated eating area open to residents for breakfast
- If dinner is offered it should be on at least five days a week, with last orders no earlier than 6.30pm
- TV in bedroom
- All rooms en suite, or private facilities with bath or shower room available at all times

★★ Two Star

As for one star, plus

- At least one restaurant or dining room open to residents for breakfast (and for dinner at least five days a week)
- Last orders for dinner no earlier than 7pm
- Easy access to both sides of beds for double occupancy

★★★ Three Star

- Management and staff smartly and professionally presented and usually uniformed
- A dedicated receptionist on duty at peak times
- At least one restaurant or dining room open to residents and non-residents for breakfast and dinner whenever the hotel is open
- Last orders for dinner no earlier than 8pm
- En suite bath or shower and WC

★★★★ Four Star

- A formal, professional staffing structure with smartly presented, uniformed staff, anticipating and responding to your needs or requests. Usually spacious, well-appointed public areas
- Reception staffed 24 hours by well-trained staff
- Express checkout facilities where appropriate
- Porterage available on request
- Night porter available
- At least one restaurant open to residents and non-residents for breakfast and dinner seven days per week, and lunch to be available in a designated eating area
- Last orders for dinner no earlier than 9pm
- En suite bath with fixed overhead shower and WC

★★★★★ Five Star

- Luxurious accommodation and public areas with a range of extra facilities
- First time guests shown to their bedroom
- Multilingual service
- Guest accounts well explained and presented
- Porterage offered
- Guests greeted at hotel entrance, full concierge service provided
- At least one restaurant open to residents and non-residents for all meals seven days per week
- Last orders for dinner no earlier than 10pm
- High-quality menu and wine list
- Evening service to turn down the beds. Direct-dial telephone at bedside and desk, a range of luxury toiletries, bath sheets and robes.
- En suite bathroom incorporating fixed overhead shower and WC.

★ Inspector's Choice

Each year we select the best hotels in each rating. These hotels stand out as the very best in the British Isles, regardless of style. Red Star hotels appear in highlighted panels throughout the guide. Inspector's Choice Restaurants with Rooms have been chosen to represent the best offerings of both dining and accommodation.

★ Highly Recommended

Hotels with Silver Stars ★ have been selected for their superior levels of quality, high standards of hotel keeping and for the quality of food within their star rating.

AA Rosette awards

Out of the many thousands of restaurants in the UK, the AA identifies over 2,000 as the best. The following is an outline of what to expect from restaurants with AA Rosette awards.

◉ Excellent local restaurants serving food prepared with care, understanding and skill, using good quality ingredients.

◉◉ The best local restaurants, which aim for and achieve higher standards, and better consistency; where a greater precision is apparent in the cooking. There will be obvious attention to the selection of quality ingredients.

◉◉◉ Outstanding restaurants that demand recognition well beyond their local area.

◉◉◉◉ Among the very best restaurants in the British Isles, where the cooking demands national recognition.

◉◉◉◉◉ The finest restaurants in the British Isles, where the cooking stands comparison with the best in the world.

Additional information

Hints and tips on booking your stay

It's always worth booking as early as possible, particularly for the peak holiday period from the beginning of June to the end of September. Bear in mind that Easter and other public holidays may be busy too and in some parts of Scotland, the ski season is a peak holiday period.

Some hotels will ask for a deposit or full payment in advance, especially for one-night bookings. Some hotels charge half-board (bed, breakfast and dinner) whether you require the meals or not, while others may only accept full-board bookings. Not all hotels will accept advance bookings for bed and breakfast, overnight or short stays. Some will not take reservations from mid week.

Once a booking is confirmed, let the hotel know at once if you are unable to keep your reservation. If the hotel cannot re-let your room you may be liable to pay about two-thirds of the room price (a deposit will count towards this payment). In Britain a legally binding contract is made when you accept an offer of accommodation, either in writing or by phone, and illness is not accepted as a release from this contract. You are advised to take out insurance against possible cancellation, for example AA Single Trip Insurance (tel: 0808 169 1195).

AA Hotels online

Locating and booking somewhere to stay can be a time-consuming process, but all the hotels inspected and rated by the AA are searchable online at: www.theaa.com/hotels

Facilities for disabled guests

The Equality Act 2010 provides legal rights for disabled people including access to goods, services and facilities, and means that service providers may have to consider making adjustments to their premises. For more information about the Act see www.gov.uk/definition-of-disability-under-equality-act-2010 or www.gov.uk/government/policies/creating-a-fairer-and-more-equal-society

The establishments in this guide should be aware of their obligations under the Act. We recommend that you always telephone in advance to ensure that the establishment you have chosen has appropriate facilities.

Please note: AA inspectors are not accredited to make inspections under the National Accessible Scheme. We indicate in entries if an establishment has ground floor rooms, walk-in showers and whether the hotel has a hearing loop system; and if a hotel tells us that they have disabled facilities this is included in the description.

Food allergies

Since December 2014, when a new EU regulation came into force, it has been easier for those with food allergies to make safer food choices when eating out. There are 14 allergens listed in the regulation, and pubs and restaurants are required to list any of these that are used in the dishes they offer. These may be highlighted on the menus or customers can ask staff for full information. Remember, if you are allergic to a food and are in any doubt speak to a member of the hotel's staff. For further information see: www.food.gov.uk/safety-hygiene/allergy-and-intolerance

Licensing laws

Licensing laws differ in England, Wales, Scotland, the Republic of Ireland, the Isle of Man, the Isles of Scilly and the Channel Islands. Public houses are generally open from mid morning to early afternoon, and from about 6 or 7pm until 11pm, although closing times may be earlier or later and some pubs are open all afternoon. Unless otherwise stated, establishments listed are licensed to serve alcohol. Hotel residents can obtain alcoholic drinks at all times, if the licensee is prepared to serve them. Non-residents eating at the hotel restaurant can have drinks with meals. Children under 14 may be excluded from bars where no food is served. Those under 18 may not purchase or consume alcoholic drinks.

Club licence means that drinks are served to club members only, 48 hours must lapse between joining and ordering.

The Fire Safety Order 2005 does not apply to the Channel Islands or the Republic of Ireland which have their own rules. As far as we are aware, all hotels listed in Great Britain have applied for and not been refused a fire certificate.

Bank and Public Holidays 2019

New Year's Day	1st January	Spring Bank Holiday	27th May
2nd January (Scotland)	2nd January	Orangemen's Day (Northern Ireland)	12th July
St Patrick's Day (NI & ROI)		Summer Bank Holiday (Scotland)	5th August
(Substitute Day)	18th March	Summer Bank Holiday	26th August
Good Friday	19th April	St Andrew's Day (Scotland)	2nd December
Easter Monday	22nd April	Christmas Day	25th December
Early May Bank Holiday	6th May	Boxing Day	26th December

AA Hotels of the Year 2018–19

Each year the AA celebrates the best among those Hotels that are part of the AA hotel rating scheme. Our inspectors nominate those places that they feel to be a cut above the rest, and award-winners are chosen from these nominations. Held this year at Grosvenor House, a JW Marriott Hotel, London, the AA Hospitality Awards 2018–19 recognised and rewarded the best that the British hospitality industry has to offer. Awards are given for the Hotel of the Year for England, London, Scotland, Wales and Northern Ireland, as well as an overall Hotel Group of the Year. Find out more about the winners of these awards over the next four pages.

The AA Hospitality Awards website features information about current and previous AA awards. Awards are also given for B&Bs, Caravan & Camping sites, and Restaurants, along with many more.

Visit www.theaa.com/hospitality-awards

ENGLAND

GREAT FOSTERS

★★★★ @@@@

EGHAM, SURREY, page 126

Over the years, Great Fosters has been on an incredible journey – the Grade I listed Tudor mansion, set in 50 acres of beautiful parkland and immaculate gardens, has risen from black stars to red stars and The Tudor Room has been awarded four AA Rosettes for Douglas Balish's outstanding cuisine, and two Rosettes in the more informal Estate Grill. Behind these accolades is, of course, a dedicated team of professional staff who are all highly guest focused and deliver attentive and intuitive service with a smile – from arrival through to departure. The main house's bedrooms are sumptuous and will make you believe you're staying in a royal palace – some have towering four-posters, some have elegant roll top baths. On a less grand scale, but still luxurious, are the more modern cloister and coach house rooms. Guests find it easy to relax here but the swimming pool, tennis courts, croquet lawn and spa treatments could easily tempt them away from reading a book in a comfortable chair. Excellence is around every corner at this wonderful hotel.

LONDON

FOUR SEASONS HOTEL LONDON AT TEN TRINITY SQUARE
★★★★★
LONDON EC3, page 218

Located in the heart of the City, this hotel has recently completed a seven-year refurbishment programme to transform it into the newest 5-star hotel on the London scene. The quality here is excellent – all of the bedrooms have the most up-to-date furnishings, technology and high levels of comfort. The majority of suites are all located on the ground floor and benefit from the hotel's original features. The dome in the Rotunda bar (see image) has been completely restored and the white walls are moulded with motifs representing earth, water, fire and air, and circles. The Spa is an excellent new asset to the hotel and the main reception, which took over eight months to be completed, features a gold leaf-backed double mosaic wall. Add to this a partnership with Anne-Sophie, one of the world's most decorated chefs, and her La Dame de Pic restaurant, plus also Mei Ume, which follows the culinary traditions of Japan and China. All-in-all an excellent hotel, with so much detail and no expense spared. In short, nothing comes close in London at this moment in time.

SCOTLAND

OLD COURSE HOTEL, GOLF RESORT & SPA
★★★★★
ST ANDREW'S, FIFE, page 456

This iconic hotel is located in one of the most enviable locations in Scotland. The hotel has continued to develop under the ownership of Kohler who have made major investment into refurbishing the bedrooms and creating a new spa. Rooms are a blend of classic and contemporary with elegance throughout, a transformation which has been overseen by the French designer Jacques Garcia. Dining at the hotel comes in many forms with the Road Hole Restaurant offering great food and stunning views of the golf course and golden beaches beyond. The new spa offers an alternative leisure activity to walking and playing the world renowned golf courses. It features a range of treatment rooms, two Kohler wet bathing rooms, a 20-metre indoor pool, hydrotherapy pool, steam room, experience showers, refreshing ice shower, cold plunge pool and a Finnish sauna. If that's not enough, then the roof-top garden has a hot tub. And to top it all, the team are caring and attentive in their approach to every day customer care, ensuring each stay is a memorable one.

AA Hotels of the Year *continued*

WALES

TREFEDDIAN HOTEL
★★★ 82%
ABERDYFI, GWYNEDD, page 468

The location of this property is perfectly summed up from a quote in its own literature 'where the mountains meet the sea', and for many this would be enough to warrant a trip to this family-run property. But there's so much more, including a swimming pool, treatment rooms, games room and a putting green (9 hole). The bedrooms and public areas have all been refurbished to a high standard and offer exceptional levels of comfort for its grading. The range of facilities offered here is more in line with larger operators and caters for all ages; giving the feeling of something for everyone. But it's the understanding of what a guest wants and needs and how the team strive to deliver this, which sees guests coming back year on year. This, combined with constant improvements to the hotel, sets this property apart from its competitors. The hotel manages to have that small homely feeling running through its veins which is why it is so coveted by guests. Throughout your stay you are made to feel like a valued guest and leave wanting to book a return visit. The hotel features a great team of committed staff.

NORTHERN IRELAND

BISHOPS GATE HOTEL
★★★★ 83% ◉
LONDONDERRY DERRY, COUNTY LONDONDERRY DERRY, page 497

Bishops Gate Hotel is located within the historic city walls in the heart of the Cathedral Quarter. It was built in 1899 for members of the local gentry who had fought in the Crimean War, and was known as the Northern Counties Club. The Grade B1 listed building has a rich history and has welcomed visits from many illustrious people, from Churchill to WB Yeats, and from Field Marshal Montgomery to artist, Derek Hill. It was the place to meet, discuss ideas and conduct business, and nothing has really changed. This fantastic boutique hotel has undergone a restoration programme that fully showcases the fine Victorian architecture; the results display high degrees of luxury and quality as can be seen in the residents' lounge, restaurant and champagne and cocktail bar. The 31 stylish bedrooms cater well for the needs of the modern guest. The service is friendly and attentive with a professional approach noted in all areas, but it is the warmth of the hospitality from all the team that really sets this hotel apart from the rest.

Harbour Hotels

HARBOUR HOTELS This group was launched in 2003 when the founder Nicolas Roche, who is a PwC-trained accountant, bought what was then the Avonmouth Hotel in Christchurch. After extending and upgrading the hotel at a cost of £8m, it was transformed from a three AA-star property into the four AA-star Christchurch Harbour Hotel. Since these early years, the group has gradually developed into a collection of prestigious hotels situated in some of the most beautiful locations throughout the south.

The collection includes the following award-winning hotels:
Brighton Harbour Hotel & Spa, East Sussex **U**
Bristol Harbour Hotel & Spa, Bristol ★★★★
Chichester Harbour Hotel, West Sussex ★★★★
Christchurch Harbour Hotel, Dorset ★★★★
The Kings Arms, Christchurch, Dorset ★★★
St Ives Harbour Hotel, Cornwall ★★★★
Salcombe Harbour Hotel, Devon ★★★★
Sidmouth Harbour Hotel, Devon ★★★★
Southampton Harbour Hotel, Hampshire ★★★★★

Mike Warren, ex-Malmaison and Hotel du Vin, joined the group in 2014 as Managing Director and under his leadership the group has gone from strength to strength.

Our inspections have identified strong physical products, professional teams delivering good service and hospitality and a real passion for quality food led by Alex Aitken, Director of Food & Beverage.

Each of their hotels features award-winning restaurant concepts; the 'Upper Deck Bar & Restaurant' and 'The Jetty', most recently in Southampton. The unique HarSPA brand will expand across all their hotels, featuring both coastal and urban spas. Chichester and Southampton have recently opened new spas, and more will follow.

Salcombe Harbour Hotel

Southampton Harbour Hotel

Southampton Harbour Hotel

Hotel groups information

ABode HOTELS	**ABode Hotels** A contemporary collection of four city centre hotels in Canterbury, Chester, Manchester and Glasgow that have a wide variety of dining outlets and are well geared to both corporate and leisure markets. Part of Andrew Brownsword Hotels.	www.abodehotels.co.uk
BW Best Western	**Best Western** Britain's largest consortia group – over 280 independently owned and managed hotels, modern and traditional, in the two-, three- and four-star range. Many have leisure facilities and AA Rosettes.	www.bestwestern.co.uk
BW Best Western PLUS	**Best Western Plus** 30 independently owned and managed hotels that offer that little something extra in the three- and four-star range. Some of these hotels have AA Rosette awards.	www.bestwestern.co.uk
BWP PREMIER | BEST WESTERN	**Best Western Premier** These hotels are selected for their beautiful settings, range of facilities and enhanced levels of service. There are currently 10 Best Western Great Britain hotels that have achieved Premier status. These join over 45 Best Western Premier accredited hotels across Europe and Asia.	www.bestwestern.co.uk
Brend Hotels	**Brend** A family owned group of 11 hotels – 7 four-star and 4 three-star – in Devon and Cornwall.	www.brendhotels.com
Andrew BROWNSWORD THE HOTELS	**Brownsword Hotels** A small group of country hotels each with unique qualities, personalised service, memorable locations and a strong focus on food and wine.	www.brownswordhotels.co.uk
CLASSIC BRITISH HOTELS	**Classic British Hotels** An exclusive upmarket collection of 1 five-star, four-star and quality three-star independent hotels throughout the UK, noted for its comfort, fine dining, spas, golf and event facilities.	www.classicbritishhotels.com
THE COACHING INN GROUP	**The Coaching Inn Group** is a small selection of historic coaching inns based in market towns within the UK. All sites are filled with character and offer a great quality in food, drink and rooms.	www.coachinginngroup.co.uk
COTSWOLD INNS & HOTELS	**Cotswold Inns & Hotels** Charming three- and four-star hotels located in the Cotswolds.	www.cotswold-inns-hotels.co.uk
CROWNE PLAZA HOTELS & RESORTS	**Crowne Plaza** Four-star hotels predominantly found in key city centre locations.	www.crowneplaza.co.uk

Days Inn Good quality modern budget hotels with good coverage across the UK.		www.daysinn.com
Eden Hotel Collection A privately owned collection of individual hotels, featuring award-winning dining in quality surroundings.		www.edenhotelcollection.com
English Lakes Hotels A collection of individually styled four-star hotels located in and around the Lake District.		www.englishlakes.co.uk
Exclusive Hotels A small, privately owned group of luxury hotels, all located in the south of England.		www.exclusive.co.uk
FBD Hotels & Resorts An Irish owned and operated group offering quality hotels in convenient locations.		www.fbdhotels.com
Focus Hotels A group of three- and four-star hotels in both city and country locations across England. All offer WiFi and a number have spa facilities.		www.focushotels.co.uk
Hallmark Hotels A collection of 8 hotels that provide comfortable accommodation; some have leisure facilities.		www.hallmarkhotels.co.uk
Hand Picked Hotels A collection of predominantly four-star, high quality country house hotels, with a real emphasis on quality food and service. Some have stylish spa facilities.		www.handpickedhotels.co.uk
Hillbrooke Hotels A growing portfolio of hotels and inns under the banner 'Quirky Luxury'. Excellent locations, comfortable surroundings, relaxed informal service.		www.hillbrookehotels.co.uk
Holiday Inn A major international group with many hotels across the UK.		www.holidayinn.co.uk
Holiday Inn Express A major international hotel brand with over 100 hotels in the UK.		www.hiexpress.co.uk
Hotel du Vin A small expanding group of high quality four-star hotels, with a strong emphasis on its destination restaurant concept and appealing menus.		www.hotelduvin.com

Hotel groups information *continued*

The Independents A consortium of independently owned, mainly two-, three- and four-star hotels across Britain.	www.theindependents.co.uk
Ireland's Blue Book A collection of country houses, historic hotels, castles and restaurants throughout Ireland.	www.irelands-blue-book.ie
Lake District Hotels A small collection of hotels situated in some beautiful parts of Lake District countryside and in some Lakeland towns.	www.lakedistricthotels.net
Legacy Hotels A small group of three- and four-star hotels growing its coverage across the UK.	www.legacy-hotels.co.uk
Leisureplex A group of 21 three-star hotels located in many popular seaside resorts.	www.leisureplex.co.uk
Macdonald A large group of predominantly four-star hotels, both traditional and modern in style and located across the UK. Many hotels enjoy rural settings and state-of-the-art spa facilities.	www.macdonaldhotels.co.uk
Malmaison A growing brand of modern, luxurious city-centre hotels that provide deeply comfortable bedrooms, exciting restaurants and carefully selected wine lists.	www.malmaison.com
Maybourne Hotels A hotel group representing the prestigious London five-star hotels – The Berkeley, Claridge's and The Connaught.	www.maybourne.com
Mercure Hotels A large group of three- and four-star hotels throughout England, Scotland and Wales.	www.mercure.com
Millennium & Copthorne Group with 10 high-quality, four-star hotels, and one five-star, mainly in central London.	www.millenniumhotels.com
Moran Hotels A privately owned group with 2 four-star hotels.	www.moranhotels.com
New Forest Hotels A collection of properties situated in the New Forest National Park, each with its own distinct character. Most have an AA Rosette award for culinary excellence.	www.newforesthotels.co.uk

Novotel Part of French group Accor, Novotel provides mainly modern three-star hotels and a new generation of four-star hotels in key locations throughout the UK.		*www.novotel.com*
Original Irish Hotels A collection of family-run hotels, all across Ireland.		*www.originalirishhotels.com*
Park Plaza Hotels A European based group increasing its presence in the UK with quality four-star hotels in primary locations.		*www.parkplaza.com*
Peel Hotels A group of mainly three- and four-star hotels located across the UK.		*www.peelhotels.co.uk*
Premier Inns The largest and fastest growing budget hotel group with over 750 hotels offering quality, modern accommodation in key locations throughout the UK and Ireland. Each hotel is located adjacent to a family restaurant and bar.		*www.premierinn.com*
Pride of Britain A consortium of privately owned high quality British hotels, often in the country house style, many of which have been awarded Red Stars and AA Rosettes.		*www.prideofbritainhotels.com*
Principal Hotel Company A collection of luxury properties from Victorian grandeur to iconic city-centre hotels.		*www.phcompany.com*
QHotels A hotel group with individually styled four star establishments located across the UK, in city locations and countryside retreats.		*www.qhotels.co.uk*
Ramada A large hotel group with many properties throughout the UK in three brands – Ramada, Ramada Hotel & Resort, and Ramada Plaza.		*www.ramada.co.uk*
Red Carnation A unique collection of prestigious four- and five-star hotels in Dorset, the Channel Islands, London and Ireland providing luxurious surroundings and attentive service.		*www.redcarnationhotels.com*
Relais et Châteaux An international consortium of rural, privately owned hotels, mainly in the country house style.		*www.relaischateaux.com*

Hotel groups information *continued*

RENAISSANCE. HOTELS & RESORTS	**Renaissance** One of the Marriott brands, Renaissance is a collection of individual hotels offering comfortable guest rooms, quality cuisine and good levels of service.	www.marriott.co.uk
ROCCO FORTE HOTELS	**Rocco Forte Hotels** A small group of luxury hotels spread across Europe. Owned by Sir Rocco Forte, with two hotels in the UK, situated in major city locations.	www.roccofortehotels.com
	Scotland's Hotels of Distinction A consortium of independent Scottish hotels.	www.hotels-of-distinction.com
Sheraton Grand	**Sheraton** Represented in the UK by a small number of hotels in London and Scotland.	www.starwoodhotels.com
SMALL LUXURY HOTELS OF THE WORLD	**Small Luxury Hotels of the World** Part of an international consortium of mainly privately-owned hotels, often in the country-house style.	www.slh.com
SURYA	**Surya Hotels** A privately owned group of hotels in East Anglia and the south-east of England	www.suryahotels.co.uk
T|A|HOTEL COLLECTION	**TA Hotel Collection** A privately owned collection of three- and four-star hotels across Suffolk	www.tahotelcollection.co.uk
THE CIRCLE	**The Circle** A consortium of independently owned hotels, across Britain.	www.circlehotels.co.uk
THWAITES	**Thwaites** A small group of four-star hotels which feature spa facilities and well-equipped bedrooms ideal for both business and leisure guests.	www.thwaites.co.uk
WARNER LEISURE HOTELS	**Warner Leisure Hotels** A collection of three- and four-star country hotels and villages, exclusively for adults. Renowned for their restaurants, daytime activities and live entertainment.	www.warnerleisurehotels.co.uk
Z HOTELS	**Z Hotels** Modern hotels in city-centre locations with out-of-town prices	www.thezhotels.com

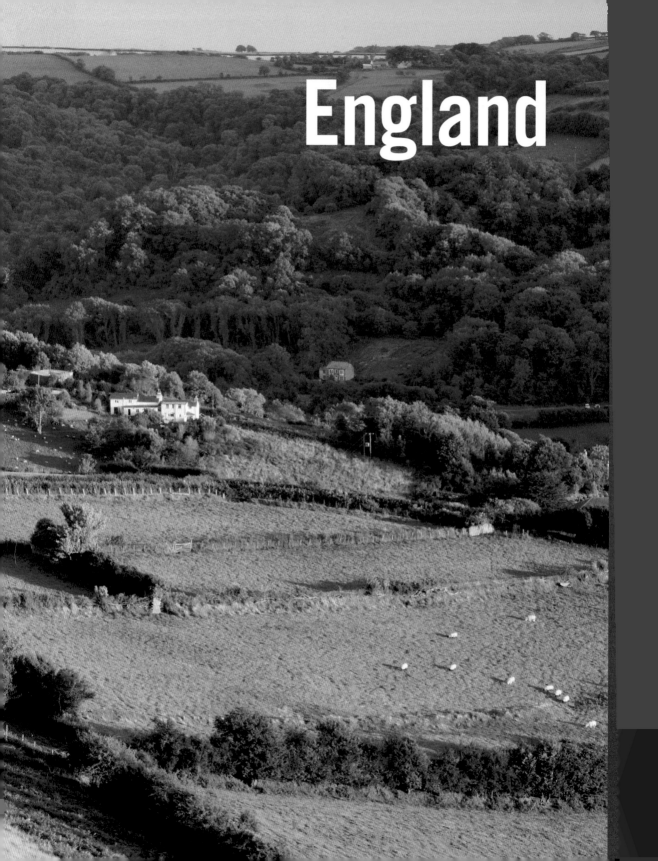

England

A

ABBERLEY   Map 10 SO76
Worcestershire

HIGHLY RECOMMENDED

The Elms Country House Hotel & Spa

★★★★ 83% HOTEL

tel: 01299 896666 **Stockton Road WR6 6AT**
email: info@theelmshotel.co.uk **web:** www.theelmshotel.co.uk
dir: *On Stockton Road in Abberley village.*

This attractive Queen Anne manor house is set in mature landscaped grounds and surrounded by open countryside. The individually decorated bedrooms are tastefully appointed with modern facilities, and most rooms have great views over the Teme Valley. The public rooms offer a wide choice of places to relax, including a choice of lounges, a restaurant and a spa.

Rooms: 23 (6 annexe) ✆ **S** fr £110 **D** fr £125 (including breakfast)*
Facilities: Spa FTV WiFi ↻ 🔕 ♨ ⛳ Gym Xmas New Year **Conf:** Class 45 Board 30 Theatre 90 **Services:** Night porter **Parking:** 150 **Notes:** LB Civ Wed 80

ABINGDON-ON-THAMES   Map 5 SU49
Oxfordshire

Premier Inn Abingdon

BUDGET HOTEL

tel: 0871 527 8014 (Calls cost 13p per minute plus your phone company's access charge) **Marcham Road OX14 1AD**
web: www.premierinn.com
dir: *On A415. Approximately 0.5 mile from A34 at Abingdon South junction Marcham Interchange.*

High quality, budget accommodation ideal for both families and business travellers. Spacious, en suite bedrooms feature free WiFi and tea and coffee making facilities, and in most hotels, Freeview TV is also available. The adjacent family restaurant features a wide and varied menu.

Rooms: 27

ACCRINGTON   Map 18 SD72
Lancashire

Mercure Blackburn Dunkenhalgh Hotel & Spa

★★★★ 74% HOTEL

tel: 01254 398021 **Blackburn Road, Clayton-le-Moors BB5 5JP**
email: H6617@accor.com **web:** www.mercure.com
dir: *M65 junction 7, left at roundabout, left at lights, hotel 100 yards on left.*

Set in delightfully tended grounds yet only a stone's throw from the M65, this fine mansion has conference and banqueting facilities that attract the wedding and corporate markets. The state-of-the-art thermal suite allows guests to relax and take it easy. Bedrooms come in a variety of styles, sizes and standards; some are located away from the main hotel building.

Rooms: 175 (119 annexe) (36 family) (43 GF) ✆ **Facilities:** Spa STV WiFi HL ↻ Gym Thermal suite Aerobics studio Xmas New Year **Conf:** Class 200 Board 100 Theatre 400 **Services:** Lift Night porter **Parking:** 400 **Notes:** Civ Wed 300

ADDLESTONE   Map 6 TQ06
Surrey

Premier inn Addlestone

Premier Inn 🌙

BUDGET HOTEL

tel: 0871 622 2416 (Calls cost 13p per minute plus your phone company's access charge) **Station Road KT15 2AH**
web: www.premierinn.com
dir: *Phone for directions.*

High quality, budget accommodation ideal for both families and business travellers. Spacious, en suite bedrooms feature free WiFi and tea and coffee making facilities, and in most hotels, Freeview TV is also available. The adjacent family restaurant features a wide and varied menu.

Rooms: 101

ALCESTER   Map 10 SP05
Warwickshire

Kings Court Hotel

★★★ 78% HOTEL

tel: 01789 763111 **Kings Coughton B49 5QQ**
email: info@kingscourthotel.co.uk **web:** www.kingscourthotel.co.uk
dir: *1 mile north on A435.*

This privately-owned hotel dates back to Tudor times and the bedrooms in the original house have oak beams. Most guests are accommodated in the well-appointed modern wings. The bar and restaurant offer very good dishes from interesting menus. The hotel is licensed to hold civil ceremonies, and the pretty garden is ideal for summer weddings.

Rooms: 61 (58 annexe) (2 family) (30 GF) ✆ **S** fr £45 **D** fr £65 (including breakfast)*
Facilities: FTV WiFi ↻ Gym Xmas New Year **Conf:** Class 60 Board 40 Theatre 100 **Parking:** 100 **Notes:** Civ Wed 100

ALDEBURGH   Map 13 TM45
Suffolk

HIGHLY RECOMMENDED

Brudenell Hotel

★★★★ 85% ◉◉ HOTEL

tel: 01728 452071 **The Parade IP15 5BU**
email: info@brudenellhotel.co.uk **web:** www.brudenellhotel.co.uk
dir: *A12, A1094. In town, right into High Street. Hotel on seafront adjoining Fort Green car park.*

Situated at the far end of the town centre just a step away from the beach, this hotel has a contemporary appearance, enhanced by subtle lighting and quality soft furnishings. Many of the bedrooms have superb sea views; they include deluxe rooms with king-sized beds and superior rooms suitable for families. The informal restaurant showcases skilfully prepared dishes that use fresh, seasonal produce, especially local fish, seafood and game.

Rooms: 44 (17 family) ✆ **Facilities:** STV WiFi Xmas New Year **Conf:** Class 20 Board 20 Theatre 20 **Services:** Lift Night porter **Parking:** 18

HIGHLY RECOMMENDED

The White Lion Hotel

★★★ 88% ⊛ HOTEL

tel: 01728 452720 **Market Cross Place IP15 5BJ**
email: info@whitelion.co.uk **web:** www.whitelion.co.uk
dir: *A12 onto A1094, follow signs to Aldeburgh at junction on left. Hotel on right.*

A popular 15th-century hotel situated at the quiet end of town overlooking the sea. Bedrooms are pleasantly decorated and thoughtfully equipped, many rooms have lovely sea views. Public areas include two lounges and an elegant restaurant, where locally-caught fish and seafood are served. There is also a modern brasserie.

Rooms: 38 **Facilities:** STV WiFi ☼ Xmas New Year **Conf:** Class 50 Board 30 Theatre 80 **Services:** Night porter **Parking:** 10 **Notes:** Civ Wed 90

ALDERLEY EDGE
Cheshire   **Map 16 SJ87**

Alderley Edge Hotel

★★★★ 80% ⊛⊛ HOTEL

tel: 01625 583033 **Macclesfield Road SK9 7BJ**
email: reservations@alderleyedgehotel.com **web:** www.alderleyedgehotel.com
dir: *From A34 in Alderley Edge onto B5087 towards Macclesfield. Hotel 200 yards on right.*

Discreetly located at the edge of town and set in some pleasant gardens, this former 'cotton kings' house now offers a contemporary and refreshing style, the public rooms here are quite stylish. The restaurant provides a great range of menu choice, featuring items cooked on the Josper Grill. A stylish and relaxing bar offers cocktails and a great range of drinks and wines. Bedrooms many of which are recently refreshed, are stylish, comfortable and very well equipped.

Rooms: 50 (4 family) (6 GF) ☎ **S** fr £100 **D** fr £120 **Facilities:** STV WiFi ☼ **Conf:** Class 40 Board 30 Theatre 120 **Services:** Lift Night porter **Parking:** 90 **Notes:** Closed 1 January RS 25–26 December Civ Wed 120

Red Stars

The AA Red Star rating denotes an Inspectors' Choice hotel. They stand out as the very best places to stay and appear in highlighted panels throughout the guide.

ALDERMINSTER
Warwickshire   **Map 10 SP24**

INSPECTOR'S CHOICE

Ettington Park Hotel

★★★★ ⊛⊛ COUNTRY HOUSE HOTEL

tel: 01789 450123 & 0845 072 7454 (Calls cost 5p per minute plus your phone company's access charge) **CV37 8BU**
email: enquiries.ettington@handpicked.co.uk
web: www.handpickedhotels.co.uk/ettingtonpark
dir: *Off A3400 5 miles south of Stratford, just outside Alderminster. M40 junction 15/ A46 towards Stratford-Upon-Avon, A439 in town centre, A3400 to Shipston, 0.5 mile on left.*

Set in 40 acres of grounds in the picturesque Stour Valley, Ettington Park offers the best of both worlds – the peace of the countryside and easy access to main roads and motorway networks. Bedrooms are spacious and individually decorated; views include the delightful grounds and gardens, or the historic chapel. Luxurious day rooms extend to the period drawing room, the oak-panelled dining room with inlays of family crests, a range of contemporary meeting rooms and an indoor leisure centre.

Rooms: 48 (20 annexe) (5 family) (10 GF) ☎ **Facilities:** STV WiFi HL ⌧ ♨ ⚊ Clay pigeon shooting Archery Sauna Steam room Xmas New Year **Conf:** Class 48 Board 48 Theatre 80 **Services:** Lift Night porter **Parking:** 100 **Notes:** Civ Wed 96

ALDERSHOT
Hampshire   **Map 5 SU85**

Potters International Hotel

★★★ 73% HOTEL

tel: 01252 344000 **1 Fleet Road GU11 2ET**
email: reservations@pottersinthotel.com **web:** www.pottersinthotel.com
dir: *Access via A325 and A321 towards Fleet.*

This modern hotel is located within easy reach of Aldershot. Extensive air-conditioned public areas include ample lounge areas, a pub and a more formal restaurant; there are also conference rooms and a very good leisure club. Bedrooms, mostly spacious, are well equipped and have been attractively decorated and furnished.

Rooms: 103 (9 family) (9 GF) **Facilities:** STV WiFi ⌧ Gym Beauty treatment room **Conf:** Class 250 Board 100 Theatre 400 **Services:** Lift Night porter **Parking:** 120

A

ALDERSHOT *continued*

Premier Inn Aldershot

Premier Inn

BUDGET HOTEL

tel: 0871 527 8018 (Calls cost 13p per minute plus your phone company's access charge) **7 Wellington Avenue GU11 1SQ**
web: www.premierinn.com
dir: *M3 junction 4, A331. A325 through Farnborough. Pass Barons BMW then Queens Roundabout. Adjacent to Willems Park Brewers Fayre.*

High quality, budget accommodation ideal for both families and business travellers. Spacious, en suite bedrooms feature free WiFi and tea and coffee making facilities, and in most hotels, Freeview TV is also available. The adjacent family restaurant features a wide and varied menu.

Rooms: 84

ALDWARK
North Yorkshire

Map 19 SE46

Aldwark Manor Golf & Spa Hotel

QHOTELS
INSPIRED
BY YOU

★★★★ 77% ⊛ HOTEL

tel: 01347 838146 **YO61 1UF**
email: aldwarkmanor@qhotels.co.uk **web:** www.qhotels.co.uk
dir: *A1/A59 towards Green Hammerton, then B6265 Little Ouseburn. Follow signs for Aldwark Bridge/Manor. A19 through Linton-on-Ouse.*

Mature parkland forms the impressive backdrop for this rambling 19th-century mansion, with the River Ure flowing gently through the hotel's own 18-hole golf course. Bedrooms vary – the rooms in the main house are traditional and those in the extension are modern in design. Impressive conference and banqueting facilities and a stylish, very well-equipped leisure club are available.

Rooms: 53 (6 family) ⦿ **S** fr £79 **D** fr £89 (including breakfast)* **Facilities:** Spa FTV WiFi ⬗ ⬙ ⬚ 18 Gym Sauna Steam room Dance studio Relaxation rooms Nail stations Xmas New Year **Conf:** Class 100 Board 80 Theatre 240 **Services:** Lift Night porter **Parking:** 250 **Notes:** Civ Wed 140

Silver Stars

The AA Silver Star rating denotes a Hotel that we highly recommend. They have a superior level of quality within their star rating, high standards of hospitality, service and cleanliness.

ALFRISTON
East Sussex

Map 6 TQ50

Deans Place

CLASSIC BRITISH HOTELS

★★★ 85% ⊛⊛ HOTEL

tel: 01323 870248 **Seaford Road BN26 5TW**
email: mail@deansplacehotel.co.uk **web:** www.deansplacehotel.co.uk
dir: *Exit A27 between Eastbourne and Brighton, signed Alfriston and Drusillas Zoo Park. South through village towards Seaford.*

Situated on the southern fringe of the village, this friendly hotel is set in attractive gardens. Bedrooms vary in size and are well appointed with good facilities. A wide range of food is offered, including an extensive bar menu and a fine dining option in The Dining Room restaurant.

Rooms: 36 (4 family) (8 GF) ⦿ **S** fr £49 **D** fr £64* **Facilities:** FTV WiFi ⬗ ⬚ ⬙ Boules Xmas New Year **Conf:** Class 100 Board 60 Theatre 200 **Services:** Night porter **Parking:** 100 **Notes:** LB Civ Wed 150

ALMONDSBURY
Gloucestershire

Map 4 ST68

Aztec Hotel & Spa

THWAITES

★★★★ 81% ⊛ HOTEL

tel: 01454 201090 **Aztec West BS32 4TS**
email: reservations@aztechotelbristol.co.uk **web:** www.thwaites.co.uk/aztec-hotel-bristol

(for full entry see Bristol)

A

ALNWICK

See **Embleton**

ALSAGER
Cheshire

Map 15 SJ75

Best Western Plus Manor House Hotel

★★★★ 75% HOTEL

tel: 01270 884000 **Audley Road ST7 2QQ**
email: res@manorhousealsager.com **web:** www.manorhousealsager.co.uk
dir: *M6 junction 16, A500 towards Stoke-on-Trent. 1st junction signed Audley, left to Alsager, hotel 2 miles on left.*

Manor House Hotel is peacefully located in the village of Alsager, with easy links to the M6 and major road networks. Modern decor and period architecture sit comfortably together to create a stylish interior. Bedrooms are appointed in attractive colour schemes and are well equipped for both business and leisure guests. Public areas include Stables bar, a large lobby lounge, and Ostler's restaurant which is set in the oldest part of the property. Complimentary WiFi is available throughout.

Rooms: 57 (2 family) (8 GF) 🐾 **S** fr £69 **D** fr £79* **Facilities:** FTV WiFi 🏊 🎣
Conf: Class 108 Board 82 Theatre 200 **Services:** Lift Night porter **Parking:** 150
Notes: Civ Wed 150

ALTRINCHAM
Greater Manchester

Map 15 SJ78

Mercure Altrincham Bowdon Hotel

focushotels
management limited

★★★ 76% HOTEL

tel: 0161 928 7121 **Langham Road, Bowdon WA14 2HT**
email: enquiries@hotels-altrincham.com **web:** www.hotels-altrincham.com
dir: *A556 towards Manchester, into Park Road at lights, hotel 1 mile on right.*

Situated within easy reach of Manchester and the airport, this hotel offers comfortable and well-equipped bedrooms. Public areas include the Café Bar and The Restaurant, both serving a good choice of dishes. A leisure centre has an indoor heated pool, spa, sauna and comprehensive air-conditioned gym. There is free WiFi throughout.

Rooms: 87 (8 family) (13 GF) **Facilities:** FTV WiFi 🎣 Gym Sauna Steam room Xmas New Year **Conf:** Class 48 Board 50 Theatre 120 **Services:** Night porter **Parking:** 125
Notes: Civ Wed 120

Premier Inn Manchester Altrincham

Premier Inn

BUDGET HOTEL

tel: 0871 527 8738 (Calls cost 13p per minute plus your phone company's access charge) **Manchester Road WA14 4PH**
web: www.premierinn.com
dir: *From north: M60 junction 7, A56 towards Altrincham. From south: M6 junction 19, A556 then A56 towards Sale.*

High quality, budget accommodation ideal for both families and business travellers. Spacious, en suite bedrooms feature free WiFi and tea and coffee making facilities, and in most hotels, Freeview TV is also available. The adjacent family restaurant features a wide and varied menu.

Rooms: 43

ALVESTON
Gloucestershire

Map 4 ST68

Alveston House Hotel

★★★ 85% 🏵 HOTEL

tel: 01454 415050 **Davids Lane BS35 2LA**
email: info@alvestonhousehotel.co.uk **web:** www.alvestonhousehotel.co.uk
dir: *M5 junction 14 from north or junction 16 from south, on A38.*

In a quiet area with easy access to the city and a short drive from both the M4 and M5, this smartly presented hotel provides an impressive combination of good service, friendly hospitality and a relaxed atmosphere. The comfortable bedrooms are well equipped for both business and leisure guests. The restaurant offers carefully prepared fresh food, and the pleasant bar and conservatory area is perfect for enjoying a pre-dinner drink.

Rooms: 29 (1 family) (6 GF) 🐾 **S** fr £75 **D** fr £95* **Facilities:** FTV WiFi 🏊 Beauty treatments Xmas New Year **Conf:** Class 38 Board 40 Theatre 85 **Parking:** 75
Notes: LB Civ Wed 75

AMBERLEY
West Sussex

Map 6 TQ01

INSPECTOR'S CHOICE

Amberley Castle

Andrews
BROWNSWORD
THE HOTELS

★★★★ 🏵🏵🏵 🍴 COUNTRY HOUSE HOTEL

tel: 01798 831992 **BN18 9LT**
email: info@amberleycastle.co.uk **web:** www.amberleycastle.co.uk
dir: *On B2139, off A29 between Bury and Storrington.*

The delightful castle hotel is idyllically set in the Sussex countryside, and boasts 900 years of history. The battlements (complete with mighty portcullis; one of the few in Europe that still works) enclose the hotel. Beyond these walls are acres of stunning parkland that feature formal gardens, koi ponds and a thatched treehouse accessed by a rope bridge. Guests can enjoy the magnificent restaurant where pre-booking is essential. Named after castles in Sussex, each of the sumptuously furnished bedrooms and suites is unique in design. Luxury amenities are provided in all rooms.

Rooms: 19 (5 annexe) (5 family) (5 GF) 🐾 **D** fr £175.50 (including breakfast)*
Facilities: FTV WiFi 🏊 ⛳ 🎾 Xmas New Year **Conf:** Class 30 Board 30 Theatre 56
Services: Night porter **Parking:** 40 **Notes:** LB No children 8 years Civ Wed 56

AMBLESIDE
Cumbria

Map 18 NY30

See also **Elterwater**

Ambleside Salutation Hotel

PREMIER | BEST WESTERN

★★★★ 78% HOTEL

tel: 015394 32244 **Lake Road LA22 9BX**
email: ambleside@hotelslakedistrict.com **web:** www.hotelslakedistrict.com
dir: *A591 to Ambleside, onto one-way system, Wansfell Road into Compston Road. Right at lights into village.*

A former coaching inn, this hotel lies squarely in the centre of Ambleside. Bedrooms are tastefully appointed and thoughtfully equipped; many boast balconies, fine views and hot tubs. Inviting public areas include an attractive restaurant and a choice of comfortable lounges for relaxing. For the more energetic there is a swimming pool and small gym, and for relaxation a spa and treatment rooms.

Ambleside Salutation Hotel

Rooms: 57 (15 annexe) (4 family) (1 GF) Facilities: Spa WiFi Gym Sauna Steam room Fountain spa Xmas New Year **Conf:** Class 36 Board 26 Theatre 80 **Services:** Lift **Parking:** 57 **Notes:** LB Closed 15–16 December

See advert below

Rothay Manor

★★★★ 76% HOTEL

tel: 015394 33605 **Rothay Bridge LA22 0EH**
email: hotel@rothaymanor.co.uk **web:** www.rothaymanor.co.uk

Originally built in 1823 for a wealthy Liverpool merchant, Rothay Manor exists today as a welcoming hotel. Perfectly located for touring the Lakes and set in its own stunning grounds, the hotel features 19 individual bedrooms. Public areas include comfortable lounges and a popular restaurant where a range of imaginative dishes is provided. Both dog-friendly and accessible bedrooms are available.

Rooms: 19 (2 family) (2 GF) ✿ **S** fr £110 **D** fr £140 (including breakfast)*
Facilities: STV FTV WiFi ➩ ⛵ Xmas New Year **Conf:** Board 18 Theatre 22 **Parking:** 30
Notes: Closed 3–21 January Civ Wed 40

Regent Hotel

★★★ 86% HOTEL

tel: 015394 32254 **Waterhead Bay LA22 0ES**
email: info@regentlakes.co.uk **web:** www.regentlakes.co.uk
dir: M6 junction 36, 13 miles south on A591.

This attractive holiday hotel, situated close to Waterhead Bay, offers a warm welcome. Bedrooms come in a variety of styles, including three suites and five bedrooms in the garden wing. Public areas are contemporary and comfortable; the light, airy restaurant is the setting for hearty, enjoyable meals.

Rooms: 32 (2 family) (9 GF) ✿ **S** fr £79 **D** fr £99 (including breakfast)*
Facilities: FTV WiFi ➩ New Year **Parking:** 38 **Notes:** Closed 21–27 December

Esseborne Manor

★★★ 82% HOTEL

tel: 01264 736444 **Hurstbourne Tarrant SP11 0ER**
email: info@esseborne-manor.co.uk **web:** www.esseborne-manor.co.uk
dir: Halfway between Andover and Newbury on A343, 1 mile north of Hurstbourne Tarrant.

Set in two acres of well-tended gardens, this attractive manor house is surrounded by the open countryside of the North Wessex Downs. Bedrooms are delightfully individual and are split between the main house, an adjoining courtyard and separate garden cottage. There's a wonderfully relaxed atmosphere throughout, and public rooms combine elegance with comfort.

Rooms: 18 (7 annexe) (5 family) (4 GF) ✿ **S** fr £92 **D** fr £112 (including breakfast)
Facilities: STV FTV WiFi ⛵ New Year **Conf:** Class 40 Board 30 Theatre 60 **Parking:** 50
Notes: LB Civ Wed 100

Premier Inn Andover

BUDGET HOTEL

tel: 0871 527 8020 (Calls cost 13p per minute plus your phone company's access charge) **West Portway Industrial Estate, Joule Road SP10 3UX**
web: www.premierinn.com
dir: From A303 follow A342/A343 signs. Hotel at roundabout junction of A342 and A343 adjacent to Portway Inn Brewers Fayre.

High quality, budget accommodation ideal for both families and business travellers. Spacious, en suite bedrooms feature free WiFi and tea and coffee making facilities, and in most hotels, Freeview TV is also available. The adjacent family restaurant features a wide and varied menu.

Rooms: 81

Macdonald Ansty Hall

★★★★ 75% HOTEL

MACDONALD
HOTELS & RESORTS

tel: 0344 879 9031 **Main Road CV7 9HZ**
email: general.ansty@macdonald-hotels.co.uk
web: www.macdonald-hotels.co.uk/anstyhall
dir: M6 junction 2 onto B4065 signed Ansty. Hotel 1.5 mile on left.

Dating back to 1678, this Grade II listed Georgian house is set in eight acres of attractive grounds and woodland. The hotel enjoys a central yet tranquil location. Spacious bedrooms feature a traditional decorative style and a range of extras; rooms are divided between the main house and the newer annexe.

Rooms: 62 (39 annexe) (4 family) (22 GF) **S** fr £69 **Facilities:** FTV WiFi ➩ Xmas New Year **Conf:** Class 60 Board 60 Theatre 150 **Services:** Lift Night porter **Parking:** 100
Notes: LB Civ Wed 100

HIGHLY RECOMMENDED

Appleby Manor Hotel & Garden Spa

★★★★ 83% COUNTRY HOUSE HOTEL

tel: 017683 51571 **Roman Road CA16 6JB**
email: reception@applebymanor.co.uk **web:** www.applebymanor.co.uk
dir: M6 junction 40, A66 towards Brough. Take Appleby turn, immediately right. 0.5 mile to hotel.

Appleby Manor Hotel & Garden Spa is an imposing country mansion, set in extensive grounds amid stunning Cumbrian scenery. The Dunbobbin family and their experienced staff ensure a warm welcome and attentive service. The comfortable and well-presented bedrooms vary in style, but all cater well for the expectations of today's guests; some rooms benefit from having patio areas. The bar stocks a wide range of malt whiskies, and the restaurant and bistro offer high-quality, award-winning food. The luxury Garden Spa boasts treatment rooms, a hydrotherapy pool, outdoor hot tubs and thermal rooms.

Rooms: 30 (7 annexe) (9 family) (10 GF) ✿ **Facilities:** Spa FTV WiFi ➩ ☒ Steam room Sauna Salt room experience shower Hydrotherapy pool Outdoor spa bath New Year **Conf:** Class 25 Board 28 Theatre 38 **Parking:** 51 **Notes:** Closed 24–26 December Civ Wed 60

A

ARUNDEL
West Sussex   Map 6 TQ00

Premier Inn Arundel
Premier Inn

BUDGET HOTEL

tel: 0871 527 8022 (Calls cost 13p per minute plus your phone company's access charge) **Crossbush Lane BN18 9PQ**
web: www.premierinn.com
dir: At junction of A27 and A284, 1 mile east of Arundel.

High quality, budget accommodation ideal for both families and business travellers. Spacious, en suite bedrooms feature free WiFi and tea and coffee making facilities, and in most hotels, Freeview TV is also available. The adjacent family restaurant features a wide and varied menu.

Rooms: 31

ASCOT
Berkshire   Map 6 SU96

INSPECTOR'S CHOICE

Coworth Park
★★★★★ ⊛⊛⊛ ⌂ COUNTRY HOUSE HOTEL

tel: 01344 876600 **Blacknest Road SL5 7SE**
email: reservations.CPA@dorchestercollection.com **web:** www.coworthpark.com
dir: M25 junction 13 south onto A30 Egham/Bagshot. Past Wentworth Golf Club turn right at lights onto Blacknest Road (A329) hotel on left.

Set in 240 acres of stunning parkland, Coworth Park is part of the luxury Dorchester Collection, sister to The Dorchester in London. The hotel offers luxurious guest rooms and suites, polo grounds, stables and a spa. Children are well cared for too, with a kids' concierge who can arrange a wide variety of activities for them. The hotel maintains a strong 'green' policy, as does the kitchen team where local quality suppliers are a priority. Award-winning cuisine is offered in Restaurant Coworth Park and there's more casual dining available in The Barn which is located in a converted stable block; The Spatisserie is located in the luxury spa.

Rooms: 70 (40 family) (27 GF) ☞ **D** fr £395 (including breakfast)* **Facilities:** Spa STV FTV WiFi ⌨ ⊛ ⌂ ⚘ Gym Polo Equestrian centre Archery Laser clays Falconry Duck herding ♫ Xmas New Year **Conf:** Class 54 Board 40 Theatre 100 **Services:** Lift Night porter Air con **Parking:** 100 **Notes:** LB Civ Wed 100

Macdonald Berystede Hotel & Spa
 MACDONALD HOTELS & RESORTS

★★★★ 80% HOTEL

tel: 01344 623311 **Bagshot Road, Sunninghill SL5 9JH**
email: general.berystede@macdonald-hotels.co.uk
web: www.macdonald-hotels.co.uk/berystede
dir: A30, B3020 (Windmill Pub). 1.25 miles to hotel on left just before junction with A330.

This impressive Victorian mansion, close to Ascot Racecourse, offers executive bedrooms that are spacious, comfortable and particularly well equipped. Public rooms include a cosy bar and an elegant restaurant which serves creative dishes. The impressive self-contained conference centre and spa facility appeal to both conference and leisure guests.

Rooms: 126 (61 family) (33 GF) **Facilities:** Spa STV WiFi ⌨ ⊛ ⚘ Gym Leisure complex (thermal and beauty treatments) Outdoor garden spa Xmas New Year **Conf:** Class 220 Board 150 Theatre 330 **Services:** Lift Night porter **Parking:** 200 **Notes:** Civ Wed 300

ASHBY-DE-LA-ZOUCH
Leicestershire   Map 11 SK31

Premier Inn Ashby De La Zouch
Premier Inn

BUDGET HOTEL

tel: 0871 527 8026 (Calls cost 13p per minute plus your phone company's access charge) **Flagstaff Island LE65 1DS**
web: www.premierinn.com
dir: M1 junction 23a, follow A42 (M42), Tamworth and Birmingham signs. Hotel at roundabout at A42 junction 13. Note for sat nav use LE65 1JP.

High quality, budget accommodation ideal for both families and business travellers. Spacious, en suite bedrooms feature free WiFi and tea and coffee making facilities, and in most hotels, Freeview TV is also available. The adjacent family restaurant features a wide and varied menu.

Rooms: 94

ASHFORD
Kent   Map 7 TR04

Ashford International Hotel
QHOTELS
INSPIRED BY YOU

★★★★ 80% HOTEL

tel: 01233 219988 **Simone Weil Avenue TN24 8UX**
email: ashford@qhotels.co.uk **web:** www.qhotels.co.uk
dir: M20 junction 9, exit for Ashford/Canterbury. Left at 1st roundabout, hotel 200 metres on left.

Situated just off the M20 and with easy links to the Eurotunnel, Eurostar and ferry terminals, this hotel has been stunningly appointed. The slick, stylishly presented bedrooms are equipped with the latest amenities. Public areas include the spacious Horizons Restaurant serving a competitively priced menu, and Quench Bar for relaxing drinks. The leisure club boasts a pool, fully-equipped gym, spa facilities and treatment rooms.

Rooms: 179 (29 family) (57 GF) ☞ **S** fr £87 **D** fr £99 (including breakfast) **Facilities:** Spa WiFi ⌨ ⊛ Gym Aroma steam room Rock Sauna Feature shower Ice fountain Xmas New Year **Conf:** Class 180 Board 26 Theatre 400 **Services:** Lift Night porter Air con **Parking:** 400 **Notes:** LB Civ Wed 400

Premier Inn Ashford Central

BUDGET HOTEL

tel: 0871 527 8030 (Calls cost 13p per minute plus your phone company's access charge) **Hall Avenue, Orbital Park TN24 0GN**
web: www.premierinn.com
dir: *M20 junction 10 southbound: 4th exit at roundabout. Northbound: 1st exit onto A2070 signed Brenzett. Hotel on right at next roundabout.*

High quality, budget accommodation ideal for both families and business travellers. Spacious, en suite bedrooms feature free WiFi and tea and coffee making facilities, and in most hotels, Freeview TV is also available. The adjacent family restaurant features a wide and varied menu.

Rooms: 60

Premier Inn Ashford (Eureka Leisure Park)

BUDGET HOTEL

tel: 0871 527 8028 (Calls cost 13p per minute plus your phone company's access charge) **Eureka Leisure Park TN25 4BN**
web: www.premierinn.com
dir: *M20 junction 9, take 1st exit on left.*

Rooms: 74

Premier Inn Ashford North

BUDGET HOTEL

tel: 0871 527 8032 (Calls cost 13p per minute plus your phone company's access charge) **Maidstone Road (A20), Hothfield Common TN26 1AP**
web: www.premierinn.com
dir: *M20 junction 9, A20 follow Lenham signs. Hotel between Ashford and Charing.*

Rooms: 60

ASHINGTON
Northumberland   **Map 21 NZ28**

Premier Inn Ashington

BUDGET HOTEL

tel: 0871 527 8034 (Calls cost 13p per minute plus your phone company's access charge) **Queen Elizabeth II Country Park, Woodhorn NE63 9AT**
web: www.premierinn.com
dir: *From A1 follow signs to Morpeth then Woodhorn Colliery Museum/Ashington. Through Ashington. Hotel in Queen Elizabeth II Country Park.*

High quality, budget accommodation ideal for both families and business travellers. Spacious, en suite bedrooms feature free WiFi and tea and coffee making facilities, and in most hotels, Freeview TV is also available. The adjacent family restaurant features a wide and varied menu.

Rooms: 61

ATTLEBOROUGH
Norfolk   **Map 13 TM09**

Sherbourne House Hotel

★★★ 76% METRO HOTEL

tel: 01953 454363 **8 Attleborough Road NR17 2JX**
email: stay@sherbourne-house.co.uk **web:** www.sherbourne-house.co.uk
dir: *A11 from London/Thetford towards Attleborough, through town centre, pass church on right, next left, hotel on right after 500 metres.*

Built in 1740, this fine manor house is set among beautifully landscaped gardens and is a short walk from the historic market town of Attleborough. The bedrooms are spacious and comfortable, and there is a light-filled conservatory lounge for guests to relax in. An extensive dinner menu is available in the evenings and freshly prepared breakfasts are served in the charming breakfast room overlooking the gardens. WiFi is available throughout the property, and the hotel is ideally placed for visitors to Snetterton motor racing circuit.

Rooms: 9 (1 family) (1 GF) ☏ **S** fr £50 **D** fr £99 (including breakfast)* **Facilities:** FTV WiFi **Conf:** Class 18 Board 22 Theatre 30 **Parking:** 20

AXMINSTER
Devon   **Map 4 SY29**

Fairwater Head Hotel

★★★ 79% ⓦ HOTEL

tel: 01297 678349 **Hawkchurch EX13 5TX**
email: stay@fairwaterheadhotel.co.uk **web:** www.fairwaterheadhotel.co.uk
dir: *From B3165 Crewkerne to Lyme Regis road, follow Hawkchurch signs.*

This elegant Edwardian country house provides a perfect location for anyone looking for a peaceful break. Surrounded by extensive gardens and rolling countryside, the setting guarantees relaxation. Bedrooms are located both within the main house and the garden wing, and all provide good levels of comfort. Public areas are very appealing and include lounge areas, a bar and an elegant restaurant. Food is a highlight, with excellent local produce prepared with care and skill.

Rooms: 16 (4 annexe) (8 GF) ☏ **S** fr £124 **D** fr £135 (including breakfast)*
Facilities: FTV WiFi Library **Conf:** Class 25 Board 20 Theatre 35 **Parking:** 30 **Notes:** LB Closed 1–30 January

Symbols and abbreviations
explained on pages 6–7

A

AYLESBURY
Buckinghamshire
Map 11 SP81

Hartwell House Hotel, Restaurant & Spa
★★★★ HOTEL

tel: 01296 747444 **Lower Hartwell HP17 8NR**
email: info@hartwell-house.com **web:** www.hartwell-house.com
dir: *From south: M40 junction 7, A329 to Thame, then A418 towards Aylesbury. After 6 miles, through Stone, hotel on left. From north: M40 junction 9 for Bicester. A41 to Aylesbury, A418 to Oxford for 2 miles. Hotel on right.*

This beautiful historic house is set in 90 acres of unspoilt parkland. The grand public rooms are truly magnificent, and feature many fine works of art. The service standards are very high; guests will find that the staff offer attentive and traditional hospitality without stuffiness. There is an elegant award-winning restaurant where carefully prepared dishes use the best local produce. Bedrooms are spacious, elegant and very comfortable. Most are in the main house, but some, including suites, are in the nearby renovated coach house, which also houses an excellent spa.

Rooms: 46 (16 annexe) (3 family) (10 GF) **S** fr £160 **D** fr £220 (including breakfast)* **Facilities:** Spa STV WiFi Gym Sauna Steam rooms ♫ Xmas New Year **Conf:** Class 40 Board 40 Theatre 100 **Services:** Lift Night porter **Parking:** 91 **Notes:** No children 6 years Civ Wed 120

Premier Inn Aylesbury
Premier Inn

BUDGET HOTEL

tel: 0871 527 8036 (Calls cost 13p per minute plus your phone company's access charge) **Buckingham Road HP19 9QL**
web: www.premierinn.com
dir: *From Aylesbury on A413 towards Buckingham. Hotel in 1 mile on left adjacent to lights.*

High quality, budget accommodation ideal for both families and business travellers. Spacious, en suite bedrooms feature free WiFi and tea and coffee making facilities, and in most hotels, Freeview TV is also available. The adjacent family restaurant features a wide and varied menu.

Rooms: 64

BABBACOMBE
See **Torquay**

BAGSHOT
Surrey
Map 6 SU96

Premier Inn Bagshot
Premier Inn

BUDGET HOTEL

tel: 0871 527 8040 (Calls cost 13p per minute plus your phone company's access charge) **1 London Road GU19 5HR**
web: www.premierinn.com
dir: *On A30 (London Road) just before junction with A322 (Bracknell Road). Adjacent to Cricketers Beefeater.*

High quality, budget accommodation ideal for both families and business travellers. Spacious, en suite bedrooms feature free WiFi and tea and coffee making facilities, and in most hotels, Freeview TV is also available. The adjacent family restaurant features a wide and varied menu.

Rooms: 53

Pennyhill Park, an Exclusive Hotel & Spa
EXCLUSIVE

AA Advertised

tel: 01276 471774 **London Road GU19 5EU**
email: enquiries@pennyhillpark.co.uk **web:** www.exclusive.co.uk
dir: *M3 junction 3, follow signs to Camberley. On A30 between Bagshot and Camberley.*

This delightful country-house hotel, set in 120 acres of grounds, provides every modern comfort. The stylish bedrooms are individually designed and have impressive bathrooms. Leisure facilities include a jogging trail, a golf course and a state-of-the-art spa with a thermal sequencing experience, ozone treated swimming and hydrotherapy pools, along with a comprehensive range of therapies and treatments. In addition there is a choice of eating options, lounges and bars to relax in.

Rooms: 123 (97 annexe) (6 family) (26 GF) **D** fr £266 (including breakfast)* **Facilities:** Spa STV WiFi Fishing Gym Archery Clay shooting Plunge pool Turkish steam room Rugby pitch Bike hire ♫ Xmas New Year **Conf:** Class 144 Board 72 Theatre 200 **Services:** Lift Night porter **Parking:** 500 **Notes:** Civ Wed 140

BALDOCK
Hertfordshire
Map 12 TL23

Days Inn Stevenage North - A1
WELCOMEBREAK

AA Advertised

tel: 01462 730598 **Baldock Extra Motorways, A1(M) Junction 10 SG7 5TR**
email: stevenage.hotel@welcomebreak.co.uk **web:** www.welcomebreak.co.uk
dir: *A1(M) junction 10 Baldock Extra Services.*

This modern, purpose built accommodation offers smartly appointed, well-equipped bedrooms, with good power showers. There is a choice of adjacent food outlets where guests may enjoy breakfast, snacks and meals.

Rooms: 62 (14 family) (30 GF) (8 smoking) **Facilities:** STV FTV WiFi
Services: Air con **Parking:** 120

B

BALSALL COMMON
West Midlands — Map 10 SP27

Nailcote Hall
★★★★ 76% ⊛ HOTEL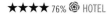

tel: 024 7646 6174 **Nailcote Lane, Berkswell CV7 7DE**
email: info@nailcotehall.co.uk web: www.nailcotehall.co.uk
dir: On B4101.

This black and white timbered 17th-century house, set in 15 acres of grounds, boasts a 9-hole championship golf course and Roman bath-style swimming pool amongst its many facilities. The bedrooms are spacious and elegantly furnished. The eating options are the fine dining Oak Room Restaurant where smart casual dress is required, or The Piano Bar where more informal meals are served.

Rooms: 49 (28 annexe) (5 family) (22 GF) S fr £99 D fr £109 (including breakfast)*
Facilities: STV FTV WiFi ⊕ ⅃ 9 ⅍ Gym ♫ Xmas New Year Conf: Class 80 Board 44 Theatre 140 Services: Lift Night porter Parking: 200 Notes: Civ Wed 250

Premier Inn Balsall Common (Near NEC)
BUDGET HOTEL Premier Inn

tel: 0871 527 8042 (Calls cost 13p per minute plus your phone company's access charge) **Kenilworth Road CV7 7EX**
web: www.premierinn.com
dir: M42 junction 6, A45 towards Coventry for 0.5 mile. A452 signed Leamington/Kenilworth. In 3 miles hotel on right.

High quality, budget accommodation ideal for both families and business travellers. Spacious, en suite bedrooms feature free WiFi and tea and coffee making facilities, and in most hotels, Freeview TV is also available. The adjacent family restaurant features a wide and varied menu.

Rooms: 66

BAMBURGH
Northumberland — Map 21 NU13

Waren House Hotel
★★★ 81% ⊛⊛ COUNTRY HOUSE HOTEL

tel: 01668 214581 **Waren Mill NE70 7EE**
email: enquiries@warenhousehotel.co.uk web: www.warenhousehotel.co.uk
dir: 2 miles east of A1 turn onto B1342 to Waren Mill, at T-junction turn right, hotel 100 yards on right.

This delightful Georgian mansion is set in six acres of woodland and offers a welcoming atmosphere and views of the coast. The individually themed bedrooms and suites include many with large bathrooms. Good, home-cooked, AA Rosette-worthy food is served in the elegant dining room. A comfortable lounge and library are also available.

Rooms: 13 (4 annexe) (3 GF) ⌂ S fr £85 D fr £100 (including breakfast)*
Facilities: FTV WiFi Xmas New Year Parking: 20 Notes: No children 14 years

BANBURY
Oxfordshire — Map 11 SP44

Best Western Plus Wroxton House Hotel
★★★★ 79% ⊛⊛ HOTEL Best Western PLUS

tel: 01295 730777 **Wroxton St Mary OX15 6QB**
email: reservations@wroxtonhousehotel.com web: www.wroxtonhousehotel.com
dir: M40 junction 11, A422 signed Banbury and Wroxton. Approximately 3 miles, hotel on right on entering Wroxton.

Dating in part from 1649, this partially thatched hotel is set just off the main road. Bedrooms, either created from cottages or situated in a contemporary wing, are comfortable and well equipped with WiFi and LCD TVs. The public areas are open plan and the low-beamed Restaurant 1649 has a peaceful atmosphere for dining.

Rooms: 32 (3 annexe) (5 family) (8 GF) ⌂ Facilities: FTV WiFi ⅃ New Year Conf: Class 40 Board 40 Theatre 90 Services: Night porter Parking: 60 Notes: Civ Wed 90

Mercure Banbury Whately Hall Hotel
★★★ 76% HOTEL Mercure

tel: 01295 253261 **Banbury Cross OX16 0AN**
email: h6633@accor.com web: www.mercure.com
dir: M40 junction 11, straight over 2 roundabouts, left at 3rd, 0.25 mile to Banbury Cross, hotel on right.

Dating back to 1677, this historic inn boasts many original features such as stone passages, priests' holes and a fine wooden staircase. Spacious public areas include the oak-panelled restaurant, which overlooks the attractive well-tended gardens, a choice of lounges and a traditional bar. Smartly appointed bedrooms vary in size and style but all are thoughtfully equipped.

Rooms: 69 (6 family) (2 GF) Facilities: FTV WiFi Xmas New Year Conf: Class 40 Board 40 Theatre 120 Services: Lift Night porter Parking: 52 Notes: Civ Wed 120

Premier Inn Banbury (M40 Jct 11)
BUDGET HOTEL Premier Inn

tel: 0871 527 9458 (Calls cost 13p per minute plus your phone company's access charge) **Stroud Park, Ermont Way OX16 4AE**
web: www.premierinn.com
dir: M40 junction 11, follow Banbury signs. Keep in left lane, take slip road on left. Hotel in Stroud Park Estate on left.

High quality, budget accommodation ideal for both families and business travellers. Spacious, en suite bedrooms feature free WiFi and tea and coffee making facilities, and in most hotels, Freeview TV is also available. The adjacent family restaurant features a wide and varied menu.

Rooms: 128

B

BARKING
Greater London

Map 6 TQ48

Premier Inn Barking

Premier Inn

BUDGET HOTEL

tel: 0871 527 8048 (Calls cost 13p per minute plus your phone company's access charge) **Highbridge Road IG11 7BA**
web: www.premierinn.com
dir: *A13 onto A406 signed Barking/Ilford. At Barking, exit at Tesco/A406 slip road. Hotel on left.*

High quality, budget accommodation ideal for both families and business travellers. Spacious, en suite bedrooms feature free WiFi and tea and coffee making facilities, and in most hotels, Freeview TV is also available. The adjacent family restaurant features a wide and varied menu.

Rooms: 88

BARNARD CASTLE
County Durham

Map 19 NZ01

The Morritt Country House Hotel & Spa

★★★★ 78% ⊛⊛ COUNTRY HOUSE HOTEL

tel: 01833 627232 **Greta Bridge DL12 9SE**
email: relax@themorritt.co.uk **web:** www.themorritt.co.uk
dir: *From M1 (east) exit at junction 57 onto A66 westbound. From M6 (west) exit at junction 40 onto A66 eastbound. Follow signs to Greta Bridge.*

In the heart of beautiful Teesdale, this 17th-century former coaching house, with connections to Charles Dickens, is full of character and is a popular meeting place. The bar area has two amazing Dickens murals — one was created in 2012 to commemorate Dickens' 200th birthday. The hotel prides itself on its traditional values which is very apparent in the quality of its service, locally-sourced food and individually styled rooms. Guests can enjoy pampering and treatments in the adjoining spa.

Rooms: 26 (6 annexe) (4 family) (4 GF) ⏻ **S** fr £95 **D** fr £115 (including breakfast)*
Facilities: Xmas New Year **Conf:** Class 60 Board 40 Theatre 120 **Notes:** LB No children Civ Wed 120

BARNBY MOOR
Nottinghamshire

Map 16 SK68

Ye Olde Bell Hotel & Spa

★★★★ 79% ⊛ HOTEL

tel: 01777 705121 **DN22 8QS**
email: enquiries@yeoldebell-hotel.co.uk **web:** www.yeoldebell-hotel.co.uk
dir: *A1(M) south near junction 34, exit Barnby Moor or A1(M) north exit A620 Retford. Hotel on A638 between Retford and Bawtry.*

This beautifully refurbished 17th-century hotel is conveniently located just off the A1 between Retford and Doncaster in the village of Barnby Moor. Public rooms have a wealth of original character including traditional log fires. Restaurant 1650 features elegant wood panelling as well as a striking contemporary bar; there is also an outdoor terrace. The tastefully appointed bedrooms are furnished to a high standard and are attractively co-ordinated; all benefit from modern bathrooms. The luxury spa has an indoor/outdoor vitality pool and 10 thermal experiences including the unique 'Snowstorm'. There are also beauty treatment rooms and a hair salon.

The gardens are a highlight here – perfect for weddings or outside entertaining in warmer weather.

Ye Olde Bell Hotel & Spa

Rooms: 59 (10 annexe) (5 family) (8 GF) ⟰ **S** fr £79 **D** fr £99 (including breakfast)*
Facilities: Spa FTV WiFi ⌕ ⟰ ⟰ Gym Beauty treatment rooms Hair salon Xmas New Year **Conf:** Class 100 Board 50 Theatre 250 **Services:** Night porter **Parking:** 200 **Notes:** LB Civ Wed 250

| **BARNSLEY** | Map 16 SE30 |
| South Yorkshire | |

Tankersley Manor

★★★★ 75% HOTEL

QHOTELS
INSPIRED BY YOU

tel: 01226 744700 **Church Lane S75 3DQ**
email: tankersleymanor@qhotels.co.uk **web:** www.qhotels.co.uk

(for full entry see Tankersley)

Premier Inn Barnsley Central M1 Jct 37

Premier Inn

BUDGET HOTEL

tel: 0871 527 9204 (Calls cost 13p per minute plus your phone company's access charge) **Gateway Plaza, Sackville Street S70 2RD**
web: www.premierinn.com
dir: *M1 junction 37, A628 (Dodworth Road) signed Barnsley. In approximately 1 mile 2nd exit at roundabout into Shambles Street, car park entrance on left.*

High quality, budget accommodation ideal for both families and business travellers. Spacious, en suite bedrooms feature free WiFi and tea and coffee making facilities, and in most hotels, Freeview TV is also available. The adjacent family restaurant features a wide and varied menu.

Rooms: 110

| **BARNSTAPLE** | Map 3 SS53 |
| Devon | |

The Imperial Hotel

★★★★ 78% HOTEL

Brend Hotels

B

tel: 01271 345861 **Taw Vale Parade EX32 8NB**
email: reservations@brend-imperial.co.uk **web:** www.brend-imperial.co.uk
dir: *M5 junction 27/A361 to Barnstaple. Follow town centre signs, passing Tesco. Straight on at next 2 roundabouts. Hotel on right.*

This smart and attractive hotel is pleasantly located at the centre of Barnstaple and overlooks the River Taw. Staff are friendly and offer attentive service. The comfortable bedrooms are of various sizes; some have balconies and many enjoy river views. Afternoon tea is available in the lounge, and the appetising cuisine is freshly prepared.

Rooms: 63 (8 annexe) (9 family) (4 GF) ⟰ **S** fr £95 **D** fr £120* **Facilities:** FTV WiFi ⌕ Leisure facilities at sister hotel Xmas New Year **Conf:** Class 40 Board 30 Theatre 60 **Services:** Lift Night porter **Parking:** 80 **Notes:** LB Civ Wed 50

See advert opposite

BARNSTAPLE *continued*

The Park Hotel
★★★★ 77% HOTEL

tel: 01271 372166 **Taw Vale EX32 9AE**
email: reservations@parkhotel.co.uk **web:** www.parkhotel.co.uk
dir: A361 to Barnstaple, 0.5 mile from town centre. Opposite Rock Park.

Enjoying views across the park and within easy walking distance of the town centre, this modern hotel offers a choice of bedrooms in both the main building and the Garden Court, just across the car park. Public rooms are open-plan in style and the friendly staff offer attentive service in a relaxed atmosphere.

Rooms: 49 (16 annexe) (3 family) (10 GF) ☎ **S** fr £80 **D** fr £90* **Facilities:** FTV WiFi ⚑ Leisure facilities at sister hotel Xmas New Year **Conf:** Class 50 Board 30 Theatre 80 **Services:** Lift Night porter **Parking:** 80 **Notes:** LB Civ Wed 100

See advert opposite

The Royal & Fortescue Hotel
★★★ 84% HOTEL

tel: 01271 342289 **Boutport Street EX31 1HG**
email: reservations@royalfortescue.co.uk **web:** www.royalfortescue.co.uk
dir: From A361 onto Barbican Road signed town centre, right into Queen Street, left into Boutport Street, hotel on left.

Formerly a coaching inn, this friendly and convivial hotel is conveniently located in the centre of town. Bedrooms vary in size and all are decorated and furnished to a consistently high standard. In addition to the formal restaurant, guests can take snacks in the popular coffee shop or dine more informally in The Bank, a bistro and café bar.

Rooms: 48 (4 family) (4 GF) ☎ **S** fr £70 **D** fr £85* **Facilities:** FTV WiFi ⚑ Leisure facilities at sister hotel Xmas New Year **Conf:** Class 25 Board 25 Theatre 25 **Services:** Lift Night porter **Parking:** 40 **Notes:** LB

The Barnstaple Hotel
★★★ 82% HOTEL

tel: 01271 376221 **Braunton Road EX31 1LE**
email: reservations@barnstaplehotel.co.uk **web:** www.barnstaplehotel.co.uk
dir: Outskirts of Barnstaple on A361.

This well-established hotel enjoys a convenient location on the edge of town. Bedrooms are spacious and well equipped, many have access to a balcony overlooking the outdoor pool and garden. In the Brasserie Restaurant, a wide choice from various menus is offered – dishes are based on local produce. There is an extensive range of leisure and conference facilities.

Rooms: 60 (4 family) (17 GF) **S** fr £90 **D** fr £95* **Facilities:** FTV WiFi ⚑ ⊛ ⚑ Gym Beauty treatment room Saunas Chill out sanctuary Xmas New Year **Conf:** Class 100 Board 50 Theatre 250 **Services:** Night porter **Parking:** 250 **Notes:** LB Civ Wed 150

B

Premier Inn Barnstaple

BUDGET HOTEL

tel: 0871 527 8052 (Calls cost 13p per minute plus your phone company's access charge) **Whiddon Drive, off Eastern Avenue EX32 8RY**
web: www.premierinn.com
dir: *Exit A361 (North Devon Link Road) towards Barnstaple. Right at Portmore roundabout.*

High quality, budget accommodation ideal for both families and business travellers. Spacious, en suite bedrooms feature free WiFi and tea and coffee making facilities, and in most hotels, Freeview TV is also available. The adjacent family restaurant features a wide and varied menu.

Rooms: 71

BARROW-IN-FURNESS	Map 18 SD26
Cumbria	

Abbey House Hotel & Gardens

★★★★ 80% ⊛ HOTEL

tel: 01229 838282 **Abbey Road LA13 0PA**
email: enquiries@abbeyhousehotel.com **web:** www.abbeyhousehotel.com
dir: *From A590 follow signs for Furness General Hospital and Furness Abbey. Hotel approximately 100 yards on left.*

Set in 14 acres of private gardens and woodland, this red stone building is a local landmark. The sharp and contemporary interior style sits well with the original architectural features and charm of the building. Bedrooms are stylish and well equipped. Service is personal, and food is a highlight of any stay. Business and function facilities also impress.

Rooms: 61 (4 annexe) (6 family) (2 GF) ✿ **Facilities:** STV FTV WiFi ⇗ Beauty treatment room Xmas New Year **Conf:** Class 120 Board 80 Theatre 300 **Services:** Lift Night porter **Parking:** 100 **Notes:** Civ Wed 120

Premier Inn Barrow-in-Furness

Premier Inn

BUDGET HOTEL

tel: 0871 527 9470 (Calls cost 13p per minute plus your phone company's access charge) **North Road LA14 2PW**
web: www.premierinn.com
dir: *M6 junction 36, A590. In 3 miles take slip road signed Barrow-in-Furness. Follow signs for Barrow-in-Furness and A590. At roundabout 2nd exit signed Walney Island and A590. Approximately 0.5 mile, hotel on right.*

High quality, budget accommodation ideal for both families and business travellers. Spacious, en suite bedrooms feature free WiFi and tea and coffee making facilities, and in most hotels, Freeview TV is also available. The adjacent family restaurant features a wide and varied menu.

Rooms: 80

BARTON	Map 18 SD53
Lancashire	

Barton Grange Hotel

★★★★ 80% HOTEL

tel: 01772 862551 **Garstang Road PR3 5AA**
email: stay@bartongrangehotel.com **web:** www.bartongrangehotel.co.uk
dir: *M6 junction 32, follow Garstang (A6) signs for 2.5 miles. Hotel on right.*

Situated close to the M6, this modern, stylish hotel benefits from extensive public areas that include leisure facilities with a swimming pool, sauna and gym. Comfortable, well-appointed bedrooms include executive rooms and family rooms, as well as attractive accommodation in an adjacent cottage. The unique Walled Garden Bistro offers all-day eating.

Rooms: 51 (8 annexe) (8 family) (4 GF) ✿ **S** fr £79 **D** fr £89* **Facilities:** STV WiFi ⇗ ⊛ Gym Sauna ♫ Xmas New Year **Conf:** Class 100 Board 80 Theatre 300 **Services:** Lift Night porter **Parking:** 250 **Notes:** LB Civ Wed 300

B

BASILDON
Essex
Map 6 TQ78

Premier Inn Basildon (East Mayne)
Premier Inn

BUDGET HOTEL

tel: 0871 527 8054 (Calls cost 13p per minute plus your phone company's access charge) **Felmores, East Mayne SS13 1BW**
web: www.premierinn.com
dir: M25 junction 29, A127 towards Southend, take A132 south signed Basildon and Wickford at Neverdon exit. Hotel on left.

High quality, budget accommodation ideal for both families and business travellers. Spacious, en suite bedrooms feature free WiFi and tea and coffee making facilities, and in most hotels, Freeview TV is also available. The adjacent family restaurant features a wide and varied menu.

Rooms: 74

Premier Inn Basildon (Festival Park)
Premier Inn

BUDGET HOTEL

tel: 0871 527 8056 (Calls cost 13p per minute plus your phone company's access charge) **Festival Leisure Park, Pipps Hill Road South SS14 3WB**
web: www.premierinn.com
dir: M25 junction 9, A217 towards Basildon. Take A17. Hotel just off A1235 adjacent to David Lloyd Leisure Club.

Rooms: 82

Premier Inn Basildon South
Premier Inn

BUDGET HOTEL

tel: 0871 527 8060 (Calls cost 13p per minute plus your phone company's access charge) **High Road, Fobbing SS17 9NR**
web: www.premierinn.com
dir: M2 junction 30/31, A13 towards Southend. 10 miles to Five Bells Roundabout junction with A176. Right into Fobbing High Road. Hotel on left.

Rooms: 61

BASINGSTOKE
Hampshire
Map 5 SU65

INSPECTOR'S CHOICE

Tylney Hall Hotel

★★★★ ◉◉ ⌚HOTEL

tel: 01256 764881 **Ridge Lane RG27 9AZ**
email: sales@tylneyhall.com **web:** www.tylneyhall.com

(for full entry see Rotherwick)

HIGHLY RECOMMENDED

Oakley Hall Hotel
★★★★ 87% ◉◉ COUNTRY HOUSE HOTEL

tel: 01256 783350 **Rectory Road, Oakley RG23 7EL**
email: enquiries@oakleyhall-park.com **web:** www.oakleyhall-park.com
dir: M3 junction 7, follow Basingstoke signs. In 500 yards before lights turn left onto A30 towards Oakley, immediately right onto unclass road towards Oakley. In 3 miles left at T-junction into Rectory Road. Left onto B3400. Hotel signed first on left.

An impressive drive leads to this country house which benefits from delightful country views across north Hampshire. Built in 1795, it was once owned by the Bramston family who were friends of Jane Austen. An ideal wedding venue, Oakley Hall also has an excellent range of conference facilities, and is a great place to spend a relaxing leisure break. The bedrooms are spacious; many are located in the impressively restored courtyard and are particularly well equipped; there is also the delightful Garden Cottage. The stylish 1795 Bar & Lounge and the Glasshouse Restaurant offer contemporary surroundings in which to relax and enjoy the excellent food and friendly service.

Rooms: 47 (18 annexe) (14 family) (23 GF) ⚑ **Facilities:** FTV WiFi ↻ ⛳ Clay pigeon shooting Archery In-room pamper treatments. Xmas New Year
Conf: Class 82 Board 50 Theatre 300 **Services:** Lift Night porter Air con
Parking: 100 **Notes:** Civ Wed 100

Audleys Wood Hotel

★★★★ 82% ◉◉ HOTEL

tel: 01256 817555 & 0845 072 7405 (Calls cost 5p per minute plus your phone company's access charge) **Alton Road RG25 2JT**
email: audleyswood@handpicked.co.uk
web: www.handpickedhotels.co.uk/hotels/audleys-wood-hotel-basingstoke
dir: M3 junction 6. From Basingstoke take A339 towards Alton, hotel on right.

A long sweeping drive leads to what was once a Victorian hunting lodge and a private family home. This traditional country house hotel offers a range of bedrooms and suites equipped with TVs, MP3 player connections and free WiFi. The smart and traditional public areas have interesting period features, log fires and comfortable sofas. The Conservatory Restaurant with its high vaulted ceiling and small minstrels' gallery serves a seasonal award-winning menu. The Garden Pavilion, within the grounds, is the prefect wedding venue. Audleys Wood also offers a range of meeting rooms for business and conferences, and ample, secure parking is available.

Rooms: 72 (23 family) (34 GF) **Facilities:** STV FTV WiFi ↻ HL ⛳ Xmas New Year
Conf: Class 80 Board 60 Theatre 200 **Services:** Night porter **Parking:** 100
Notes: Civ Wed 100

The Hampshire Court Hotel

★★★★ 79% HOTEL

tel: 01256 319700 **Centre Drive, Chineham RG24 8FY**
email: hampshirecourt@qhotels.co.uk **web:** www.qhotels.co.uk
dir: Off A33 Reading Road, behind Chineham Shopping Centre, via Great Binfields Road.

This hotel boasts a range of smart, comfortable and stylish bedrooms, and leisure facilities that are unrivalled locally. Facilities include indoor and outdoor tennis courts, two swimming pools, a gym and a number of treatment rooms.

Rooms: 90 (6 family) ⚑ **S** fr £79 **D** fr £91 (including breakfast)* **Facilities:** Spa STV WiFi ↻ HL ⊕ ⌚ Gym Steam room Sauna Exercise studios Xmas New Year
Conf: Class 800 Board 60 Theatre 1500 **Services:** Lift Night porter **Parking:** 220
Notes: LB Civ Wed 1500

B

Apollo Hotel

★★★★ 78% HOTEL

tel: 01256 796700 **Aldermaston Roundabout RG24 9NU**
email: enquiries@apollohotels.com **web:** www.apollohotels.com
dir: *M3 junction 6. Follow ring road north towards Newbury. Follow A340 Aldermaston signs. Hotel on roundabout, 5th exit into Popley Way for access.*

This modern hotel provides well-equipped accommodation and spacious public areas, appealing to both the leisure and business guest. Facilities include a smartly appointed leisure club, a business centre, along with a good choice of formal and informal eating in two restaurants; Vespers is the fine dining option.

Rooms: 125 (51 family) (34 GF) **S** fr £65 **D** fr £75 (including breakfast)
Facilities: Spa FTV WiFi ⚑ ⚒ Gym Sauna Steam room Spa pool Beauty treatments New Year **Conf:** Class 196 Board 50 Theatre 300 **Services:** Lift Night porter
Parking: 200 **Notes:** LB Civ Wed 300

Premier Inn Basingstoke Central

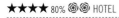

BUDGET HOTEL

tel: 0871 527 8062 (Calls cost 13p per minute plus your phone company's access charge) **Basingstoke Leisure Park, Worting Road RG22 6PG**
web: www.premierinn.com
dir: *M3 junction 6, A339 towards Newbury. A340 follow brown Leisure Park signs. At next roundabout right onto B3400 (Churchill Way West). Right on next roundabout into Leisure Park. Hotel adjacent to Spruce Goose Beefeater.*

High quality, budget accommodation ideal for both families and business travellers. Spacious, en suite bedrooms feature free WiFi and tea and coffee making facilities, and in most hotels, Freeview TV is also available. The adjacent family restaurant features a wide and varied menu.

Rooms: 99

Premier Inn Basingstoke Town Centre Hotel

BUDGET HOTEL

tel: 0871 527 9518 (Calls cost 13p per minute plus your phone company's access charge) **Victoria Street RG21 3BT**
web: www.premierinn.com
dir: *M3 junction 6 signed Basingstoke. Then follow A30 and Alton signs. At next roundabout take 3rd exit to Fairfield, left into New Road. Hotel on left after Caston's car park.*

Rooms: 81

BASLOW
Derbyshire

Map 16 SK27

Cavendish Hotel

★★★★ 80% ⚙⚙ HOTEL

CLASSIC BRITISH HOTELS

tel: 01246 582311 **Church Lane DE45 1SP**
email: info@cavendish-hotel.net **web:** www.cavendish-hotel.net
dir: *M1 junction 29/A617 west to Chesterfield and A619 to Baslow. Hotel in village centre, off main road.*

This stylish property, dating back to the 18th century, is delightfully situated on the outskirts of the Chatsworth Estate. All rooms enjoy far-reaching views across the estate and benefit from the slightly elevated position. Bedrooms are elegantly appointed and offer a host of thoughtful amenities including Temple Spa toiletries in the bathrooms. The comfortable public areas are furnished with period pieces and paintings from the Duke's extensive art collection. Guests have a choice of dining in either the informal conservatory Garden Room or the elegant Gallery Restaurant. A sun terrace overlooks the croquet lawn and estate beyond.

Rooms: 28 (4 annexe) (3 family) (4 GF) **S** fr £178.50 **D** fr £235* **Facilities:** FTV WiFi Fishing offsite can be arranged Xmas New Year **Conf:** Class 8 Board 18 Theatre 25 **Services:** Night porter **Parking:** 50 **Notes:** LB Civ Wed 50

INSPECTOR'S CHOICE

Fischer's Baslow Hall

★★★ ⚙⚙⚙ HOTEL

tel: 01246 583259 **Calver Road DE45 1RR**
email: reservations@fischers-baslowhall.co.uk
web: www.fischers-baslowhall.co.uk
dir: *On A623 between Baslow and Calver.*

Located at the end of a chestnut tree-lined drive on the edge of the Chatsworth Estate, in marvellous gardens, this beautiful Derbyshire manor house offers sumptuous accommodation and facilities. Staff provide very friendly and personally attentive service. There are two styles of bedroom available – traditional, individually-themed rooms in the main house, and spacious, more contemporary-styled rooms with Italian marble bathrooms in the Garden House. The cuisine is excellent and may prove the highlight of any stay.

Rooms: 11 (5 annexe) (4 GF) **S** fr £185 **D** fr £260 (including breakfast)*
Facilities: FTV WiFi ⚑ **Conf:** Board 15 Theatre 20 **Parking:** 40 **Notes:** No children 8 years Closed 25–26 December RS 24 and 31 December, 1 January Civ Wed 38

B

BASSENTHWAITE
Cumbria

Map 18 NY23

Armathwaite Hall Hotel and Spa
★★★★ ◎◎ COUNTRY HOUSE HOTEL

tel: 017687 76551 **CA12 4RE**
email: reservations@armathwaite-hall.com **web:** www.armathwaite-hall.com
dir: *M6 junction 40/A66 to Keswick roundabout then A591 signed Carlisle. 8 miles to Castle Inn junction, turn left. Hotel 300 yards.*

Enjoying fine views over Bassenthwaite Lake, this impressive 17th-century mansion is set in 400 acres of deer park; part of the site is the Lake District Wildlife Park. The comfortably furnished bedrooms and well-appointed bathrooms are complemented by a choice of public rooms that have many original features. The spa is an outstanding asset to the leisure facilities; it offers an infinity pool, thermal suite, sauna, state-of-the-art gym, treatments, exercise classes and a hot tub overlooking the landscaped gardens.

Rooms: 46 (8 family) (8 GF) ⟨⟩ **Facilities:** Spa STV WiFi ⟨⟩ ⟨⟩ Fishing ⟨⟩ Gym Archery Clay shooting Quad and mountain bikes Falconry Xmas New Year **Conf:** Class 50 Board 60 Theatre 200 **Services:** Lift Night porter **Parking:** 100 **Notes:** Civ Wed 150

Best Western Plus Castle Inn
★★★★ 78% HOTEL

BW Best Western **PLUS**

tel: 017687 76401 **CA12 4RG**
email: reservations@castleinncumbria.co.uk **web:** www.castleinncumbria.co.uk
dir: *A591 to Carlisle, pass Bassenthwaite village on right. Hotel on left of T-junction.*

Overlooking some of England's highest fells and Bassenthwaite Lake, this fine hotel is ideally situated for exploring Bassenthwaite, Keswick and the Lake District. The accommodation, extensive leisure facilities, and friendly service are certainly strong points here. Ritson's Restaurant and Laker's Lounge offer a range of dishes using locally sourced meats from the fells; managed, sustainable fish stocks; and international and seasonal ingredients.

Rooms: 42 (4 family) (9 GF) ⟨⟩ **Facilities:** FTV WiFi ⟨⟩ ⟨⟩ Gym Sauna Steam room Xmas New Year **Conf:** Class 108 Board 60 Theatre 200 **Services:** Night porter **Parking:** 120 **Notes:** Civ Wed 180

The Pheasant
★★★ 87% ◎◎ HOTEL

tel: 017687 76234 **CA13 9YE**
email: reception@the-pheasant.co.uk **web:** www.the-pheasant.co.uk
dir: *Midway between Keswick and Cockermouth, signed from A66.*

Enjoying a rural setting, within well-tended gardens, on the western side of Bassenthwaite Lake, this friendly 500-year-old inn is steeped in tradition. The attractive oak-panelled bar has seen few changes over the years, and features log fires and a great selection of malt whiskies. The individually decorated bedrooms are stylish and thoughtfully equipped.

Rooms: 15 (2 annexe) (2 GF) ⟨⟩ **Facilities:** FTV WiFi ⟨⟩ Use of spa pool and treatment rooms at Armathwaite Hall Hotel New Year **Parking:** 40 **Notes:** LB No children 12 years Closed 25 December

Ravenstone Lodge Country House Hotel
★★★ 84% ◎ COUNTRY HOUSE HOTEL

tel: 01768 776629 **CA12 4QG**
email: enquiries@ravenstonelodge.co.uk **web:** www.ravenstonelodge.co.uk
dir: *5 miles north of Keswick on A591.*

Close to both Keswick and Bassenthwaite, set in rolling countryside, this small country house hotel offers warm, genuine hospitality along with high quality food. Bedrooms are well equipped and appointed, benefiting from a rolling refurbishment programme. Outside garden seating and the large conservatory offer unrestricted views of the picture-postcard location.

Rooms: 9 (1 family) (2 GF) ⟨⟩ **D** fr £70 (including breakfast)* **Facilities:** FTV WiFi ⟨⟩ **Parking:** 15

BATH
Somerset

Map 4 ST76

See also **Colerne & Hinton Charterhouse**

The Bath Priory Hotel, Restaurant & Spa

★★★★★ ◎◎◎ HOTEL

tel: 01225 331922 **Weston Road BA1 2XT**
email: info@thebathpriory.co.uk **web:** www.thebathpriory.co.uk
dir: *Adjacent to Victoria Park.*

The Bath Priory Hotel is a country house set in four acres of beautiful grounds. It features a luxury spa, and the Priory Restaurant that delivers food derived from modern European cuisine; created from the very finest local produce and seasonal fruit, vegetable and herbs from the property's own garden. Opening onto the leafy gardens, the Mediterranean-style spa features an indoor heated swimming pool with a pool-side sauna and modern steam pod. Luxury beauty treatments are also available by appointment. Luxurious bedrooms have elegant decor and free WiFi access. All rooms feature period furniture and spacious en suite bathrooms with fluffy bathrobes and designer toiletries.

Rooms: 33 (6 annexe) (2 family) (1 GF) ⟋ **S** fr £140 **D** fr £140* **Facilities:** Spa STV FTV WiFi ⟲ ⟍ ⟍ Steam pod Sauna Xmas New Year **Conf:** Class 24 Board 16 Theatre 24 **Services:** Night porter **Parking:** 40 **Notes:** LB Civ Wed 70

The Royal Crescent Hotel & Spa

★★★★★ ◎◎◎ ⟐ HOTEL

tel: 01225 823333 **16 Royal Crescent BA1 2LS**
email: info@royalcrescent.co.uk **web:** www.royalcrescent.co.uk
dir: *From A4 at junction of London Road and George Street turn up Lansdowne Hill. 2nd left into Bennett Street, into The Circus, 2nd exit into Brock Street, merge into Royal Crescent.*

The Royal Crescent Hotel is set in several houses in Bath's famous Royal Crescent and is one of the country's most interesting and historic places to stay. Bedrooms offer a range of suites and sizes, all with individual style and character; many have views across the city, and all are most comfortably appointed. Public rooms make the most of the character of the houses and are styled in keeping with the elegance of the period. The hotel has a superb spa and range of leisure facilities, as well as a number of meeting rooms and private dining venues. The Montagu Bar and Dower House Restaurant offer the very best of contemporary dining and are not to be missed. Ingredients are sourced locally where possible, and elegantly presented by head chef David Campbell and his team.

Rooms: 45 (8 family) (8 GF) ⟋ **S** fr £330 **D** fr £330 (including breakfast)* **Facilities:** Spa STV FTV WiFi ⟑ ⟲ ⟍ Gym Xmas New Year **Conf:** Class 18 Board 30 Theatre 60 **Services:** Lift Night porter Air con **Parking:** 41 **Notes:** Civ Wed 50

The Gainsborough Bath Spa

★★★★★ 88% ◎◎◎ HOTEL

tel: 01225 358888 **Beau Street BA1 1QY**
web: www.thegainsboroughbathspa.co.uk
dir: *From St James Parade into Lower Borough Walls, left into Bilbury Lane.*

The Gainsborough Bath Spa offers guests a full range of facilities including a world class thermal Bath House Spa Village utilising thermal waters. Public areas, bed- and bathrooms are luxuriously furnished with high quality decor, furniture and fittings. The friendly and attentive team do everything they can to meet their guests' requirements. Meals are served in the smart and stylish Dan Moon at The Gainsborough Restaurant. Valet parking is available, though pre-booking is advised.

Rooms: 99 (10 family) (2 GF) ⟋ **S** fr £345 **D** fr £380* **Facilities:** Spa STV FTV WiFi ⟲ Gym Xmas New Year **Conf:** Board 24 Theatre 60 **Services:** Night porter **Parking:** 20 **Notes:** LB Civ Wed 60

BATH *continued*

Macdonald Bath Spa

★★★★★ 78% ◉◉ HOTEL

tel: 0344 879 9106 **Sydney Road BA2 6JF**
email: sales.bathspa@macdonald-hotels.co.uk
web: www.macdonaldhotels.co.uk/bathspa
dir: *A4, left onto A36 at 1st lights. Right at lights after pedestrian crossing left into Sydney Place. Hotel 200 yards on right.*

A delightful Georgian mansion set in seven acres of pretty landscaped grounds, just a short walk from the many and varied delights of the city centre. A timeless elegance pervades the gracious public areas and the bedrooms. Facilities include a popular leisure club, The Vellore Restaurant, and a number of meeting rooms. Ample parking is provided on site.

Rooms: 131 (3 family) (17 GF) 🐾 **Facilities:** Spa STV FTV WiFi ⌀ HL ☻ ⤳ 🏊 Gym Thermal suite Outdoor hydro pool Whirlpool Xmas New Year **Conf:** Class 100 Board 50 Theatre 130 **Services:** Lift Night porter Air con **Parking:** 160 **Notes:** Civ Wed 130

HIGHLY RECOMMENDED

Bailbrook House Hotel

★★★★ 83% ◉◉ HOTEL

tel: 01225 855100 & 0845 072 7515 (Calls cost 7p per minute plus your phone company's access charge) **Eveleigh Avenue, London Road West BA1 7JD**
email: reception.bailbrook@handpicked.co.uk **web:** www.bailbrookhouse.co.uk
dir: *M4 junction 18/A46, at bottom of long hill take slip road to city centre. At roundabout take 1st exit, London Road. Hotel 200 metres on left.*

In the last few years, Bailbrook House Hotel has seen a dramatic rebuilding programme, and offers superior accommodation, ideally situated on the edge of Bath, set in attractive grounds with ample parking. It is perfectly placed to avoid parking and driving in the city, but close enough to allow ease of access. Bedrooms are spacious and extremely well appointed. There are two dining options and a range of meeting and conference facilities.

Rooms: 94 (81 annexe) (2 family) (27 GF) 🐾 **S** fr £99 **D** fr £109 (including breakfast) **Facilities:** STV FTV WiFi ⌀ Gym New Year **Conf:** Class 72 Board 40 Theatre 160 **Services:** Lift Night porter Air con **Parking:** 120 **Notes:** LB Civ Wed 120

Find out more

about the AA's Hotel rating scheme on pages 12–13

The Queensberry Hotel

★★★★ 80% ◉◉◉ ⚜ HOTEL

tel: 01225 447928 **Russell Street BA1 2QF**
email: reservations@thequeensberry.co.uk **web:** www.thequeensberry.co.uk
dir: *100 metres from the Assembly Rooms.*

This charming family-run hotel, situated in a quiet residential street near the city centre, consists of four delightful townhouses. The spacious bedrooms offer deep armchairs, marble bathrooms and a range of modern comforts. Sumptuously furnished sitting rooms add to The Queensberry's appeal and allow access to the very attractive and peaceful walled gardens. The Olive Tree Restaurant is stylish and combines Georgian opulence with contemporary simplicity; the innovative menus are based on best quality ingredients and outstanding cooking. Valet parking proves a useful service.

Rooms: 29 (2 family) (4 GF) 🐾 **S** fr £112.50 **D** fr £125 (including breakfast)*
Facilities: FTV WiFi ⌀ **Conf:** Class 12 Board 25 Theatre 35 **Services:** Lift Night porter
Parking: 6

Abbey Hotel

★★★★ 74% HOTEL

Mercure HOTELS

tel: 01225 461603 **1 North Parade BA1 1LF**
email: reception@abbeyhotelbath.co.uk **web:** www.abbeyhotelbath.co.uk
dir: *M4 junction 18/A46 for approximately 8 miles. At roundabout right onto A4 for 2 miles. Once past Morrisons stay in left lane and turn left at lights. Over bridge and right at lights. Over roundabout and right at lights. Hotel at end of road.*

Perfectly located in the heart of Bath, just a two-minute stroll from the famous abbey, this popular hotel offers a relaxing welcome with professional, helpful service in contemporary surroundings. For eating, the Allium Restaurant offers an excellent range of the highest quality dishes with something to suit all tastes. In the warmer months, outdoor seating on the front terrace is the ideal location for coffee or lunch.

Rooms: 62 (7 family) (3 GF) 🐾 **S** fr £80 **D** fr £100* **Facilities:** WiFi ⌀ Xmas New Year **Conf:** Class 10 Board 16 Theatre 30 **Services:** Lift Night porter

Premier Inn Bath

Premier Inn

BUDGET HOTEL

tel: 0871 527 9454 (Calls cost 13p per minute plus your phone company's access charge) **James Street West BA1 2BX**
web: www.premierinn.com
dir: *M4 junction 18, A46 towards city centre. In approximately 7 miles 3rd exit A4 towards city centre. 1.5 miles left into Gay Street, through Queen Square, straight ahead into Charles Street. At 2nd lights left into James Street West. Hotel 200 metres on right.*

High quality, budget accommodation ideal for both families and business travellers. Spacious, en suite bedrooms feature free WiFi and tea and coffee making facilities, and in most hotels, Freeview TV is also available. The adjacent family restaurant features a wide and varied menu.

Rooms: 108

BATTLE
East Sussex

Map 7 TQ71

The Powder Mills Hotel

★★★ 84% ◎◎ HOTEL

tel: 01424 775511 **Powdermill Lane TN33 0SP**
email: reservations@thepowdermills.com **web:** www.powdermillshotel.com
dir: *M25 junction 5, A21 towards Hastings. At Johns Cross take A2100 to Battle. Pass Abbey on right, 1st right into Powdermill Lane. 1 mile, hotel on right.*

A delightful 18th-century country house hotel set amidst 150 acres of landscaped grounds with lakes and woodland. The individually decorated bedrooms are tastefully furnished and thoughtfully equipped; some rooms have sun terraces with lovely views over the lake. Public rooms include a cosy lounge bar, music room, drawing room, library, restaurant and conservatory.

Rooms: 48 (18 annexe) (5 GF) **S** fr £110 **D** fr £140 (including breakfast)
Facilities: FTV WiFi ↻ ⬋ ⬈ Fishing Jogging trails Woodland walks Xmas New Year
Conf: Class 50 Board 16 Theatre 250 **Services:** Night porter **Parking:** 101 **Notes:** LB
Civ Wed 100

The Brickwall Hotel & Restaurant

★★★ 80% HOTEL

tel: 01424 870253 **The Green TN33 0QA**
email: info@brickwallhotel.com **web:** www.brickwallhotel.com
dir: *A21 on B2244 at top of Sedlescombe Green.*

This is a well-maintained Tudor house, which is situated in the heart of the pretty village of Sedlescombe overlooking the green. The spacious public rooms feature a lovely wood-panelled restaurant with a wealth of oak beams, a choice of lounges and a smart bar. The popular restaurant offers a range of menus which pay homage to the Italian roots of the owner. The bedrooms are pleasantly decorated and well equipped; some have garden views. There is an outdoor swimming pool for the warmer months of the year. Ample and secure parking is available.

Rooms: 24 (2 family) (17 GF) **S** fr £70 **D** fr £100 (including breakfast)*
Facilities: FTV WiFi ↻ ⬈ Xmas New Year **Conf:** Class 40 Board 30 Theatre 30
Parking: 40 **Notes:** LB

BEANACRE
Wiltshire

Map 4 ST96

INSPECTOR'S CHOICE

Beechfield House

★★★★ ◎◎ COUNTRY HOUSE HOTEL

tel: 01225 703700 **SN12 7PU**
email: reception@beechfieldhouse.co.uk **web:** www.beechfieldhouse.co.uk
dir: *M4 junction 17, A350 south, bypass Chippenham, towards Melksham. Hotel on left in Beanacre.*

This is a charming, privately-owned hotel set within eight acres of beautiful grounds that has its own arboretum. Bedrooms are individually styled and include four-poster rooms, and ground-floor rooms in the coach house. Relaxing public areas are comfortably furnished and there is a beauty salon with a range of pampering treatments available. At dinner there is a very good selection of carefully prepared dishes with an emphasis on seasonal and local produce.

Rooms: 24 (7 family) (4 GF) **S** fr £125 **D** fr £150 (including breakfast)*
Facilities: FTV WiFi ↻ ⬈ ⬋ Xmas New Year **Conf:** Class 60 Board 36 Theatre 80
Services: Night porter **Parking:** 70 **Notes:** LB Civ Wed 70

BEAULIEU
Hampshire   Map 5 SU30

HIGHLY RECOMMENDED

The Montagu Arms Hotel
★★★★ 85% ◉◉◉ ▤HOTEL

tel: 01590 612324 **Palace Lane SO42 7ZL**
email: reservations@montaguarmshotel.co.uk
web: www.montaguarmshotel.co.uk
dir: *M27 junction 2, follow signs for Beaulieu. In Dibden Purlieu right at roundabout. Hotel on left in Beaulieu.*

Situated at the heart of this charming village and surrounded by glorious New Forest scenery, The Montagu Arms Hotel dates back to 1742, and still retains the character of a traditional country house. The individually designed bedrooms include some with four-posters. Public rooms include a choice of two dining options: the informal Monty's brasserie serving home-cooked classics, and the stylish, award-winning Terrace Restaurant. Much produce comes from the kitchen garden project which saw a derelict piece of land to the rear transformed to produce organic fruit, vegetables and herbs plus free-range eggs from the hens. In warmer weather there is a sheltered alfresco eating area overlooking the pretty terraced garden. Complimentary use of leisure and spa facilities is available to guests at a sister hotel, six miles away.

Rooms: 24 (2 annexe) (3 family) ☏ **Facilities:** FTV WiFi ⌁ Complimentary use of spa in Brockenhurst Xmas New Year **Conf:** Class 45 Board 30 Theatre 60 **Services:** Night porter **Parking:** 86 **Notes:** Civ Wed 100

The Master Builder's at Buckler's Hard
★★★ 82% ◉ HOTEL

tel: 01590 616253 **Buckler's Hard SO42 7XB**
email: enquiries@themasterbuilders.co.uk **web:** www.themasterbuilders.co.uk
dir: *M27 junction 2, follow Beaulieu signs. At T-junction left onto B3056, 1st left to Buckler's Hard. Hotel 2 miles on left before village.*

The tranquil Beaulieu River, on the Beaulieu estate, is the setting for this delightful property that dates from the time when many naval ships were built in Buckler's Hard. The main house bedrooms are full of historical features and are of individual design, and in addition there are some bedrooms in the newer wing. Public areas include a popular bar and guest lounge, while the terrace and gardens are ideal for alfresco dining in the summer months. Award-winning cuisine is served in the stylish dining room.

Rooms: 26 (18 annexe) (4 family) (8 GF) **Facilities:** FTV WiFi ⌁ Xmas New Year **Conf:** Class 30 Board 20 Theatre 40 **Services:** Night porter **Parking:** 40 **Notes:** LB Civ Wed 100

Beaulieu Hotel
★★★ 82% HOTEL

tel: 023 8029 3344 & 0800 444 441 **Beaulieu Road SO42 7YQ**
email: beaulieu@newforesthotels.co.uk **web:** www.newforesthotels.co.uk
dir: *M27 junction 1, A337 towards Lyndhurst. Left at lights, through Lyndhurst, right onto B3056, hotel in 3 miles.*

Located in the heart of the beautiful New Forest National Park and close to Beaulieu Road railway station, this popular, small hotel provides an ideal base for exploring the area. Once a coaching inn, the hotel now particularly welcomes families; children will delight in seeing the ponies on the doorstep. Bedrooms, all with free WiFi and Freeview TVs, range from cosy Keeper rooms to Crown rooms which also have four-posters and iPod docking stations. Classic dishes and local produce is served in the adjacent gastro pub, the Drift Inn.

Rooms: 35 (14 annexe) (5 family) (4 GF) ☏ **S** fr £55 **D** fr £69 (including breakfast)* **Facilities:** FTV WiFi ⌁ HL ⌖ Xmas New Year **Conf:** Class 100 Board 100 Theatre 250 **Services:** Lift **Parking:** 60 **Notes:** LB Civ Wed 200

BECCLES
Suffolk   Map 13 TM48

Waveney House Hotel
★★★ 82% HOTEL

tel: 01502 712270 **Puddingmoor NR34 9PL**
email: enquiries@waveneyhousehotel.co.uk **web:** www.waveneyhousehotel.co.uk
dir: *From A146 onto Common Lane North, left into Pound Road, left into Ravensmere, right onto Smallgate, right onto Old Market, continue to Puddingmoor.*

Waveney House is an exceptionally well presented, privately-owned hotel situated by the River Waveney on the edge of this busy little market town. The stylish public rooms include a smart lounge bar and a contemporary Riverside Restaurant with views over the river. The bar menu is sure to include something for everyone. All bedrooms have individually designed decor, and second-floor rooms include vaulted oak-beamed rafters. Some also enjoy picturesque River Waveney and Waveney Marsh views, and two bridal suites are available.

Rooms: 12 (3 family) ☏ **S** fr £90 **D** fr £100 (including breakfast)* **Facilities:** FTV WiFi Xmas New Year **Conf:** Class 100 Board 50 Theatre 160 **Services:** Night porter **Parking:** 45 **Notes:** Civ Wed 80

BEDFORD
Bedfordshire   Map 12 TL04

Barns Hotel
★★★★ 80% HOTEL

tel: 01234 270044 **Cardington Rd MK44 3SA**
email: reservations@barnshotelbedford.co.uk **web:** www.barnshotelbedford.co.uk
dir: *M1 junction 13, A421, approximately 10 miles to A603 Sandy/Bedford exit, hotel on right at 2nd roundabout.*

A tranquil location on the outskirts of Bedford, friendly staff and well-equipped bedrooms all combine to make this a good choice. Cosy day rooms and two informal bars add to the hotel's appeal, while large windows in the restaurant make the most of the view over the river. The original barn houses the conference and function suite.

Rooms: 49 (18 GF) ☏ **S** fr £95 **D** fr £99* **Facilities:** WiFi Free use of local leisure centre (1 mile) Xmas New Year **Conf:** Class 40 Board 40 Theatre 120 **Services:** Night porter **Parking:** 90 **Notes:** Civ Wed 90

The Bedford Swan Hotel
★★★★ 70% HOTEL

tel: 01234 346565 **The Embankment MK40 1RW**
email: info@bedfordswanhotel.co.uk **web:** www.bedfordswanhotel.co.uk
dir: *Towards Bedford - A421 or A1M/A428.*

This historic hotel successfully combines original features with modern comforts. The bedrooms ooze style and quality, and the needs of the modern traveller are well catered for. The River Room Restaurant offers a varied choice of freshly prepared dishes. The hotel also offers meeting and function rooms, spa facilities and secure parking.

Rooms: 113 (10 family) **S** fr £199 **D** fr £199* **Facilities:** Spa STV FTV WiFi ⌁ ⌖ Xmas New Year **Conf:** Class 40 Board 60 Theatre 250 **Services:** Lift Night porter Air con **Parking:** 80 **Notes:** LB Civ Wed 250

B

Premier Inn Bedford (Priory Marina)

Premier Inn

BUDGET HOTEL

tel: 0871 527 8066 (Calls cost 13p per minute plus your phone company's access charge) **Priory Country Park, Barkers Lane MK41 9DJ**
web: www.premierinn.com
dir: *M1 junction 13, A421, A6, A428 signed Cambridge. Cross River Ouse, right at next roundabout into Barkers Lane. Follow Priory Country Park signs. Hotel adjacent to Priory Marina Beefeater.*

High quality, budget accommodation ideal for both families and business travellers. Spacious, en suite bedrooms feature free WiFi and tea and coffee making facilities, and in most hotels, Freeview TV is also available. The adjacent family restaurant features a wide and varied menu.

Rooms: 57

Premier Inn Bedford South (A421)

Premier Inn

BUDGET HOTEL

tel: 0871 527 9410 (Calls cost 13p per minute plus your phone company's access charge) **Marsh Leys, Kempston MK42 7DN**
web: www.premierinn.com
dir: *See website for directions.*

Rooms: 60

| BELTON | Map 11 SK93 |
| Lincolnshire | |

Belton Woods

★★★★ 77% HOTEL

QHOTELS
INSPIRED BY YOU

tel: 01476 593200 **NG32 2LN**
email: beltonreception@qhotels.co.uk **web:** www.qhotels.co.uk
dir: *A1 to Gonerby Moor Services. B1174 towards Great Gonerby. At top of hill turn left towards Manthorpe/Belton. At T-junction turn left onto A607. Hotel 0.25 mile on left.*

Beautifully located amidst 475 acres of picturesque countryside, this is a destination venue for lovers of sport, especially golf, as well as a relaxing executive retreat for seminars. Comfortable and well-equipped accommodation complements the elegant and spacious public areas, which provide a good choice of drinking, dining and relaxing options.

Rooms: 136 (136 family) (68 GF) ↑ **S** fr £95 **D** fr £109 (including breakfast)*
Facilities: Spa FTV WiFi ↳ HL 🕐 ♨ 45 🏌 Gym Squash Outdoor activity centre Xmas New Year **Conf:** Class 160 Board 80 Theatre 270 **Services:** Lift Night porter **Parking:** 350 **Notes:** LB Civ Wed 200

| BEMBRIDGE | Map 5 SZ68 |
| Isle of Wight | |

Bembridge Coast Hotel

★★★ 79% HOTEL

WARNERLEISUREHOTELS
We're all grown up

tel: 01983 873931 **Fishermans Walk PO35 5TH**
web: www.warnerleisurehotels.co.uk
dir: *A3055 Ryde to Sandown, approximately 1.5 miles, left at lights into Carpenter's Road to St Helens. At mini-roundabout 2nd exit onto A3395 signed Bembridge. In Bembridge follow one-way system to right, left after bakery into Forelands Road. 1 mile, left into Lane End Road. Follow to end, right to hotel entrance.*

This hotel occupies a delightfully peaceful location on the east coast of the Isle of Wight in 23-acre grounds. The accommodation is comfortable, and there are a number of rooms with sea views for which a small supplementary charge applies. A full activities itinerary ensures that guests can make the most of what the hotel, and this beautiful island, has to offer. The helpful reservations team can also arrange ferry bookings from the UK mainland. Please note that this is an adults-only (minimum 21 years old) hotel.

Rooms: 258 (30 annexe) (76 GF) ↑ **S** fr £179 **D** fr £378 (including breakfast & dinner)* **Facilities:** Spa FTV WiFi HL 🕐 ♨ 🏊 Gym Tropicarium Archery Rifle shooting Crossbow Indoor and outdoor bowls Steam room Sauna 🎵 Xmas New Year **Services:** Lift Night porter **Parking:** 154 **Notes:** No children 21 years

| BERWICK-UPON-TWEED | Map 21 NT95 |
| Northumberland | |

HIGHLY RECOMMENDED

Queens Head

★★★ 86% SMALL HOTEL

tel: 01289 307852 **Sandgate TD15 1EP**
email: info@queensheadberwick.co.uk **web:** www.queensheadberwick.co.uk
dir: *A1 towards centre and town hall, into High Street. Right at bottom to Hide Hill.*

The Queens Head is a small hotel situated in the town centre, close to the old walls of this former garrison town. Bedrooms provide many thoughtful extras as standard. Dining remains a strong aspect with a carte menu that offers an impressive choice of tasty, freshly prepared dishes served in the comfortable lounge or dining room.

Rooms: 6 (1 family) ↑ **S** fr £84 **D** fr £99 (including breakfast)* **Facilities:** STV FTV WiFi ↳ **Services:** Night porter

| BETCHWORTH | Map 6 TQ25 |
| Surrey | |

Hartsfield Manor Hotel

[U]

tel: 01737 845300 **Sandy Lane RH3 7AA**
email: hotel@hartsfieldmanor.co.uk **web:** www.hartsfieldmanor.co.uk
dir: *Under 5 miles from Redhill train station and M25 junction 8.*

Hartsfield Manor is perfectly located in a quiet location in Betchworth and within very easy access of Dorking, Reigate and Gatwick Airport. This former Victorian Manor House still offers plenty of original charm and character yet all of the rooms are modern and well equipped for both todays corporate and leisure customer. The restaurant and bar are open daily and there are extensive conference and meeting facilities available on site.

Rooms: 50 (16 annexe) (6 family) (20 GF) ↑ **S** fr £59 **D** fr £79* **Facilities:** FTV WiFi ↳ Gym **Conf:** Class 60 Board 40 Theatre 100 **Services:** Night porter **Parking:** 100 **Notes:** Closed 1st week January Civ Wed 90

| BEVERLEY | Map 17 TA03 |
| East Riding of Yorkshire | |

Premier Inn Beverley Town Centre

Premier Inn

BUDGET HOTEL

tel: 0871 527 9490 (Calls cost 13p per minute plus your phone company's access charge) **Flemingate Centre HU17 0NQ**
web: www.premierinn.com
dir: *From north: From York on A1079, at roundabout onto A1174, follow Flemingate Centre Car Park signs. From south: M62 junction 38, B1230. 7 miles, left into Wold Road. 1 mile, right into Walkington. Left into Coppleflat Lane, to Killingwoldgraves. At roundabout 3rd exit onto A1174, follow Flemingate Centre Car Park signs.*

High quality, budget accommodation ideal for both families and business travellers. Spacious, en suite bedrooms feature free WiFi and tea and coffee making facilities, and in most hotels, Freeview TV is also available. The adjacent family restaurant features a wide and varied menu.

Rooms: 80

B

BEWDLEY
Worcestershire

Map 2100 SO77

Mercure Bewdley The Heath Hotel

★★★★ 69% COUNTRY HOUSE HOTEL

tel: 01299 406402 & 0844 815 9033 (Calls cost 7p per minute plus your phone company's access charge) **Habberley Road DY12 1LA**
email: info@mercurebewdley.co.uk **web:** www.mercurebewdley.co.uk
dir: *A456 towards Kidderminster to ring road, follow signs to Bewdley. Pass Safari Park then exit A456/Town Centre, take sharp right after 200 yards onto B4190, hotel 400 yards on right.*

This 19th-century property is set in 20 acres of neat landscaped grounds in the Worcestershire countryside, close to West Midland Safari Park. The bedrooms are modern and well equipped; some rooms have great views of the grounds. Public rooms include a choice of lounges and the brasserie restaurant; the property also boasts great leisure facilities that include a coffee shop, a hairdresser and a 25-metre swimming pool.

Rooms: 44 (9 family) (17 GF) ⚓ **S** fr £65 **D** fr £75* **Facilities:** FTV WiFi ⌕ ⌖ ♨ Gym Beauty treatment room Sauna Steam room Spa bath New Year **Conf:** Class 150 Board 80 Theatre 450 **Services:** Night porter **Parking:** 150 **Notes:** LB Civ Wed 350

BEXHILL
East Sussex

Map 6 TQ70

The Cooden Beach Hotel

★★★ 84% HOTEL

tel: 01424 842281 **Cooden Beach TN39 4TT**
email: rooms@thecoodenbeachhotel.co.uk **web:** www.thecoodenbeachhotel.co.uk
dir: *A259 towards Bexhill. Signed at roundabout in Little Common Village. Hotel at end of road in Cooden, just past railway station.*

This privately owned hotel is situated in private gardens which have direct access to the beach. With a train station within walking distance, the location is perfectly suited for both business and leisure guests. Bedrooms are comfortably appointed, and public areas include a spacious restaurant, lounge, bar and leisure centre with swimming pool.

Rooms: 41 (8 annexe) (10 family) (4 GF) ⚓ **Facilities:** FTV WiFi ⌕ ⌖ Gym Sauna Steam room Spa bath Beauty treatment room Xmas New Year **Conf:** Class 40 Board 40 Theatre 150 **Services:** Night porter **Parking:** 60 **Notes:** Civ Wed 160

BEXLEYHEATH
Greater London

Map 6 TQ47

Premier Inn London Bexleyheath

 Premier Inn

BUDGET HOTEL

tel: 0871 527 9562 (Calls cost 13p per minute plus your phone company's access charge) **51 Albion Road DA6 7AR**
web: www.premierinn.com
dir: *From M25 follow sings for M1 and M11. Take A2(W) exit towards London (southeast and central)/Bexleyheath). Merge onto A2, take A223 signed Bexley/Bexleyheath Town Centre/A220. At roundabout take 1st exit into Bourne Road, left into Albion Road (A207). At roundabout 3rd exit, hotel on left.*

High quality, budget accommodation ideal for both families and business travellers. Spacious, en suite bedrooms feature free WiFi and tea and coffee making facilities, and in most hotels, Freeview TV is also available. The adjacent family restaurant features a wide and varied menu.

Rooms: 92

BIBURY
Gloucestershire

Map 5 SP10

Swan Hotel

★★★★ 78% HOTEL

 COTSWOLD INNS & HOTELS

tel: 01285 740695 **GL7 5NW**
email: info@swanhotel.co.uk **web:** www.cotswold-inns-hotels.co.uk
dir: *9 miles south of Burford A40 onto B4425. 6 miles north of Cirencester A4179 onto B4425.*

This hotel, built in the 17th century as a coaching inn, is set in peaceful and picturesque surroundings. It provides well-equipped and smartly presented accommodation, including four luxury cottage suites set just outside the main hotel. The elegant public areas are comfortable and have feature fireplaces. There is a choice of dining options to suit all tastes.

Rooms: 22 (4 annexe) (1 family) ⚓ **S** fr £150 **D** fr £180 (including breakfast)* **Facilities:** FTV WiFi ⌕ Xmas New Year **Conf:** Class 50 Board 32 Theatre 80 **Services:** Lift Night porter **Parking:** 22 **Notes:** Civ Wed 100

BICESTER
Oxfordshire

Map 11 SP52

Premier Inn Bicester

 Premier Inn

BUDGET HOTEL

tel: 0871 527 9394 (Calls cost 13p per minute plus your phone company's access charge) **Oxford Road OX26 1BT**
web: www.premierinn.com
dir: *M40 junction 9, A41 towards Bicester. 1.5 miles, hotel on left adjacent to Brewers Fayre.*

High quality, budget accommodation ideal for both families and business travellers. Spacious, en suite bedrooms feature free WiFi and tea and coffee making facilities, and in most hotels, Freeview TV is also available. The adjacent family restaurant features a wide and varied menu.

Rooms: 84

BIDEFORD
Devon

Map 3 SS42

The Royal Hotel

★★★ 76% HOTEL

 Brend Hotels

tel: 01237 472005 **Barnstaple Street EX39 4AE**
email: reservations@royalbideford.co.uk **web:** www.royalbideford.co.uk
dir: *At eastern end of old Bideford Bridge.*

A quiet and relaxing hotel, The Royal Hotel is located near the river within a five-minute walk of the busy town centre and the quay. The bright, well maintained public areas retain much of the charm and style of the hotel's 17th-century origins, particularly in the wood-panelled Kingsley Suite. Bedrooms are well equipped and comfortable. Both the meals and lounge snacks are very good.

The Royal Hotel

Rooms: 32 (2 family) (2 GF) ☎ **S** fr £65 **D** fr £85* **Facilities:** FTV WiFi ☇ Xmas New Year **Conf:** Class 100 Board 100 Theatre 100 **Services:** Lift Night porter **Parking:** 70 **Notes:** LB Civ Wed 130

Durrant House Hotel

★★★ ⏃ HOTEL

tel: 01237 472361 **Heywood Road, Northam EX39 3QB**
email: info@durranthousehotel.com **web:** www.durranthousehotel.com
dir: *A39 to Bideford, over New Torridge Bridge, right at roundabout, hotel 500 yards on right.*

This large hotel offers bedrooms with Italian-marble bathrooms, and all include a hospitality tray, hairdryer, TV, clock radio and an iron with ironing board; superior rooms have wonderful views of the Torridge estuary and Taw Valley, plus rain showers, sofas and luxury toiletries. The fine dining, oak-panelled Olive Tree Restaurant offers dishes based on locally sourced produce.

Rooms: 125 (20 family) ☎ **S** fr £50 **D** fr £80 (including breakfast)* **Facilities:** Spa FTV WiFi ⚡ Gym Sauna Sun shower Pool table ♫ Xmas New Year **Conf:** Class 100 Board 80 Theatre 350 **Services:** Lift Night porter **Parking:** 100 **Notes:** Civ Wed 200

BILDESTON
Suffolk   Map 13 TL94

The Bildeston Crown

★★★ 88% ◉◉ HOTEL

tel: 01449 740510 **104-106 High Street IP7 7EB**
email: reception@thebildestoncrown.co.uk **web:** www.thebildestoncrown.co.uk
dir: *A12 junction 31, B1070 towards Hadleigh. At T-junction left onto A1141, right onto B1115. Hotel 0.5 mile.*

The Bildeston Crown is a delightful Grade II former coaching inn situated in a peaceful village location just a short drive from the historic town of Lavenham. The public areas feature beams, exposed brickwork and oak floors, with contemporary style decor. There is a choice of bars, a lounge and a restaurant. The individually designed bedrooms, including a romantic four-poster room, have well co-ordinated fabrics and modern facilities including internet access.

Rooms: 12 ☎ **Facilities:** STV FTV WiFi Xmas New Year **Conf:** Class 25 Board 16 Theatre 40 **Services:** Lift Night porter **Parking:** 30 **Notes:** LB

BILLINGHAM
County Durham   Map 19 NZ47

Wynyard Hall Hotel

★★★★ ◉◉ HOTEL

tel: 01740 644811 **Wynyard TS22 5NF**
email: reception@wynyardhall.co.uk **web:** www.wynyardhall.co.uk
dir: *A19, A1027 towards Stockton. At roundabout take B1274 (Junction Road). At next roundabout take A177 (Durham Road). Right onto Wynyard Road signed Wolviston. Left into estate.*

Drive through the gates, over the lion bridge, and Wynyard Hall will immediately impress with its grandeur and elegance. The opulent public areas are as much a feature of the property as are the grounds and gardens. The individually designed bedrooms and suites are stunning, with a combination of modern and period style furniture. The elegant, award-winning Wellington Restaurant is also impressive. The Essential Time Treatment Suite offers many relaxing therapies and beauty treatments. As a wedding venue, the hall provides the option for a civil ceremony, or a religious service in the chapel, followed by a memorable reception.

Rooms: 24 (5 annexe) (1 family) ☎ **S** fr £205 **D** fr £205 (including breakfast)* **Facilities:** Spa FTV WiFi ☇ Clay pigeon shooting Archery Hawk walk Boot camp Walled garden Farmshop Xmas New Year **Conf:** Class 680 Board 100 Theatre 1000 **Services:** Lift Night porter **Parking:** 500 **Notes:** LB Civ Wed 180

BILSBORROW
Lancashire   Map 18 SD53

Premier Inn Preston North

Premier Inn

BUDGET HOTEL

tel: 0871 527 8912 (Calls cost 13p per minute plus your phone company's access charge) **Garstang Road PR3 0RN**
web: www.premierinn.com
dir: *4 miles from M6 junction 32 on A6 towards Garstang. 7 miles from Preston.*

High quality, budget accommodation ideal for both families and business travellers. Spacious, en suite bedrooms feature free WiFi and tea and coffee making facilities, and in most hotels, Freeview TV is also available. The adjacent family restaurant features a wide and varied menu.

Rooms: 42

B

BINGLEY
West Yorkshire

Map 19 SE13

Mercure Bradford, Bankfield Hotel

★★★ 76% HOTEL

tel: 01274 519300 & 0844 815 9004 (Calls cost 7p per minute plus your phone company's access charge) **Bradford Road BD16 1TU**
email: info@mercurebradford.co.uk **web:** www.mercurebradford.co.uk
dir: From M62 junction 26 onto M606, at roundabout follow signs for A650 Skipton/Keighley, hotel 2 miles from Shipley.

This striking Gothic-style mansion house is set in landscaped gardens and is a short walk from the River Aire. The rural setting is peaceful, yet the hotel is also convenient for Bradford and Leeds, and is understandably a popular wedding venue; it also caters well for corporate guests, with extensive meeting facilities available in a designated conference centre. Free WiFi access is provided throughout the hotel.

Rooms: 103 (8 family) ☎ S fr £50 D fr £60* **Facilities:** FTV WiFi ॐ **Conf:** Class 200 Board 80 Theatre 350 **Services:** Lift Night porter **Parking:** 350 **Notes:** Civ Wed 350

BIRCHANGER GREEN MOTORWAY SERVICE AREA (M11)
Essex

Map 6 TL52

Days Inn London Stansted Airport - M11

AA Advertised

tel: 01279 656477 **Birchanger Services, M11 Motorway CM23 5QZ**
email: daysinnlsa@welcomebreak.co.uk **web:** www.welcomebreak.co.uk
dir: M11 junction 8.

This modern building offers accommodation in smart, spacious and well-equipped bedrooms, suitable for families and business travellers, and all with en suite bathrooms. Continental breakfast is available and other refreshments may be taken at the nearby family restaurant.

Rooms: 60 (12 family) (29 GF) (8 smoking) **Facilities:** FTV WiFi ॐ **Services:** Night porter **Parking:** 60

BIRKENHEAD
Merseyside

Map 15 SJ38

Premier Inn Birkenhead Town Centre

Premier Inn

BUDGET HOTEL

tel: 0871 527 9630 (Calls cost 13p per minute plus your phone company's access charge) **Conway Street CH41 5AP**
web: www.premierinn.com
dir: M53 junction 5, follow Birkenhead, A41 and New Chester Road signs. Straight on at 3 roundabouts. Keep left towards A41/New Ferry Bypass. Keep right, follow signs for Wallasey/All Docks. Under flyover, left into Market Street. 1st left into Hamilton Street. Hotel on right.

High quality, budget accommodation ideal for both families and business travellers. Spacious, en suite bedrooms feature free WiFi and tea and coffee making facilities, and in most hotels, Freeview TV is also available. The adjacent family restaurant features a wide and varied menu.

Rooms: 67

Premier Inn Wirral (Greasby)

Premier Inn

BUDGET HOTEL

tel: 0871 527 9176 (Calls cost 13p per minute plus your phone company's access charge) **Greasby Road, Greasby CH49 2PP**
web: www.premierinn.com
dir: 9 miles from Liverpool city centre. 2 miles from M53 junction 2. Just off B5139.

Rooms: 30

BIRMINGHAM
West Midlands

Map 10 SP08

See also **Bromsgrove, Lea Marston, Oldbury and Sutton Coldfield (Royal)**

Hotel du Vin & Bistro Birmingham

Hotel du Vin & Bistro

★★★★ 81% ◎ TOWN HOUSE HOTEL

tel: 0121 794 3005 & 0844 736 4250 (Calls cost 5p per minute plus your phone company's access charge) **Church Street B3 2NR**
email: info@birmingham.hotelduvin.com
web: www.hotelduvin.com/locations/birmingham
dir: M6 junction 6/A38(M) to city centre, over flyover. Keep left and exit at St Chads Circus signed Jewellery Quarter. At lights and roundabout take 1st exit, follow signs for Colmore Row, opposite cathedral. Right into Church Street, across Barwick Street. Hotel on right.

The former Birmingham Eye Hospital has become a chic and sophisticated hotel. The stylish, high-ceilinged rooms, all with a wine theme, are luxuriously appointed and feature stunning bathrooms, sumptuous duvets and Egyptian cotton sheets. The Bistro offers relaxed dining and a top-notch wine list, while other attractions include a champagne bar, a wine boutique and a health club.

Rooms: 66 ☎ **Facilities:** Spa STV FTV WiFi ॐ Gym Steam room Sauna Plunge shower Xmas New Year **Conf:** Class 40 Board 40 Theatre 84 **Services:** Lift Night porter Air con **Notes:** LB Civ Wed 84

Novotel Birmingham Centre

NOVOTEL
HOTELS & RESORTS

★★★★ 76% HOTEL

tel: 0121 643 2000 **70 Broad Street B1 2HT**
email: h1077@accor.com **web:** www.novotel.com
dir: M6 junction 6, A38(M) Aston Expressway, A456 towards Kidderminster.

This large, modern, purpose-built hotel benefits from an excellent city centre location, with the bonus of secure parking. Bedrooms are spacious, modern and well equipped especially for business users; four rooms have facilities for guests with disabilities. Public areas include the Garden Brasserie, function rooms and a fitness suite with sauna and steam room.

Rooms: 148 (148 family) ☎ **Facilities:** WiFi ॐ Gym Fitness room Cardiovascular equipment Sauna Steam room New Year **Conf:** Class 120 Board 90 Theatre 300 **Services:** Lift **Parking:** 53

Macdonald Burlington Hotel

MACDONALD
HOTELS & RESORTS

★★★★ 75% HOTEL

tel: 0344 879 9019 **Burlington Arcade, 126 New Street B2 4JQ**
email: events.burlington@macdonald-hotels.co.uk
web: www.macdonaldhotels.co.uk/our-hotels/macdonald-burlington-hotel/
dir: *M6 junction 6, A38, follow city centre signs.*

The Burlington's original Victorian grandeur – the marble and iron staircases and the high ceilings – blend seamlessly with modern facilities. Bedrooms are equipped to a good standard and public areas include a stylish bar and coffee lounge. The Scottish Steak Club Restaurant specialises in contemporary dishes using fresh, local produce.

Rooms: 114 (6 family) **Facilities:** FTV WiFi HL New Year **Conf:** Class 200 Board 80 Theatre 500 **Services:** Lift Night porter Air con **Notes:** Closed 24–26 December Civ Wed 400

Hallmark Birmingham

★★★★ 74% HOTEL

tel: 0330 028 3410 **225 Hagley Road, Edgbaston B16 9RY**
email: birmingham.hallmark@hallmarkhotels.co.uk **web:** www.hallmarkhotels.co.uk
dir: *From A38 follow signs for ICC into Broad Street, towards Five Ways island, take underpass to Hagley Road. Hotel 0.5 mile.*

Located just a few minutes from the city's central attractions and with the benefit of excellent parking, this hotel provides a range of comfortable and well-equipped bedrooms. A modern lounge bar and contemporary restaurant offer a good range of dining options.

Rooms: 135 (36 family) **Facilities:** STV FTV WiFi Gym Xmas New Year **Conf:** Class 90 Board 50 Theatre 170 **Services:** Lift Night porter **Parking:** 120

Malmaison Birmingham

Malmaison
hotels that dare to be different

★★★★ 73% HOTEL

tel: 0121 246 5000 **1 Wharfside Street, The Mailbox B1 1RD**
email: birmingham@malmaison.com **web:** www.malmaison.com/locations/birmingham
dir: *M6 junction 6, A38 towards Birmingham. Hotel within The Mailbox, signed from A38.*

The 'Mailbox' development, of which this stylish and contemporary hotel is a part, incorporates the very best in fashionable shopping outlets, an array of restaurants and ample parking. The air-conditioned bedrooms are stylishly decorated and feature comprehensive facilities. Public rooms include a contemporary bar and brasserie which prove a hit with guests and locals alike. Gymtonic, and a Petit Spa offering rejuvenating treatments are also available.

Rooms: 192 **Facilities:** Spa STV FTV WiFi Gym Sauna Steam room **Conf:** Class 40 Board 24 Theatre 150 **Services:** Lift Night porter Air con **Notes:** LB Civ Wed 120

Edgbaston Palace Hotel

★★★ 75% HOTEL

tel: 0121 452 1577 **198-200 Hagley Road, Edgbaston B16 9PQ**
email: enquiries@edgbastonpalacehotel.com **web:** www.edgbastonpalacehotel.com
dir: *M5 junction 3 north, A456 for 4.3 miles. Hotel on right.*

Dating back to the 19th century, this Grade II listed Victorian property has bedrooms that are modern, well appointed and offer good comfort levels. The hospitality is warm, personal and refreshing. Supervised children under 18 are welcome.

Rooms: 48 (21 annexe) (3 family) (16 GF) **Facilities:** FTV WiFi **Conf:** Class 70 Board 60 Theatre 200 **Services:** Night porter **Parking:** 70 **Notes:** Civ Wed

Great Barr Hotel & Conference Centre

★★★ 68% HOTEL

tel: 0121 357 1141 **Pear Tree Drive, Newton Road B43 6HS**
email: sales@thegreatbarrhotel.com **web:** www.thegreatbarrhotel.com
dir: *M6 junction 7, at Scott Arms crossroads right towards West Bromwich (A4010) Newton Road. Hotel 1 mile on right.*

This busy hotel, situated in a leafy residential area, is particularly popular with business clients; the hotel has excellent, state-of-the-art training and seminar facilities. There is a traditional oak-panelled bar and formal restaurant, and bedrooms are appointed to a good standard with the expected amenities.

Rooms: 92 (6 family) **S** fr £45 **D** fr £65* **Facilities:** STV WiFi New Year **Conf:** Class 90 Board 60 Theatre 200 **Services:** Night porter **Parking:** 200 **Notes:** LB Civ Wed 200

Premier Inn Birmingham Broad St Canal Side

Premier Inn

BUDGET HOTEL

tel: 0871 527 8078 (Calls cost 13p per minute plus your phone company's access charge) **20 Bridge Street B1 2JH**
web: www.premierinn.com
dir: *M6 junction 6, A38(M) towards city centre. Follow signs for city centre/ICC/A456 (Broad Street). Left at Hyatt Hotel, hotel on right at bottom of Bridge Street.*

High quality, budget accommodation ideal for both families and business travellers. Spacious, en suite bedrooms feature free WiFi and tea and coffee making facilities, and in most hotels, Freeview TV is also available. The adjacent family restaurant features a wide and varied menu.

Rooms: 116

Premier Inn Birmingham Broad Street (Brindley Place)

Premier Inn

BUDGET HOTEL

tel: 0871 527 8076 (Calls cost 13p per minute plus your phone company's access charge) **80 Broad Street B15 1AU**
web: www.premierinn.com
dir: *M6 junction 6, A38(M) (Aston Expressway). Follow City Centre, ICC and NIA signs into Broad Street. Right into Sheepcote Street. 2nd left at roundabout into Essington Street. Hotel on left. Note: for sat nav use B16 8AL.*

Rooms: 58

Premier Inn Birmingham Central East

Premier Inn

BUDGET HOTEL

tel: 0871 527 8080 (Calls cost 13p per minute plus your phone company's access charge) **Richard Street, Aston B7 4AA**
web: www.premierinn.com
dir: *M6 junction 6, signed city centre. A38(M) signed A4540 (ring road). At roundabout 1st exit 50 metres left into Richard Street, hotel on left, barrier access to car park.*

Rooms: 100

B

BIRMINGHAM *continued*

Premier Inn Birmingham Central (Hagley Road)

Premier Inn

BUDGET HOTEL

tel: 0871 527 8082 (Calls cost 13p per minute plus your phone company's access charge) **Hagley Road B16 9NY**
web: www.premierinn.com
dir: *M6 junction 6, A38(M) (Aston Express Way). Follow city centre, ICC and NIA signs, into Broad Street. From M5 junction 3, A456 for approximately 3 miles, hotel on left.*

Rooms: 65

Premier Inn Birmingham City Centre New Street

Premier Inn

BUDGET HOTEL

tel: 0871 527 9442 (Calls cost 13p per minute plus your phone company's access charge) **Birmingham Exchange Buildings, Stephenson Place B2 4NH**
web: www.premierinn.com
dir: *M6 junction 6, A38 (Corporation Street) keep right at fork. Exit towards New Street, merge into Suffolk Street Queensway. At roundabout 1st exit into Smallbrook Queensway, left into Hill Street, right into Queen's Drive. Multi-storey parking at New Street Station, The Pallasades or Bull Ring.*

Rooms: 140

Premier Inn Birmingham City Centre (Waterloo St)

Premier Inn

BUDGET HOTEL

tel: 0871 527 8074 (Calls cost 13p per minute plus your phone company's access charge) **3–6 Waterloo Street B2 5PG**
web: www.premierinn.com
dir: *M6 junction 6, A38 (Corporation Street). Follow West Bromwich/A41 signs. Merge into St Chad's Queensway. 2nd exit for Great Charles Street Queensway, becomes Livery Street. Left into Waterloo Street.*

Rooms: 152

Premier Inn Birmingham (Great Barr/M6 Jct 7)

Premier Inn

BUDGET HOTEL

tel: 0871 527 8072 (Calls cost 13p per minute plus your phone company's access charge) **Birmingham Road, Great Barr B43 7AG**
web: www.premierinn.com
dir: *M6 junction 7, A34 towards Walsall. Hotel on left behind Beacon Harvester.*

Rooms: 33

Premier Inn Birmingham South (Hall Green)

Premier Inn

BUDGET HOTEL

tel: 0871 527 8092 (Calls cost 13p per minute plus your phone company's access charge) **Stratford Road, Hall Green B28 9ES**
web: www.premierinn.com
dir: *M42 junction 4, A34 towards Shirley signed Birmingham. Straight on at 6 roundabouts. At 7th roundabout 4th exit. Hotel on left.*

Rooms: 52

Premier Inn Birmingham South (Longbridge St)

Premier Inn

BUDGET HOTEL

tel: 0871 527 9434 (Calls cost 13p per minute plus your phone company's access charge) **2 College Street, Longbridge B31 2US**
web: www.premierinn.com
dir: *M5 junction 4, A38 towards Birmingham. 3 miles (pass Morrisons and McDonald's) to roundabout. 1st exit towards A38 (Birmingham). Right at 1st lights signed Longbridge train station. 1st right at Sainsburys, hotel on right. Note: for sat nav use B31 2TW.*

Rooms: 75

BIRMINGHAM AIRPORT
West Midlands
Map 10 SP18

Novotel Birmingham Airport

★★★★ 74% HOTEL

NOVOTEL
HOTELS & RESORTS

tel: 0121 782 7000 **B26 3QL**
email: H1158@accor.com **web:** www.novotel.com
dir: *M42 junction 6, A45 to Birmingham, signed to airport. Hotel opposite main terminal.*

This smartly decorated hotel with air conditioning throughout its public areas and bedrooms, benefits from being less than a minute's walk from the main terminal of Birmingham International Airport. Spacious bedrooms are comfortable, and modern bathrooms with powerful showers are stylish. The Elements bar and restaurant has a great atmosphere and a fitness room is available on site. Long-stay car parking packages can be arranged.

Rooms: 195 (24 family) **Facilities:** FTV WiFi Gym Fitness room **Conf:** Class 10 Board 20 Theatre 35 **Services:** Lift Night porter Air con

---

BIRMINGHAM [NATIONAL EXHIBITION CENTRE]
West Midlands
Map 10 SP18

Moor Hall Hotel & Spa

★★★★ 80% @@ HOTEL

PREMIER | BEST WESTERN

tel: 0121 308 3751 **Moor Hall Drive, Four Oaks B75 6LN**
email: mail@moorhallhotel.co.uk **web:** www.moorhallhotel.co.uk

(for full entry see Sutton Coldfield (Royal))

Nailcote Hall

★★★★ 76% @ HOTEL

CLASSIC BRITISH HOTELS

tel: 024 7646 6174 **Nailcote Lane, Berkswell CV7 7DE**
email: info@nailcotehall.co.uk **web:** www.nailcotehall.co.uk

(for full entry see Balsall Common)

Arden Hotel & Leisure Club

★★★ 77% HOTEL

tel: 01675 443221 **Coventry Road, Bickenhill B92 0EH**
email: enquiries@ardenhotel.co.uk **web:** www.ardenhotel.co.uk
dir: *M42 junction 6, A45 towards Birmingham. Hotel 0.25 mile on right, just off Birmingham International railway island.*

This smart hotel neighbouring the NEC and Birmingham Airport, offers modern rooms and well-equipped leisure facilities. After dinner in the formal restaurant, the place to relax is the spacious lounge area, or the large snooker room available to resident guests. A buffet breakfast is served in the bright and airy Meeting Place. Free WiFi and on-site parking are also available.

Rooms: 216 (6 family) (6 GF) (4 smoking) **Facilities:** Spa FTV WiFi ⓧ Gym ♫ Xmas New Year **Conf:** Class 40 Board 60 Theatre 200 **Services:** Lift Night porter **Parking:** 300 **Notes:** Civ Wed 100

Premier Inn Birmingham NEC/Airport

BUDGET HOTEL

tel: 0871 527 8086 (Calls cost 13p per minute plus your phone company's access charge) **Off Bickenhill Parkway, National Exhibition Centre B40 1QA**
web: www.premierinn.com
dir: *M42 junction 6 signed NEC. Turn right towards North Way. Follow Premier Inn signs. Hotel on left at 5th roundabout.*

High quality, budget accommodation ideal for both families and business travellers. Spacious, en suite bedrooms feature free WiFi and tea and coffee making facilities, and in most hotels, Freeview TV is also available. The adjacent family restaurant features a wide and varied menu.

Rooms: 247

BISHOP AUCKLAND	Map 19 NZ22
County Durham	

Premier Inn Bishop Auckland

BUDGET HOTEL

tel: 0871 527 8096 (Calls cost 13p per minute plus your phone company's access charge) **West Auckland Road DL14 9AP**
web: www.premierinn.com
dir: *From south: A1 junction 58, left onto A68 signed Corbridge/Bishop Auckland. At 1st roundabout 2nd exit onto A6072 signed Shildon. Straight on at 4 roundabouts, follow Shildon/Bishop Auckland signs. Hotel approximately 1 mile on left.*

High quality, budget accommodation ideal for both families and business travellers. Spacious, en suite bedrooms feature free WiFi and tea and coffee making facilities, and in most hotels, Freeview TV is also available. The adjacent family restaurant features a wide and varied menu.

Rooms: 60

BISHOP'S STORTFORD	Map 6 TL42
Hertfordshire	

HIGHLY RECOMMENDED

Down Hall Hotel & Spa

★★★★ 88% ⊛ HOTEL

tel: 01279 731441 **Hatfield Heath CM22 7AS**
email: info@downhall.co.uk **web:** www.downhall.co.uk
dir: *A1060, at Hatfield Heath keep left. Right into lane opposite Hunters Meet restaurant, left at end, follow signs.*

This imposing country house hotel is set in 100 acres of mature grounds in a peaceful location just a short drive from Stansted Airport. Bedrooms are generally quite spacious; each is pleasantly decorated, tastefully furnished and equipped with modern facilities. Public rooms include a choice of restaurants, a cocktail bar, two lounges and leisure facilities.

Rooms: 100 (20 GF) ⚫ **S** fr £89 **D** fr £109 (including breakfast)* **Facilities:** Spa FTV WiFi ⚒ ⚒ Gym Giant chess Sauna Steam room Hydrotherapy pool Xmas New Year **Conf:** Class 140 Board 68 Theatre 200 **Services:** Lift Night porter **Parking:** 150 **Notes:** Civ Wed 150

The Great Hallingbury Manor Hotel

★★★★ 73% HOTEL

tel: 01279 506475 **Tilekiln Green, Great Hallingbury CM22 7TJ**
email: info@greathallingburymanor.co.uk **web:** www.greathallingburymanor.co.uk
dir: *M11 junction 8 roundabout take exit to B1256, turn immediately right at petrol station. Under bridge, sharp left bend, continue for 500 yards. Hotel on left.*

This Tudor-style manor is set in lovely landscaped grounds and is surrounded by open countryside. The property is situated close to Stansted Airport, and the major road networks are within easy reach. The interior has a very contemporary feel, and bedrooms are smartly appointed with a range of thoughtful touches; public areas include a choice of lounges, a bar and an open-plan restaurant.

Rooms: 45 (22 annexe) (3 family) (16 GF) ⚫ **Facilities:** FTV WiFi ⓧ Xmas New Year **Conf:** Class 80 Board 30 Theatre 170 **Services:** Night porter **Parking:** 50 **Notes:** LB Civ Wed 170

Ramada London Stansted Airport - M11

AA Advertised

tel: 01279 213900 **Birchanger Services, M11 Motorway CM23 5QZ**
email: ramadalsa@welcomebreak.co.uk **web:** www.welcomebreak.co.uk
dir: *M11 junction 8.*

This modern building offers accommodation in smart, spacious and well-equipped bedrooms, suitable for families and business travellers, and all with en suite bathrooms. There is an attractive lounge area and a dining room where breakfast is served and other refreshments may be taken.

Rooms: 76 (15 family) (16 GF) (8 smoking) ⚫ **Facilities:** FTV WiFi ⓧ **Services:** Lift Air con **Parking:** 100

BLACKBURN	Map 18 SD62
Lancashire	

See also **Langho**

Premier Inn Blackburn South (M65 Jct 4)

BUDGET HOTEL

tel: 0871 527 8100 (Calls cost 13p per minute plus your phone company's access charge) **Off Eccleshill Road, Riversway Drive BB3 0SN**
web: www.premierinn.com
dir: *At M65 junction 4.*

High quality, budget accommodation ideal for both families and business travellers. Spacious, en suite bedrooms feature free WiFi and tea and coffee making facilities, and in most hotels, Freeview TV is also available. The adjacent family restaurant features a wide and varied menu.

Rooms: 62

Premier Inn Blackburn Town Centre Hotel

BUDGET HOTEL

tel: 0871 527 9622 (Calls cost 13p per minute plus your phone company's access charge) **3 Cathedral Square BB1 1FB**
web: www.premierinn.com
dir: *M6 junction 29, M65 (West) towards Blackburn. At junction 4 follow signs for A666/ Blackburn Town Centre, then follow signs for Blackburn Railway Station. On Jubilee Street the car park is adjacent to railway station, hotel opposite.*

Rooms: 60

B

BLACKPOOL
Lancashire
Map 18 SD33

Imperial Hotel
★★★★ 74% HOTEL

tel: 01253 623971 **North Promenade FY1 2HB**
email: agilmore@imperialhotelblackpool.co.uk **web:** www.imperialhotelblackpool.co.uk
dir: M55 junction 2, A583 (North Shore), follow signs to North Promenade. Hotel on seafront, north of tower.

Enjoying a prime seafront location, this grand Victorian hotel offers smartly appointed, well-equipped bedrooms and spacious, elegant public areas. Facilities include a smart leisure club, a comfortable lounge, the No 10 bar and an attractive split-level restaurant that overlooks the seafront. Conferences and functions are extremely well catered for.

Rooms: 180 (16 family) ☏ **S** fr £95 **D** fr £105* **Facilities:** Spa FTV WiFi ⌕ HL ☒ Gym Sauna Hot tub Steam room Xmas New Year **Conf:** Class 240 Board 104 Theatre 600 **Services:** Lift Night porter **Parking:** 150 **Notes:** LB Civ Wed 200

Best Western Carlton Hotel Blackpool
Ⓑ Best Western.
★★★ 76% HOTEL

tel: 01253 628966 **282 North Promenade FY1 2EZ**
email: reception@bwblackpool.com **web:** www.bwblackpool.com
dir: M6 junction 32/M55, follow signs for North Shore. Between Blackpool Tower and Gynn Square.

Enjoying a prime seafront location, this hotel offers bedrooms that are attractively furnished in modern style. Refreshed public areas, including a choice of bar lounge and seaview lounge, are bright and reflect the seaside location. Well cooked meals are served in the elegant restaurant; extensive function facilities are available.

Rooms: 60 (7 family) (3 GF) ☏ **Facilities:** FTV WiFi ⌕ Xmas New Year **Conf:** Class 40 Board 40 Theatre 90 **Services:** Lift Night porter **Parking:** 40 **Notes:** LB Civ Wed 90

Carousel Hotel
★★★ 73% HOTEL

tel: 01253 402642 **663-671 New South Prom FY4 1RN**
email: carousel.reservations@sleepwellhotels.com **web:** www.sleepwellhotels.com
dir: From M55 follow signs to airport, pass airport to lights. Turn right, hotel 100 yards on right.

This friendly seafront hotel, close to the Pleasure Beach, offers smart, contemporary accommodation. Bedrooms are comfortably appointed and have a modern, stylish feel to them. An airy restaurant and a spacious bar/lounge both overlook the Promenade. The hotel has good conference and meeting facilities and its own car park.

Rooms: 92 (22 family) **S** fr £40 **D** fr £50 (including breakfast)* **Facilities:** FTV WiFi ⌕ ♫ Xmas New Year **Conf:** Class 30 Board 40 Theatre 100 **Services:** Lift Night porter **Parking:** 28 **Notes:** Civ Wed 150

Queens Hotel
★★★ 67% HOTEL

Leisureplex
HOLIDAY HOTELS

tel: 01253 342015 **469-471 South Promenade FY4 1AY**
email: queens.blackpool@leisureplex.co.uk **web:** www.leisureplex.co.uk

Queens Hotel is situated on the South Promenade overlooking the Irish Sea, close to the South Pier and Pleasure Beach. The bedrooms are well equipped and some rooms have lovely sea views. The spacious public areas include a choice of lounges, a range of bars, a conservatory and a large dining room as well as a 300-seat theatre bar.

Rooms: 117 (9 family) ☏ **Facilities:** FTV WiFi HL ☒ ♫ Xmas New Year **Conf:** Class 60 Board 60 Theatre 80 **Services:** Lift Night porter **Parking:** 55 **Notes:** Closed January to February

The Viking Hotel
★★ 77% HOTEL

tel: 0844 811 5570 (Calls cost 7p per minute plus your phone company's access charge) & 01253 348411 **479 South Promenade FY4 1AX**
email: reservations@choice-hotels.co.uk **web:** www.choicehotels.co.uk
dir: M55 junction 3, follow Pleasure Beach signs.

In a prime location at the centre of the South Promenade, this hotel offers comfortable accommodation and a warm welcome. Meals are served in the attractive sea view restaurant and entertainment is available nightly in the renowned 'Talk of the Coast' night club. Secure on-site parking is a boon and leisure facilities at sister hotels are also available free of charge.

Rooms: 100 (10 GF) ☏ **S** fr £45 **D** fr £74 (including breakfast & dinner) **Facilities:** FTV WiFi Cabaret club ♫ Xmas New Year **Services:** Lift Night porter **Parking:** 50 **Notes:** LB No children 18 years

New Guilderoy Hotel
★★ 76% SMALL HOTEL

tel: 01253 351547 **57-59 Holmfield Road, North Shore FY2 9RU**
email: simon_connelly@yahoo.com **web:** www.new-guilderoy-hotel-blackpool.co.uk
dir: M55 Blackpool. Follow signs North Shore. Located behind The Cliffs Hotel, Queens Promenade.

This pleasant, personally-run hotel caters for a wide market and sits in a quiet location, away from the hubbub of the town, yet conveniently close to attractions and the famous North Promenade (very handy for the famous illuminations). There is a relaxing lounge and a cosy bar with a very good wine list to choose from. Home-cooked food is a feature here, and menus at both dinner and breakfast offer a good choice.

Rooms: 15 (4 family) ☏ **Facilities:** FTV WiFi Xmas New Year **Notes:** LB Closed 10 November to 22 December RS 2 January to 28 February

B

The Claremont Hotel

★★ 74% HOTEL

tel: 0844 811 5570 (Calls cost 7p per minute plus your phone company's access charge)
& 01253 293122 **270 North Promenade FY1 1SA**
email: reservations@choice-hotels.co.uk **web:** www.choicehotels.co.uk
dir: *M55 junction 3 follow sign for promenade. Hotel beyond North Pier.*

Conveniently situated, the Claremont is a popular family holiday hotel. Bedrooms
are bright and attractively decorated, and extensive public areas include a
spacious air-conditioned restaurant which offers a good choice of dishes. There is a
well-equipped, supervised children's play room, and entertainment is provided
during the season.

Rooms: 143 (50 family) **S** fr £45 **D** fr £84 (including breakfast & dinner)
Facilities: FTV WiFi ⏰ ♫ Xmas New Year **Services:** Lift Night porter **Parking:** 40
Notes: LB

The Cliffs Hotel

★★ 74% HOTEL

tel: 0844 811 5570 (Calls cost 7p per minute plus your phone company's access charge)
& 01253 595559 **Queens Promenade FY2 9SG**
email: reservations@choice-hotels.co.uk **web:** www.choicehotels.co.uk
dir: *M55 junction 3, follow Promenade signs. Hotel just after Gynn roundabout.*

This large, privately owned and extremely popular promenade hotel is within easy
reach of the town centre. The well-equipped bedrooms, including spacious family
rooms, vary in size. Public areas offer an all-day coffee shop, a smart restaurant
and a suite of games rooms where children of all ages are entertained. A modern
gym and leisure pool complete the experience.

Rooms: 163 (47 family) **S** fr £34 **D** fr £68 (including breakfast & dinner)
Facilities: FTV WiFi ⏰ Gym ♫ Xmas New Year **Conf:** Class 210 Board 50 Theatre
475 **Services:** Lift Night porter **Parking:** 30 **Notes:** LB

Silver Stars

The AA Silver Star rating
denotes a Hotel that
we highly recommend.
They have a superior level of
quality within their star rating,
high standards of hospitality,
service and cleanliness.

Lyndene Hotel

★★ Ⓐ HOTEL

tel: 01253 346779 **303/315 Promenade FY1 6AN**
email: enquiries@lyndenehotel.com **web:** www.lyndenehotel.com
dir: *Phone for directions.*

Family run for over 20 years, this hotel is situated in a good location on the
promenade for the attractions. All bedrooms have LCD TVs, safes and hospitality
trays; some rooms are on the ground floor. Public rooms include two air-conditioned
lounges, two restaurants, a games room and an outside seating area and sun
terrace. Plus there's cabaret entertainment every evening, all year round.

Rooms: 141 (60 family) (17 GF) (70 smoking) **Facilities:** FTV WiFi ♫ Xmas New
Year **Services:** Lift Night porter **Parking:** 70 **Notes:** No children 5 years

Hotel Ibis Styles Blackpool

BUDGET HOTEL

tel: 01253 752478 **Talbot Square FY1 1ND**
email: H9148@accor.com **web:** www.focushotels.co.uk/hotels
dir: *M55 junction 4, follow signs for A583 Blackpool North Shore, approximately 4 miles to
seafront. Property on right opposite North Pier entrance.*

Modern, budget hotel offering comfortable accommodation in bright and practical
bedrooms. Breakfast is self-service and dinner is available in the restaurant.

Rooms: 90 (4 family) **S** fr £54 **D** fr £59 (including breakfast)

BLACKPOOL *continued*

Premier Inn Blackpool Airport

BUDGET HOTEL

tel: 0871 527 8106 (Calls cost 13p per minute plus your phone company's access charge) **Squire Gate Lane FY4 2QS**
web: www.premierinn.com
dir: *M55 junction 4, A5230, left at 1st roundabout towards airport. Hotel just before Squires Gate rail station.*

High quality, budget accommodation ideal for both families and business travellers. Spacious, en suite bedrooms feature free WiFi and tea and coffee making facilities, and in most hotels, Freeview TV is also available. The adjacent family restaurant features a wide and varied menu.

Rooms: 39

Premier Inn Blackpool (Bispham)

BUDGET HOTEL

tel: 0871 527 8102 (Calls cost 13p per minute plus your phone company's access charge) **Devonshire Road, Bispham FY2 0AR**
web: www.premierinn.com
dir: *M55 junction 4, A583. At 5th lights turn right (Whitegate Drive). Approximately 4.5 miles onto A587 Devonshire Road.*

Rooms: 67

Premier Inn Blackpool Central

BUDGET HOTEL

tel: 0871 527 8108 (Calls cost 13p per minute plus your phone company's access charge) **Yeadon Way, South Shore FY1 6BF**
web: www.premierinn.com
dir: *M55 junction 4 to Blackpool, straight on at last island onto Yeaden Way. Follow signs for Central Car Park/Coach Area. Left at Total garage.*

Rooms: 103

Premier Inn Blackpool East (M55 Jct 4)

BUDGET HOTEL

tel: 0871 527 8110 (Calls cost 13p per minute plus your phone company's access charge) **Whitehills Park, Preston New Road FY4 5NZ**
web: www.premierinn.com
dir: *Just off M55 junction 4. 1st left off roundabout. Hotel on right.*

Rooms: 81

BLAKENEY   Map 13 TG04
Norfolk

INSPECTOR'S CHOICE

Morston Hall

★★★★ ◉◉◉◉ ≋ SMALL HOTEL

tel: 01263 741041 **Morston, Holt NR25 7AA**
email: reception@morstonhall.com **web:** www.morstonhall.com
dir: *1 mile west of Blakeney on A149 – King's Lynn to Cromer road.*

This delightful flint and brick 17th-century country house hotel enjoys a tranquil setting amid beautiful, well-tended gardens. The comfortable public rooms offer a choice of attractive lounges and a sunny conservatory, while the elegant dining room, with floor to ceiling windows, is the perfect setting to enjoy chef patron Galton Blackiston's outstanding cuisine. The spacious bedrooms are individually decorated and stylishly furnished with modern opulence; there are six garden suites in the hotel's pavilion. Cookery courses and demonstrations take place throughout the year. Well-behaved children and well-behaved dogs are very welcome here.

Rooms: 13 (6 annexe) (7 GF) ⬩ **S** fr £275 **D** fr £390 (including breakfast & dinner)* **Facilities:** STV FTV WiFi ⬩ New Year **Conf:** Class 20 Board 16 **Parking:** 40 **Notes:** Closed 1 January to last Friday in January and 2 days Christmas Civ Wed 55

HIGHLY RECOMMENDED

The Blakeney Hotel

★★★★ 83% ◉ HOTEL

tel: 01263 740797 **The Quay NR25 7NE**
email: reception@blakeneyhotel.co.uk **web:** www.blakeneyhotel.co.uk
dir: *From A148 between Fakenham and Holt, take B1156 to Langham and Blakeney.*

A traditional, privately-owned hotel situated on the quayside with superb views across the estuary and the salt marshes to Blakeney Point. Public rooms feature an elegant restaurant, ground-floor lounge, a bar and a first-floor sun lounge overlooking the harbour. Bedrooms are smartly decorated and equipped with modern facilities. The leisure area is a real feature with pool, sauna, steam room and mini-gym.

Rooms: 64 (16 annexe) (20 family) (17 GF) ⬩ **Facilities:** FTV WiFi ⬩ HL ☻ Gym Billiards Snooker Table tennis Sauna Steam room spa bath Xmas New Year **Conf:** Class 100 Board 100 Theatre 150 **Services:** Lift Night porter **Parking:** 60 **Notes:** LB

BLANCHLAND
Northumberland   Map 18 NY95

The Lord Crewe Arms Blanchland
★★★ ⊛ COUNTRY HOUSE HOTEL

tel: 01434 675469 **The Square DH8 9SP**
email: enquiries@lordcrewearmsblanchland.co.uk
web: www.lordcrewearmsblanchland.co.uk
dir: *10 miles south of Hexham via B6306.*

Set in the tranquil and picturesque Northumbrian countryside, 'The Crewe' dates back to the 12th century and was built as the abbot's priory. The building has plenty of character from the pub in the vaulted crypt to the numerous, large open log fires. Bedrooms come in three styles – Cosy, Canny and Champion. The team are naturally friendly with two dining options serving, as they say, 'proper, unpretentious country grub'.

Rooms: 21 (17 annexe) (6 GF) ⊠ **D** fr £184 (including breakfast)* **Facilities:** FTV WiFi ⌇ Fishing ⌇ Xmas New Year **Conf:** Board 12 Theatre 18 **Parking:** 25 **Notes:** Civ Wed 120

BLEADON
Somerset   Map 4 ST35

Premier Inn Weston-Super-Mare (Lympsham)
Premier Inn

BUDGET HOTEL

tel: 0871 527 9154 (Calls cost 13p per minute plus your phone company's access charge) **Bridgwater Road, Lympsham BS24 0BP**
web: www.premierinn.com
dir: *M5 junction 22, A38 (Bristol Road) signed Weston-super-Mare. At 1st roundabout take 1st exit into Bridgwater Road (A370). Approximately 2 miles to hotel.*

High quality, budget accommodation ideal for both families and business travellers. Spacious, en suite bedrooms feature free WiFi and tea and coffee making facilities, and in most hotels, Freeview TV is also available. The adjacent family restaurant features a wide and varied menu.

Rooms: 45

BODMIN
Cornwall & Isles of Scilly   Map 2 SX06

Trehellas House Hotel & Restaurant
★★★ 77% ⊛ SMALL HOTEL

tel: 01208 72700 **Washaway PL30 3AD**
email: enquiries@trehellashouse.co.uk **web:** www.trehellashouse.co.uk
dir: *A389 from Bodmin towards Wadebridge. Hotel on right 0.5 mile beyond road to Camelford.*

This 18th-century former posting inn retains many original features and provides comfortable accommodation. Bedrooms are located in both the main house and adjacent coach house – all provide the same high standards. An interesting choice of dishes, with an emphasis on locally-sourced ingredients, is offered in the impressive slate-floored restaurant.

Rooms: 12 (7 annexe) (2 family) (5 GF) **S** fr £50 **D** fr £60 (including breakfast)* **Facilities:** FTV WiFi ⌇ Xmas New Year **Conf:** Board 20 Theatre 20 **Parking:** 32 **Notes:** LB No children 13 years

Premier Inn Bodmin
Premier Inn ⊙

BUDGET HOTEL

tel: 0871 527 8112 (Calls cost 13p per minute plus your phone company's access charge) **Launceston Road PL31 2AR**
web: www.premierinn.com
dir: *From A30 southbound exit onto A389, hotel 0.5 mile on right. Northbound exit onto A38, follow A389 signs. Left at T-junction.*

High quality, budget accommodation ideal for both families and business travellers. Spacious, en suite bedrooms feature free WiFi and tea and coffee making facilities, and in most hotels, Freeview TV is also available. The adjacent family restaurant features a wide and varied menu.

Rooms: 44

BOGNOR REGIS
West Sussex   Map 6 SZ99

Best Western Beachcroft Hotel
BW Best Western.

★★★ 80% HOTEL

tel: 01243 827142 **Clyde Road, Felpham PO22 7AH**
email: reservations@beachcroft-hotel.co.uk **web:** www.beachcroft-hotel.co.uk
dir: *On the seafront in Felpham.*

The Best Western Beachcroft Hotel enjoys a prominent position on the seafront. Service is attentive and guests are guaranteed a warm welcome and genuine hospitality throughout the hotel. The bedrooms are spacious and well equipped; several rooms have commanding views over the sea. Public areas include a stylish lounge bar and popular restaurant. Other facilities are free WiFi, an indoor swimming pool and convenient parking.

Rooms: 38 (7 family) (6 GF) ⊠ **S** fr £64 **D** fr £85 (including breakfast)* **Facilities:** FTV WiFi ⌇ ⌇ Xmas New Year **Conf:** Class 20 Board 20 Theatre 100 **Services:** Night porter **Parking:** 35 **Notes:** LB

B

BOGNOR REGIS *continued*

The Royal Norfolk Hotel

Leisureplex
HOLIDAY HOTELS

★★★ 73% HOTEL

tel: 01243 826222 **The Esplanade PO21 2LH**
email: royalnorfolk@leisureplex.co.uk **web:** www.leisureplex.co.uk
dir: *From A259 follow Longford Road through lights to Canada Grove to T-junction. Right, take 2nd exit at roundabout. Hotel on right.*

Located on the seafront, but set back behind well-tended lawns and gardens, is this fine Regency hotel. The bedrooms are traditionally furnished and provide guests with modern comforts. There are sea views from the bar and restaurant, as well as the lounges.

Rooms: 68 (3 family) (7 GF) ☏ **S** fr £41 **D** fr £64 (including breakfast)*
Facilities: FTV WiFi ♫ Xmas New Year **Services:** Lift Night porter **Parking:** 40
Notes: LB Closed 2 January to 14 February

Premier Inn Bognor Regis

Premier Inn

BUDGET HOTEL

tel: 0871 527 8114 (Calls cost 13p per minute plus your phone company's access charge) **Shripney Road PO22 9PA**
web: www.premierinn.com
dir: *From A27 and A29 roundabout junction follow Bognor Regis signs. Approximately 4 miles, hotel on left.*

High quality, budget accommodation ideal for both families and business travellers. Spacious, en suite bedrooms feature free WiFi and tea and coffee making facilities, and in most hotels, Freeview TV is also available. The adjacent family restaurant features a wide and varied menu.

Rooms: 46

| **BOLTON** | **Map 15 SD70** |
| Greater Manchester | |

Mercure Bolton Georgian House Hotel

★★★ 75% HOTEL

tel: 01942 850900 & 0844 815 9029 (Calls cost 7p per minute plus your phone company's access charge) **Manchester Road, Blackrod BL6 5RU**
email: info@mercurebolton.co.uk **web:** www.mercurebolton.co.uk
dir: *M61 junction 6, follow Blackrod A6027 signs. 200 metres turn right onto A6 signed Chorley. Hotel 0.5 mile on right.*

This hotel has a pleasant location and very good parking, convenient for corporate or leisure guests alike. Bedrooms are pleasantly appointed, and beds very comfortable. There is a range of meeting rooms and the hotel is popular for weddings. There is a choice of dining venues and a pleasant bar.

Rooms: 91 (6 family) **S** fr £60 **D** fr £65* **Facilities:** FTV WiFi ♿ ✋ Gym Sauna Beauty treatments Dance studio Xmas **Conf:** Class 100 Board 40 Theatre 275
Services: Night porter **Parking:** 250 **Notes:** Civ Wed 275

Premier Inn Bolton (Reebok Stadium)

Premier Inn

BUDGET HOTEL

tel: 0871 527 8116 (Calls cost 13p per minute plus your phone company's access charge) **Arena Approach 3, Horwich BL6 6LB**
web: www.premierinn.com
dir: *M61 junction 6, right at roundabout, left at 2nd roundabout.*

High quality, budget accommodation ideal for both families and business travellers. Spacious, en suite bedrooms feature free WiFi and tea and coffee making

facilities, and in most hotels, Freeview TV is also available. The adjacent family restaurant features a wide and varied menu.

Rooms: 126

Premier Inn Bolton West

Premier Inn

BUDGET HOTEL

tel: 0871 527 8118 (Calls cost 13p per minute plus your phone company's access charge) **991 Chorley New Road, Horwich BL6 4BA**
web: www.premierinn.com
dir: *M61 junction 6, follow dual carriageway signed Bolton/Horwich (Reebok Stadium on left). Hotel at 2nd roundabout.*

Rooms: 60

| **BOLTON ABBEY** | **Map 19 SE05** |
| North Yorkshire | |

The Devonshire Arms Hotel & Spa

★★★★ ◉◉◉◉ ☕ HOTEL

tel: 01756 718100 & 718111 **BD23 6AJ**
email: res@devonshirehotels.co.uk **web:** www.thedevonshirearms.co.uk
dir: *On B6160, 250 yards north of junction with A59.*

With stunning views of the Wharfedale countryside, this beautiful hotel, owned by the Duke and Duchess of Devonshire, dates back to the 17th century. A long tradition of fine hospitality continues to this day, as guests' needs are accommodated in fine style – attention to detail and friendly, personalised service are always in evidence. Bedrooms are elegantly furnished; those in the old part of the house are particularly spacious and have four-posters and fine antiques. The rest of the hotel is equally elegant, and it's a pleasure to spend time in one of the cosy sitting rooms. The Burlington Restaurant offers accomplished cuisine, while the Brasserie provides a lighter alternative. Both serve fresh, seasonal produce largely from the estate, neighbouring farms and the hotel's own kitchen garden.

Rooms: 40 (1 family) (17 GF) ☏ **S** fr £119 **D** fr £138 (including breakfast)*
Facilities: Spa STV FTV WiFi ♿ ✋ 🏊 Fishing ✋ Gym Fly fishing Cricket Xmas New Year **Conf:** Class 32 Board 30 Theatre 90 **Services:** Night porter **Parking:** 150
Notes: LB Closed 25–26 December RS 24 and 31 December, 1 January
Civ Wed 90

B

BOREHAMWOOD
Hertfordshire   Map 6 TQ19

Premier Inn London Elstree/Borehamwood

BUDGET HOTEL

tel: 0871 527 8654 (Calls cost 13p per minute plus your phone company's access charge) **Warwick Road WD6 1US**
web: www.premierinn.com
dir: Exit A1 signed Borehamwood onto A5135 (Elstree Way). Pass BP Garage, left into Warwick Road.

High quality, budget accommodation ideal for both families and business travellers. Spacious, en suite bedrooms feature free WiFi and tea and coffee making facilities, and in most hotels, Freeview TV is also available. The adjacent family restaurant features a wide and varied menu.

Rooms: 124

BOROUGHBRIDGE
North Yorkshire   Map 19 SE36

Best Western Crown Hotel

★★★ 77% HOTEL

tel: 01423 322328 **Horsefair YO51 9LB**
email: sales@crownboroughbridge.co.uk **web:** www.crownboroughbridge.co.uk
dir: A1(M) junction 48 towards Boroughbridge. Hotel 1 mile.

Situated in the centre of town but convenient for the A1(M), The Crown provides a full leisure complex, conference rooms and a secure car park. Bedrooms are well appointed. A wide range of well-prepared dishes can be enjoyed in both the restaurant and bar.

Rooms: 37 (3 family) (2 GF) **Facilities:** FTV WiFi ⓗ HL 🏊 Gym Xmas New Year
Conf: Class 80 Board 80 Theatre 150 **Services:** Night porter **Parking:** 60
Notes: Civ Wed 120

BORROWDALE
Cumbria   Map 18 NY21

See also Keswick & Rosthwaite

Lodore Falls Hotel

LAKE DISTRICT HOTELS

★★★★ 83% ⓦⓦ HOTEL

tel: 017687 77285 **CA12 5UX**
email: lodorefalls@lakedistricthotels.net **web:** www.lakedistricthotels.net/lodorefalls
dir: M6 junction 40, A66 to Keswick, B5289 to Borrowdale. Hotel on left.

This impressive hotel in an enviable location overlooking Derwentwater has now completed a major refurbishment programme. Newly appointed bedrooms and suites, many with lake or fell views, are comfortably equipped; family rooms are also available. 2018 saw the opening of a luxury spa and the addition of spa suites and deluxe spa suites. The award-winning dining room, where casual yet smart attire is requested to be worn, offers a global range of dishes cooked with precision. The hotel offers many interesting and exciting leisure breaks. Dogs are very welcome here (for a small charge) and doggie beds and bowls are available.

Rooms: 69 (11 family) (3 GF) 🐾 **S** fr £99.50 **D** fr £117 (including breakfast)*
Facilities: Spa FTV WiFi 🏊 Gym Sauna Outdoor hydrotherapy pool Xmas New Year
Conf: Class 90 Board 45 Theatre 200 **Services:** Lift Night porter **Parking:** 112
Notes: LB Civ Wed 130

Borrowdale Gates Hotel

★★★★ 80% ⓦ COUNTRY HOUSE HOTEL

tel: 017687 77204 **CA12 5UQ**
email: hotel@borrowdale-gates.com **web:** www.borrowdale-gates.com
dir: From A66 follow B5289 for approximately 4 miles. Turn right over bridge, hotel 0.25 mile beyond village.

Close to the village, this friendly hotel is peacefully located in the Borrowdale Valley, in its own three-acre wooded grounds. Public rooms include comfortable lounges and a restaurant with picture-postcard views; the award-winning cuisine is a modern take on traditional British and classic French. The stylish, contemporary bedrooms and the Millican Dalton Suite are beautifully appointed; several have balconies and others patio doors leading to the garden. Dogs can be accommodated in three of the bedrooms.

Rooms: 25 (2 family) (9 GF) 🐾 **S** fr £100 **D** fr £200 (including breakfast & dinner)*
Facilities: FTV WiFi ⓗ Xmas New Year **Services:** Lift Air con **Parking:** 25
Notes: Closed 5–25 January

Borrowdale Hotel

LAKE DISTRICT HOTELS

★★★★ 78% ⓦ HOTEL

tel: 017687 77224 **CA12 5UY**
email: borrowdale@lakedistricthotels.net
web: www.lakedistricthotels.net/borrowdalehotel
dir: 3 miles from Keswick, on B5289 at south end of Lake Derwentwater.

Situated in the beautiful Borrowdale Valley overlooking Derwentwater, this traditionally styled hotel guarantees a friendly welcome. Extensive public areas include a choice of lounges, traditional dining room, lounge bar and popular conservatory which serves more informal meals. Bedrooms vary in style and size, including two that are suitable for less able guests.

Rooms: 40 (2 family) (4 GF) 🐾 **S** fr £105 **D** fr £130 (including breakfast)*
Facilities: STV FTV WiFi ⓗ Leisure facilities at sister hotel Xmas New Year
Conf: Class 30 Board 24 Theatre 80 **Services:** Night porter **Parking:** 30

HIGHLY RECOMMENDED

Leathes Head Hotel

★★★ 87% ⓦⓦ HOTEL

tel: 017687 77247 **CA12 5UY**
email: reservations@leatheshead.co.uk **web:** www.leatheshead.co.uk
dir: 3.5 miles from Keswick on B5289 (Borrowdale road). Hotel on left 0.25 mile before Grange Bridge.

Leathes Head Hotel is a fine Edwardian building, with lovely gardens, set in the heart of the unspoilt Borrowdale Valley. The hospitality and customer care are really outstanding here. The bedrooms have commanding views and the award-winning food, including a wonderful Cumbrian breakfast, will not disappoint.

Rooms: 11 (3 GF) 🐾 **S** fr £100 **D** fr £160 (including breakfast & dinner)*
Facilities: FTV WiFi Xmas New Year **Parking:** 16 **Notes:** No children 15 years Closed 3 weeks January Civ Wed 24

BOSCASTLE
Cornwall & Isles of Scilly   Map 2 SX09

The Wellington Hotel
★★★ 80% ◉◉ HOTEL

tel: 01840 250202 **The Harbour PL35 0AQ**
email: info@wellingtonhotelboscastle.com **web:** www.wellingtonhotelboscastle.com
dir: *A30/A395 at Davidstowe follow Boscastle signs. B3266 to village. Right into Old Road.*

This 16th-century coaching inn is very much a landmark in Boscastle and has been providing rest and relaxation for weary travellers for many years. There is character in abundance which adds to its engaging charm and personality. The Long Bar is popular with visitors and locals alike and features a delightful galleried area. The stylish bedrooms come in varying sizes, including the spacious Tower Rooms; all provide contemporary comforts and the expected necessities. In addition to the bar menus, The Waterloo Restaurant is the elegant setting for accomplished cuisine.

Rooms: 17 (3 annexe) (3 family) ✦ **Facilities:** FTV WiFi ⬩ Xmas New Year
Conf: Class 40 Board 24 Theatre 50 **Parking:** 14 **Notes:** LB

BOSHAM
West Sussex   Map 5 SU80

HIGHLY RECOMMENDED

The Millstream Hotel & Restaurant
★★★ 87% ◉◉ HOTEL

tel: 01243 573234 **Bosham Lane PO18 8HL**
email: info@millstreamhotel.co.uk **web:** www.millstreamhotel.com
dir: *4 miles west of Chichester on A259, left at Bosham roundabout. After 0.5 mile right at T-junction signed to church and quay. Hotel 0.5 mile on right.*

Located in the idyllic village of Bosham, this attractive hotel provides comfortable, well-equipped and tastefully decorated bedrooms. Many guests regularly return here for the relaxed atmosphere created by the notably efficient and friendly staff. Public rooms include a cocktail bar that opens onto the garden, and a pleasant award-winning restaurant where varied and freshly prepared cuisine can be enjoyed. Markwick's Brasserie Restaurant is open all day for coffee, snacks, light lunches and dinners.

Rooms: 35 (2 annexe) (2 family) (9 GF) ✦ **Facilities:** FTV WiFi Painting and bridge breaks ♫ Xmas New Year **Conf:** Class 20 Board 20 Theatre 45 **Services:** Night porter **Parking:** 44 **Notes:** LB Civ Wed 75

BOSTON
Lincolnshire   Map 12 TF34

Supreme Inns Boston
★★★ 78% HOTEL

tel: 01205 822804 **Donnington Road, Bicker Bar Roundabout PE20 3AN**
email: enquiries@supremeinns.co.uk **web:** www.supremeinns.co.uk
dir: *At roundabout junction of A52 and A17.*

Situated south-west of Boston and surrounded by the Lincolnshire Fens, this modern, purpose-built hotel offers well-equipped bedrooms that have Freeview TVs and internet access. Food is available in the Haven Restaurant in the evenings or all day in the relaxing bar area. Wedding, private dinner and conference facilities are all available.

Rooms: 55 (27 GF) ✦ **Facilities:** FTV WiFi ⬩ Xmas New Year **Conf:** Board 30 Theatre 50 **Services:** Night porter **Parking:** 65 **Notes:** LB

White Hart Hotel and Eatery
★★★ 77% HOTEL

tel: 01205 311900 **1-5 High Street PE21 8SH**
email: whitehartboston@innmail.co.uk **web:** www.whitehartboston.com
dir: *In town centre.*

The White Hart Hotel is well appointed and attractive and is conveniently located in the centre of this market town with great views of the 700-year-old St Botolph's Church, known as the Boston Stump, from its riverside location. The hotel has spacious public areas including the Riverside Restaurant for evening meals, and the lively Courtyard Bar which is open for brunch, lunch and afternoon tea. There is a wonderful outside area for relaxing, eating and drinking. Conferences and weddings are catered for, and a private car park is also available. Bedrooms are comfortable and come complete with Sky TVs.

Rooms: 26 ✦ **Facilities:** FTV WiFi ⬩ HL Xmas New Year **Conf:** Class 26 Board 26 Theatre 80 **Services:** Night porter **Parking:** 45 **Notes:** Civ Wed 80

Premier Inn Boston

BUDGET HOTEL

tel: 0871 527 8120 (Calls cost 13p per minute plus your phone company's access charge) **Wainfleet Road PE21 9RW**
web: www.premierinn.com
dir: A52, 300 yards east of junction with A16 Boston/Grimsby road.

High quality, budget accommodation ideal for both families and business travellers. Spacious, en suite bedrooms feature free WiFi and tea and coffee making facilities, and in most hotels, Freeview TV is also available. The adjacent family restaurant features a wide and varied menu.

Rooms: 73

BOTLEY
Hampshire   Map 5 SU51

Macdonald Botley Park Hotel & Spa

★★★★ 74% HOTEL

tel: 01489 780888 **Winchester Road, Boorley Green SO32 2UA**
email: general.botleypark@macdonald-hotels.co.uk
web: www.macdonald-hotels.co.uk/botleypark
dir: M27 junction 7, A334 towards Botley. At 1st roundabout left, past M&S store, over at next 5 mini-roundabouts. At 6th mini-roundabout turn right. In 0.5 mile hotel on left.

This modern and spacious hotel has bedrooms which are comfortably appointed with a good range of extras, and extensive leisure facilities are on offer. Attractive public areas include the relaxing Winchester Restaurant and the more informal Sports Bar and Wickham Lounge.

Rooms: 130 (30 family) (34 GF) **Facilities:** Spa STV FTV WiFi Gym Squash Dance studio Sauna Steam room Relaxation lounge Xmas New Year **Conf:** Class 180 Board 140 Theatre 450 **Services:** Night porter Air con **Parking:** 310 **Notes:** Civ Wed 400

BOURNEMOUTH
Dorset   Map 5 SZ19

See also **Christchurch**

Cumberland Hotel

★★★★ 80% HOTEL

tel: 01202 290722 & 298350 **27 East Overcliffe Drive BH1 3AF**
email: sales@oceanahotels.co.uk **web:** www.cumberlandbournemouth.co.uk
dir: A35 towards East Cliff and beaches, right onto Holdenhurst Road, straight over 2 roundabouts, left at junction to East Overcliff Drive, hotel on seafront.

At this art deco hotel many of the bedrooms are appointed in keeping with the hotel's original character, while still offering all that the modern guest expects.

Front-facing bedrooms have balconies with superb sea views. The well-appointed public areas are spacious and striking in their design. The Ventana Grand Café and Mirabelle Restaurant offer cuisine with local produce at their heart.

Cumberland Hotel

Rooms: 107 (16 family) **Facilities:** Spa FTV WiFi Gym Squash Xmas New Year **Conf:** Class 80 Board 50 Theatre 120 **Services:** Lift Night porter **Parking:** 55 **Notes:** LB Civ Wed 120

See advert opposite

The Green House

★★★★ 80% TOWN HOUSE HOTEL

tel: 01202 498900 **4 Grove Road BH1 3AX**
email: reception@thegreenhousehotel.com **web:** www.thegreenhousehotel.com

This hotel has a clear commitment to the environment which goes beyond just energy efficient lighting; everything has been designed and built to be sympathetic to the environment. The beautifully appointed bedrooms and bathrooms demonstrate the 'green' principle from the locally-made 100% wool carpets and solid wood furniture, to the wallpapers and paint that have been used. The ingredients used for the menus are locally sourced and organic.

Rooms: 32 (3 family) (6 GF) **Facilities:** FTV WiFi In-room beauty treatments Xmas New Year **Conf:** Class 40 Board 40 Theatre 100 **Services:** Lift Night porter **Parking:** 32 **Notes:** LB Civ Wed 100

Hotel Miramar

★★★★ 79% HOTEL

tel: 01202 556581 **East Overcliff Drive, East Cliff BH1 3AL**
email: sales@miramar-bournemouth.com **web:** www.miramar-bournemouth.com
dir: From Wessex Way roundabout into St Pauls Road, right at next roundabout. 3rd exit at next roundabout, 2nd exit at next roundabout into Grove Road. Hotel car park on right.

Conveniently located on the East Cliff, this Edwardian hotel enjoys glorious sea views. The Miramar was a favoured destination of famed author J.R.R. Tolkien, who often stayed here. The bedrooms are comfortable and well equipped, and there are spacious public areas and a choice of lounges. The friendly staff and relaxing environment are also noteworthy.

Rooms: 43 (6 family) **S** fr £34.50 **D** fr £103 (including breakfast)* **Facilities:** FTV WiFi HL Xmas New Year **Conf:** Class 50 Board 50 Theatre 200 **Services:** Lift Night porter **Parking:** 90 **Notes:** Civ Wed 110

B

BOURNEMOUTH *continued*

Park Central Hotel

★★★★ 78% 🏵🏵 HOTEL

tel: 01202 203600 **Exeter Road BH2 5AJ**
email: reception@parkcentralhotel.co.uk **web:** www.parkcentralhotel.co.uk
dir: *A338, A35 (St Pauls Road). At roundabout 3rd exit onto B3066 (Holdenburst Road). Straight on at 3 roundabouts, hotel on right opposite Bournemouth International Centre.*

Located opposite Bournemouth International Centre, this modern, contemporary hotel is in a good location and has sea views; bedrooms are comfortable and attractively furnished. The menu features creative modern ideas based on intuitive combinations of well-sourced raw materials featuring, of course a great deal of seafood. A pre-theatre menu is also available, but be sure to book as this can prove very popular.

Rooms: 48 (6 family) (7 GF) 🐾 **S** fr £54 **D** fr £69 (including breakfast)*
Facilities: FTV WiFi ⚐ In-room spa New Year **Services:** Lift Night porter **Parking:** 29

Best Western Plus The Connaught Hotel

(BW) Best Western PLUS

★★★★ 77% 🏵🏵 HOTEL

tel: 01202 298020 **30 West Hill Road, West Cliff BH2 5PH**
email: reception@theconnaught.co.uk **web:** www.theconnaught.co.uk
dir: *Follow Town Centre West and BIC signs.*

Conveniently located on the West Cliff, close to the BIC, beaches and town centre, this privately-owned hotel offers well-equipped, neatly decorated rooms, some with balconies. The hotel boasts a very good leisure complex with a large pool and gym. Breakfast and dinner offer imaginative dishes made with quality local ingredients.

Rooms: 81 (28 annexe) 🐾 **S** fr £75 **D** fr £90 (including breakfast) **Facilities:** Spa FTV WiFi ⚐ 🌀 Gym Beauty treatments Sauna room Steam room 🎵 Xmas New Year **Conf:** Class 60 Board 35 Theatre 180 **Services:** Lift Night porter **Parking:** 66 **Notes:** Civ Wed 130

Hermitage Hotel

★★★★ 76% 🏵 HOTEL

tel: 01202 557363 **Exeter Road BH2 5AH**
email: info@hermitage-hotel.co.uk **web:** www.hermitage-hotel.co.uk
dir: *A338 Ringwood, follow signs for BIC and pier. Hotel directly opposite.*

Occupying an impressive location overlooking the seafront, at the heart of the town centre, the Hermitage offers friendly and attentive service. The majority of the smart bedrooms are comfortably appointed and all are very well equipped; many rooms have sea views. The wood-panelled lounge provides an elegant and tranquil area, as does the restaurant where well-prepared and interesting dishes are served.

Rooms: 76 (16 annexe) (9 family) (7 GF) 🐾 **S** fr £45 **D** fr £60* **Facilities:** FTV WiFi ⚐ Xmas New Year **Conf:** Class 60 Board 60 Theatre 180 **Services:** Lift Night porter **Parking:** 58 **Notes:** LB

The Orchid Hotel

★★★★ 76% 🏵 SMALL HOTEL

tel: 01202 551600 **34 Gervis Road BH1 3DH**
email: georgemiles@orchidhotel.co.uk **web:** www.orchidhotel.co.uk
dir: *Phone for directions.*

The Orchid Hotel is just a few minutes' walk from Bournemouth Pier, and has undergone a full refurbishment to reveal a contemporary atmosphere. Bedrooms are set across two main buildings connected by an internal walkway overlooking a pretty courtyard. The hotel is popular for weddings and events. No 34 offers a 'Londonesque' vibe for diners.

Rooms: 31 (2 family) (6 GF) **S** fr £70 **D** fr £120 (including breakfast)* **Facilities:** FTV WiFi **Conf:** Class 60 Board 40 Theatre 80 **Services:** Lift Night porter Air con **Parking:** 31 **Notes:** Civ Wed 96

Best Western Hotel Royale

(BW) Best Western

★★★★ 74% HOTEL

tel: 01202 554794 **16 Gervis Road BH1 3EQ**
email: patgreen@oceanahotels.com **web:** www.thehotelroyale.com
dir: *M27 junction 1, A31 onto A338 to Bournemouth, follow signs for East Cliff and seafront. Over 2 roundabouts into Gervis Road. Hotel on right.*

Located on the East Cliff, just a short walk from the seafront and local shops and amenities, is this privately-owned hotel. Public areas are contemporary in style, and facilities include a small health club and spacious function rooms. Bedrooms are comfortable and well furnished.

Rooms: 64 (8 annexe) (22 family) (8 GF) 🐾 **Facilities:** STV FTV WiFi ⚐ 🌀 Xmas New Year **Conf:** Class 60 Board 40 Theatre 100 **Services:** Lift Night porter **Parking:** 80 **Notes:** LB Civ Wed 100

B

The Norfolk Royale Hotel

★★★★ 72% HOTEL

PEEL HOTELS PLC

tel: 01202 551521 **Richmond Hill BH2 6EN**
email: rooms@norfolkroyale-hotel-bournemouth.com **web:** www.peelhotels.co.uk
dir: *A338 into Bournemouth take Richmond Hill exit to A347 Wimborne, turn left at top into Richmond Hill. Hotel on right.*

Easily recognisable by its wrought iron balconies, this Edwardian hotel is conveniently located for the centre of the town. Most of the bedrooms are contained in a modern wing at the side of the building, overlooking the pretty landscaped gardens. There is a car park at the rear of the hotel.

Rooms: 95 (23 family) (9 GF) ☎ **S** fr £56.50 **D** fr £93 (including breakfast)*
Facilities: STV FTV WiFi ⬥ HL ⬥ Membership of nearby health club Xmas New Year **Conf:** Class 50 Board 40 Theatre 150 **Services:** Lift Night porter **Parking:** 95
Notes: LB Civ Wed 150

Durley Dean Hotel

★★★ 79% HOTEL

tel: 01202 557711 **West Cliff Road BH2 5HE**
email: reservations@durleydean.co.uk **web:** www.durleydean.co.uk
dir: *Into Bournemouth, follow signs for Westcliff. Onto Durley Chine Road South to next roundabout, hotel at 2nd exit on left.*

Situated close to the seafront on the West Cliff, Durley Dean is a modern hotel with bedrooms that vary in size and style. The hotel has a restaurant, a comfortable bar and several meeting rooms. Parking is also a bonus. Additional facilities include a spa with indoor pool, gym, and treatment rooms for a touch of pampering.

Rooms: 115 (36 family) (6 GF) **Facilities:** Spa FTV WiFi ⬥ ⬥ Gym Sauna Steam room ♫ Xmas New Year **Conf:** Class 40 Board 45 Theatre 150 **Services:** Lift Night porter **Parking:** 30 **Notes:** LB Civ Wed 120

Elstead Hotel

★★★ 78% HOTEL

CLASSIC BRITISH HOTELS

tel: 01202 293071 **Knyveton Road BH1 3QP**
email: info@the-elstead.co.uk **web:** www.the-elstead.co.uk
dir: *A338 (Wessex Way) to St Pauls roundabout, left and left again.*

Ideal as a base for business and leisure travellers, Elstead Hotel is conveniently located for the town centre, seafront and BIC. An impressive range of facilities is offered, including meeting rooms, an indoor leisure centre and comfortable lounges.

Rooms: 50 (15 family) **Facilities:** Spa FTV WiFi ⬥ Gym Sauna Steam room Pool and snooker tables Xmas New Year **Conf:** Class 70 Board 35 Theatre 80
Services: Lift Night porter **Parking:** 40 **Notes:** Civ Wed 60

Hallmark Hotel Bournemouth Carlton

★★★ 78% HOTEL

tel: 0330 028 3411 **East Overcliff BH1 3DN**
email: carlton@hallmarkhotels.co.uk **web:** www.hallmarkhotels.co.uk
dir: *From M3, M27 towards Bournemouth on A338, follow signs to East Cliff, hotel on seafront.*

Enjoying a prime location on the East Cliff, and with views of the Isle of Wight and Dorset coastline, this hotel has attractive gardens and pool area. Most of the

spacious bedrooms enjoy sea views. Leisure facilities include an indoor and outdoor pool as well as a gym. Guests can enjoy an interesting range of carefully prepared dishes in Fredericks restaurant. The conference and banqueting facilities are varied.

Rooms: 76 (17 family) (8 GF) **Facilities:** Spa FTV WiFi ⬥ ⬥ Gym Hair and beauty salon Xmas New Year **Conf:** Class 110 Board 50 Theatre 200 **Services:** Lift Night porter **Parking:** 87 **Notes:** Civ Wed 200

Royal Exeter Hotel

★★★ 78% HOTEL

tel: 01202 438000 **Exeter Road BH2 5AG**
email: enquiries@royalexeterhotel.com **web:** www.royalexeterhotel.com
dir: *Opposite Bournemouth International Centre.*

Ideally located opposite the Bournemouth International Centre, and convenient for the beach and town centre, this busy hotel caters for both business and leisure guests. Public areas are smart, and there's a modern open-plan lounge bar and restaurant, together with an exciting adjoining bar complex.

Rooms: 54 (13 family) (12 smoking) **Facilities:** FTV WiFi Gym ♫ **Conf:** Class 40 Board 40 Theatre 100 **Services:** Lift Night porter **Parking:** 50 **Notes:** LB

See advert on following page

BOURNEMOUTH *continued*

Hallmark Hotel Bournemouth West Cliff

★★★ 77% HOTEL

tel: 0330 028 3413 **Durley Chine Road, West Cliff BH2 5JS**
email: westcliff@hallmarkhotels.co.uk **web:** www.hallmarkhotels.co.uk
dir: *A338 follow signs to West Cliff and Bournemouth International Centre, hotel on right.*

This property is conveniently located and offers a friendly atmosphere and attentive service. The comfortable bedrooms are tastefully appointed and are suitable for both business and leisure guests. The restaurant and bar serve a good choice of dishes, and the well-appointed lounge area is popular with both residents and locals alike. There is also a good range of conference facilities and meeting rooms.

Rooms: 83 (5 GF) **Facilities:** Spa FTV WiFi Gym Sauna Steam room Aromatherapy cave Relaxation room Xmas New Year **Conf:** Class 80 Board 40 Theatre 250 **Services:** Lift Night porter **Parking:** 80 **Notes:** LB Civ Wed 200

Hotel Collingwood

★★★ 77% HOTEL

tel: 01202 557575 **11 Priory Road, West Cliff BH2 5DF**
email: info@hotelcollingwood.co.uk **web:** www.hotelcollingwood.co.uk
dir: *A338 left at West Cliff sign, over 1st roundabout, left at 2nd roundabout. Hotel 500 yards on left.*

This privately owned and managed hotel is situated close to the BIC. The bedrooms are airy, with an emphasis on guest comfort. An excellent range of leisure facilities is available, and the public areas are spacious and welcoming. Pinks Restaurant offers carefully prepared cuisine and a fixed-price, five-course dinner.

Rooms: 53 (16 family) (6 GF) **Facilities:** FTV WiFi Gym Steam room Sauna Games room Snooker room Xmas New Year **Conf:** Class 40 Board 20 Theatre 80 **Services:** Lift Night porter **Parking:** 55 **Notes:** LB

Hallmark Hotel Bournemouth East Cliff

★★★ 76% HOTEL

tel: 01202 554545 **East Overcliff Drive BH1 3AN**
email: eastcliff@hallmarkhotels.co.uk **web:** www.hallmarkhotels.co.uk
dir: *From M3, M27 towards Bournemouth on A33 follow signs to East Cliff, hotel on seafront.*

Enjoying panoramic views across the bay, this popular hotel offers bedrooms that are modern and contemporary in style; they are appointed to a very high standard, and many have the benefit of balconies and sea views. Stylish public areas include a range of inviting lounges, a spacious restaurant and a selection of conference rooms.

Rooms: 67 (15 family) (2 GF) (5 smoking) **Facilities:** FTV WiFi Full leisure facilities at adjacent Hallmark Carlton Xmas New Year **Conf:** Class 60 Board 40 Theatre 150 **Services:** Lift Night porter **Parking:** 45 **Notes:** Civ Wed 250

Trouville Hotel

★★★ 75% HOTEL

tel: 01202 552262 **Priory Road BH2 5DH**
email: reception@trouvillehotel.com **web:** www.trouvillehotel.com
dir: *Follow Town Centre West signs. Exit at roundabout signed Bournemouth International Centre/West Cliff/Beaches. 2nd exit at next roundabout, left at next roundabout. Hotel on left near end of Priory Road.*

Located near Bournemouth International Centre, the seafront and the shops, this hotel has the advantage of indoor leisure facilities and a large car park. Bedrooms are generally a good size with comfortable furnishings, and there are plenty of family rooms. The air-conditioned restaurant offers a daily-changing menu.

Rooms: 99 (19 annexe) (21 family) (2 GF) **Facilities:** FTV WiFi Gym Sauna Beauty treatment room Xmas New Year **Conf:** Class 100 Board 80 Theatre 250 **Services:** Lift Night porter **Parking:** 70 **Notes:** Civ Wed 130

Devon Towers Hotel

Leisureplex
HOLIDAY HOTELS

★★★ 71% HOTEL

tel: 01202 553863 **58-62 St Michael's Road, West Cliff BH2 5ED**
email: devontowers@leisureplex.co.uk **web:** www.leisureplex.co.uk
dir: *A338 into Bournemouth, follow signs for BIC. Left into St Michaels Road at top of hill. Hotel 100 metres on left.*

Located in a quiet road within walking distance of the West Cliff and shops, this hotel appeals to the budget leisure market. The four-course menus offer plenty of choice and entertainment is featured most evenings. The bar and lobby area provide plenty of space for relaxing.

Rooms: 60 (3 family) (8 GF) 🐾 **S** fr £39 **D** fr £60 (including breakfast)*
Facilities: FTV WiFi 🎵 Xmas New Year **Services:** Lift Night porter **Parking:** 2
Notes: Closed January to mid February (except Christmas) RS mid to end February, March and November

Tower House Hotel

★★ 80% HOTEL

tel: 01202 290742 **West Cliff Gardens BH2 5HP**
email: towerhouse.hotel@btconnect.com **web:** www.towerhousehotelbournemouth.com

Tower House Hotel is a popular family-owned and run hotel on the West Cliff. The owners and their staff are friendly and helpful. The bedrooms are comfortable and well maintained, and the hotel provides good off-road parking.

Rooms: 32 (12 family) (3 GF) 🐾 **S** fr £30 **D** fr £60 (including breakfast)*
Facilities: FTV WiFi Xmas New Year **Services:** Lift **Parking:** 30 **Notes:** Closed 2–31 January

Premier Inn Bournemouth Central

Premier Inn

BUDGET HOTEL

tel: 0871 527 8124 (Calls cost 13p per minute plus your phone company's access charge) **Westover Road BH1 2BZ**
web: www.premierinn.com
dir: *M27 junction 1, A31. Left at Ashley Heath junction. A338 towards Bournemouth. At roundabout 1st exit. At next roundabout 3rd exit (Holdenhurst Road). At next roundabout 3rd exit (Bath Road). At next roundabout into Westover Road, right into Hinton Road, hotel on right.*

High quality, budget accommodation ideal for both families and business travellers. Spacious, en suite bedrooms feature free WiFi and tea and coffee making facilities, and in most hotels, Freeview TV is also available. The adjacent family restaurant features a wide and varied menu.

Rooms: 120

Premier Inn Bournemouth East (Lynton Court)

Premier Inn

BUDGET HOTEL

tel: 0871 527 8126 (Calls cost 13p per minute plus your phone company's access charge) **47 Christchurch Road, Boscombe BH1 3PA**
web: www.premierinn.com
dir: *M27 junction 1, A31, 9 miles, left at Ashley Heath junction, take A338 signed Bournemouth. At 1st roundabout take 1st exit into Saint Paul's Road. At 2nd roundabout 1st exit onto Christchurch Road. Hotel on right.*

Rooms: 20

Premier Inn Bournemouth Westcliffe

Premier Inn

BUDGET HOTEL

tel: 0871 527 8128 (Calls cost 13p per minute plus your phone company's access charge) **Poole Road BH2 5QU**
web: www.premierinn.com
dir: *M27 junction 1, A31. At Ashley Heath junction, left. Take A338 signed Bournemouth. At Bournemouth West roundabout 1st exit signed Ring Road, West Cliff. At next roundabout (St Michael's) 3rd exit (signed Westbourne) into Poole Road. Hotel on right.*

Rooms: 168

BOURTON-ON-THE-WATER   Map 10 SP12
Gloucestershire

Chester House Hotel

★★★ 80% SMALL HOTEL

tel: 01451 820286 **Victoria Street GL54 2BU**
email: info@chesterhousehotel.com **web:** www.chesterhousehotel.com
dir: *On A429 between Northleach and Stow-on-the-Wold.*

Chester House Hotel occupies a secluded but central location in this delightful Cotswold village. Bedrooms, some at ground-floor level, are situated in the main house and adjoining coach house. The public areas are stylish, light and airy. Breakfast is taken in the main building whereas dinner is served in the attractive restaurant just a few yards away.

Rooms: 22 (10 annexe) (3 family) (8 GF) 🐾 **D** fr £110 (including breakfast)*
Facilities: FTV WiFi ⌨ Beauty therapist New Year **Parking:** 18 **Notes:** Closed 2 January to 10 February

---

BOWNESS-ON-WINDERMERE
See **Windermere**

BRACKNELL   Map 5 SU86
Berkshire

Coppid Beech

★★★★ 74% HOTEL

tel: 01344 303333 **John Nike Way RG12 8TF**
email: sales@coppidbeech.com **web:** www.coppidbeech.com
dir: *M4 junction 10 take Wokingham/Bracknell onto A329. In 2 miles take B3408 to Binfield, at lights turn right. Hotel 200 yards on right.*

This chalet designed hotel offers extensive facilities and includes a ski-slope, ice rink, nightclub, health club and Bier Keller. Bedrooms range from suites to standard rooms – all are impressively equipped. A choice of dining is offered; there's a full bistro menu available in the Keller, and for more formal dining, Rowans restaurant provides award-winning cuisine.

Rooms: 205 (6 family) (16 GF) **S** fr £69 **D** fr £79 (including breakfast)*
Facilities: STV WiFi ⌨ 🎣 Gym Beauty treatment room Ice rink Dry ski slope Snow boarding freestyle park 🎵 New Year **Conf:** Class 161 Board 24 Theatre 350
Services: Lift Night porter Air con **Parking:** 350 **Notes:** LB Civ Wed 200

B

BRACKNELL *continued*

Stirrups Country House Hotel

★★★ 84% HOTEL

tel: 01344 882284 **Maidens Green RG42 6LD**
email: reception@stirrupshotel.co.uk web: www.stirrupshotel.co.uk
dir: *3 miles north on B3022 towards Windsor.*

Situated in a peaceful location between Maidenhead, Bracknell and Windsor, this hotel has high standards of comfort particularly in the bedrooms; some rooms have a small sitting room area. There is a popular bar, a restaurant, function rooms and delightful grounds.

Rooms: 36 (5 annexe) (6 family) (5 GF) ☎ **S** fr £90 (including breakfast)*
Facilities: FTV WiFi ☙ HL Xmas New Year **Conf:** Class 50 Board 40 Theatre 100
Services: Lift Night porter **Parking:** 100 **Notes:** Civ Wed 100

Premier Inn Bracknell Central

Premier Inn

BUDGET HOTEL

tel: 0871 527 8132 (Calls cost 13p per minute plus your phone company's access charge) **Wokingham Road RG42 1NA**
web: www.premierinn.com
dir: *M4 junction 10, A329(M) (Bracknell) to lights.1st left, 3rd exit roundabout by Morrisons to town centre. Left at roundabout, left at next roundabout. Hotel on left.*

High quality, budget accommodation ideal for both families and business travellers. Spacious, en suite bedrooms feature free WiFi and tea and coffee making facilities, and in most hotels, Freeview TV is also available. The adjacent family restaurant features a wide and varied menu.

Rooms: 80

Premier Inn Bracknell (Twin Bridges)

Premier Inn

BUDGET HOTEL

tel: 0871 527 8130 (Calls cost 13p per minute plus your phone company's access charge) **Downshire Way RG12 7AA**
web: www.premierinn.com
dir: *M4 junction 10, A329(M) towards Bracknell. Straight on at mini-roundabout. At Twin Bridges roundabout take 2nd exit. Hotel on right adjacent to Downshire Arms Beefeater.*

Rooms: 42

BRADFORD	Map 19 SE13
West Yorkshire	

See also **Gomersal**

Midland Hotel

★★★ 78% HOTEL

 PEEL HOTELS PLC

tel: 01274 735735 **Forster Square BD1 4HU**
email: info@midland-hotel-bradford.com web: www.peelhotels.co.uk
dir: *M62 junction 26, M606, past ASDA, left at roundabout onto A650. Through 2 roundabouts and 2 lights. Follow A6181/Haworth signs. Up hill, next left into Manor Row. Hotel 400 metres.*

Ideally situated in the heart of the city, this grand Victorian hotel provides modern, very well-equipped accommodation and comfortable, spacious day rooms. Ample parking is available in what was once the city's railway station, and a Victorian walkway linking the hotel to the old platform can still be used today.

Rooms: 90 (5 family) (4 smoking) ☎ **S** fr £69 **D** fr £89 (including breakfast)
Facilities: STV FTV WiFi ☙ HL Xmas New Year **Conf:** Class 150 Board 100 Theatre 450 **Services:** Lift Night porter **Parking:** 60 **Notes:** LB Civ Wed 300

Best Western Bradford Guide Post Hotel

 Best Western

★★★ 76% HOTEL

tel: 01274 607866 **Common Road, Low Moor BD12 0ST**
email: sue.barnes@guideposthotel.net web: www.guideposthotel.net
dir: *From M606 roundabout take 2nd exit. At next roundabout take 1st exit (Cleckheaton Road). 0.5 mile, turn right at bollard into Common Road.*

Situated south of the city, this hotel offers attractively styled, modern, comfortable bedrooms. The restaurant offers an extensive range of food using fresh, local produce; lighter snack meals are served in the bar. There is also a choice of well-equipped meeting and function rooms. There's disabled access to the hotel, restaurant and one function room.

Rooms: 42 (10 family) (13 GF) ☎ **S** fr £50 **D** fr £50* **Facilities:** FTV WiFi ☙ Use of nearby swimming and gym facilities at reduced rates **Conf:** Class 80 Board 60 Theatre 100 **Services:** Night porter **Parking:** 100 **Notes:** Civ Wed 100

Premier Inn Bradford Central

Premier Inn

BUDGET HOTEL

tel: 0871 527 9306 (Calls cost 13p per minute plus your phone company's access charge) **Vicar Lane BD1 5LD**
web: www.premierinn.com
dir: *M62 junction 24, M606, at junction 3 take 4th exit into Rooley Lane (A6177) towards Ring Road/A650/Leeds/A647. In 1 mile 1st exit into Wakefield Road towards City Centre. Follow Wakefield Road/A650 signs. Straight on at 2 roundabouts, right into Vicar Lane.*

High quality, budget accommodation ideal for both families and business travellers. Spacious, en suite bedrooms feature free WiFi and tea and coffee making facilities, and in most hotels, Freeview TV is also available. The adjacent family restaurant features a wide and varied menu.

Rooms: 118

BRADFORD-ON-AVON	Map 4 ST86
Wiltshire	

Widbrook Grange

★★★ 82% COUNTRY HOUSE HOTEL

tel: 01225 864750 **Trowbridge Road BA15 1UH**
email: stay@widbrookgrange.com web: www.widbrookgrange.co.uk
dir: *1 mile southeast from Bradford on A363, hotel diagonally opposite Bradford Marina and Arabian Stud.*

Widbrook Grange is an impressive Bath-stone country house offering a quiet retreat a short drive from the bustle of Bath. Spacious bedrooms are located either in the main house or in the converted farm buildings, and some rooms have four-poster beds. Leisure facilities include a small gym and indoor swimming pool with beauty treatments available on request. The brasserie focuses on local seasonal produce at breakfast and dinner.

Rooms: 19 (15 annexe) (6 family) (13 GF) ☎ **Facilities:** FTV WiFi ☙ Gym Children's weekend play room Beauty treatments Xmas New Year **Conf:** Class 35 Board 25 Theatre 50 **Parking:** 50 **Notes:** LB Civ Wed 50

B

BRAINTREE
Essex   Map 7 TL72

Premier Inn Braintree (A120)

BUDGET HOTEL   Premier Inn

tel: 0871 527 8138 (Calls cost 13p per minute plus your phone company's access charge) **Cressing Road, Galley's Corner CM77 8GG**
web: www.premierinn.com
dir: *On A120 (Stansted to Braintree link road). Adjacent to Mulberry Tree Brewers Fayre.*

High quality, budget accommodation ideal for both families and business travellers. Spacious, en suite bedrooms feature free WiFi and tea and coffee making facilities, and in most hotels, Freeview TV is also available. The adjacent family restaurant features a wide and varied menu.

Rooms: 78

Premier Inn Braintree (Freeport Village)

BUDGET HOTEL   Premier Inn

tel: 0871 527 8140 (Calls cost 13p per minute plus your phone company's access charge) **Fowlers Farm, Cressing Road CM77 8DH**
web: www.premierinn.com
dir: *M11 junction 8, follow signs to A120 Colchester and Freeport Shopping Village. At Galley's Corner roundabout, 4th exit, left into Wyevale Garden Centre. Hotel adjacent.*

Rooms: 48

BRAMPTON
Cumbria   Map 21 NY56

INSPECTOR'S CHOICE

Farlam Hall Hotel

★★★ HOTEL

tel: 016977 46234 **Hallbankgate CA8 2NG**
email: farlam@relaischateaux.com **web:** www.farlamhall.co.uk
dir: *On A689 (Brampton to Alston). Hotel 2 miles on left – not in Farlam village.*

This delightful country house has a history dating back to 1428, although the building today is very much the result of alterations carried out in the mid-19th century. The hotel is run by a friendly family team and their enthusiastic staff, and is set in beautifully landscaped Victorian gardens complete with an ornamental lake and stream. Lovingly restored over many years, it provides very high standards of comfort and hospitality. Gracious public rooms are very relaxing, and a lot of thought has gone into the beautiful bedrooms, many of which are simply stunning. Nearby are Hadrian's Wall and the Northern Pennines

Area of Outstanding Natural Beauty, which both provide endless opportunities for walking and sightseeing.

Rooms: 12 (1 annexe) (2 GF) ⌂ **S** fr £165 **D** fr £310 (including breakfast & dinner)* **Facilities:** FTV WiFi ⌂ ⌂ New Year **Conf:** Class 24 Board 12 Theatre 24 **Parking:** 25 **Notes:** LB No children 5 years Closed 24–30 December and 4–24 January Civ Wed 45

BRANCASTER STAITHE
Norfolk   Map 13 TF74

HIGHLY RECOMMENDED

The White Horse

★★★ 86% ⌂⌂ HOTEL

tel: 01485 210262 **PE31 8BY**
email: reception@whitehorsebrancaster.co.uk
web: www.whitehorsebrancaster.co.uk
dir: *On A149 (coast road) midway between Hunstanton and Wells-next-the-Sea.*

The White Horse is a charming hotel situated on the north Norfolk coast with contemporary bedrooms in two wings, some featuring an interesting cobbled fascia. Each room is attractively decorated and thoughtfully equipped. There is a large bar and a lounge area leading through to the conservatory restaurant, with stunning tidal marshland views across to Scolt Head Island.

Rooms: 15 (8 annexe) (5 family) (8 GF) ⌂ **S** fr £140 **D** fr £140 (including breakfast) **Facilities:** FTV WiFi ⌂ Holistic therapies in room Xmas New Year **Parking:** 30 **Notes:** LB

BRANDON
Warwickshire   Map 11 SP47

Mercure Coventry Brandon Hall Hotel & Spa

★★★★ 73% HOTEL   Mercure HOTELS

tel: 024 7654 6000 **Main Street CV8 3FW**
email: h6625@accor.com **web:** www.mercure.com
dir: *A45 towards Coventry south. After Peugeot-Citroen garage on left, at island take 5th exit to M1 south/London (back onto A45). After 200 yards, immediately after Texaco garage, left into Brandon Lane, hotel after 2.5 miles.*

An impressive tree-lined avenue leads to this 17th-century property which sits in 17 acres of grounds. The hotel provides a peaceful and friendly sanctuary away from the hustle and bustle. Bedrooms provide comfortable facilities and a good range of extras for guest comfort. There is a Spa Naturel with health, beauty and fitness facilities in a separate building.

Rooms: 120 (30 annexe) (10 family) (50 GF) ⌂ **S** fr £84 **D** fr £84* **Facilities:** Spa STV WiFi ⌂ Gym Steam room Sauna Xmas New Year **Conf:** Class 120 Board 112 Theatre 280 **Services:** Lift Night porter **Parking:** 200 **Notes:** Civ Wed 280

BRANKSOME
See **Poole**

BRANSFORD
Worcestershire   Map 10 SO75

Bank House Hotel, Spa & Golf Club
PREMIER | BEST WESTERN

★★★★ 78% HOTEL

tel: 01886 833 551 **WR6 5JD**
email: reception@bankhouseworcester.com **web:** www.bankhouseworcester.com
dir: *Located on A4103, 5 miles from Worcester centre, 7 miles from M5 junction 7.*

Bank House is a family-run hotel, ideally located on the outskirts of Worcester and within easy reach of both the Malvern Hills and the Cotswolds. The property has a range of well-equipped bedrooms including impressive suites. The leisure facilities include an indoor swimming pool, and spa treatments are available. A challenging 18-hole golf course and driving range can be used by guests. Menus in The Pear Tree restaurant focus on ingredients sourced whenever possible from within a 25-mile radius; casual meals are also offered in the Sportman's Bar.

Rooms: 66 (8 family) (12 GF) ☎ **S** fr £75 **D** fr £85 **Facilities:** Spa FTV WiFi ⇗ ◱ ♨ 18 Gym New Year **Conf:** Class 150 Board 70 Theatre 500 **Services:** Lift Night porter **Parking:** 250 **Notes:** LB Civ Wed 400

BRENTFORD
Greater London

Novotel London Brentford
NOVOTEL
HOTELS & RESORTS

★★★★ 81% HOTEL Plan 1 C3

tel: 020 3693 1800 **Great West Road TW8 0GP**
email: H6995@accor.com **web:** www.novotel.com
dir: *Phone for directions.*

Located just 20 minutes from Heathrow, with Richmond and Twickenham Stadium just a couple of minutes away, Novotel London Brentford offers stylish public areas throughout, and comfortably appointed rooms. There are conference facilities on site and a leisure suite on the lower ground floor. Parking is available, and South Ealing and Brentford station is less than a mile from the hotel.

Rooms: 202 (90 family) ☎ **Facilities:** FTV WiFi ⇗ HL ◱ Gym **Conf:** Class 50 Board 30 Theatre 90 **Services:** Lift Night porter Air con **Parking:** 100

Premier Inn London Kew
Premier Inn

BUDGET HOTEL Plan 1 C3

tel: 0871 527 8670 (Calls cost 13p per minute plus your phone company's access charge) **52 High Street TW8 0BB**
web: www.premierinn.com
dir: *At junction of A4 (M4), A205 and A406, Chiswick roundabout, take A205 towards Kew and Brentford. 200 yards right fork onto A315 (High Street), for 0.5 mile. Hotel on left.*

High quality, budget accommodation ideal for both families and business travellers. Spacious, en suite bedrooms feature free WiFi and tea and coffee making facilities, and in most hotels, Freeview TV is also available. The adjacent family restaurant features a wide and varied menu.

Rooms: 141

BRENTWOOD
Essex   Map 6 TQ59

De Rougemont Manor
★★★★ 77% HOTEL

tel: 01277 226418 **Great Warley Street CM13 3JP**
email: info@derougemontmanor.co.uk **web:** www.derougemontmanor.co.uk
dir: *M25 junction 29, A127 to Southend then B186 towards Great Warley.*

Expect a warm welcome at this family-owned and managed hotel, situated on the outskirts of Brentwood just off the M25. The stylish bedrooms are divided between the main hotel and a bedroom wing; each is tastefully appointed and well equipped. Public rooms include a smart lounge bar, restaurant and a choice of seating areas.

Rooms: 75 (10 annexe) (6 family) (16 GF) ☎ **Facilities:** FTV WiFi ⇗ ✦ ♨ Gym Beauty treatment rooms 3-acre nature reserve Xmas New Year **Conf:** Class 66 Board 42 Theatre 260 **Services:** Lift Night porter Air con **Parking:** 200 **Notes:** Civ Wed 90

Marygreen Manor Hotel
★★★★ 75% HOTEL

tel: 01277 225252 **London Road CM14 4NR**
email: info@marygreenmanor.co.uk **web:** www.marygreenmanor.co.uk
dir: *M25 junction 28, onto A1023 over 2 sets of lights, hotel on right.*

This 16th-century house was built by Robert Wright, who named the house 'Manor of Mary Green' after his young bride. Public rooms exude character and have a wealth of original features that include exposed beams, carved panelling and the impressive Tudors Restaurant. Bedrooms are tastefully decorated and thoughtfully equipped.

Rooms: 44 (40 annexe) (35 GF) ☎ **S** fr £85 **D** fr £115* **Facilities:** STV FTV WiFi ⇗ **Conf:** Class 20 Board 25 Theatre 50 **Services:** Night porter **Parking:** 100 **Notes:** LB Civ Wed 60

Premier Inn Brentwood
Premier Inn

BUDGET HOTEL

tel: 0871 527 8142 (Calls cost 13p per minute plus your phone company's access charge) **Brentwood House, 169 Kings Road CM14 4EG**
web: www.premierinn.com
dir: *From south: M25 junction 28 take A1023 (or from north: at Brook Street roundabout 2nd exit onto A1023). Right at lights into Kings Road, at roundabout 2nd exit into Kings Road.*

High quality, budget accommodation ideal for both families and business travellers. Spacious, en suite bedrooms feature free WiFi and tea and coffee making facilities, and in most hotels, Freeview TV is also available. The adjacent family restaurant features a wide and varied menu.

Rooms: 122

BRIDGWATER   Map 4 ST23
Somerset

Walnut Tree Hotel

★★★ 78% HOTEL

tel: 01278 662255 **North Petherton TA6 6QA**
email: reservations@walnuttreehotel.com **web:** www.walnuttreehotel.com
dir: *M5 junction 24. Follow North Petherton signs. 1.3 miles. Hotel in village centre.*

Popular with both business and leisure guests, this 18th-century former coaching inn is conveniently located within easy reach of the M5. The spacious and smartly decorated bedrooms are well furnished to ensure a comfortable and relaxing stay. An extensive selection of dishes is offered in either the restaurant, or the more informal setting of the bistro.

Rooms: 30 (3 family) (3 GF) ⬢ **S** fr £75 **D** fr £85* **Facilities:** FTV WiFi ⬧ Xmas New Year **Conf:** Class 60 Board 50 Theatre 100 **Services:** Night porter **Parking:** 70

Apple Tree Hotel

★★★ 75% HOTEL

tel: 01278 733238 **Keenthorne TA5 1HZ**
email: reservations@appletreehotel.com **web:** www.appletreehotel.com
dir: *A39 from Bridgwater towards Minehead. Hotel on left, 2 miles past Cannington.*

Once a farm cottage, dating back over 300 years, this popular hotel now provides a perfect base from which to explore the many and varied local places of interest, including the unspoilt beauty of the Quantock Hills. Whether choosing to stay for business or leisure, the warmth of welcome is always the same, with the owners ensuring guests are well looked after. Bedrooms provide all expected contemporary comforts, and are split between the main building and adjacent garden rooms. Dinner is served in the conservatory restaurant, perhaps preceded by a relaxing drink in the bar or library lounge.

Rooms: 16 (2 family) (7 GF) ⬢ **S** fr £79 **D** fr £120 (including breakfast)*
Facilities: FTV WiFi ⬧ **Conf:** Class 12 Board 12 Theatre 20 **Parking:** 30

Mercure Bridgwater Hotel

■■ LEGACY
■■ HOTELS.

Ⓤ

tel: 0871 663 0624 **55-66 Eastover TA6 5AR**
email: h9861-gm@accor.com **web:** www.accorhotels.com

Currently the rating for this establishment is not confirmed. This may be due to a change of ownership or because ot has only recently joined the AA rating scheme.

Rooms: 118 **Facilities:** WiFi ⬧ Fitness centre **Conf:** Class 20 Board 16 Theatre 30 **Services:** Night porter Air con

---

Premier Inn Bridgwater

Premier Inn 🌙

BUDGET HOTEL

tel: 0871 527 8148 (Calls cost 13p per minute plus your phone company's access charge) **Express Park, Bristol Road TA6 4RR**
web: www.premierinn.com
dir: *M5 junction 23, A38 to Bridgwater. Hotel on right in 2 miles.*

High quality, budget accommodation ideal for both families and business travellers. Spacious, en suite bedrooms feature free WiFi and tea and coffee making facilities, and in most hotels, Freeview TV is also available. The adjacent family restaurant features a wide and varied menu.

Rooms: 67

BRIDLINGTON   Map 17 TA16
East Riding of Yorkshire

Expanse Hotel

★★★ 78% HOTEL

tel: 01262 675347 **North Marine Drive YO15 2LS**
email: reservations@expanse.co.uk **web:** www.expanse.co.uk
dir: *Follow North Beach signs, pass under railway arch for North Marine Drive. Hotel at bottom of hill.*

This traditional seaside hotel overlooks the bay and has been in the same family's ownership for many years. Service is relaxed and friendly and the modern bedrooms are well equipped. Comfortable public areas include a conference suite, a choice of bars and an inviting lounge. Complimentary WiFi is available.

Rooms: 45 (2 family) ⬢ **S** fr £42.95 **D** fr £85.90 (including breakfast)*
Facilities: FTV WiFi ⬧ ♫ Xmas New Year **Conf:** Class 50 Board 50 Theatre 180 **Services:** Lift Night porter **Parking:** 17 **Notes:** Civ Wed 140

Premier Inn Bridlington Seafront

Premier Inn

BUDGET HOTEL

tel: 0871 527 9700 (Calls cost 13p per minute plus your phone company's access charge) **Albion Terrace YO15 2PJ**
web: www.premierinn.com
dir: *Leave B1255 onto Sewerby Heads. Continue along Sewerby Heads onto Fortyfoot. Continue straight along this road into B1254 (Promenade). Turn left onto Albion Terrace.*

High quality, budget accommodation ideal for both families and business travellers. Spacious, en suite bedrooms feature free WiFi and tea and coffee making facilities, and in most hotels, Freeview TV is also available. The adjacent family restaurant features a wide and varied menu.

Rooms: 82

B

BRIGHOUSE
West Yorkshire

Map 16 SE12

Premier Inn Huddersfield North

Premier Inn

BUDGET HOTEL

tel: 0871 527 8530 (Calls cost 13p per minute plus your phone company's access charge) **Wakefield Road HD6 4HA**
web: www.premierinn.com
dir: M62 junction 25, A644 signed Huddersfield, Dewsbury and Wakefield. Hotel 500 metres up hill on right.

High quality, budget accommodation ideal for both families and business travellers. Spacious, en suite bedrooms feature free WiFi and tea and coffee making facilities, and in most hotels, Freeview TV is also available. The adjacent family restaurant features a wide and varied menu.

Rooms: 99

BRIGHTON & HOVE
East Sussex

Map 6 TQ30

See also **Steyning**

Hotel du Vin Brighton

★★★★ 77% TOWN HOUSE HOTEL

Hotel du Vin & Bistro

tel: 01273 718588 **2-6 Ship Street BN1 1AD**
email: info@brighton.hotelduvin.com **web:** www.hotelduvin.com/locations/brighton/
dir: From A23 follow seafront/city centre signs. Right at seafront, right into Middle Street. Follow to end bear right into Ship Street. Hotel on right.

This tastefully converted mock-Tudor building occupies a convenient location in a quiet side street close to the seafront. The individually designed bedrooms have a wine theme, and all are comprehensively equipped. Public areas include a spacious split-level bar, an atmospheric and locally popular restaurant, and useful private dining and meeting facilities.

Rooms: 49 (2 family) (4 GF) **S** fr £95 **D** fr £95* **Facilities:** STV WiFi 🎵 Xmas New Year **Conf:** Class 50 Board 60 Theatre 80 **Services:** Night porter Air con
Notes: Civ Wed 120

Jurys Inn Brighton Waterfront

★★★★ 74% HOTEL

tel: 01273 2067700 **Kings Road BN1 2GS**
email: jurysinnbrightonwaterfront@jurysinns.com
web: www.jurysinns.com/hotels/brighton-waterfront
dir: Phone for directions.

Located on Brighton's seafront, close to the city centre and The Lanes, is this modern hotel. The bedrooms are varied and are particularly well appointed and stylishly finished; many have sea views. Guests can eat in the bar, lounge and sea-facing restaurant from a menu of crowd-pleasing dishes. There is also an impressive pool and leisure facility, meetings and events space, pamper studio and convenient underground parking (chargeable).

Rooms: 210 (64 family) 🐾 **Facilities:** STV FTV WiFi ⌨ 🏊 Gym Sauna Steam room treatments 🎵 Xmas New Year **Conf:** Class 200 Board 100 Theatre 350 **Services:** Lift Night porter Air con **Parking:** 150

The Old Ship Hotel

★★★★ 74% HOTEL

tel: 01273 329001 **Kings Road BN1 1NR**
email: reservations@oldshipbrighton.co.uk **web:** www.thecairncollection.co.uk/oldship
dir: A23 to seafront, right at roundabout along Kings Road. Hotel 200 yards on right.

This historic hotel enjoys a stunning seafront location and offers guests elegant surroundings to relax in. Bedrooms are well designed, with modern facilities ensuring comfort. Many original features have been retained, including the Paganini Ballroom. Facilities include a sleek bar, alfresco dining and a variety of conference rooms.

Rooms: 154 🐾 **D** fr £120* **Facilities:** FTV WiFi HL Gym Xmas New Year **Conf:** Class 100 Board 35 Theatre 250 **Services:** Lift Night porter **Parking:** 40 **Notes:** Civ Wed 120

Blanch House

★★★ 82% 🛏 TOWN HOUSE HOTEL

tel: 01273 603504 **17 Atlingworth Sreet BN2 1PL**
email: info@blanchhouse.co.uk **web:** www.blanchhouse.co.uk
dir: Take A23 to A259, left at the pier/seafront.

Blanch House is located in the heart of Kemp Town with the seafront and town centre just a couple of minutes' walk away. Bedrooms are individual in their design and style, yet all are comfortable and of a very good quality. The spacious function suite is ideal for private meetings, dinners or weddings. There is a bar (open daily) where guests can enjoy cocktails, champagne and afternoon tea.

Rooms: 12 🐾 **S** fr £72 **D** fr £87 (including breakfast)* **Facilities:** FTV WiFi ⌨ **Conf:** Class 16 Board 20 Theatre 40 **Notes:** No children 15 years Civ Wed 40

Best Western Princes Marine

★★★ 79% HOTEL

tel: 01273 207660 **153 Kingsway, Hove BN3 4GR**
email: princesmarine@bestwestern.co.uk **web:** www.princesmarinehotel.co.uk
dir: Right at Brighton Pier, follow seafront for 2 miles. Hotel 200 yards from King Alfred leisure centre.

This friendly hotel enjoys a seafront location and offers spacious, comfortable bedrooms equipped with a good range of facilities including free WiFi. Ten rooms on the top floor, some with private balconies, offer incredible sea views and tranquillity. There is a stylish restaurant, modern bar and a flexible meeting room. Limited and secure parking is available at the rear.

Rooms: 57 (4 family) 🐾 **Facilities:** STV FTV WiFi ⌨ **Conf:** Class 40 Board 40 Theatre 60 **Services:** Lift Night porter **Parking:** 25

Mercure Brighton Seafront Hotel

★★★ 76% HOTEL

tel: 0844 815 9061 (Calls cost 5p per minute plus your phone company's access charge) **149 Kings Road BN1 2PP**
email: info@mercurebrighton.co.uk **web:** www.mercurebrighton.co.uk
dir: A23 follow signs for seafront. Right at Brighton Pier roundabout. Hotel on right, just after West Pier.

Located right on the seafront in the heart of Brighton, this hotel offers uninterrupted sea views from all seafront-facing rooms and public areas. Brighton Pier, The Lanes and town centre are just a couple of minutes' walk away. The hotel is spacious and offers comfortably appointed accommodation, all with complimentary WiFi. Plenty of secure off-road parking is available.

Rooms: 116 (11 family) **Facilities:** FTV WiFi ⌨ **Conf:** Class 80 Board 60 Theatre 180 **Services:** Night porter **Parking:** 36 **Notes:** Civ Wed 180

Queens Hotel

★★★ 73% HOTEL

tel: 01273 321222 & 0800 970 7570 **1-3 Kings Road BN1 1NS**
email: info@queenshotelbrighton.com **web:** www.queenshotelbrighton.com
dir: *A23 to Brighton town centre, follow signs for seafront. At Brighton Pier right onto seafront, hotel 500 metres on right.*

This hotel has a fantastic location with views of the beach and pier. The modern bedrooms and bathrooms are spacious, and many benefit from uninterrupted sea views. All bedrooms have LCD TVs and free WiFi. There is a spacious bar and restaurant area plus a spa, fully-equipped gym and swimming pool.

Rooms: 94 (28 family) **S** fr £69 **D** fr £79 (including breakfast) **Facilities:** Spa FTV WiFi ▷ HL ⑨ Gym Beauty salon **Conf:** Class 50 Board 50 Theatre 150 **Services:** Lift Night porter

The Kings Hotel

★★★ 73% METRO HOTEL

tel: 01273 820854 **139-141 Kings Road BN1 2NA**
email: info@kingshotelbrighton.co.uk **web:** www.kingshotelbrighton.com
dir: *Follow signs to seafront. At Brighton Pier roundabout take 3rd exit and drive west (seafront on left). Hotel adjacent to West Pier.*

Located on the seafront adjacent to West Pier, this Grade II listed, Regency building has been restored to offer contemporary accommodation. Although the hotel does not provide a full dinner service, light snacks are available throughout the day and evening in the public areas and also in the guests' bedrooms. There is parking space which is a bonus in Brighton.

Rooms: 96 (5 family) (9 GF) 🐾 **Facilities:** FTV WiFi ▷ **Services:** Lift Night porter **Parking:** 11

Brighton Harbour Hotel

Ⓤ

tel: 01273 323221 **64 Kings Road BN1 1NA**
email: brighton@harbourhotels.co.uk **web:** www.brighton-harbour-hotel.co.uk
dir: *Phone for directions.*

Currently the rating for this establishment is not confirmed. This may be due to a change of ownership or because ot has only recently joined the AA rating scheme.

Rooms: 79 **Facilities:** Spa FTV WiFi ▷ ⑨ Gym Xmas New Year **Services:** Lift Night porter **Notes:** Civ Wed

Malmaison Brighton

Ⓤ

tel: 01273 041482 **Waterfront, Brighton Marina Village BN2 5WA**
web: www.malmaison.com/locations/brighton

Currently the rating for this establishment is not confirmed. This may be due to a change of ownership or because ot has only recently joined the AA rating scheme.

Rooms: 26 **Facilities:** WiFi

Premier Inn Brighton City Centre

Premier Inn

BUDGET HOTEL

tel: 0871 527 8150 (Calls cost 13p per minute plus your phone company's access charge) **144 North Street BN1 1RE**
web: www.premierinn.com
dir: *From A23 follow signs for city centre. Right at lights near Royal Pavilion, take road ahead on left (runs adjacent to Pavilion) into Church Street, 1st left into New Road leading to North Street.*

High quality, budget accommodation ideal for both families and business travellers. Spacious, en suite bedrooms feature free WiFi and tea and coffee making facilities, and in most hotels, Freeview TV is also available. The adjacent family restaurant features a wide and varied menu.

Rooms: 160

The Grand Brighton

AA Advertised ⓦ ⓦ

tel: 01273 224300 **97-99 Kings Road BN1 2FW**
email: reservations@grandbrighton.co.uk **web:** www.grandbrighton.co.uk
dir: *On A259 adjacent to Brighton Centre.*

Dating back to the mid-19th century, this landmark seafront hotel, with its eye-catching white facade and intricate balconies, is as grand as the name suggests. Bedrooms include a number of deluxe sea view rooms, some with balconies, and suites, also with sea views. The hotel is perhaps best known for its extensive conference and banqueting facilities; there is also an impressive conservatory adjoining the bar.

Rooms: 201 (60 family) 🐾 **Facilities:** Spa FTV WiFi Gym Thermal suite ♫ Xmas New Year **Conf:** Class 450 Board 60 Theatre 800 **Services:** Lift Night porter **Parking:** 50 **Notes:** Civ Wed 800

| **BRISTOL** | Map 4 ST57 |
| Bristol | |

Aztec Hotel & Spa

THWAITES

★★★★ 81% ⓦ HOTEL

tel: 01454 201090 **Aztec West BS32 4TS**
email: reservations@aztechotelbristol.co.uk **web:** www.thwaites.co.uk/aztec-hotel-bristol
dir: *Access via M5 junction 16 and M4.*

Situated close to Cribbs Causeway shopping centre and major motorway links, this stylish hotel offers comfortable, very well-equipped bedrooms and suites. Built in a Nordic style, public rooms boast log fires and vaulted ceilings. Leisure facilities include a popular gym and good size pool. The restaurant offers relaxed informal dining with a focus on simply prepared, quality regional foods. The hotel has a spa with a gym, pool, children's pool, whirlpool, sauna, steam room and a range of treatments.

Rooms: 128 (8 family) (29 GF) **S** fr £98 **D** fr £98* **Facilities:** Spa STV WiFi ▷ HL ⑨ Gym Steam room Sauna Children's splash pool Activity studio New Year **Conf:** Class 120 Board 36 Theatre 200 **Services:** Lift Night porter **Parking:** 240 **Notes:** LB Civ Wed 120

B

BRISTOL *continued*

DoubleTree by Hilton Bristol City Centre

fOCUShotels
management limited

★★★★ 80% HOTEL

tel: 0117 926 0041 **Redcliffe Way BS1 6NL**
email: sales@focusbristol.co.uk **web:** www.doubletree3.hilton.com
dir: *1 mile from M32. 400 yards from Temple Meads station, before church.*

This large, modern hotel is situated in the heart of the city centre and offers spacious public areas and ample parking. Bedrooms are well equipped for both business and leisure guests. Dining options include a relaxed bar and the unique Kiln Restaurant (a listed glass-kiln dating from the 17th century) where a good selection of freshly prepared dishes is available.

Rooms: 206 ☎ **S** fr £85 **D** fr £85* **Facilities:** FTV WiFi ⓘ HL Gym **Conf:** Class 120 Board 75 Theatre 300 **Services:** Lift Night porter Air con **Parking:** 150 **Notes:** LB

Hotel du Vin Bristol

Hotel
du Vin
& Bistro

★★★★ 78% ⓖ TOWN HOUSE HOTEL

tel: 0117 925 5577 & 0844 736 4252 (Calls cost 5p per minute plus your phone company's access charge) **The Sugar House, Narrow Lewins Mead BS1 2NU**
email: info.bristol@hotelduvin.com **web:** www.hotelduvin.com/locations/bristol
dir: *From A4 follow city centre signs. After 400 yards pass Rupert Street NCP on right. Hotel on opposite carriageway.*

This hotel is part of one of Britain's most innovative hotel groups, offering high standards of hospitality and accommodation. The property is a Grade II listed, converted 18th-century sugar refinery, and provides great facilities with a modern, minimalist design. The bedrooms are exceptionally well designed and the bistro offers an excellent menu and wine list.

Rooms: 40 (10 family) ☎ **Facilities:** STV FTV WiFi ⓘ ♫ New Year **Conf:** Class 36 Board 34 Theatre 72 **Services:** Lift Night porter **Parking:** 9 **Notes:** Civ Wed 65

Bristol Harbour Hotel & Spa

★★★★ 76% HOTEL

tel: 0117 203 4445 **55 Corn Street BS1 1HT**
email: bristol@harbourhotels.co.uk **web:** www.harbourhotels.co.uk
dir: *Phone for directions.*

This modern and stylish hotel fuses two iconic former bank properties in the very heart of Bristol. Bedrooms and bathrooms are very comfortably furnished and equipped and offer a range of shapes and sizes including one being the converted office of the bank manager. The adjoining Jetty restaurant is open throughout the day and has an emphasis on seafood, while evening cocktails can be taken in the contemporary Gold Bar. The grand former banking hall is now the main space for large events and meetings and the bank vaults have been transformed into the hotel spa complete with the original huge safe doors.

Rooms: 42 (3 family) (1 GF) ☎ **S** fr £145 **D** fr £145* **Facilities:** Spa FTV WiFi ⓘ ⓧ Gym Xmas New Year **Conf:** Class 220 Board 120 Theatre 300 **Services:** Lift Night porter Air con **Notes:** Civ Wed 300

Mercure Bristol North The Grange

★★★★ 74% ⓖ COUNTRY HOUSE HOTEL

tel: 01454 777333 & 0844 815 9063 (Calls cost 7p per minute plus your phone company's access charge) **Northwoods, Winterbourne BS36 1RP**
email: gm.mercurebristolnorthgrange@jupiterhotels.co.uk **web:** www.mercurebristol.co.uk
dir: *A38 towards Filton/Bristol. At roundabout 1st exit into Bradley Stoke Way, at lights 1st left into Woodlands Lane, at 2nd roundabout left into Tench Lane. In 1 mile left at T-junction, hotel 200 yards on left.*

Built in the 19th century and surrounded by 18 acres of attractive grounds, this is a pleasant hotel situated only a short drive from the city centre. The bedrooms are spacious and well equipped with a range of meeting facilities also available. The conservatory bar has a terrace which makes a delightful place to enjoy a drink under the shade of a 200-year-old cedar tree. The hotel is popular as a wedding venue.

Rooms: 68 (6 annexe) (4 family) (22 GF) ☎ **Facilities:** STV FTV WiFi ⓘ Xmas New Year **Conf:** Class 60 Board 76 Theatre 180 **Services:** Night porter **Parking:** 150 **Notes:** LB Civ Wed 150

Novotel Bristol Centre

NOVOTEL
HOTELS & RESORTS

★★★★ 73% HOTEL

tel: 0117 976 9988 **Victoria Street BS1 6HY**
email: H5622@accor.com **web:** www.novotel.com
dir: *At end of M32 follow signs for Temple Meads station to roundabout. Final exit, hotel immediately on right.*

This city centre hotel provides smart, contemporary accommodation. Most of the bedrooms demonstrate the Novotel 'Novation' style with unique swivel desk, internet access, air conditioning and a host of extras. The hotel is convenient for the mainline railway station and also has its own car park.

Rooms: 131 (34 family) ☎ **Facilities:** STV FTV WiFi ⓘ HL Gym Sauna Steam room **Conf:** Class 70 Board 35 Theatre 210 **Services:** Lift Night porter Air con **Parking:** 100 **Notes:** LB Civ Wed 100

Henbury Lodge Hotel

★★★ 80% ⓖ HOTEL

tel: 0117 950 2615 **Station Road, Henbury BS10 7QQ**
email: info@henburyhotel.com **web:** www.henburyhotel.com
dir: *M5 junction 17/A4018 (signed Westbury on Trym) follow to 3rd roundabout then 3rd exit into Crown Lane. Follow to end then right into Henbury Road, continue to mini-roundabout then right into Station Road. Hotel entrance first on left.*

Located a few miles from the city centre with easy access to the M4 and M5, this small hotel is popular with both business and leisure guests. Bedrooms come in a range of shapes and sizes and are divided between the main house and the converted, adjacent stable block. All are comfortably furnished and well equipped. The friendly team of staff offer a personal welcome and many guests are regular visitors. Top quality ingredients are used at both dinner and breakfast, both taken in the stylish restaurant.

Rooms: 12 (10 annexe) (2 family) (7 GF) **S** fr £109 **D** fr £118 (including breakfast)*
Facilities: FTV WiFi ⓘ **Services:** Night porter **Parking:** 20

Rodney Hotel

★★★ 69% HOTEL

tel: 0117 973 5422 **4 Rodney Place, Clifton BS8 4HY**
email: rodney@cliftonhotels.com **web:** www.cliftonhotels.com/bristolhotels/rodney
dir: *Off Clifton Down Road.*

With easy access from the M5, this attractive, listed building in Clifton is conveniently close to the city centre. The individually decorated bedrooms provide a useful range of extra facilities for the business traveller; the public areas include a smart bar, and a small restaurant offering enjoyable and carefully prepared dishes. A pleasant rear garden provides additional seating in the summer months.

Rooms: 31 (1 family) (2 GF) **Facilities:** FTV WiFi **Conf:** Class 20 Board 20 Theatre 30 **Services:** Night porter **Parking:** 7 **Notes:** LB Closed 22 December to 3 January RS Sunday Civ Wed 40

Clifton Hotel

★★ 75% HOTEL

tel: 0117 973 6882 **St Pauls Road, Clifton BS8 1LX**
email: clifton@cliftonhotels.com **web:** www.cliftonhotels.com/bristolhotels/clifton
dir: *M32 follow Bristol/Clifton signs, along Park Street. Left at lights into St Pauls Road.*

This popular hotel offers a relaxed, friendly service and very well-equipped bedrooms. There is a welcoming lounge by the reception, and in summer months drinks and meals can be enjoyed on the terrace. The Racks Bar and Restaurant offers an interesting selection of modern dishes in informal surroundings. There is street parking, or for a small charge, secure garage parking is available.

Rooms: 59 (2 family) (12 GF) **Facilities:** STV FTV WiFi **Services:** Lift Night porter **Parking:** 12

Premier Inn Bristol Airport (Sidcot)

Premier Inn

BUDGET HOTEL

tel: 0871 527 8154 (Calls cost 13p per minute plus your phone company's access charge) **Bridgwater Road, Winscombe BS25 1NN**
web: www.premierinn.com
dir: *Between M5 junction 21 and 22 (9 miles from Bristol Airport), onto A371 towards Banwell, Winscombe to A38. Right at lights, hotel 300 yards on left.*

High quality, budget accommodation ideal for both families and business travellers. Spacious, en suite bedrooms feature free WiFi and tea and coffee making facilities, and in most hotels, Freeview TV is also available. The adjacent family restaurant features a wide and varied menu.

Rooms: 31

Premier Inn Bristol (Alveston)

Premier Inn

BUDGET HOTEL

tel: 0871 527 8152 (Calls cost 13p per minute plus your phone company's access charge) **Thornbury Road, Alveston BS35 3LL**
web: www.premierinn.com
dir: *Just off M5. From north: exit at junction 14 onto A38 towards Bristol. From south: exit at junction 16 onto A38 towards Gloucester.*

Rooms: 75

Premier Inn Bristol City Centre (Haymarket)

Premier Inn

BUDGET HOTEL

tel: 0871 527 8156 (Calls cost 13p per minute plus your phone company's access charge) **The Haymarket BS1 3LR**
web: www.premierinn.com
dir: *M4 junction 19, M32 towards city centre. Through 2 sets of lights, at 3rd lights turn right, to roundabout, take 2nd exit. Hotel on left.*

Rooms: 224

Premier Inn Bristol City Centre King St

Premier Inn

BUDGET HOTEL

tel: 0871 527 8158 (Calls cost 13p per minute plus your phone company's access charge) **Llandoger Trow, King Street BS1 4ER**
web: www.premierinn.com
dir: *A38 into city centre. Left onto B4053 Baldwin Street. Right into Queen Charlotte Street, follow one-way system, bear right at river. Hotel on right.*

Rooms: 60

Premier Inn Bristol City Centre (Lewins Mead)

Premier Inn

BUDGET HOTEL

tel: 0871 527 9594 (Calls cost 13p per minute plus your phone company's access charge) **Lewins Mead BS1 2PY**
web: www.premierinn.com
dir: *From north: M4 junction 19, M32 (city centre/Clifton/bus station). 3rd exit at roundabout. 4th left into Lower Moulden Street, hotel on right. From south: M5 junction 19, A369. Keep right, at roundabout 1st exit, merge onto A370. Right into Hotwell Road. At roundabout 3rd exit to next roundabout. Keep right, left onto A38. Hotel on left.*

Rooms: 167

Premier Inn Bristol City (Finzels Reach)

Premier Inn

BUDGET HOTEL

tel: 0871 622 2428 (Calls cost 13p per minute plus your phone company's access charge) **Counterslip BS1 6BX**
web: www.premierinn.com
dir: *Follow Baldwin Street then right onto Bristol Bridge. Left into Bath Street, follow this road then turn right. Hotel straight ahead.*

Rooms: 168

Premier Inn Bristol Cribbs Causeway

Premier Inn

BUDGET HOTEL

tel: 0871 527 8160 (Calls cost 13p per minute plus your phone company's access charge) **Cribbs Causeway, Catbrain Lane BS10 7TQ**
web: www.premierinn.com
dir: *M5 junction 17, A4018. 1st left at roundabout into Lysander Road. Right into Catbrain Hill, leads to Catbrain Lane.*

Rooms: 177

B

BRISTOL *continued*

Premier Inn Bristol East (Emersons Green)

Premier Inn

BUDGET HOTEL

tel: 0871 527 8162 (Calls cost 13p per minute plus your phone company's access charge) **200/202 Westerleigh Road, Emersons Green BS16 7AN**
web: www.premierinn.com
dir: *M4 junction 19 onto M32 junction 1, left onto A4174 (Avon Ring Road). Hotel at 3rd roundabout.*

Rooms: 83

Premier Inn Bristol Filton

Premier Inn

BUDGET HOTEL

tel: 0871 527 8164 (Calls cost 13p per minute plus your phone company's access charge) **Shield Retail Park, Gloucester Road North BS34 7BR**
web: www.premierinn.com
dir: *M5 junction 16, A38 signed Filton/Patchway. Pass airport and Royal Mail on right. Left at 2nd roundabout, 1st left into retail park.*

Rooms: 62

Premier Inn Bristol South

Premier Inn

BUDGET HOTEL

tel: 0871 527 8166 (Calls cost 13p per minute plus your phone company's access charge) **Hengrove Leisure Park, Hengrove Way BS14 0HR**
web: www.premierinn.com
dir: *From city centre take A37 to Wells and Shepton Mallet. Right onto A4174. Hotel at 3rd lights.*

Rooms: 88

BRIXHAM	Map 3 SX95
Devon	

Berry Head Hotel

THE INDEPENDENTS
HOTEL ASSOCIATION

★★★ 81% HOTEL

tel: 01803 853225 **Berry Head Road TQ5 9AJ**
email: stay@berryheadhotel.com **web:** www.berryheadhotel.com
dir: *From marina 1 mile, hotel on left.*

Set in a stunning cliff-top location, this imposing property dates back to 1809, and has spectacular views across Torbay. Public areas include two comfortable lounges, an outdoor terrace, and a swimming pool, together with a bar serving a range of popular dishes. Many of the bedrooms have the benefit of splendid sea views.

Rooms: 32 (7 family) **Facilities:** FTV WiFi ☒ ⛵ Petanque Sailing Deep sea fishing Yacht charter ♫ Xmas New Year **Conf:** Class 250 Board 40 Theatre 300 **Services:** Lift Night porter **Parking:** 100 **Notes:** Civ Wed 200

Quayside Hotel

★★★ 79% ❀ HOTEL

tel: 01803 855751 **41-49 King Street TQ5 9TJ**
email: reservations@quaysidehotel.co.uk **web:** www.quaysidehotel.co.uk
dir: *On A380 continue towards Brixham taking the A3022.*

With views over the harbour and bay, this hotel was formerly six cottages, and the public rooms retain a certain cosiness and intimacy. These include the lounge, residents' bar and Ernie Lister's public bar. Freshly-landed fish features on the menus, alongside a number of creative and skilfully prepared dishes, served in the well-appointed restaurant. Good food is also available in the public bar. The owners and their team of local staff provide friendly and attentive service.

Rooms: 29 (2 family) **S** fr £75 **D** fr £100 (including breakfast)* **Facilities:** FTV WiFi ☒ ♫ Xmas New Year **Conf:** Class 18 Board 18 Theatre 25 **Services:** Night porter **Parking:** 30 **Notes:** LB

BROADWAY	Map 10 SP03
Worcestershire	

Foxhill Manor

★★★★★ 85% SMALL HOTEL

tel: 01386 852711 **Farncombe Estate WR12 7LJ**
email: reservations@foxhillmanor.com **web:** www.foxhillmanor.com
dir: *Off A44 between Broadway and Moreton-in-Marsh on Fish Hill. 1 mile outside Broadway village.*

Located on the sprawling Farncombe Estate, this intimate country house offers excellent accommodation with a truly personalised service experience. The team of house managers and butlers will ensure your stay is tailored for you from start to finish. The chef will introduce you to dishes that are based on the very best of seasonal produce from the estate and surrounding areas. Up-to-the-minute technology is embraced with touch-screen tablets connecting guests to the amenities throughout the estate.

Rooms: 8 (1 family) (2 GF) ↻ **S** fr £399 **D** fr £399 (including breakfast)*
Facilities: STV FTV WiFi ↻ ⊛ ♨ Gym In room treatments **Conf:** Class 40 Board 28
Theatre 70 **Services:** Night porter Air con **Parking:** 30 **Notes:** No children 12 years
Civ Wed 70

Dormy House Hotel

★★★★ ⊛⊛ HOTEL

tel: 01386 852711 **Willersey Hill WR12 7LF**
email: reservations@dormyhouse.co.uk **web:** www.dormyhouse.co.uk
dir: 2 miles east of Broadway off A44, at top of Fish Hill turn for Saintbury/Picnic area.
In 0.5 mile turn left, hotel on left.

Dormy House is a converted 17th-century farmhouse set in 400-acre grounds on
the Farncombe Estate, with stunning views over Broadway. The hotel boasts a
luxury spa offering a wide range of treatments, a swimming pool, a Veuve Clicquot
Champagne nail bar, gym and thermal suite. The best traditions are retained here
– customer care, real fires, comfortable sofas and afternoon teas. Dinner features
an interesting choice of dishes created by a skilled kitchen brigade.

Rooms: 38 (19 annexe) (8 family) (19 GF) ↻ **Facilities:** Spa STV FTV WiFi ↻ ⊛
Gym Nature and jogging trail Circular walks Champagne nail bar Xmas New
Year **Conf:** Class 16 Board 16 Theatre 16 **Services:** Night porter **Parking:** 70
Notes: LB Civ Wed 80

The Fish

★★★ 88% ⊛⊛ HOTEL

tel: 01386 858000 **Farncombe Estate WR12 7LJ**
email: reception@thefishhotel.co.uk **web:** www.thefishhotel.co.uk
dir: Follow A44 to Moreton-in-Marsh then follow signs to Evesham and Broadway. Take
Saintbury turn by Broadway Tower, estate on the left.

Part of the 400-acre Farncombe Estate, The Fish benefits from far-reaching views
across the Worcestershire countryside. The smartly appointed bedrooms are
located on the hillside in former farmhouses and converted buildings, within easy
reach of The Lodge, where all the hotel's main facilities can be found. In addition
to the use of the on-site tennis court and gym, outdoor activities can be arranged.

Rooms: 63 (59 GF) ↻ **S** fr £170 **D** fr £170 (including breakfast) **Facilities:** FTV
WiFi ↻ HL ♨ Gym Xmas New Year **Conf:** Class 50 Board 30 Theatre 80
Services: Night porter Air con **Parking:** 200 **Notes:** LB

The Broadway Hotel

★★★ 85% ⊛⊛ HOTEL

tel: 01386 852401 **The Green, High Street WR12 7AA**
email: info@broadwayhotel.info **web:** www.cotswold-inns-hotels.co.uk
dir: Follow signs to Evesham, then Broadway. Left onto Leamington Road, hotel just
off village green.

The Broadway Hotel is a half-timbered Cotswold-stone property, built in the 15th
century as a retreat for the Abbots of Pershore. It combines modern, attractive
decor with original charm and character. Bedrooms are tastefully furnished and
well equipped while public rooms include a relaxing lounge, cosy bar and
charming restaurant; alfresco all-day dining in summer months proves popular.

Rooms: 19 (1 family) (3 GF) **S** fr £120 **D** fr £150 (including breakfast)*
Facilities: FTV WiFi ↻ Xmas New Year **Parking:** 20

B

Rhinefield House Hotel

★★★★ ⊛⊛ ♨ HOTEL

tel: 01590 622922 & 0845 072 7516 (Calls cost 5p per minute plus your phone
company's access charge) **Rhinefield Road SO42 7QB**
email: rhinefieldhouse@handpicked.co.uk
web: www.handpickedhotels.co.uk/rhinefieldhouse
dir: A35 towards Christchurch. 3 miles from Lyndhurst turn left to Rhinefield,
1.5 miles to hotel.

This stunning 19th-century, mock-Elizabethan mansion is set in 40 acres of
beautifully landscaped gardens and forest. Bedrooms are spacious and great
consideration is given to guest comfort. The elegant and award-winning Armada
Restaurant is richly furnished, and features a fireplace carving (nine years in
the making) that is worth taking time to admire. If the weather permits, the
delightful terrace is just the place for enjoying alfresco eating.

Rooms: 50 (13 family) (18 GF) ↻ **D** fr £144 (including breakfast)* **Facilities:** Spa
STV FTV WiFi ↻ HL ⊛ ↻ ♨ Gym Hydrotherapy pool Plunge pool Steam room
Sauna Xmas New Year **Conf:** Class 72 Board 56 Theatre 160 **Services:** Lift Night
porter **Parking:** 100 **Notes:** LB Civ Wed 130

See advert on following page

BROCKENHURST *continued*

HIGHLY RECOMMENDED

Careys Manor Hotel & Senspa

★★★★ 84% ◉◉◉ HOTEL

tel: 01590 624467 **Lyndhurst Road SO42 7RH**
email: stay@careysmanor.com **web:** www.careysmanor.com
dir: *M27 junction 3, M271, A35 to Lyndhurst. A337 towards Brockenhurst. Hotel on left after Beaulieu sign.*

This smart property offers a host of facilities that include an Oriental-style spa and leisure suite with an excellent range of unusual treatments, as well as three contrasting restaurants that offer a choice of Thai, French or modern British cuisine. Many of the spacious and well-appointed bedrooms have balconies overlooking the gardens. Extensive function and conference facilities are also available.

Rooms: 79 (61 annexe) (31 GF) ⬦ **S** fr £139 **D** fr £159 (including breakfast)*
Facilities: Spa FTV WiFi ⬦ HL ⬦ ⬦ Gym Steam room Hydrotherapy pool Sauna herbal sauna Crystal steam room Laconicum Tepidarium Experience showers Xmas New Year **Conf:** Class 70 Board 40 Theatre 120 **Services:** Lift Night porter **Parking:** 180 **Notes:** Civ Wed 100

The Balmer Lawn Hotel

★★★★ 81% ◉◉ HOTEL

tel: 01590 623116 **Lyndhurst Road SO42 7ZB**
email: info@blh.co.uk **web:** www.balmerlawnhotel.com
dir: *Just off A337 from Brockenhurst towards Lymington.*

Situated in the heart of the New Forest, this peacefully located hotel provides comfortable public rooms and a wide range of bedrooms. A selection of carefully prepared and enjoyable dishes is offered in the spacious restaurant. The extensive function and leisure facilities make this popular with both families and conference delegates.

Rooms: 54 (10 family) ⬦ **Facilities:** Spa FTV WiFi ⬦ ⬦ Gym Squash Indoor leisure suite sauna Xmas New Year **Conf:** Class 76 Board 48 Theatre 150 **Services:** Lift Night porter **Parking:** 100 **Notes:** Civ Wed 120

THE PIG

★★★ ◉◉ ⬦ COUNTRY HOUSE HOTEL

tel: 01590 622354 **Beaulieu Road SO42 7QL**
email: info@thepighotel.com **web:** www.thepighotel.co.uk
dir: *At Brockenhurst onto B3055 Beaulieu Road. 1 mile on left up private road.*

A delightful country house where the focus is very much on the food, with the chef, gardener and forager working as a team to create menus of seasonal, locally sourced produce; all ingredients are found within a 15-mile radius. The result of this policy is that menus change daily, and sometimes even more frequently. The stylish dining room is an authentically reproduced Victorian greenhouse, and alfresco eating is possible as there is a wood-fired oven in the courtyard. The bedrooms have eclectic furnishings, good beds and views of either the forest or the garden; two suites with private courtyards are available.

Rooms: 31 (15 annexe) (3 family) (16 GF) ⬦ **D** fr £155* **Facilities:** STV FTV WiFi ⬦ ⬦ Massage treatment rooms Xmas New Year **Conf:** Board 14 **Services:** Night porter **Parking:** 30 **Notes:** Civ Wed 120

B

Forest Park Hotel

★★★ 73% HOTEL

tel: 01590 622844 **Rhinefield Road SO42 7ZG**
email: reservations@forestpark-hotel.co.uk **web:** www.forestpark-hotel.co.uk
dir: *M27 junction 1, follow signs for A337 Lyndhurst. Follow road for 3 miles, left at lights onto A35, A337 Lymington Brockenhurst, right into Meerut Road, right at T-junction.*

Located in the heart of the beautiful New Forest National Park, this popular hotel provides an ideal base for exploring this remarkable area. Bedrooms have garden or forest views, and free WiFi is available throughout. The hotel is children friendly, and they will delight in seeing the ponies on the doorstep. The restaurant has views of the lovely landscaped gardens, with delicious food to match. The bar offers a more relaxed atmosphere and food is served from midday to nine in the evening.

Rooms: 38 (6 family) (7 GF) ↸ **Facilities:** FTV WiFi HL ♬ **Conf:** Class 15 Board 20 Theatre 40 **Services:** Night porter **Parking:** 38 **Notes:** Civ Wed 70

The Cottage Hotel

★★ 75% HOTEL

tel: 01590 622296 **Sway Road SO42 7SH**
email: enquiries@cottagelodge.co.uk **web:** www.cottagelodge.co.uk
dir: *Exit A337 opposite Careys Manor Hotel into Grigg Lane, 0.25 mile over crossroads, cottage next to war memorial.*

Although it has been skilfully modernised by the resident owners, parts of this attractive small hotel date back over 300 years. On offer is a choice of well furnished, bright bedrooms reflecting the hotel's New Forest location. There is a low-beamed snug lounge with welcoming woodburner, and a licensed restaurant, White Tails, which offers a good variety of dishes to suit all.

Rooms: 15 (3 family) (7 GF) ↸ **S** fr £50 **D** fr £80 (including breakfast)*
Facilities: FTV WiFi ♑ **Conf:** Class 8 Board 8 Theatre 8 **Parking:** 15 **Notes:** LB Closed 1 week at Christmas

---

BROMBOROUGH
Merseyside
Map 15 SJ38

Premier Inn Wirral (Bromborough)

Premier Inn

BUDGET HOTEL

tel: 0871 527 9172 (Calls cost 13p per minute plus your phone company's access charge) **High Street, Bromborough Cross CH62 7EZ**
web: www.premierinn.com
dir: *On A41 (New Chester Road), 2 miles from M53 junction 5.*

High quality, budget accommodation ideal for both families and business travellers. Spacious, en suite bedrooms feature free WiFi and tea and coffee making facilities, and in most hotels, Freeview TV is also available. The adjacent family restaurant features a wide and varied menu.

Rooms: 32

BROME
Suffolk
Map 13 TM17

HIGHLY RECOMMENDED

Best Western Brome Grange Hotel

Best Western

★★★ 86% @@ ⌖ HOTEL

tel: 01379 870456 **Norwich Road, Nr Diss IP23 8AP**
email: info@bromegrangehotel.co.uk **web:** www.bromegrange.co.uk
dir: *Located on the A140 between Ipswich and Norwich in the village of Brome.*

Conveniently located between Ipswich and Norfolk the Best Western Brome Grange Hotel offers bedrooms that are spacious, well equipped and attractively presented. The charming cosy bar has lots of character and the restaurant is very popular with locals and residents. A warm welcome is assured, and ample secure parking is available for guests.

Rooms: 44 (26 annexe) (2 family) (26 GF) ↸ **S** fr £55 **D** fr £55* **Facilities:** Spa FTV WiFi ⌂ Gym Whirlpool Steam room Sauna 2 treatment rooms Xmas New Year **Conf:** Class 60 Board 40 Theatre 150 **Services:** Lift Night porter **Parking:** 100 **Notes:** Civ Wed 110

BROMLEY
Greater London

Bromley Court Hotel

★★★ 81% HOTEL Plan 1 H1

tel: 020 8461 8600 **Bromley Hill BR1 4JD**
email: enquiries@bromleycourthotel.co.uk **web:** www.bromleycourthotel.co.uk
dir: *North of town centre, off A21. Private drive opposite Volkswagen garage on Bromley Hill.*

Set amid three acres of grounds, this smart hotel enjoys a peaceful location, in a residential area on the outskirts of town. Well maintained bedrooms are smartly appointed and thoughtfully equipped. The contemporary-style restaurant offers a good choice of meals in comfortable surroundings. Extensive facilities include a leisure club and a good range of meeting rooms.

Rooms: 117 (4 family) ↸ **S** fr £50 **D** fr £70* **Facilities:** STV FTV WiFi ⌂ Gym Steam room Beauty room ♬ Xmas New Year **Conf:** Class 70 Board 40 Theatre 150 **Services:** Lift Night porter Air con **Parking:** 86 **Notes:** LB Civ Wed 180

BROMSGROVE
Worcestershire
Map 10 SO97

Premier Inn Bromsgrove Central

Premier Inn

BUDGET HOTEL

tel: 0871 527 8168 (Calls cost 13p per minute plus your phone company's access charge) **Birmingham Road B61 0BA**
web: www.premierinn.com
dir: *M42 junction 1 (southbound access only) or M5 junction 4 southbound or M5 junction 5 northbound onto A38 towards Bromsgrove. Hotel adjacent to Guild Brewers Fayre. Note: for sat nav use B60 1GJ.*

High quality, budget accommodation ideal for both families and business travellers. Spacious, en suite bedrooms feature free WiFi and tea and coffee making facilities, and in most hotels, Freeview TV is also available. The adjacent family restaurant features a wide and varied menu.

Rooms: 78

BROMSGROVE *continued*

Premier Inn Bromsgrove South (Worcester Road)

Premier Inn

BUDGET HOTEL

tel: 0871 527 8170 (Calls cost 13p per minute plus your phone company's access charge) **Worcester Road, Upton Warren B61 7ET**
web: www.premierinn.com
dir: *M5 junction 5, A38 towards Bromsgrove, 1.2 miles. Or M42 junction 1, A38 south, cross over A448.*

Rooms: 27

BROXTON
Cheshire
Map 15 SJ45

Carden Park Hotel, Golf Resort & Spa

★★★★ 82% ⊛ HOTEL

tel: 01829 731000 **Carden Park CH3 9DQ**
email: reservations@cardenpark.co.uk **web:** www.cardenpark.co.uk
dir: *M56 junction 15, M53 Chester. Take A41 signed Whitchurch. 8 miles. At Broxton roundabout right onto A534 (signed Wrexham). Hotel 1.5 miles on left.*

This impressive Cheshire estate dates back to the 17th century and consists of 1,000 acres of mature parkland. The hotel offers a choice of dining options along with superb leisure facilities that include golf courses, a fully-equipped gym, a swimming pool and popular spa. Spacious, thoughtfully equipped bedrooms have excellent business and in-room entertainment facilities.

Rooms: 196 (83 annexe) (24 family) (68 GF) ⏸ ⬤ **S** fr £99 **D** fr £99 (including breakfast)* **Facilities:** Spa STV FTV WiFi ⬠ ⬤ ⬤ 36 ⬤ Gym Archery mountain bike laser clay shooting Sauna Steam room Segway Quad bikes Xmas New Year **Conf:** Class 240 Board 125 Theatre 350 **Services:** Lift Night porter **Parking:** 700 **Notes:** LB Civ Wed 350

BRYHER
Cornwall & Isles Of Scilly
Map 2 SV81

HIGHLY RECOMMENDED

Hell Bay

★★★★ ⊛⊛⊛ HOTEL

tel: 01720 422947 **TR23 0PR**
email: contactus@hellbay.co.uk **web:** www.hellbay.co.uk
dir: *Access by boat from Penzance, plane from Exeter, Newquay or Land's End.*

Located on the smallest of the inhabited islands of the Scilly Isles on the edge of the Atlantic, this hotel makes a really special destination. The owners have filled the hotel with original works of art by artists who have connections with the islands, and the interior is decorated in cool blues and greens creating an extremely restful environment. The contemporary bedrooms are equally stylish, and many have garden access and stunning sea views. Eating here is a delight, and naturally, seafood features strongly on the award-winning, daily-changing menus.

Rooms: 25 (25 annexe) (4 family) (15 GF) ⏸ **S** fr £175 **D** fr £280 (including breakfast & dinner)* **Facilities:** Spa FTV WiFi ⬠ ⬤ ⬤ 7 ⬤ ⬤ Gym **Conf:** Class 36 Board 20 **Notes:** LB Closed November to February

---

BUCKHURST HILL
Essex
Map 6 TQ49

Premier Inn Loughton/Buckhurst Hill

Premier Inn

BUDGET HOTEL

tel: 0871 527 8686 (Calls cost 13p per minute plus your phone company's access charge) **High Road IG9 5HT**
web: www.premierinn.com
dir: *M25 junction 26 towards Loughton. A121 into Buckhurst Hill (approximately 5 miles), hotel on left.*

High quality, budget accommodation ideal for both families and business travellers. Spacious, en suite bedrooms feature free WiFi and tea and coffee making facilities, and in most hotels, Freeview TV is also available. The adjacent family restaurant features a wide and varied menu.

Rooms: 50

BUCKINGHAM
Buckinghamshire
Map 11 SP63

Buckingham Villiers Hotel

★★★★ 75% ⊛ HOTEL

tel: 01280 822444 **3 Castle Street MK18 1BS**
email: villiers@oxfordshire-hotels.co.uk **web:** www.villiers-hotel.co.uk
dir: *M1 junction 13 north or junction 15 south follow signs to Buckingham. Castle Street by Old Town Hall.*

Guests can enjoy a town centre location with a high degree of comfort at this 400-year-old former coaching inn. Relaxing public areas feature flagstone floors, oak panelling and real fires, while bedrooms are modern, spacious and equipped to a high level. Diners can unwind in the atmospheric bar before taking dinner in the award-winning restaurant.

Rooms: 49 (4 family) (3 GF) **S** fr £90 **D** fr £160 (including breakfast)* **Facilities:** STV FTV WiFi Xmas New Year **Conf:** Class 120 Board 80 Theatre 250 **Services:** Lift Night porter **Parking:** 52 **Notes:** LB Civ Wed 180

Best Western Buckingham Hotel

BW Best Western.

★★★ 75% HOTEL

tel: 01280 822622 **Buckingham Ring Road MK18 1RY**
email: info@thebuckinghamhotel.co.uk **web:** www.thebuckinghamhotel.co.uk
dir: *A421 to Buckingham, take ring road south towards Brackley and Bicester. Hotel on left.*

A purpose-built hotel, which offers comfortable and spacious rooms with well designed working spaces for business travellers. There are also extensive conference facilities. The open-plan restaurant and bar offer a good range of dishes, and the well-equipped leisure suite is popular with guests.

Rooms: 70 (6 family) (31 GF) **D** fr £80* **Facilities:** STV FTV WiFi ⬠ ⬤ Gym Sauna Steam room Xmas New Year **Conf:** Class 60 Board 60 Theatre 200 **Services:** Night porter **Parking:** 200 **Notes:** Civ Wed 120

B

BUCKLAND (NEAR BROADWAY)
Gloucestershire   Map 10 SP03

INSPECTOR'S CHOICE

Buckland Manor

★★★★ 🏵🏵🏵 ⚱ COUNTRY HOUSE HOTEL

tel: 01386 852626 **WR12 7LY**
email: info@bucklandmanor.co.uk **web:** www.bucklandmanor.co.uk
dir: 2 miles south of Broadway, off B4632.

Buckland Manor is a grand 13th-century manor house, surrounded by well-kept and beautiful gardens that feature a stream and waterfall. Everything at this hotel is geared to encourage rest and relaxation. Spacious bedrooms and public areas are furnished with high quality pieces and decorated in keeping with the style of the manor; crackling log fires warm the wonderful lounges. The elegant dining room, with views over the rolling hills, is the perfect place to enjoy dishes that use excellent local produce

Rooms: 15 (1 family) (4 GF) 🐾 **S** fr £205 **D** fr £225 (including breakfast)*
Facilities: FTV WiFi ♨ 🌤 Xmas New Year **Conf:** Board 25 Theatre 30
Services: Night porter **Parking:** 20 **Notes:** LB No children 10 years Civ Wed 40

BUDE
Cornwall & Isles Of Scilly   Map 2 SS20

Premier Inn Bude

Premier Inn 🌙

BUDGET HOTEL

tel: 0871 527 9664 (Calls cost 13p per minute plus your phone company's access charge) **The Strand EX23 8RA**
web: www.premierinn.com
dir: A39 onto A3072 (Stratton Road). At 1st roundabout take 2nd exit to A3072. At mini-roundabout take 2nd exit, right onto The Strand. Hotel on right.

High quality, budget accommodation ideal for both families and business travellers. Spacious, en suite bedrooms feature free WiFi and tea and coffee making facilities, and in most hotels, Freeview TV is also available. The adjacent family restaurant features a wide and varied menu.

Rooms: 67

BURFORD
Oxfordshire   Map 5 SP21

The Bay Tree Hotel

★★★★ 79% 🏵 ⚱ HOTEL

COTSWOLD INNS & HOTELS

tel: 01993 822791 **Sheep Street OX18 4LW**
email: info@baytreehotel.info **web:** www.cotswold-inns-hotels.co.uk
dir: A40 or A361 to Burford. From High Street turn into Sheep Street, next to old market square. Hotel on right.

The Bay Tree Hotel's modern decorative style combines seamlessly with features from this delightful inn's long history. Bedrooms are tastefully furnished and some have four-poster or half-tester beds. Public areas consist of a character bar, a sophisticated airy restaurant, a selection of meeting rooms and an attractive walled garden.

Rooms: 21 (13 annexe) (2 family) (3 GF) **S** fr £120 **D** fr £150 (including breakfast)*
Facilities: FTV WiFi 🌤 Xmas New Year **Conf:** Class 12 Board 25 Theatre 40
Parking: 50 **Notes:** Civ Wed 90

HIGHLY RECOMMENDED

The Lamb Inn

★★★ 86% 🏵🏵 SMALL HOTEL

COTSWOLD INNS & HOTELS

tel: 01993 823155 **Sheep Street OX18 4LR**
email: info@lambinn-burford.co.uk
web: www.cotswold-inns-hotels.co.uk/the-lamb-inn
dir: A40 into Burford, downhill, 1st left into Sheep Street, hotel last on right.

The Lamb is an enchanting old inn just a short walk from the centre of this delightful Cotswold village. An abundance of character and charm is found in the cosy lounge with log fire, and intimate bar with flagged floors. An elegant restaurant offers locally sourced produce in carefully prepared dishes. Bedrooms, some with original features, are comfortable and well appointed.

Rooms: 17 (1 family) (4 GF) 🐾 **S** fr £150 **D** fr £180 (including breakfast)*
Facilities: FTV WiFi ♨ Xmas New Year **Services:** Night porter

BURGESS HILL
West Sussex   Map 6 TQ31

Premier Inn Burgess Hill

Premier Inn 🌙

BUDGET HOTEL

tel: 0871 527 8172 (Calls cost 13p per minute plus your phone company's access charge) **Charles Avenue RH15 9AG**
web: www.premierinn.com
dir: M25 junction 7, M23, A23. Left at Burgess Hill follow A2300 signs. At roundabout 2nd exit onto A2300. At next roundabout 4th exit onto A273, straight on at next 2 roundabouts, at 3rd roundabout (Tesco) 1st left. Hotel 2nd left.

High quality, budget accommodation ideal for both families and business travellers. Spacious, en suite bedrooms feature free WiFi and tea and coffee making facilities, and in most hotels, Freeview TV is also available. The adjacent family restaurant features a wide and varied menu.

Rooms: 60

B

BURLEY
Hampshire

Map 5 SU20

Burley Manor
★★★★ 80% @ HOTEL

NEW FOREST HOTELS

tel: 01425 403522 **Ringwood Road BH24 4BS**
email: burley.manor@newforesthotels.co.uk **web:** www.burleymanor.com
dir: *From east – M27 end to A31 for 7 miles take Burley slip road. follow signs to hotel. From west – A31, 2nd slip road after Ringwood to Burley. Follow signs to hotel.*

Burley Manor is located in the New Forest and enjoys beautiful parkland views. Bedrooms are located in the main manor house as well as the stables, and all have been appointed to a high standard with quality furnishings and a bold use of colours. Drinks can be enjoyed in the comfortable, elegantly furnished lounge and bar, and when weather permits, on the garden patio. In the restaurant, the menu has Mediterranean influences, and some dishes are cooked in the wood-fired oven. There is also the chef's pantry for small private dinners; while the barn is ideal for larger celebrations.

Rooms: 40 (16 GF) ⟲ fr £89 **D** fr £99 (including breakfast)* **Facilities:** Spa FTV WiFi ⟲ ⟲ Treatment rooms Xmas New Year **Conf:** Class 40 Board 32 Theatre 100 **Services:** Night porter **Parking:** 50 **Notes:** No children 13 years Civ Wed 120

Moorhill House Hotel
★★★ 78% @ COUNTRY HOUSE HOTEL

NEW FOREST HOTELS

tel: 01425 403285 & 0800 444 441 **BH24 4AG**
email: moorhill@newforesthotels.co.uk **web:** www.newforesthotels.co.uk
dir: *M27, A31, follow signs to Burley, through village, up hill, right opposite school and cricket grounds.*

Situated deep in the heart of the New Forest and formerly a grand gentleman's residence, this charming hotel offers a relaxed and friendly environment. Bedrooms, which come in varying sizes, are smartly decorated. A range of facilities is provided and guests can relax by walking around the extensive grounds. Both dinner and breakfast offer a choice of interesting and freshly prepared dishes.

Rooms: 31 (13 family) (3 GF) ⟲ **S** fr £45 **D** fr £59 (including breakfast)* **Facilities:** FTV WiFi ⟲ HL ⟲ ⟲ Xmas New Year **Conf:** Class 60 Board 65 Theatre 120 **Parking:** 50 **Notes:** LB Civ Wed 90

BURNHAM
Buckinghamshire

Map 6 SU98

Burnham Beeches Hotel
★★★★ 75% @@ HOTEL

tel: 01628 429955 **Grove Road SL1 8DP**
email: burnhambeeches@corushotels.com **web:** www.corushotels.com/burnham
dir: *M40 junction 2, A355 towards Slough, right at 2nd roundabout, 1st right to Grove Road.*

Set in attractive mature grounds on the fringes of woodland, this extended Georgian manor house has spacious, comfortable and well-equipped bedrooms. Public rooms include a cosy lounge/bar offering all-day snacks and an elegant wood-panelled restaurant that serves interesting cuisine; there are also conference facilities, a fitness centre and pool.

Rooms: 82 (22 family) (12 GF) ⟲ **S** fr £75 **D** fr £75* **Facilities:** FTV WiFi ⟲ ⟲ Gym Beauty treatment room Xmas New Year **Conf:** Class 80 Board 60 Theatre 150 **Services:** Lift Night porter **Parking:** 150 **Notes:** LB Civ Wed 120

BURNLEY
Lancashire

Map 18 SD83

Best Western Higher Trapp Hotel
★★★ 77% HOTEL

BW Best Western.

tel: 01282 7772781 **Trapp Lane, Simonstone BB12 7QW**
email: highertrapp@lavenderhotels.co.uk **web:** www.lavenderhotels.co.uk/Higher-Trapp
dir: *M65 junction 8, follow signs for the A6068 towards Whalley and Clitheroe. Straight at 1st lights. Left at 2nd lights onto A671 signposted Whalley and Clitheroe for 0.3 mile. After primary school on right, turn right on to School Lane. School Lane becomes Trapp Lane, continue for 0.5 mile, over crossroads, hotel on left.*

Pleasantly located in an extensive country setting between Manchester and Blackpool, this hotel enjoys delightful views across the Pendle Valley and has a range of conference facilities. A popular wedding venue, there are pleasant landscaped gardens within a 36-acre parkland. Bedrooms offer a range of sizes and many have views across the valley, as does the popular restaurant where local classics and more adventurous dishes are available.

Rooms: 29 (10 annexe) (4 family) (5 GF) ⟲ **D** fr £70* **Facilities:** STV FTV WiFi ⟲ **Conf:** Class 40 Board 20 Theatre 80 **Parking:** 90 **Notes:** Civ Wed 120

Best Western Oaks Hotel
★★★ 71% HOTEL

tel: 01282 414141 **Colne Road BB10 2LF**
email: oaks@lavenderhotels.co.uk **web:** www.lavenderhotels.co.uk/Oaks

Formerly the grand home of a tea merchant, many of the original features are retained here including a grand staircase and magnificent stained-glass window illustrating the origins of the tea industry. Located at the edge of town, the hotel includes an impressive leisure centre, extensive meeting facilities and is a popular venue for weddings. The bedrooms are pleasantly spacious. The cuisine has a broad appeal and there is a pleasant bar.

Rooms: 51 **D** fr £69* **Conf:** Class 80 Board 30 Theatre 160

Premier Inn Burnley
BUDGET HOTEL

Premier Inn

tel: 0871 527 8174 (Calls cost 13p per minute plus your phone company's access charge) **Queen Victoria Road BB10 3EF**
web: www.premierinn.com
dir: *M65 junction 12, 5th exit at roundabout, 1st exit at roundabout, keep in right lane at lights, 2nd exit at next roundabout, 3rd at next roundabout, under bridge, left before football ground.*

High quality, budget accommodation ideal for both families and business travellers. Spacious, en suite bedrooms feature free WiFi and tea and coffee making facilities, and in most hotels, Freeview TV is also available. The adjacent family restaurant features a wide and varied menu.

Rooms: 67

BURRINGTON (NEAR PORTSMOUTH ARMS STATION)   Map 3 SS61
Devon

INSPECTOR'S CHOICE

Northcote Manor

★★★ ◉◉ COUNTRY HOUSE HOTEL

tel: 01769 560501 **EX37 9LZ**
email: rest@northcotemanor.co.uk **web:** www.northcotemanor.co.uk
dir: *From A377 opposite Portsmouth Arms, into hotel drive. Note – do not enter Burrington village.*

A warm and friendly welcome is assured at this beautiful country house hotel, built in 1716 and surrounded by 20 acres of grounds and woodlands. Guests can enjoy wonderful views over the Taw River Valley while relaxing in the delightful environment created by the attentive staff. A meal in either the intimate, more formal Manor House Restaurant or the Walled Garden Restaurant will prove a highlight; both offer menus of the finest local produce used in well-prepared dishes. Bedrooms, including some suites, are individually styled, spacious and well appointed.

Rooms: 16 (3 family) (3 GF) ➧ **S** fr £120 **D** fr £170 (including breakfast)*
Facilities: FTV WiFi ⬇ Xmas New Year **Conf:** Class 50 Board 30 Theatre 80
Parking: 50 **Notes:** Civ Wed 100

BURTON UPON TRENT   Map 10 SK22
Staffordshire

Mercure Burton Upon Trent Newton Park

★★★★ 72% COUNTRY HOUSE HOTEL

tel: 01283 703568 & 707500 **Newton Solney DE15 0SS**
email: info@mercureburton.co.uk **web:** www.mercureburton.co.uk
dir: *On B5008 past Repton to Newton Solney. Hotel on left.*

Standing in eight-acre grounds, this Grade II listed, 18th-century Italian-style country manor provides comfort in elegant surroundings. The well-equipped bedrooms are suitable for both business and leisure guests. The oak-panelled restaurant serves a good choice of dishes and overlooks the landscaped gardens. Eight fully-equipped meeting rooms are available.

Rooms: 50 (3 family) (5 GF) ➧ **S** fr £75 **D** fr £95* **Facilities:** STV FTV WiFi ⬇
Conf: Class 70 Board 60 Theatre 100 **Services:** Lift Night porter **Parking:** 100
Notes: LB Civ Wed 100

Holiday Inn Express Burton upon Trent

BUDGET HOTEL

tel: 01283 504300 **2nd Avenue, Centrum 100 DE14 2WF**
email: reservations@exhiburton.co.uk **web:** www.exhiburton.co.uk
dir: *From A38 Branston exit take A5121 signed Town Centre. At McDonald's roundabout, turn left into 2nd Avenue. Hotel on left.*

A modern hotel ideal for families and business travellers. Fresh and uncomplicated, the spacious rooms include Sky TV, power shower and tea and coffee-making facilities. Continental buffet breakfast is included in the room rate; other meals may be taken at the nearby family pub or restaurant.

Rooms: 82 (47 family) (14 GF) ➧ **S** fr £50 **D** fr £50 (including breakfast)

Premier Inn Burton upon Trent Central

BUDGET HOTEL

tel: 0871 527 9280 (Calls cost 13p per minute plus your phone company's access charge) **Wellington Road DE14 2WD**
web: www.premierinn.com
dir: *Exit A38 at Branston junction onto A5121 to Burton on Trent. Straight on at lights. At roundabout take 3rd exit, hotel on left.*

High quality, budget accommodation ideal for both families and business travellers. Spacious, en suite bedrooms feature free WiFi and tea and coffee making facilities, and in most hotels, Freeview TV is also available. The adjacent family restaurant features a wide and varied menu.

Rooms: 64

Premier Inn Burton upon Trent East

BUDGET HOTEL

Premier Inn ◉

tel: 0871 527 8176 (Calls cost 13p per minute plus your phone company's access charge) **Ashby Road East DE15 0PU**
web: www.premierinn.com
dir: *2 miles east of Burton upon Trent on A50.*

Rooms: 32

BURY   Map 15 SD81
Greater Manchester

Red Hall Hotel

★★★ 84% ◉ HOTEL

tel: 01706 822476 **Manchester Road, Walmersley BL9 5NA**
email: info@red-hall.co.uk **web:** www.red-hall.co.uk
dir: *M66 junction 1, A56. Over motorway bridge, hotel approximately 300 metres on right.*

Originally a farmhouse, this now much expanded hotel is located in the picturesque village of Warlmersley just off the M66, making it ideal for business and leisure guests alike. The bright bedrooms are comfortable, contemporary and equipped to a modern standard. Oscar's restaurant serves a wide-ranging menu. Meeting and event facilities complete the package.

Rooms: 37 (2 family) (18 GF) ➧ **S** fr £70 **D** fr £75 (including breakfast)*
Facilities: STV FTV WiFi ⬇ Xmas New Year **Conf:** Class 60 Board 30 Theatre 140
Services: Lift Night porter **Parking:** 100 **Notes:** Civ Wed 80

B

BURY *continued*

Premier Inn Manchester Bury

Premier Inn

BUDGET HOTEL

tel: 0871 527 9294 (Calls cost 13p per minute plus your phone company's access charge) **5 Knowsley Place, Duke Street BL9 0EJ**
web: www.premierinn.com
dir: *M66 junction 2, A58 towards Bolton and Bury. At roundabout in Bury centre follow A58 (Angouleme Way). Left in Knowsley Street, hotel on left.*

High quality, budget accommodation ideal for both families and business travellers. Spacious, en suite bedrooms feature free WiFi and tea and coffee making facilities, and in most hotels, Freeview TV is also available. The adjacent family restaurant features a wide and varied menu.

Rooms: 115

BURY ST EDMUNDS Suffolk	**Map 13 TL86**

HIGHLY RECOMMENDED

The Angel Hotel

★★★★ 86% ◎◎ TOWN HOUSE HOTEL

tel: 01284 714000 **Angel Hill IP33 1LT**
email: staying@theangel.co.uk **web:** www.theangel.co.uk
dir: *From A134, left at roundabout into Northgate Street. Continue to lights, right into Mustow Street, left into Angel Hill. Hotel on right.*

The Angel Hotel is an impressive building situated just a short walk from the town centre. One of the hotel's more notable guests over the last 400 years was Charles Dickens, who is reputed to have written part of *The Pickwick Papers* while in residence. The hotel offers a range of individually designed bedrooms that include a selection of four-poster rooms and a suite.

Rooms: 77 (5 family) (22 GF) ☏ **S** fr £139 **D** fr £139* **Facilities:** FTV WiFi Xmas
Conf: Board 16 **Services:** Lift Night porter **Parking:** 20

Best Western Priory Hotel

Best Western

★★★ 84% ◎ HOTEL

tel: 01284 766181 **Mildenhall Road IP32 6EH**
email: reservations@prioryhotel.co.uk **web:** www.prioryhotel.co.uk
dir: *From A14 (junction 43) take Bury St Edmunds west slip road. Follow signs to Brandon. At mini-roundabout turn right. Hotel 0.5 mile on left.*

Priory Hotel is an 18th-century Grade II listed building set in landscaped grounds on the outskirts of town. The attractively decorated, tastefully furnished and thoughtfully equipped bedrooms are split between the main house and garden wings, which have their own sun terraces. Public rooms feature a smart restaurant, a conservatory dining room and a lounge bar.

Rooms: 43 (34 annexe) (1 family) (34 GF) ☏ **S** fr £50 **D** fr £70* **Facilities:** FTV WiFi Xmas New Year **Conf:** Class 24 Board 30 Theatre 75 **Services:** Night porter **Parking:** 60 **Notes:** Civ Wed 75

The Grange Hotel

★★★ 79% COUNTRY HOUSE HOTEL

tel: 01359 231260 **Barton Road, Thurston IP31 3PQ**
email: info@grangecountryhousehotel.com **web:** www.grangecountryhousehotel.com
dir: *A14 junction 45 towards Great Barton, right at T-junction. At crossroads left into Barton Road to Thurston. At roundabout, left after 0.5 mile, hotel on right.*

The Grange Hotel is a Tudor-style country house hotel situated on the outskirts of town. The individually decorated bedrooms have co-ordinated fabrics and many thoughtful touches; some rooms have nice views of the gardens. Public areas include a smart lounge bar, two private dining rooms, the Garden Restaurant and banqueting facilities.

Rooms: 18 (5 annexe) (1 family) (3 GF) ☏ **S** fr £82.50 **D** fr £115 (including breakfast)* **Facilities:** FTV WiFi Well being and beauty clinic ♫ Xmas New Year **Conf:** Class 40 Board 30 Theatre 135 **Parking:** 70 **Notes:** Civ Wed 150

Premier Inn Bury St Edmunds Town Centre

Premier Inn

BUDGET HOTEL

tel: 0871 527 9512 (Calls cost 13p per minute plus your phone company's access charge) **Raingate Street IP33 2AR**
web: www.premierinn.com
dir: *A14 junction 44 signed Bury St Edmunds East/Sudbury A134. At roundabout 3rd exit towards Bury St Edmunds. At next roundabout 2nd exit (Town Centre/A1302). At next roundabout 3rd exit (town centre). At mini-roundabout 3rd exit into Westgate Street. At Greene King Brewery (one-way system) into Crown Street. Hotel at bottom of hill.*

High quality, budget accommodation ideal for both families and business travellers. Spacious, en suite bedrooms feature free WiFi and tea and coffee making facilities, and in most hotels, Freeview TV is also available. The adjacent family restaurant features a wide and varied menu.

Rooms: 75

BUXTON Derbyshire	**Map 16 SK07**

Best Western Lee Wood Hotel

Best Western

★★★★ 77% ◎ HOTEL

tel: 01298 23002 **The Park SK17 6TQ**
email: reservations@leewoodhotel.co.uk **web:** www.leewoodhotel.co.uk
dir: *From town centre take A5004 northeast, hotel 150 metres beyond University of Derby – Buxton Campus.*

This elegant Georgian hotel offers high standards of comfort and hospitality. The individually furnished bedrooms are generally spacious, with all of the expected modern conveniences. There is a choice of two comfortable lounges and a conservatory restaurant. The quality cooking, good service and fine hospitality are noteworthy.

Rooms: 39 (5 annexe) (4 family) **Facilities:** STV FTV WiFi ♦ Gym Serenity beauty and wellbeing New Year **Conf:** Class 65 Board 40 Theatre 120 **Services:** Lift Night porter **Parking:** 50 **Notes:** Civ Wed 120

C

CADNAM
Hampshire Map 5 SU31

HIGHLY RECOMMENDED

Bartley Lodge Hotel
★★★ 87% ◉ HOTEL

tel: 023 8081 2248 & 0800 444 441 **Lyndhurst Road SO40 2NR**
email: bartley@newforesthotels.co.uk web: www.newforesthotels.co.uk
dir: *M27 junction 1, at 1st roundabout 1st exit, at 2nd roundabout 3rd exit onto A337. Hotel sign on left.*

This 18th-century former hunting lodge is very quietly situated yet is just minutes from the M27. Bedrooms vary in size but all are well equipped. There is a selection of small lounge areas, a cosy bar and an indoor pool, together with a small fitness suite. Hunter's Restaurant offers a tempting choice of well-prepared dishes.

Rooms: 40 (15 family) (4 GF) 🐾 **S** fr £59 **D** fr £79 (including breakfast)*
Facilities: FTV WiFi ↘ HL 🐾 🏊 Xmas New Year **Conf:** Class 60 Board 60 Theatre 120 **Services:** Lift **Parking:** 60 **Notes:** LB Civ Wed 100

CALNE
Wiltshire Map 4 ST97

Bowood Hotel, Spa and Golf Resort
★★★★ 80% HOTEL

tel: 01249 822228 **Derry Hill SN11 9PQ**
email: hotelreception@bowood.org web: www.bowood.org
dir: *Located just off the A4 between Chippenham and Calne in the village of Derry Hill.*

Bowood Hotel, Spa and Golf Club has an enviable range of facilities that make it a true year-round resort. The hotel sits on the Bowood Estate – over 100 acres of 'Capability' Brown designed parkland which includes formal gardens and woodland gardens as well as a popular adventure playground. Golfers will enjoy the renowned championship course that meanders through woodland, by streams and across an undulating landscape. On site there is a golf pro shop too. The spa offers a range of de-stress treatments and packages. All the bedrooms have been designed by Lady Lansdowne with country-house styling bought right up to date. Dinner should be missed; local sourcing is the key, with the kitchen team showcasing the best Wiltshire produce.

Rooms: 47 (4 annexe) (10 GF) 🐾 **D** fr £90* **Facilities:** Spa FTV WiFi ↘ 🐾 ⚓ 18 Fishing 🏊 Gym Sauna Steam room Jacuzzi Adventure playground (April to October) complimentary access to Bowood House and gardens (April to October) Xmas New Year **Conf:** Class 100 Board 50 Theatre 160 **Services:** Lift Night porter Air con **Parking:** 100 **Notes:** LB Civ Wed 160

CAMBERLEY
Surrey Map 6 SU86

Macdonald Frimley Hall Hotel & Spa
★★★★ 79% ◉◉ HOTEL

tel: 01276 413100 **Lime Avenue GU15 2BG**
email: sales.frimleyhall@macdonald-hotels.co.uk
web: www.macdonaldhotels.co.uk/frimleyhall
dir: *M3 junction 3, A321 follow Bagshot signs. Through lights, left onto A30 signed Camberley and Basingstoke. To roundabout, 2nd exit onto A325, take 5th right.*

The epitome of classic English elegance, Macdonald Frimley Hall Hotel is an ivy-clad Victorian manor house set in two acres of immaculate grounds in the heart of Surrey. The bedrooms and public areas are smart and have a modern decorative theme. The hotel boasts an impressive health club and spa with treatment rooms, a fully equipped gym and heated indoor swimming pool.

Rooms: 98 (15 family) 🐾 **Facilities:** Spa FTV WiFi ↘ HL 🐾 Gym Technogym Sauna Steam room Relaxation room Xmas New Year **Conf:** Class 100 Board 60 Theatre 250 **Services:** Night porter **Parking:** 150 **Notes:** Civ Wed 220

Lakeside International
★★★ 73% HOTEL

tel: 01252 838000 **Wharf Road, Frimley Green GU16 6JR**
email: info@lakesideinthotel.com web: www.lakesideinternationalhotel.com
dir: *Exit A321 at mini-roundabout turn into Wharf Road. Lakeside complex on right.*

This hotel, geared towards the business market, enjoys a lakeside location with noteworthy views. Bedrooms are modern, comfortable and with a range of facilities. Public areas are spacious and include a residents' lounge, bar, games room, a smart restaurant and an established health and leisure club.

Rooms: 98 (1 family) (31 GF) 🐾 **Facilities:** FTV WiFi 🐾 Gym Squash Sauna Steam room **Conf:** Class 100 Board 40 Theatre 120 **Services:** Lift Night porter **Parking:** 250 **Notes:** Civ Wed 100

Premier Inn Camberley
BUDGET HOTEL

tel: 0871 527 9322 (Calls cost 13p per minute plus your phone company's access charge) **Park Street GU15 3SG**
web: www.premierinn.com
dir: *M3 junction 4, A331 towards Camberley. In 2 miles, at major junction into right lane, 4th exit signed A30. For parking, in 1 mile, right into Southern Road for Atrium Car Park.*

High quality, budget accommodation ideal for both families and business travellers. Spacious, en suite bedrooms feature free WiFi and tea and coffee making facilities, and in most hotels, Freeview TV is also available. The adjacent family restaurant features a wide and varied menu.

Rooms: 95

Premier Inn Sandhurst
BUDGET HOTEL

tel: 0871 527 8958 (Calls cost 13p per minute plus your phone company's access charge) **221 Yorktown Road, College Town GU47 0RT**
web: www.premierinn.com
dir: *M3 junction 4, A331 to Camberley. At large roundabout take A321 towards Bracknell. At 3rd lights, hotel on left.*

Rooms: 54

CAMBORNE
Cornwall & Isles Of Scilly   **Map 2 SW63**

Premier Inn Camborne

BUDGET HOTEL

tel: 0871 527 9308 (Calls cost 13p per minute plus your phone company's access charge) **Treswithian Road TR14 7NF**
web: www.premierinn.com
dir: *From M5 (south) junction 31, A30 to Bodmin, then to Redruth, follow signs to Camborne. Left onto A3047, to roundabout, 1st exit to hotel.*

High quality, budget accommodation ideal for both families and business travellers. Spacious, en suite bedrooms feature free WiFi and tea and coffee making facilities, and in most hotels, Freeview TV is also available. The adjacent family restaurant features a wide and varied menu.

Rooms: 110

CAMBOURNE
Cambridgeshire   **Map 12 TL35**

The Cambridge Belfry

★★★★ 81% HOTEL

tel: 01954 714600 **Back Street CB23 6BW**
email: cambridgebelfry@qhotels.co.uk **web:** www.qhotels.co.uk
dir: *M11 junction 13, A428 towards Bedford, follow signs to Cambourne. Exit at Cambourne, keep left. Left at roundabout, hotel on left.*

This exciting hotel, built beside the water, is located at the gateway to Cambourne Village and Business Park. The hotel boasts excellent leisure facilities, including Reflections Spa offering a range of therapies and treatments, and extensive conference and banqueting rooms. Meals are served in the Bridge Restaurant, and original artwork is displayed throughout the hotel.

Rooms: 120 (30 GF) **Facilities:** Spa FTV WiFi HL Gym Beauty treatments Fitness classes Xmas New Year **Conf:** Class 70 Board 70 Theatre 250 **Services:** Lift Night porter **Parking:** 200 **Notes:** LB Civ Wed 130

CAMBRIDGE
Cambridgeshire   **Map 12 TL45**

HIGHLY RECOMMENDED

Quy Mill Hotel & Spa, Cambridge

★★★★ 83% HOTEL

tel: 01223 293383 **Church Road, Stow Cum Quy CB25 9AF**
email: info@cambridgequymill.co.uk **web:** www.cambridgequymill.co.uk
dir: *Exit A14 at junction 35, east of Cambridge, onto B1102 for 50 yards. Entrance opposite church.*

Set in open countryside, this 19th-century former watermill is conveniently situated for access to Cambridge. Bedroom styles differ, yet each room is smartly appointed and brightly decorated; superior, spacious courtyard rooms are noteworthy. Well-designed public areas include several spacious bar/lounges, with a choice of casual and formal eating areas; service is both friendly and helpful. There is a smart leisure club with state-of-the-art equipment, as well as a health spa.

Rooms: 51 (30 annexe) (4 family) (24 GF) **S** fr £95 **D** fr £110* **Facilities:** Spa FTV WiFi HL Gym Sauna Steam room wellness suite New Year **Conf:** Class 30 Board 24 Theatre 80 **Services:** Night porter **Parking:** 90 **Notes:** Civ Wed 80

The Varsity Hotel & Spa

★★★★ 86% HOTEL

tel: 01223 306030 **Thompson's Lane CB5 8AQ**
email: info@thevarsityhotel.co.uk **web:** www.thevarsityhotel.co.uk
dir: *M11 junction 13, pass Park and Ride, next roundabout 1st left, right at next junction into Bridge Street, right into Thompon's Lane.*

Situated close to the River Cam and occupying a central location, The Varsity Hotel is a stylish property. The bedrooms are smartly decorated and have all the expected facilities including power showers, CD players and free internet access. The River Bar, to the side of the hotel, has a buzzing atmosphere and offers a range of popular dishes, while on the sixth floor there is another restaurant with stunning views of the city. The hotel has a health club and spa, and a roof top bar.

Rooms: 44 (2 family) **D** fr £135 (including breakfast)* **Facilities:** Spa FTV WiFi Gym Sauna Steam room valet parking New Year **Conf:** Class 40 Board 30 Theatre 60 **Services:** Lift Night porter Air con **Notes:** LB Civ Wed 60

Hotel Felix

★★★★ 82% @@ HOTEL

tel: 01223 277977 **Whitehouse Lane, Huntingdon Road CB3 0LX**
email: help@hotelfelix.co.uk **web:** www.hotelfelix.co.uk
dir: M11 junction 13. From A1 north, take A14 onto A1307. At 'City of Cambridge' sign left into Whitehouse Lane.

A beautiful Victorian mansion set amidst three acres of landscaped gardens, this property was originally built in 1852 for a surgeon from the famous Addenbrookes Hospital. The contemporary-style bedrooms have carefully chosen furniture and many thoughtful touches, while public rooms feature an open-plan bar, the adjacent Graffiti restaurant and a small quiet lounge.

Rooms: 52 (5 family) (26 GF) ☞ **S** fr £222 **D** fr £235 (including breakfast)*
Facilities: STV WiFi ☼ Xmas New Year **Conf:** Class 36 Board 34 Theatre 60
Services: Lift Night porter **Parking:** 90 **Notes:** Civ Wed 60

The Gonville Hotel

★★★★ 82% HOTEL

tel: 01223 366611 **Gonville Place CB1 1LY**
email: info@gonvillehotel.co.uk **web:** www.gonvillehotel.co.uk
dir: M11 junction 11, on A1309 follow city centre signs. At 2nd mini-roundabout right into Lensfield Road, over junction with lights. Hotel 25 yards on right.

This is a well-established hotel situated on the inner ring road, a short walk across the green from the city centre. The air-conditioned public areas are cheerfully furnished, and include a lounge bar and brasserie. Bedrooms are well appointed and appealing, offering a good range of facilities for both corporate and leisure guests.

Rooms: 84 (2 family) (8 GF) ☞ **Facilities:** FTV WiFi ☼ HL ♫ New Year **Conf:** Class 30 Board 30 Theatre 50 **Services:** Lift Night porter Air con **Parking:** 70

Hotel du Vin Cambridge

★★★★ 79% @ TOWN HOUSE HOTEL

tel: 01223 227330 & 0844 736 4253 (Calls cost 5p per minute plus your phone company's access charge) **15-19 Trumpington Street CB2 1QA**
email: info.cambridge@hotelduvin.com **web:** www.hotelduvin.com/locations/cambridge
dir: M11 junction 11 Cambridge south, pass Trumpington Park and Ride on left. Hotel 2 miles on right after double roundabout.

This beautiful building, which dates back in part to medieval times, has been transformed to enhance its many quirky architectural features. The bedrooms and suites, some with private terraces, have the company's trademark monsoon showers and Egyptian linen. The French-style bistro has an open kitchen and the bar is set in the unusual labyrinth of vaulted cellar rooms. Other parts of the hotel include a library, a specialist wine-tasting room and a private dining room.

Rooms: 41 (3 annexe) (6 GF) ☞ **Facilities:** STV WiFi Xmas New Year **Conf:** Class 18 Board 18 Theatre 30 **Services:** Lift Night porter Air con **Parking:** 24

Hallmark Hotel Cambridge

★★★★ 73% HOTEL

tel: 0330 028 3400 **Bar Hill CB23 8EU**
email: cambridge@hallmarkhotels.co.uk **web:** www.hallmarkhotels.co.uk
dir: M11 junction 13, A14, follow signs for Huntingdon. Take B1050 Bar Hill, hotel 1st exit on roundabout.

The Hallmark Hotel Cambridge is ideally situated in 200 acres of open countryside, just five miles from the university city of Cambridge. Public rooms include a brasserie restaurant and the popular Gallery Bar. The contemporary-style bedrooms are smartly decorated and equipped with a good range of useful facilities. The hotel also has a leisure club, swimming pool and golf course.

Rooms: 136 (35 family) (68 GF) **Facilities:** Spa STV FTV WiFi ☼ HL ♫ ♨ 18 ☁ Gym Hair and beauty salon Steam room Sauna Xmas New Year **Conf:** Class 90 Board 45 Theatre 220 **Services:** Lift Night porter **Parking:** 200 **Notes:** Civ Wed 200

The Lensfield Hotel

★★★ 82% METRO HOTEL

tel: 01223 355017 **53-57 Lensfield Road CB2 1EN**
email: reservations@lensfieldhotel.co.uk **web:** www.lensfieldhotel.co.uk
dir: M11 junctions 11, 12 or 13, follow signs to city centre. Access via Silver Street, Trumpington Street, left into Lensfield Road.

Located close to all the city's attractions, this constantly improving hotel provides a range of attractive bedrooms, equipped with thoughtful extras. Comprehensive breakfasts are taken in an elegant dining room, and a comfortable bar and cosy foyer lounge are also available.

Rooms: 38 (2 family) (4 GF) **S** fr £77 **D** fr £120 (including breakfast)* **Facilities:** Spa STV FTV WiFi ☼ HL Gym Thermal suite Fitness suite (in ladies spa only)
Services: Night porter Air con **Parking:** 5 **Notes:** LB Closed last 2 weeks in December to 4 January

Arundel House Hotel

★★★ 78% HOTEL

tel: 01223 367701 **Chesterton Road CB4 3AN**
email: info@arundelhousehotels.co.uk **web:** www.arundelhousehotels.co.uk
dir: In city centre on A1303.

Overlooking the River Cam and enjoying views of open parkland, this popular and smart hotel was originally a row of townhouses dating from Victorian times. Bedrooms are attractive and have a special character. The smart public areas feature a conservatory for informal snacks, a spacious bar and an elegant restaurant for more serious dining.

Rooms: 101 (22 annexe) (7 family) (14 GF) **Facilities:** FTV WiFi ☼ New Year **Conf:** Class 18 Board 22 Theatre 44 **Services:** Night porter **Parking:** 70 **Notes:** LB Closed 25–26 December

C

C

CAMBRIDGE *continued*

Centennial Hotel

★★★ 76% HOTEL

tel: 01223 314652 **63-71 Hills Road CB2 1PG**
email: reception@centennialhotel.co.uk **web:** www.centennialhotel.co.uk
dir: *M11 junction 11, A1309 to Cambridge. Right into Brooklands Avenue to end. Left, hotel 100 yards on right.*

This friendly hotel is convenient for the railway station and town centre. Well-presented public areas include a welcoming lounge, a relaxing bar and restaurant on the lower-ground level. Bedrooms are generally spacious, well maintained and thoughtfully equipped with a good range of facilities; several rooms are available on the ground floor.

Rooms: 39 (1 family) (7 GF) 🐾 **S** fr £90 **D** fr £100 (including breakfast)*
Facilities: FTV WiFi ⌕ **Conf:** Class 22 Board 22 Theatre 25 **Services:** Night porter
Parking: 28 **Notes:** Closed 23 December to 1 January

Ashley Hotel

★★ 76% METRO HOTEL

tel: 01223 350059 **74-76 Chesterton Road CB4 1ER**
email: info@arundelhousehotels.co.uk **web:** www.arundelhousehotels.co.uk
dir: *On city centre ring road.*

Expect a warm welcome at this delightful Victorian property situated just a short walk from the River Cam. The smartly decorated bedrooms are generally quite spacious and equipped with a good range of useful extras. Breakfast is served at individual tables in the smart lower ground floor dining room.

Rooms: 16 (5 family) (5 GF) **Facilities:** FTV WiFi ⌕ **Services:** Night porter **Parking:** 12
Notes: Closed 24–26 December

Premier Inn Cambridge (A14 Jct 32)

 Premier Inn

BUDGET HOTEL

tel: 0871 527 8186 (Calls cost 13p per minute plus your phone company's access charge) **Ring Fort Road CB4 2GW**
web: www.premierinn.com
dir: *A14 junction 32, follow B1049/city centre signs. At 1st lights left into Kings Hedges Road, 2nd left into Ring Fort Road.*

High quality, budget accommodation ideal for both families and business travellers. Spacious, en suite bedrooms feature free WiFi and tea and coffee making facilities, and in most hotels, Freeview TV is also available. The adjacent family restaurant features a wide and varied menu.

Rooms: 154

Premier Inn Cambridge City Centre

Premier Inn

BUDGET HOTEL

tel: 0871 527 9396 (Calls cost 13p per minute plus your phone company's access charge) **Newmarket Road CB1 3EP**
web: www.premierinn.com
dir: *M11 junction 12, A603, left at mini-roundabout then take 2nd exit at next roundabout (continue on A603). Through lights, at roundabout take 3rd exit onto A1134 signed Ring Road, Newmarket and Airport. Hotel on right.*

Rooms: 120

CAMBRIDGE SERVICES	Map 12 TL36
Cambridgeshire	

Days Inn Cambridge - A1

AA Advertised · WELCOMEBREAK

tel: 01954 267176 **Cambridge Extra Services, Junction A14/M11 CB23 4WU**
email: cambridge.hotel@welcomebreak.co.uk **web:** www.welcomebreak.co.uk
dir: *A14/M11 Cambridge Extra Services.*

This modern, purpose built accommodation offers smartly appointed, well-equipped bedrooms, with good power showers. There is a choice of adjacent food outlets where guests may enjoy breakfast, snacks and meals.

Rooms: 82 (14 family) (40 GF) (19 smoking) **Facilities:** FTV WiFi ⌕ **Services:** Air con
Parking: 120

CANNOCK	Map 10 SJ91
Staffordshire	

Premier Inn Cannock (Orbital)

Premier Inn

BUDGET HOTEL

tel: 0871 527 8190 (Calls cost 13p per minute plus your phone company's access charge) **Eastern Way WS11 8XR**
web: www.premierinn.com
dir: *Northbound: M6 (Toll) junction 7, A5. At roundabout 1st exit (A5), 4th exit onto A460, 1st exit. Southbound: (no access from M6 Toll). M6 junction 11, A460 signed Cannock. At next 2 roundabouts take 3rd exit. At next roundabout 1st exit onto service road. Hotel adjacent to Orbital Brewers Fayre.*

High quality, budget accommodation ideal for both families and business travellers. Spacious, en suite bedrooms feature free WiFi and tea and coffee making facilities, and in most hotels, Freeview TV is also available. The adjacent family restaurant features a wide and varied menu.

Rooms: 21

Premier Inn Cannock South

Premier Inn

BUDGET HOTEL

tel: 0871 527 8192 (Calls cost 13p per minute plus your phone company's access charge) **Watling Street WS11 1SJ**
web: www.premierinn.com
dir: *At junction of A5 and A460, 2 miles from M6 junctions 11 and 12.*

Rooms: 60

C

CANTERBURY
Kent

Map 7 TR15

ABode Canterbury

★★★★ 82% HOTEL

aBode HOTELS

tel: 01227 766266 **High Street CT1 2RX**
email: reservations@abodecanterbury.co.uk **web:** www.abodecanterbury.co.uk
dir: M2 junction 7. Follow Canterbury signs onto ring road. At Wincheap roundabout turn into city. Left into Rosemary Lane, into Stour Street. Hotel at end.

ABode Canterbury is a stylish hotel located on the city's main street. A range of well-appointed bedrooms and suites is available, many retaining original features, all boasting modern facilities and smart en suites. A choice of dining options and bars include The County Restaurant, a smart Champagne Bar, and the more relaxed and hip Old Brewery Tavern.

Rooms: 72 (10 family) ⚑ **S** fr £124 **D** fr £139 (including breakfast) **Facilities:** FTV WiFi ⓘ Gym Xmas New Year **Conf:** Class 48 Board 20 Theatre 140 **Services:** Lift Night porter Air con **Parking:** 44 **Notes:** Civ Wed 100

Best Western Abbots Barton Hotel

★★★ 79% HOTEL

Best Western.

tel: 01227 760341 **New Dover Road CT1 3DU**
email: info@abbotsbartonhotel.com **web:** www.abbotsbartonhotel.com
dir: Phone for directions.

Abbots Barton Hotel is in a central location, just a 10-minute walk from the city centre, and benefits from two acres of gardens and on-site parking. Bedrooms are comfortably appointed throughout, traditional in style yet with all modern amenities including free WiFi and digital TV. The bar and restaurant are open daily, and there are good function facilities with a private bar and patio – ideal for conferences and weddings.

Rooms: 53 (3 family) (6 GF) **Facilities:** FTV WiFi ⓘ Xmas New Year **Conf:** Class 60 Board 60 Theatre 130 **Services:** Lift Night porter **Parking:** 40 **Notes:** Civ Wed 80

Castle House

★★★ 73% METRO HOTEL

tel: 01227 761897 **28 Castle Street CT1 2PT**
email: info@castlehousehotel.co.uk **web:** www.castlehousehotel.co.uk
dir: Next to Canterbury Castle.

Conveniently located in the city centre opposite the imposing ruins of the ancient Norman castle; part of the building dates back to the 1730s. Bedrooms are spacious, all with en suite facilities and many useful extras, such as WiFi. There is a walled garden in which to relax during the warmer months.

Rooms: 15 (3 family) (2 GF) **D** fr £75 (including breakfast)* **Facilities:** WiFi **Services:** Night porter **Parking:** 15

Premier Inn Canterbury City Centre

Premier Inn

BUDGET HOTEL

tel: 0871 527 9408 (Calls cost 13p per minute plus your phone company's access charge) **New Dover Road CT1 1UP**
web: www.premierinn.com
dir: M2 junction 7. At Brenley Corner roundabout 4th exit onto A2. Left then merge onto A2050. At London Road roundabout 2nd exit (A2050). At St Peters roundabout 3rd exit onto A290. At Wincheap roundabout 2nd exit onto A28. At St Georges roundabout 2nd exit onto A257. At lights right (A257). At lights right onto A2050. Hotel in view.

High quality, budget accommodation ideal for both families and business travellers. Spacious, en suite bedrooms feature free WiFi and tea and coffee making facilities, and in most hotels, Freeview TV is also available. The adjacent family restaurant features a wide and varied menu.

Rooms: 120

CARBIS BAY
See **St Ives (Cornwall)**

CARLISLE
Cumbria

Map 18 NY35

Crown Hotel

★★★★ 77% HOTEL

tel: 01228 561888 **Station Road, Wetheral CA4 8ES**
email: info@crownhotelwetheral.co.uk **web:** www.crownhotelwetheral.co.uk
dir: M6 junction 42, B6263 to Wetheral, right at village shop, car park at rear of hotel.

Set in the attractive village of Wetheral, with landscaped gardens to the rear, this hotel is well suited for both business and leisure guests, as well as families. There are more than 50 bedrooms in a variety of sizes and styles, including two apartments in an adjacent house, ideal for longer stays. A choice of dining options is available, with the popular Waltons Bar as an informal alternative to the main Conservatory Restaurant. Weddings and conferences can be catered for, and there are leisure club facilities – a swimming pool, jacuzzi, squash court, two gyms and a sauna.

Rooms: 51 (2 annexe) (10 family) (3 GF) ⚑ **Facilities:** STV WiFi HL ⓘ Gym Squash Children's splash pool Steam room Sauna Dance studio Xmas New Year **Conf:** Class 60 Board 65 Theatre 140 **Services:** Night porter **Parking:** 55 **Notes:** Civ Wed 120

CARLISLE *continued*

Hallmark Hotel Carlisle

★★★★ 72% HOTEL

tel: 0330 028 3401 **Court Square CA1 1QY**
email: carlisle@hallmarkhotels.co.uk **web:** www.hallmarkhotels.co.uk
dir: *M6 junction 43, to city centre, then follow road to left and railway station.*

This hotel is at the heart of the town, opposite the railway station. The contemporary bedrooms benefit from having high ceilings, large windows and WiFi. The smart ground-floor areas include a popular bar and restaurant. Several meeting rooms are available, and at the rear of the hotel is a small car park.

Rooms: 70 (3 family) **Facilities:** FTV WiFi Xmas New Year **Conf:** Class 100 Board 30 Theatre 240 **Services:** Lift Night porter **Parking:** 26 **Notes:** Civ Wed 200

The Crown & Mitre

★★★ 81% HOTEL

PEEL HOTELS PLC

tel: 01228 525491 **4 English Street CA3 8HZ**
email: info@crownandmitre-hotel-carlisle.com
web: www.crownandmitre-hotel-carlisle.com
dir: *A6 to city centre, pass station on left. Turn left at end of English Street, then immediate right onto Blackfriars Street.*

Located in the heart of the city, this Edwardian hotel is close to the cathedral and a few minutes' walk from the castle. Bedrooms vary in size and style, from smart executive rooms to more functional standard rooms. Public rooms include a comfortable lounge area and the lovely bar with its feature stained-glass windows.

Rooms: 90 (20 annexe) (1 family) **S** fr £50 **D** fr £100 (including breakfast)*
Facilities: STV FTV WiFi Xmas New Year **Conf:** Class 250 Board 50 Theatre 400 **Services:** Lift Night porter **Parking:** 42 **Notes:** Civ Wed 200

Premier Inn Carlisle Central

Premier Inn

BUDGET HOTEL

tel: 0871 527 8210 (Calls cost 13p per minute plus your phone company's access charge) **Warwick Road CA1 2WF**
web: www.premierinn.com
dir: *M6 junction 43, on A69.*

High quality, budget accommodation ideal for both families and business travellers. Spacious, en suite bedrooms feature free WiFi and tea and coffee making facilities, and in most hotels, Freeview TV is also available. The adjacent family restaurant features a wide and varied menu.

Rooms: 65

Premier Inn Carlisle Central North

Premier Inn

BUDGET HOTEL

tel: 0871 527 8212 (Calls cost 13p per minute plus your phone company's access charge) **Kingstown Road CA3 0AT**
web: www.premierinn.com
dir: *M6 junction 44, A7 towards Carlisle, hotel 1 mile on left.*

Rooms: 49

Premier Inn Carlisle (M6 Jct 42)

Premier Inn

BUDGET HOTEL

tel: 0871 527 8206 (Calls cost 13p per minute plus your phone company's access charge) **Carleton CA4 0AD**
web: www.premierinn.com
dir: *Just off M6 junction 42, south of Carlisle.*

Rooms: 80

Premier Inn Carlisle (M6 Jct 44)

Premier Inn

BUDGET HOTEL

tel: 0871 527 8208 (Calls cost 13p per minute plus your phone company's access charge) **Parkhouse Road CA3 0JR**
web: www.premierinn.com
dir: *M6 junction 44, A7 signed Carlisle. Hotel on right at 1st set of lights.*

Rooms: 127

CARTMEL | **Map 18 SD37**
Cumbria

HIGHLY RECOMMENDED

Aynsome Manor Hotel

 ★★★ 86% COUNTRY HOUSE HOTEL

tel: 015395 36653 **LA11 6HH**
email: aynsomemanor@btconnect.com **web:** www.aynsomemanorhotel.co.uk
dir: *M6 junction 36, A590 signed Barrow-in-Furness towards Cartmel. Left at end of road, hotel before village.*

A warm and genuine welcome is guaranteed at this well-situated Lake District country house. Dating back, in part, to the early 16th century, the manor overlooks the Fells and the nearby Cartmel Priory. Spacious bedrooms, including some courtyard rooms, are comfortably furnished. Dinner in the elegant restaurant features local produce and there is a choice of deeply comfortable lounges to relax in, beside open fires.

Rooms: 12 (2 annexe) (1 family) **S** fr £85 **D** fr £99 (including breakfast)*
Facilities: FTV WiFi New Year **Parking:** 20 **Notes:** Closed 2–31 January

Find out more about
the AA Hotel Group
of the Year – see page 19

C

CASTLE COMBE
Wiltshire
Map 4 ST87

The Manor House, an Exclusive Hotel & Golf Club

AA Advertised

tel: 01249 782206 **SN14 7HR**
email: enquiries@manorhouse.co.uk **web:** www.exclusive.co.uk
dir: *M4 junction 17 follow Chippenham signs onto A420 Bristol, then right onto B4039. Through village, right after bridge. Follow brown tourist signs to Castle Combe Racing Circuit.*

This delightful hotel is situated in a secluded valley adjacent to a picturesque village where there have been no new buildings for 300 years. There are 365 acres of grounds to enjoy, complete with an Italian garden and an 18-hole golf course. Bedrooms, some in the main house and some in a row of stone cottages, are superbly furnished, and public rooms include several cosy lounges with roaring fires. The award-winning food utilises top quality local produce. Service is a pleasing blend of professionalism and friendliness.

Rooms: 48 (27 annexe) (8 family) (13 GF) ♪ **D** fr £193.50 (including breakfast)*
Facilities: STV WiFi ♂ ⚓ 18 ⛳ Fishing ♨ Beauty treatment room jogging track giant games on lawns Xmas New Year **Conf:** Class 50 Board 34 Theatre 100
Services: Night porter **Parking:** 100 **Notes:** Civ Wed 110

CASTLE DONINGTON

See **East Midlands Airport**

CASTLEFORD
West Yorkshire
Map 16 SE42

Premier Inn Castleford M62 Jct 31
Premier Inn

BUDGET HOTEL

tel: 0871 527 8216 (Calls cost 13p per minute plus your phone company's access charge) **Pioneer Way WF10 5TG**
web: www.premierinn.com
dir: *M62 junction 31, A655 towards Castleford, right at 1st lights, then left.*

High quality, budget accommodation ideal for both families and business travellers. Spacious, en suite bedrooms feature free WiFi and tea and coffee making facilities, and in most hotels, Freeview TV is also available. The adjacent family restaurant features a wide and varied menu.

Rooms: 62

Premier Inn Castleford (Xscape, M62 Jct 32)
Premier Inn

BUDGET HOTEL

tel: 0871 527 8218 (Calls cost 13p per minute plus your phone company's access charge) **Colarado Way WF10 4TA**
web: www.premierinn.com
dir: *M62 junction 32, follow signs for Xscape. Hotel adjacent to Xscape complex.*

Rooms: 119

CATTERICK
North Yorkshire
Map 19 SE29

Premier Inn Catterick Garrison
Premier Inn

BUDGET HOTEL

tel: 0871 527 9568 (Calls cost 13p per minute plus your phone company's access charge) **Princes Gate DL9 3BA**
web: www.premierinn.com
dir: *A1 towards Wetherby, right onto A6136 (Catterick Garrison). At 1st roundabout take 1st exit (A6136/Richmond), straight on at 4 mini-roundabouts. At 5th roundabout 3rd exit, hotel on left.*

High quality, budget accommodation ideal for both families and business travellers. Spacious, en suite bedrooms feature free WiFi and tea and coffee making facilities, and in most hotels, Freeview TV is also available. The adjacent family restaurant features a wide and varied menu.

Rooms: 60

CHADDESLEY CORBETT
Worcestershire
Map 10 SO87

INSPECTOR'S CHOICE

Brockencote Hall Country House Hotel
★★★★ 🍴 COUNTRY HOUSE HOTEL

tel: 01562 777876 **DY10 4PY**
email: info@brockencotehall.com **web:** www.brockencotehall.com
dir: *A38 to Bromsgrove, off A448 towards Kidderminster.*

Brockencote Hall Hotel is a Victorian country manor house set in 70 acres of stunning parkland, complete with a scenic lake, tennis courts and dovecote. A fountain adorns the approach, the terrace and gardens are beautifully landscaped, and the private dining rooms, restaurant and public areas are classically decorated with a colour palette of damson, light grey and lavender. The kitchen brigade create inspired dishes that revolve around the seasons and their local suppliers; their focus is very much on the purity of flavours.

Rooms: 21 (4 family) (5 GF) ♪ **S** fr £105 **D** fr £130 (including breakfast)*
Facilities: FTV WiFi ♂ ⛳ Fishing ♨ Xmas New Year **Conf:** Class 35 Board 35 Theatre 80 **Services:** Night porter **Parking:** 60 **Notes:** Civ Wed 90

CHAGFORD	Map 3 SX78
Devon	

Gidleigh Park

★★★★★ ◉◉◉ COUNTRY HOUSE HOTEL

tel: 01647 432367 **TQ13 8HH**
email: info@gidleigh.co.uk **web:** www.gidleigh.co.uk
dir: *From Chagford, right at the Spar shop into Mill Street. After 150 yards fork right. 2 miles to end.*

Built in 1928 as a private residence for an Australian shipping magnate, and set in 107 acres of lovingly tended grounds, this world-renowned hotel retains a timeless charm and a very endearing, homely atmosphere. The individually styled bedrooms are sumptuously furnished; some with separate seating areas, some with balconies and many enjoying panoramic views. There are spa suites, a loft suite which is ideal for families, and the stunning thatched Pavilion in the grounds. The latter has two bedrooms, two bathrooms, a lounge and kitchen diner. The spacious public areas feature antique furniture, beautiful flower arrangements and magnificent artwork. All of this is topped off with cuisine of the highest order from executive chef Chris Simpson to complete the Gidleigh experience.

Rooms: 24 (3 annexe) (4 family) (3 GF) D fr £248 (including breakfast)*
Facilities: FTV WiFi Fishing Bowls Peter Allis 18-hole putting course
Xmas New Year **Services:** Night porter **Parking:** 45 **Notes:** Civ Wed 50

Mill End Hotel

★★★ 82% ◉◉ COUNTRY HOUSE HOTEL

tel: 01647 432282 **Dartmoor National Park TQ13 8JN**
email: info@millendhotel.com **web:** www.millendhotel.com
dir: *From A30 at Whiddon Down take A382 to Moretonhampstead. In 3.5 miles hump back bridge at Sandy Park, hotel on right.*

Set on the banks of Devon's majestic River Teign, Mill End Hotel is a secluded country house hideaway. There are 20 individually-styled bedrooms, comfy lounges, log fires and beautiful riverside gardens. The hotel restaurant is open for breakfast, lunch, and dinner; and non-residents are very welcome too. After a day on the moors or a trip to the coast, guests can simply relax in front of an open fire or be tempted by the cream tea on offer. This hotel is dog friendly.

Rooms: 20 **S** fr £75 **D** fr £135 (including breakfast)* **Facilities:** FTV WiFi Fishing
Xmas New Year **Conf:** Class 20 Board 30 Theatre 30 **Parking:** 21 **Notes:** LB
Civ Wed 60

CHANDLER'S CROSS	Map 6 TQ09
Hertfordshire	

The Grove

★★★★★ ◉◉◉ HOTEL

tel: 01923 807807 **WD3 4TG**
email: info@thegrove.co.uk **web:** www.thegrove.co.uk
dir: *M25 junction 19, A411 towards Watford. Hotel on right.*

Set amid 300 acres of rolling countryside, much of which is golf course, The Grove hotel combines historic features with cutting-edge, modern design. The spacious bedrooms have the latest in temperature control, lighting technology, Bose docking stations and LED TVs; many also have balconies. Suites in the original mansion are particularly stunning. Championship golf, a world-class spa, extensive crèche facilities and family activities are available. The dining options are Collette's with 3 AA Rosettes that offers fine dining, and a more relaxed style in The Glasshouse and The Stables restaurants. The walled garden is also well worth exploring.

Rooms: 215 (69 family) (23 GF) **S** fr £265 **D** fr £290 (including breakfast)*
Facilities: Spa STV FTV WiFi 18 Gym Walk and cycle trails
Giant chess Driving range Kids club Games room Xmas New Year **Conf:** Class
300 Board 78 Theatre 450 **Services:** Lift Night porter Air con **Parking:** 400
Notes: LB Civ Wed 450

C

CHARD
Somerset
Map 4 ST30

Cricket St Thomas Hotel

WARNERLEISUREHOTELS

★★★★ 75% COUNTRY HOUSE HOTEL

tel: 01460 30111 **TA20 4DD**
email: cricket.sales@bourne-leisure.co.uk **web:** www.warnerleisurehotels.co.uk
dir: M5 junction 25, A358 towards Chard, A30 to Crewkerne. Hotel 3 miles from Chard.

This Grade II listed house has an interesting history, including the fact that Lord Nelson and Lady Hamilton were frequent visitors. The hotel is set in splendid wooded parkland with lakes and colourful gardens. Various holiday packages are available, and there are extensive leisure facilities, as well as live entertainment and various dining venues, including The Granary and Tree Tops. The bedrooms are spacious and well appointed. Please note that this is an adults-only (minimum 21 years old) hotel.

Rooms: 239 (84 GF) **Facilities:** Spa FTV WiFi HL Gym Rifle shooting Archery Xmas New Year **Conf:** Class 50 Board 25 Theatre 80 **Services:** Lift Night porter **Parking:** 351 **Notes:** No children 21 years Civ Wed 80

Lordleaze Hotel

THE INDEPENDENTS
HOTEL ASSOCIATION

★★★ 78% HOTEL

tel: 01460 61066 **Henderson Drive, Forton Road TA20 2HW**
email: info@lordleazehotel.com **web:** www.lordleazehotel.com
dir: A358 from Chard, left at St Mary's Church to Forton and Winsham on B3162. Follow signs to hotel.

Conveniently and quietly located, this hotel is close to the Devon, Dorset and Somerset borders, and only minutes from Chard. All bedrooms are well equipped and comfortable. The friendly lounge bar has a wood-burning stove and serves tempting bar meals. The conservatory restaurant offers more formal dining.

Rooms: 25 (2 family) (7 GF) **S** fr £82 **D** fr £125 (including breakfast)*
Facilities: FTV WiFi Xmas New Year **Conf:** Class 60 Board 40 Theatre 180 **Parking:** 55 **Notes:** LB Civ Wed 100

CHARMOUTH
Dorset
Map 4 SY39

Fernhill Hotel

★★★ 82% HOTEL

tel: 01297 560492 **Fernhill DT6 6BX**
email: mail@fernhill-hotel.co.uk **web:** www.fernhill-hotel.co.uk
dir: A35 onto A3052 to Lyme Regis. Hotel 0.25 mile on left.

Fernhill is a small, friendly hotel in well-tended grounds on top of a hill. It boasts an outdoor pool and treatment rooms, together with elegant public areas. Each of the comfortable bedrooms is individually styled and many have views of the Char Valley and beyond. The menus are based on seasonal, locally sourced produce.

Rooms: 10 (1 family) **Facilities:** FTV WiFi Fishing Holistic treatment centre Massage baths Xmas **Conf:** Class 20 Board 24 Theatre 100 **Parking:** 48 **Notes:** LB Closed 31 December to 30 January Civ Wed 100

CHARNOCK RICHARD MOTORWAY SERVICE AREA (M6)
Lancashire
Map 15 SD51

Days Inn Charnock Richard - M6

WELCOMEBREAK

AA Advertised

tel: 01257 791746 **Welcome Break Service Area PR7 5LR**
email: charnockhotel@welcomebreak.co.uk **web:** www.welcomebreak.co.uk
dir: Between junction 27 and 28 of M6 northbound. 500 yards from Camelot Theme Park via Mill Lane.

This modern building offers accommodation in smart, spacious and well-equipped bedrooms, suitable for families and business travellers, and all with en suite bathrooms. Continental breakfast is available and other refreshments may be taken at the nearby family restaurant.

Rooms: 100 (68 family) (32 GF) (20 smoking) **Facilities:** FTV WiFi **Conf:** Class 16 Board 24 Theatre 40 **Services:** Night porter **Parking:** 100

CHATHAM
Kent
Map 7 TQ76

Bridgewood Manor

QHOTELS
INSPIRED
BY YOU

★★★★ 80% HOTEL

tel: 01634 201333 **Bridgewood Roundabout, Walderslade Woods ME5 9AX**
email: bridgewoodmanor@qhotels.co.uk **web:** www.qhotels.co.uk
dir: Adjacent to Bridgewood roundabout on A229. Take 3rd exit signed Walderslade and Lordswood. Hotel 50 metres on left.

Bridgewood Manor is a modern, purpose-built hotel situated on the outskirts of Rochester. Bedrooms are pleasantly decorated, comfortably furnished and equipped with many thoughtful touches. The hotel has an excellent range of leisure and conference facilities. Guests can dine in the informal Terrace Bistro or experience fine dining in the more formal Squires restaurant, where the service is both attentive and friendly.

Rooms: 100 (12 family) (26 GF) **Facilities:** Spa FTV WiFi Gym Beauty treatments Xmas New Year **Conf:** Class 110 Board 80 Theatre 200 **Services:** Lift Night porter **Parking:** 170 **Notes:** Civ Wed 130

C

CHATHILL
Northumberland   Map 21 NU12

Doxford Hall Hotel & Spa
★★★★ ◉◉ COUNTRY HOUSE HOTEL

tel: 01665 589700 **NE67 5DN**
email: info@doxfordhall.com **web:** www.doxfordhall.com
dir: *8 miles north of Alnwick just off A1, signed Christon Bank and Seahouses. Take B6347 follow signs for hotel.*

A beautiful country house hotel set in a private estate, surrounded by countryside and convenient for visiting nearby historic towns and attractions. Bedrooms are spacious and luxuriously furnished, each named after Northumbrian castles. The dining room and lounges are very attractive. There is an impressive grand staircase and beautiful wood throughout the hotel. The spa adds to the range of facilities.

Rooms: 34 (3 annexe) (1 family) (11 GF) *📞* **Facilities:** Spa FTV WiFi ↘ HL 🕑 Gym Sauna Steam room Xmas New Year **Conf:** Class 100 Board 22 Theatre 250 **Services:** Lift Night porter **Parking:** 100 **Notes:** LB Civ Wed 250

CHEADLE
Greater Manchester   Map 16 SJ88

Premier Inn Manchester (Cheadle)
BUDGET HOTEL   Premier Inn 🌙

tel: 0871 527 8728 (Calls cost 13p per minute plus your phone company's access charge) **Royal Crescent SK8 3FE**
web: www.premierinn.com
dir: *Exit A34 at Cheadle Royal roundabout behind TGI Friday's.*

High quality, budget accommodation ideal for both families and business travellers. Spacious, en suite bedrooms feature free WiFi and tea and coffee making facilities, and in most hotels, Freeview TV is also available. The adjacent family restaurant features a wide and varied menu.

Rooms: 65

CHELMSFORD
Essex   Map 6 TL70

Best Western Atlantic Hotel
★★★★ 74% HOTEL   Best Western.

tel: 01245 268168 **New Street CM1 1PP**
email: info@atlantichotel.co.uk **web:** www.atlantichotel.co.uk
dir: *From Chelmsford rail station, left into Victoria Road, left at lights into New Street, hotel on right.*

Ideally situated just a short walk from the railway station with its quick links to London, this modern, purpose-built hotel has contemporary-style bedrooms equipped with up-to-date facilities. The open-plan public areas include the Italian Sapori Ristorante, a lounge bar and a conservatory.

Rooms: 61 (3 family) (27 GF) *📞* **Facilities:** STV WiFi Gym Complimentary use of facilities at Absalute Gym New Year **Conf:** Class 40 Board 10 Theatre 15 **Services:** Night porter Air con **Parking:** 60 **Notes:** Closed 23 December to 3 January

County Hotel
★★★★ 72% ◉ HOTEL

tel: 01245 455700 **29 Rainsford Road CM1 2PZ**
email: sales@countyhotelgroup.co.uk **web:** www.countyhotelchelmsford.co.uk
dir: *From city centre, past rail and bus station. Hotel 300 yards left beyond lights.*

Just three minutes from the rail and bus stations, and 10 minutes' walk from the city centre, the elegant County Hotel has an award-winning restaurant, comfortable bedrooms, banqueting and conference rooms, and three rooms licensed for civil ceremonies. There is a relaxing south-facing terrace where you can enjoy a drink, and free car parking for guests in the city centre is also a bonus. Chelmsford Museum, the Essex County Cricket Club, Riverside Ice and Leisure, Chelmsford Cathedral are all within walking distance.

Rooms: 50 (2 family) *📞* **S** fr £89 **D** fr £99* **Facilities:** FTV WiFi ↘ HL Xmas New Year **Conf:** Class 54 Board 40 Theatre 150 **Services:** Lift Night porter **Parking:** 60 **Notes:** LB Closed 27–30 December Civ Wed 80

Pontlands Park
★★★ 82% HOTEL

tel: 01245 476444 **West Hanningfield Road, Great Baddow CM2 8HR**
email: sales@pontlandsparkhotel.co.uk **web:** www.heritageleisure.co.uk
dir: *A12, A130, A1114 to Chelmsford. 1st exit at roundabout, 1st slip road on left. Left towards Great Baddow, 1st left into West Hanningfield Road. Hotel 400 yards on left.*

A Victorian country-house hotel situated in a peaceful rural location amid attractive landscaped grounds. The stylishly furnished bedrooms are generally quite spacious; each is individually decorated and equipped with modern facilities. The elegant public rooms include a tastefully furnished sitting room, a cosy lounge bar, smart conservatory restaurant and an intimate dining room.

Rooms: 35 (10 family) (11 GF) **S** fr £144.50 **D** fr £144.50 (including breakfast)* **Facilities:** FTV WiFi 🕑 ↙ Gym Beauty room Xmas New Year **Conf:** Class 40 Board 40 Theatre 100 **Services:** Night porter **Parking:** 100 **Notes:** Closed 24–30 December Civ Wed 100

C

Best Western Ivy Hill

 Best Western.

★★★ 81% HOTEL

tel: 01277 353040 **Writtle Road, Margaretting CM4 0EH**
email: sales@ivyhillhotel.co.uk **web:** www.heritageleisure.co.uk
dir: *Just off A12 junction 14. Hotel on left at top of slip road.*

A smartly appointed hotel conveniently situated just off the A12. The spacious bedrooms are tastefully decorated, have co-ordinated fabrics and all the expected facilities. Public rooms include a choice of lounges, a cosy bar, a smart conservatory and restaurant, as well as a range of conference and banqueting facilities.

Rooms: 31 (5 family) (9 GF) **S** fr £136 **D** fr £136 (including breakfast)*
Facilities: FTV WiFi ☼ Xmas New Year **Conf:** Class 80 Board 40 Theatre 180
Services: Night porter **Parking:** 200 **Notes:** Closed 24–30 December RS Contact hotel for details Civ Wed 100

Premier Inn Chelmsford (Boreham)

Premier Inn

BUDGET HOTEL

tel: 0871 527 8220 (Calls cost 13p per minute plus your phone company's access charge) **Main Road, Boreham CM3 3HJ**
web: www.premierinn.com
dir: *M25 junction 28, A12 to Colchester, B1137 to Boreham.*

High quality, budget accommodation ideal for both families and business travellers. Spacious, en suite bedrooms feature free WiFi and tea and coffee making facilities, and in most hotels, Freeview TV is also available. The adjacent family restaurant features a wide and varied menu.

Rooms: 80

Premier Inn Chelmsford City Centre

Premier Inn

BUDGET HOTEL

tel: 0871 527 9534 (Calls cost 13p per minute plus your phone company's access charge) **Victoria Road CM1 1NY**
web: www.premierinn.com
dir: *A12 junction 15 (Harlow,Chelmsford/A414). At roundabout take A414 (3 Mile Hill). At next roundabout take A41114. 1st exit at next roundabout (Moulsham Street/B1007), continue into New London Road. Left into Parkway. At roundabout 2nd exit into Victoria Street. At next roundabout 1st exit into Duke Street. At next roundabout 1st exit into Victoria Road.*

Rooms: 99

Premier Inn Chelmsford (Springfield)

Premier Inn

BUDGET HOTEL

tel: 0871 527 8222 (Calls cost 13p per minute plus your phone company's access charge) **Chelmsford Service Area, Colchester Rd CM2 5PY**
web: www.premierinn.com
dir: *At A12 junction 19, Chelmsford bypass, signed Chelmsford Service Area.*

Rooms: 91

CHELTENHAM Map 10 SO92
Gloucestershire

Ellenborough Park

★★★★★ 86% COUNTRY HOUSE HOTEL

tel: 01242 545454 **Southam Road GL52 3NH**
email: info@ellenboroughpark.com **web:** www.ellenboroughpark.com
dir: *A46 right after 3 miles onto B4079, merges with A435, 4 miles, over 3 roundabouts, left onto Southam Lane, right into Old Road, right into B4632, hotel on right.*

Set on the original Cheltenham Racecourse estate, this impressive hotel dates in part from the 16th century and has been beautifully restored. The Nina Campbell-designed bedrooms and suites are spread across the main house and adjacent buildings, and all feature superb beds, a great range of modern amenities, and luxurious bathrooms. The stylish Indian-themed spa has a gym and outdoor heated pool. There are two dining options – the Horse Box with its pub atmosphere, and the elegant, oak-panelled restaurant is more formal and offers a high standard of classic cuisine.

Rooms: 61 (44 annexe) (16 family) (19 GF) ☛ **D** fr £139 (including breakfast)*
Facilities: Spa STV FTV WiFi ☼ HL ⚡ 🏊 Gym Xmas New Year **Conf:** Class 70 Board 40 Theatre 120 **Services:** Lift Night porter Air con **Parking:** 130 **Notes:** Civ Wed 120

HIGHLY RECOMMENDED

The Greenway Hotel & Spa

★★★★ 85% ⊛⊛ COUNTRY HOUSE HOTEL

tel: 01242 862352 **Shurdington GL51 4UG**
email: info@thegreenway.co.uk **web:** www.thegreenwayhotelandspa.com
dir: *From Cheltenham centre 2.5 miles south on A46.*

This hotel, with a wealth of history, is peacefully located in a delightful setting within easy reach of the many attractions of the Cotswolds and also the M5. The Manor House bedrooms are luxuriously appointed – traditional in style yet with plasma TVs and internet access. The tranquil Coach House rooms, in the converted stable block, have direct access to the beautiful grounds. The attractive dining room overlooks the sunken garden and is the venue for excellent food, proudly served by dedicated and attentive staff.

Rooms: 21 (8 annexe) (1 family) ☛ **S** fr £115 **D** fr £145 (including breakfast)
Facilities: Spa FTV WiFi ⚡ 🏊 Gym Xmas New Year **Conf:** Board 18 Theatre 50
Services: Night porter **Parking:** 30 **Notes:** LB Civ Wed 60

CHELTENHAM *continued*

The Cheltenham Chase Hotel

★★★★ 80% HOTEL

QHOTELS
INSPIRED
BY YOU

tel: 01452 519988 **Shurdington Road, Brockworth GL3 4PB**
email: cheltenhamreservations@qhotels.co.uk **web:** www.qhotels.co.uk
dir: *M5 junction 11a onto A417 Cirencester. 1st exit A46 to Stroud, hotel 500 yards on left.*

Conveniently positioned for Cheltenham, Gloucester and the M5, this hotel is set in landscaped grounds with ample parking. Bedrooms are spacious with attractive colour schemes and excellent facilities; executive rooms and suites benefit from air conditioning. Public areas include an open-plan bar/lounge, Hardy's Restaurant (named after Hardy Eustace, a famous champion hurdle winning horse), extensive meeting and functions rooms and a well-equipped leisure club.

Rooms: 122 (19 family) (44 GF) ☏ **S** fr £99 **D** fr £111 (including breakfast)*
Facilities: Spa STV FTV WiFi ⌖ HL ☼ Gym Steam room Sauna Sun beds spa bath Xmas New Year **Conf:** Class 160 Board 80 Theatre 350 **Services:** Lift Night porter Air con **Parking:** 240 **Notes:** LB Civ Wed 344

Queen's Hotel Cheltenham-MGallery by Sofitel

★★★★ 80% HOTEL

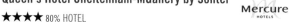
Mercure
HOTELS

tel: 01242 514754 **The Promenade GL50 1NN**
email: h6632@accor.com **web:** www.mgallery.com
dir: *Follow town centre signs. Left at Montpellier Walk roundabout. Entrance 500 metres right.*

With its spectacular position at the top of the main promenade, this landmark hotel is an ideal base from which to explore the charms of this Regency spa town and also the Cotswolds. Bedrooms are very comfortable and include two beautiful four-poster rooms. Smart public rooms include the popular Gold Cup Bar and a choice of dining options, including the Napier Restaurant & Orangery.

Rooms: 84 ☏ **S** fr £110 **D** fr £120 (including breakfast)* **Facilities:** FTV WiFi HL Xmas New Year **Conf:** Class 60 Board 40 Theatre 150 **Services:** Lift Night porter **Parking:** 70 **Notes:** Civ Wed 100

Hotel du Vin Cheltenham

★★★★ 78% ⊚ HOTEL

Hotel du Vin & Bistro

tel: 01242 588450 & 0844 736 4254 (Calls cost 5p per minute plus your phone company's access charge) **Parabola Road GL50 3AQ**
email: info@cheltenham.hotelduvin.com
web: www.hotelduvin.com/locations/cheltenham/
dir: *M5 junction 11, follow signs for city centre. At roundabout opposite Morgan Estate Agents take 2nd left, 200 metres to Parabola Road.*

This hotel, in the Montpellier area of the town, has spacious public areas that are packed with stylish features. The pewter-topped bar has comfortable seating and the spacious restaurant has the Hotel du Vin trademark design; alfresco dining is possible on the extensive terrace area. Bedrooms are very comfortable, with Egyptian linen, deep baths and power showers. The spa is the ideal place to relax and unwind. Although parking is limited, it is a definite bonus. Service is friendly and attentive.

Rooms: 49 (2 family) (5 GF) ☏ **Facilities:** Spa STV WiFi Steam room **Conf:** Class 24 Board 24 Theatre 30 **Services:** Lift Night porter Air con **Parking:** 26 **Notes:** Civ Wed 60

George Hotel

★★★ 80% ⊚⊚ HOTEL

COTSWOLD
INNS & HOTELS

tel: 01242 235751 **St Georges Road GL50 3DZ**
email: hotel@stayatthegeorge.co.uk **web:** www.cotswold-inns-hotels.co.uk
dir: *M5 junction 11 follow town centre signs. At 2nd lights left into Gloucester Road, past rail station over mini-roundabout. At lights right into St Georges Road. Hotel 0.75 mile on left.*

The George Hotel is a genuinely friendly, privately-owned hotel occupying part of a Regency terrace, just a two-minute walk from the town centre. The contemporary interior is elegant and stylish, and the well-equipped, modern bedrooms offer a relaxing haven; individually designed junior suites and deluxe double rooms are available. Lunch and dinner can be enjoyed in the lively atmosphere of Monty's Brasserie, perhaps followed by an evening in the vibrant cocktail bar which hosts live entertainment on Friday and Saturday evenings.

Rooms: 31 (1 GF) ☏ **S** fr £89 **D** fr £105* **Facilities:** FTV WiFi ⌖ Live music at weekends ♫ **Conf:** Class 18 Board 24 Theatre 30 **Services:** Night porter **Parking:** 30 **Notes:** Closed 25–26 December RS 24 December

Cotswold Grange Hotel

★★★ 78% HOTEL

tel: 01242 515119 **Pittville Circus Road GL52 2QH**
email: info@cotswoldgrange.co.uk **web:** www.cotswoldgrangehotel.co.uk
dir: *From town centre, follow Prestbury signs. Right at 1st roundabout, next roundabout straight over, hotel 100 yards on left.*

This beautifully restored Georgian property is in a quiet leafy street less than half a mile from the centre of Cheltenham. There is a range of bedroom types on offer, all are appointed to offer high levels of comfort and facilities. Original features are cleverly blended with more contemporary touches. Bathrooms are well equipped, many with both bath and separate shower facilities. Dining should not be missed, with a range of interesting dishes, prepared by the talented chef and his team, using the best local produce.

Rooms: 20 (4 family) ☏ **S** fr £85 **D** fr £99 (including breakfast)* **Facilities:** FTV WiFi ⌖ **Conf:** Class 24 Board 28 Theatre 35 **Parking:** 19

Malmaison Cheltenham

Ⓤ

tel: 01242 370655 **Bayshill Road GL50 3AS**
web: www.malmaison.com/locations/cheltenham

Currently the rating for this establishment is not confirmed. This may be due to a change of ownership or because ot has only recently joined the AA rating scheme.

Rooms: 60 **Facilities:** WiFi

Follow us on twitter
@TheAA_Lifestyle

C

Premier Inn Cheltenham Central

BUDGET HOTEL

tel: 0871 527 8224 (Calls cost 13p per minute plus your phone company's access charge) **374 Gloucester Road GL51 7AY**
web: www.premierinn.com
dir: *M5 junction 11, A40 (Cheltenham). Follow dual carriageway to end, straight on at 1st roundabout, right at 2nd roundabout.*

High quality, budget accommodation ideal for both families and business travellers. Spacious, en suite bedrooms feature free WiFi and tea and coffee making facilities, and in most hotels, Freeview TV is also available. The adjacent family restaurant features a wide and varied menu.

Rooms: 67

Premier Inn Cheltenham Town Centre

BUDGET HOTEL

tel: 0871 527 9668 (Calls cost 13p per minute plus your phone company's access charge) **The Brewery GL50 4FA**
web: www.premierinn.com
dir: *Phone for directions.*

Rooms: 104

Premier Inn Cheltenham West

BUDGET HOTEL

tel: 0871 527 8226 (Calls cost 13p per minute plus your phone company's access charge) **Tewkesbury Road, Uckington GL51 9SL**
web: www.premierinn.com
dir: *M5 junction 10 (southbound exit only), A4019, hotel in 2 miles. Or M5 junction 11, A40 towards Cheltenham. At Benhall roundabout left onto A4103 (Princess Elizabeth Way) follow racecourse signs. At roundabout left onto A4019 signed Tewkesbury/M5 North. Hotel opposite Sainsbury's.*

Rooms: 58

CHESSINGTON
Greater London

Map 6 TQ16

Premier Inn Chessington

BUDGET HOTEL

tel: 0871 527 8228 (Calls cost 13p per minute plus your phone company's access charge) **Leatherhead Road KT9 2NE**
web: www.premierinn.com
dir: *M25 junction 9, A243 towards Kingston-upon-Thames for approximately 2 miles. Hotel adjacent to Chessington World of Adventures.*

High quality, budget accommodation ideal for both families and business travellers. Spacious, en suite bedrooms feature free WiFi and tea and coffee making facilities, and in most hotels, Freeview TV is also available. The adjacent family restaurant features a wide and varied menu.

Rooms: 62

CHESTER
Cheshire

Map 15 SJ46

See also **Puddington**

The Chester Grosvenor

★★★★★  ⬛ HOTEL

tel: 01244 324024 **Bespoke Hotels Chester Ltd, Eastgate CH1 1LT**
email: reservations@chestergrosvenor.com **web:** www.chestergrosvenor.com
dir: *A56 follow signs for city centre hotels. On Eastgate Street next to the Eastgate clock.*

Located within the Roman walls of the city, this Grade II listed, half-timbered building is the essence of Englishness. Furnished with fine fabrics and queen- or king-size beds, the suites and bedrooms are of the highest standard, each designed with guest comfort as a priority. The eating options are the art deco La Brasserie, a bustling venue awarded 2 AA Rosettes; the Arkle Bar and Lounge for morning coffee, light lunches, afternoon tea and drinks; plus the fine dining restaurant, Simon Radley at The Chester Grosvenor, which offers creative cuisine with flair and style, and has been awarded 4 AA Rosettes. The hotel has a luxury spa and small fitness centre.

Rooms: 80 ⬛ **S** fr £195 **D** fr £225 (including breakfast)* **Facilities:** Spa STV FTV WiFi ⬛ HL Gym Thermal suite Relaxation room ♫ New Year **Conf:** Class 100 Board 50 Theatre 250 **Services:** Lift Night porter Air con **Notes:** Closed 25 December RS Sunday to Monday Civ Wed 250

ABode Chester

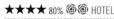

★★★★ 80% ⬛⬛ HOTEL

tel: 01244 347000 **Grosvenor Road CH1 2DJ**
email: info@abodechester.co.uk **web:** www.abodechester.co.uk
dir: *Phone for directions.*

This modern, glass-fronted property sits prominently in the centre of Chester overlooking the castle and adjacent to the racecourse. Bedrooms are well designed and equipped for the modern traveller, with a range of large spacious suites also available. Food is a highlight here, with a range of dining options and bars. The restaurant, on the fifth floor, crowns the top of the building with far-reaching views over Chester Racecourse and beyond. Additional facilities include secure parking and a gym.

Rooms: 85 (7 family) ⬛ **Facilities:** FTV WiFi ⬛ Gym ♫ Xmas New Year **Conf:** Class 24 Board 36 Theatre 90 **Services:** Lift Night porter Air con **Parking:** 39 **Notes:** LB Civ Wed 60

CHESTER *continued*

Grosvenor Pulford Hotel & Spa

★★★★ 78% ⊛ HOTEL

tel: 01244 570560 **Wrexham Road, Pulford CH4 9DG**
email: reservations@grosvenorpulfordhotel.co.uk **web:** www.grosvenorpulfordhotel.co.uk
dir: *M53, A55 at junction signed A483 Chester/Wrexham and North Wales. Left onto B5445, hotel 2 miles on right.*

Set in a rural location, this modern, stylish hotel features a magnificent spa with a large Roman-style swimming pool. Among the range of bedrooms are several executive suites, and others that have spiral staircases leading to the bedroom sections. A smart brasserie restaurant and bar provides a wide range of imaginative dishes in a relaxed atmosphere.

Rooms: 73 (10 family) (19 GF) ⬈ **S** fr £105 **D** fr £125 (including breakfast)*
Facilities: Spa STV FTV WiFi ⬇ HL ⬀ ⬤ Gym Steam room Sauna Xmas New Year **Conf:** Class 100 Board 60 Theatre 220 **Services:** Lift Night porter **Parking:** 200 **Notes:** Civ Wed 200

Hallmark Hotel Chester The Queen

★★★★ 78% ⊛ HOTEL

tel: 0330 028 3402 **City Road CH1 3AH**
email: queen@hallmarkhotels.co.uk **web:** www.hallmarkhotels.co.uk
dir: *Follow signs for railway station, hotel opposite.*

This hotel is ideally located opposite the railway station and is just a couple of minutes' walk from the city. Public areas include a restaurant, small gym, waiting room bar, separate lounge and Roman-themed gardens. The bedrooms are mostly spacious and reflect the hotel's Victorian heritage.

Rooms: 218 (11 family) (12 GF) ⬈ **Facilities:** STV FTV WiFi ⬇ HL Gym Beauty treatment room Table tennis ⬚ Xmas New Year **Conf:** Class 150 Board 60 Theatre 400 **Services:** Lift Night porter **Parking:** 150 **Notes:** Civ Wed 400

Macdonald New Blossoms Hotel

★★★★ 77% HOTEL

tel: 01244 323186 **St John Street CH1 1HL**
email: events.blossoms@macdonald-hotels.co.uk
web: www.macdonaldhotels.co.uk/blossoms
dir: *M53 junction 12 follow city centre signs for Eastgate, through pedestrian zone, hotel on left.*

Ideally located to explore the historic city of Chester, this is a modern and contemporary hotel. Bedrooms range from executive to feature four-poster rooms, with many retaining the charm of the original Victorian building. A stylish brasserie restaurant and bar offer an informal dining experience.

Rooms: 67 (1 family) ⬈ **S** fr £89 **D** fr £99* **Facilities:** FTV WiFi ⬇ Xmas New Year **Conf:** Class 50 Board 40 Theatre 90 **Services:** Lift Night porter Air con **Notes:** Civ Wed 80

Mercure Chester Abbots Well Hotel

★★★★ 74% HOTEL

tel: 0844 815 9001 (Calls cost 5p per minute plus your phone company's access charge) **Whitchurch Road, Christleton CH3 5QL**
email: gm.mercurechester@jupiterhotels.co.uk **web:** www.mercurechester.co.uk
dir: *A41 Whitchurch, hotel on right in 200 metres.*

This smart, modern hotel is located just a short drive from the city centre; with extensive meeting and function facilities, a well-equipped leisure club and ample parking, it is a popular conference venue. Bedrooms vary in size and style but all are well equipped for both business and leisure guests. Food is served in the airy restaurant and also in the large open-plan bar lounge.

Rooms: 126 (9 family) (58 GF) ⬈ **S** fr £75 **D** fr £80 (including breakfast)*
Facilities: STV WiFi ⬇ ⬀ Gym Treatment room Xmas New Year **Conf:** Class 140 Board 100 Theatre 230 **Services:** Lift Night porter **Parking:** 280 **Notes:** Civ Wed 180

Mill Hotel & Spa Destination

★★★ 78% HOTEL

tel: 01244 350035 **Milton Street CH1 3NF**
email: reservations@millhotel.com **web:** www.millhotel.com
dir: *M53 junction 12, A56, left at 2nd roundabout A5268, 1st left, 2nd left.*

There have been constant improvements at this stylish conversion of an old corn mill which enjoys an idyllic canalside location close to the city centre. The bedrooms come in a variety of styles, some accessed over the enclosed canal bridge. There are several dining and bar options, and meals are even served on a broad-beam boat that cruises Chester's canal system, to and from the hotel. A well-equipped leisure centre and spa treatments are also provided.

Rooms: 132 (49 annexe) (57 family) ⬈ **S** fr £78 **D** fr £98 (including breakfast)*
Facilities: Spa STV FTV WiFi HL ⬀ Gym Aerobic studio Sauna Steam room Kinesis studio ⬚ Xmas New Year **Conf:** Board 20 Theatre 25 **Services:** Lift Night porter **Parking:** 120 **Notes:** LB

Brookside Hotel

★★★ 77% HOTEL

tel: 01244 381943 **Brook Lane CH2 2AN**
email: info@brookside-hotel.co.uk **web:** www.brookside-hotel.co.uk
dir: *M53 junction 12, A56 towards Chester, A41. 0.5 mile left signed Newton (Plas Newton Lane). 0.5 mile right into Brook Lane. Hotel 0.5 mile. Or from Chester inner ring road follow A5116/Ellesmere Port/Hospital signs (keep in right lane to take right fork). Immediately left. At mini-roundabout 2nd right.*

This hotel is conveniently located in a residential area just north of the city centre. The attractive public areas consist of a foyer lounge, a small bar and a split-level restaurant. The homely bedrooms are thoughtfully furnished and some feature four-poster beds.

Rooms: 26 (9 family) (4 GF) **Facilities:** WiFi **Conf:** Class 20 Board 12 **Parking:** 20 **Notes:** Closed 20 December to 3 January

The Hallmark Inn

★★★ 77% METRO HOTEL

tel: 0330 028 3424 **City Road CH1 3AF**
email: westminster@hallmarkhotels.co.uk **web:** www.hallmarkhotels.co.uk
dir: *A56, 3 miles to city centre, left signed rail station. Hotel opposite station, on right.*

Situated next to the railway station and close to the city centre, The Hallmark Inn is an established hotel catering for a wide market. It has an attractive Tudor-style exterior, but bedrooms are modern and well equipped with a few luxurious touches; family rooms are also available. There is a choice of bars and lounges, and the dining room serves a broad range of dishes.

Rooms: 75 (5 family) (10 GF) **S** fr £114 **D** fr £139 (including breakfast)
Facilities: FTV WiFi Free gym facilities at sister hotel **Services:** Lift Night porter

C

Crabwall Manor Hotel & Spa

■■ LEGACY
■■ HOTELS.

[U]

tel: 01244 851666 **Parkgate Road, Mollington CH1 6NE**
email: reservations@crabwallhotel.co.uk
web: www.legacy-hotels.co.uk/hotels/crabwall-manor-hotel-spa-mollington-chester

Currently the rating for this establishment is not confirmed. This may be due to a change of ownership or because ot has only recently joined the AA rating scheme.

Rooms: 48 **Facilities:** Spa WiFi 🕙 Gym Sauna Steam room

Premier Inn Chester Central (North)

Premier Inn 🌙

BUDGET HOTEL

tel: 0871 527 8230 (Calls cost 13p per minute plus your phone company's access charge) **76 Liverpool Road CH2 1AU**
web: www.premierinn.com
dir: M53 junction 12, A56. At 2nd roundabout right signed A41 to Chester Zoo. At 1st lights left into Heath Road, leads into Mill Lane. Under small rail bridge. Hotel at end on right.

High quality, budget accommodation ideal for both families and business travellers. Spacious, en suite bedrooms feature free WiFi and tea and coffee making facilities, and in most hotels, Freeview TV is also available. The adjacent family restaurant features a wide and varied menu.

Rooms: 31

Premier Inn Chester Central (South East)

Premier Inn 🌙

BUDGET HOTEL

tel: 0871 527 8232 (Calls cost 13p per minute plus your phone company's access charge) **Caldy Valley Road, Boughton CH3 5PR**
web: www.premierinn.com
dir: M53 junction 12, A56 to Chester. At 1st lights onto A41 (Whitchurch). At 2nd roundabout exit into Caldy Valley Road (Huntington). Hotel on right.

Rooms: 93

Premier Inn Chester City Centre

Premier Inn 🌙

BUDGET HOTEL

tel: 0871 527 8234 (Calls cost 13p per minute plus your phone company's access charge) **20-24 City Road CH1 3AE**
web: www.premierinn.com
dir: M53 junction 12, follow A56/Chester City Centre signs. At roundabout 1st exit onto A5268 (St Oswalds Way) follow railway station signs. At Bar's Roundabout 1st exit. Hotel on right.

Rooms: 120

CHESTERFIELD   Map 16 SK37
Derbyshire

HIGHLY RECOMMENDED

Casa Hotel

★★★★ 83% ◎◎ HOTEL

tel: 01246 245999 **Lockoford Lane S41 7JB**
email: enquiries@casahotels.co.uk web: www.casahotels.co.uk
dir: M1 junction 29 to A617 Chesterfield/A61 Sheffield, 1st exit at roundabout, hotel on left.

Casa Hotel has a contemporary Spanish theme throughout. The stylish bedrooms feature air conditioning, Hypnos beds and bathrooms with rain showers. Four suites are equipped with their own jacuzzi hot tubs on the balconies, and two also have private saunas. Cocina Restaurant offers appealing menus featuring produce sourced from the proprietor's own farm. The conference and event facilities are excellent and offer complimentary WiFi throughout.

Rooms: 100 (6 family) 🐾 **Facilities:** STV FTV WiFi ➹ HL Gym **Conf:** Class 140 Board 50 Theatre 280 **Services:** Lift Night porter Air con **Parking:** 200 **Notes:** LB Civ Wed 280

Peak Edge Hotel

★★★★ 82% ◎◎ HOTEL

tel: 01246 566142 **Darley Road, Stone Edge S45 0LW**
email: sleep@peakedgehotel.co.uk web: www.peakedgehotel.co.uk
dir: M1 junction 29, A617 to Chesterfield. At roundabout take 1st exit onto A61, at next roundabout 2nd exit onto Whitecotes Lane, continue onto Matlock Road (A632) then Darley Road (B5057).

The Peak Edge Hotel is set in the heart of the Derbyshire countryside and benefits from great views on all sides. The modern rooms are spacious, comfortable, and all

continued

CHESTERFIELD *continued*

benefit from high quality bathrooms. The inn has a rustic, 17th-century atmosphere, with stone walls and wooden flooring. The staff are very friendly and well informed. Food is a highlight of any stay, with locally sourced produce put to good use.

Rooms: 27 (2 family) (15 GF) ♙ **S** fr £135 **D** fr £150 (including breakfast) **Facilities:** FTV WiFi ♙ Xmas New Year **Conf:** Class 175 Board 60 Theatre 145 **Services:** Lift Night porter Air con **Parking:** 70 **Notes:** LB Civ Wed 140

Ringwood Hall Hotel and Spa

★★★★ 79% HOTEL

tel: 01246 280077 **Brimington S43 1DQ**
email: reception@ringwoodhallhotel.com **web:** www.ringwoodhallhotel.com
dir: *M1 junction 30, A619 to Chesterfield through Staveley. Hotel on left.*

Ringwood Hall is a beautifully presented Georgian manor house set in 29 acres of peaceful grounds, between the M1 and Chesterfield. The stylish bedrooms include 'Feature Rooms' and three apartments within the grounds. Public areas include comfortable lounges, the Markham Bar and a cocktail lounge. The health and fitness club has a pool, sauna, steam room and gym.

Rooms: 74 (10 annexe) (32 family) (32 GF) ♙ **Facilities:** Spa FTV WiFi ☞ Gym Steam room Sauna Xmas New Year **Conf:** Class 80 Board 60 Theatre 250 **Services:** Night porter **Parking:** 150 **Notes:** LB Civ Wed 250

Premier Inn Chesterfield North

Premier Inn

BUDGET HOTEL

tel: 0871 527 8238 (Calls cost 13p per minute plus your phone company's access charge) **Tapton Lock Hill, off Rotherway S41 7NJ**
web: www.premierinn.com
dir: *Adjacent to Tesco, at A61 and A619 roundabout, 1 mile north of city centre.*

High quality, budget accommodation ideal for both families and business travellers. Spacious, en suite bedrooms feature free WiFi and tea and coffee making facilities, and in most hotels, Freeview TV is also available. The adjacent family restaurant features a wide and varied menu.

Rooms: 88

Premier Inn Chesterfield West

Premier Inn

BUDGET HOTEL

tel: 0871 527 8240 (Calls cost 13p per minute plus your phone company's access charge) **Baslow Road, Eastmoor S42 7DA**
web: www.premierinn.com
dir: *M1 junction 29, A617. At next roundabout 2nd exit. At next roundabout 1st exit into Markham Road. At next roundabout 2nd exit into Wheatbridge Road, left into Chatsworth Road. 2.5 miles to hotel.*

Rooms: 25

CHESTER-LE-STREET Map 19 NZ25
County Durham

Lumley Castle Hotel

★★★★ 74% HOTEL

tel: 0191 389 1111 **DH3 4NX**
email: reservations@lumleycastle.com **web:** www.lumleycastle.com
dir: *A1(M) junction 63, follow Chester-le-Street signs. Follow signs for Riverside then Lumley Castle.*

Dominating the landscape for the past 600 years, Lumley Castle cannot help but impress. The place has a real sense of theatre and as a guest you are left in no

doubt that you are in a genuine castle. The magnificent state rooms, along with other public areas, are very well presented in accord with all guest expectations. Bedrooms differ in style, size and type but all make good use of the available space. The staff are warm and welcoming, and quality food is served throughout.

Rooms: 73 (47 annexe) (9 family) (27 GF) ♙ **Facilities:** FTV WiFi ♙ HL Xmas New Year **Conf:** Class 60 Board 50 Theatre 150 **Services:** Lift Night porter **Parking:** 150 **Notes:** Closed 24–26 December, 1 January Civ Wed 144

CHICHESTER Map 5 SU80
West Sussex

The Goodwood Hotel

★★★★ 81% ◎◎ HOTEL

tel: 01243 775537 **PO18 0QB**
email: reservations@goodwood.com **web:** www.goodwood.com/estate/the-goodwood-hotel

(for full entry see Goodwood)

Chichester Harbour Hotel

★★★★ 77% ◎ HOTEL

tel: 01243 778000 **57 North Street PO19 1NH**
email: chichester@harbourhotels.co.uk **web:** www.chichester-harbour-hotel.co.uk
dir: *From A27, onto inner ring road to Northgate. At Northgate roundabout left into North Street, hotel on left.*

This well-presented Grade II listed, Georgian property occupies a prime position at the top of North Street. The stylish bedrooms feature Egyptian cotton linen and high-speed WiFi access. The bar and restaurant are contemporary venues for enjoying meals and refreshments which are served all day. The intimate HarSPA is tucked away underground and features treatment rooms, steam room, hydro pool and gym. The hotel is just a few minutes' away from the famous Festival Theatre, and not far from Goodwood, for motorsport and horse racing.

Rooms: 37 (1 annexe) (2 family) ♙ **S** fr £99 **D** fr £104 (including breakfast)* **Facilities:** Spa FTV WiFi ☞ Gym Hydro pool Xmas New Year **Conf:** Class 100 Board 30 Theatre 100 **Services:** Lift Night porter **Parking:** 42 **Notes:** LB Civ Wed 100

HIGHLY RECOMMENDED

Crouchers Restaurant & Hotel

★★★ 86% ◎◎ HOTEL

tel: 01243 784995 **Birdham Road PO20 7EH**
email: enquiries@crouchershotel.co.uk **web:** www.crouchershotel.co.uk
dir: *From A27 (Chichester bypass) onto A286 towards West Wittering, 2 miles, hotel on left between Chichester Marina and Dell Quay.*

This friendly, family-run hotel, situated in open countryside, is just a short drive from the harbour. The stylish and well-equipped bedrooms are situated in a separate barn, coach house and stable block, and include four-poster rooms and rooms with patios that overlook the fields. The modern oak-beamed restaurant, with country views, serves award-winning cuisine.

Rooms: 26 (23 annexe) (2 family) (15 GF) ♙ **D** fr £90* **Facilities:** STV FTV WiFi ♙ Xmas New Year **Conf:** Class 80 Board 30 Theatre 80 **Parking:** 80 **Notes:** Civ Wed 80

C

Premier Inn Chichester

Premier Inn

BUDGET HOTEL

tel: 0871 527 8242 (Calls cost 13p per minute plus your phone company's access charge) **Chichester Gate Leisure Park, Terminus Road PO19 8EL**
web: www.premierinn.com
dir: *A27 towards city centre. Follow Terminus Road Industrial Estate signs. Left at 1st lights, left at next lights into Chichester Gate Leisure Park. Hotel on right.*

High quality, budget accommodation ideal for both families and business travellers. Spacious, en suite bedrooms feature free WiFi and tea and coffee making facilities, and in most hotels, Freeview TV is also available. The adjacent family restaurant features a wide and varied menu.

Rooms: 83

CHILDER THORNTON
Cheshire   Map 15 SJ37

Premier Inn Wirral (Childer Thornton)

Premier Inn

BUDGET HOTEL

tel: 0871 527 9174 (Calls cost 13p per minute plus your phone company's access charge) **New Chester Road CH66 1QW**
web: www.premierinn.com
dir: *M53 junction 5, A41 towards Chester. Hotel on right, same entrance as Burleydam Garden Centre.*

High quality, budget accommodation ideal for both families and business travellers. Spacious, en suite bedrooms feature free WiFi and tea and coffee making facilities, and in most hotels, Freeview TV is also available. The adjacent family restaurant features a wide and varied menu.

Rooms: 68

CHIPPENHAM
Wiltshire   Map 4 ST97

Best Western Plus Angel Hotel

LEGACY HOTELS

★★★ 82% HOTEL

tel: 01249 652615 **Market Place SN15 3HD**
email: reception@angelhotelchippenham.co.uk **web:** www.angelhotelchippenham.co.uk
dir: *Follow tourist signs for Bowood House. Under railway arch, follow 'Borough Parade Parking' signs. Hotel adjacent to car park.*

Several impressive buildings combine to make this smart and comfortable hotel. The well-equipped bedrooms vary from those in the main house where character is the key, to the smart executive-style, courtyard rooms. The lounge and restaurant are bright and modern, and offer an imaginative carte and an all-day menu.

Rooms: 50 (35 annexe) (3 family) (12 GF) **S** fr £80 **D** fr £95* **Facilities:** FTV WiFi ⓒ Gym **Conf:** Class 50 Board 50 Theatre 100 **Services:** Night porter **Parking:** 50 **Notes:** LB

Premier Inn Chippenham

Premier Inn

BUDGET HOTEL

tel: 0871 527 8244 (Calls cost 13p per minute plus your phone company's access charge) **Cepen Park, West Cepen Way SN14 6UZ**
web: www.premierinn.com
dir: *M4 junction 17, A350 towards Chippenham. Hotel at 1st main roundabout.*

High quality, budget accommodation ideal for both families and business travellers. Spacious, en suite bedrooms feature free WiFi and tea and coffee making facilities, and in most hotels, Freeview TV is also available. The adjacent family restaurant features a wide and varied menu.

Rooms: 130

CHIPPING CAMPDEN
Gloucestershire   Map 10 SP13

Cotswold House Hotel & Spa

★★★★ 79% ◉◉ HOTEL

tel: 01386 840330 & 848928 **Upper High Street, The Square GL55 6AN**
email: reservations@cotswoldhouse.com **web:** www.bespokehotels.com/cotswoldhouse
dir: *A44 take B4081 to Chipping Campden. Right at T-junction into High Street. Hotel in The Square behind town hall.*

This hotel offers contemporary style within a classic townhouse set in the heart of idyllic Chipping Campden. The hotel boasts a spa and two dining outlets: The Brasserie for a relaxed casual experience and Fig, a fine dining destination. Gardens to the rear of the property offer a tranquil retreat.

Rooms: 28 (6 annexe) (4 family) (5 GF) ⌁ **S** fr £130 **D** fr £145 (including breakfast)* **Facilities:** Spa STV FTV WiFi ❧ ⓒ 🦢 Steam room Hydrotherapy pool Treatment rooms Xmas New Year **Conf:** Class 60 Board 40 Theatre 100 **Services:** Night porter Air con **Parking:** 27 **Notes:** Civ Wed 100

Three Ways House

★★★ 82% ◉ HOTEL

tel: 01386 438429 **Chapel Lane, Mickleton GL55 6SB**
email: reception@puddingclub.com **web:** www.threewayshousehotel.com
dir: *In Mickleton centre, on B4632 Stratford-upon-Avon to Broadway road.*

Built in 1870, this charming hotel has welcomed guests for over 100 years and is home to the world famous Pudding Club, formed in 1985 to promote traditional English puddings. Individuality is a hallmark here, as reflected in a number of the bedrooms that have been designed around a pudding theme. Public areas are stylish and include the air-conditioned restaurant, lounges and meeting rooms.

Rooms: 48 (7 family) (14 GF) ⌁ **S** fr £88 **D** fr £155 (including breakfast)* **Facilities:** FTV WiFi ❧ Xmas New Year **Conf:** Class 40 Board 35 Theatre 100 **Services:** Lift Night porter **Parking:** 37 **Notes:** LB Civ Wed 100

CHIPPING NORTON
Oxfordshire   Map 10 SP32

Premier Inn Chipping Norton

Premier Inn

BUDGET HOTEL

tel: 0871 527 9688 (Calls cost 13p per minute plus your phone company's access charge) **Spring Street OX7 5LM**
web: www.premierinn.com
dir: *A44/B4026/London Road/A44. At roundabout take towards B4026. At 2nd roundabout continue onto Over Norton Road/B4026. Left into Spring Street.*

High quality, budget accommodation ideal for both families and business travellers. Spacious, en suite bedrooms feature free WiFi and tea and coffee making facilities, and in most hotels, Freeview TV is also available. The adjacent family restaurant features a wide and varied menu.

Rooms: 72

C

CHITTLEHAMHOLT
Devon   Map 3 SS62

Highbullen Hotel, Golf & Country Club

★★★★ 79% ◉◉ HOTEL

tel: 01769 540561 **EX37 9HD**
email: welcome@highbullen.co.uk **web:** www.highbullen.co.uk
dir: *M5 junction 27/A361/B3227 towards South Molton. Near end of High Street bear left onto B3226. Follow road along Mole Valley for 5 miles then follow brown tourist signs.*

Highbullen Hotel offers luxury accommodation in an idyllic north Devon setting. In The Manor House, the bedrooms have different colour schemes, furniture and fittings that create individuality, and include the two-roomed Loft Suite; in other areas are the stylish Estate Rooms which offer much comfort and elegance in the peaceful surroundings. All rooms have smart TVs and internet access throughout. The food and drink options are extensive, with dinner and breakfast being served daily in the elegant Devon View Restaurant. The hotel also has a well-equipped leisure centre and spa.

Rooms: 42 (7 family) (15 GF) **Facilities:** FTV WiFi ♪ ⊗ ⤙ ⚓ 18 ⚑ Fishing ⛳ Gym Sauna Steam room shooting pilates classes fitness classes Xmas New Year **Conf:** Class 180 Board 50 Theatre 400 **Services:** Night porter **Parking:** 100 **Notes:** LB Civ Wed 200

CHORLEY
Lancashire   Map 15 SD51

Best Western Park Hall Hotel

 Best Western.

★★★ 79% ◉ HOTEL

tel: 01257 455000 **Park Hall Road, Charnock Richard PR7 5LP**
email: parkhall@lavenderhotels.co.uk **web:** www.lavenderhotels.co.uk
dir: *M6 junction 27 Chorley, south of Preston.*

This hotel is situated in wooded countryside near Preston with good links to motorways. Well equipped for both business and leisure guests, the bedrooms are comfortable, spacious and well stocked with modern amenities including complimentary WiFi. Lavender pillow sprays are thoughtfully provided too. The award-winning Brookes Restaurant serves imaginative cuisine, and more relaxed meals are also available in the bar area. Leisure facilities on site include a swimming pool, gym and spa treatments. Complimentary parking and extensive function facilities complete the package.

Rooms: 141 (30 family) (70 GF) ↻ **S** fr £70 **D** fr £80 (including breakfast)*
Facilities: Spa FTV WiFi ♪ ⊗ Gym **Conf:** Class 350 Board 60 Theatre 800
Services: Lift Night porter **Notes:** Civ Wed 120

Premier Inn Chorley North

Premier Inn 🌙

BUDGET HOTEL

tel: 0871 527 8246 (Calls cost 13p per minute plus your phone company's access charge) **Malthouse Farm, Moss Lane PR6 8AB**
web: www.premierinn.com
dir: *M61 junction 8 onto A674 (Wheelton), 400 yards on left into Moss Lane.*

High quality, budget accommodation ideal for both families and business travellers. Spacious, en suite bedrooms feature free WiFi and tea and coffee making facilities, and in most hotels, Freeview TV is also available. The adjacent family restaurant features a wide and varied menu.

Rooms: 80

Premier Inn Chorley South

Premier Inn 🌙

BUDGET HOTEL

tel: 0871 527 8248 (Calls cost 13p per minute plus your phone company's access charge) **Bolton Road PR7 4AB**
web: www.premierinn.com
dir: *From north: M61 junction 8, A6 to Chorley. From south: M6 junction 27 follow Standish signs. Left onto A5106 to Chorley, A6 towards Preston. Hotel 0.5 mile on right.*

Rooms: 29

CHRISTCHURCH
Dorset   Map 5 SZ19

HIGHLY RECOMMENDED

Captain's Club Hotel & Spa

★★★★ 83% ◉◉ HOTEL

tel: 01202 475111 **Wick Ferry, Wick Lane BH23 1HU**
email: reservations@captainsclubhotel.com **web:** www.captainsclubhotel.com
dir: *B3073 to Christchurch. On Fountain roundabout take 5th exit (Sopers Lane) 2nd left (St Margarets Avenue) 1st right into Wick Lane.*

The Captain's Club Hotel is situated in the heart of the town on the banks of the River Stour at Christchurch Quay, and only 10 minutes from Bournemouth. All bedrooms, including the suites and apartments, have views overlooking the river. Guests can relax in the hydrotherapy pool, enjoy a spa treatment or sample the cuisine in the restaurant.

Rooms: 29 (12 family) ↻ **D** fr £159 (including breakfast)* **Facilities:** Spa STV FTV WiFi ♪ Hydrotherapy pool Sauna Dry flotation ♫ **Conf:** Class 72 Board 64 Theatre 140 **Services:** Lift Night porter Air con **Parking:** 41 **Notes:** Civ Wed 100

See advert opposite

C

Christchurch Harbour Hotel

★★★★ 81% ◉◉ HOTEL

tel: 01202 483434 **95 Mudeford BH23 3NT**
email: christchurch@harbourhotels.co.uk **web:** www.christchurch-harbour-hotel.co.uk
dir: On A35 to Christchurch onto A337 to Highcliffe. Right at roundabout, hotel 1.5 miles on left.

Delightfully situated on the side of Mudeford Quay close to sandy beaches, and conveniently located for Bournemouth Airport and the BIC, this hotel boasts an impressive spa and leisure facility. The bedrooms are particularly well appointed and stylishly finished; many have excellent views, and some have balconies. Guests can eat in the award-winning Jetty Restaurant, or the Upper Deck Bar and Restaurant.

Rooms: 67 (3 annexe) (3 family) (14 GF) ⬅ **D** fr £125 (including breakfast)*
Facilities: Spa FTV WiFi ⬇ ⊗ Gym Steam room Sauna Exercise classes Hydrotherapy pool Xmas New Year **Conf:** Class 20 Board 30 Theatre 100 **Services:** Lift Night porter **Parking:** 55 **Notes:** LB Civ Wed 100

The Kings Arms

★★★ 81% HOTEL

tel: 01202 588933 **18 Castle Street BH23 1DT**
email: kings@harbourhotels.co.uk **web:** www.thekings-christchurch.co.uk

Located right in the heart of Christchurch, this elegant and stylish hotel has much to offer. There's a relaxed and welcoming ambiance, with the bar a great place for a decadent cocktail, before re-locating to the restaurant for accomplished cooking using wonderful local produce. Bedrooms combine great depth of quality with an indulgent comfort, allied with well appointed bathrooms. A number of rooms also provide lovely views across the bowling green and pavilion.

Rooms: 20 (3 family) ⬅ **S** fr £80 **D** fr £100 (including breakfast)* **Facilities:** FTV WiFi ⬇ Xmas New Year **Conf:** Class 50 Board 60 Theatre 100 **Services:** Lift Night porter **Parking:** 15 **Notes:** LB Civ Wed 96

Premier Inn Christchurch East

 Premier Inn

BUDGET HOTEL

tel: 0871 527 8250 (Calls cost 13p per minute plus your phone company's access charge) **Somerford Road BH23 3QG**
web: www.premierinn.com
dir: In Christchurch from A35 and B3059 roundabout junction take B3059 Somerford Road.

High quality, budget accommodation ideal for both families and business travellers. Spacious, en suite bedrooms feature free WiFi and tea and coffee making facilities, and in most hotels, Freeview TV is also available. The adjacent family restaurant features a wide and varied menu.

Rooms: 124

Premier Inn Christchurch West

Premier Inn

BUDGET HOTEL

tel: 0871 527 8252 (Calls cost 13p per minute plus your phone company's access charge) **Barrack Road BH23 2BN**
web: www.premierinn.com
dir: From A338 take A3060 towards Christchurch. Left onto A35. Hotel on right.

Rooms: 61

C

CHURT
Surrey

Map 5 SU83

Frensham Pond Country House Hotel & Spa
★★★★ 80% HOTEL

tel: 01252 795161 **Bacon Lane GU10 2QB**
email: info@frenshampondhotel.co.uk **web:** www.frenshampondhotel.co.uk
dir: *A3 onto A287. 4 miles left at 'Beware Horses' sign. Hotel 0.25 mile.*

This 15th-century house sits quietly on the edge of Surrey Hills, an area of natural beauty overlooking Frensham Pond. Following a multi-million pound refurbishment, it now includes a new luxury spa. Bedrooms offer style, comfort and a host of amenities. The annexe rooms have their own patio areas and private entrance. The contemporary bar and lounge offers a range of snacks while the restaurant offers a more formal menu at lunch and dinner. The newly launched conference centre is well-equipped to host range of various occasions, from business meetings to wedding celebrations and private dining. There is a well-equipped fitness room and secure parking.

Rooms: 53 (12 annexe) (16 family) (27 GF) 🐾 **S** fr £90 **D** fr £90* **Facilities:** Spa STV FTV WiFi ↕ Gym Xmas New Year **Conf:** Class 45 Board 40 Theatre 120
Services: Night porter Air con **Parking:** 120 **Notes:** LB Civ Wed 180

Silver Stars

The AA Silver Star rating denotes a Hotel that we highly recommend. They have a superior level of quality within their star rating, high standards of hospitality, service and cleanliness.

CIRENCESTER
Gloucestershire

Map 5 SP00

Barnsley House
★★★★ ◎◎ 🛎 COUNTRY HOUSE HOTEL

tel: 01285 740000 **GL7 5EE**
email: info@barnsleyhouse.com **web:** www.barnsleyhouse.com
dir: *4 miles northeast of Cirencester on B4425.*

This delightful Cotswold country house has been appointed to provide the highest levels of quality, comfort and relaxation. Individually styled bedrooms come in a range of shapes and sizes, from the large character rooms in the main house to the more contemporary-style stable rooms; all rooms have garden views and are packed with guest extras and little luxuries, including plasma TVs in the bathrooms. The delightful gardens, originally designed in the late 1950s by the previous owner and award-winning gardener Rosemary Verey and her husband, include a fruit and vegetable area which is the home of much of the produce used in the delicious cuisine on offer in The Potager restaurant. In the grounds is the Garden Spa with treatment rooms, sauna, steam room and an outdoor hydrotherapy pool. The hotel also has a cinema.

Rooms: 18 (12 annexe) (10 GF) 🐾 **S** fr £206 **D** fr £224 (including breakfast)*
Facilities: Spa STV FTV WiFi ↕ 🏊 🚣 Cinema Bicycles Hydrotherapy pool relaxation rooms Xmas New Year **Conf:** Class 20 Board 18 Theatre 30
Services: Night porter **Parking:** 30 **Notes:** No children 14 years Civ Wed 120

Corinium Hotel & Restaurant
★★★ 73% SMALL HOTEL

tel: 01285 659711 **12 Gloucester Street GL7 2DG**
email: info@coriniumhotel.co.uk **web:** www.coriniumhotel.co.uk
dir: *From A417/A419/A429 towards Cirencester. A435 at roundabout. After 500 metres turn left at lights, then 1st right, car park on left.*

This delightful, 16th-century small hotel is quietly situated just five minutes' walk from town and is an ideal base from which to explore the Cotswolds. The Corinium has a restaurant offering modern British cuisine, as well as a cosy bar full of Cotswold charm. Other benefits include free WiFi throughout the hotel, an attractive secluded garden for alfresco dining, and ample free parking.

Rooms: 15 (2 family) (2 GF) **S** fr £75 **D** fr £110 (including breakfast)* **Facilities:** FTV WiFi ↕ **Conf:** Class 25 Board 34 Theatre 60 **Parking:** 30 **Notes:** LB

Premier Inn Cirencester Town Centre

Premier Inn

BUDGET HOTEL

tel: 0871 527 9674 (Calls cost 13p per minute plus your phone company's access charge) **Kings Meadow GL7 1NP**
web: www.premierinn.com
dir: *Northwest on Cirencester Road/A419. At roundabout, take 1st exit onto Cricklade Road. At next roundabout hotel on right.*

High quality, budget accommodation ideal for both families and business travellers. Spacious, en suite bedrooms feature free WiFi and tea and coffee making facilities, and in most hotels, Freeview TV is also available. The adjacent family restaurant features a wide and varied menu.

Rooms: 62

CLACTON-ON-SEA
Essex
Map 7 TM11

The Kingscliff Hotel

★★★ 77% HOTEL

tel: 01255 812343 **55 King's Parade, Holland on Sea CO15 5JB**
email: info@thekingscliffhotel.com **web:** www.thekingscliffhotel.co.uk
dir: *A12 junction 29 onto A120, then A133, at Weeley Roundabout take 3rd exit, turn onto Marine Parade East and continue onto Kings Parade.*

The Kingscliff Hotel enjoys a prominent position along the seafront. All bedrooms are attractively presented, comfortable and very well equipped; some front-facing rooms enjoy wonderful sea views. There is a popular restaurant along with a stylish lounge bar for guests. Secure parking is available and free WiFi is offered throughout the hotel. This is also a very popular wedding and conference venue.

Rooms: 30 (2 family) (7 GF) 🐾 **S** fr £50 **D** fr £65* **Facilities:** FTV WiFi ☼ Xmas New Year **Conf:** Class 50 Board 30 Theatre 90 **Services:** Night porter **Parking:** 50 **Notes:** Civ Wed 100

Premier Inn Clacton-on-Sea

Premier Inn

BUDGET HOTEL

tel: 0871 527 8254 (Calls cost 13p per minute plus your phone company's access charge) **Crown Green Roundabout, Colchester Road CO16 9AA**
web: www.premierinn.com
dir: *A12, A120 towards Harwich. In 4 miles take A133 to Clacton-on-Sea. Hotel off Weeley Roundabout.*

High quality, budget accommodation ideal for both families and business travellers. Spacious, en suite bedrooms feature free WiFi and tea and coffee making facilities, and in most hotels, Freeview TV is also available. The adjacent family restaurant features a wide and varied menu.

Rooms: 66

Premier Inn Clacton-on-Sea (Seafront) Hotel

Premier Inn

BUDGET HOTEL

tel: 0871 527 8254 (Calls cost 13p per minute plus your phone company's access charge) **8 Marine Parade West CO15 1RD**
web: www.premierinn.com
dir: *From A12 take A120 towards Harwich. 4 miles, take A133 to Clacton-on-Sea. Hotel accessed from roundabout at Weeley. Adjacent to bowling green.*

Rooms: 66

CLAVERDON
Warwickshire
Map 10 SP16

Ardencote

★★★★ 76% HOTEL

tel: 01926 843111 **The Cumsey, Lye Green Road CV35 8LT**
email: hotel@ardencote.com **web:** www.ardencote.com
dir: *Phone or see website for directions.*

Originally built as a gentleman's residence around 1860, this hotel is set in 83 acres of landscaped grounds. Public rooms include a choice of lounge areas, a cocktail bar and conservatory breakfast room. Main meals are served in the modern Brasserie with lighter meals in the Brasserie Bar. Sunday lunch is served in the Lodge Restaurant, a separate building with a light contemporary style which sits beside a small lake. An extensive range of leisure, golf and conference facilities are provided and bedrooms are smartly decorated and tastefully furnished.

Rooms: 110 (10 family) (30 GF) 🐾 **S** fr £100 **D** fr £135 (including breakfast)* **Facilities:** Spa STV FTV WiFi ☼ HL ⊙ ⚓ ⚘ 18 ♨ ⚒ Gym Squash Sauna Steam room Dance studio Relaxation rooms Xmas New Year **Conf:** Class 70 Board 50 Theatre 175 **Services:** Lift Night porter Air con **Parking:** 350 **Notes:** Civ Wed 150

C

CLEARWELL
Gloucestershire

Map 4 SO50

Tudor Farmhouse Hotel & Restaurant

★★★ ◉◉ ☕ HOTEL

tel: 01594 833046 **High Street GL16 8JS**
email: info@tudorfarmhousehotel.co.uk **web:** www.tudorfarmhousehotel.co.uk
dir: A4136 onto B4228, through Coleford, right into Clearwell, hotel on right just
before War Memorial Cross.

Dating from the 13th century, this idyllic former farmhouse retains a host of
original features including exposed stonework, oak beams, wall panelling and
wonderful inglenook fireplaces. Bedrooms have great individuality and style and
are located either in the main house or in converted buildings in the grounds.
Creative menus offer quality cuisine, served in the intimate, candlelit
restaurant.

Rooms: 23 (18 annexe) (3 family) (10 GF) ☏ **D** fr £130 (including breakfast)*
Facilities: STV FTV WiFi ⌘ HL Xmas New Year **Conf:** Class 20 Board 12 Theatre 30
Parking: 30 **Notes:** LB Closed 2–5 January

CLECKHEATON
West Yorkshire

Map 19 SE12

Premier Inn Bradford South

 Premier Inn

BUDGET HOTEL

tel: 0871 527 8136 (Calls cost 13p per minute plus your phone company's access
charge) **Whitehall Road, Dye House Drive BD19 6HG**
web: www.premierinn.com
dir: On A58 at intersection with M62 and M606.

High quality, budget accommodation ideal for both families and business
travellers. Spacious, en suite bedrooms feature free WiFi and tea and coffee making
facilities, and in most hotels, Freeview TV is also available. The adjacent family
restaurant features a wide and varied menu.

Rooms: 60

CLEETHORPES
Lincolnshire

Map 17 TA30

Kingsway Hotel

★★★ 80% HOTEL

tel: 01472 601122 **Kingsway DN35 0AE**
email: reception@kingsway-hotel.com **web:** www.kingsway-hotel.com
dir: Exit A180 at Grimsby, to Cleethorpes seafront. Hotel at Kingsway and Queen Parade
junction – A1098.

This seafront hotel has been in the same family for four generations and continues
to provide traditional comfort and friendly service. The lounges are comfortable,
and good food is served in the pleasant dining room. The bedrooms are bright and
nicely furnished – most are comfortably proportioned.

Rooms: 46 ☏ **S** fr £79 **D** fr £96 (including breakfast)* **Facilities:** STV FTV WiFi
Conf: Board 18 Theatre 22 **Services:** Lift Night porter **Parking:** 50
Notes: No children 5 years Closed 25–26 December

Premier Inn Cleethorpes

Premier Inn

BUDGET HOTEL

tel: 0871 527 9470 (Calls cost 13p per minute plus your phone company's access
charge) **Meridian Point DN35 0PN**
web: www.premierinn.com
dir: A180 through Grimsby to Cleethorpes. At 4th roundabout take 2nd exit into Isaac's
Hill (A1098). In 0.5 mile take 2nd exit at roundabout into Alexandra Road (A1098). At next
roundabout take 1st exit into Kingsway. Hotel 1 mile on right.

High quality, budget accommodation ideal for both families and business
travellers. Spacious, en suite bedrooms feature free WiFi and tea and coffee making
facilities, and in most hotels, Freeview TV is also available. The adjacent family
restaurant features a wide and varied menu.

Rooms: 60

CLOWNE
Derbyshire

Map 16 SK47

Van Dyk

★★★★ 76% ◉ SMALL HOTEL

tel: 01246 387386 **Worksop Road S43 4TD**
email: guest.services@vandykcountryhotel.co.uk **web:** www.vandykcountryhotel.co.uk
dir: M1 junction 30, 2nd roundabout 1st exit, 3rd roundabout
straight over. Through lights, hotel 100 yards on right.

This is a small, vibrant boutique-style hotel where staff are always on hand to offer
friendly and welcoming service. Accommodation is luxurious and equipped with
many thoughtful extras. Bowdens Restaurant offers fine dining and makes the ideal
setting for a memorable evening; alternatively, there's Southgate Brasserie for
those looking for a more casual eating option.

Rooms: 15 (4 family) ☏ **Facilities:** FTV WiFi Xmas New Year **Conf:** Class 50 Board 60
Theatre 150 **Services:** Night porter **Parking:** 120 **Notes:** Civ Wed 120

COBHAM
Surrey
Map 6 TQ16

Premier Inn Cobham

Premier Inn

BUDGET HOTEL

tel: 0871 527 8256 (Calls cost 13p per minute plus your phone company's access charge) **Portsmouth Road, Fairmile KT11 1BW**
web: www.premierinn.com
dir: *M25 junction 10, A3 towards London, A245 towards Cobham. In Cobham town centre left onto A307 (Portsmouth Road). Hotel on left.*

High quality, budget accommodation ideal for both families and business travellers. Spacious, en suite bedrooms feature free WiFi and tea and coffee making facilities, and in most hotels, Freeview TV is also available. The adjacent family restaurant features a wide and varied menu.

Rooms: 48

Days Inn Cobham - M25
WELCOME BREAK

AA Advertised

tel: 01932 868958 **Cobham Services, M25 junction 9/10 Downside KT11 3DB**
email: cobham.hotel@welcomebreak.co.uk **web:** www.welcomebreak.co.uk
dir: *Between junction 9 and 10 at Extra Cobham services on M25. Accessible from both sides of motorway.*

This modern building offers accommodation in smart, spacious and well-equipped bedrooms, suitable for families and business travellers, and all with en suite bathrooms. Continental breakfast is available and other refreshments may be taken at the nearby family restaurant.

Rooms: 75 (18 family) (35 GF) **Facilities:** FTV WiFi HL **Services:** Lift Night porter Air con **Parking:** 200

COCKERMOUTH
Cumbria
Map 18 NY13

The Trout Hotel
★★★★ 84% HOTEL

tel: 01900 823591 **Crown Street CA13 0EJ**
email: reservations@trouthotel.co.uk **web:** www.trouthotel.co.uk
dir: *Adjacent to Wordsworth House.*

Dating back to 1670, this privately owned hotel has an enviable setting on the banks of the River Derwent. The well-equipped bedrooms, some contained in a wing overlooking the river, are comfortable and mostly spacious. The Terrace Bar & Bistro, serving food all day, has a sheltered patio area. There is also a cosy bar, a choice of lounge areas and an attractive, traditional-style dining room that offers a good choice of set-price dishes.

Rooms: 49 (4 family) (15 GF) **S** fr £115 **D** fr £140 (including breakfast)*
Facilities: STV FTV WiFi Fishing Xmas New Year **Conf:** Class 20 Board 20 Theatre 25 **Services:** Night porter **Parking:** 40 **Notes:** LB Civ Wed 60

COLCHESTER
Essex
Map 13 TL92

Greyfriars
★★★★ 86% HOTEL

tel: 01206 575913 **High Street CO1 1UG**
email: reservations@greyfriarscolchester.co.uk
web: www.greyfriarscolchester.co.uk
dir: *In town centre.*

This stylish hotel has 26 luxuriously appointed bedrooms, including a number of Grand Luxe Signature Suites, Deluxe Suites and Junior Suites. All rooms feature beautiful marble bathrooms or shower rooms. There's all-day dining in the lounges, the Baroque Bar and on the terrace, weather permitting. The art deco-style Cloisters restaurant is open for lunch and dinner.

Rooms: 26 (8 family) (2 GF) (2 smoking) **Facilities:** WiFi **Conf:** Class 40 Board 30 Theatre 60 **Services:** Lift Night porter Air con **Parking:** 38 **Notes:** LB Civ Wed 60

Wivenhoe House Hotel

CLASSIC BRITISH HOTELS

★★★★ 84% HOTEL

tel: 01206 863666 **Wivenhoe Park CO4 3SQ**
email: info@wivenhoehouse.co.uk **web:** www.wivenhoehouse.co.uk
dir: *From A12 take exit signed Colchester. Follow A133 towards Clacton. Take B1027 for Wivenhoe, right on Boundry Road, right on Park Road, signed.*

A superb building, this 18th-century Grade II listed country house hotel was once painted by Constable and is set in acres of magnificent parkland. Bedrooms, furnished to a very high standard, are split between the main house and the contemporary garden wing which is also home to the brasserie bar and restaurant and modern conference facilities. Public areas include the lounge and drawing room where guests can enjoy a traditional afternoon tea.

Rooms: 40 (6 family) **S** fr £85 **D** fr £85* **Facilities:** FTV WiFi Xmas New Year **Conf:** Class 70 Board 22 Theatre 180 **Services:** Lift Night porter **Parking:** 150 **Notes:** LB Civ Wed 180

C

COLCHESTER *continued*

Stoke by Nayland Hotel, Golf & Spa

★★★★ 79% HOTEL

tel: 01206 262836 **Keepers Lane, Leavenheath CO6 4PZ**
email: reservations@stokebynayland.com **web:** www.stokebynayland.com
dir: Exit A134 at Leavenheath onto B1068, hotel 0.75 mile on right.

This hotel is situated on the edge of Dedham Vale, an Area of Outstanding Natural Beauty, in 300 acres of undulating countryside with lakes and two golf courses. The spacious bedrooms are attractively decorated and equipped with modern facilities, such as free WiFi. Public rooms include a bar, a conservatory, a lounge, a smart restaurant, conference and banqueting suites, and the superb Peake Spa and Fitness Centre that offers extensive facilities including health and beauty treatments. There's even a shop that provides all the essentials, plus an array of hand-made gifts. Conveniently located for Ipswich, Bury St Edmunds and Colchester.

Rooms: 80 (6 family) (26 GF) **D** fr £76* **Facilities:** Spa STV FTV WiFi 🏊 🕭 ⚓ 36 Fishing Gym Squash Driving range Pro golf tuition 🎵 Xmas New Year **Conf:** Class 300 Board 60 Theatre 450 **Services:** Lift Night porter **Parking:** 400 **Notes:** LB Civ Wed 200

Crowne Plaza Resort Colchester - Five Lakes

★★★★ 77% HOTEL

tel: 01621 868888 **Colchester Road CM9 8HX**
email: enquiries@cpcolchester.co.uk **web:** www.cpcolchester.co.uk

(for full entry see Tolleshunt Knights)

Best Western The Rose & Crown Hotel

★★★ 77% HOTEL

tel: 01206 866677 **East Street CO1 2TZ**
email: info@rose-and-crown.com **web:** www.rose-and-crown.com
dir: From A12 follow Rollerworld signs, hotel by level crossing.

This delightful 14th-century coaching inn is situated close to the shops and is full of charm and character. Public areas feature a wealth of exposed beams and timbered walls, and include the contemporary East St Grill. Although the bedrooms vary in size, all are stylishly decorated and equipped with many thoughtful extras suitable for both business and leisure guests; luxury executive rooms are available.

Rooms: 39 (3 family) (12 GF) **Facilities:** FTV WiFi **Conf:** Class 50 Board 45 Theatre 100 **Services:** Lift Night porter **Parking:** 50 **Notes:** Civ Wed 80

Premier Inn Colchester (A12)

 Premier Inn

BUDGET HOTEL

tel: 0871 527 8260 (Calls cost 13p per minute plus your phone company's access charge) **Ipswich Road CO4 9WP**
web: www.premierinn.com
dir: From A12 exit at Colchester North/A1232 junction off towards Colchester. Hotel on right, 200 yards from roundabout. Note for sat nav use CO4 9TD.

High quality, budget accommodation ideal for both families and business travellers. Spacious, en suite bedrooms feature free WiFi and tea and coffee making facilities, and in most hotels, Freeview TV is also available. The adjacent family restaurant features a wide and varied menu.

Rooms: 104

Premier Inn Colchester Central

Premier Inn

BUDGET HOTEL

tel: 0871 527 8258 (Calls cost 13p per minute plus your phone company's access charge) **Cowdray Avenue CO1 1UT**
web: www.premierinn.com
dir: From Ipswich A12 junction 29. At roundabout onto A1232 (Ipswich road). At 2nd roundabout 2nd exit onto A133 (Cowdray Avenue). Hotel approximately 0.5 mile on right.

Rooms: 20

Premier Inn Colchester Town Centre

Premier Inn

BUDGET HOTEL

tel: 0871 527 9506 (Calls cost 13p per minute plus your phone company's access charge) **St Peter's Street CO1 1HY**
web: www.premierinn.com
dir: A12 to Colchester. Follow Colchester and A133 signs. At roundabout onto A133. At next roundabout 3rd exit signed Westway and A134. At next roundabout 2nd exit onto Middleborough, continue to St Peter's Street, hotel on left.

Rooms: 85

COLEFORD	**Map 4 SO51**
Gloucestershire	

Bells Hotel & The Forest of Dean Golf Club

★★★ 72% HOTEL

tel: 01594 832583 **Lords Hill GL16 8BE**
email: enquiries@bells-hotel.co.uk **web:** www.bells-hotel.co.uk
dir: 0.25 mile from Coleford. Off B4228.

Set in its own grounds, with an 18-hole golf course, this purpose-built establishment offers a range of facilities. Bedrooms vary in style and space, and a number are on the ground floor. There is a small gym, and a comfortable bar and lounge which is available until late. The hotel's club house, just yards away, has a bar with all-day meals and snacks, a restaurant, a games/TV room and conference and function rooms.

Rooms: 53 (12 family) (36 GF) (5 smoking) 🐾 **Facilities:** FTV WiFi ⚓ 18 Bowling green Short mat bowling room 🎵 Xmas New Year **Conf:** Class 250 Board 100 Theatre 350 **Services:** Night porter **Parking:** 100 **Notes:** Civ Wed 150

C

COLERNE
Wiltshire

Map 4 ST87

Lucknam Park Hotel & Spa
★★★★★ ◎◎◎ 🍃 COUNTRY HOUSE HOTEL

tel: 01225 742777 **SN14 8AZ**
email: reservations@lucknampark.co.uk **web:** www.lucknampark.co.uk
dir: *M4 junction 17, A350 towards Chippenham, then A420 towards Bristol for 3 miles. At Ford left to Colerne, 3 miles, right at crossroads, entrance on right.*

Approaching this Palladian mansion along a magnificent mile-long avenue of beech and lime trees builds a wonderful sense of anticipation. Surrounded by 500 acres of parkland and beautiful gardens, Lucknam Park offers a wealth of choices ranging from pampered relaxation in the indulgent spa, complete with the innovative Well-Being House, to more energetic equestrian pursuits. Elegant bedrooms and suites are split between the main building and adjacent courtyard, all of which exude quality, individuality and comfort. Dining options range from the informal Brasserie (awarded 2 AA Rosettes), to the formal and very accomplished main restaurant, The Park (with 3 AA Rosettes), where skilled, sincere and engaging staff contribute to a memorable experience. For anyone with a passion for food, the cookery school is also worth investigating.

Rooms: 42 (18 annexe) (16 GF) 🐾 **Facilities:** Spa STV FTV WiFi ⬇ ⟳ ⊇ 🏊 Gym Cross country course Mountain bikes Equestrian centre Cookery school Xmas New Year **Conf:** Class 24 Board 24 Theatre 60 **Services:** Night porter **Parking:** 80 **Notes:** Civ Wed 110

COLTISHALL
Norfolk

Map 13 TG21

Norfolk Mead Hotel
★★★★ 84% ◎◎ COUNTRY HOUSE HOTEL

tel: 01603 737531 **Church Loke NR12 7DN**
email: info@norfolkmead.co.uk **web:** www.norfolkmead.co.uk
dir: *Coltishall village, go right with petrol station on left, 200 yards church on right, go down driveway.*

This beautiful hotel enjoys a peaceful location and is set in its own extensive grounds, while still being a short walk from the pretty village of Coltishall. Bedrooms are beautifully designed, and the public areas are very well appointed. Afternoon tea can be enjoyed in the walled garden on finer days and the cosy bar is very comfortable. There is an award-winning restaurant, which benefits from garden and river views.

Rooms: 16 (5 annexe) (5 family) (4 GF) 🐾 **D** fr £135 (including breakfast)*
Facilities: Spa FTV WiFi ⬇ 🏊 Beauty treatment rooms Xmas New Year
Conf: Class 150 Board 150 Theatre 200 **Parking:** 40 **Notes:** Civ Wed 110

CONSETT
County Durham

Map 19 NZ15

Best Western Derwent Manor Hotel
🅱🅦 Best Western.

★★★★ 78% HOTEL

tel: 01207 592000 **Hole Row, Allensford DH8 9BB**
email: reservations@bw-derwentmanor.co.uk **web:** www.bw-derwentmanorhotel.co.uk
dir: *West of Consett, just off A68.*

The Best Western Derwent Manor Hotel enjoys an elevated position overlooking the Derwent Valley. Set in 20 acres, the hotel is ideally located within easy distance of both Newcastle and Durham with a wealth of visitor attractions close by. Bedrooms are generous in size and comfortable, and guests have use of a well-appointed gym and pool area as well as a welcoming bar serving food throughout the day. The main restaurant offers a full-on dining experience with local produce used to create a balanced menu.

Rooms: 53 (5 annexe) (26 family) (26 GF) 🐾 **S** fr £88 **D** fr £106 (including breakfast)* **Facilities:** FTV WiFi ⬇ ⟳ Gym Xmas New Year **Conf:** Class 170 Board 80 Theatre 350 **Services:** Lift Night porter **Parking:** 100 **Notes:** LB Civ Wed 300

COPTHORNE
See **Gatwick Airport**

C

CORBY
Northamptonshire — Map 11 SP88

Premier Inn Corby

BUDGET HOTEL

Premier Inn

---

tel: 0871 527 8264 (Calls cost 13p per minute plus your phone company's access charge) **1 Little Colliers Field NN18 8TJ**
web: www.premierinn.com
dir: *M1 junction 19, A14 eastbound. Exit at junction 7, left at roundabout onto A43. At next roundabout left onto A6003. Hotel at next roundabout. Note: for sat nav use NN18 9EX.*

High quality, budget accommodation ideal for both families and business travellers. Spacious, en suite bedrooms feature free WiFi and tea and coffee making facilities, and in most hotels, Freeview TV is also available. The adjacent family restaurant features a wide and varied menu.

Rooms: 71

CORFE CASTLE
Dorset — Map 4 SY98

HIGHLY RECOMMENDED

Mortons House Hotel

★★★ 86% ⍟⍟ HOTEL

---

tel: 01929 480988 **49 East Street BH20 5EE**
email: stay@mortonshouse.co.uk **web:** www.mortonshouse.co.uk
dir: *On A351 between Wareham and Swanage.*

Set in delightful gardens and grounds with excellent views of Corfe Castle, this impressive building dates back to Tudor times. The oak-panelled drawing room has a roaring log fire in cooler months, and an interesting range of enjoyable cuisine is available in the well-appointed dining room. Bedrooms, many with views of the castle, are comfortable and well equipped.

Rooms: 21 (7 annexe) (2 family) (4 GF) ⚓ **S** fr £95 **D** fr £170 (including breakfast)* **Facilities:** FTV WiFi HL Xmas New Year **Conf:** Class 45 Board 20 Theatre 45 **Parking:** 40 **Notes:** LB Civ Wed 60

CORLEY MOTORWAY SERVICE AREA (M6)
West Midlands — Map 10 SP38

Days Inn Corley - NEC - M6

WELCOMEBREAK

AA Advertised

---

tel: 01676 543800 **Junction 3-4, M6 North, Corley CV7 8NR**
email: corley.hotel@welcomebreak.co.uk **web:** www.welcomebreak.co.uk
dir: *On M6 between junctions 3 and 4 northbound.*

This modern building offers accommodation in smart, spacious and well-equipped bedrooms, suitable for families and business travellers, and all with en suite bathrooms. Continental breakfast is available and other refreshments may be taken at the nearby family restaurant.

Rooms: 50 (13 family) (24 GF) (8 smoking) ⚓ **Facilities:** FTV WiFi ⌨ **Parking:** 120

CORNHILL-ON-TWEED
Northumberland — Map 21 NT83

HIGHLY RECOMMENDED

Tillmouth Park Country House Hotel

★★★ 88% ⍟ COUNTRY HOUSE HOTEL

---

tel: 01890 882255 **TD12 4UU**
email: reception@tillmouthpark.f9.co.uk **web:** www.tillmouthpark.co.uk
dir: *Exit A1(M) at East Ord roundabout at Berwick-upon-Tweed. Take A698 signed Cornhill and Coldstream. Hotel 9 miles on left.*

Tillmouth Park is an imposing mansion set in landscaped grounds by the River Till. Gracious public rooms include a stunning galleried lounge with a drawing room adjacent. The quiet, elegant dining room overlooks the gardens, while lunches and early dinners are available in the bistro. Bedrooms retain much traditional character and include several magnificent master rooms.

Rooms: 14 (2 annexe) (2 family) (2 GF) (4 smoking) **S** fr £74 **D** fr £195 (including breakfast)* **Facilities:** FTV WiFi Game shooting Fishing **Conf:** Class 20 Board 20 Theatre 50 **Parking:** 50 **Notes:** LB Closed 20 December to 1 April

CORSE LAWN
Gloucestershire — Map 10 SO83

Corse Lawn House Hotel

★★★ 79% ⍟⍟ HOTEL

---

tel: 01452 780771 **GL19 4LZ**
email: enquiries@corselawn.com **web:** www.corselawn.com
dir: *On B4211 5 miles southwest of Tewkesbury.*

This gracious Grade II listed Queen Anne house, in 12 acres of grounds, has been home to the Hine family for more than 30 years. Aided by an enthusiastic and committed team, the family continues to preside over all aspects of the hotel, creating a wonderfully relaxed environment. Bedrooms offer a reassuring mix of comfort and quality and include four-poster rooms. In both The Restaurant and The Bistro, the impressive cuisine is based on excellent produce, much of it locally sourced.

Rooms: 18 (3 family) (5 GF) ⚓ **S** fr £70 **D** fr £120 (including breakfast)* **Facilities:** STV FTV WiFi ⍨ ⊗ ⚲ ⚲ Badminton Table tennis New Year **Conf:** Class 30 Board 25 Theatre 50 **Parking:** 62 **Notes:** LB Closed 26–27 December Civ Wed 70

CORSHAM
Wiltshire — Map 4 ST87

Guyers House Hotel

★★★★ 76% ⍟⍟ COUNTRY HOUSE HOTEL

---

tel: 01249 713399 **Pickwick SN13 0PS**
email: enquiries@guyershouse.com **web:** www.guyershouse.com
dir: *A4 between Pickwick and Corsham.*

This privately owned hotel retains the charm and ambience of a country house. The bedrooms are well appointed in keeping with the style of the house, and equipped with modern amenities. The award-winning restaurant is the ideal place for an intimate dinner or a family gathering; alfresco dining is possible when the weather is favourable. The gardens are a feature and are open to the public on certain days under the National Garden Scheme. The hotel is conveniently located for easy access to Bath.

Rooms: 37 (13 GF) ⚓ **Facilities:** FTV WiFi ⍨ ⚲ ⚲ Gym Xmas **Conf:** Class 34 Board 24 Theatre 75 **Services:** Night porter **Parking:** 70 **Notes:** LB Closed 30 December to 3 January Civ Wed 100

C

COVENTRY
West Midlands

Map 10 SP37

See also **Nuneaton**

Best Western Plus Windmill Village Hotel, Golf Club & Spa

★★★★ 75% HOTEL

tel: 024 7640 4040 **Birmingham Road, Allesley CV5 9AL**
email: reservations@windmillvillagehotel.co.uk **web:** www.windmillvillagehotel.co.uk
dir: *A45, close to Coventry City Centre.*

This modern hotel is conveniently located on the outskirts of Coventry and is a short drive from Birmingham and the NEC. Bedrooms are all very attractively presented and most rooms have views over the hotel's challenging golf course. The leisure facilities are first rate and include a very well-equipped gym and a swimming pool. Business guests are well catered for with a range of conference facilities including business suites, and free WiFi is available throughout the hotel.

Rooms: 105 (35 annexe) (10 family) (39 GF) ✆ **S** fr £69 **D** fr £79* **Facilities:** Spa FTV WiFi ⌕ ⊙ ⅃ 18 Gym Xmas New Year **Conf:** Class 140 Board 60 Theatre 400 **Services:** Lift Night porter **Parking:** 400 **Notes:** LB Civ Wed 100

Novotel Coventry

★★★ 77% HOTEL

tel: 024 7636 5000 **Wilsons Lane CV6 6HL**
email: h0506@accor-hotels.com **web:** www.novotel.com
dir: *M6 junction 3. Follow signs for B4113 towards Longford and Bedworth. 3rd exit on large roundabout.*

Novotel Coventry is a modern hotel convenient for Birmingham, Coventry and the motorway network, offering spacious, well-equipped accommodation. The bright brasserie has extended dining hours, alternatively there is an extensive room-service menu. Family rooms and a play area make this a child-friendly hotel, and for adults, there is also a mini-gym and a selection of meeting rooms.

Rooms: 98 (25 GF) ✆ **Facilities:** STV WiFi ⌕ Mini gym **Conf:** Class 100 Board 40 Theatre 200 **Services:** Lift Night porter **Parking:** 120 **Notes:** Civ Wed 50

The Chace Hotel

★★★ 71% HOTEL

tel: 024 7630 3398 **Toll Bar End, London Road CV3 4EQ**
email: thechace@corushotels.com **web:** www.corushotels.com/coventry
dir: *A45 or A46 follow to Toll Bar Roundabout/Coventry Airport, take B4116 to Willenhall, over mini-roundabout, hotel on left.*

Conveniently located for ease of access to the motorway network and Coventry Airport, The Chace Hotel has a long history as an important residence in Willenhall, and was once the home of Dr Charles Webb Iliffe. Rooms vary in style across the property; all are furnished to a good standard. Public areas boast many original and period features including portraits of the doctor and his wife. A popular restaurant and number of function rooms along with ample free parking are also available.

Rooms: 66 (49 annexe) (2 family) (24 GF) **S** fr £69 **D** fr £79* **Facilities:** FTV WiFi ⌕ Xmas New Year **Conf:** Class 40 Board 56 Theatre 100 **Services:** Night porter **Parking:** 100 **Notes:** LB Civ Wed 100

Premier Inn Coventry City Centre

  Premier Inn

BUDGET HOTEL

tel: 0871 527 8272 (Calls cost 13p per minute plus your phone company's access charge) **Belgrade Plaza, Bond Street CV1 4AH**
web: www.premierinn.com
dir: *A4053 (ring road) junction 9, follow Belgrade Plaza car park signs. Hotel in same complex.*

High quality, budget accommodation ideal for both families and business travellers. Spacious, en suite bedrooms feature free WiFi and tea and coffee making facilities, and in most hotels, Freeview TV is also available. The adjacent family restaurant features a wide and varied menu.

Rooms: 120

Premier Inn Coventry City Centre (Earlsdon Park)

  Premier Inn

BUDGET HOTEL

tel: 0871 527 9318 (Calls cost 13p per minute plus your phone company's access charge) **Earlsdon Park CV1 3BH**
web: www.premierinn.com
dir: *From Coventry ring road follow Ikea signs. Hotel adjacent to Coventry RFC on Butts Road. Parking in multi storey adjacent.*

Rooms: 100

Premier Inn Coventry East (Ansty)

 Premier Inn

BUDGET HOTEL

tel: 0871 527 8274 (Calls cost 13p per minute plus your phone company's access charge) **Coombe Fields Road, Ansty CV7 9JP**
web: www.premierinn.com
dir: *M6 junction 2, B4065 towards Ansty. After village right onto B4029 signed Brinklow. Right into Coombe Fields Road, hotel on right.*

Rooms: 28

Premier Inn Coventry East (Binley/A46)

 Premier Inn

BUDGET HOTEL

tel: 0871 527 8268 (Calls cost 13p per minute plus your phone company's access charge) **Rugby Road, Binley Woods CV3 2TA**
web: www.premierinn.com
dir: *M6 junction 2 follow Warwick, A46 and M40 signs. Follow 'All traffic' signs, under bridge onto A46. Left at 1st roundabout to Binley. Hotel on right at next roundabout.*

Rooms: 96

Premier Inn Coventry East (M6 Jct 2)

Premier Inn

BUDGET HOTEL

tel: 0871 527 8266 (Calls cost 13p per minute plus your phone company's access charge) **Gielgud Way, Cross Point Business Park CV2 2SZ**
web: www.premierinn.com
dir: *M6 junction 2 towards Coventry onto A4600 (Hinckley road). At roundabout 1st exit into Parkway, left at next roundabout into Olivier Way. At next roundabout straight on into retail park towards cinema, hotel on right.*

Rooms: 48

C

COVENTRY *continued*

Premier Inn Coventry South (A45)

BUDGET HOTEL

tel: 0871 527 8270 (Calls cost 13p per minute plus your phone company's access charge) **Kenpas Highway CV3 6PB**
web: www.premierinn.com
dir: *M6 junction 2, A46. Follow A45 towards Birmingham.*

Rooms: 38

COWES	Map 5 SZ49
Isle of Wight	

Best Western New Holmwood Hotel

★★★ 80% HOTEL

tel: 01983 292508 **Queens Road, Egypt Point PO31 8BW**
email: reception@newholmwoodhotel.co.uk **web:** www.newholmwoodhotel.co.uk
dir: *From A3020 at Northwood Garage lights, left and follow to roundabout. 1st left then sharp right into Baring Road, 4th left into Egypt Hill. At bottom turn right, hotel on right.*

Just by the Esplanade, this hotel has an enviable outlook. Bedrooms are comfortable and very well equipped, and the light and airy, glass-fronted restaurant looks out to sea and serves a range of interesting meals. The sun terrace is delightful in the summer and there is a choice of meeting rooms for all occasions. Parking is available on a first-come, first-serve basis.

Rooms: 26 (1 family) (9 GF) **Facilities:** STV FTV WiFi Xmas New Year **Conf:** Class 60 Board 50 Theatre 100 **Services:** Night porter **Parking:** 20 **Notes:** Civ Wed 60

CRAMLINGTON	Map 21 NZ27
Northumberland	

Premier Inn Newcastle Gosforth/Cramlington

BUDGET HOTEL

tel: 0871 527 8788 (Calls cost 13p per minute plus your phone company's access charge) **Moor Farm Roundabout, Off Front Street NE23 7QA**
web: www.premierinn.com
dir: *At roundabout junction of A19 and A189, south of Cramlington.*

High quality, budget accommodation ideal for both families and business travellers. Spacious, en suite bedrooms feature free WiFi and tea and coffee making facilities, and in most hotels, Freeview TV is also available. The adjacent family restaurant features a wide and varied menu.

Rooms: 79

CRAWLEY
See **Gatwick Airport**

CREDITON	Map 3 SS80
Devon	

Paschoe House

[U]

tel: 01363 84244 & 07769 268848 **Paschoe House LLP, Bow EX17 6JT**
email: stay@paschoehouse.co.uk **web:** www.paschoehouse.co.uk
dir: *A377, at Barnstaple Cross take junction towards Coleford, at Broomhill Cross continue for 500 yards, hotel next left.*

Currently the rating for this establishment is not confirmed. This may be due to a change of ownership or because ot has only recently joined the AA rating scheme.

Rooms: 9 (4 family) **S** fr £150 **D** fr £290 (including breakfast)* **Facilities:** STV FTV WiFi HL Xmas New Year **Conf:** Class 200 Board 100 Theatre 300 **Services:** Lift Night porter **Parking:** 250 **Notes:** LB Civ Wed 200

CREWE	Map 15 SJ75
Cheshire	

Crewe Hall

★★★★ 82% HOTEL

tel: 01270 253333 **Weston Road CW1 6UZ**
email: crewehall@qhotels.co.uk **web:** www.qhotels.co.uk
dir: *M6 junction 16, A500 to Crewe. Take A5020. 1st exit at next roundabout to Crewe. Hotel 150 yards on right.*

Standing in 500 acres of mature grounds, this historic hall dates back to the 17th century, yet retains an elaborate interior with Victorian-style architecture. Bedrooms are spacious, well equipped and comfortable with traditionally styled suites in the main hall and modern rooms in the west wing. Afternoon tea is served in The Sheridan Lounge, while The Brasserie Restaurant and Bar is contemporary and has a relaxed atmosphere. The health and beauty spa ensure that the hotel is a popular choice with both corporate and leisure guests.

Rooms: 117 (91 annexe) (5 family) (35 GF) **S** fr £87 **D** fr £99 (including breakfast)* **Facilities:** Spa STV WiFi Gym Enclosed events field **Conf:** Class 172 Board 96 Theatre 364 **Services:** Lift Night porter **Parking:** 500 **Notes:** LB Civ Wed 180

Hunters Lodge Hotel

★★★ 67% HOTEL

tel: 01270 539100 **Sydney Road, Sydney CW1 5LU**
email: info@hunterslodge.co.uk **web:** www.hunterslodge.co.uk
dir: *M6 junction 16. 1 mile from Crewe station, off A534.*

Dating back to the 18th century, the hotel has been extended and modernised over the years. Accommodation, mainly located in adjacent well-equipped bedroom wings, includes family rooms and four-poster rooms. Imaginative dishes are served in the popular bar which also offers open fires and friendly and efficient service.

Rooms: 57 (52 annexe) (4 family) (31 GF) **S** fr £45 **D** fr £56* **Facilities:** FTV WiFi Gym **Conf:** Class 100 Board 80 Theatre 160 **Services:** Night porter **Parking:** 240 **Notes:** Civ Wed 130

C

Wychwood Park Hotel and Golf Club

tel: 01270 829200 **Weston CW2 5GP**
email: wychwood.reception@wychwoodparkhotel.com
web: www.legacy-hotels.co.uk/hotels/wychwood-park-hotel-crewe-cheshire
dir: *M6 Junction 16, take the A500 toward Nantwich. At the roundabout take the A531 towards Keele and Nantwich. At the next roundabout turn left on to the A531 towards Keele. Wychwood Park is on the right-hand side and the entrance is at the right exit on the next roundabout.*

Currently the rating for this establishment is not confirmed. This may be due to a change of ownership or because ot has only recently joined the AA rating scheme.

Rooms: 108 **Facilities:** STV WiFi ♨ ⅃ 18 Xmas New Year **Conf:** Theatre 300
Parking: 400 **Notes:** Civ Wed 160

Premier Inn Crewe Central

Premier Inn

BUDGET HOTEL

tel: 0871 527 8276 (Calls cost 13p per minute plus your phone company's access charge) **Weston Road CW1 6FX**
web: www.premierinn.com
dir: *M6 Junction 16, A500, at roundabout 3rd exit onto A5020 (Old Park Road). At next roundabout 2nd exit into Western Road, at next roundabout 3rd exit, hotel on left.*

High quality, budget accommodation ideal for both families and business travellers. Spacious, en suite bedrooms feature free WiFi and tea and coffee making facilities, and in most hotels, Freeview TV is also available. The adjacent family restaurant features a wide and varied menu.

Rooms: 34

Premier Inn Crewe West

Premier Inn

BUDGET HOTEL

tel: 0871 527 8278 (Calls cost 13p per minute plus your phone company's access charge) **Coppenhall Lane, Woolstanwood CW2 8SD**
web: www.premierinn.com
dir: *At junction of A530 and A532, 9 miles from M6 junction 16 northbound.*

Rooms: 80

CROMER
Norfolk | Map 13 TG24

Sea Marge Hotel

★★★★ 75% ◎◎ HOTEL

tel: 01263 579579 **16 High Street, Overstrand NR27 0AB**
email: seamarge@mackenziehotels.com **web:** www.mackenziehotels.com
dir: *A140 from Norwich then A149 to Cromer, B1159 to Overstrand. Hotel in village centre.*

An elegant Grade II listed Edwardian mansion perched on the clifftop amidst pretty, landscaped gardens which lead down to the beach. Bedrooms are tastefully decorated and thoughtfully equipped; many have superb sea views. Public rooms offer a wide choice of areas in which to relax, including Frazer's Restaurant and a smart lounge bar.

Rooms: 25 (6 annexe) (6 family) (3 GF) ◖ **S** fr £105 **D** fr £170 (including breakfast)*
Facilities: FTV WiFi ⛲ Xmas New Year **Conf:** Class 55 Board 30 Theatre 70
Services: Lift Night porter **Parking:** 50 **Notes:** LB

The Cliftonville Hotel

★★★ 78% HOTEL

tel: 01263 512543 **Seafront NR27 9AS**
email: reservations@cliftonvillehotel.co.uk **web:** www.cliftonvillehotel.co.uk
dir: *From A149 (coast road) 500 yards from town centre, northbound on clifftop by sunken gardens.*

The Cliftonville Hotel is an imposing Edwardian building situated on the main coast road with stunning views of the sea. Public areas feature a magnificent staircase, minstrels' gallery, coffee shop, lounge bar, a further residents' lounge, Boltons Bistro and The Westcliff restaurant. The pleasantly decorated bedrooms are generally quite spacious and have lovely sea views.

Rooms: 30 (3 family) ◖ **S** fr £56 **D** fr £112 (including breakfast)* **Facilities:** FTV WiFi ♨ Xmas New Year **Conf:** Class 100 Board 60 Theatre 150 **Services:** Lift Night porter **Parking:** 20 **Notes:** LB

Hotel de Paris

Leisureplex
HOLIDAY HOTELS

★★★ 71% HOTEL

tel: 01263 513141 **High Street NR27 9HG**
email: deparis.cromer@alfatravel.co.uk **web:** www.leisureplex.co.uk
dir: *Enter Church Street (one way) after lights left straight into Jetty Street, car park at end on left.*

An imposing, traditional-style resort hotel, situated in a prominent position overlooking the pier and beach. The bedrooms are pleasantly decorated and equipped with a good range of useful extras; many rooms have lovely sea views. The spacious public areas include a large lounge bar, restaurant, games room and a further lounge.

Rooms: 67 (8 family) (4 GF) ◖ **S** fr £41 **D** fr £64 (including breakfast)*
Facilities: FTV WiFi ♫ Xmas New Year **Services:** Lift Night porter **Parking:** 14
Notes: LB Closed January to Febrary RS March, November to December

C

CROOKLANDS
Cumbria
Map 18 SD58

Crooklands Hotel
★★★ 79% HOTEL

tel: 015395 67432 **LA7 7NW**
email: reception@crooklands.com web: www.crooklands.com
dir: *M6 junction 36 onto A65. Left at roundabout. Hotel 1.5 miles on right past garage.*

This hotel is a popular stop-over for both leisure and corporate guests travelling between England and Scotland and visiting the Lakes. Although only a stone's throw from the M6, this hotel enjoys a peaceful rural location. The bedrooms vary in size, and continual updating ensures a contemporary feel throughout. Housed in a converted 200-year-old farmhouse, the restaurant retains many original features such as the beams and stone walls. Enjoyable cuisine can be enjoyed in a choice of dining areas.

Rooms: 30 (1 family) (14 GF) ☎ **S** fr £74 **D** fr £99 (including breakfast)*
Facilities: FTV WiFi New Year **Conf:** Class 50 Board 40 Theatre 80 **Services:** Lift
Parking: 80 **Notes:** LB Closed 24–28 December

CROYDON
Greater London
Map 6 TQ36

Hallmark Hotel London Croydon Aerodrome
★★★★ 74% HOTEL

tel: 0330 028 3403 **Purley Way CR9 4LT**
email: admin@hallmarkhotels.co.uk web: www.hallmarkhotels.co.uk
dir: *Follow A23 and Central London signs. Hotel on left adjacent to Airport House.*

This hotel (formerly the Aerodrome Hotel) sits in a prime location and offers comfortably appointed bedrooms, all with LCD TVs and free WiFi throughout. Public areas are stylish and modern in their design and include a spacious open-plan bar and brasserie. Ideal for both the leisure and corporate market, there are a number of fully-equipped meeting and conference facilities.

Rooms: 110 (10 family) ☎ **Facilities:** FTV WiFi ⌕ **Conf:** Class 60 Board 36 Theatre 170 **Services:** Lift Night porter Air con **Parking:** 79 **Notes:** Civ Wed 150

Croydon Park Hotel
★★★★ 70% HOTEL

tel: 020 8680 9200 **7 Altyre Road CR9 5AA**
email: info@croydonparkhotel.com web: www.croydonparkhotel.com
dir: *3 minutes walk from East Croydon Station.*

This hotel is located in the heart of the town centre, a 3-minute walk from East Croydon train station and with easy access to both Gatwick Airport and central London. Bedrooms vary in style, but all are comfortably appointed. The two dining options are Whistlers Bar with a menu available throughout the day, and Oscars Brasserie with a daily buffet and carte menu. Conference and leisure facilities are available.

Rooms: 211 (36 family) (6 GF) **Facilities:** FTV WiFi ⌕ ⓢ Gym Squash Sauna Xmas New Year **Conf:** Class 100 Board 30 Theatre 220 **Services:** Lift Night porter Air con **Parking:** 91 **Notes:** Civ Wed 220

Premier Inn Croydon (Purley A23)
Premier Inn

BUDGET HOTEL

tel: 0871 527 8282 (Calls cost 13p per minute plus your phone company's access charge) **The Colonnades Leisure Park, 619 Purley Way CR0 4RQ**
web: www.premierinn.com
dir: *From north: M1, M25, A23 towards Croydon. From south: M25 junction 7, A23 towards Purley Way, 8 miles, hotel close to junction with Waddon Way.*

High quality, budget accommodation ideal for both families and business travellers. Spacious, en suite bedrooms feature free WiFi and tea and coffee making facilities, and in most hotels, Freeview TV is also available. The adjacent family restaurant features a wide and varied menu.

Rooms: 84

Premier Inn Croydon South (A212)
Premier Inn

BUDGET HOTEL

tel: 0871 527 8280 (Calls cost 13p per minute plus your phone company's access charge) **104 Coombe Road CR0 5RB**
web: www.premierinn.com
dir: *M25 junction 7, A23 to Purley, A235 to Croydon. Pass Tree House pub on left. Right at lights onto A212.*

Rooms: 39

Premier Inn London Croydon Town Centre Hotel
Premier Inn

BUDGET HOTEL

tel: 0871 527 9438 (Calls cost 13p per minute plus your phone company's access charge) **Philips House, Lansdowne Road CR0 2BX**
web: www.premierinn.com
dir: *Phone for directions.*

Rooms: 168

CULLOMPTON
Devon
Map 3 ST00

Padbrook Park Hotel
★★★ 79% HOTEL

tel: 01884 836100 **EX15 1RU**
email: info@padbrookpark.co.uk web: www.padbrookpark.co.uk
dir: *1 mile from M5 junction 28, follow brown signs.*

Located in the heart of the Culm Valley, at the southern end of Cullompton, Padbrook Park is set in serene Devon countryside, yet benefits from good local transport links. The spacious bedrooms each have a private bathroom, tea/coffee facilities, a business desk and Freeview TV. Ripleys Restaurant serves traditional British cuisine in intimate surroundings. There is also a modern bar, offering beverages and snacks, and full English breakfasts are served daily. The hotel also offers facilities FootGolf, conferences, meetings, weddings, functions and events, with packages for all budgets.

Rooms: 40 (4 family) (11 GF) **S** fr £63 **D** fr £63* **Facilities:** STV FTV WiFi ⌕ HL Gym 3 Rink Bowling centre Crazy golf Beauty treatment room Hairdressing salon **Conf:** Class 50 Board 50 Theatre 200 **Services:** Lift Night porter **Parking:** 250 **Notes:** Civ Wed 200

D

DAGENHAM
Greater London
Map 6 TQ48

Premier Inn London Dagenham
Premier Inn

BUDGET HOTEL

tel: 0871 527 9364 (Calls cost 13p per minute plus your phone company's access charge) **Chequers Corner, 2 New Road RM9 6YS**
web: www.premierinn.com
dir: *M25 junction 30/A13 signed Barking. Continue on A13 through underpass then flyover, following directions to Central London, Barking and Docklands. Left off A13 – Dagenham East. At roundabout 4th exit, then left at traffic signals onto A1306 Dagenham. Continue at traffic signals. Inn on left.*

High quality, budget accommodation ideal for both families and business travellers. Spacious, en suite bedrooms feature free WiFi and tea and coffee making facilities, and in most hotels, Freeview TV is also available. The adjacent family restaurant features a wide and varied menu.

Rooms: 120

DARLINGTON
County Durham
Map 19 NZ21

INSPECTOR'S CHOICE

Rockliffe Hall
★★★★★ ◉◉◉◉ HOTEL

tel: 01325 729999 **Rockliffe Park, Hurworth-on-Tees DL2 2DU**
email: enquiries@rockliffehall.com **web:** www.rockliffehall.com
dir: *A66 towards Darlington, A167, through Hurworth-on-Tees. In Croft-on-Tees left into Hurworth Road.*

This impressive hotel enjoys a peaceful setting on a restored 18th-century estate by the banks of the River Tees. Luxurious, spacious bedrooms, contemporary in style, are split between the original old hall, the new hall and Tiplady Lodge. Dining options include The Orangery, The Clubhouse and The Brasserie. A state-of-the-art spa and championship golf course, with a first-class club house, complete the picture.

Rooms: 61 (5 family) (17 GF) **S** fr £185 **D** fr £210 (including breakfast)* **Facilities:** Spa STV FTV WiFi ⊗ ⊛ ↘ ↓ 18 ⊜ Fishing ⊌ Gym Nordic walking Children's play area Woodland pods ♫ Xmas New Year **Conf:** Class 100 Board 30 Theatre 180 **Services:** Lift Night porter Air con **Parking:** 200 **Notes:** LB Civ Wed 180

Headlam Hall
★★★★ 82% ◉ HOTEL

tel: 01325 730238 **Headlam, Gainford DL2 3HA**
email: admin@headlamhall.co.uk **web:** www.headlamhall.co.uk
dir: *2 miles north of A67 between Piercebridge and Gainford.*

This impressive Jacobean hall lies in farmland north east of Piercebridge and has its own 9-hole golf course. The main house retains many historical features, including flagstone floors and a pillared hall. Bedrooms are well proportioned and traditionally styled; a converted coach house contains the more modern rooms. There are extensive conference facilities, and the hotel is popular as a wedding venue. Further facilities include a stunning spa complex with a 14-metre pool, an outdoor hot spa, drench shower, sauna and steam room, as well as a gym with the latest cardio and resistance equipment, and five treatment rooms offering a range of therapies and beauty treatments.

Rooms: 38 (22 annexe) (4 family) (9 GF) ⋒ **Facilities:** Spa STV FTV WiFi ⊗ ⊛ ↓ 9 ⊜ Fishing ⊌ Gym New Year **Conf:** Class 40 Board 40 Theatre 120 **Services:** Lift Night porter **Parking:** 80 **Notes:** LB Closed 24–26 December Civ Wed 150

Hall Garth Hotel, Golf and Country Club
★★★ 81% HOTEL
CLASSIC BRITISH HOTELS

tel: 01325 300400 **Coatham Mundeville DL1 3LU**
email: gm@hallgarthdarlington.co.uk **web:** www.hallgarthdarlington.co.uk
dir: *A1(M) junction 59, A167 towards Darlington. After 600 yards left at top of hill, hotel on right.*

Peacefully situated in grounds that feature a golf course, this hotel is just a few minutes from the motorway network. The well-equipped bedrooms come in various styles – it's worth asking for one of the modern rooms. Public spaces include relaxing lounges, a fine-dining restaurant and a separate pub. The extensive leisure and conference facilities are an important focus here.

Rooms: 56 (16 annexe) (3 family) (1 GF) **S** fr £45 **D** fr £45* **Facilities:** Spa STV FTV WiFi ⊗ ⊛ ↓ 9 Gym Steam room Beauty salon Sauna Jacuzzi Xmas New Year **Conf:** Class 160 Board 80 Theatre 250 **Services:** Night porter **Parking:** 150 **Notes:** LB Civ Wed 170

Best Western Walworth Castle Hotel
★★★ 79% HOTEL
BW Best Western.

tel: 01325 485470 **Walworth DL2 2LY**
email: enquiries@walworthcastle.co.uk **web:** www.bw-walworthcastle.co.uk
dir: *A1(M) junction 58 follow signs to Corbridge. Left at The Dog pub. Hotel on left after 2 miles.*

This 12th-century castle is privately owned and has been tastefully converted. Accommodation is offered in a range of styles, including an impressive suite and more compact rooms in an adjoining wing. Dinner can be taken in the fine-dining Hansard's Restaurant or the more relaxed Farmer's Restaurant. This is a popular venue for conferences and weddings, and there is also a falconry in the grounds.

Rooms: 32 (14 annexe) (4 family) (8 GF) ⋒ **Facilities:** FTV WiFi ⊗ ⊌ Falconry centre Xmas New Year **Conf:** Class 60 Board 40 Theatre 120 **Services:** Night porter **Parking:** 100 **Notes:** Civ Wed 100

DARLINGTON *continued*

Premier Inn Darlington

Premier Inn

BUDGET HOTEL

tel: 0871 527 8286 (Calls cost 13p per minute plus your phone company's access charge) **Morton Park Way, Morton Park DL1 4PJ**
web: www.premierinn.com
dir: *A1(M) junction 57, A66(M), A66 towards Teeside. At 3rd roundabout left onto B6280. Hotel on right. From north: A1(M) junction 57 onto A167, A1150, A66 towards Darlington, right onto B6280. Hotel on right.*

High quality, budget accommodation ideal for both families and business travellers. Spacious, en suite bedrooms feature free WiFi and tea and coffee making facilities, and in most hotels, Freeview TV is also available. The adjacent family restaurant features a wide and varied menu.

Rooms: 79

Premier Inn Darlington Town Centre

Premier Inn

BUDGET HOTEL

tel: 0871 527 9650 (Calls cost 13p per minute plus your phone company's access charge) **Unit 3, Feethams Leisure, Feethams DL1 5AD**
web: www.premierinn.com
dir: *Phone for directions.*

Rooms: 80

DARTFORD	Map 6 TQ57
Kent	

HIGHLY RECOMMENDED

Rowhill Grange Hotel & Utopia Spa

★★★★ 84% @@ HOTEL

tel: 01322 615136 **Wilmington DA2 7QH**
email: admin@rowhillgrange.co.uk **web:** www.rowhillgrange.co.uk
dir: *M25 junction 3 take B2173 to Swanley, then B258 to Hextable.*

Set in nine acres of mature woodland, this hotel enjoys a tranquil setting, yet is still easily accessible to road networks. Bedrooms are stylishly and individually decorated; many have four-poster or sleigh beds. The elegant lounge is popular for afternoon teas, and the leisure and conference facilities are impressive. There is a smart, conservatory restaurant and also a more informal brasserie.

Rooms: 38 (8 annexe) (4 family) (3 GF) ⬥ **S** fr £115 **D** fr £115* **Facilities:** Spa STV FTV WiFi ⬥ ⬥ Gym Beauty treatment Hair salon Aerobic studio Japanese therapy pool Xmas New Year **Conf:** Class 64 Board 34 Theatre 160 **Services:** Lift Night porter **Parking:** 150 **Notes:** Civ Wed 150

Premier Inn Dartford

Premier Inn

BUDGET HOTEL

tel: 0871 527 9328 (Calls cost 13p per minute plus your phone company's access charge) **Halcrow Avenue DA1 5FX**
web: www.premierinn.com
dir: *M25 junction 1A , A206 towards Erith. At next roundabout right to Bridge Business Park. At next roundabout left towards Power Station. Hotel 300 yards on left.*

High quality, budget accommodation ideal for both families and business travellers. Spacious, en suite bedrooms feature free WiFi and tea and coffee making facilities, and in most hotels, Freeview TV is also available. The adjacent family restaurant features a wide and varied menu.

Rooms: 120

DARTMOUTH	Map 3 SX85
Devon	

The Dart Marina Hotel

★★★★ 81% @ HOTEL

tel: 01803 832580 **Sandquay Road TQ6 9PH**
email: reservations@dartmarina.com **web:** www.dartmarina.com
dir: *A3122 from Totnes to Dartmouth. Follow road which becomes College Way, before Higher Ferry. Hotel sharp left in Sandquay Road.*

Boasting a stunning riverside location with its own marina, this is a very special place to stay. Bedrooms vary in style, all have wonderful views, and some have private balconies where you can sit and soak up the atmosphere. The stylish public areas take full advantage of the waterside setting with opportunities to dine alfresco. The River Restaurant is the venue for accomplished cooking.

Rooms: 49 (4 annexe) (4 family) (4 GF) ⬥ **D** fr £180 **Facilities:** Spa FTV WiFi ⬥ Gym Xmas New Year **Services:** Lift Night porter **Parking:** 50

Royal Castle Hotel

★★★ 82% @ HOTEL

tel: 01803 833033 **11 The Quay TQ6 9PS**
email: enquiry@royalcastle.co.uk **web:** www.royalcastle.co.uk
dir: *In centre of town, overlooking Inner Harbour.*

At the edge of the harbour, this imposing 17th-century former coaching inn is filled with charm and character. Bedrooms are well equipped and comfortable, and many have harbour views. A choice of quiet seating areas is offered in addition to both the traditional and contemporary bars. A variety of eating options is available, including the main restaurant which has lovely views.

Rooms: 24 (3 family) ⬥ **S** fr £100 **D** fr £120* **Facilities:** FTV WiFi ⬥ ♫ Xmas New Year **Conf:** Class 30 Board 20 Theatre 50 **Services:** Night porter **Parking:** 15 **Notes:** Civ Wed 80

DAVENTRY
Northamptonshire — Map 11 SP56

INSPECTOR'S CHOICE

Fawsley Hall Hotel & Spa
★★★★ ◉◉ HOTEL

HandPICKED HOTELS

tel: 01327 892000 & 0845 072 7482 (Calls cost 5p per minute plus your phone company's access charge) **Fawsley NN11 3BA**
email: reservations.fawsley@handpicked.co.uk
web: www.handpickedhotels.co.uk/fawsleyhall
dir: *A361 south of Daventry, between Badby and Charwelton, hotel signed single track lane.*

Dating back to the 15th century, this delightful hotel is peacefully located in beautiful parkland designed by 'Capability' Brown. Spacious, individually designed bedrooms and stylish public areas are beautifully furnished with antique and period pieces. The different wings of the house – Tudor, Georgian and Victorian – all have their distinct identity. For a true sense of the past, guests can choose to stay in the Queen's Suite, where Elizabeth I slept in 1575. Afternoon tea is served in the impressive Great Hall, Tudor Bar and Lounge, and dinner is available in the award-winning Cedar Restaurant, with its original beams and stonework, an impressive inglenook fireplace and candlelit tables dressed in fine white linen. The hotel has its own cinema and the spa features an ozone pool, treatment rooms and fitness studio.

Rooms: 60 (14 annexe) (3 family) (2 GF) **S** fr £129 **D** fr £139 (including breakfast)* **Facilities:** Spa STV WiFi HL Gym Health and beauty treatment rooms Fitness studio 29-seat cinema Xmas New Year **Conf:** Class 64 Board 40 Theatre 120 **Services:** Night porter **Parking:** 140 **Notes:** Civ Wed 120

Mercure Daventry Court Hotel
★★★★ 73% HOTEL

tel: 01327 307000 **Sedgemoor Way NN11 0SG**
email: HA010@accor.com **web:** www.themercure.com/Daventrycourt
dir: *M1 junction 16, A45 to Daventry, at 1st roundabout turn right signed Kilsby/M1(North). Hotel on right in 1 mile.*

This modern, striking hotel overlooking Drayton Water boasts spacious public areas that include a good range of banqueting, meeting and leisure facilities. It is a popular venue for conferences. Bedrooms are suitable for both business and leisure guests.

Rooms: 155 (17 family) **Facilities:** Spa FTV WiFi HL Gym Steam room Sauna Health and beauty salon New Year **Conf:** Class 200 Board 100 Theatre 600 **Services:** Lift Night porter **Parking:** 350 **Notes:** Civ Wed 280

DAWLISH
Devon — Map 3 SX97

Langstone Cliff Hotel
★★★ 81% HOTEL

tel: 01626 868000 **Dawlish Warren EX7 0NA**
email: reception@langstone-hotel.co.uk **web:** www.langstone-hotel.co.uk
dir: *1.5 miles northeast off A379 – Exeter Road to Dawlish Warren.*

A family-owned and run hotel, the Langstone Cliff Hotel offers a range of leisure, conference and function facilities. Bedrooms, many with sea views and balconies, are spacious, comfortable and well equipped. The hotel has a number of attractive lounges and a well-stocked bar. Dinner is served, often carvery style, in the restaurant.

Rooms: 64 (2 annexe) (19 family) (10 GF) **Facilities:** STV FTV WiFi HL Gym Table tennis Golf practice area Hair and beauty salon Treatment room Therapy room Ballroom Xmas New Year **Conf:** Class 200 Board 80 Theatre 400 **Services:** Lift Night porter **Parking:** 200 **Notes:** Civ Wed 400

DEAL
Kent — Map 7 TR35

Dunkerleys Hotel & Restaurant
★★★ 78% ◉◉ HOTEL

tel: 01304 375016 **19 Beach Street CT14 7AH**
email: info@dunkerleys.co.uk **web:** www.dunkerleys.co.uk
dir: *From M20 or M2 follow signs for A258 Deal. Hotel close to Pier.*

Dunkerleys Hotel is located on the seafront, and offers bedrooms furnished to a high standard with a good range of amenities. The restaurant and bar is a comfortable and attractive environment in which to relax and to enjoy cuisine that makes the best use of local ingredients. Service throughout is friendly and attentive.

Rooms: 16 (2 family) **S** fr £80 **D** fr £120 (including breakfast) **Facilities:** FTV WiFi Xmas New Year **Services:** Night porter **Notes:** LB

D

DEDHAM
Essex
Map 13 TM03

Maison Talbooth
★★★ ◎◎ COUNTRY HOUSE HOTEL

tel: 01206 322367 **Stratford Road CO7 6HN**
email: maison@milsomhotels.co.uk
web: www.milsomhotels.com/maisontalbooth
dir: *A12 towards Ipswich, 1st turn signed Dedham, follow to left bend, turn right. Hotel 1 mile on right.*

Warm hospitality and quality service can be expected at this Victorian country-house hotel, situated in a peaceful rural location amid pretty landscaped grounds overlooking the Stour River Valley. Public areas include a comfortable drawing room where guests may take afternoon tea or snacks. Residents are chauffeured to the popular Le Talbooth Restaurant just a mile away for dinner. The spacious bedrooms are individually decorated and tastefully furnished with lovely co-ordinated fabrics and many thoughtful touches.

Rooms: 12 (1 family) (5 GF) ↗ **D** fr £265 (including breakfast)* **Facilities:** Spa STV WiFi ↘ ☺ ⚑ Xmas New Year **Conf:** Class 20 Board 16 Theatre 30 **Parking:** 40 **Notes:** LB Civ Wed 50

milsoms
★★★ 85% ◎ SMALL HOTEL

tel: 01206 322795 **Stratford Road CO7 6HN**
email: milsoms@milsomhotels.com **web:** www.milsomhotels.com/milsoms
dir: *6 miles north of Colchester off A12, follow Stratford St Mary/Dedham signs. Turn right over A12, hotel on left.*

Situated in the Dedham Vale, an Area of Outstanding Natural Beauty, milsoms is the perfect base to explore the countryside on the Essex-Suffolk border. This small hotel is styled along the lines of a contemporary 'gastro bar' combining good food served in an informal atmosphere with stylish and well-appointed accommodation.

Rooms: 15 (3 family) (4 GF) **D** fr £135* **Facilities:** STV WiFi Use of spa at sister hotel (Maison Talbooth) Walking Cycling Xmas **Conf:** Board 24 **Services:** Night porter **Parking:** 90

DELPH
Greater Manchester
Map 16 SD90

The Saddleworth Hotel
★★★★ 82% ◎ COUNTRY HOUSE HOTEL

tel: 01457 871888 **Huddersfield Road OL3 5LX**
email: enquiries@thesaddleworthhotel.co.uk **web:** www.thesaddleworthhotel.co.uk
dir: *M62 junction 21, A640 towards Huddersfield. At Junction Inn take A6052 towards Delph; at White Lion left onto unclassified road; in 0.5 mile left on A62 towards Huddersfield. Hotel 0.5 mile on right.*

Situated in nine acres of landscaped gardens and woodlands in the Castleshaw Valley, this lovingly restored 17th-century building, once a coaching station, has stunning views. The hotel offers comfort and opulence together with a team of staff who provide delightful customer care. Antique pieces have been acquired from far and wide, and no expense has been spared to provide guests with the latest up-to-date facilities. The restaurant, with black table linen and crystal glassware, offers an award-winning, fashionably understated, modern European menu.

Rooms: 16 (8 annexe) (4 family) (4 GF) **S** fr £120 **D** fr £180* **Facilities:** FTV WiFi ↘ ↘ Gym Xmas New Year **Conf:** Class 40 Board 40 Theatre 150 **Parking:** 140 **Notes:** Civ Wed 250

D

DERBY
Derbyshire

Map 11 SK33

See also **Morley**

Hallmark Hotel Derby Mickleover Court

★★★★ 76% HOTEL

tel: 0330 028 3404 **Etwall Road, Mickleover DE3 0XX**
email: mickleover@hallmarkhotels.co.uk **web:** www.hallmarkhotels.co.uk
dir: *A50 towards Derby, exit at junction 5. A516 towards Derby, take exit signed Mickleover.*

Located close to Derby, this modern hotel is well suited to both the conference and leisure markets. Bedrooms are spacious, air conditioned, well equipped and include some smart executive rooms and suites. The well presented leisure facilities are amongst the best in the region.

Rooms: 99 (20 family) (5 smoking) **Facilities:** STV FTV WiFi Gym Beauty salon Steam room Xmas New Year **Conf:** Class 106 Board 45 Theatre 200 **Services:** Lift Night porter Air con **Parking:** 225 **Notes:** LB Civ Wed 200

Hallmark Hotel Derby Midland

★★★★ 73% HOTEL

tel: 0330 028 3405 **Midland Road DE1 2SQ**
email: derby@hallmarkhotels.co.uk **web:** www.hallmarkhotels.co.uk
dir: *Opposite rail station.*

This early Victorian hotel situated opposite Derby Midland Station provides very comfortable accommodation. The executive rooms are ideal for business travellers as they are equipped with writing desks and high speed internet access. Public rooms include a comfortable lounge and a popular restaurant. Service is skilled, attentive and friendly. There is also a walled garden and private parking.

Rooms: 102 (6 family) **Facilities:** FTV WiFi Xmas New Year **Conf:** Class 50 Board 35 Theatre 150 **Services:** Lift Night porter **Parking:** 70 **Notes:** Civ Wed 150

Premier Inn Derby City Centre

BUDGET HOTEL

tel: 0871 527 9638 (Calls cost 13p per minute plus your phone company's access charge) **Cathedral Quarter, Full Street DE1 3AF**
web: www.premierinn.com
dir: *From north: M1 junction 25, A52. 10 miles, 2nd exit at roundabout into Eastgate. In 0.6 mile, exit for Irongate, left into Queens Street, left into Full Street. From south: From A38 onto A516 (M1 South/Nottingham). 2nd exit at roundabout into Uttoxeter New Road. 1.4 miles, 2nd exit at roundabout into Stafford Street, right into Cathedral Road, then Full Street.*

High quality, budget accommodation ideal for both families and business travellers. Spacious, en suite bedrooms feature free WiFi and tea and coffee making facilities, and in most hotels, Freeview TV is also available. The adjacent family restaurant features a wide and varied menu.

Rooms: 118

Premier Inn Derby East

BUDGET HOTEL

tel: 0871 527 8292 (Calls cost 13p per minute plus your phone company's access charge) **The Wyvern, Stanier Way DE21 6BF**
web: www.premierinn.com
dir: *M1 junction 25, A52 towards Derby. After 6.5 miles exit for Wyvern/Pride Park. 1st exit at roundabout (A52 Nottingham), straight on at next roundabout. Hotel on left.*

Rooms: 108

Premier Inn Derby North West

BUDGET HOTEL

tel: 0871 527 8294 (Calls cost 13p per minute plus your phone company's access charge) **95 Ashbourne Road, Mackworth DE22 4LZ**
web: www.premierinn.com
dir: *Exit M1 junction 25 onto A52 towards Derby. At Pentagon Island straight ahead towards city centre. Follow A52/Ashbourne signs into Mackworth.*

Rooms: 22

Premier Inn Derby South

BUDGET HOTEL

tel: 0871 527 8296 (Calls cost 13p per minute plus your phone company's access charge) **Foresters Leisure Park, Osmaston Park Road DE23 8AG**
web: www.premierinn.com
dir: *M1 junction 24, A6 towards Derby. Left onto A5111 (ring road), hotel in 2 miles.*

Rooms: 51

Premier Inn Derby West

Premier Inn

BUDGET HOTEL

tel: 0871 527 8298 (Calls cost 13p per minute plus your phone company's access charge) **Manor Park Way, Uttoxeter New Road DE22 3HN**
web: www.premierinn.com
dir: *M1 junction 25, A38 west towards Burton upon Trent (approximately 15 miles). Left at island (city hospital), right at lights, 3rd exit at city hospital island.*

Rooms: 86

DERBY SERVICE AREA (A50)
Derbyshire

Map 11 SK42

Days Inn Donington - A50

WELCOME BREAK

AA Advertised

tel: 01332 799666 **Welcome Break Services, A50 Westbound DE72 2WA**
email: derby.hotel@welcomebreak.co.uk **web:** www.welcomebreak.co.uk
dir: *M1 junction 24/24a, onto A50 towards Stoke/Derby. Hotel between junctions 1 and 2.*

This modern building offers accommodation in smart, spacious and well-equipped bedrooms, suitable for families and business travellers, and all with en suite bathrooms. Continental breakfast is available and other refreshments may be taken at the nearby family restaurant.

Rooms: 47 (38 family) (17 GF) (9 smoking) **Facilities:** FTV WiFi **Conf:** Class 20 Board 40 Theatre 40 **Parking:** 80

DIDCOT
Oxfordshire

Map 5 SU59

Premier Inn Oxford South (Didcot)

BUDGET HOTEL

tel: 0871 527 8868 (Calls cost 13p per minute plus your phone company's access charge) **Milton Heights, Milton OX14 4TX**
web: www.premierinn.com
dir: *On A4130. Just off A34 at Milton interchange, between Oxford and Newbury.*

High quality, budget accommodation ideal for both families and business travellers. Spacious, en suite bedrooms feature free WiFi and tea and coffee making facilities, and in most hotels, Freeview TV is also available. The adjacent family restaurant features a wide and varied menu.

Rooms: 135

D

DOGMERSFIELD
Hampshire   Map 5 SU75

INSPECTOR'S CHOICE

Four Seasons Hotel Hampshire
★★★★★ @ ⚓ COUNTRY HOUSE HOTEL

tel: 01252 853000 **Dogmersfield Park, Chalky Lane RG27 8TD**
email: reservations.ham@fourseasons.com
web: www.fourseasons.com/hampshire
dir: *M3 junction 5 onto A287 Farnham. After 1.5 miles left for Dogmersfield, hotel 0.6 mile on left.*

This Georgian manor house, set in 500 acres of rolling grounds and English Heritage listed gardens, offers the upmost in luxury and relaxation, just an hour from London. The spacious and stylish bedrooms are particularly well appointed and offer up-to-date technology. Fitness and spa facilities include nearly every conceivable indoor and outdoor activity, in addition to luxurious pampering. An elegant restaurant, a healthy-eating spa café and a trendy bar are popular venues.

Rooms: 133 (23 GF) 🐾 **S** fr £285 **D** fr £285* **Facilities:** Spa STV WiFi 🎾 ⛲ Fishing 🏊 Gym Clay pigeon Bikes Canal boat Falconry Horse riding Jogging trails Rope course 🎣 Xmas New Year **Conf:** Class 110 Board 60 Theatre 260 **Services:** Lift Night porter Air con **Parking:** 165 **Notes:** Civ Wed 200

DONCASTER
South Yorkshire   Map 16 SE50

Best Western Premier Mount Pleasant Hotel
★★★★ 79% HOTEL

tel: 01302 868696 **Great North Road DN11 0HW**
email: reception@mountpleasant.co.uk **web:** www.mountpleasant.co.uk

(for full entry see Rossington)

Premier Inn Doncaster Central East   Premier Inn
BUDGET HOTEL

tel: 0871 527 8304 (Calls cost 13p per minute plus your phone company's access charge) **Doncaster Leisure Park, Herten Way DN4 7NW**
web: www.premierinn.com
dir: *M18 junction 3, signed Doncaster racecourse. Left into Whiterose Way (B&Q on left). Straight on at roundabout into Wilmington Drive, right at next roundabout into Lakeside Boulevard. At next roundabout 2nd exit. Straight on at next roundabout, hotel ahead.*

High quality, budget accommodation ideal for both families and business travellers. Spacious, en suite bedrooms feature free WiFi and tea and coffee making facilities, and in most hotels, Freeview TV is also available. The adjacent family restaurant features a wide and varied menu.

Rooms: 80

Premier Inn Doncaster Central (High Fishergate)   Premier Inn
BUDGET HOTEL

tel: 0871 527 8302 (Calls cost 13p per minute plus your phone company's access charge) **High Fishergate DN1 1QZ**
web: www.premierinn.com
dir: *Off A630 Church Way.*

Rooms: 138

Premier Inn Doncaster (Lakeside)   Premier Inn
BUDGET HOTEL

tel: 0871 527 8300 (Calls cost 13p per minute plus your phone company's access charge) **Wilmington Drive, Doncaster Carr DN4 5PJ**
web: www.premierinn.com
dir: *M18 junction 3, A6182. Hotel near junction with access road.*

Rooms: 66

DORCHESTER
Dorset   Map 4 SY69

Best Western Wessex Royale Hotel   BW Best Western
★★★ 80% HOTEL

tel: 01305 262660 **High West Street DT1 1UP**
email: info@wessexroyalehotel.co.uk **web:** www.wessexroyalehotel.co.uk
dir: *From A35 follow town centre signs. Straight on, hotel at top of hill on left.*

This centrally situated Georgian townhouse dates from 1756 and successfully combines historic charm with modern comforts. The restaurant is a relaxed venue for enjoying innovative food, and the hotel offers the benefit of a smart conservatory, ideal for functions. Limited courtyard parking is available.

Rooms: 29 (4 annexe) (3 family) (2 GF) 🐾 **S** fr £69 **D** fr £89* **Facilities:** STV FTV WiFi ❧ **Conf:** Class 40 Board 40 Theatre 80 **Services:** Night porter **Parking:** 11 **Notes:** LB Closed 23 December to January Civ Wed

Premier Inn Dorchester   Premier Inn
BUDGET HOTEL

tel: 0871 527 9376 (Calls cost 13p per minute plus your phone company's access charge) **21 Weymouth Avene DT1 1GA**
web: www.premierinn.com
dir: *On A35 follow Dorchester and Weymouth signs. At roundabout take B3150 (Stinsford Hill) left into Kings Road. At roundabout 2nd exit into Prince of Wales Road (B3144). Left into Weymouth Avenue. Left into Brewery Square.*

High quality, budget accommodation ideal for both families and business travellers. Spacious, en suite bedrooms feature free WiFi and tea and coffee making facilities, and in most hotels, Freeview TV is also available. The adjacent family restaurant features a wide and varied menu.

Rooms: 76

D

DORKING
Surrey
Map 6 TQ14

Mercure Boxhill Burford Bridge Hotel

★★★★ 80% 🏅🏅 HOTEL

Mercure HOTELS

tel: 01306 884561 **Burford Bridge, Box Hill RH5 6BX**
email: h6635@accor.com **web:** www.mercure.com
dir: *M25 junction 9, A245 towards Dorking. Hotel approximately 5 miles on A24.*

Steeped in history, this hotel was reputedly where Lord Nelson and Lady Hamilton met for the last time, and it is said that the landscape around the hotel has inspired many poets. The hotel has a contemporary feel throughout. The grounds, running down to the River Mole, are extensive, and there are good transport links to major centres, including London. The elegant Emlyn Restaurant offers a modern award-winning menu.

Rooms: 57 (22 family) (3 GF) **Facilities:** STV FTV WiFi ↘ ↖ Xmas New Year **Conf:** Class 80 Board 60 Theatre 200 **Services:** Night porter Air con **Parking:** 130 **Notes:** LB Civ Wed 200

DORRIDGE
West Midlands
Map 10 SP17

HIGHLY RECOMMENDED

Hogarths Hotel

★★★★ 83% 🏅🏅 HOTEL

tel: 01564 779988 **Four Ashes Road B93 8QE**
email: reception@hogarths.co.uk **web:** www.hogarths.co.uk
dir: *M42 junction 4, 1st exit to A3400. Left to Gate Lane. Left into Four Ashes Road. Hotel 300 metres on left.*

Hogarths Hotel, with its contemporary interior design and panoramic views of the gardens from the open-plan and airy brasserie, is a stunning property. The young team here deliver high quality, relaxed and friendly service throughout. Bedrooms meet all modern requirements, and many have their own balcony or outside area. The lake area in the well-kept and managed gardens is a stunning location for weddings and also conference events.

Rooms: 49 (5 annexe) (9 family) (15 GF) ↗ **S** fr £120 **D** fr £145 (including breakfast)* **Facilities:** FTV WiFi ↘ Gym 🎵 Xmas New Year **Conf:** Class 200 Board 60 Theatre 400 **Services:** Lift Night porter **Parking:** 120 **Notes:** LB Civ Wed 270

DOVER
Kent
Map 7 TR34

Ramada Hotel Dover

★★★★ 75% HOTEL

🅡 R A M A D A.

tel: 01304 821230 **Singledge Lane, Whitfield CT16 3EL**
email: reservations@ramadadover.co.uk **web:** www.ramadadover.co.uk
dir: *From M20 follow signs to A2 towards Canterbury. Turn right after Whitfield roundabout. From A2 towards Dover, turn left before Whitfield roundabout.*

Ramada Hotel Dover is a modern purpose-built hotel situated in a quiet location between Dover and Canterbury, close to the ferry port and seaside. The open-plan public areas are contemporary in style and include a lounge, a bar and The Olive Tree Restaurant. The stylish bedrooms are simply decorated with co-ordinated soft furnishings and many thoughtful extras.

Rooms: 68 (19 family) (68 GF) ↗ **S** fr £52 **D** fr £52* **Facilities:** FTV WiFi ↘ HL Gym 🎵 Xmas New Year **Conf:** Class 150 Board 40 Theatre 400 **Services:** Night porter **Parking:** 110 **Notes:** Civ Wed 80

Best Western Plus Dover Marina Hotel & Spa
 Best Western PLUS

★★★★ 74% HOTEL

tel: 01304 203633 **Dover Waterfront CT17 9BP**
email: reservations@dovermarinahotel.co.uk **web:** www.dovermarinahotel.co.uk
dir: *M20 junction 13, A20 to Dover, straight on at 2 roundabouts, at 3rd take 2nd exit into Union Street. Cross swing bridge, next left into Marine Parade/Waterloo Cresent. Hotel 200 yards on left.*

An attractive, terraced, waterfront hotel overlooking the harbour, offering a wide range of facilities including meeting rooms, health club, hairdresser and beauty treatments. Some of the tastefully decorated bedrooms have balconies, some have broadband access and many have superb sea views. Public rooms include a large, open-plan lounge bar and a smart bistro restaurant.

Rooms: 81 (5 family) ↗ **Facilities:** Spa STV FTV WiFi ↘ HL Gym Sauna Xmas New Year **Conf:** Class 60 Board 50 Theatre 110 **Services:** Lift Night porter **Notes:** Civ Wed 100

Premier Inn Dover (A20)

 Premier Inn

BUDGET HOTEL

tel: 0871 527 8310 (Calls cost 13p per minute plus your phone company's access charge) **Folkestone Road CT15 7AB**
web: www.premierinn.com
dir: *A20 to Dover. Through tunnel, take 2nd exit onto B2011. 1st left at roundabout. In 1 mile hotel on left.*

High quality, budget accommodation ideal for both families and business travellers. Spacious, en suite bedrooms feature free WiFi and tea and coffee making facilities, and in most hotels, Freeview TV is also available. The adjacent family restaurant features a wide and varied menu.

Rooms: 64

Premier Inn Dover Central (Eastern Ferry Terminal)

Premier Inn

BUDGET HOTEL

tel: 0871 527 8306 (Calls cost 13p per minute plus your phone company's access charge) **Marine Court, Marine Parade CT16 1LW**
web: www.premierinn.com
dir: *In town centre adjacent to ferry terminal. M20 junction 13 onto A20 for 8.2 miles.*

Rooms: 100

DOVER *continued*

Premier Inn Dover East

Premier Inn

BUDGET HOTEL

tel: 0871 527 8308 (Calls cost 13p per minute plus your phone company's access charge) **Jubilee Way, Guston Wood CT15 5FD**
web: www.premierinn.com
dir: *At roundabout junction of A2 and A258.*

Rooms: 40

DUDLEY	Map 10 SO99
West Midlands	

Premier Inn Dudley Town Centre

Premier Inn

BUDGET HOTEL

tel: 0871 527 9420 (Calls cost 13p per minute plus your phone company's access charge) **Castlegate Business Park, Castlegate Way DY1 4TA**
web: www.premierinn.com
dir: *From north: M5 junction 2, A4123 signed Dudley. At roundabout onto A4123. 4th exit into Wolverhampton Road (A4123). Left to Birmingham Road (A461). At roundabout 4th exit into Castlegate Way. At next roundabout 3rd exit.*

High quality, budget accommodation ideal for both families and business travellers. Spacious, en suite bedrooms feature free WiFi and tea and coffee making facilities, and in most hotels, Freeview TV is also available. The adjacent family restaurant features a wide and varied menu.

Rooms: 63

DUMBLETON	Map 10 SP03
Gloucestershire	

Dumbleton Hall Hotel

★★★ 78% COUNTRY HOUSE HOTEL

tel: 01386 881240 **WR11 7TS**
email: dh@pofr.co.uk **web:** www.dumbletonhall.co.uk
dir: *M5 junction 9/A46. 2nd exit at roundabout signed Evesham. Through Beckford for 1 mile, turn right signed Dumbleton. Hotel at south end of village.*

Standing on the site of a 16th-century building also known as Dumbleton Hall, the current mansion, surrounded by 19 acres of landscaped gardens and parkland, was built in the mid-18th century. Panoramic views of the Vale of Evesham can be seen from every window, and the spacious public rooms make this an ideal venue for weddings, conferences or just as a hideaway retreat. The individually designed bedrooms vary in size and layout; one room is adapted for less able guests.

Rooms: 34 (9 family) **Facilities:** WiFi 🏊 Xmas New Year **Conf:** Class 60 Board 60 Theatre 100 **Services:** Lift Night porter **Parking:** 60 **Notes:** Civ Wed 100

DUNSTABLE	Map 11 TL02
Bedfordshire	

Premier Inn Dunstable South (A5)

Premier Inn

BUDGET HOTEL

tel: 0871 527 8332 (Calls cost 13p per minute plus your phone company's access charge) **Watling Street, Kensworth LU6 3QP**
web: www.premierinn.com
dir: *M1 junction 9 towards Dunstable on A5, hotel on right after Packhorse pub.*

High quality, budget accommodation ideal for both families and business travellers. Spacious, en suite bedrooms feature free WiFi and tea and coffee making facilities, and in most hotels, Freeview TV is also available. The adjacent family restaurant features a wide and varied menu.

Rooms: 40

Premier Inn Dunstable/Luton

Premier Inn

BUDGET HOTEL

tel: 0871 527 8330 (Calls cost 13p per minute plus your phone company's access charge) **350 Luton Road LU5 4LL**
web: www.premierinn.com
dir: *M1 junction 11, follow Dunstable signs. At 1st roundabout turn right. Hotel on left on A505.*

Rooms: 42

DUNSTER	Map 3 SS94
Somerset	

The Luttrell Arms Hotel

★★★ 82% ⚜⚜ HOTEL

tel: 01643 821555 **Exmoor National Park TA24 6SG**
email: enquiry@luttrellarms.co.uk **web:** www.luttrellarms.co.uk
dir: *M5 junction 24, A38 then A39 towards Minehead. Left at Dunster junction onto A396. Hotel at top of high street.*

This charming and privately owned hotel is located in the heart of the picturesque village of Dunster, right next to the famous Yarn Market. With parts dating back to the 15th century, the hotel offers plenty of character and quality throughout. Bedrooms and bathrooms come in a range of shapes and sizes including some with four-poster beds. Guests can enjoy a drink with the locals in the friendly bar or, in warmer weather, enjoy the pleasant garden to the rear. Dinner and breakfast are highlights, offering a range of carefully-prepared dishes utilising much local produce.

Rooms: 28 (2 family) (4 GF) **S** fr £105 **D** fr £150 (including breakfast)*
Facilities: FTV WiFi ♨ Xmas New Year **Conf:** Class 40 Board 30 Theatre 60 **Services:** Night porter **Notes:** LB Civ Wed 60

Dunster Castle Hotel

★★★ 75% HOTEL

tel: 01463 823030 **5 High Street TA24 6SF**
email: enquiries@dunstercastlehotel.co.uk **web:** www.dunstercastlehotel.co.uk

Perfectly located on the main cobbled street at the foot of the entrance to Dunster Castle, this newly refurbished hotel now combines contemporary style with traditional comfort and hospitality. Bedrooms and bathrooms offer a range of shapes and sizes from the luxurious larger rooms overlooking the main street, to smaller, rear-facing rooms, but all are very well decorated and comfortably furnished. High quality dishes created from much local produce are served throughout the day and evening in the main restaurant. A pleasant rear garden and a car park are also available.

Rooms: 9 (1 annexe) (1 GF) 🐾 **S** fr £70 **D** fr £100 (including breakfast)*
Facilities: FTV WiFi ♨ Xmas New Year **Conf:** Class 50 Board 36 Theatre 100 **Parking:** 26 **Notes:** LB

DURHAM
County Durham — Map 19 NZ24

HIGHLY RECOMMENDED

Ramside Hall Hotel Golf & Spa
★★★★ 84% ⊛ HOTEL

tel: 0191 386 5282 **Carrville DH1 1TD**
email: mail@ramsidehallhotel.co.uk **web:** www.ramsidehallhotel.co.uk
dir: *A1(M) junction 62, A690 to Sunderland. Straight on at lights. 200 metres after rail bridge turn right.*

With its proximity to the A1(M) and delightful parkland setting, this establishment combines the best of both worlds – convenience and tranquillity. The hotel boasts two championship golf courses, a choice of lounges, several eating options including the Rib Room, specialising in steaks; and Fusion, an Asian-inspired concept. Bedrooms are furnished and decorated to a very high standard and include some stunning suites. There is also an excellent spa and leisure facility.

Rooms: 128 (10 family) (28 GF) **Facilities:** Spa STV FTV WiFi ♂ ⊛ ✈ ↕ 36 Gym Steam room Sauna Hydro pool Golf academy Driving range ♫ Xmas New Year **Conf:** Class 160 Board 40 Theatre 500 **Services:** Lift Night porter **Parking:** 750 **Notes:** Civ Wed 500

Honest Lawyer Hotel
★★★ 81% ⊛ HOTEL

tel: 0191 378 3780 **Croxdale Bridge, Croxdale DH1 3SP**
email: enquiries@honestlawyerhotel.com **web:** www.honestlawyerhotel.com
dir: *A1(M) junction 61, A688 towards Bishops Auckland, continue on A688, right at next roundabout onto A167 towards Durham. In 2.5 miles hotel on right.*

This hotel offers a mixture of smart motel-style bedrooms along with six junior suites in the main building that have four-poster beds. 40" LCD TVs, power showers and complimentary WiFi are provided as standard. Facilities also include a beauty treatment room and a boutique. Bailey's, with its open kitchen, offers a seasonally-changing menu and friendly service. There is also a terrace and modern event facilities. There are good transportation links to Durham and the motorway.

Rooms: 51 (45 annexe) (3 family) (45 GF) **Facilities:** FTV WiFi ♂ ♫ Xmas New Year **Conf:** Class 27 Board 24 Theatre 50 **Services:** Night porter Air con **Parking:** 150

Premier Inn Durham City Centre

BUDGET HOTEL

tel: 0871 527 8338 (Calls cost 13p per minute plus your phone company's access charge) **Freemans Place, Walkergate DH1 1SQ**
web: www.premierinn.com
dir: *A1(M) junction 62, A690 (Leazes Road) towards city centre. In Durham follow Watergate signs, under bridge immediately left into Walkergate (one way). Back under A690, hotel on right.*

High quality, budget accommodation ideal for both families and business travellers. Spacious, en suite bedrooms feature free WiFi and tea and coffee making facilities, and in most hotels, Freeview TV is also available. The adjacent family restaurant features a wide and varied menu.

Rooms: 103

Premier Inn Durham East

BUDGET HOTEL

tel: 0871 527 8340 (Calls cost 13p per minute plus your phone company's access charge) **Broomside Park, Belmont Industrial Estate DH1 1GG**
web: www.premierinn.com
dir: *A1(M) junction 62, A690 west towards Durham. In 1 mile left. Hotel on left.*

Rooms: 62

Premier Inn Durham North
Premier Inn
BUDGET HOTEL

tel: 0871 527 8342 (Calls cost 13p per minute plus your phone company's access charge) **adj. Arnison Retail Centre, Pity Me DH1 5GB**
web: www.premierinn.com
dir: *A1 junction 63, A167 to Durham. Straight on at 5 roundabouts, left at 6th roundabout. Hotel on right after 200 yards.*

Rooms: 77

EAST GRINSTEAD
West Sussex — Map 6 TQ33

Premier Inn East Grinstead
Premier Inn
BUDGET HOTEL

tel: 0871 527 8348 (Calls cost 13p per minute plus your phone company's access charge) **London Road, Felbridge RH19 2QR**
web: www.premierinn.com
dir: *M25 junction 6. Hotel at junction of A22 and A264.*

High quality, budget accommodation ideal for both families and business travellers. Spacious, en suite bedrooms feature free WiFi and tea and coffee making facilities, and in most hotels, Freeview TV is also available. The adjacent family restaurant features a wide and varied menu.

Rooms: 41

EAST MIDLANDS AIRPORT
Leicestershire — Map 11 SK42

Best Western Premier Yew Lodge Hotel & Spa
BW PREMIER | BEST WESTERN
★★★★ 79% HOTEL

tel: 01509 672518 **Packington Hill DE74 2DF**
email: info@yewlodgehotel.co.uk **web:** www.yewlodgehotel.co.uk
dir: *M1 junction 24. Follow signs to Loughborough and Kegworth on A6. On entering village, right 1st lights, hotel 400 yards on right.*

This smart, family-owned hotel is close to both the motorway and airport yet is peacefully located. Modern, stylish bedrooms and public areas are thoughtfully appointed and smartly presented. The restaurant serves interesting dishes, while lounge service and extensive conference facilities are available. A very well-equipped spa and leisure centre complete the picture.

Rooms: 114 (22 family) ♠ **Facilities:** Spa STV FTV WiFi ♂ HL ⊛ Gym Beauty therapy suite Steam room Sauna Power plate Xmas New Year **Conf:** Class 150 Board 84 Theatre 330 **Services:** Lift Night porter **Parking:** 180 **Notes:** Civ Wed 260

EAST MIDLANDS AIRPORT *continued*

Premier Inn East Midlands Airport

Premier Inn

BUDGET HOTEL

tel: 0871 527 8350 (Calls cost 13p per minute plus your phone company's access charge) **Pegasus Business Park, Herald Way DE74 2TQ**
web: www.premierinn.com
dir: *From south: M1 junction 23a, A453 signed to airport. From north: M1 junction 24, A456 signed to airport. Hotel on Pegasus Business Park.*

High quality, budget accommodation ideal for both families and business travellers. Spacious, en suite bedrooms feature free WiFi and tea and coffee making facilities, and in most hotels, Freeview TV is also available. The adjacent family restaurant features a wide and varied menu.

Rooms: 80

EASTBOURNE	Map 6 TV69
East Sussex	

The Grand Hotel

★★★★★ 85% ⊛⊛ HOTEL

SMALL LUXURY HOTELS OF THE WORLD

tel: 01323 412345 **King Edwards Parade BN21 4EQ**
email: reservations@grandeastbourne.com **web:** www.grandeastbourne.com
dir: *On seafront west of Eastbourne, 1 mile from railway station.*

This famous Victorian hotel offers high standards of service and hospitality, and is in close proximity to both the beach and the South Downs National Park. The extensive public rooms feature a magnificent Great Hall, with marble columns and high ceilings, where guests can relax and enjoy afternoon tea. The spacious bedrooms provide high levels of comfort; many with stunning sea views and a number with private balconies. Guests can choose fine dining in The Mirabelle, or

the Garden Restaurant, and there are bars as well as superb spa and leisure facilities.

The Grand Hotel

Rooms: 152 (35 family) (4 GF) ☏ **S** fr £120 **D** fr £150 (including breakfast)*
Facilities: Spa STV FTV WiFi ⓑ HL ⓢ ⚲ Gym Snooker table ♫ Xmas New Year
Conf: Class 170 Board 60 Theatre 330 **Services:** Lift Night porter **Parking:** 70
Notes: LB Civ Wed 150

Langham Hotel

★★★★ 77% ⊛ HOTEL

tel: 01323 731451 **43-49 Royal Parade BN22 7AH**
email: frontdesk@langhamhotel.co.uk **web:** www.langhamhotel.co.uk
dir: *Follow seafront signs. Hotel 0.5 mile east of pier.*

This popular hotel is situated in a prominent position with superb views of the sea and pier. Bedrooms are pleasantly decorated, and equipped with modern facilities. Superior rooms, some with four-poster beds, are stylish and offer sea views. The spacious public rooms include the Grand Parade bar, a lounge and a fine dining conservatory restaurant. The hotel has 40 additional secure, charged-for parking spaces within 350 yards, available on Fridays, Saturdays and Sundays.

Rooms: 77 (2 family) ☏ **S** fr £68 **D** fr £129 (including breakfast)* **Facilities:** FTV WiFi ⓑ ♫ Xmas New Year **Conf:** Class 40 Board 30 Theatre 80 **Services:** Lift Night porter **Parking:** 9 **Notes:** Civ Wed 120

E

Hydro Hotel

★★★★ 75% HOTEL

tel: 01323 720643 **Mount Road BN20 7HZ**
email: sales@hydrohotel.com web: www.hydrohotel.com
dir: *From pier/seafront, right along Grand Parade. At Grand Hotel follow Hydro Hotel sign. Into South Cliff, 200 metres.*

This well-managed and popular hotel enjoys an elevated position with views of attractive gardens and the sea beyond. The spacious bedrooms are attractive and well equipped. In addition to the comfortable lounges, guests also have access to fitness facilities and a hairdressing salon. Service is both professional and efficient throughout.

Rooms: 82 (3 family) (3 GF) ✆ S fr £80 D fr £150 (including breakfast)*
Facilities: FTV WiFi ✈ 🏌 Beauty room Hair salon ♫ Xmas New Year Conf: Class 90 Board 40 Theatre 140 Services: Lift Night porter Parking: 40 Notes: LB Civ Wed 120

Best Western Lansdowne Hotel

 BW **Best Western**

★★★ 82% HOTEL

tel: 01323 725174 **King Edward's Parade BN21 4EE**
email: enquiries@lansdowne-hotel.co.uk web: www.bw-lansdownehotel.co.uk
dir: *At west end of seafront opposite Western Lawns, 1 mile from railway station.*

Enjoying an enviable position at the quieter end of the parade, this hotel overlooks the Western Lawns and The Wish Tower and is just a few minutes' walk from many of the town's attractions. Public rooms include a variety of lounges, a range of meeting rooms and games rooms. Bedrooms are attractively decorated and many offer sea views. The hotel has a wheelchair lift near the front entrance that operates between the pavement and one of the ground-floor public rooms.

Rooms: 102 (10 family) ✆ S fr £55 D fr £90* Facilities: FTV WiFi ♿ HL Table tennis Pool table Snooker Xmas New Year Conf: Class 40 Board 40 Theatre 80 Services: Lift Night porter Parking: 22 Notes: LB Civ Wed 60

New Wilmington Hotel

★★★ 80% HOTEL

tel: 01323 721219 **25-27 Compton Street BN21 4DU**
email: info@new-wilmington-hotel.co.uk web: www.new-wilmington-hotel.co.uk
dir: *A22 to Eastbourne seafront. Right along promenade to Wish Tower. Right, then left at end of road, hotel 2nd on left.*

This friendly, family-run hotel is conveniently located close to the seafront, the Congress Theatre and Winter Gardens. Public rooms are well presented and include a cosy bar, a small comfortable lounge and a spacious restaurant. Bedrooms are comfortably appointed and tastefully decorated; family and superior bedrooms are available.

Rooms: 40 (14 family) (3 GF) ✆ S fr £56.95 D fr £67.15* Facilities: STV FTV WiFi ♿ ♫ Xmas New Year Conf: Class 20 Board 20 Theatre 40 Services: Lift Night porter Parking: 3 Notes: LB Closed 3 January to mid February

The Devonshire Park Hotel

★★★ 79% HOTEL

tel: 01323 728144 **27-29 Carlisle Road BN21 4JR**
email: info@devonshire-park-hotel.co.uk web: www.devonshire-park-hotel.co.uk
dir: *Follow signs to seafront, exit at Wish Tower. Hotel opposite Congress Theatre.*

A handsome family-run hotel handily placed for the seafront and theatres. Attractively furnished rooms are spacious and comfortable; many boast king-size

beds and all are equipped with WiFi and satellite TV. Guests can relax in the well presented lounges, the cosy bar or, when the weather's fine, on the garden terrace.

Rooms: 35 (8 GF) ✆ Facilities: STV WiFi Xmas New Year Services: Lift Night porter Parking: 25 Notes: LB No children 12 years

Queens Hotel

Leisureplex HOLIDAY HOTELS

★★★ 72% HOTEL

tel: 01323 722822 **Marine Parade BN21 3DY**
email: queens.eastbourne@alfatravel.co.uk web: www.leisureplex.co.uk
dir: *Follow signs for seafront, hotel opposite pier.*

Popular with tour groups, this long-established hotel enjoys a central, prominent seafront location overlooking the pier. Spacious public areas include a choice of lounges, and regular entertainment is also provided. Bedrooms are suitably appointed and equipped.

Rooms: 127 (5 family) ✆ S fr £39 D fr £64 (including breakfast)* Facilities: FTV WiFi Snooker ♫ Xmas New Year Services: Lift Night porter Parking: 50 Notes: LB Closed January (except New Year) RS November, February to March

Imperial Hotel

★★★ 69% HOTEL

tel: 01323 411043 **16-32 Devonshire Place BN21 4AH**
email: info@holdsworthhotels.co.uk web: www.holdsworthhotels.co.uk/imperial.php
dir: *Phone for directions.*

The Imperial is an impressive Victorian hotel situated at the seaward end of Devonshire Place, an imposing tree-lined boulevard, less than a 15-minute walk from the facilities and amenities in the town centre, and just across the road from the promenade and the bandstand. The hotel offers a good standard of accommodation, spacious lounge areas, and a large restaurant offering hearty, home-cooked food.

Rooms: 113 (1 family) (5 GF) ✆ S fr £30 D fr £60* Facilities: FTV WiFi ♫ Xmas New Year Services: Lift Night porter Notes: Closed 3 January to 8 February

Premier Inn Eastbourne

Premier Inn

BUDGET HOTEL

tel: 0871 527 8352 (Calls cost 13p per minute plus your phone company's access charge) **Willingdon Drive BN23 8AL**
web: www.premierinn.com
dir: *From A22 or A27 at Polegate, take bypass signed Eastbourne (A22). Continue to Shinewater roundabout. Left towards Langney. Hotel 0.25 mile on left.*

High quality, budget accommodation ideal for both families and business travellers. Spacious, en suite bedrooms feature free WiFi and tea and coffee making facilities, and in most hotels, Freeview TV is also available. The adjacent family restaurant features a wide and varied menu.

Rooms: 47

Premier Inn Eastbourne (Polegate)

Premier Inn

BUDGET HOTEL

tel: 0871 527 8354 (Calls cost 13p per minute plus your phone company's access charge) **Hailsham Road, Polegate BN26 6QL**
web: www.premierinn.com
dir: *At roundabout junction of A22 and A27.*

Rooms: 56

E

EASTBOURNE *continued*

Premier Inn Eastbourne Town Centre

Premier Inn

BUDGET HOTEL

tel: 0871 527 9448 (Calls cost 13p per minute plus your phone company's access charge) **Terminus Road BN21 3DF**
web: www.premierinn.com
dir: *From Lewes on A27, A2270, right at lights (Polegate). At roundabout 1st exit onto A2021 (Eastbourne). At roundabout 2nd exit (All other routes). At roundabout 2nd exit onto A2040. At roundabout 1st exit (Upper Avenue). At end left into Cavendish Place (Seafront). At pier right into Grand Parade, next right into Terminus Road.*

Rooms: 65

EASTLEIGH	Map 5 SU41
Hampshire	

Premier Inn Southampton (Eastleigh)

Premier Inn

BUDGET HOTEL

tel: 0871 527 8994 (Calls cost 13p per minute plus your phone company's access charge) **Leigh Road SO50 9YX**
web: www.premierinn.com
dir: *M3 junction 13, A335 towards Eastleigh. Hotel on right.*

High quality, budget accommodation ideal for both families and business travellers. Spacious, en suite bedrooms feature free WiFi and tea and coffee making facilities, and in most hotels, Freeview TV is also available. The adjacent family restaurant features a wide and varied menu.

Rooms: 80

EDENBRIDGE	Map 6 TQ44
Kent	

Hever Hotel

★★★ 79% HOTEL

tel: 01732 700700 **Hever Road TN8 7NP**
email: reception@heverhotel.co.uk **web:** www.heverhotel.co.uk
dir: *Exit M25 junction 5/6, follow tourist signs for Hever Castle. Hotel 1 mile north.*

Located in the vicinity of Hever Golf Club, next door to the historic Hever Castle and Grounds, and convenient for Gatwick and the M25, this hotel is in an ideal spot. The hotel has a comfortable bar, a restaurant and a games room. All bedrooms are annexed in the original stable blocks for Hever Castle, and have been tastefully decorated throughout. Dinner, lunch and a hearty breakfast are served daily in the main restaurant.

Rooms: 81 (3 family) (59 GF) ⚓ **Facilities:** STV FTV WiFi ⌁ ⚲ Gym New Year
Conf: Class 60 Board 40 Theatre 130 **Services:** Night porter **Parking:** 70
Notes: Civ Wed 100

EDGWARE	Map 6 TQ19
Greater London	

Premier Inn London Edgware

Premier Inn

BUDGET HOTEL

tel: 0871 527 8652 (Calls cost 13p per minute plus your phone company's access charge) **435 Burnt Oak Broadway HA8 5AQ**
web: www.premierinn.com
dir: *M1 junction 4, A41, A5 towards Edgware. 3 miles to hotel.*

High quality, budget accommodation ideal for both families and business travellers. Spacious, en suite bedrooms feature free WiFi and tea and coffee making

facilities, and in most hotels, Freeview TV is also available. The adjacent family restaurant features a wide and varied menu.

Rooms: 114

EDMONTON	Map 6 TQ39
Greater London	

Premier Inn London Edmonton

Premier Inn

BUDGET HOTEL

tel: 0871 527 9404 (Calls cost 13p per minute plus your phone company's access charge) **Advent Way, N18 3AF**
web: www.premierinn.com
dir: *From A406 exit at Cooks Ferry roundabout. 1st exit into Advent Way. Left (remain on Advent Way). Right into Eley Road. Left into Nobel Road. 2nd left into Advent Way.*

High quality, budget accommodation ideal for both families and business travellers. Spacious, en suite bedrooms feature free WiFi and tea and coffee making facilities, and in most hotels, Freeview TV is also available. The adjacent family restaurant features a wide and varied menu.

Rooms: 96

EGHAM	Map 6 TQ07
Surrey	

INSPECTOR'S CHOICE

AA HOTEL OF THE YEAR FOR ENGLAND 2018–19

Great Fosters

★★★★ ◉◉◉◉ ⚲ HOTEL

tel: 01784 433822 **Stroude Road TW20 9UR**
email: reception@greatfosters.co.uk **web:** www.greatfosters.co.uk
dir: *From A30 Bagshot to Staines, right at lights by Wheatsheaf pub into Christchurch Road. Straight on at roundabout. Left at lights into Stroude Road. Hotel 0.75 mile on right.*

This Grade I listed mansion dates back to the 16th century. The main house rooms are very much in keeping with the house's original style but are, of course, up-to-date with modern amenities. The stables and cloisters provide particularly stylish and luxurious accommodation. A stimulating range of award-winning cuisine can be enjoyed in The Tudor Room and The Estate Grill. The beautiful public rooms, including the terrace during the summer months, provide the perfect setting for afternoon tea and cocktails. A host of meeting and event facilities provide the setting for a range of individual events.

Great Fosters

Rooms: 43 (22 annexe) (1 family) (13 GF) ☎ **S** fr £125 **D** fr £155 **Facilities:** STV FTV WiFi ⚓ ↖ ☕ ☜ Xmas New Year **Conf:** Class 72 Board 50 Theatre 150 **Services:** Night porter **Parking:** 200 **Notes:** LB Civ Wed 180

HIGHLY RECOMMENDED

The Runnymede on Thames

★★★★ 83% ◉ HOTEL

tel: 01784 220600 **Windsor Road TW20 0AG**
email: info@therunnymede.co.uk **web:** www.therunnymede.co.uk
dir: *M25 junction 13, onto A308 towards Windsor.*

Enjoying a peaceful location beside the River Thames, this large modern hotel, with its excellent range of facilities, balances both leisure and corporate business. The extensive function suites, with spacious lounges and stylish, well laid-out bedrooms are impressive. Superb spa facilities are available, and the food and beverage venues offer wonderful river views.

Rooms: 180 (19 family) ☎ **S** fr £135 **D** fr £160 **Facilities:** Spa STV WiFi ⚓ HL ☜ ↖ ☕ Gym Dance studio Boat hire Sauna Steam room Outdoor pool available summer only ♫ New Year **Conf:** Class 180 Board 80 Theatre 300 **Services:** Lift Night porter Air con **Parking:** 300 **Notes:** LB Closed 27–28 December, 1–2 January Civ Wed 142

ELSTREE
Hertfordshire

Map 6 TQ19

HIGHLY RECOMMENDED

Laura Ashley The Manor

★★★★ 83% ◉◉ HOTEL

tel: 020 8327 4700 **Barnet Lane WD6 3RE**
email: elstree@lauraashleyhotels.com
web: www.lauraashleyhotels.com/themanorelstree

This old Tudor house, built around 1540, is set in 10 acres of grounds and has been appointed throughout to reflect the rich design heritage of the Laura Ashley company. Public rooms include a smart bar with original features and the panelled Cavendish Restaurant. Bedrooms, in the newer wing and the main house, have modern facilities and feature Laura Ashley products.

Rooms: 49 (36 annexe) **S** fr £115 **D** fr £145* **Facilities:** FTV WiFi Gym Xmas New Year **Conf:** Class 30 Board 36 Theatre 80 **Services:** Night porter **Parking:** 100 **Notes:** LB Civ Wed 86

E

ELTERWATER
Cumbria   Map 18 NY30

HIGHLY RECOMMENDED

Langdale Hotel & Spa

★★★★ 82% ◎ COUNTRY HOUSE HOTEL

tel: 015394 38014 & 37302 **The Langdale Estate LA22 9JD**
email: info@langdale.co.uk **web:** www.langdale.co.uk
dir: *In Langdale Valley west of Ambleside.*

Built on the site of an abandoned 19th-century gunpowder works, this thoroughly modern hotel and resort is set in 35 acres of woodland and waterways. Comfortable bedrooms, many with spa baths, vary in size. Extensive public areas include the exceptional Stove restaurant and bar. The ever-improving, luxurious spa and leisure facilities are on hand, and there is also a traditional pub, run by the hotel, just along the main road.

Rooms: 52 (47 annexe) (4 family) (25 GF) ✆ **Facilities:** Spa STV FTV WiFi 🕹 🏊 Fishing Gym Steam room Solarium Aerobics studio Health and beauty salon Cycle hire Xmas New Year **Conf:** Class 20 Board 18 Theatre 40 **Services:** Night porter **Parking:** 65 **Notes:** Civ Wed 34

ELY
Cambridgeshire   Map 12 TL58

HIGHLY RECOMMENDED

Poets House

★★★★ 83% ◎ HOTEL

tel: 01353 887777 **40-44 St Mary's Street CB7 4EY**
email: reception@poetshouse.uk.com **web:** www.poetshouse.uk.com
dir: *Follow A10 into Ely, cathedral on right, hotel on left.*

Poets House is a Grade II listed building situated in the heart of Ely, just a few minutes' walk from the historic cathedral and town centre. The property features stylish, individually designed and well-equipped bedrooms. The public rooms include a smart restaurant, The Dining Room, and a bar, The Study, as well as a smart outside garden and terrace.

Rooms: 21 (4 GF) ✆ **S** fr £170 **D** fr £190 (including breakfast)* **Facilities:** FTV WiFi **Conf:** Class 30 Board 25 Theatre 60 **Services:** Lift Night porter **Notes:** LB Civ Wed 65

EMBLETON
Northumberland   Map 21 NU22

Dunstanburgh Castle Hotel

★★★ 84% HOTEL

tel: 01665 576111 **NE66 3UN**
email: stay@dunstanburghcastlehotel.co.uk **web:** www.dunstanburghcastlehotel.co.uk
dir: *From A1 take B1340 to Denwick through Rennington. Right signed Embleton, over level crossing, left at crossroads, 2 miles to Embleton, hotel on right.*

The focal point of the village, this friendly, family-run hotel has a dining room and grill room that offer different menus, plus a cosy bar and two lounges. In addition to the main bedrooms, a barn conversion houses three stunning suites, each with a lounge and gallery bedroom above.

Rooms: 18 (6 family) ✆ **S** fr £72 **D** fr £124 (including breakfast)* **Facilities:** WiFi **Parking:** 26 **Notes:** LB Closed December to January

ENFIELD
Greater London   Map 6 TQ39

Premier Inn Enfield
Premier Inn

BUDGET HOTEL

tel: 0871 527 8374 (Calls cost 13p per minute plus your phone company's access charge) **Innova Park, Corner of Solar Way EN3 7XY**
web: www.premierinn.com
dir: *M25 junction 25, A10 towards London, left into Bullsmoor Lane and Mollison Avenue. Over roundabout, right at lights into Innova Science Park.*

High quality, budget accommodation ideal for both families and business travellers. Spacious, en suite bedrooms feature free WiFi and tea and coffee making facilities, and in most hotels, Freeview TV is also available. The adjacent family restaurant features a wide and varied menu.

Rooms: 202

EPSOM
Surrey   Map 6 TQ26

Premier Inn Epsom Central
Premier Inn

BUDGET HOTEL

tel: 0871 527 8376 (Calls cost 13p per minute plus your phone company's access charge) **2-4 St Margarets Drive, off Dorking Road KT18 7LB**
web: www.premierinn.com
dir: *M25 junction 9, A24 towards Epsom, hotel on left, just before town centre.*

High quality, budget accommodation ideal for both families and business travellers. Spacious, en suite bedrooms feature free WiFi and tea and coffee making facilities, and in most hotels, Freeview TV is also available. The adjacent family restaurant features a wide and varied menu.

Rooms: 58

Premier Inn Epsom North
Premier Inn

BUDGET HOTEL

tel: 0871 527 8380 (Calls cost 13p per minute plus your phone company's access charge) **272 Kingston Road, Ewell KT19 0SH**
web: www.premierinn.com
dir: *M25 junction 8, A217 towards Sutton. A240 towards Ewell. At Beggars Hill roundabout 2nd exit into Kingston Road.*

Rooms: 29

E

The Parsonage Country House Hotel

★★★★ 76% COUNTRY HOUSE HOTEL

tel: 01904 728111 **York Road YO19 6LF**
email: reservations@parsonagehotel.co.uk **web:** www.parsonagehotel.co.uk
dir: *A64 onto A19 Selby, Follow to Escrick. Hotel by St Helens Church.*

This 19th-century, former parsonage has been carefully restored and extended, and is situated in six acres of gardens. Bedrooms are smartly appointed and well equipped for both business and leisure guests. Public areas include an elegant restaurant, conference facilities and a choice of attractive lounges. Cloisters Spa is located in the formal gardens and includes a swimming pool, jacuzzi, sauna, steam room, aromatherapy salt room and an excellent gym; please note, the spa and health club are for those aged 18 and over only. In addition to The Lascelles restaurant, The Fat Abbot gastro pub is located in the grounds and offers a more relaxed dining experience.

Rooms: 56 (19 annexe) (4 family) (12 GF) **S** fr £80 **D** fr £86 **Facilities:** Spa FTV WiFi Gym Sauna Steam room Aromatherapy room Salt room Xmas New Year **Conf:** Class 80 Board 50 Theatre 150 **Services:** Lift Night porter **Parking:** 120 **Notes:** LB Civ Wed 100

Summer Lodge Country House Hotel, Restaurant & Spa

THE
RED CARNATION
HOTEL COLLECTION

★★★★★ 84% COUNTRY HOUSE HOTEL

tel: 01935 482000 **Fore Street, EVERSHOT DT2 0JR**
email: summer@relaischateaux.com **web:** www.summerlodgehotel.co.uk
dir: *1 mile west of A37 halfway between Dorchester and Yeovil.*

This picturesque hotel is situated in the heart of Dorset and is the ideal retreat; it's worth arriving in time for the excellent afternoon tea. Bedrooms are appointed to a very high standard; each is individually designed, with upholstered walls and a wealth of luxurious facilities. Expect plasma-screen TVs, DVD players, radios, air conditioning and WiFi, plus little touches such as home-made shortbread, fresh fruit and scented candles. The delightful public areas include a sumptuous lounge complete with an open fire, and the elegant restaurant where the cuisine continues to be the high point of any stay.

Rooms: 24 (14 annexe) (6 family) (3 GF) **S** fr £182.75 **D** fr £182.75 (including breakfast)* **Facilities:** Spa STV FTV WiFi Gym Sauna Xmas New Year **Conf:** Board 12 Theatre 20 **Services:** Night porter Air con **Parking:** 41 **Notes:** LB No children 7 years Closed 2–25 January Civ Wed 30

George Albert Hotel

★★★ 82% HOTEL

tel: 01935 483430 **Wardon Hill DT2 9PW**
email: enquiries@gahotel.co.uk **web:** www.gahotel.co.uk
dir: *On A37 – between Yeovil and Dorchester.*

Situated mid-way between Dorchester and Yeovil, this hotel has much to offer for both business and leisure guests. The bedrooms offer impressive levels of comfort and many also have wonderful views across the Dorset countryside. Stylish public areas include extensive function rooms, a relaxing lounge, and a choice of dining options. Additional facilities include a spa offering a range of beauty treatments, along with a sauna, steam room and jacuzzi.

Rooms: 39 (3 family) **S** fr £70 **D** fr £80 (including breakfast)* **Facilities:** Spa FTV WiFi Kart track Xmas New Year **Conf:** Class 60 Board 90 Theatre 250 **Services:** Lift Night porter Air con **Parking:** 200 **Notes:** LB Civ Wed 405

Wood Norton Hotel

★★★★ 83% HOTEL

tel: 01386 765611 **Worcester Road WR11 4YB**
email: info@thewoodnorton.com **web:** www.thewoodnorton.com
dir: *2 miles from Evesham on A44, after Chadbury.*

Equidistant from Worcester, Stratford-upon-Avon and Cheltenham, this 19th-century former hunting lodge, originally built for European royalty, is ideally located for exploring the Cotswolds. Modern details and period architecture sit comfortably together, creating a stylish interior. Bedrooms are well equipped for both business and leisure guests, and complimentary WiFi is available throughout. Public areas encompass a stylish bar, guest lounges and an oak-panelled dining room overlooking the gardens.

Rooms: 50 (30 annexe) (6 family) (12 GF) **Facilities:** FTV WiFi Xmas New Year **Conf:** Class 60 Board 40 Theatre 200 **Services:** Lift Night porter **Notes:** LB Civ Wed

Dumbleton Hall Hotel

★★★ 78% COUNTRY HOUSE HOTEL

tel: 01386 881240 **WR11 7TS**
email: dh@pofr.co.uk **web:** www.dumbletonhall.co.uk

(for full entry see Dumbleton)

Best Western Salford Hall Hotel

 Best Western.

★★★ 76% HOTEL

tel: 01386 871300 **Abbots Salford WR11 8UT**
email: reception@salfordhall.co.uk **web:** www.salfordhall.co.uk
dir: *M40 junction 15, A46 for Evesham 16 miles, right on Bidford Roundabout towards Salford Priors, 1.4 miles, hotel on left.*

Set on the Warwickshire-Worcestershire border, Salford Hall is a Grade I listed, Tudor manor house originally built as a guest house for the monks of nearby Evesham Abbey. It has retained much of its historic charm, with inglenook fireplaces, oak beams and wood panelling. The bedrooms are comfortable and well equipped, and the hotel is popular for its weddings and events packages.

Rooms: 15 (21 annexe) (1 family) (9 GF) **S** fr £60 **D** fr £70* **Facilities:** WiFi Xmas New Year **Conf:** Class 60 Board 60 Theatre 120 **Services:** Night porter **Parking:** 60 **Notes:** Civ Wed 97

Premier Inn Evesham

Premier Inn

BUDGET HOTEL

tel: 0871 527 8384 (Calls cost 13p per minute plus your phone company's access charge) **Evesham Country Park, A46 Trunk Road WR11 4TP**
web: www.premierinn.com
dir: *At roundabout junction of A46(T) and A4184 at north end of Evesham bypass. Adjacent to Evesham Country Park.*

High quality, budget accommodation ideal for both families and business travellers. Spacious, en suite bedrooms feature free WiFi and tea and coffee making facilities, and in most hotels, Freeview TV is also available. The adjacent family restaurant features a wide and varied menu.

Rooms: 108

E

Hotel du Vin Exeter

★★★★ 75% HOTEL

tel: 01392 790120 & 288165 **Magdalen Street EX2 4HY**
email: reception.exeter@hotelduvin.com **web:** www.hotelduvin.com/location/exeter
dir: *M5 junction 29 from north and junction 30 from south. See website for detailed directions.*

Once an eye infirmary, this statuesque building in the heart of the city is now home to Hotel du Vin Exeter. The fusion of traditional and contemporary provides a fascinating environment in which to relax and enjoy some genuine hospitality from the committed team. Stylish bedrooms come in a variety of shapes and sizes with a host of thoughtful extras and wonderfully snuggly beds. Cosseting towels, fluffy robes and REN toiletries also contribute to equally impressive bathrooms. The bistro is the venue for flavoursome, French-inspired cuisine, complemented by a cosmopolitan wine list. Public areas provide a number of options in which to sink back into a sofa and soak up the unique atmosphere. A spa and swimming pool are also available, housed within the secluded walled garden.

Rooms: 59 (6 family) (3 GF) ☏ **Facilities:** Spa FTV WiFi ♨ ⊙ ⚓ Gym Xmas New Year **Conf:** Class 30 Board 16 Theatre 100 **Services:** Lift Night porter Air con **Parking:** 12 **Notes:** LB Civ Wed 100

The Devon Hotel

★★★ 80% HOTEL

tel: 01392 259268 **Exeter Bypass, Matford EX2 8XU**
email: reservations@devonhotel.co.uk **web:** www.devonhotel.co.uk
dir: *M5 junction 30 follow Marsh Barton Industrial Estate signs on A379. Hotel on Marsh Barton roundabout.*

Within easy reach of the city centre, the M5 and the city's business parks, this smart Georgian hotel offers modern, comfortable accommodation. The Carriages Bar and Brasserie is popular with guests and locals alike, offering a wide range of dishes as well as a carvery at both lunch and dinner. Service is friendly and attentive, and extensive meeting and business facilities are available.

Rooms: 60 (60 annexe) (17 family) (21 GF) ☏ **S** fr £80 **D** fr £90* **Facilities:** FTV WiFi ♨ Gym Xmas New Year **Conf:** Class 80 Board 40 Theatre 150 **Services:** Night porter **Parking:** 150 **Notes:** LB Civ Wed 100

Best Western Lord Haldon Country Hotel

★★★ 79% HOTEL

tel: 01392 832483 **Dunchideock EX6 7YF**
email: enquiries@lordhaldonhotel.co.uk **web:** www.lordhaldonhotel.co.uk
dir: *M5 junction 31, A30, 1st exit, follow signs through Ide to Dunchideock.*

Set in rural tranquillity, this is an attractive country house where guests are assured of a warm welcome from the professional team of staff. The well-equipped bedrooms are comfortable, and many have stunning views. The daily-changing menu features skilfully cooked dishes, with most of the produce sourced locally.

Rooms: 25 (3 family) ☏ **S** fr £75 **D** fr £95 (including breakfast) **Facilities:** FTV WiFi ♨ Xmas New Year **Conf:** Class 100 Board 40 Theatre 250 **Services:** Night porter **Parking:** 120 **Notes:** LB Civ Wed 120

Gipsy Hill Hotel

THE INDEPENDENTS
HOTEL ASSOCIATION

★★★ 78% HOTEL

tel: 01392 465252 **Gipsy Hill Lane, Monkerton EX1 3RN**
email: stay@gipsyhillhotel.co.uk **web:** www.gipsyhillhotel.co.uk
dir: *M5 junction 29 towards Exeter. Right at 1st roundabout, right again at next roundabout, turn left onto Pinn Lane, right into Gipsy Hill Lane.*

Located on the edge of the city, with easy access to the M5 and the airport, this popular hotel is set in attractive, well-tended gardens and boasts far-reaching country views. The hotel offers a range of conference and function rooms, comfortable bedrooms and modern facilities including free WiFi. An intimate bar and lounge are adjacent to the elegant restaurant. Secure indoor cycle storage is also provided.

Rooms: 37 (17 annexe) (4 family) (12 GF) ☏ **Facilities:** FTV WiFi ♨ Xmas New Year **Conf:** Class 80 Board 80 Theatre 300 **Services:** Night porter **Parking:** 74 **Notes:** Civ Wed 160

Premier Inn Exeter Central St Davids

Premier Inn

BUDGET HOTEL

tel: 0871 527 9278 (Calls cost 13p per minute plus your phone company's access charge) **Bonhay Road EX4 4BG**
web: www.premierinn.com
dir: *M5 junction 31, A30 towards Bodmin and Okehampton. Exit onto A377 towards Exeter and Crediton. Hotel on left.*

High quality, budget accommodation ideal for both families and business travellers. Spacious, en suite bedrooms feature free WiFi and tea and coffee making facilities, and in most hotels, Freeview TV is also available. The adjacent family restaurant features a wide and varied menu.

Rooms: 102

Premier Inn Exeter City Centre

BUDGET HOTEL

tel: 0871 527 9570 (Calls cost 13p per minute plus your phone company's access charge) **2 Southernhay Gardens EX1 1SG**
web: www.premierinn.com
dir: *M5 junction 29, A3015. Right at lights into Honiton Road. At Moor Lane roundabout 2nd exit (A3015) then B3183. At next roundabout 1st exit into Western Way (B3212). Right into Barnfield Road, left then left again into Southernhay Gardens.*

Rooms: 120

Premier Inn Exeter (Countess Wear)

BUDGET HOTEL

tel: 0871 527 8386 (Calls cost 13p per minute plus your phone company's access charge) **398 Topsham Road EX2 6HE**
web: www.premierinn.com
dir: *2 miles from M5 junction 30/A30 junction 29. Follow signs for Exeter and Dawlish (A379). On dual carriageway take 2nd slip road on left at Countess Wear roundabout. Hotel adjacent to Beefeater.*

Rooms: 44

Premier Inn Exeter M5 Jct 29

BUDGET HOTEL

tel: 0871 527 9468 (Calls cost 13p per minute plus your phone company's access charge) **Fitzroy Road EX1 3LJ**
web: www.premierinn.com
dir: *M5 junction 29, A3015 towards city centre. Straight on at 1st roundabout. 2nd right (at lights) into Fitzroy Road.*

Rooms: 102

EXMOUTH
Devon   Map 3 SY08

Lympstone Manor Hotel

★★★★★ 84% COUNTRY HOUSE HOTEL

tel: 01395 202040 **Courtlands Lane EX8 3NZ**
email: info@lympstonemanor.co.uk web: www.lympstonemanor.co.uk

Lympstone Manor is a Grade II listed Georgian manor with a fascinating history dating back many centuries. Thanks to the vision of Michael Caines, it has been transformed and now stands proud, a stunning building with breathtaking views over the Exe estuary. Comfort and quality are delivered in equal measure throughout the public areas, the styling being a fusion of classic country house with contemporary flair. Elegant and accomplished cuisine, augmented by a significant wine list, underpin the Lympstone experience, attuned to the surroundings with a choice of three exquisite dining rooms. Impressive bedrooms are luxuriously appointed with a number having either balconies or terraces with superb views.

Rooms: 21 (4 family) (6 GF) ☏ **S** fr £290 **D** fr £315 (including breakfast)*
Facilities: FTV WiFi ↕ ☙ Bicycle hire Xmas New Year **Conf:** Class 17 Board 14 Theatre 20 **Services:** Night porter **Parking:** 80 **Notes:** LB Closed 1 week January Civ Wed 100

Cavendish Hotel

★★★ 73% HOTEL

tel: 01395 272528 **11 Morton Crescent, The Esplanade EX8 1BE**
email: cavendish.exmouth@alfatravel.co.uk web: www.leisureplex.co.uk
dir: *Follow seafront signs, hotel in centre of large crescent.*

Situated on the seafront, this terraced hotel attracts many groups from around the country, and is within walking distance of the town centre. The bedrooms are neatly presented, and front-facing rooms are always popular. Entertainment is provided on most evenings during the summer.

Rooms: 81 (2 family) (21 GF) ☏ **S** fr £41 **D** fr £64 (including breakfast)*
Facilities: FTV WiFi ♫ Xmas New Year **Services:** Lift **Parking:** 25 **Notes:** Closed December to January (excluding Christmas) RS November and February to March

Premier Inn Exmouth Seafront

BUDGET HOTEL

tel: 0871 527 9400 (Calls cost 13p per minute plus your phone company's access charge) **The Esplanade EX8 2AZ**
web: www.premierinn.com
dir: *M5 junction 30, A376 signed Exeter/Exmouth. At roundabout take A376. At 4th roundabout take 2nd exit into Imperial Road. After next roundabout, right onto Alexandra Terrace. 1st left into Morton Road, left onto Esplanade. Hotel on left.*

High quality, budget accommodation ideal for both families and business travellers. Spacious, en suite bedrooms feature free WiFi and tea and coffee making facilities, and in most hotels, Freeview TV is also available. The adjacent family restaurant features a wide and varied menu.

Rooms: 60

FALFIELD
Gloucestershire   Map 4 ST69

Best Western The Gables Hotel

★★★ 77% HOTEL

tel: 01454 260502 **Bristol Road GL12 8DL**
email: mail@thegablesbristol.co.uk web: www.thegablesbristol.co.uk
dir: *M5 junction 14 northbound. Left at end of sliproad. Right onto A38, hotel 300 yards on right.*

Conveniently located just a few minutes from the motorway, this establishment is ideally suited to both business and leisure guests, with easy access to Cheltenham, Gloucester, Bristol and Bath. Bedrooms are spacious and well equipped. Relaxing public areas consist of a light and airy bar, and a restaurant where meals and all-day snacks are available; a more formal restaurant is open for dinner. There is also a range of meeting rooms.

Rooms: 46 (4 family) (18 GF) **S** fr £79 **D** fr £89 (including breakfast)* **Facilities:** FTV WiFi ↕ New Year **Conf:** Class 90 Board 50 Theatre 200 **Services:** Night porter **Parking:** 104 **Notes:** LB Civ Wed 150

F

FALMOUTH
Cornwall & Isles Of Scilly   Map 2 SW83

See also **Mawnan Smith**

HIGHLY RECOMMENDED

The Royal Duchy Hotel

★★★★ 83% @@ HOTEL

tel: 01326 313042 **Cliff Road TR11 4NX**
email: reservations@royalduchy.com **web:** www.royalduchy.com
dir: *On Cliff Road, along Falmouth seafront.*

The staff at this hotel, which looks out over the sea and towards Pendennis Castle, create a very friendly environment. The comfortable lounge and cocktail bar are well appointed and just the place for a light lunch. Leisure facilities include a beauty salon, and meeting rooms are also available. The award-winning Terrace Restaurant serves carefully prepared dishes, and guests can sit on the sea-facing terrace in warmer weather. The bedrooms vary in size and aspect, and many have sea views. Babysitting is happily arranged for families with small children and babies.

Rooms: 45 (6 family) (1 GF) ⌂ **S** fr £99 **D** fr £176 (including breakfast)*
Facilities: Spa FTV WiFi ⌂ ☺ Games room Sauna Hot stone therapy beds 🎵
Xmas New Year **Conf:** Theatre 50 **Services:** Lift Night porter **Parking:** 50 **Notes:** LB Civ Wed 100

See advert opposite

St Michael's Hotel and Spa

★★★★ 79% @@ HOTEL

tel: 01326 312707 **Gyllyngvase Beach, Seafront TR11 4NB**
email: greghenry@stmichaelshotel.co.uk **web:** www.stmichaelshotel.co.uk
dir: *A39 into Falmouth, follow beach signs, at 2nd mini-roundabout into Pennance Road. Take 2nd left and 2nd left again.*

Overlooking the bay, this hotel is in an excellent position and commands lovely views. It is appointed in a fresh, contemporary style that reflects its location by the sea. The Flying Fish restaurant has a great atmosphere and a real buzz about it. The light and bright bedrooms, some with balconies, are well equipped. There are excellent leisure facilities including a fitness and health club together with a spa offering many treatments. The attractive gardens also provide a place to relax and unwind.

Rooms: 84 (32 annexe) (7 family) (12 GF) ⌂ **S** fr £45 **D** fr £70 (including breakfast)*
Facilities: Spa FTV WiFi ⌂ ☺ ☺ Gym Sauna Steam room Aqua aerobics Fitness classes Xmas New Year **Conf:** Class 40 Board 30 Theatre 80 **Services:** Lift Night porter **Parking:** 60 **Notes:** Civ Wed 80

Merchants Manor

★★★★ 78% @@@ HOTEL

tel: 01326 312734 **1 Weston Manor TR11 4AJ**
email: info@merchantsmanor.com **web:** www.merchantsmanor.com
dir: *Phone for directions.*

Merchants Manor is an historical country house situated within walking distance of the busy town centre and pretty beaches. Beautiful original features have been sympathetically mixed with contemporary style and design. Bedrooms are modern and comfortable with a keen eye on quality and high standards. It's ideal for that special wedding or family celebration with the added benefit of leisure facilities for families, including a good sized gym. There is also generous seating in the lounge, perfect for a morning coffee or afternoon tea.

Rooms: 39 (2 family) (11 GF) ⌂ **S** fr £65 **D** fr £150 (including breakfast)*
Facilities: Spa FTV WiFi ⌂ HL ☺ Gym Sauna In-room treatments Wellbeing studio Xmas New Year **Conf:** Class 20 Board 20 Theatre 20 **Services:** Night porter **Parking:** 30 **Notes:** LB Civ Wed 40

The Greenbank Hotel

★★★★ 77% @@ HOTEL

tel: 01326 312440 **Harbourside TR11 2SR**
email: reception@greenbank-hotel.co.uk **web:** www.greenbank-hotel.co.uk
dir: *A39 to Falmouth, left at Ponsharden roundabout onto North Parade. 500 yards past Falmouth Marina on the Harbourfront.*

Located by the marina, and with its own private quay dating from the 17th century, The Greenbank Hotel has a strong maritime theme throughout. Set at the water's edge, the lounge, restaurant and many bedrooms all benefit from harbour views. The restaurant provides a choice of interesting and enjoyable dishes.

Rooms: 61 (6 family) ⌂ **S** fr £69 **D** fr £109 (including breakfast)* **Facilities:** FTV WiFi ⌂ Private beach quay and pontoons Beauty treatment room Xmas New Year **Conf:** Class 30 Board 50 Theatre 120 **Services:** Lift Night porter **Parking:** 69 **Notes:** LB Civ Wed 120

F

Penmorvah Manor

★★★ 81% 🏵 COUNTRY HOUSE HOTEL

tel: 01326 250277 **Budock Water TR11 5ED**
email: reception@penmorvah.co.uk **web:** www.penmorvah.co.uk
dir: *A39 to Hillhead roundabout, take 2nd exit. 2nd exit at next roundabout, right at Falmouth Football Club, through Budock. Hotel opposite Penjerrick Gardens.*

Situated within two miles of central Falmouth, this extended Victorian manor house is a peaceful hideaway, set in six acres of private woodland and gardens. Penmorvah is well positioned for visiting the local gardens, and offers many garden-tour breaks. Dinner features locally sourced, quality ingredients such as Cornish cheeses, meat, fish and game.

Rooms: 27 (1 family) (10 GF) 🐾 **D** fr £120 (including breakfast)* **Facilities:** FTV WiFi ⌕ Xmas New Year **Conf:** Class 100 Board 40 Theatre 100 **Parking:** 100 **Notes:** LB Civ Wed 100

Penmere Manor Hotel

★★★ 80% HOTEL

tel: 01326 211411 **Mongleath Road TR11 4PN**
email: reservations@penmere.co.uk **web:** www.penmere.co.uk
dir: *Take 2nd exit at Hillhead roundabout, over next roundabout to Union Road. Follow road and turn left into Mongleath Road.*

Set in five acres on the outskirts of town, this Georgian manor house was originally built for a ship's captain. Now a family-owned hotel it provides friendly service and a good range of facilities. Bedrooms vary in size and are located in the manor house and the garden wing. Various menus are available in the bar and the smart restaurant. There is a leisure club with an indoor heated pool, jacuzzi, sauna and a well-equipped small gym; the water in the pool is UV filtered.

Rooms: 37 (12 family) (13 GF) **S** fr £75 **D** fr £140 (including breakfast)* **Facilities:** FTV WiFi ☒ Gym Sauna Jacuzzi New Year **Conf:** Class 20 Board 30 Theatre 60 **Parking:** 50 **Notes:** LB Closed 22–27 December

Membly Hall Hotel

★★★ 69% HOTEL

tel: 01326 312869 **Sea Front, Cliff Road TR11 4NT**
email: memblyhallhotel@tiscali.co.uk **web:** www.memblyhallhotel.co.uk
dir: *A39 to Falmouth. Follow seafront and beaches signs.*

Located conveniently on the seafront and enjoying splendid views, this family-run hotel offers friendly service. Bedrooms are pleasantly spacious and well equipped. Carefully prepared and enjoyable meals are served in the spacious dining room. Live entertainment is provided on some evenings and there is also a sauna and spa pool.

Rooms: 35 (3 family) (6 GF) 🐾 **Facilities:** FTV WiFi Gym Indoor short bowls Table tennis Pool table Sauna Spa pool 🎵 New Year **Conf:** Class 130 Board 60 Theatre 150 **Services:** Lift **Parking:** 30 **Notes:** Closed Christmas week RS December to January

---

FAREHAM
Hampshire

Map 5 SU50

Solent Hotel & Spa

★★★★ 81% 🏵 HOTEL

tel: 01489 880000 **Rookery Avenue, Whiteley PO15 7AJ**
email: reservations@solenthotel.co.uk **web:** www.solenthotel.co.uk
dir: *M27 junction 9, hotel on Solent Business Park.*

Close to the M27 with easy access to Portsmouth, the New Forest and other attractions, this smart, purpose-built hotel enjoys a peaceful location. Bedrooms are spacious and very well appointed and there is a well-equipped spa with health and beauty facilities.

Rooms: 115 (9 family) (39 GF) **S** fr £95 **D** fr £95* **Facilities:** Spa STV WiFi ⌕ HL ☒ ⌕ Gym Steam room Sauna Children's splash pool Activity studio Treatment rooms Xmas New Year **Conf:** Class 100 Board 80 Theatre 200 **Services:** Lift Night porter **Parking:** 200 **Notes:** LB Civ Wed 160

FAREHAM *continued*

Lysses House Hotel

★★★ 75% HOTEL

tel: 01329 822622 **51 High Street PO16 7BQ**
email: lysses@lysses.co.uk **web:** www.lysses.co.uk
dir: *M27 junction 11 follow Fareham signs, stay in left lane to Delme roundabout. At roundabout 3rd exit into East Street, follow into High Street. Hotel at top on right.*

This attractive Georgian hotel is situated on the edge of the town in a quiet location and provides spacious and well-equipped accommodation. There are conference facilities, and a lounge bar serving a range of snacks together with the Richmond Restaurant that offers imaginative cuisine.

Rooms: 21 (2 family) (7 GF) ❨ **S** fr £70 **D** fr £102.50 (including breakfast)
Facilities: FTV WiFi Free entry to gym/pool 5 minutes walk away **Conf:** Class 42 Board 28 Theatre 95 **Services:** Lift Night porter **Parking:** 30 **Notes:** Closed 25 December to 1 January RS 24 December and bank holidays Civ Wed 100

Premier Inn Fareham

BUDGET HOTEL

Premier Inn

tel: 0871 527 8396 (Calls cost 13p per minute plus your phone company's access charge) **Southampton Road, Park Gate SO31 6AF**
web: www.premierinn.com
dir: *M27 junction 9, follow Fareham West, A27 signs. Note for sat nav use SO31 6BZ.*

High quality, budget accommodation ideal for both families and business travellers. Spacious, en suite bedrooms feature free WiFi and tea and coffee making facilities, and in most hotels, Freeview TV is also available. The adjacent family restaurant features a wide and varied menu.

Rooms: 61

FARINGDON
Oxfordshire

Map 5 SU29

Sudbury House

★★★★ 83% @@@ HOTEL

tel: 01367 241272 **56 London Street SN7 7AA**
email: reception@sudburyhouse.co.uk **web:** www.sudburyhouse.co.uk
dir: *M40 junction 9, A34. A420, London Street 0.5 mile on left.*

Set in nine acres of well-tended grounds and located on the edge of the Cotswolds, Sudbury House is a great place to relax and unwind. Restaurant 56 offers fine dining while the brasserie, with its open-plan kitchen is more relaxed. Accommodation has a contemporary design and offers great comfort.

Rooms: 50 (2 family) (10 GF) ❨ **D** fr £130 (including breakfast)* **Facilities:** FTV WiFi ⇖ Xmas New Year **Conf:** Class 16 Board 30 Theatre 100 **Services:** Lift Night porter **Parking:** 60 **Notes:** LB Civ Wed 180

FARNBOROUGH
Hampshire

Map 5 SU85

Aviator

★★★★ @@ HOTEL

tel: 01252 555890 **Farnborough Road GU14 6EL**
email: enquiries@aviatorbytag.com **web:** www.aviatorbytag.com
dir: *A325 to Aldershot, 3 miles, hotel on right.*

Aviator is a striking property with a modern, sleek interior overlooking Farnborough Airfield, and located close to the main transport networks. Bedrooms are well designed and provide complimentary WiFi. Both the Brasserie and the One Eleven source local ingredients for their menus.

Rooms: 169 (19 family) ❨ **S** fr £95 **D** fr £95* **Facilities:** Spa STV FTV WiFi ⇖ Gym Exercise studio Theraputic, holistic and beauty treatments Xmas New Year **Conf:** Class 48 Board 40 Theatre 110 **Services:** Lift Night porter Air con **Parking:** 169 **Notes:** LB Civ Wed 90

Premier Inn Farnborough

BUDGET HOTEL

Premier Inn

tel: 0871 527 8398 (Calls cost 13p per minute plus your phone company's access charge) **Ively Road, Southwood GU14 0JP**
web: www.premierinn.com
dir: *Phone for directions.*

High quality, budget accommodation ideal for both families and business travellers. Spacious, en suite bedrooms feature free WiFi and tea and coffee making facilities, and in most hotels, Freeview TV is also available. The adjacent family restaurant features a wide and varied menu.

Rooms: 82

Premier Inn Farnborough Town Centre

BUDGET HOTEL

Premier Inn

tel: 0871 527 9628 (Calls cost 13p per minute plus your phone company's access charge) **3 Kingsmead GU14 7NY**
web: www.premierinn.com
dir: *Phone for directions.*

Rooms: 80

FARNHAM	Map 5 SU84
Surrey	

Frensham Pond Country House Hotel & Spa

★★★★ 80% HOTEL

tel: 01252 795161 **Bacon Lane GU10 2QB**
email: info@frenshampondhotel.co.uk **web:** www.frenshampondhotel.co.uk

(for full entry see Churt)

Mercure Farnham Bush Hotel

★★★ 78% HOTEL

tel: 01252 234800 **The Borough GU9 7NN**
email: H6621@accor.com **web:** www.mercure.com
dir: *M3 junction 4, A31, follow town centre signs. At East Street lights turn left, hotel on right.*

Dating back to the 17th century, this extended former coaching inn is attractively presented and has a courtyard and a lawned garden. The bedrooms are well appointed, with quality fabrics and good facilities. The public areas include the panelled Oak Lounge, a smart cocktail bar and a conference facility in an adjoining building.

Rooms: 94 (3 family) (27 GF) **Facilities:** FTV WiFi Xmas **Conf:** Class 80 Board 30 Theatre 140 **Services:** Night porter **Parking:** 70 **Notes:** Civ Wed 100

The Farnham Hog's Back Hotel

★★★ 78% HOTEL

tel: 01252 782345 **Hog's Back, Seale GU10 1EX**
email: res@farnhamhogsbackhotel.co.uk **web:** www.farnhamhogsbackhotel.co.uk
dir: *On A31 Hogs Back Road 15 minutes from Farnham and Guildford.*

The Farnham Hog's Back Hotel offers a convenient location, plenty of free parking, comfortable rooms with all the required amenities, including free WiFi, and the extensive Active Life Health Club. There is also a choice of two event suites, one of which has its own exclusive entrance, designed to host a range of different occasions such as business meetings, weddings or civil partnerships.

Rooms: 96 (17 family) (24 GF) **Facilities:** Spa WiFi HL Gym Steam room Sauna Xmas New Year **Conf:** Class 120 Board 40 Theatre 180 **Services:** Night porter **Parking:** 150 **Notes:** Civ Wed 150

FAWKHAM GREEN	Map 6 TQ56
Kent	

Brandshatch Place Hotel & Spa

★★★★ 78% 🌐🌐 HOTEL

tel: 01474 875000 & 0845 072 7395 (Calls cost 5p per minute plus your phone company's access charge) **Brands Hatch Road, Fawkham Green DA3 8NQ**
email: brandshatchplace@handpicked.co.uk
web: www.handpickedhotels.co.uk/brandshatchplace
dir: *M25 junction 3, A20 West Kingsdown. Left at paddock entrance/Fawkham Green sign. 3rd left signed Fawkham Road. Hotel 500 metres on right.*

This charming 18th-century Georgian country house close to the famous racing circuit offers stylish and elegant rooms. Bedrooms are appointed to a very high standard, offering impressive facilities and excellent levels of comfort and quality. The hotel also features a comprehensive leisure club with substantial crèche facilities.

Rooms: 38 (12 annexe) (1 family) (6 GF) **Facilities:** Spa STV FTV WiFi Gym Aerobic dance studio Sauna Steam room Spin studio Xmas New Year **Conf:** Class 60 Board 50 Theatre 160 **Services:** Lift Night porter **Parking:** 100 **Notes:** Civ Wed 110

FELIXSTOWE	Map 13 TM33
Suffolk	

Best Western Brook Hotel

★★★ 77% HOTEL

tel: 01394 278441 **Orwell Road IP11 7PF**
email: welcome@brookhotel.com **web:** www.brookhotel.com

The Brook Hotel is a modern, well furnished building ideally situated in a residential area close to the town centre and the sea. Public areas include a lounge bar, a large open-plan restaurant with a bar area and a residents' lounge. Bedrooms are generally quite spacious; each one is pleasantly decorated and equipped with modern facilities.

Rooms: 25 (5 family) (3 GF) **Facilities:** FTV WiFi Xmas New Year **Conf:** Class 60 Board 60 Theatre 100 **Parking:** 20 **Notes:** Civ Wed 150

Premier Inn Felixstowe Town Centre

Premier Inn

BUDGET HOTEL

tel: 0871 527 9536 (Calls cost 13p per minute plus your phone company's access charge) **Undercliffe Rd West IP11 2AN**
web: www.premierinn.com
dir: *A14 towards Felixstowe. At roundabout (Trimley St Mary on right) follow Town Centre (A154) signs. At next roundabout right into Garrison Lane. Hotel on left before Undercliffe Road.*

High quality, budget accommodation ideal for both families and business travellers. Spacious, en suite bedrooms feature free WiFi and tea and coffee making facilities, and in most hotels, Freeview TV is also available. The adjacent family restaurant features a wide and varied menu.

Rooms: 60

FERNDOWN	Map 5 SU00
Dorset	

Premier Inn Bournemouth/Ferndown

Premier Inn

BUDGET HOTEL

tel: 0871 527 8122 (Calls cost 13p per minute plus your phone company's access charge) **Ringwood Road, Tricketts Cross BH22 9BB**
web: www.premierinn.com
dir: *Off A348 just before Tricketts Cross roundabout.*

High quality, budget accommodation ideal for both families and business travellers. Spacious, en suite bedrooms feature free WiFi and tea and coffee making facilities, and in most hotels, Freeview TV is also available. The adjacent family restaurant features a wide and varied menu.

Rooms: 32

FLAMBOROUGH
East Riding of Yorkshire   Map 17 TA27

North Star Hotel

★★ 85% SMALL HOTEL

tel: 01262 850379 **North Marine Drive YO15 1BL**
email: thenorthstarhotel@live.co.uk **web:** www.thenorthstarhotel.co.uk
dir: *B1229 or B1255 to Flamborough. Follow signs for North Landing along North Marine Drive. Hotel 100 yards from sea.*

Standing close to the North Landing of Flamborough Head, this family-run hotel overlooks delightful countryside, and provides excellent accommodation and caring hospitality. A good range of fresh local food, especially fish, is available in both the bar and the dining room.

Rooms: 9 (2 GF) ☎ **S** fr £65 **D** fr £90 (including breakfast)* **Facilities:** FTV WiFi
Parking: 60 **Notes:** LB Closed Christmas RS November to Easter

FLEET
Hampshire   Map 5 SU85

Premier Inn Fleet

 Premier Inn

BUDGET HOTEL

tel: 0871 527 9446 (Calls cost 13p per minute plus your phone company's access charge) **Waterfront Business Park, 7-11 Fleet Road GU51 3QT**
web: www.premierinn.com
dir: *On A3013.*

High quality, budget accommodation ideal for both families and business travellers. Spacious, en suite bedrooms feature free WiFi and tea and coffee making facilities, and in most hotels, Freeview TV is also available. The adjacent family restaurant features a wide and varied menu.

Rooms: 70

FLEET MOTORWAY SERVICE AREA (M3)
Hampshire   Map 5 SU75

Days Inn Fleet - M3

WELCOMEBREAK

AA Advertised

tel: 01252 815587 **Fleet Services GU51 1AA**
email: fleet.hotel@welcomebreak.co.uk **web:** www.welcomebreak.co.uk
dir: *Between junction 4a and 5 southbound on M3.*

This modern building offers accommodation in smart, spacious and well-equipped bedrooms, suitable for families and business travellers, and all with en suite bathrooms. Continental breakfast is available and other refreshments may be taken at the nearby family restaurant.

Rooms: 59 (46 family) (5 smoking) **Facilities:** STV FTV WiFi **Services:** Night porter
Parking: 60

FLITWICK
Bedfordshire   Map 11 TL03

Hallmark Hotel Flitwick Manor

★★★★ 77% ◎◎ COUNTRY HOUSE HOTEL

tel: 0330 028 3406 **Church Road MK45 1AE**
email: flitwick@hallmarkhotels.co.uk **web:** www.hallmarkhotels.co.uk
dir: *M1 junction 12, follow signs for Flitwick, turn left into Church Road, hotel on left.*

With its picturesque setting in acres of gardens and parkland, yet only minutes from the motorway, this lovely Georgian house combines the best of both worlds, being both accessible and peaceful. Bedrooms are individually decorated and furnished with period pieces; some are air conditioned. Cosy and intimate, the lounge and restaurant give the hotel a home-from-home feel.

Rooms: 18 (1 family) (5 GF) (1 smoking) ☎ **Facilities:** STV FTV WiFi ☇ ♨ ⚓ Xmas New Year **Conf:** Class 30 Board 22 Theatre 50 **Services:** Night porter **Parking:** 18
Notes: LB Civ Wed 58

FOLKESTONE
Kent   Map 7 TR23

Best Western Clifton Hotel

BW Best Western.

★★★ 76% HOTEL

tel: 01303 851231 **The Leas, 1–6 Clifton Gardens CT20 2EB**
email: reservations@thecliftonhotel.com **web:** www.thecliftonhotel.com
dir: *M20 junction 13, 0.25 mile west of town centre on A259.*

This hotel is located right in the centre of Folkestone on the famous Leas with its elevated views of the English Channel. The stylish and modern public areas of the hotel offer plenty of space for guest relaxation. There is a bar and restaurant as well as conference and event facilities. The comfortable bedrooms and bathrooms are traditional in style.

Rooms: 80 (5 family) **Facilities:** FTV WiFi ☇ Xmas New Year **Conf:** Class 30 Board 30 Theatre 80 **Services:** Lift

The Southcliff Hotel

★★ 72% METRO HOTEL

tel: 01303 850075 **22-26 The Leas CT20 2DY**
email: sales@thesouthcliff.co.uk **web:** www.thesouthcliff.co.uk
dir: *M20 junction 13, follow signs for The Leas. Left at roundabout into Sandgate Road, right into Shakespeare Terrace, right at end of road, hotel on right.*

Located on the town's panoramic promenade with a bird's eye view of the sea, this historical Victorian hotel is perfectly located for cross channel connections and is

F

only minutes from the town centre. The bedrooms are spacious and airy with some boasting balconies and sea views. Enjoy a freshly prepared breakfast in the spacious breakfast room on the lower ground floor or relax in the bar. The front lounge is perfect to peruse newspapers or get stuck into a book. Plenty of street parking is available.

Rooms: 68 ✆ **S** fr £29.50 **D** fr £49* **Facilities:** FTV WiFi ↕ **Conf:** Class 120 Board 50 Theatre 200 **Services:** Lift Night porter **Notes:** No children

Premier Inn Folkestone (Channel Tunnel)

BUDGET HOTEL

tel: 0871 527 8400 (Calls cost 13p per minute plus your phone company's access charge) **Cherry Garden Lane CT19 4AP**
web: www.premierinn.com
dir: *M20 junction 13. Follow Folkestone, A20 signs. At lights turn right, hotel on right.*

High quality, budget accommodation ideal for both families and business travellers. Spacious, en suite bedrooms feature free WiFi and tea and coffee making facilities, and in most hotels, Freeview TV is also available. The adjacent family restaurant features a wide and varied menu.

Rooms: 81

| FOREST ROW | Map 6 TQ43 |
| East Sussex | |

INSPECTOR'S CHOICE

Ashdown Park Hotel & Country Club
★★★★ HOTEL

tel: 01342 824988 **Wych Cross RH18 5JR**
email: reservations@ashdownpark.com **web:** www.ashdownpark.com
dir: *A264 to East Grinstead, then A22 to Eastbourne. 3 miles south of Forest Row at Wych Cross lights. Left to Hartfield, hotel on right 0.75 mile.*

Situated in 186 acres of landscaped gardens and parkland, this impressive country house enjoys a peaceful countryside setting in the heart of the Ashdown Forest. Bedrooms are individually styled and decorated. Public rooms include a restored 18th-century chapel, ideal for exclusive meetings and wedding parties, plus three drawing rooms, a cocktail bar and the award-winning Anderida

Restaurant. The extensive indoor and outdoor leisure facilities include the Country Club and Spa plus an 18-hole, par 3 golf course and driving range.

Ashdown Park Hotel & Country Club

Rooms: 106 (12 family) (16 GF) ✆ **D** fr £162 (including breakfast)*
Facilities: Spa FTV WiFi ↕ HL ⊛ ↧ 18 ⊝ ⊛ Gym Aerobics Snooker clay pigeon Archery Falconry Cycling Xmas New Year **Conf:** Class 100 Board 40 Theatre 160
Services: Night porter **Parking:** 200 **Notes:** Civ Wed 150

| FOWEY | Map 2 SX15 |
| Cornwall & Isles Of Scilly | |

Fowey Hall

AA Advertised ⊛⊛

tel: 01726 833866 **LFH (Fowey Hall) Ltd, Hanson Drive PL23 1ET**
email: info@foweyhallhotel.co.uk **web:** www.foweyhallhotel.co.uk
dir: *M5, A30 turn off at Bodmin, follow signs to Lostwithiel and Fowey.*

Built in 1899, this listed mansion looks out on to the English Channel. The imaginatively designed bedrooms offer charm, individuality and sumptuous comfort; the Garden Wing rooms add an extra dimension to a stay here. The beautifully appointed public rooms include the wood-panelled dining room where accomplished cuisine is served. This is a very family friendly hotel with a crèche, baby sitting and listening services, plus many other facilities for children. The luxury spa includes a swimming pool, treatment rooms and a sun deck with a glorious view.

Rooms: 36 (8 annexe) (30 family) (10 GF) **Facilities:** Spa FTV WiFi ↕ ⊛ Free crèche for children of 0–8 years Xmas New Year **Conf:** Class 20 Board 20 Theatre 40
Services: Night porter **Parking:** 40 **Notes:** Civ Wed 120

| FRADDON | Map 2 SW95 |
| Cornwall & Isles Of Scilly | |

Premier Inn Newquay (A30/Fraddon)

BUDGET HOTEL

tel: 0871 527 8816 (Calls cost 13p per minute plus your phone company's access charge) **Penhale Round TR9 6NA**
web: www.premierinn.com
dir: *On A30, 2 miles south of Indian Queens.*

High quality, budget accommodation ideal for both families and business travellers. Spacious, en suite bedrooms feature free WiFi and tea and coffee making facilities, and in most hotels, Freeview TV is also available. The adjacent family restaurant features a wide and varied menu.

Rooms: 65

F

FRANKBY
Merseyside   Map 15 SJ28

Hillbark Hotel & Spa

★★★★★ 86% ◉◉ ☷ HOTEL

tel: 0151 625 2400 **Royden Park CH48 1NP**
email: enquiries@hillbarkhotel.co.uk **web:** www.hillbarkhotel.co.uk
dir: M53 junction 3, A552 Upton, right onto A551 Arrowe Park Road. 0.6 mile at lights left into Arrowe Brook Road. 0.5 mile on left.

Originally built in 1891 on Bidston Hill, this Elizabethan-style mansion was actually moved, brick by brick, to its current site in 1931. The house now sits in a 250-acre woodland estate and enjoys delightful views towards the River Dee and to hills in north Wales. Bedrooms are luxuriously furnished and well equipped, while elegant day rooms are richly styled. There is a choice of eating options, including a fine dining restaurant, and guests also have use of a spa.

Rooms: 18 (1 family) **Facilities:** Spa STV FTV WiFi ⊹ ❦ Gym Cinema Library Games room Children's play area ♫ Xmas New Year **Conf:** Class 300 Board 60 Theatre 750 **Services:** Lift Night porter **Parking:** 160 **Notes:** LB Civ Wed 500

FRESHWATER
Isle Of Wight   Map 5 SZ38

Albion Hotel

★★★ 75% HOTEL

tel: 01983 755755 **PO40 9RA**
email: enquiries@albionhotel.info **web:** www.sandringhamhotel.co.uk/albion

In an idyllic location on the island's southern heritage coast, the Albion Hotel is right on the seafront with stunning views of Freshwater Bay. The bedrooms and bathrooms are spacious and offer guests modern, comfortable accommodation; many rooms have balconies. Breakfast and dinner are served in the traditionally styled restaurant that also enjoys the lovely views.

Rooms: 40 **Facilities:** ⊗ Xmas **Conf:** Class 30 Board 40 Theatre 60 **Parking:** 30

FROME
Somerset   Map 4 ST74

Premier Inn Frome

BUDGET HOTEL   Premier Inn

tel: 0871 527 8404 (Calls cost 13p per minute plus your phone company's access charge) **Commerce Park, Jenson Avenue BA11 2LD**
web: www.premierinn.com
dir: M4 junction 18, A46 follow Warminster and Frome signs. Hotel off A361 (Frome bypass) in Commerce Park.

High quality, budget accommodation ideal for both families and business travellers. Spacious, en suite bedrooms feature free WiFi and tea and coffee making facilities, and in most hotels, Freeview TV is also available. The adjacent family restaurant features a wide and varied menu.

Rooms: 119

GARSTANG
Lancashire   Map 18 SD44

Best Western Garstang Country Hotel & Golf Centre

★★★ 77% HOTEL

tel: 01995 600100 **Garstang Road, Bowgreave PR3 1YE**
email: reception@garstanghotelandgolf.com **web:** www.garstanghotelandgolf.com
dir: M6 junction 32 take 1st right after Shell garage on A6 onto B6430. 1 mile, hotel on left.

This smart, purpose-built hotel enjoys a peaceful location alongside its own 18-hole golf course. Comfortable and spacious bedrooms are well equipped for both business and leisure guests, while inviting public areas include quiet lounges, the Kingfisher Restaurant and the more informal Bradbeer Brasserie.

Rooms: 33 (17 GF) **Facilities:** STV FTV WiFi ⊹ ⅃ 18 Golf driving range Xmas New Year **Conf:** Class 150 Board 80 Theatre 250 **Services:** Lift Night porter **Parking:** 172 **Notes:** LB Civ Wed 200

GATESHEAD
Tyne & Wear   Map 21 NZ26

Ramada Encore Newcastle - Gateshead

★★★ 81% HOTEL

tel: 0191 481 3600 **Hawks Road, Gateshead Quays NE8 3AD**
email: enquiries@encorenewcastlegateshead.co.uk
web: www.encorenewcastlegateshead.co.uk
dir: Located Gateshead Quays.

This modern, purpose-built hotel is located at the Gateshead Quays. Bedrooms are well appointed and comfortable, with well-presented en suites. Public areas are open-plan with a relaxed all-day menu serving food in all locations. A small gym and off-road parking are added benefits.

Rooms: 200 (75 family) **S** fr £49 **D** fr £49* **Facilities:** FTV WiFi ⊹ HL Gym **Conf:** Class 14 Board 18 Theatre 20 **Services:** Lift Night porter **Parking:** 70 **Notes:** LB

Premier Inn Newcastle (Metro Centre)

Premier Inn 🌙

BUDGET HOTEL

tel: 0871 527 8792 (Calls cost 13p per minute plus your phone company's access charge) **Derwent Haugh Road, Swalwell NE16 3BL**
web: www.premierinn.com
dir: From A1and A694 junction into Derwent Haugh Road. 1 mile north of Metro Centre.

High quality, budget accommodation ideal for both families and business travellers. Spacious, en suite bedrooms feature free WiFi and tea and coffee making facilities, and in most hotels, Freeview TV is also available. The adjacent family restaurant features a wide and varied menu.

Rooms: 72

Premier Inn Newcastle South

BUDGET HOTEL

tel: 0871 527 8806 (Calls cost 13p per minute plus your phone company's access charge) **Lobley Hill Road NE11 9NA**
web: www.premierinn.com
dir: A1 onto A692.

Rooms: 42

Premier Inn Newcastle (Team Valley)

BUDGET HOTEL

tel: 0871 527 8794 (Calls cost 13p per minute plus your phone company's access charge) **Maingate, Kingsway North NE11 0BE**
web: www.premierinn.com
dir: A1 onto B1426 signed Team Valley (southbound) or Teams/Consett (northbound). Take Gateshead exit at roundabout. At bottom of hill straight on at roundabout. Hotel opposite.

Rooms: 115

GATWICK AIRPORT	Map 6 TQ24
West Sussex	

See also **Dorking, East Grinstead and Reigate**

INSPECTOR'S CHOICE

Langshott Manor

★★★★ ◉◉◉ COUNTRY HOUSE HOTEL

SMALL LUXURY HOTELS OF THE WORLD

tel: 01293 786680 **Langshott Lane RH6 9LN**
email: admin@langshottmanor.com **web:** www.langshottmanor.com
dir: From A23 take Ladbroke Road, off roundabout to Langshott, after 0.75 mile hotel on right.

On the outskirts of Horley, this charming timber-framed Tudor manor house is set amidst beautifully landscaped grounds with an ancient moat. The stylish public areas feature a choice of inviting lounges with polished oak panelling, exposed beams and crackling log fires. Each bedroom – whether in the manor itself or in one of three mews buildings in the grounds – has been designed with flair and imagination. Expect sumptuous furnishings, Egyptian linens, TVs and bathrooms with deep baths and power showers. The Mulberry Restaurant overlooks a picturesque pond and offers an imaginative menu.

Rooms: 22 (15 annexe) (2 family) (8 GF) S fr £109.48 **D** fr £109.48*
Facilities: FTV WiFi Xmas New Year **Conf:** Class 20 Board 22 Theatre 40
Services: Night porter **Parking:** 25 **Notes:** LB Civ Wed 60

Sofitel London Gatwick

★★★★ 79% ◉◉ HOTEL

tel: 01293 567070 **North Terminal RH6 0PH**
email: slg@sofitelgatwick.com **web:** www.sofitelgatwick.com
dir: M23 junction 9, follow to 2nd roundabout. Hotel straight ahead.

One of the closest to the airport, this modern, purpose-built hotel is located only minutes from the terminals. Bedrooms are contemporary and all are air-conditioned. Guests have a choice of eating options including a French-style café, a brasserie and an oriental restaurant.

Rooms: 518 (19 family) **Facilities:** FTV WiFi Gym **Conf:** Class 150 Board 90 Theatre 300 **Services:** Lift Night porter Air con **Parking:** 565

Holiday Inn London Gatwick Worth

Holiday Inn

★★★★ 79% HOTEL

tel: 01293 884806 **Crabbet Park, Turners Hill Road RH10 4SS**
email: info@higatwickworth.co.uk **web:** www.higatwickworth.co.uk
dir: M23 junction 10/A264 Copthorne Way at roundabout last exit towards Three Bridges. 1st left along Old Hollow, right at end of lane then 1st right into Crabbet Park.

This purpose-built hotel is ideally placed for access to Gatwick Airport. The bedrooms are spacious and suitably appointed with good facilities. Public areas consist of a light and airy bar area and a brasserie-style restaurant offering good value meals. Guests have use of the superb leisure club next door.

Rooms: 118 (39 family) (56 GF) **Facilities:** FTV WiFi HL Use of gym and pool next door (chargeable) Xmas New Year **Conf:** Class 80 Board 80 Theatre 250 **Services:** Lift Night porter Air con **Parking:** 150 **Notes:** Civ Wed 60

Premier Inn Gatwick Airport North

BUDGET HOTEL

tel: 0871 527 9354 (Calls cost 13p per minute plus your phone company's access charge) **Crossway, Gatwick North Terminal RH6 0PH**
web: www.premierinn.com
dir: M23 junction 9. Follow signs for Gatwick North Terminal, at North Terminal roundabout enter at Arrivals Road (2nd exit), turn right onto Northway (Drop Off point), hotel is on right.

High quality, budget accommodation ideal for both families and business travellers. Spacious, en suite bedrooms feature free WiFi and tea and coffee making facilities, and in most hotels, Freeview TV is also available. The adjacent family restaurant features a wide and varied menu.

Rooms: 701

Premier Inn Gatwick Airport South

BUDGET HOTEL

tel: 0871 527 8408 (Calls cost 13p per minute plus your phone company's access charge) **London Road, Lowfield Heath RH10 9ST**
web: www.premierinn.com
dir: M23 junction 9a towards North Terminal roundabout. Follow A23 and Crawley signs. Hotel in 2 miles.

Rooms: 105

G

GATWICK AIRPORT *continued*

Premier Inn Gatwick Crawley Town (Goffs Park)

BUDGET HOTEL

tel: 0871 527 8414 (Calls cost 13p per minute plus your phone company's access charge) **45 Goffs Park Road RH11 8AX**
web: www.premierinn.com
dir: *M23 junction 11, A23 towards Crawley. At 2nd roundabout take 3rd exit for town centre, then 2nd right into Goffs Park Road.*

Rooms: 48

Premier Inn Gatwick Crawley Town West

BUDGET HOTEL

tel: 0871 527 8412 (Calls cost 13p per minute plus your phone company's access charge) **Crawley Avenue, Gossops Green RH10 8BA**
web: www.premierinn.com
dir: *M23 junction 11, A23 towards Crawley and Gatwick Airport.*

Rooms: 83

Premier Inn London Gatwick Airport A23

BUDGET HOTEL

tel: 0871 527 8406 (Calls cost 13p per minute plus your phone company's access charge) **Longbridge Way, North Terminal RH6 0NX**
web: www.premierinn.com
dir: *M23 junction 9/9A towards North Terminal, at roundabout take 3rd exit, hotel on right.*

Rooms: 220

Premier Inn London Gatwick Airport East

BUDGET HOTEL

tel: 0871 527 8410 (Calls cost 13p per minute plus your phone company's access charge) **Balcombe Road, Worth RH10 3NL**
web: www.premierinn.com
dir: *M23 junction 10, B2036 south towards Crawley.*

Rooms: 42

Premier Inn London Gatwick Manor Royal

BUDGET HOTEL

tel: 0871 527 9214 (Calls cost 13p per minute plus your phone company's access charge) **Crawley Business Quarter, Fleming Way RH10 9DF**
web: www.premierinn.com
dir: *M23 junction 10, A2011 (Crawley Avenue). At roundabout 4th exit onto A23 (London Road), at roundabout right into Fleming Way. Hotel 300 yards on left.*

Rooms: 204

Arora Hotel Gatwick

AA Advertised

tel: 01293 530000 **Southgate Avenue, Southgate RH10 6LW**
email: gatwick@arorahotels.com **web:** www.arorahotels.com
dir: *M23 junction 10 then A2011 to Crawley. At 1st roundabout take 2nd exit towards town centre, at 2nd roundabout take 1st exit towards the County Mall. At both sets of lights proceed straight over; the County Mall on right, go straight under railway bridge, hotel on right.*

The Arora Hotel Gatwick/Crawley is situated in the heart of the town centre, perfectly placed for easy access to M23, A23 and M25; it has direct access to Crawley train station, and is a short journey from Gatwick Airport by direct bus transfer. Accommodation is stylish and there are excellent meeting, conference, training and banqueting facilities. Meals and drinks can be taken in The Grill Restaurant, a traditional pub or the bar. There is also an internet café, a luxurious health and fitness club, and on-site parking.

Rooms: 432 (120 annexe) (15 family) (24 GF) S fr £60 **D** fr £60* **Facilities:** FTV WiFi HL Gym Treatment room Xmas **Conf:** Class 150 Board 60 Theatre 270 **Services:** Lift Night porter Air con **Parking:** 245 **Notes:** LB Civ Wed 270

GERRARDS CROSS
Buckinghamshire
Map 6 TQ08

The Bull Hotel

★★★★ 78% HOTEL

tel: 01753 885995 **Oxford Road SL9 7PA**
email: bull@sarova.com **web:** www.sarova.com
dir: *M40 junction 2 follow Beaconsfield on A355. After 0.5 mile 2nd exit at roundabout signed A40 Gerrards Cross for 2 miles. The Bull is on right.*

Dating from the 17th-century, this former coaching inn has certainly expanded over the years and today offers smart, well-equipped bedrooms in a range of sizes. Public areas include the popular bar and Beeches Restaurant, serving a wide variety of dishes to suit all tastes. In addition, there is the informal Jack Shrimpton bar offering snacks and bar meals. Attractive gardens and a good range of function rooms make this a popular wedding and events venue.

Rooms: 150 (15 family) (19 GF) S fr £80 **D** fr £90 (including breakfast)*
Facilities: FTV WiFi Use of private leisure facilities Xmas New Year
Conf: Class 108 Board 40 Theatre 180 **Services:** Lift Night porter **Parking:** 150
Notes: Civ Wed 114

GILLINGHAM
Kent
Map 7 TQ76

Premier Inn Chatham/Gillingham (Victory Pier)

BUDGET HOTEL

tel: 0871 527 9510 (Calls cost 13p per minute plus your phone company's access charge) **Blake Avenue ME7 1GB**
web: www.premierinn.com
dir: *From A289 (Pier Road) in Gillingham, at lights, into Pegasus Way. 1st left.*

High quality, budget accommodation ideal for both families and business travellers. Spacious, en suite bedrooms feature free WiFi and tea and coffee making facilities, and in most hotels, Freeview TV is also available. The adjacent family restaurant features a wide and varied menu.

Rooms: 80

Premier Inn Gillingham Business Park

Premier Inn

BUDGET HOTEL

tel: 0871 527 8416 (Calls cost 13p per minute plus your phone company's access charge) **Will Adams Way ME8 6BY**
web: www.premierinn.com
dir: *M2 junction 44, A278 to A2. Left at Tesco. Hotel at next roundabout.*

Rooms: 76

Premier Inn Gillingham/Rainham

Premier Inn

BUDGET HOTEL

tel: 0871 527 9268 (Calls cost 13p per minute plus your phone company's access charge) **High Street, Rainham ME8 7JE**
web: www.premierinn.com
dir: *M25 junction 2 (Canterbury/Dover/A2), A2 to M2 (Dover). Exit at junction 4 (Rainham/ Medway Tunnel), straight on at 2 roundabouts. At 3rd roundabout take 3rd exit (Rainham High Street). Hotel on right at 3rd lights.*

Rooms: 26

GIRTON
Cambridgeshire   **Map 12 TL46**

Premier Inn Cambridge North (Girton)

Premier Inn

BUDGET HOTEL

tel: 0871 527 8188 (Calls cost 13p per minute plus your phone company's access charge) **Huntingdon Road CB3 0DR**
web: www.premierinn.com
dir: *A14 junction 31 follow signs towards Cambridge. Pass BP garage, next right. Hotel adjacent to Traveller's Rest Beefeater.*

High quality, budget accommodation ideal for both families and business travellers. Spacious, en suite bedrooms feature free WiFi and tea and coffee making facilities, and in most hotels, Freeview TV is also available. The adjacent family restaurant features a wide and varied menu.

Rooms: 20

GLASTONBURY
Somerset   **Map 4 ST53**

Premier Inn Glastonbury

Premier Inn

BUDGET HOTEL

tel: 0871 527 9398 (Calls cost 13p per minute plus your phone company's access charge) **Morland Road BA6 9FW**
web: www.premierinn.com
dir: *From A361 and A39 roundabout junction (southwest of Glastonbury) take A39 towards Street. Right at lights into Morlands Enterprise Park. Left at 1st roundabout.*

High quality, budget accommodation ideal for both families and business travellers. Spacious, en suite bedrooms feature free WiFi and tea and coffee making facilities, and in most hotels, Freeview TV is also available. The adjacent family restaurant features a wide and varied menu.

Rooms: 78

GLENRIDDING
Cumbria   **Map 18 NY31**

HIGHLY RECOMMENDED

Inn on the Lake

LAKE DISTRICT HOTELS

★★★★ 84% HOTEL

tel: 017684 82444 **Lake Ullswater CA11 0PE**
email: innonthelake@lakedistricthotels.net
web: www.lakedistricthotels.net/innonthelake
dir: *M6 juncton 40, A66 to Keswick. At roundabout take A592 to Ullswater Lake. Along lake to Glenridding. Hotel on left on entering village.*

In a picturesque lakeside setting, this restored Victorian hotel is a popular leisure destination as well as catering for weddings and conferences. Superb views can be enjoyed from the bedrooms and from the garden terrace where afternoon teas are served during warmer months. There is a popular pub in the grounds, and moorings for yachts are available to guests. Sailing tuition can be arranged.

Rooms: 47 (20 family) (1 GF) ♠ **Facilities:** FTV WiFi ♨ Gym Sauna 9-hole pitch and putt course Xmas New Year **Conf:** Class 42 Board 30 Theatre 100 **Services:** Lift Night porter **Parking:** 100 **Notes:** Civ Wed 110

Glenridding Hotel

★★★ 81% HOTEL

tel: 01768 482289 **CA11 0PB**
email: stay@theglenriddinghotel.com **web:** www.theglenriddinghotel.com
dir: *Northbound M6 junction 36, A591 Windermere then A592, for 14 miles. Southbound M6 junction 40, A592 for 13 miles.*

Like a phoenix rising from the ashes, the Glenridding Hotel has reopened after a massive refurbishment programme which shows great results. This friendly hotel benefits from a picturesque location in the village centre, and many rooms have fine views of the lake and fells. The public areas are extensive, and include a choice of dining options: the Garden Room, Let it Brew café and the fantastic Beckside Bar with great outside seating beside a babbling beck. Leisure facilities are available along with a conference room and a garden function room.

Rooms: 36 (7 family) (8 GF) **Facilities:** STV WiFi ⌕ Spa bath Sauna Snooker Table tennis Xmas New Year **Conf:** Class 30 Board 24 Theatre 30 **Services:** Lift **Parking:** 30 **Notes:** Civ Wed 120

GLOSSOP
Derbyshire   **Map 16 SK09**

Wind in the Willows Hotel

★★ 85% COUNTRY HOUSE HOTEL

tel: 01457 868001 **Derbyshire Level SK13 7PT**
email: info@windinthewillows.co.uk **web:** www.windinthewillows.co.uk
dir: *1 mile east of Glossop on A57, turn right opposite Royal Oak, hotel 400 yards on right.*

This impressive house sits in peaceful grounds with lovely views of the Peak District National Park. Individually furnished bedrooms are in keeping with the Victorian style of the house. Beautiful original oak panelling and crackling log fires add to the charm of the lounges and dining room. There is also a conference suite that is perfect for meetings, private dining or special occasions.

Rooms: 12 ♠ **S** fr £85 **D** fr £149 (including breakfast)* **Facilities:** FTV WiFi ♨ Xmas New Year **Conf:** Class 12 Board 16 Theatre 40 **Parking:** 16 **Notes:** LB No children 10 years

GLOUCESTER
Gloucestershire

Map 10 SO81

Hatherley Manor Hotel & Spa
★★★★ 76%  HOTEL

tel: 01452 730217 **Down Hatherley Lane GL2 9QA**
email: reservations@hatherleymanor.com **web:** www.hatherleymanor.com
dir: A38 into Down Hatherley Lane, signed. Hotel 600 yards on left.

Within easy striking distance of the M5, Gloucester, Cheltenham and the Cotswolds, this stylish 17th-century manor, set in attractive grounds, remains popular with both business and leisure guests. Bedrooms are well appointed and offer contemporary comforts. A particularly impressive range of meeting and function rooms is available.

Rooms: 50 (5 family) (18 GF) ✿ **Facilities:** FTV WiFi ⌿ Xmas New Year **Conf:** Class 90 Board 75 Theatre 400 **Services:** Night porter **Parking:** 250 **Notes:** Civ Wed 300

Hatton Court
★★★★ 76%  COUNTRY HOUSE HOTEL

tel: 01452 617412 **Upton Hill, Upton St Leonards GL4 8DE**
email: res@hatton-court.co.uk **web:** www.hatton-court.co.uk
dir: From Gloucester on B4073 Painswick Road. Hotel at top of hill on right.

Built in the style of a 17th-century Cotswold manor house and set in seven acres of well-kept gardens, this hotel is popular with both business and leisure guests. It stands at the top of Upton Hill and commands truly spectacular views of the Severn Valley. The bedrooms, including a four-poster room, are comfortable and tastefully furnished with many extra facilities. The elegant Tara Restaurant offers varied menus, and outdoor seating in summer; there is also a bar and foyer lounge.

Rooms: 45 (28 annexe) (6 family) ✿ **Facilities:** FTV WiFi HL ⌿ Gym Xmas New Year **Conf:** Class 100 Board 60 Theatre 200 **Services:** Night porter **Parking:** 80 **Notes:** LB Civ Wed 120

Hallmark Hotel Gloucester
★★★★ 74% HOTEL

tel: 0330 028 3408 **Matson Lane, Robinswood Hill GL4 6EA**
email: gloucester@hallmarkhotels.co.uk **web:** www.hallmarkhotels.co.uk
dir: A40 towards Gloucester onto A38. 1st exit at 4th roundabout (Painswick Road). Right into Matson Lane.

Ideally located for exploring the Cotswolds and Gloucester, this hotel offers well-appointed bedrooms and relaxing public areas. The large leisure club has a well-equipped gym, squash courts and pool. Complimentary WiFi is available throughout.

Rooms: 95 (6 family) (21 GF) ✿ **Facilities:** Spa FTV WiFi ⌿ ⛳ Gym Squash Beauty salon Xmas New Year **Conf:** Class 150 Board 18 Theatre 220 **Services:** Night porter **Parking:** 200 **Notes:** Civ Wed 120

Mercure Gloucester, Bowden Hall Hotel
★★★★ 73% COUNTRY HOUSE HOTEL

tel: 01452 614121 & 0844 815 9077 (Calls cost 7p per minute plus your phone company's access charge) **Bondend Lane, Upton St Leonards GL4 8ED**
email: info@mercuregloucester.co.uk **web:** www.mercuregloucester.co.uk
dir: A417/A38/Gloucester. At roundabout take 2nd exit. At 2nd lights left onto Abbeymead Avenue/Metz Way. 1.5 miles, 3rd left onto Upton Lane, left into Bondend Road, then left into Bondend Lane. Hotel at end.

Conveniently located a short distance from the M5, the hotel is set in delightful grounds and is an ideal venue for weddings, banquets and meetings, or for a quiet

break. Bedrooms are spacious and nicely appointed and many have lovely views of the grounds. Guests can choose to dine in the restaurant or bar.

Rooms: 72 ✿ **D** fr £89* **Facilities:** FTV WiFi ⌿ HL Xmas New Year **Conf:** Class 70 Board 35 Theatre 180 **Parking:** 180 **Notes:** Civ Wed 200

Premier Inn Gloucester (Barnwood)

BUDGET HOTEL

tel: 0871 527 8456 (Calls cost 13p per minute plus your phone company's access charge) **Barnwood GL4 3HR**
web: www.premierinn.com
dir: M5 junction 11, A40 towards Gloucester. At 1st roundabout A417 towards Cirencester, at next roundabout take 4th exit.

High quality, budget accommodation ideal for both families and business travellers. Spacious, en suite bedrooms feature free WiFi and tea and coffee making facilities, and in most hotels, Freeview TV is also available. The adjacent family restaurant features a wide and varied menu.

Rooms: 83

Premier Inn Gloucester Business Park

BUDGET HOTEL

tel: 0871 527 8462 (Calls cost 13p per minute plus your phone company's access charge) **Gloucester Business Park, Brockworth GL3 4AJ**
web: www.premierinn.com
dir: M5 junction 11a, A417 towards Cirencester. At Brockworth Roundabout follow Gloucester Business Park signs, onto dual carriageway (Valiant Way). At next roundabout left into Delta Way. Hotel adjacent to Tesco.

Rooms: 48

Premier Inn Gloucester (Little Witcombe)

BUDGET HOTEL

tel: 0871 527 8458 (Calls cost 13p per minute plus your phone company's access charge) **Witcombe GL3 4SS**
web: www.premierinn.com
dir: M5 junction 11a, A417 signed Cirencester. At 1st exit turn right onto A46 towards Stroud and Witcombe. Left at next roundabout by Crosshands pub.

Rooms: 59

Premier Inn Gloucester (Longford)

BUDGET HOTEL

tel: 0871 527 8460 (Calls cost 13p per minute plus your phone company's access charge) **Tewkesbury Road, Longford GL2 9BE**
web: www.premierinn.com
dir: M5 junction 11, A40 towards Gloucester and Ross-on-Wye. Hotel on A38 towards Gloucester.

Rooms: 60

Premier Inn Gloucester (Twigworth)

BUDGET HOTEL

tel: 0871 527 8464 (Calls cost 13p per minute plus your phone company's access charge) **Tewkesbury Road, Twigworth GL2 9PG**
web: www.premierinn.com
dir: On A38, 1 mile north from junction with A40.

Rooms: 50

G

GOATHLAND
North Yorkshire   Map 19 NZ80

HIGHLY RECOMMENDED

Mallyan Spout Hotel

★★★ 87% ◉ COUNTRY HOUSE HOTEL

tel: 01947 896486 **YO22 5AN**
email: info@mallyanspout.co.uk **web:** www.mallyanspout.co.uk
dir: A169 Pickering to Whitby. Take Goathland turn, hotel opposite St Mary's Church.

This Grade II listed building is set in the charming village of Goathland, which is well known as the setting of the village of Aidensfield in the TV series, *Heartbeat*. The hotel is privately owned and full of character and charm, and the popular seaside resort of Whitby is just a short drive away. Bedrooms provide comfortable accommodation, and the public areas include three lounges, some with open fires, and a bar boasting a selection of real ales. The restaurant serves a good mix of modern and traditional dishes.

Rooms: 20 (4 family) ⦅ **D** fr £120 (including breakfast)* **Facilities:** FTV WiFi New Year **Conf:** Class 50 Board 35 Theatre 50 **Services:** Night porter **Parking:** 24 **Notes:** LB Closed 23-27 December Civ Wed 65

GODALMING
Surrey   Map 6 SU94

Premier Inn Godalming

BUDGET HOTEL   Premier Inn

tel: 0871 527 8466 (Calls cost 13p per minute plus your phone company's access charge) **Guildford Road GU7 3BX**
web: www.premierinn.com
dir: Exit A3 onto A3000 signed Godalming. 1 mile to roundabout, turn right into Guildford Road towards Godalming. Hotel on left in 500 yards.

High quality, budget accommodation ideal for both families and business travellers. Spacious, en suite bedrooms feature free WiFi and tea and coffee making facilities, and in most hotels, Freeview TV is also available. The adjacent family restaurant features a wide and varied menu.

Rooms: 16

GOLANT
Cornwall & Isles Of Scilly   Map 2 SX15

Cormorant Hotel & Restaurant

★★★ 82% ◉◉ HOTEL

tel: 01726 833426 **PL23 1LL**
email: relax@cormoranthotel.co.uk **web:** www.cormoranthotel.co.uk
dir: A390 onto B3269 signed Fowey. In 3 miles left to Golant, through village to end of road, hotel on right.

This hotel focuses on traditional hospitality, attentive service and good food. All the bedrooms enjoy views of the river, and guests can expect goose down duvets, digital TVs and free WiFi access. Breakfast and lunch may be taken on the terrace which overlooks the river.

Rooms: 14 (4 GF) ⦅ **D** fr £80 (including breakfast)* **Facilities:** FTV WiFi ⦆ Xmas New Year **Parking:** 20 **Notes:** LB No children 16 years

GOMERSAL
West Yorkshire   Map 19 SE22

Gomersal Park Hotel

★★★ 79% HOTEL

tel: 01274 869386 **Moor Lane BD19 4LJ**
email: enquiries@gomersalparkhotel.com **web:** www.gomersalparkhotel.com
dir: A62 to Huddersfield. At junction with A65, by Greyhound Pub right, after 1 mile take 1st right after Oakwell Hall.

Constructed around a 19th-century house, this stylish, modern hotel enjoys a peaceful location and pleasant grounds. Deep sofas ensure comfort in the open-plan lounge, and the Massimo Italian Restaurant offers a wide choice of freshly prepared meals. The well-equipped bedrooms are contemporary and comfortable. Extensive public areas include a fantastic, newly built leisure spa and a wide variety of air-conditioned conference and function suites.

Rooms: 86 (3 family) (32 GF) ⦅ **S** fr £99 **D** fr £109 (including breakfast)* **Facilities:** Spa FTV WiFi ⦆ ⦆ Gym Sauna **Conf:** Class 130 Board 60 Theatre 250 **Services:** Lift Night porter **Parking:** 150 **Notes:** LB Civ Wed 200

GOODRINGTON

See **Paignton**

GOODWOOD
West Sussex   Map 6 SU81

The Goodwood Hotel

★★★★ 81% ◉◉ HOTEL

tel: 01243 775537 **PO18 0QB**
email: reservations@goodwood.com **web:** www.goodwood.com/estate/the-goodwood-hotel
dir: Off A285, 3 miles northeast of Chichester.

Set at the centre of the 12,000-acre Goodwood Estate, this attractive hotel boasts extensive indoor and outdoor leisure facilities, along with a range of meeting rooms plus conference and banqueting facilities. Bedrooms are furnished to a consistently high standard, including individually decorated character rooms located in the old coaching inn; and garden rooms, each with a patio. Eating options include The Farmer, Butcher, Chef Restaurant and Bar which sources produce extensively from the estate's very own farm, and The Goodwood Bar and Grill. The Kennels is a private sporting members' clubhouse.

Rooms: 91 (15 family) (31 GF) ⦅ **Facilities:** Spa STV FTV WiFi ⦆ ⦆ ⦆ 18 ⦆ Gym Golf Driving range Sauna Steam room Fitness studio Xmas New Year **Conf:** Class 60 Board 40 Theatre 150 **Services:** Night porter **Parking:** 150 **Notes:** Civ Wed 120

GOOLE
East Riding of Yorkshire   Map 17 SE72

Premier Inn Goole

BUDGET HOTEL   Premier Inn

tel: 0871 527 8468 (Calls cost 13p per minute plus your phone company's access charge) **Rawcliffe Road, Airmyn DN14 8JS**
web: www.premierinn.com
dir: M62 junction 36, A614 signed Rawcliffe. Hotel immediately on left.

High quality, budget accommodation ideal for both families and business travellers. Spacious, en suite bedrooms feature free WiFi and tea and coffee making facilities, and in most hotels, Freeview TV is also available. The adjacent family restaurant features a wide and varied menu.

Rooms: 73

GORDANO SERVICE AREA (M5)
Somerset   Map 4 ST57

Days Inn Bristol West - M5   WELCOMEBREAK

AA Advertised

tel: 01275 373709 **BS20 7XG**
email: gordano.hotel@welcomebreak.co.uk **web:** www.welcomebreak.co.uk
dir: *M5 junction 19, follow signs for Gordano Services.*

This modern building offers accommodation in smart, spacious and well-equipped bedrooms, suitable for families and business travellers, and all with en suite bathrooms. Continental breakfast is available and other refreshments may be taken at the nearby family restaurant.

Rooms: 60 (52 family) (29 GF) (8 smoking) **Facilities:** FTV WiFi ⟲ **Conf:** Board 10 **Parking:** 60

GORLESTON ON SEA
Norfolk   Map 13 TG50

The Pier Hotel
★★★ 86% HOTEL

tel: 01493 662631 **Harbourmouth, South Pier NR31 6PL**
email: bookings@pierhotelgorleston.co.uk **web:** www.pierhotelgorleston.co.uk
dir: *From A47 west of Great Yarmouth take A12 signed Lowestoft. At 3rd roundabout 1st left Beccles Road, signed Gorleston. At roundabout 2nd left Church Road. Next roundabout 1st left Baker Street. Right into Pier Plain, then Pier Walk to Pier Gardens.*

Ideally situated on the seafront, this hotel offers smartly appointed bedrooms that are thoughtfully equipped and have a good range of useful extras; some rooms have superb sea views. The public areas include a large restaurant and a conservatory, which leads to a terrace and bar.

Rooms: 21 (1 family) ⟋ **Facilities:** STV FTV WiFi ⟲ New Year **Services:** Night porter **Parking:** 25 **Notes:** LB

GOSFORTH
Cumbria   Map 18 NY00

Westlakes Hotel
★★★ 87% HOTEL

tel: 019467 25221 **CA20 1HP**
email: info@westlakeshotel.co.uk **web:** www.westlakeshotel.co.uk
dir: *From A595 take B5344 signed Seascale. Hotel entrance 1st right.*

Located amid the stunning scenery of the western lakes and within easy striking distance of a whole array of visitor attractions, Westlakes Hotel offers accommodation of a high standard, with many thoughtful extras provided. High quality food is served in the restaurant with relaxed and friendly service led by the hands-on owners and their team. There are excellent walking opportunities from this hotel.

Rooms: 10 (4 annexe) (1 GF) ⟋ **S** fr £100 **D** fr £100 (including breakfast)* **Facilities:** FTV WiFi **Conf:** Class 30 Board 30 Theatre 50 **Parking:** 50

GOSPORT
Hampshire   Map 5 SZ69

Premier Inn Gosport   Premier Inn

BUDGET HOTEL

tel: 0871 527 9436 (Calls cost 13p per minute plus your phone company's access charge) **Fareham Road PO13 0ZX**
web: www.premierinn.com
dir: *M27 junction 11 (westbound exit), at Wallington roundabout 1st exit onto A27 (Fareham Central Gosport and A32). At Quay Street roundabout left onto A32. At roundabout 2nd exit onto A32. Left at one-way system signed Gosport. Right at lights into Forrest Way, left into Holbrook, and Gosport Leisure Centre.*

High quality, budget accommodation ideal for both families and business travellers. Spacious, en suite bedrooms feature free WiFi and tea and coffee making facilities, and in most hotels, Freeview TV is also available. The adjacent family restaurant features a wide and varied menu.

Rooms: 99

GRANGE-OVER-SANDS
Cumbria   Map 18 SD47

Netherwood Hotel   CLASSIC BRITISH HOTELS
★★★ 76% HOTEL

tel: 015395 32552 **Lindale Road LA11 6ET**
email: enquiries@netherwood-hotel.co.uk **web:** www.netherwood-hotel.co.uk
dir: *On B5277 before station.*

This imposing hotel stands in terraced grounds, enjoys fine views of Morecambe Bay, and is also popular as a conference and wedding venue. Good levels of hospitality and service ensure all guests are well looked after. Bedrooms vary in size with the newer, refurbished rooms being bright and modern. Magnificent woodwork is a feature of the public areas.

Rooms: 34 (5 family) ⟋ **Facilities:** FTV WiFi ⟳ ⤳ Gym Steam room Fitness centre Xmas New Year **Conf:** Class 150 Board 60 Theatre 150 **Services:** Lift Night porter **Parking:** 100 **Notes:** LB Civ Wed 200

Cumbria Grand Hotel
★★★ 73% HOTEL

tel: 015395 32331 **LA11 6EN**
email: salescumbria@strathmorehotels.com **web:** www.strathmorehotels.com
dir: *M6 junction 36, A590 and follow Grange-over-Sands signs.*

Set within extensive grounds, this ever-improving, grand hotel offers fine views over Morecambe Bay. Public areas are pure nostalgia, and include comfortable lounges, a magnificent dining room, a fine ballroom, and conference suites. Bedrooms are comfortably equipped and some have views of the bay.

Rooms: 122 (10 family) (25 GF) ✿ S fr £35 D fr £75 (including breakfast)*
Facilities: STV WiFi ☺ Snooker and pool table Table tennis ♫ Xmas New Year
Conf: Class 80 Board 36 Theatre 160 **Services:** Lift Night porter **Parking:** 75
Notes: LB Civ Wed 100

INSPECTOR'S CHOICE

Clare House
★★ ◉ HOTEL

tel: 015395 33026 **Park Road LA11 7HQ**
email: info@clarehousehotel.co.uk **web:** www.clarehousehotel.co.uk
dir: A590 onto B5277, through Lindale into Grange, keep left, hotel 0.5 mile on left past Crown Hill and St Paul's Church.

A warm, genuine welcome awaits guests at this delightful hotel, proudly run by the Read family for over 40 years. Situated in its own secluded gardens, it provides a relaxed haven in which to enjoy the panoramic views across Morecambe Bay. The stylish bedrooms and public areas are comfortable and attractively furnished. Skilfully prepared dinners and hearty breakfasts are served in the elegant dining room.

Rooms: 18 (4 GF) ✿ S fr £98 D fr £196 (including breakfast & dinner)*
Facilities: FTV WiFi ☺ **Parking:** 18 **Notes:** Closed mid December to late March

GRANTHAM
Lincolnshire
Map 11 SK93

Premier Inn Grantham
Premier Inn
BUDGET HOTEL

tel: 0871 527 8470 (Calls cost 13p per minute plus your phone company's access charge) **A1/607 Junction, Harlaxton Road NG31 7UA**
web: www.premierinn.com
dir: A1 onto A607. Northbound: hotel on right. Southbound: under A1, hotel on left.

High quality, budget accommodation ideal for both families and business travellers. Spacious, en suite bedrooms feature free WiFi and tea and coffee making facilities, and in most hotels, Freeview TV is also available. The adjacent family restaurant features a wide and varied menu.

Rooms: 95

Stoke Rochford Hall
Premier | BEST WESTERN
Ⓤ

tel: 01476 530337 & 531217 **NG33 5EJ**
email: reception@stokerochfordhall.co.uk
web: www.bestwestern.co.uk/hotels/stoke-rochford-hall-bw-premier-collection-84238
dir: Phone for directions. Use NG33 5EB for sat nav.

Currently the rating for this establishment is not confirmed. This may be due to a change of ownership or because ot has only recently joined the AA rating scheme.

Rooms: 51 (31 annexe) (7 family) (36 GF) ✿ S fr £85 D fr £95 (including breakfast)*
Facilities: FTV WiFi ↕ HL ⊛ ☺ Gym Xmas New Year **Conf:** Class 80 Board 52
Theatre 300 **Services:** Lift Night porter **Parking:** 200 **Notes:** Civ Wed 150

GRASMERE
Cumbria
Map 18 NY30

HIGHLY RECOMMENDED

Forest Side
★★★★ 85% ◉◉◉◉ 🏵HOTEL

tel: 015394 35250 **Keswick Road LA22 9RN**
email: info@theforestside.com **web:** www.theforestside.com
dir: M6 junction 36, 1st exit at roundabout onto A590 to Grasmere. 2nd exit at mini-roundabout. Hotel 0.5 mile on right.

Located on the edge of Grasmere village, this former mansion house has been lovingly converted into a charming and relaxing hotel. Dinner is a must – the kitchen team working closely with local suppliers and also growing much of their own produce in the walled garden, or by foraging the local area. The 20 bedrooms have stunning views of the hills and countryside beyond.

Rooms: 20 (5 family) (2 GF) ✿ S fr £109 D fr £199 (including breakfast)*
Facilities: FTV WiFi ↕ Xmas New Year **Services:** Night porter **Parking:** 42
Notes: No children 8 years Civ Wed 60

HIGHLY RECOMMENDED

Rothay Garden Hotel
★★★★ 84% ◉◉ HOTEL

tel: 015394 35334 **Broadgate LA22 9RJ**
email: stay@rothaygarden.com **web:** www.rothaygarden.com
dir: A591, opposite Swan Hotel, into Grasmere, 300 yards on left.

Situated just on the edge of Grasmere village in two acres of riverside gardens, this stylishly designed hotel offers comfort and luxury. Bedrooms include five loft suites which are named after the fells they overlook, while upper floors have their own balconies. The Garden Spa is the perfect place to relax – it provides a steam room, sauna and heated, relaxation beds. The chic bar and lounges provide somewhere to unwind before dinner, which is served in the Garden Restaurant.

Rooms: 30 (3 family) (8 GF) ✿ S fr £120.50 D fr £161 (including breakfast)*
Facilities: Spa FTV WiFi ↕ HL Sauna Aromatherapy room Infra red loungers Spa pool Xmas New Year **Parking:** 35 **Notes:** LB No children 12 years

G

GRASMERE *continued*

HIGHLY RECOMMENDED

The Daffodil Hotel & Spa

★★★★ 83% HOTEL

tel: 015394 63550 **Keswick Road LA22 9PR**
email: stay@daffodilhotel.com **web:** www.daffodilhotel.com
dir: *M6 junction 36 then A591, past Windermere and Ambleside. Hotel on left on entering Grasmere.*

The Daffodil Hotel provides very high levels of service, comfort and luxury in a spectacular location on the edge of Grasmere. It's an easy walk both into the village and onto the local Wordsworth trail, and it is of course located in a hillwalker's paradise. Most bedrooms have either a lake or a valley view, and are equipped to high standards; several have private balconies.

Rooms: 78 (11 family) ☎ **D** fr £115 (including breakfast)* **Facilities:** Spa FTV WiFi ♨ HL Sauna Steam room Tepidarium Thermal pool Mud rasul room Xmas New Year **Conf:** Class 150 Board 32 Theatre 400 **Services:** Lift Night porter Air con **Parking:** 96 **Notes:** Civ Wed 200

HIGHLY RECOMMENDED

The Wordsworth Hotel & Spa

★★★★ 83% HOTEL

tel: 015394 35592 **Stock Lane LA22 9SW**
email: enquiry@thewordsworthhotel.co.uk **web:** www.thewordsworthhotel.co.uk
dir: *Off A591. In centre of village adjacent to St Oswald's Church.*

This historic hotel ideally situated in the heart of Grasmere provides high levels of style and luxury. The bedrooms are equipped with smart furnishings, quality accessories and comfortable beds with Egyptian cotton linen. Guests can enjoy fine dining in the modern Signature Restaurant which boasts stylish and elegant decor, while for a less formal dining experience, light meals and fine ales are offered in the Dove Bistro. The hotel has a heated swimming pool and the sauna and spa make the ideal place for relaxation.

Rooms: 38 (4 family) (3 GF) ☎ **Facilities:** Spa FTV WiFi ♨ ⊛ ⇟ Sauna Xmas New Year **Conf:** Class 80 Board 40 Theatre 120 **Services:** Lift Night porter **Parking:** 40 **Notes:** LB Civ Wed 100

HIGHLY RECOMMENDED

Oak Bank Hotel

★★★ 87% SMALL HOTEL

tel: 015394 35217 **Broadgate LA22 9TA**
email: info@lakedistricthotel.co.uk **web:** www.lakedistricthotel.co.uk
dir: *Northbound: M6 junction 36 onto A591 to Windermere, Ambleside, then Grasmere. Southbound: M6 junction 40 onto A66 to Keswick, A591 to Grasmere.*

Privately owned and personally-run by friendly proprietors, Oak Bank Hotel is a Victorian house in the very heart of the English lakes. Bedrooms are well-equipped and include one suite that has a jacuzzi. The four Superior View rooms have, as their designation suggests, fantastic views of the surrounding fells. In colder weather, welcoming log fires burn in the comfortable lounges. The dining room is the focus for food, serving technically accomplished cooking in a stylish conservatory setting overlooking the garden.

Rooms: 13 (1 GF) ☎ **S** fr £71 **D** fr £71 (including breakfast) **Facilities:** STV FTV WiFi ♨ New Year **Parking:** 13 **Notes:** LB Closed 6–25 January, 16–26 December

Macdonald Swan Hotel

 MACDONALD
HOTELS & RESORTS

★★★ 81% HOTEL

tel: 01539 435742 **LA22 9RF**
email: sales/oldengland@macdonald-hotels.co.uk **web:** www.macdonaldhotels.co.uk
dir: *M6 junction 36, A591 towards Kendal, A590 to Keswick through Ambleside. Hotel on right on entering village.*

Close to Dove Cottage and occupying a prominent position on the edge of the village, this 300-year-old inn is mentioned in Wordsworth's poem, The Waggoner. Attractive public areas are spacious and comfortable, and bedrooms are equally stylish. A modern bar and grill menu is available, while the elegant restaurant offers more formal dining.

Rooms: 37 (2 family) (21 GF) ☎ **Facilities:** FTV WiFi HL Xmas New Year **Conf:** Class 20 Board 30 Theatre 40 **Services:** Night porter **Parking:** 45 **Notes:** Civ Wed 60

GRAVESEND	Map 6 TQ67
Kent	

Premier Inn Gravesend (A2/Singlewell)

Premier Inn

BUDGET HOTEL

tel: 0871 527 8472 (Calls cost 13p per minute plus your phone company's access charge) **Hevercourt Road, Singlewell DA12 5UQ**
web: www.premierinn.com
dir: *At Gravesend East exit on A2.*

High quality, budget accommodation ideal for both families and business travellers. Spacious, en suite bedrooms feature free WiFi and tea and coffee making facilities, and in most hotels, Freeview TV is also available. The adjacent family restaurant features a wide and varied menu.

Rooms: 31

Premier Inn Gravesend Central

Premier Inn

BUDGET HOTEL

tel: 0871 527 8474 (Calls cost 13p per minute plus your phone company's access charge) **Wrotham Road DA11 7LF**
web: www.premierinn.com
dir: *A2 onto A227 towards town centre, 1 mile to hotel.*

Rooms: 55

GREAT CHESTERFORD	Map 12 TL54
Essex	

The Crown House

★★★ 77% HOTEL

tel: 01799 530515 **CB10 1NY**
email: reservations@crownhousehotel.com **web:** www.crownhousehotel.com
dir: *From north, M11 junction 9 (from south, junction 10) follow signs for Saffron Walden, then Great Chesterford B1383.*

This Georgian coaching inn, situated in a peaceful village close to the M11, has been sympathetically restored and retains much original character. The bedrooms are well equipped and individually decorated; some rooms have delightful four-poster beds. Public rooms include an attractive lounge bar, an elegant oak-panelled restaurant and an airy conservatory.

Rooms: 18 (10 annexe) (1 family) (5 GF) ☎ **Facilities:** FTV WiFi ♨ New Year **Conf:** Class 14 Board 12 Theatre 30 **Parking:** 30 **Notes:** Closed 27–30 December Civ Wed 60

GREAT MILTON
Oxfordshire

Map 5 SP60

INSPECTOR'S CHOICE

Belmond Le Manoir aux Quat'Saisons
★★★★★ ◉◉◉◉◉ ≋ HOTEL

tel: 01844 278881 **Church Road OX44 7PD**
email: manoir.mqs@belmond.com **web:** www.belmond.com/lemanoir
dir: *From A329 2nd right to Great Milton Manor, hotel 200 yards on right.*

Even though Le Manoir is now very much part of the British scene, its iconic chef patron, Raymond Blanc, still fizzes with new ideas and projects. His first loves are his kitchen and his garden and the vital link between them. The fascinating grounds feature a Japanese tea garden and two acres of vegetables and herbs that supply the kitchen with an almost never-ending supply of top-notch produce. The kitchen is the epicentre, with outstanding cooking highlighting freshness and seasonality. Bedrooms in this idyllic 'grand house on a small scale' are either in the main house or around an outside courtyard; all offer the highest levels of comfort and quality, have magnificent marble bathrooms and are equipped with a host of thoughtful extra touches. For something really special there is the 15th-century dovecot with a stunning upper-floor bedroom and a bathroom below. La Belle Epoque is the private dining room, ideal for weddings, celebrations and corporate events.

Rooms: 32 (23 annexe) (13 GF) ☏ **S** fr £695 **D** fr £695 (including breakfast)*
Facilities: STV FTV WiFi ↳ 🚣 Cookery school gardening school water gardens bikes spa treatment Xmas New Year **Conf:** Class 30 Board 24 Theatre 80
Services: Night porter **Parking:** 60 **Notes:** Civ Wed 50

GREAT YARMOUTH
Norfolk

Map 13 TG50

Imperial Hotel
★★★★ 81% ◉ HOTEL

THE INDEPENDENTS
HOTEL ASSOCIATION

tel: 01493 842000 **North Drive NR30 1EQ**
email: reservations@imperialhotel.co.uk **web:** www.imperialhotel.co.uk
dir: *Follow signs to seafront, turn left. Hotel opposite Waterways.*

This friendly, family-run hotel is situated at the quieter end of the seafront within easy walking distance of the town centre. Bedrooms are attractively decorated with co-ordinated soft furnishings and many thoughtful touches; most rooms have superb sea views. Public areas include The Terrace, the smart Bar Fizz and the Café Cru restaurant.

Rooms: 39 (4 family) ☏ **S** fr £90 **D** fr £110 (including breakfast) **Facilities:** FTV WiFi ↳ New Year **Conf:** Class 40 Board 30 Theatre 140 **Services:** Lift Night porter **Parking:** 40 **Notes:** LB Civ Wed 140

The Prom Hotel
★★★★ 78% ◉ HOTEL

tel: 01493 842308 **77 Marine Parade NR30 2DH**
email: info@promhotel.co.uk **web:** www.promhotel.co.uk
dir: *Phone for directions.*

The Prom Hotel is ideally situated on the seafront close to the bright lights and attractions of Marine Parade. The open-plan public areas include a smart lounge bar with views of the sea, and a relaxed restaurant; guests also have the use of a further quieter lounge bar with plush seating. The modern contemporary bedrooms are smartly appointed and have many thoughtful touches; many rooms have lovely sea views.

Rooms: 50 (3 family) ☏ **S** fr £80 **D** fr £90 (including breakfast)* **Facilities:** STV FTV WiFi ↳ Games room Xmas New Year **Conf:** Class 40 Board 30 Theatre 50 **Services:** Lift Night porter **Parking:** 30 **Notes:** LB Civ Wed 60

Andover House
★★★ 81% ◉◉ SMALL HOTEL

tel: 01493 843490 **28-30 Camperdown NR30 3JB**
email: bookings@andoverhouse.co.uk **web:** www.andoverhouse.co.uk
dir: *Opposite Wellington Pier turn into Shadingfield Close, right into Kimberley Terrace, follow into Camperdown. Hotel on left.*

This charming Victorian building enjoys a peaceful location on a tree-lined avenue close to the town centre and the beach, making it an ideal base from which to explore the Norfolk Broads. Andover House offers a range of individually styled, comfortable bedrooms along with a modern bar and well-appointed lounge areas. The award-winning brasserie-style restaurant offers an extensive choice of imaginative dishes and there is a smart sun terrace available for guests.

Rooms: 27 (1 GF) ☏ **S** fr £69 **D** fr £79 (including breakfast)* **Facilities:** STV WiFi ↳ **Conf:** Class 18 Board 18 Theatre 18 **Services:** Night porter **Notes:** No children 13 years

Furzedown Hotel
★★★ 80% HOTEL

tel: 01493 844138 **19-20 North Drive NR30 4EW**
email: paul@furzedownhotel.co.uk **web:** www.furzedownhotel.co.uk
dir: *At end of A47 or A12, towards seafront, left, hotel opposite Waterways.*

Expect a warm welcome at this family-run hotel situated at the northern end of the seafront overlooking the town's Venetian Waterways. Bedrooms are pleasantly decorated and thoughtfully equipped; many rooms have superb sea views. The stylish public areas include a comfortable lounge bar, a smartly appointed restaurant and a cosy TV room.

Rooms: 20 (11 family) **S** fr £65 **D** fr £84 (including breakfast)* **Facilities:** FTV WiFi New Year **Conf:** Class 80 Board 40 Theatre 75 **Parking:** 30

GREAT YARMOUTH *continued*

The Cliff Hotel

★★★ 79% HOTEL

tel: 01493 662179 **Cliff Hill, Gorleston NR31 6DH**
email: reception@thecliffhotel.co.uk **web:** www.thecliffhotel.co.uk
dir: *A47 Acle new road roundabout 3rd exit, continue A12 3rd roundabout, 1st exit onto Victoria Road, 3rd right onto Avondale Road, follow round.*

The Cliff Hotel offers an extensive choice of stylish, very well appointed bedrooms. Overlooking the harbour and Gorleston Beach, the hotel enjoys a prominent position in the town. Ample, secure parking is available, and the modern terrace, along with the contemporary lounge, is very popular with guests.

Rooms: 37 (4 family) **S** fr £65 **D** fr £65 (including breakfast) **Facilities:** FTV WiFi Children's play area ♬ Xmas New Year **Conf:** Class 60 Board 45 Theatre 160 **Services:** Night porter **Parking:** 30 **Notes:** Civ Wed 80

New Beach Hotel

★★★ 79% HOTEL

Leisureplex
HOLIDAY HOTELS

tel: 01493 332300 **67 Marine Parade NR30 2EJ**
email: newbeach.gtyarmouth@alfatravel.co.uk **web:** www.leisureplex.co.uk
dir: *Follow signs to seafront. Hotel facing Britannia Pier.*

This Victorian building is centrally located on the seafront, overlooking Britannia Pier and the sandy beach. Bedrooms are pleasantly decorated and equipped with modern facilities; many have lovely sea views. Dinner is taken in the restaurant which doubles as the ballroom, and guests can also relax in the bar or sunny lounge.

Rooms: 95 (8 family) **Facilities:** FTV WiFi ♬ Xmas New Year **Services:** Lift Night porter **Notes:** Closed January to February RS March

Knights Court Hotel

★★★ 77% HOTEL

tel: 01493 843089 **22 North Drive NR30 4EW**
email: enquiries@knights-court.co.uk **web:** www.knights-court.co.uk
dir: *Within close proximity of A12/A47, Great Yarmouth.*

Knights Court Hotel is situated on the seafront and is a small privately-owned hotel. Expect friendly service from Malcolm and the team, who will ensure all guests are welcomed. Bedrooms are comfortable and some offer good views of the sea. High quality ingredients are used at dinner, which is served in the stylish dining room. There is also a cosy lounge bar with thoughtful extras such as a library of books and magazines.

Rooms: 20 (6 annexe) (5 family) (6 GF) (6 smoking) **S** fr £50 **D** fr £60 (including breakfast) **Facilities:** FTV WiFi ↘ **Conf:** Class 24 Board 24 Theatre 24 **Services:** Night porter **Parking:** 15 **Notes:** Closed 10 December to 5 January

The Waverley Hotel

★★★ 71% HOTEL

tel: 01493 853388 **32-34 Princes Road NR30 2DG**
email: thewaverleyhotel.gy@gmail.com **web:** www.thewaverleyhotelgy.com
dir: *Follow A47 from London to Great Yarmouth or A143 from Haverhill. Hotel opposite Britannia Pier at Princes Road.*

The Waverley is situated in a side road adjacent to the seafront and close to the local amenities. The property is appointed to a very good standard. Public rooms include a large lounge bar, foyer and spacious restaurant. Bedrooms are contemporary in style and have a good range of extra facilities.

Rooms: 47 (2 family) **Facilities:** FTV WiFi Library ♬ Xmas New Year **Conf:** Class 60 Board 60 Theatre 60 **Services:** Lift Night porter

The Nelson Hotel

★★★ 69% HOTEL

tel: 01493 855551 **1 Marine Parade NR30 3AG**
email: nelsonhotel@theukholidaygroup.com
web: www.thenelsonhotelgreatyarmouth.co.uk
dir: *On right of Marine Parade, opposite Sealife Centre.*

The Nelson Hotel is ideally situated overlooking the sea, close to the pier and just a short stroll from the town centre and local amenities. It is ideal for both business and leisure guests, and all the bedrooms are well equipped; some rooms have lovely sea views. Public areas include a lounge with plush sofas, a bar and a separate dining room.

Rooms: 50 (10 family) **S** fr £25 **D** fr £50 (including breakfast)* **Facilities:** FTV WiFi ♬ Xmas New Year **Conf:** Class 60 Board 60 Theatre 100 **Services:** Lift Night porter **Notes:** LB

Premier Inn Great Yarmouth

BUDGET HOTEL

tel: 0871 527 9494 (Calls cost 13p per minute plus your phone company's access charge) **Runham Road NR30 1SH**
web: www.premierinn.com
dir: *A12 onto A149, at roundabout left into Runham Road.*

High quality, budget accommodation ideal for both families and business travellers. Spacious, en suite bedrooms feature free WiFi and tea and coffee making facilities, and in most hotels, Freeview TV is also available. The adjacent family restaurant features a wide and varied menu.

Rooms: 80

GREENFORD
Greater London

Premier Inn London Greenford

BUDGET HOTEL Plan 1 C4

tel: 0871 527 8658 (Calls cost 13p per minute plus your phone company's access charge) **Western Avenue UB6 8TE**
web: www.premierinn.com
dir: *From A40 (Western Avenue) eastbound, exit at Perivale. Right, left at 2nd lights. Hotel opposite Hoover Building.*

High quality, budget accommodation ideal for both families and business travellers. Spacious, en suite bedrooms feature free WiFi and tea and coffee making facilities, and in most hotels, Freeview TV is also available. The adjacent family restaurant features a wide and varied menu.

Rooms: 39

G

GRIMSBY
Lincolnshire

Map 17 TA21

Millfields Hotel

THE INDEPENDENTS
HOTEL ASSOCIATION

★★★ Ⓐ HOTEL

tel: 01472 356068 **53 Bargate DN34 5AD**
email: info@millfieldshotel.co.uk web: www.millfieldshotel.co.uk
dir: *A180, right at KFC roundabout then left at next roundabout. Right at 2nd lights and right onto Bargate, hotel 0.5 mile on left after Wheatsheaf pub.*

Dating from 1879 this hotel is surrounded by its own grounds and caters for both leisure and business guests. The bedrooms are individually designed and there is a four-poster room. The contemporary Bargate 53 Restaurant offers both carte and traditional bar menus. The hotel has extensive leisure facilities.

Rooms: 27 (4 annexe) (7 family) (13 GF) ☊ **S** fr £75 **D** fr £85 (including breakfast)*
Facilities: FTV WiFi Gym Squash Hairdresser beauty salon aromatherapist **Conf:** Class 25 Board 25 Theatre 50 **Services:** Night porter **Parking:** 75 **Notes:** Civ Wed 60

Premier Inn Grimsby

Premier Inn

BUDGET HOTEL

tel: 0871 527 8478 (Calls cost 13p per minute plus your phone company's access charge) **Europa Park, Appian Way DN31 2UT**
web: www.premierinn.com
dir: *M180 junction 5, A180 towards town centre. At 1st roundabout take 2nd exit. 1st left, left at mini-roundabout into Appian Way.*

High quality, budget accommodation ideal for both families and business travellers. Spacious, en suite bedrooms feature free WiFi and tea and coffee making facilities, and in most hotels, Freeview TV is also available. The adjacent family restaurant features a wide and varied menu.

Rooms: 58

GRIMSTON
Norfolk

Map 12 TF72

INSPECTOR'S CHOICE

Congham Hall Country House Hotel

★★★ ◉◉ COUNTRY HOUSE HOTEL

tel: 01485 600250 **Lynn Road PE32 1AH**
email: info@conghamhallhotel.co.uk web: www.conghamhallhotel.co.uk
dir: *At A149/A148 junction northeast of King's Lynn, take A148 towards Fakenham for 100 yards. Right to Grimston, hotel 2.5 miles on left.*

Congham Hall is an elegant 18th-century Georgian manor set amid 30 acres of mature landscaped grounds and surrounded by parkland. The inviting public

rooms provide a range of tastefully furnished areas in which to sit and relax. Imaginative cuisine is served in The Restaurant which has an intimate atmosphere and panoramic views of the gardens. The bedrooms, tastefully furnished with period pieces, have modern facilities and many thoughtful touches.

Congham Hall Country House Hotel

Rooms: 26 (6 annexe) (12 GF) ☊ **Facilities:** Spa WiFi ⓣ ♨ ♨ Sauna Steam room Herb garden Xmas New Year **Conf:** Class 60 Board 18 Theatre 100 **Services:** Night porter **Parking:** 50 **Notes:** LB Civ Wed 100

GRINDLEFORD
Derbyshire

Map 16 SK27

The Maynard

★★★ 84% ◉◉ HOTEL

tel: 01433 630321 **Main Road S32 2HE**
email: info@themaynard.co.uk web: www.themaynard.co.uk
dir: *A625 from Sheffield to Castleton. Left into Grindleford on B6521. Hotel on left after Fox House Hotel.*

This building, dating back over 100 years, is situated in a beautiful and tranquil location yet within easy reach of Sheffield and the M1. The bedrooms are contemporary in style and offer a wealth of accessories. The Peak District views from the restaurant and garden are stunning.

Rooms: 10 (1 family) ☊ **Facilities:** FTV WiFi **Conf:** Class 60 Board 40 Theatre 120 **Parking:** 60 **Notes:** Civ Wed 120

GUILDFORD
Surrey

Map 6 SU94

HIGHLY RECOMMENDED

The Mandolay Hotel

★★★★ 83% ◉◉ HOTEL

tel: 01483 303030 **36-40 London Road GU1 2AE**
email: info@guildford.com web: www.guildford.com
dir: *M25 junction 10, follow A3(south) for 7 miles. Take 3rd exit at 1st roundabout onto London Road for 1 mile.*

Situated close to the centre of Guildford, The Mandolay Hotel offers comfortable bedrooms. Free, unrestricted WiFi is available throughout the hotel and there are over 900 international TV channels free of charge. A range of dining options, from coffee shop and bar menu to full restaurant service are on offer. Extensive meeting facilities and off-street parking are available.

Rooms: 78 (4 family) (13 GF) ☊ **S** fr £90 **D** fr £100* **Facilities:** STV FTV WiFi ⓘ Xmas New Year **Conf:** Class 200 Board 100 Theatre 700 **Services:** Lift Night porter **Parking:** 41 **Notes:** Civ Wed 500

GUILDFORD *continued*

Guildford Harbour Hotel

★★★★ 78% @ HOTEL

tel: 01483 792300 **3 Alexandra Terrace, High Street GU1 3DA**
email: guildford@harbourhotels.co.uk **web:** www.harbourhotels.co.uk/hotels/guildford

Located with the heart of the town centre just off the cobled high street, this contemporary hotel offers a comfortable and luxurious environment. Bedrooms and bathrooms are well appointed and provide up-to-date amenities for business and leisure guests. Two restaurants offer a great choice, with the award-winning seafood restaurant The Jetty paired with all-day dining in the Harbar (kitchen-bar-terrace). A state-of-the-art gym and relaxing HarSPA add to the excellent facilities at this property. Secure parking is certainly an added plus for this location.

Rooms: 183 **Facilities:** Spa WiFi Gym

Premier Inn Guildford Central

BUDGET HOTEL

Premier Inn

tel: 0871 527 8482 (Calls cost 13p per minute plus your phone company's access charge) **Parkway GU1 1UP**
web: www.premierinn.com
dir: *M25 junction 10, follow Portsmouth (A3) signs. Exit for Guildford Centre/Leisure Complex (A322/A320/A25). Turn left, hotel on left.*

High quality, budget accommodation ideal for both families and business travellers. Spacious, en suite bedrooms feature free WiFi and tea and coffee making facilities, and in most hotels, Freeview TV is also available. The adjacent family restaurant features a wide and varied menu.

Rooms: 109

GUISBOROUGH
North Yorkshire
Map 19 NZ61

HIGHLY RECOMMENDED

Gisborough Hall

★★★★ 83% @ HOTEL

tel: 01287 611500 **Whitby Lane TS14 6PT**
web: www.gisborough-hall.com
dir: *A171, follow signs for Whitby to Waterfall roundabout, 3rd exit into Whitby Lane, hotel 500 yards on right.*

Dating back to the mid-19th century, this elegant country house provides a pleasing combination of original features and modern facilities. Bedrooms, including four-poster and family rooms, are richly furnished. The elegant Drawing Room is welcoming and has an open fire, while the opulent G Bar & Bistro provides a contemporary alternative. Excellent food is served in Chaloner's Restaurant.

Rooms: 71 (2 family) (12 GF) ✆ **S** fr £89 **D** fr £89* **Facilities:** Spa STV WiFi ⌨ HL ☺ ⛵ Sauna Xmas New Year **Conf:** Class 150 Board 32 Theatre 400 **Services:** Lift Night porter **Parking:** 180 **Notes:** LB Civ Wed 250

HADLEY WOOD
Greater London
Map 6 TQ29

West Lodge Park Hotel

★★★★ 82% @ HOTEL

tel: 020 8216 3900 **Cockfosters Road EN4 0PY**
email: westlodgepark@bealeshotels.co.uk **web:** www.bealeshotels.co.uk
dir: *On A111, 1 mile south of M25 junction 24.*

West Lodge Park Hotel is a stylish country house set in stunning parkland and gardens, yet only 12 miles from central London and a few miles from the M25. Bedrooms are individually decorated in traditional style and offer excellent facilities. Annexe rooms feature air conditioning and have access to an outdoor patio area. Public rooms include the award-winning Cedar Restaurant, cosy bar area and separate lounge.

Rooms: 58 (13 annexe) (4 family) (11 GF) ✆ **S** fr £65 **D** fr £85* **Facilities:** STV FTV WiFi ⌨ ⛵ Free use of nearby leisure club ♬ Xmas New Year **Conf:** Class 30 Board 30 Theatre 64 **Services:** Lift Night porter **Parking:** 200 **Notes:** Civ Wed 72

HADLOW
Kent
Map 6 TQ65

Hadlow Manor Hotel

★★★ 76% HOTEL

tel: 01732 851442 **Goose Green TN11 0JH**
email: hotel@hadlowmanor.co.uk **web:** www.hadlowmanor.co.uk
dir: *On A26 Maidstone to Tonbridge road. 1 mile east of Hadlow.*

This is a friendly, independently owned country house hotel, ideally situated between Maidstone and Tonbridge. Traditionally styled bedrooms are spacious and attractively furnished with many amenities. Public areas include a sunny restaurant, bar and lounge. The gardens are delightful and there's a seated area ideal for relaxation in warmer weather. Meeting and banqueting facilities are available.

Rooms: 29 (2 family) (8 GF) **Facilities:** STV FTV WiFi Xmas New Year **Conf:** Class 90 Board 103 Theatre 200 **Parking:** 120 **Notes:** Civ Wed 200

HAGLEY
Worcestershire
Map 10 SO98

Premier Inn Hagley

BUDGET HOTEL

Premier Inn

tel: 0871 527 8484 (Calls cost 13p per minute plus your phone company's access charge) **Birmingham Road DY9 9JS**
web: www.premierinn.com
dir: *M5 junction 3, A456 towards Kidderminster (dual carriageway). Hotel visible on opposite side of road. At next roundabout double back follow A456 Birmingham signs. Hotel on left.*

High quality, budget accommodation ideal for both families and business travellers. Spacious, en suite bedrooms feature free WiFi and tea and coffee making facilities, and in most hotels, Freeview TV is also available. The adjacent family restaurant features a wide and varied menu.

Rooms: 40

HALIFAX
West Yorkshire

Map 19 SE02

Holdsworth House Hotel
★★★★ 76% HOTEL

tel: 01422 240024 **Holdsworth Road, Holmfield HX2 9TG**
email: info@holdsworthhouse.co.uk **web:** www.holdsworthhouse.co.uk
dir: *From town centre take A629 towards Keighley. 1.5 miles right at garage, into Shay Lane. Hotel on right after 1 mile.*

This delightful 17th-century Jacobean manor house, set in well-tended gardens, offers individually decorated, thoughtfully equipped bedrooms. Public rooms, adorned with beautiful paintings and antique pieces, include a choice of inviting lounges and superb conference and function facilities. Dinner provides the highlight of any stay and is served in the elegant restaurant by friendly, attentive staff.

Rooms: 38 (9 family) (20 GF) 🐾 **Facilities:** FTV WiFi ⅃ New Year **Conf:** Class 75 Board 50 Theatre 150 **Services:** Night porter **Parking:** 60 **Notes:** Civ Wed 120

Premier Inn Halifax South

BUDGET HOTEL

tel: 0871 527 8486 (Calls cost 13p per minute plus your phone company's access charge) **Salterhebble Hill, Huddersfield Road HX3 0QT**
web: www.premierinn.com
dir: *Just off M62 junction 24 on A629 towards Halifax.*

High quality, budget accommodation ideal for both families and business travellers. Spacious, en suite bedrooms feature free WiFi and tea and coffee making facilities, and in most hotels, Freeview TV is also available. The adjacent family restaurant features a wide and varied menu.

Rooms: 31

Premier Inn Halifax Town Centre
Premier Inn

BUDGET HOTEL

tel: 0871 527 9348 (Calls cost 13p per minute plus your phone company's access charge) **Broad Street Plaza HX1 1YA**
web: www.premierinn.com
dir: *Phone for directions.*

Rooms: 100

HANDFORTH
See **Manchester Airport**

HARROGATE
North Yorkshire

Map 19 SE35

INSPECTOR'S CHOICE

Rudding Park Hotel, Spa & Golf
★★★★  HOTEL

tel: 01423 871350 **Rudding Park, Follifoot HG3 1JH**
email: reservations@ruddingpark.com **web:** www.ruddingpark.co.uk
dir: *From A61 at roundabout with A658 take York exit, follow signs to Rudding Park.*

Set in beautiful parkland, Rudding Park dates from the early 19th century and the interiors are stylishly contemporary and elegant. The bedrooms are luxurious – the Follifoot Wing features stunning suites and bedrooms with spas. Carefully prepared meals and Yorkshire tapas are served in the relaxed Clocktower which has a striking pink chandelier as its centrepiece, and the stylish bar and conservatory lead to a generous terrace which is perfect for eating alfresco. Then there's Horto (Latin for 'garden') which showcases produce from the hotel's own kitchen garden to produce innovative, award-winning dishes. The grandeur of the mansion house and grounds make this a popular wedding venue; there's also an impressive spa with treatment rooms, a gym, private cinema and extensive conference facilities, plus an adjoining 18-hole, par 72 golf course, and driving range.

Rooms: 90 (15 family) (35 GF) 🐾 **S** fr £175 **D** fr £203 (including breakfast)
Facilities: Spa STV FTV WiFi ⅃ HL ⓢ ⅃ 18 Gym Driving range Jogging trail Roof top spa garden ♫ Xmas New Year **Conf:** Class 150 Board 40 Theatre 300
Services: Lift Night porter Air con **Parking:** 350 **Notes:** LB Civ Wed 300

H

H

HARROGATE *continued*

West Park Hotel

★★★★ 82% HOTEL

tel: 01423 524471 **19 West Park HG1 1BJ**
email: enquiries@thewestparkhotel.com **web:** www.thewestparkhotel.com
dir: *A1(M) junction 47, A59 to Harrogate. 2 miles straight on A658, 3rd exit at roundabout onto A661 for 2.5 miles. 1st exit at roundabout onto A6040, 3rd exit next roundabout onto West Park. Hotel 500 metres on right.*

West Park Hotel is perfectly situated in a busy area of the popular town of Harrogate. Bedrooms are equipped with plentiful accessories and gadgets such as climate control, smart TVs and Nespresso machines as well as well-stocked hospitality trays. Many bathrooms have separate shower and bath facilities, and luxurious toiletries are provided. Meals can be enjoyed in the bustling restaurant and bar area, and outdoor seating is provided for alfresco dining in the summer months.

Rooms: 25 (8 family) ⚡ **S** fr £129 **D** fr £129* **Facilities:** FTV WiFi ⌂ Xmas New Year **Conf:** Class 24 Board 30 Theatre 60 **Services:** Lift Night porter Air con

Studley Hotel

★★★★ 78% ⚘⚘ HOTEL

tel: 01423 560425 **28 Swan Road HG1 2SE**
email: info@studleyhotel.co.uk **web:** www.studleyhotel.co.uk
dir: *Adjacent to Valley Gardens, opposite Mercer Gallery.*

This friendly, well-established hotel, close to the town centre and Valley Gardens, is well known for The Orchid restaurant, which provides a dynamic and authentic approach to Pacific Rim and Asian cuisine. Bedrooms are modern and come in a variety of styles and sizes, while the stylish bar lounge provides an excellent place for relaxing. A PC is available for guests' use.

Rooms: 28 (6 family) ⚡ **S** fr £94 **D** fr £104* **Facilities:** FTV WiFi ⌂ Free use of facilities at local health club New Year **Conf:** Class 15 Board 12 Theatre 15 **Services:** Lift Night porter **Parking:** 14 **Notes:** LB Closed 22–30 December

White Hart Hotel

★★★★ 77% ⚘ HOTEL

tel: 01423 505681 **2 Cold Bath Road HG2 0NF**
email: reception@whitehart hotelharrogate.com **web:** www.whitehart hotelharrogate.com
dir: *A59 to Harrogate. A661 3rd exit on roundabout to Harrogate. Left at roundabout onto A6040 for 1 mile. Right onto A61. Bear left down Montpellier Hill.*

Set in the heart of Harrogate's Montpellier Quarter, this fine Georgian hotel has free WiFi and luxurious bedrooms, just a few minutes' stroll from the town centre, Harrogate International Centre and the famous Valley Gardens. The Deluxe bedrooms have USB ports and soft tartan furnishings, while the Classic bedrooms retain their older shabby-chic style and antique furniture. All rooms feature TVs with Freeview, and an en suite bathroom with H2K toiletries. Guests can choose to relax in the residents' lounge or enjoy the atmosphere of The Fat Badger, an adjoining, traditional English pub. The on-site restaurant, The Fat Badger Grill, is the place for breakfast, lunch and dinner. There's parking for over 80 vehicles.

Rooms: 82 (18 annexe) ⚡ **Facilities:** FTV WiFi ⌂ Gym Xmas New Year **Conf:** Class 40 Board 25 Theatre 80 **Services:** Lift Night porter **Parking:** 80 **Notes:** Civ Wed 80

Nidd Hall Hotel

★★★★ 76% ⚘⚘ COUNTRY HOUSE HOTEL

tel: 01423 771598 **Nidd HG3 3BN**
web: www.warnerleisurehotels.co.uk
dir: *A59 through Knaresborough, follow signs for Ripley. Hotel on right.*

This fine hotel is set in 45 acres of Victorian and Edwardian gardens. Bedrooms are spacious and appointed to a high standard, while public areas are delightful and retain many original features. Leisure and spa facilities are available along with a variety of outdoor activities. This is an adults-only (minimum 21 years old) hotel.

Rooms: 193 (57 GF) ⚡ **S** fr £76 **D** fr £140 (including breakfast & dinner)* **Facilities:** Spa FTV WiFi HL ⚘ ⚘ Fishing ⚘ Gym ♫ Xmas New Year **Conf:** Class 40 Board 30 Theatre 60 **Services:** Lift Night porter **Parking:** 200 **Notes:** No children 21 years

Hotel du Vin & Bistro Harrogate

★★★★ 76% ⚘ TOWN HOUSE HOTEL

Hotel du Vin & Bistro

tel: 01423 856800 & 0844 736 4257 (Calls cost 5p per minute plus your phone company's access charge) **Prospect Place HG1 1LB**
email: info@harrogate.hotelduvin.com **web:** www.hotelduvin.com/locations/harrogate
dir: *A1(M) junction 47, A59 to Harrogate, follow town centre signs for Prince of Wales roundabout, 3rd exit, remain in right lane. Right at lights into Albert Street, right into Prospect Place.*

This town house was created from eight Georgian-style properties and overlooks The Stray, a large expanse of parkland set aside for public use. The spacious, open-plan lobby has seating, a bar, and the reception desk. Hidden downstairs is a cosy, snug cellar. The French-influenced bistro offers high quality cooking and a great choice of wines. Bedrooms face front and back, and are smart and modern, with excellent 'deluge' showers.

Rooms: 48 (4 GF) ⚡ **Facilities:** Spa STV FTV WiFi ⌂ New Year **Conf:** Class 20 Board 30 Theatre 60 **Services:** Lift Night porter **Parking:** 30 **Notes:** Civ Wed 90

The Majestic Hotel

★★★★ 74% HOTEL

tel: 01423 700300 **Ripon Road HG1 2HU**
email: majestic@majestichotelharrogate.co.uk **web:** www.majestichotelharrogate.co.uk
dir: *M1 onto A1(M) at Wetherby. Take A661 to Harrogate. Hotel in town centre adjacent to Royal Hall and next to Harrogate International Centre.*

Popular for conferences and functions, this grand Victorian hotel is set in 12 acres of landscaped grounds that is within walking distance of the town centre. It benefits from spacious public areas, and the comfortable bedrooms, including some spacious suites, come in a variety of sizes.

Rooms: 170 (8 family) ⚡ **S** fr £79 **D** fr £99* **Facilities:** Spa FTV WiFi ⌂ HL ⚘ Gym Saunas Xmas New Year **Conf:** Class 260 Board 70 Theatre 500 **Services:** Lift Night porter **Parking:** 250 **Notes:** Civ Wed 200

Cairn Hotel

★★★ 70% HOTEL

tel: 01423 504005 **HG1 2JD**
email: salescairn@strathmorehotels.com **web:** www.strathmorehotels.com

This large Victorian hotel is just a short walk from the town centre and also benefits from free on-site parking. Many of the original features have been retained and the spacious foyer lounge and bar areas are perfect for relaxing. Bedrooms are comfortable, with Club Packages offering extra accessories and luxury touches. Complimentary WiFi is also provided in public areas and there is a fitness room with a mini gym.

Rooms: 135 (7 family) ☎ **Facilities:** WiFi Gym Xmas New Year **Conf:** Class 170 Board 100 Theatre 400 **Services:** Lift Night porter **Parking:** 150 **Notes:** LB Civ Wed 150

Premier Inn Harrogate

BUDGET HOTEL

tel: 0871 527 8490 (Calls cost 13p per minute plus your phone company's access charge) **Hornbeam Park Avenue HG2 8RA**
web: www.premierinn.com
dir: A1(M) junction 46 west, A661 to Harrogate. In 2 miles left at The Woodlands lights. 1.5 miles left into Hornbeam Park Avenue.

High quality, budget accommodation ideal for both families and business travellers. Spacious, en suite bedrooms feature free WiFi and tea and coffee making facilities, and in most hotels, Freeview TV is also available. The adjacent family restaurant features a wide and varied menu.

Rooms: 68

Premier Inn Harrogate Town Centre

BUDGET HOTEL

tel: 0871 527 9432 (Calls cost 13p per minute plus your phone company's access charge) **Springfield Avenue HG1 2HY**
web: www.premierinn.com
dir: A1 junction 47, follow Ripon/A61 signs. After Ripton follow Harrogate signs. After Cairn Hotel (on right) turn left into Springfield Avenue. Hotel on right. Parking at hotel (chargeable).

Rooms: 107

HARTINGTON	Map 16 SK16
Derbyshire	

Biggin Hall Hotel

★★★ 78% ☺ COUNTRY HOUSE HOTEL

tel: 01298 84451 **Biggin-by-Hartington SK17 0DH**
email: enquiries@bigginhall.co.uk **web:** www.bigginhall.co.uk
dir: 0.5 mile off A515, midway between Ashbourne and Buxton.

Dating back to the 17th century, Biggin Hall is peacefully situated, surrounded by open countryside in the heart of the Peak District. Its location makes it ideal for exploring the Tissington Trail, which is virtually on the doorstep. There are also a host of historical market towns all within easy reach. Bedrooms are arranged across three main buildings and offer a mix of styles; all are comfortably furnished with a number benefiting from luxury bathrooms.

Rooms: 21 (13 annexe) (2 family) (6 GF) ☎ **S** fr £80 **D** fr £120 (including breakfast)*
Facilities: FTV WiFi Xmas New Year **Parking:** 25 **Notes:** No children 12 years Civ Wed 50

HARTLEPOOL	Map 19 NZ53
County Durham	

Premier Inn Hartlepool Marina

BUDGET HOTEL

tel: 0871 527 8492 (Calls cost 13p per minute plus your phone company's access charge) **Maritime Avenue, Hartlepool Marina TS24 0XZ**
web: www.premierinn.com
dir: Approximately 1 mile from A689/A179 junction. On marina.

High quality, budget accommodation ideal for both families and business travellers. Spacious, en suite bedrooms feature free WiFi and tea and coffee making facilities, and in most hotels, Freeview TV is also available. The adjacent family restaurant features a wide and varied menu.

Rooms: 98

HARTSHEAD MOOR SERVICE AREA (M62)	Map 19 SE12
West Yorkshire	

Days Inn Bradford - M62

WELCOMEBREAK

AA Advertised

tel: 01274 851706 **Hartshead Moor Service Area, Clifton HD6 4JX**
email: hartshead.hotel@welcomebreak.co.uk **web:** www.welcomebreak.co.uk
dir: M62 between junction 25 and 26.

This modern building offers accommodation in smart, spacious and well-equipped bedrooms, suitable for families and business travellers, and all with en suite bathrooms. Continental breakfast is available and other refreshments may be taken at the nearby family restaurant.

Rooms: 38 (33 family) (17 GF) **Facilities:** FTV WiFi ⊷ **Conf:** Board 10 **Parking:** 100

H

H

HARWICH
Essex

Map 13 TM23

The Pier at Harwich

★★★★ 80% @@ SMALL HOTEL

tel: 01255 241212 **The Quay CO12 3HH**
email: pier@milsomhotels.com **web:** www.milsomhotels.com/thepier
dir: *From A12 take A120 to Quay. Hotel opposite lifeboat station.*

The Pier is situated on the quay, overlooking the ports of Harwich and Felixstowe. The bedrooms are tastefully decorated, thoughtfully equipped, and furnished in a contemporary style; many rooms have superb sea views. The public rooms include the restaurant which is influenced by the best ideas in European cooking, the NAVYÄRD bar and terrace, and a plush residents' lounge.

Rooms: 14 (7 annexe) (5 family) (1 GF) ♠ **D** fr £135 (including breakfast)*
Facilities: STV WiFi Day cruises on yachts Golf breaks arranged with nearby course Xmas **Conf:** Board 16 **Services:** Lift Night porter **Parking:** 12 **Notes:** LB Civ Wed 50

Tower Hotel

★★★ 79% HOTEL

tel: 01255 504952 **Dovercourt CO12 3PJ**
email: reception@tower-hotel-harwich.co.uk **web:** www.tower-hotel-harwich.co.uk
dir: *Follow main road into Harwich. Past BP garage on left.*

The Tower Hotel is an impressive late 17th-century Italian-style building, with a wealth of ornamental ceiling cornices, beautiful architraves and an impressive balustrade. Bedrooms, many named after prominent people from Harwich's past, are spacious and furnished to a very high standard. Evening meals and breakfast are served in the decorative dining rooms, and Rigby's bar offers tempting meals and a wide range of refreshments.

Rooms: 13 (2 family) (2 GF) ♠ **S** fr £55 **D** fr £68* **Facilities:** WiFi **Conf:** Class 30 Board 30 Theatre 30 **Services:** Night porter **Parking:** 30 **Notes:** Closed 25–26 December Civ Wed 70

Premier Inn Harwich

Premier Inn 🌙

BUDGET HOTEL

tel: 0871 527 8494 (Calls cost 13p per minute plus your phone company's access charge) **Parkstone Road, Dovercourt CO12 4NX**
web: www.premierinn.com
dir: *A120 to Harwich, hotel opposite Morrisons. Right at roundabout. Hotel entrance through Lidl car park.*

High quality, budget accommodation ideal for both families and business travellers. Spacious, en suite bedrooms feature free WiFi and tea and coffee making facilities, and in most hotels, Freeview TV is also available. The adjacent family restaurant features a wide and varied menu.

Rooms: 45

HASLEMERE
Surrey

Map 6 SU93

Lythe Hill Hotel & Spa

★★★★ 77% HOTEL

tel: 01428 651251 **Petworth Road GU27 3BQ**
email: lythe@lythehill.co.uk **web:** www.lythehill.co.uk
dir: *From High Street onto B2131. Hotel 1.25 miles on right.*

This privately-owned hotel sits in 20 acres of attractive parkland. It has been described as a hamlet of character buildings, each furnished in a style that complements the age of the property; the oldest one dating back to 1475. The restaurant offers interesting, quality dishes, and is also the venue for breakfast and afternoon tea. The bedrooms are split between a 15th-century building and those in the main house. The stylish Armana Spa includes a 16-metre swimming pool, as well as various ESPA treatments and therapies, spa bath, sauna and a fully equipped gym.

Rooms: 44 (9 family) (19 GF) ♠ **S** fr £119 **D** fr £129 (including breakfast)*
Facilities: Spa FTV WiFi 🕐 ♨ 🥾 Gym Boules Giant chess Xmas New Year
Conf: Class 40 Board 30 Theatre 128 **Services:** Night porter **Parking:** 120 **Notes:** LB Civ Wed 128

HASSOCKS
West Sussex   Map 6 TV31

Wickwoods Country Club Hotel & Spa

★★★ 85% ⊛ HOTEL

tel: 01273 857567 **Shaveswood Lane, Albourne BN6 9DY**
email: reception@wickwoods.co.uk **web:** www.wickwoods.co.uk
dir: *On B2117 just off A23. From the north take Sayerscommon exit; from the south take Henfield turning.*

Wickwoods Country Club Hotel & Spa, set in 22 acres of landscaped gardens and woodland in the South Downs National Park, offers individually decorated bedrooms that provide a comfortable night's sleep along with excellent leisure and spa facilities. The Glass House restaurant serves good quality meals and is a popular venue for weddings and functions.

Rooms: 6 ⬩ **S** fr £65 **D** fr £75* **Facilities:** Spa FTV WiFi ⊗ ♨ Gym Sauna Steam room Exercise classes **Parking:** 140 **Notes:** LB No children Civ Wed 80

HASTINGS & ST LEONARDS
East Sussex   Map 7 TQ80

Bannatyne Spa Hotel Hastings

★★★★ 79% HOTEL

tel: 01424 851222 & 0844 248 3836 (Calls cost 7p per minute plus your phone company's access charge) **Battle Road TN38 8EA**
email: enquiries.hastingshotel@bannatyne.co.uk **web:** www.bannatyne.co.uk
dir: *M25 junction 5, A21 Hastings. At 5th roundabout take 2nd exit Hastings/Filmwell. After 2 roundabouts turn right Folkestone/A259/Battle/A2100. Left at A2100/The Ridge Way. At 2nd roundabout right to hotel.*

This hotel offers a range of facilities that will appeal to both leisure and business travellers. The well-appointed accommodation is available in a range of types and sizes from small doubles to superior rooms, while the public areas are a tasteful blend of contemporary design and period features. The Conservatory Restaurant has attractive views over the formal garden. There is a spa and health club plus meeting facilities. Free WiFi is available.

Rooms: 38 (7 family) (4 GF) ⬩ **S** fr £95 **D** fr £99 (including breakfast)*
Facilities: Spa FTV WiFi ⊗ Gym Xmas New Year **Conf:** Class 300 Board 50 Theatre 425 **Services:** Lift Night porter **Parking:** 150 **Notes:** Civ Wed 300

Royal Victoria Hotel

★★★ 75% HOTEL

tel: 01424 445544 **Marina, St Leonards-on-Sea TN38 0BD**
email: reception@royalvichotel.co.uk **web:** www.royalvichotel.co.uk
dir: *On A259 (seafront road) 1 mile west of Hastings pier.*

This imposing 18th-century property is situated in a prominent position overlooking the sea in the heart of St Leonards. A superb Grade II listed marble staircase leads from the lobby to the main public areas, the Piano Lounge and Bar, on the first floor. The Sea Terrace Restaurant caters for all dining occasions, including the popular Sunday lunch carvery. The spacious bedrooms, many with stunning sea views, are pleasantly decorated and well equipped, and include duplex and family suites. The hotel also offers a range of meeting rooms, including a stunning ballroom.

Rooms: 50 (15 family) **S** fr £55 **D** fr £60 **Facilities:** FTV WiFi ⊗ Xmas New Year **Conf:** Class 40 Board 40 Theatre 100 **Services:** Lift Night porter **Parking:** 6 **Notes:** LB Civ Wed 100

Premier Inn Hastings

Premier Inn

BUDGET HOTEL

tel: 0871 527 8496 (Calls cost 13p per minute plus your phone company's access charge) **1 John Macadam Way, St Leonards on Sea TN37 7DB**
web: www.premierinn.com
dir: *A21 into Hastings. Hotel on right after junction with A2100 – Battle road.*

High quality, budget accommodation ideal for both families and business travellers. Spacious, en suite bedrooms feature free WiFi and tea and coffee making facilities, and in most hotels, Freeview TV is also available. The adjacent family restaurant features a wide and varied menu.

Rooms: 73

HATFIELD
Hertfordshire   Map 6 TL20

Beales Hotel

★★★★ 82% ⊛ HOTEL

tel: 01707 288500 **Comet Way AL10 9NG**
email: hatfield@bealeshotels.co.uk **web:** www.bealeshotels.co.uk
dir: *On A1001 opposite Galleria Shopping Mall – follow signs for Galleria.*

Beales Hotel, with easy access of the M25, is a stunning contemporary property – its striking exterior incorporates giant glass panels and cedar wood slats. Bedrooms have Hypnos beds and smart bathrooms with power showers. Public areas include a small bar and an attractive restaurant which opens throughout the day. The hotel is fully air-conditioned and free broadband is available in bedrooms, conference and banqueting rooms.

Rooms: 53 (3 family) (21 GF) ⬩ **S** fr £79* **Facilities:** STV FTV WiFi ⊗ Free use of nearby leisure club Xmas New Year **Conf:** Class 124 Board 64 Theatre 300 **Services:** Lift Night porter Air con **Parking:** 126 **Notes:** LB Civ Wed 300

Mercure Hatfield Oak Hotel

fOCUS hotels
management limited

★★★ 78% HOTEL

tel: 01707 275701 **Roehyde Way AL10 9AF**
email: enquiries@hotels-hatfield.com **web:** www.hotels-hatfield.com
dir: *M25 junction 23 between junctions 2 and 3 of A1(M). Roehyde Way runs parallel to A1(M).*

This hotel enjoys an enviable location for both leisure and business guests, as it is within easy reach of major roads and central London. The University of Hertfordshire is situated nearby. The accommodation has been appointed to a good standard with Freeview TVs and WiFi, among other facilities. The hotel also caters for conferences and banqueting.

Rooms: 85 (14 family) (37 GF) ⬩ **S** fr £65 **D** fr £85* **Facilities:** FTV WiFi ⊗ Xmas New Year **Conf:** Class 60 Board 40 Theatre 100 **Services:** Night porter **Parking:** 85 **Notes:** Civ Wed 100

H

HATFIELD *continued*

Premier Inn Hatfield

Premier Inn

BUDGET HOTEL

tel: 0871 527 8498 (Calls cost 13p per minute plus your phone company's access charge) **Lemsford Road AL10 0DZ**
web: www.premierinn.com
dir: *From A1(M) junction 4, A1001 towards Hatfield. At roundabout take 2nd exit, 1st right.*

High quality, budget accommodation ideal for both families and business travellers. Spacious, en suite bedrooms feature free WiFi and tea and coffee making facilities, and in most hotels, Freeview TV is also available. The adjacent family restaurant features a wide and varied menu.

Rooms: 40

HAVANT	Map 5 SU70
Hampshire	

Premier Inn Portsmouth (Havant)

Premier Inn

BUDGET HOTEL

tel: 0871 527 8900 (Calls cost 13p per minute plus your phone company's access charge) **65 Bedhampton Hill, Bedhampton PO9 3JN**
web: www.premierinn.com
dir: *At roundabout just off A3(M) junction 5 towards Bedhampton.*

High quality, budget accommodation ideal for both families and business travellers. Spacious, en suite bedrooms feature free WiFi and tea and coffee making facilities, and in most hotels, Freeview TV is also available. The adjacent family restaurant features a wide and varied menu.

Rooms: 59

Silver Stars

The AA Silver Star rating denotes a Hotel that we highly recommend. They have a superior level of quality within their star rating, high standards of hospitality, service and cleanliness.

HAWES	Map 18 SD88
North Yorkshire	

HIGHLY RECOMMENDED

Simonstone Hall Hotel

★★★ 87% COUNTRY HOUSE HOTEL

tel: 01969 667255 **Simonstone DL8 3LY**
email: enquiries@simonstonehall.com **web:** www.simonstonehall.com
dir: *1.5 miles north of Hawes on road signed Muker and Buttertubs.*

This former hunting lodge provides professional, friendly service and a relaxed atmosphere. Public areas include an inviting drawing room, a bar and a conservatory. For dining, there is the Garden Room Brasserie which offers a lunchtime and extended afternoon menu as well as the evening à la carte.; afternoon tea is also available if pre-booked. The generally spacious bedrooms are elegantly designed to reflect the style of the house, and many offer spectacular views of the countryside.

Rooms: 18 (10 family) (2 GF) ↶ **S** fr £80 **D** fr £100 (including breakfast)
Facilities: FTV WiFi ↴ In-room beauty treatments Xmas New Year **Conf:** Class 20 Board 20 Theatre 50 **Parking:** 40 **Notes:** LB Civ Wed 100

HAYDOCK	Map 15 SJ59
Merseyside	

Premier Inn Haydock

Premier Inn

BUDGET HOTEL

tel: 0871 527 8500 (Calls cost 13p per minute plus your phone company's access charge) **Yew Tree Way, Golbourne WA3 3JD**
web: www.premierinn.com
dir: *M6 junction 23, A580 towards Manchester. Approximately 2 miles. Straight on at major roundabout. Hotel on left.*

High quality, budget accommodation ideal for both families and business travellers. Spacious, en suite bedrooms feature free WiFi and tea and coffee making facilities, and in most hotels, Freeview TV is also available. The adjacent family restaurant features a wide and varied menu.

Rooms: 60

HAYES

See **Heathrow Airport**

HAYLE
Cornwall & Isles Of Scilly   Map 2 SW53

Premier Inn Hayle

Premier Inn

BUDGET HOTEL

tel: 0871 527 8506 (Calls cost 13p per minute plus your phone company's access charge) **Carwin Rise, Loggans TR27 4PN**
web: www.premierinn.com
dir: *On A30 at Loggans Moor roundabout exit into Carwin Rise. Hotel on right.*

High quality, budget accommodation ideal for both families and business travellers. Spacious, en suite bedrooms feature free WiFi and tea and coffee making facilities, and in most hotels, Freeview TV is also available. The adjacent family restaurant features a wide and varied menu.

Rooms: 57

HAYLING ISLAND
Hampshire   Map 5 SU70

Langstone Hotel

★★★★ 77% ◉◉ HOTEL

tel: 023 9246 5011 **Northney Road PO11 0NQ**
email: info@langstonehotel.co.uk **web:** www.langstonehotel.co.uk
dir: *From A27 take A3023 signed Havant/Hayling Island. Over bridge onto Hayling Island, sharp left after bridge.*

This hotel is located on the north shore of Hayling Island yet is only minutes from the M27 with easy access to Fareham, Havant and Chichester. All the smartly designed bedrooms, including 45 superior rooms, have views over Langstone Harbour. The Brasserie offers a good choice of dishes and overlooks the harbour. A gym, indoor pool, sauna, steam room, beauty salon and fitness club are also available.

Rooms: 148 (25 family) (60 GF) (3 smoking) ⌁ **S** fr £80 **D** fr £120* **Facilities:** Spa FTV WiFi ⌁ HL ⌁ Gym Sauna Steam room Beauty room Fitness classes Xmas New Year **Conf:** Class 80 Board 50 Theatre 160 **Services:** Lift Night porter **Parking:** 220 **Notes:** LB Civ Wed 150

HAYTOR VALE
Devon   Map 3 SX77

The Moorland Hotel

ⓤ

tel: 01364 661407 **TQ13 9XT**
email: mail@tinpickleandrhum.com

Currently the rating for this establishment is not confirmed. This may be due to a change of ownership or because ot has only recently joined the AA rating scheme.

Rooms: 36

HEACHAM
Norfolk   Map 12 TF63

Heacham Manor Hotel

★★★ 86% ◉ HOTEL

tel: 01485 536030 **Hunstanton Road PE31 7JX**
email: info@heacham-manor.co.uk **web:** www.heacham-manor.co.uk
dir: *On A149 between Heacham and Hunstanton. Near Hunstanton roundabout with water tower.*

This delightful 16th-century, Grade II listed house has been beautifully restored. The property is approached via a winding driveway through landscaped grounds to the front of the hotel. Public areas include a smart dining room, a sunny conservatory and a cosy bar which leads out onto a terrace. The bedrooms are very stylish and have modern facilities such as free WiFi. Dogs are very welcome at Heacham Manor. There is a selection of dog-friendly family suites; these are limited and subject to availability, so please contact the hotel if you need one. An extra charge applies to each dog that visits.

Rooms: 45 (32 annexe) (10 family) (12 GF) ⌁ **Facilities:** Spa FTV WiFi ⌁ ⌁ 18 Sauna Steam room Relaxation room Thermal suite Swimming pools and leisure facilities available at sister resort Xmas New Year **Conf:** Class 35 Board 20 Theatre 40 **Services:** Night porter **Parking:** 55 **Notes:** LB Civ Wed 120

H

HEATHROW AIRPORT
Greater London

See also **Slough & Staines-upon-Thames**

HIGHLY RECOMMENDED

Hilton London Heathrow Airport Terminal 5

★★★★ 84% ◉◉ HOTEL PLAN 1 A3

tel: 01753 686860 **Poyle Road, Colnbrook SL3 0FF**
email: heathrowairportterminal5.info@hilton.com
web: www.hilton.com/heathrowt5
dir: *Phone for directions.*

Hilton London Heathrow Airport Terminal 5 is located just a mile from Terminal 5 with easy access to the M25. Bedrooms offer practical and modern amenities such as soundproof windows and high quality, comfortable beds. A complimentary shuttle service is available to businesses in Stockley Park and Bedfont Lakes. It is an ideal venue for conferences, meetings and banqueting events for up to 1,000 guests. There are two restaurants – The Gallery offering traditional British dishes, and Mr Todiwala's which offers Pan-Indian cuisine. Guests can relax in the state-of-the-art, on-site Imagine Spa Thames Valley and use the 24-hour fitness centre.

Rooms: 350 (4 family) 🐾 **Facilities:** Spa STV FTV WiFi ৬ Gym Hydrotherapy pool **Conf:** Class 430 Board 78 Theatre 1400 **Services:** Lift Night porter Air con **Parking:** 486 **Notes:** Civ Wed 1170

DoubleTree by Hilton London Heathrow Airport

fOCUShotels
management limited

★★★★ 79% HOTEL PLAN 1 A3

tel: 020 8564 4450 **Bath Road, Cranford TW5 9QE**
email: reservations@doubletree-heathrow.com **web:** www.doubletree3.hilton.com
dir: *M4 junction 3 follow signs to Heathrow Terminals 1, 2 and 3. Hotel on right of A4 Bath Road.*

This well presented hotel is conveniently situated just three miles from Heathrow airport. Bedrooms are located in a smart block and all are well appointed for both business and leisure guests; each has a TV, climate control and good lighting. The Arts Bar and Brasserie is adjacent to a contemporary open-plan reception area. There is a chargeable car park on site.

Rooms: 200 (21 family) (38 GF) 🐾 **D** fr £89* **Facilities:** FTV WiFi ৬ Gym **Conf:** Class 35 Board 30 Theatre 70 **Services:** Lift Night porter Air con **Parking:** 72 **Notes:** LB

Novotel London Heathrow Airport M4 Jct 4 Hotel

NOVOTEL
HOTELS & RESORTS

★★★★ 77% HOTEL PLAN 1 A3

tel: 01895 431431 **Cherry Lane UB7 9HJ**
email: H1551-gm@accor.com **web:** www.novotel.com
dir: *M4 junction 4, follow Uxbridge signs on A408. Keep left, take 2nd exit off traffic island into Cherry Lane signed West Drayton. Hotel on left.*

Conveniently located for Heathrow Airport and the motorway network, this modern hotel provides comfortable accommodation. The large, airy indoor atrium creates a sense of space in the public areas, which include an all-day restaurant and bar, meeting rooms, fitness centre and swimming pool. Ample secure parking is available.

Rooms: 178 (178 family) (10 GF) **S** fr £60 **D** fr £70 (including breakfast)* **Facilities:** FTV WiFi ৬ HL 🏊 Gym Xmas **Conf:** Class 100 Board 90 Theatre 250 **Services:** Lift Night porter Air con **Parking:** 100 **Notes:** LB Civ Wed 160

The Hyatt Place London Heathrow Airport

★★★★ 75% HOTEL PLAN 1 A3

tel: 020 8759 7777 **The Grove, Bath Road UB7 0DG**
email: lhza.reception@hyatt.com **web:** www.londonheathrowairport.place.hyatt.com

This refurbished hotel offers very modern and comfortable accommodation for business and leisure guests alike. Centrally located in Heathrow, within minutes of terminals 2, 3 and 5, the rooms have new triple-glazed windows that offer excellent soundproofing. There is a restaurant on site serving breakfast and dinner; lunch is available in the bar. Underground parking and conference facilities are also available.

Rooms: 349 **Facilities:** FTV WiFi ৬ Gym Xmas **Conf:** Class 60 Board 48 Theatre 129 **Services:** Lift Night porter Air con **Parking:** 75

Leonardo Heathrow Airport Hotel

★★★★ 74% HOTEL PLAN 1 A3

tel: 020 8990 0000 **Bath Road UB7 0DP**
email: info.heathrowair@leonardo-hotels.com **web:** www.leonardo-hotels.com
dir: *Opposite terminals 2 and 3 at Heathrow Airport.*

The Leonardo Heathrow Airport Hotel is conveniently located on Bath Road just a couple of minutes from the Heathrow Terminals and only 15 minutes by express from central London. This hotel offers modern accommodation, a good range of meeting and event rooms, a large open-plan bar and restaurant, and plenty of parking on site. Free WiFi is available throughout the hotel.

Rooms: 230 (58 GF) 🐾 **S** fr £65 **D** fr £75* **Facilities:** Spa STV FTV WiFi ৬ HL Gym Hair salon Xmas New Year **Conf:** Class 60 Board 80 Theatre 120 **Services:** Lift Night porter Air con **Parking:** 90

Mercure London Heathrow Airport

Mercure
HOTELS

★★★★ 74% HOTEL PLAN 1 A3

tel: 020 8573 6162 **Shepiston Lane UB3 1LP**
email: info@mlondonheathrow.com **web:** www.mlondonheathrow.com
dir: *M4 junction 4, follow signs to Hayes and Shepiston Lane, hotel approximately 1 mile, adjacent to fire station.*

This hotel is conveniently located just two miles from Heathrow Airport and there is a Hoppa shuttle service (chargeable) that operates from 4am until 11pm daily. Bedrooms are stylish and comfortably appointed with a good range of amenities; free WiFi is available throughout. The hotel has a restaurant, snack bar, Costa Coffee, a gym and extensive meeting facilities. Plenty of parking is available on site.

Rooms: 184 (11 family) (75 GF) **S** fr £69 **D** fr £79 **Facilities:** FTV WiFi ৬ HL Gym **Conf:** Class 84 Board 60 Theatre 160 **Services:** Lift Night porter Air con **Parking:** 160 **Notes:** Civ Wed 80

The Park Grand London Heathrow

★★★★ 73% HOTEL PLAN 1 B3

tel: 020 7479 2266 **449 Great West Road TW5 0BY**
email: john@montcalm.co.uk **web:** www.parkgrandheathrow.co.uk
dir: *From A4 Great Western Road, turn into Jersey Road, 3rd exit at roundabout, turn left. Hotel on the left.*

This modern hotel is in a convenient location just five miles from London Heathrow airport and with easy access to central London. The hotel is modern in style with spacious open-plan public areas including a stylish bar and restaurant. Bedrooms are also modern and very comfortable; all are fully air-conditioned and have digital TV and complimentary WiFi. Parking is available on site.

Rooms: 124 (14 family) ⏺ **Facilities:** STV FTV WiFi ⏶ HL Gym New Year
Conf: Class 60 Board 40 Theatre 70 **Services:** Lift Night porter Air con **Parking:** 38
Notes: Civ Wed 80

Ramada Hounslow - Heathrow East

 RAMADA.

★★★ 73% HOTEL PLAN 1 B2

tel: 020 8538 1230 **8-10 Lampton Road TW3 1JL**
email: gm@ramadahounslow.co.uk **web:** www.ramada.co.uk/hounslow
dir: A4 Bath Road, A3006, into Lampton Road A3005.

A purpose-built hotel situated in the centre of Hounslow, within walking distance of the tube station and with easy access to the motorway network. The accommodation is comfortable and offers a range of amenities. The public areas are light and airy, and parking is available.

Rooms: 96 (11 family) (4 GF) ⏺ **S** fr £69 **D** fr £79* **Facilities:** FTV WiFi ⏶ Gym Xmas New Year **Conf:** Class 50 Board 60 Theatre 100 **Services:** Lift Night porter Air con **Parking:** 20

Premier Inn Hayes Heathrow

Premier Inn

BUDGET HOTEL PLAN 1 A4

tel: 0871 527 8504 (Calls cost 13p per minute plus your phone company's access charge) **362 Uxbridge Road UB4 0HF**
web: www.premierinn.com
dir: M4 junction 3, A312 north straight across next roundbaout onto dual carriageway, at A4020 junction turn left, hotel 100 yards on right.

High quality, budget accommodation ideal for both families and business travellers. Spacious, en suite bedrooms feature free WiFi and tea and coffee making facilities, and in most hotels, Freeview TV is also available. The adjacent family restaurant features a wide and varied menu.

Rooms: 86

Premier Inn Heathrow Airport (Bath Road)

Premier Inn

BUDGET HOTEL PLAN 1 A3

tel: 0871 527 8508 (Calls cost 13p per minute plus your phone company's access charge) **15 Bath Road TW6 2AB**
web: www.premierinn.com
dir: M4 junction 4, follow signs for Heathrow Terminals 1, 2 and 3. Left onto Bath Road signed A4/London. Hotel on right after 0.5 mile.

Rooms: 594

Premier Inn Heathrow Airport Terminal 5

Premier Inn

BUDGET HOTEL PLAN 1 A3

tel: 0871 527 9344 (Calls cost 13p per minute plus your phone company's access charge) **Bath Road, Hillingdon UB7 0EB**
web: www.premierinn.com
dir: M25 junction 14, follow A3113/Heathrow T4 and Cargo signs. At roundabout 1st left onto A3044, at next roundabout 3rd exit signed Longford. Hotel approximately 250 yards on left.

Rooms: 400

Premier Inn London Brentford

BUDGET HOTEL PLAN 1 C3

tel: 0871 527 9560 (Calls cost 13p per minute plus your phone company's access charge) **Alfa Laval, Great West Road TW8 9AD**
web: www.premierinn.com
dir: M4 junction 2, to Chiswick Roundabout. Take 5th exit onto A4 (keep right to next roundabout). Take 1st exit, hotel on right.

Rooms: 124

Premier Inn London Heathrow Airport (M4 Jct 4) hotel

Premier Inn

BUDGET HOTEL PLAN 1 A3

tel: 0871 527 8510 (Calls cost 13p per minute plus your phone company's access charge) **Shepiston Lane, Heathrow Airport UB3 1RW**
web: www.premierinn.com
dir: M4 junction 4 take 3rd exit off roundabout. Hotel on right.

Rooms: 134

Premier Inn London Heathrow Airport Terminal 4

Premier Inn

BUDGET HOTEL PLAN 1 A2

tel: 0871 527 9698 (Calls cost 13p per minute plus your phone company's access charge) **Terminal 4, Sheffield Road, London Heathrow Airport TW6 3FH**
web: www.premierinn.com
dir: Phone for directions.

Rooms: 613

Renaissance London Heathrow Hotel

R RENAISSANCE LONDON HEATHROW HOTEL

AA Advertised PLAN 1 A3

tel: 020 8897 6363 **Bath Road TW6 2AQ**
email: re3@renaissanceheathrow.co.uk **web:** www.renaissancelondonheathrow.co.uk
dir: M4 junction 4 take spur road towards airport, then 2nd left. At roundabout, 2nd exit signed 'Renaissance Hotel'. Hotel adjacent to Customs House.

This spacious hotel is located on the perimeter of Heathrow airport with spectacular views of the main runway, and is within easy reach of Windsor, and motorway and rail networks to London. The hotel has excellent conference and leisure facilities.

Rooms: 710 (87 GF) ⏺ **S** fr £129 **D** fr £139 (including breakfast)* **Facilities:** Spa STV WiFi ⏶ Gym Fitness centre **Conf:** Class 300 Board 80 Theatre 500 **Services:** Lift Night porter Air con **Parking:** 700 **Notes:** Civ Wed 360

H

HEATHROW AIRPORT *continued*

Sofitel London Heathrow

SOFITEL

◉◉◉ AA Advertised PLAN 1 A3

tel: 020 8757 7777 **Terminal 5, Wentworth Drive TW6 2GD**
email: slh@sofitelheathrow.com **web:** www.sofitelheathrow.com
dir: *M25 junction 14. At roundabout take 2nd exit, after 80 metres turn left. Hotel on right.*

This is the only Heathrow airport hotel with direct access to Terminal 5 via a covered walkway and Terminals 1, 2, 3 and 4 via the Heathrow Express/Connect rail connection. It is only 21 minutes from Central London by train. Sofitel London Heathrow boasts 605 non-smoking bedrooms including 27 suites, 45 meeting rooms, 2 restaurants, 2 bars and a tea salon as well as private dining options. The hotel also offers a hair salon, a state-of-the-art health spa and gym, as well as an on-site car park.

Rooms: 605 (38 GF) ☛ **S** fr £329 **D** fr £349 (including breakfast)* **Facilities:** Spa STV FTV WiFi Gym **Conf:** Class 820 Board 80 Theatre 1200 **Services:** Lift Night porter Air con **Parking:** 360 **Notes:** LB Civ Wed 220

HELLIDON	Map 11 SP55
Northamptonshire	

Hellidon Lakes Golf & Spa Hotel

Q**HOTELS**
INSPIRED BY YOU

★★★★ 74% HOTEL

tel: 01327 262550 **NN11 6GG**
email: hellidonlakes@qhotels.co.uk **web:** www.qhotels.co.uk
dir: *Off A361 between Daventry and Banbury, signed.*

Some 220 acres of beautiful countryside, which include 27 holes of golf and 12 lakes, combine to form a rather spectacular backdrop to this impressive hotel. Bedroom styles vary, from ultra smart, modern rooms through to those in the original wing that offer superb views. There is an extensive range of facilities available, from meeting rooms to a swimming pool, gym and ten-pin bowling. Golfers of all levels can try some of the world's most challenging courses on the indoor golf simulator.

Rooms: 110 (5 family) ☛ **Facilities:** Spa FTV WiFi ⓥ HL ⓒ ♨ 27 ♒ Fishing ⛷ Gym Beauty therapist Indoor smart golf 10-pin bowling Steam room Coarse fishing lake Xmas New Year **Conf:** Class 110 Board 50 Theatre 300 **Services:** Lift Night porter **Parking:** 200 **Notes:** LB Civ Wed 176

HELMSLEY	Map 19 SE68
North Yorkshire	

Feversham Arms Hotel & Verbena Spa

★★★★ ◉◉ HOTEL

tel: 01439 770766 **1-8 High Street YO62 5AG**
email: info@fevershamarmshotel.com **web:** www.fevershamarmshotel.com
dir: *A168 signed Thirsk A1, A170 or A64 signed York from A1 to York North, B1363 to Helmsley. Hotel 125 metres from Market Place.*

This long-established hotel lies just round the corner from the main square, and under caring ownership proves to be a refined operation, yet without airs and graces. There are several lounge areas and a high-ceilinged conservatory restaurant where menus are created with skill and minimal fuss from good local ingredients. The bedrooms, including four air-conditioned poolside suites (some with wood-burners) and spa suites with balconies or French balconies, all have their own individual character and decor. Expect Egyptian cotton sheets, duck down duvets and smart TVs. The spa offers a comprehensive range of pampering treatments.

Rooms: 33 (9 family) (8 GF) ☛ **Facilities:** Spa STV FTV WiFi ⓥ ☇ Sauna Saunarium Arometherapy room Monsoon showers Relaxation lounge Xmas New Year **Conf:** Class 20 Board 24 Theatre 35 **Services:** Lift Night porter **Parking:** 50 **Notes:** Civ Wed 50

H

Black Swan Hotel

★★★★ 79% ◎◎◎ HOTEL

tel: 01439 770466 **Market Place YO62 5BJ**
email: enquiries@blackswan-helmsley.co.uk **web:** www.blackswan-helmsley.co.uk
dir: *A1 junction 49, A168, A170 east, hotel 14 miles from Thirsk.*

People have been visiting this establishment for over 200 years and it has become a landmark that dominates the market square. The hotel is renowned for its hospitality and friendliness; many of the staff are long-serving and dedicated. The bedrooms are stylish and include a junior suite and feature rooms. Dinner in the award-winning restaurant is the highlight of any stay. The hotel has a tearoom and patisserie that is open daily.

Rooms: 45 (4 family) ⟨S fr £135 **D** fr £189 (including breakfast & dinner)*
Facilities: FTV WiFi Xmas New Year **Conf:** Class 30 Board 26 Theatre 50
Services: Night porter **Parking:** 40 **Notes:** LB Civ Wed 90

The Pheasant Hotel

★★★ ◎◎ 🍽 COUNTRY HOUSE HOTEL

tel: 01439 771241 **Mill Street, Harome YO62 5JG**
email: reservations@thepheasanthotel.com **web:** www.thepheasanthotel.com
dir: *Leave A1(M) at Thirsk, follow A170 east towards Helmsley/Scarborough and then through Helmsley. Right after 0.5 mile to Harome, follow road for 2.5 miles.*

The Pheasant Hotel sits in a delightful small North Yorkshire village, overlooking the village pond. The public areas are delightful in a very country-house style, with ample outside seating areas that is ideal for enjoying a delightful afternoon tea. The rooms are spacious, very well appointed and have a luxury feel to them. The small heated pool is easily accessible, and the hotel has ample parking. Food is the highlight of the stay with the menu boasting local produce and inventive cooking.

Rooms: 16 (2 family) (3 GF) ⟨S fr £95 **D** fr £180 (including breakfast)*
Facilities: FTV WiFi 🏊 ⛳ Xmas New Year **Conf:** Class 30 Board 20 Theatre 30
Parking: 10 **Notes:** LB Civ Wed 60

HELSTON
Cornwall & Isles Of Scilly   Map 2 SW62

Premier Inn Helston

Premier Inn

BUDGET HOTEL

tel: 0871 527 8512 (Calls cost 13p per minute plus your phone company's access charge) **Clodgey Lane TR13 8FZ**
web: www.premierinn.com
dir: *A39 towards Falmouth. Right onto A394 towards Helston, 8 miles. At roundabout 1st exit (Helston bypass) signed Penzance (A394)/Lizard. Hotel at next roundabout on left. Note: for sat nav use TR13 0QD.*

High quality, budget accommodation ideal for both families and business travellers. Spacious, en suite bedrooms feature free WiFi and tea and coffee making facilities, and in most hotels, Freeview TV is also available. The adjacent family restaurant features a wide and varied menu.

Rooms: 50

H

HEMEL HEMPSTEAD
Hertfordshire   Map 6 TL00

Aubrey Park Hotel

★★★★ 80% HOTEL

tel: 01582 792105 **Hemel Hempstead Road, Redbourn AL3 7AF**
email: reception@aubreypark.co.uk **web:** www.aubreypark.co.uk
dir: *M1 junction 9 follow Hemel Hempstead and St Albans signs for 3 miles, straight across 2 roundabouts onto B487 signed Hemel Hempstead. Hotel on right.*

The hotel is conveniently located a short drive from the historic Roman city of St Albans, close to the M1 and the M25, and is an ideal venue for both corporate and leisure guests. The hotel is modern with attentive staff, good food, ample parking and extensive, well-equipped meeting areas.

Rooms: 137 (10 family) (65 GF) ☏ **S** fr £60 **D** fr £60* **Facilities:** FTV WiFi ♬ Gym Xmas New Year **Conf:** Class 96 Board 65 Theatre 200 **Services:** Lift Night porter **Parking:** 129 **Notes:** LB Civ Wed 85

The Watermill

★★★ 69% HOTEL

tel: 01442 349955 **London Road, Bourne End HP1 2RJ**
email: info@hotelwatermill.co.uk **web:** www.hotelwatermill.co.uk
dir: *From M25 and M1 follow signs to Aylesbury on A41, A4251 to Bourne End. Hotel 0.25 mile on right.*

In the heart of the county, this modern hotel has been built around an old flour mill on the banks of the River Bulbourne with water meadows adjacent. The thoughtfully equipped, contemporary bedrooms are located in three annexes situated around the complex. A good range of air-conditioned conference and meeting rooms complement the lounge bar and restaurant.

Rooms: 71 (71 annexe) (10 family) (35 GF) (8 smoking) ☏ **Facilities:** STV FTV WiFi Fishing Xmas New Year **Conf:** Class 150 Board 125 Theatre 200 **Services:** Night porter **Parking:** 100 **Notes:** Civ Wed 180

Premier Inn Hemel Hempstead Central

Premier Inn

BUDGET HOTEL

tel: 0871 527 8514 (Calls cost 13p per minute plus your phone company's access charge) **Moor End Road HP1 1BT**
web: www.premierinn.com
dir: *M1 junction 8, A414, follow town centre signs. Right at 1st mini-roundabout, right at 2nd mini-roundabout into Seldon Hill Road, follow Riverside car park signs (footbridge to hotel from floor 3).*

High quality, budget accommodation ideal for both families and business travellers. Spacious, en suite bedrooms feature free WiFi and tea and coffee making facilities, and in most hotels, Freeview TV is also available. The adjacent family restaurant features a wide and varied menu.

Rooms: 114

Premier Inn Hemel Hempstead West

Premier Inn

BUDGET HOTEL

tel: 0871 527 8516 (Calls cost 13p per minute plus your phone company's access charge) **A41 Service Area, Bourne End HP1 2SB**
web: www.premierinn.com
dir: *M25 junction 20, A41 exit at services. Or from M1 junction 8, A414, A41, exit at services.*

Rooms: 62

HENLEY-ON-THAMES
Oxfordshire   Map 5 SU78

Hotel du Vin Henley-on-Thames

★★★★ 77% TOWN HOUSE HOTEL

tel: 01491 848400 & 0844 736 4258 (Calls cost 5p per minute plus your phone company's access charge) **New Street RG9 2BP**
email: info.henley@hotelduvin.com
web: www.hotelduvin.com/locations/henley-on-thames
dir: *M4 junction 8/9 signed High Wycombe, 2nd exit onto A404 in 2 miles. A4130 to Henley, over bridge, through lights, into Hart Street, right into Bell Street, right into New Street, hotel on right.*

Situated just 50 yards from the water's edge, this hotel retains the character and much of the architecture of its former life as a brewery. Food, and naturally wine, take on a strong focus here and guests will find an interesting mix of dishes to choose from; there are three private dining rooms where the fermentation room and old malt house once were; alfresco dining is popular when the weather permits. Bedrooms provide comfort, style and a good range of facilities including power showers. Parking is available and there is a drop-off point in the courtyard.

Rooms: 43 (4 family) (4 GF) ☏ **Facilities:** STV FTV WiFi ♬ Xmas New Year **Conf:** Class 20 Board 36 Theatre 56 **Services:** Night porter Air con **Parking:** 46 **Notes:** Civ Wed 60

HEREFORD
Herefordshire   Map 10 SO54

See also **Leominster**

Holme Lacy House Hotel

WARNERLEISUREHOTELS

★★★★ 75% COUNTRY HOUSE HOTEL

tel: 01432 870870 **Holme Lacy HR2 6LP**
email: kellie.appleyard@bourne-leisure.co.uk **web:** www.warnerleisurehotels.co.uk
dir: *B4399 at Holme Lacy, take lane opposite college. Hotel 500 metres on right.*

This is a grand Grade I listed mansion with a rich history, just a short drive from Hereford, set in 20 acres of superb parkland in the heart of the Wye Valley. The well-appointed bedrooms are comfortable and vary in size and style. There's plenty to do here, with a full daily entertainment programme, an indoor pool, and health and beauty treatments. The three restaurants provide carefully selected menus of quality cuisine. This hotel is for adults only (minimum 21 years old).

Rooms: 181 (150 annexe) (53 GF) ☏ **Facilities:** Spa FTV WiFi HL 🔄 ♨ Fishing 🌊 Gym Archery Rifle shooting Aquafit Yoga ♫ Xmas New Year **Services:** Lift Night porter **Parking:** 200 **Notes:** No children 21 years

Three Counties Hotel

★★★ 77% HOTEL

tel: 01432 299955 **Belmont Road HR2 7BP**
email: enquiries@threecountieshotel.co.uk **web:** www.threecountieshotel.co.uk
dir: *On A465 Abergavenny road.*

Just a mile west of the city centre, this large, privately owned, modern complex has well-equipped, spacious bedrooms; many are located in separate single-storey buildings around the extensive car park. There is a spacious, comfortable lounge, a traditional bar and an attractive restaurant.

Rooms: 60 (32 annexe) (4 family) (46 GF) **S** fr £55 **D** fr £84 (including breakfast)* **Facilities:** STV FTV WiFi **Conf:** Class 200 Board 120 Theatre 450 **Services:** Night porter **Parking:** 250 **Notes:** Civ Wed 350

Premier Inn Hereford

Premier Inn

BUDGET HOTEL

tel: 0871 527 8518 (Calls cost 13p per minute plus your phone company's access charge) **Holmer Road, Holmer HR4 9RS**
web: www.premierinn.com
dir: *From north: M5 junction 7, A4103 to Worcester. M50 junction 4, A49 (Leominster road). Hotel 800 yards on left.*

High quality, budget accommodation ideal for both families and business travellers. Spacious, en suite bedrooms feature free WiFi and tea and coffee making facilities, and in most hotels, Freeview TV is also available. The adjacent family restaurant features a wide and varied menu.

Rooms: 101

HERNE BAY
Kent   Map 7 TR16

Premier Inn Canterbury North/Herne Bay

Premier Inn

BUDGET HOTEL

tel: 0871 527 8520 (Calls cost 13p per minute plus your phone company's access charge) **Blacksole Farm, Margate Road CT6 6LA**
web: www.premierinn.com
dir: *From M2 junction 7 follow Canterbury signs, A299 signed Ramsgate/Margate. Exit at Broomfield and Beltinge. Hotel just off roundabout.*

High quality, budget accommodation ideal for both families and business travellers. Spacious, en suite bedrooms feature free WiFi and tea and coffee making facilities, and in most hotels, Freeview TV is also available. The adjacent family restaurant features a wide and varied menu.

Rooms: 50

HESWALL
Merseyside   Map 15 SJ28

Premier Inn Wirral (Heswall)

Premier Inn

BUDGET HOTEL

tel: 0871 527 9178 (Calls cost 13p per minute plus your phone company's access charge) **Chester Road, Gayton CH60 3SD**
web: www.premierinn.com
dir: *M53 junction 4, A5137 signed Heswall. In 3 miles left at next roundabout, hotel on left.*

High quality, budget accommodation ideal for both families and business travellers. Spacious, en suite bedrooms feature free WiFi and tea and coffee making facilities, and in most hotels, Freeview TV is also available. The adjacent family restaurant features a wide and varied menu.

Rooms: 87

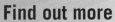

Find out more
about the AA Hotel of the Year for England on page 16

HETHERSETT
Norfolk   Map 13 TG10

Park Farm Hotel

★★★★ 81% ⊛ HOTEL

tel: 01603 810264 **NR9 3DL**
email: enq@parkfarm-hotel.co.uk **web:** www.parkfarm-hotel.co.uk
dir: *5 miles south of Norwich, exit A11 onto B1172.*

Park Farm is an elegant Georgian farmhouse set in landscaped grounds surrounded by open countryside. The property has been owned and run by the Gowing family since 1958. Bedrooms are pleasantly decorated and tastefully furnished; some rooms have patio doors with a sun terrace. Public rooms include a stylish conservatory, a lounge bar, a smart restaurant and superb leisure facilities.

Rooms: 53 (16 annexe) (15 family) (26 GF) ⌁ **S** fr £75 **D** fr £95 (including breakfast)* **Facilities:** Spa FTV WiFi ⌖ Gym Beauty salon Hairdressing Xmas New Year **Conf:** Class 50 Board 50 Theatre 120 **Services:** Night porter **Parking:** 150 **Notes:** Civ Wed 100

HEXHAM
Northumberland   Map 21 NY96

HIGHLY RECOMMENDED

Langley Castle Hotel

★★★★ 83% ⊛⊛ HOTEL

tel: 01434 688888 **Langley NE47 5LU**
email: manager@langleycastle.com **web:** www.langleycastle.com
dir: *From A69 south on A686 for 2 miles. Hotel on right.*

Langley is a magnificent 14th-century fortified castle, with its own chapel, set in 10 acres of parkland. There is an award-winning restaurant, a comfortable drawing room and a cosy bar. Bedrooms are furnished with period pieces and most feature window seats. Restored buildings in the grounds have been converted into very stylish castle-view bedrooms.

Rooms: 27 (18 annexe) (8 family) (9 GF) ⌁ **S** fr £131.50 **D** fr £167 (including breakfast) **Facilities:** STV WiFi ⌕ HL Xmas New Year **Conf:** Class 60 Board 40 Theatre 120 **Services:** Lift Night porter Air con **Parking:** 70 **Notes:** LB Civ Wed 120

Slaley Hall

★★★★ 82% HOTEL

tel: 01434 673350 & 0871 222 4688 (Calls cost 10p per minute plus your phone company's access charge) **Slaley NE47 0BX**
email: Slaleyreception@qhotels.co.uk **web:** www.qhotels.co.uk
dir: *A1 from south to A68 link road follow signs for Slaley Hall.*

One thousand acres of Northumbrian forest and parkland, two championship golf courses and indoor leisure facilities can all be found here. Spacious bedrooms are fully air-conditioned, equipped with a range of extras and the deluxe rooms offer excellent standards. Public rooms include a number of lounges and dining options, including the fine-dining Dukes Grill, informal Claret Jug and the impressive main restaurant that overlooks the golf course.

Rooms: 141 (5 family) (45 GF) ⌁ **S** fr £87 **D** fr £99 (including breakfast)* **Facilities:** Spa FTV WiFi ⌖ ⌕ 36 Gym Quad bikes Archery Clay pigeon shooting 4x4 driving Segway Xmas New Year **Conf:** Class 220 Board 150 Theatre 350 **Services:** Lift Night porter Air con **Parking:** 500 **Notes:** LB Civ Wed 250

H

HEXHAM *continued*

Battlesteads

★★★ 88% HOTEL

tel: 01434 230209 **Wark On Tyne NE48 3LS**
email: info@battlesteads.com **web:** www.battlesteads.com

Battlesteads is located in the peaceful and picturesque village of Wark in the heart of Hadrian's Wall country. Boasting an observatory to make the best of the area's Dark Skies status, and an award-winning kitchen team sourcing local produce, and even growing their own ingredients. Bedrooms are well appointed and presented with quality beds. The log-burning stove in the bar makes it the perfect place to sit while sampling one of a host of real ales on offer .The team throughout the hotel are warm and friendly, and really do strive to go that extra mile for guests.

Rooms: 22 (5 annexe) (2 family) (4 GF) ☎ **D** fr £100 (including breakfast)*
Facilities: FTV WiFi ☟ New Year **Parking:** 30 **Notes:** Closed 25 December Civ Wed 70

Santo's Higham Farm Hotel

★★★ 79% ❀ HOTEL

tel: 01773 833812 **Main Road DE55 6EH**
email: reception@santoshighamfarm.co.uk **web:** www.santoshighamfarm.co.uk
dir: *M1 junction 28, A38 towards Derby, then A61 towards Chesterfield. Onto B6013 towards Belper, hotel 300 yards on right.*

With panoramic views across the rolling Amber Valley, this 15th-century crook barn and farmhouse has been expertly restored and extended. There's an Italian wing and an international wing of themed bedrooms and mini suites. Freshly prepared dishes, especially fish, are available in Guiseppe's restaurant. This hotel makes an ideal romantic hideaway.

Rooms: 31 (3 family) (7 GF) ☎ **S** fr £101 **D** fr £125 (including breakfast)*
Facilities: FTV WiFi ☟ Xmas New Year **Conf:** Class 40 Board 34 Theatre 100
Services: Lift Night porter **Parking:** 100 **Notes:** LB Civ Wed 100

Premier Inn Christchurch/Highcliffe

Premier Inn ●

BUDGET HOTEL

tel: 0871 527 9276 (Calls cost 13p per minute plus your phone company's access charge) **266 Lymington Road BH23 5ET**
web: www.premierinn.com
dir: *From A35 (Christchurch roundabout) onto A337 towards New Milton and Lymington. Approximately 2 miles, hotel on left.*

High quality, budget accommodation ideal for both families and business travellers. Spacious, en suite bedrooms feature free WiFi and tea and coffee making facilities, and in most hotels, Freeview TV is also available. The adjacent family restaurant features a wide and varied menu.

Rooms: 62

Karma St Martin's

★★★★ 79% ❀❀ HOTEL

tel: 01720 422368 **TR25 0QW**
email: st.martins@karmaresorts.com **web:** www.karmastmartins.com
dir: *Phone for directions.*

Located a stone's throw from the beach in Lower Town, St Martin's (Isles of Scilly), from a distance the hotel appears as a small hamlet of traditional stone cottages lining the shore line. Inside, there's a contemporary hideaway hotel with all the up-to-date amenities, including a bespoke book and vinyl library. Excellent ocean views are a feature here as is the Karma Spa. On arrival, the hotel porter will meet guests (when organised in advance) and transport them to the hotel via shuttle. Award-winning cuisine is showcased in the Cloudesley Shovell Restaurant with fresh produce and foraged ingredients at its heart.

Karma St Martin's

Rooms: 30 (5 family) (16 GF) **Facilities:** Spa STV FTV WiFi ⬐ ⬐ Games room
Conf: Class 30 Board 25 Theatre 80 **Notes:** Closed 1 November to Easter Civ Wed 80

See advert below

HIGH WYCOMBE	Map 5 SU89
Buckinghamshire	

Premier Inn High Wycombe Central

BUDGET HOTEL

tel: 0871 527 9326 (Calls cost 13p per minute plus your phone company's access charge) **Arch Way HP13 5HL**
web: www.premierinn.com
dir: *M4, junction 8/9, A404(M) signed Marlow and Wycombe. Exit for High Wycombe, right at roundabout (town centre) via Marlow Hill. Left at 1st mini-roundabout, right at next roundabout, left signed Dovecot. Right at next junction into Arch Way, (Sainsburys on left) 1st left, left to hotel. Note: for sat nav use HP11 2DN.*

High quality, budget accommodation ideal for both families and business travellers. Spacious, en suite bedrooms feature free WiFi and tea and coffee making facilities, and in most hotels, Freeview TV is also available. The adjacent family restaurant features a wide and varied menu.

Rooms: 120

Premier Inn High Wycombe/Beaconsfield

BUDGET HOTEL

tel: 0871 527 8522 (Calls cost 13p per minute plus your phone company's access charge) **Thanstead Farm, London Road HP10 9YL**
web: www.premierinn.com
dir: *M40 junction 3, A40 towards High Wycombe.*

Rooms: 135

H

H

HINCKLEY
Leicestershire

Map 11 SP49

Sketchley Grange Hotel

focus hotels
management limited

★★★★ 81% HOTEL

tel: 01455 251133 **Sketchley Lane, Burbage LE10 3HU**
email: info@sketchleygrangehotel.co.uk **web:** www.sketchleygrangehotel.co.uk
dir: M69 junction 1, B4109 towards Hinckley. Left at 2nd roundabout. Into Sketchley Lane, 1st right, also Sketchley Lane.

Close to motorway connections, this hotel is peacefully set in its own grounds, and enjoys open country views. Extensive leisure facilities include a stylish health and leisure spa. There are modern meeting facilities, a choice of bars, and two dining options, together with comfortable bedrooms furnished with many extras.

Rooms: 102 (7 family) (11 GF) S fr £162.50 **D** fr £175 (including breakfast)*
Facilities: Spa FTV WiFi Gym Steam room Sauna Xmas New Year
Conf: Class 150 Board 50 Theatre 280 **Services:** Lift Night porter **Parking:** 300
Notes: Civ Wed 220

Jurys Inn Hinckley Island Hotel

★★★★ 77% HOTEL

tel: 01455 631122 **A5 Watling Street LE10 3JA**
email: hinckleyisland_reception@jurysinn.com **web:** www.jurysinns.com
dir: M69 junction 1 from Leicester, A5/B4109. Hotel 0.3 mile on left.

A modern hotel situated in the middle of Leicestershire with spacious rooms and comfortable beds. Guests can relax, drink and eat in the lounge and coffee bar, a themed bar or a Marco Pierre White restaurant. The hotel also offers a pool and gym facilities.

Rooms: 362 (125 family) (148 GF) **Facilities:** WiFi HL Gym **Conf:** Class 200 Board 40 Theatre 650 **Services:** Lift Night porter **Parking:** 650 **Notes:** Civ Wed

Premier Inn Hinckley

Premier Inn

BUDGET HOTEL

tel: 0871 527 8524 (Calls cost 13p per minute plus your phone company's access charge) **Coventry Road LE10 0NB**
web: www.premierinn.com
dir: M69 junction 1, A5 towards Nuneaton. In 2.5 miles right at roundabout onto B4666 signed Hinckley Town Centre. Hotel on right, entrance via Total petrol station.

High quality, budget accommodation ideal for both families and business travellers. Spacious, en suite bedrooms feature free WiFi and tea and coffee making facilities, and in most hotels, Freeview TV is also available. The adjacent family restaurant features a wide and varied menu.

Rooms: 91

HINTLESHAM
Suffolk

Map 13 TM04

Hintlesham Hall Hotel

★★★★ ◎◎ HOTEL

tel: 01473 652334 **George Street IP8 3NS**
email: reservations@hintleshamhall.com **web:** www.hintleshamhall.com
dir: 4 miles west of Ipswich on A1071 to Hadleigh and Sudbury.

Hospitality and service are key features at this imposing Grade I listed country house hotel, situated in 175 acres of grounds and landscaped gardens. Originally a manor house dating from the Elizabethan era, the building was extended in the 17th and 18th centuries. It was a Red Cross hospital in World War II, and has been a hotel for nearly 40 years. Individually decorated bedrooms offer a high degree of comfort; each is tastefully furnished and equipped with many thoughtful touches. The Hintlesham Spa has three treatment rooms (including one for couples), a sumptuous relaxation area, nail bar, and enclosed outdoor area with hot tub. The spacious public rooms include a series of comfortable lounges, and an elegant restaurant which serves fine classical cuisine based on top-notch and, where practical, local ingredients. WiFi is offered throughout. A helicopter landing area is also available.

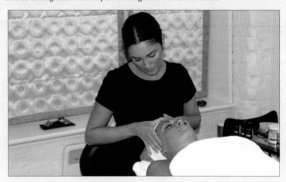

Rooms: 32 (10 annexe) (9 GF) S fr £85 **D** fr £105 (including breakfast)*
Facilities: Spa FTV WiFi HL Health and beauty services Clay pigeon shooting Xmas New Year **Conf:** Class 50 Board 32 Theatre 80 **Services:** Night porter
Parking: 60 **Notes:** LB Civ Wed 110

HINTON CHARTERHOUSE
Somerset — Map 4 ST75

HIGHLY RECOMMENDED

Homewood Park Hotel & Spa
★★★★ 83% ◉◉ HOTEL

tel: 01225 723731 **Abbey Lane BA2 7TB**
email: info@homewoodpark.co.uk **web:** www.homewoodpark.co.uk
dir: *6 miles southeast of Bath on A36, left at 2nd sign for Freshford.*

This hotel has a delightful location in attractive parkland, close to Bath and the Longleat estate. Bedrooms are stylishly and comfortably appointed, and many enjoy splendid countryside views. The spa and leisure facilities are notable, and a meal in the restaurant should not be missed.

Rooms: 21 (2 annexe) (3 family) (2 GF) ⚓ **Facilities:** Spa FTV WiFi ⚡ 🏊 Sauna Steam room Nail bar Hydrotherapy pool Xmas New Year **Conf:** Class 30 Board 25 Theatre 40 **Services:** Night porter **Parking:** 40 **Notes:** LB Civ Wed 120

HITCHIN
Hertfordshire — Map 12 TL12

Premier Inn Hitchin Town Centre
Premier Inn 🔵

BUDGET HOTEL

tel: 0871 527 9578 (Calls cost 13p per minute plus your phone company's access charge) **Portmill Lane SG5 1DJ**
web: www.premierinn.com
dir: *A1(M) junction 8, A602 (Hitchin). At 1st roundabout take 4th exit into St Johns Road, left into Hitchin Hill. At next roundabout 2nd exit into Queen Street. 4th left turn into Portmill Lane, hotel on right.*

High quality, budget accommodation ideal for both families and business travellers. Spacious, en suite bedrooms feature free WiFi and tea and coffee making facilities, and in most hotels, Freeview TV is also available. The adjacent family restaurant features a wide and varied menu.

Rooms: 60

HOAR CROSS
Staffordshire — Map 10 SK12

Hoar Cross Hall
AA Advertised ◉

tel: 01283 575671 **Maker Lane DE13 8QS**
web: www.hoarcross.co.uk

This well-established hotel has gained a reputation for its comprehensive spa offering. The Ballroom Restaurant offers a good food experience and features faultless table settings. The hall's larger luxury rooms are located in both the original stately home East Wing (with wonderful views of the formal garden) and the newer West Wing, which looks out on to the woodland or the Italian Water Garden.

Rooms: 96 **S** fr £179 **D** fr £278 (including breakfast & dinner)*
Facilities: Conf: Class 70 Board 30 Theatre 150

HOCKLEY HEATH
West Midlands — Map 10 SP17

HIGHLY RECOMMENDED

Nuthurst Grange Hotel
★★★★ 83% ◉◉ HOTEL

tel: 01564 783972 **Nuthurst Grange Lane B94 5NL**
email: info@nuthurst-grange.co.uk **web:** www.nuthurst-grange.co.uk
dir: *Exit A3400, 0.5 mile south of Hockley Heath. Turn at sign into Nuthurst Grange Lane.*

A stunning avenue is the approach to this country house hotel, set amid several acres of well-tended gardens and mature grounds, with views over rolling countryside. The spacious bedrooms and bathrooms offer considerable luxury and comfort, and public areas include restful lounges, meeting rooms and a sunny restaurant. The kitchen brigade produces highly imaginative British and French cuisine, complemented by very attentive, professional restaurant service.

Rooms: 19 (7 family) (2 GF) ⚓ **Facilities:** STV FTV WiFi 🏊 **Conf:** Class 50 Board 35 Theatre 100 **Parking:** 80 **Notes:** Civ Wed 100

HOLLINGBOURNE
Kent — Map 7 TQ85

Mercure Maidstone, Great Danes Hotel
★★★★ 72% HOTEL

tel: 0844 815 9045 (Calls cost 5p per minute plus your phone company's access charge) **ME17 1RE**
email: info@mercuremaidstone.co.uk **web:** www.mercuremaidstone.co.uk
dir: *M20 junction 8, follow Leeds Castle signs, at 2nd roundabout turn right.*

This property is set in 26 acres of private grounds just a few minutes from the M20, and close to channel ports and the Eurotunnel. The smartly appointed bedrooms are well equipped and suitable for business and leisure guests alike. Public rooms and facilities include Art's Bar and Grill as well as an indoor pool, fitness centre and a 9-hole golf course.

Rooms: 126 (15 family) **Facilities:** FTV WiFi ♿ 🎣 Gym Squash Steam room Beauty treatments **Conf:** Class 220 Board 90 Theatre 650 **Services:** Night porter **Parking:** 500 **Notes:** Civ Wed 650

HOLT
Norfolk — Map 13 TG03

HIGHLY RECOMMENDED

The Pheasant Hotel & Restaurant
★★★★ 83% ◉ HOTEL

tel: 01263 588382 **Coast Road, Kelling NR25 7EG**
email: enquiries@pheasanthotelnorfolk.co.uk
web: www.pheasanthotelnorfolk.co.uk
dir: *On A149 coast road, mid-way between Sheringham and Blakeney.*

The Pheasant is a charming country house hotel set in its own extensive grounds, enjoying a peaceful rural location in the small village of Kelling, making it an ideal base from which to explore the beautiful north Norfolk coast and the surrounding villages of Cley and Blakeney. All bedrooms are beautifully presented and very comfortable. Afternoon tea is served on the terrace on warmer days and the lounge bar is cosy.

Rooms: 32 (1 family) (24 GF) ⚓ **S** fr £120 **D** fr £145 (including breakfast)*
Facilities: FTV WiFi ♿ Xmas New Year **Conf:** Class 15 Board 20 Theatre 50 **Services:** Night porter **Parking:** 50 **Notes:** Civ Wed 200

H

HONITON
Devon   **Map 4 ST10**

The Deer Park Country House Hotel
★★★★ 80% ◉◉ COUNTRY HOUSE HOTEL

tel: 01404 41266 **Weston EX14 3PG**
email: hello@deerpark.co.uk **web:** www.deerparkcountryhotel.co.uk
dir: A30, take slip road into Honiton signed Turks Head. Next right then next left into Heathpark Industrial Estate. Hotel approximately 1.6 miles.

This country manor hotel is set in 80 acres of gardens, which includes an alfresco dining area with wood-burning oven and a walled kitchen garden. The hotel is just a short drive from Honiton and has easy access to the A30. The spacious accommodation is located in both the main house and separate garden rooms; there is even a luxurious treehouse with stunning views across the countryside. Deer Park is ideal for both business and leisure guests, and its picturesque setting makes it ideal for weddings and events. The hotel also boasts the Priory Collection, the largest collection of sporting memorabilia in the country.

Rooms: 33 (18 annexe) (2 family) (10 GF) ⟨ **S** fr £70 **D** fr £140 (including breakfast)* **Facilities:** STV FTV WiFi ⟲ Fishing Clay shooting Archery Quad bikes Segways Xmas New Year **Conf:** Class 32 Board 22 Theatre 250 **Services:** Night porter **Parking:** 70 **Notes:** LB Civ Wed 170

HIGHLY RECOMMENDED

THE PIG at Combe
★★★ 86% ◉◉ COUNTRY HOUSE HOTEL

tel: 01404 540400 & 03452 259494 **Giltisham EX14 3AD**
email: info@thepigatcombe.com **web:** www.thepighotel.com/at-combe
dir: M5 junction 29, left onto Honiton Road/A3015, at roundabout take 2nd exit and stay on Honiton Road/A3015. Take exit towards B3177/Fenton/Fairmile, turn right then left. Continue on B3177, slight right then left then right again.

This mellow, honey-coloured Elizabethan manor is situated in the beautiful Otter Valley near Honiton. The old garden folly has been semi-restored to create an atmospheric indoor-outdoor bar and dining area with its own wood-fired oven. Comfortable and cosy public areas offer guests charming places to chill out and relax; the informality is infectious here. Bedrooms range in size and are located in the main house as well as former stables and cottages in the grounds. Food is not to be missed here, with the kitchen's truly local provenance – the hotel has three walled gardens producing much of the ingredients; what cannot be grown here is sourced within a 25-miles-radius. Massage treatments are on offer in the Infusion Walled Garden area.

Rooms: 30 (13 annexe) (5 family) (6 GF) ⟨ **S** fr £145 **D** fr £145* **Facilities:** FTV WiFi ⟲ Two treatment rooms **Conf:** Class 14 Board 14 Theatre 14 **Services:** Night porter **Parking:** 50 **Notes:** Civ Wed 20

Premier Inn Honiton
BUDGET HOTEL

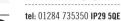

tel: 0871 527 9508 (Calls cost 13p per minute plus your phone company's access charge) **Turks Head Lane EX14 1BQ**
web: www.premierinn.com
dir: From A30 southbound, exit at 'Turks Head' junction signed Sidmouth and Cullompton. Turn left, hotel on left. Or from A30 northbound, follow Honiton and Heathpark signs. Hotel on left.

High quality, budget accommodation ideal for both families and business travellers. Spacious, en suite bedrooms feature free WiFi and tea and coffee making facilities, and in most hotels, Freeview TV is also available. The adjacent family restaurant features a wide and varied menu.

Rooms: 66

HOPE
Derbyshire   **Map 16 SK18**

Losehill House Hotel & Spa
★★★★ 77% ◉◉ HOTEL

tel: 01433 621219 **Lose Hill Lane, Edale Road S33 6AF**
email: info@losehillhouse.co.uk **web:** www.losehillhouse.co.uk
dir: A6187 into Hope. Into Edale Road opposite church. 1 mile, left and follow signs to hotel.

Situated down a quiet leafy lane, this hotel occupies a secluded spot in the Peak District National Park. Bedrooms are comfortable and beautifully appointed. The outdoor hot tub, with stunning views over the valley, is a real indulgence. A heated swimming pool, sauna and spa treatments are also on offer. The views from the Orangery Restaurant are a real delight.

Rooms: 22 (2 annexe) (4 family) (3 GF) ⟨ **S** fr £180 **D** fr £220 (including breakfast & dinner)* **Facilities:** Spa FTV WiFi ⟳ ♪ Xmas New Year **Conf:** Class 20 Board 15 Theatre 30 **Services:** Lift Night porter **Parking:** 30 **Notes:** LB Civ Wed 100

HORLEY
See **Gatwick Airport**

HORNCASTLE
Lincolnshire   **Map 17 TF26**

Admiral Rodney Hotel
★★★ 81% HOTEL

tel: 01507 523131 **North Street LN9 5DX**
email: admiralrodney@innmail.co.uk **web:** www.admiralrodney.com

The Admiral Rodney, a former coaching inn, is located in the picturesque town of Horncastle. Public areas are mostly open plan with a large lounge and bar area to relax in. The spacious bedrooms are well appointed and feature up-to-date technology including Sky TV; free WiFi is also available throughout the hotel. A brasserie-style menu is served throughout the day and evening, and guests can eat in either the Courtyard Restaurant or alfresco when the weather's warmer. Large function rooms and extensive parking are all available. The staff are very welcoming.

Rooms: 31 (4 family) (7 GF) **Facilities:** STV FTV WiFi ⟲ HL **Conf:** Class 60 Board 40 Theatre 140 **Services:** Lift Night porter **Parking:** 60 **Notes:** Civ Wed 100

HORRINGER
Suffolk   **Map 13 TL86**

The Ickworth
AA Advertised ◉◉

tel: 01284 735350 **IP29 5QE**
email: info@ickworthhotel.co.uk **web:** www.ickworthhotel.co.uk
dir: A14 exit for Bury St Edmunds, follow brown signs for Ickworth House, 4th exit at roundabout, cross staggered crossroads. Then onto T-junction, right into village, almost immediately right into Ickworth Estate.

The Ickworth is set in 1,800 acres of Suffolk parkland with opportunities for spotting deer, walking, geo-caching, cycling and just generally relaxing. The hotel interior is full of period and contemporary furnishings, marble flooring and modern chandeliers, creating a luxurious and memorable impression. The hotel is also very family-friendly, offering free childcare, a cinema room, adventure playground, lawn games, flexible mealtimes, children's menus, swimming pools, Wendy houses, a fairy garden and lots more. The ideal setting for a satisfying family break.

Rooms: 51 (23 annexe) (49 family) (5 GF) ⟨ **Facilities:** Spa FTV WiFi ⟲ ⟳ ⌕ ⚓ 1800 acres of grounds and up to 60 bikes Xmas New Year **Conf:** Class 30 Board 24 Theatre 45 **Services:** Lift Night porter **Parking:** 75 **Notes:** Civ Wed 50

HORSHAM
West Sussex — Map 6 TQ13

Premier Inn Horsham

 Premier Inn

BUDGET HOTEL

tel: 0871 527 8526 (Calls cost 13p per minute plus your phone company's access charge) **57 North Street RH12 1RB**
web: www.premierinn.com
dir: Opposite railway station, 5 miles from M23 junction 11.

High quality, budget accommodation ideal for both families and business travellers. Spacious, en suite bedrooms feature free WiFi and tea and coffee making facilities, and in most hotels, Freeview TV is also available. The adjacent family restaurant features a wide and varied menu.

Rooms: 64

HOUGHTON-LE-SPRING
Tyne & Wear — Map 19 NZ34

Chilton Country Pub & Hotel

★★★ 69% HOTEL

tel: 0191 385 2694 **Black Boy Road, Chilton Moor DH4 6PY**
email: reception@chiltoncountrypub.co.uk **web:** www.chiltoncountrypubandhotel.co.uk
dir: A1(M) junction 62, onto A690 towards Sunderland. Left at Rainton Bridge and Fencehouses sign, right at roundabout, next roundabout straight over, next left. At next junction left, hotel on right.

This country pub and hotel has been extended from the original farm cottages. Bedrooms are modern and comfortable and some rooms are particularly spacious. This hotel is popular for weddings and functions; there is also a well stocked bar, and a wide range of dishes is served in the Orangery Restaurant.

Rooms: 25 (7 family) (11 GF) 🐾 **Facilities:** STV FTV WiFi ◊ 🎵 Xmas New Year **Conf:** Class 50 Board 30 Theatre 150 **Services:** Night porter **Parking:** 200 **Notes:** LB Civ Wed 100

HOUNSLOW
See **Heathrow Airport**

HOVE
See **Brighton & Hove**

HOVINGHAM
North Yorkshire — Map 19 SE67

The Worsley Arms Hotel

★★★ 79%  SMALL HOTEL

tel: 01653 628234 **High Street YO62 4LA**
email: enquiries@worsleyarms.co.uk **web:** www.worsleyarms.co.uk
dir: On B1257 between Malton and Helmsley. 4 miles from Castle Howard.

This proprietor-run hotel offers a truly gastronomic experience. Food and wine are taken seriously here, and there is a strong commitment to local provenance. Guests can enjoy the restaurant menu in either the restaurant or in the less formal Cricket Bar. The hotel has very attractive gardens, and the village is a delightfully tranquil location, close to many of North Yorkshire's tourist attractions. Rooms are located in the main house, or cottages across the road; all are pleasantly appointed and comfortable.

Rooms: 20 (2 family) (4 GF) **S** fr £65 **D** fr £85 (including breakfast)* **Facilities:** WiFi ◊ Xmas New Year **Conf:** Class 30 Board 20 Theatre 20 **Notes:** LB Civ Wed

HOYLAKE
Merseyside — Map 15 SJ28

Holiday Inn Express Liverpool - Hoylake

 Holiday Inn Express

BUDGET HOTEL

tel: 0151 632 2073 **The Kings Gap CH47 1HE**
email: info@hiexpresshoylake.co.uk **web:** www.hiexpresshoylake.co.uk
dir: M53 towards Liverpool junction 2, then A551 towards Hoylake, at roundabout turn right onto The King's Gap. Hotel on right.

A modern hotel ideal for families and business travellers. Fresh and uncomplicated, the spacious rooms include Sky TV, power shower and tea and coffee-making facilities. Continental buffet breakfast is included in the room rate; other meals may be taken at the nearby family pub or restaurant.

Rooms: 56 (24 family) (10 GF) 🐾

HUCKNALL
Nottinghamshire — Map 16 SK54

Premier Inn Nottingham North West (Hucknall)

  Premier Inn

BUDGET HOTEL

tel: 0871 527 8852 (Calls cost 13p per minute plus your phone company's access charge) **Nottingham Road NG15 7PY**
web: www.premierinn.com
dir: A611, A6002, straight on at 2 roundabouts. Hotel 500 yards on right.

High quality, budget accommodation ideal for both families and business travellers. Spacious, en suite bedrooms feature free WiFi and tea and coffee making facilities, and in most hotels, Freeview TV is also available. The adjacent family restaurant features a wide and varied menu.

Rooms: 34

HUDDERSFIELD
West Yorkshire — Map 16 SE11

The Huddersfield Central Lodge

★★★ 77% METRO HOTEL

tel: 01484 515551 **11/15 Beast Market HD1 1QF**
email: joe@centrallodge.com **web:** www.centrallodge.com
dir: Off main Huddersfield Inner Ring Road turn for Kirkgate, town centre. Turn 1st right and then 1st right again into Beast Market. Hotel on left.

This friendly, family-run Metro Hotel offers smart, spacious en suite bedrooms. Across a private courtyard from the main building are more rooms, many with kitchenettes. Public rooms include a fully licensed bar and lounge, a 40 square-metre conservatory and an outdoor, covered and heated smoking area; large-screen TVs are placed in all these areas. Many recommended restaurants with a wide variety of cuisine are within a 10-minute walk from this hotel. On-site, secure free parking is available to all guests along with free WiFi.

Rooms: 22 (4 family) (4 smoking) 🐾 **Facilities:** FTV WiFi ◊ **Services:** Night porter **Parking:** 50

H

HUDDERSFIELD *continued*

Premier Inn Huddersfield Central

BUDGET HOTEL

tel: 0871 527 8528 (Calls cost 13p per minute plus your phone company's access charge) **St Andrews Way HD1 3AQ**
web: www.premierinn.com
dir: *Phone or see website for directions.*

High quality, budget accommodation ideal for both families and business travellers. Spacious, en suite bedrooms feature free WiFi and tea and coffee making facilities, and in most hotels, Freeview TV is also available. The adjacent family restaurant features a wide and varied menu.

Rooms: 52

Premier Inn Huddersfield West

BUDGET HOTEL

tel: 0871 527 8532 (Calls cost 13p per minute plus your phone company's access charge) **New Hey Road, Ainley Top HD2 2EA**
web: www.premierinn.com
dir: *Just off M62 junction 24. From M62 take Brighouse exit from roundabout (A643). 1st left into Grimescar Road, right into New Hey Road.*

Rooms: 42

| **HUGH TOWN** | **Map 2 SV91** |
| Cornwall & Isles Of Scilly | |

HIGHLY RECOMMENDED

St Mary's Hall Hotel

★★★ 86% HOTEL

tel: 01720 422316 **Church Street, St Marys TR21 0JR**
email: contactus@stmaryshallhotel.co.uk **web:** www.stmaryshallhotel.co.uk
dir: *Phone for directions.*

An elegant town house, originally built by Count Leon de Ferrari and surrounded by beautiful Mediterranean gardens, St Mary's Hall Hotel offers contemporary style and comfort in a traditional setting. Situated just two minutes from Porthcressa beach, and only five minutes' level walking from the quay, it reflects the relaxed lifestyle of the Isles of Scilly. A range of comfortable accommodation is available with breakfast, lunch and dinner offered daily.

Rooms: 27 (4 family) (4 GF) ⋒ **S** fr £84 **D** fr £168 (including breakfast)*
Facilities: FTV WiFi ⓦ **Notes:** Closed 18 October to 18 March

| **HUNGERFORD** | **Map 5 SU36** |
| Berkshire | |

Littlecote House Hotel

★★★★ 79% ⓦⓦ COUNTRY HOUSE HOTEL

tel: 01488 682509 **Chilton Foliat RG17 0SU**
email: phil.howden@bourne-leisure.co.uk **web:** www.warnerleisurehotels.co.uk
dir: *M4 junction 14, A338, right onto A4, right onto B4192, left into Littlecote Road, hotel 0.5 mile on right at top of hill.*

This hotel provides comfortable, spacious accommodation and is located in stunning grounds close to the Cotswolds, only a 10-minute drive from Hungerford. There are traditional-style bedrooms in the ornate Grade I listed Tudor building and more contemporary rooms in the main building. Facilities include a regular programme of entertainment, beauty treatments and a choice of dining locations in either Oliver's Bistro or the all-day Warner's Café. This is an adults-only (minimum 21 years old) hotel.

Rooms: 208 (19 annexe) (57 GF) ⋒ **S** fr £149 **D** fr £298 (including breakfast & dinner)* **Facilities:** Spa FTV WiFi HL ⓦ ⓦ ⓦ Gym Bowling Table tennis Snooker Archery Rifle shooting ♫ Xmas New Year **Services:** Lift Night porter **Notes:** LB No children 21 years

Three Swans Hotel

★★★ 71% HOTEL

tel: 01488 682721 **117 High Street RG17 0LZ**
email: swans.hungerford@innmail.co.uk **web:** www.threeswans.net
dir: *M4 junction 14 follow signs to Hungerford. Hotel in High Street on left.*

Centrally located in the bustling market town of Hungerford, this is a charming, former inn dates back some 700 years. Visitors will still see the original arch under which the horse-drawn carriages once passed. There is a wood-panelled bar, a spacious lounge, coffee shop and attractive rear garden to relax in. The informal restaurant is decorated with works by local artists. The bedrooms are well appointed and comfortable.

Rooms: 26 (10 annexe) (2 family) (5 GF) (3 smoking) ⋒ **Facilities:** FTV WiFi Access to local private gym Xmas New Year **Conf:** Class 40 Board 30 Theatre 55
Services: Night porter **Parking:** 30 **Notes:** LB

| **HUNSTANTON** | **Map 12 TF64** |
| Norfolk | |

Le Strange Arms Hotel

★★★★ 75% HOTEL

tel: 01485 534411 **Golf Course Road, Old Hunstanton PE36 6JJ**
email: reception@lestrangearms.co.uk **web:** www.abacushotels.co.uk
dir: *Off A149 1 mile north of Hunstanton. Left at sharp right bend by pitch and putt course.*

Le Strange Arms is an impressive hotel with superb views from the wide lawns down to the sandy beach and across The Wash. Bedrooms in the main house are individually decorated. Public rooms include the comfortable Oak Bar and a conference and banqueting suite. There is a choice of dining options beside the Oak Bar – The Brasserie, and the Ancient Mariner, a traditional inn adjacent to the hotel, serving good food and real ales.

Rooms: 46 (10 annexe) (2 family) ⋒ **S** fr £102.50 **D** fr £120* **Facilities:** FTV WiFi ⓦ Xmas New Year **Conf:** Class 150 Board 50 Theatre 180 **Services:** Lift Night porter **Parking:** 80 **Notes:** LB Civ Wed 70

Caley Hall Hotel

★★★ 85% ⓦ HOTEL

tel: 01485 533486 **Old Hunstanton Road PE36 6HH**
email: mail@caleyhallhotel.co.uk **web:** www.caleyhallhotel.co.uk
dir: *1 mile from Hunstanton, on A149.*

Situated within easy walking distance of the seafront, Caley Hall Hotel offers tastefully decorated bedrooms in a series of converted outbuildings. Each is smartly furnished and thoughtfully equipped. Public rooms feature a large open-plan lounge/bar with plush leather seating, and a restaurant offering an interesting choice of dishes.

Rooms: 39 (20 family) (30 GF) ⋒ **S** fr £79 **D** fr £89 (including breakfast)*
Facilities: STV FTV WiFi ⓦ New Year **Parking:** 50 **Notes:** Closed 23–26 December, 7–18 January Civ Wed 80

HUNSTRETE
Somerset   Map 4 ST66

THE PIG near Bath
★★★ ◉◉ HOTEL

tel: 01761 490490 **Hunstrete House, Pensford BS39 4NS email:** reservations@thepighotel.com **web:** www.thepighotel.com
dir: *From Bath take A4 to Bristol. At Globe Inn roundabout 2nd left onto A368 to Wells. 1 mile after Marksbury turn right for Hunstrete. Hotel next left.*

A beautiful country house set in delightful grounds with its own deer park, livestock and walled garden, the latter providing the kitchen with much of its excellent produce. Alfresco eating is possible in the warmer months as there is a wood-fired oven in the courtyard. Bedrooms come in an array of shapes and sizes; some located in the main house, some around the courtyard, and others in beautifully converted garden sheds. All are spacious, have high quality fixtures, and come with their own larders and Nespresso machines. There are plenty of comfortable lounges. The old dining room can accommodate meetings, and treatments can be taken in the potting shed.

Rooms: 29 (5 annexe) (10 GF) ✿ **Facilities:** FTV WiFi ⇗ ♨ Treatment rooms Xmas New Year **Conf:** Board 22 **Services:** Night porter **Parking:** 100 **Notes:** Civ Wed

HUNTINGDON
Cambridgeshire   Map 12 TL27

The Old Bridge Hotel
★★★ 88% ◉ ☕ HOTEL

tel: 01480 424300 **1 High Street PE29 3TQ**
email: oldbridge@huntsbridge.co.uk **web:** www.huntsbridge.com
dir: *From A14 or A1 follow Huntingdon signs. Hotel visible from inner ring road.*

The Old Bridge Hotel is an imposing 18th-century building prominently situated close to shops and amenities. On offer is superb accommodation in stylish and individually decorated bedrooms that include many useful extras. Guests can choose from the same menu whether dining in the restaurant or on the terrace in favourable weather. There is also an excellent business centre.

Rooms: 24 (2 family) (2 GF) ✿ **S** fr £89 **D** fr £148 (including breakfast)*
Facilities: STV FTV WiFi ⇗ Fishing Private mooring for boats Xmas New Year **Conf:** Class 16 Board 24 Theatre 50 **Services:** Night porter Air con **Parking:** 50 **Notes:** LB Civ Wed 100

Premier Inn Huntingdon (A1/A14)
BUDGET HOTEL   Premier Inn

tel: 0871 527 8540 (Calls cost 13p per minute plus your phone company's access charge) **Great North Road, Brampton PE28 4NQ**
web: www.premierinn.com
dir: *At junction of A1 and A14. (Note: from north do not use junction 14. Take exit for Huntingdon and Brampton). Access to hotel via Services.*

High quality, budget accommodation ideal for both families and business travellers. Spacious, en suite bedrooms feature free WiFi and tea and coffee making facilities, and in most hotels, Freeview TV is also available. The adjacent family restaurant features a wide and varied menu.

Rooms: 104

HYDE
Greater Manchester   Map 16 SJ99

Premier Inn Manchester (Hyde)
BUDGET HOTEL   Premier Inn

tel: 0871 527 8712 (Calls cost 13p per minute plus your phone company's access charge) **Stockport Road, Mottram SK14 3AU**
web: www.premierinn.com
dir: *At end of M67 between A57 and A560.*

High quality, budget accommodation ideal for both families and business travellers. Spacious, en suite bedrooms feature free WiFi and tea and coffee making facilities, and in most hotels, Freeview TV is also available. The adjacent family restaurant features a wide and varied menu.

Rooms: 83

HYTHE
Kent   Map 7 TR13

Hythe Imperial
★★★★ 82% ◉ HOTEL

tel: 01303 267441 **Princes Parade CT21 6AE**
email: reception@hytheimperialhotel.com **web:** www.hytheimperial.co.uk
dir: *M20, junction 11 onto A261. In Hythe follow Folkestone signs. Right into Twiss Road to hotel.*

This imposing seafront hotel is enhanced by impressive grounds that inlcude a 13-green golf course and delightful gardens. The bedrooms offer modern facilities with pleasant interiors; many enjoy stunning sea views. Award-winning cuisine is served in Coast Restaurant, while a varied afternoon tea menu is offered in the Afternoon Tea Parlour. The leisure club includes a gym, a squash court, an indoor pool, and a spa offering a range of luxury treatments. The new Champagne Bar is the latest addition to the hotel.

Rooms: 92 (11 family) (6 GF) ✿ **S** fr £60 **D** fr £70* **Facilities:** Spa FTV WiFi ⇗ ⊛ ♨ 9 Gym Squash Aerobic studio Sauna Steam room Xmas New Year **Conf:** Class 120 Board 80 Theatre 220 **Services:** Lift Night porter **Parking:** 207 **Notes:** LB Civ Wed 120

HYTHE *continued*

Stade Court

★★★ 73% HOTEL

tel: 01303 268263 **Stade Street, West Parade CT21 6DT**
email: info@stadecourthotel.co.uk **web:** www.stadecourthotel.co.uk
dir: *M20 junction 11 follow signs for Hythe town centre. Follow brown tourist sign for hotel.*

Stade Court is situated right on the seafront with many bedrooms having the benefit of uninterrupted views of the English Channel. The comfortable bedrooms are tastefully decorated and provide free WiFi and in-room beverage-making facilities. Guests can enjoy traditional English or Indian cuisine in the sea-facing restaurant.

Rooms: 41 (5 family) **Facilities:** STV FTV WiFi Xmas New Year **Conf:** Class 20 Board 30 Theatre 40 **Services:** Lift Night porter **Parking:** 11 **Notes:** Civ Wed 100

ILFORD
Greater London

Premier Inn Ilford

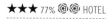

BUDGET HOTEL PLAN 1 H5

tel: 0871 527 8542 (Calls cost 13p per minute plus your phone company's access charge) **Redbridge Lane East IG4 5BG**
web: www.premierinn.com
dir: *At end of M11 follow London East, A12 and Chelmsford signs onto A12, hotel on left at bottom of slip road.*

High quality, budget accommodation ideal for both families and business travellers. Spacious, en suite bedrooms feature free WiFi and tea and coffee making facilities, and in most hotels, Freeview TV is also available. The adjacent family restaurant features a wide and varied menu.

Rooms: 44

ILFRACOMBE   Map 3 SS54
Devon

Sandy Cove Hotel

★★★ 77% ◉◉ HOTEL

tel: 01271 882 243 **Old Coast Road, Combe Martin Bay EX34 9SR**
email: info@sandycove-hotel.co.uk **web:** www.sandycove-hotel.co.uk
dir: *A339 to Combe Martin, through village towards Ilfracombe for approximately 1 mile. Turn right just over brow of hill marked Sandy Cove.*

This hotel enjoys a truly spectacular position, with front-facing bedrooms that benefit from uninterrupted views of the north Devon coastline. In addition, guests can relax on the sea decks or in the terraced garden, and really appreciate the peace and tranquillity. Locally sourced produce is a feature of the menus offered in the dining room, which makes the perfect setting for a romantic dinner or a family gathering.

Rooms: 36 (15 family) (7 GF) **Facilities:** Spa WiFi Sauna Steam room Heated relaxation loungers Xmas New Year **Conf:** Class 20 Board 30 Theatre 30 **Parking:** 45 **Notes:** Civ Wed 150

Imperial Hotel

Leisureplex
HOLIDAY HOTELS

★★★ 70% HOTEL

tel: 01271 862536 **Wilder Road EX34 9AL**
email: imperial.ilfracombe@alfatravel.co.uk **web:** www.leisureplex.co.uk
dir: *Opposite Landmark Theatre.*

This popular hotel is just a short walk from the shops and harbour, overlooking gardens and the sea. Public areas include the spacious sun lounge, where guests can relax and enjoy the excellent views. Comfortable bedrooms are well equipped, with several having the added bonus of sea views.

Rooms: 104 (6 family) **Facilities:** FTV WiFi Xmas New Year **Services:** Lift Night porter **Parking:** 7 **Notes:** Closed December to February (excluding Christmas/New Year) RS March, November

ILKLEY   Map 19 SE14
West Yorkshire

Best Western Plus Craiglands Hotel

★★★ 75% HOTEL

tel: 01943 430001 **Cowpasture Road LS29 8RQ**
email: reservations@craiglands.co.uk **web:** www.craiglands.co.uk
dir: *A65 into Ilkley. Left at T-junction. Past rail station, fork right into Cowpasture Road. Hotel opposite school.*

This grand Victorian hotel is situated close to the town centre. Spacious public areas and a good range of services are ideal for business or leisure. Extensive conference facilities are available along with an elegant restaurant and traditionally styled bar and lounge. Bedrooms, varying in size and style, are comfortably furnished and well equipped.

Rooms: 63 (5 family) **D** fr £69 (including breakfast)* **Facilities:** FTV WiFi Xmas New Year **Conf:** Class 200 Board 100 Theatre 500 **Services:** Lift Night porter **Parking:** 100 **Notes:** LB Civ Wed 500

ILSINGTON   Map 3 SX77
Devon

Ilsington Country House Hotel

★★★ 88% ◉◉ COUNTRY HOUSE HOTEL

tel: 01364 661452 **Ilsington Village TQ13 9RR**
email: hotel@ilsington.co.uk **web:** www.ilsington.co.uk
dir: *M5 onto A38 to Plymouth. Exit at Bovey Tracey. 3rd exit from roundabout to Ilsington, then 1st right. Hotel in 5 miles by Post Office.*

This friendly, family-owned hotel, offers tranquillity and far-reaching views from its elevated position on the southern slopes of Dartmoor. The stylish suites and bedrooms, some on the ground floor, are individually furnished. The restaurant provides a stunning backdrop for the innovative, daily-changing menus which feature local fish, meat and game. Additional facilities include an indoor pool and the Blue Tiger Inn, where a pint, a bite to eat and convivial conversation can all be enjoyed.

Rooms: 25 (4 family) (6 GF) **S** fr £85 **D** fr £125 (including breakfast)* **Facilities:** Spa FTV WiFi Gym Steam room Sauna Beauty treatment rooms Hydrotherapy pool Xmas New Year **Conf:** Class 60 Board 40 Theatre 100 **Services:** Lift **Parking:** 70 **Notes:** LB Civ Wed 100

INSTOW
Devon   Map 3 SS43

Commodore Hotel

★★★ 85% HOTEL

tel: 01271 860347 **Marine Parade EX39 4JN**
email: admin@commodore-instow.co.uk **web:** www.commodore-instow.co.uk
dir: *M5 junction 27 follow north Devon link road to Bideford. Right before bridge, hotel in 3 miles.*

Maintaining its links with the local maritime and rural communities, The Commodore provides an interesting place to stay. Situated at the mouth of the Taw and Torridge rivers and overlooking a sandy beach, it offers well-equipped bedrooms, many with balconies. There are five ground-floor suites. Eating options include the restaurant, the Quarterdeck bar, or the terrace in the warmer months.

Rooms: 25 (1 family) (5 GF) 🐾 **Facilities:** FTV WiFi ⇘ Xmas New Year **Services:** Night porter **Parking:** 200 **Notes:** LB No children 3 years

IPSWICH
Suffolk   Map 13 TM14

INSPECTOR'S CHOICE

Hintlesham Hall Hotel

★★★★ @@ HOTEL

tel: 01473 652334 **George Street IP8 3NS**
email: reservations@hintleshamhall.com **web:** www.hintleshamhall.com

(for full entry see Hintlesham)

INSPECTOR'S CHOICE

Salthouse Harbour Hotel

★★★★ @@ TOWN HOUSE HOTEL

tel: 01473 226789 **No 1 Neptune Quay IP4 1AX**
email: reception@salthouseharbour.co.uk **web:** www.salthouseharbour.co.uk
dir: *From A14 junction 56 follow signs for town centre, then Salthouse signs.*

Situated just a short walk from the town centre, this waterfront warehouse conversion is a clever mix of contemporary styles and original features. The hotel is stylishly designed throughout with modern art, sculptures, interesting artefacts and striking colours. The spacious bedrooms provide luxurious comfort; some have feature bathrooms and some have balconies. Two air-conditioned penthouse suites, with stunning views, have extras such as state-of-the-art sound systems and telescopes. Award-winning food is served in the busy, ground-floor brasserie, and alfresco eating is possible in warmer weather.

Rooms: 70 (6 family) 🐾 **D** fr £108.75 (including breakfast)* **Facilities:** STV FTV WiFi ⇘ **Services:** Lift Night porter **Parking:** 30

HIGHLY RECOMMENDED

milsoms Kesgrave Hall

★★★★ 83% @@ HOTEL

tel: 01473 333741 **Hall Road, Kesgrave IP5 2PU**
email: reception@kesgravehall.com **web:** www.milsomhotels.com/kesgravehall
dir: *A12 north of Ipswich, left at Ipswich/Woodbridge roundabout onto A1214. Right after 0.5 mile into Hall Road. Hotel 200 yards on left.*

Kesgrave Hall is a superb 18th-century, Grade II listed Georgian mansion set amidst 38 acres of mature grounds. Appointed in a contemporary style, the large open-plan public areas include a smart bar, a lounge with plush sofas, and a restaurant where guests can watch the chefs in action. Bedrooms are tastefully appointed and thoughtfully equipped.

Rooms: 23 (9 annexe) (3 family) (8 GF) 🐾 **D** fr £145 (including breakfast)*
Facilities: STV FTV WiFi ⇘ ⚓ Xmas **Conf:** Class 200 Board 24 Theatre 600
Services: Night porter **Parking:** 200 **Notes:** LB Civ Wed 300

Best Western Ipswich Hotel

★★★★ 76% HOTEL

tel: 01473 209988 **Old London Road, Copdock IP8 3JD**
email: reception@hotelipswich.co.uk **web:** www.hotelipswich.co.uk
dir: *Phone for directions.*

Ideally situated on the outskirts of Ipswich within easy access of the town centre and major routes via the Copdock interchange. Bedrooms are modern and well equipped with up-to-date facilities; public areas include a large open-plan lounge/bar area and a restaurant overlooking the neat garden to the rear; a range of meeting rooms is also available.

Rooms: 76 (29 annexe) (23 GF) **Facilities:** FTV WiFi ⇘ 🕐 ♫ Xmas New Year
Conf: Class 120 Board 90 Theatre 450 **Services:** Lift Night porter **Parking:** 350
Notes: LB Civ Wed 85

IPSWICH *continued*

Novotel Ipswich Centre

★★★★ 75% HOTEL

tel: 01473 232400 **Greyfriars Road IP1 1UP**
email: h0995@accor.com **web:** www.novotel.com
dir: *From A14 towards Felixstowe. Left onto A137, 2 miles into town centre. Hotel on double roundabout by Stoke Bridge.*

This modern, red brick hotel is perfectly placed in the centre of town close to shops, bars and restaurants. The open-plan public areas include a Mediterranean-style restaurant and a bar with a small games area. The bedrooms are smartly appointed and have many thoughtful touches; three rooms are suitable for less mobile guests.

Rooms: 101 (8 family) ☎ **Facilities:** STV FTV WiFi ☟ HL Gym Xmas New Year **Conf:** Class 100 Board 45 Theatre 180 **Services:** Lift Night porter Air con **Parking:** 53 **Notes:** Civ Wed 150

Best Western Claydon Hotel

★★★ 82% HOTEL

tel: 01473 830382 **16-18 Ipswich Road, Claydon IP6 0AR**
email: enquiries@hotelsipswich.com **web:** www.hotelsipswich.com
dir: *From A14, northwest of Ipswich. After 4 miles take Great Blakenham Road B1113 to Claydon, hotel on left.*

A delightful hotel situated just off the A14 and within easy driving distance of the town centre. The pleasantly decorated bedrooms are thoughtfully equipped and one room has a lovely four-poster bed. An interesting choice of freshly prepared dishes is available in the smart restaurant, and guests have the use of a relaxing lounge bar.

Rooms: 36 (12 GF) ☎ **Facilities:** FTV WiFi ☟ New Year **Conf:** Class 50 Board 40 Theatre 80 **Services:** Night porter Air con **Parking:** 85 **Notes:** Civ Wed 65

Best Western Gatehouse Hotel

★★★ 82% HOTEL

tel: 01473 741897 **799 Old Norwich Road IP1 6LH**
email: enquiries@gatehousehotel.com **web:** www.gatehousehotel.com
dir: *A14 junction 53, A1156 signed Ipswich, left at lights into Norwich Road, hotel on left.*

A Regency-style property set amidst three acres of landscaped grounds, on the outskirts of town in a quiet road just a short drive from the A14. The spacious bedrooms have co-ordinated soft furnishings and many thoughtful touches. Public rooms include a smart lounge bar, an intimate restaurant and a cosy drawing room with plush leather sofas.

Rooms: 15 (4 annexe) (1 family) (6 GF) ☎ **Facilities:** FTV WiFi ☟ **Parking:** 25

Premier Inn Ipswich (Chantry Park)

BUDGET HOTEL

tel: 0871 527 8548 (Calls cost 13p per minute plus your phone company's access charge) **Old Hadleigh Road IP8 3AR**
web: www.premierinn.com
dir: *From A12/A14 junction take A1214 to Ipswich town centre. Left at lights by Holiday Inn, left onto A1071. At mini-roundabout turn right. Hotel on right.*

High quality, budget accommodation ideal for both families and business travellers. Spacious, en suite bedrooms feature free WiFi and tea and coffee making facilities, and in most hotels, Freeview TV is also available. The adjacent family restaurant features a wide and varied menu.

Rooms: 74

Premier Inn Ipswich North

BUDGET HOTEL

tel: 0871 527 8550 (Calls cost 13p per minute plus your phone company's access charge) **Paper Mill Lane, Claydon IP6 0BE**
web: www.premierinn.com
dir: *A14 junction 52. At roundabout exit into Paper Mill Lane. Hotel 1st left.*

Rooms: 90

Premier Inn Ipswich South

BUDGET HOTEL

tel: 0871 527 8552 (Calls cost 13p per minute plus your phone company's access charge) **Bourne Hill, Wherstead IP2 8ND**
web: www.premierinn.com
dir: *From A14 follow Ipswich Central A137 signs, then Ipswich Central and Docks signs. At bottom of hill at roundabout 2nd exit. Hotel on right.*

Rooms: 40

Premier Inn Ipswich South East

BUDGET HOTEL

tel: 0871 527 8554 (Calls cost 13p per minute plus your phone company's access charge) **Augusta Close, Ransomes Euro Park IP3 9SS**
web: www.premierinn.com
dir: *A14 junction 57, stay in right lane. At roundabout 2nd exit, then 1st left. Hotel adjacent to Swallow Restaurant.*

Rooms: 36

Premier Inn Ipswich Town Centre (Quayside)

BUDGET HOTEL

tel: 0871 527 9388 (Calls cost 13p per minute plus your phone company's access charge) **33 Key Street IP4 1BZ**
web: www.premierinn.com
dir: *Phone for directions.*

Rooms: 85

KEGWORTH

See **East Midlands Airport**

KEIGHLEY
West Yorkshire

Map 19 SE04

Dalesgate Hotel

★★ 73% HOTEL

tel: 01535 664930 **406 Skipton Road, Utley BD20 6HP**
email: info@dalesgate.co.uk **web:** www.dalesgate.co.uk
dir: *In town centre follow A629 over roundabout onto B6265. Right after 0.75 mile into St John's Road. 1st right into hotel car park.*

Originally the residence of a local chapel minister, this modern, well-established hotel provides well-equipped, comfortable bedrooms. It also boasts a cosy bar and pleasant restaurant, serving an imaginative range of dishes. A large car park is provided to the rear.

Rooms: 20 (2 family) (3 GF) **Parking:** 25

Premier Inn Bradford North (Bingley)

Premier Inn

BUDGET HOTEL

tel: 0871 527 8134 (Calls cost 13p per minute plus your phone company's access charge) **502 Bradford Road, Sandbeds BD20 5NG**
web: www.premierinn.com
dir: M62 junctions 26 or 27 follow A650/Keighley and Skipton signs. From Bingley Bypass (A650 Cottingley) right at 1st roundabout signed Crossflatts and Micklethwaite. Hotel 50 yards on left. Note: for sat nav use BD20 5NH.

High quality, budget accommodation ideal for both families and business travellers. Spacious, en suite bedrooms feature free WiFi and tea and coffee making facilities, and in most hotels, Freeview TV is also available. The adjacent family restaurant features a wide and varied menu.

Rooms: 61

KENDAL
Cumbria
Map 18 SD59

See also **Crooklands**

Castle Green Hotel in Kendal

Premier | BEST WESTERN

★★★★ 80% ⊛⊛ HOTEL

tel: 01539 734000 **Castle Green Lane LA9 6RG**
email: reception@castlegreen.co.uk **web:** www.castlegreen.co.uk
dir: M6 junction 37, A684 towards Kendal. Hotel on right in 5 miles.

This smart, modern hotel enjoys a peaceful location and is conveniently situated for access to both the town centre and the M6. Stylish bedrooms are thoughtfully equipped for both the business and leisure guest. The Greenhouse Restaurant provides imaginative dishes and boasts a theatre kitchen; alternatively, Alexander's pub, in the old stable block, serves food all day. The hotel has a fully equipped business centre and leisure club.

Rooms: 99 (3 family) (25 GF) ⤷ **S** fr £90 **D** fr £120 (including breakfast)*
Facilities: Spa FTV WiFi ⓑ ⓧ Gym Steam room Aerobics Yoga Beauty salon Xmas New Year **Conf:** Class 120 Board 100 Theatre 300 **Services:** Lift Night porter **Parking:** 200 **Notes:** LB Civ Wed 250

Premier Inn Kendal Central

Premier Inn

BUDGET HOTEL

tel: 0871 527 8562 (Calls cost 13p per minute plus your phone company's access charge) **Maude Street LA9 4QD**
web: www.premierinn.com
dir: M6 junction 36, A591 to Kendal. (Note: ignore exit for Kendal South). At Plumbgarm Roundabout take 3rd exit, 0.5 mile to Kendal. Hotel on right.

High quality, budget accommodation ideal for both families and business travellers. Spacious, en suite bedrooms feature free WiFi and tea and coffee making facilities, and in most hotels, Freeview TV is also available. The adjacent family restaurant features a wide and varied menu.

Rooms: 92

KENILWORTH
Warwickshire
Map 10 SP27

Chesford Grange

QHOTELS
INSPIRED BY YOU

★★★★ 80% HOTEL

tel: 01926 859331 **Chesford Bridge CV8 2LD**
email: chesfordreservations@qhotels.co.uk **web:** www.qhotels.co.uk
dir: 0.5 mile southeast of junction A46/A452. At roundabout turn right signed Leamington Spa, follow signs to hotel.

This much-extended hotel set in 17 acres of private grounds is well situated for Birmingham International Airport, the NEC and major routes. Bedrooms range from traditional style to contemporary rooms featuring state-of-the-art technology. Public areas include a leisure club and extensive conference and banqueting facilities.

Rooms: 205 (20 family) (43 GF) ⤷ **S** fr £99 **D** fr £111 (including breakfast)*
Facilities: Spa STV WiFi ⓑ HL ⓧ Gym Steam room Solarium Xmas New Year **Conf:** Class 350 Board 50 Theatre 710 **Services:** Lift Night porter **Parking:** 650 **Notes:** Civ Wed 700

KENTISBURY
Devon
Map 3 SS64

HIGHLY RECOMMENDED

Kentisbury Grange

★★★★ 84% ⊛⊛⊛ HOTEL

tel: 01271 882295 **Kentisbury EX31 4NL**
email: reception@kentisburygrange.co.uk **web:** www.kentisburygrange.com
dir: From Barnstaple take A3125. At roundabout take 2nd exit onto A39 to Burrington through Shirwell and Arlington. After Kentisbury Ford, follow signs for hotel for approximately 0.75 mile.

Good quality and comfort are in generous supply at this Victorian country house which offers an impressive blend of traditional elegance and contemporary luxury. Bedrooms and bathrooms offer pampering touches which make all the difference, ensuring a relaxing and rewarding stay. The Coach House restaurant is the venue for dining, where a skilled kitchen team maximise the excellent local produce. Surrounded by the stunning north Devon countryside and a short drive from superb beaches, this is a great base from which to explore all the area has to offer.

Rooms: 21 (10 annexe) (14 GF) ⤷ **S** fr £125 **D** fr £125 (including breakfast)*
Facilities: FTV WiFi ⓑ Xmas New Year **Conf:** Class 12 Board 20 Theatre 30 **Services:** Night porter **Parking:** 50 **Notes:** LB Civ Wed 50

K

K

KENTON
Greater London

Premier Inn London Harrow

Premier Inn

BUDGET HOTEL PLAN 1 C5

tel: 0871 527 8664 (Calls cost 13p per minute plus your phone company's access charge) **Kenton Road HA3 8AT**
web: www.premierinn.com
dir: *M1 junction 5, follow Harrow and Kenton signs. Hotel between Harrow and Wembley on A4006 opposite Kenton railway station.*

High quality, budget accommodation ideal for both families and business travellers. Spacious, en suite bedrooms feature free WiFi and tea and coffee making facilities, and in most hotels, Freeview TV is also available. The adjacent family restaurant features a wide and varied menu.

Rooms: 119

KESWICK
Cumbria   Map 18 NY22

Inn on the Square

LAKE DISTRICT HOTELS

★★★★ 81% ☺ HOTEL

tel: 017687 73333 **Main Street CA12 5JF**
email: innonthesquare@lakedistricthotels.net **web:** www.innonthesquare.co.uk
dir: *A66 to Keswick centre then follow signs to Bell Close car park. Rear entrance to hotel can be accessed from the car park.*

This luxury hotel enjoys a great location on the square in the centre of Keswick. The contemporary and funky design is matched by high levels of comfort. Public areas include the Brossen Steakhouse and a choice of bars simply named, the Front and Back Bars. The bedrooms are impressive – deeply luxurious beds and modern, colourful furniture feature; bathrooms also reflect the same up-to-the-minute style. Friendly staff ensure warm Lakes hospitality and dogs are welcome here too.

Rooms: 34 (1 family) ☍ **S** fr £120 **D** fr £140 (including breakfast)* **Facilities:** STV FTV WiFi ☖ ♫ Xmas New Year **Conf:** Class 10 Board 16 Theatre 30 **Services:** Lift Night porter **Parking:** 7 **Notes:** LB

Skiddaw Hotel

LAKE DISTRICT HOTELS

★★★ 84% HOTEL

tel: 017687 72071 **Main Street CA12 5BN**
email: skiddawhotel@lakedistricthotels.net **web:** www.lakedistricthotels.net/skiddawhotel
dir: *A66 to Keswick, follow town centre signs. Hotel in market square.*

Occupying a central position overlooking the market square, this hotel provides smartly furnished bedrooms that include several family suites and a room with a four-poster bed. In addition to the restaurant, food is served all day in the bar and in the conservatory. There is also a quiet residents' lounge and two conference rooms.

Rooms: 43 (7 family) ☍ **S** fr £75 **D** fr £100 (including breakfast)* **Facilities:** FTV WiFi ☖ Use of leisure facilities at sister hotels (3 miles) ♫ Xmas New Year **Conf:** Class 60 Board 40 Theatre 90 **Services:** Lift Night porter **Parking:** 35 **Notes:** Civ Wed 90

Dale Head Hall Lakeside Hotel

★★★ 82% COUNTRY HOUSE HOTEL

tel: 017687 72478 **Lake Thirlmere CA12 4TN**
email: onthelakeside@daleheadhall.co.uk **web:** www.daleheadhall.co.uk
dir: *Between Keswick and Grasmere. Exit A591 onto private drive.*

Set in attractive, private grounds on the shores of Lake Thirlmere, this historic lakeside residence dates from the 16th century. Comfortable and inviting public areas include a choice of lounges and a traditionally furnished restaurant featuring a daily-changing menu. Bedrooms have views of the lake or surrounding mountains.

Rooms: 12 (1 family) (2 GF) ☍ **Facilities:** STV FTV WiFi ☋ Fishing ☌ Fishing permits Boating Xmas New Year **Conf:** Class 20 Board 20 Theatre 20 **Parking:** 34 **Notes:** Closed 3–30 January Civ Wed 60

Keswick Country House Hotel

★★★ 81% HOTEL

tel: 0844 811 5580 (Calls cost 5p per minute plus your phone company's access charge) & 017687 72020 **Station Road CA12 4NQ**
email: reservations@choicehotels.co.uk **web:** www.thekeswickhotel.co.uk
dir: *M6 junction 40, A66, 1st slip road into Keswick, then follow signs for leisure pool.*

This impressive Victorian hotel is set amid attractive gardens close to the town centre. Eight superior bedrooms are available in the Station Wing, which is accessed through a conservatory. The attractively appointed main house rooms are modern in style and offer a good range of amenities. Public areas include a well-stocked bar, a spacious and relaxing lounge, and a restaurant serving interesting dinners.

Rooms: 70 (6 family) (4 GF) ☍ **S** fr £59 **D** fr £104 (including breakfast & dinner) **Facilities:** FTV WiFi ☌ Xmas New Year **Conf:** Class 25 Board 25 Theatre 50 **Services:** Lift Night porter **Parking:** 70 **Notes:** LB

Kings Arms Hotel

LAKE DISTRICT HOTELS

★★★ 80% HOTEL

tel: 017687 72083 **27 Main Street CA12 5BL**
email: kingsarms@lakedistricthotels.net **web:** www.lakedistricthotels.net/kingsarms
dir: *M6 junction 40, follow A66 to Keswick then follow signs to town centre.*

Located in the heart of Keswick, the Kings Arms Hotel offers modern, tastefully appointed bedrooms and en suites, alongside intimate public spaces and a choice of two restaurants. The bar offers some great local real ales and changing guest beers. The small hands-on team offer friendly and relaxed service.

Rooms: 13 ☍ **S** fr £76 **D** fr £89 (including breakfast)* **Facilities:** FTV WiFi ☖ Complimentary leisure club membership at sister hotel Xmas **Parking:** 13

Keswick Park Hotel

★★★ 72% HOTEL

tel: 017687 72072 **33 Station Road CA12 4NA**
email: info@keswickparkhotel.co.uk **web:** www.keswickparkhotel.co.uk
dir: *Phone for directions.*

Keswick Park Hotel dates from 1880 and enjoys a prominent central position in the town. Built in a traditional Lakeland style, the hotel has gone through extensive refurbishment over the last few years. Bedrooms are of a good size and well appointed with thoughtful extras including free WiFi. There is a small cosy bar and a restaurant specialising in seafood. Limited free off-road parking is available on a first-come, first-served basis.

Rooms: 17 (2 family) (1 GF) **S** fr £60 **D** fr £115 (including breakfast)* **Facilities:** FTV WiFi ◊ **Conf:** Class 10 Board 10 Theatre 15 **Services:** Night porter **Parking:** 8 **Notes:** Closed 24–26 December

KETTERING
Northamptonshire   Map 11 SP87

Rushton Hall Hotel and Spa
★★★★ ◉◉◉ COUNTRY HOUSE HOTEL

tel: 01536 713001 **Rushton NN14 1RR**
email: enquiries@rushtonhall.com **web:** www.rushtonhall.com
dir: A14 junction 7, A43 to Corby then A6003 to Rushton, turn after bridge.

Ruston Hall is an elegant country house hotel set amidst 30 acres of parkland and surrounded by open countryside. The stylish public rooms include a library, a superb open-plan lounge bar with a magnificent vaulted ceiling and plush sofas, and an oak-panelled dining hall, where Adrian Coulthard oversees a very high quality operation. The tastefully appointed bedrooms have co-ordinated fabrics and many thoughtful touches.

Rooms: 51 (5 family) (6 GF) ⬧ **S** fr £150 **D** fr £170 (including breakfast)* **Facilities:** Spa FTV WiFi ◊ ⓢ ⬧ Gym Billiard table Sauna Steam room Xmas New Year **Conf:** Class 100 Board 62 Theatre 300 **Services:** Lift Night porter **Parking:** 140 **Notes:** LB Civ Wed 220

Kettering Park Hotel & Spa
★★★★ 81% ◉ HOTEL

THWAITES

tel: 01536 416666 **Kettering Parkway NN15 6XT**
email: reseravtions@ketteringparkhotel.co.uk **web:** www.ketteringparkhotel.co.uk
dir: Exit A14 junction 9 (M1 to A1 link road), hotel in Kettering Venture Park.

Expect a warm welcome at this stylish hotel situated just off the A14. The spacious, smartly decorated bedrooms are well equipped and meticulously maintained. Guests can choose from classical or contemporary dishes in the restaurant and lighter meals that are served in the bar. The extensive leisure facilities are impressive.

Rooms: 119 (29 family) (35 GF) **S** fr £85 **D** fr £85* **Facilities:** Spa STV FTV WiFi ◊ HL ⓢ Gym Steam room Sauna Children's splash pool Activity studio Treatment rooms New Year **Conf:** Class 120 Board 40 Theatre 260 **Services:** Lift Night porter Air con **Parking:** 200 **Notes:** LB Civ Wed 120

Barton Hall Hotel
★★★ 88% ◉◉ HOTEL

tel: 01536 515505 **Barton Road, Barton Seagrave NN15 6SG**
email: enquiries@bartonhall.com **web:** www.bartonhall.com
dir: From A14 junction 10 onto Barton Road. Hotel on right, approximately 0.5 mile.

Barton Hall Hotel offers modern and comfortable accommodation to suit both business and leisure guests. All of the rooms include 40" smart TVs, with complementary WiFi throughout. Dinner can be enjoyed in Vines Brasserie, which serves a traditional menu in a relaxing and friendly environment.

Rooms: 29 (3 family) (8 GF) ⬧ **D** fr £120 (including breakfast)* **Facilities:** FTV WiFi ◊ **Conf:** Class 150 Board 60 Theatre 300 **Services:** Night porter **Parking:** 150 **Notes:** Civ Wed 160

K

KETTERING *continued*

Premier Inn Kettering

BUDGET HOTEL

tel: 0871 527 8564 (Calls cost 13p per minute plus your phone company's access charge) **Rothwell Road NN16 8XF**
web: www.premierinn.com
dir: *Off A14 junction 7.*

High quality, budget accommodation ideal for both families and business travellers. Spacious, en suite bedrooms feature free WiFi and tea and coffee making facilities, and in most hotels, Freeview TV is also available. The adjacent family restaurant features a wide and varied menu.

Rooms: 83

KIDDERMINSTER
Worcestershire   **Map 10 SO87**

Stone Manor Hotel

★★★★ 72% @ HOTEL

tel: 01562 777555 **Stone DY10 4PJ**
email: reception.stonemanor@hogarths.co.uk
web: www.hogarths.co.uk/hogarths-stone-manor
dir: *2.5 miles from Kidderminster on A448, on right.*

This converted and much-extended former manor house, set in 25 acres, has a history that dates back as far as the Domesday Book. Bedrooms are comfortably furnished and equipped with modern essentials, and many of them benefit from far-reaching views across the Worcestershire countryside. This property is well placed for the Midlands motorway network and many local attractions, making it a popular venue for both corporate and leisure guests.

Rooms: 56 (5 annexe) (4 family) (6 GF) ♠ **S** fr £62.10 **D** fr £62.10* **Facilities:** STV WiFi ↔ HL 🏊 🍴 Xmas New Year **Conf:** Class 40 Board 40 Theatre 130 **Services:** Night porter **Parking:** 400 **Notes:** LB Civ Wed 170

The Granary Hotel & Restaurant

★★★ 79% @ HOTEL

tel: 01562 777535 **Heath Lane, Shenstone DY10 4BS**
email: info@granary-hotel.co.uk **web:** www.granary-hotel.co.uk
dir: *On A450 between Stourbridge and Worcester, 1 mile from Kidderminster.*

This modern hotel offers spacious, well-equipped accommodation with many rooms enjoying views towards Great Witley and the Amberley Hills. Public areas include a bar and a residents' lounge. The attractive, modern restaurant serves dishes created from locally sourced produce that is cooked with flair and imagination. There are also extensive conference facilities, and the hotel is popular as a wedding venue.

Rooms: 18 (1 family) (18 GF) ♠ **Facilities:** FTV WiFi ↔ **Conf:** Class 80 Board 70 Theatre 200 **Services:** Night porter **Parking:** 96 **Notes:** LB Closed 2–8 January Civ Wed 120

Gainsborough House Hotel

★★★ 79% HOTEL

tel: 01562 820041 **Bewdley Hill DY11 6BS**
email: reservations@gainsboroughhousehotel.com
web: www.gainsboroughhousehotel.com
dir: *Follow A456 to Kidderminster (West Midlands Safari Park) pass hospital, hotel 500 yards on left.*

This listed Georgian property provides a wide range of thoughtfully furnished bedrooms that have smart modern bathrooms. The contemporary decor and furnishing throughout the public areas highlights the many retained period features. A large function suite and several meeting rooms are available.

Rooms: 42 (16 family) (12 GF) **S** fr £73 **D** fr £73* **Facilities:** STV FTV WiFi ↔ Xmas New Year **Conf:** Class 70 Board 60 Theatre 250 **Services:** Night porter Air con **Parking:** 90 **Notes:** LB Civ Wed 250

Premier Inn Kidderminster

BUDGET HOTEL

tel: 0871 527 9350 (Calls cost 13p per minute plus your phone company's access charge) **Slingfield Mill, Weavers Wharf DY10 1AA**
web: www.premierinn.com
dir: *M5 junction 3, A456 towards Kidderminster, 5.5 miles. Straight on at 1st roundabout, left into Lower Mill Street. Straight on into Crown Lane.*

High quality, budget accommodation ideal for both families and business travellers. Spacious, en suite bedrooms feature free WiFi and tea and coffee making facilities, and in most hotels, Freeview TV is also available. The adjacent family restaurant features a wide and varied menu.

Rooms: 56

KINGSBRIDGE
Devon   **Map 3 SX74**

Buckland-Tout-Saints

★★★ 82% @@ COUNTRY HOUSE HOTEL

tel: 01548 853055 **Goveton TQ7 2DS**
email: info@bucklandtoutsaints.co.uk **web:** www.tout-saints.co.uk
dir: *Turn off A381 to Goveton. Follow brown tourist signs to St Peter's Church. Hotel 2nd right after church.*

It is well worth navigating the winding country lanes to dine at this delightful Queen Anne manor house that has been host to many famous guests over the years. Set in over four acres of gardens the hotel is a peaceful retreat. Bedrooms are tastefully furnished and attractively decorated; the majority are very spacious. Local produce is used with care and imagination to create the dishes offered. This is a popular choice for weddings.

Rooms: 16 (6 family) ♠ **S** fr £89 **D** fr £89 (including breakfast)* **Facilities:** STV WiFi ↔ 🍴 Xmas New Year **Conf:** Class 40 Board 26 Theatre 80 **Services:** Night porter **Parking:** 25 **Notes:** Civ Wed 120

KINGSCLERE
Hampshire   Map 5 SU55

Sandford Springs Hotel and Golf Club
★★★★ 78% HOTEL

tel: 01635 291500 & 296800 **RG26 5RT**
email: info@sandfordsprings.co.uk **web:** www.sandfordsprings.co.uk
dir: M3 junction 6, A339 for 9 miles, hotel on right; M4 junction 13, A34 to Newbury then A339 for 11 miles, hotel on left.

This modern hotel is located in a lovely country location between Newbury and Basingstoke and offers a super range of facilities with three 9-hole golf courses, woods and lakes. In addition there are also conference and meeting rooms. Bedrooms are spacious and have good facilities. There is a choice of restaurants – the dining room in the hotel and the first-floor Kingsclere Restaurant & Bar in the clubhouse which overlooks the golf course and offers all-day dining.

Rooms: 40 (4 family) (21 GF) ⌇ **S** fr £79 **D** fr £89 (including breakfast)
Facilities: FTV WiFi ⌇ ⌇ 27 New Year **Conf:** Class 80 Board 40 Theatre 180
Services: Lift Night porter Air con **Parking:** 150 **Notes:** LB Civ Wed 100

KINGS LANGLEY
Hertfordshire   Map 6 TL00

Premier Inn Kings Langley
BUDGET HOTEL

tel: 0871 527 8568 (Calls cost 13p per minute plus your phone company's access charge) **Hempstead Road WD4 8BR**
web: www.premierinn.com
dir: 1 mile from M25 junction 20 on A4251 after King's Langley.

High quality, budget accommodation ideal for both families and business travellers. Spacious, en suite bedrooms feature free WiFi and tea and coffee making facilities, and in most hotels, Freeview TV is also available. The adjacent family restaurant features a wide and varied menu.

Rooms: 86

KING'S LYNN
Norfolk   Map 12 TF62

The Duke's Head Hotel
★★★★ 84% ◉ HOTEL

tel: 01553 774996 **5-6 Tuesday Market Place PE30 1JS**
email: reception@dukeshead.com **web:** www.dukesheadhotel.com
dir: From A10/A47/A17 enter King's Lynn via South Gates roundabout. Hotel opposite Corn Exchange.

Occupying a central location and overlooking the market square, this hotel is a beautiful property. The bedrooms are smartly decorated, and include widescreen TVs, free WiFi and bathrooms with walk-in showers. Parking is also available.

Rooms: 79 (6 family) ⌇ **S** fr £67 **D** fr £89* **Facilities:** FTV WiFi ⌇ Gym available from quarter 4 2018 External laundry facility available Xmas New Year **Conf:** Class 80 Board 100 Theatre 220 **Services:** Lift Night porter **Parking:** 40 **Notes:** LB Civ Wed 200

Knights Hill Hotel and Spa
★★★★ 75% HOTEL

tel: 01553 675566 **Knights Hill Village, South Wootton PE30 3HQ**
email: reception@knightshill.co.uk **web:** www.abacushotels.co.uk
dir: At junction A148 and A149.

This hotel village complex is set on a 16th-century site on the outskirts of King's Lynn. The smartly decorated, well-equipped bedrooms are situated in extensions of the original hunting lodge. Public areas have a wealth of historic charm including the Garden Brasserie & Bar and the Farmers Arms, which serves good food and real ales. The hotel also has conference and leisure facilities, including the Imagine Spa.

Rooms: 79 (12 annexe) (1 family) (38 GF) ⌇ **S** fr £102.50 **D** fr £120* **Facilities:** Spa STV WiFi ⌇ ⌇ ⌇ ⌇ Gym Xmas New Year **Conf:** Class 150 Board 30 Theatre 200 **Services:** Night porter **Parking:** 350 **Notes:** LB Civ Wed 90

Congham Hall Country House Hotel
★★★ ◉◉ COUNTRY HOUSE HOTEL

tel: 01485 600250 **Lynn Road PE32 1AH**
email: info@conghamhallhotel.co.uk **web:** www.conghamhallhotel.co.uk

(for full entry see Grimston)

Bank House
★★★ 84% ◉ HOTEL

tel: 01553 660492 **King's Staithe Square PE30 1RD**
email: info@thebankhouse.co.uk **web:** www.thebankhouse.co.uk
dir: In King's Lynn Old Town follow quay, through floodgates, hotel on right opposite Custom House.

This Grade II listed, 18th-century town house is situated on the quayside in the heart of King's Lynn's historical quarter. Bedrooms are individually decorated and have high quality fabrics and furnishings along with a range of useful facilities. Public rooms include the Counting House coffee shop, a wine bar and brasserie restaurant, as well as a residents' lounge.

Rooms: 12 (5 family) ⌇ **S** fr £95 **D** fr £120 (including breakfast)* **Facilities:** FTV WiFi ⌇ Half size billiards table Xmas New Year **Conf:** Class 20 Board 15 Theatre 30 **Notes:** LB

Grange Hotel
★★ 75% HOTEL

tel: 01553 673777 **Willow Park, South Wootton Lane PE30 3BP**
email: info@thegrangehotelkingslynn.co.uk **web:** www.thegrangehotelkingslynn.co.uk
dir: A148 towards King's Lynn for 1.5 miles. At lights left into Wootton Road, 400 yards, on right into South Wootton Lane. Hotel 1st on left.

Expect a warm welcome at this Edwardian house which is situated in a quiet residential area in its own grounds. Public rooms include a smart lounge bar and a cosy restaurant. The spacious bedrooms are pleasantly decorated and equipped with many thoughtful touches; some are located in an adjacent wing.

Rooms: 9 (4 annexe) (2 family) (4 GF) **Facilities:** WiFi Xmas **Conf:** Class 15 Board 12 Theatre 20 **Parking:** 15

K

KING'S LYNN *continued*

Premier Inn King's Lynn

BUDGET HOTEL

tel: 0871 527 8570 (Calls cost 13p per minute plus your phone company's access charge) **Clenchwarton Road, West Lynn PE34 3LJ**
web: www.premierinn.com
dir: *At junction of A47 and A17.*

High quality, budget accommodation ideal for both families and business travellers. Spacious, en suite bedrooms feature free WiFi and tea and coffee making facilities, and in most hotels, Freeview TV is also available. The adjacent family restaurant features a wide and varied menu.

Rooms: 149

KINGSTON UPON HULL	Map 17 TA02
East Riding of Yorkshire	

Best Western Willerby Manor Hotel

★★★ 82% HOTEL

tel: 01482 652616 **Well Lane HU10 6ER**
email: info@willerbymanor.co.uk **web:** www.willerbymanor.co.uk

(for full entry see Willerby)

Premier Inn Hull City Centre

BUDGET HOTEL

tel: 0871 527 8534 (Calls cost 13p per minute plus your phone company's access charge) **Tower Street HU9 1TQ**
web: www.premierinn.com
dir: *M62, A63 into Hull city centre. At roundabout left onto A1165 (Great Union Street), left into Citadel Way. Hotel at end on right.*

High quality, budget accommodation ideal for both families and business travellers. Spacious, en suite bedrooms feature free WiFi and tea and coffee making facilities, and in most hotels, Freeview TV is also available. The adjacent family restaurant features a wide and varied menu.

Rooms: 136

Premier Inn Hull North

BUDGET HOTEL

tel: 0871 527 8536 (Calls cost 13p per minute plus your phone company's access charge) **Ashcombe Road, Kingswood Park HU7 3DD**
web: www.premierinn.com
dir: *A63 to town centre, take A1079 north for approximately 5 miles. Right at roundabout onto A1033. Hotel at 2nd roundabout in New Kingswood Park.*

Rooms: 93

Premier Inn Hull West

BUDGET HOTEL

tel: 0871 527 8538 (Calls cost 13p per minute plus your phone company's access charge) **Ferriby Road, Hessle HU13 0JA**
web: www.premierinn.com
dir: *A63 onto A15 to Humber Bridge (Beverley and Hessle Viewpoint). Hotel at 1st roundabout.*

Rooms: 83

KINGSTON UPON THAMES	Map 6 TQ26
Greater London	

Premier Inn London Kingston upon Thames

BUDGET HOTEL PLAN 1 C1

tel: 0871 527 9586 (Calls cost 13p per minute plus your phone company's access charge) **Combined House, 15 Wheatfield Way KT1 2PA**
web: www.premierinn.com
dir: *M25 juncton 13, A30 (signed Staines), A308 towards Kingston upon Thames. Pass Bentalls shopping centre, stay in right lane, left at Odeon cinema. On one-way system pass Cattle Market car park on left. Right after car park, left into Eden Street. Left into Lady Booth Road.*

High quality, budget accommodation ideal for both families and business travellers. Spacious, en suite bedrooms feature free WiFi and tea and coffee making facilities, and in most hotels, Freeview TV is also available. The adjacent family restaurant features a wide and varied menu.

Rooms: 160

Premier Inn London Tolworth hotel

BUDGET HOTEL

tel: 0871 622 2421 (Calls cost 13p per minute plus your phone company's access charge) **12 Kingston Road, Tolworth KT5 9NU**
web: www.premierinn.com
dir: *A3/A240 (Kingston Road) past Tolworth Station on your right. Follow road past hotel, take left onto Worcester Park Road. Immediately turn right and right again at lights to head back onto A240 (Kingston Road). Follow road back towards hotel which will be on your left.*

Rooms: 137

KINGSWINFORD	Map 10 SO88
West Midlands	

Premier Inn Dudley (Kingswinford)

BUDGET HOTEL

tel: 0871 527 8314 (Calls cost 13p per minute plus your phone company's access charge) **Dudley Road DY6 8WT**
web: www.premierinn.com
dir: *A4123 to Dudley, A461 follow signs for Russell's Hall Hospital. On A4101 to Kingswinford, hotel opposite Pensnett Trading Estate.*

High quality, budget accommodation ideal for both families and business travellers. Spacious, en suite bedrooms feature free WiFi and tea and coffee making facilities, and in most hotels, Freeview TV is also available. The adjacent family restaurant features a wide and varied menu.

Rooms: 60

K

KNUTSFORD
Cheshire   Map 15 SJ77

The Mere Golf Resort & Spa
★★★★ 80% HOTEL

tel: 01565 830155 **Chester Road, Mere WA16 6LJ**
web: www.themereresort.co.uk
dir: *M6 junction 19 or M56 junction 7.*

This hotel sits alongside Mere Lake and is close to the picturesque town of Knutsford; there are excellent transport links with Manchester International Airport which is only 10 minutes away. The resort's historic main Victorian building conveys the classic charm of that era, and offers stylish, luxury accommodation. The championship golf course designed by James Braid is both beautiful and challenging. The spa features an extensive range of treatments and facilities including a Thermal Zone. The staff are professional and very friendly, offering personal service.

Rooms: 81 **Facilities:** Spa ⚓ 18 **Conf:** Class 350 Board 40 Theatre 700

Cottons Hotel & Spa
★★★★ 80% HOTEL   **THWAITES**

tel: 01565 650333 **Manchester Road WA16 0SU**
email: reservations@cottonshotel.co.uk **web:** www.cottonshotel.co.uk
dir: *On A50, 1 mile from M6 junction 19.*

The superb leisure facilities and quiet location are main attractions at this hotel which is just a short distance from Manchester Airport. The bedrooms are smartly appointed in various styles, and executive rooms have very good working areas. The hotel has spacious lounges and an excellent leisure centre.

Rooms: 138 (14 family) (48 GF) ⌇ **S** fr £90 **D** fr £90* **Facilities:** Spa STV WiFi ⌇ ⊗ Gym Steam room Activity studio for exercise classes Sauna Children's splash pool Xmas New Year **Conf:** Class 100 Board 36 Theatre 200 **Services:** Lift Night porter Air con **Parking:** 180 **Notes:** LB Civ Wed 120

Mere Court Hotel & Conference Centre
★★★★ 76% HOTEL

tel: 01565 831000 **Warrington Road, Mere WA16 0RW**
email: ops@merecourt.co.uk **web:** www.merecourt.co.uk
dir: *A50, 1 mile west of junction with A556, on right.*

This is a smart and attractive hotel, set in extensive, well-tended gardens. The elegant and spacious bedrooms are individually styled and offer a host of thoughtful extras. Conference facilities are particularly impressive and there is a large, self contained, conservatory function suite. Modern British dishes are served in the fine dining Arboreum Restaurant.

Rooms: 35 (12 GF) **S** fr £100 **D** fr £100 **Facilities:** STV FTV WiFi Xmas New Year **Conf:** Class 75 Board 50 Theatre 200 **Services:** Lift Night porter **Parking:** 150 **Notes:** LB Civ Wed 150

The Longview Hotel
★★ 80% HOTEL

tel: 01565 632119 **55 Manchester Road WA16 0LX**
email: enquiries@longviewhotel.com **web:** www.longviewhotel.com
dir: *M6 junction 19 take A556 west towards Chester. Left at lights onto A5033, 1.5 mile to roundabout then left. Hotel 200 yards on right.*

This friendly, personally-run hotel is part of a Victorian terrace near the centre of Knutsford, offering high standards of hospitality and attractive public areas including a cellar bar. The restaurant serves a range of dishes. Bedrooms, located either in a superb renovation of a nearby house or within the main building, are individually styled and offer comfortable, modern appointment.

Rooms: 32 (19 annexe) (1 family) (5 GF) **S** fr £94 **D** fr £115 (including breakfast)*
Facilities: FTV WiFi ⌇ **Conf:** Class 20 Board 20 **Services:** Night porter **Parking:** 20
Notes: Closed 21 December to 6 January

Premier Inn Knutsford (Bucklow Hill)
BUDGET HOTEL   Premier Inn 🌓

tel: 0871 527 8572 (Calls cost 13p per minute plus your phone company's access charge) **Bucklow Hill WA16 6RD**
web: www.premierinn.com
dir: *M6 junction 19, A556 towards Manchester Airport and Stockport.*

High quality, budget accommodation ideal for both families and business travellers. Spacious, en suite bedrooms feature free WiFi and tea and coffee making facilities, and in most hotels, Freeview TV is also available. The adjacent family restaurant features a wide and varied menu.

Rooms: 68

Premier Inn Knutsford (Mere)
BUDGET HOTEL   Premier Inn 🌓

tel: 0871 527 8574 (Calls cost 13p per minute plus your phone company's access charge) **Warrington Road, Hoo Green WA16 0PZ**
web: www.premierinn.com
dir: *M6 junction 19, A556, follow Manchester signs. At 1st lights left onto A50 towards Warrington. Hotel 1 mile on right.*

Rooms: 28

LACEBY
Lincolnshire   Map 17 TA20

Best Western Oaklands Hall Hotel
★★★ 80% HOTEL   BW Best Western.

tel: 01472 872248 **Barton Street DN37 7LF**
email: reception@oaklandshallhotel.co.uk **web:** www.oaklandshallhotel.co.uk
dir: *At junction of A46 and A18 at Laceby, on edge of Grimsby.*

This attractive 19th-century property is located on a private estate in five acres of parkland. It appointed in a contemporary style yet retains beautiful period features. The Comfy Duck bistro is stylish, and food is a highlight of any stay, with a strong emphasis on local produce. Bedrooms are comfortable and complimentary WiFi is provided.

Rooms: 46 (5 family) (10 GF) ⌇ **Facilities:** FTV WiFi ⌇ ♫ New Year **Conf:** Class 150 Board 50 Theatre 180 **Services:** Night porter **Parking:** 80 **Notes:** Civ Wed 150

L

L

LANCASTER
Lancashire   Map 18 SD46

Lancaster House
★★★★ 76% HOTEL   English Lakes
Hotels Resorts & Venues

tel: 01524 844822 **Green Lane, Ellel LA1 4GJ**
email: lancasterhouse@englishlakes.co.uk **web:** www.englishlakes.co.uk
dir: *M6 junction 33 north towards Lancaster. Through Galgate into Green Lane. Hotel before university on right.*

This modern hotel enjoys a rural setting south of the city and close to the university. The attractive open-plan reception and lounge boast a roaring log fire in colder months. Bedrooms are spacious, and include 19 rooms that are particularly well equipped for business guests. There are leisure facilities with a hot tub and a function suite.

Rooms: 99 (29 family) (44 GF) ⌁ **Facilities:** Spa STV WiFi ⌁ HL ⌁ Gym Beauty salon Xmas New Year **Conf:** Class 60 Board 48 Theatre 250 **Services:** Night porter
Parking: 120 **Notes:** Civ Wed 140

Premier Inn Lancaster
BUDGET HOTEL   Premier Inn

tel: 0871 527 8576 (Calls cost 13p per minute plus your phone company's access charge) **Lancaster Business Park, Caton Road LA1 3PE**
web: www.premierinn.com
dir: *M6 junction 34, A683 towards Lancaster. Hotel 0.25 mile on left at entrance to Business Park.*

High quality, budget accommodation ideal for both families and business travellers. Spacious, en suite bedrooms feature free WiFi and tea and coffee making facilities, and in most hotels, Freeview TV is also available. The adjacent family restaurant features a wide and varied menu.

Rooms: 85

LAND'S END
Cornwall & Isles Of Scilly   Map 2 SW32

The Land's End Hotel
★★★ 81% HOTEL

tel: 01736 871844 **TR19 7AA**
email: reservations@landsendhotel.co.uk **web:** www.landsendhotel.co.uk
dir: *From Penzance take A30, follow Land's End signs. After Sennen 1 mile to Land's End.*

This famous location provides a memorable setting for The Land's End Hotel. Bedrooms, many with stunning views of the Atlantic, are pleasantly decorated and comfortable. Public areas provide plenty of style and comfort with a relaxing lounge and convivial bar. The restaurant is equally impressive with accomplished cuisine complementing the amazing views out to sea.

Rooms: 30 (4 family) **S** fr £75 **D** fr £100 (including breakfast)* **Facilities:** FTV WiFi Free entry to Land's End Visitor Centre and attractions Xmas **Conf:** Class 50 Board 30 Theatre 100 **Services:** Night porter **Parking:** 100 **Notes:** Civ Wed 120

LANGHO
Lancashire   Map 18 SD73

INSPECTOR'S CHOICE

Northcote
★★★★ ◉◉◉◉ ⌁ SMALL HOTEL
RELAIS & CHATEAUX

tel: 01254 240555 **Northcote Road BB6 8BE**
email: reception@northcote.com **web:** www.northcote.com
dir: *M6 junction 31, 9 miles to Northcote. Follow Clitheroe A59 signs, Hotel on left before roundabout.*

This is a gastronomic haven, and guests frequently return to sample the delights of its famous kitchen. The outstanding, seasonally-based cooking includes Lancashire's finest fare, and fruit and herbs from the hotel's own beautifully laid-out organic gardens. Drinks can be enjoyed in the comfortable, elegantly furnished lounges and bar. Each of the luxury bedrooms has its own identity with sumptuous fabrics and soft furnishings, sophisticated lighting and ultra-modern bathrooms; some have a garden patio. New annexe rooms are particularly impressive.

Rooms: 26 (8 annexe) (3 family) (8 GF) ⌁ **S** fr £165 **D** fr £255 (including breakfast)* **Facilities:** STV FTV WiFi ⌁ Xmas New Year **Conf:** Class 40 Board 20 Theatre 40 **Services:** Lift Night porter **Parking:** 50 **Notes:** LB Civ Wed 60

LASTINGHAM
North Yorkshire   Map 19 SE79

Lastingham Grange Hotel
★★★ 80% HOTEL

tel: 01751 417345 **YO62 6TH**
email: reservations@lastinghamgrange.com **web:** www.lastinghamgrange.com
dir: *From A170 follow signs for Appleton-le-Moors, continue into Lastingham, pass church on left, right, then left up hill. Hotel on right.*

A warm welcome and sincere hospitality have been the hallmarks of this hotel for over 60 years. Antique furniture is plentiful, and the lounge and the dining room both look out onto the terrace and sunken rose garden below. There is a large play area for older children and the moorland views are breathtaking

Rooms: 12 (2 family) **Facilities:** FTV WiFi ⌁ Large adventure playground **Parking:** 30 **Notes:** LB Closed December to February

LAVENHAM
Suffolk   Map 13 TL94

INSPECTOR'S CHOICE

The Swan at Lavenham Hotel and Spa
★★★★ ◎◎ HOTEL   T|A|HOTEL COLLECTION

tel: 01787 247477 **High Street CO10 9QA**
email: info@theswanatlavenham.co.uk **web:** www.theswanatlavenham.co.uk
dir: *From Bury St Edmunds take A134 south, then A1141 to Lavenham.*

This hotel is a delightful collection of listed buildings, dating back to the 14th century, lovingly restored to retain their original charm. Public rooms include comfortable lounge areas, a charming rustic bar, an informal brasserie and a fine-dining restaurant. Bedrooms are tastefully furnished and equipped with many thoughtful touches. The friendly staff are helpful, attentive and offer professional service. Facilities in the award-winning spa include six rooms offering over 30 treatments, a hot stone sauna, steam room, manicure and pedicure area, a beautiful spa boutique, outdoor terrace and a vitality pool.

Rooms: 45 (7 family) (9 GF) **S** fr £105 **D** fr £125 (including breakfast)*
Facilities: Spa FTV WiFi Steam room Sauna Vitality pool Xmas New Year
Conf: Class 36 Board 30 Theatre 50 **Services:** Night porter **Parking:** 30
Notes: Civ Wed 100

LEA MARSTON
Warwickshire   Map 10 SP29

Lea Marston Hotel & Spa
★★★★ 78% ◎ HOTEL   CLASSIC BRITISH HOTELS

tel: 01675 470468 **Haunch Lane B76 0BY**
email: info@leamarstonhotel.co.uk **web:** www.leamarstonhotel.co.uk
dir: *M42 junction 9, A4097 to Kingsbury. Hotel signed 1.5 mile on right.*

Excellent access to the motorway network and a good range of sports facilities make this hotel a popular choice for conferences and leisure breaks. Bedrooms are set mostly around an attractive quadrangle and are generously equipped. Diners can choose between the popular Hathaway's Bar and the elegant Adderley Restaurant.

Rooms: 118 (16 family) (66 GF) **Facilities:** Spa STV FTV WiFi
Gym Golf driving range Golf simulator Sauna Steam room Rasul Xmas New Year
Conf: Class 70 Board 35 Theatre 120 **Services:** Lift Night porter **Parking:** 220

LEAMINGTON SPA (ROYAL)
Warwickshire   Map 10 SP36

INSPECTOR'S CHOICE

Mallory Court Country House Hotel & Spa
★★★★ ◎◎◎ HOTEL

tel: 01926 330214 **Harbury Lane, Bishop's Tachbrook CV33 9QB**
email: info@mallory.co.uk **web:** www.mallory.co.uk
dir: *M40 junction 13 northbound left, left again towards Bishops Tachbrook, right into Harbury Lane after 0.5 mile. M40 junction 14 southbound A452 to Leamington, at 2nd roundabout left into Harbury Lane.*

Mallory Court Country House Hotel is part of the Eden Hotel Collection, and with its tranquil rural setting, this elegant Lutyens-style country house is an idyllic retreat, set in 10 acres of landscaped gardens with immaculate lawns and an orchard. Relaxation is easy in the two sumptuous lounges, drawing room and conservatory, and dining is a treat in either the elegant restaurant or the brasserie. Bedrooms in the main house are luxuriously decorated and most have wonderful views; those in the Knights Suite are more contemporary and have their own access via a smart conference and banqueting facility. The hotel also has a state-of-the-art Elan Spa.

Rooms: 43 (23 annexe) (2 family) (5 GF) **D** fr £145 (including breakfast)*
Facilities: Spa FTV WiFi Gym Xmas New Year **Conf:** Class 160 Board 50
Theatre 200 **Services:** Lift Night porter **Parking:** 120 **Notes:** LB Civ Wed 160

Premier Inn Leamington Spa Town Centre
BUDGET HOTEL   Premier Inn

tel: 0871 527 9380 (Calls cost 13p per minute plus your phone company's access charge) **Regency Arcade, The Parade CV32 4BQ**
web: www.premierinn.com
dir: *From north: M40 junction 15/A452. Through 4 roundabouts. At next roundabout take 4th exit, at final roundabout, take 1st exit A452 (Adelaide Road). Right onto Dormer Place and left onto St Peters Road into St Peters car park. Follow directional signage to Premier Inn. From south: M40 junction 13 then follow directions as above.*

High quality, budget accommodation ideal for both families and business travellers. Spacious, en suite bedrooms feature free WiFi and tea and coffee making facilities, and in most hotels, Freeview TV is also available. The adjacent family restaurant features a wide and varied menu.

Rooms: 82

L

LEDBURY
Herefordshire

Map 10 SO73

Feathers Hotel

★★★ 82% HOTEL

THE COACHING INN GROUP

tel: 01531 635266 **High Street HR8 1DS**
email: feathers.ledbury@innmail.co.uk **web:** www.feathers-ledbury.co.uk
dir: *South from Worcester on A449, east from Hereford on A438, north from Gloucester on A417. Hotel in town centre.*

A wealth of authentic features can be found at this historic timber-framed hotel, situated in the middle of town. The comfortably equipped bedrooms are tastefully decorated; there is also Eve's Cottage, in the grounds, and Lanark House, a two-bedroom apartment that is ideal for families and self-catering use. Well-prepared meals can be taken in Fuggles Brasserie with its adjoining bar, and breakfast is served in Quills Restaurant. A swimming pool and gym are available for guests.

Rooms: 20 (1 annexe) (2 family) ☎ **S** fr £99 **D** fr £240 (including breakfast & dinner)* **Facilities:** STV FTV WiFi ⬡ ⊕ Gym Steam room New Year **Conf:** Class 80 Board 40 Theatre 140 **Services:** Night porter **Parking:** 30 **Notes:** Civ Wed 100

Leadon House Hotel

★★ ⚠ SMALL HOTEL

tel: 01531 631199 **Ross Road HR8 2LP**
email: leadon.house@btconnect.com **web:** www.leadonhouse.com
dir: *M5 junction 8/M50/A417 exit Ledbury. Left at 1st roundabout then take A449. Hotel 400 yards on right by Ledbury Rugby Club.*

This family-run hotel, which has been tastefully appointed in an Edwardian style, offers an idyllic environment and a peaceful night's stay. Many interesting architectural features add to its unique charm and elegance. All bedrooms are en suite and finished to a high standard - plenty of attention is paid to the little details. Also available is the Coach House, a two-bedroom apartment.

Rooms: 8 (2 annexe) (1 family) (1 GF) **Facilities:** FTV WiFi **Parking:** 10 **Notes:** No children 16 years

LEEDS
West Yorkshire

Map 19 SE23

See also **Gomersal & Wakefield**

Thorpe Park Hotel & Spa

★★★★ 84% HOTEL

THWAITES

tel: 0113 264 1000 **Century Way, Thorpe Park LS15 8ZB**
email: reservations@thorpeparkhotel.co.uk **web:** www.thorpeparkhotel.co.uk
dir: *M1 junction 46, follow signs for Thorpe Park.*

Conveniently close to the M1, this hotel offers bedrooms that are modern in both style and facilities. The Terrace and courtyard offer all-day casual dining and refreshments, and the restaurant features a Mediterranean-themed menu. There is also a state-of-the-art spa and leisure facilities.

Thorpe Park Hotel & Spa

Rooms: 117 (13 family) (25 GF) ☎ **S** fr £89 **D** fr £89* **Facilities:** Spa STV WiFi ⬡ HL ⊕ Gym Activity studio Steam room Sauna New Year **Conf:** Class 100 Board 50 Theatre 200 **Services:** Lift Night porter Air con **Parking:** 200 **Notes:** LB Civ Wed 150

Oulton Hall

★★★★ 82% HOTEL

QHOTELS
INSPIRED
BY YOU

tel: 0113 282 1000 & 0845 034 5777 (Calls cost 2p per minute plus your phone company's access charge) **Rothwell Lane, Oulton LS26 8HN**
email: oultonreception@qhotels.co.uk **web:** www.qhotels.co.uk/oultonhall
dir: *2 miles from M62 junction 30, follow Rothwell signs, then 'Oulton 1 mile' sign. 1st exit at next 2 roundabouts. Hotel on left. Or 1 mile from M1 junction 44, follow Castleford and Pontefract sign on A639.*

Surrounded by the beautiful Yorkshire Dales, yet only 15 minutes from the city centre, this elegant 19th-century house offers the best of both worlds. Impressive features include stylish, opulent day rooms and delightful formal gardens, which have been restored to their original design. The hotel boasts a choice of dining options, and extensive leisure facilities. Golfers can book preferential tee times at the adjacent golf club.

Rooms: 152 **S** fr £97 **D** fr £109 (including breakfast)* **Facilities:** Spa STV FTV WiFi HL ⊕ ⚲ 27 ⛳ Gym Beauty therapy Sauna Steam room Juice bar Xmas New Year **Conf:** Class 160 Board 40 Theatre 350 **Services:** Lift Night porter Air con **Parking:** 300 **Notes:** LB Civ Wed 250

Park Plaza Leeds

★★★★ 78% HOTEL

Park Plaza
Hotels & Resorts

tel: 0113 380 4000 & 0333 4006144 **Boar Lane LS1 5NS**
email: pplinfo@pphe.com **web:** www.parkplaza.com
dir: *Follow signs for city centre.*

Chic, stylish, ultra modern, city-centre hotel located just opposite City Square. Chino Latino, located on the first floor, is a fusion Far East and modern Japanese restaurant with a Latino bar. Stylish, air-conditioned bedrooms are spacious and have a range of modern facilities, including high-speed internet connection.

Rooms: 187 ☎ **Facilities:** STV FTV WiFi ⬡ Gym Xmas New Year **Conf:** Class 70 Board 60 Theatre 220 **Services:** Lift Night porter Air con **Parking:** 6 **Notes:** Civ Wed 120

L

The Queens

INSPIRED BY YOU

★★★★ 78% HOTEL

tel: 0113 243 1323 **City Square LS1 1PJ**
email: queensreservations@qhotels.co.uk **web:** www.qhotels.co.uk
dir: M621, M1 and M62 follow signs for city centre and rail station, along Neville Street towards City Square. Under rail bridge, at lights left into slip road in front of hotel.

A legacy from the golden age of railways and located in the heart of Leeds, overlooking City Square, this grand Victorian hotel retains much of its original splendour. Public rooms include the spacious lounge bar, a range of conference and function rooms along with the grand ballroom. Bedrooms vary in size but all are very well equipped, and there is a choice of suites available.

Rooms: 215 (16 family) **Facilities:** STV WiFi New Year **Conf:** Class 200 Board 80 Theatre 500 **Services:** Lift Night porter Air con **Parking:** 55 **Notes:** Civ Wed 500

Malmaison Leeds

★★★★ 77% HOTEL

tel: 0113 398 1000 & 0844 693 0654 (Calls cost 7p per minute plus your phone company's access charge) **1 Swinegate LS1 4AG**
email: leeds@malmaison.com **web:** www.malmaison.com/locations/leeds
dir: M621/M1 junction 3, follow city centre signs. At KPMG building, right into Sovereign Street. Hotel at end on right.

Close to the waterfront, this stylish property offers striking bedrooms with CD players and air conditioning. The popular bar and brasserie feature vaulted ceilings and intimate lighting, and offer a choice of a full three-course meal or a substantial snack. Service is both willing and friendly. A small fitness centre and impressive meeting rooms complete the package.

Rooms: 100 (4 family) **S** fr £79 **D** fr £79* **Facilities:** STV WiFi Xmas New Year **Conf:** Class 100 Board 70 Theatre 150 **Services:** Lift Night porter Air con **Notes:** Civ Wed 70

Novotel Leeds Centre

NOVOTEL
HOTELS & RESORTS

★★★★ 74% HOTEL

tel: 0113 242 6446 **4 Whitehall, Whitehall Quay LS1 4HR**
email: H3270@accor.com **web:** www.novotel.com
dir: M621 junction 3, follow signs to rail station. Into Aire Street and left at lights.

With a minimalist style, this contemporary hotel provides a quality experience close to the city centre and within walking distance of the train station. Spacious, climate-controlled bedrooms are provided, while public areas are smartly presented. The bar is modern and airy, and The Soap Factory Cocktail Lounge and Kitchen offers an informal brasserie style of dining. Facilities also include a fitness suite and a sauna. There is complimentary WiFi throughout the hotel.

Rooms: 196 (50 family) **Facilities:** STV FTV WiFi HL Gym Steam room Sauna **Conf:** Class 50 Board 50 Theatre 100 **Services:** Lift Night porter **Parking:** 80

The Cosmopolitan

PEEL HOTELS PLC

★★★ 80% HOTEL

tel: 0113 243 6454 **2 Lower Briggate LS1 4AE**
email: info@cosmopolitan-hotel-leeds.com **web:** www.cosmopolitan-hotel-leeds.com
dir: M621 junction 3. Keep in right lane. Follow until road splits into 4 lanes. Keep right, right at lights. (ASDA House on left). Left at lights. Over bridge, left, hotel opposite. Parking in 150 metres.

This smartly presented, Victorian building is located on the south side of the city. The well-equipped bedrooms offer both standard and executive grades. Staff are

friendly and helpful ensuring a warm and welcoming atmosphere. Discounted overnight parking is provided in the adjacent 24-hour car park.

Rooms: 89 (5 family) (14 smoking) **Facilities:** STV FTV WiFi Xmas New Year **Conf:** Class 45 Board 40 Theatre 120 **Services:** Lift Night porter

Chevin Country Park Hotel & Spa

CRERAR
HOTELS WITH HEART & SOUL

★★★ 78% HOTEL

tel: 01943 467818 **Yorkgate LS21 3NU**
email: chevin@crerarhotels.com **web:** www.crerarhotels.com

(for full entry see Otley)

Mercure Leeds Parkway Hotel

★★★ 76% HOTEL

tel: 0844 815 9020 (Calls cost 5p per minute plus your phone company's access charge) & 0113 269 9000 **Otley Road LS16 8AG**
email: sales.mercureleedsparkway@jupiterhotels.co.uk **web:** www.mercureleeds.co.uk
dir: From A1 take A58 towards Leeds, then right onto A6120. At A660 turn right towards Airport/Skipton. Hotel 2 miles on right.

This hotel is conveniently located and caters well for both business and leisure guests. It is close to Leeds yet has a quiet spot near to the Yorkshire Dales. The lovely gardens lead on to wildlife walks that can be continued directly into Golden Acre Park (a beautiful 179-acre park and wildlife sanctuary). The hotel is a popular wedding venue and also has extensive conference facilities in the adjacent Summit Centre. A leisure club with indoor pool and fitness centre is also available and the hotel offers complimentary WiFi.

Rooms: 118 (4 family) (18 GF) **Facilities:** Spa STV FTV WiFi Gym Beauty facilities Hair salon Physiotherapy Xmas New Year **Conf:** Class 100 Board 65 Theatre 280 **Services:** Lift Night porter **Parking:** 250 **Notes:** Civ Wed 200

Holiday Inn Express Leeds - East

BUDGET HOTEL

tel: 0113 288 0574 **Aberford Road, Oulton LS26 8EJ**
email: reservations@hiexpressleedseast.co.uk **web:** www.hiexpressleedseast.co.uk
dir: M62 junction 29, east towards Pontefract. Exit at junction 30, A642 signed Rothwell. Hotel opposite at 1st roundabout.

A modern hotel ideal for families and business travellers. Fresh and uncomplicated, the spacious rooms include Sky TV, power shower and tea and coffee-making facilities. Continental buffet breakfast is included in the room rate; other meals may be taken at the nearby family pub or restaurant.

Rooms: 77 (50 family) (32 GF) **S** fr £49 **D** fr £49 (including breakfast)*

Premier Inn Leeds/Bradford Airport

Premier Inn

BUDGET HOTEL

tel: 0871 527 8578 (Calls cost 13p per minute plus your phone company's access charge) **Victoria Avenue, Yeadon LS19 7AW**
web: www.premierinn.com
dir: On A658, near Leeds Bradford Airport.

High quality, budget accommodation ideal for both families and business travellers. Spacious, en suite bedrooms feature free WiFi and tea and coffee making facilities, and in most hotels, Freeview TV is also available. The adjacent family restaurant features a wide and varied menu.

Rooms: 76

LEEDS *continued*

Premier Inn Leeds City Centre

BUDGET HOTEL

tel: 0871 527 8582 (Calls cost 13p per minute plus your phone company's access charge) **Citygate, Wellington Street LS3 1LW**
web: www.premierinn.com
dir: *At A65 and A58 junction.*

Rooms: 140

Premier Inn Leeds City Centre (Leeds Arena)

BUDGET HOTEL

tel: 0871 527 9356 (Calls cost 13p per minute plus your phone company's access charge) **Hepworth Point, Claypit Lane LS2 8BQ**
web: www.premierinn.com
dir: *On foot from Leeds rail station cross road into Park Row, continue into Cookridge Street to Clay Pit Lane. Hotel on left at top of lane.*

Rooms: 131

Premier Inn Leeds City Centre (Whitehall Road)

BUDGET HOTEL

tel: 0871 622 2412 (Calls cost 13p per minute plus your phone company's access charge) **1 Whitehall Riverside, Lower Wortley LS1 4EQ**
web: www.premierinn.com
dir: *Phone for directions.*

Rooms: 136

Premier Inn Leeds City West

BUDGET HOTEL

tel: 0871 527 8584 (Calls cost 13p per minute plus your phone company's access charge) **City West One Office Park, Gelderd Road LS12 6LX**
web: www.premierinn.com
dir: *M621 junction 1 take ring road towards Leeds. At 1st lights right into Gelderd Road, right at roundabout.*

Rooms: 126

Premier Inn Leeds East

BUDGET HOTEL

tel: 0871 527 8586 (Calls cost 13p per minute plus your phone company's access charge) **Selby Road, Whitkirk LS15 7AY**
web: www.premierinn.com
dir: *M1 junction 46 towards Leeds. At 2nd roundabout follow Temple Newsam signs. Hotel 500 metres on right.*

Rooms: 88

Premier Inn Leeds Headingley

BUDGET HOTEL

tel: 0871 527 8000 (Calls cost 13p per minute plus your phone company's access charge) **Arndale House, Otley Road LS6 2UU**
web: www.premierinn.com
dir: *Phone for directions.*

Rooms: 98

Premier Inn Leeds South (Birstall)

BUDGET HOTEL

tel: 0871 527 8580 (Calls cost 13p per minute plus your phone company's access charge) **Wakefield Road, Drighlington BD11 1EA**
web: www.premierinn.com
dir: *On Drighlington bypass, adjacent to M62 junction 27. Take A650, right to Drighlington, right, hotel on left.*

Rooms: 60

LEEK
Staffordshire   Map 16 SJ95

Premier Inn Leek Town Centre

BUDGET HOTEL

tel: 0871 527 9330 (Calls cost 13p per minute plus your phone company's access charge) **Ashbourne Road ST13 5AS**
web: www.premierinn.com
dir: *M6 junction 16, A500. In 6 miles left at Eturia junction onto A53 signed Leek to the town centre. At lights in town centre turn right onto A523 (Ashbourne Road). Hotel adjacent to war memorial on left.*

High quality, budget accommodation ideal for both families and business travellers. Spacious, en suite bedrooms feature free WiFi and tea and coffee making facilities, and in most hotels, Freeview TV is also available. The adjacent family restaurant features a wide and varied menu.

Rooms: 63

LEEK WOOTTON
Warwickshire   Map 10 SP26

The Warwickshire Hotel & Country Club

★★★★ 79% HOTEL

tel: 01926 409409 & 622550 **CV35 7QT**
email: g.rayner@theclubcompany.com **web:** www.thewarwickshire.com
dir: *M40 junction 15 towards Coventry A46, then B4115 towards Leek Wootton. At roundabout 1st exit towards Leek Wootton, at next roundabout 1st exit to hotel.*

This well-established venue, known for the golf and leisure facilities, includes a 56-bedroom hotel. The comfortable accommodation offered is very high quality – the rooms are equipped for both the leisure or corporate guests. Dining options are a casual café and lounge area, and for a quieter spot, the club lounge.

Rooms: 56 (12 family) (28 GF) **Facilities:** Spa FTV WiFi ❨❩ 45 Gym Sauna Solarium Steam room New Year **Conf:** Class 100 Board 80 Theatre 200 **Services:** Lift Night porter Air con **Parking:** 264 **Notes:** Civ Wed 173

L

LEICESTER
Leicestershire

Map 11 SK50

Belmont Hotel

★★★★ 78% ◉◉ HOTEL

tel: 0116 254 4773 **De Montfort Street LE1 7GR**
email: info@belmonthotel.co.uk **web:** www.belmonthotel.co.uk
dir: *From A6 take 1st right after rail station. Hotel 200 yards on left.*

This well-established hotel, under the same family ownership, has been welcoming guests for over 70 years. It is conveniently situated within easy walking distance of the railway station and city centre though it sits in a quiet leafy residential area. Extensive public rooms are smartly appointed and include Jamie's Bar with its relaxed atmosphere and the more formal David Ferguson's at the Belmont.

Rooms: 74 (7 family) (8 GF) (2 smoking) ☎ S fr £70 D fr £89* **Facilities:** FTV WiFi ⌂ Gym Xmas New Year **Conf:** Class 75 Board 65 Theatre 175 **Services:** Lift Night porter **Parking:** 70 **Notes:** LB Civ Wed 100

Mercure Leicester The Grand Hotel

★★★★ 72% HOTEL

tel: 0844 815 9012 (Calls cost 5p per minute plus your phone company's access charge) **Granby Street LE1 6ES**
email: info@mercureleicester.co.uk **web:** www.mercureleicester.co.uk
dir: *A5460 into city. Follow Leicester Central Station signs. Left off St Georges Way, A594 into Charles Street. 1st left into Northampton Street, right into Granby Street. Hotel on left.*

Located in the heart of Leicester's city centre, this hotel offers well-appointed bedrooms and spacious public areas. Conferences and weddings are catered for. On-site parking is a plus and free WiFi is available throughout.

Rooms: 104 ☎ S fr £69 D fr £79* **Facilities:** FTV WiFi ⌂ Xmas New Year **Conf:** Class 200 Board 90 Theatre 350 **Services:** Lift Night porter **Parking:** 120 **Notes:** Civ Wed 200

Premier Inn Leicester (Braunstone)

Premier Inn

BUDGET HOTEL

tel: 0871 527 8590 (Calls cost 13p per minute plus your phone company's access charge) **Meridian Business Park, Thorpe Astley LE19 1LU**
web: www.premierinn.com
dir: *M1 junction 21, follow A563 (outer ring road) signs west to Thorpe Astley. At slip road after Texaco garage. Hotel on left.*

High quality, budget accommodation ideal for both families and business travellers. Spacious, en suite bedrooms feature free WiFi and tea and coffee making facilities, and in most hotels, Freeview TV is also available. The adjacent family restaurant features a wide and varied menu.

Rooms: 75

Premier Inn Leicester Central (A50)

Premier Inn

BUDGET HOTEL

tel: 0871 527 8594 (Calls cost 13p per minute plus your phone company's access charge) **Heathley Park, Groby Road LE3 9QE**
web: www.premierinn.com
dir: *Off A50, city centre side of County Hall and Glenfield General Hospital.*

Rooms: 76

Premier Inn Leicester City Centre

Premier Inn

BUDGET HOTEL

tel: 0871 527 8596 (Calls cost 13p per minute plus your phone company's access charge) **1 St Georges Way LE1 1AA**
web: www.premierinn.com
dir: *Phone for directions.*

Rooms: 135

Premier Inn Leicester (Forest East)

Premier Inn

BUDGET HOTEL

tel: 0871 527 8592 (Calls cost 13p per minute plus your phone company's access charge) **Hinckley Road, Leicester Forest East LE3 3GD**
web: www.premierinn.com
dir: *M1 junction 21, A5460. At major junction (Holiday Inn on right), left into Braunstone Lane. In 2 miles left onto A47 towards Hinckley. Hotel 400 yards on left.*

Rooms: 60

Premier Inn Leicester Fosse Park

Premier Inn

BUDGET HOTEL

tel: 0871 527 8588 (Calls cost 13p per minute plus your phone company's access charge) **Braunstone Lane East LE3 2FW**
web: www.premierinn.com
dir: *M1 junction 21, at M69 junction take A5460 towards city. After 1 mile right at lights to hotel.*

Rooms: 176

Premier Inn Leicester North West

Premier Inn

BUDGET HOTEL

tel: 0871 527 8598 (Calls cost 13p per minute plus your phone company's access charge) **Leicester Road, Glenfield LE3 8HB**
web: www.premierinn.com
dir: *M1 junction 21a northbound, A46. Onto A50 for Glenfield and County Hall. Or M1 junction 22 southbound onto A50 towards Glenfield. Into County Hall. Hotel on left adjacent to Gynsills.*

Rooms: 68

Premier Inn Leicester South (Oadby)

Premier Inn

BUDGET HOTEL

tel: 0871 527 8600 (Calls cost 13p per minute plus your phone company's access charge) **Glen Rise, Oadby LE2 4RG**
web: www.premierinn.com
dir: *M1 junction 21, A563 signed South. Right at Leicester racecourse. Follow Market Harborough signs. Dual carriageway, straight on at roundabout. Into single lane, hotel on right.*

Rooms: 30

L

L

LEICESTER FOREST EAST MOTORWAY SERVICE AREA — Map 11 SK50
Leicestershire

Days Inn Leicester Forest East - M1

WELCOMEBREAK

AA Advertised

tel: 0116 239 0534 **Leicester Forest East, M1 junction 21 LE3 3GB**
email: leicester.hotel@welcomebreak.co.uk **web:** www.welcomebreak.co.uk
dir: *On M1 northbound between junction 21 and 21A.*

This modern building offers accommodation in smart, spacious and well-equipped bedrooms, suitable for families and business travellers, and all with en suite bathrooms. Continental breakfast is available, and other refreshments may be taken at the nearby family restaurant.

Rooms: 86 (71 family) (10 smoking) **Facilities:** FTV WiFi ⌨ **Conf:** Board 10
Services: Lift **Parking:** 100

LENHAM — Map 7 TQ85
Kent

INSPECTOR'S CHOICE

Chilston Park Hotel

Hand PICKED HOTELS

★★★★ ◉◉ ⌘ HOTEL

tel: 01622 859803 & 0845 072 7426 (Calls cost 5p per minute plus your phone company's access charge) **Sandway ME17 2BE**
email: chilstonpark@handpicked.co.uk
web: www.handpickedhotels.co.uk/chilstonpark
dir: *Exit A20 to Lenham, right into High Street, pass station on right, 1st left, over crossroads, hotel 0.25 mile on left.*

This elegant Grade I listed country house is set in 23 acres of immaculately landscaped gardens and parkland. An impressive collection of original paintings and antiques creates a unique environment. The sunken Venetian-style restaurant serves modern British food with French influences. Bedrooms are individual in design, some have four-poster beds and many have garden views.

Rooms: 53 (23 annexe) (2 family) (3 GF) ⌨ **D** fr £109 (including breakfast)
Facilities: STV FTV WiFi ⌨ HL Fishing 🚣 Xmas New Year **Conf:** Class 60 Board 50 Theatre 100 **Services:** Lift Night porter **Parking:** 100 **Notes:** LB Civ Wed 90

LEOMINSTER — Map 10 SO45
Herefordshire

Talbot Hotel

★★★ 73% HOTEL

tel: 01568 616347 **West Street HR6 8EP**
email: info@talbothotelleominster.com **web:** www.talbothotelleominster.com
dir: *From A49, A44 or A4112, hotel in town centre.*

This charming former coaching inn is located in the town centre and makes an ideal base for exploring the area. Public areas feature original beams and antique furniture, and include an atmospheric bar and elegant restaurant. The bedrooms vary in size, but all are comfortably furnished and equipped. Facilities are available for private functions and conferences.

Rooms: 28 (3 family) (2 GF) **Facilities:** FTV WiFi **Conf:** Class 60 Board 30 Theatre 130 **Parking:** 26

LETCHWORTH GARDEN CITY — Map 12 TL23
Hertfordshire

Mercure Letchworth Hall Hotel

★★★★ 73% HOTEL

tel: 01462 683747 **Letchworth Lane SG6 3NP**
email: mlreservations@mercureletchworth.com **web:** www.fairviewhotels.com

This hotel has an interesting history and is set in peaceful eight-acre grounds overlooking a golf course; it retains much original country-house style. There is a leisure facility as well as a host of meeting and function rooms. Bedrooms are spacious and well equipped and include air conditioning, Freeview TVs and complimentary WiFi. Lytton's offers international cuisine features produce from local suppliers.

Rooms: 87 (10 GF) ⌨ **Facilities:** Spa FTV WiFi ⌨ Gym Xmas New Year **Conf:** Class 100 Board 60 Theatre 200 **Services:** Lift Night porter Air con **Parking:** 200 **Notes:** LB Civ Wed 80

Premier Inn Letchworth Garden City

Premier Inn

BUDGET HOTEL

tel: 0871 527 8000 (Calls cost 13p per minute plus your phone company's access charge) **39-41 Station Road SG6 3BG**
web: www.premierinn.com
dir: *Phone for directions.*

High quality, budget accommodation ideal for both families and business travellers. Spacious, en suite bedrooms feature free WiFi and tea and coffee making facilities, and in most hotels, Freeview TV is also available. The adjacent family restaurant features a wide and varied menu.

Rooms: 57

LEVENS
Cumbria
Map 18 SD48

The Villa Levens
★★★★ 79% @@ HOTEL

tel: 01539 980980 **Brettargh Holt LA8 8EA**
email: reception@thevillalevens.co.uk **web:** www.thevillalevens.co.uk
dir: *M6 junction 36, A590 signed Barrow. At next roundabout (Brettargh Holt Roundabout), 1st left signed Barrow, hotel 200 yards on left.*

This former family home and convent on the edge of the Lake District is now a charming hotel. Bedrooms are spacious, with the feature room having a copper bath in the bedroom. Two dining options are available; the brasserie is open throughout the day while the restaurant offers a more formal dining option to guests at lunch and dinner. Conference facilities are also available.

Rooms: 22 (3 family) (4 GF) ↟ **S** fr £70 **D** fr £80* **Facilities:** FTV WiFi ↡ ⚘ Xmas New Year **Conf:** Class 250 Board 100 Theatre 300 **Services:** Night porter **Parking:** 130 **Notes:** LB Civ Wed 300

LEWES
East Sussex
Map 6 TQ41

Premier Inn Lewes Town Centre
Premier Inn 🌙

BUDGET HOTEL

tel: 0871 527 9524 (Calls cost 13p per minute plus your phone company's access charge) **BN7 2FT**
web: www.premierinn.com
dir: *From A27 take Lewes, East Grinstead, Tunbridge Wells exit onto A26 at Southerham Roundabout. Through Cuilfail Tunnel, take 1st exit left at roundabout after tunnel onto Malling Street/A2029. Continue over next roundabout onto Phoenix Causeway, at lights continue onto Friars Walk B2193. Hotel on left.*

High quality, budget accommodation ideal for both families and business travellers. Spacious, en suite bedrooms feature free WiFi and tea and coffee making facilities, and in most hotels, Freeview TV is also available. The adjacent family restaurant features a wide and varied menu.

Rooms: 61

LEYLAND
Lancashire
Map 15 SD52

Hallmark Hotel Preston Leyland
★★★ 78% HOTEL

tel: 0330 028 3420 **Leyland Way PR25 4JX**
email: leyland@hallmarkhotels.co.uk **web:** www.hallmarkhotels.co.uk
dir: *M6 junction 28, left at end of slip road, hotel 100 metres on left.*

This purpose-built hotel enjoys a convenient location, just off the M6, within easy reach of Preston and Blackpool. Spacious public areas include extensive conference and banqueting facilities as well as a smart leisure club.

Rooms: 93 (4 family) (31 GF) ↟ **Facilities:** FTV WiFi ↡ HL ⊛ Xmas New Year **Conf:** Class 100 Board 40 Theatre 220 **Services:** Night porter **Parking:** 150 **Notes:** LB Civ Wed 200

LICHFIELD
Staffordshire
Map 10 SK10

Swinfen Hall Hotel
★★★★ @@@ HOTEL

tel: 01543 481494 **Swinfen WS14 9RE**
email: info@swinfenhallhotel.co.uk **web:** www.swinfenhallhotel.co.uk
dir: *Set back from A38, 2.5 miles outside Lichfield, towards Birmingham.*

Dating from 1757, this lavishly decorated mansion has been painstakingly restored by the present owners. It is set in 100 acres of parkland which includes a deer park. Public rooms are particularly stylish, with intricately carved ceilings and impressive oil portraits. Bedrooms on the first floor boast period features and tall sash windows; those on the second floor (the former servants' quarters) are smaller and more contemporary by comparison. Service in the award-winning restaurant is both professional and attentive.

Rooms: 17 (5 family) ↟ **S** fr £135 **D** fr £155 (including breakfast)* **Facilities:** STV FTV WiFi ↡ ⚲ Fishing ⚘ Jogging trail 100 acre park New Year **Conf:** Class 50 Board 50 Theatre 160 **Services:** Night porter **Parking:** 80 **Notes:** Civ Wed 120

Best Western The George Hotel
Ⓑ Best Western.
★★★ 81% HOTEL

tel: 01543 414822 **12-14 Bird Street WS13 6PR**
email: mail@thegeorgelichfield.co.uk **web:** www.thegeorgelichfield.co.uk
dir: *From Bowling Green Island on A461 take Lichfield exit. Left at next island into Swan Road, as road bears left, turn right into Bird Street for hotel car park.*

Situated in the city centre, this privately-owned hotel provides good quality, well-equipped accommodation which includes a room with a four-poster bed. Facilities here include a large ballroom, plus several other rooms for meetings and functions.

Rooms: 45 (5 family) **S** fr £45 **D** fr £65 (including breakfast)* **Facilities:** FTV WiFi ↡ HL Gym **Conf:** Class 60 Board 40 Theatre 110 **Services:** Lift Night porter **Parking:** 45 **Notes:** LB Civ Wed 110

L

LICHFIELD *continued*

Premier Inn Lichfield City Centre

BUDGET HOTEL

tel: 0871 527 9440 (Calls cost 13p per minute plus your phone company's access charge) **Swan Road WS13 6QZ**
web: www.premierinn.com
dir: *From M6 Toll junction T5 take A5148. Take A5206 ramp to Lichfield. At roundabout 1st exit (London Road/A5206) into Upper St John Street (A51). Left into The Friary. 3rd exit at roundabout (Swan Road). Hotel on right.*

High quality, budget accommodation ideal for both families and business travellers. Spacious, en suite bedrooms feature free WiFi and tea and coffee making facilities, and in most hotels, Freeview TV is also available. The adjacent family restaurant features a wide and varied menu.

Rooms: 79

Premier Inn Lichfield North East (A38)

Premier Inn

BUDGET HOTEL

tel: 0871 527 8602 (Calls cost 13p per minute plus your phone company's access charge) **Fine Lane, Fradley WS13 8RD**
web: www.premierinn.com
dir: *On A38, 3 miles northeast of Lichfield.*

Rooms: 30

LIFTON
Devon
Map 3 SX38

HIGHLY RECOMMENDED

Arundell Arms

★★★ 87% HOTEL

tel: 01566 784666 **Fore Street PL16 0AA**
email: reservations@arundellarms.co.uk **web:** www.arundellarms.co.uk
dir: *1 mile off A30, 3 miles east of Launceston.*

This former coaching inn, boasting a long history, sits in the heart of a quiet Devon village, and is internationally famous for its country pursuits such as winter shooting and angling. The bedrooms offer individual style and comfort. Public areas are full of character with a relaxed atmosphere, particularly around the open log fire during colder evenings. Award-winning cuisine is a celebration of local produce.

Rooms: 27 (6 annexe) (3 family) (4 GF) **Facilities:** FTV WiFi Fishing Game shooting (in winter) Fly fishing school Riding Xmas New Year **Conf:** Class 30 Board 40 Theatre 100 **Services:** Night porter **Parking:** 70 **Notes:** Closed 24–27 December

LINCOLN
Lincolnshire
Map 17 SK97

Best Western Plus Bentley Hotel & Spa

Best Western PLUS

★★★★ 73% HOTEL

tel: 01522 878000 **Newark Road, South Hykeham LN6 9NH**
email: info@bentleyhotellincoln.co.uk **web:** www.bentleyhotellincoln.co.uk
dir: *A1 onto A46 E towards Lincoln for 10 miles. Over 1st roundabout on Lincoln Bypass to hotel 50 yards on left.*

This conveniently located hotel is perfect for business and leisure guests alike. Staff are friendly, and adopt a personal approach to hospitality. Bedrooms and bathrooms are comfortably appointed and modern accessories such as complimentary WiFi are provided. Leisure facilities including swimming pool, sauna, steam room and gym are included for residential guests. A good range of meal options is available in both the bar and the restaurant. Ample parking is provided.

Rooms: 80 (5 family) (23 GF) (4 smoking) **S** fr £57 **D** fr £65* **Facilities:** Spa STV FTV WiFi HL Gym Steam room Sauna Jacuzzi Thermal suite Rasul New Year **Conf:** Class 150 Board 30 Theatre 300 **Services:** Lift Night porter Air con **Parking:** 170 **Notes:** Civ Wed 120

HIGHLY RECOMMENDED

Washingborough Hall Hotel

★★★ 87% COUNTRY HOUSE HOTEL

tel: 01522 790340 **Church Hill, Washingborough LN4 1BE**
email: enquiries@washingboroughhall.com **web:** www.washingboroughhall.com
dir: *B1190 into Washingborough. Right at roundabout, hotel 500 yards on left.*

This Georgian manor stands on the edge of the quiet village of Washingborough and is set in attractive gardens. Public rooms are pleasantly furnished and comfortable, while the restaurant offers interesting menus. Bedrooms are individually designed and most have views out over the grounds to the countryside beyond.

Rooms: 20 (6 annexe) (2 family) (3 GF) **S** fr £85 **D** fr £135* **Facilities:** FTV WiFi **Conf:** Class 70 Board 30 Theatre 100 **Parking:** 40 **Notes:** LB Civ Wed 100

The White Hart

★★★ 81% HOTEL

tel: 01522 526222 **Bailgate LN1 3AR**
email: info@whitehart-lincoln.co.uk **web:** www.whitehart-lincoln.co.uk
dir: *A46 onto B1226, through Newport Arch. Hotel 0.5 mile on left as road bends left.*

Sitting in the shadow of Lincoln's magnificent cathedral, this hotel is perfectly positioned for exploring the shops and sights of this medieval city. The attractive bedrooms are furnished and decorated in a traditional style and many have views of the cathedral. Given the hotel's central location, parking is a real benefit.

Rooms: 50 (3 family) **S** fr £75 **D** fr £85 (including breakfast)* **Facilities:** FTV WiFi **Conf:** Class 70 Board 50 Theatre 160 **Services:** Lift Night porter **Parking:** 50 **Notes:** Civ Wed 120

L

The Lincoln Hotel

★★★ 79% ◉ HOTEL

tel: 01522 520348 **Eastgate LN2 1PN**
email: reservations@thelincolnhotel.com **web:** www.thelincolnhotel.com
dir: *Adjacent to cathedral.*

This privately-owned, modern hotel enjoys superb uninterrupted views of Lincoln Cathedral. There are ruins of the Roman wall and Eastgate in the grounds. Bedrooms are contemporary with up-to-the-minute facilities. An airy restaurant and bar, a cellar bar, plus a comfortable lounge are provided. There are substantial conference and meeting facilities.

Rooms: 71 (4 family) (10 GF) ⚓ **S** fr £79 **D** fr £89* **Facilities:** FTV WiFi Gym New Year **Conf:** Class 50 Board 40 Theatre 100 **Services:** Lift Night porter **Parking:** 54 **Notes:** LB Civ Wed 150

Tower Hotel

★★★ 77% ◉ HOTEL

tel: 01522 529999 **38 Westgate LN1 3BD**
email: tower.hotel@btclick.com **web:** www.lincolntowerhotel.com
dir: *From A46 follow signs to Lincoln north then to Bailgate area. Through arch, 2nd right.*

This hotel faces the Norman castle wall and is in a very convenient location for the city. The relaxed and friendly atmosphere is very noticeable here. There's a modern conservatory bar and a stylish restaurant where contemporary dishes are available throughout the day.

Rooms: 15 (1 family) ⚓ **S** fr £70 **D** fr £95 (including breakfast)* **Facilities:** STV FTV WiFi **Conf:** Class 24 Board 16 Theatre 24 **Services:** Night porter **Notes:** Closed 24–27 December, 1 January

Branston Hall Hotel

★★★ 75% ◉ COUNTRY HOUSE HOTEL

tel: 01522 793305 **Branston Park, Branston LN4 1PD**
email: info@branstonhall.com **web:** www.branstonhall.com
dir: *On B1188, 3 miles southeast of Lincoln.*

Dating back to 1885, this country house sits in 88 acres of beautiful grounds complete with a lake. There is an elegant restaurant, a spacious bar and a beautiful lounge in addition to impressive conference and leisure facilities. Individually styled bedrooms vary in size and include several with four-poster beds. The hotel is a popular wedding venue.

Rooms: 50 (7 annexe) (3 family) (4 GF) **Facilities:** Spa STV FTV WiFi ◉ Gym Jogging circuit Xmas New Year **Conf:** Class 54 Board 40 Theatre 200 **Services:** Lift Night porter **Parking:** 100 **Notes:** Civ Wed 160

Premier Inn Lincoln (Canwick)

BUDGET HOTEL

tel: 0871 527 8604 (Calls cost 13p per minute plus your phone company's access charge) **Lincoln Road, Canwick Hill LN4 2RF**
web: www.premierinn.com
dir: *Approximately 1 mile south of city centre at junction of B1188 and B1131.*

High quality, budget accommodation ideal for both families and business travellers. Spacious, en suite bedrooms feature free WiFi and tea and coffee making facilities, and in most hotels, Freeview TV is also available. The adjacent family restaurant features a wide and varied menu.

Rooms: 98

Premier Inn Lincoln City Centre

Premier Inn

BUDGET HOTEL

tel: 0871 527 9418 (Calls cost 13p per minute plus your phone company's access charge) **Broadgate LN2 5AQ**
web: www.premierinn.com
dir: *From north: from A57 left into Mint Street B1003. Right into Broadgate A15. From south: on A46 to A1434/Newark Road roundabout. Straight on next roundabout into St Catherines A15, straight on at next roundabout. Left into St Swithins Square. Right into Silver Street B1003. Right into Broadgate A15.*

Rooms: 131

LIPHOOK
Hampshire   Map 5 SU83

Old Thorns Manor Hotel Golf & Country Estate

★★★★ 79% HOTEL

tel: 01428 724555 **Griggs Green GU30 7PE**
email: reservations@oldthorns.com **web:** www.oldthorns.com
dir: *At Griggs Green exit A3, hotel 0.5 mile.*

Old Thorns is a modern, relaxed and welcoming hotel, set in 400 acres of peaceful Hampshire countryside. The bedrooms are spacious and stylish and offer high levels of comfort. The leisure facilities are extensive and include a health club, wellness centre and spa; in addition there is also a sports bar, champagne and cocktail bar, Kings Restaurant and all-day dining is also available.

Rooms: 175 (2 family) (64 GF) ⚓ **Facilities:** Spa STV FTV WiFi ⓠ ◉ ♨ 18 ⛳ Gym Xmas New Year **Conf:** Class 100 Board 30 Theatre 300 **Services:** Lift Night porter **Parking:** 278 **Notes:** Civ Wed 250

LISKEARD
Cornwall & Isles Of Scilly   Map 2 SX26

Premier Inn Liskeard

Premier Inn

BUDGET HOTEL

tel: 0871 527 8608 (Calls cost 13p per minute plus your phone company's access charge) **Liskeard Retail Park, Haviland Road PL14 3PR**
web: www.premierinn.com
dir: *Off A38, on A390 southwest of Liskeard.*

High quality, budget accommodation ideal for both families and business travellers. Spacious, en suite bedrooms feature free WiFi and tea and coffee making facilities, and in most hotels, Freeview TV is also available. The adjacent family restaurant features a wide and varied menu.

Rooms: 51

L

LITTLEHAMPTON   Map 6 TQ00
West Sussex

Premier Inn Littlehampton

BUDGET HOTEL

tel: 0871 527 8610 (Calls cost 13p per minute plus your phone company's access charge) **Roundstone Lane, East Preston BN16 1EB**
web: www.premierinn.com
dir: *A27 onto A280 signed Littlehampton/Rustington and Angmering. At next roundabout follow Littlehampton, Rustington/A259 signs. At next roundabout 1st exit signed East Preston. Hotel on left.*

High quality, budget accommodation ideal for both families and business travellers. Spacious, en suite bedrooms feature free WiFi and tea and coffee making facilities, and in most hotels, Freeview TV is also available. The adjacent family restaurant features a wide and varied menu.

Rooms: 39

LIVERPOOL   Map 15 SJ39
Merseyside

Thornton Hall Hotel and Spa

★★★★ 82% ◉◉ HOTEL

tel: 0151 336 3938 **Neston Road CH63 1JF**
email: reservations@thorntonhallhotel.com **web:** www.thorntonhallhotel.com

(for full entry see Thornton Hough)

Hope Street Hotel

★★★★ 79% ◉ HOTEL

tel: 0151 709 3000 **40 Hope Street L1 9DA**
email: sleep@hopestreethotel.co.uk **web:** www.hopestreethotel.co.uk
dir: *Follow Cathedral and University signs on entering city. Telephone for detailed directions.*

This stylish property is located in the Georgian quarter within easy walking distance of the city's cathedrals, theatres, major shops and attractions. Stylish bedrooms and suites, many with far-reaching views across the city, have DVD players, internet access and comfy beds with Egyptian cotton sheets. Bathrooms have rain showers and deep tubs. The London Carriage Works Restaurant specialises in local, seasonal produce, and the adjacent lounge bar offers lighter all-day dining and wonderful cocktails. A current development will provide an additional 60 bedrooms,

terraced suites and penthouses. Complementing this will be a destination spa to include thermal cabins, outdoor vitality pool, heated indoor swimming pool, gym, and six treatment rooms.

Hope Street Hotel

Rooms: 89 (16 family) (5 GF) ✆ **S** fr £89 **D** fr £89* **Facilities:** STV FTV WiFi ↳ Gym In-room massage and beauty treatments Xmas New Year **Conf:** Class 40 Board 30 Theatre 70 **Services:** Lift Night porter Air con **Parking:** 10 **Notes:** LB Civ Wed 70

Malmaison Liverpool

★★★★ 76% ◉ HOTEL

tel: 0151 229 5000 & 0844 693 0655 (Calls cost 5p per minute plus your phone company's access charge) **7 William Jessop Way, Princes Dock L3 1QZ**
email: reception.liverpool@malmaison.com **web:** www.malmaison.com/locations/liverpool
dir: *A5080 follow signs for Pier Head/Southport/Bootle. Into Baln Street to roundabout, 1st exit at roundabout, immediately left onto William Jessop Way.*

This is a purpose-built hotel with cutting edge and contemporary style. 'Mal' Liverpool, as its known, has a stunning location, alongside the river and docks, and in the heart of the city's regeneration. Bedrooms are stylish and comfortable and are provided with lots of extra facilities. The public areas are packed with fun and style, and there are a number of meeting rooms as well as private dining, including a chef's table.

Rooms: 130 ✆ **S** fr £79 **D** fr £79* **Facilities:** STV FTV WiFi ↳ Gym ♫ Xmas New Year **Conf:** Class 85 Board 80 Theatre 100 **Services:** Lift Night porter Air con **Notes:** LB Civ Wed 120

Novotel Liverpool Centre

★★★★ 76% HOTEL

tel: 0151 702 5100 **40 Hanover Street L1 4LN**
email: h6495@accor.com **web:** www.novotel.com

This attractive and stylish city centre hotel is convenient for Liverpool Echo Arena, Liverpool One shopping centre and the Albert Dock; it is also adjacent to a car park. Novotel Liverpool Centre has a range of conference and leisure facilities which include an indoor heated pool and fitness suite. Rope Walks restaurant offers a contemporary-style menu and relaxed lounge bar concept, taking influences from Liverpool's industrial and shipping history. The open-plan bar has many seating options, from high stools to button-backed benches, soft sofas and armchairs. The bedrooms are comfortable and stylishly designed.

Rooms: 209 (127 family) ✆ **Facilities:** FTV WiFi ↳ ⊛ Gym Steam room ♫ **Conf:** Class 60 Board 50 Theatre 90 **Services:** Lift Night porter

Hard Days Night Hotel

★★★★ 72% HOTEL

tel: 0151 236 1964 **Central Buildings, North John Street L2 6RR**
email: info@harddaysnighthotel.com **web:** www.harddaysnighthotel.com
dir: *Phone for directions.*

In the heart of Liverpool and close to Liverpool One, a shoppers' delight, and less than a stone's throw from the iconic Cavern Club, Hard Days Night Hotel is a very tasteful celebration of Beatle Mania. Guests travel from far and wide to stay at this hotel. Each attractively furnished, modern bedroom is very well equipped, and all feature a Beatles-inspired, specially commissioned piece of artwork. Blakes Restaurant provides a relaxed and informal dining venue and cocktails are served nightly in the Fab Four bar.

Rooms: 110 ☏ **S** fr £79 **D** fr £79* **Facilities:** STV FTV WiFi ⌕ HL ♫ **Conf:** Class 40 Board 20 Theatre 120 **Services:** Lift Night porter Air con **Notes:** LB Civ Wed 60

Hallmark Hotel Liverpool Alicia

★★★ 76% HOTEL

tel: 0330 028 3416 & 0151 727 4411 **3 Aigburth Drive, Sefton Park L17 3AA**
email: alicia@hallmarkhotels.co.uk **web:** www.hallmarkhotels.co.uk
dir: *From end of M62 take A5058 to Sefton Park, then left, follow park around.*

This stylish and friendly hotel overlooks Sefton Park and is just a few minutes' drive from both the city centre and Liverpool John Lennon Airport. Bedrooms are well equipped and comfortable. Day rooms include a striking modern restaurant and bar. Extensive, stylish function facilities make this a popular wedding venue.

Rooms: 41 (8 family) ☏ **Facilities:** STV WiFi HL Xmas New Year **Conf:** Class 80 Board 40 Theatre 120 **Services:** Lift Night porter **Parking:** 40 **Notes:** Civ Wed 120

Hallmark Inn Liverpool

★★ 78% METRO HOTEL

tel: 0330 028 3426 **115-125 Mount Pleasant L3 5TF**
email: liverpool.inn@hallmarkhotels.co.uk **web:** www.hallmarkhotels.co.uk
dir: *In city centre.*

This stylish and friendly metro hotel has a prime city centre location close to both cathedrals, universities, and local eateries. Bedrooms come in a variety of distinctive styles and are well equipped and comfortable. Limited secure parking is available on a first come-first served basis.

Rooms: 81 ☏ **Facilities:** FTV WiFi **Parking:** 24

Premier Inn Liverpool (Aintree)

BUDGET HOTEL

tel: 0871 527 8612 (Calls cost 13p per minute plus your phone company's access charge) **Ormskirk Road, Aintree L9 5AS**
web: www.premierinn.com
dir: *M58, A57, A59 towards Liverpool. Pass Aintree Retail Park, left at lights into Aintree Racecourse. Hotel on left.*

High quality, budget accommodation ideal for both families and business travellers. Spacious, en suite bedrooms feature free WiFi and tea and coffee making facilities, and in most hotels, Freeview TV is also available. The adjacent family restaurant features a wide and varied menu.

Rooms: 40

Premier Inn Liverpool Albert Dock

BUDGET HOTEL

tel: 0871 527 8622 (Calls cost 13p per minute plus your phone company's access charge) **East Britannia Building, Albert Dock L3 4AD**
web: www.premierinn.com
dir: *Follow signs for Liverpool City Centre and Albert Dock.*

Rooms: 186

Premier Inn Liverpool City Centre

BUDGET HOTEL

tel: 0871 527 8624 (Calls cost 13p per minute plus your phone company's access charge) **Vernon Street L2 2AY**
web: www.premierinn.com
dir: *From M62 follow Liverpool City Centre and Birkenhead Tunnel signs. At roundabout 3rd exit into Dale Street, right into Vernon Street. Hotel on left.*

Rooms: 165

Premier Inn Liverpool City Centre (Liverpool 1)

BUDGET HOTEL

tel: 0871 527 9382 (Calls cost 13p per minute plus your phone company's access charge) **48 Hanover Street L1 4AF**
web: www.premierinn.com
dir: *A5047 follow signs for city centre. At lights left onto A5048, at next lights right onto A5047. A5038 signed Toxteth, Airport. Right into Renshaw Street and right onto Ranelagh Street. Hotel on left opposite BBC Radio Merseyside.*

Rooms: 183

Premier Inn Liverpool John Lennon Airport

BUDGET HOTEL

tel: 0871 527 8626 (Calls cost 13p per minute plus your phone company's access charge) **57 Speke Hall Avenue L24 1YQ**
web: www.premierinn.com
dir: *A561 towards Liverpool follow 'Liverpool John Lennon Airport' signs into Seake Hall Avenue, at 1st roundabout take 2nd left. Hotel 300 metres on left.*

Rooms: 101

Premier Inn Liverpool North

BUDGET HOTEL

tel: 0871 527 8628 (Calls cost 13p per minute plus your phone company's access charge) **Northern Perimeter Road L30 7PT**
web: www.premierinn.com
dir: *0.25 mile from end of M58/M5, on A5207.*

Rooms: 83

L

LIVERPOOL *continued*

Premier Inn Liverpool (Roby)

Premier Inn

BUDGET HOTEL

tel: 0871 527 8616 (Calls cost 13p per minute plus your phone company's access charge) **Roby Road, Huyton L36 4HD**
web: www.premierinn.com
dir: *Just off M62 junction 5 on A5080.*

Rooms: 56

Premier Inn Liverpool (Tarbock)

Premier Inn

BUDGET HOTEL

tel: 0871 527 8618 (Calls cost 13p per minute plus your phone company's access charge) **Wilson Road, Tarbock L36 6AD**
web: www.premierinn.com
dir: *At M62 and M57 junction, take M62 junction 6, take A5080 (Huyton).1st right into Wilson Road.*

Rooms: 41

Premier Inn Liverpool (West Derby)

Premier Inn

BUDGET HOTEL

tel: 0871 527 8620 (Calls cost 13p per minute plus your phone company's access charge) **Queens Drive, West Derby L13 0DL**
web: www.premierinn.com
dir: *At end of M62 right under flyover onto A5058 (follow football stadium signs). Hotel 1.5 miles on left, just past Esso garage.*

Rooms: 85

The Z Hotel Liverpool

AA Advertised

tel: 0151 556 1770 **2 North John Street L2 4SA**
email: liverpool@thezhotels.com **web:** www.thezhotels.com
dir: *M62 junction 7, continue onto Bowring Park Road/A5080, then Edge Lane/A5047. Right into Low Hill, continue into Erskine Street, then Churchill Way/A57. Left into North John Street, hotel on right.*

The Z Hotel Liverpool has 92 rooms set over the top three floors, with stunning views over the city. This budget, boutique hotel is perfectly located for all the city has to offer. Bedrooms have en suite wet rooms, crisp bed linen, 40" Sky TVs and complimentary WiFi. Key local attractions include Albert Dock (home to Tate Liverpool and the Merseyside Maritime Museum), Pier Head, Mann Island and the Liverpool Echo Arena.

Rooms: 92 ⟟ **D** fr £35* **Facilities:** STV FTV WiFi ⇘ **Services:** Lift Night porter Air con

---

LIVERSEDGE Map 16 SE12
West Yorkshire

Healds Hall Hotel & Restaurant

THE INDEPENDENTS
HOTEL ASSOCIATION

★★★ 80% ⊛ HOTEL

tel: 01924 409112 **Leeds Road WF15 6JA**
email: enquire@healdshall.co.uk **web:** www.healdshall.co.uk
dir: *On A62 between Leeds and Huddersfield. 50 yards on left after lights at Swan Pub.*

This 18th-century house, in the heart of West Yorkshire, provides comfortable and well-equipped accommodation and excellent hospitality. The hotel has earned a good local reputation for the quality of its food and offers a choice of casual or more formal dining styles, alongside a wide range of dishes on the various menus.

Rooms: 24 (4 family) (3 GF) ⟟ **S** fr £75 **D** fr £95 (including breakfast)*
Facilities: FTV WiFi ⇘ **Conf:** Class 60 Board 45 Theatre 100 **Services:** Night porter
Parking: 90 **Notes:** LB Closed 1 January, Bank holiday Mondays RS Sunday evenings Civ Wed 100

London

Central and Greater London hotel index

Hotels are listed in alphabetical order with their postal district. Plan/Map refers to London plans 1–9 (pages 202–214) or the maps at the back of the book. The page number refers to each hotel's full guide entry.

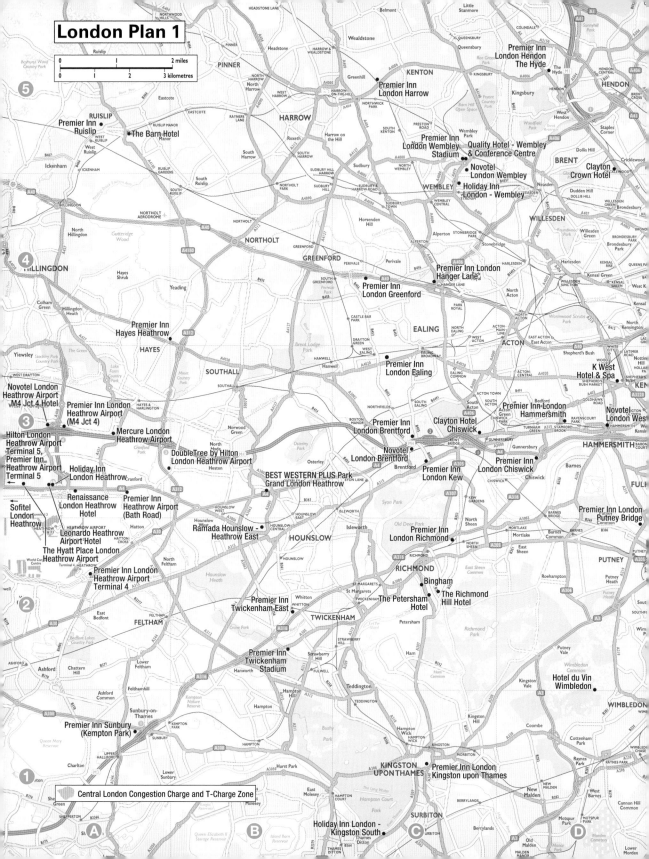

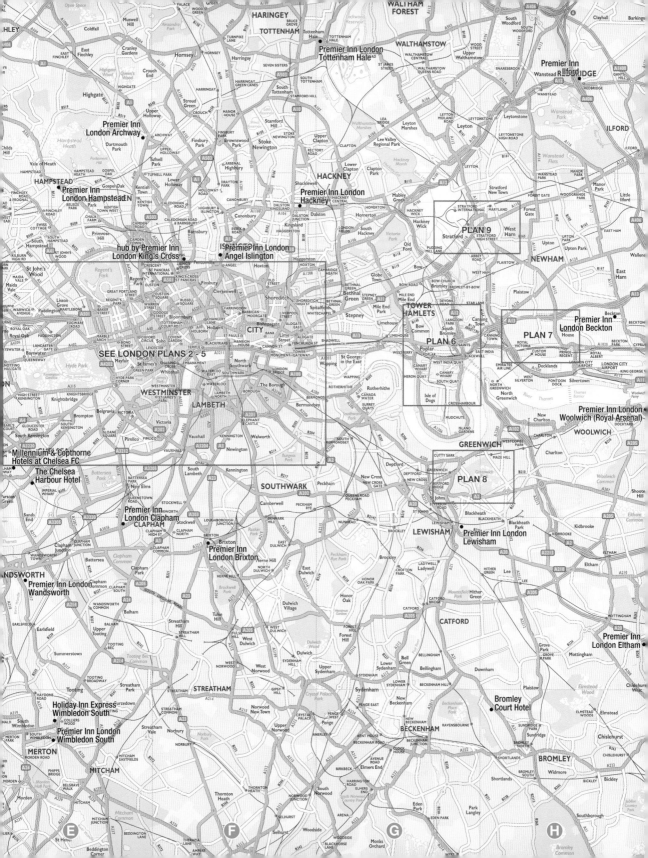

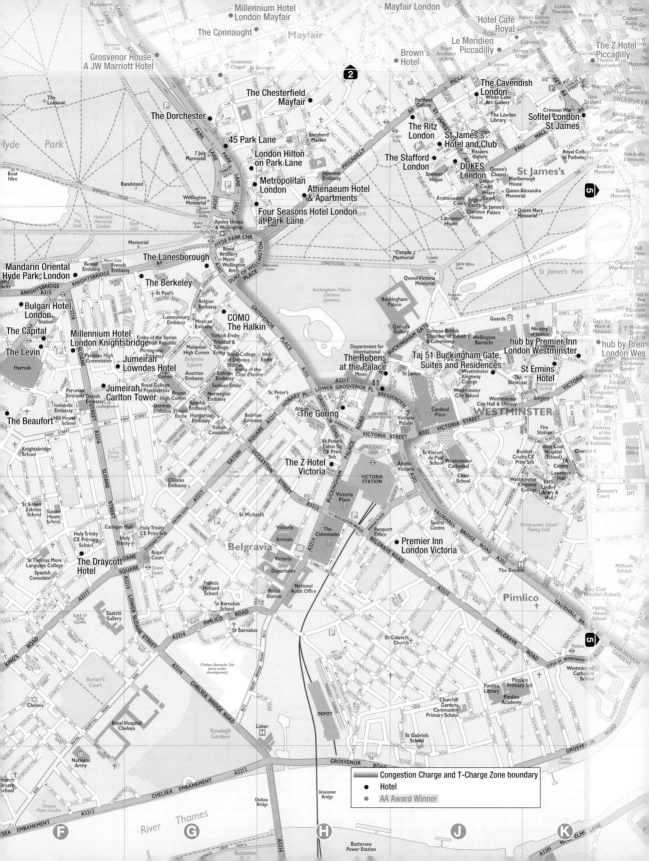

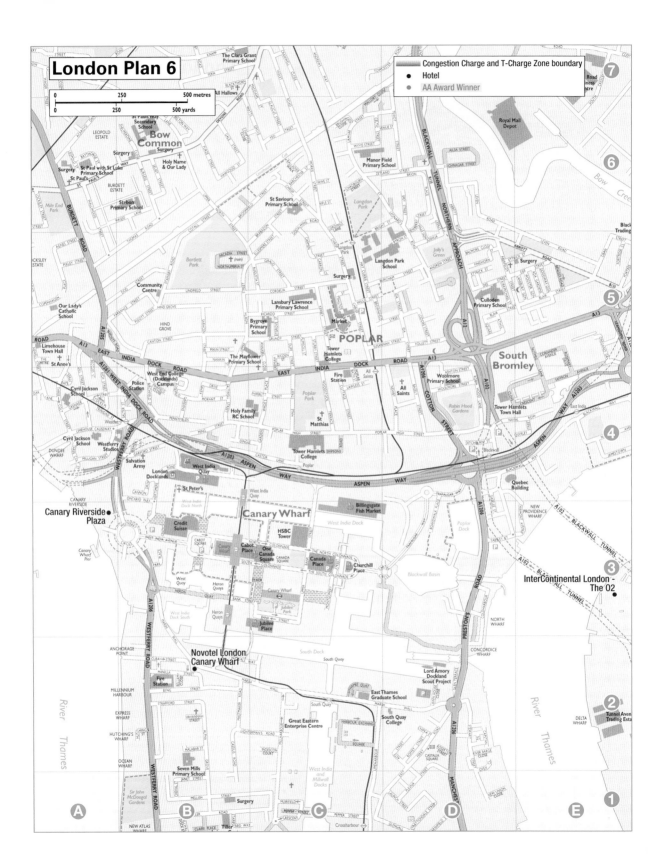

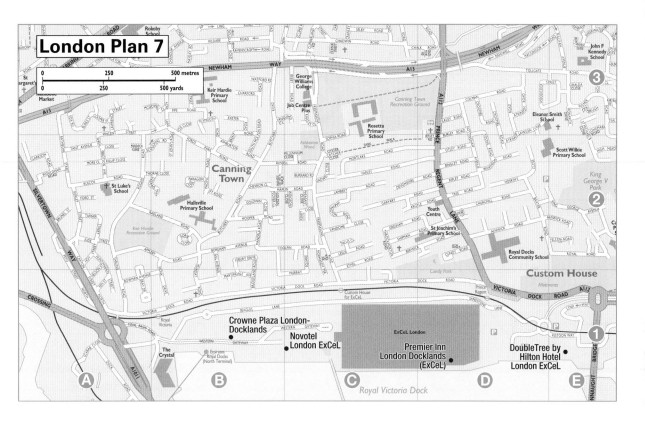

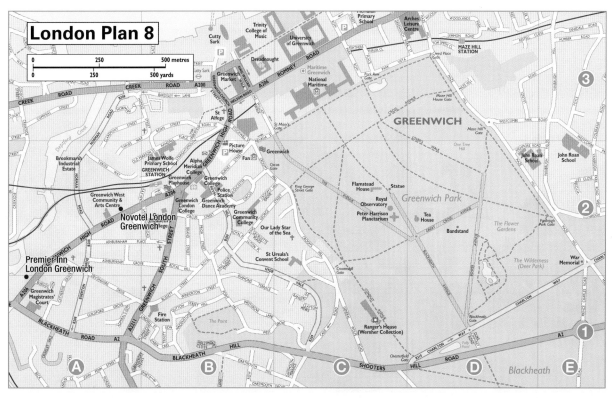

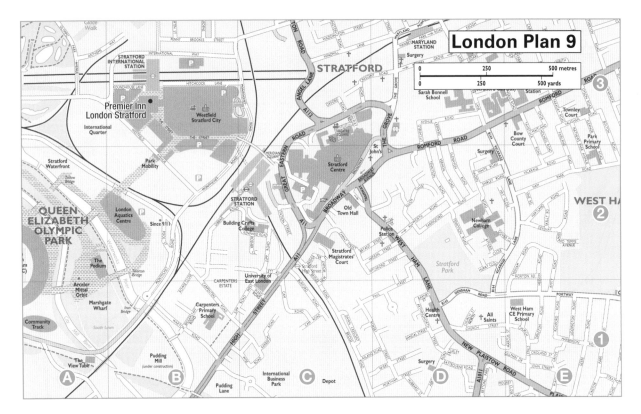

LONDON

Hotels are listed below in postal district order, commencing East, then North, South and West. Detailed plans 2–9 (204–214) show the locations of AA-appointed hotels within the Central London postal districts. If you do not know the postal district of the hotel you want, please refer to the index preceding the street plans for the entry and map pages on pages 198–201. The plan reference (or small-scale map reference – see maps 6–7 at back of the book) for each AA-appointed hotel also appears within its directory entry.

LONDON E1

hub by Premier Inn London Spitalfields

BUDGET HOTEL PLAN 3 J3

tel: 0871 527 9588 (Calls cost 13p per minute plus your phone company's access charge) **86 Brick Lane, Spitalfields E1 6RL**
web: www.premierinn.com
dir: *Nearest tube stations Aldgate East and Liverpool Street.*

This modern hotel offers self-check-in kiosks, superfast free WiFi, and cleverly designed and compact bedrooms with all the entertainment and comfort you need: 40" flat-screen smart TV, temperature and lighting controlled by a special Premier Inn app, Hypnos bed, and monsoon shower. The Deli+Bar is open for grab-and-go breakfast boxes, pastries, grilled sandwiches, Costa Coffee, beer, wine and more.

Rooms: 189

Premier Inn London City (Aldgate)

BUDGET HOTEL PLAN 3 K2

tel: 0871 527 9526 (Calls cost 13p per minute plus your phone company's access charge) **66 Alie Street, Aldgate E1 8PX**
web: www.premierinn.com
dir: *Exit Aldgate East tube station, south along Leman Street. Left into Alie Street, hotel on right.*

High quality, budget accommodation ideal for both families and business travellers. Spacious, en suite bedrooms feature free WiFi and tea and coffee making facilities, and in most hotels, Freeview TV is also available. The adjacent family restaurant features a wide and varied menu.

Rooms: 250

Premier Inn London City (Tower Hill)

BUDGET HOTEL PLAN 3 J1

tel: 0871 527 8646 (Calls cost 13p per minute plus your phone company's access charge) **22-24 Prescott Street, Tower Hill E1 8BB**
web: www.premierinn.com
dir: *Nearest tube: Tower Hill. 3 minutes walk from Docklands Light Rail DLR.*

Rooms: 165

LONDON E4

Map 6 TQ39

Premier Inn Chingford

BUDGET HOTEL

tel: 0871 527 9836 (Calls cost 13p per minute plus your phone company's access charge) **Rangers Road, Chingford E4 7QH**
web: www.premierinn.com
dir: *M25 junction 26, A121 (Loughton) At next roundabout 1st exit (A121). At Wake Arms roundabout 2nd exit onto A104 (Woodford). Right onto A1069 (Rangers Road). 1 mile, hotel on right.*

High quality, budget accommodation ideal for both families and business travellers. Spacious, en suite bedrooms feature free WiFi and tea and coffee making facilities, and in most hotels, Freeview TV is also available. The adjacent family restaurant features a wide and varied menu.

Rooms: 24

LONDON E6

Premier Inn London Beckton

BUDGET HOTEL PLAN 3 K2

tel: 0871 527 8644 (Calls cost 13p per minute plus your phone company's access charge) **1 Woolwich Manor Way, Beckton E6 5NT**
web: www.premierinn.com
dir: *A13 onto A117 (Woolwich Manor Way) towards City Airport, hotel on left after 1st roundabout.*

High quality, budget accommodation ideal for both families and business travellers. Spacious, en suite bedrooms feature free WiFi and tea and coffee making facilities, and in most hotels, Freeview TV is also available. The adjacent family restaurant features a wide and varied menu.

Rooms: 156

LONDON E8

Premier Inn London Hackney

BUDGET HOTEL PLAN 1 F4

tel: 0871 527 9582 (Calls cost 13p per minute plus your phone company's access charge) **27 Dalston Lane E8 3DF**
web: www.premierinn.com
dir: *A406, A10 onto Kingsland High Street, left onto A104, hotel approximately 200 yards on left.*

High quality, budget accommodation ideal for both families and business travellers. Spacious, en suite bedrooms feature free WiFi and tea and coffee making facilities, and in most hotels, Freeview TV is also available. The adjacent family restaurant features a wide and varied menu.

Rooms: 90

LONDON

LONDON

LONDON E14

Canary Riverside Plaza

★★★★★ 86% @ HOTEL PLAN 6 A3

tel: 020 7510 1999 **46 Westferry Circus, Canary Wharf E14 8RS**
web: www.canaryriversideplaza.com

Located in Canary Wharf by the river, this modern and elegant hotel has a popular bar and restaurant, small 24-hour gym and an open-air terrace. Bedrooms and bathrooms are very spacious and equipped to a very high standard; some have stunning riverside views. There is also a business centre and meeting and banquet facilities.

Rooms: 142 ☎ **Facilities:** Spa STV FTV WiFi ⚑ ⛻ ⛲ Gym Xmas New Year **Conf:** Class 135 Board 50 Theatre 220 **Services:** Lift Night porter Air con **Notes:** LB Civ Wed 220

HIGHLY RECOMMENDED

Novotel London Canary Wharf

★★★★ 83% @@ HOTEL PLAN 6 B2

NOVOTEL
HOTELS & RESORTS

tel: 020 3530 0500 **40 Marsh Wall E14 9TP**
email: H9057@accor.com
web: www.novotel.com/gb/hotel-9057-novotel-london-canary-wharf/index.shtml
dir: Contact for directions.

This brand new hotel in Canary Wharf offers guests very stylish accommodation and is the flagship hotel for the Accor Brand with new concepts and style throughout. There are leisure facilities on the lower ground, plus a Leclub members' area in addition to the modern roof-top terrace on the 39th floor with amazing views of London.

Rooms: 313 ☎ **S** fr £120 **D** fr £130 (including breakfast)* **Facilities:** WiFi ⚑ HL ⛲ Gym Sauna ♫ Xmas New Year **Conf:** Board 12 Theatre 40 **Services:** Night porter Air con

---

LONDON E15

Premier Inn London Stratford

Premier Inn 🏅

BUDGET HOTEL PLAN 9 B3

tel: 0871 527 9286 (Calls cost 13p per minute plus your phone company's access charge) **International Square, Westfield Stratfield City E15 1AZ**
web: www.premierinn.com
dir: From A11 or A12 follow signs for Westfield Shopping City and Stratford International and Car Park A.

High quality, budget accommodation ideal for both families and business travellers. Spacious, en suite bedrooms feature free WiFi and tea and coffee making facilities, and in most hotels, Freeview TV is also available. The adjacent family restaurant features a wide and varied menu.

Rooms: 267

LONDON E16

DoubleTree by Hilton Hotel London ExCel

★★★★ 80% HOTEL PLAN 7 E1

tel: 020 7540 4820 **Excel 2 Festoon Way, Royal Victoria Dock E16 1RH**
web: www.doubletree.com
dir: Follow signs for ExCeL East and London City Airport. Over Connaught Bridge then immediately left at roundabout.

This hotel benefits from a stunning waterfront location and is close to the events venue, ExCeL, the O2 Arena, Canary Wharf and London City Airport. The accommodation comprises a mix of spacious bedrooms and suites. The relaxed public areas consist of a modern restaurant and informal lounge area. Parking, a fitness room and meeting rooms are available on site. Free WiFi is available.

Rooms: 287 (25 family) ☎ **S** fr £84 **D** fr £84* **Facilities:** FTV WiFi ⚑ HL Gym **Conf:** Class 20 Board 25 Theatre 30 **Services:** Lift Air con **Parking:** 45 **Notes:** LB

Novotel London ExCeL

★★★★ 80% HOTEL PLAN 7 C1

NOVOTEL
HOTELS & RESORTS

tel: 020 7540 9700 **7 Western Gateway, Royal Victoria Docks E16 1AA**
email: H3656@accor.com **web:** www.novotel.com/3656
dir: M25 junction 30, A13 follow City signs, exit at Canning Town. Follow ExCeL West signs. Hotel adjacent.

This hotel is situated adjacent to the ExCeL exhibition centre and overlooks the Royal Victoria Dock. Design throughout the hotel is contemporary and stylish. Public rooms include a range of meeting rooms, a modern coffee station, indoor leisure facilities and a smart bar and restaurant, both with a terrace overlooking the dock. Bedrooms feature modern decor, bathrooms with separate bath and shower, and an extensive range of extras.

Rooms: 257 (176 family) ☎ **S** fr £95 **D** fr £105* **Facilities:** STV FTV WiFi HL Gym Sauna Steam room Relaxation room with massage bed **Conf:** Class 55 Board 30 Theatre 70 **Services:** Lift Night porter Air con **Parking:** 72 **Notes:** LB Civ Wed 40

Crowne Plaza London Docklands

★★★★ 78% HOTEL PLAN 7 B1

CROWNE PLAZA
HOTELS & RESORTS

tel: 020 7055 2100 **Western Gateway E16 1AL**
email: sales@cpdocklands.co.uk **web:** www.cpdocklands.co.uk
dir: 30 seconds from Royal Victoria DLR, 30 seconds from Emirates Cable Car.

Ideally located for the ExCeL exhibition centre, Canary Wharf and London City Airport, this unique, contemporary hotel overlooking Royal Victoria Dock offers accommodation suitable for both leisure and business travellers. Rooms are spacious and equipped with all modern facilities. Front-facing corner suites offer interesting far-reaching views. The hotel has a busy bar, a contemporary restaurant, and health and fitness facilities with an indoor pool, jacuzzi and sauna. A secure and easily accessible parking area is located at the rear of the property.

Rooms: 210 (65 family) (3 smoking) ☎ **Facilities:** Spa STV FTV WiFi ⚑ HL ⛲ Gym Xmas New Year **Conf:** Class 126 Board 40 Theatre 250 **Services:** Lift Night porter Air con **Parking:** 75 **Notes:** LB Civ Wed 250

Premier Inn London Docklands (ExCeL)

BUDGET HOTEL PLAN 7 B1

tel: 0871 527 8650 (Calls cost 13p per minute plus your phone company's access charge) **Excel East E16 1SJ**
web: www.premierinn.com
dir: A13 onto A1020. At Connaught roundabout take 2nd exit into Connaught Road. Hotel on right.

High quality, budget accommodation ideal for both families and business travellers. Spacious, en suite bedrooms feature free WiFi and tea and coffee making facilities, and in most hotels, Freeview TV is also available. The adjacent family restaurant features a wide and varied menu.

Rooms: 203

LONDON EC1

Malmaison Charterhouse Square

★★★★ 80% ⦾ HOTEL PLAN 3 E3

tel: 020 70123700 **18-21 Charterhouse Square, Clerkenwell EC1M 6AH**
email: reception@malmaison.com **web:** www.malmaison.com/locations/london
dir: Exit Barbican Station turn left, take 1st left. Hotel on far left corner of Charterhouse Square.

Situated in a leafy and peaceful square, Malmaison Charterhouse maintains the same focus on quality service and food as the other hotels in the group. The bedrooms, stylishly decorated in calming tones, have all the expected facilities including power showers, CD players and free internet access. The brasserie and bar at the hotel's centre has a buzzing atmosphere and offers traditional French cuisine.

Rooms: 97 (5 GF) 🐾 **Facilities:** STV FTV WiFi ↕ HL Gym Xmas **Conf:** Board 20 Theatre 45 **Services:** Lift Night porter Air con **Parking:** 5 **Notes:** LB

M by Montcalm Tech City

AA Advertised PLAN 3 G5

tel: 020 3837 3000 **151-157 City Road EC1V 1JH**
email: reservations@mbymontcalm.co.uk **web:** www.mbymontcalm.co.uk

Located in the heart of Shoreditch, this hotel offers excellent-sized rooms which are modern and comfortably appointed. The hotel benefits from leisure and spa facilities as well as meeting space for corporate guests. The Plate restaurant and bar offers a trendy environment for guests to relax and enjoy both cocktails and dinner.

Rooms: 269 **Facilities:** Spa WiFi 🕹 Gym Steam room Sauna **Notes:** No children

The Montcalm London City at The Brewery

AA Advertised ⦾ PLAN 3 F3

tel: 020 7614 0100 **52 Chiswell Street EC1Y 4SB**
email: info@themontcalmlondoncity.co.uk **web:** www.themontcalmlondoncity.co.uk
dir: From Gatwick M23 north to M25 signed Heathrow Airport/Central London to M4. From Heathrow M4 east 9 miles.

Situated in the heart of The City, this luxury hotel is a Grade II listed building that has maintained many original features. As its name implies there's a brewing connection – this was formerly the site of Britain's first purpose-built mass production brewery, Whitbread & Co. The last beer brewed here was in 1976, when the property was turned into the company's head office. With luxurious suites, deluxe studios and City or Club rooms, this hotel is ideal for business or leisure. Chiswell Street Dining Rooms and The Jugged Hare are the eating options.

Rooms: 236 🐾 **Facilities:** STV FTV WiFi ↕ HL Gym Xmas New Year **Conf:** Class 40 Board 40 Theatre 60 **Services:** Lift Night porter Air con

The Z Hotel Shoreditch

AA Advertised PLAN 3 G5

tel: 020 3551 3700 **136-144 City Road EC1V 2RL**
email: shoreditch@thezhotels.com **web:** www.thezhotels.com

Z Hotel Shoreditch, a conversion of an office building, offers over 100 bedrooms; it is part of The Bower, a new landmark quarter for Old Street, comprising offices, restaurants and retail units. As with the others in the Z Hotel chain, bedrooms have en suite wet rooms, crisp bed linen, 40" TV with Sky, and complimentary WiFi.

Rooms: 111 🐾 **Facilities:** STV FTV WiFi ↕ HL **Services:** Lift Night porter Air con

LONDON EC2

ANdAZ Liverpool Street

★★★★★ 86% ⦾ HOTEL PLAN 3 H

tel: 020 7961 1234 **40 Liverpool Street EC2M 7QN**
email: guestservices.londonliv@andaz.com **web:** www.london.liverpoolstreet.andaz.com
dir: On corner of Liverpool Street and Bishopsgate, attached to Liverpool Street station.

ANdAZ is an exciting and contemporary place to stay – there's no reception desk here so guests are checked-in by staff with laptops. Bedrooms are stylish, and designed very much with the executive in mind, with iPods and WiFi as well as a mini-bar stocked with healthy choices. The dining options are varied and many; Japanese cuisine in Miyako, 1901 Restaurant and Wine Bar, Eastway Brasserie, and the newest addition is Lady Abercorn's Pub & Kitchen for roasts. There are also rooms for private dining and other events.

Rooms: 267 🐾 **Facilities:** Spa STV FTV WiFi ↕ Gym Steam room Beauty treatment rooms New Year **Conf:** Class 120 Board 60 Theatre 250 **Services:** Lift Night porter Air con **Notes:** Civ Wed 230

EC2 *continued*

Montcalm Royal London House

AA Advertised PLAN 3 G4

tel: 020 3873 4000 **22–25 Finsbury Square EC2A 1DX**
email: reservations@montcalmroyallondoncity.co.uk
web: www.montcalmroyallondoncity.co.uk

This is the newest hotel to the Montcalm Selection in a great location overlooking Finsbury Square. Bedrooms and bathrooms are stylish and offer both corporate and leisure guests a very comfortable stay. There's a good range of food and drink offerings with two bars and a coffee shop on the ground floor. The Aviary Restaurant on the 10th floor offers all-day dining and benefits from an excellent roof terrace with some superb London views.

Rooms: 253

LONDON EC3

**AA HOTEL OF THE YEAR
FOR LONDON 2018–19**

INSPECTOR'S CHOICE

Four Seasons Hotel London at Ten Trinity Square

★★★★★ HOTEL PLAN 3 H1

tel: 020 3297 9200 & 7319 5188 **10 Trinity Square EC3N 4AJ**
web: www.fourseasons.com/tentrinity
dir: *Phone for directions.*

Overlooking Tower Bridge and the Tower of London, this new hotel is the fully restored and refurbished former Port of London Authority HQ. The spacious bdrooms are of the highest of quality and have all the up-to-date technology. There is an excellent spa with treatment rooms, a swimming pool, steam and sauna. There's a choice of restaurants including La Dame de Pic London offering authentic French cuisine and Mei Ume, an Asian restaurant showcasing a mix of sharing dishes from China and Japan. This is a truly fantastic hotel, oozing quality, style and comfort.

Rooms: 100 (4 family) (9 GF) ☏ **D** fr £390* **Facilities:** Spa STV FTV WiFi ⌨ ☂ Gym ♫ Xmas New Year **Conf:** Class 100 Board 48 Theatre 245 **Services:** Lift Night porter Air con **Parking:** 14

Novotel London Tower Bridge

★★★★ 79% HOTEL PLAN 3 J1

tel: 020 7265 6000 **10 Pepys Street EC3N 2NR**
email: H3107@accor.com **web:** www.novotel.com
dir: *Phone for directions.*

Located near the Tower of London, this smart hotel is convenient for Docklands, The City, Heathrow and London City airports. Air-conditioned bedrooms are spacious, modern, and offer a great range of facilities. There is a smart bar and restaurant, a small gym, children's play area and extensive meeting and conference facilities.

Rooms: 203 (130 family) ☏ **D** fr £135 (including breakfast)* **Facilities:** FTV WiFi ⌨ Gym Steam room Sauna Fitness room ♫ Xmas New Year **Conf:** Class 56 Board 25 Theatre 100 **Services:** Lift Night porter

hub by Premier Inn London Tower Bridge

Premier Inn

BUDGET HOTEL PLAN 3 H1

tel: 0871 527 9576 (Calls cost 13p per minute plus your phone company's access charge) **28 Great Tower Street EC3R 5AT**
web: www.premierinn.com
dir: *Nearest tube stations: Tower Hill and Monument.*

This modern hotel offers self-check-in kiosks, superfast free WiFi, and cleverly designed and compact bedrooms with all the entertainment and comfort you need: 40" flat-screen smart TV, temperature and lighting controlled by a special Premier Inn app, Hypnos bed, and monsoon shower. The Deli+Bar is open for grab-and-go breakfast boxes, pastries, grilled sandwiches, Costa Coffee, beer, wine and more.

Rooms: 112

Premier Inn London City (Monument)

Premier Inn

BUDGET HOTEL PLAN 3 H1

tel: 0871 527 9452 (Calls cost 13p per minute plus your phone company's access charge) **20 St Mary at Hill EC3R 8EE**
web: www.premierinn.com
dir: *Nearest tube stations: Monument and Bank.*

High quality, budget accommodation ideal for both families and business travellers. Spacious, en suite bedrooms feature free WiFi and tea and coffee making facilities, and in most hotels, Freeview TV is also available. The adjacent family restaurant features a wide and varied menu.

Rooms: 184

LONDON EC4

Crowne Plaza London - The City

CROWNE PLAZA
HOTELS & RESORTS

★★★★ 83% HOTEL PLAN 3 E1

tel: 0871 942 9190 (Calls cost 13p per minute plus your phone company's access charge) & 020 7438 8000 **19 New Bridge Street EC4V 6DB**
email: loncy.info@ihg.com **web:** www.cplondoncityhotel.co.uk
dir: *Opposite Blackfriars station.*

With a 1919 facade and a modern, stylish interior, Crowne Plaza London - The City is located in London's historic Square Mile near Blackfriars station, minutes away from some of London's very famous attractions such as The London Eye, St Paul's Cathedral and Covent Garden. At the hotel, guests can enjoy great dining in two destination restaurants: the celebrated Italian Diciannove or the Chinese Cricket Club, offering a mouth-watering range of Sichuan and dim sum specialities with a

LONDON

modern twist. In addition, you can enjoy all-day dining in the comfortable City Lounge, or relax in the stylish champagne bar and cigar terrace, Voltaire.

Rooms: 204 (60 family) (7 smoking) 🛏 **S** fr £175 **D** fr £185* **Facilities:** STV WiFi ⌨ HL Gym Sauna 🎵 Xmas New Year **Conf:** Class 100 Board 50 Theatre 160 **Services:** Lift Night porter Air con **Notes:** LB Civ Wed 160

Premier Inn London Blackfriars

BUDGET HOTEL PLAN 3 E2   Premier Inn

tel: 0871 527 9362 (Calls cost 13p per minute plus your phone company's access charge) **1-2 Dorset Rise EC4Y 8EN**
web: www.premierinn.com
dir: *Phone for directions.*

High quality, budget accommodation ideal for both families and business travellers. Spacious, en suite bedrooms feature free WiFi and tea and coffee making facilities, and in most hotels, Freeview TV is also available. The adjacent family restaurant features a wide and varied menu.

Rooms: 310

The Z Hotel City

AA Advertised PLAN 3 D2   **Z** HOTELS

tel: 020 3551 3718 **24-28 Fleet Street EC4Y 1AA**
email: city@thezhotels.com **web:** www.thezhotels.com/z-city
dir: *Within Temple between Aldwych and Ludgate Circus.*

Z City is in the Temple area, between Aldwych and Ludgate Circus; Immediately behind the hotel is Temple Church, built by the Knights Templar. This hotel is a designer conversion of a former office building, with 109 bedrooms arranged over lower ground, ground and three upper floors. The bedrooms are functional and each offers an en suite wet room, crisp bed linen, a 48" TV with Sky channels,and complimentary WiFi. Some rooms are internal, and therefore windowless.

Rooms: 109 (10 family) (7 GF) 🛏 **Facilities:** STV FTV WiFi HL **Services:** Lift Air con

■ LONDON N1

hub by Premier Inn London King's Cross

BUDGET HOTEL PLAN 1 F4   Premier Inn

tel: 0871 527 9608 (Calls cost 13p per minute plus your phone company's access charge) **50 Wharfdale Road, Kings Cross N1 9AG**
web: www.premierinn.com
dir: *When leaving Kings Cross St Pancras Station, turn left onto York Way. Continue to follow York Way. Hotel on right. The closest tube station is Kings Cross St Pancras.*

This modern hotel offers self-check-in kiosks, superfast free WiFi, and cleverly designed and compact bedrooms with all the entertainment and comfort you need: 40" flat-screen smart TV, temperature and lighting controlled by a special Premier Inn app, Hypnos bed, and monsoon shower. The Deli+Bar is open for grab-and-go breakfast boxes, pastries, grilled sandwiches, Costa Coffee, beer, wine and more.

Rooms: 389

Premier Inn London Angel Islington

BUDGET HOTEL PLAN 1 F4

tel: 0871 527 8558 (Calls cost 13p per minute plus your phone company's access charge) **Parkfield Street, Islington N1 0PS**
web: www.premierinn.com
dir: *From A1 (Islington High Street) into Berners Road bear left into Parkfield Street. N1 car park opposite hotel.*

High quality, budget accommodation ideal for both families and business travellers. Spacious, en suite bedrooms feature free WiFi and tea and coffee making

facilities, and in most hotels, Freeview TV is also available. The adjacent family restaurant features a wide and varied menu.

Rooms: 95

Premier Inn London City (Old Street)

BUDGET HOTEL PLAN 3 G5   Premier Inn

tel: 0871 527 9312 (Calls cost 13p per minute plus your phone company's access charge) **1 Silicon Way N1 6AT**
web: www.premierinn.com
dir: *From Old Street tube station exit 1 (on foot) onto A501 (City Road). Right into East Street. 2nd right into Brunswick Place (Three Crowns pub on corner), 1st left into Corsham Street.*

Rooms: 251

Premier Inn London Kings Cross

BUDGET HOTEL PLAN 3 B6   Premier Inn

tel: 0871 527 8672 (Calls cost 13p per minute plus your phone company's access charge) **26-30 York Way N1 9AA**
web: www.premierinn.com
dir: *M25 junction 16 onto M40 (becomes A40). Follow City signs, exit at Euston Road, follow one-way system to York Way.*

Rooms: 281

■ LONDON N14   Map 6 TQ29

Premier Inn London Southgate

BUDGET HOTEL   Premier Inn

tel: 0871 527 9748 (Calls cost 13p per minute plus your phone company's access charge) **John Bradshaw Road, Southgate N14 6BN**
web: www.premierinn.com
dir: *Leave A10 or North Circular Road at roundabout onto Hedge Lane (A111). Follow Hedge Lane, into Bourne Hill and The Bourne. At roundabout with Southgate station directly in front, take 1st exit onto High Street. Left onto John Bradshaw Road.*

High quality, budget accommodation ideal for both families and business travellers. Spacious, en suite bedrooms feature free WiFi and tea and coffee making facilities, and in most hotels, Freeview TV is also available. The adjacent family restaurant features a wide and varied menu.

Rooms: 90

■ LONDON N17

Premier Inn London Tottenham Hale hotel

BUDGET HOTEL PLAN 1 G5   Premier Inn

tel: 0871 527 9614 (Calls cost 13p per minute plus your phone company's access charge) **N17 9LR**
web: www.premierinn.com
dir: *From the A10, turn onto Monument Way/A503. Stay in right lane to stay on Monument Way. Continue onto The Hale. Turn left onto Station Road, hotel on left.*

High quality, budget accommodation ideal for both families and business travellers. Spacious, en suite bedrooms feature free WiFi and tea and coffee making facilities, and in most hotels, Freeview TV is also available. The adjacent family restaurant features a wide and varied menu.

Rooms: 96

LONDON N19

Premier Inn London Archway

Premier Inn

BUDGET HOTEL PLAN 1 E5

tel: 0871 527 9598 (Calls cost 13p per minute plus your phone company's access charge) **Hamlyn House, Highgate Hill N19 5PA**
web: www.premierinn.com
dir: *M1 junction 2, follow Barnet Bypass/Great North Way/A1 signs towards central London. From A406 to A1 junction. Follow Archway Road until it becomes MacDonald Road. Hotel on left.*

High quality, budget accommodation ideal for both families and business travellers. Spacious, en suite bedrooms feature free WiFi and tea and coffee making facilities, and in most hotels, Freeview TV is also available. The adjacent family restaurant features a wide and varied menu.

Rooms: 163

LONDON NW1

INSPECTOR'S CHOICE

The Landmark London

★★★★★ ⊛⊛ 🍴 HOTEL PLAN 2 F3

tel: 020 7631 8000 **222 Marylebone Road NW1 6JQ**
email: reservations@thelandmark.co.uk **web:** www.landmarklondon.co.uk
dir: *Adjacent to Marylebone Station. Hotel on Marylebone Road.*

Once one of the last truly grand railway hotels, The Landmark London boasts several stunning features, the most spectacular being the naturally lit central atrium forming the hotel's focal point. When it comes to eating and drinking there are many choices, including the Mirror Bar for expertly crafted cocktails and the Great Central Bar and Restaurant – ideal for a business meeting or a celebration. Then there's the Winter Garden Restaurant, with very tall palm trees, that takes centre stage in the atrium and is a great place to watch the world go by, and the twotwentytwo restaurant and bar which is a cosy, relaxing place to meet, eat and drink. The air-conditioned bedrooms are luxurious and have large, stylish bathrooms. There is also a health club that offers a complete wellbeing experience.

Rooms: 300 (71 family) (52 smoking) 🐾 **S** fr £294 **D** fr £294* **Facilities:** Spa STV FTV WiFi ⊗ 🎾 Gym Beauty treatments Massages ♫ Xmas New Year **Conf:** Class 364 Board 72 Theatre 568 **Services:** Lift Night porter Air con **Parking:** 25 **Notes:** Civ Wed 360

Meliã White House

★★★★ 82% ⊛⊛ HOTEL PLAN 2 H4

tel: 020 7391 3000 **Albany Street, Regents Park NW1 3UP**
email: melia.white.house@melia.com **web:** www.melia.com/london/white-house
dir: *Opposite Great Portland Street underground station and next to Regents Park/Warren Street underground.*

Owned by the Spanish Solmelia company, this impressive art deco property is located opposite Great Portland Street tube station. Spacious public areas offer a high degree of comfort and include the award-winning fine dining Spanish restaurant, L' Albufera, The Place Restaurant where tapas-style dishes are served in an informal setting, and the cocktail bar 'Dry Martini by Javier de las Muelas' where guests can enjoy classic cocktails alongside Javier de las Muelas' signature drinks. Stylish bedrooms come in a variety of sizes and styles, but all offer high levels of comfort and are thoughtfully equipped. For longer stays, the larger apartments are an obvious choice.

Rooms: 580 (28 family) 🐾 **S** fr £130 **D** fr £180* **Facilities:** STV FTV WiFi ⊗ Gym Beauty treatment room ♫ Xmas New Year **Conf:** Class 80 Board 60 Theatre 140 **Services:** Lift Night porter Air con **Notes:** LB

Pullman London St Pancras

pullman

★★★★ 80% ⊛ HOTEL PLAN 3 A5

tel: 020 7666 9000 **100-110 Euston Road NW1 2AJ**
email: H5309@accor.com **web:** www.accorhotels.com/5309
dir: *Between St Pancras and Euston stations, entrance opposite British Library.*

This hotel enjoys a central location adjacent to the British Library and close to some of London's main transport hubs. The style is modern and contemporary throughout. Bedrooms vary in size but are all very well equipped and many have views over the city. Open-plan public areas include a leisure suite and extensive conference facilities including the Shaw Theatre. Free WiFi is available.

Rooms: 312 🐾 **Facilities:** STV FTV WiFi ⊗ HL Gym Sauna ♫ Xmas New Year **Conf:** Class 220 Board 80 Theatre 446 **Services:** Lift Night porter Air con

Premier Inn London St Pancras

Premier Inn

BUDGET HOTEL PLAN 3 B5

tel: 0871 527 9492 (Calls cost 13p per minute plus your phone company's access charge) **Euston House, 81-103 Euston Street NW1 2EZ**
web: www.premierinn.com
dir: *Nearest tube: London Euston, King's Cross, St Pancras.*

High quality, budget accommodation ideal for both families and business travellers. Spacious, en suite bedrooms feature free WiFi and tea and coffee making facilities, and in most hotels, Freeview TV is also available. The adjacent family restaurant features a wide and varied menu.

Rooms: 266

LONDON NW2

Clayton Crown Hotel

MORAN HOTELS

★★★★ 76% HOTEL PLAN 1 D5

tel: 020 8452 4175 **142-152 Cricklewood Broadway, Cricklewood NW2 3ED**
email: info.crown@claytonhotels.com **web:** www.claytonhotels.com
dir: *M1 junction 1 follow signs onto North Circular west A406. Junction with A5 Staples Corner. At roundabout take 1st exit onto A5 to Cricklewood.*

This striking hotel is connected by an impressive glass atrium to the popular Crown Pub. Features include excellent function and conference facilities, a leisure club, a choice of stylish lounges and bars and a contemporary restaurant. The air-conditioned bedrooms are appointed to a high standard and include a number of trendy suites.

Rooms: 152 (63 family) (35 GF) **Facilities:** STV WiFi Gym Xmas New Year **Conf:** Class 150 Board 80 Theatre 300 **Services:** Lift Night porter Air con **Parking:** 39 **Notes:** Civ Wed 300

LONDON NW3

Premier Inn London Hampstead

BUDGET HOTEL PLAN 1 E4

tel: 0871 527 8662 (Calls cost 13p per minute plus your phone company's access charge) **215 Haverstock Hill, Hampstead NW3 4RB**
web: www.premierinn.com
dir: A41 to Swiss Cottage. Before junction take feeder road left into Buckland Cresent into Belsize Avenue. Left into Haverstock Hill.

High quality, budget accommodation ideal for both families and business travellers. Spacious, en suite bedrooms feature free WiFi and tea and coffee making facilities, and in most hotels, Freeview TV is also available. The adjacent family restaurant features a wide and varied menu.

Rooms: 143

LONDON NW9

Premier Inn London Hendon The Hyde

BUDGET HOTEL PLAN 1 D5

tel: 0871 527 9450 (Calls cost 13p per minute plus your phone company's access charge) **Hyde House NW9 6LH**
web: www.premierinn.com
dir: M1 junction 4, A41, A5 towards Edgware. Hotel opposite junction of A4006 and Kingsbury.

High quality, budget accommodation ideal for both families and business travellers. Spacious, en suite bedrooms feature free WiFi and tea and coffee making facilities, and in most hotels, Freeview TV is also available. The adjacent family restaurant features a wide and varied menu.

Rooms: 99

LONDON SE1

INSPECTOR'S CHOICE

Shangri-La Hotel, at The Shard, London

★★★★★ HOTEL PLAN 5 G6

tel: 020 7234 8000 **31 St Thomas Street SE1 9QU**
email: info.slln@shangri-la.com **web:** www.shangri-la.com/london
dir: Phone for directions.

This hotel, in the iconic London Shard, occupies floors 34 to 52 so it won't come as a surprise that every room has a stupendous view, as does the bar, sky pool and Tīng Restaurant. The bedrooms and suites, with floor-to-ceiling windows, are fully equipped for business and leisure travellers alike – free WiFi, climate control, ample work space and binoculars are standard. Fully automatic black-out blinds prevent those with vertigo from suffering too much. There are luxurious toiletries in the well-proportioned marble bathrooms that have heated floors and walk-in showers. Gŏng on the 52nd floor is the highest bar in western Europe.

Rooms: 202 (202 family) **D** fr £500* **Facilities:** STV WiFi Gym Spa treatments available in room or spa residences **Conf:** Class 60 Board 50 Theatre 120 **Services:** Lift Night porter Air con **Parking:** 15 **Notes:** Civ Wed 120

Plaza on the River London

Park Plaza
Hotels & Resorts

★★★★★ 83% TOWN HOUSE HOTEL PLAN 5 B2

tel: 020 7620 8656 & 0844 854 5295 (Calls cost 7p per minute plus your phone company's access charge) **18 Albert Embankment SE1 7TJ**
email: guestrelations@plazaontheriver.co.uk **web:** www.plazaontheriver.co.uk
dir: From Houses of Parliament turn into Millbank, at roundabout left into Lambeth Bridge. At roundabout 3rd exit into Albert Embankment.

This is a superb modern townhouse overlooking London from the south bank of the Thames, with outstanding views of the capital's landmarks. The bedrooms are large and many are full suites with state-of-the-art technology and kitchen facilities; all are decorated in an elegant modern style. Service includes a full range of in-room dining options; additionally, the bar and restaurant in the adjacent Park Plaza are available to guests.

Rooms: 127 (127 family) **Facilities:** Spa WiFi Gym **Conf:** Class 450 Board 40 Theatre 650 **Services:** Lift Night porter Air con **Notes:** Civ Wed 660

London Bridge Hotel

★★★★ 83% HOTEL PLAN 5 G6

tel: 020 7855 2200 **8-18 London Bridge Street SE1 9SG**
email: sales@londonbridgehotel.com **web:** www.londonbridgehotel.com
dir: Access through London Bridge Station, past taxi rank, towards Shard into London Bridge Street (one way). Hotel on left.

This elegant, independently owned hotel enjoys a prime location adjacent to London Bridge station. Smartly appointed, well-equipped bedrooms include a number of spacious deluxe rooms and suites. Free WiFi is available throughout. The Quarter Bar & Lounge is the ideal place for light bites, old favourites and cocktails. The Londinium Restaurant offers a seasonal British menu.

Rooms: 138 (10 family) (5 smoking) **Facilities:** STV FTV WiFi Gym **Conf:** Class 36 Board 36 Theatre 80 **Services:** Lift Night porter Air con

LONDON

SE1 *continued*

Park Plaza Westminster Bridge London

★★★★ 81% HOTEL PLAN 5 C5

tel: 020 7620 1110 & 0844 415 6790 (Calls cost 7p per minute plus your phone company's access charge) **SE1 7UT**
email: ppwlres@pphe.com **web:** www.parkplaza.com

A very smart hotel located in The City, close to Waterloo Station, featuring eye-catching, contemporary decor, a state-of-the-art indoor leisure facility, and extensive conference and banqueting facilities. There is the awarding-winning Brasserie Joël as well as the popular Ichi Sushi and Sashimi Bar. The bedrooms are also up-to-the-minute in style and feature a host of extras including mini bars, safes and modem points.

Rooms: 1019 (575 family) ⋒ **S** fr £159 **D** fr £169* **Facilities:** Spa STV FTV WiFi ↕ HL ⏂ Gym ♫ Xmas New Year **Conf:** Class 800 Board 50 Theatre 2000 **Services:** Lift Night porter Air con **Notes:** LB Civ Wed 1400

Park Plaza London Riverbank

★★★★ 80% HOTEL PLAN 5 C3

tel: 020 7958 8000 & 0844 854 5292 (Calls cost 7p per minute plus your phone company's access charge) **18 Albert Embankment SE1 7SP**
email: rppres@pphe.com **web:** www.parkplaza.com/riverbank
dir: *From Houses of Parliament turn onto Millbank, at roundabout left onto Lambeth Bridge. At roundabout take 3rd exit onto Albert Embankment.*

Situated on the south side of the River Thames, this hotel offers guests the convenience of a central London location and high levels of comfort. Contemporary design coupled with a host of up-to-date facilities, the hotel is home to the Chino Latino brasserie. The air-conditioned bedrooms have smart LED TVs and large work desks; some rooms and suites have stunning views of the Houses of Parliament. Other facilities include WiFi throughout, high-tech conference rooms, a business centre, and a fitness centre with cardiovascular equipment.

Rooms: 498 ⋒ **Facilities:** Spa STV FTV WiFi ↕ HL ⏂ Gym **Conf:** Class 450 Board 40 Theatre 650 **Services:** Lift Night porter Air con **Notes:** Civ Wed 660

Park Plaza London Waterloo

★★★★ 80% HOTEL PLAN 5 D4

tel: 0845 450 2145 **6 Hercules Road SE1 7DP**
email: ppwainfo@pphe.com

Located close to Waterloo train station and just across the road from North Lambert tube station, stands this modern purpose-built hotel. The bedrooms are varied, including many family rooms, and are particularly well appointed and stylishly finished; all have city views. All-day dining is available in the Florentine Restaurant & Bar and light snacks are available from the Illy caffè. There is also a 15-metre indoor pool, sauna/steam room and fitness centre.

Rooms: 494 **S** fr £207 **D** fr £207* **Facilities:** ⏂ Sauna Steam room **Conf:** Class 110 Board 48 Theatre 190

Park Plaza County Hall London

★★★★ 79% HOTEL PLAN 5 C5

tel: 020 7021 1800 & 0333 4006116 **1 Addington Street SE1 7RY**
email: ppchinfo@pphe.com **web:** www.parkplazacountyhall.com
dir: *From Houses of Parliament cross Westminster Bridge A302. At roundabout take 4th right at dedicated lights.*

This hotel is located just south of Westminster Bridge near Waterloo International Rail Station. A contemporary design-led, air-conditioned establishment, Park Plaza County Hall London features studios and suites, most with kitchenettes and seating areas with TV. There are six meeting rooms, an executive lounge, a restaurant and bar, plus a fully-equipped gym with sauna and steam room. WiFi is available.

Rooms: 399 (304 family) ⋒ **Facilities:** Spa STV FTV WiFi ↕ HL Gym Sauna Steam room Beauty therapy room Xmas New Year **Conf:** Class 60 Board 40 Theatre 100 **Services:** Lift Night porter Air con

Novotel London Blackfriars

★★★★ 79% HOTEL PLAN 5 E6

tel: 020 7660 0834 **46 Blackfriars Road SE1 8NZ**
email: H7942@accor.com **web:** www.novotel.com

This Novotel is just south of the Thames and utilises the latest in hotel and bedroom technology. There are media hubs in each bedroom, as well as air conditioning and glass walls to the bathroom that become opaque in an instant for privacy. There is also a swimming pool, gym and sauna in the basement, and a bar and restaurant on the ground floor.

Rooms: 182 (39 family) ⋒ **Facilities:** FTV WiFi HL ⏂ Gym Saunarium ♫ **Conf:** Class 50 Board 40 Theatre 90 **Services:** Lift Air con

Novotel London City South

★★★★ 79% HOTEL PLAN 5 F6

tel: 020 7660 0676 **Southwark Bridge Road SE1 9HH**
email: H3269@accor.com **web:** www.novotel.com
dir: *At junction at Thrale Street, off Southwark Street.*

Conveniently located for both business and leisure guests, with The City just across the Thames; other major attractions are also easily accessible. The hotel is contemporary in design with smart, modern bedrooms and spacious public rooms. There is a gym, sauna and steam room on the 6th floor, and limited parking is available at the rear of the hotel.

Rooms: 182 (164 family) ⋒ **S** fr £125 **D** fr £135* **Facilities:** STV FTV WiFi ↕ HL Gym Steam room Sauna **Conf:** Class 45 Board 40 Theatre 100 **Services:** Lift Night porter Air con **Parking:** 50 **Notes:** LB

Mercure London Bridge

★★★★ 78% HOTEL PLAN 5 E6

tel: 020 7660 0683 **71-79 Southwark Street SE1 0JA**
email: H2814@accor.com **web:** www.mercure.com
dir: *A200 to London Bridge. Left into Southwark Street.*

This smart, contemporary hotel forms part of the rejuvenation of the South Bank. With the City of London just over the river and a number of tourist attractions within easy reach, the hotel is well located for business and leisure visitors alike. Facilities include spacious air-cooled bedrooms, a modern bar and Marco's New York Italian restaurant.

Rooms: 144 (15 family) (5 GF) **Facilities:** STV FTV WiFi ↕ HL Gym Xmas **Conf:** Class 40 Board 30 Theatre 60 **Services:** Lift Night porter Air con

LONDON

Novotel London Waterloo

★★★★ 77% HOTEL PLAN 5 C3

tel: 020 7793 1010 **113 Lambeth Road SE1 7LS**
email: h1785@accor.com **web:** www.novotel.com/1785
dir: *Opposite Houses of Parliament on south bank of River Thames.*

This hotel is in an excellent location, with Lambeth Palace, the Houses of Parliament and Waterloo Station all within a short walk. The bedrooms are spacious and benefit from air conditioning. Open-plan public areas include a bar, Elements Restaurant and a children's play area. There's also a fitness room, well-equipped conference facilities and secure parking.

Rooms: 187 (80 family) **Facilities:** STV WiFi HL Gym Steam room Sauna **Conf:** Class 24 Board 24 Theatre 40 **Services:** Lift Air con **Parking:** 40

Days Hotel London Waterloo

BUDGET HOTEL PLAN 5 D4

tel: 020 7922 1331 **54 Kennington Road SE1 7BJ**
email: book@hotelwaterloo.com **web:** www.hotelwaterloo.com
dir: *On corner of Kennington Road and Lambeth Road. Opposite Imperial War Museum.*

This modern building offers accommodation in smart, spacious and well-equipped bedrooms, suitable for families and business travellers, and all with en suite bathrooms. Continental breakfast is available and other refreshments may be taken at the nearby family restaurant.

Rooms: 162 (15 family) (13 GF) **S** fr £129 **D** fr £129*

Premier Inn London Bridge hotel

BUDGET HOTEL PLAN 5 G6

tel: 0871 527 9690 (Calls cost 13p per minute plus your phone company's access charge) **135 Borough High Street SE1 1NP**
web: www.premierinn.com
dir: *Phone for directions.*

High quality, budget accommodation ideal for both families and business travellers. Spacious, en suite bedrooms feature free WiFi and tea and coffee making facilities, and in most hotels, Freeview TV is also available. The adjacent family restaurant features a wide and varied menu.

Rooms: 99

Premier Inn London County Hall

BUDGET HOTEL PLAN 5 C5

tel: 0871 527 8648 (Calls cost 13p per minute plus your phone company's access charge) **Belvedere Road SE1 7PB**
web: www.premierinn.com
dir: *In County Hall building. Nearest tube: Waterloo.*

Rooms: 316

Premier Inn London Southwark (Borough Market)

BUDGET HOTEL PLAN 5 F6

tel: 0871 527 8676 (Calls cost 13p per minute plus your phone company's access charge) **Bankside, 34 Park Street SE1 9EF**
web: www.premierinn.com
dir: *A3200 onto A300 (Southwark Bridge Road), 1st left into Sumner Street, right into Park Street. From south: M3, A3 follow Central London signs.*

Rooms: 59

Premier Inn London Southwark (Tate Modern)

BUDGET HOTEL PLAN 5 E6

tel: 0871 527 9332 (Calls cost 13p per minute plus your phone company's access charge) **15A Great Suffolk Street, Southwark SE1 0FL**
web: www.premierinn.com
dir: *Phone for directions.*

Rooms: 122

Premier Inn London Tower Bridge

BUDGET HOTEL PLAN 5 H5

tel: 0871 527 8678 (Calls cost 13p per minute plus your phone company's access charge) **159 Tower Bridge Road SE1 3LP**
web: www.premierinn.com
dir: *South of Tower Bridge on A100.*

Rooms: 196

Premier Inn London Waterloo

BUDGET HOTEL PLAN 5 C5

tel: 0871 527 9412 (Calls cost 13p per minute plus your phone company's access charge) **York Road, Waterloo SE1 7NJ**
web: www.premierinn.com
dir: *Nearest station: Waterloo.*

Rooms: 234

citizenM London Bankside

AA Advertised PLAN 5 E6

tel: 020 3519 1680 **20 Lavington Street SE1 0NZ**
email: supportlba@citizenm.com **web:** www.citizenm.com
dir: *Phone for directions.*

Just a short walk from Tate Modern and Shakespeare's Globe, citizenM London Bankside is the height of urban, stylish, business-and-pleasure, boutique accommodation. From the '1 minute check in/out' promise to the new-media friendly meeting rooms and lobby, this is something different. The bedrooms are stylishly economical, making the most of limited space, with super-sized beds, blackout blinds, free WiFi, ambient mood lighting, a rain shower and a wall-to-wall window above the bed. CanteenM serves breakfast, lunch and dinner, and also has as a 24-hour bar.

Rooms: 192 **Facilities:** STV FTV WiFi **Services:** Lift

LONDON SE9

Premier Inn London Eltham hotel

 Premier Inn

BUDGET HOTEL PLAN 1 H2

tel: 0871 527 9604 (Calls cost 13p per minute plus your phone company's access charge) **SE9 3NS**
web: www.premierinn.com
dir: *Sidcup Road meets Green Lane. Hotel is on corner; entrance to car park on Green Lane.*

High quality, budget accommodation ideal for both families and business travellers. Spacious, en suite bedrooms feature free WiFi and tea and coffee making facilities, and in most hotels, Freeview TV is also available. The adjacent family restaurant features a wide and varied menu.

Rooms: 91

LONDON SE10

Novotel London Greenwich

 NOVOTEL HOTELS & RESORTS

★★★★ 77% HOTEL PLAN 8 A2

tel: 020 8312 6800 **173-185 Greenwich High Road, Greenwich SE10 8JA**
email: H3476@accor.com **web:** www.novotel.com
dir: *Adjacent to Greenwich Station.*

This purpose-built hotel is conveniently located for rail and DLR stations, as well as major attractions such as the Royal Maritime Museum and the Royal Observatory. Air-conditioned bedrooms are spacious and equipped with a host of extras, and public areas include a small gym, contemporary lounge bar and restaurant.

Rooms: 151 (34 family) ☏ **Facilities:** STV FTV WiFi ☒ HL Gym Steam room Xmas
Conf: Class 40 Board 32 Theatre 92 **Services:** Lift Night porter Air con **Parking:** 30

Premier Inn London Greenwich

 Premier Inn

BUDGET HOTEL PLAN 8 A1

tel: 0871 527 9208 (Calls cost 13p per minute plus your phone company's access charge) **43-81 Greenwich High Road, Greenwich SE10 8JL**
web: www.premierinn.com
dir: *Phone for directions.*

High quality, budget accommodation ideal for both families and business travellers. Spacious, en suite bedrooms feature free WiFi and tea and coffee making facilities, and in most hotels, Freeview TV is also available. The adjacent family restaurant features a wide and varied menu.

Rooms: 156

InterContinental London - The O2

AA Advertised ⊛⊛⊛ PLAN 6 E3

tel: 020 8463 6868 **1 Waterview Drive SE10 0TW**
email: info@iclondon-theo2.com **web:** www.iclondon-theo2.com
dir: *Greenwich Peninsula, 5 minute walk from North Greenwich tube station.*

Situated between the O2 Arena and the Thames, this InterContinental offers the perfect location for those attending any kind of event at the Arena; it is directly linked via a walkway. The views from the hotel are impressive whichever direction you look. The bedrooms are spacious, contemporary and luxurious. There is also a state-of-the-art spa, an exclusive club lounge, and a range of eating and drinking options including a roof-top bar.

Rooms: 453 (59 family) ☏ **D** fr £175* **Facilities:** Spa FTV WiFi ☒ HL ☒ Gym Xmas New Year **Conf:** Class 1800 Theatre 3000 **Services:** Lift Night porter Air con **Parking:** 250

LONDON SE13

Premier Inn London Lewisham

 Premier Inn

BUDGET HOTEL PLAN 1 G2

tel: 0871 527 9480 (Calls cost 13p per minute plus your phone company's access charge) **1-13 Lewisham High Street SE13 5AF**
web: www.premierinn.com
dir: *From A2 at lights into Lewisham Road, under rail bridge, inn on left. Or from Lewisham Station (walking), left into Station Road. At road end, left into Lewisham Road (A2211). 1st right into Lewisham High Street, 1st left into Kings Hall Mews.*

High quality, budget accommodation ideal for both families and business travellers. Spacious, en suite bedrooms feature free WiFi and tea and coffee making facilities, and in most hotels, Freeview TV is also available. The adjacent family restaurant features a wide and varied menu.

Rooms: 60

LONDON SE18

Premier Inn London Woolwich (Royal Arsenal)

 Premier Inn

BUDGET HOTEL PLAN 1 H3

tel: 0871 097 1087 (Calls cost 13p per minute plus your phone company's access charge) **Beresford Street, Woolwich SE18 6BF**
web: www.premierinn.com
dir: *Leave A2 onto South Circular Road and continue towards Woolwich Ferry Centre. At end of this road, take 3rd exit onto A206 (Woolwich High Street). At next roundabout take 2nd exit onto A206 (Beresford Street). Hotel on left.*

High quality, budget accommodation ideal for both families and business travellers. Spacious, en suite bedrooms feature free WiFi and tea and coffee making facilities, and in most hotels, Freeview TV is also available. The adjacent family restaurant features a wide and varied menu.

Rooms: 128

LONDON

INSPECTOR'S CHOICE

The Berkeley

MAYBOURNE
HOTEL GROUP

★★★★★ ◎◎◎◎◎ ⌘ HOTEL PLAN 4 G5

tel: 020 7235 6000 **Wilton Place, Knightsbridge SW1X 7RL**
email: info@the-berkeley.co.uk web: www.the-berkeley.co.uk
dir: *300 metres from Hyde Park Corner along Knightsbridge.*

This stylish hotel, just off Knightsbridge, boasts an excellent range of bedrooms, each furnished with care and a host of thoughtful extras. Newer rooms feature trendy, spacious, glass and marble bathrooms, and some of the private suites have their own roof terrace. The striking Blue Bar enhances the reception rooms, all of which are adorned with magnificent flower arrangements. Various eating options include the Collins Room which offers breakfast, all-day dining, and a wonderful afternoon tea. Marcus Wareing at The Berkeley has attained five AA Rosettes for stunning French cuisine, and a chef's table is available. The health spa offers a range of treatment rooms and includes a stunning open-air, roof-top pool.

Rooms: 190 (34 smoking) **S** fr £450 **D** fr £540* **Facilities:** Spa STV FTV WiFi
Gym Beauty/therapy treatments Personal training Xmas New Year
Conf: Class 133 Board 54 Theatre 250 **Services:** Lift Night porter Air con
Parking: 8 **Notes:** Civ Wed 250

INSPECTOR'S CHOICE

Mandarin Oriental Hyde Park, London

★★★★★ ◎◎◎◎ ⌘ HOTEL PLAN 4 F5

tel: 020 7235 2000 **66 Knightsbridge SW1X 7LA**
email: molon-reservations@mohg.com web: www.mandarinoriental.com/london
dir: *Harrods 400 metres on right and Harvey Nichols directly opposite hotel.*

Situated in fashionable Knightsbridge and overlooking Hyde Park, this iconic venue is a popular destination for highfliers, celebrities and the young and fashionable. Bedrooms, many with park views, are appointed to the highest standards with luxurious features such as the finest Irish linen and goose down pillows. Guests have a choice of dining options – Bar Boulud (with two AA Rosettes) offering a contemporary bistro menu of seasonal, rustic French dishes; and Dinner by Heston Blumenthal where the dishes are based on recipes that date back as far as the 14th century, but with Heston's legendary modern twist. The Mandarin Bar serves light snacks and cocktails. The stylish spa is a destination in its own right and offers a range of innovative treatments.

Rooms: 181 (30 smoking) **D** fr £540* **Facilities:** Spa STV FTV WiFi Gym
Sanarium Steam room Vitality pool Zen colour therapy Relaxation area Xmas
New Year **Conf:** Class 140 Board 70 Theatre 300 **Services:** Lift Night porter
Air con **Parking:** 25 **Notes:** Civ Wed 250

LONDON

SW1 *continued*

St James's Hotel and Club

★★★★★ ⚫⚫⚫⚫ TOWN HOUSE HOTEL PLAN 4 J6

tel: 020 7316 1600 **7-8 Park Place SW1A 1LP**
email: info@stjameshotelandclub.com **web:** www.stjameshotelandclub.com
dir: *On A4 near Piccadilly Circus and St James's Street.*

Dating back to 1857, this elegant property with its distinctive neo-Gothic exterior is discreetly set in the heart of St James's. Inside there is impressive decor created by interior designer Anne Maria Jagdfeld. Air-conditioned bedrooms are appointed to a very high standard and feature luxurious beds alongside a range of modern facilities. Stylish open-plan public areas offer a smart bar/lounge and the fine dining restaurant, Seven Park Place by William Drabble, which serves modern French dishes based mainly on British ingredients.

Rooms: 60 (8 family) (15 GF) S fr £330 **D** fr £330* **Facilities:** STV FTV WiFi New Year **Conf:** Class 22 Board 25 Theatre 40 **Services:** Lift Night porter Air con **Notes:** LB Civ Wed 40

COMO The Halkin

★★★★★ ⚫⚫⚫ TOWN HOUSE HOTEL PLAN 4 G5

tel: 020 7333 1000 **Halkin Street, Belgravia SW1X 7DJ**
email: res.thehalkin@comohotels.com **web:** www.comohotels.com/thehalkin
dir: *Between Belgrave Square and Grosvenor Place. Via Chapel Street into Headfort Place, left into Halkin Street.*

Set in an enviable and peaceful position just a short stroll from both Hyde Park and the designer shops of Knightsbridge, COMO The Halkin can claim pride of place in Belgravia, and combines timelessness with contemporary. The hotel's Georgian-styled facade of weathered bricks, Portland stone and arching windows blend comfortably into its surroundings. Inside, the Milan-based architecture studio Laboratorio Associati has created a scheme imbued with a warm, modern vibe. For dining, Ametsa with Arzak Instruction, offers award-winning Basque cuisine, while The Halkin Bar offers all-day eating including an Ametsa afternoon tea menu.

Rooms: 41 S fr £350 **D** fr £350* **Facilities:** STV FTV WiFi Gym Complimentary use of spa at sister hotel Como Metropolitan London **Conf:** Class 20 Board 26 Theatre 40 **Services:** Lift Night porter Air con **Notes:** LB

Red Stars The AA Red Star rating denotes an Inspectors' Choice hotel. They stand out as the very best places to stay and appear in highlighted panels throughout the guide.

INSPECTOR'S CHOICE

The Goring

★★★★★ ⚛⚛⚛ ☕ HOTEL PLAN 4 H4

tel: 020 7396 9000 **Beeston Place SW1W 0JW**
email: reception@thegoring.com **web:** www.thegoring.com
dir: *Off Lower Grosvenor Place, just prior to Royal Mews.*

An icon of British hospitality for over 100 years, The Goring is centrally located and within walking distance of the Royal Parks and principal shopping areas. Spacious bedrooms and suites – some contemporary in style with state-of-the-art technology, and others more classically furnished – all boast high levels of comfort and quality. Elegant day rooms include the Garden Bar and the drawing room, both popular for afternoon tea and cocktails. The stylish, airy restaurant offers a popular menu of contemporary British cuisine, and delightful private dining rooms are also available. Guests will experience a personalised service from the attentive and friendly team.

Rooms: 69 (9 family) ♠ **Facilities:** STV WiFi ⬧ ⬧ Gym Free membership of nearby health club Xmas New Year **Conf:** Board 20 Theatre 50 **Services:** Lift Night porter Air con **Parking:** 16 **Notes:** Civ Wed 50

INSPECTOR'S CHOICE

The Lanesborough

★★★★★ ⚛⚛⚛ ☕ HOTEL PLAN 4 G5

tel: 020 7259 5599 **Hyde Park Corner SW1X 7TA**
email: mryan@lanesborough.com
web: www.oetkercollection.com/destinations/the-lanesborough/
dir: *At Hyde Park corner.*

Set in prestigious Knightsbridge, with panoramic views of Hyde Park, this elegant and luxurious hotel offers nearly 100 rooms, including almost 50 suites, with a personal butler service for all guests 24 hours a day. Public areas include the award-winning Céleste restaurant, The Library Bar and the very elegant Withdrawing Room. The Garden Room, a lounge for cigar connoisseurs, and the Club & Spa for adults complete the first-class facilities. Children are very welcome at The Lanesborough and even receive a gift on arrival. For the staff here, no detail is too small.

Rooms: 93 (7 family) (6 GF) (38 smoking) ♠ **Facilities:** Spa STV FTV WiFi ⬧ Gym Hydropool Rasul ♫ Xmas New Year **Conf:** Class 60 Board 45 Theatre 100 **Services:** Lift Night porter Air con **Parking:** 48 **Notes:** Civ Wed 100

INSPECTOR'S CHOICE

Corinthia Hotel London

★★★★★ ⚛⚛ HOTEL PLAN 5 B6

tel: 020 7930 8181 **Whitehall Place SW1A 2BD**
email: london@corinthia.com **web:** www.corinthia.com/london
dir: *M4 onto A4, follow Central London signs. Pass Green Park, right into Coventry Street, 1st right into Haymarket, left into Pall Mall East, right into Trafalgar Square, 3rd exit into Whitehall Place.*

Steeped in history, this elegant hotel is reputed to be one of London's oldest, having opened in 1885. The team are welcoming and friendly, and all requests are skilfully dealt with. Bedrooms, including suites and penthouses, are equipped to very high standards and offer all modern amenities. Eating options are The Northall with British cuisine, and The Massimo Restaurant offering Mediterranean seafood. The Bassoon Bar is the place for cocktails and it's worth noting the counter which is actually an elongated piano. Afternoon tea is another highlight, served in the stunning lobby lounge. The Espa Spa offers world-class facilities. Valet parking is available.

Rooms: 294 (10 family) (46 smoking) ♠ **Facilities:** Spa STV WiFi ⬧ ⬧ Gym Vitality pool Nail studio Hair salon Relaxation sleep pod Xmas New Year **Conf:** Class 120 Board 50 Theatre 250 **Services:** Lift Night porter Air con **Notes:** Civ Wed 250

Find out more

about the AA Hotel of the Year for London on page 17

SW1 *continued*

LONDON

The Stafford London

★★★★★ ◉◉ HOTEL PLAN 4 J6

tel: 020 7493 0111 **16-18 St James's Place SW1A 1NJ**
email: reservations@thestaffordlondon.com **web:** www.thestaffordlondon.com
dir: *Exit Pall Mall into St James's Street 2nd left into St James's Place.*

Tucked away in a quiet corner of St James's, this classically styled boutique hotel has an air of understated luxury. The restaurant, Game Bird, serves wonderful modern British food, and the American Bar is a fabulous venue in its own right, festooned with an eccentric array of celebrity photos, caps and ties. Also, afternoon tea is a long established tradition here. From the pristine, tastefully decorated and air-conditioned bedrooms, to the highly professional, yet friendly service, this exclusive hotel maintains the highest standards. 26 stunning mews suites are available.

Rooms: 107 (39 annexe) (8 GF) (2 smoking) ↻ **D** fr £348* **Facilities:** STV WiFi ↻ Gym Use of fitness club Xmas New Year **Conf:** Class 24 Board 32 Theatre 40 **Services:** Lift Night porter Air con **Notes:** Civ Wed 44

Taj 51 Buckingham Gate, Suites and Residences

★★★★★ ◉◉ TOWN HOUSE HOTEL PLAN 4 J4

tel: 020 7769 7766 **SW1E 6AF**
email: info.london@tajhotels.com **web:** www.taj51buckinghamgate.co.uk
dir: *From Buckingham Palace into Spur Road. Right into Birdcage Walk, 1st left into Buckingham Gate, 100 metres, hotel on right.*

This all-suites hotel is a favourite with those who desire a quiet, sophisticated

environment. Each of the suites has its own butler on hand plus a kitchen, and most have large lounge areas furnished in a contemporary style with modern accessories. There are one, two, three and four-bedroom suites to choose from, which include the stunning Jaguar Suite and the spectacular Cinema Suite. The hotel has a spa and a well-equipped gym.

Rooms: 85 (85 family) (3 GF) ↻ **Facilities:** Spa STV FTV WiFi ↻ HL Gym Sauna Steam room Xmas New Year **Conf:** Class 90 Board 60 Theatre 180 **Services:** Lift Night porter Air con **Notes:** Civ Wed 150

41

★★★★★ ◉ TOWN HOUSE HOTEL PLAN 4 H4

THE
RED CARNATION
HOTEL COLLECTION

tel: 020 7300 0041 **41 Buckingham Palace Road SW1W 0PS**
email: book41@rchmail.com **web:** www.41hotel.com
dir: *Opposite Buckingham Palace Mews entrance.*

Small, intimate and very private, this stunning townhouse is located opposite the Royal Mews. Decorated in stylish black and white, bedrooms successfully combine comfort with state-of-the-art technology such as iPod docking stations, interactive TV and free high-speed internet access. Thoughtful touches such as fresh fruit, flowers and scented candles add to the welcoming atmosphere. The large lounge is the focal point; food and drinks are available as are magazines and newspapers from around the world plus internet access. Attentive personal service and a host of thoughtful extra touches make 41 really special.

Rooms: 30 (2 family) ↻ **S** fr £395* **Facilities:** STV FTV WiFi ↻ Local health club Beauty treatments in-room Spa **Conf:** Board 8 **Services:** Lift Night porter Air con **Notes:** LB

Symbols and abbreviations
explained on pages 6–7

LONDON

DUKES London

★★★★★ HOTEL PLAN 4 J6

SMALL LUXURY HOTELS OF THE WORLD

tel: 020 7491 4840 **35 St James's Place SW1A 1NY**
email: bookings@dukeshotel.com **web:** www.dukeshotel.com
dir: *From Pall Mall into St James's Street. 2nd left into St James's Place. Hotel in courtyard on left.*

Discreetly tucked away in St James's, DUKES London is over 100 years old. Its style is understated, with smart, well-equipped bedrooms and public areas. The Penthouse Suite has its own balcony with views over Green Park. Facilities include a gym, marble steam room and body-care treatments. GBR (Great British Restaurant) is the all-day dining concept here, offering many British classics using the very best ingredients. A smart lounge and a sophisticated and buzzing cocktail bar add to guests' enjoyment, and the martinis are a must.

Rooms: 90 (40 family) (4 GF) S fr £311.10 D fr £311.10* **Facilities:** STV FTV WiFi Gym Steam room Health club Personal training Beauty treatment room Xmas New Year **Conf:** Class 30 Board 30 Theatre 70 **Services:** Lift Night porter Air con **Notes:** Civ Wed 60

Jumeirah Carlton Tower

★★★★★ HOTEL PLAN 4 F4

tel: 020 7235 1234 **Cadogan Place SW1X 9PY**
email: jctinfo@jumeirah.com **web:** www.jumeirah.com
dir: *A4 towards Knightsbridge, right onto Sloane Street. Hotel on left before Cadogan Place.*

This impressive hotel enjoys an enviable position in the heart of Knightsbridge, overlooking Cadogan Gardens. The stunningly designed bedrooms, including a

number of suites, vary in size and style. Many have wonderful city views and all have free WiFi. Leisure facilities include a glass-roofed swimming pool, a well-equipped gym and a number of treatment rooms. The renowned Rib Room Bar & Restaurant provides excellent dining, together with the other options of the Club Room, and Chinoiserie.

Rooms: 216 (76 smoking) **Facilities:** Spa STV FTV WiFi Gym Sauna Steam room **Conf:** Class 250 Board 90 Theatre 400 **Services:** Lift Night porter Air con **Parking:** 30 **Notes:** Civ Wed 400

Sofitel London St James

★★★★★ 88% HOTEL PLAN 4 K6

SOFITEL

tel: 020 7747 2200 **6 Waterloo Place SW1Y 4AN**
email: H3144@sofitel.com **web:** www.sofitelstjames.com
dir: *3 minutes walk from Piccadilly Circus and Trafalgar Square.*

Located moments away from Trafalgar Square, Sofitel London St James offers a sophisticated yet relaxed welcome, enhanced by a spa, The Balcon all-day brasserie, the Rose Lounge ideal for afternoon tea and St James Bar. With 12 meeting rooms and a private dining room, the hotel can also cater for all manners of functions.

Rooms: 183 (102 family) S fr £336 D fr £336* **Facilities:** Spa STV WiFi Gym So FIT So SPA Xmas New Year **Conf:** Class 125 Board 45 Theatre 200 **Services:** Lift Night porter Air con **Notes:** Civ Wed 140

The Royal Horseguards

★★★★★ 82% HOTEL PLAN 5 B6

tel: 0871 376 9033 (Calls cost 7p per minute plus your phone company's access charge) **2 Whitehall Court SW1A 2EJ**
email: royalhorseguards@guoman.co.uk **web:** www.theroyalhorseguards.com
dir: *Trafalgar Square to Whitehall, left to Whitehall Place, turn right.*

This majestic hotel in the heart of Whitehall sits beside the Thames and enjoys unrivalled views of the London Eye and the city skyline. Bedrooms, appointed to a high standard, are well equipped and some of the luxurious bathrooms are finished in marble. Impressive public areas and outstanding meeting facilities are also available.

Rooms: 282 (7 family) **Facilities:** STV WiFi Gym Xmas New Year **Conf:** Class 180 Board 84 Theatre 240 **Services:** Lift Night porter Air con **Notes:** Civ Wed 228

St Ermins Hotel

★★★★ 87% HOTEL PLAN 4 K4

tel: 020 7222 7888 **2 Caxton Street, St James Park SW1H 0QW**
email: reservations@sterminshotel.co.uk **web:** www.sterminshotel.co.uk
dir: *Just off Victoria Street, directly opposite New Scotland Yard.*

Located in an enviable London location, the delightful courtyard offers a sanctuary from the hustle and bustle of the city. St Ermins' day rooms are fresh, modern and innovative, with a respectful nod to the hotel's former character. No detail has been overlooked. Food is served in the popular Caxton Grill. Limited valet parking is available by arrangement.

Rooms: 331 (18 family) (12 GF) S fr £299 D fr £299* **Facilities:** STV FTV WiFi HL Gym Xmas New Year **Conf:** Class 80 Board 60 Theatre 160 **Services:** Lift Night porter Air con **Parking:** 5 **Notes:** LB Civ Wed 160

SW1 *continued*

The Rubens at the Palace

★★★★ 87% ◉◉ HOTEL PLAN 4 H4

tel: 020 7834 6600 **39 Buckingham Palace Road SW1W 0PS**
email: bookrb@rchmail.com **web:** www.rubenshotel.com
dir: *Opposite Royal Mews, 100 metres from Buckingham Palace.*

This hotel enjoys an enviable location close to Buckingham Palace. Stylish, air-conditioned bedrooms include the pinstripe-walled Savile Row rooms, which follow a tailoring theme, and the opulent Royal rooms, named after different monarchs. The English Grill offers contemporary brasserie food while the Curry Room offers a more intimate dining experience. The comfortable, stylish cocktail bar and lounge provide afternoon teas and a place to relax and unwind. The team here pride themselves on their warmth and friendliness.

Rooms: 161 (25 family) ☎ **S** fr £239 **D** fr £251* **Facilities:** STV FTV WiFi↕ Health club and beauty treatment available nearby ♫ Xmas New Year **Conf:** Class 50 Board 30 Theatre 90 **Services:** Lift Night porter Air con **Notes:** LB Civ Wed 80

The Cavendish London

★★★★ 82% ◉◉ HOTEL PLAN 4 J6

tel: 020 7930 2111 **81 Jermyn Street SW1Y 6JF**
email: info@thecavendishlondon.com **web:** www.thecavendish-london.co.uk
dir: *From Piccadilly, pass The Ritz, 1st right into Dukes Street after Fortnum & Mason.*

This smart, stylish hotel enjoys an enviable location in the prestigious St James's area, just a short walk from Green Park and Piccadilly. Bedrooms have a fresh, contemporary feel, and there are several spacious executive rooms, studios and suites. Elegant public areas include a spacious first-floor lounge and well-appointed conference and function facilities. The popular Petrichor Restaurant is committed to sourcing sustainable ingredients, especially from British producers. A good value, pre-theatre menu is available.

Rooms: 230 (7 family) ☎ **S** fr £225 **D** fr £255* **Facilities:** STV FTV WiFi HL **Conf:** Class 50 Board 40 Theatre 80 **Services:** Lift Night porter Air con **Parking:** 50 **Notes:** LB

Millennium Hotel London Knightsbridge

★★★★ 79% ◉ HOTEL PLAN 4 F4

tel: 020 7235 4377 **17 Sloane Street, Knightsbridge SW1X 9NU**
email: reservations.knightsbridge@millenniumhotels.co.uk
web: www.millenniumhotels.co.uk
dir: *From Knightsbridge tube station towards Sloane Street. Hotel 70 metres on right.*

This fashionable hotel boasts an enviable location in Knightsbridge's chic shopping district. Air-conditioned, thoughtfully equipped bedrooms are complemented by a popular lobby lounge and the Tangerine Café Bar that serves food throughout the day. Le Chinois Restaurant and Bar offers modern Chinese cuisine. Valet parking is available if pre-booked.

Rooms: 222 (41 family) **Facilities:** STV FTV WiFi↕ Xmas **Conf:** Class 80 Board 50 Theatre 120 **Services:** Lift Night porter Air con **Parking:** 11

hub by Premier Inn London Westminster

 Premier Inn

BUDGET HOTEL PLAN 4 K4

tel: 0871 527 9608 (Calls cost 13p per minute plus your phone company's access charge) **St James's Park, 15 Dacre Street SW1H 0DJ**
web: www.premierinn.com
dir: *Phone for directions.*

This modern hotel offers self-check-in kiosks, superfast free WiFi, and cleverly designed and compact bedrooms with all the entertainment and comfort you need: 40" flat-screen smart TV, temperature and lighting controlled by a special Premier Inn app, Hypnos bed, and monsoon shower. The Deli+Bar is open for grab-and-go breakfast boxes, pastries, grilled sandwiches, Costa Coffee, beer, wine and more.

Rooms: 137

hub by Premier Inn London Westminster Abbey

 Premier Inn

BUDGET HOTEL PLAN 5 A4

tel: 0871 527 8000 (Calls cost 13p per minute plus your phone company's access charge) **21 Tothill Street, Westminster SW1H 9LL**
web: www.premierinn.com
dir: *Closest tube station is St James's Park on the District and Circle line. Use the Park and Broadway exit where Broadway meets Tothill Street. Continue along Tothill Street, passing Costa Pronto on the corner. Hotel will be on your right.*

Rooms: 339

Premier Inn London Victoria

Premier Inn

BUDGET HOTEL PLAN 4 J3

tel: 0871 527 8680 (Calls cost 13p per minute plus your phone company's access charge) **82-83 Eccleston Square SW1V 1PS**
web: www.premierinn.com
dir: *From Victoria Station, right into Wilton Road, 3rd right into Gillingham Street, hotel 150 metres.*

High quality, budget accommodation ideal for both families and business travellers. Spacious, en suite bedrooms feature free WiFi and tea and coffee making facilities, and in most hotels, Freeview TV is also available. The adjacent family restaurant features a wide and varied menu.

Rooms: 110

Jumeirah Lowndes Hotel

AA Advertised PLAN 4 F4

tel: 020 7823 1234 **21 Lowndes Street SW1X 9ES**
email: jlhinfo@jumeirah.com **web:** www.jumeirah.com
dir: *M4 onto A4 into London. Left from Brompton Road into Sloane Street. Left into Pont Street, Lowndes Street next left. Hotel on right.*

This chic, contemporary hotel is a smart modern townhouse set in timelessly stylish Belgravia. Guests can enjoy a meal in the international bistro Lowndes Bar & Kitchen or relax outside on The Terrace with an open-air barbecue. Bedrooms and suites all have a contemporary style with high-spec facilities such as iPads and WiFi. There are also extensive leisure facilities at the nearby Jumeirah Carlton Tower, which includes access to The Peak Health Club & Spa.

Rooms: 88 (12 family) ☎ **Facilities:** Spa STV FTV WiFi↕ 🏊 Gym **Conf:** Class 15 Board 16 Theatre 25 **Services:** Lift Night porter Air con **Notes:** LB

The Z Hotel Victoria

AA Advertised PLAN 4 H4

tel: 020 3589 3990 **5 Lower Belgrave Street SW1W 0NR**
email: victoria@thezhotels.com **web:** www.thezhotels.com
dir: *Near Victoria Station, via Buckingham Palace Road/A3214.*

The Z Hotel Victoria is the ideal location for London Victoria station, one of the UK's busiest transport interchanges, as well as the Apollo Victoria Theatre, Belgrave Square, Sloane Square and Knightsbridge. The hotel was converted from a Victorian townhouse which has resulted in a mix of complementary architectural styles. The stylish, modern bedrooms are spread over eight floors. Each room has an en suite wet room, crisp bed linen, 40" Sky TV and complimentary WiFi.

Rooms: 106 (8 GF) 🛏 **D** fr £70* **Facilities:** STV WiFi **Services:** Lift Air con

LONDON SW3

The Capital

★★★★★ 🏵🏵🏵 TOWN HOUSE HOTEL PLAN 4 F5

tel: 020 7589 5171 **Basil Street, Knightsbridge SW3 1AT**
email: reservations@capitalhotel.co.uk **web:** www.capitalhotel.co.uk
dir: *20 yards from Harrods and Knightsbridge tube station.*

Personal service is assured at this small, family-owned hotel set in the heart of Knightsbridge. Beautifully designed bedrooms come in a number of styles, but all rooms feature antique furniture, a marble bathroom and a thoughtful range of extras. Cocktails are a speciality in the delightful, stylish bar, while afternoon tea in the elegant, bijou lounge is a must. The signature restaurant, Outlaw's at The Capital provides stunning dishes, featuring the best in British seafood from Nathan Outlaw and his head chef here, Andrew Sawye.

Rooms: 49 (4 family) 🛏 **S** fr £251 **D** fr £297* **Facilities:** STV FTV WiFi ☒
Conf: Class 24 Board 24 Theatre 30 **Services:** Lift Night porter Air con **Parking:** 7
Notes: LB

The Egerton House Hotel

★★★★★ 🍽 TOWN HOUSE HOTEL PLAN 4 E4

THE
RED CARNATION
HOTEL COLLECTION

tel: 020 7589 2412 **17 Egerton Terrace, Knightsbridge SW3 2BX**
email: bookeg@rchmail.com **web:** www.egertonhousehotel.com
dir: *Just off Brompton Road, between Harrods and Victoria & Albert Museum, opposite Brompton Oratory.*

This delightful town house enjoys a prestigious Knightsbridge location, a short walk from Harrods and close to the Victoria & Albert Museum. Air-conditioned bedrooms and public rooms are appointed to the highest standards, with luxurious furnishings and quality antique pieces; an exceptional range of facilities include iPods, safes, mini bars and flat-screen TVs. Staff offer the highest levels of personalised, attentive service.

Rooms: 28 (5 family) (2 GF) 🛏 **S** fr £315 **D** fr £315 **Facilities:** STV WiFi ☒ HL Xmas New Year **Conf:** Class 12 Board 10 Theatre 14 **Services:** Lift Night porter Air con

LONDON

Silver Stars

The AA Silver Star rating denotes a Hotel that we highly recommend. They have a superior level of quality within their star rating, high standards of hospitality, service and cleanliness.

LONDON

SW3 *continued*

The Draycott Hotel

★★★★★ 81% TOWN HOUSE HOTEL PLAN 4 F3

tel: 020 7730 6466 **26 Cadogan Gardens SW3 2RP**
email: reservations@draycotthotel.com **web:** www.draycotthotel.com
dir: *From Sloane Square station towards Peter Jones, keep to left. At Kings Road take 1st right into Cadogan Gardens, 2nd right, hotel on left corner.*

Enjoying a prime location just yards from Sloane Square, this town house provides an ideal base in one of the most fashionable areas of London. Many regular guests regard this as their London residence and staff pride themselves on their hospitality. Beautifully appointed bedrooms include a number of very spacious suites and all are equipped to a high standard. Attractive day rooms, furnished with antique and period pieces, include a choice of lounges, one with access to a lovely sheltered garden.

Rooms: 35 (9 family) (2 GF) ↖ **Facilities:** STV FTV WiFi Beauty treatments Massage
Services: Lift Night porter Air con

INSPECTOR'S CHOICE

The Levin

★★★★ TOWN HOUSE HOTEL PLAN 4 F4

tel: 020 7589 6286 **28 Basil Street, Knightsbridge SW3 1AS**
email: reservations@thelevinhotel.co.uk **web:** www.thelevinhotel.co.uk
dir: *20 yards from Harrods and Knightsbridge tube station.*

This sophisticated town house is the sister property to the adjacent Capital Hotel and enjoys a prime location on the doorstep of Knightsbridge's stylish department and designer stores. Bedrooms and en suites offer timeless elegance alongside a host of up-to-date modern comforts; extra touches include

champagne bars, state-of-the-art audio-visual systems, and complimentary WiFi. Guests can enjoy all-day dining in the stylish, popular, lower ground-floor Metro Restaurant.

Rooms: 12 (1 GF) **D** fr £232* **Facilities:** STV FTV WiFi ↘ **Services:** Lift Night porter Air con **Parking:** 7 **Notes:** LB

The Beaufort

★★★★ 80% TOWN HOUSE HOTEL PLAN 4 F4

tel: 020 7584 5252 **33 Beaufort Gardens SW3 1PP**
email: reservations@thebeaufort.co.uk **web:** www.thebeaufort.co.uk
dir: *100 yards past Harrods on left of Brompton Road.*

This friendly, attractive town house enjoys a peaceful location in a tree-lined cul-de-sac just a few minutes' walk from Knightsbridge. Air-conditioned bedrooms are thoughtfully furnished and equipped with CD player, movie channel access, safe, and free WiFi. Guests are offered complimentary drinks and afternoon cream tea with home-made scones and clotted cream. A good continental breakfast is served in bedrooms.

Rooms: 29 (3 GF) **Facilities:** STV FTV WiFi **Conf:** Theatre 10 **Services:** Lift Night porter Air con

LONDON SW5

Best Western Burns Hotel

★★★ 75% METRO HOTEL PLAN 4 B3

tel: 020 7373 3151 **18-26 Barkston Gardens, Kensington SW5 0EN**
email: info@burnshotel.co.uk **web:** www.burnshotel.co.uk
dir: *From A4, right to Earls Court Road (A3220), 2nd left.*

This friendly Victorian hotel overlooks a leafy garden in a quiet residential area not far from the Earls Court tube station. Bedrooms are attractively appointed, with modern facilities. Public areas, although not extensive, are stylish.

Rooms: 105 (10 family) **Facilities:** STV WiFi ↘ **Services:** Lift Night porter

Premier Inn London Kensington (Earl's Court)

BUDGET HOTEL PLAN 4 B3

tel: 0871 527 8666 (Calls cost 13p per minute plus your phone company's access charge) **11 Knaresborough Place SW5 0TJ**
web: www.premierinn.com
dir: *Just off A4 (Cromwell Road). Nearest tube: Earls Court.*

High quality, budget accommodation ideal for both families and business travellers. Spacious, en suite bedrooms feature free WiFi and tea and coffee making facilities, and in most hotels, Freeview TV is also available. The adjacent family restaurant features a wide and varied menu.

Rooms: 184

Premier Inn London Kensington (Olympia)

BUDGET HOTEL PLAN 4 A3

tel: 0871 527 8668 (Calls cost 13p per minute plus your phone company's access charge) **22-32 West Cromwell Road SW5 9QJ**
web: www.premierinn.com
dir: *On north side of West Cromwell Road, between junctions of Cromwell Road, Earls Court Road and Warwick Road.*

Rooms: 90

LONDON SW6

Millennium & Copthorne Hotels at Chelsea FC

★★★★ 78% HOTEL PLAN 1 E3

MILLENNIUM
HOTELS AND RESORTS

tel: 020 7565 1400 **Stamford Bridge, Fulham Road SW6 1HS**
email: reservations@chelseafc.com **web:** www.millenniumhotels.com
dir: *4 minutes walk from Fulham Broadway tube station.*

A unique destination in a fashionable area of the city. Situated at Chelsea's famous Stamford Bridge ground, the accommodation offered here is very up-to-the-minute. Bedroom facilities include LCD TVs, video-on-demand, broadband, WiFi and good-sized desk space; larger Club rooms have additional features. For eating and drinking there's Frankie's Sports Bar & Diner, Delta 360° Lounge, 55 Restaurant, 55 Lounge and Bar, and for corporate guests a flexible arrangement of meeting and event rooms is available.

Rooms: 273 (64 family) **Facilities:** STV WiFi Stadium and museum tours **Conf:** Board 10 **Services:** Lift Night porter Air con

Premier Inn London Putney Bridge

BUDGET HOTEL PLAN 1 D2

Premier Inn

tel: 0871 527 8674 (Calls cost 13p per minute plus your phone company's access charge) **3 Putney Bridge Approach SW6 3JD**
web: www.premierinn.com
dir: *Nearest tube: Putney Bridge. Hotel on A219, north of River Thames.*

High quality, budget accommodation ideal for both families and business travellers. Spacious, en suite bedrooms feature free WiFi and tea and coffee making facilities, and in most hotels, Freeview TV is also available. The adjacent family restaurant features a wide and varied menu.

Rooms: 179

LONDON SW7

INSPECTOR'S CHOICE

Bulgari Hotel, London

★★★★★ @@@ HOTEL PLAN 4 F5

tel: 020 7151 1010 **171 Knightsbridge SW7 1DW**
email: london@bulgarihotels.co.uk **web:** www.bulgarihotels.com/london
dir: *Almost opposite Hyde Park Knightsbridge.*

This striking, contemporary hotel, in the heart of Knightsbridge, has sister hotels in Milan and Bali. The luxury accommodation is stylish and deeply comfortable, complete with Bulgari Trunk mini-bars and Nespresso machines; bathrooms are equally lavish with deep baths and rain showers. Spacious public areas include a stunning spa complete with a 25-metre swimming pool, separate vitality pool and a range of treatment rooms. A unique, hammered metal oval bar top provides the focal point in the bar that has a sweeping staircase taking guests down to the Rivea London restaurant which is overseen by Alain Ducasse and his protégé Alexandre Nicolas. Immaculately attired staff offer high standards of service and hospitality.

Rooms: 85 (17 smoking) **D** fr £588* **Facilities:** Spa STV FTV WiFi HL Gym The Screening Room cinema Xmas New Year **Conf:** Class 80 Board 40 Theatre 100 **Services:** Lift Night porter Air con **Parking:** 6

INSPECTOR'S CHOICE

Baglioni Hotel London

★★★★★ @ HOTEL PLAN 4 C5

tel: 020 7368 5700 **60 Hyde Park Gate, Kensington Road SW7 5BB**
email: info.london@baglionihotels.com **web:** www.baglionihotels.com
dir: *On corner of Hyde Park Gate and De Vere Gardens.*

Located in the heart of Kensington and overlooking Hyde Park, this small hotel buzzes with Italian style and chic. Bedrooms, mostly suites, are generously sized and designed in bold dark colours; they have Illy espresso machines, interactive TVs and a host of other excellent touches. Service is both professional and friendly. Public areas include the main open-plan space with a lounge and Brunello Bar and Restaurant, all merging together with great elan; there is a spa with four treatment rooms and a techno-gym, and a fashionable private club bar downstairs.

Rooms: 67 (7 family) (30 smoking) **S** fr £270 **D** fr £270* **Facilities:** Spa STV FTV WiFi Gym Steam room Relaxation area Xmas New Year **Conf:** Class 48 Board 34 Theatre 65 **Services:** Lift Night porter Air con **Parking:** 4 **Notes:** Civ Wed 60

SW7 *continued*

The Gore

★★★★ 83% TOWN HOUSE HOTEL PLAN 4 C4

tel: 020 7584 6601 **190 Queen's Gate SW7 5EX**
email: reservations.thegore@starhotels.com **web:** www.gorehotel.com
dir: *Adjacent to Royal Albert Hall.*

Convenient for many of London's attractions including the Royal Albert Hall, and close to Gloucester Road tube station, stands this character town house. The lounge serves afternoon tea, and 190 Queens Gate restaurant and bar is popular with the pre-theatre crowd. Bedrooms are varied in size, from the cosy classics to more spacious suites.

Rooms: 50 **S** fr £170 **D** fr £199 (including breakfast)* **Facilities:** WiFi
Conf: Class 30 Board 30 Theatre 80 **Services:** Night porter Air con
Notes: Civ Wed 80

Crowne Plaza London - Kensington

★★★★ 79% HOTEL PLAN 4 C3

tel: 020 7373 2222 **100 Cromwell Road SW7 4ER**
email: lonke.reservations@ihg.com **web:** www.cplondonkensingtonhotel.co.uk
dir: *Opposite Gloucester Road tube station. From M4 follow Central London signs. At Cromwell Road hotel is visible on left.*

A contemporary hotel with a grand Victorian townhouse facade offering accommodation that meets the needs of both leisure and business travellers. The spilt-level Superior Suites are ideal for families and for long stays. The many facilities include complimentary high-speed WiFi, a state-of-the-art fitness suite and sauna. The ground-floor Umami Restaurant offers a real taste of pan-Asian cooking and a relaxed atmosphere. The one-acre landscaped private garden is an oasis of peace and tranquillity. There are two public car parks in the vicinity.

Rooms: 162 (74 family) **Facilities:** STV FTV WiFi Gym **Conf:** Class 64 Board 60 Theatre 150 **Services:** Lift Night porter Air con

The Rembrandt Hotel

★★★★ 79% HOTEL PLAN 4 E4

tel: 020 7589 8100 **11 Thurloe Place, Knightsbridge SW7 2RS**
email: rembrandt@sarova.com **web:** www.sarova.com
dir: *M4 onto A4 Cromwell Road into central London. Hotel opposite Victoria and Albert Museum.*

In the heart of South Kensington and Knightsbridge, not far from Harrods, this attractive hotel has elegant Edwardian architecture and sits opposite the V&A. All of the elegantly designed rooms include a complimentary Handy smartphone for guests to use during their stay – this includes free calls to selected countries, unlimited 3G data, Google Maps, tube and travel updates and much more. Guests can enjoy fine dining in the sophisticated Palette restaurant, or relax with a drink in the glamorous 1606 lounge bar. All overnight guests receive a free full English breakfast, and enjoy reduced-rate access to Aquilla Health and Fitness, a private health club adjacent to the hotel.

Rooms: 194 **S** fr £179 **D** fr £189 (including breakfast)* **Facilities:** Spa STV FTV WiFi Gym **Conf:** Class 84 Board 80 Theatre 200 **Services:** Lift Night porter Air con **Notes:** Civ Wed 200

Millennium Bailey's Hotel London Kensington

★★★★ 78% HOTEL PLAN 4 C3

tel: 020 7373 6000 **140 Gloucester Road SW7 4QH**
email: reservations.baileys@millenniumhotels.co.uk **web:** www.thebaileyshotel.co.uk
dir: *From A4, at Cromwell Hospital, into Knaresborough Place, to Courtfield Road to corner of Gloucester Road, hotel opposite tube station.*

This elegant hotel has a town-house atmosphere and enjoys a prime London location. The bedrooms and bathrooms have been appointed to a high standard; each floor has a different theme reflecting the history of the building; all rooms feature large TVs, minibars and air conditioning. The public spaces include the stylish, contemporary Olives Restaurant, and alfresco dining is available during the warmer months. Guests may also use the facilities at the larger sister hotel, which is adjacent.

Rooms: 212 (27 family) **Facilities:** FTV WiFi HL Xmas New Year **Services:** Lift Night porter Air con **Parking:** 60

Millennium Gloucester Hotel London Kensington

★★★★ 76% HOTEL PLAN 4 C3

tel: 020 7373 6030 **4-18 Harrington Gardens SW7 4LH**
email: reservations.gloucester@millenniumhotels.co.uk
web: www.millenniumhotels.co.uk
dir: *Opposite Gloucester Road underground station.*

This spacious, stylish hotel is centrally located, close to The Victoria & Albert Museum and Gloucester Road tube station. Air-conditioned bedrooms are furnished in a variety of contemporary styles, and Clubrooms benefit from a dedicated club lounge with complimentary breakfast and snacks. A wide range of eating options includes Singaporean and Mediterranean cuisine.

Rooms: 610 (10 family) **Facilities:** STV WiFi HL Gym **Conf:** Class 300 Board 100 Theatre 500 **Services:** Lift Night porter Air con **Parking:** 110 **Notes:** Civ Wed 500

Park International Hotel

★★★★ 76% HOTEL PLAN 4 B3

tel: 020 7370 5711 **117–129 Cromwell Road SW7 4DS**
email: reservations@parkinternationalhotel.com **web:** www.parkinternationalhotel.com
dir: *2 minutes walk from Gloucester Road station.*

The Park International Hotel is within easy reach of all major attractions in Kensington and Chelsea. The hotel offers a range of well designed rooms to meet the needs of the modern traveller, and the Heritage Suites are individually styled for that extra bit of opulence. Afternoon tea is served in the Checkmate Bar, cocktails in the Piano Bar, and breakfast in the Orchid Room. The menu offers a blend of carefully chosen Thai and modern British dishes.

Rooms: 171 (18 family) (15 GF) **S** fr £90 **D** fr £110 (including breakfast)* **Facilities:** STV FTV WiFi HL Gym Xmas New Year **Conf:** Board 12 **Services:** Lift Night porter Air con

LONDON SW8

Premier Inn London Clapham hotel

Premier Inn

BUDGET HOTEL PLAN 1 E2

tel: 0871 527 9678 (Calls cost 13p per minute plus your phone company's access charge) **638-640 Wandsworth Road, Clapham SW8 3JW**
web: www.premierinn.com
dir: *Phone for directions.*

High quality, budget accommodation ideal for both families and business travellers. Spacious, en suite bedrooms feature free WiFi and tea and coffee making facilities, and in most hotels, Freeview TV is also available. The adjacent family restaurant features a wide and varied menu.

Rooms: 92

LONDON SW9

Premier Inn London Brixton

Premier Inn

BUDGET HOTEL PLAN 1 F2

tel: 0871 527 9530 (Calls cost 13p per minute plus your phone company's access charge) **457-461 Brixton Road SW9 8HH**
web: www.premierinn.com
dir: *From South Circular Road, turn onto Brixton Hill/A23. Slight right onto Coldharbour Lane/A2217, hotel on left.*

High quality, budget accommodation ideal for both families and business travellers. Spacious, en suite bedrooms feature free WiFi and tea and coffee making facilities, and in most hotels, Freeview TV is also available. The adjacent family restaurant features a wide and varied menu.

Rooms: 736

LONDON SW10

The Chelsea Harbour Hotel

MILLENNIUM

★★★★★ 83% HOTEL PLAN 1 E3

tel: 020 7823 3000 **Chelsea Harbour SW10 0XG**
email: reservations.chelseaharbour@millenniumhotels.com
web: www.thechelseaharbourhotel.co.uk
dir: *A4 to Earls Court Road south towards river. Right into Kings Road, left into Lots Road.*

Against the picturesque backdrop of Chelsea Harbour's small marina, this modern hotel offers spacious, comfortable accommodation. All rooms are suites, which are superbly equipped; many enjoy splendid views of the marina. In addition, there are also several luxurious penthouse suites. Public areas include a modern bar and restaurant, excellent leisure facilities (including a spa) and extensive meeting and function rooms.

Rooms: 158 (158 family) **Facilities:** Spa STV FTV WiFi Gym Sauna Steam room Relaxation lounge Hair salon Xmas New Year **Conf:** Class 250 Board 50 Theatre 500 **Services:** Lift Night porter Air con **Parking:** 2000 **Notes:** Civ Wed 450

LONDON SW18

Premier Inn London Wandsworth

Premier Inn

BUDGET HOTEL PLAN 1 E2

tel: 0871 527 9486 (Calls cost 13p per minute plus your phone company's access charge) **45 Garratt Lane SW18 4AD**
web: www.premierinn.com
dir: *From A3 (Wandsworth High Street) at lights into Garratt Lane. Hotel on left.*

High quality, budget accommodation ideal for both families and business travellers. Spacious, en suite bedrooms feature free WiFi and tea and coffee making facilities, and in most hotels, Freeview TV is also available. The adjacent family restaurant features a wide and varied menu.

Rooms: 120

LONDON SW19

Hotel du Vin Wimbledon

Hotel du Vin & Bistro

★★★★ 80% COUNTRY HOUSE HOTEL PLAN 1 D2

tel: 020 8879 1464 **Cannizaro House, West Side SW19 4UE**
email: reservations@hotelduvin.com **web:** www.hotelduvin.com/locations/wimbledon
dir: *From A3 follow A219 signed Wimbledon into Parkside, right into Cannizaro Road, sharp right into West Side.*

This unique, 18th-century house located opposite Wimbledon Common and set within 34 acres of Cannizaro Park, offers a tranquil setting, just a short distance from central London. The hotel has a large, stylish bar and dining options including the main restaurant, and the Orangery which enjoys excellent views of the terrace and common. Bedrooms are spacious and stylish with feature walls, high quality furnishings and a good range of amenities including coffee machines, WiFi and Sky TV. Function facilities are available and there is complimentary parking.

Rooms: 48 (5 family) (5 GF) **D** fr £124* **Facilities:** STV FTV WiFi **Conf:** Class 50 Board 40 Theatre 120 **Services:** Lift Night porter Air con **Parking:** 95 **Notes:** Civ Wed 200

Holiday Inn Express Wimbledon South

Holiday Inn Express

BUDGET HOTEL PLAN 1 E1

tel: 020 8545 7300 **Miller's Meadhouse, 200 High Street SW19 2BH**
email: reservations@exhiwimbledon.co.uk **web:** www.exhiwimbledon.co.uk
dir: *A238 Kingston Road, at lights into Merton High Street, signed Colliers Wood. Hotel directly opposite Colliers Wood underground station.*

A modern hotel ideal for families and business travellers. Fresh and uncomplicated, the spacious rooms include Sky TV, power shower and tea and coffee-making facilities. Continental buffet breakfast is included in the room rate; other meals may be taken at the nearby family pub or restaurant.

Rooms: 139 (92 family) (12 GF)

LONDON

SW19 *continued*

Premier Inn London Wimbledon South

Premier Inn

BUDGET HOTEL PLAN 1 E1

tel: 0871 527 8684 (Calls cost 13p per minute plus your phone company's access charge) **27 Chapter Way, Off Merantun Way SW19 2RF**
web: www.premierinn.com
dir: *M25 junction 10, A3 towards London. Exit A298 (Wimbledon) onto A238. Right onto A219, left onto A24 (Merantun Way). At roundabout 3rd exit signed Merton Abbey Mills.*

High quality, budget accommodation ideal for both families and business travellers. Spacious, en suite bedrooms feature free WiFi and tea and coffee making facilities, and in most hotels, Freeview TV is also available. The adjacent family restaurant features a wide and varied menu.

Rooms: 134

LONDON W1

INSPECTOR'S CHOICE

The Connaught

MAYBOURNE
HOTEL GROUP

★★★★★ ◎◎◎◎◎◎ 🍴 HOTEL PLAN 2 G1

tel: 020 7499 7070 **Carlos Place W1K 2AL**
email: info@the-connaught.co.uk **web:** www.the-connaught.com
dir: *Between Grosvenor Square and Berkeley Square.*

This iconic hotel is truly spectacular, with stunning interior design. There are sumptuous day rooms and stylish bedrooms with state-of-the-art facilities and marble en suites with deep tubs, TV screens and power showers. Butlers are available at the touch of a button and guests are pampered by friendly, attentive staff offering intuitive service. There is a choice of bars and restaurants including the Espelette bistro, and the award-winning cuisine of Hélène Darroze which is imaginative, inspired and truly memorable. The excellent Aman Spa at the hotel offers health and beauty treatments, a swimming pool and fitness centre.

Rooms: 122 (4 smoking) 🌑 **S** fr £930 **D** fr £1080* **Facilities:** Spa STV FTV WiFi ⬦ 🕸 Gym Xmas New Year **Conf:** Class 70 Board 60 Theatre 120 **Services:** Lift Night porter Air con **Notes:** Civ Wed 200

INSPECTOR'S CHOICE

45 Park Lane

★★★★★ ◎◎◎ 🍴 HOTEL PLAN 4 G6

tel: 020 7493 4545 **45 Park Lane W1K 1PN**
email: reservations.45L@dorchestercollection.com **web:** www.45parklane.com
dir: *Park Lane, near The Dorchester.*

This hotel offers luxurious and contemporary interiors. The bedrooms, including ten suites, all have a view of Hyde Park; the Penthouse Suite has its own roof terrace. A striking central staircase leads to a mezzanine featuring Bar 45, a library and a private media room. Other public areas include a lounge area and CUT at 45 Park Lane, a modern American steak restaurant.

Rooms: 46 🌑 **S** fr £575 **D** fr £575* **Facilities:** STV WiFi ⬦ HL Gym 🎵 New Year **Services:** Lift Night porter Air con **Parking:** 12 **Notes:** Civ Wed 60

INSPECTOR'S CHOICE

Claridge's

MAYBOURNE
HOTEL GROUP

★★★★★ ◎◎◎ 🍴 HOTEL PLAN 2 H1

tel: 020 7629 8860 **Brook Street W1K 4HR**
email: info@claridges.co.uk **web:** www.claridges.co.uk
dir: *First turn after Green Park tube station to Berkeley Square and fourth exit into Davies Street. Third right into Brook Street.*

Once renowned as a resort of kings and princes, Claridge's today continues to set the standards by which other hotels are judged. The sumptuous, air-conditioned bedrooms are elegantly themed to reflect the Victorian or art deco architecture of the building. Fera at Claridge's is now well established, and like the stylish cocktail bar, is a hit with residents and non-residents alike. Service throughout is meticulous and thoroughly professional.

Rooms: 190 ✆ **S** fr £510 **D** fr £510* **Facilities:** Spa STV WiFi Gym Beauty and health treatments use of sister hotel's swimming pool ♫ Xmas New Year **Conf:** Class 150 Board 60 Theatre 260 **Services:** Lift Night porter Air con **Notes:** Civ Wed 240

INSPECTOR'S CHOICE

The Ritz London

★★★★★ ⊚⊚⊚ ⧈ HOTEL PLAN 4 J6

tel: 020 7493 8181 **150 Piccadilly W1J 9BR**
email: enquire@theritzlondon.com **web:** www.theritzlondon.com
dir: *From Hyde Park Corner east on Piccadilly. Hotel on right after Green Park.*

This renowned, stylish hotel offers guests the ultimate in sophistication while still managing to retain all its former historic glory. Bedrooms and suites are exquisitely furnished in Louis XVI style, with fine marble bathrooms and every imaginable comfort. Elegant reception rooms include the Palm Court with its legendary afternoon teas, the beautiful fashionable Rivoli Bar and the sumptuous Ritz Restaurant, complete with gold chandeliers and extraordinary trompe-l'oeil decoration. The Ritz London offers complimentary high-speed WiFi.

Rooms: 136 (65 family) (24 smoking) ✆ **S** fr £370 **D** fr £445* **Facilities:** STV FTV WiFi ⧈ Gym The Ritz Club and Casino The Ritz Salon ♫ Xmas New Year **Conf:** Class 40 Board 30 Theatre 70 **Services:** Lift Night porter Air con **Parking:** 10 **Notes:** Civ Wed 60

INSPECTOR'S CHOICE

The Athenaeum Hotel & Residences

★★★★★ ⊚⊚ HOTEL PLAN 4 H6

tel: 020 7640 3557 **116 Piccadilly W1J 7BJ**
email: info@athenaeumhotel.com **web:** www.athenaeumhotel.com
dir: *Located between Green Park and Hyde Park Corner tube stations, an easy 5–7 minute stroll from either.*

This independent family-run hotel is located in the heart of Mayfair, making it easy to discover London's attractions including Buckingham Palace, the West End and Oxford Street. Following a multi-million pound refurbishment, the spacious rooms and suites in this art deco hotel offer the highest levels of comfort and all include Bose speakers, a pillow menu and WiFi. There's also a spectacular penthouse with a private balcony and 180-degree views of the city. For ultimate luxury there are 18 private residences accessed via a private entrance. Guests can enjoy 24-hour in-room dining, gym access and the spa's hot tubs, sauna and steam room. The hotel bar is renowned for its range of whiskies and cocktails, while fine-dining Galvin at the Athenaeum offers wonderful French-inspired dishes with a British slant.

Rooms: 164 (18 family) (12 GF) ✆ **Facilities:** Spa STV FTV WiFi Gym REN Spa with hot tubs Sauna Steam room and treatment area Free bike hire **Conf:** Class 35 Board 47 Theatre 80 **Services:** Lift Night porter Air con **Notes:** LB No children Civ Wed 80

LONDON

Silver Stars The AA Silver Star rating denotes a Hotel that we highly recommend. They have a superior level of quality within their star rating, high standards of hospitality, service and cleanliness.

W1 *continued*

INSPECTOR'S CHOICE

Four Seasons Hotel London at Park Lane

★★★★★ ◎◎ ≋ HOTEL PLAN 4 G6

tel: 020 7499 0888 **Hamilton Place, Park Lane W1J 7DR**
email: reservations@fourseasons.com **web:** www.fourseasons.com/london
dir: *From Piccadilly into Old Park Lane, into Hamilton Place.*

This long-established popular hotel is discreetly located near Hyde Park Corner, in the heart of Mayfair. It successfully combines modern efficiencies with traditional luxury. Guest care is consistently of the highest order, even down to the smallest detail of the personalised wake-up call. The bedrooms are elegant and spacious, and the unique conservatory rooms are particularly special. Spacious public areas include extensive conference and banqueting facilities, Lane's bar and fine-dining restaurant, and an elegant lounge where wonderful afternoon teas are served.

Rooms: 193 (49 smoking) **Facilities:** Spa STV FTV WiFi ↘ Gym Fitness centre ♫ Xmas New Year **Conf:** Class 174 Board 108 Theatre 375 **Services:** Lift Night porter Air con **Parking:** 10 **Notes:** Civ Wed 350

INSPECTOR'S CHOICE

The Dorchester

★★★★★ ◎◎ ≋ HOTEL PLAN 4 G6

tel: 020 7629 8888 **Park Lane W1K 1QA**
email: reservations.TDL@dorchestercollection.com **web:** www.thedorchester.com
dir: *Halfway along Park Lane between Hyde Park Corner and Marble Arch.*

One of London's finest, The Dorchester remains one of the best-loved hotels in the country and always delivers. The spacious bedrooms and suites are beautifully appointed and feature fabulous marble bathrooms. Leading off from the foyer, The Promenade is the perfect setting for afternoon tea or drinks. In the evening guests can relax to the sound of live jazz, while enjoying a cocktail in the stylish bar. Dining options include the sophisticated Chinese restaurant, China Tang; Alain Ducasse at The Dorchester from the world-renowned French chef of the same name; and of course, The Grill.

Rooms: 250 **Facilities:** Spa STV FTV WiFi ↘ HL Gym Steam rooms Fitness suite ♫ Xmas New Year **Conf:** Class 300 Board 42 Theatre 400 **Services:** Lift Night porter Air con **Notes:** LB Civ Wed 432

INSPECTOR'S CHOICE

Brown's Hotel

★★★★★ ≋ HOTEL PLAN 2 J1

ROCCO FORTE HOTELS

tel: 020 7493 6020 **Albemarle Street, Mayfair W1S 4BP**
email: reservations.browns@roccofortehotels.com
web: www.roccofortehotels.com
dir: A short walk from Green Park, Bond Street, Piccadilly and Buckingham Palace.

Brown's is a London hospitality icon that maintains its charm through the successful balance of traditional and contemporary. Bedrooms are luxurious, furnished to the highest standard and come with all the modern comforts expected of such a grand Mayfair hotel. The hotel has 29 suites including two Royal Suites and two Presidential Suites. The restaurant, Beck at Brown's, serves a casual dining menu of classic Italian dishes, and it is also home to a collection of works by leading British artists. The English Tea Room proves a great meeting place for afternoon tea.

Rooms: 115 (33 family) ☎ **Facilities:** Spa STV WiFi ⇘ Gym 𝄢 Xmas New Year **Conf:** Class 30 Board 30 Theatre 70 **Services:** Lift Night porter Air con **Parking:** 4 **Notes:** Civ Wed 70

Hyatt Regency London - The Churchill

★★★★★ 87% ◉◉◉ HOTEL PLAN 2 F2

tel: 020 7486 5800 **30 Portman Square W1H 7BH**
email: london.churchill@hyatt.com **web:** www.londonchurchill.regency.hyatt.com
dir: From Marble Arch roundabout, follow signs for Oxford Circus into Oxford Street. Left after 2nd lights into Portman Street. Hotel on left.

This smart hotel enjoys a central location overlooking Portman Square. Excellent conference and in-room facilities, plus a fitness room make this the ideal choice for both corporate and leisure guests. To set the style, guests are greeted by stunning floral displays in the sophisticated lobby. The Montagu restaurant offers contemporary dining, plus the option to sit at the Chef's Table for a front row seat to watch all the action in the kitchen.

Rooms: 440 ☎ **S** fr £259 **D** fr £259* **Facilities:** STV FTV WiFi ⇘ ᷒ Gym Jogging track 𝄢 Xmas New Year **Conf:** Class 180 Board 48 Theatre 250 **Services:** Lift Night porter Air con **Notes:** Civ Wed 250

COMO Metropolitan London

★★★★★ 87% ◉◉ HOTEL PLAN 4 G6

tel: 020 7447 1000 **Old Park Lane W1K 1LB**
email: res.met.lon@comohotels.com **web:** www.comohotels.com/metropolitanlondon
dir: On corner of Old Park Lane and Hertford Street.

Overlooking Hyde Park this hotel is located within easy reach of the fashionable stores of Knightsbridge and Mayfair. The hotel's contemporary style allows freedom and space to relax. Understated luxury is the key here with bedrooms enjoying great natural light. There is also a Shambhala Spa, steam room and fully equipped gym. For those seeking a culinary experience, Nobu offers innovative Japanese cuisine with an upbeat atmosphere.

Rooms: 144 (23 smoking) ☎ **D** fr £330* **Facilities:** Spa STV FTV WiFi ⇘ Gym Steam rooms **Conf:** Class 25 Board 30 Theatre 80 **Services:** Lift Night porter Air con **Parking:** 8 **Notes:** Civ Wed 80

The Langham, London

★★★★★ 87% ◉◉ HOTEL PLAN 2 H3

tel: 020 7636 1000 & 7965 0187 **Portland Place W1B 1JA**
email: tllon.info@langhamhotels.com **web:** www.langhamhotels.com/london
dir: North of Regent Street, left opposite All Soul's Church.

This hotel has a grand entrance which leads into restored interior elegance. Dating back to 1865 the building displays a contemporary, luxurious style. Situated near Regent Street it is ideally located for both theatreland and the principal shopping areas. Bedrooms are delightfully appointed and many have excellent views. The Landau restaurant and Artesian bar offer high standards of service, delivered by a friendly team. Palm Court is a great place for afternoon tea or a glass of champagne. There is also an extensive health club complete with a 16-metre pool.

Rooms: 380 (5 family) ☎ **S** fr £400 **D** fr £400* **Facilities:** Spa STV WiFi ⇘ HL ⊕ Gym Health club Sauna Steam room 𝄢 Xmas New Year **Conf:** Class 144 Board 80 Theatre 300 **Services:** Lift Night porter Air con **Notes:** LB Civ Wed 250

The Beaumont

★★★★★ 86% ◉ ≋ HOTEL PLAN 2 G1

tel: 020 7499 1001 **8 Balderton Street, Mayfair W1K 6TF**
email: info@thebeaumont.com **web:** www.thebeaumont.com
dir: M1 junction 1/A41/A501, Oxford Street into North Audley Street. 1st left into North Row, 1st right into Balderton Street.

The Beaumont is a beautifully renovated hotel in the Mayfair area, just a stone's throw from Oxford Street. The art deco-style bedrooms vary in size but are deeply comfortable, with marble bathrooms and up-to-the-minute technology. The art deco theme runs through the stylish public spaces which include the popular Colony Grill Room restaurant, Jimmy's American bar and residents' club lounge. A unique feature is ROOM, an installation space by Antony Gormley. From the outside, ROOM looks like a crouching figure, perched on one part of the original building; inside is an unusual suite of rooms – sculpture you can sleep in. The hotel also has a small spa, meeting room, gym and hair salon. A courtesy car is available, subject to availability.

Rooms: 73 (31 family) ☎ **S** fr £395 **D** fr £395* **Facilities:** Spa STV FTV WiFi ⇘ HL Gym Sauna Steam room Cold plunge pool Barber shop Xmas New Year **Conf:** Board 18 Theatre 40 **Services:** Lift Night porter Air con **Parking:** 3

LONDON

W1 *continued*

The Westbury Mayfair, A Luxury Collection Hotel London

★★★★★ 85% ◉ ◉ ◉ ◉ HOTEL PLAN 2 H1

tel: 020 7629 7755 **37 Conduit Street, Mayfair W1S 2YF**
email: reservations@westburymayfair.com **web:** www.westburymayfair.com
dir: *From Oxford Circus south down Regent Street, right onto Conduit Street, hotel at junction of Conduit Street and Bond Street.*

A well-known London favourite with an international clientele, The Westbury is located in the heart of the capital's finest shopping district, neighbour to the world's most exclusive fashion brands, restaurants and nightlife destinations. The standards of accommodation are very high throughout with the bedrooms and suites offering stunning panoramic views of picturesque Mayfair. Foodies and cocktail fanatics will find plenty to enjoy in-house – at the art deco designed Polo Bar, at Tsukiji Sushi for Japanese cuisine, and at the award-winning restaurant, Alyn Williams at The Westbury (4 AA Rosettes). Private dining is also available.

Rooms: 225 (102 family) ❧ **S** fr £279 **D** fr £279* **Facilities:** STV FTV WiFi ↻ Gym Live entertainment in the Polo Bar on Friday and Saturday evenings Fitness centre ♫ Xmas New Year **Conf:** Class 45 Board 35 Theatre 100 **Services:** Lift Night porter Air con **Parking:** 10 **Notes:** Civ Wed 90

Grosvenor House, A JW Marriott Hotel

★★★★★ 85% ◉ HOTEL PLAN 2 G1

GROSVENOR HOUSE
A JW MARRIOTT HOTEL
LONDON

tel: 020 7499 6363 **Park Lane W1K 7TN**
email: grosvenor.house@marriotthotels.com **web:** www.londongrosvenorhouse.co.uk
dir: *Centrally located on Park Lane, between Hyde Park Corner and Oxford Street.*

This quintessentially British hotel, overlooking Hyde Park, offers luxurious accommodation, warm hospitality and exemplary service that epitomises the fine hotel culture of London. The property boasts the largest ballroom in Europe, and there is a steakhouse and a cocktail bar. The Park Room and The Library make perfect settings for afternoon tea.

Rooms: 496 (10 family) ❧ **Facilities:** STV WiFi ↻ Gym Fitness centre ♫ Xmas New Year **Conf:** Class 800 Board 140 Theatre 1500 **Services:** Lift Night porter Air con **Parking:** 48 **Notes:** Civ Wed 1500

The London EDITION

★★★★★ 84% ◉ ◉ HOTEL PLAN 2 J2

tel: 020 7781 0000 **10 Berners Street W1T 3NP**
email: reservations.london@editionhotels.com **web:** www.editionhotels.com/london
dir: *Located in Fitzrovia on the edges of London's Soho neighbourhood, Central London.*

This hotel is the latest from the EDITION portfolio, transforming a landmark building with the company's innovation and truly great design. The public spaces are a dynamic fusion of past and present. Service is personal and friendly, ensuring a flawless and memorable stay. Outstanding cuisine is provided in the Berners Tavern, under direction of award-winning chef, Jason Atherton. The reservations-only Punch Room is a great place to unwind with a traditional punch bowl. Bedrooms are finished in either light oak or dark walnut creating a cosy, cabin-like feel, perhaps akin to that of a private yacht.

Rooms: 173 (17 family) ❧ **Facilities:** STV FTV WiFi ↻ Gym Xmas New Year **Conf:** Class 48 Board 30 Theatre 70 **Services:** Lift Night porter Air con

Hotel Café Royal

★★★★★ 84% HOTEL PLAN 2 J1

tel: 020 7406 3333 **68 Regent Street W1B 4DY**
email: enquiries@hotelcaferoyal.com **web:** www.hotelcaferoyal.com
dir: *Phone for directions.*

This impressive and imposing hotel has an enviable location in Piccadilly. Public rooms are impressive, and successfully blend modern and classic styles well. There is a popular café, the opulent Oscar Wilde Lounge for that traditional afternoon tea, and the Ten Room for all-day dining. The Green Bar specialises in cocktails and there is even a members' club. The contemporary, amply proporationed bedrooms are appointed to an extremely high standard, and have marble bathrooms. The luxurious spa is where guests can swim, use the gym or enjoy a range of treatments.

Rooms: 160 (111 family) ☊ **Facilities:** Spa STV FTV WiFi ⌕ HL ⊛ Gym ♫ Xmas New Year **Conf:** Class 60 Board 57 Theatre 160 **Services:** Lift Night porter Air con **Notes:** Civ Wed 120

The Montcalm

★★★★★ 83% HOTEL PLAN 2 F2

tel: 020 7402 4288 **Great Cumberland Place W1H 7TW**
email: reservations@montcalm.co.uk **web:** www.montcalm.co.uk
dir: *2 minutes walk north from Marble Arch station.*

The Montcalm is ideally situated in the heart of London, just a short walk from Marble Arch, Oxford Street, Park Lane, Mayfair, Hyde Park and Theatreland. The elegantly decorated bedrooms are tastefully appointed and have many thoughtful touches. Public areas include a contemporary lounge bar and The Crescent restaurant which serves modern European cuisine. The hotel has a range of private rooms and conference suites, as well as spa, sauna, steam room, gym and exercise pool.

Rooms: 143 (17 family) (7 GF) ☊ **Facilities:** Spa STV WiFi ⊛ Gym **Conf:** Class 250 Board 250 Theatre 500 **Services:** Lift Night porter Air con **Notes:** Civ Wed 60

The Arch London

★★★★★ 82% HOTEL PLAN 2 F2

tel: 020 7724 4700 **50 Great Cumberland Place W1H 7FD**
email: info@thearchlondon.com **web:** www.thearchlondon.com
dir: *200 yards from Marble Arch.*

Convenient for many of London's attractions and close to Marble Arch Tube station, stands this luxurious hotel. The Martini Library serves afternoon tea, along with light-bites all day, and Hunter 486 offers relaxed dining at lunch and dinner. Cocktails can be taken in Le Salon de Champagne. Bedrooms vary in size from the cosy standards to more spacious suites, but all are well equipped and high quality. There is also a well-equipped gym for guests' use.

Rooms: 82 (29 family) (8 GF) ☊ **S** fr £270 **D** fr £282* **Facilities:** STV FTV WiFi ⌕ Gym Xmas New Year **Conf:** Class 48 Board 18 Theatre 30 **Services:** Lift Night porter Air con

London Hilton on Park Lane

★★★★★ 82% HOTEL PLAN 4 G6

tel: 020 7493 8000 **22 Park Lane W1K 1BE**
email: reservations.parklane@hilton.com **web:** www.parklanehilton.com
dir: *From north: M1/A41 towards central London and West End. West along Oxford Street, into Park Lane. From south: A23 for central London and West End, cross Vauxhall Bridge (A202) and into Park Lane.*

Located in the heart of Park Lane, this landmark hotel offers a luxury environment overlooking Hyde Park. A dedicated team of staff is available to meet their guests' every need. Bedrooms are designed with quality appointments and luxury fabrics. Several eating options are available – from the renowned Galvin at Windows to the all-day dining of Podium Restaurant & Bar, which also serves a splendid afternoon tea.

Rooms: 453 (52 smoking) ☊ **Facilities:** Spa STV FTV WiFi ⌕ Gym ♫ Xmas New Year **Conf:** Class 600 Board 60 Theatre 1100 **Services:** Lift Night porter Air con **Parking:** 242 **Notes:** Civ Wed 1000

Le Meridien Piccadilly

★★★★★ 80% ⊛ HOTEL PLAN 2 J1

tel: 020 7734 8000 **21 Piccadilly W1J 0BH**
email: reservations.piccadilly@lemeridien.com **web:** www.lemeridien.com/piccadilly
dir: *100 metres from Piccadilly Circus.*

Situated in the heart of Piccadilly, this well established hotel is ideally located for the West End and Theatreland. The well-equipped, air-conditioned bedrooms, varying in shape and size, are modern and contemporary in style. Public areas include extensive leisure facilities, with a state-of-the-art gym, pool and sauna, the trendy Longitude 0° 8' cocktail bar, and the popular Terrace Restaurant which overlooks Piccadilly.

Rooms: 283 (16 family) ☊ **S** fr £250 **D** fr £250* **Facilities:** Spa STV WiFi ⌕ ⊛ Gym Squash ♫ Xmas New Year **Conf:** Class 160 Board 80 Theatre 250 **Services:** Lift Night porter Air con **Notes:** LB Civ Wed 200

INSPECTOR'S CHOICE

The Chesterfield Mayfair

★★★★ ◉◉ ⍾ HOTEL PLAN 4 H6

THE
RED CARNATION
HOTEL COLLECTION

tel: 020 7491 2622 **35 Charles Street, Mayfair W1J 5EB**
email: bookch@rchmail.com **web:** www.chesterfieldmayfair.com
dir: *Hyde Park Corner along Piccadilly, left into Half Moon Street. At end left and 1st right into Queens Street, then right into Charles Street.*

Quiet elegance and an atmosphere of exclusivity characterise this stylish Mayfair hotel where attentive, friendly service is paramount. The bedrooms, each with a marble-clad bathroom, have contemporary styles – perhaps with floral fabric walls, an African theme or with Savile Row stripes. In addition to these deluxe bedrooms there are 13 individually designed suites; some with four-poster beds and some with jacuzzis. The Butler's Restaurant is the fine dining option, and The Conservatory, with views over the garden, is just the place for cocktails, light lunches and afternoon teas. The hotel is air-conditioned throughout.

Rooms: 107 ☊ **Facilities:** STV FTV WiFi ⌕ ♫ **Conf:** Class 45 Board 45 Theatre 100 **Services:** Lift Night porter Air con **Notes:** LB Civ Wed 120

LONDON

W1 *continued*

The Mandeville Hotel

★★★★ 83% @ HOTEL PLAN 2 G2

tel: 020 7935 5599 **Mandeville Place W1U 2BE**
email: sales@mandeville.co.uk **web:** www.mandeville.co.uk
dir: *3 minutes walk from Bond Street tube station.*

This is a stylish and attractive boutique-style hotel with a very contemporary feel. Bedrooms are high in quality, are air-conditioned and large, and have very comfortable beds. One of the suites, The Penthouse, has a patio with views over London. The Reform Social & Grill offers award-winning modern British cuisine, and the cocktail bar is always popular.

Rooms: 142 (6 family) ♠ **Facilities:** STV FTV WiFi ⓑ Xmas New Year **Conf:** Class 20 Board 20 Theatre 40 **Services:** Lift Night porter Air con

DoubleTree by Hilton Hotel, Marble Arch

★★★★ 80% HOTEL PLAN 2 F2

tel: 020 7935 2361 **4 Bryanston Street W1H 7BY**
email: lonma.res@hilton.com **web:** www.londonmarblearch.doubletreebyhilton.com
dir: *Walking distance from Oxford Street, Marble Arch and Hyde Park.*

This historic 18th-century building has now been refurbished throughout and is centrally located just steps from Oxford Street, Marble Arch and Hyde Park. The bedrooms, including executive and deluxe club floor rooms, vary in size but all are smartly equipped, boast bright trendy soft furnishings and are air-conditioned; the en suites are equally modern and stylish. The public areas include the Indigo Bar & Lounge, and Fire & Spice Bar & Kitchen. The hotel offers free WiFi throughout.

Rooms: 122 (12 family) (5 GF) ♠ **Facilities:** STV FTV WiFi ⓑ HL Gym **Conf:** Class 45 Board 34 Theatre 90 **Services:** Lift Night porter Air con

Millennium Hotel London Mayfair

★★★★ 80% HOTEL PLAN 2 G1

tel: 020 7629 9400 **Grosvenor Square W1K 2HP**
email: reservations@millenniumhotels.co.uk **web:** www.millenniumhotels.co.uk
dir: *South side of Grosvenor Square, 5 minutes walk from Oxford Street and Bond Street stations.*

This hotel benefits from a prestigious location in the heart of Mayfair, close to Bond Street. The smart bedrooms are generally spacious and club-floor rooms have exclusive use of their own lounge with complimentary refreshments. A choice of bars and dining options is available along with conference facilities and a fitness room.

Rooms: 336 ♠ **Facilities:** STV FTV WiFi ⓑ HL Gym Fitness suite ♫ Xmas New Year **Conf:** Class 250 Board 70 Theatre 500 **Services:** Lift Night porter Air con **Notes:** LB Civ Wed 250

Park Plaza Sherlock Holmes

★★★★ 71% HOTEL PLAN 2 F3

tel: 020 7486 6161 & 0844 415 6740 (Calls cost 7p per minute plus your phone company's access charge) **108 Baker Street W1U 6LJ**
email: info@sherlockholmeshotel.com **web:** www.sherlockholmeshotel.com
dir: *From Marylebone Flyover into Marylebone Road. At Baker Street turn right for hotel on left.*

Chic and modern, this boutique-style hotel is near a number of London underground and rail stations. Public rooms include a popular bar, sited just inside the main entrance, and Sherlock's Grill, where the mesquite-wood burning stove is a feature of the cooking. The hotel also features an indoor health suite and a relaxing lounge.

Rooms: 119 (20 family) ♠ **Facilities:** STV WiFi ⓑ Gym Beauty treatment room Xmas **Conf:** Class 35 Board 30 Theatre 80 **Services:** Lift Night porter Air con **Notes:** Civ Wed 80

Z at Gloucester Place

AA Advertised PLAN 2 F3

tel: 020 3551 3719 **23 Gloucester Place W1U 8JF**
email: gloucesterplace@thezhotels.com **web:** www.thezhotels.com

Z at Gloucester Place is a conversion of five town houses – 23, 33, 51-55 Gloucester Place; reception and check-in are at No 51. The hotel is ideally located between Portman Square and Marylebone Road. There's a wide range of rooms – each has an en suite shower room, 48" Sky TV and complimentary WiFi. A comprehensive breakfast buffet is available and the hotel has a 24/7, full alcohol license.

Rooms: 114

The Z Hotel Soho

AA Advertised PLAN 3 A2

tel: 020 3551 3701 **17 Moor Street W1D 5AP**
email: soho@thezhotels.com **web:** www.thezhotels.com

The Z Hotel Soho offers a central London stay for an 'out-of-town price'. The conversion of 12 Georgian town houses combines classic architectural proportions with designer-led contemporary style. The bedrooms are situated around a central courtyard, set between Charing Cross Road and Old Compton Street. They have en suite wet rooms, crisp bed linen, 40" Sky TV and complimentary WiFi.

Rooms: 85 ♠ **Facilities:** STV FTV WiFi ⓑ HL **Services:** Lift Air con

LONDON

LONDON W2

HIGHLY RECOMMENDED

Roseate House London

★★★★ 85% ⊚ TOWN HOUSE HOTEL PLAN 2 D2

tel: 020 7479 6600 **3 Westbourne Terrace W2 3UL**
web: www.roseatehouselondon.com

The Royal Park Hotel was once private residences in Westbourne Terrace, now converted into an quintessential town house hotel within walking distance of Hyde Park and all major attractions and fashionable restaurants. The elegant public areas have been appointed in a classic yet contemporary style, while the bedrooms offer comfort and a reassuring homely feel. The award-winning restaurant offers a tapas-style menu for all dining occasions. Afternoon teas are served in bespoke china, and cocktails are expertly prepared in the evening. The rear terrace is a haven of tranquility. Limited parking is available.

Rooms: 48 (5 GF) 🐾 **D** fr £129* **Facilities:** WiFi 🏊 **Services:** Lift Night porter Air con **Parking:** 8

Novotel London Paddington

★★★★ 76% HOTEL PLAN 2 C3

NOVOTEL
HOTELS & RESORTS

tel: 020 7266 6000 **3 Kingdom Street, Paddington W2 6BD**
email: h6455@accor.com **web:** www.novotel.com
dir: *Easy access from Westway A40 and Bishops Bridge Road A4206.*

Located in the Paddington Central area, this hotel is easily accessible by road, and is only a few minutes' walk from Paddington Station. Ideal for business or leisure guests. The facilities include the Elements Restaurant, a bar, conference facilities, a swimming pool, sauna, plus steam and fitness rooms. An NCP car park is a five-minute walk away.

Rooms: 206 (24 family) **Facilities:** STV WiFi 🏊 ☺ Gym Steam room Sauna **Conf:** Class 70 Board 40 Theatre 150 **Services:** Lift Night porter

Hotel Indigo

★★★★ 75% HOTEL PLAN 2 D2

tel: 020 7706 4444 **16 London Street, Paddington W2 1HL**
email: info@indigopaddington.com **web:** www.indigopaddington.com

This smart hotel is located within a stone's throw of Paddington Station. Contemporary and stylish, bedrooms vary in size but are equipped with all modern extras; they boast high quality comfy beds, and en suites with power showers and quality toiletries. Delightful public areas include a restaurant, bar and a coffee shop offering tempting cakes. The cosy and tranquil seating area at the back of the property can be accessed from the first floor's corridor. Parking is available at the nearby public car park.

Rooms: 64 🐾 **S** fr £99 **D** fr £119* **Facilities:** STV FTV WiFi HL Gym **Conf:** Class 22 Board 22 Theatre 30 **Services:** Lift Night porter Air con

Mercure London Hyde Park

★★★★ 75% HOTEL PLAN 2 D2

Mercure
HOTELS

tel: 020 7262 6699 & 7835 2000 **8-14 Talbot Square W2 1TS**
email: stay@mercurehydepark.com
web: www.accorhotels.com/gb/hotel-A002-mercure-london-hyde-park-hotel/index.shtml
dir: *3 minute walk from Paddington Station.*

This recently refurbished hotel located just a two minute walk from Paddington Tube Station offers guests very modern and stylish accommodation which is well equipped for both business and leisure guests alike. Some of the first floor rooms have private terraces with excellent views over the central gardens. The hotel has a new restaurant, London Street Brasserie, which is open for breakfast, lunch and dinner.

Rooms: 72 (5 family) (5 GF) **S** fr £159 **D** fr £169* **Facilities:** WiFi 🏊 Gym **Conf:** Class 16 Board 26 Theatre 30 **Services:** Lift Night porter Air con

Lancaster Gate Hotel

★★★ 78% HOTEL PLAN 2 C1

tel: 020 7479 2500 & 7262 5090 **66 Lancaster Gate W2 3NA**
email: info@lghhydepark.co.uk **web:** www.lancastergatehotelhydepark.co.uk
dir: *Just off Bayswater Road.*

This hotel offers a convenient location between Oxford Street and Knightsbridge and is also close to Hyde Park and Kensington Gardens. Bedrooms are well equipped with broadband and safes, as well as TVs with a wide selection of channels. There is a comfortable bar and stylish restaurant, and the hotel also has a range of meeting rooms.

Rooms: 188 (7 family) (13 GF) (5 smoking) 🐾 **S** fr £69 **D** fr £74* **Facilities:** STV FTV WiFi Off-site leisure facilities available **Conf:** Class 24 Board 28 Theatre 50 **Services:** Lift Night porter Air con

Mitre House Hotel

★★ 76% METRO HOTEL PLAN 2 D2

tel: 020 7723 8040 **178-184 Sussex Gardens, Hyde Park W2 1TU**
email: reservations@mitrehousehotel.com **web:** www.mitrehousehotel.com
dir: *Parallel to Bayswater Road and one block from Paddington Station.*

This family-run hotel continues to offers a warm welcome and attentive service. It is ideally located, close to Paddington Station and near the West End and its major attractions. Bedrooms include a number of family suites and there is a lounge bar. Limited parking is available.

Rooms: 69 (7 family) (7 GF) (69 smoking) **Facilities:** STV WiFi 🏊 **Services:** Lift Night porter **Parking:** 20

Royal Lancaster London

AA Advertised ⊚⊚ PLAN 2 D1

tel: 020 7551 6000 **Lancaster Terrace W2 2TY**
email: info@royallancaster.com **web:** www.royallancaster.com
dir: *Adjacent to Lancaster Gate tube station, 5 minutes from Paddington Heathrow Express, 10 minutes from A40, opposite Hyde Park.*

Located adjacent to Hyde Park, this large hotel offers a wide range of facilities. There are many room types; higher floors have excellent panoramic views of the city and park, and the suites are truly impressive. The hotel also offers two contrasting award-winning restaurants – the contemporary Island Grill, and Nipa Thai restaurant with authentic Thai cuisine. There are spacious state-of-the-art, flexible conference and banqueting facilities, a 24-hour business centre and secure parking. This is an environmentally conscious hotel which has instigated many initiatives including a honey farm on the roof.

Rooms: 411 (40 family) (28 smoking) 🐾 **S** fr £259 **D** fr £259* **Facilities:** STV FTV WiFi 🏊 Gym Xmas New Year **Conf:** Class 550 Board 46 Theatre 1000 **Services:** Lift Night porter Air con **Parking:** 20 **Notes:** Civ Wed 1000

LONDON

LONDON W4

Clayton Hotel Chiswick

★★★★ 79% HOTEL PLAN 1 C3

tel: 020 8996 5200 **626 Chiswick High Road W4 5RY**
email: info.chiswick@claytonhotels.com **web:** www.claytonhotelchiswick.com
dir: *Located 0.2 mile from Chiswick roundabout/London M4.*

This stylish, modern hotel is conveniently located for Heathrow and central London, with Gunnersbury tube station just a few minutes' walk away. Airy, spacious public areas include a modern restaurant, a popular bar and excellent meeting facilities. Fully air-conditioned bedrooms are stylish and extremely well appointed with broadband, laptop safes and LCD TVs. All boast spacious, modern bathrooms, many with walk-in rain showers.

Rooms: 227 (10 family) (9 GF) **Facilities:** STV FTV WiFi ॐ Gym Xmas New Year
Conf: Class 45 Board 40 Theatre 300 **Services:** Lift Night porter Air con **Parking:** 100
Notes: LB Civ Wed 300

Premier Inn London Chiswick

Premier Inn

BUDGET HOTEL PLAN 1 D3

tel: 0871 527 9728 (Calls cost 13p per minute plus your phone company's access charge) **Hogarth Roundabout, Great West Road W4 2TH**
web: www.premierinn.com
dir: *Continue to end of M4 onto A4. At roundabout take 5th exit onto A4 (Hogarth Lane). Take first left.*

High quality, budget accommodation ideal for both families and business travellers. Spacious, en suite bedrooms feature free WiFi and tea and coffee making facilities, and in most hotels, Freeview TV is also available. The adjacent family restaurant features a wide and varied menu.

Rooms: 167

LONDON W5

Premier Inn London Ealing

Premier Inn

BUDGET HOTEL PLAN 1 C3

tel: 0871 527 9368 (Calls cost 13p per minute plus your phone company's access charge) **22-24 Uxbridge Road, Ealing W5 2SR**
web: www.premierinn.com
dir: *M4 junction 1, A406 (signed North Circular and M1). Left onto A4020 (signed Ealing and Southall). Hotel on right after Ealing Broadway tube station.*

High quality, budget accommodation ideal for both families and business travellers. Spacious, en suite bedrooms feature free WiFi and tea and coffee making facilities, and in most hotels, Freeview TV is also available. The adjacent family restaurant features a wide and varied menu.

Rooms: 165

Premier Inn London Hanger Lane

Premier Inn

BUDGET HOTEL PLAN 1 C4

tel: 0871 527 8346 (Calls cost 13p per minute plus your phone company's access charge) **1-6 Ritz Parade, Ealing W5 3RA**
web: www.premierinn.com
dir: *M4 junction 2, A4 follow North Circular/A406 signs, for 0.5 mile. Take A406 for approximately 2.5 miles. Right into Ashbourne Road, immediately left into Ashbourne Parade, right into Ritz Parade. Hotel on right.*

Rooms: 167

LONDON W6

Novotel London West

★★★★ 76% HOTEL PLAN 1 D3

tel: 020 8741 1555 **1 Shortlands W6 8DR**
email: H0737@accor.com **web:** www.novotellondonwest.co.uk
dir: *M4 (A4) and A316 junction at Hogarth roundabout. Along Great West Road, left for Hammersmith before flyover. On Hammersmith Bridge Road to roundabout, take 5th exit. 1st left into Shortlands, 1st left to hotel main entrance.*

A Hammersmith landmark, this substantial hotel is a popular base for both business and leisure travellers. Spacious, air-conditioned bedrooms have a good range of extras and many have additional beds, making them suitable for families. The comfort of the bedrooms is complemented by a choice of dining options – the Aroma Restaurant and the Artisan Grill. The hotel also has its own car park, business centre and shop, and boasts one of the largest convention centres in Europe.

Rooms: 630 (148 family) **S** fr £98 **D** fr £98* **Facilities:** FTV WiFi ⌨ HL Gym Xmas New Year **Conf:** Class 540 Board 75 Theatre 1000 **Services:** Lift Night porter **Parking:** 240 **Notes:** LB Civ Wed 1000

Premier Inn London Hammersmith

Premier Inn

BUDGET HOTEL PLAN 1 D3

tel: 0871 527 8660 (Calls cost 13p per minute plus your phone company's access charge) **255 King Street, Hammersmith W6 9LU**
web: www.premierinn.com
dir: *From central London on A4 to Hammersmith, follow A315 towards Chiswick.*

High quality, budget accommodation ideal for both families and business travellers. Spacious, en suite bedrooms feature free WiFi and tea and coffee making facilities, and in most hotels, Freeview TV is also available. The adjacent family restaurant features a wide and varied menu.

Rooms: 119

LONDON W8

Royal Garden Hotel

★★★★★  HOTEL PLAN 4 B5

tel: 020 7937 8000 **2-24 Kensington High Street W8 4PT**
email: reservations@royalgardenhotel.co.uk **web:** www.royalgardenhotel.co.uk
dir: *Adjacent to Kensington Palace.*

This landmark hotel, just a short walk from the Royal Albert Hall, has airy, stylish public rooms that include the Park Terrace Restaurant, Lounge and Bar; Bertie's cocktail bar and the contemporary 10th-floor Min Jiang Restaurant; the latter offers authentic Chinese cuisine and enjoys breathtaking views of the city. The stylish and contemporary bedrooms are equipped with up-to-date facilities and include a number of spacious, air-conditioned rooms and suites with super views over Kensington Gardens. All rooms have high-speed internet access, interactive TVs and triple-glazed windows as standard.

Rooms: 394 (59 family) ⌨ **S** fr £220 **D** fr £220* **Facilities:** STV FTV WiFi ⌨ HL Gym Health club Treatment rooms ♫ Xmas New Year **Conf:** Class 320 Board 100 Theatre 550 **Services:** Lift Night porter Air con **Parking:** 200 **Notes:** Civ Wed 400

See advert opposite

W8 *continued*

The Milestone Hotel and Residences

★★★★★ ◉◉ ◎ HOTEL PLAN 4 B5

THE
RED CARNATION
HOTEL COLLECTION

---

tel: 020 7917 1000 **1 Kensington Court W8 5DL**
email: bookms@rchmail.com **web:** www.milestonehotel.com
dir: *From Warwick Road right into Kensington High Street. Hotel 400 yards past Kensington tube station. Adjacent to Kensington Palace.*

This delightful town house enjoys a wonderful location opposite Kensington Palace and is near some seriously elegant shops. The individually themed bedrooms include a selection of stunning suites that are equipped with every conceivable extra – fruit, fresh flowers, cookies, chocolates, complimentary newspapers to name but a few, and 24-hour butler service in the Deluxe Suites. Up-to-the-minute technology includes high speed WiFi, iPod docks and interactive Sky TV. Public areas include the luxurious Park Lounge where afternoon tea is served, the delightful split-level Stables Bar, a conservatory, the sumptuous Cheneston's Restaurant and a fully-equipped, small gym, resistance pool and spa treatment room.

Rooms: 62 (12 family) (1 GF) ✆ **S** fr £375 **D** fr £415* **Facilities:** STV FTV WiFi ⚲ HL ⊕ Gym Beauty treatment room Sauna Yoga ♫ Xmas New Year **Conf:** Class 20 Board 20 Theatre 50 **Services:** Lift Night porter Air con **Parking:** 1 **Notes:** LB Civ Wed 30

Copthorne Tara Hotel London Kensington

★★★★ 77% HOTEL PLAN 4 B4

MILLENNIUM
HOTELS AND RESORTS

---

tel: 020 7937 7211 **Scarsdale Place, Wrights Lane W8 5SR**
email: reservations.tara@millenniumhotels.co.uk **web:** www.millenniumhotels.com
dir: *From Kensington High Street into Wrights Lane. Note for sat nav use W8 5SY.*

This expansive hotel is ideally placed for Kensington High Street shops and tube station. Smart public areas include a trendy coffee shop, a gym, a stylish brasserie and bar, plus extensive conference facilities. Bedrooms include several well-equipped rooms for less mobile guests, in addition to a number of Connoisseur rooms that have the use of a club lounge as one of its many complimentary facilities.

Rooms: 833 (3 family) ✆ **Facilities:** FTV WiFi ⚲ HL Fitness room Xmas New Year **Conf:** Class 160 Board 90 Theatre 280 **Services:** Lift Night porter Air con **Parking:** 126 **Notes:** Civ Wed 280

London Lodge Hotel

★★★ 75% TOWN HOUSE HOTEL PLAN 4 A3

---

tel: 020 7244 8444 **134-136 Lexham Gardens, Kensington W8 6JE**
email: info@londonlodgehotel.com **web:** www.londonlodgehotel.com
dir: *Located in the heart of Kensington, close to Olympia exhibition centre. At junction of A4 and Cromwell Road.*

The London Lodge Hotel was created from two beautiful Victorian town houses, sympathetically converted to form a home-away-from-home. It is located in a quiet residential area of Kensington, close to public transport and within walking distance of major attractions. All bedrooms are nicely appointed and offer all modern facilities.

Rooms: 28 (1 family) (6 GF) **S** fr £125 **D** fr £165* **Facilities:** FTV WiFi ⚲ **Conf:** Class 15 Board 10 Theatre 25 **Services:** Lift Night porter Air con

---

K West Hotel & Spa

★★★★ 80% HOTEL PLAN 1 D3

---

tel: 020 8008 6600 **Richmond Way W14 0AX**
email: info@k-west.co.uk **web:** www.k-west.co.uk
dir: *From A40(M) take Shepherd's Bush exit. At Holland Park roundabout 3rd exit. 1st left and left again. Hotel straight ahead.*

This stylish, contemporary hotel is conveniently located for Notting Hill, the exhibition halls and the BBC; Bond Street is only a 10-minute tube journey away. Funky, minimalist public areas include a trendy lobby bar and mezzanine-style restaurant. Spacious bedrooms and suites are extremely well appointed and offer luxurious bedding and a host of thoughtful extras such as CD and DVD players. WiFi is available throughout. The spa offers a comprehensive range of health, beauty and relaxation treatments.

Rooms: 219 (31 GF) ✆ **S** fr £109 **D** fr £109* **Facilities:** Spa STV FTV WiFi ⚲ Gym Hydrotherapy pool Sauna Steam room Snow room Solarium ♫ Xmas New Year **Conf:** Class 20 Board 25 Theatre 55 **Services:** Lift Night porter Air con **Parking:** 50 **Notes:** LB

Rosewood London

★★★★★ ◉◉ ◎ HOTEL PLAN 3 C3

tel: 020 7781 8888 **252 High Holborn WC1V 7EN**
email: london@rosewoodhotels.com **web:** www.rosewoodhotels.com/london
dir: *200 metres east from Holborn underground station.*

Situated in the heart of Holborn, this impressive hotel was originally built from 1912–1914 and designed by H Percy Monckton in an ostentatious Edwardian style. Today, the interior design is striking, stylish and unconventional in parts. Spacious public areas include the very popular Scarfes Bar, Holborn Dining Room and the elegant Mirror Room salon, complete with stunning flower displays, where afternoon tea is served. The contemporary accommodation is luxurious with many super features – 46" LED TVs, Nespresso coffee machines, a sound system with iPod and iPhone docking stations, pillow selection and twice-daily housekeeping services; the impressive suite includes even more facilities.

Rooms: 306 (24 family) (10 smoking) ✆ **S** fr £390 **D** fr £390* **Facilities:** Spa STV FTV WiFi ⚲ Gym Amethyst steam rooms Sauna Relaxation lounge ♫ Xmas New Year **Conf:** Class 285 Board 82 Theatre 430 **Services:** Lift Night porter Air con **Parking:** 10 **Notes:** LB Civ Wed 340

HIGHLY RECOMMENDED

The Montague on the Gardens

★★★★ 87% HOTEL PLAN 3 B3

THE RED CARNATION HOTEL COLLECTION

tel: 020 7637 1001 **15 Montague Street, Bloomsbury WC1B 5BJ**
email: bookmt@rchmail.com **web:** www.montaguehotel.com
dir: *Just off Russell Square, adjacent to British Museum.*

This stylish hotel, a Georgian town house, is situated right next to the British Museum and boasts an alfresco terrace overlooking a delightful garden. Other public rooms include the Blue Door Bistro, a bar, a lounge and a conservatory where traditional afternoon teas are served. The bedrooms are beautifully appointed and range from split-level suites to more compact rooms.

Rooms: 100 (10 family) (19 GF) 🐾 **S** fr £192 **D** fr £216* **Facilities:** STV FTV WiFi ⌖ HL Gym 🎵 Xmas New Year **Conf:** Class 50 Board 50 Theatre 120 **Services:** Lift Night porter Air con **Notes:** LB Civ Wed 90

Crowne Plaza London - Kings Cross

★★★★ 78% HOTEL PLAN 3 C5

CROWNE PLAZA HOTELS & RESORTS

tel: 020 7833 3900 **1 Kings Cross Road WC1X 9HX**
email: reservations@cplondon.co.uk **web:** www.ihg.com/crowneplaza/hotels
dir: *On corner of King Cross Road and Calthorpe Street.*

Conveniently located for Kings Cross station and The City, this modern hotel offers smart, spacious air-conditioned accommodation with a wide range of facilities. There are versatile meeting rooms, a bar, a well-equipped fitness centre and a choice of restaurants including one serving Indian cuisine.

Rooms: 405 (163 family) (126 smoking) 🐾 **Facilities:** Spa STV FTV WiFi HL ⌖ Gym **Conf:** Class 120 Board 30 Theatre 220 **Services:** Lift Night porter Air con **Parking:** 14

The Principal London

PRINCIPAL

★★★★ 76% HOTEL PLAN 3 B4

tel: 020 7123 5000 **Russell Square WC1B 5BE**
email: londonreservations@theprincipalhotel.com
web: www.phcompany.com/principal/london-hotel
dir: *From A501 into Woburn Place. Hotel 500 metres on left.*

This stunning landmark Grade II, Victorian hotel has been restored and updated to its former glory. Located on Russell Square and within easy walking distance of the West End and London's theatre district. Spacious public areas include the impressive foyer with a magnificent restored mosaic floor, while a choice of food and beverage areas include the popular neighbourhood restaurant, Neptune, Fitz's cocktail bar and lounge, (the impressive social hub of the hotel), the palm court and the all-day coffee house/wine bar Burr & Co. A true landmark property, brought up-to-date through considered refurbishment.

Rooms: 334 (2 family) 🐾 **S** fr £195 **D** fr £225* **Facilities:** STV FTV WiFi ⌖ HL Gym **Conf:** Class 160 Board 75 Theatre 370 **Services:** Lift Night porter Air con **Notes:** Civ Wed 300

hub by Premier Inn London Goodge Street

BUDGET HOTEL PLAN 2 K3

Premier Inn

tel: 0333 321 3104 (Calls cost 13p per minute plus your phone company's access charge) **Brook House, Torrington Place WC1E 7HN**
web: www.premierinn.com
dir: *Phone for directions.*

This modern hotel offers self-check-in kiosks, superfast free WiFi, and cleverly designed and compact bedrooms with all the entertainment and comfort you need: 40" flat-screen smart TV, temperature and lighting controlled by a special Premier Inn app, Hypnos bed, and monsoon shower. The Deli+Bar is open for grab-and-go breakfast boxes, pastries, grilled sandwiches, Costa Coffee, beer, wine and more.

Rooms: 168

Premier Inn London Euston

BUDGET HOTEL PLAN 3 A5

tel: 0871 527 8656 (Calls cost 13p per minute plus your phone company's access charge) **1 Duke's Road, Euston WC1H 9PJ**
web: www.premierinn.com
dir: *On corner of Euston Road and Duke's Road, between Kings Cross/St Pancras and Euston stations.*

High quality, budget accommodation ideal for both families and business travellers. Spacious, en suite bedrooms feature free WiFi and tea and coffee making facilities, and in most hotels, Freeview TV is also available. The adjacent family restaurant features a wide and varied menu.

Rooms: 265

Premier Inn London Holborn

BUDGET HOTEL PLAN 3 C3

Premier Inn

tel: 0871 527 9496 (Calls cost 13p per minute plus your phone company's access charge) **27 Red Lion Street WC1R 4PS**
web: www.premierinn.com
dir: *Nearest tube: Holborn and Chancery Lane.*

Rooms: 150

Follow us on twitter
@TheAA_Lifestyle

LONDON WC2

INSPECTOR'S CHOICE

The Savoy

★★★★★ @ ≗ HOTEL PLAN 3 C1

tel: 020 7836 4343 **Strand WC2R 0EU**
email: savoy@fairmont.com **web:** www.fairmont.com/savoy
dir: *Halfway along The Strand between Trafalgar Square and Aldwych and steps from Covent Garden.*

The Savoy has been at the forefront of the London hotel scene since it opened in 1889, and is located on the banks of the Thames and within walking distance of vibrant Covent Garden. Rooms and suites are decorated in either Edwardian or art deco style, and vary in style and size. Many overlook the river. The Savoy Grill and American Bar remain as well-loved favourites; Kaspar's offers informal yet luxury all-day dining; the Thames Foyer is renowned for its afternoon teas; and the Beaufort Bar offers cocktails that push the boundaries of mixology. Immaculately presented staff offer excellent standards of hospitality.

Rooms: 267 (5 family) (10 smoking) ✿ **Facilities:** Spa STV FTV WiFi ⇘ ⊛ Gym Fitness gallery Health and beauty treatments Personal training ♬ Xmas New Year **Conf:** Class 300 Board 60 Theatre 500 **Services:** Lift Night porter Air con **Parking:** 20 **Notes:** Civ Wed 300

Premier Inn London Leicester Square

BUDGET HOTEL PLAN 3 A1

tel: 0871 527 9334 (Calls cost 13p per minute plus your phone company's access charge) **1 Leicester Place, Leicester Square WC2H 7BP**
web: www.premierinn.com
dir: *Nearest tube station: Leicester Square. From Cranbourne Street into Leicester Square. Hotel on right (Leicester Place). Car parks: China Town and Witcombe Street, approximately 10 minutes walk.*

High quality, budget accommodation ideal for both families and business travellers. Spacious, en suite bedrooms feature free WiFi and tea and coffee making facilities, and in most hotels, Freeview TV is also available. The adjacent family restaurant features a wide and varied menu.

Rooms: 83

The Z Hotel Piccadilly

AA Advertised PLAN 3 A1

tel: 020 3551 3720 **2 Orange Street WC2H 7DF**
email: piccadilly@thezhotels.com **web:** www.thezhotels.com
dir: *Phone for directions.*

Z Piccadilly is just a short walk from Piccadilly Circus, and offers a West End location for an out-of-town price. This is a converted office building, with 112 bedrooms arranged over lower ground, ground and five upper floors. Each room has an en suite wet room, crisp bed linen, 48" TV with Sky, and complimentary WiFi.

Rooms: 112 (10 GF) ✿ **Facilities:** STV FTV WiFi **Services:** Lift Night porter Air con

LONDON GATEWAY MOTORWAY SERVICE AREA (M1)   Map 6 TQ19

Ramada London North - M1

WELCOMEBREAK

AA Advertised

tel: 020 8906 7000 **Welcome Break Services Area, M1 junction 2–4 NW7 3HU**
email: ramadaln@welcomebreak.co.uk **web:** www.welcomebreak.co.uk
dir: *On M1 between junction 2/4 northbound and southbound.*

This modern building offers accommodation in smart, spacious and well-equipped bedrooms, suitable for families and business travellers, and all with en suite bathrooms. Continental breakfast is available and other refreshments may be taken at the nearby family restaurant.

Rooms: 200 (190 family) (80 GF) (20 smoking) **Facilities:** FTV WiFi ⇘ Gym **Conf:** Class 30 Board 50 Theatre 70 **Services:** Lift Night porter Air con **Parking:** 160 **Notes:** Civ Wed 80

LONGHORSLEY
Northumberland   Map 21 NZ19

Macdonald Linden Hall, Golf & Country Club
 MACDONALD HOTELS & RESORTS

★★★★ 77% @ HOTEL

tel: 01670 500000 **NE65 8XF**
email: lindenhall@macdonald-hotels.co.uk **web:** www.macdonaldhotels.co.uk
dir: Northbound on A1 take A697 towards Coldstream. Hotel 1 mile north of Longhorsley.

This impressive Georgian mansion lies in 400 acres of parkland and offers extensive indoor and outdoor leisure facilities including a golf course. The elegant Dobson Restaurant provides a fine dining experience, or guests can eat in the more informal Linden Tree Pub. The good-sized bedrooms have a restrained modern style. The team of staff are enthusiastic and professional.

Rooms: 50 (3 family) (16 GF) **Facilities:** Spa STV FTV WiFi ♦ ⌖ ♿ 18 ♨ ⛳ Gym Steam room Sauna Xmas New Year **Conf:** Class 120 Board 50 Theatre 300 **Services:** Lift Night porter **Parking:** 300 **Notes:** Civ Wed 120

LOOE
Cornwall & Isles Of Scilly   Map 2 SX25

Trelaske Hotel & Restaurant

★★★ 83% @@ HOTEL

tel: 01503 262159 **Polperro Road PL13 2JS**
email: info@trelaske.co.uk **web:** www.trelaske.co.uk
dir: B252 signed Looe. Over Looe bridge signed Polperro. 1.9 miles, hotel signed on left, turn right.

This small and welcoming hotel offers comfortable accommodation, professional and friendly service plus award-winning food. Set in its own very well-tended and pretty grounds, it is only two miles from Polperro and Looe.

Rooms: 7 (4 annexe) (2 family) (2 GF) **S** fr £110 **D** fr £130 (including breakfast)* **Facilities:** FTV WiFi **Conf:** Class 30 Board 40 Theatre 100 **Parking:** 50 **Notes:** LB Closed 17 October to 1 March

Hannafore Point Hotel & Spa
THE INDEPENDENTS HOTEL ASSOCIATION

★★★ 77% HOTEL

tel: 01503 263273 **Marine Drive, West Looe PL13 2DG**
email: stay@hannaforepointhotel.com **web:** www.hannaforepointhotel.com
dir: A38, left onto A385 to Looe. Over bridge turn left. Hotel 0.5 mile on left.

With panoramic coastal views of St George's Island around to Rame Head, this popular hotel provides a warm welcome. The wonderful view is certainly a feature of the spacious restaurant and bar, creating a scenic backdrop for both dinners and breakfasts. Additional facilities include a heated indoor pool and a gym.

Rooms: 37 (5 family) **S** fr £64 **D** fr £128 (including breakfast)* **Facilities:** Spa FTV WiFi ♦ ♿ Gym Steam room Sauna Hydropool and shower ♫ Xmas New Year **Conf:** Class 80 Board 40 Theatre 120 **Services:** Lift Night porter **Parking:** 32 **Notes:** LB Civ Wed 150

LOUGHBOROUGH
Leicestershire   Map 11 SK51

Burleigh Court Hotel and Conference Centre

★★★★ A HOTEL

tel: 01509 211515 **Off Ashby Road LE11 3TD**
email: info@welcometoimago.com **web:** www.burleigh-court.co.uk
dir: M1 junction 23 then A512 Ashby Road to Loughborough. At 1st roundabout right into Holywell Way, signed Burleigh Court and Holywell Park. Obtain visitors badge from gatehouse then turn left at next roundabout and enter Loughborough University Campus using West Entrance. Hotel car park on 2nd right.

Set in the grounds of Loughborough University, with modern design, clean lines, and bright, airy public areas, Burleigh Court is an ideal choice for anyone planning a conference in the East Midlands or visiting the university. Accommodation ranges from luxury suites and executive rooms to high quality, economy lodge rooms. Guests can enjoy extensive spa facilities, with a well-equipped gym, a swimming pool, a whirlpool spa, a steam room, and a sauna. The conference facilities are extensive.

Rooms: 225 (40 annexe) (8 family) (79 GF) **S** fr £98 **D** fr £110 (including breakfast)* **Facilities:** Spa FTV WiFi ♦ HL ♿ Gym **Conf:** Class 90 Board 56 Theatre 200 **Services:** Lift Night porter **Parking:** 189 **Notes:** Closed 25–30 December Civ Wed 200

Link Hotel

★★★ 79% HOTEL

tel: 01509 211800 **New Ashby Road LE11 4EX**
email: info@linkhotel.co.uk **web:** www.linkhotelloughborough.co.uk
dir: M1 junction 23, follow A512 signed Loughborough. Continue on A512, turn left onto slip road to reach hotel.

Ideally located, close to Loughborough University, and only half a mile away from junction 23 on the M1, this hotel offers modern and stylish accommodation, with warm hospitality at the forefront. A modern restaurant, bar and lounge area are available. A small gym is also on site.

Rooms: 94 (12 family) (47 GF) **S** fr £79 **D** fr £89 (including breakfast)* **Facilities:** FTV WiFi ♦ Gym Xmas New Year **Conf:** Class 40 Board 30 Theatre 180 **Services:** Night porter Air con **Parking:** 164 **Notes:** Closed 25–27 December Civ Wed 154

Premier Inn Loughborough
 Premier Inn

BUDGET HOTEL

tel: 0871 527 9314 (Calls cost 13p per minute plus your phone company's access charge) **Southfields Road LE11 9SA**
web: www.premierinn.com
dir: M1 junction 23, A512 towards Loughborough. Left into Greenclose Lane. Right onto A6, Right into Southfield Road, hotel on left.

High quality, budget accommodation ideal for both families and business travellers. Spacious, en suite bedrooms feature free WiFi and tea and coffee making facilities, and in most hotels, Freeview TV is also available. The adjacent family restaurant features a wide and varied menu.

Rooms: 112

LOUTH
Lincolnshire

Map 17 TF38

HIGHLY RECOMMENDED

Brackenborough Hotel

★★★ 87% HOTEL

tel: 01507 609169 **Cordeaux Corner, Brackenborough LN11 0SZ**
email: reception@brackenborough.co.uk **web:** www.oakridgehotels.co.uk
dir: On A16, Louth to Grimsby road, 1 mile from Louth.

In an idyllic setting amid well-tended gardens, this hotel offers attractive bedrooms, each individually decorated with co-ordinated furnishings and many extras. The award-winning bistro offers informal dining and the menu is based on locally sourced produce. The hotel specialises in weddings, events and private functions and has excellent conference facilities. Free WiFi is available. Guests have free access to state-of-the-art leisure facilities (less than half a mile away) that includes a swimming pool, tennis courts and a gym.

Rooms: 24 (2 family) (6 GF) **S** fr £66 **D** fr £80 (including breakfast)*
Facilities: FTV WiFi Gym Xmas New Year **Conf:** Class 150 Board 50 Theatre 300 **Services:** Night porter Air con **Parking:** 90 **Notes:** LB Civ Wed 220

Best Western Plus Kenwick Park Hotel

Best Western PLUS

★★★ 79% HOTEL

tel: 01507 608806 **Kenwick Park Estate LN11 8NR**
email: enquiries@kenwick-park.co.uk **web:** www.kenwick-park.co.uk
dir: A16 from Grimsby, then A157 Mablethorpe/Manby Road. Hotel 400 metres down hill on right.

This elegant Georgian house is situated on the 320-acre Kenwick Park estate, overlooking its own golf course. Bedrooms are spacious and comfortable, and provide modern facilities. Public areas include a restaurant and a conservatory bar that overlook the grounds. There is also an extensive leisure centre and state-of-the-art conference and banqueting facilities.

Rooms: 34 (5 annexe) (10 family) (11 GF) **S** fr £75 **D** fr £99* **Facilities:** Spa FTV WiFi 18 Gym Health and beauty centre Xmas New Year **Conf:** Class 40 Board 90 Theatre 250 **Services:** Night porter **Parking:** 100 **Notes:** LB Civ Wed 200

LOWER BARTLE
Lancashire

Map 18 SD43

Bartle Hall Hotel

★★★★ 78% HOTEL

tel: 01772 690506 **Lea Lane PR4 0HA**
email: info@bartlehall.co.uk **web:** www.bartlehall.co.uk
dir: M6 junction 32 into Tom Benson Way, follow signs for Woodplumpton/Bartle Hall.

Ideally situated between Preston and Blackpool, Bartle Hall Hotel is within easy access of the M6 and the Lake District. Set in its own extensive grounds, the hotel offers comfortable and well-equipped accommodation. The restaurant cuisine uses local produce and there is a large comfortable bar and lounge. There are also extensive conference facilities, and the hotel is a popular wedding venue.

Rooms: 15 (2 annexe) (3 family) (2 GF) **Facilities:** FTV WiFi HL Xmas New Year **Conf:** Class 50 Board 40 Theatre 200 **Services:** Night porter **Parking:** 150 **Notes:** LB Civ Wed 130

LOWER BEEDING
West Sussex

Map 6 TQ22

South Lodge, an Exclusive Hotel

AA Advertised

EXCLUSIVE

tel: 01403 891711 **Brighton Road RH13 6PS**
email: enquiries@southlodgehotel.co.uk **web:** www.exclusive.co.uk
dir: A23, onto B2110. Right, through Handcross to A281 junction. Left, hotel on right.

This impeccably presented 19th-century lodge with stunning views of the rolling South Downs is an ideal retreat. There is the traditional and elegant Camellia Restaurant; as well as a more innovative take on the chef's table concept, The Pass – a mini-restaurant within the kitchen itself. Guests can take a tour of the restored Victorian wine cellar, either with a sommelier or on their own. The elegant lounge is popular for afternoon teas. Bedrooms are individually designed with character and quality throughout. The conference facilities are impressive.

Rooms: 85 (11 family) (19 GF) **D** fr £175.50 (including breakfast)* **Facilities:** STV WiFi Fishing Gym Mountain bikes Archery Clay pigeon shooting Wine tasting Xmas New Year **Conf:** Class 100 Board 50 Theatre 180 **Services:** Lift Night porter **Parking:** 200 **Notes:** Civ Wed 130

LOWER SLAUGHTER
Gloucestershire

Map 10 SP12

INSPECTOR'S CHOICE

The Slaughters Manor House

BROWNSWORD
THE HOTELS

★★★★ COUNTRY HOUSE HOTEL

tel: 01451 820456 **GL54 2HP**
email: info@slaughtersmanor.co.uk **web:** www.slaughtersmanor.co.uk
dir: Exit A429 signed 'The Slaughters'. Manor 0.5 mile on right on entering village.

The Slaughters Manor House offers a contemporary interpretation of country living, boasting well defined rooms, including a snug, billiards room, library and lounge, and a bar in partnership with the Sipsmith distillery. These alluring rooms are unified by the use of natural materials and finishes and a simple colour palette. The elegant restaurant is run by award-winning head chef Nik Chappell whose dishes are often picture-perfect explorations of flavour and texture.

Rooms: 19 (8 annexe) (5 family) (4 GF) **Facilities:** STV FTV WiFi Xmas New Year **Conf:** Class 40 Board 30 Theatre 70 **Services:** Night porter **Parking:** 20 **Notes:** Civ Wed 74

LOWESTOFT
Suffolk   Map 13 TM59

HIGHLY RECOMMENDED

Ivy House Country Hotel

★★★ 87% ◉◉ HOTEL

tel: 01502 501353 **Ivy Lane, Beccles Road NR33 8HY**
email: info@ivyhousecountryhotel.co.uk **web:** www.ivyhousecountryhotel.co.uk
dir: *On A146 southwest of Oulton Broad turn into Ivy Lane beside Esso petrol station. Over railway bridge, follow private drive.*

A peacefully located, family-run hotel set in 21 acres of mature, landscaped grounds, just a short walk from Oulton Broad. Public rooms include an 18th-century thatched barn restaurant where an interesting choice of dishes is served. The attractively decorated bedrooms are housed in garden wings, and many have lovely views of the grounds to the countryside beyond.

Rooms: 21 (10 annexe) (2 family) (17 GF) **S** fr £99 **D** fr £140 (including breakfast)* **Facilities:** FTV WiFi ↳ Xmas New Year **Conf:** Class 250 Board 100 Theatre 250 **Parking:** 300 **Notes:** LB Civ Wed 250

Premier Inn Lowestoft

BUDGET HOTEL   Premier Inn

tel: 0871 527 8688 (Calls cost 13p per minute plus your phone company's access charge) **249 Yarmouth Road NR32 4AA**
web: www.premierinn.com
dir: *On A12, 2 miles north of Lowestoft.*

High quality, budget accommodation ideal for both families and business travellers. Spacious, en suite bedrooms feature free WiFi and tea and coffee making facilities, and in most hotels, Freeview TV is also available. The adjacent family restaurant features a wide and varied menu.

Rooms: 99

★ ## Symbols and abbreviations
explained on pages 6–7

LUDLOW
Shropshire   Map 10 SO57

INSPECTOR'S CHOICE

Fishmore Hall

★★★ SMALL HOTEL

tel: 01584 875148 **Fishmore Road SY8 3DP**
email: reception@fishmorehall.co.uk **web:** www.fishmorehall.co.uk
dir: *A49 into Henley Road. 1st right, Weyman Road, at bottom of hill right into Fishmore Road.*

Located in a rural area within easy reach of the town centre, this Palladian-style Georgian house has been sympathetically renovated and extended to provide high standards of comfort and facilities. The contemporary interior highlights many period features, and public areas include a comfortable lounge and restaurant, the setting for imaginative cooking.

Rooms: 15 (1 GF) **S** fr £135 **D** fr £175 (including breakfast)* **Facilities:** Spa FTV WiFi ↳ ✦ Sauna Steam room Xmas New Year **Conf:** Class 60 Board 40 Theatre 130 **Services:** Lift Night porter **Parking:** 48 **Notes:** LB Civ Wed 130

L

LUDLOW *continued*

The Feathers Hotel

★★★ 82% ⊛ HOTEL

tel: 01584 875261 **The Bull Ring SY8 1AA**
email: enquiries@feathersatludlow.co.uk **web:** www.feathersatludlow.co.uk
dir: *From A49 follow town centre signs to centre. Hotel on left.*

Famous for the carved woodwork outside and in, this picture-postcard 17th-century hotel is one of the town's best-known landmarks and is in an excellent location. Bedrooms are traditional both in style and decor. The public areas have retained much of the traditional charm, and the first-floor lounge is particularly stunning. Modern British menus are offered in the smart restaurant which has wooden beams and exposed brickwork.

Rooms: 40 (3 family) ⟨ **S** fr £95 **D** fr £120 (including breakfast)* **Facilities:** STV FTV WiFi ⟩ Xmas New Year **Conf:** Class 40 Board 40 Theatre 80 **Services:** Lift Night porter **Parking:** 33 **Notes:** LB

LUTON	Map 6 TL02
Bedfordshire	

Luton Hoo Hotel, Golf & Spa

★★★★★ 86% ⊛⊛ ≋ HOTEL

SMALL LUXURY HOTELS OF THE WORLD

tel: 01582 734437 & 698888 **The Mansion House LU1 3TQ**
email: reservations@lutonhoo.com **web:** www.lutonhoo.com
dir: *M1 junction 10 towards Harpenden and St Albans. Hotel approximately 1 mile on left.*

Luton Hoo is a luxury hotel set in more than 1,000 acres of 'Capability' Brown designed parkland and formal gardens, with an 18-hole, par 73 golf course and the River Lea meandering through. The centrepiece is the Grade I listed mansion house that has influences from many famous architects including Robert Adams. There are three sumptuous lounges where guests can enjoy afternoon tea and pre-dinner drinks, and two eating options – The Wernher Restaurant and the Adams Brasserie. The spacious bedrooms and impressive suites combine historic character with modern amenities. The Robert Adams Club House is the perfect place for relaxation. There is also a brasserie, a spa, golf, pool and gym, together with two bars. Warren

Weir, at the foot of the estate, on the river bank is an exclusive retreat for weddings and meetings.

Luton Hoo Hotel, Golf & Spa

Rooms: 228 (50 family) (65 GF) ⟨ **S** fr £190 **D** fr £210 (including breakfast)* **Facilities:** Spa FTV WiFi ⟩ HL ⊛ ⌇ 18 ⌣ Fishing ⌣ Gym Bird watching Clay pigeon shooting Archery Falconry Cycling Snooker ♬ Xmas New Year **Conf:** Class 220 Board 60 Theatre 388 **Services:** Lift Night porter **Parking:** 316 **Notes:** LB Civ Wed 380

Icon Hotel

★★★★ 76% HOTEL

tel: 01582 722123 **15 Stuart Street LU1 2SA**
email: reservations@iconhotelluton.com **web:** www.iconhotelluton.com
dir: *M1 junction 10 and 10A, A1081 signed Luton, left follow Luton Retail Park and station signs. Left at roundabout, left at next roundabout onto A505 Park Viaduct. Straight on at next roundabout, left into Hastings Street.*

This modern, purpose-built hotel occupies a prominent position close to the town centre and is a short drive from the international airport. The contemporary, open-plan bar is very comfortable and Capello's Restaurant offers a modern Mediterranean menu. The bedrooms are attractively presented and feature the latest technology along with large LCD TVs and complimentary WiFi. There is a range of business suites and a well-equipped gym.

Rooms: 62 (7 family) (6 GF) ⟨ **S** fr £69 **D** fr £79* **Facilities:** FTV WiFi ⟩ Gym ♬ Xmas New Year **Conf:** Class 20 Board 26 Theatre 45 **Services:** Lift Night porter Air con **Parking:** 18

Premier Inn Luton Town Centre

Premier Inn

BUDGET HOTEL

tel: 0871 527 9542 (Calls cost 13p per minute plus your phone company's access charge) **Regent Street LU1 5FA**
web: www.premierinn.com
dir: *M1 junction 10 (southbound), A1081 (Luton Airport). At 1st roundabout left onto London Road (A1081). Into Castle Street, left into Windsor Street. 1st right into Chapel Street. 1st left into Regent Street. Hotel on left.*

High quality, budget accommodation ideal for both families and business travellers. Spacious, en suite bedrooms feature free WiFi and tea and coffee making facilities, and in most hotels, Freeview TV is also available. The adjacent family restaurant features a wide and varied menu.

Rooms: 120

LUTON AIRPORT
Bedfordshire   Map 6 TL12

Premier Inn Luton Airport

BUDGET HOTEL

tel: 0871 527 8690 (Calls cost 13p per minute plus your phone company's access charge) **Osborne Road LU1 3HJ**
dir: *M1 junction 10, A1081 follow signs for Luton, at 3rd roundabout left into Gypsy Lane, left at next roundabout.*

High quality, budget accommodation ideal for both families and business travellers. Spacious, en suite bedrooms feature free WiFi and tea and coffee making facilities, and in most hotels, Freeview TV is also available. The adjacent family restaurant features a wide and varied menu.

Rooms: 134

LYME REGIS
Dorset   Map 4 SY39

Royal Lion Hotel
★★★ 81% HOTEL

tel: 01297 445622 **Broad Street DT7 3QF**
email: enquiries@royallionhotel.com **web:** www.royallionhotel.com
dir: *From west on A35 take A3052, or from east take B3165 to Lyme Regis. Hotel in town centre, opposite The Fossil Shop.*

This 17th-century, former coaching inn is full of character and charm, and is just a short walk from the seafront. Bedrooms vary in size; those in the newer wing are more spacious and some have balconies, sea views or a private terrace. In addition to the elegant dining room and guest lounges, a heated pool, jacuzzi, sauna and small gym are available. A good selection of enjoyable, well-prepared dishes is offered in either the bar and the main restaurant. There is a car park at the rear of the hotel.

Rooms: 33 (8 family) (4 GF) 🐾 **D** fr £122 (including breakfast)* **Facilities:** FTV WiFi 🏊 Sauna Games room Snooker tables Table tennis Xmas New Year **Conf:** Class 20 Board 20 Theatre 50 **Parking:** 33

LYMINGTON
Hampshire   Map 5 SZ39

Macdonald Elmers Court Hotel & Resort
MACDONALD HOTELS & RESORTS

★★★★ 76% HOTEL

tel: 0344 879 9060 **South Baddesley Road SO41 5ZB**
email: elmerscourt@macdonald-hotels.co.uk **web:** www.macdonaldhotels.co.uk
dir: *M27 junction 1, through Lyndhurst, Brockenhurst to Lymington, hotel 200 yards right after Lymington ferry terminal.*

Originally known as The Elms, this Tudor manor house dates back to the 1820s. Ideally located at the edge of the New Forest and overlooking The Solent with views towards the Isle of Wight, the hotel offers suites and self-catering accommodation in the grounds, along with a host of leisure facilities.

Rooms: 42 (42 annexe) (8 family) (22 GF) 🐾 **Facilities:** Spa FTV WiFi 🏊 ⛷ ♨ 🏌 Gym Squash Steam room Aerobics classes Sauna Table tennis Xmas New Year **Conf:** Class 70 Board 40 Theatre 120 **Services:** Night porter **Parking:** 100 **Notes:** LB Civ Wed 120

HIGHLY RECOMMENDED

Stanwell House Hotel
★★★ 88% ◉◉ HOTEL

tel: 01590 677123 **14-15 High Street SO41 9AA**
email: enquiries@stanwellhouse.com **web:** www.stanwellhouse.com
dir: *M27 junction 1, follow signs to Lyndhurst then Lymington.*

Stanwell House Hotel is a privately owned Georgian building situated on the wide high street only a few minutes from the marina, and a short drive from the New Forest. Styling itself as a boutique hotel, the bedrooms are individually designed; there are Terrace rooms with garden access, four-poster rooms, and Georgian rooms in the older part of the building. The four suites include two with their own roof terrace. Dining options include the informal bistro and the intimate Seafood Restaurant. Service is friendly and attentive. A meeting room is available.

Rooms: 29 (7 family) (7 GF) 🐾 **S** fr £145 **D** fr £145 (including breakfast)* **Facilities:** FTV WiFi 🐾 Xmas New Year **Conf:** Class 35 Board 30 Theatre 70 **Services:** Night porter **Parking:** 12 **Notes:** Civ Wed 100

Premier Inn Lymington (New Forest Hordle)
Premier Inn

BUDGET HOTEL

tel: 0871 527 8692 (Calls cost 13p per minute plus your phone company's access charge) **Silver Street, Hordle SO41 0FN**
web: www.premierinn.com
dir: *M27 junction 1, A337. 3.5 miles, left into High Street (A35) right into Gosport Lane. Left into Clay Hill (A337). Right into Grigg Lane (B3055). Approximately 8 miles, left into Barrows Lane, right into Silver Street.*

Rooms: 20

Find out more
about the AA's Hotel rating scheme on pages 12–13

L

LYNDHURST
Hampshire

Map 5 SU30

INSPECTOR'S CHOICE

Lime Wood

★★★★★ 🏵🏵🏵 ⌁ COUNTRY HOUSE HOTEL

tel: 023 8028 7177 **Beaulieu Road SO43 7FZ**
email: info@limewood.co.uk **web:** www.limewood.co.uk
dir: Exit A35 onto B3056 towards Beaulieu, hotel 1 mile on right.

This meticulously restored country house situated deep in the New Forest, provides a wealth of facilities and much opulence. The hotel prides itself on its relaxed, friendly and attentive service, and has lots to interest and captivate. The luxurious bedrooms are notable; some are in the pavilion and some in the main house. A major attraction at Lime Wood is the restaurant, Hartnett Holder & Co which is headed up by Luke Holder and, as you'd expect, Angela Hartnett. The Herb House spa offers a hydrotherapy pool and many other excellent facilities along with a gym and steam room.

Rooms: 33 (17 annexe) (7 family) (6 GF) 🐾 **S** fr £385 **D** fr £385* **Facilities:** Spa STV FTV WiFi ⊾ 🏵 Gym Xmas New Year **Conf:** Board 30 Theatre 50 **Services:** Lift Night porter **Parking:** 60 **Notes:** Civ Wed 60

Forest Lodge Hotel

NEW FOREST HOTELS

★★★ 85% 🏵🏵 HOTEL

tel: 023 8028 3677 & 0800 444441 **Pikes Hill, Romsey Road SO43 7AS**
email: forest@newforesthotels.co.uk **web:** www.newforesthotels.co.uk
dir: M27 junction 1, A337 towards Lyndhurst. In village, with police station and courts on right, take 1st right into Pikes Hill.

Situated on the edge of Lyndhurst, this hotel is set well back from the main road. The smart, contemporary bedrooms include four-poster rooms and family rooms; children are very welcome here. The eating options are the Forest Restaurant and the fine-dining Glasshouse Restaurant. There is an indoor swimming pool and Nordic sauna.

Rooms: 36 (11 family) (10 GF) 🐾 **S** fr £59 **D** fr £79 (including breakfast)*
Facilities: FTV WiFi ⊾ HL 🕃 Xmas New Year **Conf:** Class 70 Board 60 Theatre 120
Parking: 50 **Notes:** LB Civ Wed 90

Ormonde House Hotel

★★★ 73% METRO HOTEL

tel: 023 8028 2806 **Southampton Road SO43 7BT**
email: enquiries@ormondehouse.co.uk **web:** www.ormondehouse.co.uk
dir: M27/M271/A35 east through Ashurst, hotel on right on entering Lyndhurst.

Ormonde House Hotel is located on the edge of bustling Lyndhurst in the heart of the New Forest, and provides comfortable en suite accommodation, with breakfast served in the dining room and conservatory. It is a dog friendly hotel and has ample off-street parking. It is ideally placed for visiting all New Forest activities and attractions.

Rooms: 21 (4 annexe) (2 family) (7 GF) 🐾 **S** fr £75 **D** fr £85 (including breakfast)*
Facilities: FTV WiFi New Year **Parking:** 21 **Notes:** LB Closed 13–27 December

The Crown Manor House Hotel

AA Advertised 🏵🏵

tel: 02380 282 922 **High Street SO43 7NF**
email: stay@crownhotel-lyndhurst.co.uk **web:** www.crownhotel-lyndhurst.co.uk
dir: M27 junction 1, follow signs to Lyndhurst for 4 miles.

The Crown Manor House Hotel occupies a prime location in Lyndhurst. Bedrooms vary in size, but all are comfortable and equipped to a high standard. Public areas include the comfortable lounges, popular restaurant and airy breakfast room, all retaining many of the original features of the property. On-site parking and quiet gardens with terrace seating are further features.

Rooms: 50 (4 family) **Facilities:** FTV WiFi ⊾ Xmas New Year **Conf:** Class 40 Board 30 Theatre 80 **Services:** Lift Night porter **Parking:** 50 **Notes:** LB Closed Civ Wed 100

LYTHAM ST ANNES
Lancashire   Map 18 SD32

Clifton Arms Hotel
★★★★ 80% HOTEL

---

tel: 01253 739898 **West Beach, Lytham FY8 5QJ**
email: welcome@cliftonarms-lytham.com **web:** www.cliftonarmslytham.com
dir: On A584 along seafront.

This long established hotel occupies a prime position overlooking Lytham Green and the Ribble Estuary beyond. Bedrooms vary in size and are appointed to a high standard; front-facing rooms are particularly spacious and enjoy splendid views. There is an elegant restaurant, a stylish open-plan lounge and cocktail bar, as well as modern function and conference facilities. Afternoon teas are a highlight and served daily, as is imaginative cuisine in the restaurant.

Rooms: 48 (2 family) ☏ **S** fr £95 **D** fr £150 (including breakfast)* **Facilities:** STV FTV WiFi ⌇ Xmas New Year **Conf:** Class 100 Board 60 Theatre 150 **Services:** Lift Night porter **Parking:** 40 **Notes:** LB Civ Wed 100

Bedford Hotel
★★★ 82% HOTEL

---

tel: 01253 724636 **307-313 Clifton Drive South FY8 1HN**
email: reservations@bedford-hotel.com **web:** www.bedford-hotel.com
dir: From M55 follow signs for airport to last lights. Left through 2 sets of lights. Hotel 300 yards on left.

This popular family-run hotel is close to the town centre and the seafront. Bedrooms vary in size and style, and include superior and club class rooms. Newer bedrooms are particularly elegant and tastefully appointed. Spacious public areas include a choice of lounges, a coffee shop, fitness facilities and an impressive function suite. The Restaurant offers imaginative dishes, skilfully prepared.

Rooms: 44 (6 GF) ☏ **S** fr £65 **D** fr £110 (including breakfast)* **Facilities:** FTV WiFi ⌇ Gym Hydrotherapy spa bath Xmas New Year **Conf:** Class 140 Board 60 Theatre 160 **Services:** Lift Night porter **Parking:** 25 **Notes:** LB

Best Western Glendower Hotel

★★★ 80% HOTEL

---

tel: 01253 723241 **North Promenade FY8 2NQ**
email: recp@theglendowerhotel.co.uk **web:** www.glendowerhotel.co.uk
dir: M55 follow airport signs. Left at Promenade to St Annes. Hotel 500 yards from pier.

Located on the seafront and with easy access to the town centre, this popular, friendly hotel offers comfortably furnished, well-equipped accommodation. Bedrooms vary in size and style including suites and very popular, spacious family rooms. Public areas feature a choice of smart, comfortable lounges, a bright, modern leisure club and function facilities.

Rooms: 61 (17 family) ☏ **Facilities:** FTV WiFi ⌇ Gym Snooker room Table tennis room ♫ Xmas New Year **Conf:** Class 120 Board 50 Theatre 150 **Services:** Lift Night porter **Parking:** 45 **Notes:** LB Civ Wed 150

MACCLESFIELD
Cheshire   Map 16 SJ97

Premier Inn Macclesfield North

BUDGET HOTEL

---

tel: 0871 527 8694 (Calls cost 13p per minute plus your phone company's access charge) **Tytherington Business Park, Springwood Way SK10 2XA**
web: www.premierinn.com
dir: On A523 in Tytherington Business Park.

High quality, budget accommodation ideal for both families and business travellers. Spacious, en suite bedrooms feature free WiFi and tea and coffee making facilities, and in most hotels, Freeview TV is also available. The adjacent family restaurant features a wide and varied menu.

Rooms: 55

Premier Inn Macclesfield South West

BUDGET HOTEL

---

tel: 0871 527 8696 (Calls cost 13p per minute plus your phone company's access charge) **Congleton Road, Gawsworth SK11 7XD**
web: www.premierinn.com
dir: M6 junction 17, A534 towards Congleton, A536 towards Macclesfield to Gawsworth. Hotel on left.

Rooms: 28

MAIDENCOMBE
See **Torquay**

MAIDENHEAD
Berkshire   Map 6 SU88

Fredrick's Hotel and Spa
★★★★ 80% ◉◉ HOTEL

---

tel: 01628 581000 **Shoppenhangers Road SL6 2PZ**
email: reservations@fredricks-hotel.co.uk **web:** www.fredricks-hotel.co.uk
dir: M4 junction 8/9, 1st exit off M404 signed Cox Green. Hotel on right, 300 yards after garage.

Set in attractive grounds on the fringes of Maidenhead, this stylish hotel has comfortable and well-equipped bedrooms. Public rooms include the Wintergarden restaurant, which serves afternoon tea as well as varied bar menus; and Fredrick's Restaurant which has a wide selection for lunch and dinner. There are also conference facilities, a fitness room, pool and spa. Fredrick's is a very popular venue for weddings.

Rooms: 37 (5 family) (14 GF) ☏ **S** fr £129 **D** fr £139 (including breakfast)* **Facilities:** Spa FTV WiFi ⌇ ⊛ ⚲ Gym Xmas New Year **Conf:** Class 65 Board 46 Theatre 100 **Services:** Night porter **Parking:** 80 **Notes:** LB Civ Wed 150

M

MAIDENHEAD *continued*

Premier Inn Maidenhead Town Centre

Premier Inn

BUDGET HOTEL

tel: 0871 527 9520 (Calls cost 13p per minute plus your phone company's access charge) **Kidwells Park Drive SL6 8AQ**
web: www.premierinn.com
dir: *From A308(M) towards Maidenhead. 1st exit at next roundabout onto A308. 2nd exit signed Braywick Road/A308. 1st exit at next roundabout into Bad Godesberg Way. 3rd exit at next roundabout into Market Street, right into West Street, right into Kidwells Park Drive, hotel on right.*

High quality, budget accommodation ideal for both families and business travellers. Spacious, en suite bedrooms feature free WiFi and tea and coffee making facilities, and in most hotels, Freeview TV is also available. The adjacent family restaurant features a wide and varied menu.

Rooms: 124

MAIDSTONE Kent **Map 7 TQ75**

Grange Moor Hotel

Premier Inn

★★★ A HOTEL

tel: 01622 677623 **4-8 St Michael's Road ME16 8BS**
email: reservations@grangemoor.co.uk **web:** www.grangemoor.co.uk
dir: *From town centre towards A26 Tonbridge road. Hotel 0.25 mile on left, just after church.*

Grange Moor Hotel is easily recognised in summer by its colourful hanging baskets. On offer are 50 well-appointed bedrooms that have TV, radio alarm clock, hairdryer, and tea- and coffee-making facilities. There is a guest lounge area and a Tudor-style bar and restaurant.

Rooms: 50 (11 annexe) (5 family) (7 GF) **S** fr £55 **D** fr £61* **Facilities:** FTV WiFi **Conf:** Class 60 Board 40 Theatre 100 **Services:** Night porter **Parking:** 75 **Notes:** Closed 23–30 December Civ Wed 120

Premier Inn Maidstone (A26/Wateringbury)

BUDGET HOTEL

tel: 0871 527 8706 (Calls cost 13p per minute plus your phone company's access charge) **103 Tonbridge Road, Wateringbury ME18 5NS**
web: www.premierinn.com
dir: *M25 junction 3 onto M20. Exit at junction 4 onto A228 towards West Malling. A26 towards Maidstone, approximately 3 miles.*

Rooms: 39

Premier Inn Maidstone (Allington)

Premier Inn

BUDGET HOTEL

tel: 0871 527 8698 (Calls cost 13p per minute plus your phone company's access charge) **London Road ME16 0HG**
web: www.premierinn.com
dir: *M20 junction 5, 0.5 mile on London Road towards Maidstone.*

Rooms: 65

Premier Inn Maidstone (Leybourne)

Premier Inn

BUDGET HOTEL

tel: 0871 527 8702 (Calls cost 13p per minute plus your phone company's access charge) **Castle Way, Leybourne ME19 5TR**
web: www.premierinn.com
dir: *M20 junction 4, A228, hotel on left.*

Rooms: 56

Premier Inn Maidstone (Sandling)

Premier Inn

BUDGET HOTEL

tel: 0871 527 8704 (Calls cost 13p per minute plus your phone company's access charge) **Allington Lock, Sandling ME14 3AS**
web: www.premierinn.com
dir: *M20 junction 6, follow Museum of Kent Life signs.*

Rooms: 40

Premier Inn Maidstone Town Centre

Premier Inn

BUDGET HOTEL

tel: 0871 527 9392 (Calls cost 13p per minute plus your phone company's access charge) **5-11 London Road ME16 8HR**
web: www.premierinn.com
dir: *M20 junction 5, A20 signed Maidstone (West) and Aylesford. At next roundabout 1st exit (Maidstone). Straight on at next roundabout.*

Rooms: 99

MALMESBURY
Wiltshire

Map 4 ST98

Whatley Manor Hotel and Spa
★★★★★ 🏵🏵🏵 ⌂ HOTEL

tel: 01666 822888 **Easton Grey SN16 0RB**
email: reservations@whatleymanor.com **web:** www.whatleymanor.com
dir: M4 junction 17, follow signs to Malmesbury, continue over two roundabouts. Follow B4040 and signs for Sherston, hotel 2 miles on left.

Sitting in 12 acres of beautiful countryside, this impressive country house provides the most luxurious accommodation. Spacious bedrooms, most with views over the attractive gardens, are individually appointed with excellent high-tech features and unique works of art. Several eating options are available under the direction of Executive Chef Niall Keating – Grey's, a relaxed brasserie, The Dining Room that serves modern British cuisine with Asian influences, and the Kitchen Garden Terrace for alfresco breakfasts, lunches and dinners. Guests might even like to take a hamper and a picnic rug and find a quiet spot in the grounds. The old Loggia Barn is ideal for wedding ceremonies, and the Aquarius Spa is magnificent.

Rooms: 23 (4 GF) 🐾 **D** fr £260 (including breakfast)* **Facilities:** Spa STV FTV WiFi ⌂ ⊛ Fishing 🏊 Gym Cinema Hydropool (indoor/outdoor) Xmas New Year **Conf:** Class 20 Board 24 Theatre 60 **Services:** Lift Night porter **Parking:** 100 **Notes:** LB No children 12 years Civ Wed 100

The Old Bell Hotel
★★★★ 80% 🏵 HOTEL

tel: 01666 822 344 **Abbey Row SN16 0BW**
email: info@oldbellhotel.com **web:** www.oldbellhotel.co.uk

The oldest purpose-built hotel in Britain, The Old Bell dates back to 1220 and originally provided accommodation to illustrious guests visiting the adjacent Malmesbury Abbey. Many features survive to tell its story – the original stone fireplace dating back to 1220 is a real focal point. Today, the hotel has been fully refurbished and offers high-quality, spacious accommodation and is well equipped for modern day travellers. Dining is not to be missed, whether a casual bite from the small plates menu served in the bar or the innovative and exciting menu served in the restaurant. A hearty breakfast sets guests up for a day exploring the surrounding Cotswolds.

Rooms: 34 **Facilities:** FTV WiFi

Best Western Mayfield House Hotel

★★★ 73% HOTEL

tel: 01666 577409 **Crudwell SN16 9EW**
email: reception@mayfieldhousehotel.co.uk **web:** www.mayfieldhousehotel.co.uk
dir: M4 junction 17, A429 to Cirencester. 2 miles north of Malmesbury on left in Crudwell village.

This popular hotel is in an ideal location for exploring many of the attractions that Wiltshire and The Cotswolds have to offer. Bedrooms come in a range of shapes and sizes, and include some on the ground-floor level in a cottage adjacent to the main building. In addition to outdoor seating, guests can relax with a drink in the comfortable lounge area, where orders are taken for the carefully prepared dinner to follow.

Rooms: 28 (8 annexe) (4 family) (8 GF) 🐾 **Facilities:** FTV WiFi ⌂ 🏊 Xmas New Year **Conf:** Class 30 Board 25 Theatre 40 **Parking:** 50

MALVERN
Worcestershire

Map 10 SO74

The Abbey Hotel
★★★★ 77% HOTEL

SAROVA HOTELS

tel: 01684 892332 **Abbey Road WR14 3ET**
email: abbey@sarova.com **web:** www.sarova.com
dir: In Great Malvern town centre, opposite theatres.

This large, impressive, ivy-clad hotel stands in the centre of Great Malvern, at the foot of the Malvern Hills, next to the Abbey and close to the theatre. It provides well-equipped modern accommodation equally suitable for business guests and tourists. Facilities include a good range of function rooms, making the hotel a popular venue for meetings and events.

Rooms: 103 (14 family) (23 GF) 🐾 **S** fr £70 **D** fr £79 (including breakfast) **Facilities:** STV FTV WiFi ⌂ Xmas New Year **Conf:** Class 90 Board 85 Theatre 300 **Services:** Lift Night porter **Parking:** 85 **Notes:** LB Civ Wed 300

M

MALVERN *continued*

The Malvern

★★★★ 76% ◎ HOTEL

tel: 01684 898290 **Grovewood Road WR14 1GD**
email: enquiries@themalvernspa.com **web:** www.themalvernspa.com
dir: *A4440 to Malvern. Over 2 roundabouts, at 3rd roundabout turn left. 6 miles, left at roundabout, over 1st roundabout, hotel on right.*

This modern, friendly hotel is set on the outskirts of the famous spa town. The bedrooms are contemporary with sumptuous beds, and many guest extras are provided; the bathrooms have quality fixtures and fittings. There is a brasserie restaurant which offers quality seasonal menus that include healthy options and vegetarian dishes. The Malvern Spa, designed exclusively for adults, includes a hydrotherapy pool which goes from inside to outside, heat experiences, a range of saunas, crystal steam room, salt grotto, and adventure showers, along with a host of treatments. There is also a 50-station gym with state-of-the-art equipment. There is ample parking around the hotel.

Rooms: 33 ↄ **S** fr £110 **D** fr £119 (including breakfast)* **Facilities:** Spa FTV WiFi ↄ ⊛ ↄ Gym Exercise classes Xmas New Year **Services:** Lift Night porter Air con **Parking:** 82 **Notes:** LB No children 18 years

The Cotford Hotel & L'Amuse Bouche Restaurant

★★★ 81% ◎◎ HOTEL

tel: 01684 572427 **51 Graham Road WR14 2HU**
email: reservations@cotfordhotel.co.uk **web:** www.cotfordhotel.co.uk
dir: *From Worcester follow signs to Malvern on A449. Left into Graham Road signed town centre, hotel on right.*

This delightful house, built in 1851, reputedly for the Bishop of Worcester, stands in attractive gardens with stunning views of The Malverns. Bedrooms have been stylishly appointed, retaining many of the original features and with a good

selection of welcome extras. Food, service and hospitality are all major strengths – it features L'Amuse Bouche Restaurant serving classic French cuisine.

The Cotford Hotel & L'Amuse Bouche Restaurant

Rooms: 15 (3 family) (1 GF) ↄ **S** fr £75 **D** fr £140 (including breakfast)* **Facilities:** STV FTV WiFi ↄ ↄ **Parking:** 15 **Notes:** LB

The Cottage in the Wood

★★★ 81% ◎◎ HOTEL

tel: 01684 588860 **Holywell Road, Malvern Wells WR14 4LG**
email: reception@cottageinthewood.co.uk **web:** www.cottageinthewood.co.uk
dir: *On Ledbury side of Great Malvern on A449 Worcester – Ledbury road.*

Set high on the hillside with stunning, far-reaching views across the Worcestershire countryside, The Cottage in The Wood offers a variety of accommodation styles – bedrooms are available in the main house, Beech Cottage where the rooms are cosier and The Coach House where larger rooms are available, some have semi-private terraces or balconies. The main house public areas have been refurbished to become a modern open-plan space with touch of London sophistication. Dinner, with menus of innovative dishes based on high quality produce, should not be missed.

Rooms: 30 (23 annexe) (10 GF) ↄ **S** fr £85 **D** fr £90 (including breakfast)* **Facilities:** FTV WiFi ↄ HL Xmas New Year **Conf:** Class 14 Board 14 Theatre 20 **Parking:** 45

Colwall Park Hotel

★★★ 80% ◎◎ HOTEL

tel: 01684 540000 **Walwyn Road, Colwall WR13 6QG**
email: hotel@colwallpark.com **web:** www.colwall.co.uk
dir: *Phone for directions.*

Located in the rural Herefordshire, the purpose-built Colwall Park Hotel has been welcoming visitors to the Malvern Hills for over a century. Guest rooms are comfortable and well equipped. The newly refurbished bar and wood burning stove are a welcome sight in winter months, while the mature gardens are a hidden gem for warmer days. Colwall Station is just a stone's throw from the property for those arriving by train. Dinner should not be missed and the dishes utilise produce of high quality from the local area wherever possible.

Rooms: 22 **S** fr £75 **D** fr £115 (including breakfast)* **Facilities:** FTV WiFi Leisure facilities at sister hotel (chargeable) Xmas New Year **Conf:** Class 40 Board 50 Theatre 120 **Services:** Night porter **Parking:** 36 **Notes:** LB Civ Wed 80

M

M

Holdfast Cottage Hotel

★★ 83% HOTEL

tel: 01684 310288 **Marlbank Road, Welland WR13 6NA**
email: enquiries@holdfast-cottage.co.uk **web:** www.holdfast-cottage.co.uk
dir: *M50 junction 1, follow Upton Three Counties/A38 signs, onto A4104 to Welland.*

At the base of the Malvern Hills, this delightful wisteria-covered hotel sits in attractive, manicured grounds. Charming public areas include an intimate bar, a log fire-enhanced lounge and an elegant dining room. Bedrooms vary in size but all are comfortable and well appointed. Fresh local and seasonal produce are the basis for the cuisine.

Rooms: 8 (1 family) **Facilities:** FTV WiFi ⚡ Xmas New Year **Parking:** 16
Notes: Civ Wed 50

The Great Malvern Hotel

★★ 79% HOTEL

tel: 01684 563411 **Graham Road WR14 2HN**
email: sutton@great-malvern-hotel.co.uk **web:** www.great-malvern-hotel.co.uk
dir: *From Worcester on A449, left after fire station into Graham Road. Hotel at end on right.*

Close to the town centre, this privately owned and managed hotel is ideally situated for many of Malvern's attractions. The accommodation is spacious and well equipped. Public areas include quiet lounge areas, and a cosy bar which is popular with locals.

Rooms: 13 (1 family) **Facilities:** STV FTV WiFi ⚡ 🎵 **Conf:** Class 20 Board 20 Theatre 20 **Services:** Lift **Parking:** 9

Premier Inn Malvern

Premier Inn

BUDGET HOTEL

tel: 0871 527 9406 (Calls cost 13p per minute plus your phone company's access charge) **Townsend Way WR14 1GD**
web: www.premierinn.com
dir: *M5 junction 7, A44 (1st exit from south; 3rd exit from north). At roundabout 1st exit onto A440. 1st exit at 3rd roundabout onto A449 (Malvern Road). At next roundabout 1st exit into Townsend Way (B4208). At next roundabout 2nd exit into Grove Wood Road.*

High quality, budget accommodation ideal for both families and business travellers. Spacious, en suite bedrooms feature free WiFi and tea and coffee making facilities, and in most hotels, Freeview TV is also available. The adjacent family restaurant features a wide and varied menu.

Rooms: 66

MANCHESTER	Map 16 SJ89
Greater Manchester	

See also **Manchester Airport & Sale**

The Lowry Hotel

★★★★★ 84% HOTEL

tel: 0161 827 4000 **50 Dearmans Place, Chapel Wharf M3 5LH**
email: enquiries@thelowryhotel.com **web:** www.thelowryhotel.com
dir: *M6 junction 19, A556/M56/A5103 for 4.5 miles. At roundabout take A57(M) to lights, right into Water Street. Left to New Quay Street/Trinity Way. At 1st lights right into Chapel Street for hotel.*

This modern, contemporary hotel, set beside the River Irwell in the centre of the city, offers spacious bedrooms equipped to meet the needs of business and leisure visitors alike. Many of the rooms look out over the river, as do the sumptuous suites. The River Room restaurant produces good brasserie cooking. Extensive business and function facilities are available, together with a spa to provide extra pampering.

Rooms: 165 **Facilities:** Spa STV FTV WiFi ⚡ Gym Sauna Relaxation rooms 🎵 Xmas New Year **Conf:** Class 250 Board 38 Theatre 400 **Services:** Lift Night porter Air con **Parking:** 88 **Notes:** Civ Wed 200

Hotel Gotham

★★★★★ 83% HOTEL

tel: 0161 4130000 **100 King Street M2 4WU**
email: reservations@hotelgotham.co.uk **web:** www.bespokehotels.com/hotelgotham
dir: *Phone for directions.*

Hotel Gotham is a beautifully renovated former bank designed by Edwin Lutyens, with art deco themes throughout. The Brass Club is a popular cocktail bar with balconies overlooking the city, while the hotel's restaurant, Honey, offers guests innovative dishes. Bedrooms and bathrooms are spacious and stylish, and there are subtle references to the property's former life everywhere.

Rooms: 60 (8 family) **S** fr £125 **D** fr £139 (including breakfast) **Facilities:** STV FTV WiFi ⚡ 🎵 Xmas New Year **Conf:** Class 14 Board 14 Theatre 20 **Services:** Lift Night porter Air con **Parking:** 40

HIGHLY RECOMMENDED

The Midland

QHOTELS
INSPIRED
BY YOU

★★★★ 85% HOTEL

tel: 0161 236 3333 **Peter Street M60 2DS**
email: themidland@qhotels.co.uk **web:** www.qhotels.co.uk
dir: *M602 junction 3, follow Manchester Central Convention Complex signs, hotel opposite.*

This much-loved, centrally located, well-established Edwardian-style hotel (Grade II listed) offers stylish, thoughtfully equipped bedrooms that have a contemporary feel. Elegant public areas are equally impressive and facilities include extensive function and meeting rooms. Eating options include Adam Reid at The French and Mr Cooper's.

Rooms: 312 (13 family) **S** fr £109 **D** fr £109* **Facilities:** Spa STV FTV WiFi ⚡ HL ⚡ Gym Hair and beauty salon 🎵 **Conf:** Class 300 Board 120 Theatre 600 **Services:** Lift Night porter Air con **Notes:** Civ Wed 600

ABode Manchester

ABode
HOTELS

★★★★ 80% HOTEL

tel: 0161 247 7744 **107 Piccadilly M1 2DB**
email: info@abodemanchester.co.uk **web:** www.abodemanchester.co.uk
dir: *M62/M602 follow signs for city centre/Piccadilly.*

Located in the heart of Piccadilly, this Grade II listed, former wholesale textile warehouse has embraced its industrial heritage. Exposed steel beams and structural iron columns together with an ornate, wrought iron and walnut staircase are striking features. Beds are low and comfortable, while feature walls, a tuck box filled with regional food and drink, and complimentary WiFi can be found in all rooms. A relaxed, all-day brasserie menu features plats du jour with a comfortingly nostalgic nod, and time-honoured classics.

Rooms: 61 **Facilities:** STV WiFi ⚡ Xmas New Year **Conf:** Class 16 Board 26 Theatre 30 **Services:** Lift Night porter Air con

MANCHESTER *continued*

The Principal Manchester

PRINCIPAL

★★★★ 80% HOTEL

tel: 0161 288 1111 **Oxford Street M60 7HA**
email: ManchesterReservations@theprincipalhotel.com
web: www.phcompany.com/principal/manchester-hotel
dir: *Opposite Manchester Oxford Road rail station.*

Formerly the offices of the Refuge Life Assurance Company, this impressive neo-Gothic building occupies a central location. There is a vast lobby, spacious open-plan bar lounge and restaurant, and extensive conference and function facilities. Bedrooms vary in size and style but are all spacious and well equipped.

Rooms: 275 (59 family) **Facilities:** STV WiFi **Conf:** Class 650 Board 200 Theatre 1000 **Services:** Lift Night porter **Notes:** Civ Wed 600

Macdonald Manchester Hotel

 MACDONALD HOTELS & RESORTS

★★★★ 78% HOTEL

tel: 0161 272 3200 **London Road M1 2PG**
email: general.manchester@macdonald-hotels.co.uk web: www.macdonaldhotels.co.uk
dir: *Opposite Piccadilly Station.*

Ideally situated just a short walk from Piccadilly Station, this hotel provides a handy location for both business and leisure travellers. Stylish, modern rooms have plasma TVs and iPod docking stations, and the bathrooms offer walk-in power showers and luxury baths. The first-floor restaurant serves skilfully prepared dinners and hearty breakfasts. Staff throughout are cheerful and keen to please.

Rooms: 338 (14 family) **Facilities:** Spa FTV WiFi HL Gym Sauna New Year **Conf:** Class 150 Board 80 Theatre 250 **Services:** Lift Night porter Air con **Parking:** 85 **Notes:** Civ Wed 200

Malmaison Manchester

 Malmaison
hotels that dare to be different

★★★★ 77% HOTEL

tel: 0161 278 1000 & 0844 693 0657 (Calls cost 5p per minute plus your phone company's access charge) **Piccadilly M1 3AQ**
email: manchester@malmaison.com web: www.malmaison.com/locations/manchester
dir: *Follow city centre signs, then signs to Piccadilly station. Hotel at bottom of station approach.*

Stylish and chic, Malmaison Manchester offers the best contemporary hotel-keeping in a relaxed and comfortable environment. Converted from a former warehouse, it features a range of bright meeting rooms, a gym, and treatment rooms. The Mal Bar here is impressive and understandably popular. Air-conditioned suites combine comfort with stunning design. Expect the unusual in some of the rooms, for instance the Red and Blue Manchester Suites.

Rooms: 167 **Facilities:** Spa STV WiFi HL Gym Sauna Relaxation area Solarium Massage chairs Xmas New Year **Conf:** Class 40 Board 30 Theatre 100 **Services:** Lift Night porter Air con **Notes:** Civ Wed 100

Holiday Inn Manchester - MediaCityUK

  Holiday Inn

★★★★ 76% HOTEL

tel: 0161 813 1040 **MediaCityUK, Salford M50 2HT**
email: reservations@himediacityuk.co.uk web: www.holidayinn.com/mediacity
dir: *M602 junction 2 onto A576 to Salford Quays signed MediaCityUK.*

Located in the heart of the exciting media district on Salford Quays, this hotel is adjacent to the main production studios and only minutes from Old Trafford and The Lowry Centre. The stylish Hub Bar features TV-themed murals. Food is served from Marco Pierre Whites' New York Italian on the mezzanine floor. Bedrooms are well equipped with safes and mini-bars, and many have views of the Manchester Shipping Canal. There's complimentary WiFi throughout, and a mini-gym is available to guests.

Rooms: 218 (10 family) **Facilities:** FTV WiFi HL Gym Xmas New Year **Conf:** Class 25 Board 30 Theatre 44 **Services:** Lift Night porter Air con **Parking:** 2300 **Notes:** Civ Wed 70

Hotel Football

★★★★ 75% HOTEL

tel: 0161 751 0430 **99 Sir Matt Busby Way M16 0SZ**
email: info@hotelfootball.com web: www.hotelfootball.com
dir: *Follow A56 unitl Sir Matt Busby Way. Hotel opposite Manchester Utd football stadium.*

Hotel Football is a stylish, contemporary hotel offering comfortable accommodation with relaxed and friendly service. All-day dining is available in Café Football where dishes are themed around footballers, managers and match day treats. The hotel also offers a gym and five-a-side football pitch on the top floor.

Rooms: 133 **Facilities:** STV FTV WiFi HL Gym Xmas New Year **Conf:** Class 250 Board 40 Theatre 350 **Services:** Lift Night porter Air con **Notes:** Civ Wed 300

Novotel Manchester Centre

  NOVOTEL HOTELS & RESORTS

★★★★ 75% HOTEL

tel: 0161 235 2200 **21 Dickinson Street M1 4LX**
email: H3145@accor.com web: www.novotel.com
dir: *From Oxford Street into Portland Street, left into Dickinson Street. Hotel on right.*

This smart, modern property enjoys a central location convenient for theatres, shops, China Town and Manchester's business district. Spacious bedrooms are thoughtfully equipped and brightly decorated. Open-plan public areas include an all-day restaurant and a stylish bar. Extensive conference and meeting facilities are available.

Rooms: 164 (15 family) **Facilities:** STV FTV WiFi HL Gym Steam room Sauna Aromatherapy **Conf:** Class 50 Board 36 Theatre 90 **Services:** Lift Night porter Air con

Mercure Manchester Piccadilly Hotel

★★★★ 73% HOTEL

tel: 0844 815 9024 (Calls cost 5p per minute plus your phone company's access charge)
Portland Street M1 4PH
email: info@mercuremanchester.co.uk **web:** www.jupiterhotels.co.uk
dir: *Opposite Piccadilly Gardens.*

Overlooking Piccadilly Gardens and views of the city, this hotel is located within the heart of Manchester. Bedrooms and bathrooms are tastefully appointed, with a range of rooms for both leisure and business guests. Contemporary dining can be enjoyed within the Brasserie and popular bar areas. A range of spacious meetings and events spaces is also available. Free WiFi across the hotel is a plus.

Rooms: 280 ♜ **Facilities:** FTV WiFi ⌕ **Conf:** Class 320 Board 60 Theatre 800
Services: Lift Night porter Air con **Parking:** 80 **Notes:** Civ Wed 800

Princess St. Hotel

★★★★ 72% HOTEL

tel: 0161 236 8999 **18-24 Princess Street M1 4LG**
email: rooms@princess-st.com **web:** www.princess-st.com
dir: *Phone for directions.*

Conveniently located close to the city centre and ideal for both shops and theatres, this hotel provides comfortable accommodation. The hotel also has meeting room facilities, a small gym with good facilities and a contemporary dining room, the 24 Bar and Grill.

Rooms: 140 (32 family) (15 GF) ♜ **S** fr £99* **Facilities:** FTV WiFi ⌕ Gym **Conf:** Class 40 Board 45 Theatre 100 **Services:** Lift Night porter Air con

Chancellors Hotel & Conference Centre

★★★ 75% HOTEL

tel: 0161 907 7414 **Moseley Road, Fallowfield M14 6NN**
email: chancellors@manchester.ac.uk **web:** www.chancellorshotel.co.uk
dir: *Moseley Road leading to Chancellors Way. Follow signs to Armitage Centre and Chancellors Conference Centre.*

This Grade II listed manor house is set in five acres of landscaped gardens hidden in the heart of Fallowfield, and is well located for the city's shopping, business and commercial centres. Bedrooms offer modern facilities and the cuisine is enjoyable. WiFi and secure parking are available.

Rooms: 72 (4 family) (16 GF) ♜ **S** fr £60 **D** fr £60* **Facilities:** FTV WiFi ⌕ HL
Conf: Class 100 Board 50 Theatre 125 **Services:** Lift Night porter **Parking:** 70
Notes: LB Closed 25 December Civ Wed 125

Novotel Manchester West

★★★ 75% HOTEL

tel: 0161 799 3535 **Worsley Brow M28 2YA**
email: H0907@accor.com **web:** www.novotel.com

(for full entry see Worsley)

Hallmark Inn, Manchester South

★★★ 73% METRO HOTEL

tel: 0330 028 3427 **340-342 Wilmslow Road, Fallowfield M14 6AF**
email: machesterinn@hallmarkhotels.co.uk **web:** www.hallmarkhotels.co.uk
dir: *M60 junction 5, A5103, left onto B5093. Hotel 2.5 miles on left.*

This popular hotel is conveniently located three miles from the city centre, close to the universities. Bedrooms vary in size and style but all are appointed to

impressively high standards; they are well equipped and many rooms benefit from CD players and PlayStations. Spacious, elegant public areas include a bar, a restaurant and meeting rooms.

Rooms: 116 (4 family) **S** fr £45 **D** fr £55* **Facilities:** FTV WiFi Xmas New Year
Conf: Class 20 Board 20 Theatre 50 **Services:** Night porter **Parking:** 100
Notes: Civ Wed 100

Holiday Inn Express Manchester - Oxford Road

BUDGET HOTEL

tel: 0161 238 6660 **Ensco 1160 Ltd, 2 Oxford Road M1 5QA**
email: info@hiemanchester.co.uk **web:** www.hiemanchester.co.uk
dir: *From A57(M) follow signs for Peters Fields and A5103, into Cambridge Street. 2nd right into Hulme Street, ahead onto Charles Street. Opposite BBC building.*

A modern hotel ideal for families and business travellers. Fresh and uncomplicated, the spacious rooms include power shower and tea and coffee-making facilities. Continental buffet breakfast is included in the room rate; other meals may be taken at the nearby family pub or restaurant. The hotel is within walking distance of The Arndale shopping centre, Manchester Art Gallery, The Palace Theatre and Manchester Metropolitan University. It also has easy access to the Trafford Centre and both the Old Trafford and City of Manchester stadiums.

Rooms: 147 **S** fr £65 **D** fr £65 (including breakfast)*

Premier Inn Manchester Central

BUDGET HOTEL

tel: 0871 527 8742 (Calls cost 13p per minute plus your phone company's access charge) **Bishopsgate, 7-11 Lower Mosley Street M2 3DW**
web: www.premierinn.com
dir: *M56 to end, A5103 towards city. Right at 2nd lights. At next lights left into Oxford Road, left at junction of St Peters Square. Hotel on left.*

High quality, budget accommodation ideal for both families and business travellers. Spacious, en suite bedrooms feature free WiFi and tea and coffee making facilities, and in most hotels, Freeview TV is also available. The adjacent family restaurant features a wide and varied menu.

Rooms: 197

Premier Inn Manchester City Centre (Arena/Printworks)

BUDGET HOTEL

tel: 0871 527 8744 (Calls cost 13p per minute plus your phone company's access charge) **North Tower, Victoria Bridge Street M3 5AS**
web: www.premierinn.com
dir: *Exit M602 junction 3, left into A5063 towards Salford. Right at 2nd lights onto A6. Hotel 100 yards on right after 6th set of lights.*

Rooms: 170

Premier Inn Manchester City Centre (Piccadilly)

Premier Inn

BUDGET HOTEL

tel: 0871 527 9390 (Calls cost 13p per minute plus your phone company's access charge) **72 Dale Street M1 2HR**
web: www.premierinn.com
dir: *Phone for directions.*

Rooms: 193

MANCHESTER *continued*

Premier Inn Manchester City Centre (Portland Street)

 Premier Inn

BUDGET HOTEL

tel: 0871 527 8746 (Calls cost 13p per minute plus your phone company's access charge) **The Circus, 112-114 Portland Street M1 4WB**
web: www.premierinn.com
dir: *M6 junction 19, A556. M56, exit junction 3 onto A5103 to Medlock Street, right into Whitworth Street, left into Oxford Street, right into Portland Street.*

Rooms: 232

Premier Inn Manchester (Deansgate Locks)

 Premier Inn

BUDGET HOTEL

tel: 0871 527 8740 (Calls cost 13p per minute plus your phone company's access charge) **Medlock Street M15 5FJ**
web: www.premierinn.com
dir: *M60 junction 24, A57(M) (Mancunian Way) towards city centre. Hotel adjacent, on A5103 Medlock Street.*

Rooms: 199

Premier Inn Manchester (Denton)

 Premier Inn

BUDGET HOTEL

tel: 0871 527 8708 (Calls cost 13p per minute plus your phone company's access charge) **Alphagate Drive, Manchester Road South M34 3SH**
web: www.premierinn.com
dir: *M60 junction 24, A57 signed Denton. 1st right at lights, right at next lights, hotel on left.*

Rooms: 58

Premier Inn Manchester (Heaton Park)

 Premier Inn

BUDGET HOTEL

tel: 0871 527 8710 (Calls cost 13p per minute plus your phone company's access charge) **Middleton Road, Crumpsall M8 4NB**
web: www.premierinn.com
dir: *M60 junction 19, A576 towards Manchester, through 2 sets of lights. Hotel on left.*

Rooms: 45

Premier Inn Manchester Old Trafford

 Premier Inn

BUDGET HOTEL

tel: 0871 527 8750 (Calls cost 13p per minute plus your phone company's access charge) **Waters Reach, Trafford Park M17 1WS**
web: www.premierinn.com
dir: *M6 junction 19, A556 towards Altrincham. Follow Stretford and Manchester City Centre signs (road becomes A56). Follow Manchester United Football Stadium signs. At stadium left at lights. Into Sir Matt Busby Way, after 1st lights hotel on right.*

Rooms: 172

Premier Inn Manchester (Salford Quays)

 Premier Inn

BUDGET HOTEL

tel: 0871 527 8718 (Calls cost 13p per minute plus your phone company's access charge) **11 The Quays, Salford Quays M50 3SQ**
web: www.premierinn.com
dir: *M602 junction 3, A5063, on Salford Quays.*

Rooms: 80

Premier Inn Manchester Trafford Centre North

 Premier Inn

BUDGET HOTEL

tel: 0871 527 8752 (Calls cost 13p per minute plus your phone company's access charge) **18-20 Trafford Boulevard M41 7JE**
web: www.premierinn.com
dir: *M6, onto M62 at junction 21a, towards Manchester. M62 junction 1, M60 towards south. M60 junction 10, take B5214. Hotel on left just before Ellesmere Circle.*

Rooms: 62

Premier Inn Manchester Trafford Centre South

 Premier Inn

BUDGET HOTEL

tel: 0871 527 8754 (Calls cost 13p per minute plus your phone company's access charge) **Wilderspool Wood, Trafford Centre M17 8WW**
web: www.premierinn.com
dir: *M6 onto M62 junction 21a towards Manchester. Or M62 junction 1 onto M60 south. Or M60 junction 10, B5124 towards Trafford Park. At 1st roundabout take last exit for Trafford Centre parking. At 2nd roundabout straight on. Hotel on left.*

Rooms: 60

Premier Inn Manchester Trafford Centre West

 Premier Inn

BUDGET HOTEL

tel: 0871 527 8756 (Calls cost 13p per minute plus your phone company's access charge) **Old Park Lane M17 8PG**
web: www.premierinn.com
dir: *M60 junction 10 towards The Trafford Centre.*

Rooms: 234

Premier Inn Manchester (West Didsbury)

 Premier Inn

BUDGET HOTEL

tel: 0871 527 8722 (Calls cost 13p per minute plus your phone company's access charge) **Christies Field Office Park, Derwent Ave M21 7QS**
web: www.premierinn.com
dir: *M60 junction 5, A5103 (Princess Parkway) towards Manchester on A5103. Hotel approximately 1 mile.*

Rooms: 112

Premier Inn Manchester (Wilmslow)

Premier Inn

BUDGET HOTEL

tel: 0871 527 8736 (Calls cost 13p per minute plus your phone company's access charge) **Racecourse Road, Wilmslow SK9 5LR**
web: www.premierinn.com
dir: *M6 junction 19 to Knutsford, follow Wilmslow signs. Left at 1st and 2nd lights towards Wilmslow. Through Mobberley, left just before Bird in Hand pub. At T-junction, right. Hotel 150 yards on right.*
Rooms: 37

MANCHESTER AIRPORT
Greater Manchester   Map 15 SJ88

See also **Altrincham**

The Stanneylands
★★★★ 79% 🏵🏵 HOTEL

tel: 01625 525225 **Stanneylands Road SK9 4EY**
email: reservations@stanneylands.co.uk **web:** www.stanneylands.co.uk
dir: *From M56 at airport exit, follow signs to Wilmslow. Left towards Handforth. Left at lights into Stanneylands Road, hotel on left.*

This traditional country house hotel, just three miles from Manchester Airport, offers well-equipped bedrooms that include suites, prestige and executive rooms together with delightful, comfortable day rooms. The cuisine in the restaurant is of a high standard, and ranges from traditional favourites to more imaginative modern dishes. There is also the contemporary Calico café bar in a conservatory setting offering all-day menus, including afternoon tea, and live music played on the baby grand piano. The hotel makes an ideal wedding venue, and the staff throughout are friendly and obliging.

Rooms: 52 (2 family) (10 GF) 🔌 **S** fr £89 **D** fr £89* **Facilities:** STV FTV WiFi ⌨ 🎵 Xmas New Year **Conf:** Class 50 Board 40 Theatre 120 **Services:** Lift Night porter **Parking:** 108 **Notes:** Civ Wed 90

Best Western Plus Pinewood on Wilmslow
★★★★ 77% 🏵 HOTEL   Ⓑ Best Western PLUS

tel: 01625 529211 **180 Wilmslow Road SK9 3LF**
email: pinewood.res@pinewood-hotel.co.uk **web:** www.pinewood-hotel.co.uk
dir: *Phone for directions.*

This stylish hotel is conveniently situated for the M60, Trafford Park, Trafford Centre and Manchester Airport. Bedrooms provide very good quality accommodation; all come with WiFi. The modern public areas include Restaurant One Eighty, open every night with a choice of menus. Ample parking is available.

Rooms: 89 (3 family) 🔌 **Facilities:** FTV WiFi HL Use of nearby Total Fitness Club Xmas New Year **Conf:** Class 60 Board 60 Theatre 120 **Services:** Lift Night porter **Parking:** 120 **Notes:** Civ Wed 120

Hallmark Hotel Manchester
★★★★ 76% HOTEL

tel: 0330 028 3419 **Stanley Road SK9 3LD**
email: manchester@hallmarkhotels.co.uk **web:** www.hallmarkhotels.co.uk
dir: *M60 junction 3/A34 signed Cheadle/Wilmslow. Right at 3rd roundabout into Stanley Road (B5094). Hotel on left.*

Ideally located for Manchester Airport and just a few miles from both the Trafford Centre and the city's many shops, the Hallmark Hotel offers well appointed bedrooms. Guests can relax and unwind in the hotel's 20-metre pool, jacuzzi and

steam rooms. The brasserie is open for both lunch and dinner, and offers a range of international dishes.

Rooms: 88 (8 family) (12 GF) 🔌 **S** fr £165* **Facilities:** Spa FTV WiFi ⌨ 🅣 Gym Steam room Sauna Treatment rooms New Year **Conf:** Class 250 Board 60 Theatre 500 **Services:** Lift Night porter **Parking:** 220 **Notes:** Civ Wed 300

Premier Inn Manchester Airport Hotel (M56 Jct 6 South)

Premier Inn

BUDGET HOTEL

tel: 0871 527 8726 (Calls cost 13p per minute plus your phone company's access charge) **Runger Lane, Wilmslow Road M90 5DL**
web: www.premierinn.com
dir: *M56 junction 6, follow Wilmslow and Hale signs. Merge onto M56 signed Warrington, Macclesfield and Hale. Left into Runger Lane signed Freight Terminal.*
Rooms: 195

Premier Inn Manchester Airport (M56 Jct 6) Runger Lane North

Premier Inn

BUDGET HOTEL

tel: 0871 527 8730 (Calls cost 13p per minute plus your phone company's access charge) **Runger Lane, Wilmslow Road M90 5DL**
web: www.premierinn.com
dir: *M56 junction 6, follow Airport signs. 2nd exit at roundabout. Hotel on left. Through Travelodge car park. Hotel on right.*
Rooms: 165

Premier Inn Manchester (Handforth)

Premier Inn

BUDGET HOTEL

tel: 0871 527 8732 (Calls cost 13p per minute plus your phone company's access charge) **30 Wilmslow Road SK9 3EW**
web: www.premierinn.com
dir: *M56 junction 6, A538 towards Wilmslow. At main junction into town centre bear left. In 2 miles hotel at top of hill on right just after Wilmslow Garden Centre.*
Rooms: 35

MARGATE
Kent   Map 7 TR37

Sands Hotel
★★★★ 80% 🏵🏵 🏛 TOWN HOUSE HOTEL

tel: 01843 228228 **16 Marine Drive CT9 1DH**
email: reservations@sandshotelmargate.co.uk **web:** www.sandshotelmargate.co.uk
dir: *From London M2, A299 to A28 to Margate.*

Located in the centre of Margate, Sands Hotel enjoys uninterrupted sea views. The award-winning Bay Restaurant which is open for breakfast, lunch, afternoon tea and dinner also has great views, and hotel guests can relax on the private roof terrace when the weather is fine. The smart bedrooms and bathrooms are contemporary in style, and many rooms have private balconies.

Rooms: 20 (6 family) 🔌 **Facilities:** STV FTV WiFi ⌨ HL 🎵 Xmas New Year **Conf:** Class 55 Board 30 Theatre 80 **Services:** Lift Night porter Air con **Notes:** LB Civ Wed 80

M

MARGATE *continued*

Premier Inn Margate

BUDGET HOTEL

tel: 0871 527 8762 (Calls cost 13p per minute plus your phone company's access charge) **Station Green, Station Road CT9 5AF**
web: www.premierinn.com
dir: *M2, A299, A28 to Margate seafront. Hotel adjacent to Margate station.*

High quality, budget accommodation ideal for both families and business travellers. Spacious, en suite bedrooms feature free WiFi and tea and coffee making facilities, and in most hotels, Freeview TV is also available. The adjacent family restaurant features a wide and varied menu.

Rooms: 64

MARKET DRAYTON
Shropshire

Map 15 SJ63

INSPECTOR'S CHOICE

Goldstone Hall

★★★ ◉◉ HOTEL

tel: 01630 661202 **Goldstone Road TF9 2NA**
email: enquiries@goldstonehall.com **web:** www.goldstonehall.com
dir: *4 miles south of Market Drayton, 4 miles north of Newport. Hotel signed from A529 and A41.*

Situated in extensive grounds, this period property is a family-run hotel. It provides traditionally furnished, well-equipped accommodation with outstanding en suite bathrooms and lots of thoughtful extras. The public rooms are extensive and include a choice of lounges, a snooker room and a conservatory. The kitchen has a well deserved reputation for good food that utilises home-grown produce, and a warm welcome is assured.

Rooms: 12 (2 GF) **Facilities:** STV FTV WiFi ☂ ⛵ Snooker table New Year
Conf: Class 30 Board 30 Theatre 50 **Parking:** 60 **Notes:** Civ Wed 100

MARKET HARBOROUGH
Leicestershire

Map 11 SP78

Three Swans Hotel

★★★ 82% ◉ HOTEL

tel: 01858 466644 **21 High Street LE16 7NJ**
email: threeswans@innmail.co.uk **web:** www.threeswans.co.uk
dir: *M1 junction 20, A304 to Market Harborough. Through town centre on A6 from Leicester, hotel on right.*

Public areas in this former coaching inn include an elegant fine dining restaurant and cocktail bar, a smart foyer lounge and popular public bar areas. Bedroom styles and sizes vary, but are very well appointed and equipped. Those in the wing are particularly impressive, offering high quality and spacious accommodation. Sky TV in rooms comes as standard.

Rooms: 59 (46 annexe) (10 family) (20 GF) **Facilities:** STV FTV WiFi ☂ Xmas New Year **Conf:** Class 90 Board 50 Theatre 250 **Services:** Lift Night porter **Parking:** 70 **Notes:** Civ Wed 140

Premier Inn Market Harborough

BUDGET HOTEL

tel: 0871 527 8764 (Calls cost 13p per minute plus your phone company's access charge) **Melton Road, East Langton LE16 7TG**
web: www.premierinn.com
dir: *On A6, north of Market Harborough. Hotel on roundabout junction of A6 and B6047.*

Rooms: 58

MARLOW
Buckinghamshire

Map 5 SU88

Macdonald Compleat Angler
★★★★ ◎◎ ⓢ HOTEL

tel: 01628 484444 **Marlow Bridge SL7 1RG**
email: compleatangler@macdonald-hotels.co.uk
web: www.macdonaldhotels.co.uk/compleatangler
dir: M4 junction 8/9 or M40 junction 4, A404(M) to roundabout, Bisham exit, 1 mile to Marlow Bridge, hotel on right.

This well-established hotel enjoys an idyllic location overlooking the River Thames and the delightful Marlow weir. The bedrooms, which differ in size and style, are individually decorated and are equipped with satellite TVs, high-speed internet and air conditioning; some rooms have balconies with views of the weir and some have four-posters. The Riverside Restaurant provides outstanding and award-winning cuisine. In summer guests can use two boats that the hotel has moored on the river, and fishing is, of course, a popular activity – a ghillie can accompany guests if arranged in advance. Staff throughout are keen to please and nothing is too much trouble.

Rooms: 64 (6 family) (6 GF) **S** fr £149 **D** fr £159 **Facilities:** FTV WiFi ⓐ HL Fishing Fly and coarse fishing River trips (April to September) Xmas New Year
Conf: Class 65 Board 36 Theatre 150 **Services:** Lift Night porter **Parking:** 100
Notes: Civ Wed 120

Danesfield House Hotel & Spa
★★★★ 87% ◎◎ HOTEL

tel: 01628 891010 **Henley Road SL7 2EY**
email: reservations@danesfieldhouse.co.uk **web:** www.danesfieldhouse.co.uk
dir: 2 miles from Marlow on A4155 towards Henley.

Set in 65 acres of elevated grounds just 45 minutes from central London and 30 minutes from Heathrow, this hotel enjoys spectacular views across the River Thames. Impressive public rooms include the cathedral-like Great Hall, an impressive spa, and The Orangery for informal dining. The beautiful Oak Room restaurant is also an ideal setting to enjoy superb, imaginative modern British cuisine. Some bedrooms have balconies and stunning views. Nothing is too much trouble for the team of committed staff.

Rooms: 78 (3 family) (27 GF) 🐾 **S** fr £250 **D** fr £250* **Facilities:** Spa STV FTV WiFi ⓐ ⓣ ⓢ ⓨ Gym Jogging trail Steam room Hydrotherapy room Sauna Xmas New Year **Conf:** Class 60 Board 50 Theatre 100 **Services:** Lift Night porter **Parking:** 100 **Notes:** Civ Wed 120

Crowne Plaza Marlow
★★★★ 79% ◎ HOTEL

tel: 01628 496800 **Field House Lane SL7 1GJ**
email: enquiries@cpmarlow.co.uk **web:** www.cpmarlow.co.uk
dir: A404 exit to Marlow, left at mini-roundabout, left into Field House Lane.

This hotel is in the Thames Valley not far from Windsor and Henley-on-Thames. The public areas are air conditioned and include the Agua Café and Bar and Glaze Restaurant. Leisure facilities include an up-to-the-minute gym and large pool. Bedrooms, including six contemporary suites, enjoy plenty of natural light and have excellent workstations; the Club Rooms have European and US power points.

Rooms: 168 (47 family) (56 GF) 🐾 **S** fr £75 **D** fr £95 (including breakfast)*
Facilities: Spa FTV WiFi ⓐ HL ⓣ ⓨ Gym Sauna Steam room dance studio nail bar Xmas New Year **Conf:** Class 180 Board 76 Theatre 450 **Services:** Lift Night porter Air con **Parking:** 300 **Notes:** LB Civ Wed 250

Premier Inn Marlow
BUDGET HOTEL

tel: 0871 527 8766 (Calls cost 13p per minute plus your phone company's access charge) **The Causeway SL7 2AA**
web: www.premierinn.com
dir: M40 junction 4, A404 signed Marlow/Maidenhead. Left, follow A4155 signs to Marlow. At 3rd roundabout 1st exit into High Street, signed Bisham. Straight on at mini-roundabout. Hotel on left.

High quality, budget accommodation ideal for both families and business travellers. Spacious, en suite bedrooms feature free WiFi and tea and coffee making facilities, and in most hotels, Freeview TV is also available. The adjacent family restaurant features a wide and varied menu.

Rooms: 17

M

MARSTON
Lincolnshire

Map 11 SK84

Ramada Resort Grantham

★★★ 75% HOTEL

tel: 01400 250909 **Toll Bar Road NG32 2HT**
email: reservations@ramadaresortgrantham.co.uk
web: www.ramadaresortgrantham.co.uk
dir: *From A1 north: left to Marston adjacent to petrol station. From A1 south: 1st right after Allington/Belton exit.*

Located in the countryside one mile from the A1, this sympathetically renovated and extended former period barn provides a range of thoughtfully furnished bedrooms, ideal for both business and leisure customers. Imaginative food is offered in the attractive beamed restaurant, and extensive leisure facilities include a swimming pool, sauna, steam room and a well-equipped gym.

Rooms: 103 (11 family) (46 GF) ⋔ **S** fr £50 **D** fr £60 (including breakfast)
Facilities: Spa STV FTV WiFi ⬠ HL ⬡ Gym Sauna Steam room Solarium Spa bath Xmas New Year **Conf:** Class 180 Board 100 Theatre 300 **Services:** Lift Night porter **Parking:** 280 **Notes:** LB Civ Wed 250

MASHAM
North Yorkshire

Map 19 SE28

Swinton Park

★★★★ ⊛ HOTEL

tel: 01765 680900 **Swinton HG4 4JH**
email: reservations@swintonpark.com **web:** www.swintonestate.com
dir: *Phone for directions.*

Although extended during the Victorian and Edwardian eras, the original part of this welcoming castle dates from the 17th century. Bedrooms are luxuriously furnished and come with a host of thoughtful extras. Samuel's restaurant serves food sourced from the 20,000-acre Swinton Estate, as the hotel, winner of several green awards, is committed to keeping the 'food miles' to a minimum. The gardens, including a four-acre walled garden, have been gradually restored. The Deerhouse is the venue for the hotel's alfresco food festivals, summer BBQs and weddings.

Rooms: 32 (6 family) ⋔ **S** fr £195 **D** fr £195 (including breakfast)*
Facilities: Spa FTV WiFi ⬠ ⬡ ⬥ ⬦ 9 Fishing ⬧ Gym Shooting Falconry Birds of prey Pony trekking Cookery school Xmas New Year **Conf:** Class 60 Board 40 Theatre 110 **Services:** Lift Night porter **Parking:** 50 **Notes:** LB Civ Wed 120

MATFEN
Northumberland

Map 21 NZ07

Matfen Hall

★★★★ 80% ⊛⊛ HOTEL

tel: 01661 886500 **NE20 0RH**
email: info@matfenhall.com **web:** www.matfenhall.com
dir: *A69 onto B6318. Hotel just before village.*

Matfen Hall is a luxurious and elegant stately home set in 300 acres of beautiful Northumbrian countryside. The hotel offers individually decorated bedrooms in both traditional and contemporary styles, while the impressive public rooms include the Library Restaurant, the Keepers Lodge and the Conservatory Bistro; the Great Hall is perfect for weddings and private dining. The golf estate includes a 27-hole course, a par 3 course and a driving range. Relax in the stylish spa, leisure and conference facilities.

Rooms: 53 (11 family) ⋔ **S** fr £124 **D** fr £140 (including breakfast)* **Facilities:** Spa STV FTV WiFi ⬠ HL ⬡ ⬦ 27 Gym Sauna Steam room Salt grotto Ice fountain Aerobics Driving range Golf academy Xmas New Year **Conf:** Class 46 Board 40 Theatre 120 **Services:** Lift Night porter **Parking:** 150 **Notes:** LB Civ Wed 120

MATLOCK
Derbyshire

Map 16 SK35

Premier Inn Matlock

Premier Inn

BUDGET HOTEL

tel: 0871 527 9612 (Calls cost 13p per minute plus your phone company's access charge) **DE4 3AZ**
web: www.premierinn.com
dir: *Phone for directions.*

High quality, budget accommodation ideal for both families and business travellers. Spacious, en suite bedrooms feature free WiFi and tea and coffee making facilities, and in most hotels, Freeview TV is also available. The adjacent family restaurant features a wide and varied menu.

Rooms: 58

MAWGAN PORTH
Cornwall & Isles Of Scilly

Map 2 SW86

The Scarlet Hotel

★★★★ 84% ⊛⊛ HOTEL

tel: 01637 861800 **Tredragon Road TR8 4DQ**
email: stay@scarlethotel.co.uk **web:** www.scarlethotel.co.uk
dir: *A39, A30 towards Truro. At Trekenning roundabout take A3059, follow Newquay Airport signs. Right after garage signed St Mawgan and Airport. Right after airport, at T-junction signed Padstow B3276. At Mawgan Porth left. Hotel 250 yards.*

Built as an eco hotel, this strikingly modern property has a stunning cliff-top location with magnificent views, and offers something a little different. The very stylish and well-equipped bedrooms are categorised in five types: Just Right, Generous, Unique, Spacious and Indulgent. The Ayurvedic spa is exceptional and encompasses the rejuvenation of the whole body and mind; relaxation is the key here. Cuisine is equally important, and in tune with the hotel's environment policies, daily-changing menus feature fresh, seasonal and local produce. The team of 'hosts' offer a high level of hospitality and service.

Rooms: 37 (5 GF) **S** fr £200 **D** fr £220 (including breakfast)* **Facilities:** Spa FTV WiFi ᐯ ᐯ ᐯ Yoga room Meditation and relaxation room Library Outside sauna Outdoor nature swimming pool ♫ Xmas New Year **Conf:** Board 20 **Services:** Lift Night porter **Parking:** 37 **Notes:** LB No children 18 years Closed 3–28 January RS 25 and 31 December Civ Wed 74

Bedruthan Hotel and Spa

★★★★ 79% HOTEL

tel: 01637 861200 **TR8 4BU**
email: stay@bedruthan.com web: www.bedruthan.com
dir: *From A39 or A30 follow signs to Newquay Airport. Pass airport, right at T-junction to Mawgan Porth. Hotel at top of hill on left.*

Bedruthan Hotel and Spa features stunning views over Mawgan Porth beach from its public areas, restaurants and the majority of the bedrooms. The hotel is a homage to the architecture of the 1970s, with a comfortable, contemporary feel. It also has a spa and conference facilities and holds a variety of events and workshops throughout the year. There are two restaurants – the simple and contemporary Wild Café, and the quiet and intimate, The Herring. Both offer food made from local Cornish produce. This is a very child-friendly hotel, including kids' clubs for various ages, play areas, childcare, baby-listening service and equipment such as pushchairs that guests can borrow for free.

Rooms: 101 (60 family) (1 GF) **D** fr £166 (including breakfast)* **Facilities:** Spa FTV WiFi ᐯ ᐯ ᐯ ᐯ Gym Sauna Steam room Hydropool Pool table Outdoor sensory spa garden Weekly entertainment during school holidays Workshops Surf lessons fairs ♫ Xmas New Year **Conf:** Class 60 Board 40 Theatre 150 **Services:** Lift Night porter **Parking:** 120 **Notes:** LB Closed 2 January to 2 February Civ Wed 150

MAWNAN SMITH	Map 2 SW72
Cornwall & Isles Of Scilly	

Budock Vean Hotel

★★★★ 79% COUNTRY HOUSE HOTEL

tel: 01326 252100 & 250288 **TR11 5LG**
email: relax@budockvean.co.uk web: www.budockvean.co.uk
dir: *From A39 follow tourist signs to Trebah Gardens. 0.5 mile to hotel.*

Set in 65 acres of attractive, well-tended grounds, this peaceful hotel offers an impressive range of facilities. It is convenient for visiting the Helford River estuary and many local gardens, or simply as a tranquil venue for a leisure break. The bedrooms are spacious and come in a choice of styles; some overlook the grounds and the golf course.

Rooms: 57 (2 family) **S** fr £73 **D** fr £146 (including breakfast)* **Facilities:** Spa FTV WiFi ᐯ ᐯ 9 ᐯ Fishing ᐯ Kayaking Boat trips ♫ Xmas New Year **Services:** Lift Night porter **Parking:** 100 **Notes:** LB Closed 1st 3 weeks January Civ Wed 60

Meudon Hotel

★★★★ 77% COUNTRY HOUSE HOTEL

tel: 01326 250541 **TR11 5HT**
email: wecare@meudon.co.uk web: www.meudon.co.uk
dir: *From Truro A39 towards Falmouth at Hillhead – Anchor & Cannons roundabout, follow signs to Mabe then Mawnan Smith, left at Red Lion, hotel on right.*

This charming late Victorian mansion is a relaxing place to stay, with friendly hospitality and attentive service. It sits in impressive 9-acre gardens that lead down to a private beach. The spacious and comfortable bedrooms are situated in a more modern building. The cuisine features the best local Cornish produce and is served in the conservatory restaurant.

Rooms: 30 (2 family) (15 GF) **S** fr £80 **D** fr £100 (including breakfast)* **Facilities:** FTV WiFi ᐯ Fishing Private beach Hair salon Beauty treatment room **Conf:** Class 30 Board 30 Theatre 30 **Services:** Lift **Parking:** 50 **Notes:** LB Closed 24 December to January

Trelawne Hotel

★★★ 84% HOTEL

tel: 01326 250226 **Maenporth Road TR11 5HT**
email: info@trelawnehotel.co.uk web: www.trelawnehotel.co.uk
dir: *A39 to Falmouth, right at Hillhead roundabout signed Maenporth. Past beach, up hill, hotel on left.*

This hotel is surrounded by attractive lawns and gardens, and enjoys superb coastal views. An informal atmosphere prevails, and many guests return year after year. Bedrooms, many with sea views, are of varying sizes, but all are well equipped. Dinner features quality local produce used in imaginative dishes.

Rooms: 12 (3 family) (4 GF) **S** fr £55 **D** fr £90 (including breakfast)* **Facilities:** FTV WiFi ᐯ **Parking:** 16 **Notes:** LB

MELKSHAM	Map 4 ST96
Wiltshire	

Shaw Country Hotel

★★ 78% SMALL HOTEL

tel: 01225 702836 **Bath Road, Shaw SN12 8EF**
email: info@shawcountryhotel.com web: www.shawcountryhotel.com
dir: *1 mile from Melksham, 9 miles from Bath on A365.*

Located within easy reach of both Bath and the M4, this relaxed and friendly hotel sits in its own gardens and includes a patio area ideal for enjoying a drink during the summer months. The house boasts very well-appointed bedrooms, a comfortable lounge and bar, and a restaurant where a wide selection of innovative dishes make up both carte and set menus. A spacious function room is a useful addition.

Rooms: 13 (2 family) **S** fr £65 **D** fr £90 (including breakfast)* **Facilities:** FTV WiFi **Conf:** Class 40 Board 20 Theatre 60 **Parking:** 30 **Notes:** Closed 26–28 December, 1 January Civ Wed 70

M

MELTON MOWBRAY
Leicestershire

Map 11 SK71

INSPECTOR'S CHOICE

Stapleford Park
★★★★ ◉◉ COUNTRY HOUSE HOTEL

tel: 01572 787000 **Stapleford LE14 2EF**
email: reservations@staplefordpark.com **web:** www.staplefordpark.com
dir: *1 mile southwest of B676, 4 miles east of Melton Mowbray and 9 miles west of Colsterworth.*

This stunning mansion, dating back to the 14th century, sits in over 500 acres of beautiful grounds. Spacious, sumptuous public rooms include a choice of lounges and an elegant restaurant. An additional brasserie-style restaurant is located in the golf complex. The hotel also boasts a spa with health and beauty treatments and gym, plus horse riding and many other country pursuits. Bedrooms are individually styled and furnished to a high standard. Attentive service is delivered with a relaxed yet professional style. Dinner, in the impressive dining room, is a highlight of any stay.

Rooms: 55 (7 annexe) (10 family) (3 GF) ⌇ **S** fr £170 **D** fr £170 (including breakfast)* **Facilities:** Spa STV FTV WiFi ⌇ ⊛ ⚲ 18 ⚲ ⚲ Gym Archery Falconry Horse riding Petanque Shooting Billiards ⥮ Xmas New Year **Conf:** Class 140 Board 80 Theatre 200 **Services:** Lift Night porter **Parking:** 120 **Notes:** LB Civ Wed 200

Quorn Lodge Hotel
★★★ 73% HOTEL

tel: 01664 566660 **46 Asfordby Road LE13 0HR**
email: quornlodge@aol.com **web:** www.quornlodge.co.uk
dir: *From town centre take A6006. Hotel 300 yards from junction of A606/A607 on right.*

Centrally located, this smart, privately-owned and managed hotel offers a comfortable and welcoming atmosphere. Bedrooms are individually decorated and thoughtfully designed. The public rooms consist of a bright restaurant overlooking the garden, a cosy lounge bar and a modern function suite. High standards are maintained throughout and parking is a bonus.

Rooms: 21 (4 family) (3 GF) ⌇ **Facilities:** STV FTV WiFi ⌇ Gym **Conf:** Class 70 Board 80 Theatre 100 **Services:** Night porter **Parking:** 38 **Notes:** Civ Wed 80

Premier Inn Melton Mowbray

Premier Inn

BUDGET HOTEL

tel: 0871 527 9584 (Calls cost 13p per minute plus your phone company's access charge) **5 Norman Way LE13 1JE**
web: www.premierinn.com
dir: *On A607, north of town centre.*

High quality, budget accommodation ideal for both families and business travellers. Spacious, en suite bedrooms feature free WiFi and tea and coffee making facilities, and in most hotels, Freeview TV is also available. The adjacent family restaurant features a wide and varied menu.

Rooms: 55

MEMBURY MOTORWAY SERVICE AREA (M4)
Berkshire

Map 5 SU37

Days Inn Membury - M4

WELCOMEBREAK

AA Advertised

tel: 01488 72336 **Membury Service Area RG17 7TZ**
email: membury.hotel@welcomebreak.co.uk **web:** www.welcomebreak.co.uk
dir: *M4 between junction 14 and 15.*

This modern building offers accommodation in smart, spacious and well-equipped bedrooms, suitable for families and business travellers, and all with en suite bathrooms. Continental breakfast is available and other refreshments may be taken at the nearby family restaurant.

Rooms: 38 (32 family) (17 GF) (5 smoking) **Facilities:** FTV WiFi ⌇ Game zone amusements **Conf:** Board 10 **Parking:** 200

MEVAGISSEY
Cornwall & Isles Of Scilly

Map 2 SX04

Trevalsa Court Hotel
★★★ 82% ◉◉ HOTEL

tel: 01726 842468 **School Hill, Polstreath PL26 6TH**
email: stay@trevalsa-hotel.co.uk **web:** www.trevalsa-hotel.co.uk
dir: *From St Austell take B3273 to Mevagissey. Pass sign to Pentewan. At top of hill left at crossroad. Hotel signed.*

Very well located above the town of Mevagissey, with easy access to nearby attractions, this establishment is an Arts & Crafts style property appointed to a high standard throughout with lots of original features. Bedrooms, many with sea views, are comfortable and well presented; there is also a stylish guests' sitting room with views across the bay.

Rooms: 14 (1 annexe) (1 family) (4 GF) ⌇ **Facilities:** FTV WiFi ⌇ **Parking:** 20 **Notes:** LB Closed December to January

MEXBOROUGH
South Yorkshire   Map 16 SE40

Best Western Plus Pastures Hotel
Best Western PLUS.

★★★ 81% HOTEL

tel: 01709 577707 **Pastures Road S64 0JJ**
email: info@pastureshotel.co.uk **web:** www.pastureslodge.co.uk/hotel
dir: *0.5 mile from town centre on A6023, left by CLS Mot, signed Denaby Ings and Cadeby. Hotel on right.*

This private hotel is in a rural setting beside a working canal with views of Conisbrough Castle in the distance; it is convenient for Doncaster or the Dearne Valley with its nature reserves and leisure centre. Guests can dine in the family-friendly Pastures Lodge Pub and Restaurant situated opposite the hotel, or in Reeds restaurant in the hotel. Bedrooms, in a modern, purpose-built block, are quiet, comfortable and equipped with many modern facilities including smart TVs and in-room safes.

Rooms: 60 (5 family) (28 GF) ✆ **S** fr £72 **D** fr £84 (including breakfast)*
Facilities: STV FTV WiFi Xmas New Year **Conf:** Class 170 Board 100 Theatre 250
Services: Lift Night porter **Parking:** 179 **Notes:** LB Civ Wed 200

MICHAEL WOOD MOTORWAY SERVICE AREA (M5)
Gloucestershire   Map 4 ST79

Days Inn Michaelwood - M5
WELCOMEBREAK

AA Advertised

tel: 01454 261513 **Michaelwood Service Area GL11 6DD**
email: michaelwood.hotel@welcomebreak.co.uk **web:** www.welcomebreak.co.uk
dir: *M5 northbound between junction 13 and 14.*

This modern building offers accommodation in smart, spacious and well-equipped bedrooms, suitable for families and business travellers, and all with en suite bathrooms. Continental breakfast is available and other refreshments may be taken at the nearby family restaurant.

Rooms: 38 (15 family) (7 smoking) **Facilities:** FTV WiFi **Conf:** Board 10
Parking: 40

MIDDLESBROUGH
North Yorkshire   Map 19 NZ41

Premier Inn Middlesbrough Central South
Premier Inn

BUDGET HOTEL

tel: 0871 527 8770 (Calls cost 13p per minute plus your phone company's access charge) **Marton Way TS4 3BS**
web: www.premierinn.com
dir: *Off A172 opposite South Cleveland Hospital complex.*

High quality, budget accommodation ideal for both families and business travellers. Spacious, en suite bedrooms feature free WiFi and tea and coffee making facilities, and in most hotels, Freeview TV is also available. The adjacent family restaurant features a wide and varied menu.

Rooms: 74

Premier Inn Middlesbrough Town Centre
Premier Inn

BUDGET HOTEL

tel: 0871 527 8000 (Calls cost 13p per minute plus your phone company's access charge) **Wilson Road TS1 1JL**
web: www.premierinn.com
dir: *Leave the A19 and merge onto A66. Continue to follow the A66 then take the slip road towards Middlesbrough Centre (east). At the roundabout, take the 3rd exit and take the 2nd exit at the roundabout immediately after onto Wilson Street. Note: for sat nav use postcode TS1 1JL.*

MIDDLETON STONEY
Oxfordshire   Map 11 SP52

Best Western The Jersey Arms
Best Western.

★★ 76% HOTEL

tel: 01869 343234 **OX25 4AD**
email: jerseyarms@bestwestern.co.uk **web:** www.jerseyarms.com
dir: *3 miles from A34, on B430, 10 miles north of Oxford, between junction 9 and 10 of M40.*

With a history dating back to the 13th century, The Jersey Arms combines old-fashioned charm with contemporary style and elegance. The individually designed bedrooms are well equipped and comfortable. The lounge has an open fire, and the smart and spacious restaurant provides a calm atmosphere in which to enjoy the popular cuisine.

Rooms: 20 (9 GF) **S** fr £69 **D** fr £89* **Facilities:** FTV WiFi **Parking:** 55
Notes: No children

MIDSOMER NORTON
Somerset   Map 4 ST65

Best Western Plus Centurion Hotel
Best Western PLUS.

★★★★ 79% @@ HOTEL

tel: 01761 417711 **Charlton Lane BA3 4BD**
email: enquiries@centurionhotel.co.uk **web:** www.centurionhotel.co.uk
dir: *Just off A367, 10 miles south of Bath. Once in Radstock follow signs at mini-roundabout for Shepton Mallet/Wells, follow for 2 miles, left at small roundabout.*

The Best Western Plus Centurion Hotel is located just nine miles from Bath, in a peaceful area with a golf course in its own grounds. Bedrooms and bathrooms have been completely refurbished and offer good levels of quality and comfort. In addition to the relaxing public areas, a range of leisure facilities is available including a gym, swimming pool and the Centurion Health Club and Spa. Dinner may be taken in the relaxed Jays Bar or the stylish restaurant, with the option of dining in the conservatory area.

Rooms: 45 (2 family) (18 GF) ✆ **S** fr £60 **D** fr £90* **Facilities:** Spa FTV WiFi 9 Gym Sauna Steam room Spa pool New Year **Conf:** Class 50 Board 50 Theatre 180
Services: Night porter **Parking:** 160 **Notes:** LB Closed 24–26 December Civ Wed 110

M

MILTON COMMON
Oxfordshire   Map 5 SP60

The Oxfordshire
★★★★ 81% ⊛ HOTEL

tel: 01844 278300 **Rycote Lane OX9 2PU**
email: gm@theoxfordshire.com **web:** www.theoxfordshire.com
dir: *M40 junction 7 northbound (junction 8 southbound), A329 towards Thame.*

Located within easy reach of the M40 in the heart of the beautiful Chilterns, this hotel has a championship golf course. The accommodation offers impressive levels of comfort and quality, and all rooms are air-conditioned and have access onto a balcony. The Tempus Spa includes a 15-metre pool, modern gym and three treatment rooms. This resort makes an ideal location for a relaxing break, especially for golf enthusiasts.

Rooms: 50 (18 GF) **S** fr £89 **D** fr £99 (including breakfast)* **Facilities:** Spa FTV WiFi ↻ ⑭ ♿ 18 Gym Sauna Steam room New Year **Conf:** Class 66 Board 54 Theatre 180 **Services:** Lift Night porter Air con **Parking:** 150 **Notes:** LB Civ Wed 180

The Oxford Belfry

★★★★ 80% HOTEL

tel: 01844 279381 **OX9 2JW**
email: oxfordbelfry@qhotels.co.uk **web:** www.qhotels.co.uk
dir: *M40 junction 7 onto A329 to Thame. Left onto A40, hotel 300 yards on right.*

This modern hotel has a relatively rural location and enjoys lovely views of the countryside to the rear. The hotel is built around two very attractive courtyards and has a number of lounges and conference rooms, as well as indoor leisure facilities and outdoor tennis courts. Bedrooms are large and feature a range of extras.

Rooms: 154 (20 family) (66 GF) ⌇ **S** fr £99 **D** fr £109 (including breakfast) **Facilities:** Spa FTV WiFi ↻ HL ⑭ ♨ Gym Steam room Sauna Xmas New Year **Conf:** Class 180 Board 100 Theatre 450 **Services:** Lift Night porter **Parking:** 350 **Notes:** LB Civ Wed 300

MILTON KEYNES
Buckinghamshire   Map 11 SP83

Mercure Milton Keynes

★★★★ 74% HOTEL

tel: 01908 561666 **The Approach, Monks Way MK8 8LY**
email: h8876@accor.com **web:** www.mercure-milton-keynes-abbey-hill.com
dir: *M1 junction 14/A509, 3rd exit at roundabout onto London Road. 1st exit at roundabout onto A422, straight across 7 roundabouts, 3rd exit onto Monks Way, left to The Approach.*

This Mecure hotel is located close to Milton Keynes Central railway station and is within easy access to the M1 and Luton Airport. The bedrooms have a contemporary design, and the hotel provides a relaxing setting for meetings and events. Guests can enjoy a selection of freshly cooked meals in the bar and restaurant. Free parking and free WiFi are available.

Rooms: 92 (14 family) (44 GF) ⌇ **Facilities:** STV FTV WiFi ↻ HL Gym Xmas New Year **Conf:** Class 120 Board 80 Theatre 250 **Services:** Night porter Air con **Parking:** 120 **Notes:** Civ Wed 120

Novotel Milton Keynes

★★★ 76% HOTEL

tel: 01908 322212 **Saxon Street, Layburn Court MK13 7RA**
email: H3272@accor.com **web:** www.novotel.com
dir: *M1 junction 14, follow Childsway signs towards city centre. Right into Saxon Way, straight across all roundabouts, hotel on left.*

Contemporary in style, this purpose-built hotel is situated on the outskirts of the town, just a few minutes' drive from the centre and mainline railway station. Bedrooms provide ample workspace and a good range of facilities for the modern traveller, and public rooms include a children's play area and indoor leisure centre.

Rooms: 124 (40 family) (33 GF) ⌇ **Facilities:** FTV WiFi ↻ ⑭ Gym Sauna **Conf:** Class 75 Board 40 Theatre 120 **Services:** Lift Night porter **Parking:** 130 **Notes:** Civ Wed 100

Premier Inn Milton Keynes Central

BUDGET HOTEL

tel: 0871 527 8774 (Calls cost 13p per minute plus your phone company's access charge) **Secklow Gate West MK9 3BZ**
web: www.premierinn.com
dir: *M1 junction 14 follow H6 route over 6 roundabouts, at 7th (South Secklow) turn right, hotel on left.*

High quality, budget accommodation ideal for both families and business travellers. Spacious, en suite bedrooms feature free WiFi and tea and coffee making facilities, and in most hotels, Freeview TV is also available. The adjacent family restaurant features a wide and varied menu.

Rooms: 38

Premier Inn Milton Keynes East (Willen Lake)

BUDGET HOTEL

tel: 0871 527 8778 (Calls cost 13p per minute plus your phone company's access charge) **Brickhill Street, Willen Lake MK15 9HQ**
web: www.premierinn.com
dir: *M1 junction 14, H6 (Childsway). Right at 3rd roundabout into Brickhill Street. Right at 1st mini roundabout, hotel 1st left.*

Rooms: 41

Premier Inn Milton Keynes South
BUDGET HOTEL

tel: 0871 527 8780 (Calls cost 13p per minute plus your phone company's access charge) **Lakeside Grove, Bletcham Way, Caldecotte MK7 8HP**
web: www.premierinn.com
dir: *M1 junction 14, towards Milton Keynes on H6 (Childs Way). Straight on at 2 roundabouts. Left at 3rd onto V10 (Brickhill Street). Straight on at 5 roundabouts, at 6th right onto H10 Bletcham Way.*

Rooms: 61

Premier Inn Milton Keynes South West (Furzton Lake)

Premier Inn

BUDGET HOTEL

tel: 0871 527 8776 (Calls cost 13p per minute plus your phone company's access charge) **Shirwell Crescent, Furzton MK4 1GA**
web: www.premierinn.com
dir: M1 junction 14, A509 to Milton Keynes. Straight on at 8 roundabouts, at 9th roundabout (North Grafton) left onto V6. Right at next onto H7. Over The Bowl roundabout, hotel on left.

Rooms: 120

Premier Inn Milton Keynes (Theatre District)

Premier Inn

BUDGET HOTEL

tel: 0871 622 2426 (Calls cost 13p per minute plus your phone company's access charge) **801 Avebury Boulevard MK9 3JT**
web: www.premierinn.com
dir: A5 onto A509 Portway. Continue straight over 4 roundabouts, at 5th roundabout, take 3rd exit onto Secklow Gate. Left onto Avebury Boulevard. Hotel will be on left.

Rooms: 763

MINEHEAD
Somerset
Map 3 SS94

Premier Inn Minehead

Premier Inn

BUDGET HOTEL

tel: 0871 527 9696 (Calls cost 13p per minute plus your phone company's access charge) **Seaward Way TA24 6DF**
web: www.premierinn.com
dir: Leave A39 onto Seaward Way. Continue on Seaward Way. Hotel on left.

Rooms: 102

MINSTER
Kent
Map 7 TR36

Premier Inn Ramsgate

Premier Inn

BUDGET HOTEL

tel: 0871 527 9270 (Calls cost 13p per minute plus your phone company's access charge) **Tothill Street CT12 4HY**
web: www.premierinn.com
dir: M25 onto A2 (signed Dover) merge onto M2 (signed Canterbury). Onto A299 (signed Margate/Ramsgate). Hotel at Minister roundabout.

Rooms: 71

MONK FRYSTON
North Yorkshire
Map 19 SE52

Monk Fryston Hall Hotel

★★★ 82% COUNTRY HOUSE HOTEL

tel: 01977 682369 **LS25 5DU**
email: reception@monkfrystonhallhotel.co.uk **web:** www.monkfrystonhallhotel.co.uk
dir: A1(M) junction 42, A63 towards Selby. Monk Fryston 2 miles, hotel on left.

This delightful 16th-century mansion house enjoys a peaceful location in 30 acres of grounds yet is only minutes' drive from the A1(M). Many original features have been retained and the public rooms are furnished with antique and period pieces. Bedrooms are individually styled and thoughtfully equipped for both business and leisure guests.

Rooms: 30 (2 family) (6 GF) **Facilities:** FTV WiFi Xmas New Year **Conf:** Class 30 Board 25 Theatre 100 **Services:** Night porter **Parking:** 80 **Notes:** LB Civ Wed 100

MORECAMBE
Lancashire
Map 18 SD46

The Midland

 English Lakes
Hotels Resorts & Venues

★★★★ 78% HOTEL

tel: 01524 424000 **Marine Road West LA4 4BU**
email: themidland@englishlakes.co.uk **web:** www.englishlakes.co.uk/hotels/midland
dir: A589 towards Morecambe, follow seafront signs, left on B5321 Lancaster Road, then Easton Road, left into Central Drive. Right at roundabout on seafront. Left to hotel entrance.

This art deco hotel sits on the seafront and commands stunning views across Morecambe Bay to the mountains of the Lake District. Stylish and modern accommodation is provided in the well-appointed bedrooms. Spa facilities are available on site, and guests can use the leisure club at the nearby sister hotel.

Rooms: 44 (16 family) **Facilities:** FTV WiFi Xmas New Year **Conf:** Class 30 Board 48 Theatre 140 **Services:** Lift Night porter **Parking:** 70 **Notes:** Civ Wed 140

Best Western Lothersdale Hotel

 Best Western.

★★★ 79% HOTEL

tel: 01524 416404 **320-323 Marine Road LA4 5AA**
email: hello@bfhotels.com **web:** www.bfhotels.com
dir: M6 junction 34 follow signs for Morecambe and Heysham. Straight over 3 roundabouts following sign for Promenade. At seafront turn left, hotel 0.5 mile on left.

Located in a central position on Morecambe's promenade, the Lothersdale Hotel offers enviable views across the bay and the Lakeland hills beyond. For eating there's Aspects Bistro & Bistro with its modern British menu. Conference and function rooms are available, with parking located to the rear of the hotel. Free WiFi is provided too.

Rooms: 40 (1 family) (5 GF) **Facilities:** FTV WiFi New Year **Conf:** Class 100 Board 60 Theatre 120 **Services:** Lift Night porter **Parking:** 20 **Notes:** LB Closed 22–27 December Civ Wed 110

M

MORETONHAMPSTEAD	Map 3 SX78
Devon	

Bovey Castle

★★★★★ ◉◉◉ ⬚ HOTEL

tel: 01647 445000 **Dartmoor National Park TQ13 8RE**
email: info@boveycastle.com **web:** www.boveycastle.com
dir: *M5 junction 31 signed A30 Okehampton, stay on A30 until Whitton Down. Follow signs to Morehampton A382, stay on A382 until roundabout, turn right for Postbridge and Princetown B3212. Stay on B3212 for approximately 1.5 miles. Bovey Castle is on left.*

Bovey Castle is a relaxed and welcoming hotel, located in 275 acres of peaceful Devonshire countryside, which includes an award-winning 18-hole championship golf course. The bedrooms are elegant, spacious and stylish and offer high levels of comfort. Leisure facilities are extensive and include a health club, pool, spa and shop. Fine-dining is available in the Great Western Restaurant and a more casual style of eating is available in Smith's Brasserie. Cocktail bar, lounges and plenty of parking are also available.

Rooms: 60 (5 annexe) (9 family) (2 GF) ⬚ **Facilities:** Spa STV FTV WiFi ⬚ ⬚ ⬚ 18 ⬚ Fishing ⬚ Gym Falconry Archery Clay pigeon shooting Table tennis Cider & gin making 4x4 driving Xmas New Year **Conf:** Class 64 Board 50 Theatre 120 **Services:** Lift Night porter **Parking:** 100 **Notes:** Civ Wed 150

The White Hart Hotel

★★★ 81% HOTEL

tel: 01647 440500 **The Square TQ13 8NQ**
email: enquiries@whitehartdartmoor.co.uk **web:** www.whitehartdartmoor.co.uk
dir: *A30 towards Okehampton. At Whiddon Down take A382 for Moretonhampstead.*

Dating back to the 1700s, this former coaching inn is located on the edge of Dartmoor. A relaxed and friendly atmosphere prevails, with the staff providing attentive service. Comfortable bedrooms have a blend of traditional and contemporary styles with thoughtful extras provided. Dining is in either the brasserie restaurant or more informally in the bar; in both quality cuisine is served.

Rooms: 28 (8 annexe) (3 family) (4 GF) ⬚ **Facilities:** FTV WiFi ⬚ Xmas New Year **Conf:** Class 30 Board 20 Theatre 50 **Notes:** Civ Wed 60

MORETON-IN-MARSH	Map 10 SP23
Gloucestershire	

Manor House Hotel

★★★★ 83% ◉◉ ⬚ HOTEL

COTSWOLD
INNS & HOTELS

tel: 01608 650501 **High Street GL56 0LJ**
email: info@manorhousehotel.info **web:** www.cotswold-inns-hotels.co.uk
dir: *Off A429 at south end of town. Take East Street off High Street, hotel car park 3rd right.*

Dating back to the 16th century, this charming Cotswold coaching inn retains much of original character, with stone walls, impressive fireplaces and a relaxed, country-house atmosphere. Bedrooms vary in size and reflect the individuality of the building; all are well equipped and some are particularly opulent. Comfortable public areas include a popular bar, a brasserie and the stylish Mulberry Restaurant where an opportunity to enjoy an evening meal should not be missed.

Rooms: 35 (1 annexe) (3 family) (1 GF) ⬚ **S** fr £150 **D** fr £180 (including breakfast)* **Facilities:** FTV WiFi ⬚ Xmas New Year **Conf:** Class 48 Board 54 Theatre 120 **Services:** Lift Night porter **Parking:** 24 **Notes:** Civ Wed 120

White Hart Royal Hotel

★★★ 82% ◉ HOTEL

THE
COACHING
INN GROUP

tel: 01608 650731 **High Street GL56 0BA**
email: whr@innmail.co.uk **web:** www.whitehartroyal.co.uk
dir: *On High Street at junction with Oxford Road.*

This historic hotel has been providing accommodation for hundreds of years and today offers high standards of quality and comfort. Public areas are full of character, and the bedrooms, in a wide range of shapes and sizes, include several very spacious and luxurious rooms situated adjacent to the main building. A varied range of well prepared dishes is available throughout the day and evening in the main bar and the relaxing restaurant.

Rooms: 28 (8 annexe) (2 family) (9 GF) ⬚ **Facilities:** FTV WiFi ⬚ HL Xmas New Year **Conf:** Class 40 Board 20 Theatre 55 **Services:** Night porter **Parking:** 6 **Notes:** Civ Wed 50

Redesdale Arms

★★★ 79% ◉ HOTEL

tel: 01608 650308 **High Street GL56 0AW**
email: info@redesdalearms.com **web:** www.redesdalearms.com
dir: On A429, 0.5 mile from rail station.

This fine old inn has played a central role in the town for centuries. Traditional features combine successfully with contemporary comforts; bedrooms are located in the main building and in an annexe. Guests can choose from an imaginative menu in either the stylish restaurant or the conservatory.

Rooms: 34 (26 annexe) (6 family) (16 GF) **Facilities:** STV FTV WiFi Xmas New Year **Parking:** 17

MORLEY	Map 11 SK34
Derbyshire	

The Morley Hayes Hotel

★★★★ 81% ◉◉ HOTEL

tel: 01332 780480 **Main Road DE7 6DG**
email: hotel@morleyhayes.com **web:** www.morleyhayes.com
dir: 4 miles north of Derby on A608.

Located in rolling countryside, this modern golfing destination provides extremely comfortable, stylish bedrooms with wide-ranging facilities, plasma TVs and state-of-the-art bathrooms; the plush suites are particularly eye-catching. Creative cuisine is offered in the Dovecote Restaurant, and both Roosters and the Spikes sports bar provide informal eating options.

Rooms: 32 (4 family) (15 GF) **Facilities:** STV FTV WiFi HL 27 Golf driving range **Conf:** Class 50 Board 40 Theatre 120 **Services:** Lift Night porter Air con **Parking:** 245 **Notes:** Civ Wed 90

MORPETH	Map 21 NZ28
Northumberland	

Eshott Hall

★★★★ 77% ◉◉ COUNTRY HOUSE HOTEL

tel: 01670 787454 **Eshott NE65 9EN**
email: info@eshotthall.co.uk **web:** www.eshotthall.co.uk
dir: A1 Northbound from Morpeth 5 miles. A1 Southbound from Alnwick 15 miles.

Eshott Hall dates back to the 16th century and is set behind walled gardens in the heart of Northumberland, just a few miles from the A1. Bedrooms are extremely comfortable and very well appointed in keeping with the style and character of the house. Award-winning food uses the best from the local larder with public areas offering a real 'wow' factor.

Rooms: 17 (3 family) (3 GF) **Facilities:** **Conf:** Class 70 Board 50 Theatre 120 **Notes:** Civ Wed 80

MOTTRAM ST ANDREW	Map 16 SJ87
Cheshire	

Mottram Hall

★★★★ 83% ◉ HOTEL

tel: 01625 828135 **Wilmslow Road SK10 4QT**
email: mottramevents@qhotels.co.uk
web: www.qhotels.co.uk/our-locations/mottram-hall
dir: M6 junction 18 from south, M6 junction 20 from north, M56 junction 6, A538 Prestbury.

Set in 272 acres of some of Cheshire's most beautiful parkland, this 18th-century Georgian country house is certainly an idyllic retreat. The hotel boasts extensive leisure facilities, including a championship golf course, swimming pool, gym and spa. Bedrooms are well equipped and elegantly furnished, and include a number of superior rooms and suites.

Rooms: 120 (37 family) (28 GF) **S** fr £107 **D** fr £119 (including breakfast)* **Facilities:** Spa FTV WiFi 18 Gym FA approved football pitch Xmas New Year **Conf:** Class 120 Board 60 Theatre 180 **Services:** Lift Night porter **Parking:** 300 **Notes:** LB Civ Wed 160

MUCH WENLOCK	Map 10 SO69
Shropshire	

Raven Hotel

★★★ 80% ◉◉ HOTEL

tel: 01952 727251 **30 Barrow Street TF13 6EN**
email: enquiry@ravenhotel.com **web:** www.ravenhotel.com
dir: M54 junction 4 or 5, take A442 south, then A4169 to Much Wenlock.

This town-centre hotel spreads across several historic buildings with a 17th-century coaching inn at its centre. The accommodation is well furnished and equipped to offer modern comfort; some ground-floor rooms are available. Public areas feature an interesting collection of prints and memorabilia connected with the modern-day Olympic Games – an idea which was, interestingly, born in Much Wenlock.

Rooms: 20 (13 annexe) (5 GF) **Facilities:** FTV WiFi New Year **Conf:** Board 16 Theatre 16 **Parking:** 30 **Notes:** Closed 25–26 December

---

Gaskell Arms

★★★ 76% SMALL HOTEL

tel: 01952 727212 **Bourton Road TF13 6AQ**
email: maxine@gaskellarms.co.uk **web:** www.gaskellarms.co.uk
dir: M6 junction 10A onto M54, exit at junction 4, follow signs for Ironbridge / Much Wenlock and A4169.

This 17th-century former coaching inn has exposed beams and log fires in the public areas, and much original charm and character is retained throughout. In addition to the lounge bar and restaurant offering a wide range of meals and snacks, there is a small bar which is popular with locals. Well-equipped bedrooms, some located in stylishly renovated stables, provide good standards of comfort.

Rooms: 14 (3 family) (5 GF) **S** fr £79 **D** fr £99 (including breakfast)* **Facilities:** FTV WiFi **Conf:** Class 30 Board 20 Theatre 30 **Parking:** 40

M

MUDEFORD

See **Christchurch**

MULLION
Cornwall & Isles Of Scilly

Map 2 SW61

HIGHLY RECOMMENDED

Mullion Cove Hotel

★★★ ◎◎ HOTEL

tel: 01326 240328 **TR12 7EP**
email: enquiries@mullion-cove.co.uk **web:** www.mullion-cove.co.uk
dir: *A3083 towards The Lizard. Through Mullion towards Mullion Cove. Hotel in approximately 1 mile.*

Built at the turn of the last century and set high above the working harbour of Mullion, this hotel has spectacular views of the rugged coastline; seaward facing rooms are always popular. The elegant restaurant offers some carefully prepared dishes using local produce, while an alternative option is to eat less formally in the stylish bistro. After dinner, guests might like to relax in one of the charming lounges.

Rooms: 30 (3 family) (3 GF) S fr £85 **D** fr £100 (including breakfast)*
Facilities: FTV WiFi Xmas New Year **Conf:** Class 20 Board 30 Theatre 50
Services: Lift Night porter **Parking:** 60 **Notes:** LB

Polurrian Bay Hotel

AA Advertised ◎◎

tel: 01326 240421 **TR12 7EN**
email: info@polurrianhotel.com **web:** www.polurrianhotel.com
dir: *A394 to Helston. Follow The Lizard and Mullion signs onto A3083. Approximately 5 miles, right onto B3296 to Mullion. Follow one-way system to T-junction, left signed Mullion Cove. 0.5 mile right, follow hotel sign.*

Polurrian Bay Hotel boasts a stunning cliff-top position with spectacular views across St Mount's Bay. It is very much a family-friendly establishment with a range of facilities available. Small children can be entertained in the crèche, while the spa provides some rest and relaxation for mum and dad. Bedrooms provide impressive levels of comfort and quality, and many also enjoy wonderful sea views. Public areas include the Vista, a wonderful area in which to relax and take in the breathtaking scenery while enjoying a light lunch.

Rooms: 41 (12 family) (8 GF) **D** fr £120 (including breakfast)* **Facilities:** Spa FTV WiFi Gym Xmas New Year **Conf:** Class 12 Board 30 Theatre 90
Services: Night porter **Notes:** LB Civ Wed 80

NANTWICH
Cheshire

Map 15 SJ65

INSPECTOR'S CHOICE

Rookery Hall Hotel & Spa

★★★★ ◎◎ HOTEL

*Hand*PICKED
HOTELS

tel: 01270 610016 & 0845 072 7533 (Calls cost 5p per minute plus your phone company's access charge) **Main Road, Worleston CW5 6DQ**
email: rookeryhall@handpicked.co.uk
web: www.handpickedhotels.co.uk/rookeryhall
dir: *From A51 north of Nantwich take B5074 Winsford, signed Rookery Hall. Hotel 1.5 miles on right.*

This fine 19th-century mansion is set in 38 acres of gardens, pasture and parkland. Bedrooms are spacious and appointed to a high standard with wide-screen plasma TVs and DVD players; many rooms have separate walk-in showers as well as deep tubs. Public areas are delightful and retain many original features. There is an extensive, state-of-the art spa and leisure complex.

Rooms: 70 (39 annexe) (6 family) (23 GF) S fr £119 **D** fr £134 (including breakfast)* **Facilities:** Spa STV FTV WiFi HL Gym Sauna Crystal steam room Hydrotherapy pool Xmas New Year **Conf:** Class 90 Board 60 Theatre 200
Services: Lift Night porter **Parking:** 120 **Notes:** Civ Wed 160

Alvaston Hall Hotel

WARNER LEISURE HOTELS

★★★★ 75% HOTEL

tel: 01270 624341 **Middlewich Road CW5 6PD**
web: www.warnerleisurehotels.co.uk
dir: *Phone for directions.*

Alvaston Hall is a Grade II listed Victorian property located in the delightful Cheshire countryside and set in extensive grounds. A variety of very well-equipped bedrooms is available; some have spacious seating areas and some have outdoor terraces. Outdoor and indoor leisure facilities include a 9-hole golf course, hair and beauty treatments, and a great range of entertainment and activities including an impressive cabaret facility. Please note that this is an adults-only (minimum 21 years old) hotel.

Rooms: 245 (15 annexe) (101 GF) **Facilities:** Spa FTV WiFi HL 🅗 ⚲ 9 🏌 Gym Archery Bowling green 🎵 Xmas New Year **Services:** Lift Night porter **Parking:** 300
Notes: LB No children 21 years

Premier Inn Crewe/Nantwich

Premier Inn

BUDGET HOTEL

tel: 0871 527 8782 (Calls cost 13p per minute plus your phone company's access charge) **221 Crewe Road CW5 6NE**
web: www.premierinn.com
dir: *M6 junction 16, A500 towards Chester, A534 towards Nantwich. Hotel approximately 100 yards on right.*

High quality, budget accommodation ideal for both families and business travellers. Spacious, en suite bedrooms feature free WiFi and tea and coffee making facilities, and in most hotels, Freeview TV is also available. The adjacent family restaurant features a wide and varied menu.

Rooms: 37

NEW ALRESFORD
Hampshire
Map 5 SU53

Swan Hotel

THE INDEPENDENTS
HOTEL ASSOCIATION

★★★ 80% HOTEL

tel: 01962 732302 **11 West Street SO24 9AD**
email: swanhotel@btinternet.com **web:** www.swanhotelalresford.com
dir: *Exit A31 onto B3047.*

This former coaching inn dates back to the 18th century and remains a busy and popular destination for travellers and locals alike. Bedrooms are situated in both the main building and the more modern wing. The lounge bar and adjacent restaurant are open all day; for more traditional dining there is another restaurant which overlooks the busy village street.

Rooms: 23 (11 annexe) (2 family) (5 GF) **S** fr £80 **D** fr £110 (including breakfast)*
Facilities: FTV WiFi ↳ New Year **Conf:** Class 60 Board 40 Theatre 90 **Parking:** 25

NEWARK-ON-TRENT
Nottinghamshire
Map 17 SK75

Premier Inn Newark

Premier Inn

BUDGET HOTEL

tel: 0871 527 8784 (Calls cost 13p per minute plus your phone company's access charge) **Lincoln Road NG24 2DB**
web: www.premierinn.com
dir: *At junction of A1, A46 and A17, follow B6166 signs.*

High quality, budget accommodation ideal for both families and business travellers. Spacious, en suite bedrooms feature free WiFi and tea and coffee making facilities, and in most hotels, Freeview TV is also available. The adjacent family restaurant features a wide and varied menu.

Rooms: 70

NEWBURY
Berkshire
Map 5 SU46

See also **Andover**

INSPECTOR'S CHOICE

The Vineyard

★★★★★ 🌸🌸🌸 🍴 HOTEL

RELAIS & CHATEAUX

tel: 01635 528770 **Stockcross RG20 8JU**
email: general@the-vineyard.co.uk **web:** www.the-vineyard.co.uk
dir: *From M4 junction 13, A34 towards Newbury, exit at 3rd junction for Speen. Right at roundabout then right again at 2nd roundabout.*

The Vineyard is a haven of style in the Berkshire countryside, where only perfect will do. Bedrooms and suites come in a variety of styles, including many split-level suites that are exceptionally well equipped with indulgent features that ensure a wonderful stay. Comfortable lounges lead into the stylish award-winning restaurant – at the helm of the kitchen is Robby Jenks, an inspirational chef who recreates classical British dishes using modern techniques, delivering a simple yet perfect dining experience. The hotel has an impressive 30,000 bottle wine cellar which includes wines from California and around the world, including bottles from the award-winning estate of owner Sir Peter Michael. The hotel also prides itself on a superb art collection, which can be seen throughout the building. The welcome throughout the hotel is warm and sincere, the service professional yet relaxed.

Rooms: 49 (18 GF) **S** fr £215 **D** fr £236 (including breakfast) **Facilities:** Spa STV WiFi ↳ 🅗 ⚲ 9 Gym 🎵 Xmas New Year **Conf:** Class 70 Board 30 Theatre 140 **Services:** Lift Night porter Air con **Parking:** 100 **Notes:** LB Civ Wed 100

N

NEWBURY *continued*

HIGHLY RECOMMENDED

Donnington Valley Hotel & Spa

★★★★ 82% HOTEL

tel: 01635 551199 **Old Oxford Road, Donnington RG14 3AG**
email: general@donningtonvalley.co.uk **web:** www.donningtonvalley.co.uk
dir: *M4 junction 13, A34 signed Newbury. Take exit signed Donnington/Services, at roundabout 2nd exit signed Donnington. Left at next roundabout. Hotel 2 miles on right.*

In its own grounds complete with an 18-hole golf course, this stylish hotel boasts excellent facilities for both corporate and leisure guests; from the state-of-the-art spa offering excellent treatments, to an extensive range of meeting and function rooms. Air-conditioned bedrooms are stylish, spacious and particularly well equipped with fridges, lap-top safes and internet access. The Wine Press restaurant offers imaginative food complemented by a superb wine list.

Rooms: 111 (4 family) (36 GF) **D** fr £85* **Facilities:** Spa STV WiFi ↕ 🕙 ♨ 18 Gym Aromatherapy Sauna Steam room Studio Xmas New Year **Conf:** Class 50 Board 65 Theatre 160 **Services:** Lift Night porter Air con **Parking:** 150 **Notes:** LB Civ Wed 85

Regency Park Hotel

★★★★ 80% HOTEL

tel: 01635 871555 **Bowling Green Road, Thatcham RG18 3RP**
email: info@regencyparkhotel.co.uk **web:** www.regencyparkhotel.co.uk
dir: *From Newbury take A4 signed Thatcham and Reading. 2nd roundabout exit signed Cold Ash. Hotel 1 mile on left.*

This smart, stylish hotel is ideal for both business and leisure guests. Spacious, well-equipped bedrooms include a number of contemporary, tasteful executive rooms. Smart, airy public areas include a state-of-the-art spa and leisure club, plus the Watermark Restaurant which offers appealing cuisine.

Rooms: 108 (10 family) (9 GF) **S** fr £78 **D** fr £78* **Facilities:** Spa STV FTV WiFi ↕ HL 🕙 Gym Beauty treatments Sauna Steam room Xmas **Conf:** Class 80 Board 70 Theatre 200 **Services:** Lift Night porter **Parking:** 200 **Notes:** LB Civ Wed 100

Mercure Newbury Elcot Park

★★★★ 74% COUNTRY HOUSE HOTEL

tel: 0844 815 9060 (Calls cost 5p per minute plus your phone company's access charge) **Elcot RG20 8NJ**
email: gm.mercurenewburyelcotpark@jupiterhotels.co.uk
web: www.mercurenewbury.co.uk
dir: *M4 junction 13, A338 to Hungerford, A4 to Newbury. Hotel 4 miles from Hungerford.*

Enjoying a peaceful location within easy reach of both the A4 and M4, this country-house hotel is set in 16 acres of gardens and woodland. Bedrooms are comfortably appointed and include some located in an adjacent mews. Public areas include the Orangery Restaurant which enjoys views over the Kennet Valley and a range of conference rooms.

Rooms: 73 (17 annexe) (6 family) (25 GF) **Facilities:** FTV WiFi ↕ 🌭 💆 Gym New Year **Conf:** Class 60 Board 50 Theatre 140 **Services:** Night porter **Parking:** 120 **Notes:** LB Civ Wed 140

Donnington Grove Country Club

★★★ 76% HOTEL

tel: 01635 581000 **Grove Road, Donnington RG14 2LA**
email: enquiries@donnington-grove.com **web:** www.donnington-grove.com
dir: *Phone for directions.*

Situated on the outskirts of Newbury, overlooked by the ruins of Donnington Castle, this splendid manor house, a popular wedding venue, offers comfortable bedrooms in a variety of styles, all tastefully appointed to meet the needs of the leisure and business traveller. The estate comprises some 550 acres featuring a popular championship golf course designed by Dave Thomas. Fishing on the River Lambourn and clay-pigeon shooting are offered here.

Rooms: 39 (19 annexe) (27 GF) **S** fr £87 **D** fr £97* **Facilities:** FTV WiFi ↕ ↥ 18 Fishing Beauty treatment rooms New Year **Conf:** Class 30 Board 36 Theatre 100 **Services:** Lift Night porter **Parking:** 90 **Notes:** LB Civ Wed 100

Best Western West Grange Hotel

★★★ 75% HOTEL

tel: 01635 273074 **Cox's Lane, Bath Road RG7 5UP**
email: reservations@westgrangehotel.co.uk **web:** www.westgrangehotel.co.uk
dir: *M4 junction 12, A4 Bath Road, follow Newbury signs. Through Woolhampton, hotel on right in approximately 2 miles.*

Conveniently situated between Reading and Newbury, this modern hotel has well-appointed, spacious bedrooms; executive rooms are beautifully presented and have a host of additional features. The contemporary open-plan lounge and restaurant area serves an extensive choice of British cuisine. There is a range of business suites along with a larger conference room. The gardens are a real feature and the central courtyard is popular with guests.

Rooms: 62 (1 family) (21 GF) **S** fr £55 **D** fr £65* **Facilities:** FTV WiFi ↕ Xmas New Year **Conf:** Class 25 Board 30 Theatre 50 **Services:** Lift Night porter **Parking:** 50 **Notes:** Civ Wed 60

NEWBY BRIDGE	Map 18 SD38
Cumbria	

HIGHLY RECOMMENDED

Lakeside Hotel Lake Windermere

★★★★ 85% ◉◉ HOTEL

tel: 015395 30001 **Lakeside LA12 8AT**
email: sales@lakesidehotel.co.uk **web:** www.lakesidehotel.co.uk
dir: *M6 junction 36, A590 to Barrow, follow signs to Newby Bridge. Right over bridge, hotel 1 mile on right.*

This impressive hotel enjoys an enviable location on the southern edge of Lake Windermere and has easy access to the Lakeside & Haverthwaite Steam Railway, as well as the ferry terminal. Bedrooms are individually styled, and many enjoy delightful lake views. Spacious lounges and a choice of restaurants are available. The state-of-the-art spa is exclusive to residents and provides a range of treatment suites. Staff throughout are friendly and nothing is too much trouble.

Rooms: 74 (8 family) (8 GF) ♪ **D** fr £145 (including breakfast)* **Facilities:** Spa STV WiFi ⊳ ⊗ Gym Private jetty Rowing boats ♫ Xmas New Year **Conf:** Class 70 Board 40 Theatre 100 **Services:** Lift Night porter **Parking:** 200 **Notes:** Civ Wed 80

The Swan Hotel & Spa

★★★★ 79% HOTEL

tel: 015395 31681 **LA12 8NB**
email: enquiries@swanhotel.com **web:** www.swanhotel.com
dir: *M6 junction 36, A591, merge onto A590. At roundabouts follow A590, left at Newby Bridge roundabout, 1st right for hotel.*

The Swan Hotel & Spa is set in idyllic surroundings and offers something to suit every taste, from the gym and spa therapies for adults to the dedicated children's lounge. The well-equipped bedrooms are thoroughly modern, but each has a vintage touch. Good quality meals are served in the River Room; in good weather guests can eat on the riverside terrace.

Rooms: 54 (8 family) (14 GF) ♪ **Facilities:** Spa FTV WiFi ⊳ ⊗ Fishing Gym Sauna Steam room Xmas New Year **Conf:** Class 60 Board 40 Theatre 100 **Services:** Lift Night porter Air con **Parking:** 100 **Notes:** LB Civ Wed 100

NEWCASTLE-UNDER-LYME	Map 10 SJ84
Staffordshire	

Premier Inn Newcastle-under-Lyme

Premier Inn

BUDGET HOTEL

tel: 0871 527 8808 (Calls cost 13p per minute plus your phone company's access charge) **Talke Road, Chesterton ST5 7AL**
web: www.premierinn.com
dir: *M6 junction 12, A500, A34 to Newcastle-under-Lyme. Hotel 0.5 mile on right.*

High quality, budget accommodation ideal for both families and business travellers. Spacious, en suite bedrooms feature free WiFi and tea and coffee making facilities, and in most hotels, Freeview TV is also available. The adjacent family restaurant features a wide and varied menu.

Rooms: 83

NEWCASTLE UPON TYNE	Map 21 NZ26
Tyne & Wear	

INSPECTOR'S CHOICE

Jesmond Dene House

★★★★ ◉◉ HOTEL

tel: 0191 212 3000 **Jesmond Dene Road NE2 2EY**
email: info@jesmonddenehouse.co.uk **web:** www.jesmonddenehouse.co.uk
dir: *A167 north to A184. Right, right again into Jesmond Dene Road, hotel on left.*

This grand house overlooks the wooded valley of Jesmond Dene yet is just five minutes from the centre of town. It has been sympathetically converted into a stylish, contemporary hotel destination. The bedrooms are beautifully designed and boast TVs with Sky channels including HD Sky Sports, sumptuous beds with Egyptian cotton linen, digital radios, well-stocked mini bars, free broadband, desk space and safes. Equally eye-catching bathrooms with underfloor heating are equipped with high quality bespoke amenities. The stylish restaurant is the venue for innovative cooking which will prove a highlight of any stay.

Rooms: 40 (8 annexe) (1 family) (6 GF) ♪ **S** fr £114 **D** fr £114 (including breakfast)* **Facilities:** STV FTV WiFi ⊳ HL **Conf:** Class 40 Board 40 Theatre 120 **Services:** Lift Night porter **Parking:** 64 **Notes:** LB Civ Wed 100

HIGHLY RECOMMENDED

Hotel du Vin Newcastle

★★★★ 83% ◉ TOWN HOUSE HOTEL

Hotel du Vin & Bistro

tel: 0191 229 2200 **Allan House, City Road NE1 2BE**
email: reception.newcastle@hotelduvin.com
web: www.hotelduvin.com/locations/newcastle
dir: *A1 junction 65 onto A184 Gateshead/Newcastle, Quayside to City Road.*

The former maintenance depot of the Tyne Tees Shipping Company, this is a landmark building on the Tyne which has been transformed into a modern and stylish hotel. Bedrooms are well equipped and deeply comfortable with all the Hotel du Vin trademark features such as Egyptian cotton sheets, plasma TVs, DVD players and monsoon showers. Guests can dine in the bistro, or alfresco if the weather allows in the courtyard.

Rooms: 42 (6 GF) ♪ **Facilities:** STV WiFi HL **Conf:** Board 20 Theatre 26 **Services:** Lift Night porter Air con **Parking:** 10 **Notes:** Civ Wed 40

N

NEWCASTLE UPON TYNE *continued*

Malmaison Newcastle

★★★★ 81%  HOTEL

tel: 0191 389 8627 & 0844 693 0658 (Calls cost 5p per minute plus your phone company's access charge) **104 Quayside NE1 3DX**
email: newcastle@malmaison.com **web:** www.malmaison.com/locations/newcastle/
dir: *Follow signs for city centre, then for Quayside/Law Courts. Hotel 100 yards past Law Courts.*

The Malmaison Newcastle overlooks the river and the Millennium Bridge, in a prime position in the very popular quayside district. Bedrooms and suites have striking decor as well as mini bars, storm showers and free WiFi. Food and drink are an integral part of the operation here, with a stylish brasserie-style restaurant overlooking the river and bridge. The bar is modern and lively, attracting locals as well as the overnight guests. At the main entrance, there's a Starbucks bar to set you up with a coffee fix for the morning.

Rooms: 122 (10 family) ☛ **Facilities:** Spa STV FTV WiFi Gym ♫ **Conf:** Class 50 Board 40 Theatre 80 **Services:** Lift Night porter Air con **Parking:** 50 **Notes:** Civ Wed 80

Holiday Inn Newcastle Gosforth Park

★★★★ 79% HOTEL

tel: 0191 201 9988 & 0871 423 4818 **Great North Road, Seaton Burn NE13 6BP**
email: info@hinewcastlegosforthpark.co.uk **web:** www.hinewcastlegosforthpark.co.uk
dir: *A1 junction 80, at roundabout 1st left signed Blagdon. Hotel 500 yards on right.*

The Holiday Inn Newcastle Gosforth Park continues to undergo significant investment on a rolling programme, with leisure facilities, public spaces and bedrooms already benefiting from the work. Ample parking is offered along with a pool, gym and spa facilities.

Rooms: 151 (65 family) (69 GF) ☛ **S** fr £69 **D** fr £69* **Facilities:** Spa FTV WiFi ⮂ Gym Sauna Steam room New Year **Conf:** Class 180 Board 40 Theatre 450 **Services:** Lift Night porter **Parking:** 240 **Notes:** LB Civ Wed 200

The Vermont Hotel

★★★★ 79% HOTEL

tel: 0191 233 1010 **Castle Garth NE1 1RQ**
email: info@vermonthotel.co.uk **web:** www.vermont-hotel.com
dir: *Phone for directions.*

This iconic building offers some great views of the city. Centrally located and benefiting from an off-road car park, The Vermont Hotel is accessible from both the Quayside and from the castle.

Rooms: 101 ☛ **S** fr £80 **D** fr £90* **Facilities:** FTV WiFi ⮂ Gym Sauna Steam room Xmas New Year **Conf:** Class 80 Board 60 Theatre 220 **Services:** Lift Night porter **Parking:** 40 **Notes:** LB Civ Wed 220

Holiday Inn Newcastle Jesmond

★★★★ 78% HOTEL

tel: 0191 281 5511 **Jesmond Road NE2 1PR**
email: enquiries@hinewcastle.co.uk **web:** www.hinewcastle.co.uk

Holiday Inn Newcastle Jesmond is located next to the Metro Station and benefits from off-road parking. The interior is modern, and there is a vibrant restaurant and bar operation. This is a great location for enjoying the café culture of Jesmond or the upbeat pace of the city centre.

Rooms: 116 ☛ **Facilities:** STV FTV WiFi ⮂ HL Gym ♫ New Year **Conf:** Class 160 Board 46 Theatre 250 **Services:** Lift Night porter Air con **Parking:** 80 **Notes:** Civ Wed

County Hotel Newcastle

★★★★ 75% HOTEL

tel: 0191 731 6670 **Neville Street NE1 5DF**
email: info@countyhotel.co.uk **web:** www.countyhotel.co.uk

Built in 1874 and located in the centre of Newcastle opposite the train station, this hotel was one of the original hotels of the city and the grandeur of the architecture continues to set it aside from newer buildings. Recent and ongoing refurbishments have transformed the public areas. Exquisite cocktails are served in the bar followed by dinner in the well-presented Hudson Restaurant.

Rooms: 127 **S** fr £55 **D** fr £135* **Facilities: Conf:** Class 100 Board 100 Theatre 280

The Caledonian Hotel, Newcastle

★★★ 80% HOTEL

tel: 0191 281 7881 **64 Osborne Road, Jesmond NE2 2AT**
email: info@caledonian-hotel-newcastle.com **web:** www.peelhotels.co.uk
dir: *From A1 follow signs to Newcastle City, cross Tyne Bridge to Tynemouth. Left at lights at Osborne Road, hotel on right.*

This hotel is located in the Jesmond area of the city and offers comfortable bedrooms that are well equipped. The public areas include the trendy Billabong Bistro which serves food all day, and the terrace where a cosmopolitan atmosphere prevails. Alfresco dining is available.

Rooms: 89 (6 family) (7 GF) ☛ **Facilities:** WiFi Xmas New Year **Conf:** Class 50 Board 50 Theatre 100 **Services:** Lift Night porter **Parking:** 35 **Notes:** Civ Wed 70

Horton Grange Country House Hotel

★★★ 78% ◉◉ HOTEL

tel: 01661 860686 **Berwick Hill, Ponteland NE13 6BU**
email: info@hortongrange.co.uk **web:** www.hortongrange.co.uk
dir: *A1/A19 junction at Seaton Burn take 1st exit at 1st roundabout, after 1 mile, left signed Ponteland/Dinnington. Hotel on right approximately 2 miles.*

Horton Grange is a Grade II listed building set in its own grounds just a short distance from Newcastle Airport and Ponteland. The main house has traditionally styled executive bedrooms, and in addition there are four contemporary garden rooms that are elegant and spacious. All bedrooms have Freeview TVs, digital radios and broadband access. Food is served in the light and airy restaurant and the lounge, both of which overlook the gardens.

Rooms: 9 (4 annexe) (1 family) (4 GF) ☛ **S** fr £65 **D** fr £75 (including breakfast) **Facilities:** FTV WiFi HL Xmas New Year **Conf:** Class 40 Board 30 Theatre 120 **Parking:** 50 **Notes:** LB Civ Wed 120

Best Western New Kent Hotel

★★★ Ⓐ HOTEL

tel: 0191 281 7711 **127 Osborne Road NE2 2TB**
email: reservations@newkenthotel.co.uk **web:** www.newkenthotel.co.uk
dir: *On B1600, opposite St Georges Church.*

This popular business hotel offers relaxed service and typical Geordie hospitality. The bright, modern bedrooms are well equipped and the hotel's bar is an ideal meeting place. A range of generous, good value dishes are served in the restaurant, which doubles as a wedding venue.

Rooms: 32 (4 family) **Facilities:** STV FTV WiFi ⮂ Xmas New Year **Conf:** Class 30 Board 40 Theatre 60 **Services:** Night porter **Parking:** 22 **Notes:** LB Civ Wed 90

Premier Inn Newcastle Central

BUDGET HOTEL

tel: 0871 527 8802 (Calls cost 13p per minute plus your phone company's access charge) **New Bridge Street West NE1 8BS**
web: www.premierinn.com
dir: *Follow Gateshead and Newcastle signs on A167(M), over Tyne Bridge. A193 signed Wallsend and city centre, left to Carliol Square, hotel on corner.*

High quality, budget accommodation ideal for both families and business travellers. Spacious, en suite bedrooms feature free WiFi and tea and coffee making facilities, and in most hotels, Freeview TV is also available. The adjacent family restaurant features a wide and varied menu.

Rooms: 186

Premier Inn Newcastle City Centre (Millennium Bridge)

BUDGET HOTEL

tel: 0871 527 8800 (Calls cost 13p per minute plus your phone company's access charge) **City Road, Quayside NE1 2AN**
web: www.premierinn.com
dir: *At corner of City Road (A186) and Crawhall Road.*

Rooms: 82

Premier Inn Newcastle (Holystone)

BUDGET HOTEL

tel: 0871 527 8790 (Calls cost 13p per minute plus your phone company's access charge) **The Stonebrook, Edmund Road NE27 0UN**
web: www.premierinn.com
dir: *3 miles north of Tyne Tunnel. From A19 take A191 signed Gosforth. Hotel on left.*

Rooms: 112

Premier Inn Newcastle Quayside

BUDGET HOTEL

tel: 0871 527 8804 (Calls cost 13p per minute plus your phone company's access charge) **The Quayside NE1 3AE**
web: www.premierinn.com
dir: *Southbound: A1, A167(M), A186 signed Walker and Wallsend follow B1600 Quayside signs. Northbound: A1, A184, A189 (cross river). 1st exit, follow B1600 Quayside signs. Hotel at foot of Tyne Bridge in Exchange building.*

Rooms: 152

Novotel Newcastle Airport

★★★ 81% HOTEL

tel: 028 4345 2800 **Ponteland Road, Kenton NE3 3HZ**
email: H1118@accor.com **web:** www.novotel.com
dir: *A1(M) airport junction onto A696, take Kingston Park exit.*

This modern, well-proportioned hotel lies just off the bypass and is a five-minute drive from the airport. The hotel has a scheduled shuttle service and flight information screens for air passengers. Bedrooms are spacious with a range of extras. The Elements Restaurant offers a flexible dining option and is open until late. There is a contemporary lounge bar and also a small leisure centre for the more energetic guests. Secure parking is available.

Rooms: 126 (36 family) **Facilities:** FTV WiFi Gym Sauna Xmas New Year **Conf:** Class 150 Board 100 Theatre 200 **Services:** Lift **Parking:** 200
Notes: Civ Wed 200

Premier Inn Newcastle Airport

BUDGET HOTEL

tel: 0871 527 8796 (Calls cost 13p per minute plus your phone company's access charge) **Newcastle Int Airport, Ponteland Rd NE20 9DB**
web: www.premierinn.com
dir: *A1 onto A696, follow Airport signs. At roundabout take turn immediately after airport exit.*

High quality, budget accommodation ideal for both families and business travellers. Spacious, en suite bedrooms feature free WiFi and tea and coffee making facilities, and in most hotels, Freeview TV is also available. The adjacent family restaurant features a wide and varied menu.

Rooms: 88

Premier Inn Newcastle Airport (South)

BUDGET HOTEL

tel: 0871 527 8798 (Calls cost 13p per minute plus your phone company's access charge) **Callerton Lane Ends, Woolsington NE13 8DF**
web: www.premierinn.com
dir: *Just off A696 on B6918, 0.3 mile from airport.*

Rooms: 53

Premier Inn Newhaven

BUDGET HOTEL

tel: 0871 527 8810 (Calls cost 13p per minute plus your phone company's access charge) **Avis Road BN9 0AG**
web: www.premierinn.com
dir: *From A26 (New Road) through Drove Industrial Estate, left after underpass. Hotel in same complex as Sainsbury's.*

Rooms: 83

N

NEWMARKET
Suffolk

Map 12 TL66

INSPECTOR'S CHOICE

Bedford Lodge Hotel & Spa

★★★★ ◎◎ HOTEL

tel: 01638 663175 **Bury Road CB8 7BX**
email: info@bedfordlodgehotel.co.uk **web:** www.bedfordlodgehotel.co.uk
dir: *From town centre take A1304 towards Bury St Edmunds, hotel 0.5 mile on left.*

Bedford Lodge Hotel is an imposing 18th-century Georgian hunting lodge with more modern additions, set in three acres of secluded landscaped gardens. Public rooms feature the AA Rosette-worthy Squires Restaurant, Roxana Bar and a small lounge. The hotel also features superb leisure facilities including a health and fitness club, as well as self-contained conference and banqueting suites. Contemporary bedrooms have a light, airy feel, and each is tastefully furnished and well equipped.

Rooms: 80 (3 annexe) (6 family) (21 GF) (3 smoking) ✆ **S** fr £99 **D** fr £109 (including breakfast)* **Facilities:** Spa STV FTV WiFi ↺ ⊕ Gym Steam room Sauna Hydrotherapy pool Rasul Dry floatation New Year **Conf:** Class 80 Board 50 Theatre 180 **Services:** Lift Night porter Air con **Parking:** 120 **Notes:** LB Civ Wed 150

HIGHLY RECOMMENDED

Tuddenham Mill

★★★★ 83% ◎◎◎ HOTEL

tel: 01638 713552 **High Street, Tuddenham St Mary IP28 6SQ**
email: info@tuddenhammill.co.uk **web:** www.tuddenhammill.co.uk
dir: *M11 junction 9, merge A14. Left lane junction 38 towards Thetford/Norwich. Signed Tuddenham.*

Tuddenham Mill is a beautifully converted old watermill set amidst landscaped grounds between Newmarket and Bury St Edmunds. The contemporary bedrooms are situated in separate buildings adjacent to the main building, and each is tastefully appointed with co-ordinated fabrics and soft furnishings. The public areas have a wealth of original features such as the water wheel and exposed beams; they include a lounge bar, a smart restaurant, a meeting room and choice of terraces.

Rooms: 20 (17 annexe) (13 GF) ✆ **Facilities:** STV FTV WiFi ↺ Spa treatment room Xmas New Year **Conf:** Class 16 Board 16 Theatre 40 **Services:** Night porter **Parking:** 40 **Notes:** Civ Wed 60

Best Western Heath Court Hotel

 Best Western

★★★ 79% HOTEL

tel: 01638 667171 **Moulton Road CB8 8DY**
email: quality@heathcourthotel.com **web:** www.heathcourthotel.com
dir: *Phone for directions.*

Heath Court Hotel enjoys a very convenient location close to the town centre and overlooks the Newmarket gallops. Bedrooms are all well-equipped and spacious, and free WiFi is available throughout the hotel. Ample, secure parking is available and there is a popular restaurant and bar.

Rooms: 43 (2 family) **S** fr £78 **D** fr £93* **Facilities:** STV FTV WiFi ↺ New Year **Conf:** Class 45 Board 40 Theatre 130 **Services:** Lift Night porter **Parking:** 60 **Notes:** Civ Wed 120

Premier Inn Newmarket

Premier Inn

BUDGET HOTEL

tel: 0871 527 9296 (Calls cost 13p per minute plus your phone company's access charge) **Fred Archer Way CB8 7XN**
web: www.premierinn.com
dir: *A14 junction 37, A142 (Fordham Road). 2.3 miles, straight on at 2 roundabouts. At end of Fordham Road, into right lane, turn right. Hotel on right.*

High quality, budget accommodation ideal for both families and business travellers. Spacious, en suite bedrooms feature free WiFi and tea and coffee making facilities, and in most hotels, Freeview TV is also available. The adjacent family restaurant features a wide and varied menu.

Rooms: 75

NEW MILTON
Hampshire   Map 5 SZ29

Chewton Glen
★★★★★ ◉◉ ⓘ COUNTRY HOUSE HOTEL

tel: 01425 275341 & 282212 **Christchurch Road BH25 6QS**
email: reservations@chewtonglen.com **web:** www.chewtonglen.com
dir: *A35 from Lyndhurst for 10 miles, left at staggered junction. Follow tourist sign for hotel through Walkford, take 2nd left.*

Chewton Glen has been revitalised in recent years and the eco-friendly treehouses point the hotel in a fresh and exciting direction. The extensive grounds include – in addition to activities like golf and croquet – a walled garden, which provides for the hotel kitchen, and is a feature in its own right. Bedrooms are luxurious and delightfully appointed, while public areas are stylish and comfortable, the perfect place for traditional afternoon tea. Cuisine, as ever, is at the forefront, and in The Dining Room restaurant there is something for every diner. A new addition to the range of facilities is The Kitchen by James Martin, a relaxed and informal setting to dine in, but it's also a cookery school.

Rooms: 72 (14 annexe) (43 family) (11 GF) ☏ **D** fr £325* **Facilities:** Spa STV FTV WiFi ▵ ⌖ ⚲ ⅃ 9 ▣ ♨ Gym Hydrotherapy spa Dance studio Cycling and jogging trail Clay shooting Archery ♫ Xmas New Year **Conf:** Class 70 Board 40 Theatre 150 **Services:** Night porter Air con **Parking:** 150 **Notes:** LB Civ Wed 140

NEWPORT
Isle Of Wight   Map 5 SZ58

Premier Inn Isle of Wight (Newport)
Premier Inn

BUDGET HOTEL

tel: 0871 527 8556 (Calls cost 13p per minute plus your phone company's access charge) **Seaclose, Fairlee Road PO30 2DN**
web: www.premierinn.com
dir: *From Newport take A3054 signed Ryde. In 0.75 mile at Seaclose lights, turn left. Hotel adjacent to council offices.*

High quality, budget accommodation ideal for both families and business travellers. Spacious, en suite bedrooms feature free WiFi and tea and coffee making facilities, and in most hotels, Freeview TV is also available. The adjacent family restaurant features a wide and varied menu.

Rooms: 68

NEWPORT
Shropshire   Map 15 SJ71

Premier Inn Newport/Telford
Premier Inn

BUDGET HOTEL

tel: 0871 527 8808 (Calls cost 13p per minute plus your phone company's access charge) **Stafford Road TF10 9BY**
web: www.premierinn.com
dir: *From A41 east of Newport take A518 towards Stafford. Hotel on right adjacent to Mere Park Garden Centre.*

High quality, budget accommodation ideal for both families and business travellers. Spacious, en suite bedrooms feature free WiFi and tea and coffee making facilities, and in most hotels, Freeview TV is also available. The adjacent family restaurant features a wide and varied menu.

Rooms: 50

NEWPORT PAGNALL MOTORWAY SERVICE AREA (M1)   Map 11 SP84
Buckinghamshire

Days Inn Milton Keynes
WELCOMEBREAK

AA Advertised

tel: 01908 610878 **Newport Pagnell Services, M1 junction 14/15 MK16 9DS**
email: miltonkeynes.hotelmanager@welcomebreak.co.uk
web: www.welcomebreak.co.uk/hotels/milton-keynes
dir: *M1 northbound junction 14/15. Hotel is located in Welcome Break services off Little Linford Lane.*

This modern building offers accommodation in smart, spacious and well-equipped bedrooms, suitable for families and business travellers, and all with en suite bathrooms. Continental breakfast is available and other refreshments may be taken at the nearby family restaurant.

Rooms: 87 (14 family) (25 GF) (4 smoking) **Facilities:** STV FTV WiFi **Conf:** Class 12 Board 16 Theatre 40 **Services:** Night porter **Parking:** 90

N

NEWQUAY
Cornwall & Isles Of Scilly

Map 2 SW86

The Headland Hotel and Spa
★★★★ 86% ◉◉ HOTEL

tel: 01637 872211 **Fistral Beach TR7 1EW**
email: reception@headlandhotel.co.uk **web:** www.headlandhotel.co.uk
dir: *A30 onto A392 at Indian Queens, approaching Newquay follow signs for Fistral Beach, hotel adjacent.*

This Victorian hotel enjoys a stunning location overlooking Fistral Bay on three sides, and these views can be enjoyed from most windows. The individually designed rooms and suites are comfortable and spacious. The grand public spaces include various lounges, the formal Samphire restaurant and The Terrace that offers a relaxed food option. Guest can enjoy pampering at the spa and take advantage of the leisure facilities that include a relaxation pool, steam room, aromatherapy showers and sauna. Self-catering cottages are available, and guests staying in these are welcome to use the hotel facilities.

Rooms: 95 (30 family) ☏ **S** fr £70 **D** fr £120 (including breakfast)*
Facilities: Spa STV FTV WiFi ⌕ ⊛ ⚲ ⚲ 9 Gym Pitch & putt Fitness centre Wellness centre Xmas New Year **Conf:** Class 200 Board 40 Theatre 300
Services: Lift Night porter **Parking:** 300 **Notes:** Civ Wed 200

Atlantic Hotel
★★★★ 81% ◉ HOTEL

tel: 01637 872244 **Dane Road TR7 1EN**
email: info@atlantichotelnewquay.co.uk **web:** www.atlantichotelnewquay.co.uk
dir: *A30 onto A392 to Indian Queens, approaching Newquay. Follow signs for Fistral Beach, hotel on hill overlooking sea and harbour.*

Glamour, grandeur and a warm welcome await at the Atlantic Hotel. Set in ten acres of private headland, this stunning art-deco hotel offers sweeping views of the Atlantic Ocean. Each room is unique, comfortably furnished and comes with a glorious sea view. Diners can enjoy a range of contemporary dishes that offer the best local seafood and seasonal produce, in the relaxed, elegant atmosphere at Silks Bistro and Champagne Bar. The south-facing terrace, sun-trap pool and spa treatment room offer a range of spaces to relax and indulge. Just a short stroll from Newquay, and the South West Coast Path, the Atlantic Hotel is the perfect base for exploring the dramatic north Cornwall coast.

Rooms: 57 (4 annexe) (10 family) ☏ **S** fr £97 **D** fr £116 (including breakfast)*
Facilities: Spa STV FTV WiFi ⌕ ⊛ ⚲ Surf school Steam room Sauna Billiard room ♫ Xmas New Year **Conf:** Class 350 Board 150 Theatre 350 **Services:** Lift Night porter **Parking:** 57 **Notes:** LB Civ Wed 360

N

Best Western Hotel Bristol

 Best Western

★★★ 82% HOTEL

tel: 01637 875181 **Narrowcliff TR7 2PQ**
email: info@hotelbristol.co.uk web: www.hotelbristol.co.uk
dir: *A30 onto A392, then A3058. Hotel 2.5 miles on left.*

This hotel is conveniently situated, and many of the bedrooms enjoy fine sea views. Staff are friendly and provide a professional and attentive service. There is a range of comfortable lounges, ideal for relaxing prior to eating in the elegant dining room. There are also leisure and conference facilities.

Rooms: 74 (23 family) ✿ **S** fr £45 **D** fr £55* **Facilities:** FTV WiFi HL ⊛ Table tennis Xmas New Year **Conf:** Class 80 Board 30 Theatre 200 **Services:** Lift Night porter **Parking:** 105 **Notes:** LB Civ Wed 300

The Legacy Hotel Victoria

 LEGACY HOTELS

★★★ 75% HOTEL

tel: 0844 411 9025 (Calls cost 7p per minute plus your phone company's access charge) & 0330 333 2825 **East Street TR7 1DB**
email: bookings@hotel-victoria.co.uk web: www.legacy-hotels.co.uk
dir: *A30 towards Bodmin following signs to Newquay. Hotel next to Newquay's main post office.*

Standing on the cliffs, overlooking Newquay Bay, the hotel is situated at the centre of this vibrant town. The spacious lounges and bar areas all benefit from glorious views. Varied menus, using the best of local produce, are offered in the restaurant, and there's Senor Dicks serving Mexican food. Bedrooms vary from spacious superior rooms and suites to standard inland-facing rooms. Berties pub, a nightclub, and indoor leisure facilities are also available.

Rooms: 71 (23 family) (1 GF) ✿ **Facilities:** FTV WiFi ⊛ Gym Beauty treatment room Sauna Steam room **Conf:** Class 130 Board 50 Theatre 200 **Services:** Lift Night porter **Parking:** 50 **Notes:** LB Civ Wed 270

Eliot Hotel

Leisureplex HOLIDAY HOTELS

★★★ 71% HOTEL

tel: 01637 878177 **Edgcumbe Avenue TR7 2NH**
email: eliot.newquay@alfatravel.co.uk web: www.leisureplex.co.uk
dir: *A30 onto A392 towards Quintrell Downs. Right at roundabout onto A3058. 4 miles to Newquay, left at amusements onto Edgcumbe Avenue. Hotel on left.*

Located in a quiet residential area just a short walk from the beaches and the varied attractions of the town, this long-established hotel offers comfortable accommodation. Entertainment is provided most nights throughout the season and guests can relax in the spacious public areas.

Rooms: 79 (10 family) (3 GF) ✿ **S** fr £34 **D** fr £50* **Facilities:** FTV WiFi ⊁ Pool table Table tennis ♬ Xmas New Year **Services:** Lift Night porter **Parking:** 20 **Notes:** Closed December to January (excluding Christmas/New Year) RS February to March

Hotel California

★★★ 67% HOTEL

tel: 01637 879292 **Pentire Crescent TR7 1PU**
email: info@hotel-california.co.uk web: www.hotel-california.co.uk
dir: *A392 to Newquay, follow signs for Pentire Hotels and Guest Houses.*

This hotel is tucked away in a delightful location, close to Fistral Beach and adjacent to the River Gannel. Many bedrooms have views across the river towards

the sea, and some have balconies. There is an impressive range of leisure facilities, including ten-pin bowling and both indoor and outdoor pools. The cuisine is enjoyable and menus offer a range of interesting dishes.

Rooms: 70 (27 family) (13 GF) **S** fr £45 **D** fr £97 (including breakfast)* **Facilities:** FTV WiFi HL ⊛ ⊁ Squash 4-lane American bowling alley hairdresser Snooker and pool room Sauna Solarium ♬ Xmas New Year **Conf:** Class 100 Board 30 Theatre 100 **Services:** Lift Night porter **Parking:** 66 **Notes:** LB Closed 3–25 January Civ Wed 300

Priory Lodge Hotel

★★ 80% HOTEL

tel: 01637 874111 **30 Mount Wise TR7 2BN**
email: fionapocklington@tiscali.co.uk web: www.priorylodgehotel.co.uk
dir: *From lights in town centre onto Berry Road, right onto B3282 Mount Wise, 0.5 mile on right.*

This hotel enjoys a central location close to the town centre, the harbour and the local beaches. Secure parking is available at the hotel along with a range of leisure facilities including a heated pool, sauna, games room and hot tub. Attractively decorated bedrooms vary in size and style – many have sea views over Towan Beach.

Rooms: 28 (6 annexe) (13 family) (1 GF) **S** fr £50 **D** fr £80 (including breakfast) **Facilities:** FTV WiFi ⊁ ♬ **Parking:** 30 **Notes:** Closed December to March

Premier Inn Newquay (Quintrell Downs)

 Premier Inn

BUDGET HOTEL

tel: 0871 527 8818 (Calls cost 13p per minute plus your phone company's access charge) **Quintrell Downs TR8 4LE**
web: www.premierinn.com
dir: *From A30 take A39. At roundabout 2nd exit signed Newquay A392. 4 miles, in Quintrell Downs take 1st exit at roundabout. Hotel on left.*

High quality, budget accommodation ideal for both families and business travellers. Spacious, en suite bedrooms feature free WiFi and tea and coffee making facilities, and in most hotels, Freeview TV is also available. The adjacent family restaurant features a wide and varied menu.

Rooms: 74

NEWTON ABBOT
Devon

Map 3 SX87

See also **Islington**

Best Western Passage House Hotel

Best Western

★★★ 75% HOTEL

tel: 01626 355515 **Hackney Lane, Kingsteignton TQ12 3QH**
email: mail@passagehousegroup.co.uk web: www.bw-passagehousehotel.co.uk
dir: *A380 onto A381, follow racecourse signs.*

With memorable views of the Teign Estuary, this popular hotel provides spacious, well-equipped bedrooms. An impressive range of leisure and meeting facilities is offered and a conservatory provides a pleasant extension to the bar and lounge. A choice of eating options is available, either in the main restaurant, or the adjacent Passage House Inn for less formal dining.

Rooms: 90 (52 annexe) (64 family) (26 GF) **S** fr £69 **D** fr £79 (including breakfast)* **Facilities:** Spa FTV WiFi ⊛ Gym **Conf:** Class 50 Board 40 Theatre 120 **Services:** Lift Night porter **Parking:** 300 **Notes:** LB Civ Wed 75

N

NEWTON ABBOT *continued*

Premier Inn Newton Abbot

Premier Inn

BUDGET HOTEL

tel: 0871 527 9300 (Calls cost 13p per minute plus your phone company's access charge) **Newton Abbott Racecourse, Newton Road TQ12 3AF**
web: www.premierinn.com
dir: *A380 exit at Ware Barton signed A383/Ashburton, follow brown signs for Newton Abbot Racecourse through Kingsteignton. Then follow Officials Entrance sign to hotel.*

High quality, budget accommodation ideal for both families and business travellers. Spacious, en suite bedrooms feature free WiFi and tea and coffee making facilities, and in most hotels, Freeview TV is also available. The adjacent family restaurant features a wide and varied menu.

Rooms: 84

NEWTON AYCLIFFE
County Durham
Map 19 NZ22

Premier Inn Durham (Newton Aycliffe)

Premier Inn

BUDGET HOTEL

tel: 0871 527 8336 (Calls cost 13p per minute plus your phone company's access charge) **Ricknall Lane, Great North Road DL5 6JG**
web: www.premierinn.com
dir: *On A167 east of Newton Aycliffe, 3 miles from A1(M).*

Rooms: 44

NORMAN CROSS
Cambridgeshire
Map 12 TL19

Premier Inn Peterborough (A1(M) Jct 16)

Premier Inn

BUDGET HOTEL

tel: 0871 527 8870 (Calls cost 13p per minute plus your phone company's access charge) **Norman Cross, A1(M) Junction 16 PE7 3TB**
web: www.premierinn.com
dir: *A1(M) junction 16, A15 towards Yaxley, hotel in 100 yards.*

Rooms: 99

NORMANTON
Rutland
Map 11 SK90

Best Western Normanton Park Hotel

 Best Western.

★★★ 69% HOTEL

tel: 01780 720315 **Oakham LE15 8RP**
email: info@normantonpark.co.uk **web:** www.bw-normantonparkhotel.co.uk
dir: *From A1 follow A606 towards Oakham, 5 miles. Turn left, 1.5 miles. Hotel on right.*

This hotel offers some of Rutland Water's best views over the south shore. The comfortable bedrooms are located in the main house and the courtyard. Public rooms include a conservatory dining room overlooking the water, and a cosy lounge is available for guests to relax in.

Rooms: 30 (7 annexe) (6 family) (11 GF) **Facilities:** FTV WiFi Xmas New Year **Conf:** Class 60 Board 80 Theatre 200 **Services:** Night porter **Parking:** 100 **Notes:** Civ Wed 80

NORTHAMPTON
Northamptonshire
Map 11 SP76

Westone Manor Hotel

★★★ 68% HOTEL

tel: 01604 739955 **Ashley Way, Weston Favell NN3 3EA**
email: enquiries@westonemanor.com **web:** www.westonemanor.com
dir: *A43 Kettering for 0.5 mile. Then A4500 for Town Centre/Earls Barton/Weston Favell. Left at lights onto A4500 for 100 yards. 1st right at sign Westone Manor Hotel Northampton, over small roundabout, hotel on left.*

Built in 1914 as the home of the local shoe manufacturer William Sears, this property has since been expanded, and now offers comfortable accommodation to the rear. A lounge, bar, and conservatory restaurant are available. Free WiFi is available throughout the hotel.

Rooms: 69 (38 annexe) (3 family) (19 GF) **S** fr £50 **D** fr £60* **Facilities:** FTV WiFi Xmas New Year **Conf:** Class 60 Board 60 Theatre 120 **Services:** Lift Night porter **Parking:** 70 **Notes:** Civ Wed 120

Premier Inn Northampton Bedford Road/A428

Premier Inn

BUDGET HOTEL

tel: 0871 527 8822 (Calls cost 13p per minute plus your phone company's access charge) **The Lakes, Bedford Road NN4 7YD**
web: www.premierinn.com
dir: *M1 junction 15, follow A508 (A45) signs to Northampton. A428 at roundabout take 4th exit (signed Bedford). Left at next roundabout. Hotel on right.*

Rooms: 44

Premier Inn Northampton Great Billing/A45

Premier Inn

BUDGET HOTEL

tel: 0871 527 8824 (Calls cost 13p per minute plus your phone company's access charge) **Crow Lane, Great Billing NN3 9DA**
web: www.premierinn.com
dir: *M1 junction 15, A508, A45 follow Billing Aquadrome signs.*

Rooms: 60

Premier Inn Northampton South (Wootton)

Premier Inn

BUDGET HOTEL

tel: 0871 527 8826 (Calls cost 13p per minute plus your phone company's access charge) **Newport Pagnell Road West, Wootton NN4 7JJ**
web: www.premierinn.com
dir: *M1 junction 15, A508 towards Northampton, exit at junction with A45. At roundabout take B526. Hotel on right.*

Rooms: 70

Premier Inn Northampton Town Centre

Premier Inn

BUDGET HOTEL

tel: 0871 527 9590 (Calls cost 13p per minute plus your phone company's access charge) **St. Johns Street NN1 1FA**
web: www.premierinn.com
dir: *From north: M1 junction 16, A45, signed Northampton West. At roundabout onto A4 (Northampton). Pass Northampton Rugby Ground on right. At Northampton Rail Station turn right at lights, (stay in left lane) 2nd exit at roundabout left at 2nd.*

Rooms: 104

Premier Inn Northampton West (Harpole) Premier Inn

BUDGET HOTEL

tel: 0871 527 8828 (Calls cost 13p per minute plus your phone company's access charge) **Harpole Turn, Weedon Rd NN7 4DD**
web: www.premierinn.com
dir: *M1 junction 16, A45 towards Northampton. In 1 mile left into Harpole Turn. Hotel on left.*
Rooms: 75

NORTH FERRIBY
East Riding of Yorkshire   **Map 17 SE92**

Hallmark Hotel Hull

★★★★ 76% HOTEL

tel: 0330 028 3414 & 07482 645212 **Ferriby High Road HU14 3LG**
email: hull@hallmarkhotels.co.uk **web:** www.hallmarkhotels.co.uk
dir: *M62 onto A63 towards Hull. Exit at Humber Bridge signage. Follow North Ferriby signs, hotel 0.5 mile on left.*

This property is situated just outside Hull city centre, with breathtaking views of the Humber Bridge. Service is attentive and the atmosphere friendly. The comfortable bedrooms are tastefully appointed and are suitable for both business and leisure guests. The restaurant and bar serve a good choice of dishes. Conference facilities are available along with free WiFi and private parking.

Rooms: 95 (3 family) (16 GF) ☞ **Facilities:** Spa FTV WiFi ⊁ Fitness suite Sauna Xmas New Year **Conf:** Class 85 Board 86 Theatre 200 **Services:** Night porter **Parking:** 150 **Notes:** LB Civ Wed 200

NORTH KILWORTH
Leicestershire   **Map 11 SP68**

> ### INSPECTOR'S CHOICE

Kilworth House Hotel & Theatre

★★★★ ◎◎ HOTEL

tel: 01858 880058 **Lutterworth Road LE17 6JE**
email: info@kilworthhouse.co.uk **web:** www.kilworthhouse.co.uk
dir: *A4304 towards Market Harborough, after Walcote, hotel 1.5 miles on right.*

Kilworth House Hotel is a restored Victorian country house located in 38 acres of private grounds offering state-of-the-art conference rooms. The gracious public areas feature many period pieces and original art works. The bedrooms are very

comfortable and well equipped, and the large Orangery is the place for informal dining, while the opulent Wordsworth Restaurant has a more formal air. Close to the lake there's an open-air theatre which seats 540; professional productions are performed, and picnics can be arranged, or dinner back at the hotel is also an option.

Rooms: 44 (2 family) (13 GF) ☞ **S** fr £125 **D** fr £135 (including breakfast)*
Facilities: FTV WiFi ⊁ Fishing ⇜ Gym Beauty therapy rooms Xmas New Year
Conf: Class 30 Board 30 Theatre 80 **Services:** Lift Night porter **Parking:** 140
Notes: Civ Wed 180

NORTH SHIELDS
Tyne & Wear   **Map 21 NZ36**

Premier Inn North Shields (Ferry Terminal) Premier Inn

BUDGET HOTEL

tel: 0871 527 8818 (Calls cost 13p per minute plus your phone company's access charge) **Coble Dene Road NE29 6DL**
web: www.premierinn.com
dir: *From all directions follow signs for Royal Quays (Outlet Centre) and International Ferry Terminal. From A187 take Coble Dene Road. At 3rd roundabout right, 1st right at mini-roundabout.*

High quality, budget accommodation ideal for both families and business travellers. Spacious, en suite bedrooms feature free WiFi and tea and coffee making facilities, and in most hotels, Freeview TV is also available. The adjacent family restaurant features a wide and varied menu.

Rooms: 74

NORTH WALSHAM
Norfolk   **Map 13 TG23**

N

> ### HIGHLY RECOMMENDED

Beechwood Hotel

★★★ 88% ◎◎ HOTEL

tel: 01692 403231 **20 Cromer Road NR28 0HD**
email: info@beechwood-hotel.co.uk **web:** www.beechwood-hotel.co.uk
dir: *B1150 from Norwich. At North Walsham left at 1st lights, then right at next.*

Beechwood Hotel offers a friendly and informal atmosphere, comfortable and well-appointed bedrooms, and a creative head chef sourcing produce from local farms and Cromer fishermen. Near to the North Norfolk Heritage Coast, the Norfolk Broads and the cathedral city of Norwich, this is a great place for a short break.

Rooms: 18 (4 GF) ☞ **S** fr £70 **D** fr £100 (including breakfast)* **Facilities:** FTV WiFi ⊁ ⇜ Xmas New Year **Conf:** Class 20 Board 20 Theatre 20 **Parking:** 20 **Notes:** LB

NORTHWICH
Cheshire | Map 15 SJ67

Premier Inn Northwich (Sandiway)

BUDGET HOTEL

tel: 0871 527 8830 (Calls cost 13p per minute plus your phone company's access charge) **520 Chester Road, Sandiway CW8 2DN**
web: www.premierinn.com
dir: *M6 junction 19, A556 towards Chester. Hotel in 11 miles.*

High quality, budget accommodation ideal for both families and business travellers. Spacious, en suite bedrooms feature free WiFi and tea and coffee making facilities, and in most hotels, Freeview TV is also available. The adjacent family restaurant features a wide and varied menu.

Rooms: 42

Premier Inn Northwich South

BUDGET HOTEL

tel: 0871 527 8832 (Calls cost 13p per minute plus your phone company's access charge) **London Road, Leftwich CW9 8EG**
web: www.premierinn.com
dir: *Just off M6 junction 19. Follow A556 towards Chester. Right at sign for Northwich and Davenham.*

Rooms: 61

NORWICH
Norfolk | Map 13 TG20

HIGHLY RECOMMENDED

Maids Head Hotel
★★★★ 83% ⚫⚫ HOTEL

tel: 01603 209955 **Tombland NR3 1LB**
email: reservations@maidsheadhotel.co.uk **web:** www.maidsheadhotel.co.uk
dir: *In city centre. Phone or see website for detailed directions.*

The Maids Head Hotel is an impressive 13th-century building situated close to the impressive Norman cathedral, and within easy walking distance of the city centre. The bedrooms are pleasantly decorated and thoughtfully equipped; some rooms have original oak beams. The spacious public rooms include a Jacobean bar, a range of seating areas and the WinePress Restaurant.

Rooms: 84 (10 family) ⚫ **S** fr £85 **D** fr £95* **Facilities:** FTV WiFi ⚫ Beauty treatment room Use of nearby gym Xmas New Year **Conf:** Class 30 Board 50 Theatre 100 **Services:** Lift Night porter **Parking:** 83 **Notes:** LB Civ Wed 100

St Giles House Hotel
★★★★ 81% ⚫⚫ HOTEL

tel: 01603 275180 **41-45 St Giles Street NR2 1JR**
email: reception@stgileshousehotel.com **web:** www.stgileshousehotel.com
dir: *A11 into central Norwich. Left at roundabout (Chapelfield Shopping Centre). 3rd exit at next roundabout. Left onto St Giles Street. Hotel on left.*

St Giles House Hotel is a stylish 19th-century, Grade II listed building situated in the heart of the city. The property has a wealth of magnificent original features such as wood-panelling, ornamental plasterwork and marble floors. Public areas include an open-plan lounge bar/restaurant, a smart lounge with plush sofas and a Parisian-style terrace. The spacious, contemporary bedrooms are individually designed and have many thoughtful touches.

Rooms: 24 (3 GF) ⚫ **Facilities:** Spa FTV WiFi ⚫ Xmas New Year **Conf:** Class 20 Board 24 Theatre 45 **Services:** Lift Night porter **Parking:** 30 **Notes:** LB Civ Wed 60

Dunston Hall
★★★★ 81% HOTEL

tel: 01508 470444 **Ipswich Road NR14 8PQ**
email: dunstonreception@qhotels.co.uk **web:** www.qhotels.co.uk
dir: *From A47 take A140 (Ipswich road). 0.25 mile, hotel on left.*

Dunston Hall is an imposing Grade II listed building set amidst 170 acres of landscaped grounds just a short drive from the city centre. The spacious bedrooms are smartly decorated, tastefully furnished and equipped to a high standard. The attractively appointed public rooms offer a wide choice of areas in which to relax, and the hotel also boasts a superb range of leisure facilities including an 18-hole PGA golf course, floodlit tennis courts and a football pitch.

Rooms: 169 (16 family) (16 GF) (2 smoking) **Facilities:** Spa WiFi ⚫ ⚫ 18 Gym Floodlit driving range Xmas New Year **Conf:** Class 140 Board 80 Theatre 300 **Services:** Lift Night porter **Parking:** 500 **Notes:** LB Civ Wed 200

Park Farm Hotel
★★★★ 81% ⚫ HOTEL

tel: 01603 810264 **NR9 3DL**
email: enq@parkfarm-hotel.co.uk **web:** www.parkfarm-hotel.co.uk

(for full entry see Hethersett)

Mercure Norwich Hotel
★★★★ 76% HOTEL

tel: 0844 815 9036 (Calls cost 5p per minute plus your phone company's access charge) & 01603 786400 **121-131 Boundary Road NR3 2BA**
email: fo.mercurenorwich@jupiterhotels.co.uk **web:** www.mercurenorwich.co.uk
dir: *Approximately 2 miles from airport on A140 Norwich ring road.*

This purpose-built property is situated on the outer ring road within easy striking distance of the city centre. Bedrooms are spacious and well equipped with modern facilities. Public rooms include an open-plan lounge bar and a smart restaurant. The hotel has leisure facilities, meeting rooms and a banqueting suite.

Rooms: 107 (10 family) (39 GF) ⚫ **S** fr £90 **D** fr £100 **Facilities:** FTV WiFi ⚫ Gym Sauna Steam room Xmas New Year **Conf:** Class 160 Board 80 Theatre 400 **Services:** Night porter **Parking:** 225 **Notes:** Civ Wed 400

HIGHLY RECOMMENDED

Best Western Annesley House Hotel
★★★ 88% ⚫⚫ HOTEL

tel: 01603 624553 **6 Newmarket Road NR2 2LA**
email: reception@annesleyhouse.co.uk **web:** www.bw-annesleyhouse.co.uk
dir: *On A11, 0.5 mile before city centre.*

This delightful Georgian property is set in three acres of landscaped gardens close to the city centre. Bedrooms are split between three separate houses, two of which are linked by a glass walkway. Each is attractively decorated, tastefully furnished and thoughtfully equipped. Public rooms include a comfortable lounge/bar and a smart conservatory restaurant which overlooks the gardens.

Rooms: 31 (13 annexe) (1 family) (9 GF) ⚫ **S** fr £64.50 **D** fr £92.50*
Facilities: FTV WiFi ⚫ **Parking:** 28 **Notes:** LB Closed 24–27 December

N

Best Western Brook Hotel Norwich

 Best Western.

★★★ 76% HOTEL

tel: 01603 741161 **2 Barnard Road, Bowthorpe NR5 9JB**
email: welcome@brookhotelnorwich.com **web:** www.brookhotelnorwich.com
dir: *A47 towards Swaffham then A1074. Over double roundabout, to next roundabout, hotel on last exit.*

Brook Hotel Norwich is a modern, purpose-built hotel situated to the west of the city centre, just off the A47. The open-plan public areas include a lounge bar with TV, a foyer with plush sofas and a large dining room. The spacious bedrooms are equipped for both leisure and business guests alike.

Rooms: 81 (13 family) (40 GF) **S** fr £50 **D** fr £50* **Facilities:** FTV WiFi Gym Xmas New Year **Conf:** Class 90 Board 60 Theatre 200 **Services:** Night porter Air con **Parking:** 100 **Notes:** LB Civ Wed 200

Premier Inn Norwich Airport

 Premier Inn

BUDGET HOTEL

tel: 0871 527 8836 (Calls cost 13p per minute plus your phone company's access charge) **Delft Way NR6 6BB**
web: www.premierinn.com
dir: *From Norwich take A140 signed Cromer and Airport. Right at lights into Amsterdam Way. At mini-roundabout turn right. Hotel on right.*

High quality, budget accommodation ideal for both families and business travellers. Spacious, en suite bedrooms feature free WiFi and tea and coffee making facilities, and in most hotels, Freeview TV is also available. The adjacent family restaurant features a wide and varied menu.

Rooms: 80

Premier Inn Norwich (Broadlands Park)

 Premier Inn

BUDGET HOTEL

tel: 0871 527 8838 (Calls cost 13p per minute plus your phone company's access charge) **Broadlands Business Park, Old Chapel Way NR7 0WG**
web: www.premierinn.com
dir: *A47 onto A1042, 3 miles east of city centre.*

Rooms: 92

Premier Inn Norwich City Centre (Duke Street)

 Premier Inn

BUDGET HOTEL

tel: 0871 527 8840 (Calls cost 13p per minute plus your phone company's access charge) **Duke Street NR3 3AP**
web: www.premierinn.com
dir: *From A1074, straight on at lights into St Benedict's Street (or from A147, A140, A11) right at lights. At next lights into Duke Street. Car park in St Andrews multi-storey on right – free to guests.*

Rooms: 117

Premier Inn Norwich Nelson City Centre

 Premier Inn

BUDGET HOTEL

tel: 0871 527 8842 (Calls cost 13p per minute plus your phone company's access charge) **Prince of Wales Road NR1 1DX**
web: www.premierinn.com
dir: *Follow city centre, football ground and railway station signs. Hotel opposite station.*

Rooms: 185

Premier Inn Norwich (Showground A47)

Premier Inn

BUDGET HOTEL

tel: 0871 527 8834 (Calls cost 13p per minute plus your phone company's access charge) **Longwater Interchange, Dereham Road NR5 0TP**
web: www.premierinn.com
dir: *A47 towards Dereham, take A1074 to City Centre. At roundabout 2nd exit, hotel on right. From north: A47 through Dereham. Straight on at 1st roundabout, at 2nd roundabout take 3rd exit. Hotel on left.*

Rooms: 62

NOTTINGHAM
Nottinghamshire
Map 11 SK53

N

HIGHLY RECOMMENDED

Hart's Hotel

★★★★ 84% ◉◉ HOTEL

tel: 0115 988 1900 **Standard Hill, Park Row NG1 6GN**
email: reception@hartshotel.co.uk **web:** www.hartsnottingham.co.uk
dir: *At junction of Park Row and Ropewalk.*

This outstanding modern building stands on the site of the ramparts of the medieval castle, overlooking the city. Many of the bedrooms enjoy splendid views; all are well appointed and stylish. The Park Bar is the focal point of the public areas. Service is professional and caring and fine dining is offered at nearby Hart's Restaurant. Secure parking and private gardens are an added bonus.

Rooms: 32 (1 family) (7 GF) **S** fr £134 **D** fr £134* **Facilities:** STV FTV WiFi Small unsupervised exercise room Beauty treatments Use of local tennis club Xmas New Year **Conf:** Class 75 Board 30 Theatre 100 **Services:** Lift Night porter **Parking:** 16 **Notes:** Civ Wed 100

NOTTINGHAM *continued*

The Nottingham Belfry

★★★★ 80% HOTEL

tel: 0115 973 9393 **Mellor's Way, Off Woodhouse Way NG8 6PY**
email: reservations@thenottinghambelfry.co.uk **web:** www.qhotels.co.uk
dir: *From M1 junction 26 take A610 towards Nottingham. A6002 to Stapleford/Strelley. 0.75 mile, last exit at roundabout, hotel on right.*

Set conveniently close to the motorway links, yet not far from the city centre attractions, this modern hotel has a stylish and impressive interior. Bedrooms and bathrooms are spaciously appointed and very comfortable. There are two restaurants and two bars that offer interesting and satisfying cuisine. Staff are friendly and helpful.

Rooms: 120 (20 family) (36 GF) ⟡ **S** fr £65 **D** fr £77 (including breakfast)*
Facilities: Spa FTV WiFi ♨ HL ⟲ Gym Sauna Steam room Aerobic studio Xmas New Year **Conf:** Class 360 Board 60 Theatre 700 **Services:** Lift Night porter Air con **Parking:** 250 **Notes:** LB Civ Wed 500

Park Plaza Nottingham

★★★★ 73% ◉◉ HOTEL

tel: 0115 947 7200 & 0844 415 6730 (Calls cost 7p per minute plus your phone company's access charge) **41 Maid Marian Way NG1 6GD**
email: ppnsales@pphe.com **web:** www.parkplaza.com/nottinghamuk
dir: *A6200 Derby Road into Wollaton Street. 2nd exit into Maid Marian Way. Hotel on left.*

This modern hotel is located in the centre of the city within walking distance of retail, commercial and tourist attractions. Bedrooms are spacious and comfortable, with many extras, including laptop safes and air conditioning. Service is discreetly attentive in the foyer lounge and the Chino Latino Restaurant, where pan-Asian cooking is a feature.

Rooms: 178 (10 family) ⟡ **S** fr £69 **D** fr £79 (including breakfast)* **Facilities:** STV FTV WiFi ♨ Gym Complimentary use of fitness suite **Conf:** Class 90 Board 30 Theatre 200 **Services:** Lift Night porter Air con **Parking:** 30 **Notes:** LB

Best Western Plus Nottingham Westminster Hotel

★★★★ 71% HOTEL

tel: 0115 955 5000 **312 Mansfield Road, Nottingham NG5 2EF**
email: mail@westminster-hotel.co.uk
dir: *Phone for directions.*

The hotel has been created from a number of red-bricked Victorian properties and refurbishment has added a modern twist to the decor. Expect a friendly welcome and comfortable bedrooms. The hotel has parking facilities and is only a 10-minute walk from the city centre.

Rooms: 73 (21 annexe) (19 family) (3 GF) ⟡ **S** fr £50 **D** fr £60*
Facilities: **Conf:** Class 32 Board 30 Theatre 60 **Parking:** 51

The Strathdon

★★★ 68% HOTEL

tel: 0115 941 8501 **Derby Road NG1 5FT**
email: info@strathdon-hotel-nottingham.com **web:** www.peelhotels.co.uk
dir: *From M1 follow city centre signs. At Canning Circus into one-way system into Wollaton Street, keep right, next right to hotel.*

This city-centre hotel has modern facilities and is very convenient for all city attractions. A popular themed bar has a large-screen TV and serves an extensive

range of popular fresh food, while more formal dining is available in Bobbins Restaurant.

Rooms: 69 (4 family) (16 smoking) **S** fr £50 **D** fr £65* **Facilities:** FTV WiFi ♨ Xmas New Year **Conf:** Class 60 Board 40 Theatre 150 **Services:** Lift Night porter **Notes:** Civ Wed 85

Premier Inn Nottingham Arena (London Rd)

BUDGET HOTEL

tel: 0871 527 8848 (Calls cost 13p per minute plus your phone company's access charge) **Island Site, London Road NG2 4UU**
web: www.premierinn.com
dir: *M1 junction 25, A52 into city centre. Follow signs for A60 to Loughborough. Hotel adjacent to BBC building.*

High quality, budget accommodation ideal for both families and business travellers. Spacious, en suite bedrooms feature free WiFi and tea and coffee making facilities, and in most hotels, Freeview TV is also available. The adjacent family restaurant features a wide and varied menu.

Rooms: 87

Premier Inn Nottingham Castle Marina

BUDGET HOTEL

tel: 0871 527 8844 (Calls cost 13p per minute plus your phone company's access charge) **Castle Marina Park, Castle Bridge Road NG7 1GX**
web: www.premierinn.com
dir: *M1 junction 24, A453. Follow ring road and signs for Queen's Drive Industrial Estate. After Homebase left into Castle Bridge Road, opposite Pizza Hut restaurant. Hotel adjacent to Boathouse Beefeater.*

Rooms: 61

Premier Inn Nottingham City Centre Chapel Bar

BUDGET HOTEL

tel: 0871 527 9658 (Calls cost 13p per minute plus your phone company's access charge) **7 Chapel Quarter, Chapel Bar NG1 6JS**
web: www.premierinn.com
dir: *M1 junction 26, follow Nottingham City Centre signs. Into Maid Marian Way (A6008). 1st right into Friar Lane.*

Rooms: 60

Premier Inn Nottingham City Centre (Goldsmith Street)

BUDGET HOTEL

tel: 0871 527 8846 (Calls cost 13p per minute plus your phone company's access charge) **Goldsmith Street NG1 5LT**
web: www.premierinn.com
dir: *A610 to city centre. Follow signs for Nottingham Trent University into Talbot Street. 1st left into Clarendon Street. Right at lights. Hotel on right.*

Rooms: 161

Premier Inn Nottingham North (Daybrook)

Premier Inn

BUDGET HOTEL

tel: 0871 527 8850 (Calls cost 13p per minute plus your phone company's access charge) **101 Mansfield Road, Daybrook NG5 6BH**
web: www.premierinn.com
dir: *M1 junction 26, A610 towards Nottingham. Left onto A6514. Left onto A60 towards Mansfield. Hotel 0.25 mile on left.*

Rooms: 64

Premier Inn Nottingham South

Premier Inn

BUDGET HOTEL

tel: 0871 527 8854 (Calls cost 13p per minute plus your phone company's access charge) **Loughborough Road, Ruddington NG11 6LS**
web: www.premierinn.com
dir: *M1 junction 24, follow A453 signs to Nottingham, A52 to Grantham. Hotel at 1st roundabout on left.*

Rooms: 60

Premier Inn Nottingham West

Premier Inn

BUDGET HOTEL

tel: 0871 527 8856 (Calls cost 13p per minute plus your phone company's access charge) **The Phoenix Centre, Millennium Way West NG8 6AS**
web: www.premierinn.com
dir: *M1 junction 26, 1 mile on A610 towards Nottingham.*

Rooms: 99

Lace Market Hotel

AA Advertised ⊕

tel: 0115 948 4414 **29-31 High Pavement NG1 1HE**
web: www.lacemarkethotel.co.uk
dir: *Phone for directions.*

This superb Georgian town house has undergone a total refurbishment and offers a choice of individually decorated and tastefully appointed bedrooms equipped with modern facilities. The property is situated on one of the oldest streets in Nottingham just a short walk from the city centre. Public rooms include a smart cocktail lounge, Merchants Restaurant, Saint Bar and the Cock and Hoop Pub.

Rooms: 42 **S** fr £70 **D** fr £75* **Facilities:** FTV WiFi **Conf:** Class 20 Board 20 Theatre 60 **Notes:** Civ Wed 54

NUNEATON	Map 11 SP39
Warwickshire	

Best Western Weston Hall Hotel

 Best Western

★★★ 75% HOTEL

tel: 024 7631 2989 **Weston Lane, Bulkington CV12 9RU**
email: info@westonhallhotel.co.uk **web:** www.bw-westonhallhotel.co.uk
dir: *M6 junction 2, B4065 through Ansty. Left in Shilton, from Bulkington follow Nuneaton signs, into Weston Lane at 30mph sign.*

This Grade II listed hotel, with origins dating back to the reign of Elizabeth I, sits within seven acres of peaceful grounds. The original three-gabled building retains many original features, such as the carved wooden fireplace in the library. Friendly service is provided; and the bedrooms, that vary in size, are thoughtfully equipped.

Rooms: 38 (1 family) (14 GF) **Facilities:** FTV WiFi ⤵ New Year **Conf:** Class 100 Board 60 Theatre 200 **Parking:** 250 **Notes:** Civ Wed 200

Premier Inn Nuneaton/Coventry

Premier Inn

BUDGET HOTEL

tel: 0871 527 8858 (Calls cost 13p per minute plus your phone company's access charge) **Coventry Road CV10 7PJ**
web: www.premierinn.com
dir: *M6 junction 3, A444 towards Nuneaton. Hotel on B4113 on right, just off Griff roundabout towards Bedworth.*

High quality, budget accommodation ideal for both families and business travellers. Spacious, en suite bedrooms feature free WiFi and tea and coffee making facilities, and in most hotels, Freeview TV is also available. The adjacent family restaurant features a wide and varied menu.

Rooms: 50

OAKHAM	Map 11 SK80
Rutland	

INSPECTOR'S CHOICE

Hambleton Hall

★★★★ ⊕⊕⊕⊕ ⌕ COUNTRY HOUSE HOTEL

tel: 01572 756991 **Hambleton LE15 8TH**
email: hotel@hambletonhall.com **web:** www.hambletonhall.com
dir: *3 miles east of Oakham. 8 miles west of A1 Stamford junction (A606).*

Established over 30 years ago by Tim and Stefa Hart this delightful country house enjoys tranquil and spectacular views over Rutland Water. The beautifully manicured grounds are a delight to walk in. The bedrooms in the main house are stylish, individually decorated, and equipped with a range of thoughtful extras. A two-bedroom folly, with its own sitting and breakfast room, is only a short walk away. Day rooms include a cosy bar and a sumptuous drawing room, both featuring open fires. The elegant restaurant serves very accomplished, award-winning cuisine with menus highlighting locally sourced, seasonal produce — some of which is grown in the hotel's own grounds.

Rooms: 17 (2 annexe) ⤳ **S** fr £200 **D** fr £290 (including breakfast)*
Facilities: STV FTV WiFi ⤹ ⤺ ♨ ⤵ Private access to lake Xmas New Year
Conf: Board 24 Theatre 40 **Services:** Lift **Parking:** 40 **Notes:** LB Civ Wed 60

OAKHAM *continued*

Barnsdale Lodge Hotel

★★★ 78% ◉ HOTEL

tel: 01572 724678 **The Avenue, Rutland Water LE15 8AH**
email: enquiries@barnsdalelodge.co.uk **web:** www.barnsdalelodge.co.uk
dir: *A1 onto A606. Hotel 5 miles on right, 2 miles east of Oakham.*

A popular and interesting hotel converted from a farmstead overlooking Rutland Water. The public areas are dominated by a successful food operation with a good range of appealing meals on offer for either formal or informal dining. Bedrooms are comfortably appointed with excellent beds enhanced by contemporary soft furnishings and thoughtful extras.

Rooms: 46 (2 family) (17 GF) ♠ **Facilities:** FTV WiFi ⓑ Fishing ⚓ Archery Beauty treatment room Sailing Shooting Hair salon Xmas New Year **Conf:** Class 120 Board 76 Theatre 330 **Services:** Night porter **Parking:** 250 **Notes:** Civ Wed 200

OKEHAMPTON
Devon   Map 3 SX59

Manor House Hotel

★★★ 73% HOTEL

tel: 01837 53053 **Fowley Cross EX20 4NA**
email: reception@manorhousehotel.co.uk **web:** www.manorhousehotel.co.uk
dir: *Exit A30 at Sourton Cross flyover, right onto A386. Hotel 1.5 miles on right.*

Enjoying views to Dartmoor in the distance, this hotel specialises in short breaks and is set in 17 acres of grounds, close to the A30. The superb range of sporting and craft facilities has been enhanced by an impressive swimming pool and relaxation spa; golf is also offered at the adjacent sister hotel. Bedrooms, many located on the ground floor, are comfortable and well equipped.

Rooms: 204 (92 family) (93 GF) ♠ **Facilities:** Spa FTV WiFi ⓑ ⓧ ⚡ 99 ⚓ Fishing ⚓ Gym Squash Craft centre Indoor bowls Shooting ranges Indoor tennis Exercise classes Ice skating Roller skating Snooker table Adventure golf Ten-pin bowling ♫ Xmas New Year **Conf:** Class 60 Board 40 Theatre 250 **Services:** Night porter **Parking:** 204

Ashbury Hotel

★★★ 71% HOTEL

tel: 01837 55453 **Higher Maddaford, Southcott EX20 4NL**
email: reception@manorhousehotel.co.uk **web:** www.ashburygolfhotel.co.uk
dir: *Exit A30 at Sourton Cross onto A386. Left onto A3079 to Bude at Fowley Cross. After 1 mile right to Ashbury. Hotel 0.5 mile on right.*

With no fewer than seven courses and a clubhouse with lounge, bar and dining facilities, The Ashbury is a golfers' paradise. The majority of the well-equipped bedrooms are located in the farmhouse and the courtyard-style development around the putting green. Guests can enjoy the many on-site leisure facilities or join the activities available at the nearby sister hotel.

Rooms: 222 (115 family) (89 GF) ♠ **Facilities:** Spa FTV WiFi ⓑ ⓧ ⚡ 99 ⚓ Fishing Gym Badminton Shooting ranges Ten-pin bowling Indoor bowls 5-a-side Craft centre Sports simulators Snooker table Exercise classes ♫ New Year **Conf:** Class 60 Board 40 Theatre 250 **Services:** Night porter **Parking:** 200

OLDBURY   Map 10 SO98
West Midlands

Premier Inn Birmingham Oldbury M5 Jct 2

Premier Inn

BUDGET HOTEL

tel: 0871 527 8090 (Calls cost 13p per minute plus your phone company's access charge) **Wolverhampton Road B69 2BH**
web: www.premierinn.com
dir: *M5 junction 2, A4123 (Wolverhampton Road) north towards Dudley.*

High quality, budget accommodation ideal for both families and business travellers. Spacious, en suite bedrooms feature free WiFi and tea and coffee making facilities, and in most hotels, Freeview TV is also available. The adjacent family restaurant features a wide and varied menu.

Rooms: 78

OLDHAM   Map 16 SD90
Greater Manchester

Best Western Hotel Smokies Park

Best Western

★★★ 77% HOTEL

tel: 0161 785 5000 **Ashton Road, Bardsley OL8 3HX**
email: sales@smokies.co.uk **web:** www.smokies.co.uk
dir: *On A627 between Oldham and Ashton-under-Lyne.*

This modern, stylish hotel offers smart, comfortable bedrooms and spacious suites. A wide range of international dishes is offered in the main restaurant, Eat@ Smokies and there is also a lounge bar catering for all tastes. A small yet well equipped, residents-only fitness centre for the more active, and extensive function facilities are available.

Rooms: 73 (10 family) (22 GF) ♠ **S** fr £67 **D** fr £67* **Facilities:** FTV WiFi ⓑ Gym Xmas New Year **Conf:** Class 100 Board 40 Theatre 400 **Services:** Lift Night porter **Parking:** 120 **Notes:** Civ Wed 400

Premier Inn Oldham (Broadway)

Premier Inn

BUDGET HOTEL

tel: 0871 527 8860 (Calls cost 13p per minute plus your phone company's access charge) **Broadway/Hollinwood Avenue, Chadderton OL9 8DW**
web: www.premierinn.com
dir: *M60 (anti-clockwise) junction 21, signed Manchester city centre. Take A663, hotel 400 yards on left.*

High quality, budget accommodation ideal for both families and business travellers. Spacious, en suite bedrooms feature free WiFi and tea and coffee making facilities, and in most hotels, Freeview TV is also available. The adjacent family restaurant features a wide and varied menu.

Rooms: 58

Premier Inn Oldham Central

Premier Inn

BUDGET HOTEL

tel: 0871 527 8862 (Calls cost 13p per minute plus your phone company's access charge) **Westwood Park, Chadderton Way OL1 2NA**
web: www.premierinn.com
dir: *M62 junction 20, A627(M) to Oldham. Take A627 (Chadderton Way). Hotel on left opposite B&Q Depot.*

Rooms: 58

OLD HARLOW
Essex
Map 4 TL41

Premier Inn Harlow

Premier Inn

BUDGET HOTEL

tel: 0871 527 8488 (Calls cost 13p per minute plus your phone company's access charge) **Cambridge Road CM20 2EP**
web: www.premierinn.com
dir: *M11 junction 7, A414, A1184 Sawbridgeworth to Bishop's Stortford road.*

High quality, budget accommodation ideal for both families and business travellers. Spacious, en suite bedrooms feature free WiFi and tea and coffee making facilities, and in most hotels, Freeview TV is also available. The adjacent family restaurant features a wide and varied menu.

Rooms: 81

OLLERTON
Nottinghamshire
Map 16 SK66

Thoresby Hall Hotel

WARNER LEISURE HOTELS

★★★★ 79% COUNTRY HOUSE HOTEL

tel: 01623 821000 **Thoresby Park NG22 9WH**
email: reception.thoresbyhall@bourne-leisure.co.uk **web:** www.warnerleisurehotels.co.uk
dir: *Phone for directions.*

Thoresby Hall is a magnificent Grade I Victorian country house, set in acres of rolling parklands on the edge of Sherwood Forest. Guests can choose to relax in the spa, stroll around the beautiful gardens or relax in the Great Hall. Bedrooms vary in style and size. This is an adults-only (minimum 21 years old) hotel.

Rooms: 221 (168 annexe) (72 GF) **Facilities:** Spa FTV WiFi HL 🦢 Gym Rifle shooting archery outdoor bowls yoga 🎵 Xmas New Year **Conf:** Class 200 Board 30 Theatre 400 **Services:** Lift Night porter **Parking:** 240 **Notes:** No children 21 years

ORMSKIRK
Lancashire
Map 15 SD40

Premier Inn Southport (Ormskirk)

Premier Inn

BUDGET HOTEL

tel: 0871 527 9010 (Calls cost 13p per minute plus your phone company's access charge) **544 Southport Road, Scarisbrick L40 9RG**
web: www.premierinn.com
dir: *From Southport follow Ormskirk/A570 signs. Hotel on right off A570 Southport Road at 1st lights, entrance just after lights.*

High quality, budget accommodation ideal for both families and business travellers. Spacious, en suite bedrooms feature free WiFi and tea and coffee making facilities, and in most hotels, Freeview TV is also available. The adjacent family restaurant features a wide and varied menu.

Rooms: 20

ORPINGTON
Greater London
Map 6 TQ46

Premier Inn London Orpington

Premier Inn

BUDGET HOTEL

tel: 0871 527 9606 (Calls cost 13p per minute plus your phone company's access charge) **BR6 0TW**
web: www.premierinn.com
dir: *M25 junction 4 then northwest on A224 Court Road. Left onto Spur Road/A232 then right onto Gravel Pit Way. Left onto Homefield Rise, at roundabout take 1st exit onto High Street. Hotel near Sainsburys on right.*

High quality, budget accommodation ideal for both families and business travellers. Spacious, en suite bedrooms feature free WiFi and tea and coffee making facilities, and in most hotels, Freeview TV is also available. The adjacent family restaurant features a wide and varied menu.

Rooms: 63

ORSETT
Essex
Map 6 TQ68

Orsett Hall Hotel, Restaurant & Spa

★★★★ 80% COUNTRY HOUSE HOTEL

tel: 01375 891402 & 893096 **Prince Charles Avenue RM16 3HS**
email: accounts@orsetthall.co.uk **web:** www.orsetthall.co.uk
dir: *M25 junction 29, A127 Southend, A128. Hotel 3 miles on right.*

This beautiful country house hotel, conveniently located for the M25, is set in 12 acres of landscaped gardens, and has individually designed, luxurious bedrooms. The award-winning Garden Brasserie is a fabulous dining venue and the stylish modern bar is popular with guests for afternoon tea. Orsett Hall has a first-rate spa, and a very well-equipped gym along with a range of business suites. Free WiFi is available throughout.

Rooms: 56 (24 annexe) (2 family) (14 GF) **S** fr £79 **D** fr £79* **Facilities:** Spa FTV WiFi 🛁 Gym Hair salon Sauna Steam room Heated spa pool Xmas New Year **Conf:** Class 200 Board 50 Theatre 450 **Services:** Lift Night porter Air con **Parking:** 250 **Notes:** Civ Wed 400

O

OSWESTRY
Shropshire

Map 15 SJ22

Wynnstay Hotel

★★★★ 80% ◉ ◉ HOTEL

tel: 01691 655261 **Church Street SY11 2SZ**
email: info@wynnstayhotel.com **web:** www.wynnstayhotel.com
dir: B4083 to town, fork left at Honda Garage, right at lights. Hotel opposite church.

This Georgian property was once a coaching inn and posting house and surrounds a unique 200-year-old bowling green. Elegant public areas include a health, leisure and beauty centre, which is housed in a former coach house. Well-equipped bedrooms are individually styled and include several suites, four-poster rooms and a self-catering apartment. The Four Seasons Restaurant has a well-deserved reputation for its food, and the adjacent Wilsons Bar and Courtyard is a stylish, informal alternative.

Rooms: 31 (5 family) ☞ **Facilities:** Spa FTV WiFi ⓧ Gym Crown bowling green Beauty suite ♫ New Year **Conf:** Class 150 Board 50 Theatre 290 **Services:** Night porter **Parking:** 80 **Notes:** Civ Wed 90

Lion Quays Hotel & Spa

★★★★ 77% ◉ HOTEL

tel: 01691 684300 **Weston Rhyn SY11 3EN**
email: info@lionquays.com **web:** www.lionquays.com
dir: On A5, 3 miles north of Oswestry.

Located in beautiful countryside, north of Oswestry and close to the Llangollen branch of the Shropshire Union Canal, this peaceful retreat offers easy access to Shrewsbury, Chester and Manchester. It features the contemporary Waterside Restaurant, which boasts fine views of the tranquil surroundings and there are good alfresco dining options on sunnier days.

Rooms: 82 (3 family) (25 GF) ☞ **Facilities:** Spa FTV WiFi ♨ ⓧ ☺ Gym Xmas New Year **Conf:** Theatre 400 **Services:** Lift Night porter **Parking:** 300 **Notes:** Civ Wed 400

HIGHLY RECOMMENDED

Pen-y-Dyffryn Country Hotel

★★★ 86% ◉ ◉ COUNTRY HOUSE HOTEL

tel: 01691 653700 **Rhydycroesau SY10 7JD**
email: stay@peny.co.uk **web:** www.peny.co.uk
dir: A5 into town centre. Follow signs to Llansilin on B4580, hotel 3 miles west of Oswestry before Rhydycroesau.

Peacefully situated in five acres of grounds, this charming old house dates back to around 1840, when it was built as a rectory. The tastefully appointed public rooms have real fires, lit in colder weather, and the accommodation includes several mini-cottages, each with its own patio. Many guests are attracted to this hotel for the excellent food and attentive, friendly service.

Rooms: 12 (4 annexe) (1 family) (1 GF) ☞ **S** fr £99 **D** fr £140 (including breakfast)* **Facilities:** STV FTV WiFi ♨ Fishing Guided walks In-room treatments available New Year **Parking:** 18 **Notes:** LB No children 3 years Closed 18 December to 19 January (excluding New Year)

Sweeney Hall Hotel

★★★ 77% COUNTRY HOUSE HOTEL

tel: 01691 652450 **Morda SY10 9EU**
email: hello@thesweeneyhotel.com **web:** www.thesweeneyhotel.com
dir: From A5 on outskirts of Oswestry, take A483 towards Welshpool, hotel 2 miles on left.

This Grade I Listed, friendly family-owned hotel was built in 1805 although previous settlements on this site date back to the 16th century; at one time it was used as a refuge for the Protestant dissenters. Sweeney Hall is set amidst several acres of mature parkland and makes an ideal base for exploring the Shropshire countryside. A log fire welcomes guests on arrival in the colder months and the smart terrace area is ideal for whiling away a summer evening. Bedrooms are spacious and well equipped. The comfortable restaurant is open for breakfast, lunch and dinner.

Rooms: 13 (1 annexe) (4 family) ☞ **S** fr £72.50 **D** fr £97.50 (including breakfast)* **Facilities:** FTV WiFi New Year **Conf:** Class 20 Board 24 Theatre 72 **Parking:** 50 **Notes:** LB Civ Wed 72

Premier Inn Oswestry

Premier Inn 🌙

BUDGET HOTEL

tel: 0871 527 8864 (Calls cost 13p per minute plus your phone company's access charge) **SY10 8NN**
web: www.premierinn.com
dir: From roundabout junction of A483 and A5 (southeast of Oswestry) take A5 signed Oswestry B4579. Hotel 500 yards.

High quality, budget accommodation ideal for both families and business travellers. Spacious, en suite bedrooms feature free WiFi and tea and coffee making facilities, and in most hotels, Freeview TV is also available. The adjacent family restaurant features a wide and varied menu.

Rooms: 98

OTLEY
West Yorkshire

Map 19 SE24

Chevin Country Park Hotel & Spa

CRERAR

★★★ 78% HOTEL

tel: 01943 467818 **Yorkgate LS21 3NU**
email: chevin@crerarhotels.com **web:** www.crerarhotels.com
dir: From Leeds Bradford Airport roundabout take A658 north towards Harrogate, 0.75 mile to lights. Left, 2nd left into Yorkgate. Hotel 0.5 mile on left.

Chevin Country Park Hotel & Spa is peacefully located in its own woodland yet is convenient for major road links and the airport. Bedrooms are split between the original main building and chalet-style accommodation in the extensive grounds. Public areas include a bar and several lounges. The Lakeside Restaurant provides views over the small lake, and good leisure facilities are available.

Rooms: 49 (30 annexe) (7 family) (45 GF) **Facilities:** Spa FTV WiFi ⓧ ☺ Fishing Gym Steam room Xmas New Year **Conf:** Class 90 Board 50 Theatre 120 **Services:** Night porter **Parking:** 100 **Notes:** LB Civ Wed 100

OTTERSHAW	**Map 6 TQ06**
Surrey	

Foxhills Club & Resort

★★★★ 84% HOTEL

tel: 01932 872050 **Stonehill Road KT16 0EL**
email: reservations@foxhills.co.uk **web:** www.foxhills.co.uk
dir: *M25 junction 11, A320 to Woking. 2nd roundabout last exit into Chobham Road. Right into Foxhills Road, left into Stonehill Road.*

Foxhills is a welcome retreat, set on a 400-acre Surrey estate just 25 minutes from Waterloo and Heathrow, with easy access to major road networks including the M25. The entire resort is bursting with things to do, including golf, tennis, swimming pools and impressive indoor leisure facilities. At the heart of the estate and just a short walk from the spacious well-appointed bedrooms, stands the 19th-century manor house, home to the popular Manor Restaurant.

Rooms: 70 (8 family) (39 GF) ☎ **Facilities:** Spa STV FTV WiFi ↻ ☺ ⚡ ♨ 45 ♟ ⚑ Gym Squash Children's adventure playground Country pursuits Hairdresser ♫ Xmas New Year **Conf:** Class 60 Board 30 Theatre 150 **Services:** Night porter **Parking:** 500 **Notes:** Civ Wed 90

OUNDLE	**Map 11 TL08**
Northamptonshire	

The Talbot Hotel

★★★ 80% HOTEL

tel: 01832 273621 **New Street PE8 4EA**
email: talbot@innmail.co.uk **web:** www.thetalbot-oundle.com
dir: *A605 Northampton/Oundle at roundabout exit Oundle A427 – Station Road turn onto New Street.*

This Grade I listed property is steeped in history and is reputed to house the staircase that Mary, Queen of Scots walked down to her execution in 1587. The hotel offers an open-plan eatery and coffee shop for relaxed dining. Accommodation is a mix of traditional and contemporary, but all rooms provide up-to-date amenities for guest comfort.

Rooms: 34 (2 family) (12 GF) ☎ **S** fr £79 **D** fr £99 (including breakfast)*
Facilities: FTV WiFi Xmas New Year **Conf:** Class 50 Board 30 Theatre 100 **Services:** Night porter **Parking:** 30 **Notes:** LB Civ Wed 80

OXFORD	**Map 5 SP50**
Oxfordshire	

Belmond Le Manoir aux Quat'Saisons

★★★★★ ◎◎◎◎◎ ⊜ HOTEL

tel: 01844 278881 **Church Road OX44 7PD**
email: manoir.mqs@belmond.com **web:** www.belmond.com/lemanoir

(for full entry see Great Milton)

Macdonald Randolph Hotel

★★★★★ 80% HOTEL

tel: 01865 256400 **Beaumont Street OX1 2LN**
email: sales.randolph@macdonald-hotels.co.uk
web: www.macdonaldhotels.co.uk/Randolph
dir: *M40 junction 8, A40 signed Oxford/Cheltenham, 5 miles, at lights to ring road roundabout. Right signed Kidlington/North Oxford. At next roundabout left towards city centre – A4165/Banbury road. Through Summertown to lights at end of St Giles. Hotel on right.*

Superbly located near the city centre, The Randolph boasts impressive neo-Gothic architecture and tasteful decor. The spacious and traditional restaurant, complete with picture windows, is the ideal place to watch the world go by while enjoying freshly prepared, modern dishes. Bedrooms include a mix of classical and contemporary wing rooms, which have been appointed to a high standard. On-site chargeable parking is a real bonus; pre-booking is required.

Rooms: 151 ☎ **Facilities:** Spa STV FTV WiFi Gym Beauty treatment rooms Thermal suite Mini gym Xmas New Year **Conf:** Class 130 Board 60 Theatre 300 **Services:** Lift Night porter **Parking:** 45 **Notes:** LB Civ Wed 120

Malmaison Oxford

★★★★ 79% HOTEL

tel: 01865 268400 **Oxford Castle, 3 New Road OX1 1AY**
email: oxford@malmaison.com **web:** www.malmaison.com/locations/oxford
dir: *M40 junction 9, A34 north to Botley interchange. Follow city centre and rail station signs. At rail station take the 2nd exit at roundabout, then 1st exit into Park End Street. Straight on at next lights, hotel 2nd right.*

Once the city's prison, this is definitely a hotel with a difference. Many of the rooms are actually converted from the old cells. Not to worry though as there have been many improvements in facilities, services and decor since the prisoners left over 20 years ago. Exceedingly comfortable beds and luxury bathrooms are just two of the changes. The hotel has a popular brasserie with quality and value much in evidence. Limited parking space is available.

Rooms: 95 (5 GF) ☎ **Facilities:** STV FTV WiFi ↻ Xmas New Year **Conf:** Class 40 Board 40 Theatre 80 **Services:** Lift Night porter **Parking:** 30 **Notes:** Civ Wed 120

O

OXFORD *continued*

Mercure Oxford Eastgate Hotel

★★★★ 78% HOTEL

Mercure HOTELS

tel: 01865 248332 **73 High Street OX1 4BE**
email: h6668@accor.com **web:** www.mercure.com
dir: *A40 follow signs to Headington and Oxford city centre, over Magdalen Bridge, stay in left lane, through lights, left into Merton Street, entrance to car park on left.*

The Mercure Eastgate Hotel has a range of beautifully presented bedrooms and stylish public areas. This 17th-century building enjoys a great location in the centre of historic Oxford and occupies a site at the city's East Gate. The stylish Marco's New York Italian restaurant at the hotel is very popular and afternoon tea served in the comfortable lounge is another favourite with guests. Secure parking is available at the hotel.

Rooms: 64 (3 family) (4 GF) S fr £77 **D** fr £106* **Facilities:** FTV WiFi Xmas New Year **Services:** Lift Night porter Air con **Parking:** 40

Oxford Spires Hotel

★★★★ 78% HOTEL

PRINCIPAL

tel: 0800 374692 **Abingdon Road OX1 4PS**
email: SpiresReservations@oxfordspireshotel.co.uk
web: www.oxfordspireshotel.co.uk/partner/oxford-spires
dir: *From M40 junction 8 towards Oxford. Left towards Cowley. At 3rd roundabout follow city centre signs. Hotel in 1 mile. From A34 Hinksey Hill junction towards Oxford. Left at 1st roundabout. Hotel in 1 mile.*

This purpose-built hotel is surrounded by extensive parkland, yet is only a short walk from the city centre. Bedrooms are attractively furnished, well-equipped and include several apartments. Public areas include a spacious restaurant, open-plan bar/lounge, leisure club and extensive conference facilities.

Rooms: 181 (10 annexe) (1 family) (54 GF) **Facilities:** Spa FTV WiFi Gym Steam room Sauna Xmas New Year **Conf:** Class 96 Board 76 Theatre 266 **Services:** Lift Night porter **Parking:** 160 **Notes:** Civ Wed 200

Cotswold Lodge Hotel

★★★★ 76% HOTEL

tel: 01865 512121 **66a Banbury Road OX2 6JP**
email: enquiries@cotswoldlodgehotel.co.uk **web:** www.cotswoldlodgehotel.co.uk
dir: *A40 Oxford ring road onto A4165 Banbury road signed city centre/Summertown. Hotel 2 miles on left.*

This Victorian property is located close to the centre of Oxford and offers smart, comfortable accommodation. Stylish bedrooms and suites are attractively presented and some have balconies. The public areas have an elegant country-house feel. The hotel is popular with business guests and caters for conferences and banquets.

Rooms: 49 (14 GF) S fr £75 **D** fr £125 (including breakfast)* **Facilities:** FTV WiFi Xmas New Year **Conf:** Class 45 Board 40 Theatre 100 **Services:** Night porter **Parking:** 40 **Notes:** Civ Wed 100

Jurys Inn Oxford Hotel & Conference Centre

★★★★ 75% HOTEL

tel: 01865 489988 **Godstow Road OX2 8AL**
web: www.jurysinns.com
dir: *Phone for directions.*

Located just on the edge of the city centre, this large hotel offers smart, modern bedrooms. Public rooms include a lounge area with a coffee bar, a bar offering food and a Marco Pierre White restaurant. The contemporary-style bedrooms are smartly decorated and equipped with a range of useful facilities. The hotel also has a gym and pool.

Rooms: 240 (35 family) (111 GF) S fr £70 **D** fr £70* **Facilities:** WiFi Gym Squash Xmas **Conf:** Class 200 Board 50 Theatre 350 **Services:** Night porter **Parking:** 200 **Notes:** Civ Wed 300

Hawkwell House

★★★★ 72% HOTEL

tel: 01865 749988 **Church Way, Iffley Village OX4 4DZ**
email: reservations@hawkwellhouse.co.uk **web:** www.hawkwellhouse.co.uk
dir: *A34 follow signs to Cowley. At Littlemore roundabout A4158 exit into Iffley Road. After lights left to Iffley.*

Set in a peaceful residential location, Hawkwell House is just a few minutes' drive from the Oxford ring road. The spacious rooms are modern, attractively decorated and well equipped. Public areas are tastefully appointed and the conservatory-style restaurant offers an interesting choice of dishes. The hotel also has a range of conference and function facilities.

Rooms: 77 (16 annexe) (4 family) (15 GF) S fr £79 **D** fr £89* **Facilities:** FTV WiFi Xmas New Year **Conf:** Class 80 Board 60 Theatre 160 **Services:** Lift Night porter **Parking:** 60 **Notes:** Civ Wed 150

Bath Place Hotel

★★ 71% METRO HOTEL

tel: 01865 791812 **4-5 Bath Place, Holywell Street OX1 3SU**
email: info@bathplace.co.uk **web:** www.bathplace.co.uk
dir: *On south side of Holywell Street, parallel to High Street.*

The hotel has been created from a group of 17th-century cottages originally built by Flemish weavers who were permitted to settle outside the city walls. This lovely hotel is very much at the heart of the city today and offers individually designed bedrooms, including some with four-posters.

Rooms: 16 (3 family) (5 GF) S fr £110 **D** fr £135 (including breakfast)* **Facilities:** FTV WiFi **Services:** Night porter **Parking:** 16

Premier Inn Oxford

BUDGET HOTEL

tel: 0871 527 8866 (Calls cost 13p per minute plus your phone company's access charge) **Oxford Business Park, Garsington Road OX4 2JZ**
web: www.premierinn.com
dir: *On Oxford Business Park, just off A4142 and B480 junction.*

High quality, budget accommodation ideal for both families and business travellers. Spacious, en suite bedrooms feature free WiFi and tea and coffee making facilities, and in most hotels, Freeview TV is also available. The adjacent family restaurant features a wide and varied menu.

Rooms: 143

OXFORD MOTORWAY SERVICE AREA (M40)   Map 5 SP60
Oxfordshire

Ramada Oxford

AA Advertised

tel: 01865 877000 **M40 junct 8a, Waterstock OX33 1LJ**
email: oxford.hotel@welcomebreak.co.uk **web:** www.welcomebreak.co.uk
dir: *M40 junction 8a, at Welcome Break service area.*

This modern building offers accommodation in smart, spacious and well-equipped bedrooms, suitable for families and business travellers, and all with en suite bathrooms. Continental breakfast is available and other refreshments may be taken at the nearby family restaurant.

Rooms: 59 (56 family) (25 GF) (10 smoking) **Facilities:** FTV WiFi ⓑ **Parking:** 100

PADSTOW   Map 2 SW97
Cornwall & Isles Of Scilly

HIGHLY RECOMMENDED

Treglos Hotel

★★★★ 84% ⊚⊚ HOTEL

tel: 01841 520727 **Constantine Bay PL28 8JH**
email: stay@tregloshotel.com **web:** www.tregloshotel.com
dir: *From Okehampton A30, follow A39 towards Wadebridge, then B3274 to Padstow. After 2 miles turn left to St Merryn. After 3 miles, at St Merryn crossroads turn left. Take next right to Treglos. After 1 mile turn right after Constantine Bay Stores. Hotel is on left.*

This long-established hotel is situated on the edge of the stunning Cornish coast with breathtaking views. The atmosphere is all about sophistication and elegance. Bedrooms are soundly appointed and well equipped, and there is a contemporary dining room with enjoyable cuisine and wonderful views over the coast. Guests will find a superb bar and lounges to relax and unwind in. On-site parking is a bonus.

Rooms: 42 (8 family) (1 GF) ⓡ **S** fr £78 **D** fr £157 (including breakfast)*
Facilities: Spa FTV WiFi ⓑ ⓧ ⓛ 18 Whirlpool beauty treatments Games room Childrens playground ♫ **Services:** Lift Night porter **Parking:** 40 **Notes:** LB Closed December to February

---

PAIGNTON   Map 3 SX86
Devon

Redcliffe Hotel

★★★ 81% HOTEL

tel: 01803 526397 **Marine Drive TQ3 2NL**
email: reception@redcliffehotel.co.uk **web:** www.redcliffehotel.co.uk
dir: *On seafront at Torquay end of Paignton Green.*

Set at the water's edge in three acres of well-tended grounds, this popular hotel enjoys uninterrupted views across Tor Bay. On offer is a diverse range of facilities including a leisure complex, beauty treatments and lots of outdoor family activities in the summer. Bedrooms are pleasantly appointed and comfortably furnished, while public areas offer ample space for rest and relaxation.

Rooms: 70 (8 family) (3 GF) ⓡ **S** fr £62 **D** fr £124 (including breakfast)*
Facilities: Spa FTV WiFi ⓑ ⓧ ⓧ Fishing Gym Table tennis Putting green Children's play area Xmas New Year **Conf:** Class 50 Board 50 Theatre 150 **Services:** Lift Night porter **Parking:** 80 **Notes:** LB Civ Wed 150

The Queens Hotel

★★★ 78% HOTEL

tel: 01803 551048 **2-6 Queens Road TQ4 6AT**
email: gm@queenspaignton.com **web:** www.queenspaignton.com
dir: *Phone for directions.*

This popular hotel enjoys a central location close to the town centre and is within walking distance of the beaches. The attractively decorated bedrooms vary in size, but all offer good levels of quality and comfort. Wholesome, traditional food is served in the spacious dining room. Secure parking is available at the hotel along with a range of leisure facilities including a heated pool.

Rooms: 76 (5 family) (6 GF) ⓡ **Facilities:** FTV WiFi ⓧ Free use of gym at sister hotel ♫ Xmas New Year **Services:** Lift Night porter **Parking:** 36 **Notes:** LB

Premier Inn Paignton Seafront (Goodrington Sands)

BUDGET HOTEL

tel: 0871 527 9206 (Calls cost 13p per minute plus your phone company's access charge) **Tanners Road, Goodrington TQ4 6LP**
web: www.premierinn.com
dir: *From Newton Abbot take A380 south. Left into A3022 (Totnes Road), right at Hayes Road into Penwill Way, right at B3199 into Dartmouth Road, at lights left into Tanners Road.*

High quality, budget accommodation ideal for both families and business travellers. Spacious, en suite bedrooms feature free WiFi and tea and coffee making facilities, and in most hotels, Freeview TV is also available. The adjacent family restaurant features a wide and varied menu.

Rooms: 33

P

PAIGNTON continued

Premier Inn Paignton South (Brixham Road)

Premier Inn

BUDGET HOTEL

tel: 0871 527 9324 (Calls cost 13p per minute plus your phone company's access charge) **White Rock, Long Road South TQ4 7AZ**
web: www.premierinn.com
dir: *From A3022 (Brixham Road) between Tweenaway and Galmpton Warborough, right into Long Road.*

Rooms: 61

PAINSWICK	Map 4 SO80
Gloucestershire	

The Painswick

[U]

tel: 01452 813688 **Kemps Lane GL6 6YB**
email: enquiries@thepainswick.co.uk **web:** www.thepainswick.co.uk
dir: *From A46 in centre of Painswick, into Victoria Street, then into Tibbiwell Lane. Right into Kemps Lane, hotel on right.*

Currently the rating for this establishment is not confirmed. This may be due to a change of ownership or because ot has only recently joined the AA rating scheme.

Rooms: 16 (7 annexe) (4 family) **Facilities:** Spa STV FTV WiFi Xmas New Year
Conf: Board 16 **Services:** Night porter **Parking:** 20 **Notes:** Civ Wed 60

PALTERTON	Map 16 SK46
Derbyshire	

Twin Oaks Hotel

★★★ 77% HOTEL

tel: 01246 855455 **Church Lane S44 6UZ**
email: book@twinoakshotel.co.uk **web:** www.twinoakshotel.co.uk
dir: *M1 junction 29, take Palterton turn, hotel 100 metres down road on left.*

This hotel began life as a picturesque row of colliery cottages, but it has been meticulously redesigned and configured to meet the expectations of the modern business or leisure traveller. The bedrooms provide contemporary accommodation and the attractive public areas include a brasserie and bistro providing a range of dining options. The hotel is a popular wedding destination and enjoys very good transport links as it is near the M1.

Rooms: 36 (4 annexe) (4 family) (19 GF) **S** fr £80 **D** fr £80* **Facilities:** FTV WiFi
Conf: Class 25 Board 25 Theatre 40 **Parking:** 80 **Notes:** Civ Wed 80

PATTERDALE	Map 18 NY31
Cumbria	

Patterdale Hotel

★★ 80% HOTEL

tel: 01768 482231 **CA11 0NN**
email: reservations@choice-hotels.co.uk **web:** www.patterdalehotel.co.uk
dir: *M6 junction 40, A592 towards Ullswater. 10 miles to Patterdale.*

Patterdale is a real tourist destination and this hotel makes a good base for those taking part in the many activities available in this area. The hotel enjoys delightful views of the valley and fells, being located at the southern end of Ullswater. The modern bedrooms vary in style. In busier periods accommodation is let for a minimum period of two nights.

Rooms: 56 (15 family) (6 GF) **S** fr £40 **D** fr £82 (including breakfast & dinner)
Facilities: FTV WiFi Xmas New Year **Services:** Lift **Parking:** 30 **Notes:** LB

PECKFORTON	Map 15 SJ55
Cheshire	

Peckforton Castle

★★★★ @@@ HOTEL

tel: 01829 260930 **Stone House Lane CW6 9TN**
email: info@peckfortoncastle.co.uk **web:** www.peckfortoncastle.co.uk
dir: *A49. At Beeston Castle pub take right signed Peckforton Castle. Approximately 2 miles, entrance on right.*

Built in the mid 19th century by parliamentarian and landowner Lord John Tollemache, and now lovingly cared for by The Naylor Family, this Grade I medieval-style castle has been sympathetically renovated to provide high standards of comfort without losing its original charm and character. Bedrooms and public areas retain many period features, and dining in the 1851 Restaurant is a memorable experience. The kitchen team is passionate about using only the finest ingredients, sourced locally where possible. There are a host of excellent outdoor leisure activities; falconry and off-road Land Rover courses to name just two. The Tranquility Spa caters for those seeking a more serene experience.

Rooms: 48 (7 family) (2 GF) **Facilities:** Spa FTV WiFi HL Falconry Outdoor pursuits Land Rover experience Abseiling Beauty salon Xmas New Year
Conf: Class 80 Board 40 Theatre 180 **Services:** Lift Night porter **Parking:** 400
Notes: LB Civ Wed 165

PENDLEBURY	Map 15 SD70
Greater Manchester	

Premier Inn Manchester (Swinton)

Premier Inn

BUDGET HOTEL

tel: 0871 527 8720 (Calls cost 13p per minute plus your phone company's access charge) **219 Bolton Road M27 8TG**
web: www.premierinn.com
dir: *M60 junction 13 towards A572, at roundabout take 3rd exit towards Swinton. At next roundabout take A572. In 2 miles right onto A580. After 2nd lights A666 Kearsley, 1st left at roundabout. Pass fire station on right, 1st right.*

High quality, budget accommodation ideal for both families and business travellers. Spacious, en suite bedrooms feature free WiFi and tea and coffee making facilities, and in most hotels, Freeview TV is also available. The adjacent family restaurant features a wide and varied menu.

Rooms: 31

PENRITH
Cumbria
Map 18 NY53

See also **Glenridding & Shap**

North Lakes Hotel & Spa
★★★★ 80% ⚜ HOTEL

tel: 01768 868111 **Ullswater Road CA11 8QT**
email: reservations@northlakeshotel.co.uk **web:** www.northlakeshotel.co.uk
dir: *M6 junction 40 at junction with A66.*

With a great location, it's no wonder that this modern hotel is perpetually busy. Amenities include a good range of meeting and function rooms and excellent health and leisure facilities including a full spa. Themed public areas have a contemporary, Scandinavian country style and offer plenty of space and comfort. High standards of service are provided by a friendly team of staff.

Rooms: 84 (6 family) (22 GF) **S** fr £104 **D** fr £104* **Facilities:** Spa STV WiFi ⬙ ⟳ Gym Children's splash pool Steam room Activity and wellness studios Sauna Treatment rooms New Year **Conf:** Class 140 Board 30 Theatre 200 **Services:** Lift Night porter **Parking:** 150 **Notes:** LB Civ Wed 200

The George Hotel
LAKE DISTRICT HOTELS
★★★ 83% ⚜⚜ HOTEL

tel: 01768 862696 **Devonshire Street CA11 7SU**
email: georgehotel@lakedistricthotels.net **web:** www.lakedistricthotels.net/georgehotel
dir: *M6 junction 40, 1 mile to town centre. From A6/A66 to Penrith.*

This inviting and popular hotel was once visited by 'Bonnie' Prince Charlie. Extended over the years, it currently offers well-equipped bedrooms, and spacious public areas that retain a timeless charm. There is a choice of lounge areas that are ideal for morning coffee and afternoon tea.

Rooms: 35 (4 family) **S** fr £75 **D** fr £90 (including breakfast)* **Facilities:** FTV WiFi ⬙ ♫ Xmas New Year **Conf:** Class 80 Board 50 Theatre 120 **Services:** Night porter **Parking:** 40 **Notes:** Civ Wed 120

PENZANCE
Cornwall & Isles Of Scilly
Map 2 SW43

Hotel Penzance
★★★★ 80% ⚜⚜ TOWN HOUSE HOTEL

tel: 01736 363117 **Britons Hill TR18 3AE**
email: reception@hotelpenzance.com **web:** www.hotelpenzance.com
dir: *From A30, left at last roundabout for town centre. 3rd right onto Britons Hill. Hotel on right.*

Hotel Penzance is an Edwardian house that has been tastefully redesigned, particularly in the contemporary Bay Restaurant. The focus on style is not only limited to the decor, but is also apparent in the award-winning cuisine that is based on fresh Cornish produce. Bedrooms have been appointed to modern standards and are particularly well equipped; many have views across Mounts Bay.

Rooms: 25 (2 GF) 🐾 **S** fr £85 **D** fr £125 (including breakfast)* **Facilities:** FTV WiFi ⤳ Xmas New Year **Conf:** Class 50 Board 25 Theatre 80 **Services:** Night porter **Parking:** 11

Queens Hotel
★★★ 79% HOTEL

tel: 01736 362371 **The Promenade TR18 4HG**
email: enquiries@queens-hotel.com **web:** www.queens-hotel.com
dir: *A30 to Penzance, follow signs for seafront pass harbour onto promenade, hotel on right.*

With great views across Mount's Bay, this impressive family-owned and run Victorian hotel offers high levels of comfort and style while still reflecting a long and distinguished history. Many of the bedrooms, which vary in style and size, have sea views and there is free Wi-Fi throughout the property; ample on-site parking is provided.

Rooms: 70 (10 family) 🐾 **S** fr £50 **D** fr £99 (including breakfast)* **Facilities:** FTV WiFi ⬙ Hair and beauty salon Xmas New Year **Conf:** Class 200 Board 120 Theatre 200 **Services:** Lift Night porter **Parking:** 50 **Notes:** Civ Wed 250

PETERBOROUGH
Cambridgeshire
Map 12 TL19

Bull Hotel
★★★★ 81% ⚜ HOTEL
PEEL HOTELS PLC

tel: 01733 561364 **Westgate PE1 1RB**
email: rooms@bull-hotel-peterborough.com **web:** www.peelhotels.co.uk
dir: *From A1 follow city centre signs. Hotel opposite Queensgate shopping centre. Car park on Broadway adjacent to library.*

This pleasant city-centre hotel offers well-equipped, modern accommodation, which includes several wings of deluxe bedrooms. Public rooms include a popular bar and a brasserie-style restaurant serving a flexible range of dishes, with further informal dining available in the lounge. There is a good range of meeting rooms and conference facilities.

Rooms: 118 (2 family) (5 GF) 🐾 **S** fr £65 **D** fr £75* **Facilities:** STV WiFi Xmas New Year **Conf:** Class 120 Board 40 Theatre 200 **Services:** Night porter **Parking:** 100 **Notes:** LB Civ Wed 200

P

PETERBOROUGH *continued*

Best Western Plus Orton Hall Hotel & Spa

★★★★ 73% HOTEL

tel: 01733 391111 **The Village, Orton Longueville PE2 7DN**
email: reception@ortonhall.co.uk **web:** www.abacushotels.co.uk
dir: *Off A605 east, opposite Orton Mere.*

Orton Hall is an impressive country house hotel set in 20 acres of woodland on the outskirts of town and with easy access to the A1. The spacious and relaxing public areas include the baronial Great Room and the Orton Suite for banqueting and meetings, and the oak-panelled, award-winning Huntly Restaurant. The on-site pub, Ramblewood Inn, is an alternative, informal dining option.

Rooms: 70 (2 family) (15 GF) **S** fr £47.50 **D** fr £60* **Facilities:** Spa FTV WiFi ↪ ☒ Sauna Steam room Xmas New Year **Conf:** Class 70 Board 60 Theatre 160 **Services:** Night porter **Parking:** 200 **Notes:** LB Civ Wed 150

Bell Inn Hotel

★★★ 85% ◉◉ HOTEL

tel: 01733 241066 **Great North Road PE7 3RA**
email: reception@thebellstilton.co.uk **web:** www.thebellstilton.co.uk

(for full entry see Stilton)

Premier Inn Peterborough (Ferry Meadows)

Premier Inn

BUDGET HOTEL

tel: 0871 527 8872 (Calls cost 13p per minute plus your phone company's access charge) **Ham Lane, Orton Meadows PE2 5UU**
web: www.premierinn.com
dir: *A1(M) southbound: A605 signed Alwalton/Chesterton Business Park/Elton and Showground, left at T-junction. Or A1(M) northbound: after junction 17, follow Showround/Chesterton/Alwalton and Elton signs. Left at T-junction signed A605/Peterborough. For both routes: at 4th roundabout 1st exit, then 1st right.*

High quality, budget accommodation ideal for both families and business travellers. Spacious, en suite bedrooms feature free WiFi and tea and coffee making facilities, and in most hotels, Freeview TV is also available. The adjacent family restaurant features a wide and varied menu.

Rooms: 40

Premier Inn Peterborough (Hampton)

Premier Inn

BUDGET HOTEL

tel: 0871 527 8874 (Calls cost 13p per minute plus your phone company's access charge) **Ashbourne Road, off London Rd PE7 8BT**
web: www.premierinn.com
dir: *A1(M) (southbound) junction 16, A15 through Yaxley, left at roundabout. Or A1(M) (northbound) junction 17, A1139 junction 3 right to Yaxley, right at 2nd roundabout.*

Rooms: 143

Premier Inn Peterborough North

Premier Inn

BUDGET HOTEL

tel: 0871 527 8876 (Calls cost 13p per minute plus your phone company's access charge) **1023 Lincoln Road, Walton PE4 6AH**
web: www.premierinn.com
dir: *A1, A47 towards Peterborough. In 7 miles exit at junction 17 signed city centre. At roundabout (bottom of slip road) straight on signed city centre. At next roundabout left onto dual carriageway. At next roundabout double back, follow signs for city centre. Hotel in 200 metres.*

Rooms: 68

Days Inn Peterborough - A1

AA Advertised

tel: 01733 371540 **Peterborough Extra Services, A1 Junction 17 PE7 3UQ**
email: peterborough.hotel@welcomebreak.co.uk **web:** www.welcomebreak.co.uk
dir: *A1(M) junction 17.*

This modern, purpose-built accommodation offers smartly appointed, particularly well-equipped bedrooms with good power showers. There is a choice of adjacent food outlets where guests can enjoy breakfast, snacks and meals.

Rooms: 82 (16 family) (40 GF) (11 smoking) ☎ **Facilities:** FTV WiFi ↪ **Services:** Air con **Parking:** 120

PETERSFIELD	Map 5 SU72
Hampshire	

Premier Inn Petersfield

Premier Inn

BUDGET HOTEL

tel: 0871 527 8878 (Calls cost 13p per minute plus your phone company's access charge) **Winchester Road GU32 3BS**
web: www.premierinn.com
dir: *At junction of A3 and A272 westbound signed Services.*

High quality, budget accommodation ideal for both families and business travellers. Spacious, en suite bedrooms feature free WiFi and tea and coffee making facilities, and in most hotels, Freeview TV is also available. The adjacent family restaurant features a wide and varied menu.

Rooms: 81

P

PICKERING
North Yorkshire
Map 19 SE78

The White Swan Inn
★★★ 83% ◎◎ HOTEL

tel: 01751 472288 **Market Place YO18 7AA**
email: welcome@white-swan.co.uk **web:** www.white-swan.co.uk
dir: In town, between church and steam railway station.

This 16th-century coaching inn offers well-equipped, comfortable bedrooms, including suites, either of a more traditional style in the main building or modern in the annexe. Service is friendly and attentive. Good food is served in the attractive restaurant, in the cosy bar and in the lounge, where a log fire burns in cooler months. A private dining room is also available. The comprehensive wine list focuses on many fine vintages.

Rooms: 21 (9 annexe) (3 family) (8 GF) 🐾 **S** fr £129 **D** fr £159 (including breakfast)* **Facilities:** FTV WiFi Secure bike storage with drying facilities Xmas New Year **Conf:** Class 18 Board 25 Theatre 35 **Parking:** 45

Best Western Forest & Vale Hotel
 Best Western
★★★ 85% HOTEL

tel: 01751 472722 **Malton Road YO18 7DL**
email: info@forestandvalehotel.co.uk **web:** www.bw-forestandvalehotel.co.uk
dir: On A169 towards York at roundabout on outskirts of Pickering.

This lovely 18th-century manor house hotel makes an excellent base from which to explore the east coast resorts and the North Yorkshire Moors National Park, one of England's most beautiful areas. A dedicated approach to upgrading means that the hotel is particularly well maintained, inside and out. In addition to standard bedrooms there are more spacious deluxe, superior and executive rooms; they are more traditional in the main house while the ones in the wing are contemporary; one has a four-poster bed.

Rooms: 22 (5 annexe) (7 family) (5 GF) 🐾 **S** fr £98 **D** fr £130 (including breakfast)* **Facilities:** FTV WiFi ↘ **Conf:** Class 40 Board 30 Theatre 100 **Parking:** 40 **Notes:** LB Closed 23–28 December Civ Wed 90

The Beansheaf Hotel
★★★ 71% HOTEL

tel: 01653 668614 **Malton Road YO17 6UE**
email: enquiries@beansheafhotel.com **web:** www.beansheafhotel.com
dir: On A169 between Malton and Pickering at the Flamingo Land turning.

This modern hotel is conveniently located on the A169 between Pickering and Malton. It's ideal for exploring the North York Moors or visiting Flamingo Land. A range of bedrooms is available, including singles, doubles, twins and family rooms; ground floor rooms are also available. A wide range of home-made meals are served in the bar and restaurant.

Rooms: 18 (8 GF) 🐾 **S** fr £55 **D** fr £75* **Facilities:** FTV WiFi ↘ **Conf:** Class 50 Board 25 Theatre 60 **Parking:** 35

PLYMOUTH
Devon
Map 3 SX45

Boringdon Hall Hotel
★★★★★ 84% ◎◎◎ COUNTRY HOUSE HOTEL

tel: 01752 344455 **Boringdon Hill, Plympton PL7 4DP**
email: info@boringdonhall.co.uk **web:** www.boringdonhall.co.uk
dir: A38 at Marsh Mills roundabout follow Plympton signs to small island. Left over bridge and follow tourist signs.

With a history going back to the Domesday Book, this grand manor house enjoys easy access to Dartmoor and Plymouth. Quality and comfort are delivered in equal measure, and public areas exude character, charm and sophistication. The committed team is entirely focused on making your stay both relaxing and rewarding. The Gallery restaurant is the venue for accomplished cooking; menus incorporate the best quality, seasonal produce. The Gaia Spa is simply stunning with a range of treatments available alongside facilities such as infinity pool, gym, relaxation rooms, saunas and hydrotherapy pool.

Rooms: 40 **Facilities:** Spa WiFi ↘ ③ Gym Hydrotherapy pool Heat experiences Xmas New Year **Conf:** Class 40 Board 50 Theatre 120 **Services:** Night porter **Notes:** LB Civ Wed 90

Langdon Court Hotel & Restaurant
★★★★ 78% ◎◎ COUNTRY HOUSE HOTEL

tel: 01752 862358 **Adams Lane, Down Thomas PL9 0DY**
email: enquiries@langdoncourt.com **web:** www.langdoncourt.com
dir: From Plymouth follow Kingsbridge signs Elberton roundabout. Signs to Langdon Court.

A Grade II listed building, this stylish Tudor mansion is in a super location in the South Hams, just a short stroll from Wembury Cove and the coastal path. It is set in seven acres of grounds with an ornamental lake, and although it's only four miles from Plymouth, it feels a million miles from the hubbub of the city. The lovely gardens include a Jacobean walled garden and a vineyard being developed by the hotel management. Bedrooms are stylishly appointed, comfortably furnished, and have lovely views of the grounds. The restaurant and bar areas offer enjoyable meals featuring fresh and local produce.

Rooms: 19 (3 family) 🐾 **S** fr £109 **D** fr £129 (including breakfast)* **Facilities:** STV FTV WiFi ↘ Fishing Xmas New Year **Conf:** Class 20 Board 20 Theatre 60 **Services:** Night porter **Parking:** 60 **Notes:** LB Civ Wed 100

Best Western Duke of Cornwall Hotel
 Best Western
★★★ 84% ◎◎ HOTEL

tel: 01752 275850 **Millbay Road PL1 3LG**
email: enquiries@thedukeofcornwall.co.uk **web:** www.thedukeofcornwall.co.uk
dir: Follow city centre, then Plymouth Pavilions Conference and Leisure Centre signs. Hotel opposite Plymouth Pavilions.

A historic landmark, this city centre hotel is conveniently located. The spacious public areas include a popular bar, comfortable lounge and multi-functional ballroom. Bedrooms, many with far-reaching views, are individually styled and comfortably appointed. The range of dining options includes meals in the bar, or the elegant dining room for a more formal atmosphere.

Rooms: 71 (4 family) 🐾 **S** fr £55 **D** fr £80 (including breakfast)* **Facilities:** STV FTV WiFi ↘ Xmas New Year **Conf:** Class 125 Board 84 Theatre 300 **Services:** Lift Night porter **Parking:** 25 **Notes:** Civ Wed 300

P

PLYMOUTH *continued*

Invicta Hotel

★★★ 81% HOTEL

tel: 01752 664997 **11-12 Osborne Place, Lockyer Street PL1 2PU**
email: invictahotel@btconnect.com **web:** www.invictahotel.co.uk
dir: *A38 to Plymouth, follow city centre signs, then signs to The Hoe & Barbican. Hotel opposite Hoe Park on Lockyer Street at junction with Citadel Road.*

Just a short stroll from the city centre, this elegant Victorian establishment stands opposite the famous bowling green. The atmosphere is relaxed and friendly and bedrooms are neatly presented, well-equipped and attractively decorated. Eating options include meals in the bar or in the more formal setting of the dining room.

Rooms: 23 (3 family) (1 GF) 🛏 **S** fr £70 **D** fr £85* **Facilities:** FTV WiFi ⌕ **Conf:** Class 30 Board 45 Theatre 45 **Services:** Night porter **Parking:** 14 **Notes:** Closed 25–26 December

Premier Inn Plymouth Centre (Sutton Harbour)

BUDGET HOTEL

Premier Inn

tel: 0871 527 8882 (Calls cost 13p per minute plus your phone company's access charge) **Sutton Road, Shepherds Wharf PL4 0HX**
web: www.premierinn.com
dir: *A38, A374 towards Plymouth. Follow Coxside and National Marine Aquarium signs. Right at lights after leisure park. Hotel adjacent to Lockyers Quay. Note: there are 2 Premier Inns on this site, this hotel is the larger.*

High quality, budget accommodation ideal for both families and business travellers. Spacious, en suite bedrooms feature free WiFi and tea and coffee making facilities, and in most hotels, Freeview TV is also available. The adjacent family restaurant features a wide and varied menu.

Rooms: 107

Premier Inn Plymouth City Centre (Lockyers Quay)

BUDGET HOTEL

Premier Inn

tel: 0871 527 8880 (Calls cost 13p per minute plus your phone company's access charge) **1 Lockyers Quay, Coxside PL4 0DX**
web: www.premierinn.com
dir: *From A38 (Marsh Mills roundabout) take A374 into Plymouth. Follow Coxside and National Marine Aquarium signs.*

Rooms: 62

Premier Inn Plymouth East

BUDGET HOTEL

Premier Inn

tel: 0871 527 8884 (Calls cost 13p per minute plus your phone company's access charge) **300 Plymouth Road, Crabtree PL3 6RW**
web: www.premierinn.com
dir: *From east: Exit A38 at Marsh Mill junction. Straight on at roundabout, exit slip road 100 metres on left. From west: Exit A38 at Plympton junction, at roundabout exit slip road adjacent to A38.*

Rooms: 81

Feathers Hotel

★★ 77% HOTEL

tel: 01759 303155 **56 Market Place YO42 2AH**
email: info@thefeathers-hotel.co.uk **web:** www.thefeatherspocklington.co.uk
dir: *From York, B1246 signed Pocklington. Hotel just off A1079.*

This busy, traditional inn provides comfortable, well-equipped and spacious accommodation. Public areas are smartly presented. Enjoyable meals are served in the bar and the conservatory restaurant; the wide choice of dishes makes excellent use of local and seasonal produce.

Rooms: 26 (20 annexe) (3 family) (15 GF) 🛏 **S** fr £60 **D** fr £75 (including breakfast)* **Facilities:** FTV WiFi **Parking:** 25

Talland Bay Hotel

★★★★ 81% ⑩⑩ COUNTRY HOUSE HOTEL

tel: 01503 272667 **Porthallow PL13 2JB**
email: info@tallandbayhotel.com **web:** www.tallandbayhotel.co.uk
dir: *From Looe over bridge towards Polperro on A387, 2nd turn to hotel.*

This hotel has the benefit of a wonderful location with far-reaching views, situated in its own extensive gardens that run down almost to the cliff edge. The bedrooms come in a range of styles – classic twins and doubles, and rooms and suites with sea views. There is also cottage accommodation, and one is particularly suitable for families or those with dogs. The public areas of the hotel are impressive and stylish. Eating options include a brasserie and the Terrace Restaurant, where guests will find accomplished cooking, with an emphasis on carefully prepared local produce.

Rooms: 23 (2 family) (5 GF) 🛏 **Facilities:** FTV WiFi ⌕ 🍴 Xmas New Year **Conf:** Class 20 Board 20 Theatre 20 **Parking:** 23 **Notes:** Civ Wed 60

HIGHLY RECOMMENDED

Wentbridge House Hotel

★★★★ 83% ⑩⑩ HOTEL

tel: 01977 620444 **The Great North Road, Wentbridge WF8 3JJ**
email: info@wentbridgehouse.co.uk **web:** www.wentbridgehouse.co.uk
dir: *M62 junction 33 onto A1 south, hotel in 4 miles.*

This well-established hotel sits in 20 acres of landscaped gardens and offers spacious, well-equipped bedrooms and a choice of dining styles. Service in the Fleur de Lys restaurant is polished and friendly, and a varied menu offers a good choice of interesting dishes. The Brasserie has a more relaxed style of modern dining.

Rooms: 41 (4 annexe) (4 family) (4 GF) 🛏 **Facilities:** FTV WiFi Xmas New Year **Conf:** Class 100 Board 60 Theatre 130 **Services:** Lift Night porter **Parking:** 100 **Notes:** Civ Wed 130

P

Premier Inn Pontefract North

BUDGET HOTEL

tel: 0871 527 8886 (Calls cost 13p per minute plus your phone company's access charge) **Pontefract Road, Knottingley WF11 0BU**
web: www.premierinn.com
dir: M62 junction 33 onto A1 north. Exit at Pontefract junction (A645) to T-junction, right towards Pontefract. Hotel on right.

High quality, budget accommodation ideal for both families and business travellers. Spacious, en suite bedrooms feature free WiFi and tea and coffee making facilities, and in most hotels, Freeview TV is also available. The adjacent family restaurant features a wide and varied menu.

Rooms: 101

POOLE
Dorset

Map 4 SZ09

Harbour Heights Hotel

★★★★ 78% @@ HOTEL

tel: 0800 484 0048 **73 Haven Road, Sandbanks BH13 7LW**
email: reservations@fjbhotels.co.uk **web:** www.fjbhotels.co.uk/harbour-heights-hotel
dir: Follow signs for Sandbanks, hotel on left after Canford Cliffs.

Enjoying stunning panoramic vistas across the Sandbanks Peninsula and Poole Harbour, Harbour Heights is an unassuming yet stylish and innovative boutique hotel. Attention to detail is very apparent, as state-of-the-art facilities blend with traditional comforts. The Harbar Bistro is at the heart of the hotel, and offers excellent cuisine complemented by a fine and diverse wine cellar. The south-facing sun deck is the perfect setting for watching the cross-channel ferries come and go.

Rooms: 38 **S** fr £84 **D** fr £94 (including breakfast)* **Facilities:** FTV WiFi ⊠ Spa bath in all rooms Spa available at sister hotel (Haven Hotel) Xmas New Year **Conf:** Class 30 Board 30 Theatre 100 **Services:** Lift Night porter Air con **Parking:** 38 **Notes:** LB Civ Wed 100

Hotel du Vin Poole

★★★★ 77% @ HOTEL

tel: 01202 785578 & 0844 748 9265 (Calls cost 5p per minute plus your phone company's access charge) **Mansion House, Thames Street BH15 1JN**
email: info.poole@hotelduvin.com **web:** www.hotelduvin.com/locations/poole
dir: A31 to Poole, follow channel ferry signs. Left at Poole bridge onto Poole Quay, 1st left into Thames Street. Hotel opposite St James Church.

Offering a fresh approach to the well-established company style, this property boasts some delightful rooms packed with comfort and all the expected Hotel du Vin features. Situated near the harbour, the hotel offers nautically-themed bedrooms and suites that have plasma TVs, DVD players and bathrooms with power showers. The public rooms are light, open spaces, and as with the other hotels in this group, the bar and restaurant take centre stage.

Rooms: 38 (4 GF) **Facilities:** STV WiFi Xmas New Year **Conf:** Class 20 Board 20 Theatre 60 **Services:** Night porter Air con **Parking:** 8 **Notes:** LB Civ Wed 100

Haven Hotel

★★★★ 76% @@ HOTEL

tel: 0800 484 0048 **161 Banks Road, Sandbanks BH13 7QL**
email: reservations@fjbhotels.co.uk **web:** www.fjbhotels.co.uk
dir: B3065 towards Poole Bay, left onto the Peninsula. Hotel 1.5 miles on left adjacent to Swanage Toll Ferry.

Enjoying an enviable location at the water's edge with views of Poole Bay, this well established hotel was once the home of radio pioneer, Guglielmo Marconi. A friendly team of staff provide good levels of customer care. Bedrooms vary in size and style; many have balconies and wonderful sea or harbour views. The leisure facilities are noteworthy – the Harmony at the Haven is where guests can find spa treatments, a fully-equipped gym and indoor and outdoor heated pools. The hotel is a popular venue for conferences and weddings.

Rooms: 84 (5 family) **S** fr £54 **D** fr £84 (including breakfast)* **Facilities:** Spa FTV WiFi ⊠ ⊛ ⚲ Gym Sauna Steam room Treatment rooms Fitness studio Xmas New Year **Conf:** Class 50 Board 30 Theatre 150 **Services:** Lift Night porter **Parking:** 117 **Notes:** LB Civ Wed 100

Premier Inn Poole Centre (Holes Bay)

BUDGET HOTEL

tel: 0871 527 8892 (Calls cost 13p per minute plus your phone company's access charge) **Holes Bay Road BH15 2BD**
web: www.premierinn.com
dir: South of A35 and A349 on A350 (dual carriageway). Follow Poole Channel Ferry signs.

High quality, budget accommodation ideal for both families and business travellers. Spacious, en suite bedrooms feature free WiFi and tea and coffee making facilities, and in most hotels, Freeview TV is also available. The adjacent family restaurant features a wide and varied menu.

Rooms: 146

Premier Inn Poole North

BUDGET HOTEL

tel: 0871 527 8894 (Calls cost 13p per minute plus your phone company's access charge) **Cabot Lane BH17 7DA**
web: www.premierinn.com
dir: Follow Poole/Channel Ferries signs. At Darby's Corner roundabout take 2nd exit. At 2nd lights right into Cabot Lane. Hotel on right.

Rooms: 126

P

PORTISHEAD
Somerset

Map 4 ST47

Premier Inn Portishead

Premier Inn

BUDGET HOTEL

tel: 0871 527 8898 (Calls cost 13p per minute plus your phone company's access charge) **Wyndham Way BS20 7GA**
web: www.premierinn.com
dir: *M5 junction 19, A369 towards Portishead. Over 1st roundabout, hotel at next roundabout.*

High quality, budget accommodation ideal for both families and business travellers. Spacious, en suite bedrooms feature free WiFi and tea and coffee making facilities, and in most hotels, Freeview TV is also available. The adjacent family restaurant features a wide and varied menu.

Rooms: 95

PORTSCATHO
Cornwall & Isles Of Scilly

Map 2 SW83

INSPECTOR'S CHOICE

Driftwood

★★★ @ @ @ @ HOTEL

tel: 01872 580644 **Rosevine TR2 5EW**
email: info@driftwoodhotel.co.uk **web:** www.driftwoodhotel.co.uk
dir: *A390 towards St Mawes. On A3078 turn left to Rosevine at Trewithian.*

Poised on the cliff side with panoramic views, this contemporary hotel has a peaceful and secluded location. A warm welcome is guaranteed, and professional standards of service are provided in an effortless and relaxed manner. Cuisine is at the heart of any stay, with quality local produce used in a sympathetic and highly skilled manner. The extremely comfortable and elegant bedrooms are decorated in soft shades reminiscent of the seashore. There is a sheltered terraced garden that has a large deck for sunbathing.

Rooms: 15 (1 annexe) (3 family) (3 GF) **S** fr £242 **D** fr £285 (including breakfast)
Facilities: FTV WiFi ↻ Private beach Beauty treatments on request **Parking:** 20
Notes: LB Closed 10 December to 1 February

PORTSMOUTH & SOUTHSEA
Hampshire

Map 5 SU60

Best Western Royal Beach Hotel

 Best Western.

★★★ 79% HOTEL

tel: 023 9273 1281 **South Parade, Southsea PO4 0RN**
email: enquiries@royalbeachhotel.co.uk **web:** www.royalbeachhotel.co.uk
dir: *M27 to M275, follow signs to seafront. Hotel on seafront.*

This former Victorian seafront hotel is a smart and comfortable venue suitable for leisure and business guests alike. Bedrooms and public areas are well presented and generally spacious, and the smart Coast Bar is an ideal venue for a relaxing drink.

Rooms: 124 (12 family) ♠ **S** fr £75 **D** fr £105 (including breakfast)* **Facilities:** STV FTV WiFi ↻ Xmas New Year **Conf:** Class 180 Board 40 Theatre 280 **Services:** Lift Night porter **Parking:** 50 **Notes:** Civ Wed 85

Premier Inn Portsmouth City Centre

Premier Inn

BUDGET HOTEL

tel: 0871 527 9522 (Calls cost 13p per minute plus your phone company's access charge) **1 Isambard Brunel Road PO1 2TR**
web: www.premierinn.com
dir: *M275 onto A3 (Portsmouth (west)/Isle of Wight Ferries). At roundabout 2nd left (City Centre/Seafront/Historic Waterfront). At next roundabout 2nd left into Marketway. After next roundabout left signed Station into Unicorn Road. At 2nd roundabout right into Isambard Brunel Road. Under rail bridge, hotel on left.*

High quality, budget accommodation ideal for both families and business travellers. Spacious, en suite bedrooms feature free WiFi and tea and coffee making facilities, and in most hotels, Freeview TV is also available. The adjacent family restaurant features a wide and varied menu.

Rooms: 84

Premier Inn Portsmouth (Horndean)

Premier Inn

BUDGET HOTEL

tel: 0871 527 8902 (Calls cost 13p per minute plus your phone company's access charge) **2 Havant Road PO8 0DT**
web: www.premierinn.com
dir: *A3(M) junction 2, take B2149 signed Emsworth, Horndean. At roundabout left onto B2149, follow Horndean signs. At next roundabout left onto A3 towards Waterlooville. Hotel on left behind Red Lion.*

High quality, budget accommodation ideal for both families and business travellers. Spacious, en suite bedrooms feature free WiFi and tea and coffee making facilities, and in most hotels, Freeview TV is also available. The adjacent family restaurant features a wide and varied menu.

Rooms: 46

P

Premier Inn Portsmouth (Port Solent)

Premier Inn

BUDGET HOTEL

tel: 0871 527 8906 (Calls cost 13p per minute plus your phone company's access charge) **Binnacle Way PO6 4FB**
web: www.premierinn.com
dir: M27 junction 12, left at lights onto Southampton Road. Left after 200 metres at lights onto Compass Road. At mini-roundabout right onto Binnacle Way, hotel on right.

Rooms: 108

Premier Inn Portsmouth (Port Solent East)

Premier Inn

BUDGET HOTEL

tel: 0871 527 8904 (Calls cost 13p per minute plus your phone company's access charge) **1 Southampton Road, North Harbour PO6 4SA**
web: www.premierinn.com
dir: M27 junction 12, A3, left onto A27. Hotel on left.

Rooms: 64

Premier Inn Southsea

Premier Inn

BUDGET HOTEL

tel: 0871 527 9014 (Calls cost 13p per minute plus your phone company's access charge) **Long Curtain Road, Southsea PO5 3XX**
web: www.premierinn.com
dir: M27, M275, A3, follow signs for Hovercraft and Southsea Seafront. Hotel adjacent to funfair at Clarence Pier (Note: for sat nav use PO5 3AA).

Rooms: 48

PORT SUNLIGHT
Merseyside

Map 15 SJ38

HIGHLY RECOMMENDED

Leverhulme Hotel

★★★★ 85% ◉◉ HOTEL

tel: 0151 644 6655 **Central Road CH62 5EZ**
email: enquiries@leverhulmehotel.co.uk **web:** www.leverhulmehotel.co.uk
dir: From Chester: M53 junction 5, A41 Birkenhead, in approximately 4 miles left into Bolton Road, straight on at roundabout, 0.1 mile right into Church Drive. 0.2 mile hotel on right. From Liverpool: A41 Chester, 2.7 miles, 3rd exit at 3rd roundabout into Bolton Road then follow directions as above.

Built in 1907, this Grade II listed, former cottage hospital is set in the picturesque garden village of Port Sunlight, which was created by Lord Leverhulme for his soap-factory workers in the late 19th century. This art deco hotel has stylish bedrooms, appointed to a very high standard; all have impressive facilities including bathrooms with separate showers and LCD TVs; the suites have roof-top terraces and hot tubs. A games room, cosy bar with open fire, and the striking Riviera restaurant occupy the various wings.

Rooms: 23 (8 annexe) (1 family) (8 GF) **Facilities:** STV FTV WiFi♭ HL ♨ Gym Games room Children's play area Xmas New Year **Conf:** Class 140 Board 30 Theatre 300 **Services:** Night porter **Parking:** 70 **Notes:** LB Civ Wed 240

PRESTON
Lancashire

Map 18 SD52

See also **Garstang**

Barton Grange Hotel

★★★★ 80% HOTEL

tel: 01772 862551 **Garstang Road PR3 5AA**
email: stay@bartongrangehotel.com **web:** www.bartongrangehotel.co.uk

(for full entry see Barton)

Macdonald Tickled Trout

 MACDONALD HOTELS & RESORTS

★★★★ 74% HOTEL

tel: 01772 877 671 **Preston New Road, Samlesbury PR5 0UJ**
email: general.tickledtrout@macdonald-hotels.co.uk **web:** www.macdonaldhotels.co.uk
dir: M6 junction 31, A59 towards Preston.

On the banks of the River Ribble, this hotel is conveniently located for the motorway, making it a popular venue for both business and leisure guests. Smartly appointed bedrooms are tastefully decorated and equipped to a modern standard. The hotel boasts a stylish wing of meeting rooms. Dining is in MacDonald's Scottish Steakhouse where guests will find a superb range of steaks and a relaxed vibe.

Rooms: 98 (6 family) (10 GF) **Facilities:** FTV WiFi♭ Fishing Xmas New Year **Conf:** Class 35 Board 20 Theatre 100 **Services:** Lift Night porter **Parking:** 180 **Notes:** Civ Wed 90

Premier Inn Preston Central

Premier Inn

BUDGET HOTEL

tel: 0871 527 8908 (Calls cost 13p per minute plus your phone company's access charge) **Fox Street PR1 2AB**
web: www.premierinn.com
dir: Off Ridgway (A59). Phone for directions.

High quality, budget accommodation ideal for both families and business travellers. Spacious, en suite bedrooms feature free WiFi and tea and coffee making facilities, and in most hotels, Freeview TV is also available. The adjacent family restaurant features a wide and varied menu.

Rooms: 140

Premier Inn Preston East

Premier Inn

BUDGET HOTEL

tel: 0871 527 8910 (Calls cost 13p per minute plus your phone company's access charge) **Bluebell Way, Preston East Link Rd PR2 5PZ**
web: www.premierinn.com
dir: M6 junction 31a, follow ring road under motorway, hotel on left. Note: no exit for southbound traffic – exit at M6 junction 31, join M6 northbound, exit at junction 31a.

Rooms: 67

Premier Inn Preston South (Craven Drive)

Premier Inn

BUDGET HOTEL

tel: 0871 527 8914 (Calls cost 13p per minute plus your phone company's access charge) **Lostock Lane, Bamber Bridge PR5 6BZ**
web: www.premierinn.com
dir: M6 junction 29, A582 (Lostock Lane). Straight on at 1st lights, into left lane, hotel on left adjacent to B&Q.

Rooms: 75

P

PRESTON *continued*

Premier Inn Preston South (Cuerden Way)

Premier Inn

BUDGET HOTEL

tel: 0871 527 8916 (Calls cost 13p per minute plus your phone company's access charge) **Lostock Lane, Bamber Bridge PR5 6BA**
web: www.premierinn.com
dir: *Off M65 junction 1 (0.5 mile from M6 junction 29) close to roundabout junction of A582 and A6.*

Rooms: 42

Premier Inn Preston West

Premier Inn

BUDGET HOTEL

tel: 0871 527 8918 (Calls cost 13p per minute plus your phone company's access charge) **Blackpool Road, Lea PR4 0XB**
web: www.premierinn.com
dir: *Off A583, opposite Texaco garage.*

Rooms: 38

PRESTWICH	Map 15 SD80
Greater Manchester	

Premier Inn Manchester (Prestwich)

Premier Inn

BUDGET HOTEL

tel: 0871 527 8714 (Calls cost 13p per minute plus your phone company's access charge) **Bury New Road M25 3AJ**
web: www.premierinn.com
dir: *M60 junction 17, A56 signed Manchester City Centre, Prestwich and Whitefield. Hotel on left.*

High quality, budget accommodation ideal for both families and business travellers. Spacious, en suite bedrooms feature free WiFi and tea and coffee making facilities, and in most hotels, Freeview TV is also available. The adjacent family restaurant features a wide and varied menu.

Rooms: 83

PUDDINGTON	Map 15 SJ37
Cheshire	

Macdonald Craxton Wood Hotel

★★★★ 78% HOTEL

tel: 0151 347 4000 **Parkgate Road, Ledsham CH66 9PB**
email: craxton@macdonald-hotels.co.uk **web:** www.macdonaldhotels.co.uk
dir: *From M6 take M56 towards North Wales, then A5117/A540 to Hoylake. Hotel on left 200 yards past lights.*

Set in extensive grounds, this hotel offers a variety of spacious and comfortable rooms, well equipped with modern amenities. The restaurant features a range of dishes including signature grills and locally sourced ingredients. An extensive spa facility and a choice of function suites complete the package.

Rooms: 72 (8 family) (30 GF) ⚫ **Facilities:** Spa FTV WiFi ⚡ HL ⚫ Gym Sauna Steam room Thermal spa including rasul Xmas New Year **Conf:** Class 200 Board 160 Theatre 300 **Services:** Lift Night porter **Parking:** 220 **Notes:** Civ Wed 350

Premier Inn Wirral (Two Mills)

Premier Inn

BUDGET HOTEL

tel: 0871 527 9180 (Calls cost 13p per minute plus your phone company's access charge) **Parkgate Road, Two Mills CH66 9PD**
web: www.premierinn.com
dir: *5 miles from M56 junction 16 and M53 junction 5. On crossroads of A550 and A540.*

Rooms: 31

QUORN	Map 11 SK51
Leicestershire	

Quorn Country Hotel

★★★★ 76% HOTEL

tel: 01509 415050 **66 Leicester Road, Charnwood House LE12 8BB**
email: reception@quorncountryhotel.co.uk **web:** www.quorncountryhotel.info
dir: *Phone for directions.*

With easy access to the M1, this country house style of hotel offers comfort and good food to its guests. Situated by the River Soar, the gardens are a feature of the property as is the pleasant Orangery where you can take afternoon tea. Guests can expect friendly and pleasant hospitality.

Rooms: 36 (2 family) (11 GF) ⚫ **D** fr £89* **Facilities:** FTV WiFi ⚡ **Conf:** Class 120 Board 40 Theatre 300 **Services:** Lift Night porter Air con **Parking:** 100 **Notes:** Civ Wed 260

RADLETT	Map 6 TL10
Hertfordshire	

Premier Inn St Albans/Bricket Wood

Premier Inn

BUDGET HOTEL

tel: 0871 527 9016 (Calls cost 13p per minute plus your phone company's access charge) **Smug Oak Lane, Bricket Wood AL2 3PN**
web: www.premierinn.com
dir: *M1 junction 6 (or M25 junction 21a) follow Watford signs, left at lights signed M1/ Bricket Wood. 2nd left into Mount Pleasant Lane, straight on at 2 mini-roundabouts, right at The Gate pub. Hotel at end.*

High quality, budget accommodation ideal for both families and business travellers. Spacious, en suite bedrooms feature free WiFi and tea and coffee making facilities, and in most hotels, Freeview TV is also available. The adjacent family restaurant features a wide and varied menu.

Rooms: 56

RAINHAM	Map 6 TQ58
Greater London	

Premier Inn Rainham

Premier Inn

BUDGET HOTEL

tel: 0871 527 8920 (Calls cost 13p per minute plus your phone company's access charge) **New Road, Wennington RM13 9ED**
web: www.premierinn.com
dir: *M25 junction 30/31, A13 for Dagenham/Rainham, A1306 towards Wennington, Aveley and Rainham. Hotel 0.5 mile on right.*

High quality, budget accommodation ideal for both families and business travellers. Spacious, en suite bedrooms feature free WiFi and tea and coffee making facilities, and in most hotels, Freeview TV is also available. The adjacent family restaurant features a wide and varied menu.

Rooms: 82

RAINHILL
Merseyside   Map 15 SJ49

Premier Inn Liverpool (Rainhill)

 Premier Inn

BUDGET HOTEL

tel: 0871 527 8614 (Calls cost 13p per minute plus your phone company's access charge) **804 Warrington Road L35 6PE**
web: www.premierinn.com
dir: *Just off M62 junction 7, A57 towards Rainhill.*

High quality, budget accommodation ideal for both families and business travellers. Spacious, en suite bedrooms feature free WiFi and tea and coffee making facilities, and in most hotels, Freeview TV is also available. The adjacent family restaurant features a wide and varied menu.

Rooms: 34

RAMSBOTTOM
Lancashire   Map 15 SD71

Best Western The Old Mill Hotel

 BW Best Western.

★★★ 70% HOTEL

tel: 01706 82991 **Springwood Street BL0 9DS**
email: oldmill@lavenderhotels.co.uk **web:** www.lavenderhotels.co.uk/The-Old-Mill
dir: *M66 junction 1, follow signs to hotel through centre of Ramsbottom, turn right onto Springwood Street. Hotel 100 yards on left.*

Delightfully located in attractive grounds and some very pleasant forest and gardens, this small hotel offers a range of bedrooms, meeting and wedding facilities. There's also a pool, sauna and gym. The hotel also offers occasional party nights and entertainment.

Rooms: 29 **D** fr £69* **Facilities:** 🏊 Xmas New Year **Conf:** Class 30 Board 20 Theatre 60 **Services:** Night porter **Parking:** 65 **Notes:** Civ Wed

RAMSGATE
Kent   Map 7 TR36

The Pegwell Bay Hotel

★★★ 81% HOTEL

tel: 01843 599590 **81 Pegwell Road, Pegwell CT11 0NJ**
email: pegwellbay.reception@thorleytaverns.co.uk **web:** www.pegwellbayhotel.co.uk
dir: *Phone for directions.*

Boasting stunning views over the Channel, this historic cliff-top hotel is suitable for guests staying either on business or for leisure. Spacious, comfortable bedrooms are well equipped and include WiFi. A modern lounge, majestic dining room and traditional pub offer a variety of options for eating and for relaxation.

Rooms: 42 (5 family) (5 GF) **Facilities:** FTV WiFi Xmas New Year **Conf:** Class 65 Board 65 Theatre 100 **Services:** Lift Night porter **Parking:** 80 **Notes:** Civ Wed 70

Comfort Inn Ramsgate

★★★ 75% HOTEL

tel: 01843 592345 **Victoria Parade, East Cliff CT11 8DT**
email: reservations@comfortinnramsgate.co.uk **web:** www.comfortinnramsgate.co.uk
dir: *From M2 take A299 signed Ramsgate, B2054 to Victoria Parade, follow sign to harbour and carry on past the harbour.*

This Comfort Inn is a beautiful Victorian building, high on the cliff top, with views over the sea and beyond. It offers a range of well-appointed accommodation; each room has air conditioning, free WiFi and Hypnos beds. Some of the front rooms come with a balcony and sea views. There is a range of amenities such as sauna, gym, beauty salon and meeting rooms. The popular bar is well stocked whilst the restaurant offers a seasonal menu; afternoon teas are popular too. There is small, free car park at the rear plus a garden to enjoy in the warmer months.

Rooms: 44 (8 family) 🐾 **S** fr £40 **D** fr £55 (including breakfast) **Facilities:** FTV WiFi 🔌 Gym Beauty salon Sauna Xmas New Year **Conf:** Class 30 Board 30 Theatre 70 **Services:** Lift Night porter Air con **Parking:** 10

The Oak Hotel

★★ 85% HOTEL

tel: 01843 583686 **66 Harbour Parade CT11 8LN**
email: oak.reception@thorleytaverns.co.uk **web:** www.oakhotel.co.uk
dir: *Follow road around harbour, right into Harbour Parade.*

Located within easy reach of the railway station, ferry terminal and the town centre's shops, this unpretentious hotel enjoys spectacular views of the marina and harbour. The comfortable bedrooms are attractively presented and very well equipped. The Restaurant Sixty-Six, Caffe Roma and The Lounge Bar offer a variety of dining options along with a selection of wines, beers and spirits.

Rooms: 34 (9 family) 🐾 **S** fr £57 **D** fr £75 (including breakfast)* **Facilities:** FTV WiFi **Conf:** Class 60 Board 50 Theatre 100 **Services:** Night porter

Holiday Inn Express Ramsgate

Holiday Inn Express

BUDGET HOTEL

tel: 01843 820250 **Tothill Street CT12 4AU**
email: reservations.ramsgate@holidayinnexpress.org.uk **web:** www.hiexramsgate.co.uk
dir: *On A299, off roundabout junction with B2048.*

A modern hotel ideal for families and business travellers. Fresh and uncomplicated, the spacious rooms include Sky TV, power shower and tea and coffee-making facilities. Continental buffet breakfast is included in the room rate; other meals may be taken at the nearby family pub or restaurant.

Rooms: 105 (70 family) (33 GF) 🐾

R

RAVENGLASS	Map 18 SD09
Cumbria	

HIGHLY RECOMMENDED

The Pennington Hotel

★★★ 86% HOTEL

tel: 01229 717222 & 0845 450 6445 (Calls cost 7p per minute plus your phone company's access charge) **CA18 1SD**
email: info@penningtonhotels.com **web:** www.penningtonhotels.com
dir: *In village centre.*

This hotel has a very relaxed atmosphere throughout and the public areas are open-plan with high quality fabrics and artwork. Bedrooms are modern in design and have high spec fixtures and fittings in the bathrooms. Honest cooking, based on local and fine quality ingredients, is offered on the seasonal menus. Staff show exceptional customer awareness and provide very attentive and friendly service.

Rooms: 22 (4 annexe) (6 family) (5 GF) ⌁ **S** fr £100 **D** fr £110 (including breakfast)* **Facilities:** FTV WiFi ⌁ Xmas New Year **Conf:** Class 40 Board 40 Theatre 80 **Services:** Night porter **Parking:** 50

RAVENSCAR	Map 19 NZ90
North Yorkshire	

Raven Hall Country House Hotel

★★★ 80% HOTEL

tel: 01723 870353 **YO13 0ET**
email: enquiries@ravenhall.co.uk **web:** www.ravenhall.co.uk
dir: *A171 towards Whitby. At Cloughton turn right onto unclassified road to Ravenscar.*

This impressive cliff-top mansion enjoys breathtaking views over Robin Hood's Bay. Extensive well-kept grounds include tennis courts, putting green, swimming pools and historic battlements. The bedrooms vary in size but all are comfortably equipped, and many offer panoramic views. There are also eight environmentally-friendly Finnish lodges that have been furnished to a high standard.

Rooms: 63 (8 annexe) (23 family) (5 GF) ⌁ **S** fr £60 **D** fr £102 (including breakfast)* **Facilities:** FTV WiFi ⌁ ⌁ 9 ⌁ ⌁ Bowls Table tennis Xmas New Year **Conf:** Class 80 Board 40 Theatre 100 **Services:** Lift Night porter **Parking:** 100 **Notes:** LB Civ Wed 100

RAYLEIGH	Map 7 TQ89
Essex	

Premier Inn Basildon (Rayleigh)

Premier Inn

BUDGET HOTEL

tel: 0871 527 8058 (Calls cost 13p per minute plus your phone company's access charge) **Rayleigh Weir, Arterial Road (A127) SS6 7XJ**
web: www.premierinn.com
dir: *M25 junction 29, A127 towards Southend. Approximately 13 miles exit at Rayleigh Weir junction onto A129 to Rayleigh. Straight on at 2 lights, 1st left.*

High quality, budget accommodation ideal for both families and business travellers. Spacious, en suite bedrooms feature free WiFi and tea and coffee making facilities, and in most hotels, Freeview TV is also available. The adjacent family restaurant features a wide and varied menu.

Rooms: 50

READING	Map 5 SU77
Berkshire	

HIGHLY RECOMMENDED

Holiday Inn Reading M4 Jct 10

★★★★ 83%  HOTEL

tel: 0118 944 0444 **Wharfedale Road, Winnersh Triangle RG41 5TS**
email: reservations@hireadinghotel.com **web:** www.hireadinghotel.com
dir: *M4 junction 10/A329(M) towards Reading (east), 1st exit signed Winnersh/Woodley/A329, left at lights into Wharfedale Road. Hotel on left.*

Situated in the Winnersh Triangle within close proximity of the M4, Reading, Bracknell and Wokingham, this hotel offers a range of air-conditioned, contemporary and stylish bedrooms, eight state-of-the-art meeting rooms and the Esprit Spa & Wellness with extensive leisure facilities including a 19-metre indoor pool and Dermalogica Spa. The Caprice Restaurant offers relaxed dining throughout the day. Complimentary underground parking is provided.

Rooms: 174 (23 family) ⌁ **S** fr £63 **D** fr £63* **Facilities:** Spa FTV WiFi ⌁ HL ⌁ Gym Sauna Steam room ⌁ Xmas New Year **Conf:** Class 160 Board 64 Theatre 260 **Services:** Lift Night porter Air con **Parking:** 120 **Notes:** Civ Wed 260

Millennium Madejski Hotel Reading

★★★★ 80% ◉◉ HOTEL

tel: 0118 925 3500 **Madejski Stadium RG2 0FL**
email: reservations.reading@millenniumhotels.com **web:** www.millenniumhotels.com
dir: *M4 junction 11 onto A33, follow signs for Madejski Stadium Complex.*

A stylish hotel, that features an atrium lobby with specially commissioned water sculpture, is part of the Madejski stadium complex, home to both Reading FC and the London Irish rugby team. Bedrooms are appointed with spacious workstations and plenty of amenities; there is also a choice of suites and a club floor with its own lounge. The hotel also has a fine dining restaurant.

Rooms: 201 (39 family) ✆ **S** fr £75 **D** fr £85* **Facilities:** STV WiFi ↕ ⊗ Gym
Conf: Class 36 Board 30 Theatre 66 **Services:** Lift Night porter Air con **Parking:** 250
Notes: LB

Novotel Reading Centre

★★★★ 79% HOTEL

tel: 0118 952 2600 **25b Friar Street RG1 1DP**
email: h5432@accor.com **web:** www.novotel.com
dir: *M4 junction 11 or A33 towards Reading, left for Garrard Street car park, at roundabout 3rd exit on Friar Street.*

This attractive and stylish central hotel is convenient for Reading's business area and shopping centre; it is adjacent to a town centre car park and has a range of conference facilities and excellent leisure options. The restaurant offers a contemporary-style menu and a good wine list. Bedrooms are comfortable and stylishly designed.

Rooms: 178 (154 family) **Facilities:** FTV WiFi HL ⊗ Gym Steam room Sauna
Conf: Class 50 Board 36 Theatre 90 **Services:** Lift Night porter **Parking:** 15

Malmaison Reading

★★★★ 75% ◉ HOTEL

tel: 0844 693 0660 (Calls cost 5p per minute plus your phone company's access charge)
Great Western House, 18–20 Station Road RG1 1JX
email: reading@malmaison.com **web:** www.malmaison.com/locations/reading/
dir: *Opposite rail station.*

This historic property reflects a funky Malmaison style that also conveys its proximity and long-standing relationship with the nearby railway. Public areas feature rail memorabilia and excellent pictures and include a Café Mal and a meeting room. The bedrooms here have all the amenities a modern guest would expect, plus comfort and quality in abundance. Dining is interesting too, with a menu that features home-grown and local produce accompanied by an impressive wine list.

Rooms: 75 (6 family) (4 GF) ✆ **Facilities:** FTV WiFi ↕ HL Xmas New Year **Conf:** Class 18 Board 22 Theatre 30 **Services:** Lift Night porter Air con

Best Western Calcot Hotel

★★★ 77% HOTEL

tel: 0118 941 6423 **98 Bath Road, Calcot RG31 7QN**
email: reservations@calcothotel.co.uk **web:** www.calcothotel.co.uk
dir: *M4 junction 12, A4 towards Reading, hotel in 0.5 mile.*

This hotel is conveniently located in a residential area just off the motorway. Bedrooms are well equipped with good business facilities, such as data ports and good workspace. There are attractive public rooms and function suites, and the informal restaurant offers enjoyable food in welcoming surroundings.

Rooms: 78 (3 family) (6 GF) ✆ **Facilities:** FTV WiFi ♫ New Year **Conf:** Class 35 Board 35 Theatre 120 **Services:** Night porter **Parking:** 130 **Notes:** Closed 24–30 December RS 2 December to 6 January Civ Wed 200

Premier Inn Reading (Caversham Bridge)

Premier Inn

BUDGET HOTEL

tel: 0871 527 8922 (Calls cost 13p per minute plus your phone company's access charge) **Richfield Avenue RG1 8EQ**
web: www.premierinn.com
dir: *M4 junction 11, A33 to Reading. A329 towards Caversham. Left at TGI Friday's. Left at Crowne Plaza. Hotel 200 yards on right.*

High quality, budget accommodation ideal for both families and business travellers. Spacious, en suite bedrooms feature free WiFi and tea and coffee making facilities, and in most hotels, Freeview TV is also available. The adjacent family restaurant features a wide and varied menu.

Rooms: 75

Premier Inn Reading Central

Premier Inn

BUDGET HOTEL

tel: 0871 527 8924 (Calls cost 13p per minute plus your phone company's access charge) **Letcombe Street RG1 2HN**
web: www.premierinn.com
dir: *M4 junction 11, A33 towards town centre, straight on at 3 roundabouts (approximately 3.5 miles). Right onto A329 signed The Oracle, Riverside Shopping Centre. Branch immediately left, hotel opposite The Oracle shopping centre.*

Rooms: 151

Premier Inn Reading South

Premier Inn

BUDGET HOTEL

tel: 0871 527 8926 (Calls cost 13p per minute plus your phone company's access charge) **Goring Lane, Grazeley Green RG7 1LS**
web: www.premierinn.com
dir: *M4 junction 11, A33 towards Basingstoke. At roundabout take exit towards Burghfield and Mortimer. 3rd right into Grazeley Green. Under rail bridge turn left. Hotel on left.*

Rooms: 44

R

REDDITCH
Worcestershire
Map 10 SP06

The Abbey Hotel Golf and Spa

★★★★ 77% HOTEL

tel: 01527 406600 **Hither Green Lane, Dagnell End Road B98 9BE**
email: info@theabbeyhotel.co.uk **web:** www.theabbeyhotel.co.uk
dir: *M42 junction 2, A441 to Redditch. End of carriageway turn left A441, Dagnell End Road on left. Hotel 600 yards on right.*

With convenient access to the motorway and a proximity to many attractions, this modern hotel is popular with both business and leisure travellers. Bedrooms are well equipped and attractively decorated; the executive corner rooms are especially spacious. Facilities include an 18-hole golf course, pro shop, large indoor pool and extensive conference facilities.

Rooms: 99 (20 family) (23 GF) ✆ **Facilities:** Spa FTV WiFi ↕ ⊗ ♨ 18 Gym Flood lit golf driving range Xmas New Year **Conf:** Class 90 Board 52 Theatre 180
Services: Lift Night porter **Parking:** 200 **Notes:** Civ Wed 100

REDDITCH *continued*

Holiday Inn Express Birmingham - Redditch

BUDGET HOTEL

tel: 01527 584658 **2 Hewell Road, Enfield B97 6AE**
email: reservations@hieredditchhotel.com **web:** www.hieredditchhotel.com
dir: *M42 junction 2. 1st exit from roundabout to A44. 1st exit from roundabout to Bordesleigh. 4th exit from roundabout to Middelhouse Lane. Left at lights into Birmingham Road. 1st right into Clive Road. 1st exit from roundabout to Hewell Road. 1st right into Gloucester Close.*

This modern town centre hotel, adjacent to the station, is ideal for families and business travellers. The spacious tranquil rooms include flat-screen TVs with Freeview channels, and bathrooms with power showers. Complimentary hot buffet breakfast and free WiFi are included in the room rate. Freshly prepared meals are served in the GR Restaurant daily from 6pm-10pm. There are two air-conditioned meeting rooms, with natural light, available.

Rooms: 100 (75 family) (10 GF) ☎ **D** fr £50 (including breakfast)*

Premier Inn Redditch North (A441)

BUDGET HOTEL

tel: 0871 527 9372 (Calls cost 13p per minute plus your phone company's access charge) **Bordesley Lane B97 6AQ**
web: www.premierinn.com
dir: *M42 junction 3, A435 (Alcester road). In 3 miles take A4023 towards Redditch and Bromsgrove. Exit 1st roundabout towards Birmingham (A441). At next roundabout 3rd exit onto Alvechurch Highway (A441). At next roundabout 4th exit into Millrace Road, left into Bordesley Lane. Note: for sat nav use B97 6RR.*

High quality, budget accommodation ideal for both families and business travellers. Spacious, en suite bedrooms feature free WiFi and tea and coffee making facilities, and in most hotels, Freeview TV is also available. The adjacent family restaurant features a wide and varied menu.

Rooms: 80

Premier Inn Redditch West (A448)

BUDGET HOTEL

tel: 0871 527 8928 (Calls cost 13p per minute plus your phone company's access charge) **Birchfield Road B97 6PX**
web: www.premierinn.com
dir: *M5 junction 4, A38 towards Bromsgrove. At roundabout take A448 to Redditch. 1st exit for Webheath. At next roundabout 3rd exit, 1st right into Birchfield Road.*

Rooms: 33

REDHILL
Surrey

Map 6 TQ25

HIGHLY RECOMMENDED

Nutfield Priory Hotel & Spa

★★★★ 82% ◎◎ HOTEL

tel: 01737 824400 & 0845 072 7485 (Calls cost 5p per minute plus your phone company's access charge) **Nutfield RH1 4EL**
email: nutfieldpriory@handpicked.co.uk
web: www.handpickedhotels.co.uk/nutfieldpriory
dir: *M25 junction 6, follow Redhill signs via Godstone on A25. Hotel 1 mile on left after Nutfield Village. Or M25 junction 8, A25 through Reigate and Redhill. Hotel on right 1.5 miles after rail bridge.*

This Victorian country house dates back to 1872 and is set in 40 acres of grounds with stunning views over the Surrey countryside. The hotel offers a range of individually appointed bedrooms, including 15 feature bedrooms located in the oldest part of the house. All are equipped with an excellent range of facilities. The public areas include the impressive grand hall, the award-winning Cloisters Restaurant, the library, and a cosy lounge bar area. The Nutfield Priory Health Club and Spa is the place to relax and unwind. The hotel also offers a choice of private rooms for weddings, events and business meetings. Additionally, this magnificent country house can be hired for exclusive use.

Rooms: 60 (4 family) ☎ **Facilities:** Spa STV FTV WiFi ✇ HL ☺ Gym Squash Steam room Beauty therapy Aerobic and step classes Saunas Xmas New Year
Conf: Class 50 Board 42 Theatre 90 **Services:** Lift Night porter **Parking:** 130
Notes: LB Civ Wed 90

Premier Inn Redhill Reigate

BUDGET HOTEL

tel: 0871 527 8930 (Calls cost 13p per minute plus your phone company's access charge) **Brighton Road, Salfords RH1 5BT**
web: www.premierinn.com
dir: *On A23, 2 miles south of Redhill; 3 miles north of Gatwick Airport.*

High quality, budget accommodation ideal for both families and business travellers. Spacious, en suite bedrooms feature free WiFi and tea and coffee making facilities, and in most hotels, Freeview TV is also available. The adjacent family restaurant features a wide and varied menu.

Rooms: 48

R

REDRUTH
Cornwall & Isles Of Scilly   Map 2 SW64

Penventon Park Hotel
★★★★ 80% @ @ HOTEL

tel: 01209 203000 **West End TR15 1TE**
email: enquiries@penventon.com **web:** www.penventon.co.uk
dir: Exit A30 at Redruth. Follow signs for Redruth West, hotel 1 mile south.

Set in attractive parkland, this Georgian mansion is ideal for both business and leisure guests, and is well placed for visiting the glorious Cornish coastal areas. The smart bedrooms include 20 garden suites with patio doors that give access to a decking area and the garden beyond. The menus offer a wide choice of Cornish, British, Italian and French dishes. Leisure facilities include a pool, fitness suite, and health spa with beauty and holistic therapies, as well as function rooms and bars.

Rooms: 63 (8 family) (23 GF) ♠ **S** fr £69 **D** fr £89 (including breakfast)*
Facilities: Spa FTV WiFi ⊗ Gym Sauna Solarium Personal trainer ♫ Xmas New Year **Conf:** Class 100 Board 60 Theatre 200 **Services:** Night porter **Parking:** 100
Notes: LB Civ Wed 150

REDWORTH
County Durham   Map 19 NZ22

The Redworth Hall Hotel
★★★★ 78% COUNTRY HOUSE HOTEL

tel: 01388 770600 **DL5 6NL**
email: reservations@redworthhalldurham.co.uk
web: www.thecairncollection.co.uk/redworth
dir: From A1(M) junction 58, A68 signed Corbridge. Follow hotel signs.

This imposing Georgian building includes a health club with state-of-the-art equipment and impressive conference facilities, making this hotel a popular destination for business travellers. There are several spacious lounges to relax in along with the Conservatory Restaurant. Bedrooms are very comfortable and well equipped.

Rooms: 143 (12 family) (8 GF) ♠ **S** fr £50 **D** fr £60* **Facilities:** STV FTV WiFi ⊗ HL ⊗ ⊗ ⊛ Gym Health and leisure club Beauty and hair salons **Conf:** Class 144 Board 90 Theatre 300 **Services:** Lift Night porter **Parking:** 300 **Notes:** LB Civ Wed 180

REIGATE
Surrey   Map 6 TQ25

Best Western Reigate Manor Hotel
BW Best Western.
★★★ 79% HOTEL

tel: 01737 240125 **Reigate Hill RH2 9PF**
email: hotel@reigatemanor.co.uk **web:** www.reigatemanor.co.uk
dir: On A217, 1 mile south of M25 junction 8.

On the slopes of Reigate Hill, the hotel is ideally located for access to the town and for motorway links. A range of public rooms is provided along with a variety of function rooms. Bedrooms are either traditional in style in the old house, or of contemporary design in the wing.

Rooms: 50 (1 family) **Facilities:** FTV WiFi ⊗ **Conf:** Class 80 Board 50 Theatre 200
Services: Night porter **Parking:** 130 **Notes:** Civ Wed 200

RENISHAW
Derbyshire   Map 16 SK47

Sitwell Arms Hotel
★★★ 72% HOTEL

tel: 01246 435226 **Station Road S21 3WF**
email: info@sitwellarms.co.uk **web:** www.sitwellarms.co.uk
dir: On A6135 to Sheffield, west of M1 junction 30.

Parts of this attractive stone building date from the 18th century when it was a coaching inn. It has been extended to provide spacious comfortable bedrooms with modern facilities. A wide range of meals is served in the Wild Boar Restaurant; there is also a cocktail bar, informal lounge bar and a smart beer garden with patio and children's play area. The hotel has a gym and a hair and beauty salon.

Rooms: 31 (8 family) (9 GF) **S** fr £40 **D** fr £89 (including breakfast) **Facilities:** FTV WiFi Gym Fitness studio Hair and beauty salon Treatment room Xmas New Year **Conf:** Class 60 Board 60 Theatre 160 **Services:** Lift Night porter **Parking:** 150
Notes: LB Civ Wed 150

RETFORD
Nottinghamshire   Map 17 SK78

Ye Olde Bell Hotel & Spa
★★★★ 79% @ HOTEL

tel: 01777 705121 **DN22 8QS**
email: enquiries@yeoldebell-hotel.co.uk **web:** www.yeoldebell-hotel.co.uk

(for full entry see Barnby Moor)

Best Western Plus West Retford Hotel
BW Best Western PLUS.
★★★ 81% HOTEL

tel: 01777 706333 **24 North Road DN22 7XG**
email: reservations@westretfordhotel.co.uk **web:** www.westretfordhotel.co.uk
dir: From A1 take A620 to Ranby/Retford. Left at roundabout into North Road A638. Hotel on right.

Stylishly appointed throughout, and set in very attractive gardens close to the town centre, this 18th-century manor house offers a good range of well-equipped meeting rooms. The spacious, well-laid out bedrooms and suites are located in separate buildings and all offer modern facilities and comforts.

Rooms: 63 (15 family) (32 GF) ♠ **S** fr £105 **D** fr £105 **Facilities:** FTV WiFi ⊗ Xmas New Year **Conf:** Class 80 Board 40 Theatre 150 **Services:** Night porter **Parking:** 150
Notes: Civ Wed 150

RICHMOND
North Yorkshire   Map 19 NZ10

Kings Head
U

tel: 01748 850220 **Market Place DL10 4HS**
email: kingshead@innmail.co.uk

Currently the rating for this establishment is not confirmed. This may be due to a change of ownership or because ot has only recently joined the AA rating scheme.

Rooms: 24 **S** fr £69 **D** fr £79* **Conf:** Class 80 Board 40 Theatre 120

R

RICHMOND UPON THAMES
Greater London

The Petersham Hotel

★★★★ 81% ◎◎ HOTEL Plan 1 C2

tel: 020 8108 5403 **Nightingale Lane TW10 6UZ**
email: enq@petershamhotel.co.uk **web:** www.petershamhotel.co.uk
dir: *From Richmond Bridge roundabout A316 follow Ham and Petersham signs. Hotel in Nightingale Lane on left off Petersham Road.*

Managed by the same family for over 25 years, this attractive hotel is located on a hill overlooking water meadows and a sweep of the River Thames. Bedrooms and suites are comfortably furnished, while public areas combine elegance and some fine architectural features. High quality produce features in dishes offered in the restaurant that looks out over the Thames below.

Rooms: 58 (6 family) (3 GF) ✿ **S** fr £110 **D** fr £139.50* **Facilities:** STV FTV WiFi ⌂ Xmas New Year **Conf:** Board 25 Theatre 35 **Services:** Lift Night porter **Parking:** 60 **Notes:** Civ Wed 40

Richmond Hill Hotel

★★★★ 79% HOTEL Plan 1 C2

tel: 020 8940 2247 **Richmond Hill TW10 6RW**
email: info.richmond@kewgreen.co.uk **web:** www.richmondhill-hotel.co.uk
dir: *1 mile from Richmond Station at the top of Richmond Hill.*

This attractive Georgian manor is situated on Richmond Hill, enjoying elevated views over the Thames, and the town and the park are within walking distance. Bedrooms vary in size and style but all are comfortable and contemporary in style. All rooms are very well equipped. The Pembroke Restaurant serves a daily market menu amongst other options. "Tea on the Hill" is must do experience. There is a well-designed heath club, and extensive conference and banqueting facilities. Secure parking available on site..

Rooms: 142 (1 family) (15 GF) ✿ **Facilities:** Spa STV FTV WiFi ✦ Gym Steam room Health and beauty suite Sauna Xmas New Year **Conf:** Class 80 Board 50 Theatre 180 **Services:** Lift Night porter Air con **Parking:** 97 **Notes:** Civ Wed 182

R

Find out more
about the AA's Hotel rating
scheme on pages 12–13

Bingham

★★★ 86% ◎◎◎ ♔ TOWN HOUSE HOTEL Plan 1 C2

tel: 020 8940 0902 **61-63 Petersham Road TW10 6UT**
email: info@thebingham.co.uk **web:** www.thebingham.co.uk
dir: *On A307.*

This Georgian building, dating back to 1740, overlooks the River Thames and is within easy reach of the town centre, Kew Gardens and Hampton Court. The contemporary bedrooms feature bespoke art deco-style furniture and up-to-the-minute facilities such as WiFi and iPod docking station with DAB radio; most of the rooms have marble walk-in showers. Public rooms have views of the pretty garden and river. Guests can choose from a selection of meals that range from light snacks to two or three-course dinners.

Rooms: 15 (8 family) ✿ **Facilities:** FTV WiFi ⌂ Free membership at sister well-being centre Xmas New Year **Conf:** Class 70 Board 40 Theatre 90 **Services:** Lift Night porter Air con **Parking:** 20 **Notes:** Civ Wed 90

Premier Inn London Richmond

BUDGET HOTEL Plan 1 C2

tel: 0871 527 9346 (Calls cost 13p per minute plus your phone company's access charge) **136-138 Lower Mortlake Road, TW9 2JZ**
web: www.premierinn.com
dir: *Phone for directions.*

High quality, budget accommodation ideal for both families and business travellers. Spacious, en suite bedrooms feature free WiFi and tea and coffee making facilities, and in most hotels, Freeview TV is also available. The adjacent family restaurant features a wide and varied menu.

Rooms: 92

RIPLEY
Derbyshire

Map 16 SK35

Premier Inn Ripley

BUDGET HOTEL

tel: 0871 527 8935 (Calls cost 13p per minute plus your phone company's access charge) **Nottingham Road DE5 3QP**
web: www.premierinn.com
dir: *From south: M1 junction 26, A610 towards Ripley. Hotel off roundabout adjacent to Butterley Park. From north: M1 junction 28, A38, A610 towards Nottingham. Hotel on right at roundabout.*

High quality, budget accommodation ideal for both families and business travellers. Spacious, en suite bedrooms feature free WiFi and tea and coffee making facilities, and in most hotels, Freeview TV is also available. The adjacent family restaurant features a wide and varied menu.

Rooms: 78

ROCHDALE
Greater Manchester

Map 16 SD81

Premier Inn Rochdale

BUDGET HOTEL

tel: 0871 527 8936 (Calls cost 13p per minute plus your phone company's access charge) **Newhey Road, Milnrow OL16 4JF**
web: www.premierinn.com
dir: *M62 junction 21, at roundabout right towards Shaw, under motorway bridge, and 1st left.*

Rooms: 79

ROCHESTER
Kent

Map 6 TQ76

Premier Inn Rochester

BUDGET HOTEL

tel: 0871 527 8938 (Calls cost 13p per minute plus your phone company's access charge) **Medway Valley Leisure Park, Chariot Way ME2 2SS**
web: www.premierinn.com
dir: *M2 junction 2, follow Rochester and West Malling signs. At roundabout onto A228 signed Rochester and Strood. At next roundabout 2nd exit into Roman Way signed Medway Valley Park. At next roundabout 1st exit into Chariot Way, hotel in 100 metres.*

Rooms: 121

ROMALDKIRK
County Durham

Map 19 NY92

The Rose & Crown

★★★ ⚜⚜ HOTEL

tel: 01833 650213 **DL12 9EB**
email: hotel@rose-and-crown.co.uk **web:** www.rose-and-crown.co.uk
dir: *6 miles northwest from Barnard Castle on B6277.*

This charming 18th-century country inn is located in the heart of the village, overlooking beautiful dale scenery. The attractively furnished bedrooms, including suites, are split between the main house and the rear courtyard. After returning from a long walk, guests might like to have a drink in the cosy bar with its welcoming log fire. Good local produce features extensively on the menus that can be enjoyed in the oak-panelled restaurant, or more informally in the bar. Service is both friendly and attentive.

Rooms: 14 (7 annexe) (2 family) (5 GF) **Facilities:** FTV WiFi ⌁ Spa and golf available at nearby Headlam Hall **New Year Conf:** Board 12 **Parking:** 20 **Notes:** LB Closed 23–27 December

---

ROMFORD
Greater London

Map 6 TQ58

Premier Inn Romford Central

BUDGET HOTEL

tel: 0871 527 8940 (Calls cost 13p per minute plus your phone company's access charge) **Mercury Gardens RM1 3EN**
web: www.premierinn.com
dir: *M25 junction 28, A12 to Gallows Corner. Take A118 to next roundabout, turn left.*

High quality, budget accommodation ideal for both families and business travellers. Spacious, en suite bedrooms feature free WiFi and tea and coffee making facilities, and in most hotels, Freeview TV is also available. The adjacent family restaurant features a wide and varied menu.

Rooms: 103

Premier Inn Romford West

BUDGET HOTEL

tel: 0871 527 8942 (Calls cost 13p per minute plus your phone company's access charge) **Whalebone Lane North, Chadwell Heath RM6 6QU**
web: www.premierinn.com
dir: *6 miles from M25 junction 28 on A12 at junction with A1112.*

Rooms: 44

R

ROMSEY	Map 5 SU32
Hampshire	

The White Horse Hotel & Brasserie

★★★★ 81% ◉◉ HOTEL

tel: 01794 512431 **19 Market Place SO51 8ZJ**
email: thewhitehorsesales@twhromsey.com
web: www.thewhitehorseromsey.co.uk
dir: *M27 junction 3, follow signs for Romsey, right at Broadlands. In town centre.*

This family-friendly hotel is located overlooking the town's market square. The White Horse is a traditional, former coaching inn that provides comfortable and stylish, individually designed bedrooms, including loft suites and a penthouse. Public areas boast relaxing day rooms and an elegant contemporary bar. The Brasserie offers award-winning cuisine, with alfresco dining a possibility during the warmer summer months. Public car parks can be found close by.

Rooms: 29 (6 family) ☏ **S** fr £95 **D** fr £125* **Facilities:** FTV WiFi ⌦ Xmas New Year **Conf:** Class 40 Board 45 Theatre 60 **Services:** Night porter **Notes:** LB Civ Wed 40

See advert opposite

Potters Heron Hotel

★★★ 79% HOTEL

tel: 023 8027 7800 **Winchester Road, Ampfield SO51 9ZF**
email: reception@potters-heron.co.uk **web:** www.potters-heron.co.uk
dir: *M3 junction 12 follow Chandler's Ford signs. 2nd exit at 3rd roundabout follow Ampfield signs, over crossroads. Hotel on left in 1 mile.*

This distinctive thatched hotel retains many original features. In a convenient location for easy access to Winchester, Southampton and the M3, Potters Heron Hotel has modern accommodation and stylish, spacious public areas. Most of the bedrooms have their own balcony or terrace. The pub and restaurant both offer an interesting range of dishes that will suit a variety of tastes.

Rooms: 53 (1 family) (29 GF) ☏ **S** fr £60 **D** fr £60* **Facilities:** FTV WiFi ⌦ Xmas New Year **Conf:** Class 40 Board 30 Theatre 100 **Services:** Lift Night porter **Parking:** 120 **Notes:** Civ Wed 100

Premier Inn Southampton West

Premier Inn

BUDGET HOTEL

tel: 0871 527 9004 (Calls cost 13p per minute plus your phone company's access charge) **Romsey Road, Ower SO51 6ZJ**
web: www.premierinn.com
dir: *Just off M27 junction 2. Take A36 towards Salisbury. Follow brown tourist signs 'Vine Inn'.*

High quality, budget accommodation ideal for both families and business travellers. Spacious, en suite bedrooms feature free WiFi and tea and coffee making facilities, and in most hotels, Freeview TV is also available. The adjacent family restaurant features a wide and varied menu.

Rooms: 83

ROSSINGTON	Map 16 SK69
South Yorkshire	

Best Western Premier Mount Pleasant Hotel

PREMIER | BEST WESTERN

★★★★ 79% HOTEL

tel: 01302 868696 **Great North Road DN11 0HW**
email: reception@mountpleasant.co.uk **web:** www.mountpleasant.co.uk
dir: *On A638 Great North Road, between Bawtry and Doncaster.*

This charming 18th-century house stands in 100 acres of wooded parkland between Doncaster and Bawtry, near Robin Hood Airport. Spacious public areas include well furnished lounges and the elegant Garden Restaurant. There are also a health and wellbeing centre, modern conference facilities and beautiful grounds, ideal for weddings. Bedrooms are individually designed; some have four-poster beds and the spa suites are even more impressive with luxurious bathrooms.

Rooms: 84 (22 family) (40 GF) ☏ **S** fr £79 **D** fr £99 (including breakfast) **Facilities:** Spa STV WiFi ⌦ Beauty salon **Conf:** Class 70 Board 70 Theatre 200 **Services:** Lift Night porter **Parking:** 140 **Notes:** LB Civ Wed 180

R

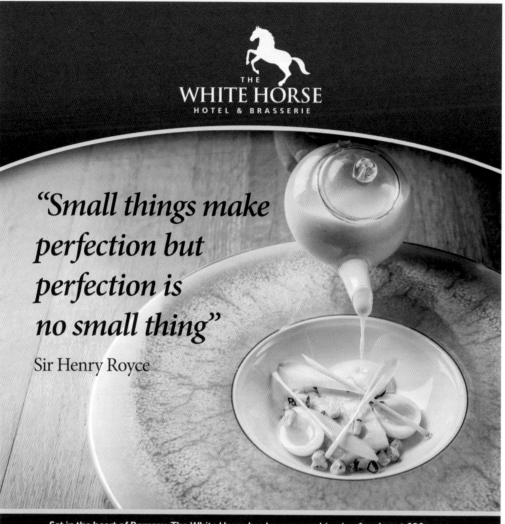

THE WHITE HORSE
HOTEL & BRASSERIE

"Small things make perfection but perfection is no small thing"

Sir Henry Royce

Set in the heart of Romsey, The White Horse has been a coaching inn for almost 600 years. The 2 AA rosette awarded Brasserie & Grill is a wonderful place to enjoy every occasion from a romantic dinner for two to a robust family lunch, during the summer months the courtyard offers a perfect retreat for al fresco dining. A stay here with us is a time to unwind – relax in one of our individually designed bedrooms, enjoy a cocktail in our delightful bar or even sample one of our delicious afternoon teas in the historic Tudor or Palmerston lounges. The hotel is also fully licensed for wedding ceremonies and offers the most romantic and intimate venue for your wedding day. **Historic charm meets modern classic chic.**

RESTAURANT AA Hotel

Market Place, Romsey, Hampshire SO51 8ZJ
T 01794 512431 **F** 01794 517485 **E** thewhitehorse@twhromsey.com
www.thewhitehorseromsey.com

ROSS-ON-WYE
Herefordshire

Map 10 SO52

The Chase Hotel

★★★ 85% HOTEL

tel: 01989 763161 **Gloucester Road HR9 5LH**
email: res@chasehotel.co.uk **web:** www.chasehotel.co.uk
dir: M50 junction 4, 1st left exit towards roundabout, left at roundabout towards A40, across next roundabout, right at 3rd roundabout towards town centre, hotel 0.5 mile on left.

This attractive Georgian mansion sits in its own landscaped grounds and is only a short walk from the town centre. Bedrooms, including two four-poster rooms, vary in size and character; all rooms are appointed to impressive standards. There is a light and spacious bar, and also Harry's restaurant which offers an excellent selection of enjoyable dishes.

Rooms: 38 (2 family) **S** fr £64 **D** fr £79 (including breakfast)* **Facilities:** FTV WiFi ↳ New Year **Conf:** Class 100 Board 80 Theatre 300 **Services:** Night porter **Parking:** 75 **Notes:** LB Closed 24–27 December Civ Wed 150

Glewstone Court Country House

★★★ 84% COUNTRY HOUSE HOTEL

tel: 01989 770367 **Glewstone HR9 6AW**
email: info@glewstonecourt.com **web:** www.glewstonecourt.com
dir: From Ross-on-Wye market place follow A40/A49 Monmouth/Hereford signs, over Wilton Bridge to roundabout, left onto A40 towards Monmouth, in 1 mile right for hotel.

This charming country house enjoys an elevated position with views over Ross-on-Wye, and is set in well-tended gardens. The owners ensure guests are well looked after from the moment of arrival. Bedrooms come in a variety of sizes and are tastefully furnished and well equipped. An excellent choice of dishes utilising high quality ingredients should not be missed at dinner.

Rooms: 9 (2 family) **Facilities:** ⚑ **Conf:** Class 50 Board 24 Theatre 50 **Notes:** Closed 2–18 January RS November to February Civ Wed 70

King's Head Hotel

★★★ 77% HOTEL

tel: 01989 763174 **8 High Street HR9 5HL**
email: enquiries@kingshead.co.uk **web:** www.kingshead.co.uk
dir: In town centre, past market building on right.

This establishment dates back to the 14th century and has a wealth of charm and character. Bedrooms are well equipped and comfortable with thoughtful guest extras provided; both four-poster and family rooms are available. The restaurant offers menus and a specials board that reflect a varied selection of local produce including fresh fish, free-range beef and lamb. There is also a well-stocked bar serving hand-pulled, real ales.

Rooms: 15 (1 family) **S** fr £60 **D** fr £85 (including breakfast)* **Facilities:** FTV WiFi **Parking:** 15

Premier Inn Ross-on-Wye

BUDGET HOTEL

tel: 0871 527 8944 (Calls cost 13p per minute plus your phone company's access charge) **Ledbury Road HR9 7QJ**
web: www.premierinn.com
dir: M50 junction 4, 1 mile from town centre.

High quality, budget accommodation ideal for both families and business travellers. Spacious, en suite bedrooms feature free WiFi and tea and coffee making facilities, and in most hotels, Freeview TV is also available. The adjacent family restaurant features a wide and varied menu.

Rooms: 59

ROSTHWAITE
Cumbria

Map 18 NY21

See also **Borrowdale**

Scafell Hotel

★★★ 86% COUNTRY HOUSE HOTEL

tel: 017687 77208 **CA12 5XB**
email: info@scafell.co.uk **web:** www.scafell.co.uk
dir: M6 junction 40 to Keswick on A66. Take B5289 to Rosthwaite.

Scafell Hotel is a friendly establishment which enjoys a peaceful location and is popular with walkers. Bedrooms have been tastefully appointed in a warm country-house style with a contemporary twist; some have traditional antique furniture. Public areas include a residents' cocktail bar, lounge and spacious restaurant as well as the popular Riverside Inn, offering all-day menus in summer months.

Rooms: 23 (3 family) (8 GF) **Facilities:** FTV WiFi Guided walks Xmas New Year **Parking:** 50 **Notes:** LB Civ Wed 75

ROTHERHAM
South Yorkshire

Map 16 SK49

Carlton Park Hotel
★★★ 77% HOTEL

tel: 01709 849955 **102/104 Moorgate Road S60 2BG**
email: reservations@carltonparkhotel.com **web:** www.carltonparkhotel.com
dir: *M1 junction 33, onto A631, then A618. Hotel 800 yards past District General Hospital.*

This modern hotel is situated in a pleasant residential area of the town, close to the hospital, yet within minutes of the M1. Bedrooms and bathrooms offer very modern facilities; three have separate sitting rooms. The restaurant and bar provide a lively atmosphere and there is a pool and leisure centre.

Rooms: 80 (20 family) (16 GF) **S** fr £80 **D** fr £90 (including breakfast)*
Facilities: STV FTV WiFi ⟲ ⏅ Gym ♫ **Conf:** Class 120 Board 60 Theatre 300
Services: Lift Night porter **Parking:** 120 **Notes:** LB Civ Wed 150

Premier Inn Rotherham East (M18/M1)
BUDGET HOTEL

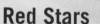

tel: 0871 527 8946 (Calls cost 13p per minute plus your phone company's access charge) **Bawtry Road S65 3JB**
web: www.premierinn.com
dir: *On A631 towards Wickersley, between M18 junction 1 and M1 junction 33.*

High quality, budget accommodation ideal for both families and business travellers. Spacious, en suite bedrooms feature free WiFi and tea and coffee making facilities, and in most hotels, Freeview TV is also available. The adjacent family restaurant features a wide and varied menu.

Rooms: 61

ROTHERWICK
Hampshire

Map 5 SU75

INSPECTOR'S CHOICE

Tylney Hall Hotel
★★★★ ◉◉ ⌂ HOTEL

tel: 01256 764881 **Ridge Lane RG27 9AZ**
email: sales@tylneyhall.com **web:** www.tylneyhall.com
dir: *M3 junction 5, A287 to Basingstoke, over junction with A30, over rail bridge, towards Newnham. Right at Newnham Green. Hotel 1 mile on left.*

Tylney Hall is a grand Victorian country house set in 66 acres of beautiful parkland. The hotel offers high standards of comfort in relaxed yet elegant surroundings, featuring magnificently restored water gardens, originally laid out by the famous gardener, Gertrude Jekyll. Spacious public rooms include Italian and Wedgwood styled drawing rooms and the panelled Oak Room Restaurant that offers cuisine based on locally sourced ingredients. The spacious bedrooms are traditionally furnished and offer individual style and high degrees of comfort. The excellent leisure facilities include indoor and outdoor swimming pools, tennis courts, jogging trails, croquet lawns and a spa.

Rooms: 112 (77 annexe) (1 family) (40 GF) ⟲ **S** £150 **D** fr £170 (including breakfast)* **Facilities:** Spa STV FTV WiFi ⟲ HL ⏅ ⟲ ♨ ⌂ Gym Clay pigeon shooting Archery Falconry Balloon rides Laser shooting Jogging trail Xmas New Year **Conf:** Class 70 Board 40 Theatre 120 **Services:** Night porter **Parking:** 120 **Notes:** Civ Wed 120

R

ROWSLEY Derbyshire	Map 16 SK26

The Peacock at Rowsley

★★★ ◉◉◉ HOTEL

tel: 01629 733518 **Bakewell Road, DE4 2EB**
email: reception@thepeacockatrowsley.com **web:** www.thepeacockatrowsley.com
dir: *A6, 3 miles before Bakewell, 6 miles from Matlock towards Bakewell.*

Set in the beautiful Peak District National Park, and owned by Lord and Lady Manners of Haddon Hall, this hotel combines stylish contemporary design with original period and antique features. Bedrooms are individually designed and boast DVD players, Apple TV, complimentary WiFi and air conditioning. One bedroom has a delightful four-poster bed. Imaginative cuisine, using local, seasonal produce, is a highlight. Guests are warmly welcomed and service is attentive. Fly fishing is popular in this area and the hotel has its own fishing rights on seven miles of the Rivers Wye and Derwent.

Rooms: 15 (6 family) 🐾 **S** fr £165 **D** fr £285 (including breakfast & dinner)*
Facilities: WiFi ⌁ Fishing 🎣 Free use of Woodlands Fitness Centre Free membership to Bakewell Golf Club ♫ New Year **Conf:** Class 8 Board 16
Services: Night porter **Parking:** 25 **Notes:** No children 10 years Civ Wed 20

See advert opposite

RUBERY West Midlands	Map 10 SO97

Premier Inn Birmingham South (Rubery)
 Premier Inn

BUDGET HOTEL

tel: 0871 527 8094 (Calls cost 13p per minute plus your phone company's access charge) **Birmingham Great Park, Ashbrook Drive B45 9FP**
web: www.premierinn.com
dir: *M5 junction 4, A38 towards Birmingham. Left at lights before Morrisons signed Great Park. Right at roundabout. Right at next roundabout, hotel on right.*

High quality, budget accommodation ideal for both families and business travellers. Spacious, en suite bedrooms feature free WiFi and tea and coffee making facilities, and in most hotels, Freeview TV is also available. The adjacent family restaurant features a wide and varied menu.

Rooms: 62

RUGBY Warwickshire	Map 11 SP57

Brownsover Hall Hotel
 CLASSIC BRITISH HOTELS

★★★ 77% HOTEL

tel: 01788 546100 **Brownsover Lane, Old Brownsover CV21 1HU**
email: reservations@brownsoverhall.co.uk **web:** www.brownsoverhall.co.uk
dir: *M6 junction 1, A426 to Rugby. After 0.5 mile at roundabout follow Brownsover signs, right into Brownsover Road, right again into Brownsover Lane. Hotel 250 yards on left.*

Brownsover Hall is a Grade II listed, Victorian Gothic building designed by Sir Gilbert Scott, set in seven acres of wooded parkland. Bedrooms vary in size and style, including spacious and contemporary rooms in the converted stable block. The former chapel makes a stylish restaurant, and for a less formal meal or a relaxing drink, the Whittle Bar is popular.

Rooms: 47 (20 annexe) (3 family) (11 GF) **Facilities:** STV FTV WiFi ⌁ Xmas New Year **Conf:** Class 36 Board 40 Theatre 70 **Services:** Night porter **Parking:** 100 **Notes:** Civ Wed 56

Premier Inn Rugby North M6 Jct 1
 Premier Inn

BUDGET HOTEL

tel: 0871 527 8948 (Calls cost 13p per minute plus your phone company's access charge) **Central Park Drive, Central Park CV23 0WE**
web: www.premierinn.com
dir: *M6 junction 1, southbound onto A426. Hotel approximately 1 mile on left at roundabout.*

High quality, budget accommodation ideal for both families and business travellers. Spacious, en suite bedrooms feature free WiFi and tea and coffee making facilities, and in most hotels, Freeview TV is also available. The adjacent family restaurant features a wide and varied menu.

Rooms: 82

Premier Inn Rugby North (Newbold)
 Premier Inn

BUDGET HOTEL

tel: 0871 527 8950 (Calls cost 13p per minute plus your phone company's access charge) **Brownsover Road CV21 1HL**
web: www.premierinn.com
dir: *M6 junction 1, A426 follow Rugby signs. Straight on at 2 roundabouts. At 3rd roundabout, hotel on right. Note: for sat nav use CV21 1NX.*

Rooms: 50

RUGELEY
Staffordshire   Map 10 SK01

Premier Inn Rugeley

BUDGET HOTEL

tel: 0871 527 9272 (Calls cost 13p per minute plus your phone company's access charge) **Tower Business Park WS15 2HJ**
web: www.premierinn.com
dir: *M6 junction 14, A5013 towards Stafford. At roundabout 2nd exit onto A34. Take A513 signed Rugeley. At roundabout take 2nd exit onto A51. Left into Wolsley Road, left into Powerstation Road. Hotel off roundabout. Note: for sat nav use WS15 1PR.*

High quality, budget accommodation ideal for both families and business travellers. Spacious, en suite bedrooms feature free WiFi and tea and coffee making facilities, and in most hotels, Freeview TV is also available. The adjacent family restaurant features a wide and varied menu.

Rooms: 50

RUISLIP
Greater London

The Barn Hotel
★★★ 80% ◉◉ HOTEL Plan 1 A5

tel: 01895 636057 **West End Road HA4 6JB**
email: info@thebarnhotel.co.uk web: www.thebarnhotel.co.uk
dir: *A40 onto A4180 (Polish War Memorial) exit to Ruislip. 2 miles to hotel entrance at mini-roundabout before Ruislip tube station.*

A mix of old and new, with parts dating back to the 17th century, this impressive property sits in three acres of gardens. Bedrooms vary in style, from contemporary to traditional with oak beams; all are comfortable and well appointed. The public areas provide a high level of quality and luxury.

Rooms: 73 (3 family) (33 GF) (20 smoking) 🐾 **S** fr £67 **D** fr £92* **Facilities:** FTV WiFi ▷ Xmas New Year **Conf:** Class 50 Board 30 Theatre 80 **Services:** Night porter **Parking:** 42 **Notes:** Civ Wed 64

Premier Inn Ruislip

BUDGET HOTEL Plan 1 A5

tel: 0871 527 8952 (Calls cost 13p per minute plus your phone company's access charge) **Ickenham Road HA4 7DR**
web: www.premierinn.com
dir: *From Ruislip High Street into Ickenham Road (B466). At mini-roundabout 1st exit, The Orchard on left.*

High quality, budget accommodation ideal for both families and business travellers. Spacious, en suite bedrooms feature free WiFi and tea and coffee making facilities, and in most hotels, Freeview TV is also available. The adjacent family restaurant features a wide and varied menu.

Rooms: 20

RUNCORN
Cheshire   Map 15 SJ58

Premier Inn Runcorn

BUDGET HOTEL

tel: 0871 527 8954 (Calls cost 13p per minute plus your phone company's access charge) **Chester Road, Preston Brook WA7 3BB**
web: www.premierinn.com
dir: *1 mile from M56 junction 11, at Preston Brook.*

High quality, budget accommodation ideal for both families and business travellers. Spacious, en suite bedrooms feature free WiFi and tea and coffee making facilities, and in most hotels, Freeview TV is also available. The adjacent family restaurant features a wide and varied menu.

Rooms: 88

R

RUSPER
West Sussex

Map 6 TQ23

Ghyll Manor

★★★ 82% @ COUNTRY HOUSE HOTEL

tel: 0330 123 0371 **High Street RH12 4PX**
email: enquiries@ghyllmanor.co.uk **web:** www.ghyllmanor.co.uk
dir: A24 onto A264. Exit at Faygate, follow signs for Rusper, 2 miles to village.

Located in the quiet village of Rusper, this traditional mansion house is set in 45 acres of idyllic, peaceful grounds. Accommodation is in either the main house or a range of courtyard-style cottages. A pre-dinner drink can be taken beside the fire, followed by an imaginative meal in the charming restaurant.

Rooms: 29 (20 annexe) (7 family) (21 GF) **Facilities:** FTV WiFi ☒ Xmas New Year **Conf:** Class 60 Board 40 Theatre 120 **Services:** Night porter **Parking:** 50 **Notes:** LB Civ Wed 120

RYDE
Isle Of Wight

Map 5 SZ59

Lakeside Park Hotel & Spa

★★★★ 77% HOTEL

tel: 01983 882266 **High Street PO33 4LJ**
email: reception@lakesideparkhotel.com **web:** www.lakesideparkhotel.com
dir: A3054 towards Newport. Hotel on left after crossing Wotton Bridge.

This hotel has picturesque views of the tidal lake and surrounding countryside. Bedrooms are well appointed with modern amenities and stylish design. Public areas feature a comfortable open-plan bar and lounge, and two restaurants that showcase the best of island produce. Sizable conference and banqueting facilities are available, while the leisure area includes an indoor pool and spa therapy.

Rooms: 44 (2 family) (15 GF) **D** fr £160 (including breakfast)* **Facilities:** Spa FTV WiFi ☒ ⊕ Sauna Steam room Relaxation room Thermal spa garden **Conf:** Class 60 Board 40 Theatre 150 **Services:** Lift Night porter Air con **Parking:** 140 **Notes:** LB Closed 1–10 January Civ Wed 120

Yelf's Hotel

★★★ 72% HOTEL

tel: 01983 564062 **Union Street PO33 2LG**
email: manager@yelfshotel.com **web:** www.yelfshotel.com
dir: From Esplanade into Union Street. Hotel on right.

This former coaching inn has smart public areas including a busy bar, a separate lounge and an attractive dining room. Bedrooms are comfortably furnished and well equipped; some are located in an adjoining wing and some in an annexe. A conservatory lounge bar and stylish terrace are ideal for relaxing.

Rooms: 40 (9 annexe) (5 family) (3 GF) (3 smoking) **Facilities:** STV FTV WiFi Spa and treatments at sister hotel nearby **Conf:** Class 30 Board 50 Theatre 100 **Services:** Lift Night porter **Parking:** 23 **Notes:** Civ Wed 100

RYE
East Sussex

Map 7 TQ92

Mermaid Inn

★★★ 84% @@ HOTEL

tel: 01797 223065 **Mermaid Street TN31 7EY**
email: info@mermaidinn.com **web:** www.mermaidinn.com
dir: A259, follow signs to town centre, then into Mermaid Street.

Situated near the top of a cobbled side street, this famous smugglers' inn is steeped in history, dating back to 1450 with 12th-century cellars. The charming interior has many architectural features such as attractive stone work. The bedrooms vary in size and style but all are tastefully furnished; there are no fewer than eight four-posters, and the Elizabethan and Dr Syn's Bedchambers are particularly noteworthy. Delightful public rooms include a choice of lounges, cosy bar and smart restaurant.

Rooms: 31 (5 family) **S** fr £90 **D** fr £140 (including breakfast)* **Facilities:** FTV WiFi ☒ Xmas New Year **Conf:** Class 40 Board 30 Theatre 50 **Services:** Night porter **Parking:** 25 **Notes:** LB

The Hope Anchor Hotel

★★★ 79% SMALL HOTEL

tel: 01797 222216 **Watchbell Street TN31 7HA**
email: info@thehopeanchor.co.uk **web:** www.thehopeanchor.co.uk
dir: From A268, Quayside, right into Wish Ward, into Mermaid Street, right into West Street, right into Watchbell Street, hotel at end.

This historic inn sits high above the town with enviable views out over the harbour and Romney Marsh, and is accessible via delightful cobbled streets. There is a relaxed and friendly atmosphere within the cosy public rooms, while the attractively furnished bedrooms are well equipped and many enjoy good views over the marshes.

Rooms: 16 (3 family) (1 GF) **S** fr £80 **D** fr £120 (including breakfast)* **Facilities:** FTV WiFi Xmas New Year **Conf:** Class 30 Board 25 Theatre 40 **Parking:** 12

ST AGNES
Cornwall & Isles Of Scilly   Map 2 SW75

Rose-in-Vale Country House Hotel
★★★★ 77% ◉◉ COUNTRY HOUSE HOTEL

tel: 01872 552202 **Mithian TR5 0QD**
email: reception@roseinvalehotel.co.uk **web:** www.roseinvalehotel.co.uk
dir: *A30 south towards Redruth. At Chiverton Cross at roundabout take B3277 signed St Agnes. In 500 metres follow tourist sign for Rose-in-Vale. Into Mithian, right at Miners Arms, down hill. Hotel on left.*

Peacefully located in a wooded valley, this Georgian manor house has a wonderfully relaxed atmosphere and abundant charm. Guests are assured of a warm welcome. Accommodation varies in size and style; several rooms are situated on the ground floor. An imaginative fixed-price menu featuring local produce is served in the spacious restaurant.

Rooms: 23 (3 annexe) (1 family) (6 GF) ✿ **S** fr £75 **D** fr £109 (including breakfast)*
Facilities: FTV WiFi ♘ ⚲ Xmas New Year **Conf:** Class 50 Board 40 Theatre 75
Services: Lift **Parking:** 50 **Notes:** No children 12 years Closed 4 January to 1 February Civ Wed 80

Beacon Country House Hotel
★★★ 77% SMALL HOTEL

tel: 01872 552318 **Goonvrea Road TR5 0NW**
email: info@beaconhotel.co.uk **web:** www.beaconhotel.co.uk
dir: *A30 onto B3277 to St Agnes. At roundabout left into Goonvrea Road. Hotel 0.75 mile on right.*

Set in a quiet and attractive area away from the busy village, this family-run, relaxed hotel has splendid views over the countryside and along the coast to St Ives. Hospitality and customer care are great strengths, with guests assured of a very warm and friendly stay. Bedrooms are comfortable and well equipped, and many benefit from glorious views.

Rooms: 11 (2 family) (2 GF) ✿ **S** fr £110 **D** fr £125 (including breakfast)*
Facilities: FTV WiFi ♘ New Year **Conf:** Class 20 Board 20 **Parking:** 12 **Notes:** LB No children 8 years Closed 4–31 January, November

Rosemundy House Hotel
★★★ 72% HOTEL

tel: 01872 552101 **Rosemundy Hill TR5 0UF**
email: info@rosemundy.co.uk **web:** www.rosemundy.co.uk
dir: *A30 to St Agnes, approximately 3 miles. On entering village 1st right signed Rosemundy, hotel at foot of hill.*

This elegant Georgian house has been carefully restored and extended to provide comfortable bedrooms and spacious, inviting public areas. The hotel is set in well-maintained gardens complete with an outdoor pool which is available in warmer months. There is a choice of relaxing lounges and a cosy bar.

Rooms: 46 (3 family) (9 GF) ✿ **S** fr £56.50 **D** fr £113 (including breakfast)*
Facilities: FTV WiFi ⚲ ♨ ♫ Xmas New Year **Conf:** Board 80 **Parking:** 50
Notes: No children 5 years Closed 12–23 December, 2 January to 12 February

ST ALBANS
Hertfordshire   Map 6 TL10

Sopwell House
★★★★ 81% ◉◉ HOTEL

tel: 01727 864477 **Cottonmill Lane, Sopwell AL1 2HQ**
email: enquiries@sopwellhouse.co.uk **web:** www.sopwellhouse.co.uk
dir: *M25 junction 21a, 1st exit roundabout to A405. A414 towards St Albans/Hatfield. Slip road Shenley, mini-roundabout left.*

This fine country hotel is situated in 12 acres of beautifully landscaped gardens and the house overlooks the hotel's golf course. Sopwell House was once the country home of Lord Mountbatten, and offers bedrooms that are all very well appointed, as well as impressive leisure facilities. Afternoon tea is served in the comfortable lounges and there is a choice of restaurants for dinner.

Rooms: 128 (16 annexe) (28 family) (7 GF) ✿ **S** fr £129 (including breakfast)*
Facilities: Spa STV FTV WiFi ♘ ⊙ Gym Sauna Steam room Dance studio ♫ Xmas New Year **Conf:** Class 180 Board 110 Theatre 450 **Services:** Lift Night porter Air con **Parking:** 250 **Notes:** LB Civ Wed 380

St Michael's Manor
★★★★ 80% ◉◉ HOTEL

tel: 01727 864444 **Fishpool Street AL3 4RY**
email: reservations@stmichaelsmanor.com **web:** www.stmichaelsmanor.com
dir: *From St Albans Abbey follow Fishpool Street towards St Michael's village. Hotel 0.5 mile on left.*

Hidden from the street, adjacent to listed buildings, mills and ancient inns, this hotel, with a history dating back 500 years, is set in five acres of beautiful landscaped grounds. Inside there is a real sense of luxury, the high standard of decor and attentive service is complemented by award-winning food; the elegant restaurant overlooks the gardens and lake. Bedrooms are individually styled and have satellite TVs, DVDs and free internet access.

Rooms: 30 (8 annexe) (3 family) (4 GF) ✿ **S** fr £115 **D** fr £155 (including breakfast)*
Facilities: STV FTV WiFi ♨ Xmas New Year **Conf:** Class 20 Board 22 Theatre 30
Services: Night porter Air con **Parking:** 80 **Notes:** Civ Wed 140

Premier Inn Luton South M1 Jct 9
BUDGET HOTEL

tel: 0871 527 8334 (Calls cost 13p per minute plus your phone company's access charge) **London Road, Flamstead AL3 8HT**
web: www.premierinn.com
dir: *M1 junction 9, A5 towards Dunstable.*

High quality, budget accommodation ideal for both families and business travellers. Spacious, en suite bedrooms feature free WiFi and tea and coffee making facilities, and in most hotels, Freeview TV is also available. The adjacent family restaurant features a wide and varied menu.

Rooms: 76

Premier Inn St Albans City Centre
BUDGET HOTEL

tel: 0871 527 9464 (Calls cost 13p per minute plus your phone company's access charge) **1 Adelaide Street AL3 5BH**
web: www.premierinn.com
dir: *M25 junction 21A, A405 signed St Albans/London/M1 South. At junction 9 onto A5 towards St Albans. At roundabout 1st exit into Dunstable Road towards St Albans Redbourn. At roundabout 2nd exit onto A5183. At roundabout 1st exit into St Albans Road. In 3 miles take 2nd exit into Redbourn Road. Right into Drovers Way, hotel on left.*

Rooms: 123

S

ST ANNES

See **Lytham St Annes**

ST AUSTELL

Cornwall & Isles Of Scilly

Map 2 SX05

Carlyon Bay Hotel

★★★★ 81% ❀ HOTEL

tel: 01726 812304 **Sea Road, Carlyon Bay PL25 3RD**
email: reservations@carlyonbay.com **web:** www.carlyonbay.com
dir: *From St Austell, follow signs for Charlestown. Carlyon Bay signed on left, hotel at end of Sea Road.*

Built in the 1920s, this long-established hotel sits on the cliff top in 250 acres of grounds which include indoor and outdoor pools, a golf course and a spa. Bedrooms are well maintained, and many have marvellous views across St Austell Bay. A good choice of comfortable lounges is available, while facilities for families include kids' clubs and entertainment.

Carlyon Bay Hotel

Rooms: 86 (14 family) ✆ **S** fr £95 **D** fr £160* **Facilities:** Spa FTV WiFi ⚐ ⊛ ⅍ ⚓ 18 ♨ Gym Hydrotherapy Spa pool Hot stone beds ♫ Xmas New Year **Conf:** Theatre 150 **Services:** Lift Night porter **Parking:** 100 **Notes:** LB Civ Wed 100

See advert below

S

The Cornwall Hotel, Spa & Estate

★★★★ 80% COUNTRY HOUSE HOTEL

tel: 01726 874050 **Pentewan Road, Tregorrick PL26 7AB**
email: enquiries@thecornwall.com **web:** www.thecornwall.com
dir: A391 to St Austell then B3273 towards Mevagissey. Hotel approximately 0.5 mile on right.

Set in 43 acres of wooded parkland, this manor house offers guests a real retreat. The restored White House has suites and traditionally styled bedrooms, and adjoining are the contemporary Woodland Rooms – standard, family, accessible and also deluxe which have private balcony areas overlooking Pentewan Valley. The superb leisure facilities include the spa with luxury treatments, an infinity pool and state-of-the-art fitness centre. For dining, there's The Elephant Bar & Brasserie, with alfresco eating and drinking on the terrace in warmer months, and afternoon tea is taken very seriously here – Cornish, vegan-friendly and gluten-free options are on offer.

Rooms: 65 (4 family) **S** fr £70 **D** fr £115* **Facilities:** Spa STV FTV WiFi ⓦ HL ⓣ ☻ ⛱
Gym Xmas New Year **Conf:** Class 30 Board 20 Theatre 40 **Services:** Lift Night porter
Parking: 200 **Notes:** Civ Wed 60

HIGHLY RECOMMENDED

Boscundle Manor

★★★ 86% ◉◉ HOTEL

tel: 01726 813557 **Boscundle PL25 3RL**
email: reservations@boscundlemanor.co.uk **web:** www.boscundlemanor.co.uk
dir: M5 to Exeter then A30 until Bodmin. A391 to St Austell. Turn Left onto A390 then left towards Tregrehan. Hotel drive is 300 metres on left.

This is a charming and delightful family-run manor house full of charm, located on the edge of Boscundle, set within five acres of its own private, well maintained and beautiful grounds and gardens. Friendly and attentive staff are eager to ensure guests have a relaxing and enjoyable stay. Accommodation is warm, comfortable and inviting, with a stylish and contemporary feel, yet still cosy. Food is of a high quality, with a good selection of wines and beers to match. Additional seating is offered in the relaxing lounge with open fireplaces; an indoor swimming pool is part of the excellent leisure facilities.

Rooms: 14 (4 annexe) (4 family) **Facilities:** WiFi ⓦ ⓣ ⛱ Beauty treatments
Xmas New Year **Notes:** Civ Wed 150

Premier Inn St Austell

BUDGET HOTEL

Premier Inn

tel: 0871 527 9018 (Calls cost 13p per minute plus your phone company's access charge) **St Austell Enterprise Park, Treverbyn Road PL25 4EL**
web: www.premierinn.com
dir: A30 onto A391 signed St Austell. Through Bugle. Continue on A391 at roundabout. Continue to follow St Austell signs. 1st exit at Carclaze roundabout. Hotel at St Austell Enterprise Park.

High quality, budget accommodation ideal for both families and business travellers. Spacious, en suite bedrooms feature free WiFi and tea and coffee making facilities, and in most hotels, Freeview TV is also available. The adjacent family restaurant features a wide and varied menu.

Rooms: 77

ST HELENS	Map 15 SJ59
Merseyside	

Premier Inn St Helens (A580/East Lancs)

Premier Inn

BUDGET HOTEL

tel: 0871 527 9020 (Calls cost 13p per minute plus your phone company's access charge) **Garswood Old Road, East Lancs Road WA11 7LX**
web: www.premierinn.com
dir: 3 miles from M6 junction 23, on A580 towards Liverpool.

High quality, budget accommodation ideal for both families and business travellers. Spacious, en suite bedrooms feature free WiFi and tea and coffee making facilities, and in most hotels, Freeview TV is also available. The adjacent family restaurant features a wide and varied menu.

Rooms: 44

Premier Inn St Helens South

Premier Inn

BUDGET HOTEL

tel: 0871 527 9022 (Calls cost 13p per minute plus your phone company's access charge) **Eurolink, Lea Green WA9 4TT**
web: www.premierinn.com
dir: M62 junction 7, A570 towards St Helens.

Rooms: 40

ST IVES	Map 12 TL37
Cambridgeshire	

Golden Lion

★★★ 75% HOTEL

COACHING
INN GROUP

tel: 01480 492100 **Market Hill PE27 5AL**
email: goldenlion@innmail.co.uk

The Golden Lion is situated at the heart of the historic town of St Ives, where markets are held every Monday and Friday – the award-winning Farmers Market is well worth attending. The original coaching inn dates from the 19th century, but today this hotel has been tastefully refurbished to provide guests with smart accommodation and up-to-date comfort and amenities. A restaurant, bar and coffee house offer a great selection of food, wines and beers throughout the day and evening.

Rooms: 27 **S** fr £49 **D** fr £59* **Conf:** Class 30 Board 20 Theatre 50

ST IVES	Map 2 SW54
Cornwall & Isles Of Scilly	

St Ives Harbour Hotel

★★★★ 80% HOTEL

tel: 01736 795221 **The Terrace TR26 2BN**
email: stives@harbourhotels.co.uk **web:** www.stives-harbour-hotel.co.uk
dir: On A3074.

This friendly hotel enjoys an enviable location with spectacular views of St Ives Bay. Extensive leisure facilities, a versatile function suite and a number of elegant and stylish lounges are available. The majority of bedrooms are appointed to a very high standard, and many rooms have spectacular sea views, as does the restaurant which looks out over the bay and golden sands below.

Rooms: 46 (6 family) ⓝ **Facilities:** Spa FTV WiFi ⓣ Gym Steam room Sauna Xmas
New Year **Conf:** Class 20 Board 35 Theatre 130 **Services:** Lift Night porter
Parking: 60 **Notes:** LB Civ Wed 160

S

ST IVES *continued*

Carbis Bay Hotel

★★★★ 79% 🏵 🏵 HOTEL

tel: 01736 795311 **Carbis Bay TR26 2NP**
email: info@carbisbayhotel.co.uk **web:** www.carbisbayhotel.co.uk
dir: *A3074, through Lelant. 1 mile, at Carbis Bay 30 yards before lights, right into Porthrepta Road to hotel.*

In a peaceful location with access to its own white-sand beach, this hotel offers comfortable accommodation. The attractive public areas feature a smart bar and lounge, and a sun lounge overlooking the sea. Bedrooms, many with fine views, are well equipped. Interesting cuisine and particularly enjoyable breakfasts are offered. A small complex of luxury, self-catering apartments is available.

Rooms: 47 (16 family) (3 GF) ꕔ **S** fr £150 **D** fr £230 (including breakfast)*
Facilities: Spa WiFi ꕔ ꕔ Fishing Private beach Watersports centre Hot tub 🎵 Xmas New Year **Conf:** Class 80 Board 60 Theatre 120 **Services:** Night porter **Parking:** 200
Notes: LB Civ Wed 150

The Garrack

★★★ 82% 🏵 HOTEL

tel: 01736 796199 **Burthallan Lane TR26 3AA**
email: reception@thegarrack.co.uk **web:** www.thegarrack.co.uk
dir: *Exit A30 for St Ives. From B3311 follow brown signs for Tate Gallery, then Garrack signs.*

The Garrack is set in two-acre gardens on a hill top, with coastal views stretching some 30 miles. The bedrooms in the original house are in keeping with the original granite architecture, whereas those in the sea-facing lower-ground floor wing are more modern in design. Dinner and breakfast are served in the restaurant which overlooks the stunning grounds. The small leisure centre, in a separate building, consists of an indoor swimming pool with sauna. The Garrack's location is ideal for families and walkers wanting to explore Cornwall.

Rooms: 19 (4 family) (3 GF) ꕔ **S** fr £69 **D** fr £145 (including breakfast)*
Facilities: FTV WiFi HL ꕔ Sauna New Year **Conf:** Class 10 Board 20 **Parking:** 20

Tregenna Castle Hotel

★★★ 80% HOTEL

tel: 01736 795254 **TR26 2DE**
email: hotel@tregenna-castle.co.uk **web:** www.tregenna-castle.co.uk
dir: *A30 from Exeter to Penzance, at Lelant take A3074 to St Ives, through Carbis Bay, main entrance signed on left.*

Sitting at the top of town in beautiful landscaped sub-tropical gardens with woodland walks, this popular hotel boasts spectacular views of St Ives. Many leisure facilities are available, including indoor and outdoor pools, a gym and a

sauna. Families are particularly welcome. The individually designed bedrooms are generally spacious. The brasserie offers modern British dishes in an informal atmosphere.

Rooms: 84 (33 family) (16 GF) ꕔ **Facilities:** Spa STV FTV WiFi HL 🕃 ꕔ ⚲ 18 ⚲ ⚲ Gym Squash Sauna Steam room Badminton Woodland walks 🎵 Xmas New Year **Conf:** Class 150 Board 50 Theatre 250 **Services:** Lift Night porter **Parking:** 200
Notes: Civ Wed 160

Cottage Hotel

Leisureplex
HOLIDAY HOTELS

★★★ 73% HOTEL

tel: 01736 795252 **Boskerris Road, Carbis Bay TR26 2PE**
email: cottage@leisureplex.co.uk **web:** www.leisureplex.co.uk
dir: *From A30 take A3074 to Carbis Bay. Right into Porthreptor Road. Just before rail bridge, left through railway car park into hotel car park.*

Set in quiet, lush gardens, this pleasant hotel offers friendly and attentive service. Smart bedrooms are pleasantly spacious and many rooms enjoy splendid views. Public areas are varied and include a snooker room, a comfortable lounge and a spacious dining room with sea views over the beach and Carbis Bay.

Rooms: 80 (18 family) (2 GF) ꕔ **S** fr £39 **D** fr £68 (including breakfast)*
Facilities: FTV WiFi ꕔ Snooker 🎵 Xmas New Year **Services:** Lift **Parking:** 20
Notes: Closed December to February (excluding Christmas/New Year) RS November, March

HIGHLY RECOMMENDED

The Queens

★★ 85% 🏵 HOTEL

tel: 01736 796468 **2 High Street TR26 1RR**
email: info@queenshotelstives.com **web:** www.queenshotelstives.com
dir: *A3074 to town centre. Hotel is located opposite Boots the chemist.*

Handily located in the centre of town, just a short stroll from the harbour, this is an ideal location for exploring the charms of St Ives. The bedrooms offer style and comfort with local Cornish artwork and lovely comfy beds. Bathrooms are also light, bright and modern. The relaxing bar and lounge is the venue for enjoyable award-winning cuisine with excellent local produce utilised in simple yet delicious dishes.

Rooms: 10 **S** fr £39 **D** fr £62 (including breakfast)* **Facilities:** FTV WiFi

ST-LEONARDS-ON-SEA

See **Hastings & St Leonards**

ST MARY CHURCH

See **Torquay**

ST MELLION
Cornwall & Isles Of Scilly
Map 3 SX36

St Mellion International Resort

★★★★ 77% 🏵 🏵 HOTEL

tel: 01579 351351 **PL12 6SD**
email: stmellion@crown-golf.co.uk **web:** www.st-mellion.co.uk
dir: *From M5, A38 towards Plymouth and Saltash. St Mellion off A38 on A388 towards Callington and Launceston.*

Set in 450 acres of Cornish countryside, this impressive golfing and leisure complex has much to offer. A vast range of leisure facilities is provided, including three pools, spa facilities and a health club. In addition, the hotel also boasts a choice of championship golf courses; the Jack Nicklaus signature course has hosted many PGA tour events. The bedrooms provide contemporary comforts and many have views across the course. Public areas are equally stylish with a choice of dining options including An Boesti, a fine-dining restaurant overlooking the 18th green.

Rooms: 80 (20 family) (18 GF) **Facilities:** Spa FTV WiFi ⚡ ⚓ 36 ⌂ Gym Studio classes Lawn bowls Xmas New Year **Conf:** Class 200 Board 80 Theatre 400 **Services:** Lift Night porter Air con **Parking:** 450 **Notes:** Civ Wed 300

ST NEOTS
Cambridgeshire
Map 12 TL16

HIGHLY RECOMMENDED

The George Hotel & Brasserie

★★★ 88% HOTEL

tel: 01480 812300 **High Street, Buckden PE19 5XA**
email: mail@thegeorgebuckden.com **web:** www.thegeorgebuckden.com
dir: *2 miles south of A1 and A14 junction at Buckden.*

The George Hotel is ideally situated in the heart of this historic town centre and is just a short drive from the A1. Public rooms feature a bustling ground-floor brasserie, which offers casual dining throughout the day and evening; there is also an informal lounge bar with an open fire and comfy seating. Bedrooms are stylish, tastefully appointed and thoughtfully equipped.

Rooms: 12 (1 family) **S** fr £95 **D** fr £120 (including breakfast)* **Facilities:** STV WiFi ⚡ **Conf:** Class 30 Board 20 Theatre 50 **Services:** Lift Night porter **Parking:** 25 **Notes:** Civ Wed 60

Premier Inn St Neots (A1/Wyboston)

Premier Inn

BUDGET HOTEL

tel: 0871 527 9024 (Calls cost 13p per minute plus your phone company's access charge) **Great North Road, Eaton Socon PE19 8EN**
web: www.premierinn.com
dir: *Just off A1 at roundabout of A428 and B1428 before St Neots. 1 mile from St Neots rail station.*

High quality, budget accommodation ideal for both families and business travellers. Spacious, en suite bedrooms feature free WiFi and tea and coffee making facilities, and in most hotels, Freeview TV is also available. The adjacent family restaurant features a wide and varied menu.

Rooms: 67

Premier Inn St Neots (Colmworth Park)

Premier Inn

BUDGET HOTEL

tel: 0871 527 9026 (Calls cost 13p per minute plus your phone company's access charge) **2 Marlborough Road, Colmworth Business Park PE19 8YP**
web: www.premierinn.com
dir: *From A1 northbound: A428 towards Cambridge. 2nd exit at roundabout onto A4128 signed St Neots. Hotel on right. From A1 southbound: follow A428 Cambridge signs. At roundabout 1st exit onto A4128 signed St Neots, hotel on right.*

Rooms: 71

SALCOMBE
Devon
Map 3 SX73

HIGHLY RECOMMENDED

Soar Mill Cove Hotel

★★★★ 85% HOTEL

tel: 01548 561566 **Soar Mill Cove, Malborough TQ7 3DS**
email: info@soarmillcove.co.uk **web:** www.soarmillcove.co.uk
dir: *3 miles west of town off A381 at Malborough. Follow Soar signs.*

Situated amid spectacular scenery with dramatic sea views, this hotel is ideal for a relaxing stay. Family-run, with a committed team, keen standards of hospitality and service are upheld. Bedrooms are well equipped and many have private terraces. There are different seating areas where, if guests wish, impressive cream teas can be enjoyed, and for the more active, there's a choice of swimming pools. Local produce and seafood are used to good effect in the restaurant.

Rooms: 22 (5 family) (21 GF) **Facilities:** Spa FTV WiFi ⚡ ⚓ ⌂ Gym Table tennis Games room Leisure complex Salt water pool ♪ Xmas **Conf:** Class 50 Board 50 Theatre 100 **Services:** Night porter **Parking:** 30 **Notes:** Civ Wed 150

HIGHLY RECOMMENDED

Thurlestone Hotel

★★★★ 84% HOTEL

tel: 01548 560382 **TQ7 3NN**
email: reception@thurlestone.co.uk **web:** www.thurlestone.co.uk

(for full entry see Thurlestone)

HIGHLY RECOMMENDED

Salcombe Harbour Hotel

★★★★ 83% HOTEL

tel: 01548 844444 **Cliff Road TQ8 8JH**
email: salcombe@harbourhotels.co.uk **web:** www.salcombe-harbour-hotel.co.uk
dir: *From A38 Exeter – Plymouth dual carriageway take A384 to Totnes then follow A381 to Kingsbridge and onto Salcombe. On entering Salcombe carry along Main Road, do not take town signs. Follow road down hill into Bennett Road. Hotel is 0.25 mile on right.*

Situated on the side of the estuary in Salcombe stands this beautiful hotel. It enjoys stunning views, and is home to an attractive spa and leisure facility. Bedrooms are particularly well appointed and stylishly finished; many have excellent views, and some have balconies. Guests can eat in the Jetty Restaurant, which serves popular dishes and local seafood. There is also a function room, spacious bar/lounge and cinema.

Rooms: 50 (6 family) (6 GF) **S** fr £175 **D** fr £185 (including breakfast)* **Facilities:** Spa FTV WiFi ⚡ HL ⚓ Gym Sauna Steam room Xmas New Year **Conf:** Class 120 Board 40 Theatre 120 **Services:** Lift Night porter **Parking:** 50 **Notes:** LB Civ Wed 120

S

SALCOMBE continued

South Sands Hotel

★★★★ 78% ◉◉ HOTEL

tel: 01548 845900 **Bolt Head TQ8 8LL**
email: enquiries@southsands.com **web:** www.southsands.com
dir: M5 onto A38 signed Plymouth, at Buckfastleigh take A384 to Totnes. In Totnes take A381 to Kingsbridge then Salcombe.

South Sands Hotel is a contemporary boutique hotel on the beach in South Sands bay, just outside Salcombe. Well-equipped, comfortable rooms and beach suites sit above the beachside restaurant and terrace that offer stunning views of the estuary. Diverse, more relaxed meals can be taken in the bar and lounge with the restaurant offering sound cuisine which reflects a foraging approach. A warm and friendly atmosphere, attention to detail, and attentive yet unobtrusive service is on offer throughout.

Rooms: 27 (5 family) (2 GF) ♠ **S** fr £200 **D** fr £215 (including breakfast)*
Facilities: FTV WiFi ♨ Xmas New Year **Services:** Night porter **Parking:** 39
Notes: Civ Wed 75

SALE	Map 15 SJ79
Greater Manchester	

Premier Inn Manchester (Sale)

BUDGET HOTEL

tel: 0871 527 8716 (Calls cost 13p per minute plus your phone company's access charge) **Carrington Lane, Ashton-upon-Mersey M33 5BL**
web: www.premierinn.com
dir: M60 junction 8, A6144(M) towards Carrington. Left at 1st lights, hotel on left.

High quality, budget accommodation ideal for both families and business travellers. Spacious, en suite bedrooms feature free WiFi and tea and coffee making facilities, and in most hotels, Freeview TV is also available. The adjacent family restaurant features a wide and varied menu.

Rooms: 61

SALFORD	Map 15 SJ89
Greater Manchester	

The Ainscow Hotel

★★★★ 76% HOTEL

tel: 0161 827 1650 **Trinity Way M3 5HY**
email: gm@theainscow.com **web:** www.theainscow.com
dir: Phone for directions.

Dating from 1878, this striking, centrally located hotel has had a varied history as a brewery and then a jam factory. Major investment has resulted in a thoroughly modern and stylish interior. Bedrooms and suites are individually decorated but all are well equipped with up-to-date accessories and comforts; some rooms are split level and some have air conditioning. Complimentary WiFi is provided. On-site parking is charged on a nightly basis. There are gym facilities and a basement spa, The Parlour, for guests to use.

Rooms: 70 (8 family) (14 GF) ♠ **Facilities:** FTV WiFi ♨ HL Personal training Gym Cardio suite Cryotherapy chamber suite **Conf:** Class 60 Board 24 Theatre 60
Services: Lift Night porter **Parking:** 32 **Notes:** Civ Wed 120

Premier Inn Manchester Salford Media City

BUDGET HOTEL

tel: 0871 527 9652 (Calls cost 13p per minute plus your phone company's access charge) **Blue, Media City UK M50 2BA**
web: www.premierinn.com
dir: At end of M602 (heading towards Salford) take 3rd exit on roundabout onto Trafford Road. Turn right onto Broadway. At roundabout take 2nd exit and stay on Broadway. Hotel on left. For car park turn left immediately after hotel and car park is on left.

Rooms: 112

Premier Inn Manchester Salford Spinningfields

BUDGET HOTEL

tel: 0871 527 9550 (Calls cost 13p per minute plus your phone company's access charge) **Irwell Street M3 5EN**
web: www.premierinn.com
dir: Northbound: M60 junction 12, M602 (city centre). A57(M) into Mancunian Way. 1.5 miles, left onto A6042. Right at lights into Irwell Street.

Rooms: 143

SALISBURY	Map 5 SU12
Wiltshire	

The Legacy Rose & Crown Hotel

★★★★ 74% HOTEL

tel: 0844 411 9046 (Calls cost 7p per minute plus your phone company's access charge) & 0330 333 2846 **Harnham Road SP2 8JQ**
email: res-roseandcrown@legacy-hotels.co.uk **web:** www.legacy-hotels.co.uk
dir: M3 junction 8, A303 and follow Salisbury Ring Road or M27 junction 2, A36 to Salisbury. A338 towards Harnham then Harnham Road. Hotel on right.

This 13th-century coaching inn, situated beside the river, enjoys picturesque views of Salisbury Cathedral, especially from the River Edge which provides a good range of dishes. Many original features are still retained in the heavy oak-beamed bars. All bedrooms and bathrooms are beautifully appointed. Excellent conference and banqueting facilities are available.

Rooms: 34 (23 family) (10 GF) ♠ **Facilities:** FTV WiFi Xmas New Year **Conf:** Class 60 Board 60 Theatre 90 **Services:** Night porter **Parking:** 60 **Notes:** LB Civ Wed 100

Mercure Salisbury White Hart Hotel

★★★★ 73% HOTEL

tel: 01722 327476 **St John Street SP1 2SD**
email: H6616@accor.com **web:** www.mercure.com
dir: *M3 junctions 7/8, A303 to A343 for Salisbury then A30. Follow city centre signs on ring road, into Exeter Street, leading into St John Street. Car park at rear on Brown Street.*

There has been a hotel on this site for hundreds of years, and the current building dates from the 17th century. Bedrooms vary in style, from contemporary to traditional, but all boast a comprehensive range of facilities. The bar and lounge areas are popular with guests and locals alike for morning coffees and afternoon teas.

Rooms: 68 (6 family) **Facilities:** STV WiFi Xmas New Year **Conf:** Class 40 Board 40 Theatre 100 **Services:** Night porter **Parking:** 60 **Notes:** Civ Wed 100

Best Western Red Lion Hotel

★★★★ 72% HOTEL

tel: 01722 323334 **4 Milford Street SP1 2AN**
email: reception@the-redlion.co.uk **web:** www.the-redlion.co.uk
dir: *In city centre close to Guildhall Square.*

This 750-year-old hotel is full of character, with a mix of bedrooms and suites; The Seamstress Room in the eves is their very stylish master suite and includes a cast iron tub taking centre stage; other bedrooms are individually designed including one with a medieval fireplace dating back to 1220. The public areas include a bar and a lounge. The elegant Vine Restaurant serves an interesting mix of modern and traditional dishes.

Rooms: 60 (1 family) (1 GF) **S** fr £70 **D** fr £75* **Facilities:** FTV WiFi Xmas New Year **Conf:** Class 40 Board 40 Theatre 110 **Services:** Lift Night porter **Parking:** 7 **Notes:** LB Civ Wed 110

Grasmere House Hotel

★★★ 75% HOTEL

tel: 01722 338388 **Harnham Road SP2 8JN**
email: info@grasmerehotel.com **web:** www.grasmerehotel.com
dir: *On A3094 on south side of Salisbury adjacent to Harnham church.*

This popular hotel, dating from 1896, has gardens that overlook the water meadows and the cathedral. The attractive bedrooms vary in size; all offer excellent quality and comfort, while some rooms are specially equipped for less mobile guests. In summer there is the option of dining on the pleasant outdoor terrace.

Rooms: 38 (31 annexe) (16 family) (9 GF) **S** fr £90 **D** fr £125* **Facilities:** STV FTV WiFi Fishing Xmas New Year **Conf:** Class 45 Board 45 Theatre 110 **Parking:** 64 **Notes:** LB Civ Wed 120

Premier Inn Salisbury North Bishopdown

BUDGET HOTEL

tel: 0871 527 8956 (Calls cost 13p per minute plus your phone company's access charge) **Pearce Way, Bishopsdown SP1 3YU**
web: www.premierinn.com
dir: *From Salisbury take A30 towards Marlborough. 1 mile. Hotel off Hampton Park at roundabout.*

High quality, budget accommodation ideal for both families and business travellers. Spacious, en suite bedrooms feature free WiFi and tea and coffee making facilities, and in most hotels, Freeview TV is also available. The adjacent family restaurant features a wide and varied menu.

Rooms: 120

SALTASH	Map 3 SX45
Cornwall & Isles Of Scilly	

China Fleet Country Club

★★★★ 75% HOTEL

tel: 01752 848668 **PL12 6LJ**
email: res@china-fleet.co.uk **web:** www.china-fleet.co.uk
dir: *A38 towards Plymouth/Saltash. Cross Tamar Bridge, take slip road before tunnel. Right at lights, 1st right follow signs, 0.5 mile.*

Set in 180 acres of stunning Cornish countryside overlooking the beautiful Tamar estuary, this hotel has easy access to Plymouth and the countryside. It offers an extensive range of leisure facilities including a golf course. The one and two-bedroom apartments are located in annexe buildings; each has a kitchen, lounge and flexible sleeping arrangements. The dining options are the brasserie and the Upper Deck Bistro. Guests can relax at the hotel's state-of the-art Aqua Spa.

Rooms: 41 (40 family) (22 GF) **S** fr £100 **D** fr £100* **Facilities:** Spa STV FTV WiFi 18 Gym Squash Floodlit driving range health and beauty suite Hairdresser Badminton Waterslide Xmas New Year **Conf:** Class 160 Board 60 Theatre 300 **Services:** Lift Night porter **Parking:** 400 **Notes:** LB Civ Wed 300

SALTBURN-BY-THE-SEA	Map 19 NZ62
North Yorkshire	

Brockley Hall Boutique Hotel & Fine Dining Restaurant

★★★★ 78% ⊛⊛ HOTEL

tel: 01287 622179 **Glenside TS12 1JS**
email: reception@brockleyhallhotel.com **web:** www.brockleyhallhotel.com
dir: *Phone for directions.*

Brockley Hall is ideally located in the heart of Saltburn, within easy walking distance to the seafront, and well positioned to tour Teeside and North Yorkshire. This property now a boutique hotel was built in 1865, and today offers high quality and comfort, with a stylish restaurant offering award-winning food. There is a range of well-appointed bedrooms to choose from.

Rooms: 22 (1 family) (3 GF) **S** fr £68 **D** fr £95 (including breakfast)*
Facilities: FTV WiFi Beauty treatment rooms **Conf:** Class 60 Board 24 Theatre 60 **Services:** Lift Night porter **Parking:** 15 **Notes:** Closed 25–26 December Civ Wed 120

S

SANDBANKS

See **Poole**

SANDIWAY
Cheshire

Map 15 SJ67

Nunsmere Hall Hotel

★★★★ @@ COUNTRY HOUSE HOTEL

tel: 01606 889100 **Tarporley Road, Oakmere CW8 2ES**
email: reception@nunsmere.co.uk **web:** www.nunsmere.co.uk
dir: *M6 junction 18, A54 to Chester, at crossroads with A49 turn left towards Tarporley, hotel 2 miles on left.*

In an idyllic and peaceful setting of well-kept grounds, including a 60-acre lake, this delightful house dates back to 1900. Spacious bedrooms are individually styled, tastefully appointed to a very high standard, and thoughtfully equipped. Guests can relax in the elegant lounges, the library or the oak-panelled bar. Dining in the Crystal Restaurant is a highlight and both a traditional carte and a gourmet menu are offered.

Rooms: 36 (8 family) (2 GF) ✿ **Facilities:** FTV WiFi ⓑ ✸ Xmas New Year
Conf: Class 150 Board 30 Theatre 200 **Services:** Lift Night porter **Parking:** 200
Notes: Civ Wed 150

SANDOWN
Isle Of Wight

Map 5 SZ58

Bayshore Hotel

Leisureplex
HOLIDAY HOTELS

★★★ 72% HOTEL

tel: 01983 403154 **12-16 Pier Street PO36 8JX**
email: bayshore.sandown@alfatravel.co.uk **web:** www.leisureplex.co.uk
dir: *From Broadway into Melville Street, follow Tourist Information Office signs. Across High Street, right opposite pier. Hotel on right.*

This large hotel is located on the seafront opposite the pier and offers extensive public rooms where live entertainment is provided in season. There is a range of bedrooms to meet a variety of needs, all are well equipped; front rooms also offer incredible sea views and are priced differently. The team is very friendly and helpful. Free WiFi is provided in the public areas.

Rooms: 77 (18 family) ✿ **Facilities:** FTV WiFi 🎵 Xmas New Year **Services:** Lift Night porter **Notes:** Closed December to February (excluding Christmas/New Year) RS March, November

Wight Bay Hotel

★★ 75% HOTEL

tel: 01983 402518 **2 Royal Street PO36 8LP**
email: booking@wightbayhotel.com **web:** www.wightbayhotel.com
dir: *At top of High Street, beyond Post Office.*

Guests return year after year to this friendly and welcoming family-run hotel. It is located near to the High Street and just a short stroll from the beach, pier and shops. Bedrooms, including several at ground floor level, are very well furnished and comfortably equipped. Enjoyable home-cooked meals are served in the spacious dining room.

Rooms: 43 (6 family) (11 GF) ✿ **S** fr £40 **D** fr £50* **Facilities:** FTV WiFi ⓑ 🎵 Xmas New Year **Parking:** 30 **Notes:** LB

Premier Inn Isle of Wight Sandown

Premier Inn

BUDGET HOTEL

tel: 0871 527 9558 (Calls cost 13p per minute plus your phone company's access charge) **Merrie Gardens, Newport Road PO36 9PE**
web: www.premierinn.com
dir: *From Fishbourne Ferry Terminal right onto B3731, right onto A3054. Next left into Station Road. 2 miles to roundabout. 1st exit into Briddlesford Road, at next roundabout into Downend Road. 4 miles, left onto A3056. 2nd exit at roundabout. At next roundabout 2nd exit into Whitcross Lane.*

High quality, budget accommodation ideal for both families and business travellers. Spacious, en suite bedrooms feature free WiFi and tea and coffee making facilities, and in most hotels, Freeview TV is also available. The adjacent family restaurant features a wide and varied menu.

Rooms: 100

SANDWICH
Kent

Map 7 TR35

The Lodge at Prince's

★★★ 84% @@ HOTEL

tel: 01304 611118 **Prince's Drive, Sandwich Bay CT13 9QB**
email: info@princesgolfclub.co.uk **web:** www.princesgolfclub.co.uk
dir: *M2 onto A299 Thanet Way to Manston Airport, A256 to Sandwich, follow sign to golf course.*

Created from the old clubhouse, The Lodge at Prince's is in one of the most sought-after locations on the south-east coast. There is a choice of bedrooms within three adjoining houses, and most rooms offer enviable views of the golf course or the Bay of Sandwich. All rooms have been carefully designed and offer a range of practical amenities including club storage. Award-winning cuisine is served in The Brasserie on the Bay.

Rooms: 38 (24 annexe) (24 family) (12 GF) ✿ **Facilities:** FTV WiFi ⓑ HL ♨ 27 Gym New Year **Conf:** Class 60 Board 50 Theatre 120 **Services:** Lift Night porter **Parking:** 50 **Notes:** LB

S

SAUNTON
Devon   Map 3 SS43

HIGHLY RECOMMENDED

Saunton Sands Hotel
★★★★ 83% ◉◉ HOTEL

tel: 01271 890212 **EX33 1LQ**
email: reservations@sauntonsands.com **web:** www.sauntonsands.com
dir: Exit A361 at Braunton, signed Croyde B3231, hotel 2 miles on left.

Stunning sea views and direct access to three miles of sandy beach are just two of the highlights at this popular hotel. The majority of sea-facing rooms have balconies, and splendid views can be enjoyed from all the public areas, which include comfortable lounges. In addition to the dining room, an outside grill has tables on the terrace overlooking the sea, which is ideal for alfresco dining. Alternatively, The Sands café/bar, an informal eating option, is a successful innovation located on the beach.

Rooms: 87 (39 family) 🐾 **S** fr £75 **D** fr £144 (including breakfast)*
Facilities: Spa STV FTV WiFi ⬧ ❄ ⬧ Gym Spa and wellness area Vitality pool Sauna Steam room Ice pit 9 treatment rooms ♫ Xmas New Year **Conf:** Class 180 Board 50 Theatre 200 **Services:** Lift Night porter **Parking:** 140 **Notes:** LB Civ Wed 200

See advert on following page

SCARBOROUGH
North Yorkshire   Map 17 TA08

Crown Spa Hotel
★★★★ 79% HOTEL

tel: 01723 357400 **Esplanade YO11 2AG**
email: info@crownspahotel.com **web:** www.crownspahotel.com
dir: On A64 follow town centre signs to lights opposite railway station, turn right over Valley Bridge, 1st left, right into Belmont Road to cliff top.

This well-known hotel has an enviable position overlooking the harbour and South Bay, and most of the front-facing bedrooms have excellent views. All the bedrooms, including suites, are contemporary and have the latest amenities including feature bathrooms. An extensive range of treatments is available in the outstanding spa.

Rooms: 115 (42 family) 🐾 **S** fr £60 **D** fr £70* **Facilities:** Spa FTV WiFi ⬧ HL ⬧ Gym Fitness classes Massage Sauna Steam room Xmas New Year **Conf:** Class 100 Board 80 Theatre 260 **Services:** Lift Night porter **Parking:** 17 **Notes:** LB Civ Wed 260

HIGHLY RECOMMENDED

Palm Court Hotel
★★★ 85% ◉ HOTEL

tel: 01723 368161 **St Nicholas Cliff YO11 2ES**
email: info@palmcourt-scarborough.co.uk
web: www.palmcourtscarborough.co.uk
dir: Follow signs for town centre and town hall, hotel before town hall on right.

The public rooms are spacious and comfortable at this modern, town centre hotel. Traditional cooking is provided in the attractive restaurant and staff are friendly and helpful. Bedrooms are quite delightfully furnished and well equipped. Extra facilities include a swimming pool and free, covered parking.

Rooms: 40 (11 family) 🐾 **S** fr £60 **D** fr £95 (including breakfast)* **Facilities:** FTV WiFi ⬧ Xmas New Year **Conf:** Class 70 Board 60 Theatre 80 **Services:** Lift Night porter **Parking:** 40 **Notes:** LB Civ Wed 80

Red Lea Hotel
★★★ 76% HOTEL

tel: 01723 362431 **Prince of Wales Terrace YO11 2AJ**
email: info@redleahotel.co.uk **web:** www.redleahotel.co.uk
dir: Follow South Cliff signs. Prince of Wales Terrace is off Esplanade opposite cliff lift.

This friendly, family-run hotel is situated close to the cliff lift. Bedrooms are well equipped and comfortably furnished, and many at the front have picturesque views of the coast. There are two large lounges and a spacious dining room where good-value, traditional food is served.

Rooms: 66 (7 family) 🐾 **S** fr £60 **D** fr £120 (including breakfast)* **Facilities:** FTV WiFi ⬧ Gym 2 treatment rooms Xmas New Year **Conf:** Class 25 Board 25 Theatre 40 **Services:** Lift Night porter **Notes:** LB

S

SCARBOROUGH *continued*

The Cumberland

★★★ 71% HOTEL

tel: 01723 361826 **Belmont Road YO11 2AB**
email: cumberland.scarborough@leisureplex.co.uk **web:** www.leisureplex.co.uk
dir: *A64 onto B1437, left at A165 towards town centre. Right into Ramshill Road, right into Belmont Road.*

On the South Cliff, convenient for the spa complex, beach and town centre shops, this hotel offers comfortably appointed bedrooms; each floor can be accessed by lift. Entertainment is provided most evenings and the meals are carefully prepared.

Rooms: 86 (7 family) ☏ **S** fr £41 **D** fr £64 (including breakfast)* **Facilities:** FTV WiFi ♫ Xmas New Year **Services:** Lift Night porter **Notes:** Closed January RS November to December and 1–9 February

Premier Inn Scarborough

BUDGET HOTEL

tel: 0871 527 9292 (Calls cost 13p per minute plus your phone company's access charge) **Falconer Road YO11 2EN**
web: www.premierinn.com
dir: *From A64 into Seamer Road, follow rail station signs. Right into Valley Bridge Road. At 1st lights follow Town Hall signs into Somerset Street (towards Brunswick shopping centre). At lights follow Town Hall signs into Falconers Road.*

High quality, budget accommodation ideal for both families and business travellers. Spacious, en suite bedrooms feature free WiFi and tea and coffee making facilities, and in most hotels, Freeview TV is also available. The adjacent family restaurant features a wide and varied menu.

Rooms: 74

SCUNTHORPE
Lincolnshire
Map 17 SE81

Forest Pines Hotel & Golf Resort

★★★★ 81% ⊛ HOTEL

tel: 01652 650770 **Ermine Street, Broughton DN20 0AQ**
email: forestpines@qhotels.co.uk **web:** www.qhotels.co.uk
dir: *200 yards from M180 junction 4, on Brigg-Scunthorpe roundabout.*

This smart hotel provides a comprehensive range of leisure facilities. Extensive conference rooms, a modern health and beauty spa, and a championship golf course ensure that it is a popular choice with both corporate and leisure guests. The well-equipped bedrooms are modern, spacious, and appointed to a good standard. Extensive public areas include a choice of dining options, with fine dining available in The Eighteen57 fish restaurant, and more informal eating in The Grill.

Rooms: 188 (66 family) (65 GF) ☏ **Facilities:** Spa STV FTV WiFi HL ⊕ ⅃ 27 Gym Mountain bikes Jogging track Xmas New Year **Conf:** Class 170 Board 96 Theatre 370 **Services:** Lift Night porter **Parking:** 400 **Notes:** Civ Wed 250

Premier Inn Scunthorpe

Premier Inn
BUDGET HOTEL

tel: 0871 527 8960 (Calls cost 13p per minute plus your phone company's access charge) **Lakeside Retail Park, Lakeside Parkway DN16 3UA**
web: www.premierinn.com
dir: *M180 junction 4, A18 towards Scunthorpe. At Morrisons roundabout left onto Lakeside Retail Park, hotel behind Morrisons petrol station.*

High quality, budget accommodation ideal for both families and business travellers. Spacious, en suite bedrooms feature free WiFi and tea and coffee making facilities, and in most hotels, Freeview TV is also available. The adjacent family restaurant features a wide and varied menu.

Rooms: 101

S

SEAHAM
County Durham
Map 19 NZ44

Seaham Hall

★★★★★ 85% ◎◎ HOTEL

tel: 0191 516 1400 **Lord Byron's Walk SR7 7AG**
email: hotel@seaham-hall.com **web:** www.seaham-hall.co.uk
dir: *From A19 take B1404 to Seaham. At lights straight over level crossing. Hotel approximately 0.25 mile on right.*

Seaham Hall benefits from a wonderful coastal location. Its interior is sumptuously furnished, with all rooms boasting the highest quality fixtures, fittings and furniture. Many have feature bathrooms, and the garden rooms have their own patio and garden areas. Public rooms boast quality and luxury throughout. The hotel boasts an award-winning Serenity Spa where you can unwind in the pool and hydrotherapy facilities, not forgetting the outside hot tubs; or book a treatment with one of the dedicated team of therapists. Seaham is home to two award-winning restaurants. Whether you choose the relaxed pan-Asian Ozone restaurant in the Serenity Spa or the opulent setting of The Dining Room restaurant, you can be sure of excellent food.

Rooms: 21 (4 GF) ✿ **S** fr £195 **D** fr £195 (including breakfast)* **Facilities:** Spa STV FTV WiFi ⓦ HL ⓧ ⓨ Gym Games room Sports lounge Xmas New Year **Conf:** Class 48 Board 40 Theatre 100 **Services:** Lift Night porter Air con **Parking:** 120 **Notes:** LB Civ Wed 100

SEAHOUSES
Northumberland
Map 21 NU23

The Links Hotel

★★ 85% SMALL HOTEL

tel: 01665 720062 **8 King Street NE68 7XP**
email: linkshotel@hotmail.com **web:** www.linkshotel-seahouses.co.uk
dir: *Off A1 at Browleside and follow signs along country road.*

This family-owned small hotel is in the heart of Seahouses. The restaurant is popular with residents and locals alike, offering relaxed and informal dining with quality home cooking and generous portions. Bedrooms are well presented and equipped and some off-road parking is available.

Rooms: 17 (7 annexe) (1 family) (2 GF) ✿ **S** fr £64 **D** fr £88 (including breakfast)* **Facilities:** STV FTV WiFi ⓦ **Parking:** 17

SEASCALE
Cumbria
Map 18 NY00

Sella Park House Hotel

★★★★ 75% COUNTRY HOUSE HOTEL

tel: 0845 450 6445 (Calls cost 7p per minute plus your phone company's access charge) **Calderbridge CA20 1DW**
email: info@penningtonhotels.com **web:** www.penningtonhotels.co.uk
dir: *From A595 at Calderbridge, follow sign for North Gate. Hotel 0.5 mile on left.*

This property, parts of which date back to at least the 16th century, is set in six acres of mature grounds which lead down to the River Calder. The individually designed bedrooms are very well appointed and have many extras; public areas are comfortable and welcoming. Food in the Priory Restaurant is a highlight, with local produce at the heart of each menu selection.

Rooms: 16 (5 annexe) (2 GF) ✿ **S** fr £91.50 **D** fr £110 (including breakfast)* **Facilities:** FTV WiFi ⓦ HL Fishing Xmas New Year **Conf:** Class 20 Board 30 Theatre 40 **Services:** Night porter **Parking:** 30 **Notes:** LB Civ Wed 150

SEAVIEW
Isle Of Wight
Map 5 SZ69

Seaview Hotel

★★★ 82% ◎◎ HOTEL

tel: 01983 612711 **High Street PO34 5EX**
email: reception@seaviewhotel.co.uk **web:** www.seaviewhotel.co.uk
dir: *Phone for directions.*

There is an enduring appeal about Seaview, a quiet seaside village where time has reassuringly stood still and the pace of life is unhurried. The hotel is just a few steps from the water's edge, a perfect place to relax and unwind with welcoming staff making every effort to ensure a rewarding experience. A choice of dining options is offered, with fish being a speciality; there is also the Pump Bar, a traditional pub situated in the heart of the hotel. A variety of bedroom styles are offered, both in the main hotel and within separate adjacent buildings, all of which provide contemporary comforts.

Rooms: 28 (12 annexe) (6 family) (6 GF) ✿ **S** fr £95 **D** fr £135 (including breakfast)* **Facilities:** FTV WiFi New Year **Conf:** Class 16 Board 20 Theatre 16 **Services:** Lift Night porter **Parking:** 10 **Notes:** LB Closed 23–27 December

SEDGEFIELD
County Durham
Map 19 NZ32

Hardwick Hall Hotel

BW PREMIER | BEST WESTERN

★★★★ 77% HOTEL

tel: 01740 620253 **TS21 2EH**
email: info@hardwickhallhotel.co.uk **web:** www.hardwickhallhotel.co.uk
dir: *Exit A1(M) junction 60 towards Sedgefield, left at 1st roundabout, hotel 400 metres on left.*

Set in extensive parkland, this 18th-century house suits both leisure and corporate guests. It is a top conference and function venue offering an impressive meeting and banqueting complex. Luxurious accommodation includes contemporary rooms, and some with antique furnishings. All are appointed to the same high standard, many have feature bathrooms, and some have stunning views over the lake. Both the modern lounge bar and cellar bistro have a relaxed atmosphere.

Rooms: 51 (6 family) (12 GF) ✿ **Facilities:** STV FTV WiFi ⓦ Xmas New Year **Conf:** Class 300 Board 80 Theatre 700 **Services:** Lift Night porter **Parking:** 300 **Notes:** LB Civ Wed 450

SEDGEMOOR MOTORWAY SERVICE AREA (M5)
Somerset
Map 4 ST35

Days Inn Sedgemoor - M5

WELCOMEBREAK

AA Advertised

tel: 01934 750831 **Sedgemoor BS24 0JL**
email: sedgemoor.hotel@welcomebreak.co.uk **web:** www.welcomebreak.co.uk
dir: *M5 northbound junction 21/22.*

This modern building offers accommodation in smart, spacious and well-equipped bedrooms, suitable for families and business travellers, and all with en suite bathrooms. Continental breakfast is available and other refreshments may be taken at the nearby family restaurant.

Rooms: 40 (22 family) (19 GF) (8 smoking) **Facilities:** WiFi ⓦ **Parking:** 40

S

Donnington Manor Hotel

★★★★ 73% HOTEL

tel: 01732 462681 **London Road, Dunton Green TN13 2TD**
email: mail@donningtonmanor.com **web:** www.donningtonmanorhotel.co.uk
dir: *M25 junction 4, follow signs for Bromley/Orpington to roundabout. Left onto A224 (Dunton Green), left at 2nd roundabout. Left at Rose & Crown, hotel 300 yards on right.*

Donnington Manor Hotel offers comfortable rooms, modern in style. There is a range of function rooms ideal for conferences and weddings. Guests can enjoy dinner in the Osteria Chartwell Italian Restaurant; breakfast is served here daily too. There's plenty of parking on site and the hotel is in close proximity to the M25, Sevenoaks and Brands Hatch.

Rooms: 63 (17 GF) **Facilities:** STV FTV WiFi Gym **Conf:** Class 70 Board 50 Theatre 120 **Services:** Lift Night porter Air con **Parking:** 80 **Notes:** LB Civ Wed 120

Best Western The Royal Chase Hotel

★★★ 73% HOTEL

tel: 01747 853355 **Royal Chase Roundabout SP7 8DB**
email: reception@theroyalchasehotel.co.uk **web:** www.theroyalchasehotel.co.uk
dir: *A303 to A350 signed Blandford Forum. Avoid town centre, follow road to 3rd roundabout.*

Equally suitable for both leisure and business guests, this well-known local landmark is situated close to the famous Gold Hill. Both Standard and Crown bedrooms offer good levels of comfort and quality. In addition to the fixed-price menu in the Byzant Restaurant, guests have the option of eating more informally in the convivial bar.

Rooms: 33 (13 family) (6 GF) **S** fr £65 **D** fr £100 (including breakfast)*
Facilities: FTV WiFi Sauna Xmas New Year **Conf:** Class 90 Board 50 Theatre 180 **Services:** Night porter **Parking:** 100 **Notes:** LB Civ Wed 80

Channel View Hotel

★★★ 79% HOTEL

tel: 01983 862309 **Hope Road PO37 6EH**
email: enquiries@channelviewhotel.co.uk **web:** www.channelviewhotel.co.uk
dir: *Exit A3055 at Esplanade and Beach sign. Hotel 250 metres on left.*

With an elevated cliff-top location overlooking Shanklin Bay, several rooms at this hotel enjoy pleasant views and all are very well decorated and furnished. The hotel is family run, and guests can enjoy efficient service, regular evening entertainment, a heated indoor swimming pool and holistic therapy.

Rooms: 56 (15 family) **S** fr £50 **D** fr £100 (including breakfast)* **Facilities:** FTV WiFi Holistic therapies Aromatherapy **Services:** Lift Night porter **Parking:** 32 **Notes:** Closed January to February

Shanklin Hotel

★★★ 73% HOTEL

tel: 01983 862286 **Clarendon Road PO37 6DP**
email: shanklin@leisureplex.co.uk **web:** www.leisureplex.co.uk
dir: *From Fishbourne ferry take A3054/A3056/A3055 south towards Shanklin. Left into Clarendon Road.*

Shanklin Hotel enjoys an enviable location with views over Sandown Bay and beyond. The accommodation is well configured and well appointed; a choice of beds is offered to meet the needs of a varied clientele. The hotel offers an indoor pool, game facilities, free WiFi in the public areas, entertainment most evenings and secure parking.

Rooms: 89 (3 family) (2 GF) **Facilities:** FTV WiFi Xmas New Year **Services:** Lift Night porter **Parking:** 32 **Notes:** Closed 2 January to 16 February RS February to March, November to December

Ocean View Hotel

★★★ 69% HOTEL

tel: 01983 863262 **1-5 Park Road PO37 6BB**
email: info@holdsworthhotels.co.uk **web:** www.holdsworthhotels.co.uk/ocean-view.php

The Ocean View is a charming, well-appointed hotel, situated in a premier location with an idyllic seaside position just a pebble's throw away from Shanklin Beach. With a number of spacious bedrooms, many with sea views and balconies, guests can sit and relax while enjoying the views.

Rooms: 100 (41 family) (8 GF) **Facilities:** FTV WiFi Xmas New Year **Services:** Lift Night porter **Parking:** 9 **Notes:** LB Closed 3 January to 8 February

Shap Wells Hotel

★★★ 78% HOTEL

tel: 01931 716628 **CA10 3QU**
email: reservations@shapwellshotel.com **web:** www.shapwells.com
dir: *Between A6 and B6261, 4 miles south of Shap.*

This hotel occupies a wonderful secluded position amid trees and waterfalls. Extensive public areas include function and meeting rooms, a well-stocked bar, a choice of lounges and a spacious restaurant. Bedrooms vary in size and style but all are equipped with the expected facilities.

Rooms: 99 (8 annexe) (10 family) (10 GF) **Facilities:** FTV WiFi Games room Cardiovascular gym Xmas New Year **Conf:** Class 150 Board 60 Theatre 400 **Services:** Lift Night porter **Parking:** 200 **Notes:** LB Closed 2–24 January Civ Wed 150

S

SHEFFIELD
South Yorkshire

Map 16 SK38

Whitley Hall Hotel

★★★★ 79%  HOTEL

tel: 0114 245 4444 **Elliott Lane, Grenoside S35 8NR**
email: reservations@whitleyhall.com **web:** www.whitleyhall.com
dir: *A61 past football ground, 2 miles, right just before Norfolk Arms, left at bottom of hill. Hotel on left.*

This 16th-century house stands in 20 acres of landscaped grounds and gardens. Public rooms are full of character and interesting architectural features and command the best views of the gardens. The individually styled bedrooms are furnished in keeping with the country-house setting, as are the oak-panelled restaurant and bar.

Rooms: 32 (3 annexe) (2 family) (8 GF) ⌂ **Facilities:** STV FTV WiFi ⌁ **Conf:** Class 50 Board 34 Theatre 70 **Services:** Lift Night porter **Parking:** 100 **Notes:** Civ Wed 100

Mercure Sheffield St Paul's Hotel & Spa

★★★★ 79% HOTEL

tel: 0114 278 2000 **119 Norfolk Street S1 2JE**
email: h6628@accor.com **web:** www.mercure.com
dir: *M1 junction 33, 4th exit at roundabout, left at 1st lights, right at 2nd in front of Crucible Theatre.*

This modern, luxury hotel enjoys a central location close to key attractions in the city. Open-plan public areas are situated in a steel and glass atrium and include a popular Champagne Bar, and the Yard Restaurant offering international dishes. Bedrooms are superbly presented and richly furnished. The Vital health and beauty treatment centre provides a fabulous thermal suite.

Rooms: 163 (40 family) **Facilities:** Spa WiFi ⌁ Sauna Steam room Snail shower Ice fountain Fitness classes Xmas New Year **Conf:** Class 400 Board 30 Theatre 600 **Services:** Lift Night porter Air con **Notes:** Civ Wed 350

Copthorne Hotel Sheffield

★★★★ 78% HOTEL

tel: 0114 252 5480 **Sheffield United Football Club, Bramall Lane S2 4SU**
email: reservations.sheffield@millenniumhotels.co.uk
web: www.millenniumhotels.co.uk/copthornesheffield
dir: *M1 junction 33/A57. At Park Square roundabout follow A61 Chesterfield Road. Follow brown signs for Bramall Lane.*

This modern and stylish hotel is situated in the centre of Sheffield. Right next to the home of Sheffield United FC, it offers contemporary public areas and an award-winning restaurant on the ground floor. A well-equipped gym is situated on the first floor. Bedrooms are spacious and comfortable. Ample parking is a plus in this central location.

Rooms: 158 (29 family) ⌂ **Facilities:** STV FTV WiFi ⌁ HL Gym **Conf:** Class 150 Board 24 Theatre 250 **Services:** Lift Night porter Air con **Parking:** 250

Mercure Sheffield Parkway Hotel

★★★★ 75% HOTEL

tel: 0114 261 5690 & 0845 485 4528 (Calls cost 7p per minute plus your phone company's access charge) **Brittania Way, Catcliffe S60 5BD**
email: fo@mercuresheffieldparkway.com **web:** www.mercuresheffieldparkway.com
dir: *M1 junction 33, just off A630 Parkway, 4 miles from city centre.*

A modern property situated just a short drive from the city centre; the smartly appointed bedrooms are equipped with modern facilities and are ideally suited for the business or leisure guest. The open-plan public areas feature a bar and Brasserie 59, where a good choice of home-made dishes is available.

Rooms: 78 (12 family) ⌂ **S** fr £59 **D** fr £59* **Facilities:** FTV WiFi ⌁ Gym Xmas New Year **Conf:** Class 80 Board 40 Theatre 120 **Services:** Lift Night porter Air con **Parking:** 100 **Notes:** LB

Novotel Sheffield Centre

★★★★ 73% HOTEL

tel: 0114 278 1781 **50 Arundel Gate S1 2PR**
email: h1348@accor.com **web:** www.novotel.com
dir: *Opposite Sheffield Hallam University follow signs to Town Hall/Theatres and Hallam University.*

In the heart of the city centre, this hotel has stylish public areas including a very modern restaurant, indoor swimming pool and a range of meeting rooms. Spacious bedrooms are suitable for families, and the Novation rooms are ideal for business users.

Rooms: 144 (134 family) ⌂ **Facilities:** STV FTV WiFi ⌁ Gym Steam room Xmas **Conf:** Class 180 Board 100 Theatre 220 **Services:** Lift Night porter **Parking:** 110 **Notes:** Civ Wed 180

Best Western Plus Aston Hall Hotel

★★★ 81% HOTEL

tel: 0114 287 2309 **Worksop Road, Aston S26 2EE**
email: reservations@astonhallhotel.co.uk **web:** www.astonhallhotel.co.uk
dir: *M1 junction 31, follow A57 to Sheffield and follow signs to hotel.*

Originally built as a manor house and set in spacious grounds with open views across the countryside to the south of the city, this hotel is well located for the M1, Meadowhall, the city, and for touring the area. Extensive conference and banqueting facilities, along with picturesque grounds, make it an ideal wedding venue. Bedrooms are comfortable and well equipped.

Rooms: 52 (6 annexe) (13 GF) ⌂ **S** fr £70 **D** fr £70* **Facilities:** FTV WiFi ⌁ Gym Xmas New Year **Conf:** Class 200 Board 60 Theatre 300 **Services:** Lift Night porter **Parking:** 90 **Notes:** LB Civ Wed 300

Best Western Plus Mosborough Hall Hotel

★★★ 79% HOTEL

tel: 0114 248 4353 **High Street, Mosborough S20 5EA**
email: hotel@mosboroughhall.co.uk **web:** www.mosboroughhall.co.uk
dir: *M1 junction 30, A6135 towards Sheffield. Follow Eckington/Mosborough signs 2 miles. Sharp bend at top of hill, hotel on right.*

This 16th-century, Grade II listed manor house is set in gardens not far from the M1 and is convenient for the city centre. The bedrooms offer very high quality furnishings and good amenities; some are very spacious. There is a galleried lounge and conservatory bar, and freshly prepared dishes are served in the traditional-style dining room.

Rooms: 46 (17 GF) ⌂ **Facilities:** FTV WiFi ⌁ Xmas New Year **Conf:** Class 125 Board 70 Theatre 220 **Services:** Night porter **Parking:** 100 **Notes:** Civ Wed 250

S

SHEFFIELD *continued*

Premier Inn Sheffield (Arena)

Premier Inn

BUDGET HOTEL

tel: 0871 527 8964 (Calls cost 13p per minute plus your phone company's access charge) **Attercliffe Common Road S9 2LU**
web: www.premierinn.com
dir: *M1 junction 34, follow signs to city centre. Hotel opposite Arena.*

High quality, budget accommodation ideal for both families and business travellers. Spacious, en suite bedrooms feature free WiFi and tea and coffee making facilities, and in most hotels, Freeview TV is also available. The adjacent family restaurant features a wide and varied menu.

Rooms: 95

Premier Inn Sheffield City Centre Angel St

Premier Inn

BUDGET HOTEL

tel: 0871 527 8970 (Calls cost 13p per minute plus your phone company's access charge) **Angel Street, (Corner of Bank Street) S3 8LN**
web: www.premierinn.com
dir: *M1 junction 33, follow city centre, A630, A57 signs. At Park Square roundabout 4th exit (A61 Barnsley). Left at 4th lights into Snig Hill, right at lights into Bank Street.*

Rooms: 160

Premier Inn Sheffield City Centre (St Mary's Gate)

Premier Inn

BUDGET HOTEL

tel: 0871 527 8972 (Calls cost 13p per minute plus your phone company's access charge) **Young Street, St Marys Gate S1 4LA**
web: www.premierinn.com
dir: *M1 junction 33, A630, A57 follow Sheffield City Centre signs. At Park Square roundabout 3rd exit signed A61/Chesterfield. At Granville Square right onto A61 signed Ring Road. Keep in left lane. At roundabout 3rd exit signed A621. Left into Cumberland Street. Left into South Lane. Right into Young Street.*

Rooms: 122

Premier Inn Sheffield (Meadowhall)

Premier Inn

BUDGET HOTEL

tel: 0871 527 8966 (Calls cost 13p per minute plus your phone company's access charge) **Sheffield Road, Meadowhall S9 2YL**
web: www.premierinn.com
dir: *On A6178 approximately 6 miles from city centre.*

Rooms: 103

SHEPTON MALLET   Map 4 ST64
Somerset

Charlton House Spa Hotel

★★★★ 80% HOTEL

tel: 0344 248 3830 **Charlton Road BA4 4PR**
email: gm.charltonhousehotel@bannatyne.co.uk **web:** www.bannatyne.co.uk
dir: *On A361 towards Frome, 1 mile from town centre.*

A peaceful location with grounds and relaxing spa facilities is just part of the charm of this interesting hotel. Individually designed bedrooms include larger suites and a luxurious lodge in the garden. Guests can relax in the 'shabby chic'

lounges or bar area, or in the warmer months there's plenty of outdoor seating. Dinner in the stylish restaurant offers a selection of carefully prepared, high quality dishes. The spa offers a wide range of facilities including treatment rooms, hydrotherapy pool, crystal room, sauna and a fitness studio. The hotel is a popular wedding venue.

Rooms: 28 (6 annexe) (3 family) (12 GF) ✆ **D** fr £140 (including breakfast)*
Facilities: Spa FTV WiFi 🏊 Gym Laconium Experience showers Sauna Steam room Hot tub Hydrotherapy Heated pool Xmas New Year **Conf:** Class 50 Board 25 Theatre 100 **Services:** Night porter **Parking:** 70 **Notes:** LB Civ Wed 120

SHERBORNE   Map 4 ST61
Dorset

Eastbury Hotel

★★★ 82%  HOTEL

tel: 01935 813131 **Long Street DT9 3BY**
email: enquiries@theeastburyhotel.co.uk **web:** www.theeastburyhotel.co.uk
dir: *From A30 westbound, left into North Road, then St Swithin's, left at bottom, hotel 800 yards on right.*

Much of the building's original Georgian charm and elegance is maintained at this smart, comfortable hotel. Just five minutes' stroll from the abbey and close to the town centre, the Eastbury's friendly and attentive staff ensure a relaxed and enjoyable stay. Award-winning cuisine is served in the attractive dining room, overlooking the walled garden, with an alfresco bistro option also available.

Rooms: 22 (1 family) (3 GF) ✆ **Facilities:** FTV WiFi ⛳ ⛵ **Conf:** Class 40 Board 28 Theatre 80 **Parking:** 30 **Notes:** LB Civ Wed 80

See advert opposite

Long Street, Sherborne, Dorset D19 3BY
Tel: 01935 813131

THE EASTBURY

The Georgian townhouse hotel was recently acquired by top-drawer hoteliers Peter and Lana de Savary. And as part of its reinvigoration, the hotel will soon enjoy the addition of a new spa and extra bedrooms set within its walled gardens.

Esteemed regional producers play a starring role in the hotel's 2 AA rosette Seasons restaurant and in a seven course tasting menu served in the conservatory. Edible flowers, herbs and its wonderful chef's garden demonstrate the kitchen's dedication to keeping things fresh.

www.theeastburyhotel.co.uk   @eastbury_hotel @theeastbury

S

SHERBORNE *continued*

Best Western The Grange at Oborne

★★★ 80% HOTEL

tel: 01935 813463 **Oborne DT9 4LA**
email: reception@thegrange.co.uk **web:** www.thegrangeatoborne.co.uk
dir: *Exit A30, follow signs through village.*

Set in beautiful gardens in a quiet hamlet, this 200-year-old, family-run hotel has a wealth of charm and character. It offers friendly hospitality together with attentive service. Bedrooms are comfortable and tastefully appointed, public areas are elegantly furnished, and the popular restaurant offers a good selection of dishes.

Rooms: 18 (3 family) (2 GF) ♠ **D** fr £129 (including breakfast) **Facilities:** STV WiFi ♧ Xmas New Year **Conf:** Class 40 Board 30 Theatre 80 **Parking:** 45 **Notes:** LB Civ Wed 120

SHERINGHAM
Norfolk

Map 13 TG14

HIGHLY RECOMMENDED

Dales Country House Hotel

★★★★★ 84% ⊛⊛ HOTEL

tel: 01263 824555 **Lodge Hill, Upper Sheringham NR26 8TJ**
email: dales@mackenziehotels.com **web:** www.mackenziehotels.com
dir: *From Sheringham take B1157 to Upper Sheringham. Through village, hotel on left.*

Dales Country House is a superb Grade II listed building situated in extensive landscaped grounds on the edge of Sheringham Park. The attractive public rooms are full of original character; they include a choice of lounges as well as an intimate restaurant and a cosy lounge bar. The spacious bedrooms are individually decorated with co-ordinated soft furnishings and many thoughtful touches.

Rooms: 21 (5 GF) ♠ **S** fr £113 **D** fr £186 (including breakfast)* **Facilities:** FTV WiFi ⅏ Giant garden chess and jenga Xmas New Year **Conf:** Class 20 Board 27 Theatre 40 **Services:** Lift Night porter **Parking:** 50 **Notes:** LB No children 14 years

SHIFNAL
Shropshire

Map 10 SJ70

Park House Hotel

★★★★ 72% HOTEL

tel: 01952 460128 **Park Street TF11 9BA**
email: reception@parkhousehotel.net **web:** www.parkhousehotel.net
dir: *M54 junction 4, A464 (Wolverhampton road) for approximately 2 miles, under railway bridge, hotel 100 yards on left.*

Set in attractive grounds, Park House Hotel features two distinct architectural styles, having once been two separate houses. Located on the edge of the historic market town of Shifnal, it offers guests easy access to the motorway network; Shrewsbury, Ironbridge and Telford are also within easy reach. Butlers Bar and Restaurant is the setting for imaginative food. A range of meeting rooms, leisure facilities and ample parking are also provided, together with complimentary WiFi.

Rooms: 54 (16 annexe) (17 family) (8 GF) ♠ **S** fr £55 **D** fr £70* **Facilities:** STV FTV WiFi ♧ ⅏ Jacuzzi Xmas New Year **Conf:** Class 80 Board 40 Theatre 160 **Services:** Lift Night porter **Parking:** 90 **Notes:** Civ Wed 160

SHREWSBURY
Shropshire

Map 15 SJ41

Mercure Shrewsbury Albrighton Hall Hotel & Spa

★★★★ 77% COUNTRY HOUSE HOTEL

tel: 01939 291000 & 291701 **Albrighton SY4 3AG**
email: H6629@accor.com **web:** www.mercureshrewsbury.co.uk
dir: *From south M6 junction 10a to M54 to end. From north M6 junction 12 to M5 then M54. Follow signs Harlescott and Ellesmere to A528.*

Dating back to 1630, this former ancestral home is set in 15 acres of attractive gardens. The bedrooms are generally spacious and the stable rooms are particularly popular. Elegant public rooms have rich oak panelling and there is a modern, well-equipped health and fitness centre.

Rooms: 87 (24 annexe) (7 family) (21 GF) **S** fr £99 **D** fr £109 (including breakfast)* **Facilities:** Spa STV WiFi ♧ ⅏ Gym Thermal suite Relaxation room Spray tan Exercise classes Sauna Steam room Ice room Xmas New Year **Conf:** Class 100 Board 80 Theatre 250 **Services:** Lift Night porter **Parking:** 200 **Notes:** LB Civ Wed 250

Prince Rupert Hotel

★★★★ 76% ⊛ HOTEL

tel: 01743 499955 **Butcher Row SY1 1UQ**
email: reservations@princeruperthotel.co.uk **web:** www.princeruperthotel.co.uk
dir: *Follow town centre signs, over English Bridge and Wyle Cop Hill. Right into Fish Street, hotel 200 yards.*

Parts of this popular town centre hotel date back to medieval times and many bedrooms have exposed beams and other original features. Luxury suites, family rooms and rooms with four-poster beds are all available. The oak-panelled Royalist Restaurant is the place for award-winning cuisine and adjacent is The Camellias Tea Rooms providing snacks and afternoon teas. The hotel's valet parking service is also commendable.

Rooms: 70 ♠ **Facilities:** FTV WiFi ♧ Gym Weight training Sauna Snooker room Hair salon Xmas New Year **Conf:** Class 80 Board 40 Theatre 120 **Services:** Lift Night porter **Parking:** 70 **Notes:** LB

HIGHLY RECOMMENDED

Lion & Pheasant Hotel

★★★ 86% ⊛⊛ TOWN HOUSE HOTEL

tel: 01743 770345 **49-50 Wyle Cop SY1 1XJ**
email: info@lionandpheasant.co.uk **web:** www.lionandpheasant.co.uk
dir: *From south and east: pass abbey, cross river on English Bridge to Wyle Cop, hotel on left. From north and west: follow Town Centre signs on one-way system to Wyle Cop. Hotel at bottom of hill on right.*

This 16th-century property stands on Wyle Cop, part of the historic centre of Shrewsbury. The interior decor is minimalist and uses natural materials such as limed oak, linens and silks. The bedrooms are of a high standard and include twin, double and family rooms. Award-winning food is offered in the first-floor restaurant and also in the ground-floor bar area.

Rooms: 22 (2 family) ♠ **Facilities:** FTV WiFi ♧ **Conf:** Class 30 Board 30 Theatre 30 **Parking:** 15 **Notes:** Closed 25–26 December

Abbots Mead Hotel

★★ 77% METRO HOTEL

tel: 01743 235281 **9 St Julian's Friars SY1 1XL**
email: res@abbotsmeadhotel.co.uk **web:** www.abbotsmeadhotel.co.uk
dir: *From south into town, 2nd left after English Bridge.*

This well maintained Georgian town house is located in a quiet cul-de-sac, near the English Bridge and close to both the River Severn and town centre with its many restaurants. Bedrooms are compact, neatly decorated and well equipped. Two lounges are available in addition to an attractive dining room, the setting for breakfasts, and dinner parties by prior arrangement.

Rooms: 16 (2 family) **S** fr £60 **D** fr £80 (including breakfast)* **Facilities:** WiFi
Services: Night porter **Parking:** 10 **Notes:** Closed certain days at Christmas

Premier Inn Shrewsbury (Harmers Hill)

BUDGET HOTEL

tel: 0871 527 8974 (Calls cost 13p per minute plus your phone company's access charge) **Wem Road, Harmer Hill SY4 3DS**
web: www.premierinn.com
dir: *M54 junction 7, A5 signed Telford for approximately 7 miles, at roundabout take A49, approximately 3 miles. At next 2 roundabouts 2nd exit, at next roundabouts 4th exit signed Ellesmere and A528. In approximately 3 miles hotel on left.*

Rooms: 20

Premier Inn Shrewsbury Town Centre

BUDGET HOTEL

tel: 0871 527 9402 (Calls cost 13p per minute plus your phone company's access charge) **Smithfield Road SY1 1QB**
web: www.premierinn.com
dir: *Phone for directions.*

Rooms: 136

SIDCUP
Greater London

Map 6 TQ47

Premier Inn London Sidcup Hotel

BUDGET HOTEL

tel: 0871 527 9640 (Calls cost 13p per minute plus your phone company's access charge) **101-108 Station Road DA15 7BS**
web: www.premierinn.com
dir: *From Sidcup station left into Station Road, under rail bridge. Hotel on right at lights.*

High quality, budget accommodation ideal for both families and business travellers. Spacious, en suite bedrooms feature free WiFi and tea and coffee making facilities, and in most hotels, Freeview TV is also available. The adjacent family restaurant features a wide and varied menu.

Rooms: 100

SIDMOUTH
Devon

Map 3 SY18

HIGHLY RECOMMENDED

Hotel Riviera

★★★★ 83% ◉◉ ⌂ HOTEL

tel: 01395 515201 **The Esplanade EX10 8AY**
email: enquiries@hotelriviera.co.uk **web:** www.hotelriviera.co.uk
dir: *M5 junction 30 and follow A3052.*

Overlooking the sea and close to the town centre, the Riviera is a fine example of Regency architecture. The large number of guests that become regular visitors here are testament to the high standards of service and hospitality offered. The front-facing bedrooms benefit from wonderful sea views, and the daily-changing menu places an emphasis on fresh, local produce.

Rooms: 26 (6 family) **S** fr £116 **D** fr £210 (including breakfast & dinner)*
Facilities: FTV WiFi ↻ ♫ Xmas New Year **Conf:** Class 60 Board 30 Theatre 85
Services: Lift Night porter **Parking:** 26 **Notes:** LB

See advert on following page

S

SIDMOUTH *continued*

The Victoria Hotel

★★★★ 83% ⊛ HOTEL

tel: 01395 512651 **The Esplanade EX10 8RY**
email: reservations@victoriahotel.co.uk **web:** www.victoriahotel.co.uk
dir: *On seafront.*

This imposing building, with manicured gardens, is situated overlooking the town. Wonderful sea views can be enjoyed from many of the comfortable

bedrooms and elegant lounges. With indoor and outdoor leisure facilities, the hotel caters to a year-round clientele. Carefully prepared meals are served in the restaurant. Staff provide a professional and friendly service.

The Victoria Hotel

Rooms: 61 (6 family) ⟨ **S** fr £160 **D** fr £215* **Facilities:** FTV WiFi ⟨ ⟨ ⟨ ⟨ Hot stone relaxation beds Spa bath Sauna Beauty treatment room Games room ♫ Xmas New Year **Conf:** Theatre 60 **Services:** Lift Night porter **Parking:** 100 **Notes:** LB Civ Wed 100

See advert opposite

S

SIDMOUTH *continued*

The Belmont Hotel

★★★★ 81% HOTEL

tel: 01395 512555 **The Esplanade EX10 8RX**
email: reservations@belmont-hotel.co.uk **web:** www.belmont-hotel.co.uk
dir: *On seafront.*

Prominently positioned on the seafront just a few minutes' walk from the town centre, this traditional hotel has many returning guests. A choice of comfortable lounges provides ample space for relaxation, and the air-conditioned restaurant has a pianist playing most evenings. Bedrooms are attractively furnished and many have fine views over the esplanade. Leisure facilities are available at the adjacent sister hotel, The Victoria.

Rooms: 50 (1 family) (2 GF) ⌁ **S** fr £165 **D** fr £190* **Facilities:** STV WiFi ⌁ Leisure facilities at sister hotel ♫ Xmas New Year **Conf:** Theatre 50 **Services:** Lift Night porter **Parking:** 45 **Notes:** LB Civ Wed 80

See advert on previous page

Sidmouth Harbour Hotel

★★★★ 76% HOTEL

tel: 01395 513252 **Manor Road EX10 8RU**
email: sidmouth@harbourhotels.co.uk **web:** www.sidmouth-harbour-hotel.co.uk
dir: *Exit A3052 to Sidmouth then to seafront and esplanade, turn right, hotel directly ahead.*

This charming hotel is ideally located within walking distance of Sidmouth's elegant promenade and beaches. The spacious lounges and the cocktail bar open onto a terrace which leads to the pool and croquet lawn. Bedrooms, several with balconies and glorious sea views, are spacious and comfortable, while the restaurant offers a choice of well-prepared dishes.

Rooms: 57 (1 family) (10 GF) ⌁ **S** fr £120 **D** fr £150 (including breakfast)* **Facilities:** Spa FTV WiFi ⌁ ⌁ Gym Xmas New Year **Conf:** Class 65 Board 50 Theatre 150 **Services:** Lift Night porter **Parking:** 40 **Notes:** LB Civ Wed 100

Royal Glen Hotel

★★★ 79% HOTEL

tel: 01395 513221 **Glen Road EX10 8RW**
email: info@royalglenhotel.co.uk **web:** www.royalglenhotel.co.uk
dir: *A303 to Honiton, A375 to Sidford, follow seafront signs, right onto esplanade, right at end into Glen Road.*

This historic 17th-century, Grade I listed hotel has been owned by the same family for several generations. The comfortable bedrooms are furnished in period style. Guests may use the well-maintained gardens and a heated indoor pool, and can enjoy well-prepared food in the elegant dining room.

Rooms: 32 (3 family) (3 GF) ⌁ **S** fr £60 **D** fr £120 (including breakfast)* **Facilities:** FTV WiFi ⌁ Gym Massage and aromatherapy room **Services:** Lift **Parking:** 22 **Notes:** LB Closed December to 21 February

The Royal York & Faulkner Hotel

★★★ 78% HOTEL

tel: 01395 513043 & 0800 220714 **The Esplanade EX10 8AZ**
email: stay@royalyorkhotel.co.uk **web:** www.royalyorkhotel.co.uk
dir: *M5 junction 30 take A3052, 10 miles to Sidmouth, hotel on centre of Esplanade.*

This seafront hotel, owned and run by the same family for over 60 years, maintains its Regency charm and grandeur. The attractive bedrooms vary in size, and many have balconies and sea views. Public rooms are spacious, and traditional dining is offered, alongside Blinis Café-Bar, which is more contemporary in style and offers coffees, lunch and afternoon tea. The spa facilities include a hydrotherapy pool, steam room, sauna and a variety of treatments.

Rooms: 72 (2 annexe) (8 family) (5 GF) ⌁ **S** fr £63 **D** fr £126 (including breakfast & dinner)* **Facilities:** Spa FTV WiFi ⌁ Hydrotherapy pool Steam room Sauna Complimentary use of nearby indoor pool ♫ Xmas New Year **Services:** Lift **Parking:** 20 **Notes:** LB Closed January

Mount Pleasant Hotel

★★ 85% HOTEL

tel: 01395 514694 **Salcombe Road EX10 8JA**
email: philip_gleave@btconnect.com **web:** www.mountpleasant-hotel.co.uk
dir: *Exit A3052 at Sidford crossroads, in 1.25 miles turn left into Salcombe Road, opposite Radway Cinema. Hotel on right after bridge.*

Quietly located within almost an acre of gardens, this modernised Georgian hotel is minutes from the town centre and seafront. Bedrooms and public areas provide good levels of comfort and high quality furnishings. Guests return on a regular basis, especially to experience the friendly, relaxed atmosphere. The light and airy restaurant overlooks the pleasant garden and offers a daily-changing menu of traditional, yet imaginative home-cooked dishes.

Rooms: 17 (1 family) (3 GF) **S** fr £61 **D** fr £102 (including breakfast)* **Facilities: Parking:** 20 **Notes:** No children 8 years Closed December to February

SILVERSTONE
Northamptonshire   Map 11 SP64

Premier Inn Silverstone

BUDGET HOTEL

tel: 0871 527 8976 (Calls cost 13p per minute plus your phone company's access charge) **Brackley Hatch, Syresham NN13 5TX**
web: www.premierinn.com
dir: *On A43 near Silverstone.*

High quality, budget accommodation ideal for both families and business travellers. Spacious, en suite bedrooms feature free WiFi and tea and coffee making facilities, and in most hotels, Freeview TV is also available. The adjacent family restaurant features a wide and varied menu.

Rooms: 79

SITTINGBOURNE
Kent   Map 7 TQ96

Premier Inn Sittingbourne Kent

BUDGET HOTEL

tel: 0871 527 8978 (Calls cost 13p per minute plus your phone company's access charge) **Bobbing Corner, Sheppy Way ME9 8RZ**
web: www.premierinn.com
dir: *M2 junction 5, A249 towards Sheerness, approximately 2 miles. Take 1st slip road after A2 underpass. At roundabout take 1st exit, hotel on left.*

High quality, budget accommodation ideal for both families and business travellers. Spacious, en suite bedrooms feature free WiFi and tea and coffee making facilities, and in most hotels, Freeview TV is also available. The adjacent family restaurant features a wide and varied menu.

Rooms: 62

SKEGNESS
Lincolnshire   Map 17 TF56

Best Western The Vine Hotel

BW Best Western.

★★★ 79% HOTEL

tel: 01754 763018 **Vine Road, Seacroft PE25 3DB**
email: info@thevinehotel.com **web:** www.bw-vinehotel.co.uk
dir: *A52 to Skegness, south towards Gibraltar Point, right into Drummond Road, 0.5 mile, right into Vine Road.*

With its long history, this traditional hotel is something of a local landmark. The smartly decorated bedrooms are well equipped and comfortably appointed. Public areas include two character bars that serve excellent local beers. Freshly prepared dishes are offered in the bar and the restaurant; service is both friendly and helpful.

Rooms: 25 (3 family) **Facilities:** FTV WiFi Xmas New Year **Conf:** Class 25 Board 30 Theatre 100 **Services:** Night porter **Parking:** 50 **Notes:** Civ Wed 100

SKIPTON
North Yorkshire   Map 18 SD95

The Coniston Hotel Country Estate and Spa

★★★★ 78% HOTEL

tel: 01756 748080 **Coniston Cold BD23 4EA**
email: info@theconistonhotel.com **web:** www.theconistonhotel.com
dir: *On A65, 7 miles northwest of Skipton, 8 miles from Settle.*

This privately owned hotel set on a 1,400 acres estate which proves a haven for both leisure and corporate guests. All bedrooms and bathrooms are appointed to a very high standard; the bedroom wing offers large rooms with balconies. The reception, bar and restaurant have style and elegance, and the stunning spa adds to the impressive list of activities for guests.

Rooms: 71 (13 family) (35 GF) ⌂ **S** fr £115.40 **D** fr £130.90 (including breakfast)*
Facilities: Spa FTV WiFi ⌕ ⊗ ⌇ Fishing Gym Clay pigeon shooting Falconry 4 x 4 off-road experience Fly fishing Archery ♫ Xmas New Year **Conf:** Class 80 Board 50 Theatre 200 **Services:** Lift Night porter Air con **Parking:** 170 **Notes:** LB Civ Wed 120

S

SKIPTON *continued*

Premier Inn Skipton North (Gargrave)

BUDGET HOTEL

tel: 0871 527 8980 (Calls cost 13p per minute plus your phone company's access charge) **Hellifield Road, Gargrave BD23 3NB**
web: www.premierinn.com
dir: *Northwest of Skipton at roundabout junction of A59 and A65, take A65 signed Kendal, Settle and Gargrave. 3.5 miles. Through Gargrave. Hotel on left.*

High quality, budget accommodation ideal for both families and business travellers. Spacious, en suite bedrooms feature free WiFi and tea and coffee making facilities, and in most hotels, Freeview TV is also available. The adjacent family restaurant features a wide and varied menu.

Rooms: 464

SLOUGH
Berkshire

Map 6 SU97

Premier Inn Slough

BUDGET HOTEL

tel: 0871 527 8982 (Calls cost 13p per minute plus your phone company's access charge) **76 Uxbridge Road SL1 1SU**
web: www.premierinn.com
dir: *2 miles from M4 junction 5, 3 miles from junction 6. Just off A4.*

High quality, budget accommodation ideal for both families and business travellers. Spacious, en suite bedrooms feature free WiFi and tea and coffee making facilities, and in most hotels, Freeview TV is also available. The adjacent family restaurant features a wide and varied menu.

Rooms: 129

Premier Inn Slough Central South (Windsor Road)

BUDGET HOTEL

tel: 0871 527 9656 (Calls cost 13p per minute plus your phone company's access charge) **Windsor Road SL1 2EL**
web: www.premierinn.com
dir: *M4 junction 6 onto Tuns Lane (Slough A355). At next roundabout take 3rd exit onto Church Street. Follow Church Street into Chalvey Road. Left onto Windsor Road. Hotel on right.*

Rooms: 131

Premier Inn Slough West (Slough Trading Estate)

BUDGET HOTEL

tel: 0871 527 8000 (Calls cost 13p per minute plus your phone company's access charge) **40 Liverpool Road SL1 4QZ**
dir: *Phone for directions.*

Rooms: 127

SOLIHULL
West Midlands

Map 10 SP17

See also **Dorridge**

The Regency Hotel

★★★ 76% @ HOTEL

tel: 0121 745 6119 **Stratford Road, Shirley B90 4EB**
email: solihull@corushotels.com **web:** www.corushotels.com/solihull
dir: *M42 junction 4 onto A34 for Shirley, cross 1st 3 roundabouts, then double back along dual carriageway, hotel on left.*

This much extended property is ideally located for access to the motorway network and Solihull's Touchwood centre. Rooms vary in style and size across the hotel; each is simply furnished and offers a good standard of comfort. The Circle health and fitness club is well equipped and includes an indoor pool. Ample free parking and WiFi are available.

Rooms: 111 (7 family) (13 GF) **S** fr £75 **D** fr £100* **Facilities:** FTV WiFi ⊘ ⊛ Gym Steam room Sauna Xmas New Year **Conf:** Class 80 Board 60 Theatre 180 **Services:** Lift Night porter **Parking:** 240 **Notes:** Civ Wed 100

Premier Inn Solihull (Hockley Heath, M42)

BUDGET HOTEL

tel: 0871 527 8984 (Calls cost 13p per minute plus your phone company's access charge) **Stratford Road, Hockley Heath B94 6NX**
web: www.premierinn.com
dir: *On A3400, 2 miles south of M42 junction 4.*

High quality, budget accommodation ideal for both families and business travellers. Spacious, en suite bedrooms feature free WiFi and tea and coffee making facilities, and in most hotels, Freeview TV is also available. The adjacent family restaurant features a wide and varied menu.

Rooms: 78

Premier Inn Solihull (Shirley)

BUDGET HOTEL

tel: 0871 527 8988 (Calls cost 13p per minute plus your phone company's access charge) **Stratford Road, Shirley B90 3AG**
web: www.premierinn.com
dir: *M42 junction 4 follow signs for Birmingham. Hotel in Shirley town centre on A34.*

Rooms: 43

Premier Inn Solihull South (M42)

BUDGET HOTEL

tel: 0871 527 8986 (Calls cost 13p per minute plus your phone company's access charge) **Stratford Road, Shirley B90 4EP**
web: www.premierinn.com
dir: *M42 junction 4, A34 north. Hotel in 1 mile.*

Rooms: 69

Premier Inn Solihull Town Centre
BUDGET HOTEL

tel: 0871 527 9366 (Calls cost 13p per minute plus your phone company's access charge) **Station Road B91 3RX**
web: www.premierinn.com
dir: M42 junction 5. At roundabout, take 3rd exit onto A41. At lights, turn left onto Lode Lane. At roundabout, take 2nd exit and continue down Lode Lane. At roundabout take 1st exit onto Station Road.
Rooms: 115

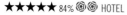
SOUTHAMPTON
Hampshire   Map 5 SU41

See also **Botley**

Southampton Harbour Hotel
★★★★★ 84% @@ HOTEL

tel: 02381 103456 **5 Maritime Way, Ocean Village SO14 3QT**
email: southampton@harbourhotels.co.uk **web:** www.southampton-harbour-hotel.co.uk
dir: Phone for directions.

This contemporary, purpose-built luxury hotel is located in Ocean Village and has wonderful views of the marina. There are multiple bars and restaurants, including the award-winning Jetty with an outside terrace area on the ground floor and the HarBAR on 6th that serves a range of crowd-pleasing dishes and cocktails. Bedrooms and bathrooms are spacious, all are equipped to a very high standard. There is also meeting and event space, excellent spa facilities including a café, eight treatment rooms, a spacious gym, pool, sauna, steam and relaxation rooms. There is also a small cinema. Complimentary parking and transfers are also provided to and from Southampton station.

Rooms: 85 (6 family) **D** fr £135 (including breakfast)* **Facilities:** Spa FTV WiFi HL Gym Xmas New Year **Conf:** Class 130 Board 50 Theatre 250 **Services:** Lift Night porter Air con **Parking:** 150 **Notes:** Civ Wed 220

Novotel Southampton
★★★★ 77% HOTEL   **NOVOTEL**

tel: 023 8033 0550 **1 West Quay Road SO15 1RA**
email: H1073@accor.com **web:** www.novotel.com
dir: M27 junction 3, follow city centre/A33 signs. In 1 mile take right lane for West Quay and Dock Gates 4-10. Hotel entrance on left. Turn at lights by McDonalds, left at roundabout, hotel straight ahead.

Novotel Southampton is a modern, purpose-built hotel situated close to the city centre, railway station, ferry terminal and major road networks. The brightly decorated bedrooms are ideal for families and business guests; four rooms have facilities for the less mobile. The open-plan public areas include the Garden Brasserie, a bar and a leisure complex.

Rooms: 121 (50 family) **S** fr £85 **D** fr £95* **Facilities:** STV FTV WiFi Gym Dry sauna **Conf:** Class 250 Board 150 Theatre 450 **Services:** Lift Night porter **Parking:** 300 **Notes:** Civ Wed 300

Mercure Southampton Centre Dolphin Hotel
★★★★ 71% HOTEL

tel: 023 8038 6460 **34-35 High Street SO14 2HN**
email: H7876@accor.com **web:** www.mercure.com
dir: From A33 follow signs for Docks, Old Town and Isle of Wight ferry. At ferry terminal right into High Street, hotel 400 yards on left.

Originally a coaching inn, this hotel enjoys a central location set almost in the heart of the town, yet close to the ferry terminals. The bedrooms are appointed to a high standard, and public areas include a traditional bar, popular restaurant and two meeting rooms. Parking at the rear of the hotel is an added bonus.

Rooms: 99 (9 annexe) (6 family) (27 GF) **Facilities:** FTV WiFi Xmas New Year **Conf:** Class 50 Board 40 Theatre 120 **Services:** Lift Night porter **Parking:** 80 **Notes:** Civ Wed 120

Best Western Chilworth Manor
★★★ 81% HOTEL

tel: 023 8076 7333 **Chilworth SO16 7PT**
email: sales@chilworth-manor.co.uk **web:** www.chilworth-manor.co.uk
dir: 1 mile from M3/M27 junction on A27 Romsey Road north from Southampton. Pass Chilworth Arms on left, in 200 metres turn left at Southampton Science Park sign. Hotel immediately right.

Set in 12 acres of delightful grounds, this attractive Edwardian manor house is conveniently located for Southampton and also the New Forest National Park. Bedrooms are located in both the main house and an adjoining wing. The hotel is particularly popular as both a conference and a wedding venue.

Rooms: 97 (4 family) (23 GF) **Facilities:** Spa FTV WiFi Gym Trail walking Conservation area Xmas New Year **Conf:** Class 60 Board 40 Theatre 150 **Services:** Lift Night porter **Parking:** 200 **Notes:** Civ Wed 105

HIGHLY RECOMMENDED

The Elizabeth House Hotel
★★ 85% HOTEL

tel: 023 8022 4327 **42-44 The Avenue SO17 1XP**
email: mail@elizabethhousehotel.com **web:** www.elizabethhousehotel.com
dir: On A33, hotel on left after Southampton Common, before main lights.

This hotel is conveniently situated close to the city centre, so provides an ideal base for both business and leisure guests. The bedrooms are well equipped and are attractively furnished with comfort in mind. There is a cosy and atmospheric bistro in the cellar where evening meals are served, and an attractive and versatile function room is also available. Complimentary parking is provided for guests.

Rooms: 27 (7 annexe) (9 family) (8 GF) **S** fr £88.50 **D** fr £98.50 (including breakfast)* **Facilities:** FTV WiFi **Conf:** Class 22 Board 24 Theatre 40 **Services:** Night porter **Parking:** 31

S

SOUTHAMPTON *continued*

New Place

U

tel: 01329 833543 **High Street, Shirrell Heath SO32 2JY**
email: sales@newplacehotel.com
web: www.legacy-hotels.co.uk/hotels/new-place-southampton
dir: *Follow signs to Wickham A334. Turn left onto B2177 signed Bishops Waltham then right signed Shirrell Heath/Swanmore/New Place. Entrance is on the left.*

Currently the rating for this establishment is not confirmed. This may be due to a change of ownership or because ot has only recently joined the AA rating scheme.

Rooms: 29 **Facilities:** FTV WiFi ⟳ 🐾 Gym Cricket pitch Tennis Xmas New Year **Conf:** Class 34 Board 28 Theatre 130 **Notes:** Civ Wed 150

Premier Inn Southampton Airport

BUDGET HOTEL

tel: 0871 527 8998 (Calls cost 13p per minute plus your phone company's access charge) **Mitchell Way SO18 2XU**
web: www.premierinn.com
dir: *M27 junction 5, A335 towards Eastleigh. Right at roundabout into Wide Lane. 1st exit at next roundabout into Mitchell Way.*

High quality, budget accommodation ideal for both families and business travellers. Spacious, en suite bedrooms feature free WiFi and tea and coffee making facilities, and in most hotels, Freeview TV is also available. The adjacent family restaurant features a wide and varied menu.

Rooms: 121

Premier Inn Southampton City Centre

BUDGET HOTEL

tel: 0871 527 9266 (Calls cost 13p per minute plus your phone company's access charge) **6 Dials, New Road SO14 0YN**
web: www.premierinn.com
dir: *M27 junction 5, A335 signed City Centre. At Charlotte Place roundabout take 3rd exit into East Park Terrace, 1st left into New Road. Hotel on right.*

Rooms: 172

Premier Inn Southampton (Cumberland Place)

BUDGET HOTEL

tel: 0871 527 8000 (Calls cost 13p per minute plus your phone company's access charge) **12-13 Cumberland SO15 2WY**
web: www.premierinn.com
dir: *From A3057: Leave A3057 (Shirley Road) onto Commercial Road then left onto Cumberland Place. Hotel on left. From A335: Follow A335 (Onslow Road). At roundabout take 4th exit onto A3024 (Cumberland Place). Hotel on right.*

Rooms: 146

Premier Inn Southampton North

BUDGET HOTEL

tel: 0871 527 9002 (Calls cost 13p per minute plus your phone company's access charge) **Romsey Road, Nursling SO16 0XJ**
web: www.premierinn.com
dir: *M27 junction 3, M271 towards Romsey. At next roundabout take 3rd exit towards Southampton (A3057). Hotel 1.5 miles on right.*

Rooms: 80

Premier Inn Southampton West Quay

BUDGET HOTEL

tel: 0871 527 9298 (Calls cost 13p per minute plus your phone company's access charge) **Harbour Parade SO15 1ST**
web: www.premierinn.com
dir: *M27 junction 3, follow M271(south)/Southampton/The Docks signs, onto M271, at Redbridge roundabout onto A35 follow Southampton/The Docks/A3024 signs. Merge onto A35 (Redbridge Road), continue onto Millbrook Flyover/A3024, right at West Quay Road/A3057, left after Ikea into Harbour Parade.*

Rooms: 155

SOUTH CAVE   **Map 17 SE93**
East Riding of Yorkshire

Cave Castle Hotel & Country Club

★★★ 81% HOTEL

tel: 01430 422245 **Church Hill HU15 2EU**
email: info@cavecastlehotel.com **web:** www.cavecastlehotel.com
dir: *In village, opposite school.*

This beautiful Victorian manor retains original turrets, stone features and much charm, together with modern comforts and style. It stands in 150 acres of meadow and parkland that provide a peaceful setting. Bedrooms are a careful mix of traditional and contemporary styles. Public areas include a well-equipped leisure complex and pool.

Rooms: 70 (5 family) (14 GF) ✆ **S** fr £75 **D** fr £85 (including breakfast)*
Facilities: Spa FTV WiFi ⟳ ✎ ⚘ 18 Fishing Gym New Year **Conf:** Class 150 Board 100 Theatre 250 **Services:** Lift Night porter **Parking:** 100 **Notes:** LB Civ Wed 150

SOUTHEND-ON-SEA   **Map 7 TQ88**
Essex

HIGHLY RECOMMENDED

The Roslin Beach Hotel

★★★★ 83% ◉ HOTEL

tel: 01702 586375 **Thorpe Esplanade, Thorpe Bay SS1 3BG**
email: info@roslinhotel.com **web:** www.roslinhotel.com
dir: *A127, follow Southend-on-Sea signs. Hotel between Walton Road and Clieveden Road on seafront.*

This friendly hotel is situated at the quiet end of the esplanade, overlooking the beach and sea. The spacious bedrooms are pleasantly decorated and thoughtfully equipped; some rooms have superb sea views. Public rooms include a large lounge bar, an AA Rosette restaurant and a smart conservatory which overlooks the sea.

Rooms: 62 (5 family) (11 GF) ✆ **Facilities:** Spa FTV WiFi Gym Manicure/pedicure bar Xmas New Year **Conf:** Class 65 Board 45 Theatre 90 **Services:** Night porter **Parking:** 48 **Notes:** LB Civ Wed 120

S

Holiday Inn Southend

★★★★ 76%  HOTEL

tel: 01702 543001 **77 Eastwoodbury Crescent SS2 6XG**
email: reservations@hisouthend.com **web:** www.hisouthend.com
dir: *M25 junction 29, A127 follow signs to London Southend Airport. Hotel 2 minutes away.*

Holiday Inn Southend offers a range of modern, well-appointed, stylish bedrooms. The open-plan, contemporary public areas look very smart and the lounges are fitted out with designer furniture and seating. The award-winning 1935 Rooftop Restaurant & Bar is situated on the fifth floor and overlooks the main runway of Southend airport. There are a range of conference facilities and business suites available along with secure parking for guests.

Rooms: 129 (17 family) **Facilities:** STV FTV WiFi HL Gym Xmas New Year
Conf: Class 50 Board 40 Theatre 140 **Services:** Lift Night porter Air con **Parking:** 250
Notes: LB Civ Wed 140

Premier Inn Southend Airport

BUDGET HOTEL

tel: 0871 527 9008 (Calls cost 13p per minute plus your phone company's access charge) **Thanet Grange SS2 6GB**
web: www.premierinn.com
dir: *At A127 and B1013 junction.*

High quality, budget accommodation ideal for both families and business travellers. Spacious, en suite bedrooms feature free WiFi and tea and coffee making facilities, and in most hotels, Freeview TV is also available. The adjacent family restaurant features a wide and varied menu.

Rooms: 80

Premier Inn Southend on Sea Eastern Esplanade

BUDGET HOTEL

tel: 0871 527 9504 (Calls cost 13p per minute plus your phone company's access charge) **Eastern Esplanade SS99 1YY**
web: www.premierinn.com
dir: *A127 to Southend rail station. At lights, left onto A13 (signed Shoeburyness). At roundabout 3rd exit (signed Seafront). At end of road, left onto Eastern Esplanade (B1016). Hotel on left.*

Rooms: 81

Premier Inn Southend-on-Sea (Thorpe Bay)

BUDGET HOTEL

tel: 0871 527 9006 (Calls cost 13p per minute plus your phone company's access charge) **213 Eastern Esplanade SS1 3AD**
web: www.premierinn.com
dir: *Follow signs for A1159 (A13) Shoebury onto dual carriageway. At roundabout, follow signs for Thorpe Bay and seafront, at seafront turn right. Hotel on right.*

Rooms: 43

Premier Inn South Mimms/Potters Bar

BUDGET HOTEL

tel: 0871 527 8990 (Calls cost 13p per minute plus your phone company's access charge) **Swanland Road EN6 3NH**
web: www.premierinn.com
dir: *M25 junction 23 and A1 take services exit off main roundabout then 1st left and follow hotel signs.*

High quality, budget accommodation ideal for both families and business travellers. Spacious, en suite bedrooms feature free WiFi and tea and coffee making facilities, and in most hotels, Freeview TV is also available. The adjacent family restaurant features a wide and varied menu.

Rooms: 142

Days Inn South Mimms - M25

AA Advertised

tel: 01707 665440 **Bignells Corner, Potters Bar EN6 3QQ**
email: south.mimms.hotel@welcomebreak.co.uk **web:** www.welcomebreak.co.uk
dir: *M25 junction 23, at roundabout follow signs.*

This modern building offers accommodation in smart, spacious and well-equipped bedrooms, suitable for families and business travellers, and all with en suite bathrooms. Continental breakfast is available and other refreshments may be taken at the nearby family restaurant.

Rooms: 75 (37 family) (23 GF) (10 smoking) **Facilities:** FTV WiFi **Services:** Lift Night porter **Parking:** 100

Premier Inn Mansfield

BUDGET HOTEL

tel: 0871 527 8758 (Calls cost 13p per minute plus your phone company's access charge) **Carter Lane East DE55 2EH**
web: www.premierinn.com
dir: *M1 junction 28, A38 signed Mansfield. Entrance 200 yards on left.*

Rooms: 138

Vincent Hotel

★★★★ 82% TOWN HOUSE HOTEL

tel: 01704 883800 **98 Lord Street PR8 1JR**
email: manager@thevincenthotel.com **web:** www.thevincenthotel.com
dir: *M58 junction 3, follow signs to Ormskirk and Southport.*

This stylish and popular hotel sits most conveniently in the centre of town and is adjacent to many attractions and boutique shops. The rooms come in a range of sizes and many have excellent views. There is a choice of dining options including Asian as well as contemporary choices. The staff are friendly and attentive; valet parking is also available.

Rooms: 59 (2 family) **Facilities:** Spa STV FTV WiFi Gym **Conf:** Class 90 Board 74 Theatre 180 **Services:** Lift Night porter Air con **Parking:** 50 **Notes:** Civ Wed 130

S

SOUTHPORT *continued*

Best Western Royal Clifton Hotel & Spa

★★★ 73% HOTEL

tel: 01704 533771 **Promenade PR8 1RB**
email: sales@royalclifton.co.uk web: www.royalclifton.co.uk
dir: *Adjacent to Marine Lake.*

This grand, traditional hotel benefits from a prime location on the promenade. Bedrooms range in size and style, but all are comfortable and thoughtfully equipped. Public areas include a choice of dining venues; the lively Conservatory Bistro or the Pavilion Restaurant. A modern, well-equipped leisure club is also available. Extensive conference and banqueting facilities make this hotel a popular function venue.

Rooms: 120 (23 family) (6 GF) ✆ **S** fr £45 **D** fr £65* **Facilities:** Spa FTV WiFi ⬇ HL ⊗ Gym Beauty treatments Sauna Steam room Aromatherapy ♫ Xmas New Year **Conf:** Class 100 Board 65 Theatre 250 **Services:** Lift Night porter **Parking:** 60 **Notes:** Civ Wed 150

Premier Inn Southport Central

BUDGET HOTEL

tel: 0871 527 9012 (Calls cost 13p per minute plus your phone company's access charge) **Marine Drive PR8 1RY**
web: www.premierinn.com
dir: *From Southport follow Promenade and Marine Drive signs. Hotel at junction of Marine Parade and Marine Drive.*

Rooms: 94

| SOUTHSEA |
See **Portsmouth & Southsea**

| SOUTH SHIELDS | Map 21 NZ36 |
Tyne & Wear

Best Western The Sea Hotel

★★★ 76% HOTEL

tel: 0191 427 0999 **Sea Road NE33 2LD**
email: info@seahotel.co.uk web: www.seahotel.co.uk
dir: *A1(M), past Washington Services onto A194. Then A183 through town centre along Ocean Road. Hotel on seafront.*

Dating from the 1930s, this long-established business hotel overlooks the boating lake and the Tyne estuary. Bedrooms are generally spacious and well equipped and include five annexe rooms with wheelchair access. A range of generously portioned meals is served in both the bar and restaurant.

Rooms: 37 (5 annexe) (5 family) (5 GF) ✆ **S** fr £49 **D** fr £65 (including breakfast)* **Facilities:** FTV WiFi ⬇ New Year **Conf:** Class 100 Board 50 Theatre 200 **Services:** Night porter **Parking:** 70

Premier Inn South Shields (Port of Tyne)

Premier Inn

BUDGET HOTEL

tel: 0871 527 8992 (Calls cost 13p per minute plus your phone company's access charge) **Hobson Avenue, Newcastle Road NE34 9PQ**
web: www.premierinn.com
dir: *A1(M) onto A194(M). 2nd exit at roundabout into Leam Lane (A194). At next roundabout 2nd exit, next roundabout 3rd exit, next roundabout 2nd exit (A194), next roundabout 2nd exit. Hotel on left adjacent to Taybarns.*

Rooms: 66

| SOUTHWOLD | Map 13 TM57 |
Suffolk

The Swan

[U]

tel: 01502 722186 **Market Place IP18 6EG**
email: theswan@adnams.co.uk

Currently the rating for this establishment is not confirmed. This may be due to a change of ownership or because ot has only recently joined the AA rating scheme.

Rooms: 42

| SPALDING | Map 12 TF22 |
Lincolnshire

Woodlands Hotel

★★★ 78% SMALL HOTEL

tel: 01775 769933 **80 Pinchbeck Road PE11 1QF**
email: reservations@woodlandshotelspalding.com
web: www.woodlandshotelspalding.com
dir: *10 minutes walk from city centre.*

A delightful Victorian house ideally situated just a short walk from the town centre. The public areas have many original features; they include the Oakleaf dining room, the Silver Birch meeting room and the Willows bar. The smartly decorated bedrooms have lovely co-ordinated soft furnishings and many thoughtful touches.

Rooms: 17 (5 GF) ✆ **Facilities:** FTV WiFi ⬇ HL **Conf:** Class 30 Board 30 Theatre 60 **Parking:** 30 **Notes:** Civ Wed 65

| SPENNYMOOR | Map 19 NZ23 |
County Durham

Best Western Whitworth Hall Hotel

★★★ 81% HOTEL

tel: 01388 811772 **Whitworth Hall Country Park DL16 7QX**
email: enquiries@whitworthhall.co.uk web: www.whitworthhall.co.uk
dir: *A688 to Spennymoor, then Bishop Auckland. At roundabout right to Middlestone Moor. Left at lights, hotel on right.*

This hotel, peacefully situated in its own grounds in the centre of the deer park, offers comfortable accommodation. Spacious bedrooms, some with excellent views, have stylish and elegant decor. Public areas include a choice of restaurants and bars, a bright conservatory and well-equipped function and conference rooms.

Rooms: 29 (2 family) (17 GF) ✆ **S** fr £75 **D** fr £80 (including breakfast)* **Facilities:** FTV WiFi ⬇ Fishing **Conf:** Class 40 Board 30 Theatre 100 **Services:** Night porter **Parking:** 100 **Notes:** LB Civ Wed 100

STAFFORD
Staffordshire   Map 10 SJ92

The Moat House
★★★★ 80% @@ HOTEL

tel: 01785 712217 **Lower Penkridge Road, Acton Trussell ST17 0RJ**
email: info@moathouse.co.uk **web:** www.moathouse.co.uk
dir: *M6 junction 13 onto A449 through Acton Trussell. Hotel on right on exiting village.*

This 17th-century timbered building, with an idyllic canal-side setting, has been skilfully extended. Bedrooms are stylishly furnished, well equipped and comfortable. The bar offers a range of snacks and the restaurant boasts a popular fine dining option where the head chef displays his skills using top quality produce.

Rooms: 41 (4 family) (15 GF) ☎ **S** fr £80 **D** fr £95 (including breakfast)*
Facilities: FTV WiFi New Year **Conf:** Class 60 Board 50 Theatre 200 **Services:** Lift Night porter **Parking:** 200 **Notes:** LB Closed 25 December Civ Wed 150

Best Western Tillington Hall Hotel

★★★ 75% HOTEL

tel: 01785 253531 **Eccleshall Road ST16 1JJ**
email: reservations@tillingtonhall.co.uk **web:** www.tillingtonhall.co.uk
dir: *M6 junction 14, A5013 towards Stafford. Hotel 0.5 mile on left.*

Located close to the M6, this modern hotel is ideal for both business and leisure guests. There is a spacious restaurant, relaxing coffee lounge and smart bar, alongside a range of function rooms for meetings and events, including the Garden Suite. Complimentary WiFi is available.

Rooms: 91 (4 family) (25 GF) ☎ **Facilities:** STV FTV WiFi HL Xmas New Year **Conf:** Class 150 Board 75 Theatre 300 **Services:** Lift Night porter **Parking:** 200 **Notes:** LB Civ Wed 300

Premier Inn Stafford North (Hurricane)
 Premier Inn
BUDGET HOTEL

tel: 0871 527 9030 (Calls cost 13p per minute plus your phone company's access charge) **1 Hurricane Close ST16 1GZ**
web: www.premierinn.com
dir: *M6 junction 14, A34 towards Stafford. Hotel approximately 2 miles northwest of town centre.*

High quality, budget accommodation ideal for both families and business travellers. Spacious, en suite bedrooms feature free WiFi and tea and coffee making facilities, and in most hotels, Freeview TV is also available. The adjacent family restaurant features a wide and varied menu.

Rooms: 102

Premier Inn Stafford North (Spitfire)
Premier Inn
BUDGET HOTEL

tel: 0871 527 9032 (Calls cost 13p per minute plus your phone company's access charge) **1 Spitfire Close ST16 1GX**
web: www.premierinn.com
dir: *M6 junction 14, A34 north. Hotel approximately 1 mile on left.*

Rooms: 87

STAINES-UPON-THAMES
Surrey   Map 6 TQ07

Mercure London Staines Upon Thames
Mercure
HOTELS
★★★ 76% HOTEL

tel: 01784 464433 **Thames Street TW18 4SJ**
email: h6620@accor.com **web:** www.mercure.com
dir: *M25 junction 13. Follow A30/town centre signs (bus station on right). Hotel straight ahead.*

Located on the banks of the River Thames in a bustling town, this hotel is well positioned for both business and leisure travellers. Meals are served in The Riverside Restaurant, and snacks are available in the spacious lounge/bar; weather permitting, the terrace provides a good place for a drink on a summer evening. On-site parking is an additional bonus.

Rooms: 88 (17 family) (31 GF) **Facilities:** STV FTV WiFi Moorings Xmas New Year **Conf:** Class 40 Board 20 Theatre 40 **Services:** Night porter **Parking:** 40

STALLINGBOROUGH
Lincolnshire   Map 17 TA11

Stallingborough Grange Hotel
★★★ 76% @ HOTEL

tel: 01469 561302 **Riby Road DN41 8BU**
email: reception@stallingboroughgrange.co.uk **web:** www.stallingboroughgrange.co.uk
dir: *From A180 take Stallingborough interchange, through village. At roundabout take 2nd exit onto A1173, hotel 1 mile on left.*

Dating back to the 18th century, this independent hotel is not short of character and charm. Bedrooms are furnished with a traditional appeal although modern accessories such as free WiFi are provided. The spacious restaurant offers an interesting choice of meals, alongside the bar area where more relaxed dishes can be enjoyed. Gym facilities are available and ample parking is provided. The location is convenient for ports such as Grimsby, a short distance away.

Rooms: 42 (9 GF) ☎ **S** fr £70 **D** fr £95 (including breakfast)* **Facilities:** STV FTV WiFi ☼ HL Gym Xmas New Year **Conf:** Class 30 Board 28 Theatre 60 **Services:** Night porter **Parking:** 80 **Notes:** Civ Wed 70

S

STAMFORD
Lincolnshire

Map 11 TF00

HIGHLY RECOMMENDED

The George of Stamford

★★★★ 83% ⊛ HOTEL

tel: 01780 750750 **71 St Martins PE9 2LB**
email: reservations@georgehotelofstamford.com
web: www.georgehotelofstamford.com
dir: *A1, 15 miles north of Peterborough onto B1081, hotel 1 mile on left.*

Steeped in hundreds of years of history, this delightful coaching inn provides spacious public areas that include a choice of dining options, inviting lounges, and a business centre. A highlight is afternoon tea, taken in the colourful courtyard when the weather permits. Bedrooms are stylishly appointed and range from traditional to contemporary in design.

Rooms: 45 ☎ **S** fr £130 **D** fr £215 (including breakfast)* **Facilities:** STV FTV WiFi ⌕ 🏊 Complimentary membership to local gym Xmas New Year **Conf:** Class 18 Board 27 Theatre 50 **Services:** Night porter **Parking:** 110 **Notes:** LB Civ Wed 50

The William Cecil

★★★★ 81% ⊛⊛ HOTEL

Hillbrooke
QUIRKYLUXURY

tel: 01780 750070 **High Street, St Martins PE9 2LJ**
email: enquiries@thewilliamcecil.co.uk **web:** www.thewilliamcecil.co.uk
dir: *Exit A1 signed Stamford and Burghley Park. Hotel 1st building on right on entering town.*

This lovely property is situated on the edge of town within the Burghley Estate. The stylish bedrooms are spacious, individually decorated and have lots of extra little touches. The public rooms include a lounge bar with plush seating and a panelled restaurant. A smart terrace is available for alfresco dining when the weather permits.

Rooms: 27 (2 family) (5 GF) ☎ **Facilities:** FTV WiFi ⌕ Xmas New Year **Conf:** Class 60 Board 40 Theatre 120 **Services:** Night porter **Parking:** 60 **Notes:** Civ Wed 120

Crown Hotel

★★★ 85% HOTEL

tel: 01780 763136 **All Saints Place PE9 2AG**
email: reservations@thecrownhotelstamford.co.uk
web: www.kneadpubs.co.uk/our-pubs/the-crown-hotel
dir: *A1 onto A43, through town to Red Lion Square, hotel behind All Saints Church.*

This small, privately owned hotel where hospitality is spontaneous and sincere, is ideally situated in the town centre. Unpretentious British food is served in the modern dining areas and the spacious bar is popular with locals. Bedrooms, appointed to a very high standard, are quite contemporary in style and very well equipped; some have four-poster beds. Additional 'superior' rooms are located in a renovated Georgian town house just a short walk up the street.

Rooms: 28 (10 annexe) (1 family) (1 GF) ☎ **S** fr £110 **D** fr £120 (including breakfast)* **Facilities:** FTV WiFi ⌕ Xmas New Year **Conf:** Class 12 Board 12 Theatre 20 **Services:** Night porter **Parking:** 21

STANDISH
Greater Manchester

Map 15 SD51

Premier Inn Wigan North (M6 Jct 27)

BUDGET HOTEL

Premier Inn

tel: 0871 527 9166 (Calls cost 13p per minute plus your phone company's access charge) **Almond Brook Road WN6 0SS**
web: www.premierinn.com
dir: *M6 junction 27 follow signs for Standish. Left at T-junction, then 1st right.*

High quality, budget accommodation ideal for both families and business travellers. Spacious, en suite bedrooms feature free WiFi and tea and coffee making facilities, and in most hotels, Freeview TV is also available. The adjacent family restaurant features a wide and varied menu.

Rooms: 36

STANSTED AIRPORT
Essex

Map 6 TL52

See also **Birchanger Green Motorway Service Area (M11)**

Premier Inn Stansted Airport

BUDGET HOTEL

Premier Inn

tel: 0871 527 9352 (Calls cost 13p per minute plus your phone company's access charge) **Thremhall Avenue, CM24 1PY**
web: www.premierinn.com
dir: *M11 junction 8/8a, follow signs Stansted Airport Terminal. Main roundabout 3rd exit follow signs mid-stay car park. Adjacent BP Petrol Station.*

Rooms: 303

STEVENAGE
Hertfordshire — Map 12 TL22

Novotel Stevenage

★★★★ 76% HOTEL

tel: 01438 346100 & 346250 **Knebworth Park SG1 2AX**
email: reception@novotel-stevenage.com **web:** www.novotel.com
dir: *A1(M) junction 7, at entrance to Knebworth Park.*

Ideally situated just off the A1(M) is this purpose-built hotel, which is a popular business and conference venue. Bedrooms are pleasantly decorated and equipped with a good range of useful extras. Public rooms include a large open-plan lounge bar serving a range of snacks, and a smartly appointed restaurant.

Rooms: 102 (20 family) (30 GF) S fr £69 D fr £69* **Facilities:** STV FTV WiFi Use of local health club Xmas New Year **Conf:** Class 80 Board 70 Theatre 150 **Services:** Lift Night porter Air con **Parking:** 120 **Notes:** Civ Wed 120

Holiday Inn Stevenage

★★★★ 75% HOTEL

tel: 01438 722727 **St George's Way SG1 1HS**
email: reservations@histevenage.com **web:** www.histevenage.com
dir: *A1(M) junction 7 take A602 to Stevenage, across 1st roundabout, 1st exit at 2nd roundabout, 2nd exit at next roundabout along St George's Way. Hotel 100 yards on right.*

Holiday Inn Stevenage is situated in the heart of the town centre and just 25 minutes from central London by train. Bedrooms are air-conditioned and well equipped; ideal for business and leisure. Public areas are smart, capacious and stylish, and as well as a comfortable bar and restaurant, there is a mini gym. Parking is limited.

Rooms: 140 (8 family) **Facilities:** STV FTV WiFi HL Gym Xmas New Year **Conf:** Class 200 Board 200 Theatre 400 **Services:** Lift Night porter Air con **Parking:** 23 **Notes:** Civ Wed 400

Premier Inn Stevenage

BUDGET HOTEL

tel: 0871 527 9036 (Calls cost 13p per minute plus your phone company's access charge) **Corey's Mill Lane SG1 4AA**
web: www.premierinn.com
dir: *A1(M) junction 8, at intersection with A602 – Hitchin Road and Corey's Mill Lane.*

High quality, budget accommodation ideal for both families and business travellers. Spacious, en suite bedrooms feature free WiFi and tea and coffee making facilities, and in most hotels, Freeview TV is also available. The adjacent family restaurant features a wide and varied menu.

Rooms: 56

Premier Inn Stevenage Central

BUDGET HOTEL

tel: 0871 527 9034 (Calls cost 13p per minute plus your phone company's access charge) **Six Hills Way, Horizon Technology Park SG1 2DD**
web: www.premierinn.com
dir: *A1(M) junction 7, follow Stevenage signs. Left into Gunnels Wood Road. (Note: do not use underpass). Left at next roundabout. Hotel in Horizon Technology Park on left.*

Rooms: 115

STEYNING
West Sussex — Map 6 TQ11

Best Western Plus Old Tollgate Hotel & Restaurant

★★★ 78% HOTEL

tel: 01903 879494 **The Street, Bramber BN44 3WE**
email: info@oldtollgatehotel.com **web:** www.oldtollgatehotel.com
dir: *From A283 at Steyning roundabout to Bramber. Hotel 200 yards on right.*

As part of its name suggests, this well-presented hotel is built on the site of the old toll house. The spacious bedrooms are smartly designed and are furnished to a high standard; eight rooms are air-conditioned and have power showers. Open for both lunch and dinner, the popular carvery-style restaurant offers an extensive choice of dishes.

Rooms: 38 (28 annexe) (5 family) (14 GF) D fr £65 (including breakfast)* **Facilities:** STV WiFi HL New Year **Conf:** Class 32 Board 24 Theatre 50 **Services:** Lift Night porter **Parking:** 60 **Notes:** LB Civ Wed 70

STILTON
Cambridgeshire — Map 12 TL18

Bell Inn Hotel
★★★ 85% ◉◉ HOTEL

tel: 01733 241066 **Great North Road PE7 3RA**
email: reception@thebellstilton.co.uk **web:** www.thebellstilton.co.uk
dir: *A1(M) junction 16, follow Stilton signs. Hotel in village centre.*

This delightful inn is steeped in history and retains many original features, with imaginative food served in both the character village bar/brasserie and the elegant beamed first-floor restaurant; refreshments can be enjoyed in the attractive courtyard and rear gardens when weather permits. Individually designed bedrooms are stylish and equipped to a high standard.

Rooms: 22 (3 annexe) (1 family) (3 GF) S fr £89.50 D fr £115 (including breakfast)* **Facilities:** STV FTV WiFi **Conf:** Class 46 Board 50 Theatre 130 **Services:** Night porter **Parking:** 30 **Notes:** Closed 25 December (pm) RS 26 December (pm), 1 January (pm) Civ Wed 130

S

STOCK
Essex

Map 6 TQ69

Greenwoods Hotel & Spa
★★★★ 79% @ HOTEL

tel: 01277 829990 **Stock Road CM4 9BE**
email: info@greenwoodshotel.co.uk **web:** www.greenwoodshotel.co.uk
dir: A12 junction 16 take B1007 signed Billericay. Hotel on right on entering village.

Greenwoods is a beautiful 17th-century, Grade II listed manor house set in extensive landscaped gardens. All bedrooms are tastefully appointed, with marble bathrooms and a wide range of extras; the premier rooms have spa baths and antique beds. The spa facilities are impressive offering the latest beauty treatments, together with saunas, a jacuzzi, steam rooms and a 20-metre pool.

Rooms: 39 (6 GF) ✆ **S** Pr £135 **D** fr £200* **Facilities:** Spa STV FTV WiFi ⬦ ⬢ Gym Steam room Sauna Monsoon shower Relaxation suite New Year **Conf:** Class 150 Board 110 Theatre 200 **Services:** Lift Night porter **Parking:** 100 **Notes:** LB No children 16 years Closed 26 December, 1 January Civ Wed 250

STOCKPORT
Greater Manchester

Map 16 SJ89

See also **Manchester Airport**

The Wycliffe Hotel
★★★ 79% HOTEL

tel: 0161 477 5395 **74 Edgeley Road, Edgeley SK3 9NQ**
email: reception@wycliffe-hotel.com **web:** www.wycliffe-hotel.com
dir: M60 junction 2, follow A560 Stockport signs, right at 1st lights, hotel 0.5 mile on left.

The Wycliffe is a family-run hotel close to the town centre and convenient for Manchester Airport. The contemporary bedrooms are very well maintained and equipped, with king-size beds and LCD TVs. Complimentary WiFi is provided throughout the hotel. There is a well-stocked bar and a popular restaurant where the menu has an Italian slant. There is also a large car park.

Rooms: 14 (3 family) (2 GF) **S** fr £75 **D** fr £95.50 (including breakfast)*
Facilities: FTV WiFi **Conf:** Class 20 Board 20 Theatre 30 **Services:** Night porter **Parking:** 46 **Notes:** Closed 25–27 December RS Bank holidays

---

Alma Lodge Hotel
★★★ 75% HOTEL

tel: 0161 483 4431 **149 Buxton Road SK2 6EL**
email: reception@almalodgehotel.com **web:** www.almalodgehotel.com
dir: M60 junction 1 at roundabout take 2nd exit under rail viaduct at lights opposite. At Debenhams turn right onto A6. Hotel approximately 1.5 miles on left.

Alma Lodge is a large hotel located on the main road close to the town, offering modern and well-equipped bedrooms. It is family-owned and run and serves a good range of quality Italian cooking in Luigi's Restaurant. Good function rooms and free internet access are also available.

Rooms: 52 (32 annexe) (2 family) **S** fr £60 **D** fr £65 (including breakfast)*
Facilities: FTV WiFi **Conf:** Class 100 Board 60 Theatre 250 **Services:** Night porter **Parking:** 120 **Notes:** Civ Wed 200

Premier Inn Manchester Airport Heald Green

Premier Inn

BUDGET HOTEL

tel: 0871 527 8734 (Calls cost 13p per minute plus your phone company's access charge) **Finney Lane, Heald Green SK8 3QH**
web: www.premierinn.com
dir: *M56 junction 5 follow signs to Terminal 1, at roundabout take 2nd exit, at next roundabout follow Cheadle signs. Left at lights, right at next lights.*

High quality, budget accommodation ideal for both families and business travellers. Spacious, en suite bedrooms feature free WiFi and tea and coffee making facilities, and in most hotels, Freeview TV is also available. The adjacent family restaurant features a wide and varied menu.

Rooms: 87

Premier Inn Stockport Central

Premier Inn

BUDGET HOTEL

tel: 0871 527 9040 (Calls cost 13p per minute plus your phone company's access charge) **Churchgate SK1 1YG**
web: www.premierinn.com
dir: *M60 junction 27, A626 towards Marple. Right at Spring Gardens.*

Rooms: 46

Premier Inn Stockport South

Premier Inn

BUDGET HOTEL

tel: 0871 527 9042 (Calls cost 13p per minute plus your phone company's access charge) **Buxton Road, Heaviley SK2 6NB**
web: www.premierinn.com
dir: *On A6, 1.5 miles from town centre.*

Rooms: 66

STOCKTON-ON-TEES	Map 19 NZ41
County Durham	

Premier Inn Stockton-on-Tees/Hartlepool

Premier Inn

BUDGET HOTEL

tel: 0871 527 9044 (Calls cost 13p per minute plus your phone company's access charge) **Coal Lane, Wolviston TS22 5PZ**
web: www.premierinn.com
dir: *A1(M) junction 60, A689, follow Teeside then Hartlepool signs. Hotel on left at A89 and A19 junction.*

Rooms: 98

Premier Inn Stockton-on-Tees/Middlesbrough

Premier Inn

BUDGET HOTEL

tel: 0871 527 9048 (Calls cost 13p per minute plus your phone company's access charge) **Whitewater Way, Thornaby TS17 6QB**
web: www.premierinn.com
dir: *A19, A66 towards Stockton and Darlington. Take 1st exit signed Teeside Park/Teesdale. Right at lights over viaduct bridge roundabout and Tees Barrage.*

Rooms: 110

Premier Inn Stockton-on-Tees West

Premier Inn

BUDGET HOTEL

tel: 0871 527 9046 (Calls cost 13p per minute plus your phone company's access charge) **Yarm Road TS18 3RT**
web: www.premierinn.com
dir: *A1(M) junction 60, A689 towards Teeside. Follow Hartlepool signs. Hotel on left at A689 and A19 interchange.*

High quality, budget accommodation ideal for both families and business travellers. Spacious, en suite bedrooms feature free WiFi and tea and coffee making facilities, and in most hotels, Freeview TV is also available. The adjacent family restaurant features a wide and varied menu.

Rooms: 87

STOKE-BY-NAYLAND	Map 13 TL93
Suffolk	

HIGHLY RECOMMENDED

The Crown

★★★ 88% SMALL HOTEL

tel: 01206 262001 **CO6 4SE**
email: info@crowninn.net **web:** www.crowninn.net
dir: *Follow Stoke-by-Nayland signs from A12 and A134. Hotel in village off B1068 towards Higham.*

Situated in a picturesque village, The Crown, with an award-winning restaurant, has a reputation for making everyone feel welcome. It offers quiet, individually decorated rooms that look out over the countryside. Ground floor rooms, including three with a terrace, are of a contemporary design while upstairs rooms are in a country-house style; each room has WiFi, DVDs and luxury toiletries.

Rooms: 11 (1 family) (8 GF) ✆ S fr £110 **D** fr £145 (including breakfast)
Facilities: STV FTV WiFi ↳ New Year **Conf:** Board 12 **Services:** Night porter
Parking: 49 **Notes:** Closed 25–26 December

STOKE D'ABERNON	Map 6 TQ15
Surrey	

Woodlands Park Hotel

Hand PICKED HOTELS

★★★★ 81% HOTEL

tel: 01372 843933 & 0845 072 7581 (Calls cost 5p per minute plus your phone company's access charge) **Woodlands Lane KT11 3QB**
email: woodlandspark@handpicked.co.uk
web: www.handpickedhotels.co.uk/woodlandspark
dir: *A3 exit at Cobham. Through town centre and Stoke D'Abernon, left at garden centre into Woodlands Lane, hotel 0.5 mile on right.*

Originally built for the Bryant family, of the matchmaking firm Bryant & May, this lovely Victorian mansion enjoys an attractive parkland setting in ten and a half acres of Surrey countryside. Bedrooms in the wing are contemporary in style while those in the main house are more traditionally decorated. The hotel boasts two dining options, Benson's Brasserie and the Oak Room Restaurant.

Rooms: 57 (4 family) ✆ S fr £99 **D** fr £125 (including breakfast)* **Facilities:** FTV WiFi ↳ HL ☺ ☺ Gym Xmas New Year **Conf:** Class 100 Board 60 Theatre 200 **Services:** Lift Night porter Air con **Parking:** 150 **Notes:** LB Civ Wed 200

S

STOKE-ON-TRENT
Staffordshire

Map 10 SJ84

Best Western Plus Stoke-on-Trent Moat House

 Best Western PLUS

★★★★ 72% HOTEL

tel: 01782 609988 **Etruria Hall, Festival Way ST1 5BQ**
email: info@bwstoke.co.uk **web:** www.bw-stokeontrentmoathouse.co.uk
dir: *M6 junction 15 (or junction 16), A500, follow A53 and Festival Park signs. Keep in left lane, take 1st slip road on left. Left at island, hotel opposite at next island.*

This large, modern hotel is located in Stoke's Festival Park which adjoins Etruria Hall, the former home of Josiah Wedgwood. Bedrooms are spacious and well equipped and include family rooms, suites and executive rooms. Public areas include a spacious lounge bar and restaurant as well as a business centre, extensive conference facilities and a leisure club.

Rooms: 147 **S** fr £59 **D** fr £59* **Facilities:** Spa FTV WiFi Gym **Conf:** Class 400 Board 40 Theatre 650 **Services:** Lift Night porter Air con **Parking:** 250
Notes: Civ Wed 400

Premier Inn Stoke-on-Trent (Hanley)

 Premier Inn

BUDGET HOTEL

tel: 0871 527 9476 (Calls cost 13p per minute plus your phone company's access charge) **Etruria Road, Hanley ST1 5NH**
web: www.premierinn.com
dir: *M6 junction 15, A500. 4.3 miles, take 5th slip road for A53 (City Centre, Hanley). At roundabout take 4th exit signed Etruria and A53. Keep in left lane until passing flyover entrance. At roundabout take 3rd exit, hotel on right.*

High quality, budget accommodation ideal for both families and business travellers. Spacious, en suite bedrooms feature free WiFi and tea and coffee making facilities, and in most hotels, Freeview TV is also available. The adjacent family restaurant features a wide and varied menu.

Rooms: 96

Premier Inn Stoke/Trentham Gardens

 Premier Inn

BUDGET HOTEL

tel: 0871 527 9050 (Calls cost 13p per minute plus your phone company's access charge) **Stone Road, Trentham ST4 8JG**
web: www.premierinn.com
dir: *M6 junction 15, A500, follow Trentham signs. At roundabout 3rd exit onto A34, 2 miles to hotel on right in Trentham Gardens.*

Rooms: 119

STOKE POGES
Buckinghamshire

Map 6 SU98

INSPECTOR'S CHOICE

Stoke Park

★★★★★ HOTEL

tel: 01753 717171 **Park Road SL2 4PG**
email: info@stokepark.com **web:** www.stokepark.com
dir: *M4 junction 6, A355 towards Slough, B416 Park Road. Hotel 1.25 miles on right.*

Located within 300 acres of beautiful parkland created by 'Capability' Brown and Humphry Repton, this hotel offers outstanding leisure and sporting facilities. Inside the stunning mansion house, designed by George III's architect, the public areas display lavish opulence throughout and the bedrooms have a luxurious and classic feel. In contrast, the Pavilion features more contemporary bedrooms and public areas; as well as extensive state-of-the-art health and beauty facilities. The hotel has a championship golf course, tennis courts, and three restaurants, including the award-winning Humphry's and the more informal Italian brasserie, San Marco. There are bars, lounges and meeting rooms as well.

Rooms: 49 (28 annexe) (6 family) **Facilities:** Spa STV FTV WiFi 27 Fishing Gym Indoor golf Games room Nail bar Spa Boutique Garden lounge Sauna Steam rooms Yoga Indoor tennis New Year **Conf:** Class 30 Board 34 Theatre 80 **Services:** Lift Night porter **Parking:** 460 **Notes:** LB Closed 24–26 December Civ Wed 146

STON EASTON
Somerset
Map 4 ST65

Ston Easton Park Hotel

★★★★ @@ COUNTRY HOUSE HOTEL

tel: 01761 241631 **BA3 4DF**
email: reception@stoneaston.co.uk **web:** www.stoneaston.co.uk
dir: *On A37.*

Surrounded by The Mendips, this outstanding Palladian mansion lies in extensive parklands that were landscaped by Humphrey Repton. The architecture and decorative features are stunning. The state rooms include one of England's earliest surviving Print Rooms, and the Palladian Saloon is considered one of Somerset's finest rooms. There is even an Edwardian kitchen that guests might like to take a look at. The helpful and attentive team provide a very efficient service, and the award-winning cuisine uses organic produce from the hotel's own kitchen garden. The bedrooms and bathrooms are all appointed to an excellent standard.

Rooms: 23 (3 annexe) (2 family) (1 GF) **Facilities:** FTV WiFi ▷ ⓢ ⚐ Archery clay pigeon shooting Quad bikes Hot air ballooning Xmas New Year **Conf:** Class 60 Board 30 Theatre 100 **Services:** Night porter **Parking:** 120 **Notes:** Civ Wed 120

STOURBRIDGE
West Midlands
Map 10 SO88

Premier Inn Stourbridge Town Centre

Premier Inn

BUDGET HOTEL

tel: 0871 527 9482 (Calls cost 13p per minute plus your phone company's access charge) **Birmingham Street DY8 1JR**
web: www.premierinn.com
dir: *On A458.*

High quality, budget accommodation ideal for both families and business travellers. Spacious, en suite bedrooms feature free WiFi and tea and coffee making facilities, and in most hotels, Freeview TV is also available. The adjacent family restaurant features a wide and varied menu.

Rooms: 80

STOURPORT-ON-SEVERN
Worcestershire
Map 10 SO87

Hallmark Hotel Stourport Manor

★★★★ 76% HOTEL

tel: 0330 028 3421 **35 Hartlebury Road DY13 9JA**
email: stourport@hallmarkhotels.co.uk **web:** www.hallmarkhotels.co.uk
dir: *M5 junction 6, A449 towards Kidderminster, B4193 towards Stourport. Hotel on right.*

Once the home of Prime Minister Sir Stanley Baldwin, this much extended country house is set in attractive grounds. A number of bedrooms and suites are located in the original building, although the majority are in a more modern, purpose-built section. Spacious public areas include a range of lounges, a popular restaurant, a leisure club and conference facilities.

Rooms: 72 (33 family) (31 GF) **Facilities:** FTV WiFi ▷ ⓢ ⚐ Gym Squash Xmas New Year **Conf:** Class 110 Board 100 Theatre 400 **Services:** Night porter **Parking:** 300 **Notes:** Civ Wed 300

STOWMARKET
Suffolk
Map 13 TM05

Cedars Hotel

BW **Best Western**

★★★ 73% HOTEL

tel: 01449 612668 **Needham Road IP14 2AJ**
email: info@cedarshotel.co.uk **web:** www.cameronventuresgroup.co.uk/cedars-home
dir: *A14 junction 50 onto A1120 towards Stowmarket. Right at end onto A1308, come back on oneself at roundabout, hotel car park on left. From Stowmarket/Station take Glipping Way towards Needham Market, take 2nd exit at roundabout. Car park on left.*

This 16th-century farmhouse is situated a short drive from Stowmarket and close to the major road networks; the property has a bar/lounge with a wealth of character that includes oak beams and an open fire place, as well as a separate restaurant. Over the years the property has been extended; all rooms are well equipped with modern facilities.

Rooms: 23 (3 family) (10 GF) **S** fr £50 **D** fr £55 (including breakfast)*
Facilities: FTV WiFi HL Xmas New Year **Conf:** Class 50 Board 30 Theatre 100 **Parking:** 75

STOW-ON-THE-WOLD
Gloucestershire
Map 10 SP12

Wyck Hill House Hotel & Spa

★★★★ 75% @@ HOTEL

tel: 01451 831936 **Burford Road GL54 1HY**
email: info@wyckhillhousehotel.co.uk **web:** www.wyckhillhousehotel.co.uk
dir: *Exit A429. Hotel 1 mile on right.*

This charming 18th-century house enjoys superb views across the Windrush Valley and is ideally positioned for a relaxing weekend exploring the Cotswolds. The spacious and thoughtfully equipped bedrooms provide high standards of comfort and quality, located both in the main house and also the original coach house. Elegant public rooms include a cosy bar, library, and the magnificent front hall with crackling log fire. The imaginative cuisine makes extensive use of local produce.

Rooms: 60 (22 annexe) (4 GF) **S** fr £85 **D** fr £115 (including breakfast)*
Facilities: Spa FTV WiFi Sauna Steam room 6 treatment rooms Xmas New Year **Conf:** Class 50 Board 50 Theatre 150 **Services:** Lift Night porter **Parking:** 100 **Notes:** LB Civ Wed 120

S

STOW-ON-THE-WOLD *continued*

Number Four at Stow

★★★ 82% HOTEL

tel: 01451 830297 **Fosse Way GL54 1JX**
email: office@hotelnumberfour.co.uk **web:** www.hotelnumberfour.co.uk
dir: *Phone for directions.*

Situated on the edge of the picturesque Cotswold town on Stow-on-the-Wold, Number 4 at Stow is only a one or two minute drive from its heart. It is also very well placed for visiting the other nearby 'chocolate box' villages in the area. All of the well-appointed bedrooms benefit from air-conditioning, with some larger family rooms also available. The split-level restaurant complete with wood burning stove serves freshly prepared dishes using locally sourced produce wherever possible. Secure overnight parking and WiFi are provided.

Rooms: 18 (1 family) (12 GF) **S** fr £110 **D** fr £120 (including breakfast)
Facilities: FTV WiFi ⌁ Xmas New Year **Conf:** Class 30 Board 16 Theatre 30
Parking: 40

Stow Lodge Hotel

★★★ 78% SMALL HOTEL

tel: 01451 830485 **The Square GL54 1AB**
email: enquiries@stowlodge.co.uk **web:** www.stowlodge.co.uk
dir: *In town centre.*

Situated in smart grounds, this family-run hotel has direct access to the market square and provides high standards of customer care. Bedrooms are offered both within the main building and in the converted coach house – all provide similar standards of homely comfort. Extensive menus and an interesting wine list make for an enjoyable dining experience.

Rooms: 21 (10 annexe) (1 family) ☏ **Facilities:** WiFi **Services:** Night porter
Parking: 30 **Notes:** No children 5 years Closed Christmas to January

STRATFORD-UPON-AVON	Map 10 SP25
Warwickshire	

INSPECTOR'S CHOICE

Ettington Park Hotel

*Hand*PICKED
HOTELS

★★★★ ◉◉ COUNTRY HOUSE HOTEL

tel: 01789 450123 & 0845 072 7454 (Calls cost 5p per minute plus your phone company's access charge) **CV37 8BU**
email: enquiries.ettington@handpicked.co.uk
web: www.handpickedhotels.co.uk/ettingtonpark

(for full entry see Alderminster)

HIGHLY RECOMMENDED

The Arden Hotel

★★★★ 84% ◉◉ HOTEL

tel: 01789 298682 **Waterside CV37 6BA**
email: enquiries@theardenhotelstratford.com
web: www.theardenhotelstratford.com
dir: *M40 junction 15 follow signs to town centre. At Barclays Bank roundabout left onto High Street, 2nd left onto Chapel Lane (Nash's House on left). Hotel car park on right in 40 yards.*

This property is on the same road as the world famous Royal Shakespeare and Swan theatres, and just a short walk from the town centre. The bedrooms and bathrooms have been tastefully designed and have quality fixtures and fittings. The dedicated team provide polite and professional service. Award-winning cuisine is served in the popular restaurant. Ample secure parking is available.

Rooms: 45 (6 family) (1 GF) ☏ **S** fr £132.50 **D** fr £165 (including breakfast)*
Facilities: FTV WiFi Xmas New Year **Conf:** Class 18 Board 28 Theatre 40
Services: Night porter Air con **Parking:** 50 **Notes:** Civ Wed 90

HIGHLY RECOMMENDED

Hallmark Hotel The Welcombe

★★★★ 83% ◉ HOTEL

tel: 0330 028 3422 **Warwick Road CV37 0NR**
email: welcombe@hallmarkhotels.co.uk **web:** www.hallmarkhotels.co.uk
dir: *M40 junction 15, A46 towards Stratford-upon-Avon, at roundabout follow signs for A439. Hotel 3 miles on right.*

This Jacobean manor house is set in 157 acres of landscaped parkland. Public rooms are impressive, especially the lounge with its wood panelling and ornate marble fireplace, and the gentleman's club-style bar. Bedrooms in the original building are stylish and gracefully proportioned; those in the garden wing are comfortable and thoughtfully equipped. The spa development incorporates advanced, luxurious facilities and treatments.

Rooms: 85 (12 family) (11 GF) ☏ **Facilities:** Spa STV FTV WiFi ⌁ ☞ ⚓ ⛳ 18 ⛳ Gym Xmas New Year **Conf:** Class 65 Board 40 Theatre 200 **Services:** Night porter
Parking: 200 **Notes:** Civ Wed 120

Stratford Manor

QHOTELS
INSPIRED
BY YOU

★★★★ 83% HOTEL

tel: 01789 731173 **Warwick Road CV37 0PY**
email: stratfordmanor@qhotels.co.uk **web:** www.qhotels.co.uk
dir: *M40 junction 15, A46 signed Stratford. At 2nd roundabout take A439 signed Stratford Town Centre. Hotel 1 mile on left. Or from Stratford centre take A439 signed Warwick and M40. Hotel 3 miles on right.*

Just outside Stratford, this hotel is set against a rural backdrop with lovely gardens and ample parking. Public areas include a stylish lounge bar and a contemporary restaurant. Service is both professional and helpful. Bedrooms are smartly appointed, spacious and have generously sized beds and a range of useful facilities. The leisure centre boasts a large indoor pool.

Rooms: 104 (8 family) (24 GF) ☏ **Facilities:** Spa FTV WiFi ⌁ HL ☞ Gym Sauna Steam room Xmas New Year **Conf:** Class 120 Board 100 Theatre 350 **Services:** Lift Night porter **Parking:** 220 **Notes:** Civ Wed 150

Macdonald Alveston Manor

★★★★ 80% HOTEL

tel: 01789 205478 **Clopton Bridge CV37 7HP**
email: sales.alvestonmanor@macdonald-hotels.co.uk **web:** www.macdonaldhotels.co.uk
dir: *On roundabout, south of Clopton Bridge.*

A striking red-brick and timbered facade, well-tended grounds, and a giant cedar tree all contribute to the charm of this well-established hotel, just five minutes from Stratford. The bedrooms vary in size and character, and the coach house conversion offers an impressive mix of full and junior suites. The superb leisure complex offers a 20-metre swimming pool, steam room, sauna, a high-tech gym and a host of beauty treatments.

Rooms: 113 (8 family) (45 GF) **D** fr £79* **Facilities:** Spa FTV WiFi Gym Technogym Beauty treatments Sauna Steam room Xmas New Year **Conf:** Class 80 Board 40 Theatre 140 **Services:** Night porter Air con **Parking:** 150 **Notes:** LB Civ Wed 110

The Stratford

★★★★ 79% HOTEL

tel: 01789 271000 **Arden Street CV37 6QQ**
email: stratfordsreservations@qhotels.co.uk **web:** www.qhotels.co.uk
dir: *A439 into Stratford. In town follow A3400/Birmingham, at lights left into Arden Street, hotel 150 yards on right.*

Situated adjacent to the hospital, within walking distance of the town centre, The Stratford is an eye-catching, contemporary hotel with a red-brick facade. It offers modern, well-equipped and spacious bedrooms. The open-plan public areas include a comfortable lounge, a small, atmospheric bar and a spacious restaurant with exposed beams.

Rooms: 102 (7 family) (14 GF) **Facilities:** FTV WiFi HL Gym Free use of Stratford Manor's leisure facilities Xmas New Year **Conf:** Class 72 Board 60 Theatre 200 **Services:** Lift Night porter Air con **Parking:** 92 **Notes:** Civ Wed 132

Macdonald Swan's Nest Hotel

★★★★ 76% HOTEL

tel: 01789 266804 **Bridgefoot CV37 7LT**
email: general.swansnest@macdonald-hotels.co.uk **web:** www.macdonald-hotels.co.uk
dir: *A439 towards Stratford, follow one-way system, left over bridge (A3400), hotel on right.*

Dating back to the 17th century, this hotel is said to be one of the earliest brick-built houses in Stratford. It occupies a prime position on the banks of the River Avon and is ideally situated for exploring the town. Bedrooms and bathrooms are appointed to a high standard with some thoughtful guest extras provided.

Rooms: 71 (2 family) (28 GF) **D** fr £107* **Facilities:** FTV WiFi Use of facilities at Macdonald Alveston Manor New Year **Services:** Night porter **Parking:** 80 **Notes:** LB

Mercure Stratford-upon-Avon Shakespeare Hotel

★★★★ 74% HOTEL

tel: 01789 294997 **Chapel Street CV37 6ER**
email: h6630@accor.com **web:** www.mercure.com
dir: *M40 junction 15. Follow signs for Stratford town centre on A439. Follow one-way system into Bridge Street. Left at roundabout, hotel 200 yards on left opposite HSBC bank.*

Dating back to the early 17th century, The Shakespeare is one of the oldest hotels in this historic town. The hotel name represents one of the earliest exploitations of Stratford as the birthplace of one of the world's leading playwrights. With exposed beams and open fires, the public rooms retain an ambience reminiscent of this era. Bedrooms are appointed to a good standard and remain in keeping with the style of the property.

Rooms: 78 (11 annexe) (4 family) (3 GF) **Facilities:** WiFi Xmas New Year **Conf:** Class 45 Board 40 Theatre 90 **Services:** Lift Night porter **Parking:** 31 **Notes:** Civ Wed 100

Premier Inn Stratford-upon-Avon Central

Premier Inn

BUDGET HOTEL

tel: 0871 527 9282 (Calls cost 13p per minute plus your phone company's access charge) **Payton Road CV37 6UQ**
web: www.premierinn.com
dir: *A439, A4300 signed Stratford-upon-Avon. Hotel on left.*

High quality, budget accommodation ideal for both families and business travellers. Spacious, en suite bedrooms feature free WiFi and tea and coffee making facilities, and in most hotels, Freeview TV is also available. The adjacent family restaurant features a wide and varied menu.

Rooms: 87

Premier Inn Stratford-upon-Avon Waterways

Premier Inn

BUDGET HOTEL

tel: 0871 527 9316 (Calls cost 13p per minute plus your phone company's access charge) **The Waterways, Birmingham Road CV37 0AZ**
web: www.premierinn.com
dir: *A3400 (Birmingham Road) towards town centre, pass large retail park on left. Straight over mini-roundabout, approximately 150 yards. Hotel on right.*

Rooms: 130

STREET
Somerset

Map 4 ST43

Wessex Hotel

★★★ 68% HOTEL

tel: 01458 443383 **High Street BA16 0EF**
email: info@wessexhotel.com **web:** www.wessexhotel.com
dir: *From A303, onto B3151 to Somerton. Then 7 miles, pass lights by Millfield School. Left at mini-roundabout.*

The Wessex Hotel is centrally located in this popular town, with easy access to all the shops and attractions. The bedrooms and bathrooms vary slightly in size but all provide good levels of quality and comfort. A wide range of snacks and refreshments is available throughout the day, including a regular carvery at dinner. Entertainment is often offered in the main season.

Rooms: 51 (9 family) **S** fr £60 **D** fr £80 (including breakfast)* **Facilities:** FTV WiFi HL Xmas New Year **Conf:** Class 120 Board 80 Theatre 400 **Services:** Lift Night porter **Parking:** 70

S

STROUD
Gloucestershire

Map 4 SO80

The Bear of Rodborough

★★★ 84% HOTEL

COTSWOLD
INNS & HOTELS

tel: 01453 878522 **Rodborough Common GL5 5DE**
email: info@bearofrodborough.info web: www.cotswold-inns-hotels.co.uk
dir: *M5 junction 13, A419 to Stroud. Follow signs to Rodborough. Up hill, left at top at T-junction. Hotel on right.*

This popular 17th-century coaching inn is situated high above Stroud in acres of National Trust parkland. Character abounds in the lounges and cocktail bar, and in the Box Tree Restaurant where the cuisine utilises fresh local produce. Bedrooms offer equal measures of comfort and style with plenty of extra touches. There is also a traditional and well-patronised public bar.

Rooms: 46 (18 annexe) (2 family) **S** fr £99 **D** fr £120 (including breakfast)*
Facilities: FTV WiFi ⬙ Xmas New Year **Conf:** Class 35 Board 30 Theatre 60
Services: Night porter **Parking:** 70 **Notes:** Civ Wed 90

Burleigh Court Hotel

★★★ 82% HOTEL

tel: 01453 883804 **Burleigh, Minchinhampton GL5 2PF**
email: burleighcourt@aol.com web: www.burleighcourthotel.co.uk
dir: *From Stroud A419 towards Cirencester. Right after 2.5 miles signed Burleigh and Minchinhampton. Left after 500 yards signed Burleigh Court. Hotel 300 yards on right.*

Dating back to the 18th century, this former gentleman's manor house is in a secluded and elevated, though accessible, position with some wonderful countryside views. Public rooms are elegantly styled and include an oak-panelled bar for pre-dinner drinks beside a crackling fire. Combining comfort and quality, no two bedrooms are alike; some are in an adjoining coach house.

Rooms: 18 (7 annexe) (2 family) (3 GF) ⬙ **S** fr £110 **D** fr £175 (including breakfast)*
Facilities: WiFi ⬙ ⬙ New Year **Conf:** Class 30 Board 30 Theatre 50 **Parking:** 40
Notes: LB Closed 24–26 December Civ Wed 50

Premier Inn Stroud

BUDGET HOTEL

Premier Inn

tel: 0871 527 9052 (Calls cost 13p per minute plus your phone company's access charge) **Stratford Lodge, Stratford Road GL5 4AF**
web: www.premierinn.com
dir: *M5 junction 13, A419 to town centre, follow Leisure Centre signs. Hotel adjacent to Tesco superstore.*

High quality, budget accommodation ideal for both families and business travellers. Spacious, en suite bedrooms feature free WiFi and tea and coffee making facilities, and in most hotels, Freeview TV is also available. The adjacent family restaurant features a wide and varied menu.

Rooms: 32

STUDLAND
Dorset

Map 5 SZ08

INSPECTOR'S CHOICE

THE PIG on the Beach

★★★  HOTEL

tel: 01929 450288 **The Manor House, Manor Road BH19 3AU**
email: info@thepigonthebeach.com web: www.thepighotel.com
dir: *A338 from Bournemouth, follow signs to Sandbanks ferry, cross on ferry, then 3 miles to Studland.*

This former summer house set in beautiful grounds has a dramatic coastal location. They rear their own livestock, including pigs and chickens, and there is a walled garden which provides much of the produce for the popular restaurant, an authentic reproduction greenhouse; alfresco eating is possible in the warmer months as there is a wood-fired oven in the grounds. The bedrooms come in an array of shapes and sizes – some are in the main house and some feature rooms are to be found in outbuildings. All are spacious, have high quality fixtures and come with their own larders and Nespresso machines. There are plenty of comfortable lounges where guests can make themselves at home, including a cosy cocktail lounge. Treatments can be taken in the two attractively converted shepherd's huts, and there's The Roundhouse which is ideal for private dining in a peaceful garden setting.

Rooms: 23 (3 annexe) (6 GF) ⬙ **Facilities:** STV FTV WiFi ⬙ Treatment rooms Beach hut Round house Xmas New Year **Services:** Night porter **Parking:** 30

SUDBURY
Suffolk

Map 13 TL84

The Mill Hotel

★★★★ 75% HOTEL

SURYA
Stay • Explore • Discover

tel: 01787 375544 **Walnut Tree Lane CO10 1BD**
email: info@themillhotelsudbury.co.uk web: www.themillhotelsudbury.co.uk
dir: *A12 direction Harwich from London, exit junction 27 onto A134, 2nd exit into A133, roundabout 1st exit onto A134, straight over 7 roundabouts, 2nd exit onto Newton Road, A131, turn right.*

Situated on the banks of the River Stour in the Suffolk countryside, close to the town of Sudbury, The Mill Hotel features an original working water mill which is a main feature in the bar/restaurant. The modern bedrooms are well equipped; many rooms have lovely views of the meadow and surrounding countryside. Public rooms include a lounge bar and a restaurant with an outdoor terrace.

Rooms: 62 (10 annexe) (4 family) (12 GF) ⬙ **S** fr £109 **D** fr £119* **Facilities:** FTV WiFi ⬙ Xmas New Year **Conf:** Class 56 Board 40 Theatre 80 **Services:** Night porter **Parking:** 45 **Notes:** LB

S

SUNBURY-ON-THAMES
Surrey

Premier Inn Sunbury (Kempton Park)

BUDGET HOTEL Plan 1 A1

tel: 0871 527 9054 (Calls cost 13p per minute plus your phone company's access charge) **Staines Road West, Sunbury Cross TW16 7AT**
web: www.premierinn.com
dir: *M25 junction 12, onto M3 signed London and Richmond. Exit at junction 1, take 1st exit at roundabout into Staines Road West (A308). 1st left into Crossways. Hotel on right.*

High quality, budget accommodation ideal for both families and business travellers. Spacious, en suite bedrooms feature free WiFi and tea and coffee making facilities, and in most hotels, Freeview TV is also available. The adjacent family restaurant features a wide and varied menu.

Rooms: 109

SUNDERLAND
Tyne & Wear Map 19 NZ35

Best Western Roker Hotel

★★★★ 77% HOTEL

tel: 0191 567 1786 **Roker Terrace SR6 9ND**
email: reception@rokerhotel.co.uk **web:** www.rokerhotel.co.uk
dir: *Follow A1231 from A9, east to Sunderland, then A1290 to Church Street north. Left onto A183 for 0.9 mile. Hotel is located left, coast to the right.*

This modern hotel offers stunning views of the coastline. Well-equipped bedrooms come in a variety of sizes, several have feature bathrooms. Functions, conferences and weddings are all well catered for with a variety of rooms and spaces available. The late-opening Poetic License Bar serves real ales from a local micro-brewery. The Italian Farmhouse Ristorante also provides lunch and dinner, while Let There Be Crumbs is a wonderful teashop operation overlooking the seafront.

Rooms: 43 (4 family) ♠ S fr £70 **D** fr £90* **Facilities:** FTV WiFi ♦ ♫ Xmas New Year **Conf:** Class 150 Board 100 Theatre 300 **Services:** Lift Night porter **Parking:** 150
Notes: Civ Wed 350

Quality Hotel Boldon

★★★★ 75% HOTEL

tel: 0191 519 1999 **Witney Way, Boldon NE35 9PE**
email: gm@hotels-sunderland.com **web:** www.hotels-sunderland.com
dir: *From Tyne Tunnel (A19), 2.5 miles south take 1st exit to roundabout with A184.*

The Quality Hotel Boldon is a well presented modern hotel located just minutes from the A19, with Newcastle and Sunderland easily accessible. Spacious well-appointed bedrooms cater well for the needs of the modern traveller and the leisure centre is well equipped for any gym enthusiast with a pool, sauna, steam room and jacuzzi. The bar and restaurant both offer informal dining with a wide and varied menu.

Rooms: 83 (4 family) (42 GF) ♠ S fr £70 (including breakfast)* **Facilities:** STV FTV WiFi ♦ ❄ Xmas New Year **Conf:** Class 100 Board 100 Theatre 230 **Services:** Lift Night porter **Notes:** LB Civ Wed 150

Hilton Garden Inn Sunderland

[U]

tel: 01915 009494 **Vaux Brewery Way SR5 1SN**
email: enquiries@hgisunderland.com
web: www.legacy-hotels.co.uk/hotels/hilton-garden-inn-sunderland
dir: *Located just off the A1290 Kier Hardie Way adjacent to the Stadium of Light and the Sunderland Aquatic Centre.*

Currently the rating for this establishment is not confirmed. This may be due to a change of ownership or because ot has only recently joined the AA rating scheme.

Rooms: 141 **Facilities:** WiFi ♦ Gym **Conf:** Class 28 Board 50 Theatre 12 **Services:** Air con

Premier Inn Sunderland A19/A1231

BUDGET HOTEL

tel: 0871 527 9058 (Calls cost 13p per minute plus your phone company's access charge) **Wessington Way, Castletown SR5 3HR**
web: www.premierinn.com
dir: *From A19 take A1231 towards Sunderland. Hotel 100 yards.*

High quality, budget accommodation ideal for both families and business travellers. Spacious, en suite bedrooms feature free WiFi and tea and coffee making facilities, and in most hotels, Freeview TV is also available. The adjacent family restaurant features a wide and varied menu.

Rooms: 91

Premier Inn Sunderland City Centre

BUDGET HOTEL

tel: 0871 527 9482 (Calls cost 13p per minute plus your phone company's access charge) **1-3 Hind Street SR1 3QD**
web: www.premierinn.com
dir: *From south: A1, A23 towards Sunderland. At 1st roundabout, right. Right at 6th roundabout, hotel on right. From north: A1, A6900, A19. Approximately 1 mile, take A1231 towards Sunderland. Right at roundabout. Right at 4th roundabout. Hotel on right.*

Rooms: 125

Premier Inn Sunderland North West

BUDGET HOTEL

tel: 0871 527 9056 (Calls cost 13p per minute plus your phone company's access charge) **Timber Beach Road, off Wessington Way SR5 3XG**
web: www.premierinn.com
dir: *A1(M) junction 65, A1231 towards Sunderland, cross over A19.*

Rooms: 63

S

SURBITON
Greater London

Holiday Inn London - Kingston South

★★★★ 77% HOTEL Plan 1 C1

tel: 020 8786 6565 **Kingston Tower, Portsmouth Road KT6 5QQ**
email: enquiries@hikingston.co.uk **web:** www.hikingston.co.uk
dir: M25 junction 10, A3, left onto A243, 3rd exit at roundabout. At lights left onto A307.

This hotel occupies a convenient location overlooking the River Thames just outside Kingston-upon-Thames and close to Surbiton. Many front-facing bedrooms have beautiful river views; all are comfortable and stylish. The public areas include a small, well-equipped fitness room. Complimentary parking and WiFi are also available.

Rooms: 121 (3 family) ✆ **Facilities:** FTV WiFi ⓑ HL Mini gym Discounted price for guests at nearby gym and pool Xmas New Year **Conf:** Class 125 Board 60 Theatre 250 **Services:** Lift Night porter Air con **Parking:** 60 **Notes:** Civ Wed 210

SUTTON COLDFIELD (ROYAL)
West Midlands   Map 10 SP19

New Hall Hotel & Spa

★★★★ ◉◉ HOTEL

tel: 0121 378 2442 & 0845 072 7577 (Calls cost 5p per minute plus your phone company's access charge) **Walmley Road B76 1QX**
email: newhall@handpicked.co.uk **web:** www.handpickedhotels.co.uk/newhall
dir: M42 junction 9, A4097, 2 miles to roundabout, take 2nd exit signed Walmley. Take 2nd exit from next 5 roundabouts follow Sutton Coldfield signs. At 6th roundabout take 3rd exit follow Sutton Coldfield signs. Hotel on left.

Situated in 26 acres of beautiful grounds, this hotel is reputed to be the oldest inhabited, moated house in the country. The house's medieval charm and character combine well with 21st-century guest facilities. Executive and luxury suites are available. Public areas, with their fine panelling and mullioned stained-glass windows include the magnificent Great Chamber.

Rooms: 60 (14 family) (25 GF) ✆ **Facilities:** Spa STV FTV WiFi ⓑ ♨ ♥ ⛳ Gym Steam room Pitch and putt Outdoor trim trail Xmas New Year **Conf:** Class 75 Board 35 Theatre 150 **Services:** Night porter **Parking:** 80 **Notes:** LB Civ Wed 75

Moor Hall Hotel & Spa

★★★★ 80% ◉◉ HOTEL

tel: 0121 308 3751 **Moor Hall Drive, Four Oaks B75 6LN**
email: mail@moorhallhotel.co.uk **web:** www.moorhallhotel.co.uk
dir: A38 onto A453 towards Sutton Coldfield, right at lights into Weeford Road. Hotel 150 yards on left.

Although only a short distance from the city centre, this hotel enjoys a peaceful setting, overlooking extensive grounds and an adjacent golf course. Bedrooms are well equipped and executive rooms are particularly spacious. Public rooms include the formal two AA Rosette Oak Room Restaurant, and the informal Country Kitchen which offers a carvery and blackboard specials. The hotel also has a well-equipped spa with pool, sauna, steam room, jacuzzi and treatment rooms. Free WiFi is available in all rooms and throughout the hotel.

Rooms: 83 (5 family) (33 GF) ✆ **S** fr £70 **D** fr £95 (including breakfast)*
Facilities: Spa FTV WiFi ⓑ HL ⓑ Gym Aerobics studio Sauna Steam room Jacuzzi **Conf:** Class 100 Board 60 Theatre 250 **Services:** Lift Night porter **Parking:** 170 **Notes:** LB Civ Wed 180

Premier Inn Birmingham North (Sutton Coldfield)

BUDGET HOTEL

tel: 0871 527 8088 (Calls cost 13p per minute plus your phone company's access charge) **Whitehouse Common Road B75 6HD**
web: www.premierinn.com
dir: M42 junction 9, A446 towards Lichfield, then A453 to Sutton Coldfield. Left into Whitehouse Common Road, hotel on left.

High quality, budget accommodation ideal for both families and business travellers. Spacious, en suite bedrooms feature free WiFi and tea and coffee making facilities, and in most hotels, Freeview TV is also available. The adjacent family restaurant features a wide and varied menu.

Rooms: 57

SUTTON SCOTNEY
Hampshire   Map 5 SU43

Norton Park

★★★★ 80% HOTEL

tel: 01962 763000 **SO21 3NB**
email: nortonpark@qhotels.co.uk **web:** www.qhotels.co.uk
dir: From A303 and A34 junction follow signs to Sutton Scotney. Hotel on Micheldever Station Road (old A30), 1 mile from Sutton Scotney.

Set in 54 acres of beautiful parkland in the heart of Hampshire, Norton Park offers both business and leisure guests a great range of amenities. Dating from the 16th century, the hotel is complemented by extensive buildings housing the bedrooms, and public areas which include a superb leisure club and numerous conference facilities. Ample parking is available.

Rooms: 165 (11 family) (72 GF) ✆ **S** fr £87 **D** fr £99 (including breakfast)*
Facilities: Spa FTV WiFi ⓑ ⓑ ♥ Gym Steam room Sauna Experience shower Ice fountain Xmas New Year **Conf:** Class 250 Board 80 Theatre 340 **Services:** Lift Night porter **Parking:** 220 **Notes:** Civ Wed 340

S

SWAFFHAM
Norfolk
Map 13 TF80

Best Western George Hotel

★★★ 75% HOTEL

tel: 01760 721238 **Station Street PE37 7LJ**
email: george@hotelswaffham.com **web:** www.georgehotelswaffham.co.uk
dir: *From south: M11 junction 9, merge onto A11, continue on A14 exit 38, join A11, at roundabout 2nd exit A1065. From the north: A1, A17, A47.*

Located in the centre of historic Swaffham and originally a 16th-century coaching inn, the hotel offers a range of bedroom styles and sizes. Meals are served every day in The Green Room restaurant, or in the bar for a more informal dining experience. A suitable base for those exploring the north Norfolk coast.

Rooms: 28 (2 family) (8 GF) ↻ **S** fr £73.50 **D** fr £83.50 (including breakfast)*
Facilities: FTV WiFi ↻ **Conf:** Class 60 Board 50 Theatre 160 **Services:** Night porter
Parking: 60

SWANAGE
Dorset
Map 5 SZ07

Purbeck House Hotel

★★★ 76% METRO HOTEL

tel: 01929 422872 **91 High Street BH19 2LZ**
email: reservations@purbeckhousehotel.co.uk **web:** www.purbeckhousehotel.co.uk
dir: *A351 to Swanage via Wareham, right into Shore Road, into Institute Road, right into High Street.*

Originally built in 1875 as a private residence for businessman and builder George Burt, (known as 'The King of Swanage'), this family-run hotel has plenty of history, including wonderful mosaic floors, original servants' bells and ornate ceilings. Bedrooms vary in style but all offer the expected comforts; they are located both in the main house and in Louisa Lodge which is just a short stroll through the wonderful Victorian gardens. The impressive cuisine, served within the grandeur of the former chapel, is well worth sampling. Ample parking is provided, and the hotel is just a short walk from the seafront and town centre.

Rooms: 38 **Conf:** Class 36 Board 25 Theatre 100 **Parking:** 57 Closed 23–29 December Civ Wed 100

SWANLEY
Kent
Map 6 TQ56

Premier Inn Swanley

BUDGET HOTEL

tel: 0871 527 9288 (Calls cost 13p per minute plus your phone company's access charge) **London Road BR8 7QD**
web: www.premierinn.com
dir: *M25 junction 3, B2173 towards Swanley. At roundabout 2nd exit onto B258 (High Street). At next roundabout 4th exit into Swanley Lane, 1st exit into Bartholomew Way, at next roundabout 3rd exit into London Road.*

High quality, budget accommodation ideal for both families and business travellers. Spacious, en suite bedrooms feature free WiFi and tea and coffee making facilities, and in most hotels, Freeview TV is also available. The adjacent family restaurant features a wide and varied menu.

Rooms: 62

SWINDON
Wiltshire
Map 5 SU18

Blunsdon House Hotel

★★★★ 76% HOTEL

tel: 01793 721701 **Blunsdon SN26 7AS**
email: reservations@blunsdonhouse.co.uk **web:** www.blunsdonhouse.co.uk
dir: *M4 junction 15, A419 towards Cirencester. Exit at Blunsdon/Swindon, follow brown hotel signs.*

Located just to the north of Swindon, Blunsdon House Hotel is set in 30 acres of well-kept grounds and offers extensive leisure facilities and spacious day rooms. The hotel has a choice of eating and drinking options, including the spacious Carrie's Bar and the contemporary Flame Restaurant that also offers a lunchtime carvery. Bedrooms are comfortably furnished and include family rooms with bunk beds and the modern, spacious Pavilion rooms.

Rooms: 108 (48 annexe) (13 family) (27 GF) ↻ **S** fr £89 **D** fr £99 (including breakfast)* **Facilities:** Spa STV FTV WiFi ↻ HL ⏱ ⚓ 9 ⚘ Gym Beauty therapy Spin studio Xmas New Year **Conf:** Class 200 Board 55 Theatre 300 **Services:** Lift Night porter **Parking:** 300 **Notes:** Civ Wed 200

Chiseldon House Hotel

★★★ 81% ⊛ HOTEL

tel: 01793 741010 **New Road, Chiseldon SN4 0NE**
email: welcome@chiseldonhouse.com **web:** www.chiseldonhouse.com
dir: *M4 junction 15, A346 signed Marlborough. In 0.5 mile right onto B4500, 0.25 mile, hotel on right.*

Conveniently located for access to the M4, Chiseldon House is in a quiet location and has a relaxed ambience. Bedrooms include a number of larger rooms but all are comfortably furnished. The award-winning restaurant offers a selection of carefully prepared dishes utilising high quality produce. Guests are welcome to enjoy the pleasant garden with outdoor seating.

Rooms: 21 (4 family) ↻ **D** fr £100 (including breakfast)* **Facilities:** FTV WiFi ↻
Conf: Class 20 Board 32 Theatre 65 **Services:** Night porter **Parking:** 50
Notes: Civ Wed 100

Stanton House Hotel

★★★ 77% HOTEL

tel: 01793 861779 & 0843 507 1388 (Calls cost 7p per minute plus your phone company's access charge) **The Avenue, Stanton Fitzwarren SN6 7SD**
email: reception@stantonhouse.co.uk **web:** www.stantonhouse.co.uk
dir: *A419 onto A361 towards Highworth, left towards Stanton Fitzwarren about 600 yards, hotel on left.*

Extensive grounds and superb gardens surround this Cotswold-stone manor house, and the park and Stanton Lake are accessible for some great walks. Smart, well-maintained bedrooms have been equipped with modern comforts. Public areas include a conservatory, a bar and two eating options – The Rosemary Restaurant offering a wide choice of Japanese and European dishes, and the Mt Fuji Restaurant specialising in authentic Japanese food in traditional surroundings. The friendly, multi-lingual staff create a relaxing atmosphere for guests.

Rooms: 78 (27 GF) **S** fr £65 **D** fr £95* **Facilities:** STV FTV WiFi Xmas New Year
Conf: Class 70 Board 40 Theatre 110 **Services:** Lift Night porter **Parking:** 110
Notes: LB Civ Wed 110

S

SWINDON *continued*

Premier Inn Swindon Central

Premier Inn

BUDGET HOTEL

tel: 0871 527 9064 (Calls cost 13p per minute plus your phone company's access charge) **Kembrey Business Park, Kembrey Street SN2 8YS**
web: www.premierinn.com
dir: *M4 junction 15, A419 (Swindon bypass) towards Cirencester. In 6 mile at Turnpike Roundabout 1st left. Hotel on left in 2 miles.*

High quality, budget accommodation ideal for both families and business travellers. Spacious, en suite bedrooms feature free WiFi and tea and coffee making facilities, and in most hotels, Freeview TV is also available. The adjacent family restaurant features a wide and varied menu.

Rooms: 50

Premier Inn Swindon North

Premier Inn

BUDGET HOTEL

tel: 0871 527 9066 (Calls cost 13p per minute plus your phone company's access charge) **Broad Bush, Blunsdon SN26 8DJ**
web: www.premierinn.com
dir: *North of Swindon. 5 miles from M4 junction 15. At junction of A419 and B4019.*

Rooms: 62

Premier Inn Swindon West

Premier Inn

BUDGET HOTEL

tel: 0871 527 9068 (Calls cost 13p per minute plus your phone company's access charge) **Great Western Way SN5 8UY**
web: www.premierinn.com
dir: *M4 junction 16, A3102 to Lydiard Fields. Past Hilton, entrance on left. Note for sat nav use SN5 8UB.*

Rooms: 89

| TADWORTH | Map 6 TQ25 |
| Surrey | |

Premier Inn Epsom South

Premier Inn

BUDGET HOTEL

tel: 0871 527 8382 (Calls cost 13p per minute plus your phone company's access charge) **Brighton Road, Burgh Heath KT20 6BW**
web: www.premierinn.com
dir: *Just off M25 junction 8 on A217 towards Sutton.*

Rooms: 78

| TAMWORTH | Map 10 SK20 |
| Staffordshire | |

Premier Inn Tamworth Central

Premier Inn

BUDGET HOTEL

tel: 0871 527 9070 (Calls cost 13p per minute plus your phone company's access charge) **Bonehill Road, Bitterscote B78 3HQ**
web: www.premierinn.com
dir: *M42 junction 10, A5 towards Tamworth. Left in 3 miles onto A51 signed Tamworth. Straight on at 1st roundabout. At next roundabout 3rd exit. Hotel adjacent to Ladybridge Beefeater.*

Rooms: 74

Premier Inn Tamworth South

Premier Inn

BUDGET HOTEL

tel: 0871 527 9072 (Calls cost 13p per minute plus your phone company's access charge) **Watling Street, Wilnecote B77 5PN**
web: www.premierinn.com
dir: *M42 junction 10, A5 towards Tamworth. Left in 200 yards signed Wilnecote/B5404. Left at next roundabout, hotel on left.*

Rooms: 32

| TANKERSLEY | Map 16 SK39 |
| South Yorkshire | |

Tankersley Manor

QHOTELS
INSPIRED BY YOU

★★★★ 75% HOTEL

tel: 01226 744700 **Church Lane S75 3DQ**
email: tankersleymanor@qhotels.co.uk **web:** www.qhotels.co.uk
dir: *M1 junction 36, A61 Sheffield Road.*

High on the moors with views over the countryside, this 17th-century residence is well located for major cities, tourist attractions and motorway links. Where appropriate, bedrooms retain original features such as exposed beams or Yorkshire-stone window sills. The hotel has a bar and brasserie which has old beams and open fires. A well-equipped leisure centre is also available.

Rooms: 98 (10 family) (16 GF) ❢ **S** fr £65 **D** fr £89 (including breakfast)*
Facilities: Spa STV FTV WiFi ⤢ ❅ Gym Swimming lessons Beauty treatments New Year **Conf:** Class 200 Board 100 Theatre 400 **Services:** Lift Night porter **Parking:** 350 **Notes:** LB Civ Wed 250

Premier Inn Sheffield/Barnsley M1 Jct 36

Premier Inn

BUDGET HOTEL

tel: 0871 527 8968 (Calls cost 13p per minute plus your phone company's access charge) **Maple Road S75 3DL**
web: www.premierinn.com
dir: *M1 junction 35A (northbound exit only), A616 for 2 miles. From M1 junction 36, A61 towards Sheffield.*

Rooms: 62

S

TAPLOW
Buckinghamshire

Map 6 SU98

Cliveden

★★★★★ ◉◉◉ ⚜ COUNTRY HOUSE HOTEL

tel: 01628 668561 **Cliveden Estate SL6 0JF**
email: info@clivedenhouse.co.uk **web:** www.clivedenhouse.co.uk
dir: M4 junction 7, A4 towards Maidenhead, 1.5 miles, onto B476 towards Taplow, 2.5 miles, hotel on left.

Cliveden is an impressive stately home standing at the end of a long, gravelled boulevard. Now restored to its former glory, Cliveden welcomes guests in luxury and style. Visitors are treated as house guests and staff recapture the tradition of fine hospitality. The range of suites and bedrooms have individual style, and the reception rooms retain a timeless elegance. Restaurant André Garrett at Cliveden has been awarded three AA Rosettes for its outstanding cuisine, and guests can also dine at the Astor Grill, housed in the old stable block. Hidden behind the garden's brick walls and enveloped by lavender and tumbling, scented roses is the Cliveden Spa – a tranquil, relaxing oasis that provides the perfect place to escape, renew and refresh.

Rooms: 48 (1 annexe) (19 family) (13 GF) ♠ **S** fr £445 **D** fr £445 (including breakfast)* **Facilities:** Spa STV FTV WiFi ⊗ ↘ ☺ ⛳ Gym 2 boats Xmas New Year **Conf:** Class 48 Board 40 Theatre 120 **Services:** Lift Night porter **Parking:** 60 **Notes:** LB Civ Wed 120

Taplow House Hotel

★★★★ 77% ◉ HOTEL

tel: 01628 670056 **Berry Hill SL6 0DA**
email: reception@taplowhouse.com **web:** www.taplowhouse.com
dir: Exit A4 onto Berry Hill, hotel 0.5 mile on right.

This elegant Georgian manor is set amid beautiful gardens and has been skilfully restored. Character public rooms are pleasing and include a number of air-conditioned conference rooms and an elegant, award-winning restaurant. Comfortable bedrooms are individually decorated and furnished to a high standard.

Rooms: 32 (5 family) (2 GF) ♠ **Facilities:** STV FTV WiFi ↘ ⛳ **Conf:** Class 50 Board 42 Theatre 100 **Services:** Night porter Air con **Parking:** 100 **Notes:** Civ Wed 100

TARPORLEY
Cheshire

Map 15 SJ56

Macdonald Portal Hotel Golf & Spa

★★★★ 79% ◉ HOTEL

tel: 01829 734100 **Cobblers Cross Lane CW6 0DJ**
email: general.portal@macdonaldhotels.co.uk
web: www.macdonaldhotels.co.uk/theportal
dir: M6 junction 18, A54 towards Middlewich/Winsford. Left onto A49, through Cotebrook. In approximately 1 mile follow signs for hotel.

Located in beautiful rolling countryside, this hotel provides a luxury base for business and leisure guests. The spacious and well-equipped bedrooms have en suites with baths and power showers. Extensive leisure facilities include a superb spa, well-equipped gym and thermal suite, three golf courses and a golf academy. The Scottish Steakhouse, as the name suggests, serves great steaks alongside innovative seasonal dishes. Staff throughout are very friendly and welcoming.

Rooms: 85 (29 GF) ♠ **Facilities:** Spa STV FTV WiFi ↘ HL ⊗ ⛳ 45 Gym Golf academy Outdoor pursuits New Year **Conf:** Class 180 Board 60 Theatre 250 **Services:** Lift Night porter **Parking:** 250 **Notes:** Civ Wed 250

TAUNTON
Somerset

Map 4 ST22

The Mount Somerset Hotel & Spa

★★★★ ◉◉◉ COUNTRY HOUSE HOTEL

tel: 01823 442500 **Lower Henlade TA3 5NB**
email: info@mountsomersethotel.co.uk
web: www.themountsomersethotelandspa.com
dir: M5 junction 25, A358 towards Chard/Ilminster, at Henlade right into Stoke Road, left at T-junction at end, then right into drive.

From its elevated and rural position, this impressive Regency house has wonderful views over Taunton Vale. There are impressive quality and comfort levels throughout in the stylish bedrooms and bathrooms. The elegant public rooms combine style and flair with an engaging and intimate atmosphere. In addition to the daily-changing, fixed-price menu, a carefully selected seasonal carte is available in the restaurant.

Rooms: 19 (1 family) ♠ **S** fr £99 **D** fr £109 **Facilities:** Spa FTV WiFi ⛳ Gym Hydrotherapy pool Sauna Steam room Experience showers Foot spas Xmas New Year **Conf:** Class 60 Board 35 Theatre 70 **Services:** Lift Night porter **Parking:** 100 **Notes:** LB Civ Wed 80

T

TAUNTON *continued*

The Castle at Taunton

★★★★ 80% HOTEL

tel: 01823 272671 **Castle Green TA1 1NF**
email: reception@the-castle-hotel.com **web:** www.the-castle-hotel.com
dir: *Phone for directions.*

This well-established, delightful hotel is in a very central location in the heart of Taunton. Combining the character and charm of a castle with stylish public areas, it offers a wide range of comfortable bedrooms and bathrooms, from larger feature rooms to smaller but well-equipped standard rooms. Dining here is a treat with the option of two restaurants – the fine dining selection in The Castle Bow restaurant or the more relaxed setting of Brazz – a combination of brasserie, bar and café. Adjacent parking is another welcome bonus.

Rooms: 44 ⬧ **S** fr £100 **D** fr £130 (including breakfast)* **Facilities:** FTV WiFi
Conf: Class 40 Board 35 Theatre 100 **Services:** Lift Night porter **Parking:** 44
Notes: LB Civ Wed 80

Corner House Hotel

★★★ 75% HOTEL

tel: 01823 284683 **Park Street TA1 4DQ**
email: res@corner-house.co.uk **web:** www.corner-house.co.uk
dir: *0.3 mile from town centre. Hotel on junction of Park Street and A38 – Wellington Road.*

The unusual Victorian facade of the Corner House Hotel, with its turrets and stained-glass windows, belies the wealth of modern innovation, quality and style to be found inside. The contemporary bedrooms have state-of-the-art facilities including Freeview TVs, ample working space, and fridges with complimentary water and fresh milk. The smart public areas include the relaxed and enjoyable Retreat pub and dining rooms. Free WiFi is available throughout.

Rooms: 45 (10 annexe) (4 family) (4 GF) ⬧ **S** fr £69 **D** fr £79 **Facilities:** FTV WiFi
Xmas New Year **Conf:** Class 32 Board 30 Theatre 60 **Services:** Night porter
Parking: 30

Taunton House Hotel

★★★ 75% METRO HOTEL

tel: 01823 272083 **14 Billetfield TA1 3NN**
email: info@tauntonhousehotel.co.uk **web:** www.tauntonhousehotel.co.uk
dir: *Phone for directions.*

Centrally and conveniently located, this elegant establishment dates back to the 1850s and retains many original features such as stained-glass windows and a wonderful oak staircase. Bedrooms provide impressive levels of comfort and quality with well-equipped, modern bathrooms. Public areas reflect the same high standards that are a hallmark throughout this hotel.

Rooms: 17 (4 family) (6 GF) (2 smoking) ⬧ **Facilities:** FTV WiFi **Parking:** 17

Premier Inn Taunton Central (North)

Premier Inn

BUDGET HOTEL

tel: 0871 527 9076 (Calls cost 13p per minute plus your phone company's access charge) **Massingham Park, Priorswood Road TA2 7RX**
web: www.premierinn.com
dir: *M5 junction 25, A358 into Taunton, at 2nd roundabout right onto Obridge Viaduct. Hotel at next roundabout.*

High quality, budget accommodation ideal for both families and business travellers. Spacious, en suite bedrooms feature free WiFi and tea and coffee making facilities, and in most hotels, Freeview TV is also available. The adjacent family restaurant features a wide and varied menu.

Rooms: 40

Premier Inn Taunton East

Premier Inn

BUDGET HOTEL

tel: 0871 527 9080 (Calls cost 13p per minute plus your phone company's access charge) **81 Bridgwater Road TA1 2DU**
web: www.premierinn.com
dir: *M5 junction 25 follow signs to Taunton. Straight on at 1st roundabout, keep left at Creech Castle lights, hotel 200 yards on right.*

Rooms: 60

Premier Inn Taunton (Ruishton)

Premier Inn

BUDGET HOTEL

tel: 0871 527 9074 (Calls cost 13p per minute plus your phone company's access charge) **Ruishton Lane, Ruishton TA3 5LU**
web: www.premierinn.com
dir: *Just off M5 junction 25 on A38.*

Rooms: 77

TAVISTOCK
Devon

Map 3 SX47

The Horn of Plenty

★★★★ 81% HOTEL

tel: 01822 832528 **Gulworthy PL19 8JD**
email: enquiries@thehornofplenty.co.uk **web:** www.thehornofplenty.co.uk
dir: *From Tavistock take A390 west for 3 miles. Right at Gulworthy Cross. In 400 yards turn left, hotel in 400 yards on right.*

With stunning views over the Tamar Valley on the Devon-Cornwall border, The Horn of Plenty maintains its reputation as one of Britain's best country house hotels. Bedrooms are well equipped and have many thoughtful extras; the garden rooms offer impressive levels of both quality and comfort. The award-winning cuisine is created with accomplished skill and reflects a passion for local produce.

Rooms: 16 (12 annexe) (3 family) (8 GF) ⬧ **S** fr £110 **D** fr £120 (including breakfast)* **Facilities:** FTV WiFi Falconry Xmas New Year **Conf:** Class 22 Board 16 Theatre 40 **Parking:** 35 **Notes:** LB Civ Wed 90

Bedford Hotel

★★★ 81% HOTEL

tel: 01822 613221 **1 Plymouth Road PL19 8BB**
email: reception@bedford-hotel.co.uk **web:** www.bedford-hotel.co.uk
dir: *M5 junction 31, A30 Launceston/Okehampton. Then A386 to Tavistock, follow town centre signs. Hotel opposite church.*

Built on the site of a Benedictine abbey, this impressive castellated building has been welcoming visitors for over 200 years. Very much a local landmark, the hotel offers comfortable and relaxing public areas, all reflecting charm and character throughout. Bedrooms are traditionally styled with contemporary comforts, while the Woburn Restaurant provides a refined setting for enjoyable cuisine.

Rooms: 31 (2 family) (5 GF) ⬧ **Facilities:** FTV WiFi Xmas New Year **Conf:** Class 100 Board 60 Theatre 160 **Services:** Lift Night porter **Parking:** 52 **Notes:** Civ Wed 120

TELFORD
Shropshire
Map 10 SJ60

Telford Hotel & Golf Resort

QHOTELS
INSPIRED BY YOU

★★★★ 81% HOTEL

tel: 01952 429977 Great Hay Drive, Sutton Heights TF7 4DT
email: telford@qhotels.co.uk web: www.qhotels.co.uk
dir: M54 junction 4, A442. Follow signs for Telford Golf Club.

Set on the edge of Telford with panoramic views of the famous Ironbridge Gorge, this hotel sets high standards. Smart bedrooms are complemented by spacious public areas, large conference facilities, a spa with treatment rooms, a golf course and a driving range. Ample parking is available.

Rooms: 114 (8 family) (50 GF) ⌇ S fr £91 D fr £103 (including breakfast)*
Facilities: Spa STV WiFi ⌇ ⌇ ⌇ 18 Gym Xmas New Year Conf: Class 220 Board 100 Theatre 350 Services: Lift Night porter Parking: 200 Notes: LB Civ Wed 250

Hadley Park House

★★★★ 75% ⓖ HOTEL

tel: 01952 677269 Hadley Park TF1 6QJ
email: info@hadleypark.co.uk web: www.hadleypark.co.uk
dir: Off Hadley Park Island exit A442 to Whitchurch.

Located in Telford, but close to Ironbridge, this elegant Georgian mansion is situated in three acres of its own grounds. Bedrooms are spacious and well equipped. There is a comfortable bar and lounge, and meals are served in the attractive conservatory-style restaurant.

Rooms: 22 (6 family) (5 GF) ⌇ Facilities: STV FTV WiFi ⌇ Xmas New Year Conf: Class 60 Board 40 Theatre 200 Services: Night porter Parking: 60 Notes: Civ Wed 200

The Valley Hotel

★★★ 81% ⓖⓖ HOTEL

tel: 01952 432247 Buildwas Road, Ironbridge TF8 7DW
email: info@thevalleyhotel.co.uk web: www.thevalleyhotel.co.uk
dir: M6, M54 junction 6 onto A5223 to Ironbridge.

This privately owned hotel is situated in attractive gardens, close to the famous Iron Bridge. It was once the home of the Maws family who manufactured ceramic tiles, and fine examples of their craft are found throughout the house. Bedrooms vary in size and are split between the main house and a mews development; imaginative meals are served in the attractive Chez Maws restaurant.

Rooms: 44 (3 family) (6 GF) ⌇ S fr £60 D fr £80 (including breakfast)*
Facilities: FTV WiFi ⌇ Conf: Class 49 Board 30 Theatre 100 Services: Lift Night porter Parking: 70 Notes: LB Closed 24 December to 2 January RS 25 December Civ Wed 120

Premier Inn Telford Central

Premier Inn

BUDGET HOTEL

tel: 0871 527 9082 (Calls cost 13p per minute plus your phone company's access charge) Euston Way TF3 4LY
web: www.premierinn.com
dir: M54 junction 5 follow Central Railway Station signs. Hotel at 2nd exit off roundabout signed railway station.

High quality, budget accommodation ideal for both families and business travellers. Spacious, en suite bedrooms feature free WiFi and tea and coffee making facilities, and in most hotels, Freeview TV is also available. The adjacent family restaurant features a wide and varied menu.

Rooms: 89

Premier Inn Telford International Centre

Premier Inn

BUDGET HOTEL

tel: 0871 527 9500 (Calls cost 13p per minute plus your phone company's access charge) Southwater Square, Saint Quentin Gate TF3 4EJ
web: www.premierinn.com
dir: M6 junction, M54. Exit at junction 5, take 2nd exit at 1st roundabout into Forge Gate. Merge into middle lane of one-way system. At next roundabout take 3rd exit into Grange Central. Right into St Quentin Gate.

Rooms: 85

Premier Inn Telford North

Premier Inn

BUDGET HOTEL

tel: 0871 527 9084 (Calls cost 13p per minute plus your phone company's access charge) Donnington Wood Way, Donnington TF2 8LE
web: www.premierinn.com
dir: From Telford M54 junction 4, B5060 (Redhill Way) signed Donnington. At roundabout straight on (becomes Donnington Wood Way then School Road). At mini-roundabout take 1st left into Wellington Road. Hotel adjacent to McDonalds and Shell garage.

Rooms: 20

TELFORD SERVICE AREA (M54)
Shropshire
Map 10 SJ70

Days Inn Telford - M54

WELCOMEBREAK

AA Advertised

tel: 01952 238400 Telford Services, Priorslee Road TF11 8TG
email: telford.hotel@welcomebreak.co.uk web: www.welcomebreak.co.uk
dir: At M54 junction 4.

This modern building offers accommodation in smart, spacious and well-equipped bedrooms, suitable for families and business travellers, and all with en suite bathrooms. Continental breakfast is available, and other refreshments may be taken at the nearby family restaurant.

Rooms: 48 (45 family) (21 GF) (9 smoking) Facilities: FTV WiFi ⌇ Conf: Board 8 Parking: 100

TENTERDEN
Kent
Map 6 TQ83

Little Silver Country Hotel

★★★ 80% HOTEL

tel: 01233 850321 Ashford Road, St Michael's TN30 6SP
email: enquiries@little-silver.co.uk web: www.little-silver.co.uk
dir: M20 junction 8, A274 signed Tenterden.

Located just outside the charming town of Tenterden and within easy reach of many Kent attractions, this welcoming hotel is ideal for leisure and business guests, as well as being a popular wedding venue. Bedrooms are spaciously appointed and well equipped; many boast spa baths. There is a spacious lounge, a small bar and a modern restaurant that overlooks beautifully tended gardens.

Rooms: 16 (1 family) (6 GF) ⌇ S fr £65 D fr £99 (including breakfast)*
Facilities: FTV WiFi ⌇ Xmas Conf: Class 50 Board 25 Theatre 75 Parking: 70 Notes: Civ Wed 120

T

TENTERDEN *continued*

London Beach Country Hotel, Spa & Golf Club

★★★ 76% HOTEL

tel: 01580 766279 **Ashford Road TN30 6HX**
email: enquiries@londonbeach.com **web:** www.londonbeach.com
dir: *M20 junction 9, A28 follow signs to Tenterden (10 miles). Hotel on right 1 mile before Tenterden.*

This modern, purpose-built hotel is situated in mature grounds on the outskirts of Tenterden. The spacious bedrooms are smartly decorated with co-ordinated soft furnishings, and most rooms have balconies with superb views over the golf course. The open-plan public rooms feature a brasserie-style restaurant, where a good choice of dishes is served.

Rooms: 26 (5 family) ⌁ **S** fr £85 **D** fr £95 (including breakfast)* **Facilities:** Spa FTV WiFi ⌁ ⊙ ♪ 9 Fishing Gym Driving range Health club Xmas New Year **Conf:** Class 75 Board 40 Theatre 100 **Services:** Lift Night porter **Parking:** 100 **Notes:** LB Civ Wed 100

TETBURY	Map 4 ST89
Gloucestershire	

INSPECTOR'S CHOICE

Calcot

★★★★ ◎◎ HOTEL

tel: 01666 890391 **Calcot GL8 8YJ**
email: receptionists@calcot.co **web:** www.calcot.co
dir: *3 miles west of Tetbury at A4135 and A46 junction.*

Cistercian monks built the ancient barns and stables around which this lovely English farmhouse is set. No two rooms are identical, and each is beautifully decorated and equipped with modern comforts. Sumptuous sitting rooms, with crackling log fires in the winter, look out over immaculate gardens. There are two dining options: the elegant conservatory restaurant and the informal Gumstool Inn. There are also ample function rooms. The health and leisure spa includes an indoor pool, high-tech gym, massage tables, complementary therapies and much more. For children, a supervised crèche and 'playzone' are a great attraction.

Rooms: 35 (23 annexe) (13 family) (17 GF) ⌁ **Facilities:** Spa STV WiFi ⌁ ⊙ ➔ ⌁ ♪ Gym Clay pigeon shooting Archery Cycling Running track Segways Disc golf Xmas New Year **Conf:** Class 70 Board 30 Theatre 120 **Services:** Night porter **Parking:** 150 **Notes:** Civ Wed 100

Hare & Hounds Hotel

★★★★ 80% ◎◎ ⌁ HOTEL

COTSWOLD
INNS & HOTELS

tel: 01666 881000 **Westonbirt GL8 8QL**
email: reception@hareandhoundshotel.com **web:** www.cotswold-inns-hotels.co.uk
dir: *2.5 miles southwest of Tetbury on A433.*

This popular hotel, set in extensive grounds, is situated close to the Westonbirt Arboretum. The stylish bedrooms are individually designed; those in the main house are more traditional and the cottage rooms are more contemporary in style. The public rooms include an informal bar and light, airy lounges – one has a welcoming log fire lit in colder months. Guests can eat either in the relaxed bar or the award-winning Beaufort Restaurant.

Rooms: 42 (21 annexe) (8 family) (13 GF) ⌁ **S** fr £120 **D** fr £150 (including breakfast)* **Facilities:** FTV WiFi ⌁ ♪ Xmas New Year **Conf:** Class 80 Board 40 Theatre 120 **Services:** Night porter **Parking:** 85 **Notes:** Civ Wed 120

The Close Hotel

★★★★ 79% ◎◎ ⌁ HOTEL

COTSWOLD
INNS & HOTELS

tel: 01666 502272 **8 Long Street GL8 8AQ**
email: info@theclose.com **web:** www.cotswold-inns-hotels.co.uk
dir: *M4 junction 17 onto A429 or M5 junction 14 onto B4509, follow Tetbury signs.*

Even with its town centre location, The Close Hotel retains a country-house feel that has made this a favourite with many for years. Bedrooms are striking and well equipped, with thoughtful touches such as home-made biscuits and bottled water. The public rooms provide a choice of relaxing areas with log fires lit in the winter. In the summer, guests can enjoy the terrace in the attractive walled garden.

Rooms: 18 ⌁ **S** fr £180 **D** fr £210 (including breakfast)* **Facilities:** FTV WiFi ⌁ Xmas New Year **Conf:** Board 22 Theatre 50 **Services:** Night porter **Parking:** 10

Snooty Fox

★★★ 78% SMALL HOTEL

tel: 01666 502436 **Market Place GL8 8DD**
email: res@snooty-fox.co.uk **web:** www.snooty-fox.co.uk
dir: *In town centre.*

Centrally situated, this 16th-century coaching inn retains original features and is a popular venue for weekend breaks. The relaxed and friendly atmosphere, the high standard of accommodation, and the food offered in the bar and restaurant are all very good reasons why many guests return here time and again.

Rooms: 12 **Facilities:** FTV WiFi ⌁ Xmas New Year **Conf:** Class 12 Board 16 Theatre 24

TEWKESBURY	Map 10 SO83
Gloucestershire	

Premier Inn Tewkesbury

Premier Inn

BUDGET HOTEL

tel: 0871 527 9088 (Calls cost 13p per minute plus your phone company's access charge) **Shannon Way, Ashchurch GL20 8ND**
web: www.premierinn.com
dir: *M5 junction 9, A438 towards Tewkesbury, hotel 400 yards on right.*

High quality, budget accommodation ideal for both families and business travellers. Spacious, en suite bedrooms feature free WiFi and tea and coffee making facilities, and in most hotels, Freeview TV is also available. The adjacent family restaurant features a wide and varied menu.

Rooms: 59

THETFORD
Norfolk — Map 13 TL88

Premier Inn Thetford

BUDGET HOTEL

tel: 0871 527 9090 (Calls cost 13p per minute plus your phone company's access charge) **Lynn Wood, Maine Street IP24 3PG**
web: www.premierinn.com
dir: *From A11 north follow Thetford signs. At 3rd roundabout 1st exit for town centre into Brandon Road. 1st exit into Maine Street.*

High quality, budget accommodation ideal for both families and business travellers. Spacious, en suite bedrooms feature free WiFi and tea and coffee making facilities, and in most hotels, Freeview TV is also available. The adjacent family restaurant features a wide and varied menu.

Rooms: 88

THIRSK
North Yorkshire — Map 19 SE48

Golden Fleece
★★★ 81% HOTEL

tel: 01845 523108 **Market Place YO7 1LL**
email: goldenfleece@innmail.co.uk

This is a modern hotel situated in Thirsk and part of The Coaching Inn Group. Main building bedrooms and bathrooms have a modern feel while those in The Mews block are more traditional. All are well equipped with modern accessories such as complimentary WiFi and Sky TV. Dinner can be enjoyed in the restaurant where menus offer an interesting range of dishes. Pizzas can also be enjoyed alfresco from the on-site wood-fired oven. Complimentary parking is a big asset in this busy town centre location.

Rooms: 26 **Facilities:** Wifi **Conf:** Class 30 Board 20 Theatre 50

Premier Inn Thirsk

BUDGET HOTEL

tel: 0871 622 2319 (Calls cost 13p per minute plus your phone company's access charge) **Sowerby Gateway YO7 3HF**
web: www.premierinn.com
dir: *Leave A168 onto B1448 (Topcliffe Road). Follow B1448. Hotel on left.*

High quality, budget accommodation ideal for both families and business travellers. Spacious, en suite bedrooms feature free WiFi and tea and coffee making facilities, and in most hotels, Freeview TV is also available. The adjacent family restaurant features a wide and varied menu.

Rooms: 65

THORNBURY
Gloucestershire — Map 4 ST69

INSPECTOR'S CHOICE

Thornbury Castle
★★★ ◉◉ COUNTRY HOUSE HOTEL

tel: 01454 281182 **Castle Street BS35 1HH**
email: info@thornburycastle.co.uk web: www.thornburycastle.co.uk
dir: *On A38 northbound from Bristol take 1st turn to Thornbury. At end of High Street left into Castle Street, follow brown sign, entrance to Castle on left behind St Mary's Church.*

History fans may be interested to learn that Henry VIII ordered the first owner of this castle to be beheaded! Guests today have the opportunity of sleeping in historical surroundings fitted out with all the modern amenities. Most rooms have four-poster or coronet beds and real fires, and guests can even choose to sleep in the Duke's Bedchamber where King Henry and Anne Boleyn once slept, or in the Tower Suite that reputedly has the widest four-poster bed in England. Tranquil lounges enjoy views over the wonderful gardens, while elegant, wood-panelled dining rooms make a memorable setting for a leisurely award-winning meal. Activities include falconry and archery and the castle has its own vineyard. Thornbury is, of course, a popular wedding venue.

Rooms: 27 (3 family) (4 GF) **Facilities:** STV FTV WiFi Archery Helicopter rides Clay pigeon shooting Massage treatment Xmas New Year **Conf:** Class 40 Board 30 Theatre 70 **Services:** Night porter **Parking:** 50 **Notes:** Civ Wed 70

T

THORNHAM
Norfolk

Map 12 TF74

The Chequers Inn
★★★ 88% ☺ SMALL HOTEL

tel: 01485 512229 **High Street PE36 6LY**
email: info@chequersinnthornham.com **web:** www.chequersinnthornham.com
dir: A149 coastal road between Hunstanton and Brancaster. Thornham village High Street, next to All Saints Church.

This lovely 16th-century inn is ideally situated for exploring the north Norfolk coast with its lovely beaches. The RSPB reserve at Titchwell Marsh, and Holme Dunes National Nature Reserve are just a stone's throw away. The individually designed bedrooms are stylish and equipped with modern facilities, while public areas feature a traditional bar with an open fire and low beams. There is also a restaurant to the rear and a lovely outdoor area with individual, heated pavilions allowing dining all year round.

Rooms: 11 **Facilities:** FTV WiFi ⌕

The Lifeboat Inn
★★★ 86% ☺ HOTEL

tel: 01485 512236 **Ship Lane PE36 6LT**
email: info@lifeboatinnthornham.com **web:** www.lifeboatinnthornham.com
dir: From A149 in Thornham village, turn into Staithe Lane, The Lifeboat Inn signed from A149.

A cosy traditional-style inn, set in the sleepy village of Thornham. There's the option of alfresco dining in the warmer months, and the property also benefits from quirky outdoor pavilion dining, perfect for private groups of 10-14 people. Stylish and very comfortable bedrooms with neutral colour palettes are on offer; each room is named after a crew member of the last pulling Hunstanton lifeboat. The hotel is dog friendly.

Rooms: 13 (1 annexe) (1 GF) ☏ **Facilities:** FTV WiFi Xmas New Year **Conf:** Class 16 Board 12 Theatre 24 **Services:** Night porter **Parking:** 30

THORNTON HOUGH
Merseyside

Map 15 SJ38

Thornton Hall Hotel and Spa
★★★★ 82% ☺☺ HOTEL

tel: 0151 336 3938 **Neston Road CH63 1JF**
email: reservations@thorntonhallhotel.com **web:** www.thorntonhallhotel.com
dir: M53 junction 4, B5151/Neston onto B5136 to Thornton Hough, signed.

Dating back to the mid 1800s, this country-house hotel has been extended, restored and updated. An impressive leisure spa boasting excellent facilities and a separate clinical retreat is a key feature. A choice of eateries is available including the Lawn Restaurant. Bedrooms vary in style and include character rooms in the main house and more contemporary rooms in the garden wings. Delightful grounds and extensive banqueting facilities make this a popular wedding and conference venue.

Rooms: 62 (12 family) (28 GF) ☏ **S** fr £89 **D** fr £89* **Facilities:** Spa STV FTV WiFi ⌕ ✹ ⌿ Gym Rasul Clinical spa treatments Outdoor spa pools Steam room Snow cave Aerobics Studio hairdressers New Year **Conf:** Class 225 Board 80 Theatre 650 **Services:** Night porter **Parking:** 250 **Notes:** LB Civ Wed 500

THORPE
Derbyshire

Map 16 SK15

The Izaak Walton Hotel
★★★ 86% ☺☺ HOTEL

tel: 01335 350981 **Dovedale DE6 2AY**
email: reception@izaakwaltonhotel.com **web:** www.izaakwaltonhotel.com
dir: A515 onto B5054 to Thorpe, over cattle grid and 2 small bridges, 1st right, sharp left.

Often it is claimed that a property is in an idyllic location; this could not be truer than for the Izaak Walton Hotel. The 17th-century property named after the author of *The Compleat Angler* sits in the picturesque Dove Valley, dwarfed by the surrounding peaks known as 'Thorpe Cloud' and 'Bunster Hill', on the Derbyshire-Staffordshire border. Bedrooms are attractively furnished and comfortably appointed. There are several small private sittings rooms and an oak-beamed bar in which to relax. Meals are served in the Haddon Restaurant or Dovedale Bar.

Rooms: 38 (3 annexe) (6 family) (7 GF) ☏ **Facilities:** WiFi Fishing Xmas New Year **Conf:** Class 80 Board 40 Theatre 100 **Services:** Night porter **Parking:** 40 **Notes:** Civ Wed 120

THORPENESS
Suffolk

Map 13 TM45

Thorpeness Hotel
★★★ 85% ☺ HOTEL

T | A | HOTEL
COLLECTION

tel: 01728 452176 **Lakeside Avenue IP16 4NH**
email: info@thorpeness.co.uk **web:** www.thorpeness.co.uk
dir: A1094 towards Aldeburgh, take coast road north for 2 miles.

Thorpeness Hotel is ideally situated in an unspoilt, tranquil setting close to Aldeburgh and Snape Maltings. The extensive public rooms include a choice of lounges, a restaurant overlooking the golf course, a smart bar, a snooker room, clubhouse and meeting rooms. The spacious bedrooms are pleasantly decorated, tastefully furnished and equipped with modern facilities. A James Braid 18-hole heathland golf course, and tennis courts, are available.

Rooms: 36 (36 annexe) (10 family) (10 GF) ☏ **S** fr £90 **D** fr £100 (including breakfast)* **Facilities:** WiFi ⌕ HL ⌿ 18 ⌣ Rowing Boat hire Birdwatching Adventure golf Xmas New Year **Conf:** Class 30 Board 24 Theatre 130 **Services:** Night porter **Parking:** 80 **Notes:** Civ Wed 130

THURLASTON
Warwickshire   Map 11 SP47

Draycote Hotel
★★★ 73% HOTEL

tel: 01788 521800 **London Road CV23 9LF**
email: mail@draycotehotel.co.uk **web:** www.draycotehotel.co.uk
dir: M1 junction 17 onto M45, A45. Hotel 500 metres on left.

Located in the picturesque Warwickshire countryside and within easy reach of motorway networks, this hotel offers modern, comfortable and well-equipped accommodation with a relaxed and friendly welcome. The hotel has a challenging golf course.

Rooms: 49 (2 family) (24 GF) **S** fr £65 **D** fr £65* **Facilities:** FTV WiFi ⬡ ⚲ 18 Golf driving range Chipping green Xmas New Year **Conf:** Class 78 Board 30 Theatre 250 **Services:** Night porter **Parking:** 150 **Notes:** LB Civ Wed 170

THURLESTONE
Devon   Map 3 SX64

HIGHLY RECOMMENDED

Thurlestone Hotel
★★★★ 84% ◉◉ HOTEL

tel: 01548 560382 **TQ7 3NN**
email: reception@thurlestone.co.uk **web:** www.thurlestone.co.uk
dir: A38, A384 into Totnes, A381 towards Kingsbridge, A379 towards Churchstow, onto B3197. Into lane signed to Thurlestone.

This perennially popular hotel has been in the same family-ownership since 1896 and continues to go from strength to strength. Set in 19 acres of gardens with extensive leisure facilities including a par 3 golf course, tennis courts, an outdoor heated swimming pool and the Voyage Spa Complex. Bedrooms are equipped to ensure a comfortable stay with many having wonderful views of the south Devon coast. The range of eating options includes the elegant and stylish Trevilder Restaurant with its stunning views.

Rooms: 65 (23 family) ⬡ **S** fr £102.50 **D** fr £205 (including breakfast)*
Facilities: Spa STV FTV WiFi ⬡ ⬡ ⚲ 9 ⚲ ⚲ Gym Squash Badminton Table tennis Toddler room Beauty treatment room Xmas New Year **Conf:** Class 100 Board 40 Theatre 150 **Services:** Lift Night porter **Parking:** 121 **Notes:** LB Closed 1st 2 weeks January Civ Wed 160

TICEHURST
East Sussex   Map 6 TQ63

Dale Hill Hotel & Golf Club
★★★★ 81% ◉ HOTEL

tel: 01580 200112 **TN5 7DQ**
email: info@dalehill.co.uk **web:** www.dalehill.co.uk
dir: M25 junction 5, A21. 5 miles after Lamberhurst, right at lights onto B2087 to Flimwell. Hotel 1 mile on left.

This modern hotel is situated just a short drive from the village. Extensive public rooms include a lounge and clubhouse bar, the 18th Restaurant, the formal, award-winning Wealden View Restaurant and the Spike Bar, which is mainly frequented by golf club members and has a lively atmosphere. The hotel also has two superb 18-hole golf courses, a swimming pool and gym.

Rooms: 35 (8 family) (23 GF) ⬡ **Facilities:** FTV WiFi ⬡ ⚲ 36 Gym Covered driving range Pool table Xmas New Year **Conf:** Class 50 Board 50 Theatre 120 **Services:** Lift Night porter **Parking:** 220 **Notes:** Civ Wed 150

TINTAGEL
Cornwall & Isles Of Scilly   Map 2 SX08

Atlantic View Hotel
★★ 82% SMALL HOTEL

tel: 01840 770221 **Treknow PL34 0EJ**
email: atlantic-view@eclipse.co.uk **web:** www.atlanticviewhoteltintagel.co.uk
dir: B3263 to Tregatta, turn left into Treknow, hotel on road to Trebarwith Strand Beach.

Conveniently located for all the attractions of Tintagel, this family-run hotel has a wonderfully relaxed and welcoming atmosphere. Public areas include a bar, comfortable lounge and a TV/games room. Bedrooms are generally spacious and some have the added advantage of distant sea views.

Rooms: 9 (1 family) ⬡ **D** fr £120 (including breakfast) **Facilities:** FTV WiFi Pool table **Parking:** 10 **Notes:** LB Closed November to February RS March

TITCHWELL
Norfolk   Map 13 TF74

HIGHLY RECOMMENDED

Titchwell Manor Hotel
★★★ 88% ◉◉◉ HOTEL

tel: 01485 210221 **PE31 8BB**
email: eric@titchwellmanor.com **web:** www.titchwellmanor.com
dir: On A149 coast road, between Brancaster and Thornham.

Titchwell Manor Hotel is a friendly, family-run hotel ideally placed for touring the north Norfolk coastline. The tastefully appointed bedrooms are very comfortable; some in the adjacent annexe offer ground floor access. Smart public rooms include a lounge area, The Eating Rooms and the delightful Conservatory restaurant, overlooking the walled garden. Chef and owner Eric Snaith and his head chef produce imaginative menus that feature quality local produce and fresh fish.

Rooms: 26 (18 annexe) (4 family) (15 GF) ⬡ **Facilities:** FTV WiFi ⬡ Xmas New Year **Conf:** Class 50 Board 30 Theatre 30 **Parking:** 50 **Notes:** Civ Wed 90

T

TOLLESHUNT KNIGHTS
Essex   Map 7 TL91

Crowne Plaza Resort Colchester - Five Lakes
★★★★ 77% HOTEL

tel: 01621 868888 **Colchester Road CM9 8HX**
email: enquiries@cpcolchester.co.uk **web:** www.cpcolchester.co.uk
dir: Exit A12 at Kelvedon, follow brown signs through Tiptree to hotel.

This hotel is set amidst 320 acres of open countryside, featuring two golf courses. The spacious bedrooms are furnished to a high standard and have excellent facilities. The public rooms offer a high degree of comfort and include five bars, two restaurants and a large lounge. The property also boasts extensive leisure facilities.

Rooms: 194 (80 annexe) (4 family) (40 GF) ↸ **S** fr £89 **D** fr £89 (including breakfast & dinner)* **Facilities:** Spa STV FTV WiFi ↻ ⊛ ♨ 36 ☃ Gym Squash Sauna Steam room Badminton Aerobics studio Nail lounge Relaxation room Xmas New Year **Conf:** Class 700 Board 60 Theatre 2000 **Services:** Lift Night porter **Parking:** 550 **Notes:** LB Civ Wed 250

TONBRIDGE
Kent   Map 6 TQ54

Best Western Rose & Crown Hotel
 Best Western

★★★ 79% HOTEL

tel: 01732 357966 **125 High Street TN9 1DD**
email: rose.crown@bestwestern.co.uk **web:** www.roseandcrowntonbridge.co.uk
dir: Phone for directions.

A 15th-century coaching inn situated in the heart of this bustling town centre. The public areas are light and airy yet still retain much original character such as oak beams and Jacobean panelling. Food is served throughout the day in the Oak Room Bar & Grill. Bedrooms are stylishly decorated, spacious and well presented; amenities include free WiFi.

Rooms: 56 (3 family) (10 GF) ↸ **S** fr £75 **D** fr £85* **Facilities:** FTV WiFi ↻ **Conf:** Class 60 Board 60 Theatre 80 **Services:** Night porter **Parking:** 43 **Notes:** LB

Premier Inn Tonbridge
Premier Inn

BUDGET HOTEL

tel: 0871 527 9096 (Calls cost 13p per minute plus your phone company's access charge) **Pembury Road TN11 0NA**
web: www.premierinn.com
dir: 11 miles from M25 junction 5. Follow A21 towards Hastings, pass A26 (Tunbridge Wells) junction. Exit at next junction, 1st exit at roundabout.

High quality, budget accommodation ideal for both families and business travellers. Spacious, en suite bedrooms feature free WiFi and tea and coffee making facilities, and in most hotels, Freeview TV is also available. The adjacent family restaurant features a wide and varied menu.

Rooms: 40

Premier Inn Tonbridge North
Premier Inn

BUDGET HOTEL

tel: 0871 527 9098 (Calls cost 13p per minute plus your phone company's access charge) **Hilden Manor, London Road TN10 3AN**
web: www.premierinn.com
dir: From A21 follow Seven Oaks and Hildenborough signs. At roundabout take 2nd exit onto B245 signed Hildenborough. In 2 miles hotel on right.

Rooms: 41

TORBAY
See Brixham, Paignton & Torquay

TORQUAY
Devon   Map 3 SX96

Belgrave Sands Hotel & Spa
★★★★ 82% HOTEL

tel: 01803 226366 **Belgrave Road TQ2 5HF**
email: info@belgravesands.com **web:** www.belgravesands.com
dir: Phone for directions.

Located a stone's throw from the seafront, this hotel has been appointed to a very high standard. Classic, Signature and Suite rooms are offered – all have comfortable beds and some have a sea view. Food forms an important part of a stay here – a relaxed fine-dining experience is offered in the award-winning Seasons restaurant, open for breakfast, lunch and dinner; regularly-changing dishes are cooked with style and flair. The hotel also has on-site spa facilities.

Rooms: 50 (2 family) (4 GF) ↸ **S** fr £75 **D** fr £150 (including breakfast)* **Facilities:** Spa FTV WiFi ↻ ⊛ Gym Sauna Steam room Beauty treatments ♪ Xmas New Year **Conf:** Class 70 Board 30 Theatre 90 **Services:** Lift Night porter **Parking:** 65 **Notes:** LB Civ Wed 100

The Imperial Hotel
★★★★ 82% ⊛ HOTEL

tel: 01803 294301 **Park Hill Road TQ1 2DG**
email: info@theimperialtorquay.co.uk **web:** www.theimperialtorquay.co.uk
dir: A380 towards seafront. Turn left to harbour, right at clocktower. Hotel 300 yards on right.

This hotel has an enviable location with extensive views of the coastline. Traditional in style, the public areas are elegant and offer a choice of dining options including the Regatta Restaurant, with its stunning views over the bay. Bedrooms are spacious, most with private balconies, and the hotel has an extensive range of indoor and outdoor leisure facilities.

Rooms: 152 (14 family) ↸ **Facilities:** Spa FTV WiFi ↻ HL ⊛ ⤫ ☃ Gym Beauty salon Sauna Steam room Xmas New Year **Conf:** Class 200 Board 30 Theatre 350 **Services:** Lift Night porter **Parking:** 140 **Notes:** Civ Wed 250

Lincombe Hall Hotel
★★★★ 73% HOTEL

tel: 01803 213361 **Meadfoot Road TQ1 2JX**
email: stay@lincombehallhotel.co.uk **web:** www.lincombehallhotel.co.uk
dir: From harbour into Torwood Street, at lights after 100 yards, turn right into Meadfoot Road. Hotel 200 yards on left.

Lincombe Hall Hotel offers a range of tastefully decorated rooms, many benefiting from views of Torquay Harbour and the sea beyond. Accommodation is exclusively for over-16s, located in a quiet leafy area just a short walk from the amenities of the town centre and marina. Leisure facilities include a heated outdoor pool and small indoor pool and jacuzzi. Complimentary WiFi is available throughout the property. There are landscaped grounds and ample parking.

Rooms: 44 (19 annexe) (2 GF) **S** fr £60 **D** fr £100 (including breakfast)* **Facilities:** FTV WiFi ⊛ ⤫ ♪ Xmas New Year **Services:** Night porter **Parking:** 60 **Notes:** LB No children 16 years Closed 2–27 January

The Headland Hotel and Spa

★★★ 82% HOTEL

tel: 01803 295666 **Daddyhole Road TQ1 2EF**
email: info@headlandtorquay.com **web:** www.headlandtorquay.com
dir: *A380 to Torquay seafront, left then far side of harbour, up hill, 500 metres and turn right.*

This hotel has a delightful location set apart from the bustle of town, but within easy walking distance of the numerous attractions. With its splendid grounds and an elevated view of the bay, the hotel has an enviable position. Bedrooms are very comfortably appointed, many with sea views. Cuisine is a highlight, and the friendly team offer attentive service.

Rooms: 78 (16 family) (7 GF) ✆ **S** fr £53 **D** fr £180 (including breakfast & dinner)*
Facilities: FTV WiFi ⓣ ♨ Gym Sauna Steam room 🎵 Xmas New Year **Conf:** Class 50 Board 40 Theatre 150 **Services:** Lift Night porter **Parking:** 42 **Notes:** LB Civ Wed 150

Best Western Livermead Cliff Hotel

★★★ 76% HOTEL

 Best Western

tel: 01803 299666 **Torbay Road TQ2 6RQ**
email: info@livermeadcliff.co.uk **web:** www.livermeadcliff.co.uk
dir: *A379, A3022 to Torquay, towards seafront, turn right towards Paignton. Hotel 600 yards on seaward side.*

Situated at the water's edge, this long-established hotel offers friendly service and traditional hospitality. The splendid views can be enjoyed from the lounge, bar and dining room. Alternatively, guests can take advantage of refreshment on the wonderful terrace and enjoy one of the best outlooks in the bay. Bedrooms, many with sea views and some with balconies, are comfortable and well equipped; a range of room sizes is available.

Rooms: 64 (17 family) ✆ **Facilities:** FTV WiFi Fishing Use of facilities at sister hotel Xmas New Year **Conf:** Class 60 Board 40 Theatre 120 **Services:** Lift Night porter **Parking:** 80 **Notes:** Civ Wed 200

Livermead House Hotel

★★★ 76% HOTEL

tel: 01803 294361 **Torbay Road TQ2 6QJ**
email: info@livermead.com **web:** www.livermead.com
dir: *From seafront turn right, follow A379 towards Paignton and Livermead, hotel opposite Institute Beach.*

Having a splendid waterfront location, this hotel dates back to the 1820s, and is where Charles Kingsley is said to have written *The Water Babies*. Bedrooms vary in size and style; excellent public rooms are popular for private parties and meetings, and a range of leisure facilities is provided. Enjoyable cuisine is served in the impressive restaurant.

Rooms: 67 (6 family) (1 GF) ✆ **Facilities:** FTV WiFi ⚡ Gym Squash Sauna Solarium snooker 🎵 Xmas New Year **Conf:** Class 175 Board 80 Theatre 250 **Services:** Lift Night porter **Parking:** 131 **Notes:** Civ Wed 250

Abbey Lawn Hotel

★★★ 73% HOTEL

tel: 01803 299199 **Scarborough Road TQ2 5UQ**
email: info@holdsworthhotels.co.uk **web:** www.holdsworthhotels.co.uk/the-abbey-lawn
dir: *Phone for directions.*

Conveniently located for both the seafront and town centre, this is an ideal base for visiting the attractions of the 'English Riviera'. Many of the bedrooms, including the four-poster suite, benefit from lovely sea views. Facilities include a health club with extensive leisure activities, plus an indoor swimming pool. Traditional cuisine is served in the elegant restaurant, and evening entertainment is a regular feature in the ballroom.

Rooms: 60 (3 family) (3 GF) ✆ **S** fr £30 **D** fr £60* **Facilities:** FTV WiFi ⓣ 🎵 Xmas New Year **Services:** Lift Night porter **Parking:** 20 **Notes:** Closed 3 January to 8 February

Anchorage Hotel

★★★ 73% HOTEL

tel: 01803 326175 **Cary Park, Aveland Road TQ1 3PT**
email: enquiries@anchoragehotel.co.uk **web:** www.anchoragehotel.co.uk
dir: *Phone for directions.*

Quietly located in a residential area and providing a friendly welcome, this family-run establishment enjoys a great deal of repeat business. Bedrooms come in a range of sizes but all rooms are neatly presented. Evening entertainment is provided regularly in the large and comfortable lounge. A beauty treatment room has now opened and offers a comprehensive range of treatments.

Rooms: 55 (5 family) (17 GF) ✆ **Facilities:** FTV WiFi ⚡ Beauty room 🎵 Xmas New Year **Services:** Lift Night porter **Parking:** 26

Symbols and abbreviations
explained on pages 6–7

T

TORQUAY *continued*

Regina Hotel

Leisureplex
HOLIDAY HOTELS

★★★ 70% HOTEL

tel: 01803 292904 **Victoria Parade TQ1 2BE**
email: regina@leisureplex.co.uk **web:** www.leisureplex.co.uk
dir: *Into Torquay, follow harbour signs, hotel on outer corner of harbour.*

This hotel enjoys a pleasant and convenient location right on the harbourside, a short stroll from the town's attractions. Bedrooms, some with harbour views, vary in size. Entertainment is provided on most nights and there is a choice of bars.

Rooms: 68 (5 family) **Facilities:** FTV ♫ Xmas New Year **Services:** Lift Night porter **Parking:** 6 **Notes:** Closed January, part February RS November to December (excluding Christmas), February to March

Seascape Hotel

★★ 71% HOTEL

tel: 01803 292617 & 07767 738697 **TQ2 5UT**
email: stay@seascapehoteltorquay.com **web:** www.seascapehoteltorquay.com
dir: *A380 Torquay, at English Riviera roundabout follow A380 signed Torquay, at Torre station turn right, left at 2nd lights. Through lights, hotel 100 yards on right.*

This long-established hotel is centrally located and handy for the town centre and the seafront. The long tradition of hospitality makes guests feel genuinely welcome. Bedrooms offer consistent levels of comfort and quality – some have lovely views across the bay. Regular evening entertainment is offered during the season in the spacious lounge area.

Rooms: 57 (26 annexe) (8 family) (6 GF) ♠ **Facilities:** FTV WiFi ♫ Xmas New Year **Services:** Lift Night porter **Parking:** 16

Ashley Court Hotel

★★ 68% HOTEL

tel: 01803 292417 **107 Abbey Road TQ2 5NP**
email: reception@ashleycourt.co.uk **web:** www.ashleycourt.co.uk
dir: *A380 to seafront, left to Shedden Hill to lights, hotel opposite.*

Located close to the town centre and within easy strolling distance of the seafront, this hotel offers a warm welcome to guests. Bedrooms are pleasantly appointed and some have sea views. The outdoor pool and patio are popular with guests wishing to soak up some sunshine. Live entertainment is provided every night throughout the season.

Rooms: 83 (12 family) (8 GF) (14 smoking) ♠ **Facilities:** ⚲ Games room ♫ Xmas New Year **Services:** Lift Night porter **Parking:** 42 **Notes:** Closed 3 January to 1 February

The Osborne Hotel

[U]

tel: 01803 213311 **Hesketh Crescent TQ1 2LL**
email: enq@osborne-torquay.co.uk
dir: *Phone for directions.*

Currently the rating for this establishment is not confirmed. This may be due to a change of ownership or because ot has only recently joined the AA rating scheme.

Rooms: 32 (2 family) ♠ **S** fr £50 **D** fr £60* **Facilities:** FTV WiFi ⚲ ⚲ ⚲ Gym Pool table Foosball table Sauna **Conf:** Class 100 Board 40 Theatre 120 **Services:** Lift Night porter **Parking:** 120 **Notes:** Civ Wed 100

Premier Inn Torquay

Premier Inn

BUDGET HOTEL

tel: 0871 527 9102 (Calls cost 13p per minute plus your phone company's access charge) **Seafront, Belgrave Road TQ2 5HE**
web: www.premierinn.com
dir: *On A380 into Torquay, continue to lights (Torre Station on right). Right into Avenue Road to Kings Drive. Left at seafront, hotel at lights.*

High quality, budget accommodation ideal for both families and business travellers. Spacious, en suite bedrooms feature free WiFi and tea and coffee making facilities, and in most hotels, Freeview TV is also available. The adjacent family restaurant features a wide and varied menu.

Rooms: 143

TOTNES	Map 3 SX86
Devon	

The Royal Seven Stars Hotel

★★★ 79% HOTEL

tel: 01803 862125 **The Plains TQ9 5DD**
email: enquiry@royalsevenstars.co.uk **web:** www.royalsevenstars.co.uk
dir: *A38 Buckfastleigh junction onto A385 towards Dartington, 6.5 miles towards Totnes town centre. On corner of Fore Street and Coronation Road.*

Situated in the vibrant town of Totnes, this engaging hotel has plenty to offer both visitors and locals alike. The style is an appealing blend of originality and stylish flourishes. The TQ9 restaurant, in the old stables, offers a seasonal menu of local produce and fish from Brixham, and has an adjoining champagne bar. Bedrooms are individually designed, quirky and full of character with quality and comfort assured; dogs are welcome at this hotel which makes a great base for exploring this beautiful part of south Devon.

Rooms: 21 (1 family) ♠ **S** fr £60 **D** fr £130 (including breakfast)* **Facilities:** FTV WiFi ♫ Xmas New Year **Conf:** Class 60 Board 40 Theatre 120 **Services:** Night porter **Parking:** 10 **Notes:** LB Civ Wed 120

TRING	Map 6 SP91
Hertfordshire	

Pendley Manor Hotel

★★★★ 74% ⚫⚫ HOTEL

tel: 01442 891891 **Cow Lane HP23 5QY**
email: info@pendley-manor.co.uk **web:** www.pendley-manor.co.uk
dir: *M25 junction 20, A41 Tring exit. At roundabout follow Berkhamsted/London signs. 1st left signed Tring Station and Pendley Manor.*

Pendley Manor Hotel is an impressive Victorian mansion set in extensive and mature landscaped grounds where peacocks roam. The spacious bedrooms are situated in both the manor house and the wing, and offer a useful range of facilities. Public areas include a cosy bar, a conservatory lounge and an intimate restaurant as well as a leisure centre.

Rooms: 86 (15 family) (17 GF) **Facilities:** Spa FTV WiFi ⚲ ⚲ ⚲ Gym Steam room Dance studio Sauna **Conf:** Class 80 Board 80 Theatre 250 **Services:** Lift Night porter Air con **Parking:** 150 **Notes:** Civ Wed 160

Premier Inn Tring

BUDGET HOTEL

tel: 0871 527 9104 (Calls cost 13p per minute plus your phone company's access charge) **Tring Hill HP23 4LD**
web: www.premierinn.com
dir: *M25 junction 20, A41 towards Aylesbury, at end of Hemel Hempstead/Tring bypass straight on at roundabout, hotel approximately 100 yards on right.*

High quality, budget accommodation ideal for both families and business travellers. Spacious, en suite bedrooms feature free WiFi and tea and coffee making facilities, and in most hotels, Freeview TV is also available. The adjacent family restaurant features a wide and varied menu.

Rooms: 42

TROWBRIDGE	Map 4 ST85
Wiltshire	

The Moonraker Hotel

★★★ 76% HOTEL

tel: 01225 777393 **Trowle Common BA14 9BL**
email: reservations@moonrakerhotel.com **web:** www.moonrakerhotel.com

Dating back 500 years, The Moonraker Hotel is a Grade II listed manor house set in four acres of land. Within the grounds are a walled garden, paddock, ponds and converted outbuildings from its days as a farm. A relaxed atmosphere has been retained including in the milking barn restaurant. Bedrooms come in range of shapes and sizes either in the main building or in newly converted outbuildings. Dinner is a highlight here with top quality produce often used in the hotel's own smokery. The tasting menu with wine flight is very tempting

Rooms: 23 **Facilities:** ⌨

Premier Inn Trowbridge

Premier Inn

BUDGET HOTEL

tel: 0871 527 9444 (Calls cost 13p per minute plus your phone company's access charge) **St Stephens Place BA14 8AH**
web: www.premierinn.com
dir: *M4 junction 17, A429 (Chippenham). A350 (Warminster and Poole). 12 miles. After Seminton roundabout, at 2nd lights right into West Ashton Road (Trowbridge). At 1st mini-roundabout 2nd exit, at 2nd mini-roundabout into County Way. At major roundabout 5th exit into Castle Street. At mini-roundabout 3rd exit, hotel on right.*

Rooms: 80

TRURO	Map 2 SW84
Cornwall & Isles of Scilly	

HIGHLY RECOMMENDED

The Alverton Hotel

★★★★ 83% HOTEL

tel: 01872 276633 **Tregolls Road TR1 1ZQ**
email: stay@thealverton.co.uk **web:** www.thealverton.co.uk
dir: *From A30 at Carland Cross take A39 to Truro. At lights right onto A39 (Tregolls Road) signed Truro/Falmouth.*

The Alverton Hotel is a beautiful Grade II listed building which was previously a convent. The bedrooms are smartly decorated, and there is a comfortable lounge/cocktail bar, as well as an attractive restaurant that serves popular meals using locally-sourced produce. Parking is available.

Rooms: 50 (15 annexe) (7 family) (11 GF) ⌨ **S** fr £69 **D** fr £99 (including breakfast)* **Facilities:** FTV WiFi ⌨ Xmas New Year **Conf:** Class 50 Board 50 Theatre 140 **Services:** Night porter **Parking:** 71 **Notes:** LB Civ Wed 120

HIGHLY RECOMMENDED

Mannings Hotel

★★★ 88% HOTEL

tel: 01872 270345 **Lemon Street TR1 2QB**
email: reception@manningshotels.co.uk **web:** www.manningshotels.co.uk
dir: *A30 to Carland Cross then Truro. Follow brown signs to hotel in city centre.*

This popular hotel is located in the heart of Truro and offers an engaging blend of traditional and contemporary. Public areas have a stylish atmosphere, with the bar and restaurant proving popular with locals and residents alike. A wide choice of appetizing dishes is available as well as daily specials. Bedrooms are pleasantly appointed.

Rooms: 43 (9 annexe) (4 family) (3 GF) ⌨ **S** fr £85 **D** fr £115 (including breakfast) **Facilities:** FTV WiFi ⌨ **Services:** Night porter **Parking:** 43 **Notes:** LB Closed 24–26 December

Premier Inn Truro

Premier Inn

BUDGET HOTEL

tel: 0871 527 9106 (Calls cost 13p per minute plus your phone company's access charge) **Old Carnon Hill, Carnon Downs TR3 6JT**
web: www.premierinn.com
dir: *On A39 (Truro to Falmouth road), 3 miles southwest of Truro.*

Rooms: 86

T

TUNBRIDGE WELLS (ROYAL)
Kent

Map 6 TQ53

One Warwick Park Hotel

★★★★ 84% HOTEL

tel: 01892 520587 **1 Warwick Park TN2 5TA**
email: info@onewarwickpark.co.uk **web:** www.onewarwickpark.co.uk
dir: *A21 at Pembury junction follow signs to Tunbridge Wells, then town centre. Adjacent to The Pantiles.*

This new hotel is just a few minutes' walk from the Pantiles of Tunbridge Wells, and offers a choice of stylish bedrooms; some in the main building and some in annexes alongside. All are very well equipped, have air conditioning and come with many useful extras including top-quality toiletries. Contemporary in style, the hotel has been finished to a very high standard throughout. The onsite restaurant, Seventeen, offers classic British dishes with a weekly changing menu. Car parking is available close by; please check when booking.

Rooms: 39 (7 family) 🐾 **S** fr £80 **D** fr £80 (including breakfast)* **Facilities:** FTV WiFi 🏃 ♫ New Year **Conf:** Class 56 Board 85 Theatre 130 **Services:** Lift Night porter Air con **Notes:** Civ Wed 120

The Spa Hotel

★★★★ 80% ◉◉ HOTEL

tel: 01892 520331 **Mount Ephraim TN4 8XJ**
email: reservations@spahotel.co.uk **web:** www.spahotel.co.uk
dir: *A21 to A26, follow A264 East Grinstead signs, hotel on right.*

Set in 14 acres of beautifully tended grounds, this imposing 18th-century mansion offers spacious, modern bedrooms that are stylishly decorated and thoughtfully equipped. The public rooms include the Chandelier Restaurant, Zagatos Bar & Brasserie and The Orangery which complements the stunning lobby. There are extensive meeting and health club facilities, and a spa offering treatment rooms. The hotel is also licensed for civil wedding ceremonies.

Rooms: 70 (4 family) (1 GF) 🐾 **S** fr £80 **D** fr £99* **Facilities:** Spa STV FTV WiFi 🏃 ⚾ 🏊 Gym Sauna Steam room Xmas New Year **Conf:** Class 63 Board 60 Theatre 300 **Services:** Lift Night porter **Parking:** 150 **Notes:** Civ Wed 150

Hotel du Vin Tunbridge Wells

★★★★ 78% ◉ TOWN HOUSE HOTEL

tel: 01892 232 0749 & 526 455 **Crescent Road TN1 2LY**
email: reception.tunbridgewells@hotelduvin.com
web: www.hotelduvin.com/locations/tunbridge-wel
dir: *Follow town centre, to main junction of Mount Pleasant Road and Crescent Road/Church Road. Hotel 150 yards on right just past Phillips House.*

This impressive Grade II listed building dates from 1762, and as a princess, Queen Victoria often stayed here. The spacious bedrooms are available in a range of sizes, beautifully and individually appointed, and equipped with a host of thoughtful extras. Public rooms include a bistro-style restaurant, two elegant lounges and a small bar.

Rooms: 34 (2 GF) 🐾 **Facilities:** WiFi ♫ Xmas New Year **Conf:** Class 40 Board 36 Theatre 85 **Services:** Lift Night porter **Parking:** 30 **Notes:** Civ Wed 84

Mercure Tunbridge Wells

★★★★ 69% HOTEL

tel: 01892 823567 & 0844 815 9074 (Calls cost 7p per minute plus your phone company's access charge) **8 Tonbridge Road TN2 4QL**
email: sales.mercuretunbridgewells@jupiterhotels.co.uk
web: www.mercuretunbridgewells.co.uk
dir: *M25 junction 5, A21 south. Left at 1st roundabout signed Pembury Hospital. Hotel on left, 400 yards past hospital.*

Built in the style of a traditional Kentish oast house, this well presented hotel is conveniently located just off the A21 with easy access to the M25. Bedrooms are comfortably appointed for both business and leisure guests. Public areas include a leisure club and a range of meeting rooms.

Rooms: 84 (12 family) (40 GF) 🐾 **Facilities:** STV FTV WiFi 🏃 HL 🏊 Steam room Sauna Beauty treatment room Xmas New Year **Conf:** Class 80 Board 50 Theatre 150 **Services:** Night porter **Parking:** 100 **Notes:** Civ Wed 180

Russell Hotel

★★ 65% METRO HOTEL

tel: 01892 544833 **80 London Road TN1 1DZ**
email: sales@russell-hotel.com **web:** www.russell-hotel.com
dir: *From Tunbridge Wells A26 junction with Lime Hill Road turn.*

This detached Victorian property is situated just a short walk from the centre of town. The generously proportioned bedrooms in the main house are pleasantly decorated and well equipped. In addition, there are several smartly appointed, self-contained suites in an adjacent building. The public rooms include a lounge and cosy bar.

Rooms: 26 (5 annexe) (5 family) (1 GF) **Facilities:** FTV WiFi **Conf:** Class 10 Board 10 Theatre 10 **Services:** Night porter **Parking:** 14

TURNERS HILL
West Sussex

Map 6 TQ33

Alexander House Hotel & Utopia Spa

★★★★★ 88% ◉◉◉ ▤ HOTEL

tel: 01342 714914 **East Street RH10 4QD**
email: admin@alexanderhouse.co.uk **web:** www.alexanderhouse.co.uk
dir: *6 miles from M23 junction 10, on B2110 between Turners Hill and East Grinstead.*

Set in 175 acres of parkland and landscaped gardens, this delightful country house hotel dates back to the 17th century. Most of the bedrooms are very spacious and all have luxurious bathrooms; the rooms in the most recent wing are particularly stunning. There are two award-winning restaurants to choose from – AG's Restaurant (3 AA Rosettes) for inspired modern British cuisine, and Reflections (2 AA Rosettes) is their bistro-style operation. The Utopia Spa has a state-of-the-art pool and gym, as well as specialised treatments.

Rooms: 58 (20 annexe) (13 family) (10 GF) **Facilities:** Spa FTV WiFi 🐾 🧖 🏊 Gym Clay shooting Archery Mountain bikes Pony trekking Xmas New Year **Conf:** Class 70 Board 40 Theatre 150 **Services:** Lift Night porter **Parking:** 100 **Notes:** Civ Wed 100

TWICKENHAM
Greater London

Premier Inn Twickenham East

Premier Inn

BUDGET HOTEL Plan 1 B2

tel: 0871 527 9108 (Calls cost 13p per minute plus your phone company's access charge) **Corner Sixth Cross, Staines Road TW2 5PE**
web: www.premierinn.com
dir: M25 junction 12 onto M3, follow Central London signs, at end of M3 becomes A316. Straight on at 1st roundabout. Hotel 500 yards on left.

High quality, budget accommodation ideal for both families and business travellers. Spacious, en suite bedrooms feature free WiFi and tea and coffee making facilities, and in most hotels, Freeview TV is also available. The adjacent family restaurant features a wide and varied menu.

Rooms: 17

Premier Inn Twickenham Stadium

Premier Inn

BUDGET HOTEL Plan 1 B2

tel: 0871 527 9110 (Calls cost 13p per minute plus your phone company's access charge) **Chertsey Road, Whitton TW2 6LS**
web: www.premierinn.com
dir: From M3 onto A316, then A305 signed Twickenham. At Hospital Bridge Roundabout 3rd exit into Hospital Bridge Road. Take B358 signed Teddington. Becomes Sixth Cross Road. Hotel on left.

Rooms: 39

TWO BRIDGES
Devon

Map 3 SX67

Two Bridges Hotel

★★★ 82% @@ HOTEL

tel: 01822 892300 **PL20 6SW**
email: reception@twobridges.co.uk **web:** www.twobridges.co.uk
dir: At junction of B3212 and B3357.

This wonderfully relaxing hotel is set in the heart of the Dartmoor National Park, in a beautiful riverside location. Three standards of comfortable rooms provide every modern convenience, and include four-poster rooms. There is a choice of lounges, and fine dining is available in the restaurant, where menus feature local game and other seasonal produce.

Rooms: 32 (2 family) (10 GF) **S** fr £69 **D** fr £99 (including breakfast)*
Facilities: FTV WiFi Fishing Xmas New Year **Conf:** Class 60 Board 40 Theatre 130 **Services:** Night porter **Parking:** 100 **Notes:** LB Civ Wed 130

TYNEMOUTH
Tyne & Wear

Map 21 NZ36

Grand Hotel

★★★ 85% HOTEL

tel: 0191 293 6666 **Grand Parade NE30 4ER**
email: reservations@grandhotel-uk.com **web:** www.grandhotel-uk.com
dir: A1058 for Tynemouth. At coast roundabout turn right. Hotel on right approximately 0.5 mile.

This grand Victorian building offers stunning views of the coast. Bedrooms come in a variety of styles and are well equipped, tastefully decorated and have impressive bathrooms. In addition to the restaurant there are two bars. The elegant and imposing staircase is a focal point, and is a favourite spot for the bride and groom to have their photograph taken after their wedding here.

Rooms: 46 (6 annexe) (14 family) **S** fr £79 **D** fr £89* **Facilities:** STV FTV WiFi Xmas New Year **Conf:** Class 40 Board 40 Theatre 130 **Services:** Lift Night porter **Parking:** 16 **Notes:** LB Civ Wed 120

UCKFIELD
East Sussex

Map 6 TQ42

INSPECTOR'S CHOICE

Buxted Park Hotel

★★★★ @@ HOTEL

 HANDPICKED HOTELS

tel: 01825 733333 & 0845 072 7412 (Calls cost 5p per minute plus your phone company's access charge) **Buxted TN22 4AY**
email: buxtedpark@handpicked.co.uk
web: www.handpickedhotels.co.uk/buxtedpark
dir: From A26 Uckfield bypass take A272 signed Buxted. Through lights, hotel 1 mile on right.

Buxted Park Hotel is an attractive Grade II listed Georgian mansion dating back to the 17th century, set amidst 300 acres of beautiful countryside and landscaped gardens. The stylish, thoughtfully equipped bedrooms are split between the main house and the modern Garden Wing. An interesting choice of dishes is served in the restaurant.

Rooms: 44 (7 family) (16 GF) **S** fr £88 **D** fr £98 (including breakfast)*
Facilities: STV WiFi HL Fishing Gym Orienteering Walking trail Snooker room Xmas New Year **Conf:** Class 80 Board 42 Theatre 180 **Services:** Lift Night porter **Parking:** 100 **Notes:** Civ Wed 120

U

UCKFIELD *continued*

Horsted Place

★★★★ 82% HOTEL

tel: 01825 750581 **Little Horsted TN22 5TS**
email: hotel@horstedplace.co.uk **web:** www.horstedplace.co.uk
dir: *From Uckfield 2 miles south on A26 towards Lewes.*

This property is one of Britain's finest examples of Gothic revivalist architecture, and much of the 1850s building was designed by Augustus Pugin. The hotel is situated in extensive landscaped grounds, with a tennis court and croquet lawn, and is adjacent to the East Sussex National Golf Club. The spacious bedrooms, in a range of both sizes and designs, are attractively decorated, tastefully furnished, and equipped with many thoughtful touches such as flowers and books. Most bedrooms also have a separate sitting area. Formal dining can be enjoyed in the elegant dining room (no children after 7pm) where the menus are based on quality seasonal produce. Pre-dinner drinks and after-dinner coffees can be enjoyed either in the Drawing Room or on the terrace overlooking the garden.

Rooms: 20 (3 annexe) (5 family) (2 GF) **S** fr £145 **D** fr £145 (including breakfast)* **Facilities:** STV FTV WiFi 36 Free use of gym and indoor pool at nearby hotel Xmas **Conf:** Class 50 Board 40 Theatre 80 **Services:** Lift Night porter **Parking:** 32 **Notes:** LB No children 7 years Closed 1–7 January Civ Wed 100

East Sussex National Golf Resort & Spa

★★★★ 81% HOTEL

tel: 01825 880088 **Little Horsted TN22 5ES**
email: reception@eastsussexnational.co.uk **web:** www.eastsussexnational.co.uk
dir: *M25 junction 6, A22 signed East Grinstead and Eastbourne. Straight on at roundabout junction of A22 and A26 (Little Horsted). At next roundabout right to hotel.*

This modern hotel is located in a lovely country location and offers a super range of facilities with two golf courses and an impressive leisure suite. In addition there are also conference and meeting facilities. The bedrooms are spacious and have good facilities; all have delightful views across the golf course to the countryside beyond. The cuisine is enjoyable; particularly at breakfast, which is served in the restaurant that overlooks the course.

Rooms: 104 (3 family) (36 GF) **S** fr £99 **D** fr £109 (including breakfast)* **Facilities:** Spa STV FTV WiFi HL 36 Gym Academy of Golf Xmas New Year **Conf:** Class 200 Board 50 Theatre 450 **Services:** Lift Night porter Air con **Parking:** 500 **Notes:** Civ Wed 250

ULLESTHORPE
Leicestershire   **Map 11 SP58**

Best Western Plus Ullesthorpe Court Hotel & Golf Club

Best Western PLUS

★★★★ 76% HOTEL

tel: 01455 209023 **Frolesworth Road LE17 5BZ**
email: bookings@ullesthorpecourt.co.uk **web:** www.ullesthorpecourt.co.uk
dir: *M1 junction 20 towards Lutterworth. Follow brown tourist signs.*

Complete with its own golf club, this impressively equipped hotel is within easy reach of the motorway network, NEC and Birmingham Airport. Public areas include both formal and informal eating options and extensive conference and leisure facilities. Spacious bedrooms are thoughtfully equipped for both the business and leisure guest, and a four-poster room is available.

Rooms: 72 (3 family) (16 GF) **Facilities:** Spa FTV WiFi 18 Gym Beauty room Steam room Sauna Snooker room New Year **Conf:** Class 48 Board 30 Theatre 80 **Services:** Lift Night porter **Parking:** 280 **Notes:** Closed RS 25–26 December Civ Wed 120

ULLSWATER

See **Glennridding & Patterdale**

ULVERSTON
Cumbria   **Map 18 SD27**

Premier Inn Ulverston

Premier Inn

BUDGET HOTEL

tel: 0871 527 9714 (Calls cost 13p per minute plus your phone company's access charge) **Lonsdale Terrace LA12 9AU**
web: www.premierinn.com
dir: *Leave the A590 (Canal Street/County Road) onto North Lonsdale Terrace. Continue to follow this road. The hotel will be on your left.*

High quality, budget accommodation ideal for both families and business travellers. Spacious, en suite bedrooms feature free WiFi and tea and coffee making facilities, and in most hotels, Freeview TV is also available. The adjacent family restaurant features a wide and varied menu.

Rooms: 79

U

UPPER SLAUGHTER
Gloucestershire   Map 10 SP12

INSPECTOR'S CHOICE

Lords of the Manor
★★★★ ◉◉ COUNTRY HOUSE HOTEL

tel: 01451 820243 **GL54 2JD**
email: reservations@lordsofthemanor.com **web:** www.lordsofthemanor.com
dir: *2 miles west of A429. Exit A40 onto A429, take 'The Slaughters' turn. Through Lower Slaughter for 1 mile to Upper Slaughter. Hotel on right.*

This wonderfully welcoming 17th-century manor house hotel sits in eight acres of gardens and parkland surrounded by beautiful Cotswold countryside. A relaxed atmosphere, underpinned by professional and attentive service is the hallmark here, so that guests are often reluctant to leave. The hotel has elegant public rooms that overlook the immaculate lawns, and the restaurant is the venue for consistently impressive cuisine. Bedrooms have much character and charm, combined with the extra touches expected of a hotel of this stature.

Rooms: 26 (4 family) (9 GF) ⋒ **S** fr £150 **D** fr £195 (including breakfast)*
Facilities: FTV WiFi Fishing 🎣 Xmas New Year **Conf:** Class 20 Board 20 Theatre 30 **Services:** Night porter **Parking:** 40 **Notes:** LB Civ Wed 80

UTTOXETER
Staffordshire   Map 10 SK03

Premier Inn Uttoxeter
Premier Inn

BUDGET HOTEL

tel: 0871 527 9112 (Calls cost 13p per minute plus your phone company's access charge) **Derby Road ST14 5AA**
web: www.premierinn.com
dir: *At junction of A50 and B5030 on outskirts of Uttoxeter, 7 miles south of Alton Towers Theme Park.*

High quality, budget accommodation ideal for both families and business travellers. Spacious, en suite bedrooms feature free WiFi and tea and coffee making facilities, and in most hotels, Freeview TV is also available. The adjacent family restaurant features a wide and varied menu.

Rooms: 75

UXBRIDGE
Greater London   Map 6 TQ08

See also **Ruislip**

Lancaster Hotel & Spa
★★★ 79% HOTEL

tel: 01895 268006 **Brunel University, Kingston Lane UB8 3PH**
email: lancaster-suite@brunel.ac.uk **web:** www.brunelcommercial.london
dir: *Follow signs for Brunel University. Hotel is situated inside the university grounds.*

The Lancaster Hotel & Spa is conveniently located in the grounds of Brunel University London. The complex has been appointed to a very high standard and offers a range of bedrooms to suit all budgets. The public areas include a comfortable lounge with a well-stocked bar and a secluded terrace for the summer. Freshly prepared dishes are served in the restaurant which is adjacent to the lounge area. The spa has a pool, sauna and steam room. Multifunctional meeting rooms are available. On-site parking is offered, and the area is patrolled 24 hours a day.

Rooms: 70 ⋒ **Facilities:** FTV WiFi ♨ Sports facilities Shops Bank **Conf:** Board 16 **Services:** Lift **Parking:** 50

Premier Inn London Uxbridge
Premier Inn

BUDGET HOTEL

tel: 0871 527 9574 (Calls cost 13p per minute plus your phone company's access charge) **Phase 500, Riverside Way UB8 2UX**
web: www.premierinn.com
dir: *M40 junction 1 follow A412/Uxbridge/A4020 signs. At Denham Roundabout 1st exit then 2nd exit into Oxford Road. 3rd exit at roundabout, left into Cross Street. Right into Cowley Road, right into Trumper Way. Left into New Windsor Street, right into Riverside Way.*

Rooms: 80

VENTNOR
Isle Of Wight   Map 5 SZ57

The Royal Hotel
★★★★ 81% ◉◉ HOTEL

tel: 01983 852186 **Belgrave Road PO38 1JJ**
email: enquiries@royalhoteliow.co.uk **web:** www.royalhoteliow.co.uk
dir: *A3055 into Ventnor follow one-way system, after lights left into Church Street. Top of hill left into Belgrave Road. Hotel on right.*

This smart hotel enjoys a central yet peaceful location in its own gardens, complete with an outdoor pool. Spacious, elegant public areas include a bright conservatory, bar and lounge. Bedrooms, appointed to a high standard, vary in size and style. Staff are friendly and efficient, particularly in the smart restaurant, where modern British cuisine is offered.

Rooms: 51 (9 family) ⋒ **S** fr £135 **D** fr £265 (including breakfast & dinner)*
Facilities: FTV WiFi ♨ ⚲ Beauty treatment room Xmas New Year **Conf:** Class 40 Board 24 Theatre 100 **Services:** Lift Night porter **Parking:** 50 **Notes:** LB Civ Wed 120

V

VERYAN
Cornwall & Isles Of Scilly

Map 2 SW93

The Nare
★★★★ ◎◎ COUNTRY HOUSE HOTEL

tel: 01872 501111 **Carne Beach TR2 5PF**
email: stay@narehotel.co.uk web: www.narehotel.co.uk
dir: *A3078 from Tregony, approximately 1.5 miles. Left at Veryan sign, through village towards sea and hotel.*

The only four AA Red Star hotel in Cornwall, The Nare offers a relaxed, country-house atmosphere in a spectacular coastal setting. The elegantly designed bedrooms, many with balconies, have fresh flowers, carefully chosen artwork and antiques that contribute to their engaging individuality. A choice of dining options is available, from light snacks to superb local seafood.

Rooms: 37 (7 family) (7 GF) ↾ **S** fr £155 **D** fr £295 (including breakfast)*
Facilities: Spa FTV WiFi ⊗ ↻ ☺ ✤ Gym Health and beauty clinic Sauna Steam room Hotel sailing boat Shooting Xmas New Year **Services:** Lift Night porter
Parking: 80

WAKEFIELD
West Yorkshire

Map 16 SE32

See also **Liversedge**

Waterton Park Hotel
★★★★ 81% ◎ HOTEL

tel: 01924 257911 **Walton Hall, The Balk WF2 6PW**
email: info@watertonparkhotel.co.uk web: www.watertonparkhotel.co.uk
dir: *3 miles southeast off B6378. Exit M1 junction 39 towards Wakefield. At 3rd roundabout right for Crofton. At 2nd lights right and follow signs.*

This Georgian mansion, built on an island in the centre of a 26-acre lake, has a truly idyllic setting. The main house contains many feature bedrooms, and the annexe houses more spacious rooms, all equally well equipped with modern facilities; most have views over the lake or the 18-hole golf course. The delightful beamed restaurant, two bars and leisure club are located in the old hall, and the hotel is licenced for civil weddings. The spa is located in the annexed section of the hotel.

Rooms: 63 (41 annexe) (5 family) (21 GF) ↾ **S** fr £105 **D** fr £175 (including breakfast)* **Facilities:** Spa STV FTV WiFi ↻ ⊗ Fishing Gym Steam room Sauna New Year **Conf:** Class 80 Board 80 Theatre 150 **Services:** Lift Night porter **Parking:** 200
Notes: LB Civ Wed 130

Best Western Hotel St Pierre
★★★ 78% HOTEL

tel: 01924 255596 **733 Barnsley Road, Newmillerdam WF2 6QG**
email: enq@hotelstpierre.co.uk web: www.bw-hotelstpierre.co.uk
dir: *M1 junction 39, A636 to Wakefield, right at 2nd roundabout into Asdale Road to lights. Right onto A61 towards Barnsley. Hotel just after lake on left.*

Located in the award-winning village of Newmillerdam, this property provides comfortable, modern accommodation; all bedrooms are well appointed with quality accessories and complimentary WiFi. The restaurant menu offers a good choice of dishes, and a more relaxed bar menu is also available. Ample on-site parking is available.

Rooms: 54 (1 family) (4 GF) ↾ **Facilities:** Spa FTV WiFi ↻ New Year **Conf:** Class 60 Board 60 Theatre 100 **Services:** Lift Night porter **Parking:** 74 **Notes:** Civ Wed 100

Premier Inn Wakefield Central
BUDGET HOTEL

tel: 0871 527 9114 (Calls cost 13p per minute plus your phone company's access charge) **Thornes Park, Denby Dale Road WF2 8DY**
web: www.premierinn.com
dir: *M1 junction 41, A650 towards Wakefield. Approximately 1.5 miles. Hotel on right.*

High quality, budget accommodation ideal for both families and business travellers. Spacious, en suite bedrooms feature free WiFi and tea and coffee making facilities, and in most hotels, Freeview TV is also available. The adjacent family restaurant features a wide and varied menu.

Rooms: 42

Premier Inn Wakefield City North
BUDGET HOTEL

tel: 0871 527 9116 (Calls cost 13p per minute plus your phone company's access charge) **Paragon Business Park, Herriot Way WF1 2UJ**
web: www.premierinn.com
dir: *M1 junction 41, A650 (Bradford Road) for approximately 1.5 miles towards Wakefield centre. Hotel on right adjacent to Bannatynes Health Club.*

Rooms: 47

Premier Inn Wakefield South M1 Jct 39
BUDGET HOTEL

tel: 0871 527 9118 (Calls cost 13p per minute plus your phone company's access charge) **Calder Park, Denby Dale Road WF4 3BB**
web: www.premierinn.com
dir: *M1 junction 39, A636 towards Wakefield. At 1st roundabout 1st exit into Calder Park. Hotel on right.*

Rooms: 75

Ramada Hotel Wakefield
AA Advertised

tel: 01924 274200 **Silkwood Business Park, M1 junction 40 WF5 9TJ**
email: wakefield.hotel@welcomebreak.co.uk
web: www.welcomebreak.co.uk/hotels/days-hotel-wakefield
dir: *M1 junction 40, follow signs to Wakefield, hotel 400 yards on left.*

This modern building offers accommodation in smart, spacious and well-equipped bedrooms, suitable for families and business travellers, and all with en suite bathrooms. Continental breakfast is available and other refreshments may be taken at the nearby family restaurant.

Rooms: 99 🐾 **Facilities:** FTV WiFi ➤ Gym **Conf:** Class 15 Board 15 Theatre 25
Services: Lift Night porter **Parking:** 80 **Notes:** LB

WALLASEY	**Map 15 SJ29**
Merseyside	

Grove House Hotel

★★★ 82% SMALL HOTEL

tel: 0151 639 3947 & 630 4558 **Grove Road CH45 3HF**
email: reception@thegrovehouse.co.uk **web:** www.thegrovehouse.co.uk
dir: *M53 junction 1, A554 (Wallasey New Brighton), right after church into Harrison Drive, left after Windsors Garage into Grove Road.*

Ideally situated for Liverpool and the M53, this friendly hotel offers attractive and comfortable bedrooms which come with a wealth of extras. Well-cooked meals are served in the elegant, panelled dining room. Weddings and conferences also catered for.

Rooms: 14 (7 family) 🐾 **S** fr £79 **D** fr £89* **Facilities:** FTV WiFi **Conf:** Class 60 Board 50 Theatre 100 **Services:** Night porter **Parking:** 28 **Notes:** Civ Wed 100

Leasowe Castle Hotel

tel: 0151 606 9191 **Leasowe Road CH46 3RF**
email: info@leasowecastle.com
dir: *M53 junction 1, follow signs to New Brighton (A5545) and Wallasey (A551). Merge onto Leasowe Road via ramp to Leasowe. Straight at roundabout, at next lights turn right into castle.*

Currently the rating for this establishment is not confirmed. This may be due to a change of ownership or because it has only recently joined the AA rating scheme.

Rooms: 47 (6 family) 🐾 **S** fr £60 **D** fr £75* **Facilities:** FTV WiFi 🐾 **Conf:** Class 175 Board 40 Theatre 350 **Services:** Lift Night porter **Parking:** 200 **Notes:** Civ Wed 300

WALLINGFORD	**Map 5 SU68**
Oxfordshire	

The George

★★★ 77% HOTEL

PEEL HOTELS PLC

tel: 01491 836665 **High Street OX10 0BS**
email: info@george-hotel-wallingford.com **web:** www.peelhotels.co.uk
dir: *East side of A329, north end of Wallingford.*

Old world charm and modern facilities merge seamlessly in this former coaching inn. Bedrooms in the main house have character in abundance. Those in the wing have a more contemporary style, but all are well equipped and attractively decorated. Diners can choose between the bistro or the cosy bar. The internal courtyard is perfect during the warm months of the year. There is secure parking at the rear of the hotel.

Rooms: 39 (1 family) (9 GF) 🐾 **S** fr £110 **D** fr £130* **Facilities:** STV WiFi Xmas New Year **Conf:** Class 60 Board 50 Theatre 150 **Services:** Night porter **Parking:** 40 **Notes:** LB Civ Wed 100

WALSALL	**Map 10 SP09**
West Midlands	

Fairlawns Hotel & Spa

★★★★ 78% ⍟⍟ HOTEL

CLASSIC BRITISH HOTELS

tel: 01922 455122 **178 Little Aston Road, Aldridge WS9 0NU**
email: reception@fairlawns.co.uk **web:** www.fairlawns.co.uk
dir: *Exit A452 towards Aldridge at crossroad with A454. Hotel 600 yards on right.*

In a rural location with immaculate landscaped grounds, this constantly improving hotel offers a wide range of facilities and modern, comfortable bedrooms. Family rooms, one with a four-poster bed, and suites are also available. The Fairlawns Restaurant serves a wide range of award-winning seasonal dishes. The extensive, comprehensively equipped leisure complex is mainly for adult use as there is restricted availability to young people.

Rooms: 60 (8 family) (1 GF) (3 smoking) 🐾 **Facilities:** Spa STV FTV WiFi ➤ 🌀 ⎐ Gym Dance studio Beauty salon Bathing suite Floatation suite Sauna Aromatherapy room New Year **Conf:** Class 40 Board 30 Theatre 80 **Services:** Lift Night porter **Parking:** 150 **Notes:** Civ Wed 100

Mercure Birmingham North Baron's Court Hotel

★★★ 76% HOTEL

Mercure HOTELS

tel: 01543 452020 **Walsall Road, Walsall Wood WS9 9AH**
email: sales@talashhotels.com
dir: *3.5 miles out of Walsall town centre, just north of Birmingham, close to M6 Toll.*

This hotel prides itself on warm hospitality and is conveniently situated for business guests visiting this area. The lounge, bar and restaurant are modern and thoughtfully designed. Conference facilities are available, along with ample parking.

Rooms: 97 (7 family) **S** fr £50* **Facilities:** FTV WiFi ➤ Xmas New Year **Conf:** Class 64 Board 45 Theatre 110 **Services:** Lift Night porter **Parking:** 123 **Notes:** Civ Wed 120

Premier Inn Walsall M6 Jct 10

BUDGET HOTEL

Premier Inn

tel: 0871 527 9120 (Calls cost 13p per minute plus your phone company's access charge) **Bentley Green, Bentley Road North WS2 0WB**
web: www.premierinn.com
dir: *M6 junction 10, A454 signed Wolverhampton. 2nd exit (Ansons junction). Left at roundabout, 1st left at next roundabout, hotel on right.*

High quality, budget accommodation ideal for both families and business travellers. Spacious, en suite bedrooms feature free WiFi and tea and coffee making facilities, and in most hotels, Freeview TV is also available. The adjacent family restaurant features a wide and varied menu.

Rooms: 60

Premier Inn Walsall Town Centre

BUDGET HOTEL

Premier Inn

tel: 0871 527 9374 (Calls cost 13p per minute plus your phone company's access charge) **Waterfront, Wolverhampton Street WS2 8LR**
web: www.premierinn.com
dir: *M6 junction 10/A454 Wolverhampton Road to Walsall. Continue on A454. Follow signs for Crown Wharf Shopping Centre. Hotel on right on Wolverhampton Street.*

Rooms: 100

W

WALTHAM ABBEY
Essex

Map 6 TL30

Premier Inn Waltham Abbey

Premier Inn

BUDGET HOTEL

tel: 0871 527 9122 (Calls cost 13p per minute plus your phone company's access charge) **Sewardstone Road EN9 3QF**
web: www.premierinn.com
dir: M25 junction 26, A121 towards Waltham Abbey. Left onto A112, hotel 0.5 mile on left.

High quality, budget accommodation ideal for both families and business travellers. Spacious, en suite bedrooms feature free WiFi and tea and coffee making facilities, and in most hotels, Freeview TV is also available. The adjacent family restaurant features a wide and varied menu.

Rooms: 99

WANSFORD
Cambridgeshire

Map 12 TL09

The Haycock Hotel

 MACDONALD
HOTELS & RESORTS

★★★ 82% HOTEL

tel: 01780 782223 **London Road PE8 6JA**
email: reception.haycock@macdonald-hotels.co.uk
web: www.macdonaldhotels.co.uk/haycock
dir: A1 junction to A47 Leicester/Peterborough.

The Haycock Hotel is a charming 17th-century coaching inn set in attractive landscaped grounds in a peaceful village location. The smartly decorated bedrooms are tastefully furnished and thoughtfully equipped. Public rooms include a choice of restaurants, a lounge bar, a cocktail bar and a stylish lounge. The hotel has a staffed business centre, and banqueting facilities are also available.

Rooms: 48 (1 family) (14 GF) ↑ **S** fr £97 **D** fr £107 (including breakfast)*
Facilities: FTV WiFi ↳ Beauty treatment room New Year **Conf:** Class 100 Board 45 Theatre 300 **Services:** Night porter **Parking:** 300 **Notes:** LB Civ Wed 200

WARMINSTER
Wiltshire

Map 4 ST84

HIGHLY RECOMMENDED

The Bishopstrow Hotel & Spa

★★★★ 84% ◉◉ HOTEL

tel: 01985 212312 **Borenam Road BA12 9HH**
email: info@bishopstrow.com **web:** www.bishopstrow.co.uk
dir: From roundabout on A36 take B3414 towards Warminster. Follow brown hotel signs.

The Bishopstrow Hotel is set in 27 acres of delightful grounds which include modern spa facilities, tennis courts and country walks. Bedrooms are comfortable and stylish, and all are well appointed. Public areas offer several day rooms, and retain the style of the original house. Cuisine is a feature here, and the menus offer fresh, local produce.

Rooms: 32 (2 annexe) (26 family) (9 GF) ↑ **Facilities:** Spa STV FTV WiFi ↳ ⊛ ↘ ⌣ Fishing Gym Thermal rooms Relaxation room Dual treatment room Xmas New Year **Conf:** Class 40 Board 36 Theatre 60 **Services:** Night porter **Parking:** 70 **Notes:** Civ Wed 82

WARRINGTON
Cheshire

Map 15 SJ68

The Park Royal

 QHOTELS
INSPIRED
BY YOU

★★★★ 82% ◉ HOTEL

tel: 01925 730706 **Stretton Road, Stretton WA4 4NS**
email: parkroyalreservations@qhotels.co.uk **web:** www.qhotels.co.uk
dir: M56 junction 10, A49 to Warrington, at lights turn right to Appleton Thorn, 1st right into Spark Hall Close, hotel on left.

This modern hotel enjoys a peaceful setting, yet is conveniently located just minutes from the M56. The bedrooms are contemporary, well furnished and attractively co-ordinated. Spacious, stylish public areas include extensive conference and function facilities and a comprehensive leisure centre complete with outdoor tennis courts and a spa. Complimentary WiFi is also provided.

Rooms: 146 (31 family) (31 GF) ↑ **D** fr £85 (including breakfast)* **Facilities:** Spa FTV WiFi ↳ HL ⊛ ⌣ Gym Dance studio Sauna Steam room Xmas New Year **Conf:** Class 180 Board 90 Theatre 400 **Services:** Lift Night porter **Parking:** 400 **Notes:** LB Civ Wed 300

Hallmark Hotel Warrington Fir Grove

★★★ 81% HOTEL

tel: 0330 028 3423 **Knutsford Old Road WA4 2LD**
email: warrington@hallmarkhotels.co.uk **web:** www.hallmarkhotels.co.uk
dir: M6 junction 20, follow signs for A50 to Warrington for 2.4 miles, before swing bridge over canal, turn right and right again.

Situated in a quiet residential area, this hotel is convenient for both the town centre and the motorway network. Comfortable bedrooms, including spacious executive rooms are appointed to a good standard. Public areas include a smart and contemporary lounge/bar, a neatly appointed restaurant, and excellent function and meeting facilities.

Rooms: 52 (4 family) (20 GF) ↑ **S** fr £49 **D** fr £59* **Facilities:** FTV WiFi ↳ Xmas New Year **Conf:** Class 100 Board 50 Theatre 200 **Services:** Night porter **Parking:** 57 **Notes:** Civ Wed 180

Premier Inn Warrington A49/M62 Jct 9

Premier Inn

BUDGET HOTEL

tel: 0871 527 9132 (Calls cost 13p per minute plus your phone company's access charge) **Winwick Road WA2 8RN**
web: www.premierinn.com
dir: M62 junction 9 towards Warrington, hotel 100 yards.

High quality, budget accommodation ideal for both families and business travellers. Spacious, en suite bedrooms feature free WiFi and tea and coffee making facilities, and in most hotels, Freeview TV is also available. The adjacent family restaurant features a wide and varied menu.

Rooms: 40

Premier Inn Warrington Central North

Premier Inn

BUDGET HOTEL

tel: 0871 527 9128 (Calls cost 13p per minute plus your phone company's access charge) **Floyd Drive WA2 8DB**
web: www.premierinn.com
dir: M62 junction 9, A49 signed Warrington. At next roundabout follow Town Centre signs. Straight on at next roundabout, left into Warrington Collegiate Camp.

Rooms: 75

W

Premier Inn Warrington Centre

BUDGET HOTEL

tel: 0871 527 9126 (Calls cost 13p per minute plus your phone company's access charge) **1430 Centre Park, Park Boulevard WA1 1PR**
web: www.premierinn.com
dir: *Take A49 to Brian Beven Island Roundabout, into Park Boulevard (Centre Park). Over bridge. Hotel on right.*

Rooms: 42

Premier Inn Warrington (M6 Jct 21)

BUDGET HOTEL

tel: 0871 527 9124 (Calls cost 13p per minute plus your phone company's access charge) **Manchester Road, Woolston WA1 4GB**
web: www.premierinn.com
dir: *Just off M6 junction 21 on A57 to Warrington.*

Rooms: 105

Premier Inn Warrington North East

BUDGET HOTEL

tel: 0871 527 9130 (Calls cost 13p per minute plus your phone company's access charge) **Golborne Road, Winwick WA2 8LF**
web: www.premierinn.com
dir: *M6 junction 22, A573 towards Newton-le-Willows. Dual carriageway to end, take 3rd exit at roundabout. Hotel adjacent to church.*

Rooms: 42

Premier Inn Warrington South

BUDGET HOTEL

tel: 0871 527 9134 (Calls cost 13p per minute plus your phone company's access charge) **Tarporley Road, Stretton WA4 4NB**
web: www.premierinn.com
dir: *Just off M56 junction 10. Follow A49 to Warrington, left at 1st lights.*

Rooms: 29

WARWICK   Map 10 SP26
Warwickshire

See also **Leamington Spa (Royal) and Wroxall**

Chesford Grange

QHOTELS
INSPIRED BY YOU

★★★★ 80% HOTEL

tel: 01926 859331 **Chesford Bridge CV8 2LD**
email: chesfordreservations@qhotels.co.uk **web:** www.qhotels.co.uk

(for full entry see Kenilworth)

Ardencote

★★★★ 76% ⊕ HOTEL

tel: 01926 843111 **The Cumsey, Lye Green Road CV35 8LT**
email: hotel@ardencote.com **web:** www.ardencote.com

(for full entry see Claverdon)

Premier Inn Warwick

BUDGET HOTEL

tel: 0871 527 9320 (Calls cost 13p per minute plus your phone company's access charge) **Opus 40, Birmingham Road CV34 5JL**
web: www.premierinn.com
dir: *M40 junction 15, A46 (Warwick bypass) towards Warwick. Follow A425 signs. From A425 1st left into industrial estate (Opus 40). Hotel 200 yards, opposite IBM office.*

High quality, budget accommodation ideal for both families and business travellers. Spacious, en suite bedrooms feature free WiFi and tea and coffee making facilities, and in most hotels, Freeview TV is also available. The adjacent family restaurant features a wide and varied menu.

Rooms: 124

WARWICK MOTORWAY SERVICE AREA (M40)   Map 11 SP35
Warwickshire

Days Inn Warwick North - M40

WELCOMEBREAK

AA Advertised

tel: 01926 651681 **Warwick Services, M40 Northbound Junction 12-13 CV35 0AA**
email: warwick.north.hotel@welcomebreak.co.uk **web:** www.welcomebreak.co.uk
dir: *M40 northbound between junction 12 and 13.*

This modern building offers accommodation in smart, spacious and well-equipped bedrooms, suitable for families and business travellers, and all with en suite bathrooms. Continental breakfast is available and other refreshments may be taken at the nearby family restaurant.

Rooms: 54 (45 family) (8 smoking) **Facilities:** FTV WiFi ⊵ **Conf:** Board 30 **Services:** Night porter **Parking:** 100

Days Inn Warwick South - M40

WELCOMEBREAK

AA Advertised

tel: 01926 652081 **Warwick Services, M40 Southbound CV35 0AA**
email: warwick.south.hotel@welcomebreak.co.uk **web:** www.welcomebreak.co.uk
dir: *M40 southbound between junction 14 and 12.*

This modern building offers accommodation in smart, spacious and well-equipped bedrooms, suitable for families and business travellers, and all with en suite bathrooms. Continental breakfast is available and other refreshments may be taken at the nearby family restaurant.

Rooms: 40 (30 family) (19 GF) (4 smoking) **Facilities:** FTV WiFi ⊵ **Parking:** 500

W

WASHINGTON
Tyne & Wear

Map 19 NZ35

Mercure George Washington Hotel, Golf & Spa

★★★★ 78% HOTEL

tel: 0191 402 9988 **Stone Cellar Road, High Usworth NE37 1PH**
email: reservations@georgewashington.co.uk **web:** www.georgewashington.co.uk
dir: A1(M) junction 65 onto A194(M). Take A195 signed Washington North. Take last exit from roundabout for Washington then right at mini-roundabout. Hotel 0.5 mile on right.

The Mercure George Washington Hotel, Golf & Spa is popular with business and leisure guests alike. It is a purpose-built hotel that boasts an 18-hole championship golf course and a driving range. The bedrooms are generally spacious and comfortably equipped. Public areas include extensive conference facilities, a business centre and spa. Carter and Fitch, a pizzeria, smokehouse and bar concept offers s a great menu of informal dishes and a friendly service to match.

Rooms: 125 (13 family) (41 GF) **S** fr £80 **D** fr £90 **Facilities:** Spa FTV WiFi ⌨ ☉ ⚓ 18 Gym Driving range Par 3 course Xmas New Year **Conf:** Class 100 Board 60 Theatre 200 **Services:** Lift Night porter **Parking:** 600 **Notes:** LB Civ Wed 150

Premier Inn Newcastle (Washington)

BUDGET HOTEL

tel: 0871 527 9136 (Calls cost 13p per minute plus your phone company's access charge) **Emerson Road NE37 1LB**
web: www.premierinn.com
dir: A1(M) junction 64, A195, follow Emerson signs. Left at roundabout, hotel 250 yards on left.

High quality, budget accommodation ideal for both families and business travellers. Spacious, en suite bedrooms feature free WiFi and tea and coffee making facilities, and in most hotels, Freeview TV is also available. The adjacent family restaurant features a wide and varied menu.

Rooms: 74

WATERMILLOCK
Cumbria

Map 18 NY42

HIGHLY RECOMMENDED

Macdonald Leeming House

★★★★ 83% ⊛ HOTEL

tel: 01768 486674 **CA11 0JJ**
email: leeminghouse@macdonald-hotels.co.uk
web: www.macdonaldhotels.co.uk
dir: M6 junction 40, A66 to Keswick. At roundabout take A592 (Ullswater). 5 miles to T-junction, right (A592). Hotel on left.

This hotel enjoys a superb location, being set in 20 acres of mature wooded gardens in the Lake District National Park, and overlooking Ullswater and the towering fells. Many rooms offer views of the lake and the rugged mountains beyond, with more than half having their own balcony. Public rooms include three sumptuous lounges, a cosy bar and library.

Rooms: 40 (1 family) (10 GF) **S** fr £149 **D** fr £169 (including breakfast)*
Facilities: FTV WiFi Fishing ⌨ Xmas New Year **Conf:** Class 40 Board 30 Theatre 80 **Services:** Night porter **Parking:** 50 **Notes:** Civ Wed 80

WATFORD
Hertfordshire

Map 6 TQ19

Mercure London Watford Hotel

★★★★ 69% HOTEL

tel: 020 8901 0000 & 0844 815 9056 (Calls cost 7p per minute plus your phone company's access charge) **A41, Watford Bypass WD25 8JH**
email: info@mercurewatford.co.uk **web:** www.mercurewatford.co.uk
dir: M1 junction 5, A41 south to London. Straight on at island, hotel 1 mile on left.

This hotel is situated on the outskirts of London close to the M1, M25, A1(M) and Luton and London Heathrow airports. The bedrooms are smartly appointed and equipped with modern facilities including WiFi and satellite TV. Public rooms include The Brasserie restaurant and bar; guests also have the use of the leisure facilities with a heated pool.

Rooms: 218 (3 family) **Facilities:** WiFi ⌨ ☉ ⚓ Gym Sauna Steam room Beauty treatment room **Conf:** Class 120 Board 58 Theatre 200 **Services:** Night porter **Parking:** 300 **Notes:** Civ Wed 200

Best Western White House

★★★ 75% HOTEL

tel: 01923 237316 **Upton Road WD18 0JF**
email: info@whitehousehotel.co.uk **web:** www.bw-whitehousehotel.co.uk
dir: From centre ring road, exit left into Upton Road, hotel on left.

This popular commercial hotel is situated within easy walking distance of the town centre. Bedrooms are pleasantly decorated and offer a good range of facilities that include interactive TV with internet. The public areas are open plan; they include a comfortable lounge/bar, cosy snug and an attractive conservatory restaurant with a sunny open terrace for summer dining. Function suites are also available.

Rooms: 68 (6 family) (17 GF) **S** fr £60 **D** fr £80* **Facilities:** FTV WiFi HL **Services:** Lift Night porter **Parking:** 40

Premier Inn Watford Central

BUDGET HOTEL

tel: 0871 527 9140 (Calls cost 13p per minute plus your phone company's access charge) **Timms Meadow, Water Lane WD17 2NJ**
web: www.premierinn.com
dir: M1 junction 5, A41 into town centre. At roundabout take 3rd exit, stay in left lane through lights. Take 1st left into Water Lane. Hotel on left.

Rooms: 105

Premier Inn Watford (Croxley Green)

BUDGET HOTEL

tel: 0871 527 9138 (Calls cost 13p per minute plus your phone company's access charge) **2 Ascot Road WD18 8AD**
web: www.premierinn.com
dir: M25 junction 18, A404 signed Watford/Rickmansworth, left at 1st roundabout signed A412 Watford. Follow Croxley Green Business Park/Watford signs, at 4th roundabout, 3rd exit. M1 junction 5, A41 towards Watford, follow Watford West and Rickmansworth A412 signs. Then Croxley Green Business Park signs.

Rooms: 126

W

Premier Inn Watford North

Premier Inn

BUDGET HOTEL

tel: 0871 527 9142 (Calls cost 13p per minute plus your phone company's access charge) **859 St Albans Road, Garston WD25 0LH**
web: www.premierinn.com
dir: M1 junction 6, A405 towards Watford. At 2nd lights onto A412 (St Albans Road). Into TGI Friday's car park. Hotel directly behind.

Rooms: 60

WATTON	**Map 13 TF90**
Norfolk	

Broom Hall Country Hotel

★★★ 81% COUNTRY HOUSE HOTEL

tel: 01953 882125 **Richmond Road, Saham Toney IP25 7EX**
email: enquiries@broomhallhotel.co.uk **web:** www.broomhallhotel.co.uk
dir: From A11 at Thetford onto A1075 to Watton, B1108 towards Swaffham, in 0.5 mile at roundabout turn right to Saham Toney, hotel 0.5 mile on left. From A47 take A1075, left onto B1108.

A delightful Victorian country house situated down a private drive and set in mature landscaped gardens surrounded by parkland. The well-equipped bedrooms are split between the main house and an adjacent building. Public rooms include a relaxing lounge, a brasserie restaurant, a lounge bar, a conservatory and a smart restaurant. There is an indoor swimming pool.

Rooms: 15 (4 annexe) (3 family) (4 GF) ✆ **Facilities:** Spa FTV WiFi ⌕ ⊗ Massage Beauty treatments **Conf:** Class 30 Board 22 Theatre 80 **Parking:** 30 **Notes:** LB Closed 24 December to 4 January Civ Wed 70

WELLINGBOROUGH	**Map 11 SP86**
Northamptonshire	

Premier Inn Wellingborough

Premier Inn

BUDGET HOTEL

tel: 0871 527 9144 (Calls cost 13p per minute plus your phone company's access charge) **London Road NN8 2DP**
web: www.premierinn.com
dir: 0.5 mile from town centre on A5193, near Dennington Industrial Estate.

High quality, budget accommodation ideal for both families and business travellers. Spacious, en suite bedrooms feature free WiFi and tea and coffee making facilities, and in most hotels, Freeview TV is also available. The adjacent family restaurant features a wide and varied menu.

Rooms: 64

WELLS	**Map 4 ST54**
Somerset	

Best Western Plus Swan Hotel

★★★★ 78% ⊛⊛ HOTEL

tel: 01749 836300 **Sadler Street BA5 2RX**
email: info@swanhotelwells.co.uk **web:** www.swanhotelwells.co.uk
dir: A39, A371, on entering Wells follow signs for Hotels and Deliveries. Hotel on right opposite cathedral.

Situated in the shadow of Wells Cathedral, this privately-owned hotel enjoys a truly stunning location, and its owners extend a genuinely friendly welcome. Full of character and with a rich history, the hotel has been restored and extended to provide high levels of quality and comfort. Guests can choose between the larger,

period bedrooms in the main building or the more contemporary coach house rooms. Dinner in the oak-panelled restaurant should not be missed.

Rooms: 50 (3 family) (4 GF) ✆ **S** fr £104 **D** fr £140 (including breakfast)*
Facilities: FTV WiFi Gym In room treatments **Conf:** Class 45 Board 40 Theatre 120
Services: Night porter **Parking:** 30 **Notes:** LB Civ Wed 90

Premier Inn Wells

Premier Inn

BUDGET HOTEL

tel: 0871 527 9730 (Calls cost 13p per minute plus your phone company's access charge) **BA5 1UA**
web: www.premierinn.com
dir: A37/A361 towards Shepton Mallet. Follow A361/A371 (Wells Road). Continue on A371 for 4 miles towards Wells. Hotel on left.

Rooms: 69

WELWYN GARDEN CITY	**Map 6 TL21**
Hertfordshire	

HIGHLY RECOMMENDED

Tewin Bury Farm Hotel

★★★★ 83% ⊛⊛ HOTEL

tel: 01438 717793 **Hertford Road (B1000) AL6 0JB**
email: reservations@tewinbury.co.uk **web:** www.tewinbury.co.uk
dir: From north: A1(M) junction 6, 1st exit signed A1000, at next roundabout 1st exit towards Digswell. 0.1 mile straight on at roundabout. 1 mile on B100. Hotel on left.

Situated not far from the A1(M) and within easy reach of Stevenage and Knebworth House, this delightful country house hotel is part of a thriving farm. Stylish, well-equipped bedrooms of varying sizes are perfectly suited for both leisure and business guests. An award-winning restaurant and meeting rooms are all part of this family-run establishment.

Rooms: 36 (20 annexe) (4 family) (26 GF) ✆ **Facilities:** FTV WiFi ⌕ Fishing Cycling Xmas New Year **Conf:** Class 300 Board 40 Theatre 500 **Services:** Lift Night porter **Parking:** 400 **Notes:** Civ Wed 300

Best Western Homestead Court Hotel

BW Best Western.

★★★ 79% HOTEL

tel: 01707 324336 **Homestead Lane AL7 4LX**
email: reservations@homesteadcourt.co.uk **web:** www.bw-homesteadcourt.co.uk
dir: Exit A1000, left at lights at Bushall Hotel. Right at roundabout into Howlands, 2nd left at Hollybush public house into Hollybush Lane. 2nd right at War Memorial into Homestead Lane.

This family-run hotel enjoys a quiet location and is a short drive from the centre of Welwyn Garden City and the major road network. All bedrooms are attractively presented and very well equipped. An extensive choice is offered on the restaurant menu, and the cosy lounge is a popular, casual dining venue. Free WiFi is available throughout the hotel and there is ample secure parking.

Rooms: 81 (9 annexe) (6 family) (7 GF) ✆ **S** fr £59 **D** fr £69* **Facilities:** STV FTV WiFi ⌕ HL Free gym nearby Xmas **Conf:** Class 120 Board 100 Theatre 200 **Services:** Lift Night porter **Parking:** 75 **Notes:** Civ Wed 200

W

WELWYN GARDEN CITY *continued*

Premier Inn Welwyn Garden City

Premier Inn

BUDGET HOTEL

tel: 0871 527 9146 (Calls cost 13p per minute plus your phone company's access charge) **Stanborough Road AL8 6DQ**
web: www.premierinn.com
dir: *A1(M) junction 4, A6129.*

High quality, budget accommodation ideal for both families and business travellers. Spacious, en suite bedrooms feature free WiFi and tea and coffee making facilities, and in most hotels, Freeview TV is also available. The adjacent family restaurant features a wide and varied menu.

Rooms: 120

WEMBLEY
Greater London

Novotel London Wembley

NOVOTEL
HOTELS & RESORTS

★★★★ 77% HOTEL Plan 1 C5

tel: 020 8069 1200 **5 Olympic Way, Wembley HA9 0NP**
email: h9389@accor.com **web:** www.novotel.com
dir: *Phone for directions.*

Located on Olympic Way, Novotel London Wembley is just a seven-minute walk from the SSE Arena; Wembley Park tube station is only a short walk away and connects directly to the Eurostar Terminal and central London. Facilities include free WiFi throughout the hotel, Freeview TV channels in each bedroom and a fitness centre with panoramic views. The restaurant offers a tempting, international menu.

Rooms: 235 (27 family) S fr £159 D fr £169 (including breakfast)* **Facilities:** FTV WiFi HL Gym **Conf:** Class 60 Board 40 Theatre 120 **Services:** Lift Air con **Parking:** 29

Holiday Inn London – Wembley

Holiday Inn

★★★★ 74% HOTEL Plan 1 C4

tel: 020 8902 8839 **Empire Way HA9 8DS**
email: info@hiwembley.co.uk **web:** www.hiwembley.co.uk
dir: *Within easy reach of North Circular, M1, M4 and M40.*

This large hotel is ideally situated for the arena, stadium and conference centre. It's also great for local shopping at Wembley Market (England's largest Sunday market), while Brent Cross and Westfield shopping centres are not far away. The hotel has a range of modern public areas and well-equipped meeting rooms. Secure parking and good leisure facilities add to this hotel's appeal.

Rooms: 336 (42 family) D fr £149 **Facilities:** Spa STV WiFi HL Gym Steam room Sauna Beauty treatment room **Conf:** Class 450 Board 80 Theatre 500 **Services:** Lift Night porter Air con **Parking:** 250 **Notes:** LB Civ Wed 500

Wembley International Hotel

★★★ 73% HOTEL Plan 1 C5

tel: 020 8733 9000 & 8903 4426 **Empire Way HA9 0NH**
email: reservations@hotels-wembley.com **web:** www.wembleyinternationalhotel.co.uk
dir: *M1 junction 6, A406, right onto A404. Right onto Empire Way, after roundabout at lights. Hotel on right.*

Conveniently situated within walking distance of both the Arena and conference centres, this modern hotel offers smart, comfortable and spacious bedrooms; many are air conditioned. All rooms offer an excellent range of amenities. Air-conditioned public areas include a large restaurant serving a wide range of contemporary dishes.

Rooms: 165 (70 family) (3 GF) (10 smoking) S fr £49 D fr £59* **Facilities:** STV FTV WiFi **Conf:** Class 90 Board 90 Theatre 150 **Services:** Lift Air con **Parking:** 65

Premier Inn London Wembley Stadium

Premier Inn

BUDGET HOTEL Plan 1 C5

tel: 0871 527 8682 (Calls cost 13p per minute plus your phone company's access charge) **151 Wembley Park Drive HA9 8HQ**
web: www.premierinn.com
dir: *A406 (North Circular) take A404 towards Wembley. 2 miles right into Wembley Hill Road, keep right into Empire Way (B4565), pass Wembley Arena on right, keep right around petrol station. Hotel 200 yards on left.*

High quality, budget accommodation ideal for both families and business travellers. Spacious, en suite bedrooms feature free WiFi and tea and coffee making facilities, and in most hotels, Freeview TV is also available. The adjacent family restaurant features a wide and varied menu.

Rooms: 154

WEST BROMWICH
West Midlands
Map 10 SP09

Premier Inn West Bromwich

Premier Inn

BUDGET HOTEL

tel: 0871 527 9148 (Calls cost 13p per minute plus your phone company's access charge) **New Gas Street B70 0NP**
web: www.premierinn.com
dir: *M5 junction 1, A41 (Expressway) towards Wolverhampton. At 3rd roundabout, hotel on right.*

High quality, budget accommodation ideal for both families and business travellers. Spacious, en suite bedrooms feature free WiFi and tea and coffee making facilities, and in most hotels, Freeview TV is also available. The adjacent family restaurant features a wide and varied menu.

Rooms: 62

Premier Inn West Bromwich Central

Premier Inn

BUDGET HOTEL

tel: 0871 527 9150 (Calls cost 13p per minute plus your phone company's access charge) **144 High Street B70 6JJ**
web: www.premierinn.com
dir: *M5 junction 1 towards town centre, hotel 2 miles.*

High quality, budget accommodation ideal for both families and business travellers. Spacious, en suite bedrooms feature free WiFi and tea and coffee making facilities, and in most hotels, Freeview TV is also available. The adjacent family restaurant features a wide and varied menu.

Rooms: 85

W

WEST DRAYTON
See **Heathrow Airport**

WEST HOATHLY
West Sussex   Map 6 TV33

Gravetye Manor Hotel
★★★★ ◎◎◎ ☺ COUNTRY HOUSE HOTEL

tel: 01342 810567 **Vowels Lane RH19 4LJ**
email: info@gravetyemanor.co.uk web: www.gravetyemanor.co.uk
dir: *B2028 to Haywards Heath. 1 mile after Turners Hill fork left towards Sharpthorne, 1st left into Vowels Lane.*

Gravetye Manor is a beautiful Elizabethan mansion, built in 1598 and enjoying a tranquil setting. One of the first country house hotels in Britain, it remains an excellent example of its type. Bedrooms and bathrooms have been sympathetically appointed with style and luxurious finishing touches. The day rooms, each with oak-panelling, fresh flower arrangements and open fires, create a relaxing atmosphere. Guests should take time to explore the impressive gardens and grounds; a perfect spot for afternoon tea. 2018 sees the re-opening of the restaurant, designed with floor-to-ceiling windows overlooking the garden. The excellent, seasonal, award-winning cuisine based on ingredients from the kitchen garden and local suppliers and producers should not be missed.

Rooms: 17 D fr £275 (including breakfast)* **Facilities:** STV WiFi Fishing Deer stalking Xmas New Year **Conf:** Board 15 **Services:** Night porter **Parking:** 30 **Notes:** LB No children 7 years Civ Wed 60

WESTLETON
Suffolk   Map 13 TM46

The Westleton Crown
★★★ 81% ◎◎ HOTEL

tel: 01728 648777 **The Street IP17 3AD**
email: info@westletoncrown.co.uk web: www.westletoncrown.co.uk
dir: *A12 north, turn right for Westleton just after Yoxford. Hotel opposite on entering Westleton.*

The Westleton Crown is a charming coaching inn situated in a peaceful village location just a few minutes from the A12. Public rooms include a smart, award-winning restaurant, comfortable lounge, and busy bar with exposed beams and open fireplaces. The stylish bedrooms are tastefully decorated and equipped with many thoughtful little extras.

Rooms: 34 (22 annexe) (5 family) (13 GF) **Facilities:** FTV WiFi Xmas New Year **Services:** Night porter **Parking:** 34 **Notes:** Civ Wed 90

Silver Stars
The AA Silver Star rating denotes a Hotel that we highly recommend. They have a superior level of quality within their star rating, high standards of hospitality, service and cleanliness.

W

WESTON-SUPER-MARE
Somerset   Map 4 ST36

The Royal Hotel
★★★ 80% HOTEL

tel: 01934 423100 1 South Parade BS23 1JP
email: reservations@royalhotelweston.com web: www.royalhotelweston.com
dir: M5 junction 21, follow signs to seafront. Hotel next to Winter Gardens Pavillion.

The Royal, which opened in 1810, was the first hotel in Weston and occupies a prime seafront position. It is a grand building and many of the bedrooms, including some with sea views, are spacious and comfortable; family apartments are also available. Public areas include a choice of bars and a restaurant which offers a range of dishes to meet all tastes. Entertainment is provided during the season.

Rooms: 44 (3 annexe) (8 family) S fr £70 D fr £100 (including breakfast)
Facilities: FTV WiFi HL Beauty treatment room Hair salon Solarium ♫ Xmas New Year Conf: Class 100 Board 60 Theatre 200 Services: Lift Night porter Parking: 152
Notes: LB Civ Wed 200

See advert opposite

Beachlands Hotel
★★★ 78% HOTEL

tel: 01934 621401 17 Uphill Road North BS23 4NG
email: info@beachlandshotel.com web: www.beachlandshotel.com
dir: M5 junction 21, follow signs for hospital. At hospital roundabout follow signs for beach. Hotel 300 yards before beach.

This popular hotel is very close to the 18-hole links course and a short walk from the seafront. Elegant public areas include a bar, a choice of lounges and a bright dining room. Bedrooms vary slightly in size, but all are well equipped for both the business and leisure guest. There is the added bonus of a 10-metre indoor pool and a sauna.

Rooms: 21 (6 family) (11 GF) Facilities: FTV WiFi Sauna Beauty treatment room New Year Conf: Class 20 Board 30 Theatre 60 Parking: 28 Notes: Closed 24–27 December Civ Wed 110

Anchor Head Hotel
★★★ 64% HOTEL

Leisureplex
HOLIDAY HOTELS

tel: 01934 620880 19 Claremont Crescent, Birnbeck Road BS23 2EE
email: anchor.weston@alfatravel.co.uk web: www.leisureplex.co.uk
dir: M5 junction 21, A370 to seafront, right, past Grand Pier towards Brimbeck Pier. Hotel at end of terrace on left.

Enjoying a very pleasant location with views across the bay, the Anchor Head offers a varied choice of comfortable lounges and a relaxing outdoor patio area. Bedrooms and bathrooms are traditionally furnished and include several ground-floor rooms. Dinner and breakfast are served in the spacious dining room that also benefits from sea views.

Rooms: 52 (1 family) (5 GF) Facilities: FTV WiFi ♫ Xmas New Year Services: Lift Night porter Notes: Closed December to February (excluding Christmas/New Year) RS March and November

Premier Inn Weston-Super-Mare East (A370)
BUDGET HOTEL
Premier Inn

tel: 0871 527 9156 (Calls cost 13p per minute plus your phone company's access charge) Hutton Moor Road BS22 8LY
web: www.premierinn.com
dir: M5 junction 21, A370 towards Weston-super-Mare. After 3rd roundabout right at lights into Hutton Moor Leisure Centre. Left, into car park.

High quality, budget accommodation ideal for both families and business travellers. Spacious, en suite bedrooms feature free WiFi and tea and coffee making facilities, and in most hotels, Freeview TV is also available. The adjacent family restaurant features a wide and varied menu.

Rooms: 88

Premier Inn Weston-Super-Mare (Seafront)
BUDGET HOTEL
Premier Inn

tel: 0871 527 9378 (Calls cost 13p per minute plus your phone company's access charge) Dolphin Square, Beach Road BS23 1TT
web: www.premierinn.com
dir: M5 junction 21, A370 towards Weston-super-Mare town centre. At double mini-roundabout 2nd exit, 1st exit into Oxford Street. At end, left into Beach Road. Left into Carlton Street. Hotel on left.

Rooms: 112

WEST THURROCK
Essex   Map 6 TQ57

Premier Inn Thurrock East
BUDGET HOTEL
Premier Inn

tel: 0871 527 9092 (Calls cost 13p per minute plus your phone company's access charge) Fleming Road, Unicorn Estate RM16 6YJ
web: www.premierinn.com
dir: From A13 follow Lakeside Shopping Centre signs. Right at 1st roundabout, straight on at next roundabout, then 1st slip road. Left at next roundabout.

High quality, budget accommodation ideal for both families and business travellers. Spacious, en suite bedrooms feature free WiFi and tea and coffee making facilities, and in most hotels, Freeview TV is also available. The adjacent family restaurant features a wide and varied menu.

Rooms: 104

W

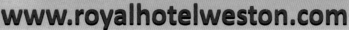
W

WEST THURROCK *continued*

Premier Inn Thurrock West

Premier Inn

BUDGET HOTEL

tel: 0871 527 9094 (Calls cost 13p per minute plus your phone company's access charge) **Stonehouse Lane RM19 1NS**
web: www.premierinn.com
dir: *From north: M25 junction 31, A1090 to Purfleet. (Note: do not cross Dartford Bridge or follow signs for Lakeside). From south: M25 junction 31. On approach to Dartford Tunnel, bear far left signed Dagenham. After tunnel, hotel at top of slip road.*

Rooms: 161

WETHERBY
West Yorkshire
Map 16 SE44

INSPECTOR'S CHOICE

Wood Hall Hotel & Spa

★★★★ ⍟⍟ ⌗ HOTEL

Hand PICKED
HOTELS

tel: 01937 587271 & 0845 072 7564 (Calls cost 5p per minute plus your phone company's access charge) **Trip Lane, Linton LS22 4JA**
email: woodhall@handpicked.co.uk web: www.handpickedhotels.co.uk/woodhall
dir: *From Wetherby take Harrogate road north (A661) for 0.5 mile, left to Sicklinghall and Linton. Cross bridge, left to Linton and Wood Hall. Turn right opposite Windmill Inn, 1.25 miles to hotel.*

A long sweeping drive leads to this delightful Georgian house situated in 100 acres of parkland. Spacious bedrooms are appointed to an impressive standard and feature comprehensive facilities, including large plasma-screen TVs. Public rooms reflect the same elegance and include a smart drawing room and dining room, both with fantastic views.

Rooms: 44 (30 annexe) (5 family) ☎ **Facilities:** Spa STV FTV WiFi ⇲ HL ⍟ Fishing Gym Steam room Xmas New Year **Conf:** Class 70 Board 40 Theatre 100 **Services:** Lift Night porter **Parking:** 200 **Notes:** Civ Wed 100

Bridge Hotel & Spa

★★★★ 76% HOTEL

tel: 01937 580115 **Walshford LS22 5HS**
email: info@bridgewetherby.co.uk web: www.bridgewetherby.co.uk
dir: *From north exit A1(M) at junction 47 York or south junction 46 Wetherby Race Centre, 1st left Walshford, follow brown tourist signs.*

The Bridge Hotel is located hotel close to the A1, with spacious public areas and a good range of services, making this an ideal venue for business or leisure. The stylish bedrooms are comfortable and well equipped. There is a choice of bars and a large open-plan restaurant. Conference and banqueting suites are also available.

Rooms: 30 (2 family) (10 GF) **S** fr £70 **D** fr £100 (including breakfast) **Facilities:** Spa FTV WiFi ⇲ Gym Xmas New Year **Conf:** Class 50 Board 50 Theatre 200 **Services:** Night porter **Parking:** 150 **Notes:** LB Civ Wed 150

Mercure Wetherby Hotel

★★★ 71% HOTEL

tel: 01937 583881 & 0844 815 9067 (Calls cost 7p per minute plus your phone company's access charge) **Leeds Road LS22 5HE**
email: info@mercurewetherby.co.uk web: www.mercurewetherby.co.uk
dir: *A1/A659, then follow A168. Hotel on roundabout.*

This modern hotel is well located for motorway access and as well as being close to the historic market town of Wetherby, it is also convenient for Leeds, Harrogate and York. Leeds Bradford Airport is just eight miles away. There is a spacious restaurant and adjacent bar. The Brasserie menu features bistro dishes and daily chef's specials. Extensive conference facilities are provided with 13 naturally lit meeting rooms available. Complimentary WiFi access is offered.

Rooms: 103 (51 GF) ☎ **S** fr £55 **D** fr £65 (including breakfast)* **Facilities:** FTV WiFi ⇲ New Year **Conf:** Class 60 Board 50 Theatre 150 **Services:** Lift Night porter **Parking:** 167 **Notes:** LB Civ Wed 100

Days Inn Wetherby

BUDGET HOTEL

DAYSINN

tel: 01937 547557 **Junction 46 A1(M), Kirk Deighton LS22 5GT**
email: reservations@daysinnwetherby.co.uk web: www.daysinnwetherby.co.uk
dir: *A1(M) junction 46 at Moto Service Area.*

This modern building offers accommodation in smart, spacious and well-equipped bedrooms, suitable for families and business travellers, and all with en suite bathrooms. Continental breakfast is available and other refreshments may be taken at the nearby family restaurant.

Rooms: 129 (33 family) (35 GF) ☎

WEYBRIDGE
Surrey
Map 6 TQ06

HIGHLY RECOMMENDED

Brooklands Hotel

★★★★ 83% ⍟⍟ HOTEL

tel: 01932 335700 **Brooklands Operations Limited, Brooklands Drive KT13 0SL**
email: info@brooklandshotelsurrey.com web: www.brooklandshotelsurrey.com
dir: *Phone for directions.*

Overlooking the historic motoring racing circuit, this hotel has stunning design that reflects the art deco style of the Mercedes Benz racetrack's heyday in the 1920s and 30s. The bedrooms are notably spacious and comfortable, with many contemporary facilities; all have floor-to-ceiling windows, and many come with balconies overlooking the racetrack. There is a wealth of public areas including leisure and meeting rooms as well as a spa. The contemporary 1907 Restaurant, Bar and Grill offers imaginative menus.

Rooms: 139 (5 family) ☎ **S** fr £139 **D** fr £139* **Facilities:** Spa STV FTV WiFi ⇲ Gym Xmas New Year **Conf:** Class 86 Board 90 Theatre 174 **Services:** Lift Night porter Air con **Parking:** 120 **Notes:** LB Civ Wed 174

Oatlands Park Hotel

★★★★ 80% HOTEL

tel: 01932 847242 **146 Oatlands Drive KT13 9HB**
email: info@oatlandsparkhotel.com **web:** www.oatlandsparkhotel.com
dir: *Through High Street to Monument Hill mini-roundabout. Left into Oatlands Drive. Hotel 500 yards on left.*

Once a palace for Henry VIII, this impressive building sits in extensive grounds encompassing tennis courts, a gym and a 9-hole golf course. The spacious lounge and bar create a wonderful first impression with tall marble pillars and plush comfortable seating. Most of the bedrooms are very spacious, and all are well equipped.

Rooms: 160 (24 family) (30 GF) 🕭 **Facilities:** STV FTV WiFi ⚑ HL ⚱ 9 🏊 🏌 Gym Jogging course Fitness suite ♫ Xmas New Year **Conf:** Class 170 Board 90 Theatre 400 **Services:** Lift Night porter Air con **Parking:** 208 **Notes:** Civ Wed 370

Best Western Ship Hotel

★★★ 79% HOTEL

tel: 01932 848364 **Monument Green KT13 8BQ**
email: reservations@desboroughhotels.com **web:** www.shiphotel.co.uk
dir: *M25 junction 11, at 3rd roundabout left into High Street. Hotel 300 yards on left.*

This former coaching inn has retained much of its period charm and is now a comfortable and welcoming hotel. Bedrooms, some overlooking a delightful courtyard, are spacious and cheerfully decorated. Public areas include a lounge and cocktail bar, restaurant and a popular pub. The high street location and private parking are a bonus.

Rooms: 76 (2 family) 🕭 **S** fr £50 **D** fr £65 **Facilities:** FTV WiFi ⚑ Xmas New Year **Conf:** Class 70 Board 60 Theatre 180 **Services:** Lift Night porter **Parking:** 65 **Notes:** Civ Wed 120

WEYMOUTH
Dorset   Map 4 SY67

Best Western Hotel Rembrandt

★★★ 78% HOTEL   BW Best Western.

tel: 01305 764000 **12-18 Dorchester Road DT4 7JU**
email: reception@hotelrembrandt.co.uk **web:** www.hotelrembrandt.co.uk
dir: *On A354 from Dorchester, turn left at Manor roundabout and proceed for 0.75 mile.*

Only a short distance from the seafront and the town centre, this hotel is ideal for visiting local attractions. Facilities include a spa, gym, heated pool, a bar and extensive meeting rooms. The restaurant offers an impressive carvery and carte menu, which proves popular with locals and residents alike.

Rooms: 78 (27 family) (5 GF) 🕭 **S** fr £45 **D** fr £65* **Facilities:** STV FTV WiFi ⚑ ⊛ Gym Steam room Sauna Beautician Beauty treatment room **Conf:** Class 100 Board 60 Theatre 200 **Services:** Lift Night porter **Parking:** 60 **Notes:** LB Civ Wed 150

Hotel Rex

★★★ 73% HOTEL

tel: 01305 760400 **29 The Esplanade DT4 8DN**
email: rex@kingshotels.co.uk **web:** www.kingshotels.co.uk
dir: *On seafront opposite Alexandra Gardens.*

Originally built as the summer residence for the Duke of Clarence, this hotel benefits from a seafront location with stunning views across Weymouth Bay. Bedrooms, including several sea-facing rooms, are well equipped. A wide range of imaginative dishes is served in the popular and attractive restaurant.

Rooms: 31 (2 family) 🕭 **S** fr £50 **D** fr £90 (including breakfast)* **Facilities:** FTV WiFi New Year **Conf:** Class 30 Board 25 Theatre 40 **Services:** Lift Night porter **Parking:** 9 **Notes:** Closed Christmas

Crown Hotel

★★ 78% HOTEL

tel: 01305 760800 **51-53 St Thomas Street DT4 8EQ**
email: crown@kingshotels.co.uk **web:** www.kingshotels.co.uk
dir: *From Dorchester, A354 to Weymouth. Follow Back Water on left and cross 2nd bridge.*

This popular hotel is conveniently located adjacent to the old harbour and is ideal for shopping, local attractions and transportation links, including the ferry. Public areas include an extensive bar, ballroom, and comfortable residents' lounge on the first floor. Themed events, such as mock cruises, are a speciality.

Rooms: 86 (15 family) 🕭 **S** fr £42 **D** fr £75 (including breakfast)* **Facilities:** WiFi New Year **Services:** Lift Night porter **Parking:** 11 **Notes:** Closed Christmas

Fairhaven Hotel

★★ 76% HOTEL

tel: 01305 760200 **37 The Esplanade DT4 8DH**
email: fairhaven@kingshotels.co.uk **web:** www.kingshotels.co.uk
dir: *On right just before Alexandra Gardens.*

Fairhaven Hotel is a popular sea-facing, family-run hotel with a friendly young team of staff. Bedrooms are comfortable and well maintained, and there are two bars, one with panoramic views of the bay. Entertainment is provided most nights during the season.

Rooms: 81 (21 family) (1 GF) 🕭 **S** fr £45 **D** fr £80 (including breakfast)* **Facilities:** WiFi ♫ **Services:** Lift Night porter **Parking:** 5 **Notes:** Closed November to 1 March

Hotel Central

★★ 72% HOTEL

tel: 01305 760700 **17-19 Maiden Street DT4 8BB**
email: central@kingshotels.co.uk **web:** www.kingshotels.co.uk
dir: *In town centre.*

Well located for the town, the beach and the ferries to the Channel Islands, and with off-road parking, this privately-owned hotel has friendly staff and comfortable bedrooms. Three rooms are designed for guests with limited mobility. The pleasant dining room offers a varied menu, and live entertainment is provided during the season.

Rooms: 28 (5 family) (4 GF) 🕭 **D** fr £70* **Facilities:** ♫ **Services:** Lift Night porter **Parking:** 5 **Notes:** Closed mid December to 1 March

W

WEYMOUTH *continued*

Premier Inn Weymouth

BUDGET HOTEL

tel: 0871 527 9384 (Calls cost 13p per minute plus your phone company's access charge) **Gateway Business Park, Mercury Road DT3 5HJ**
web: www.premierinn.com
dir: *M27 junction 1, A31 towards Bournemouth, A35 towards Dorchester. 1st exit at roundabout onto A354 (Weymouth road). At 3rd roundabout take 1st exit into Dorchester Road. Left into Mercery Road.*

High quality, budget accommodation ideal for both families and business travellers. Spacious, en suite bedrooms feature free WiFi and tea and coffee making facilities, and in most hotels, Freeview TV is also available. The adjacent family restaurant features a wide and varied menu.

Rooms: 60

Premier Inn Weymouth Seafront

BUDGET HOTEL

tel: 0871 527 9158 (Calls cost 13p per minute plus your phone company's access charge) **Lodmoor Country Park, Preston Beach Road DT4 7SX**
web: www.premierinn.com
dir: *Follow signs to Weymouth then brown route signs to Lodmoor Country Park (height restriction 9' 4" at barrier). Hotel adjacent to Lodmoor Brewers Fayre. Note: for sat nav use DT4 7SL.*

Rooms: 106

Moonfleet Manor Hotel

AA Advertised ⊛

tel: 01305 786948 **Fleet Road DT3 4ED**
email: info@moonfleetmanorhotel.co.uk **web:** www.moonfleetmanor.co.uk
dir: *Take Fleet Road just off B1357 at Chickerell. Hotel at end of road.*

This enchanting hideaway, where children are especially welcome, is peacefully located at the end of the village of Fleet and enjoys a wonderful sea-facing position. The hotel is furnished with a great deal of style, individuality and panache, particularly in the sumptuous lounges. Bedrooms are equally special with a range of sizes; all are well-equipped and many overlook Chesil Beach. Accomplished cuisine makes use of quality local produce and is served in the elegant restaurant. A host of additional facilities are also offered for all the family, including an indoor pool.

Rooms: 36 (6 annexe) (21 family) (3 GF) **Facilities:** Spa FTV WiFi ⓧ ⌁ Squash Indoor play area Creche Xmas New Year **Conf:** Class 36 Board 30 Theatre 70 **Services:** Lift Night porter **Parking:** 48 **Notes:** Civ Wed 100

WHITBY — Map 19 NZ81
North Yorkshire

The Cliffemount Hotel

★★★ 81% SMALL HOTEL

tel: 01947 840103 **Bank Top Lane, Runswick Bay TS13 5HU**
email: info@cliffemounthotel.co.uk **web:** www.cliffemounthotel.co.uk
dir: *Exit A174, 8 miles north of Whitby, 1 mile to end.*

The Cliffemount Hotel enjoys stunning picture postcard views across rugged Runswick Bay. It offers a relaxed and romantic atmosphere with open fires and individual, carefully-designed bedrooms, some of which boast their own private balcony overlooking the bay. Dining is a real strength; food is modern British in style, using locally sourced fresh seafood and game from the nearby estates. The team are relaxed and informal but provide attentive service with warm hospitality.

Rooms: 18 **Facilities: Conf:** Class 25 Board 16 Theatre 2

WHITCHURCH — Map 15 SJ54
Shropshire

Macdonald Hill Valley Spa, Hotel & Golf

MACDONALD HOTELS & RESORTS

★★★★ 79% HOTEL

tel: 01948 660700 **Tarporley Road SY13 4JH**
email: general.hillvalley@macdonald-hotels.co.uk
web: www.macdonald-hotels.co.uk/hillvalley
dir: *2nd exit off A41 towards Whitchurch.*

Located in rural surroundings on the town's outskirts, this modern hotel is surrounded by two golf courses, and a very well equipped leisure spa is also available. Spacious bedrooms, with country views, are furnished in minimalist style and public areas include a choice of bar lounges and extensive conference facilities.

Rooms: 80 (15 family) (27 GF) ⟋ **S** fr £70 **D** fr £80* **Facilities:** Spa STV FTV WiFi ⓧ ⓧ ⌁ 36 Gym Rasul mud Xmas New Year **Conf:** Class 150 Board 150 Theatre 300 **Services:** Lift Night porter **Parking:** 300 **Notes:** LB Civ Wed 300

WHITEHAVEN — Map 18 NX91
Cumbria

Premier Inn Whitehaven

Premier Inn

BUDGET HOTEL

tel: 0871 527 9160 (Calls cost 13p per minute plus your phone company's access charge) **Howgate CA28 6PL**
web: www.premierinn.com
dir: *On A595 just outside Whitehaven.*

Rooms: 117

W

WHITLEY BAY
Tyne & Wear

Map 21 NZ37

Premier Inn Whitley Bay

BUDGET HOTEL

tel: 0871 097 1085 (Calls cost 13p per minute plus your phone company's access charge) **9 Spanish City Plaza NE26 1BG**
web: www.premierinn.com
dir: *Leave Earsdon Road/Seatonville Road onto Cauldwell Lane. Follow road into Front Street and Marine Avenue. At end of road, turn right onto Promenade. Hotel on left.*

High quality, budget accommodation ideal for both families and business travellers. Spacious, en suite bedrooms feature free WiFi and tea and coffee making facilities, and in most hotels, Freeview TV is also available. The adjacent family restaurant features a wide and varied menu.

Rooms: 68

WHITSTABLE
Kent

Map 7 TR16

Crescent Turner Hotel

★★★ 81% HOTEL

tel: 01227 263506 **Wraik Hill CT5 3BY**
email: info@crescentturner.co.uk **web:** www.crescentturner.co.uk
dir: *A299 exit for Whitstable.*

Located just a couple of miles from Whitstable on Wraik Hill, the Crescent Turner Hotel benefits from fantastic countryside and sea views. The individually designed bedrooms are stylish with contemporary furnishings; many benefit from extensive views across to Whitstable. There is a bar and restaurant onsite which is open daily for breakfast, lunch and dinner.

Rooms: 17 (2 family) (5 GF) ✆ **S** fr £67.50 **D** fr £99 (including breakfast)*
Facilities: FTV WiFi ⓑ Xmas New Year **Conf:** Class 32 Board 30 Theatre 40
Services: Night porter **Parking:** 30 **Notes:** Civ Wed 56

Premier Inn Whitstable

Premier Inn

BUDGET HOTEL

tel: 0871 527 9162 (Calls cost 13p per minute plus your phone company's access charge) **Thanet Way CT5 3DB**
web: www.premierinn.com
dir: *2 miles west of town centre on B2205.*

Rooms: 73

WHITTLEBURY
Northamptonshire

Map 11 SP64

Whittlebury Hall

★★★★ 80% ◉◉ ◉ HOTEL

tel: 01327 857857 **NN12 8QH**
email: reservations@whittleburyhall.co.uk **web:** www.whittleburyhall.co.uk
dir: *A43, A413 towards Buckingham, through Whittlebury, turn for hotel on right, signed.*

Whittlebury Hall is a purpose-built, Georgian-style country house hotel with excellent spa and leisure facilities and pedestrian access to the Silverstone circuit. Grand public areas feature F1 racing memorabilia, and the accommodation includes some lavishly appointed suites. Food is a strength, with a choice of various dining options. Particularly noteworthy are the afternoon teas in the spacious, comfortable lounge and the fine dining in Murray's Restaurant.

Rooms: 254 (41 annexe) (4 family) (13 GF) **Facilities:** Spa FTV WiFi ⓑ HL ⓧ ♨ 36 Gym Beauty treatments Relaxation room Hair salon Heat and ice experience Leisure club ♫ Xmas New Year **Conf:** Class 175 Board 40 Theatre 500 **Services:** Lift Night porter **Parking:** 700 **Notes:** Civ Wed

WIDNES
Cheshire

Map 15 SJ58

Best Western Everglades Park Hotel

BW Best Western.

★★★ 76% HOTEL

tel: 0151 4955500 **Derby Road, Halton WA8 3UJ**
email: everglades@lavenderhotels.co.uk **web:** www.lavenderhotels.co.uk/Everglades-Park

Best Western Everglades Park Hotel offers a convenient location, close to motorway, rail and air links, as well as the Mersey Gateway Bridge. The hotel has a range of room sizes, and is a popular venue for meetings and weddings. Dining is available in the restaurant and bar and offers a good range of food.

Rooms: 65 **D** fr £69* **Facilities:** **Conf:** Class 90 Board 30 Theatre 160

WIDNES *continued*

Premier Inn Widnes

Premier Inn

BUDGET HOTEL

tel: 0871 527 9306 (Calls cost 13p per minute plus your phone company's access charge) **Venture Fields WA8 0GY**
web: www.premierinn.com
dir: *M62 junction 7. At Rainhill Stoops roundabout 2nd exit onto A557 (Widnes). Left into Earle Road (Widnes Waterfront), into Venture Field Leisure Entertainment complex. Hotel on left.*

High quality, budget accommodation ideal for both families and business travellers. Spacious, en suite bedrooms feature free WiFi and tea and coffee making facilities, and in most hotels, Freeview TV is also available. The adjacent family restaurant features a wide and varied menu.

Rooms: 87

WIGAN **Map 15 SD50**
Greater Manchester

HIGHLY RECOMMENDED

Haigh Hall Hotel

★★★★ 89% COUNTRY HOUSE HOTEL

tel: 01942 832895 **School Lane, Haigh WN2 1PF**
email: enquiries@haighhallhotel.co.uk **web:** www.haighhallhotel.co.uk
dir: *M6 junction 27, right onto A5209 to Standish. Straight at lights towards Haigh and Aspull on B5239. Left at roundabout. Right at next roundabout following signs to Haigh Hall and Country Park. Turn right at Red Rock Lodge on sharp bend signed Haigh Woodland Park. Right past Latham House. At Mowpin lodge, turn into hotel gate and follow driveway to hotel.*

This recently developed hotel sits in delightfully peaceful grounds and has many notable features. The bedrooms are extremely comfortable and offer high levels of style and quality. There's a roof terrace for warmer times that offers a rather pleasant BBQ menu, and dining in the Riviera restaurant has a relaxed and continental style – dishes have great clarity and the wine list has an 'all by the glass' availability. Equally, the bar has some impressive temptations and the cocktails are a serious offering. The spa is will be opening later in 2018.

Rooms: 30 (3 family) ✆ **S** fr £200 **D** fr £220 (including breakfast)*
Facilities: Spa FTV WiFi ⌁ HL ⌁ 18 ⛳ Gym Miniature golf High ropes ♫ Xmas New Year **Conf:** Class 100 Board 80 Theatre 300 **Services:** Lift Night porter
Parking: 120

Macdonald Kilhey Court Hotel

MACDONALD
HOTELS & RESORTS

★★★★ 77% HOTEL

tel: 0344 879 9045 **Chorley Road, Standish WN1 2XN**
email: general.kilheycourt@macdonald-hotels.co.uk
web: www.macdonaldhotels.co.uk/kilheycourt
dir: *M6 junction 27, A5209 Standish, over at lights, past church on right, left at roundabout 1st exit, hotel on right 350 yards. M61 junction 6, signed Wigan and Haigh Hall. 3 miles and right at roundabout 2nd exit. Hotel 0.5 mile on right.*

Macdonald Kilhey Court Hotel is peacefully located in its own grounds yet is convenient for the motorway network. Bedrooms are divided between the Victorian house and the modern extension, while public areas have original features, and the split-level restaurant has views over the Worthington Lakes. There are 11 meeting

rooms, ideal for exhibitions, and extensive landscaped grounds available for weddings. Facilities also include an indoor pool and spa.
Rooms: 62 (18 family) (8 GF) ✆ **Facilities:** Spa FTV WiFi ⌁ HL ⌁ Gym Aerobics classes Beauty treatments Xmas New Year **Conf:** Class 180 Board 60 Theatre 400
Services: Lift Night porter **Parking:** 300 **Notes:** Civ Wed 300

Wrightington Hotel & Country Club

CLASSIC BRITISH HOTELS

★★★★ 75% HOTEL

tel: 01257 425803 **Moss Lane, Wrightington WN6 9PB**
email: info@wrightingtonhotel.co.uk **web:** www.wrightingtonhotel.co.uk
dir: *M6 junction 27, 0.25 mile west, hotel on right after church.*

Situated in open countryside close to the M6, this privately-owned hotel offers friendly hospitality. Accommodation is well equipped and spacious, and public areas include an extensive leisure complex complete with hair salon, pool and sports injury lab. Bennetts Restaurant, Blazers bar and extensive, fully air-conditioned banqueting facilities appeal to a broad market, with weddings a key focus.
Rooms: 73 (6 family) (36 GF) ✆ **Facilities:** Spa STV FTV WiFi ⌁ Gym Squash Hair salon Sports injury clinic New Year **Conf:** Class 50 Board 40 Theatre 150
Services: Lift Night porter **Parking:** 240 **Notes:** LB Civ Wed 100

Premier Inn Wigan M6 Jct 25

Premier Inn

BUDGET HOTEL

tel: 0871 527 9164 (Calls cost 13p per minute plus your phone company's access charge) **Warrington Road, Marus Bridge WN3 6XB**
web: www.premierinn.com
dir: *M6 junction 25 (northbound). At roundabout left, hotel on left.*

Rooms: 40

Premier Inn Wigan Town Centre

Premier Inn

BUDGET HOTEL

tel: 0871 527 9502 (Calls cost 13p per minute plus your phone company's access charge) **Harrogate Street WN1 1BL**
web: www.premierinn.com
dir: *Northbound: M6 junction 25, A49 (Warrington Road). 3rd exit at next roundabout into Poolstock Lane (B5238). Left into Chapel Lane, continue into River Way (A49). At lights left into King Street, then into Rodney Street. Stay in right lane, through lights into Harrogate Street.*

Rooms: 83

Premier Inn Wigan West (M6 Jct 26)

Premier Inn

BUDGET HOTEL

tel: 0871 527 9168 (Calls cost 13p per minute plus your phone company's access charge) **Orrell Road, Orrell WN5 8HQ**
web: www.premierinn.com
dir: *M6 junction 26 follow signs for Upholland and Orrell. At 1st lights turn left. Hotel on right behind Priory Wood Beefeater.*

Rooms: 40

WILLERBY
East Riding of Yorkshire

Map 17 TA03

Mercure Hull Grange Park Hotel

★★★★ 72% HOTEL

tel: 01482 672801 & 0844 815 9037 (Calls cost 7p per minute plus your phone company's access charge) **Grange Park Lane HU10 6EA**
email: info@mercurehull.co.uk **web:** www.mercurehull.co.uk
dir: A164 to Beverley signed Willerby Shopping Park. Left at roundabout into Grange Park Lane, hotel at end.

Originally a 19th-century manor house, this modern hotel provides comfortable accommodation tucked away in 12 acres of landscaped gardens. The location is peaceful yet convenient for the historic market town of Beverley. Hull city centre is only five miles away. Extensive meeting rooms are in a self contained conference centre with complimentary WiFi throughout. The hotel also boasts a health club with indoor swimming pool.

Rooms: 100 (4 family) (15 GF) **Facilities:** Spa FTV WiFi ↳ ☒ Gym Sauna Steam room Xmas New Year **Conf:** Class 250 Board 80 Theatre 550 **Services:** Lift Night porter **Parking:** 600 **Notes:** Civ Wed 550

Best Western Willerby Manor Hotel

BW Best Western

★★★ 82% HOTEL

tel: 01482 652616 **Well Lane HU10 6ER**
email: info@willerbymanor.co.uk **web:** www.willerbymanor.co.uk
dir: Exit A63, signed Humber Bridge. Right at roundabout by Waitrose. At next roundabout hotel signed.

Set in a quiet residential area, amid well-tended gardens, this hotel was originally a private mansion; it has now been thoughtfully extended to provide very comfortable bedrooms, equipped with many useful extras. There are extensive leisure facilities and a wide choice of meals offered in the contemporary Figs Brasserie which has an impressive heated outdoor area.

Rooms: 63 (10 family) (20 GF) **S** fr £60 **D** fr £90 (including breakfast)*
Facilities: Spa STV FTV WiFi HL ☒ ⅃ Gym Steam room Beauty treatment room Aerobic classes New Year **Conf:** Class 200 Board 100 Theatre 500 **Services:** Night porter **Parking:** 300 **Notes:** LB Closed 24–26 December Civ Wed 150

WILMSLOW

See **Manchester Airport**

WINCHESTER
Hampshire

Map 5 SU42

Holiday Inn Winchester

★★★★ 79% ◉◎ HOTEL

tel: 01962 670700 **Telegraph Way, Morn Hill SO21 1HZ**
email: info@hiwinchester.co.uk **web:** www.hiwinchester.co.uk
dir: M3 junction 9, A31 signed Alton, A272 and Petersfield. 1st exit at roundabout onto A31, 1.6 miles, take 1st exit into Alresford Road, left into Telegraph Way.

Located a few miles from the historic city of Winchester and within easy reach of the south's transport links, this modern, purpose-built property is presented to a high standard. Bedrooms are spacious and well-equipped for both the business and leisure guest. Enjoyable cuisine is served in the restaurant and there is a very good range of freshly prepared dishes to choose from. Conference facilities and ample parking are available.

Rooms: 141 (7 family) (60 GF) **S** fr £95 **D** fr £295* **Facilities:** STV FTV WiFi ↳ HL Gym Xmas New Year **Conf:** Class 110 Board 120 Theatre 250 **Services:** Lift Night porter Air con **Parking:** 167 **Notes:** LB Civ Wed 200

Hotel du Vin Winchester

★★★★ 77% TOWN HOUSE HOTEL

tel: 01962 841414 **14 Southgate Street SO23 9EF**
email: info.winchester@hotelduvin.com **web:** www.hotelduvin.com
dir: M3 junction 11 towards Winchester, follow signs. Hotel in approximately 2 miles on left just past cinema.

Continuing to set high standards, this inviting hotel is best known for its high profile bistro. The individually designed bedrooms have all the Hotel du Vin signature touches including fine Egyptian cotton linen, power showers and WiFi. The bistro serves imaginative yet simply-cooked dishes from a seasonal, daily-changing menu.

Rooms: 24 (4 annexe) (4 GF) **Facilities:** STV WiFi ↳ Xmas New Year **Conf:** Class 30 Board 20 Theatre 40 **Services:** Night porter Air con **Parking:** 35 **Notes:** Civ Wed 60

Mercure Winchester Wessex Hotel

Mercure HOTELS

★★★★ 75% HOTEL

tel: 01962 861611 **Paternoster Row SO23 9LQ**
email: H6619@accor.com **web:** www.mercure.com
dir: M3 junction 10, 2nd exit at roundabout signed Winchester/B3330. Right at lights, left at 2nd roundabout. Over small bridge, straight on at next roundabout into Broadway. Past Guildhall, 1st left into Colebrook Street. Hotel 50 yards on right.

Occupying an enviable location in the centre of this historic city and adjacent to the spectacular cathedral, Mercure Winchester Wessex Hotel is quietly situated on a side street. Inside, the atmosphere is restful and welcoming, with public areas and some bedrooms enjoying unrivalled views of the hotel's centuries-old neighbour.

Rooms: 94 (6 family) **S** fr £75 **D** fr £75* **Facilities:** FTV WiFi Xmas New Year **Conf:** Class 25 Board 40 Theatre 100 **Services:** Lift Night porter **Parking:** 30 **Notes:** LB Civ Wed 80

Marwell Hotel

★★★ 80% ◉◎ HOTEL

tel: 01962 777681 **Thompsons Lane, Colden Common SO21 1JY**
email: info@marwellhotel.co.uk **web:** www.marwellhotel.co.uk
dir: B3354 through Twyford. 1st exit at roundabout B3354, left onto B2177 signed Bishop Waltham. Left into Thompsons Lane after 1 mile, hotel on left.

Taking its theme from the adjacent zoo, this unusual hotel is based on the famous TreeTops safari lodge in Kenya. The well-equipped bedrooms, split between four lodges, convey a safari style, while the smart public areas include an airy lobby bar and an 'Out of Africa' themed restaurant. There is also a selection of meeting and leisure facilities.

Rooms: 68 (10 family) (38 GF) **S** fr £64 **D** fr £79 (including breakfast)*
Facilities: STV WiFi ↳ ☒ ⅃ 45 Sauna Spa pool Running machine Xmas New Year **Conf:** Class 60 Board 60 Theatre 200 **Services:** Night porter **Parking:** 120 **Notes:** LB Civ Wed 200

W

WINCHESTER *continued*

Premier Inn Winchester

BUDGET HOTEL

Premier Inn

tel: 0871 527 9424 (Calls cost 13p per minute plus your phone company's access charge) **Caledonia House, Winnal Manor Road SO23 0RS**
web: www.premierinn.com
dir: *M3 junction 9, A272 to Winchester. At roundabout 3rd exit into Easton Lane. Hotel on left at next roundabout.*

High quality, budget accommodation ideal for both families and business travellers. Spacious, en suite bedrooms feature free WiFi and tea and coffee making facilities, and in most hotels, Freeview TV is also available. The adjacent family restaurant features a wide and varied menu.

Rooms: 101

Lainston House, an Exclusive Hotel

AA Advertised ⊛⊛⊛

EXCLUSIVE

tel: 01962 776088 **Woodman Lane, Sparsholt SO21 2LT**
email: enquiries@lainstonhouse.co.uk **web:** www.exclusive.co.uk
dir: *2 miles northwest off B3049 towards Stockbridge.*

This graceful example of a William and Mary house enjoys a countryside location amidst mature grounds and gardens. Staff provide good levels of courtesy and care with a polished, professional service. Bedrooms are tastefully appointed and include some spectacular, spacious rooms with stylish handmade beds and stunning bathrooms. Public rooms include a cocktail bar built entirely from a single cedar and stocked with an impressive range of rare drinks and cigars.

Rooms: 50 (6 family) (18 GF) ✿ **D** fr £166.50 (including breakfast)* **Facilities:** STV FTV WiFi ↘ ⚘ Fishing ⚲ Gym Archery Clay pigeon shooting Cycling Hot air ballooning Falconer Cookery school Xmas New Year **Conf:** Class 80 Board 40 Theatre 166 **Services:** Night porter **Parking:** 200 **Notes:** Civ Wed 200

| **WINCHESTER MOTOR SERVICE AREA** | Map 5 SU53 |
| Hampshire | |

Days Inn Winchester

AA Advertised

WELCOMEBREAK

tel: 01962 791135 **Winchester Moto Service Area, M3 south, junction 14/15 SO21 1PP**
email: winchester.hotel@welcomebreak.co.uk **web:** www.welcomebreak.co.uk
dir: *M3 southbound (between junctions 8 and 9). There is no access from M3 northbound.*

This modern building offers accommodation in smart, spacious and well-equipped bedrooms, suitable for families and business travellers, and all with en suite bathrooms. Continental breakfast is available and other refreshments may be taken at the nearby family restaurant.

Rooms: 40 (14 family) (20 GF) **Facilities:** FTV WiFi **Conf:** Class 20 Theatre 20 **Services:** Night porter **Parking:** 40 **Notes:** Closed 24–26 December

| **WINDERMERE** | Map 18 SD49 |
| Cumbria | |

Gilpin Hotel & Lake House

★★★★★ 85% ⊛⊛⊛ ⚑ HOTEL

RELAIS & CHATEAUX

tel: 015394 88818 **Crook Road LA23 3NE**
email: hotel@thegilpin.co.uk **web:** www.thegilpin.co.uk
dir: *M6 junction 36, A590, A591 to roundabout north of Kendal, onto B5284, hotel 5 miles on right.*

This smart Victorian residence is set in delightful gardens leading to the fells, and is just a short drive from the lake. The individually designed bedrooms are stylish, and a number benefit from private terraces. All are spacious and thoughtfully equipped, and each has a private sitting room. In addition there are luxury garden suites that lead onto private gardens with cedarwood hot tubs. The welcoming atmosphere is notable and the attractive day rooms are perfect for relaxation. Eating in any of the quartet of dining rooms is a must, while Gilpin Spice restaurant is located within the grounds and well worth a visit. The Lake House situated a mile from the main hotel offers an additional six suites, spa and stunning lakeside views.

Rooms: 31 (17 annexe) (1 family) (12 GF) ✿ **S** fr £225 **D** fr £285 (including breakfast) **Facilities:** STV WiFi ↘ ⚲ Spa treatments Private spa facilities for Lake House guests Xmas New Year **Conf:** Board 160 Theatre 12 **Services:** Night porter **Parking:** 40 **Notes:** No children 7 years Civ Wed 120

The Samling

★★★★ ⊛⊛⊛ ⚑ HOTEL

tel: 015394 31922 **Ambleside Road LA23 1LR**
email: info@thesamlinghotel.co.uk **web:** www.thesamlinghotel.co.uk
dir: *M6 junction 36, A591 through Windermere towards Ambleside. 2 miles. 300 yards past Low Wood Water Sports Centre just after sharp bend turn right into hotel entrance.*

This stylish 18th-century house, is set in 67 acres of grounds, and enjoys an elevated position overlooking Lake Windermere. The spacious, beautifully furnished bedrooms and suites, some in adjacent buildings, are thoughtfully equipped and all have superb bathrooms. Public rooms include a small library and an elegant dining room.

Rooms: 12 (6 annexe) (6 family) (6 GF) ✿ **S** fr £310 **D** fr £310 (including breakfast)* **Facilities:** STV FTV WiFi ↘ ⚲ Xmas New Year **Conf:** Class 80 Board 40 Theatre 80 **Services:** Night porter **Parking:** 45 **Notes:** Civ Wed 50

W

HOLBECK GHYLL

MOMENTS TO SAVOUR

Holbeck Ghyll Country House Hotel,
Holbeck Lane, Windermere, Cumbria LA23 1LU
+44 (0)1539 432 375
www.holbeckghyll.com stay@holbeckghyll.com
f /holbeck.ghyll @holbeckghyll

W

WINDERMERE *continued*

Holbeck Ghyll Country House Hotel

★★★★ COUNTRY HOUSE HOTEL

tel: 015394 32375 **Holbeck Lane LA23 1LU**
email: stay@holbeckghyll.com **web:** www.holbeckghyll.com
dir: *3 miles north of Windermere on A591, right into Holbeck Lane signed Troutbeck, hotel 0.5 mile on left.*

Holbeck Ghyll sits high up overlooking the majestic Lake Windermere surrounded by well-maintained grounds. The original house was bought in 1888 by Lord Lonsdale, the first president of the AA, who used it as a hunting lodge. Guests today will find that this is a delightful place where the service is professional and attentive. There are beautifully designed, spacious bedrooms situated in the main house and also in lodges in the grounds; each has lake views and some have patios. There are also The Shieling and Miss Potter suites. Each bedroom has Egyptian cotton linen, fresh flowers, LCD satellite TV, CD/ DVD players, bathrobes and a decanter of damson gin. The restaurant impresses with its award-winning cuisine. The hotel also has a health spa, gym and boutique store.

Rooms: 30 (17 annexe) (5 family) (12 GF) 🐾 **S** fr £149 **D** fr £169 (including breakfast)* **Facilities:** Spa FTV WiFi 🐾 💆 Sauna Steam room Beauty massage Xmas New Year **Conf:** Class 40 Board 30 Theatre 60 **Services:** Night porter **Parking:** 34 **Notes:** LB Civ Wed 60

See advert on previous page

Linthwaite House Hotel & Restaurant

★★★★ COUNTRY HOUSE HOTEL

tel: 015394 88600 **Crook Road LA23 3JA**
email: reception@linthwaitehouse.com **web:** www.linthwaitehouse.com
dir: *A591 towards The Lakes for 8 miles to large roundabout, take 1st exit B5284, 6 miles, hotel on left. 1 mile past Windermere golf club.*

Linthwaite House, part of the Leeu Collection, enjoys stunning views over Lake Windermere and offers a peaceful Lake District retreat. Inviting public rooms include an attractive conservatory and adjoining lounge, and an elegant restaurant which occupies three rooms and offers menus based on the finest local ingredients. The welcoming and intimate atmosphere allows visitors to relax and careful attention to detail can be seen throughout. The result is a crisp, modern space with a sense of history. With 14 acres of grounds there are plenty of activities on site including boats to hire on the private tarn or various garden games. Service and hospitality are attentive and friendly.

Rooms: 36 (1 family) (7 GF) 🐾 **Facilities:** FTV WiFi 🐾 💆 Beauty treatments Massage Access to nearby spa with pool and gym Xmas New Year **Services:** Night porter **Parking:** 40 **Notes:** LB

Storrs Hall Hotel

★★★★ 83% ◉◉ HOTEL

tel: 015394 47111 **Storrs Park LA23 3LG**
email: reception@storrshall.com **web:** www.storrshall.com
dir: *On A592, 2 miles south of Bowness, on Newby Bridge road.*

Set in 17 acres of landscaped grounds by the lakeside, this imposing Georgian mansion is delightful. There are numerous lounges to relax in, furnished with fine art and antiques. Individually styled bedrooms are generally spacious and boast impressive bathrooms. The elegant restaurant offers fine views across the lawn to the lake and fells beyond.

Rooms: 30 🐾 **S** fr £130 **D** fr £140 (including breakfast)* **Facilities:** FTV WiFi Fishing 💆 Xmas New Year **Conf:** Class 20 Board 20 Theatre 40 **Services:** Night porter **Parking:** 50 **Notes:** LB Civ Wed 80

W

HIGHLY RECOMMENDED

Macdonald Old England Hotel & Spa

★★★★ 83% ⊛ HOTEL

tel: 0344 879 9144 **23 Church Street, Bowness LA23 3DF**
email: sales.oldengland@macdonald-hotels.co.uk
web: www.macdonaldhotels.co.uk
dir: *Through Windermere to Bowness, straight across at mini-roundabout. Hotel behind church on right.*

This hotel stands right on the shore of England's largest lake and boasts superb views, especially through the floor-to-ceiling windows in the restaurant. There are several bedroom types – standard, executive and suites – some rooms have been designed for wheelchair users. The spa has a 20-metre pool, a gym, sauna and steam room.

Rooms: 106 (6 family) (14 GF) ⊛ **Facilities:** Spa STV WiFi ⊳ ⊛ Gym Private jetties Rock Sauna Aromatherapy shower Steam room Ice room Xmas New Year **Conf:** Class 60 Board 25 Theatre 150 **Services:** Lift Night porter **Parking:** 90 **Notes:** LB Civ Wed 100

HIGHLY RECOMMENDED

Langdale Chase

★★★★ 81% ⊛⊛ HOTEL

tel: 015394 32201 **Ambleside Road LA23 1LW**
email: relax@langdalechase.co.uk **web:** www.langdalechase.co.uk
dir: *M6 junction 36, follow A590 towards Windermere, pick up A591, through Windermere toward Ambleside for approximately 3 miles.*

With a superb location, this charming hotel has elevated views and lake-side walks. There are a number of bedroom styles, many with lake views and balconies. Dining is a must, with Lakeland produce and skilfully created cuisine. The hotel has a number of meeting rooms, and along with ample parking, there are some notable gardens and parkland too.

Rooms: 29 (9 annexe) (2 family) (5 GF) ⊛ **S** fr £86 **D** fr £100 (including breakfast)* **Facilities:** FTV WiFi ⊳ Fishing ⊛ Xmas New Year **Conf:** Class 20 Board 15 Theatre 30 **Services:** Night porter **Parking:** 50 **Notes:** Civ Wed 30

Merewood Country House Hotel

★★★★ 82% ⊛⊛ COUNTRY HOUSE HOTEL

tel: 015394 46484 **Ambleside Road, Ecclerigg LA23 1LH**
email: info@merewoodhotel.co.uk
web: www.lakedistrictcountryhotels.co.uk/merewood-hotel
dir: *M6 junction 36, follow A591 for 15 miles past Windermere, hotel on right.*

A country house in the traditional Lakeland mould, Merewood provides a relaxed environment and polished service to match. The bar and lounges overlook Windermere and the Cumbrian mountains beyond. Bedrooms vary in size and include some superb feature rooms. Food is notable here, with dinner being a highlight of any stay. Weddings and functions are ably catered for too.

Rooms: 20 (2 family) **Facilities:** FTV WiFi ⊳ Xmas New Year **Conf:** Class 45 Board 50 Theatre 150 **Services:** Night porter **Parking:** 100 **Notes:** LB Civ Wed 122

Briery Wood Country House Hotel

★★★★ 80% ⊛ COUNTRY HOUSE HOTEL

tel: 015394 33316 **Ambleside Road, Ecclerigg LA23 1ES**
email: info@brierywood.co.uk **web:** www.lakedistrictcountryhotels.co.uk/briery-wood-hotel
dir: *M6 junction 36, follow A591 for 15 miles past Windermere, hotel on right (do not use postcode for sat nav).*

This small country house hideaway is part of a small group all located on the banks of Windermere. In its own well-tended grounds, Briery Wood is a charming white house that offers 23 individually-styled bedrooms and a warren of public rooms. Cuisine is a highlight at dinner, though not overly-formal, and the warm welcome and rapport from the team is noteworthy.

Rooms: 23 (4 family) (12 GF) **Facilities:** FTV WiFi ⊳ Xmas New Year **Conf:** Class 30 Board 30 Theatre 80 **Parking:** 40 **Notes:** Civ Wed 113

Lindeth Howe Country House Hotel & Restaurant

★★★★ 79% ⊛⊛ COUNTRY HOUSE HOTEL

tel: 015394 45759 **Lindeth Drive, Longtail Hill LA23 3JF**
email: hotel@lindeth-howe.co.uk **web:** www.lindeth-howe.co.uk
dir: *Exit A592, 1 mile south of Bowness onto B5284 Longtail Hill signed Kendal and Lancaster, hotel last driveway on right.*

Historic photographs commemorate the fact that this delightful house was once the family home of Beatrix Potter. Secluded in landscaped grounds, it enjoys views across the valley and Lake Windermere. Public rooms are plentiful and inviting, with the restaurant being the perfect setting for modern country-house cooking. Deluxe and superior bedrooms are spacious and smartly appointed.

Rooms: 35 (3 family) (3 GF) ⊛ **S** fr £115 **D** fr £180 (including breakfast)* **Facilities:** FTV WiFi Xmas New Year **Conf:** Class 20 Board 18 Theatre 30 **Services:** Night porter **Parking:** 50 **Notes:** LB Closed 4–16 January Civ Wed 100

Cragwood Country House Hotel

★★★★ 77% ⊛ COUNTRY HOUSE HOTEL

tel: 01539 488177 **Ambleside Road LA23 1LQ**
email: info@cragwoodhotel.co.uk
web: www.lakedistrictcountryhotels.co.uk/cragwood-hotel
dir: *M6 junction 36 then A591 for 15 miles, past Kendal and Windermere, hotel on left.*

A typical Lakeland country house, Cragwood is a very attractive property set in 20 acres of woodland and landscaped gardens that lead down to the shores of Lake Windermere. The views are delightful. There's a range of individually designed, modern bedrooms and guests can relax in a choice of richly decorated lounges and bars. Cuisine is a highlight in the AA Rosetted restaurant.

Rooms: 23 (3 family) (4 GF) ⊛ **Facilities:** FTV WiFi ⊳ ⊛ Xmas New Year **Conf:** Class 30 Board 30 Theatre 50 **Services:** Night porter **Parking:** 50 **Notes:** Civ Wed 83

W

WINDERMERE *continued*

Laura Ashley The Belsfield Hotel

★★★★ 75% ◉ HOTEL

tel: 015394 42448 & 0844 736 8604 **Kendal Road LA23 3EL**
email: belsfield@lauraashleyhotels.com **web:** www.lauraashleyhotels.com
dir: *M6 junction 36, A591 Windermere, follow signs for Bowness. At mini-roundabout bear left and take 1st left (Kendal Road). Hotel 200 yards on right.*

Sitting in six-acre grounds and affording some of the finest views of Lake Windermere from its elevated position, this imposing hotel offers comfortable accommodation. A number of the bedrooms and the restaurant have stunning lake views, and the bistro offers a more informal dining option. Relax and take afternoon tea in the elegant drawing room or library.

Rooms: 62 (5 family) (10 GF) ↑ **S** fr £169 **D** fr £179 (including breakfast)*
Facilities: FTV WiFi ↕ Gym Xmas New Year **Conf:** Class 60 Board 30 Theatre 100
Services: Lift Night porter **Parking:** 68 **Notes:** LB Civ Wed 130

Beech Hill Hotel & Spa

★★★★ 74% ◉ HOTEL

tel: 015394 42137 **Newby Bridge Road LA23 3LR**
email: reservations@beechhillhotel.co.uk **web:** www.beechhillhotel.co.uk
dir: *M6 junction 36, A591 to Windermere. Left onto A592 towards Newby Bridge. Hotel 4 miles from Bowness-on-Windermere.*

Beech Hill Hotel is situated overlooking Windermere, with the impressive panoramic views across the lake to the Cumbrian fells beyond from most bedrooms – these are well appointed and some have balconies or terraces. The open areas, for enjoying coffee or drinks, prove very popular in the summer, and there are cosy lounges with log fires, a fine restaurant and landscaped gardens. High standards of service can be expected from the attentive, informative and very friendly staff. The hotel also has a pool and small spa.

Rooms: 57 (5 family) (4 GF) ↑ **Facilities:** Spa FTV WiFi ⊗ ↗ Fishing Sauna Steam room Xmas New Year **Services:** Night porter **Parking:** 70 **Notes:** Civ Wed 130

Cedar Manor Hotel & Restaurant

★★★ ◉ SMALL HOTEL

tel: 015394 43192 **Ambleside Road LA23 1AX**
email: info@cedarmanor.co.uk **web:** www.cedarmanor.co.uk
dir: *From A591 follow signs to Windermere. Hotel on left just beyond St Mary's Church.*

Built in 1854 as a country retreat, this lovely old house enjoys a peaceful location, tucked away within easy walking distance of the town centre. Bedrooms, some on the ground floor, are deeply comfortable and very well equipped, with a luxurious annexe suite available for longer stays or romantic getaways. There is a choice of lounges and bars where guests can relax before enjoying dinner in the well-appointed dining room.

Rooms: 10 (1 annexe) (1 family) (3 GF) ↑ **S** fr £125 **D** fr £145 (including breakfast)* **Facilities:** FTV WiFi New Year **Conf:** Board 10 **Parking:** 11 **Notes:** LB No children 10 years Closed 2–19 January

See advert opposite

HIGHLY RECOMMENDED

Miller Howe Hotel

★★★ 87% ◎◎ ⊜ COUNTRY HOUSE HOTEL

tel: 015394 42536 **Rayrigg Road LA23 1EY**
email: info@millerhowe.com **web:** www.millerhowe.com
dir: *M6 junction 36, A591 past Windermere, left at roundabout towards Bowness.*

This long established hotel enjoys a lakeside setting amidst delightful landscaped gardens. The bright and welcoming day rooms include sumptuous lounges, a conservatory and an opulently decorated restaurant. Imaginative dinners make use of fresh, local produce where possible and there is an extensive, well-balanced wine list. Stylish bedrooms, many with fabulous lake views, include well-equipped cottage rooms and a number with whirlpool baths.

Rooms: 15 (3 annexe) (1 GF) ⋒ **Facilities:** FTV WiFi ⇗ HL Xmas New Year
Parking: 35 **Notes:** Civ Wed 75

The Ryebeck

★★★ 86% ◎◎ ⊜ COUNTRY HOUSE HOTEL

tel: 015394 88195 **Lyth Valley Road LA23 3JP**
email: info@ryebeck.com **web:** www.ryebeck.com
dir: *M6 junction 46, follow A591. Right at Plumgarth's roundabout and follow Crooked to end. Left, hotel 300 yards on right.*

The Ryebeck, offering warm Lakeland hospitality, sits majestically above the shores of Lake Windermere in its own extensive, well-maintained gardens. Just a few minutes' drive from the lake and the ferry but within easy access of the M6, guests can enjoy this wonderful location without necessarily joining the crush in the town. Originally built in 1904 as a private home, the property has seen a number of different uses before it was lovingly transformed into this hotel. Luxuriously appointed bedrooms, some dog-friendly and on the ground floor, range from 'cosy' to 'grand'. Award-winning, imaginative food is served in the informal conservatory dining room.

Rooms: 26 (2 annexe) (9 GF) ⋒ **S** fr £80 **D** fr £120 (including breakfast)*
Facilities: FTV WiFi Xmas New Year **Conf:** Class 12 Board 12 Theatre 30
Services: Night porter **Parking:** 50 **Notes:** LB Civ Wed 74

Craig Manor

★★★ 77% HOTEL

tel: 015394 88877 **Lake Road LA23 2JF**
email: info@craigmanor.co.uk **web:** www.craigmanor.co.uk
dir: *A590, then A591 into Windermere, left at Windermere Hotel, through village, pass Magistrates Court/Police Station, hotel on right.*

Situated in the heart of the Lake District, Craig Manor has a relaxed and friendly atmosphere with professional staff providing attentive service. Bedrooms are comfortable and well equipped, and some rooms offer stunning views across Windermere to the Cumbrian fells beyond. This view is most notable from the attractive restaurant, which serves a wide choice of quality dishes. The large car park is a further benefit in this popular tourist resort.

Rooms: 26 ⋒ **D** fr £89 (including breakfast)* **Facilities:** FTV WiFi ⇗ **Parking:** 39

W

WINDSOR
Berkshire

Map 6 SU97

HIGHLY RECOMMENDED

The Oakley Court
★★★★ 82% @ @ ⓢ HOTEL

tel: 01753 609988 **Windsor Road, Water Oakley SL4 5UR**
email: reservations@oakleycourt.co.uk **web:** www.oakleycourt.co.uk
dir: *M4 junction 6, A355, then A332 towards Windsor, right onto A308 towards Maidenhead. Pass racecourse, hotel 2.5 miles on right.*

Built in 1859, this splendid Victorian Gothic mansion is enviably situated in extensive grounds leading down to the Thames. All bedrooms are spacious and beautifully furnished, and many enjoy river views. Extensive public areas include a range of comfortable lounges and the Dining Room Restaurant. The comprehensive leisure facilities include a fully equipped gym, indoor swimming pool, jacuzzi, sauna, steam room, tennis court, and 9-hole golf course

Rooms: 118 (108 annexe) (6 family) (42 GF) **S** fr £168 **D** fr £168* **Facilities:** FTV WiFi ⓑ HL ⓣ ⓛ 9 ⓢ ⓢ Gym Boating Sauna Steam room Snooker Bicycles Xmas New Year **Conf:** Class 90 Board 50 Theatre 170 **Services:** Night porter Air con **Parking:** 200 **Notes:** Civ Wed 170

Macdonald Windsor Hotel
★★★★ 82% ⓢ HOTEL

MACDONALD
HOTELS & RESORTS

tel: 01753 483100 **23 High Street SL4 1LH**
email: gm.windsor@macdonald-hotels.co.uk **web:** www.macdonaldhotels.co.uk/windsor
dir: *M4 junction 6 A355, take A332, roundabout 1st exit signed town centre. In 0.7 mile turn left into Bachelors Acre.*

Just across the street from Windsor Castle, this hotel is an ideal base for visiting that, and all the other famous attractions of the town. It has well-appointed contemporary, designer-led bedrooms, some overlooking the castle, that are decorated in soft shades to create a calm atmosphere; they include TVs and Bose iPod docks. The Scottish Steak Club @ Caleys restaurant offers a relaxed and informal dining venue, and 24-hour room service is also available. There is complimentary WiFi in the bedrooms and the conference rooms. The hotel has excellent wedding facilities.

Rooms: 120 (4 family) ⓕ **Facilities:** FTV WiFi ⓑ HL Xmas New Year **Conf:** Class 80 Board 35 Theatre 100 **Services:** Lift Night porter Air con **Parking:** 42 **Notes:** LB Civ Wed 100

Sir Christopher Wren Hotel and Spa
★★★★ 81% ⓢ HOTEL

SAROVA
HOTELS

tel: 01753 442400 **Thames Street SL4 1PX**
email: wrens@sarova.com **web:** www.sarova.com
dir: *M4 junction 6, at 1st exit follow signs to Windsor, 1st major exit on left, left at lights.*

Located by the side of the Thames and close to the Eton Bridge stands this well-presented hotel. Bedrooms vary – with both traditional and contemporary tastes catered for. There are comfortable lounges, a popular restaurant with great views of the river, and also a well-equipped leisure club. Limited parking is available.

Rooms: 139 (83 annexe) (5 family) (10 GF) ⓕ **S** fr £120 **D** fr £130 (including breakfast)* **Facilities:** Spa FTV WiFi ⓑ Gym Sauna Treatment rooms ♫ Xmas New Year **Conf:** Class 50 Board 45 Theatre 90 **Services:** Night porter Air con **Parking:** 40 **Notes:** LB Civ Wed 90

Find out more about the AA Hotel Group of the Year – see page 19

Castle Hotel Windsor MGallery by Sofitel

★★★★ 81% HOTEL

tel: 01753 851577 & 252800 **18 High Street SL4 1LJ**
email: h6618@accor.com **web:** www.castlehotelwindsor.com
dir: *M4 junction 6/M25 junction 15, follow signs to Windsor town centre and castle. Hotel at top of hill opposite Guildhall.*

This is one of the oldest hotels in Windsor, beginning life as a coaching inn in the 16th century. Located opposite Windsor Castle, it is an ideal base from which to explore the town and its royal connections. Stylish bedrooms are thoughtfully equipped and include four-poster and executive rooms. Public areas are spacious and tastefully decorated.

Rooms: 108 (70 annexe) (3 GF) ⚫ **S** fr £139 **D** fr £149* **Facilities:** STV FTV WiFi ⊠ Xmas New Year **Conf:** Class 150 Board 50 Theatre 400 **Services:** Lift Night porter Air con **Parking:** 133 **Notes:** Civ Wed 300

Christopher Hotel

★★★ 80% HOTEL

tel: 01753 852359 **110 High Street, Eton SL4 6AN**
email: reservations@thechristopher.co.uk **web:** www.thechristopher.co.uk
dir: *M4 junction 5 Slough east, Colnbrook Datchet Eton, B470. At roundabout 2nd exit for Datchet. Right at mini-roundabout, Eton, left into Eton Road, 3rd roundabout. Left, hotel on right.*

This hotel benefits from an ideal location in Eton, being only a short stroll across the pedestrian bridge from historic Windsor Castle and the many other attractions the town has to offer. The hotel has comfortable and smartly decorated accommodation, and a wide range of dishes is available in the informal bar and grill. A stylish room is available for private dining or for meetings.

Rooms: 34 (23 annexe) (10 family) (22 GF) ⚫ **S** fr £99 **D** fr £140* **Facilities:** FTV WiFi ⊠ Xmas New Year **Conf:** Board 10 Theatre 30 **Services:** Night porter **Parking:** 19 **Notes:** LB

WISBECH
Cambridgeshire

Map 12 TF40

HIGHLY RECOMMENDED

Crown Lodge Hotel

THE INDEPENDENTS
HOTEL ASSOCIATION

★★★ 87% ⊕ HOTEL

tel: 01945 773391 **Downham Road, Outwell PE14 8SE**
email: office@thecrownlodgehotel.co.uk **web:** www.thecrownlodgehotel.co.uk
dir: *On A1122, approximately 5 miles from Wisbech.*

Crown Lodge Hotel is a friendly, privately-owned hotel situated in a peaceful location on the banks of Well Creek, a short drive from Wisbech. The bedrooms are pleasantly decorated, with co-ordinated fabrics and modern facilities. The public areas are very stylish; they include a lounge bar, brasserie restaurant and a large seating area with plush leather sofas.

Rooms: 10 (1 family) (10 GF) ⚫ **Facilities:** FTV WiFi ⊠ Squash **Conf:** Class 60 Board 40 Theatre 80 **Services:** Air con **Parking:** 55 **Notes:** Closed 25–26 December, 1 January

WISHAW
Warwickshire

Map 10 SP19

HIGHLY RECOMMENDED

The Belfry

★★★★ 83% ⊛ HOTEL

tel: 0844 980 0600 (Calls cost 7p per minute plus your phone company's access charge) **Lichfield Road B76 9PR**
email: enquiries@thebelfry.com **web:** www.thebelfry.com
dir: *M42 junction 9, A446 towards Lichfield, hotel 1 mile on right.*

The Belfry is ideally situated within easy striking distance of the M6, Birmingham and Birmingham Airport. The property is set in 550 acres of countryside and features three golf courses, including the Ryder Cup course, The Brabazon. The facilities include the Ryder Grill, the Brabazon Bar, Leisure Café, Sam's, a Starbucks, a spa, leisure facilities and a golf shop. The bedrooms are modern and well equipped; many of the rooms have views of the surrounding countryside.

Rooms: 319 (4 family) (98 GF) ⚫ **Facilities:** Spa FTV WiFi ⊠ HL ⊛ ♨ 54 ⊜ Gym Squash Ryder legends Mini golf Children's playground Xmas New Year **Conf:** Class 435 Theatre 830 **Services:** Lift Night porter **Parking:** 1000 **Notes:** Civ Wed 300

WITNEY
Oxfordshire

Map 5 SP31

Oxford Witney Hotel

fOCUS hotels
management limited

★★★★ 75% HOTEL

tel: 01993 779777 **Ducklington Lane OX28 4TJ**
email: reception@oxfordwitneyhotel.co.uk **web:** www.oxfordwitneyhotel.co.uk
dir: *M40 junction 9, A34 to A40, exit A415 Witney/Abingdon. Hotel on left, 2nd exit for Witney.*

This attractive modern hotel is close to Oxford and Burford and offers spacious, well-equipped bedrooms. The cosy Spinners Bar has comfortable seating areas and the popular Weavers Restaurant offers a good range of dishes. Other amenities include extensive function and leisure facilities, complete with indoor swimming pool.

Rooms: 93 (14 family) (27 GF) ⚫ **S** fr £80 **D** fr £80* **Facilities:** FTV WiFi ⊠ ⊛ Gym Steam room Sauna Xmas New Year **Conf:** Class 76 Board 44 Theatre 150 **Services:** Night porter **Parking:** 120 **Notes:** LB Civ Wed 150

Premier Inn Witney

Premier Inn

BUDGET HOTEL

tel: 0871 527 9488 (Calls cost 13p per minute plus your phone company's access charge) **Beech House, Ducklington Lane OX28 4JF**
web: www.premierinn.com
dir: *M40 junction 8/9 follow Oxford signs, A40 towards Cheltenham. Take A415 (Witney and Abingdon). At bottom of slip road follow Witney signs. Straight on at lights, hotel on right.*

High quality, budget accommodation ideal for both families and business travellers. Spacious, en suite bedrooms feature free WiFi and tea and coffee making facilities, and in most hotels, Freeview TV is also available. The adjacent family restaurant features a wide and varied menu.

Rooms: 57

W

WOBURN
Bedfordshire   Map 11 SP93

The Woburn Hotel

★★★★ 82% HOTEL

tel: 01525 290441 **George Street MK17 9PX**
email: info@thewoburnhotel.co.uk **web:** www.thewoburnhotel.co.uk
dir: *M1 junction 13, towards Woburn. In Woburn left at T-junction, hotel in village.*

At the heart of the picturesque Georgian village of Woburn, standing proudly at the gateway to the Woburn Abbey Estate with its 3,000 acres of deer park and Humphry Repton inspired landscape, you will find The Woburn Hotel. It provides a high standard of accommodation and bedrooms are divided between the original house, a modern extension and stunning cottage suites. Public areas include the beamed, club-style Tavistock Bar, a range of meeting rooms and an attractive award-winning restaurant with interesting dishes on offer.

Rooms: 55 (7 annexe) (4 family) (25 GF) S fr £124.50 D fr £157 (including breakfast)* **Facilities:** FTV WiFi 54 Concessionary rate to access Woburn Safari Park and Woburn Abbey Xmas New Year **Conf:** Class 30 Board 35 Theatre 60 **Services:** Night porter **Parking:** 75 **Notes:** LB Civ Wed 60

WOKING
Surrey   Map 6 TQ05

Premier Inn Woking Town Centre

Premier Inn

BUDGET HOTEL

tel: 0871 527 9462 (Calls cost 13p per minute plus your phone company's access charge) **Eurobet House, Church Street West GU21 6HT**
web: www.premierinn.com
dir: *See website for directions.*

High quality, budget accommodation ideal for both families and business travellers. Spacious, en suite bedrooms feature free WiFi and tea and coffee making facilities, and in most hotels, Freeview TV is also available. The adjacent family restaurant features a wide and varied menu.

Rooms: 105

Premier Inn Woking West (A324)

Premier Inn

BUDGET HOTEL

tel: 0871 527 9182 (Calls cost 13p per minute plus your phone company's access charge) **Bridge Barn Lane, Horsell GU21 6NL**
web: www.premierinn.com
dir: *From A324 at roundabout into Parley Drive. Left at next roundabout into Goldsworth Road.*

Rooms: 56

WOKINGHAM
Berkshire   Map 5 SU86

Cantley House Hotel

★★★ 76% COUNTRY HOUSE HOTEL

tel: 0118 989 5100 **Milton Road RG40 1JY**
email: reception@cantleyhotel.co.uk **web:** www.cantleyhotel.co.uk
dir: *M4 junction 10, A329(M) to A329 towards Wokingham, then A321, hotel signed.*

Cantley House Hotel, surrounded by acres of parkland, is a Victorian mansion offering a number of conference and meeting rooms together with bedrooms that vary from the comfortable, cosy doubles to impressively-sized suites and executive rooms. The award-winning Milton's restaurant is housed in a beautifully converted 17th-century barn with its own secluded courtyard garden.

Rooms: 36 (20 GF) **Facilities:** FTV WiFi Hairdresser Massage treatments Xmas New Year **Conf:** Class 50 Board 50 Theatre 80 **Services:** Night porter **Parking:** 100 **Notes:** LB Civ Wed 150

WOLVERHAMPTON
West Midlands   Map 10 SO99

The Mount Hotel Country Manor

★★★★ 74% HOTEL

tel: 01902 752055 **Mount Road, Tettenhall Wood WV6 8HL**
email: sales@themount.co.uk **web:** www.themount.co.uk
dir: *M54 junction 5, follow A41 down to Yew Tree Lane which becomes Mount Road, left at lights.*

This historic hotel is peacefully located on the outskirts of the city. Modern decor and period architecture sit comfortably together, creating a stylish interior. Bedrooms are contemporary, with attractive colour schemes and are suitable for both business and leisure guests. Complimentary WiFi is available throughout, as is free secure parking. Public areas include a stylish bar and lounge, Drawing Room restaurant overlooking terrace and gardens, and extensive meeting and function rooms including the impressive Great Hall.

The Mount Hotel Country Manor

Rooms: 67 (10 annexe) (20 family) (31 GF) **Facilities:** FTV WiFi ⌕ Gym Xmas New Year **Conf:** Class 50 Board 80 Theatre 180 **Services:** Night porter **Parking:** 100 **Notes:** Civ Wed 140

Holiday Inn Wolverhampton - Racecourse

★★★ 79% HOTEL

Holiday Inn

tel: 01902 390004 & 390001 **Dunstall Park, Gorse Brook Road WV6 0PE**
email: holidayinn@wolverhampton-racecourse.com **web:** www.holidayinn.co.uk
dir: *Off A449, 1.5 miles from city centre. Follow brown sign for Dunstall Park. Adjacent to Wolverhampton Racecourse.*

This hotel forms an integral part of Wolverhampton Racecourse. Well-appointed, air-conditioned bedrooms have views across the course and stables. Open-plan public areas are modern and bright, with outdoor seating available during summer months. Free WiFi and ample parking are available.

Rooms: 54 (18 family) **S** fr £49* **Facilities:** STV WiFi ⌕ HL Gym Private location within Wolverhampton Racecourse Outdoor playground **Conf:** Class 260 Theatre 600 **Services:** Lift Air con **Parking:** 1500 **Notes:** Closed Civ Wed 60

Novotel Wolverhampton

★★★ 79% HOTEL

NOVOTEL
HOTELS & RESORTS

tel: 01902 871100 **Union Street WV1 3JN**
email: H1188@accor.com **web:** www.novotel.com
dir: *6 miles from M6 junction 10. A454 to Wolverhampton. Hotel on main ring road.*

This large, modern, purpose-built hotel stands close to the town centre. It provides spacious, smartly presented and well-equipped bedrooms, all of which have convertible bed settees for family occupancy. In addition to the open-plan lounge and bar area, there is an attractive brasserie-style restaurant, which overlooks an attractive patio garden.

Rooms: 132 (9 family) **Facilities:** FTV WiFi ⌕ **Conf:** Class 100 Board 80 Theatre 200 **Services:** Lift Night porter **Parking:** 120 **Notes:** Civ Wed 170

Premier Inn Wolverhampton City Centre

 Premier Inn

BUDGET HOTEL

tel: 0871 527 9186 (Calls cost 13p per minute plus your phone company's access charge) **Broad Gauge Way WV10 0BA**
web: www.premierinn.com
dir: *M6 junction 10, A454 signed Wolverhampton for approximately 2 miles. Right into Neachalls Lane (signed Wednesfield) for 0.75 mile. At roundabout 1st exit onto A4124 (Wednesfield Way). 1st exit at next roundabout. 2nd exit at 3rd roundabout. At 2nd lights left into Sun Street. 1st right, hotel at end of road.*

High quality, budget accommodation ideal for both families and business travellers. Spacious, en suite bedrooms feature free WiFi and tea and coffee making facilities, and in most hotels, Freeview TV is also available. The adjacent family restaurant features a wide and varied menu.

Rooms: 109

Premier Inn Wolverhampton North

Premier Inn

BUDGET HOTEL

tel: 0871 527 9184 (Calls cost 13p per minute plus your phone company's access charge) **Greenfield Lane, Stafford Road WV10 6TA**
web: www.premierinn.com
dir: *M54 junction 2. Hotel at lights in approximately 100 yards.*

Rooms: 80

WOMBWELL Map 16 SE40
South Yorkshire

Premier Inn Barnsley (Dearne Valley)

 Premier Inn

BUDGET HOTEL

tel: 0871 527 8050 (Calls cost 13p per minute plus your phone company's access charge) **Meadow Gate, Dearne Valley S73 0UN**
web: www.premierinn.com
dir: *M1 junction 36 eastbound, A6195 towards Doncaster (5 miles). Hotel at roundabout adjacent to Meadows Brewers Fayre.*

High quality, budget accommodation ideal for both families and business travellers. Spacious, en suite bedrooms feature free WiFi and tea and coffee making facilities, and in most hotels, Freeview TV is also available. The adjacent family restaurant features a wide and varied menu.

Rooms: 63

W

W

WONERSH
Surrey
Map 6 TQ04

Barnett Hill Country House Hotel

★★★★ 81% @@ COUNTRY HOUSE HOTEL

tel: 01483 893361 & 899274 **Blackheath Lane, GU5 0RF**
email: reservations@barnetthillhotel.co.uk **web:** www.barnetthillhotel.co.uk
dir: *M25 junction 10 take A3 south then B3000 to Compton/Godalming. A3100 Guildford then A248 Dorking. After 1 mile enter Wonersh village, turn left into Blackheath Lane. Hotel at top of lane.*

In the heart of the Surrey Hills, Barnett Hill is a beautiful Queen Anne-style mansion dating back to 1905; it sits in 26 acres of lovingly maintained gardens and woodland, a tranquil and peaceful setting. The hotel offers the formal Oak Hall Restaurant and also Butlers Brasserie and Bar; private dining is available too. Afternoon tea can be taken overlooking the elegant gardens and fountains. Bedrooms are individually and stylishly designed. This is a popular venue for weddings, and the conference facilities are impressive.

Rooms: 44 (26 annexe) (18 GF) **S** fr £99 **D** fr £109* **Facilities:** FTV WiFi Gym Xmas New Year **Conf:** Class 40 Board 32 Theatre 70 **Services:** Night porter **Parking:** 55 **Notes:** LB Civ Wed 80

WOOBURN
Buckinghamshire
Map 6 SU98

Chequers Inn

★★★ 80% @@ HOTEL

tel: 01628 529575 **Kiln Lane, Wooburn Common HP10 0JQ**
email: info@chequers-inn.com **web:** www.chequers-inn.com
dir: *M40 junction 2, A40 through Beaconsfield Old Town towards High Wycombe. 2 miles from town left into Broad Lane. Inn 2.5 miles.*

This 17th-century inn enjoys a peaceful, rural location beside the common. Bedrooms feature stripped-pine furniture, co-ordinated fabrics and an excellent range of extra facilities. The bar has a massive oak post, beams and flagstone floors, while the restaurant overlooks a pretty patio.

Rooms: 18 (8 GF) **Facilities:** FTV WiFi **Conf:** Class 30 Board 20 Theatre 50 **Parking:** 60 **Notes:** LB

WOODALL MOTORWAY SERVICE AREA (M1)
South Yorkshire
Map 16 SK48

Days Inn Sheffield - M1

WELCOMEBREAK

AA Advertised

tel: 0114 248 7992 **Woodall Service Area S26 7XR**
email: woodall.hotel@welcomebreak.co.uk **web:** www.welcomebreak.co.uk
dir: *M1, between junctions 30 and 31 southbound, at Woodall Services.*

This modern building offers accommodation in smart, spacious and well-equipped bedrooms, suitable for families and business travellers, and all with en suite bathrooms. Continental breakfast is available and other refreshments may be taken at the nearby family restaurant.

Rooms: 38 (32 family) (16 GF) (6 smoking) **Facilities:** FTV WiFi **Conf:** Board 10 **Parking:** 40

WOODBRIDGE
Suffolk
Map 13 TM24

Seckford Hall Hotel

★★★★ 79% @@ HOTEL

CLASSIC BRITISH HOTELS

tel: 01394 385678 **IP13 6NU**
email: reception@seckford.co.uk **web:** www.seckford.co.uk
dir: *Signed on A12. Note do not follow signs for town centre.*

Seckford Hall is an elegant Tudor manor house set amid landscaped grounds just off the A12. It is reputed that Queen Elizabeth I visited this property, and it retains much of its original character. Public rooms include a superb panelled lounge, a cosy bar and an intimate restaurant. The spacious bedrooms are attractively decorated, tastefully furnished and thoughtfully equipped.

Rooms: 32 (10 annexe) (4 family) (7 GF) **S** fr £100 **D** fr £130* **Facilities:** Spa WiFi Fishing Gym Beauty salon Xmas New Year **Conf:** Class 46 Board 40 Theatre 120 **Services:** Night porter **Parking:** 100 **Notes:** Civ Wed 120

HIGHLY RECOMMENDED

The Crown at Woodbridge

T | A | HOTEL COLLECTION

★★★ 86% @@ HOTEL

tel: 01394 384242 **The Thoroughfare IP12 1AD**
email: info@thecrownatwoodbridge.co.uk **web:** www.thecrownatwoodbridge.co.uk
dir: *A12 follow signs for Woodbridge onto B1438. 1.25 miles from roundabout left into Quay Street. Hotel on right approximately 100 yards.*

This 17th-century property offers contemporary-style accommodation throughout. The open-plan public areas are tastefully appointed and include a large lounge bar, a restaurant and a private dining room. The stylish bedrooms are tastefully appointed and equipped with modern facilities.

Rooms: 10 (2 family) **S** fr £120 **D** fr £120 (including breakfast)* **Facilities:** STV WiFi **Conf:** Class 8 Board 12 Theatre 15 **Services:** Night porter **Parking:** 40 **Notes:** LB

WOODBURY
Devon
Map 3 SY08

Woodbury Park Hotel and Golf Club

★★★★ 77% HOTEL

tel: 01395 233382 **Woodbury Castle EX5 1JJ**
email: enquiries@woodburypark.co.uk **web:** www.woodburypark.co.uk
dir: *M5 junction 30, A376 then A3052 towards Sidmouth, onto B3180, hotel signed.*

Situated in 500 acres of beautiful, unspoilt countryside, yet within easy reach of Exeter and the M5, this hotel offers smart, well-equipped and immaculately presented accommodation together with a host of sporting and banqueting facilities. There is a choice of golf courses, a Bodyzone beauty centre and enjoyable dining in the Atrium Restaurant.

Rooms: 60 (4 annexe) (4 family) (28 GF) **Facilities:** Spa STV FTV WiFi 27 Fishing Gym Squash Beauty salon Football pitch Driving range Fitness studio cinema suite Xmas New Year **Conf:** Class 100 Board 40 Theatre 250 **Services:** Lift Night porter **Parking:** 400 **Notes:** Civ Wed 150

WOODFORD BRIDGE
Greater London

Map 6 TQ49

Hallmark Hotel London Chigwell Prince Regent

★★★★ 76% HOTEL

tel: 0330 028 3418 **Manor Road IG8 8AE**
email: princeregent@hallmarkhotels.co.uk **web:** www.hallmarkhotels.co.uk
dir: *From A113 Chigwell Road south of Chigwell into B173 Manor Road.*

Situated on the edge of Woodford Bridge and Chigwell, this hotel with delightful rear gardens, offers easy access into London as well as to the M11 and M25. There is a good range of spacious, well-equipped bedrooms. Extensive conference and banqueting facilities are particularly well appointed, and are suitable for weddings or business events.

Rooms: 61 (4 family) (15 GF) (6 smoking) **Facilities:** STV FTV WiFi Xmas New Year **Conf:** Class 180 Board 80 Theatre 400 **Services:** Lift Night porter **Parking:** 225 **Notes:** LB Civ Wed 350

WOODFORD GREEN
Greater London

Map 6 TQ49

Best Western Plus Epping Forest

Best Western PLUS

★★★ 73% HOTEL

tel: 020 8787 9988 **30 Oak Hill IG8 9NY**
email: enquiries@eppingforesthotel.co.uk **web:** www.bestwestern.co.uk
dir: *M25 junction 27 take M11 southbound, at end of M11 follow A406 towards west end, stay in left hand lane and take the 1st exit to Woodford, at roundabout take 3rd exit, turn left at petrol station, hotel 150 yards on right.*

This hotel enjoys a very good location on the outskirts of London in Epping Forest – there is a real relaxed atmosphere and the woodland setting has real impact. Contemporary open-plan public areas are attractively presented and the stylish bar is very well appointed and comfortable. Spacious bedrooms look very smart with some eye-catching bold colours used in their design. Free WiFi is available throughout the hotel and secure parking is available.

Rooms: 99 (18 family) (24 GF) **Facilities:** FTV WiFi Xmas New Year **Services:** Lift Night porter **Parking:** 68 **Notes:** Civ Wed 200

Who are
the AA's award-winning hotels?
For details see pages 16–18

WOODHALL SPA
Lincolnshire

Map 17 TF16

Petwood

★★★ 79% HOTEL

tel: 01526 352411 **Stixwould Road LN10 6QG**
email: reception@petwood.co.uk **web:** www.petwood.co.uk
dir: *From Sleaford take A153 signed Skegness. At Tattershall turn left on B1192. Hotel is signed from village.*

This lovely Edwardian house, set in 30 acres of gardens and woodlands, is adjacent to Woodhall Golf Course. Built in 1905, the house was used by 617 Squadron, the famous Dambusters, as an officers' mess during World War II. Bedrooms and public areas are spacious, comfortable and retain many original features. Weddings and conferences are well catered for in modern facilities.

Rooms: 53 (6 family) (3 GF) **S** fr £75 **D** fr £140 (including breakfast)* **Facilities:** FTV WiFi Beauty treatments Xmas New Year **Conf:** Class 100 Board 50 Theatre 250 **Services:** Lift Night porter **Parking:** 140 **Notes:** LB Civ Wed 200

See advert on following page

W

WOODLANDS
Hampshire — Map 5 SU31

Woodlands Lodge Hotel
★★★ 79% ● HOTEL

tel: 023 8029 2257 **Bartley Road, Woodlands SO40 7GN**
email: reception@woodlands-lodge.co.uk **web:** www.woodlands-lodge.co.uk
dir: M27 junction 2, left at roundabout towards Fawley. 2nd roundabout right towards Cadnam. 1st left at White Horse pub onto Woodlands Road, over cattle grid.

An 18th-century former hunting lodge, this hotel is set in four acres of impressive and well-tended grounds on the edge of the New Forest. Well-equipped bedrooms come in varying sizes and styles and a number of bathrooms have a jacuzzi bath. Public areas include a pleasant lounge and intimate cocktail bar.

Rooms: 17 (3 family) (3 GF) ⚲ S fr £79 (including breakfast)* **Facilities:** FTV WiFi ⚲ Xmas New Year **Conf:** Class 20 Board 20 Theatre 65 **Parking:** 60 **Notes:** LB Civ Wed 100

WOODSTOCK
Oxfordshire — Map 11 SP41

Macdonald Bear Hotel
★★★★ 80% ●● HOTEL

 MACDONALD HOTELS & RESORTS

tel: 01993 811124 **Park Street OX20 1SZ**
email: general.bear@macdonald-hotels.co.uk **web:** www.macdonaldhotels.co.uk
dir: M40 junction 9 follow signs for Oxford and Blenheim Palace. A44 to town centre, hotel on left.

With its ivy-clad facade, oak beams and open fireplaces, this 13th-century coaching inn exudes charm and cosiness. The bedrooms are decorated in a modern style that remains in keeping with the historic character of the building. Public rooms include a variety of function rooms, an intimate bar area and an attractive restaurant where attentive service and good food are offered.

Rooms: 54 (18 annexe) (1 family) (8 GF) ⚲ **Facilities:** FTV WiFi Xmas New Year **Conf:** Class 12 Board 24 Theatre 40 **Services:** Night porter **Parking:** 40

The Feathers Hotel
★★★★ 76% ●● TOWN HOUSE HOTEL

PRIDE OF BRITAIN HOTELS

tel: 01993 812291 **Market Street OX20 1SX**
email: reception@feathers.co.uk **web:** www.feathers.co.uk
dir: From A44 Oxford to Woodstock, 1st left after lights. Hotel on left.

This intimate and unique hotel enjoys a town centre location with easy access to nearby Blenheim Palace. Public areas are elegant and full of traditional character. Individually styled bedrooms are appointed to a high standard and are furnished with attractive period and reproduction furniture. The dining options are the restaurant, Dinner by Dominic Chapman, and the Courtyard Terrace; the gin bar is worth a visit with its astonishing 400 gins from around the world on offer.

Rooms: 21 (5 annexe) (4 family) (2 GF) ⚲ S fr £99 **D** fr £109 (including breakfast)* **Facilities:** FTV WiFi ⚲ Xmas New Year **Conf:** Class 18 Board 20 Theatre 40 **Services:** Night porter **Notes:** LB

WOOLACOMBE
Devon — Map 3 SS44

Watersmeet Hotel
★★★★ 78% ●● HOTEL

tel: 01271 870333 **Mortehoe EX34 7EB**
email: info@watersmeethotel.co.uk **web:** www.watersmeethotel.co.uk
dir: B3343 into Woolacombe, right onto esplanade, hotel 0.75 mile on left.

With magnificent views, and steps leading directly to the beach, this popular hotel offers guests attentive service and a relaxing atmosphere. Bedrooms benefit from the wonderful sea views and some have private balconies. Diners in the attractive tiered restaurant can admire the beautiful sunsets while enjoying an innovative range of dishes offered on the fixed-price menu. Both indoor and outdoor pools are available.

Rooms: 25 (4 family) (3 GF) ⚲ **Facilities:** FTV WiFi ⚲ ⚲ ⚲ ⚲ Steam room ♫ Xmas New Year **Conf:** Board 20 Theatre 20 **Services:** Lift **Parking:** 38 **Notes:** LB Civ Wed 60

The Woolacombe Bay Hotel

★★★★ 78% HOTEL

tel: 01271 870388 **South Street EX34 7BN**
email: enquiries@woolacombebayhotel.co.uk **web:** www.woolacombebayhotel.co.uk
dir: A361 onto B3343 to Woolacombe. Hotel in centre.

Overlooking one of the finest beaches in England, this privately-owned hotel offers a warm welcome. Public areas are spacious and comfortable, and many of the stylishly furnished and well-equipped bedrooms have balconies with splendid views over the bay. Elegant bathroom suites certainly add to the feeling of luxury. In addition to the elegant surroundings of Doyle's Restaurant, The Bay Brasserie is available as an informal alternative. Extensive leisure facilities are also provided, including a health club, a spa and a very stylish lido.

Rooms: 64 (26 family) (2 GF) 🐾 **S** fr £97 **D** fr £164 (including breakfast)*
Facilities: Spa FTV WiFi 🐾 🔄 🛶 9 🏊 Gym Squash Paddling pool Table tennis Snooker Steam room Sauna Spa bath Xmas New Year **Conf:** Class 100 Board 50 Theatre 150 **Services:** Lift Night porter **Parking:** 150 **Notes:** Closed 2 January to 9 February Civ Wed 150

WORCESTER Map 10 SO85
Worcestershire

Premier Inn Worcester City Centre

Premier Inn

BUDGET HOTEL

tel: 0871 527 9456 (Calls cost 13p per minute plus your phone company's access charge) **Cricket Ground, New Road WR2 4QQ**
web: www.premierinn.com
dir: M5 junction 7 (Worcester South), A44 signed Worcester City Centre. At next roundabout 2nd exit (A44 and Worcester City Centre) keep in left lane. At Worcester Cathedral continue on A44, straight on at 3 sets of lights.

High quality, budget accommodation ideal for both families and business travellers. Spacious, en suite bedrooms feature free WiFi and tea and coffee making facilities, and in most hotels, Freeview TV is also available. The adjacent family restaurant features a wide and varied menu.

Rooms: 120

Premier Inn Worcester (M5 Jct 6)

Premier Inn

BUDGET HOTEL

tel: 0871 527 9188 (Calls cost 13p per minute plus your phone company's access charge) **Wainwright Way, Warndon WR4 9FA**
web: www.premierinn.com
dir: M5 junction 6. At entrance of Warndon commercial development area.

Rooms: 87

WORKINGTON Map 18 NY02
Cumbria

Hunday Manor Country House Hotel

★★★★ 77% COUNTRY HOUSE HOTEL

tel: 01900 61798 **Winscales CA14 4JF**
email: info@hundaymanorhotel.co.uk **web:** www.hundaymanorhotel.co.uk
dir: M6 junction 40, A66 towards Keswick/Workington for 30 miles until Cockermouth. At 2 roundabouts follow A66, at 3rd roundabout take 1st exit to A595, hotel 3 miles further on right.

Hunday Manor Country House Hotel has the western lakes and the Cumbrian coast both in easy reach. Benefiting from its elevated location, the hotel offers some wonderful views of the surrounding countryside, and the gardens are a delightful feature. The hotel has enjoyed extensive refurbishment over the past few years. Bedrooms are well appointed and a professional team provide attentive service and warm hospitality.

Rooms: 27 **Facilities:** WiFi 🐾 🔄 🛶 Xmas New Year **Conf:** Class 160 Board 60 Theatre 200 **Services:** Night porter **Parking:** 100 **Notes:** Civ Wed 200

W

WORKINGTON *continued*

Washington Central Hotel

★★★★ 73% HOTEL

tel: 01900 65772 **Washington Street CA14 3AY**
email: info@washingtoncentralhotel.co.uk **web:** www.washingtoncentralhotel.co.uk
dir: *M6 junction 40, A66 to Workington. Left at lights, hotel on right.*

Enjoying a prominent town centre location, this modern hotel boasts memorably hospitable staff. The well-maintained and comfortable bedrooms are equipped with a range of thoughtful extras. Public areas include numerous lounges, a spacious bar, Caesars leisure club, a smart restaurant and a popular coffee shop. The comprehensive conference facilities are ideal for meetings and weddings.

Rooms: 57 (12 family) ⫫ **S** fr £105 **D** fr £155 (including breakfast)* **Facilities:** FTV WiFi ⫫ ⫫ Gym Sauna Steam room New Year **Conf:** Class 200 Board 100 Theatre 300 **Services:** Lift Night porter **Parking:** 23 **Notes:** LB Civ Wed 300

| **WORKSOP** | Map 16 SK57 |
| Nottinghamshire | |

Best Western Lion Hotel

★★★ 80% HOTEL   **Best Western**

tel: 01909 477925 **112 Bridge Street S80 1HT**
email: reception@thelionworksop.co.uk **web:** www.bw-lionhotel.co.uk
dir: *A57 to town centre, turn right at Sainsburys, follow to Norfolk Arms, turn left.*

This former coaching inn lies on the edge of the main shopping precinct, with a car park to the rear. It has been extended to offer modern accommodation that includes excellent executive rooms. A wide range of interesting dishes are offered in both the 114 bar and grill and the 108 restaurant.

Rooms: 46 (3 family) (7 GF) ⫫ **S** fr £71 **D** fr £84 (including breakfast)*
Facilities: STV FTV WiFi ⫫ Xmas New Year **Conf:** Class 80 Board 70 Theatre 160 **Services:** Lift Night porter **Parking:** 50 **Notes:** Civ Wed 150

| **WORSLEY** | Map 15 SD70 |
| Greater Manchester | |

Novotel Manchester West

★★★ 75% HOTEL   **NOVOTEL** HOTELS & RESORTS

tel: 0161 799 3535 **Worsley Brow M28 2YA**
email: H0907@accor.com **web:** www.novotel.com
dir: *Adjacent to M60 junction 13.*

Well placed for access to the Peak District and the Lake District, as well as Manchester, this modern hotel successfully caters for both families and business guests. The spacious bedrooms have sofa beds and a large work area; the hotel has a children's play area and secure parking.

Rooms: 119 (10 family) (41 GF) ⫫ **S** fr £50 **D** fr £50* **Facilities:** STV FTV WiFi ⫫ HL Gym Xmas New Year **Conf:** Class 130 Board 60 Theatre 220 **Services:** Lift Night porter **Parking:** 95 **Notes:** Civ Wed 140

| **WORTHING** | Map 6 TQ10 |
| West Sussex | |

Ardington Hotel

★★★ 84% ⊚ HOTEL

tel: 01903 230451 **Steyne Gardens BN11 3DZ**
email: reservations@ardingtonhotel.co.uk **web:** www.ardingtonhotel.co.uk
dir: *A27 to Lancing, to seafront. Follow signs for Worthing. Left at church into Steyne Gardens.*

Overlooking Steyne Gardens adjacent to the seafront, this popular hotel offers well-appointed bedrooms with a good range of facilities. There's a stylishly modern lounge/bar with ample seating, where a light menu is available throughout the day. The popular restaurant offers local seafood and a choice of modern dishes. Free WiFi is available.

Rooms: 45 (4 family) (12 GF) **Facilities:** STV FTV WiFi **Conf:** Class 60 Board 35 Theatre 140 **Services:** Night porter **Notes:** Closed 25 December to 4 January

Premier Inn Worthing Seafront

BUDGET HOTEL   Premier Inn

tel: 0871 527 9556 (Calls cost 13p per minute plus your phone company's access charge) **127 Marine Parade BN11 3FN**
web: www.premierinn.com
dir: *From A24 and A27 Grove Lodge roundabout follow A24/South signs. At 4th roundabout 1st exit, follow seafront signs. At seafront, right into Marine Parade, pass pier, hotel approximately 1 mile on right.*

High quality, budget accommodation ideal for both families and business travellers. Spacious, en suite bedrooms feature free WiFi and tea and coffee making facilities, and in most hotels, Freeview TV is also available. The adjacent family restaurant features a wide and varied menu.

Rooms: 81

| **WORTLEY** | Map 16 SK39 |
| South Yorkshire | |

Wortley Hall

★★★ 76% ⊚⊚ HOTEL

tel: 0114 288 2100 **S35 7DB**
email: info@wortleyhall.org.uk **web:** www.wortleyhall.org.uk
dir: *Phone for directions.*

Situated in splendid parkland, this hotel was built in 1586 as a stately home. Now it is very popular for weddings and conferences, as well as for visiting guests. The Ruddy Duck restaurant is open Tuesday to Saturday, offering exciting dining and an open kitchen. There's a choice of bars too, a range of lounges, and outdoor seating.

Rooms: 49 (2 family) (4 GF) ⫫ **S** fr £44 **D** fr £65 (including breakfast)*
Facilities: FTV WiFi HL **Conf:** Class 100 Board 50 Theatre 200 **Services:** Lift Night porter **Parking:** 120 **Notes:** Closed 25–26 December, 1 January RS 24 December Civ Wed 200

W

WREA GREEN
Lancashire

Map 18 SD33

HIGHLY RECOMMENDED

The Spa Hotel at Ribby Hall Village
★★★★ 84% ◎◎ HOTEL

tel: 01772 671111 **Ribby Hall Village, Ribby Road PR4 2PR**
email: enquiries@ribbyhall.co.uk **web:** www.ribbyhall.co.uk/spa-hotel
dir: *M55 junction 33 follow A585 towards Kirkham and brown tourist signs for Ribby Hall Village. Straight across 3 roundabouts. Ribby Hall Village 200 yards on left.*

Set in 100 acres of rolling countryside, Ribby Hall is a tranquil and relaxing place to stay. The luxurious bedrooms are comfortable and come in a range of sizes. The spa is very much the focus here, offering guests a wide selection of treatments and their signature Aqua Thermal Journey. Food is another highlight, whether eaten in The Orangery restaurant or any of the nine outlets within the village.

Rooms: 38 (10 GF) ⟡ **S** fr £110 **D** fr £110* **Facilities:** Spa STV FTV WiFi ♨ ⚓ 9 ⛳ Fishing Gym Squash Aqua thermal journey Champagne bar Cycling Woodland trail Xmas New Year **Services:** Lift Night porter Air con **Parking:** 124 **Notes:** LB No children 18 years

The Villa Country House Hotel
★★★★ 77% ◎◎ COUNTRY HOUSE HOTEL

tel: 01772 804040 & 684347 **Moss Side Lane PR4 2PE**
email: info@thevilla.co.uk **web:** www.thevilla.co.uk
dir: *M55 junction 3 follow signs to Kirkham at Wrea Green follow signs to Lytham.*

Dating back to the 19th century, this former gentlemen's residence is packed full of original character and charm. Situated within the peaceful, picturesque village of Wrea Green but convenient for the motorway, it is the ideal location for a relaxing stay for both business and leisure guests. Rooms are thoughtfully appointed for the modern day traveller but still retain some of their original charm. An interesting range of dishes can be tried in the restaurant or alternatively there's all-day menus in the bar. Ample parking is available. Weddings, conferences and special events are well catered for.

Rooms: 31 (2 family) (10 GF) ⟡ **S** fr £70 **D** fr £80 (including breakfast)* **Facilities:** FTV WiFi Xmas New Year **Conf:** Class 100 Board 40 Theatre 300 **Services:** Lift Night porter **Parking:** 120 **Notes:** LB Civ Wed 300

WROTHAM HEATH
Kent

Map 6 TQ65

Premier Inn Sevenoaks/Maidstone
BUDGET HOTEL

Premier Inn

tel: 0871 527 8962 (Calls cost 13p per minute plus your phone company's access charge) **London Road TN15 7RX**
web: www.premierinn.com
dir: *M26 junction 2a, A20 south. At lights left onto A20 towards West Malling. Hotel on right.*

High quality, budget accommodation ideal for both families and business travellers. Spacious, en suite bedrooms feature free WiFi and tea and coffee making facilities, and in most hotels, Freeview TV is also available. The adjacent family restaurant features a wide and varied menu.

Rooms: 59

WROXALL
Warwickshire

Map 10 SP27

Wroxall Abbey Hotel & Estate
★★★★ 71% HOTEL

tel: 01926 484470 **Birmingham Road CV35 7NB**
email: reservation@wroxall.com **web:** www.wroxall.com
dir: *Between Solihull and Warwick on A4141.*

Situated in 27 acres of open parkland, yet only 10 miles from the NEC and Birmingham International Airport, this hotel is a magnificent Victorian mansion. Some of the individually designed bedrooms have traditional decor but there are modern loft rooms as well; some rooms have four-posters. Sonnets Restaurant, with its impressive fireplace and oak panelling, makes the ideal setting for fine dining.

Rooms: 72 (24 annexe) (10 GF) ⟡ **S** fr £79 **D** fr £99 (including breakfast)* **Facilities:** Spa FTV WiFi ⚓ ⚓ Fishing ⚓ Gym Xmas New Year **Conf:** Class 80 Board 60 Theatre 160 **Services:** Lift Night porter **Parking:** 200 **Notes:** LB No children 12 years Civ Wed 171

WYBOSTON
Bedfordshire

Map 12 TL15

Wyboston Lakes
★★★★ 80% ◎ HOTEL

tel: 0333 700 7667 **Great North Road MK44 3BA**
email: reservations@wybostonlakes.co.uk **web:** www.wybostonlakes.co.uk
dir: *From A1 and A428 junction, follow brown Cambridge signs. Wyboston Lakes and hotel on right, marked by flags.*

Wyboston Lakes is situated just off the A1(M), a short drive from Cambridge and Milton Keynes. The hotel is situated in extensive landscaped grounds and surrounded by a lake; the modern bedrooms are well equipped with a range of extra facilities that include coffee machines and large TVs. The hotel has a spa, golf course, and leisure facilities that include a gym and swimming pool.

Rooms: 103 (103 annexe) (4 family) (50 GF) ⟡ **D** fr £79* **Facilities:** Spa FTV WiFi ♨ HL ⚓ Fishing Gym Golf driving range Nature reserve Watersports New Year **Conf:** Class 120 Board 68 Theatre 270 **Services:** Lift Night porter **Parking:** 200 **Notes:** LB Civ Wed 250

W

INSPECTOR'S CHOICE

Crathorne Hall Hotel
★★★★ ◉ HOTEL

tel: 01642 700398 & 0845 072 7440 (Calls cost 5p per minute plus your phone company's access charge) **Crathorne TS15 0AR**
email: crathornehall@handpicked.co.uk
web: www.handpickedhotels.co.uk/crathorne-hall
dir: *From A19 take slip road signed Teesside Airport and Kirklevington, right signed Crathorne to hotel.*

This grand Edwardian hall sits in its own landscaped grounds and enjoys fine views of the Leven Valley and rolling Cleveland Hills. The impressively equipped bedrooms and delightful public areas offer sumptuous levels of comfort, with elegant antique furnishings that complement the hotel's architectural style. All bedrooms and suites (some now refurbished after a major refurbishment of the east wing) offer large TVs, DVD and CD players, and high-speed internet access among their many facilities. The elegant Leven Restaurant is a traditional setting for fine dining; there's also the Drawing Room for lighter food options. Weather permitting, alfresco eating is available on the terrace, and afternoon tea is always popular. Conference and banqueting facilities are available.

Rooms: 37 (10 family) **Facilities:** STV FTV WiFi HL Jogging track Clay pigeon shooting Xmas **Conf:** Class 75 Board 60 Theatre 120 **Services:** Lift Night porter **Parking:** 88 **Notes:** LB Civ Wed 90

Judges Country House Hotel
★★★ ◉◉ COUNTRY HOUSE HOTEL

tel: 01642 789000 **Kirklevington Hall TS15 9LW**
email: enquiries@judgeshotel.co.uk **web:** www.judgeshotel.co.uk
dir: *1.5 miles from A19. At A67 junction, follow Yarm road, hotel on left.*

Formerly a lodging for local circuit judges, this gracious mansion lies in landscaped grounds that has a stream running through it. Stylish bedrooms are individually decorated and come with plenty of extras; four-poster bedrooms and suites are available. Meals are offered in Judges Restaurant and private dining for a small number of guests is available in the wine cellar. Judges is a popular wedding venue. The genuinely caring and attentive service from the staff is truly memorable.

Rooms: 21 (3 family) (5 GF) **S** fr £99 **D** fr £145 (including breakfast)*
Facilities: FTV WiFi Gym Mountain bikes Nature trails Xmas New Year **Conf:** Class 50 Board 38 Theatre 80 **Services:** Night porter **Parking:** 102 **Notes:** LB Civ Wed 200

YARMOUTH
Isle Of Wight

Map 5 SZ38

INSPECTOR'S CHOICE

The George Hotel
★★★ ◉◉ HOTEL

tel: 01983 760331 **Quay Street PO41 0PE**
email: info@thegeorge.co.uk **web:** www.thegeorge.co.uk
dir: *Between castle and pier.*

This elegant 17th-century hotel enjoys a wonderful location at the water's edge, adjacent to the castle and the pier. Public areas include Isla's fine dining restaurant, where organic and local produce are utilised; The Conservatory, for modern brasserie dining and views over the Solent; a cosy bar and an inviting lounge. Individually styled bedrooms, with many thoughtful extras, are beautifully appointed; some benefit from spacious balconies. The hotel's motor yacht is available for guests to hire.

Rooms: 17 (1 GF) ✆ **S** fr £125 **D** fr £140 (including breakfast)* **Facilities:** STV WiFi ⌔ Sailing from Yarmouth Mountain biking Xmas New Year **Conf:** Class 18 Board 18 Theatre 20 **Services:** Night porter **Notes:** LB Civ Wed 120

Norton Grange Coastal Village

WARNERLEISUREHOTELS

AA Advertised

tel: 01983 760 323 **PO41 0SD**
web: www.warnerleisurehotels.co.uk
dir: *From Yarmouth Ferry Terminal leaving Yarmouth harbour, turn right at roundabout, follow road across Yarmouth bridge A3054. After approximately 0.5 mile hotel on right after bend.*

Sitting pretty in one of the UK's sunniest spots just five minutes from Yarmouth ferry port, with access to scenic coastal walks, this friendly chalet village is a favourite for sunseekers. A wide range of leisure activities is on offer, and there is nightly entertainment on the popular half-board breaks. This is an adults-only (minimum 21 years old) hotel.

Rooms: 208 ✆ **D** fr £250 (including breakfast & dinner)* **Facilities:** FTV WiFi ⌔ ⊗ ⚓ Gym ♪ Xmas New Year **Services:** Night porter **Parking:** 208 **Notes:** LB No children 21 years Closed January to February

YEALMPTON
Devon

Map 3 SX55

Kitley House Hotel

[U]

tel: 01752 881555 **PL8 2NW**
email: info@kitleyhousehotel.com **web:** www.kitleyhousehotel.com
dir: *A38 follow signs to Yealmpton. Take the A379 Plymouth to Kingsbridge road. The hotel is just outside Yealmpton. Follow the driveway for 1 mile.*

Currently the rating for this establishment is not confirmed. This may be due to a change of ownership or because ot has only recently joined the AA rating scheme.

Rooms: 19 (2 family) (1 GF) ✆ **Facilities:** WiFi **Conf:** Class 80 Board 30 Theatre 120 **Services:** Night porter **Parking:** 100 **Notes:** Civ Wed 150

YELVERTON
Devon

Map 3 SX56

Moorland Garden Hotel
★★★★ 77% ◉ HOTEL

tel: 01822 852245 **PL20 6DA**
email: stay@moorlandgardenhotel.co.uk **web:** www.moorlandgardenhotel.co.uk
dir: *A38 from Exeter to Plymouth, then A386 towards Tavistock. 5 miles onto open moorland, hotel 1 mile on left.*

This hotel has a great location for either Plymouth or Dartmoor and sits in delightful gardens. Bedrooms are spacious, all have garden views and some have impressive balconies. There is a choice of dining as well as a range of meeting and function rooms. Pleasant Devon cream teas are served in the garden in warmer months.

Rooms: 44 (5 family) (17 GF) ✆ **S** fr £70 **D** fr £80 (including breakfast)* **Facilities:** FTV WiFi ⌔ HL Reduced fees for residents at golf club Xmas New Year **Conf:** Class 60 Board 50 Theatre 170 **Services:** Night porter **Parking:** 75 **Notes:** LB Civ Wed 160

YEOVIL
Somerset

Map 4 ST51

The Yeovil Court Hotel & Restaurant
★★★ 76% HOTEL

tel: 01935 863746 **West Coker Road BA20 2HE**
email: unwind@yeovilhotel.com **web:** www.yeovilhotel.com
dir: *2.5 miles west of town centre on A30.*

This comfortable, family-run hotel offers a very relaxed atmosphere. Bedrooms are well equipped and neatly presented; some are located in an adjacent building. Public areas consist of a smart lounge, a popular bar and an attractive restaurant. Menus combine an interesting selection that includes lighter options, and dishes suited to special occasion dining.

Rooms: 30 (12 annexe) (3 family) (8 GF) ✆ **S** fr £72 **D** fr £102 (including breakfast)* **Facilities:** FTV WiFi ⌔ **Conf:** Class 18 Board 30 Theatre 50 **Services:** Night porter **Parking:** 65 **Notes:** Civ Wed 70

Y

YEOVIL *continued*

Premier Inn Yeovil

Premier Inn

BUDGET HOTEL

tel: 0871 527 9192 (Calls cost 13p per minute plus your phone company's access charge) **Alvington Lane, Brympton BA22 8UX**
web: www.premierinn.com
dir: *M5 junction 25, A358, A303 follow Yeovil signs. At roundabout onto A3088. At next roundabout 1st left, at next roundabout turn left. Hotel on left.*

High quality, budget accommodation ideal for both families and business travellers. Spacious, en suite bedrooms feature free WiFi and tea and coffee making facilities, and in most hotels, Freeview TV is also available. The adjacent family restaurant features a wide and varied menu.

Rooms: 20

Premier Inn Yeovil Town Centre

Premier Inn

BUDGET HOTEL

tel: 0871 527 9426 (Calls cost 13p per minute plus your phone company's access charge) **Key Market House, Middle Street BA20 1LT**
web: www.premierinn.com
dir: *From north: A37 to end, take A30 (Reckleford). Keep right, take 1st right. Into Sherborne Road left into Newton Road. Left into South Western Terrace, join Old Station Road. Hotel on right. From south: A30, at roundabout into Brunswick Street. Then Park Street, Taunusstein Way, Summer House Terrace, Old Station Road.*

Rooms: 80

YORK	**Map 16 SE65**
North Yorkshire	

See also **Aldwark & Escrick**

The Grand Hotel & Spa, York

★★★★★ 86% ◉◉◉ HOTEL

tel: 01904 380038 **Station Rise YO1 6HT**
email: info@thegrandyork.co.uk **web:** www.thegrandyork.co.uk
dir: *In city centre, near station.*

Located in the heart of the city, this majestic Edwardian building, built in 1906, has been transformed into a luxury hotel. Spacious, air-conditioned accommodation offers deeply comfortable rooms with luxurious bathrooms. Public areas are equally impressive with a range of delightful lounges, a modern spa in the former vaults and excellent meeting rooms. Hudson's offers award-winning dining with modern and classic dishes on offer, all delivered with both flair and a touch of fun. Afternoon tea is presented on a silver stand in a relaxing, tranquil environment. Valet parking is a great asset given the hotel's central location.

Rooms: 207 (14 GF) ↑ **S** fr £139 **D** fr £139* **Facilities:** Spa STV FTV WiFi ↕ ☜ Gym Sauna Steam room Beauty treatments Relaxation lounge Xmas New Year
Conf: Class 60 Board 50 Theatre 120 **Services:** Lift Night porter Air con **Notes:** LB Civ Wed 110

Middlethorpe Hall & Spa

★★★★ ◉◉ HOTEL

PRIDE OF BRITAIN HOTELS

tel: 01904 641241 **Bishopthorpe Road, Middlethorpe YO23 2GB**
email: info@middlethorpe.com **web:** www.middlethorpe.com
dir: *A1/A64 follow York West A1036 signs, then Bishopthorpe, Middlethorpe racecourse signs.*

This fine house, dating from the reign of William and Mary, sits in acres of beautifully landscaped gardens. The bedrooms vary in size but all are comfortably furnished; some are located in the main house, and others are in a cottage and converted courtyard stables. Public areas include a small spa and a stately drawing room where afternoon tea is quite an event. The delightful panelled restaurant is a perfect setting for enjoying the imaginative cuisine.

Rooms: 29 (19 annexe) (2 family) (10 GF) ↑ **S** fr £143 **D** fr £205 (including breakfast)* **Facilities:** Spa FTV WiFi ↕ ☜ ⚓ Gym Xmas New Year **Conf:** Class 30 Board 25 Theatre 56 **Services:** Lift Night porter **Parking:** 71 **Notes:** LB No children 6 years Civ Wed 56

The Grange Hotel

★★★★ 80% ◉◉ HOTEL

tel: 01904 644744 **1 Clifton YO30 6AA**
email: info@grangehotel.co.uk **web:** www.grangehotel.co.uk
dir: *On A19 York/Thirsk road, approximately 500 yards from city centre.*

This bustling Regency town house is just a few minutes' walk from the centre of York. Professional service is efficiently delivered by caring staff in a very friendly and helpful manner. Public rooms are comfortable and have been stylishly furnished; these include the traditional library and drawing room, and The Ivy Brasserie, which offers fine dining in a lavishly decorated environment. The individually designed bedrooms are comfortably appointed and have been thoughtfully equipped.

Rooms: 41 (1 family) (11 GF) ↑ **S** fr £110 **D** fr £140 (including breakfast)* **Facilities:** STV FTV WiFi ↕ Use of nearby health club (chargeable) Xmas New Year **Conf:** Class 24 Board 24 Theatre 40 **Services:** Lift Night porter **Parking:** 20 **Notes:** LB Civ Wed 90

Hotel du Vin & Bistro York

★★★★ 80% HOTEL

tel: 01904 557350 & 0844 748 9268 (Calls cost 7p per minute plus your phone company's access charge) 89 The Mount YO24 1AX
email: info.york@hotelduvin.com web: www.hotelduvin.com/locations/york
dir: A1036 towards city centre, 6 miles. Hotel on right through lights.

This Hotel du Vin offers luxury and quality that will cosset even the most discerning guest. Bedrooms are decadent in design and the bathrooms have huge monsoon showers and feature baths. Dinner in the bistro provides a memorable highlight thanks to exciting menus and a superb wine list. Staff throughout are naturally friendly and nothing is too much trouble.

Rooms: 44 (3 family) (14 GF) Facilities: STV FTV WiFi Conf: Class 10 Board 22 Theatre 60 Services: Lift Night porter Air con Parking: 18 Notes: Civ Wed 80

Dean Court Hotel

★★★★ 78% HOTEL

tel: 01904 625082 Duncombe Place YO1 7EF
email: sales@deancourt-york.co.uk web: www.deancourt-york.co.uk
dir: In city centre opposite York Minster.

This smart hotel enjoys a central location overlooking The Minster, and guests will find the service is particularly friendly and efficient. Bedrooms are stylishly appointed and vary in size. Public areas are elegant in a contemporary style and include the popular D.C.H. restaurant which enjoys wonderful views of the cathedral, and the D.C.H. bar. Valet parking is available.

Rooms: 40 (4 family) (3 GF) S fr £115 D fr £150 (including breakfast)*
Facilities: STV FTV WiFi Xmas New Year Conf: Class 12 Board 32 Theatre 50
Services: Lift Night porter Parking: 30 Notes: LB

Marmadukes Town House Hotel

★★★★ 77% TOWN HOUSE HOTEL

tel: 01904 640101 4-5 St Peters Grove, Bootham YO30 6AQ
email: reservations@marmadukestownhousehotelyork.com
web: www.marmadukestownhousehotelyork.com
dir: A1036 signed York for approximately 6 miles past train station then signed Inner Ring Road. Over Lendal bridge, at lights left onto A19 Bootham Bar for 0.4 mile, right into St Peters Grove.

Set in secluded gardens, this Georgian hotel has free WiFi and luxurious rooms with handmade beds. Marmadukes Town House Hotel is just a 10-minute walk from York Minster, the Shambles and the Theatre Royal. The rooms are individually decorated with antique furniture and Egyptian linens, and all have tea- and coffee-making facilities, DVD player and stylish bathrooms with designer toiletries. Guests can relax in the elegant lounge bar or leafy garden. There is also a sun lounge with antique sofas, where traditional full English breakfasts are served daily.

Rooms: 21 (11 annexe) (2 family) (3 GF) Facilities: FTV WiFi Conf: Class 25 Board 25 Theatre 50 Services: Night porter Parking: 14 Notes: Civ Wed 50

The Churchill Hotel

★★★★ 77% HOTEL

tel: 01904 644456 65 Bootham YO30 7DQ
email: info@churchillhotel.com web: www.churchillhotel.com
dir: On A19 (Bootham), west from York Minster, hotel 250 yards on right.

The Churchill Hotel is a late Georgian manor house set in its own grounds, just a short walk from York Minster and other attractions. Period features and interesting artefacts relating to Winston Churchill are incorporated into smart contemporary

design and up-to-date technology. Public areas include the Wellington Bar and Dewsnaps Brasserie where innovative menus feature high quality, local produce.

Rooms: 32 (4 family) (5 GF) Facilities: WiFi Xmas New Year Conf: Class 50 Board 30 Theatre 100 Services: Lift Night porter Parking: 40 Notes: Civ Wed 70

The Principal York

PRINCIPAL

★★★★ 77% HOTEL

tel: 01904 653681 Station Rd YO24 1AA
email: yorkreservations@theprincipalhotel.com
web: www.phcompany.com/principal/york-hotel
dir: Adjacent to railway station.

Situated in three acres of landscaped grounds in the very heart of the city, this Victorian railway hotel has views over the city and York Minster. Contemporary bedrooms are divided between those in the main hotel and the air-conditioned garden mews. Relax and enjoy afternoon tea in the Garden Room or take a meal in the Refectory Kitchen and Terrace. There is also a leisure complex and state-of-the-art conference centre.

Rooms: 155 (34 annexe) (1 family) Facilities: FTV WiFi Gym Steam room Weights room Xmas New Year Conf: Class 250 Board 80 Theatre 410 Services: Lift Night porter Parking: 90 Notes: Civ Wed 160

The Parsonage Country House Hotel

★★★★ 76% COUNTRY HOUSE HOTEL

tel: 01904 728111 York Road YO19 6LF
email: reservations@parsonagehotel.co.uk web: www.parsonagehotel.co.uk

(for full entry see Escrick)

Novotel York Centre

NOVOTEL
HOTELS & RESORTS

★★★★ 75% HOTEL

tel: 01904 611660 Fishergate YO10 4FD
email: H0949@accor.com web: www.novotel.com
dir: A19 north to city centre, hotel set back on left.

Set just outside the ancient city walls, this modern, family-friendly hotel is conveniently located for visitors to the city. Bedrooms feature bathrooms with a separate toilet room, plus excellent desk space and sofa beds. Four rooms are equipped for less mobile guests. The hotel's facilities include indoor and outdoor children's play areas and an indoor pool.

Rooms: 124 (124 family) Facilities: FTV WiFi HL Xmas New Year Conf: Class 100 Board 120 Theatre 210 Services: Lift Night porter Parking: 140

The DoubleTree by Hilton York

★★★★ 74% HOTEL

tel: 01904 638086 St Maurices Road, Monkbar YO31 7JA
email: sales@dtyork.co.uk web: www.dtyork.doubletreebyhilton.com
dir: A64 onto A1079 to city, turn right at city walls, take middle lane at lights. Hotel on right.

This smart hotel enjoys a prominent position adjacent to the city walls and is just a few minutes' walk from York Minster. Monkbar offers individually-styled bedrooms that are well equipped for both business and leisure guests. Spacious public areas include comfortable lounges, a traditional Yorkshire bar, an airy restaurant and state-of-the-art meeting and training facilities.

Rooms: 143 (8 family) (12 GF) S fr £90 D fr £100* Facilities: FTV WiFi Gym Xmas New Year Conf: Class 100 Board 60 Theatre 250 Services: Lift Night porter Air con Notes: LB Civ Wed 150

Y

YORK *continued*

Mercure York Fairfield Hotel

★★★★ 72% COUNTRY HOUSE HOTEL

tel: 01904 225012 & 0844 815 9038 (Calls cost 7p per minute plus your phone company's access charge) **Shipton Road, Skelton YO30 1XW**
email: gm.mercureyork@jupiterhotels.co.uk **web:** www.mercureyork.co.uk
dir: *Exit A1237 onto A19, hotel 0.5 mile on left.*

This stylish Georgian mansion stands in six acres of private grounds on the outskirts of the city. The contemporary bedrooms, styled in reds or blues, have broadband access; some rooms have garden and courtyard views. The suites have either four-poster or king-size beds and a separate seating area. Kilby's Restaurant serves bistro food, and 24-hour room service is available. There are good conference facilities.

Rooms: 89 (20 family) (24 GF) 🏠 🛇 **S** fr £69 **D** fr £69* **Facilities:** FTV WiFi ⤋ HL Use of nearby health club Xmas New Year **Conf:** Class 60 Board 60 Theatre 180 **Services:** Lift Night porter **Parking:** 120 **Notes:** LB Civ Wed 180

Mount Royale

★★★ 81% 🏵🏵 ⬚ HOTEL

tel: 01904 628856 **The Mount YO24 1GU**
email: reservations@mountroyale.co.uk **web:** www.mountroyale.co.uk
dir: *West on A1036, 0.5 mile after racecourse. Hotel on right after lights.*

This friendly hotel, a listed building from the 1830s, offers comfortable bedrooms in a variety of styles, several leading onto the delightful gardens. Public rooms include a lounge, a meeting room and a cosy bar; the hotel has an outdoor pool, a sauna and a hot tub plus a beauty therapist. There is a separate restaurant called Oxo's on The Mount, and a cocktail lounge overlooking the gardens. Limited car parking is also available.

Rooms: 24 (3 family) (6 GF) 🏠 🛇 **S** fr £95 **D** fr £135 (including breakfast)*
Facilities: Spa FTV WiFi ⤋ Sauna Steam room Xmas New Year **Conf:** Class 16 Board 22 Theatre 35 **Services:** Night porter **Parking:** 24 **Notes:** LB

Best Western Kilima Hotel

BW Best Western.

★★★ 77% HOTEL

tel: 01904 625787 **129 Holgate Road YO24 4AZ**
email: sales@kilima.co.uk **web:** www.bw-kilimahotel.co.uk
dir: *Phone for directions.*

Situated close to the heart of York and very handy for transport links, the racecourse and, of course, the historical centre and its attractions, this hotel has much to offer guests. Bedrooms vary in space and ably cater for the needs of the modern guest. The cellar bar and restaurant provides a bright and comfortable dining venue.

Rooms: 26 (4 family) (9 GF) **S** fr £80 **D** fr £120 (including breakfast) **Facilities:** WiFi ⤋ 🏊 Gym **Conf:** Class 14 Board 14 Theatre 14 **Parking:** 30 **Notes:** LB

Middletons Hotel

THWAITES

★★★ 74% HOTEL

tel: 01904 611570 **Skeldergate YO1 6DS**
email: reception@middletonsyork.co.uk **web:** www.middletonsyork.co.uk
dir: *From A64 Leeds, A1036 towards city centre. Right at City Walls lights, keep left, 1st left before bridge, then 1st left into Cromwell Road. Hotel on right.*

This hotel has been created from several listed buildings and is very well located in the centre of York. Bedrooms are comfortably equipped. Among its amenities is a

bar-lounge and a dining room where a satisfying range of food is served. An extensive fitness club is also available along with private parking.

Rooms: 56 (19 annexe) (6 family) (17 GF) 🏠 **Facilities:** FTV WiFi ⤋ Gym Fitness centre **Conf:** Class 36 Board 36 Theatre 60 **Services:** Night porter **Parking:** 40 **Notes:** Civ Wed 60

Premier Inn York City (Blossom St North)

Premier Inn 🌙

BUDGET HOTEL

tel: 0871 527 9196 (Calls cost 13p per minute plus your phone company's access charge) **20 Blossom Street YO24 1AJ**
web: www.premierinn.com
dir: *12 miles from A1 junction 47, off A59.*

High quality, budget accommodation ideal for both families and business travellers. Spacious, en suite bedrooms feature free WiFi and tea and coffee making facilities, and in most hotels, Freeview TV is also available. The adjacent family restaurant features a wide and varied menu.

Rooms: 102

Premier Inn York City (Blossom St South)

Premier Inn 🌙

BUDGET HOTEL

tel: 0871 527 9194 (Calls cost 13p per minute plus your phone company's access charge) **28-40 Blossom Street YO24 1AJ**
web: www.premierinn.com
dir: *From south, east and west: A64, A1036 (signed York West). From north: A1 (or A19), A59, follow city centre signs. At lights left onto A1036. Hotel on left just after cinema. Note: no drop-off point, parking at NCP, Queens Street.*

Rooms: 91

Premier Inn York North (Maritime Park)

Premier Inn 🌙

BUDGET HOTEL

tel: 0871 527 9198 (Calls cost 13p per minute plus your phone company's access charge) **Shipton Road YO30 5PA**
web: www.premierinn.com
dir: *From A1237 (ring road), A19 (Shipton Road South) signed York Centre. Hotel on right in Clifton Park.*

Rooms: 49

Premier Inn York North West (Ring Road)

Premier Inn 🌙

BUDGET HOTEL

tel: 0871 527 9200 (Calls cost 13p per minute plus your phone company's access charge) **White Rose Close, York Business Park YO26 6RL**
web: www.premierinn.com
dir: *On A1237 between A19 Thirsk road and A59 Harrogate road.*

Rooms: 82

Premier Inn York South West (A64)

Premier Inn 🌙

BUDGET HOTEL

tel: 0871 527 9202 (Calls cost 13p per minute plus your phone company's access charge) **Bilbrough Top, Colton YO23 3PP**
web: www.premierinn.com
dir: *On A64 between Tadcaster and York.*

Rooms: 62

Channel Islands

GUERNSEY

CASTEL
Map 24

Le Friquet Hotel

★★★ 80% HOTEL

tel: 01481 256509 **Rue du Friquet GY5 7ST**
email: stay@lefriquethotel.co.uk **web:** www.lefriquethotel.com
dir: *Phone for directions.*

Le Friquet (French for 'sparrow') is located in a quiet setting with extensive grounds, an outdoor swimming pool and plenty of private parking. The hotel offers traditional and comfortably appointed accommodation; all rooms are well equipped with a good range of amenities, including WiFi. Guests can enjoy alfresco dining on the terrace or in the main Lobster and Grill Restaurant which is contemporary in style; this is the only hotel in Guernsey to have a live lobster tank. Great hospitality and service can be expected from the friendly team.

Rooms: 33 (1 family) (3 GF) **S** fr £52.54 **D** fr £78.10 (including breakfast)*
Facilities: STV FTV WiFi ⌂ ⚆ Xmas New Year **Services:** Air con **Parking:** 40

FOREST
Map 24

Le Chene Hotel

★★ 76% HOTEL

tel: 01481 235566 **Forest Road GY8 0AH**
email: info@lechene.co.uk **web:** www.lechene.co.uk
dir: *Between airport and St Peter Port. From airport left to St Peter Port. Hotel on right after 1st lights.*

This Victorian manor house is well located for guests wishing to explore Guernsey's spectacular south coast. The building has been skilfully extended to house a range of well-equipped, modern bedrooms. There is a swimming pool, a cosy cellar bar and a varied range of enjoyable freshly-cooked dishes at dinner.

Rooms: 26 (2 family) (1 GF) (1 smoking) **Facilities:** WiFi ⚆ Library outdoor sauna **Parking:** 20 **Notes:** LB Closed October to March

ST MARTIN
Map 24

Bella Luce Hotel, Restaurant & Spa

★★★★ 78% ⚝⚝ SMALL HOTEL

tel: 01481 238764 **La Fosse GY4 6EB**
email: wakeup@bellalucehotel.com **web:** www.bellalucehotel.com
dir: *From airport, turn left to St Martin. At 3rd set of lights continue 30 yards, turn right, straight on to hotel.*

This delightful hotel is both contemporary and luxurious; the stylish bedrooms have comfortable beds and designer furnishings, superb bathrooms and up-to-the-minute technology. The restaurant offers the best Guernsey produce, and the head chef has a keen sense of adventure. Gin tasting and special dining experiences can be enjoyed in the hotel's Bella Luce Small Batch Distillery. Staff are friendly and attentive, and always make sure guests feel welcome.

Rooms: 23 (4 family) (2 GF) ⚆ **S** fr £120 **D** fr £130 (including breakfast)*
Facilities: Spa STV FTV WiFi ⌂ ⚆ Xmas New Year **Conf:** Class 18 Board 25 Theatre 40 **Services:** Night porter Air con **Parking:** 33 **Notes:** LB Closed 1st 2 weeks January

La Barbarie Hotel

★★★ 82% ⚝ HOTEL

tel: 01481 235217 **Saints Road, Saints Bay GY4 6ES**
email: reservations@labarbariehotel.com **web:** www.labarbariehotel.com
dir: *At lights in St Martin take road to Saints Bay. Hotel on right at end of Saints Road.*

This former priory dates back to the 17th century and retains much charm and style. Staff help to create a very friendly and attentive atmosphere, and the modern facilities offer guests a relaxing stay. Excellent choices and fresh local ingredients form the basis of the interesting menus in the attractive restaurant and bar.

La Barbarie Hotel

Rooms: 35 (8 GF) ⌂ **S** fr £75 **D** fr £100 (including breakfast)* **Facilities:** STV WiFi ⚹ **Parking:** 50 **Notes:** LB Closed November to February

Hotel Jerbourg

★★★ 79% HOTEL

tel: 01481 238826 **Jerbourg Point GY4 6BJ**
email: stay@hoteljerbourg.com **web:** www.hoteljerbourg.com
dir: *From airport turn left to St Martin, right at filter, straight on at lights, hotel at end of road on right.*

This hotel boasts excellent sea views from its cliff-top location. Public areas are smartly appointed and include an extensive bar/lounge and bright conservatory-style restaurant. In addition to the fairly extensive carte, a daily-changing menu is available. Bedrooms are well presented and comfortable, and the luxury bay rooms are generally more spacious.

Rooms: 32 (4 family) (5 GF) **Facilities:** FTV WiFi ⚹ Petanque Xmas New Year **Parking:** 50 **Notes:** LB Closed 5 January to 1 March

La Villette Hotel & Leisure Suite

★★★ 79% HOTEL

tel: 01481 235292 **GY4 6QG**
email: reservations@lavillettehotel.co.uk **web:** www.lavillettehotel.co.uk
dir: *Turn left from airport. Follow road past La Trelade Hotel. Take next right, hotel on left.*

Set in spacious grounds, this peacefully located, family-run hotel has a friendly atmosphere. The well-equipped bedrooms are spacious and comfortable. Live music is a regular feature in the large bar, while in the separate restaurant a fixed-price menu is provided. Residents have use of the excellent indoor leisure facilities, and there are also beauty treatments and a hairdressing salon.

Rooms: 35 (3 family) (14 GF) ⌂ **Facilities:** FTV WiFi ⓧ ⚹ Gym Steam room Leisure suite Beauty salon Hairdresser Petanque Xmas New Year **Conf:** Board 40 Theatre 80 **Services:** Lift **Parking:** 50

Saints Bay Hotel

★★★ 77% HOTEL

tel: 01481 238888 **Icart Road GY4 6JG**
email: info@saintsbayhotel.com **web:** www.saintsbayhotel.com
dir: *From St Martin take Saints Road into Icart Road.*

Ideally situated in an elevated position near Icart Point headland and above the fishing harbour at Saints Bay, this hotel has superb views. The spacious public rooms include a smart lounge bar, a first-floor lounge and a smart conservatory restaurant that overlooks the swimming pool. Bedrooms are pleasantly decorated and thoughtfully equipped.

Rooms: 35 (1 family) (13 GF) **S** fr £52 **D** fr £74 (including breakfast)* **Facilities:** FTV WiFi ⚹ Xmas New Year **Parking:** 15

ST PETER PORT | Map 24

The Old Government House Hotel & Spa

RED CARNATION
HOTEL COLLECTION

★★★★★ 82% ⓦ ⓢ HOTEL

tel: 01481 724921 **St Ann's Place GY1 2NU**
email: ogh@theoghhotel.com **web:** www.theoghhotel.com
dir: *At junction of St Julian's Avenue and St Ann's Place.*

Affectionately known as the OGH, this is one of the island's leading hotels. Located in the heart of St Peter Port, it is the perfect base from which to explore Guernsey and the other islands of the Bailiwick. Bedrooms vary in size but all are comfortable and offer high quality accommodation. There is an indulgent health club and spa, and the eating options are The Brasserie, the Olive Grove and the Curry Room.

Rooms: 62 (3 annexe) (6 family) ⌂ **S** fr £193 **D** fr £193 (including breakfast)* **Facilities:** Spa STV WiFi ⓝ HL ⚹ Gym Steam room Sauna Relaxation room ♫ Xmas New Year **Conf:** Class 69 Board 66 Theatre 200 **Services:** Lift Night porter Air con **Parking:** 20

The Duke of Richmond Hotel

RED CARNATION
HOTEL COLLECTION

★★★★ 82% ⓦ HOTEL

tel: 01481 726221 **Cambridge Park GY1 1UY**
email: manager@dukeofrichmond.com **web:** www.dukeofrichmond.com
dir: *On corner of Cambridge Park and L'Hyvreuse Avenue, opposite leisure centre.*

The luxurious Duke of Richmond Hotel offers unparalleled service in elegant surroundings. Located just up the hill from the bustling town centre and an easy stroll from the beautiful harbour, the position is peaceful, overlooking a park with views across the town to the sea beyond. Guests will be warmly welcomed with exceptional service that supports the ethos, 'No request is too large, no detail too small'.

Rooms: 73 (11 family) ⌂ **Facilities:** STV WiFi ⓝ HL ⚹ Xmas New Year **Conf:** Class 80 Board 40 Theatre 300 **Services:** Lift Night porter Air con **Parking:** 5 **Notes:** LB

ST PETER PORT *continued*

St Pierre Park Hotel, Spa and Golf Resort

HandPICKED HOTELS

★★★★ 79% ⊛ ⌂ HOTEL

tel: 01481 728282 **Rohais GY1 1FD**
email: reservations.stpierrepark@handpicked.co.uk **web:** www.handpickedhotels.co.uk
dir: *From harbour straight over roundabout, up hill through 3 sets of lights. Right at filter, to lights. Straight ahead, hotel 100 metres on left.*

Peacefully located on the outskirts of town in 45 acres of grounds, this well established hotel also features a 9-hole golf course. Most of the bedrooms overlook the pleasant gardens and have either a balcony or a terrace. Public areas include a choice of restaurants and a stylish bar which opens onto a spacious terrace, overlooking an elegant water feature.

Rooms: 131 (5 family) (17 GF) ✆ **Facilities:** Spa STV FTV WiFi ⓦ HL ⒯ ⌀ 9 ⌂ ⌂ Gym Exercise studio with classes Children's playground Crazy golf Xmas **Conf:** Class 120 Board 70 Theatre 200 **Services:** Lift Night porter **Parking:** 150

Best Western Hotel de Havelet

BW Best Western.

★★★ 84% HOTEL

tel: 01481 722199 **Havelet GY1 1BA**
email: stay@dehaveletguernsey.com **web:** www.dehaveletguernsey.com
dir: *From airport follow signs for St Peter Port through St. Martins. At bottom of 'Val de Terres' hill turn left at top of hill, hotel on right.*

This extended Georgian hotel looks over the harbour to Castle Cornet. Many of the well-equipped bedrooms are set around a pretty colonial-style courtyard. Day rooms in the original building have period elegance; the restaurant and bar are on the other side of the car park in converted stables.

Rooms: 34 (4 family) (9 GF) ✆ **S** fr £70 **D** fr £130 (including breakfast)*
Facilities: FTV WiFi ⓦ ⒯ Sauna Steam room EV car charger (free) Xmas New Year **Conf:** Class 20 Board 18 Theatre 30 **Parking:** 40 **Notes:** LB

Les Rocquettes Hotel

★★★ 82% HOTEL

tel: 01481 722146 **Les Gravees GY1 1RN**
email: stay@lesrocquettesguernsey.com **web:** www.lesrocquettesguernsey.com
dir: *From ferry terminal take 2nd exit at roundabout, through 5 sets of lights. After 5th lights into Les Gravees. Hotel on right opposite church.*

This late 18th-century country mansion is in a good location close to St Peter Port and Beau Sejour. Bedrooms come in three grades – Deluxe, Superior and Standard,

but all have plenty of useful facilities. Guests can eat in Oaks restaurant and bar. The hotel has attractive lounge areas on three levels; there is a health suite with a gym and swimming pool with an integrated children's pool.

Rooms: 51 (5 family) ✆ **S** fr £65 **D** fr £110 (including breakfast)* **Facilities:** FTV WiFi ⓦ ⒯ Gym Beauty treatment room Sauna Steam room Xmas New Year **Conf:** Class 60 Board 60 Theatre 100 **Services:** Lift Night porter **Parking:** 60 **Notes:** LB

Best Western Moores Hotel

BW Best Western.

★★★ 81% HOTEL

tel: 01481 724452 **Pollet GY1 1WH**
email: stay@mooresguernsey.com **web:** www.mooresguernsey.com
dir: *Left at airport, follow signs to St Peter Port. Fort Road to seafront, straight on, turn left before roundabout, to hotel.*

This elegant granite town house is situated in the heart of St Peter Port among its shops and amenities. Public rooms feature a smart conservatory restaurant which leads out onto a first-floor terrace for alfresco dining; there is also a choice of lounges and bars as well as a patisserie. Bedrooms are pleasantly decorated and thoughtfully equipped.

Rooms: 49 (3 annexe) (8 family) ✆ **S** fr £65 **D** fr £110 (including breakfast)* **Facilities:** FTV WiFi ⓦ Gym Sauna Xmas New Year **Conf:** Class 20 Board 18 Theatre 40 **Services:** Lift Night porter **Notes:** LB

Duke of Normandie Hotel

★★★ 81% HOTEL

tel: 01481 721431 **Lefebvre Street GY1 2JP**
email: enquiries@dukeofnormandie.com **web:** www.dukeofnormandie.com
dir: *From harbour roundabout St Julians Avenue, 3rd left into Anns Place, continue to right, up hill, then left into Lefebvre Street, archway entrance on right.*

The Duke of Normandie is an 18th-century hotel situated close to the high street and just a short stroll from the harbour. Bedrooms vary in style and include some that have their own access from the courtyard. Public areas feature a smart brasserie, a contemporary lounge-lobby area and a busy bar with beams and an open fireplace.

Rooms: 38 (18 annexe) (9 GF) ✆ **S** fr £49 **D** fr £92* **Facilities:** STV WiFi ⓦ **Parking:** 10 **Notes:** LB

▌ VALE Map 24

Peninsula Hotel

★★★ 80% HOTEL

tel: 01481 248400 **Les Dicqs GY6 8JP**
email: info@peninsula.gg **web:** www.peninsulahotelguernsey.com
dir: *On coast road at Grand Havre Bay.*

Adjacent to the sandy beach and set in five acres of grounds, this modern hotel provides comfortable accommodation. Bedrooms have an additional sofa bed to suit families and good workspace for the business traveller. Both fixed-price and carte menus are served in the restaurant, or guests can eat informally in the bar.

Rooms: 99 (99 family) (27 GF) ✆ **Facilities:** STV WiFi ⌀ Petanque Children's playground Table tennis Xmas New Year **Conf:** Class 100 Board 105 Theatre 250 **Services:** Lift Night porter **Parking:** 120 **Notes:** Closed January

HERM

HERM
Map 24

White House Hotel
★★★ 84% ◉◉ HOTEL

tel: 01481 750075 **GY1 3HR**
email: hotel@herm.com **web:** www.herm.com
dir: *Transport to island by catamaran ferry from St Peter Port, Guernsey.*

Enjoying a unique island setting, this attractive hotel is just 20 minutes from Guernsey by sea. Set in well-tended gardens, the hotel offers neatly decorated bedrooms, located in either the main house or adjacent cottages; the majority of rooms have sea views. Guests can relax in one of several lounges, enjoy a drink in one of two bars and choose from two dining options.

Rooms: 40 (23 annexe) (23 family) (7 GF) ⌁ **S** fr £72 **D** fr £144 (including breakfast)* **Facilities:** WiFi ⌁ ☺ ⛵ Fishing trips Yacht and motor boat charters New Year **Conf:** Class 100 Board 30 Theatre 100 **Notes:** LB Closed November to March

JERSEY

GOREY
Map 24

The Moorings Hotel & Restaurant
★★★ 79% ◉◉ HOTEL

tel: 01534 853633 **Gorey Pier JE3 6EW**
email: reservations@themooringshotel.com **web:** www.themooringshotel.com
dir: *At foot of Mont Orgueil Castle.*

Enjoying an enviable position by the harbour, the heart of this hotel is the restaurant where a selection of menus offers an extensive choice of dishes. Other public areas include a bar, coffee shop and a comfortable first-floor residents' lounge. Bedrooms at the front have a fine view of the harbour; three have access to a balcony. A small sun terrace at the back of the hotel is also available to guests.

Rooms: 15 ⌁ **Facilities:** FTV WiFi ⌁ Xmas New Year **Conf:** Class 20 Board 20 Theatre 20 **Services:** Night porter **Notes:** LB

The Dolphin Hotel and Restaurant
★★ 79% HOTEL

tel: 01534 853370 **Gorey Pier JE3 6EW**
email: dolphinhoteljersey@outlook.com **web:** www.dolphinhoteljersey.com
dir: *At foot of Mont Orgueil Castle.*

Located on the main harbour at Gorey, many bedrooms at this popular hotel enjoy views over the sea and beaches. The relaxed and friendly style is apparent from the moment of arrival, and the busy restaurant and bar are popular with locals and tourists alike. Outdoor seating is available in season, and fresh fish and seafood are included on the menu.

Rooms: 16 **S** fr £54 **D** fr £108 (including breakfast)* **Facilities:** STV WiFi ⌁ ♫ Xmas New Year **Conf:** Class 20 Board 20 Theatre 20 **Services:** Night porter **Notes:** LB

ROZEL
Map 24

Château la Chaire
★★★★ 84% ◉◉◉ HOTEL

tel: 01534 863354 **La Vallee De Rozel JE3 6AJ**
email: res@chateau-la-chaire.co.uk **web:** www.chateau-la-chaire.co.uk
dir: *From St Helier on B38 turn left in village by Rozel Bay Inn, hotel 100 yards on right.*

Built as a gentleman's residence in 1843, Château la Chaire is a haven of peace and tranquillity, set in a secluded wooded valley. Picturesque Rozel Harbour is within easy walking distance, and the house is surrounded by terraced gardens and woods. The helpful staff deliver high standards of guest care, and imaginative dishes, making the best use of local produce, are served in the oak-panelled dining room, the conservatory, or on the terrace when the weather permits. Bedroom and suite styles and sizes vary, but all are beautifully appointed and include many nice touches such as towelling robes, slippers, flowers and DVD players. Free WiFi is available throughout the hotel.

Rooms: 13 (2 family) (1 GF) ⌁ **D** fr £105 (including breakfast)* **Facilities:** FTV WiFi ⌁ Xmas New Year **Conf:** Class 60 Board 40 Theatre 60 **Services:** Night porter **Parking:** 30 **Notes:** LB No children 7 years Civ Wed 60

ST BRELADE
Map 24

L'Horizon Beach Hotel and Spa
Hand PICKED HOTELS
★★★★ ◉◉ HOTEL

tel: 01534 743101 **St Brelade's Bay JE3 8EF**
email: lhorizon@handpicked.co.uk **web:** www.handpickedhotels.co.uk/lhorizon
dir: *From airport right at roundabout towards St Brelades and Red Houses. Through Red Houses, hotel 300 metres on right in centre of bay.*

The combination of a truly wonderful setting on the golden sands of St Brelade's Bay, a relaxed atmosphere and excellent facilities prove a winning formula here. Bedrooms are stylish and have a real contemporary feel, all with plasma TVs and a host of extras; many have balconies or terraces and superb sea views. Spacious public areas include a spa and leisure club, a choice of dining options and relaxing lounges.

Rooms: 106 (1 family) (15 GF) ⌁ **S** fr £85 **D** fr £120 (including breakfast)* **Facilities:** Spa STV FTV WiFi ⌁ ☺ ☺ Gym Windsurfing Water skiing Sailing Sauna Steam room ♫ Xmas New Year **Conf:** Class 100 Board 50 Theatre 250 **Services:** Lift Night porter Air con **Parking:** 125 **Notes:** LB Civ Wed 240

ST BRELADE *continued*

INSPECTOR'S CHOICE

The Atlantic Hotel

★★★★ ◉◉◉ ☐ HOTEL

tel: 01534 744101 **Le Mont de la Pulente JE3 8HE**
email: info@theatlantichotel.com **web:** www.theatlantichotel.com
dir: *From Petit Port turn right into Rue de la Sergente, right again, hotel signed.*

Adjoining the manicured fairways of La Moye championship golf course, this hotel enjoys a peaceful setting with breathtaking views over St Ouen's Bay. Stylish bedrooms look onto the course or the sea, and offer a blend of high quality and reassuring comfort. An air of understated luxury is apparent throughout, and the attentive service achieves the perfect balance of friendliness and professionalism. The Ocean restaurant uses the best island produce to create outstanding and impeccably modern cuisine, now benefiting from the newly created tasting room, offering Chef Will Hollands tasting menu experience alongside some excellent wine pairings.

Rooms: 50 (8 GF) ⌂ **S** fr £120 **D** fr £140 (including breakfast)* **Facilities:** STV FTV WiFi ⌂ ⌖ ⌖ ☺ Gym Saunas Xmas New Year **Conf:** Class 40 Board 20 Theatre 60 **Services:** Lift Night porter **Parking:** 60 **Notes:** LB Closed 3–31 January Civ Wed 80

St Brelade's Bay Hotel

★★★★ 81% HOTEL

tel: 01534 746141 **JE3 8EF**
email: info@stbreladesbayhotel.com **web:** www.stbreladesbayhotel.com
dir: *Southwest corner of island.*

The hotel, set in five-acres of gardens, enjoys a fabulous location with unobstructed views overlooking St Brelade's Bay, and a sandy beach right on the doorstep. Bedrooms are beautifully presented and equipped to a very high standard. They include two-bedroom suites, family rooms and superb penthouse suites that have large balconies, and even telescopes. The relaxing public areas include a stylish, comfortable lounge along with a spacious bar. The gardens feature a pool area, terraces for relaxing and eating, and a tennis court. A superb leisure and fitness centre with state-of-the-art equipment is another attraction. Attentive friendly service is guaranteed in the elegant restaurant with its sea views.

Rooms: 77 (8 family) ⌂ **Facilities:** Spa FTV WiFi ⌖ ⌖ ☺ Gym Beauty treatment rooms ♪ Xmas New Year **Conf:** Class 30 Board 12 Theatre 60 **Services:** Lift Night porter **Parking:** 90 **Notes:** Civ Wed 70

Highlands Hotel

★★★ 79% HOTEL

tel: 01534 744288 **Corbiere JE3 8HN**
email: enquiries@highlandshotel.com **web:** www.highlandshotel.com
dir: *3 miles from Jersey airport. Very close to Corbiere Lighthouse.*

This hotel has an enviable location, ideally suited to touring and walking the island, close to the coast and beaches of St Brelade's Bay. There are several leisure facilities, including a swimming pool and games room. The restaurant and many of the bedrooms have delightful views. Bedrooms and bathrooms are very pleasantly appointed in a bright and attractive style.

Rooms: 50 (1 family) (11 GF) ⌂ **S** fr £70 **D** fr £110 (including breakfast)* **Facilities:** FTV WiFi ⌂ ⌖ Gym **Services:** Lift Night porter **Parking:** 60 **Notes:** LB No children 5 years Closed October to April

Beau Rivage Hotel

★★★ 76% HOTEL

tel: 01534 745983 **St Brelade's Bay JE3 8EF**
email: beau@welcome.je **web:** www.jersey.co.uk/hotels/beau
dir: *Sea side of coast road in centre of St Brelade's Bay, 1.5 miles south of airport.*

With direct access to one of Jersey's most popular beaches, residents and non-residents alike are welcome to this hotel's bar and terrace. All the accommodation is in the form of suites, most have wonderful sea views, some have the bonus of balconies. Residents have a choice of lounges, plus a sun deck exclusively for their use. A range of dishes, featuring English and Continental cuisine, is available from a selection of menus in either the bar or the main bistro restaurant.

Rooms: 12 (12 family) (12 smoking) ⌂ **Facilities:** STV FTV WiFi Games room **Services:** Lift Night porter **Parking:** 16 **Notes:** Civ Wed 80

ST CLEMENT   Map 24

Pontac House Hotel

★★★ 78% HOTEL

tel: 01534 857771 **St Clements Bay JE2 6SE**
email: admin@pontachouse.com **web:** www.pontachouse.com
dir: *10 minutes from St Helier.*

Overlooking the sandy beach of St Clement's Bay, this hotel is located on the south-east corner of Jersey. Many guests return on a regular basis to experience the friendly, relaxed style of service. The bedrooms, most with splendid views, are comfortable and well equipped. Varied menus, featuring local seafood, are on offer each evening.

Rooms: 27 (1 family) (5 GF) ⌂ **S** fr £47 **D** fr £94 (including breakfast)* **Facilities:** FTV WiFi ⌖ **Parking:** 35 **Notes:** Closed December to 1 April

ST HELIER
Map 24

Grand Jersey
HandPICKED HOTELS

★★★★★ 82% ◉◉◉◉ HOTEL

tel: 01534 722301 **The Esplanade JE2 3QA**
email: reservations.grandjersey@handpicked.co.uk
web: www.handpickedhotels.co.uk/grandjersey
dir: *Located on St Helier seafront. 15 minutes from airport.*

A local landmark, the Grand Jersey has pleasant views across St Aubin's Bay to the front, and the bustling streets of St Helier to the rear. The hotel is elegant and contemporary in design with a real touch of grandeur throughout. The air-conditioned bedrooms, including six suites, come in a variety of designs, but all have luxurious beds, ottomans and LCD TVs. The spacious public areas, many looking out onto the bay, include the very popular Champagne Lounge, Victoria's brasserie, and the impressive and intimate Tassili fine-dining restaurant. There is a large terrace for alfresco eating in the summer months, and the spa offers an indoor pool, gym and treatment rooms.

Rooms: 123 (18 family) (6 GF) 🐾 **S** fr £89 **D** fr £109 (including breakfast)*
Facilities: Spa STV FTV WiFi ⌕ 🐾 Gym Xmas New Year **Conf:** Class 90 Board 50 Theatre 160 **Services:** Lift Night porter Air con **Parking:** 27 **Notes:** LB Civ Wed 180

INSPECTOR'S CHOICE

The Club Hotel & Spa

★★★★ ◉◉◉◉◉ TOWN HOUSE HOTEL

tel: 01534 876500 **Green Street JE2 4UH**
email: reservations@theclubjersey.com **web:** www.theclubjersey.com
dir: *5 minutes walk from main shopping centre.*

This swish, town house hotel is conveniently located close to the centre of town and features stylish, contemporary decor throughout. All the guest rooms and suites have power showers and state-of-the-art technology including wide-screen LCD TVs, DVDs and CD systems. The choice of restaurants includes Bohemia, a sophisticated eating option that continues to offer outstanding cuisine. For relaxation there is an elegant spa with a luxurious range of treatments.

Rooms: 46 (4 family) (4 GF) **S** fr £99 **D** fr £99* **Facilities:** Spa STV FTV WiFi ⌕ 🐾
🐾 Steam room Salt cabin Hydrothermal bench Rasul room New Year **Conf:** Class 60 Board 34 Theatre 80 **Services:** Lift Night porter Air con **Parking:** 32 **Notes:** LB Closed 24–30 December Civ Wed 84

HIGHLY RECOMMENDED

The Royal Yacht

★★★★ 85% ◉◉◉ HOTEL

tel: 01534 720511 **The Weighbridge JE2 3NF**
email: reception@theroyalyacht.com **web:** www.theroyalyacht.com
dir: *In town centre, opposite marina and harbour.*

Overlooking the marina and steam clock, The Royal Yacht is thought to be the oldest established hotel on the island. Although it has a long history, it is very much a 21st-century hotel, with state-of-the-art technology in all the bedrooms and the two penthouse suites. There is a range of impressive dining options to suit all tastes including the award-winning Sirocco restaurant and all-day menus in Zephyr. In addition, there is a choice of bars, a luxury spa with an indoor pool and gym and conference facilities.

Rooms: 110 🐾 **S** fr £168 **D** fr £289 (including breakfast)* **Facilities:** Spa STV WiFi ⌕ 🐾 Gym 🎵 Xmas New Year **Conf:** Class 70 Board 48 Theatre 400 **Services:** Lift Night porter Air con **Notes:** LB Civ Wed 250

See advert on following page

MODERN LUXURY SITUATED IN THE HEART OF JERSEY

At The Royal Yacht, a truly memorable experience awaits you. Modern decor with a cosmopolitan flair flows throughout the hotel, complemented by tasteful nautical elements. Whether you are celebrating something special, catching up with friends over lunch or planning a weekend getaway, there really is something for everyone.

Our award-winning Spa Sirene is a haven of tranquility with beautiful surroundings and our popular restaurants cater to every taste from local seafood, Asian-inspired exotic delights or the finest cut of steak.

BOOK YOUR STAY

CALL:

01534 720 511

EMAIL:

RECEPTION@THEROYAL YACHT.COM

★★★★
THE ROYAL YACHT
HOTEL · SPA · RESTAURANTS

CHANNEL ISLANDS

ST HELIER *continued*

Radisson Blu Waterfront Hotel, Jersey

★★★★ 81% HOTEL

tel: 01534 671100 **The Waterfront, La Rue de L'Etau JE2 3WF**
email: info.jersey@radissonblu.com **web:** www.radissonblu.com/hotel-jersey
dir: *Follow signs to St Helier. From A2 follow signs to harbour. At roundabout just before harbour take 2nd exit, continue to hotel.*

Most of the bedrooms at this purpose-built hotel have fabulous views of the coastline. Facilities include a popular brasserie, cocktail bar, lounges, indoor heated pool, gym, sauna, and steam room. A wide range of meeting rooms provides conference facilities for delegates.

Rooms: 195 🐾 **S** fr £105 **D** fr £115* **Facilities:** Spa STV FTV WiFi ⌨ HL ⊙ Gym Sauna Steam room Hair salon ♫ Xmas New Year **Conf:** Class 184 Board 30 Theatre 400 **Services:** Lift Night porter Air con **Parking:** 80 **Notes:** Civ Wed 400

Pomme d'Or Hotel

★★★★ 80% HOTEL

tel: 0845 800 5555 (Calls cost 7p per minute plus your phone company's access charge)
Liberation Square JE1 3UF
email: reservations@pommedorhotel.com **web:** www.pommedorhotel.com
dir: *Opposite harbour.*

This historic hotel overlooks Liberation Square and the marina, and offers comfortably furnished, well-equipped bedrooms. Popular with the business fraternity, a range of conference facilities and meeting rooms are available. Dining options include The Harbour Room carvery and The Café Bar.

Rooms: 143 (3 family) 🐾 **S** fr £105 **D** fr £105* **Facilities:** STV FTV WiFi ⌨ Free use of The Aquadome at The Merton Hotel Xmas New Year **Conf:** Class 100 Board 50 Theatre 220 **Services:** Lift Night porter Air con **Notes:** Civ Wed 100

Best Western Royal Hotel

★★★ 86% ⊛ HOTEL

tel: 01534 726521 **David Place JE2 4TD**
email: enquiries@royalhoteljersey.com **web:** www.royalhoteljersey.com
dir: *From Airport: In St Helier on Victoria Avenue, left by Grand Hotel into Peirson Road. Follow one-way system into Cheapside. Left at filter, follow Ring Road signs into Rouge Bouillon (A14). At roundabout right, stay in right lane, right at lights into Midvale Road. Through 2 lights, hotel on left.*

This long established hotel is located in the centre of town and is within walking distance of the business district and shops. Seasons Restaurant offers a modern approach to dining, and the adjoining bar provides a relaxed venue for residents and locals alike. The bedrooms are individually styled. Extensive conference facilities are available.

Rooms: 89 (4 family) 🐾 **S** fr £74 **D** fr £104* **Facilities:** FTV WiFi ⌨ Xmas New Year **Conf:** Class 120 Board 80 Theatre 300 **Services:** Lift Night porter **Parking:** 15 **Notes:** LB Civ Wed 30

The Norfolk Lodge Hotel

★★★ 78% HOTEL

tel: 01534 722950 **Rouge Bouillon JE2 3ZB**
email: admin@morvanhotels.com **web:** www.morvanhotels.com

Centrally located and just a short walk from the main town, this popular hotel has a large number of regularly returning guests. Bedrooms are well decorated and equipped, and include some on the ground floor. In addition to an indoor swimming pool, the hotel offers regular evening entertainment during the main season. A range of well-prepared dishes is offered at dinner in the spacious restaurant.

Rooms: 101 (11 annexe) (8 family) (15 GF) 🐾 **Facilities:** FTV WiFi ⊙ Children's pool **Services:** Lift Night porter **Parking:** 40 **Notes:** LB Closed November to March

Hampshire Hotel

★★★ 77% ⊛ HOTEL

tel: 01534 724115 **53 Val Plaisant JE2 4TB**
email: info@hampshirehotel.je **web:** www.hampshirehotel.je
dir: *Phone for directions.*

Located a short walk from the town centre, this hotel features spacious public areas and comfortable bedrooms. There are premier, standard and family rooms available. The spacious restaurant features seasonally-changing dinner menus of popular dishes; at breakfast a wide choice is offered. The outdoor swimming pool and sun terrace are popular in the summer months.

Rooms: 42 (2 family) (5 GF) **S** fr £45 **D** fr £140 (including breakfast)* **Facilities:** STV WiFi ⌨ ⚲ Xmas New Year **Services:** Lift Night porter **Parking:** 30 **Notes:** LB

The Monterey Hotel

★★★ 77% HOTEL

tel: 01534 724762 **St Saviour's Road JE2 7LA**
email: bookings@morvanhotels.com **web:** www.morvanhotels.com
dir: *1 mile from Jersey Harbour.*

Conveniently located for the town, this comfortable hotel has the added benefit of ample parking and a range of leisure facilities including an indoor pool. Bedrooms are well decorated and furnished, and include a number of superior rooms. The relaxing bar area is open all day, and a good range of freshly prepared dishes is offered each evening.

Rooms: 73 (6 family) (9 GF) 🐾 **S** fr £59 **D** fr £85* **Facilities:** FTV WiFi ⌨ ⊙ ⚲ Gym Steam room Xmas New Year **Conf:** Class 12 Board 22 Theatre 40 **Services:** Lift Night porter **Parking:** 40 **Notes:** LB Closed January

Fort D'Auvergne Hotel

★★★ 76% HOTEL

tel: 01534 879960 **Harve des Pas JE2 4UQ**
email: fort@morvanhotels.com **web:** www.morvanhotels.com

The Fort D'Auvergne Hotel is bordered by the sea and sandy beach on two sides and occupies what is one of the best maritime positions in Jersey's capital. The hotel itself is traditional in style but offers modern amenities including an air-conditioned seafront table d'hôte restaurant and an outstanding luxury indoor pool complex with unrivalled views over the bay. There is only a pedestrian promenade separating the hotel from the sea shore. Dinner is served daily in the restaurant with tables benefiting from uninterrupted sea views.

Rooms: 65 (4 family) (9 GF) **Facilities:** FTV WiFi ⌨ ⊙ ♫ **Services:** Lift Night porter **Notes:** Closed 16 October to 20 April

ST HELIER *continued*

The Hotel Revere

★★★ 75% HOTEL

tel: 01534 611111 **Kensington Place JE2 3PA**
email: reservations@revere.co.uk **web:** www.revere.co.uk
dir: *From Esplanade left after Grand Hotel.*

Situated on the west side of the town and convenient for the centre and harbour side, this hotel dates back to the 17th century and retains many period features. The style here is engagingly different, and bedrooms are individually decorated. There are three dining options and a small sun terrace.

Rooms: 56 (2 family) (4 GF) 🐾 **S** fr £40.50 **D** fr £48.60* **Facilities:** FTV WiFi ⤻ 🎵 **Services:** Night porter **Notes:** LB Closed January Civ Wed 50

Westhill Country Hotel

★★★ 75% COUNTRY HOUSE HOTEL

tel: 01534 723260 **Mont-a-l'abbe JE2 3HB**
email: info@westhillhoteljersey.com **web:** www.westhillhoteljersey.com
dir: *See website for directions.*

Set in its own beautifully landscaped gardens, this hotel enjoys a prominent position just on the outskirts of St Helier. Service is attentive and guests are guaranteed a warm welcome and genuine hospitality throughout the hotel. The bedrooms are spacious and well equipped; several rooms have commanding views over the gardens to the countryside beyond. Public areas include a stylish lounge bar and popular restaurant. Free WiFi is available in the public areas and the swimming pool proves very popular with guests.

Rooms: 90 (20 family) (16 GF) 🐾 **S** fr £55 **D** fr £110 (including breakfast)* **Facilities:** FTV WiFi ⤻ ⤻ Nature trail Children's adventure play area 🎵 **Conf:** Class 80 Board 40 Theatre 60 **Services:** Night porter **Parking:** 75 **Notes:** Closed early October to early April

Apollo Hotel

★★★ 73% HOTEL

tel: 01534 725441 **St Saviours Road JE2 4GJ**
email: reservations@huggler.com **web:** www.apollojersey.com
dir: *On St Saviours Road at junction with La Motte Street.*

Centrally located, this popular hotel has a relaxed, informal atmosphere. Bedrooms are comfortably furnished and include useful extras. Many guests return regularly to enjoy the variety of leisure facilities, including an outdoor pool with water slide and indoor pool with separate jacuzzi. The cocktail bar is an ideal place for a pre-dinner drink.

Rooms: 85 (5 family) **S** fr £42 **D** fr £49* **Facilities:** FTV WiFi ⤻ 🐾 ⤻ Gym Xmas New Year **Conf:** Class 100 Board 80 Theatre 150 **Services:** Lift Night porter **Parking:** 40

Millbrook House Hotel

★★ 77% HOTEL

tel: 01534 733036 **Rue De Trachy, Millbrook JE2 3JN**
email: millbrook.house@jerseymail.co.uk **web:** www.millbrookhousehotel.com
dir: *1.5 miles west of town off A1.*

Peacefully located in its own grounds, this small, personally-run hotel offers a friendly welcome and relaxing ambience. Bedrooms and bathrooms vary in size; many have pleasant, countryside views. In addition to outdoor seating in the warmer months, guests can relax in the library, maybe with a drink before dinner.

Rooms: 24 (2 family) (6 GF) **S** fr £40 **D** fr £75 (including breakfast)* **Facilities:** WiFi ⤻ **Services:** Lift **Parking:** 20 **Notes:** Closed October to 13 May

Sarum Hotel

★★ 72% METRO HOTEL

tel: 01534 758163 **19/21 New St Johns Road JE2 3LD**
email: sarum@welcome.je **web:** www.jersey.co.uk/hotels/sarum
dir: *On northwest edge of St Helier, 0.5 mile from town centre.*

This hotel, just 600 yards from the beach, offers self-catering bedrooms and a number of suites. The friendly staff provide a warm welcome, and there is a spacious recreational lounge with pool tables, plasma-screen TV and internet access. A garden and outdoor pool are also available. Local restaurants are just a short walk away, and bar snacks are available throughout the day.

Rooms: 52 (5 annexe) (6 family) (2 GF) (52 smoking) **Facilities:** STV FTV WiFi Games room **Services:** Lift **Parking:** 10 **Notes:** LB

ST PETER   Map 24

HIGHLY RECOMMENDED

Greenhills Country Hotel

★★★★ 83% ⊛ COUNTRY HOUSE HOTEL

tel: 0845 800 555 & 01534 481042 **Mont de L'Ecole JE3 7EL**
email: reservations@greenhillshotel.com **web:** www.greenhillshotel.com
dir: *Follow signs to St Peter's Village, the A11, turn into Le Mont de L'ecole, hotel on left.*

Located in the rural centre of Jersey, this relaxing country house hotel, with delightful gardens, has a lovely atmosphere. Bedrooms extend from the main building around the courtyard; all are modern and well equipped with satellite LED TVs, luxurious bathrobes and duck down duvets. A varied menu, based on fresh local produce, is served in the restaurant, and guests also have use of the Aquadome at the Merton Hotel.

Rooms: 33 (2 family) (11 GF) 🐾 **S** fr £87 **D** fr £112 (including breakfast)* **Facilities:** STV FTV WiFi ⤻ ⤻ Free use of Merton Hotel's Aquadome and Leisure Centre **Conf:** Class 12 Board 16 Theatre 20 **Services:** Night porter **Parking:** 40 **Notes:** LB Closed mid December to early February Civ Wed 40

ST SAVIOUR
Map 24

INSPECTOR'S CHOICE

Longueville Manor Hotel
★★★★★ ◎◎◎ HOTEL

tel: 01534 725501 **JE2 7WF**
email: info@longuevillemanor.com web: www.longuevillemanor.com
dir: *A3 east from St Helier towards Gorey. Hotel 1 mile on left.*

Dating back to the 13th century, there is something very special about Longueville Manor, which is why so many guests return time and again. It is set in 16 acres of grounds including woodland walks, a spectacular rose garden, Victorian kitchen garden and a lake. Bedrooms have great style and individuality boasting fresh flowers, fine embroidered bed linen and a host of extras. The very accomplished cuisine is also a highlight of any stay. In summer the pool and terrace are popular spots, plus there are also croquet and tennis courts. Families are particularly welcome, and there are extra activities arranged for children, including an adventure zone to explore. They also have their own menus and DVD library. The committed team of staff create a welcoming atmosphere and every effort is made to ensure a memorable stay.

Rooms: 30 (1 annexe) (7 GF) S fr £175 **D** fr £200 (including breakfast)*
Facilities: Spa STV WiFi Gym Xmas New Year **Conf:** Class 30 Board 30 Theatre 45 **Services:** Lift Night porter **Parking:** 40 **Notes:** LB Civ Wed 40

Merton Hotel
★★★ 77% HOTEL

tel: 0845 800 5555 (Calls cost 7p per minute plus your phone company's access charge)
Belvedere Hill JE4 9PG
email: reservations@mertonhotel.com web: www.mertonhotel.com
dir: *Phone for directions.*

Located in the heart of Jersey, the Merton Hotel offers a huge variety of facilities. Guests can enjoy the Aquadome with its indoor and outdoor pools and flow-rider surf wave. There are six restaurant options on site and plenty of children's organised activities, in addition to evening entertainment. Bedrooms offer good levels of comfort with all modern amenities.

Rooms: 286 (39 family) (14 GF) S fr £75 **D** fr £85 (including breakfast)*
Facilities: STV WiFi HL Gym **Conf:** Class 60 Board 40 Theatre 120
Services: Lift Night porter **Parking:** 150 **Notes:** LB Closed 16 December to 28 March

SARK

SARK
Map 24

Stocks Hotel
★★★★ 81% ◎◎ SMALL HOTEL

tel: 01481 832001 & 832444 **GY10 1SD**
email: reception@stockshotel.com web: www.stockshotel.com
dir: *Ferry to Guernsey then to Sark. Tractor bus from harbour to top of island. Chargeable horse and carriage available for transfer to hotel or walk – approximately 20 minutes.*

The island of Sark is a delight. With no cars permitted, transport is provided by horse and cart, tractor or bicycle, making this a very tranquil place. Stocks Hotel has spacious, comfortable rooms, which are attractively appointed. There are several lounges, and a cosy bar, as well as two dining options; the Brasserie is at the poolside and offers alfresco dining, while the main restaurant is more formal. The hotel gardens provide many ingredients for the kitchen, and the stables house the hotel's own team of cart pullers.

Rooms: 23 (11 annexe) (2 family) (3 GF) S fr £120 **D** fr £260 (including breakfast)* **Facilities:** STV FTV WiFi Gym Massage treatment room Xmas New Year **Conf:** Class 70 Board 12 Theatre 70 **Notes:** LB Closed 3 January to 1 March RS March and November to December

CHANNEL ISLANDS

Scotland

ABERDEEN
Aberdeen

Map 23 NJ90

See also **Aberdeen Airport**

HIGHLY RECOMMENDED

The Chester Hotel

★★★★ 83% ◉◉ HOTEL

tel: 01244 327777 **59-63 Queens Road AB15 4YP**
email: enquiries@chester-hotel.com **web:** www.chester-hotel.com
dir: *From Aberdeen Airport follow signs to Perth A90, at Queens Road roundabout take first exit left. Hotel is on the right.*

The Chester Hotel offers modern and well-equipped bedrooms with lovely beds and quality bedding, along with useful extras for the modern traveller – robes, slippers and quality branded toiletries are provided as standard. Dining options include comfort food in the relaxed bar area and the award-winning restaurant that offers high quality dishes using the best local produce. There is a well-equipped gym available to residents. The hotel is ideally located for the city centre as well as the airport and numerous golf courses.

Rooms: 50 (6 annexe) (21 GF) ⌘ **S** fr £129 **D** fr £149 (including breakfast)
Facilities: WiFi ♨ Gym ♫ **Conf:** Class 80 Board 45 Theatre 220 **Services:** Lift Night porter **Parking:** 46 **Notes:** LB Civ Wed 200

Mercure Aberdeen Ardoe House Hotel & Spa

★★★★ 81% ◉ HOTEL

tel: 01224 860600 **South Deeside Road, Blairs AB12 5YP**
email: h6626@accor.com **web:** www.mercure.com/AberdeenHotels
dir: *4 miles west of city off B9077, follow for 3 miles, hotel on left.*

From its elevated position on the banks of the River Dee, this 19th-century baronial-style mansion commands excellent countryside views. Beautifully decorated, thoughtfully equipped bedrooms are located in the main house, and in the more modern extension. Public rooms include a spa and leisure club, a cosy lounge and whisky bar and impressive function facilities.

Rooms: 120 (7 family) ⌘ **S** fr £79 **D** fr £109 (including breakfast)*
Facilities: Spa FTV WiFi ♨ HL ❄ ⛱ Gym Sauna Steam room Dance studio Xmas New Year **Conf:** Class 200 Board 150 Theatre 600 **Services:** Lift Night porter **Parking:** 225 **Notes:** LB Civ Wed 500

Norwood Hall Hotel

★★★★ 79% ◉◉ HOTEL

MACDONALD HOTELS & RESORTS

tel: 01224 868951 **Garthdee Road, Cults AB15 9FX**
email: info@norwood-hall.co.uk **web:** www.norwood-hall.co.uk
dir: *Off A90, at 1st roundabout cross Bridge of Dee, left at roundabout onto Garthdee Road, B&Q and Sainsburys on left, continue to hotel sign.*

This imposing Victorian mansion has retained many of its original features, most notably the fine oak staircase, stained glass and ornately decorated walls and ceilings. Accommodation varies in style from individually designed bedrooms in the main house to the newest contemporary bedrooms. The extensive grounds ensure the hotel is popular as a wedding venue.

Rooms: 73 (14 GF) **Facilities:** STV FTV WiFi ♨ Xmas New Year **Conf:** Class 100 Board 70 Theatre 200 **Services:** Lift Night porter **Parking:** 140 **Notes:** Civ Wed 150

Malmaison Aberdeen

★★★★ 77% ◉ HOTEL

tel: 01224 327370 & 0844 693 0649 (Calls cost 5p per minute plus your phone company's access charge) **49-53 Queens Road AB15 4YP**
email: info.aberdeen@malmaison.com **web:** www.malmaison.com/locations/aberdeen
dir: *A90, 3rd exit into Queens Road at 3rd roundabout, hotel on right.*

Popular with business travellers and as a function venue, this well-established hotel lies east of the city centre. Public areas include an attractive reception lounge and an intimate restaurant featuring a Josper Grill, plus the modern bar which remains a popular choice for many regulars whether it be for a bar meal or bottle of wine from the extensive cellar. There are two styles of accommodation, with the superior rooms being particularly comfortable and well equipped.

Rooms: 79 (10 GF) ⌘ **S** fr £79 **D** fr £89 **Facilities:** Spa STV FTV WiFi ♨ Gym Steam room Xmas New Year **Conf:** Class 12 Board 25 Theatre 30 **Services:** Lift Night porter Air con **Parking:** 30 **Notes:** Civ Wed 30

The Aberdeen Altens Hotel

★★★★ 76% HOTEL

tel: 01224 877000 **Souterhead Road, Altens AB12 3LF**
email: reception@aberdeenaltenshotel.co.uk **web:** www.aberdeenaltenshotel.co.uk
dir: *Follow A90 and take A956 signed Aberdeen Harbour. 1st exit at roundabout onto Souterhead Road. Hotel on right.*

A great venue for business travellers attending conferences, or those visiting the Granite City on a leisure break, this hotel enjoys a quiet setting and ample parking. An interesting range of dishes is available in the Cairngorm Bar and Restaurant, while guests with time to spare can enjoy the extensive leisure and beauty facilities. All bedrooms feature a number of thoughtful accessories; a small number of apartments is available for guests on longer breaks.

Rooms: 216 (71 family) (48 GF) ⌘ **S** fr £45* **Facilities:** FTV WiFi ♨ HL ❄ Gym Sauna Steam room Treatment rooms Hairdresser Xmas New Year **Conf:** Class 144 Board 70 Theatre 400 **Services:** Lift Night porter **Notes:** LB Civ Wed

The Craighaar Hotel

★★★★ 75% HOTEL

tel: 01224 712275 **Waterton Road, Bucksburn AB21 9HS**
email: info@craighaar.co.uk **web:** www.craighaarhotel.com
dir: *From A96 Airport/Inverness onto A947, hotel signed.*

Conveniently located for the airport, this welcoming hotel is a popular base for business people and tourists alike. Guests can make use of a range of the public areas that include the popular brasserie and a welcoming lounge bar with open fire. All bedrooms are well equipped, plus there is a wing of duplex suites that provide additional comfort.

Rooms: 53 (6 family) (16 GF) ⌘ **S** fr £59 **D** fr £69 (including breakfast)*
Facilities: FTV WiFi ♨ Library **Conf:** Class 33 Board 30 Theatre 90 **Services:** Night porter **Parking:** 80 **Notes:** LB Closed 25–26 December RS 24 December Civ Wed 40

Premier Inn Aberdeen (Anderson Drive)

BUDGET HOTEL

tel: 0871 527 8006 (Calls cost 13p per minute plus your phone company's access charge) **North Anderson Drive AB15 6DW**

web: www.premierinn.com

dir: *Into Aberdeen from south on A90, follow airport signs. Hotel 1st left after fire station. Note: for sat nav use AB15 6TP.*

High quality, budget accommodation ideal for both families and business travellers. Spacious, en suite bedrooms feature free WiFi and tea and coffee making facilities, and in most hotels, Freeview TV is also available. The adjacent family restaurant features a wide and varied menu.

Rooms: 62

Premier Inn Aberdeen City Centre

BUDGET HOTEL

tel: 0871 527 8008 (Calls cost 13p per minute plus your phone company's access charge) **Inverlair House, West North Street AB24 5AS**

web: www.premierinn.com

dir: *A90 onto A9013 into city centre. Take A956 towards King Street, 1st left into Meal Market Street.*

Rooms: 190

Premier Inn Aberdeen North (Bridge of Don)

BUDGET HOTEL

tel: 0871 527 8010 (Calls cost 13p per minute plus your phone company's access charge) **Ellon Road, Murcar AB23 8BP**

web: www.premierinn.com

dir: *From city centre take A90 north follow Peterhead signs. At roundabout 2 miles after Aberdeen Exhibition and Conference Centre, left onto B999. Hotel on right.*

Rooms: 91

Premier Inn Aberdeen South (Portlethen)

BUDGET HOTEL

tel: 0871 527 8012 (Calls cost 13p per minute plus your phone company's access charge) **Mains of Balquharn, Portlethen AB12 4QS**

web: www.premierinn.com

dir: *From A90 follow Portlethen and Badentoy Park signs. Hotel on right.*

Rooms: 92

Premier Inn Aberdeen (Westhill)

BUDGET HOTEL

tel: 0871 527 8004 (Calls cost 13p per minute plus your phone company's access charge) **Straik Road, Westhill AB32 6HF**

web: www.premierinn.com

dir: *On A944 towards Alford, hotel adjacent to Tesco.*

Rooms: 103

ABERDEEN AIRPORT
Aberdeen
Map 23 NJ81

Hallmark Hotel Aberdeen Airport

★★★ 73% HOTEL

tel: 0330 028 3409 **Farburn Terrace, Dyce AB21 7DW**

email: aberdeen@hallmarkhotels.co.uk **web:** www.hallmarkhotels.co.uk

dir: *A96/A947 airport east after 1 mile turn left at lights. Hotel in 250 yards.*

This hotel is very convenient for air travellers and for those wishing to explore this lovely Highland area. The spacious, well-equipped bedrooms have all the expected up-to-date amenities. The public areas are welcoming and include a contemporary brasserie. Secure parking and WiFi are also provided.

Rooms: 212 (212 annexe) (20 family) (107 GF) **S** fr £45 **D** fr £55* **Facilities:** STV FTV WiFi ♨ Xmas New Year **Conf:** Class 160 Board 120 Theatre 400 **Services:** Night porter **Parking:** 150 **Notes:** LB Civ Wed 220

Premier Inn Aberdeen Airport (Dyce)

BUDGET HOTEL

tel: 0871 527 9460 (Calls cost 13p per minute plus your phone company's access charge) **Aberdeen Airport Main Terminal, Argyll Way AB21 0BN**

web: www.premierinn.com

dir: *From north on A96 follow Aberdeen signs. At roundabout 1st exit into Dyce Drive signed Airport. At 2nd lights right into Argyll Road. Hotel on right. From south on A90 follow Airport and A96 signs. Take A96 (Inverurie road) at 2nd roundabout 3rd exit into Dyce Drive then proceed as above.*

High quality, budget accommodation ideal for both families and business travellers. Spacious, en suite bedrooms feature free WiFi and tea and coffee making facilities, and in most hotels, Freeview TV is also available. The adjacent family restaurant features a wide and varied menu.

Rooms: 100

ABERFOYLE
Stirling
Map 20 NN50

Macdonald Forest Hills Hotel & Resort

MACDONALD HOTELS & RESORTS

★★★★ 80% ⊛ HOTEL

tel: 01877 389500 **Kinlochard FK8 3TL**

email: general.foresthills@macdonald-hotels.co.uk

web: www.macdonald-hotels.co.uk/foresthills

dir: *A84, A873, A81 to Aberfoyle onto B829.*

Situated in the heart of The Trossachs with wonderful views of Loch Ard, this popular hotel forms part of a resort complex offering a range of indoor and outdoor facilities. The main hotel has relaxing lounges and a restaurant that all overlook the landscaped gardens. A separate building houses the leisure centre, lounge bar and bistro.

Rooms: 55 (16 family) (12 GF) ⚑ **Facilities:** Spa STV FTV WiFi ⊛ ♨ Gym Children's club Snooker Watersports Quad biking Archery Clay pigeon shooting ♫ Xmas New Year **Conf:** Class 60 Board 20 Theatre 120 **Services:** Lift Night porter **Parking:** 100 **Notes:** Civ Wed 100

ABINGTON MOTORWAY SERVICE AREA (M74)   Map 21 NS92
South Lanarkshire

Days Inn Abington - M74   WELCOMEBREAK

AA Advertised

tel: 01864 502782 **ML12 6RG**
email: abington.hotel@welcomebreak.co.uk **web:** www.welcomebreak.co.uk
dir: *M74 junction 13, accessible from northbound and southbound carriageways.*

This modern building offers accommodation in smart, spacious and well-equipped bedrooms, suitable for families and business travellers, and all with en suite bathrooms. Continental breakfast is available and other refreshments may be taken at the nearby family restaurant.

Rooms: 54 (50 family) (4 smoking) **Facilities:** FTV WiFi ❧ **Conf:** Board 10 **Parking:** 100

AUCHENCAIRN   Map 21 NX75
Dumfries & Galloway

HIGHLY RECOMMENDED

Balcary Bay Hotel

★★★ 88% ◉◉ HOTEL

tel: 01556 640217 **Shore Road DG7 1QZ**
email: reservations@balcary-bay-hotel.co.uk **web:** www.balcary-bay-hotel.co.uk
dir: *On A711 between Dalbeattie and Kirkcudbright, hotel 2 miles from Auchencairn.*

Taking its name from the bay on which it lies, this hotel has lawns running down to the shore. The larger bedrooms enjoy stunning views over the bay, while others overlook the gardens. The comfortable public areas are very relaxing. Imaginative dishes feature at dinner, accompanied by a good wine list.

Rooms: 20 (1 family) (3 GF) ✆ **S** fr £86 **D** fr £160 (including breakfast)
Facilities: FTV WiFi **Parking:** 50 **Notes:** Closed 1st Sunday in December to 1st Friday in February

Silver Stars

The AA Silver Star rating denotes a Hotel that we highly recommend. They have a superior level of quality within their star rating, high standards of hospitality, service and cleanliness.

AUCHTERARDER   Map 21 NN91
Perth & Kinross

INSPECTOR'S CHOICE

The Gleneagles Hotel

★★★★★ ◉◉◉◉ HOTEL

tel: 01764 662231 **PH3 1NF**
email: resort.sales@gleneagles.com **web:** www.gleneagles.com
dir: *Off A9 at exit for A823 follow signs for Gleneagles Hotel.*

With its international reputation for high standards, this grand hotel provides something for everyone. Set in 850 acres of glorious countryside, Gleneagles offers a peaceful retreat, as well as many sporting activities, including the famous championship golf courses. All bedrooms are appointed to a high standard, and offer both traditional and contemporary styles and decor. Stylish public areas include various dining options: The Strathearn, with two AA Rosettes; as well as inspired cooking at Andrew Fairlie at Gleneagles, a restaurant with four AA Rosettes. There's also the Clubhouse, and many bars. The award-winning ESPA spa offers the very latest treatments to restore both body and soul. Service is always professional, the staff are friendly, and nothing is too much trouble.

Rooms: 232 (115 family) (11 GF) **S** fr £390 **D** fr £390 (including breakfast)*
Facilities: Spa STV FTV WiFi ❧ ⊛ ⚓ ♨ 54 ⛳ Fishing ⚑ Gym Falconry Off-road driving Archery Clay shooting Gundog school Horse riding Xmas New Year
Conf: Class 240 Board 60 Theatre 360 **Services:** Lift Night porter **Parking:** 300
Notes: Civ Wed 360

AULTBEA   Map 22 NG88
Highland

Aultbea Hotel

★★★ 77% HOTEL

tel: 01445 731201 **Sea Front IV22 2HX**
email: aultbeahotel@btconnect.com **web:** www.aultbeahotel.co.uk
dir: *Off A832.*

Aultbea is a hotel with both charm and character. It sits just off the North Coast 500 route and enjoys fine views across Loch Ewe. Bedrooms are individually designed and retain a bespoke style. Public rooms are cosy and inviting, and the restaurant offers innovative menus showcasing the best local produce, especially seafood and game.

Rooms: 8 ✆ **Facilities:** FTV WiFi ❧ **Parking:** 30 **Notes:** Closed November to 1 March

A

AVIEMORE
Highland   Map 23 NH81

Macdonald Aviemore Resort

 MACDONALD HOTELS & RESORTS

★★★★ 73% HOTEL

tel: 01479 815100 **PH22 1PN**
email: general@aviemorehighlandresort.com **web:** www.macdonald-hotels.co.uk
dir: *From north: Exit A9 to Aviemore (B970). Right at T-junction, through village. Right (2nd exit) at 1st roundabout into Macdonald Aviemore Resort, follow reception signs. From south: Exit A9 to Aviemore, left at T-junction. Immediately after Esso garage, turn left into Resort.*

The Highlands Hotel is part of the Macdonald Aviemore Resort, which boasts a wide range of activities including a championship golf course. The modern, well-equipped bedrooms suit business, leisure guests and families, and the Scottish Steakhouse offers a fantastic selection of grilled dishes. In addition there is a state-of-the-art gym, spa treatments and a 25-metre pool with a wave machine and flume.

Rooms: 151 (10 family) (44 GF) **Facilities:** Spa STV FTV WiFi ↕ ⏱ ⚓ 18 Fishing Gym Steam room Sauna Children's indoor and outdoor playgrounds Xmas New Year **Conf:** Class 610 Board 38 Theatre 1000 **Services:** Lift Night porter **Parking:** 500 **Notes:** Civ Wed 300

AYR
South Ayrshire   Map 20 NS32

Fairfield House Hotel

★★★★ 80% ⊛ HOTEL

tel: 01292 267461 **12 Fairfield Road KA7 2AS**
email: reservations@fairfieldhotel.co.uk **web:** www.fairfieldhotel.co.uk
dir: *From A77 towards Ayr South (A30). Follow town centre signs, down Miller Road, left, then right into Fairfield Road.*

Situated in a leafy cul-de-sac close to the esplanade, this hotel enjoys stunning seascapes towards the Isle of Arran. Bedrooms are in either modern or classical styles, the latter featuring impressive bathrooms. Public areas provide stylish, modern rooms in which to relax. Skilfully prepared meals are served in the casual brasserie and elegant restaurant.

Rooms: 44 (4 annexe) (3 family) (9 GF) **S** fr £70 **D** fr £80 (including breakfast) **Facilities:** FTV WiFi ↕ ⚓ Gym Fitness room Sauna Steam room Xmas New Year **Conf:** Class 80 Board 40 Theatre 120 **Services:** Lift Night porter **Parking:** 50 **Notes:** LB Civ Wed 150

Enterkine Country House

★★★ 80% ⊛⊛ COUNTRY HOUSE HOTEL

tel: 01292 520580 **Annbank KA6 5AL**
email: mail@enterkine.com **web:** www.enterkine.com
dir: *5 miles east of Ayr on B743.*

This luxurious art deco country mansion dates from the 1930s and retains many original features, notably some splendid bathroom suites. The focus is very much on dining, and in country house tradition there is no bar, drinks being served in the elegant lounge and library. The well-proportioned bedrooms are furnished and equipped to high standards, many with lovely countryside views.

Rooms: 14 (8 annexe) (2 family) (3 GF) ⚓ **S** fr £95 **D** fr £125 (including breakfast) **Facilities:** FTV WiFi ⚓ Xmas New Year **Conf:** Class 140 Board 140 Theatre 220 **Services:** Lift Night porter **Parking:** 95 **Notes:** Civ Wed 250

Mercure Ayr Hotel

★★★ 78% HOTEL

tel: 0844 815 9005 (Calls cost 5p per minute plus your phone company's access charge) **Dalblair Road KA7 1UG**
email: info@mercureayr.co.uk **web:** www.mercureayr.co.uk
dir: *M77 towards Prestwick Airport, then A77 Ayr, 1st roundabout 3rd exit, 2nd roundabout straight over, left at lights, then 2nd lights turn left, bottom of road turn right, hotel on left.*

This hotel is situated in a central location in Ayr, and many bedrooms benefit from sea views. The property is ideally located for both business and leisure travellers and the area boasts many golf courses within easy reach; indeed the hotel even has its own golf simulator. Bedrooms and bathrooms are presented to a modern standard with a range of extras including free WiFi. A leisure club and brasserie restaurant are also provided for guests.

Rooms: 118 (4 family) ⚓ **Facilities:** FTV WiFi ↕ ⚓ Gym Beauty treatment room **Conf:** Class 45 Board 45 Theatre 200 **Services:** Lift Night porter **Parking:** 45 **Notes:** Civ Wed 75

Premier Inn Ayr A77/Racecourse

 Premier Inn

BUDGET HOTEL

tel: 0871 527 9416 (Calls cost 13p per minute plus your phone company's access charge) **Wheatpark Place KA8 9RT**
web: www.premierinn.com
dir: *Phone for directions.*

High quality, budget accommodation ideal for both families and business travellers. Spacious, en suite bedrooms feature free WiFi and tea and coffee making facilities, and in most hotels, Freeview TV is also available. The adjacent family restaurant features a wide and varied menu.

Rooms: 84

Premier Inn Ayr/Prestwick Airport

 Premier Inn

BUDGET HOTEL

tel: 0871 527 8038 (Calls cost 13p per minute plus your phone company's access charge) **Kilmarnock Road, Monkton KA9 2RJ**
web: www.premierinn.com
dir: *At Dutch House roundabout (at junction of A77 and A78) at Monkton.*

Rooms: 64

B

BALLANTRAE
South Ayrshire

Map 20 NX08

INSPECTOR'S CHOICE

Glenapp Castle
★★★★★ ◉◉◉ COUNTRY HOUSE HOTEL

tel: 01465 831212 **KA26 0NZ**
email: enquiries@glenappcastle.com **web:** www.glenappcastle.com
dir: South through Ballantrae, cross bridge over River Stinchar, 1st right, hotel gates 1 mile.

Friendly hospitality and attentive service prevail at this stunning Victorian castle, set in extensive private grounds to the south of the village. Impeccably furnished bedrooms are graced with antiques and period pieces, and include two master bedrooms and a ground-floor family suite. Breathtaking views of Arran and Ailsa Craig can be enjoyed from the delightful, sumptuous day rooms and from many of the bedrooms. Guests should make a point of walking round the wonderful 36-acre grounds, and take a look at the azalea pond, walled vegetable gardens and restored Victorian greenhouses.

Rooms: 20 (2 family) (7 GF) ☏ **S** fr £195 **D** fr £245 (including breakfast)*
Facilities: FTV WiFi ⌕ ⊛ ⛲ Woodland walks Falconry Archery Photography Stargazing Xmas New Year **Conf:** Class 12 Board 25 Theatre 25 **Services:** Lift Night porter **Parking:** 20 **Notes:** LB Closed 2–17 January Civ Wed 40

BALLATER
Aberdeenshire

Map 23 N039

Loch Kinord Hotel
★★★ 79% ◉ HOTEL

tel: 01339 885229 **Ballater Road, Dinnet AB34 5JY**
email: stay@lochkinord.com **web:** www.lochkinord.com
dir: Between Aboyne and Ballater, on A93, in Dinnet.

Family-run, this roadside hotel is well located for leisure and sporting pursuits. It has lots of character and a friendly atmosphere. There are two bars, one outside and a cosy one inside, plus a dining room with a bold colour scheme. Bedrooms are stylish and have smart bathrooms.

Rooms: 20 (3 family) (4 GF) ☏ **Facilities:** FTV WiFi ⌕ Xmas **Conf:** Class 30 Board 30 Theatre 40 **Parking:** 20 **Notes:** Civ Wed 50

BALLOCH
West Dunbartonshire

Map 20 NS38

Cameron House on Loch Lomond
★★★★★ 85% ◉◉◉◉ HOTEL

tel: 01389 755565 **G83 8QZ**
email: reservations@cameronhouse.co.uk **web:** www.cameronhouse.co.uk
dir: M8 west junction 30 for Erskine Bridge. A82 for Crainlarich. 14 miles, at roundabout signed Luss, hotel on right.

Cameron House is currently undergoing an extensive refurbishment project which will see the main hotel closed until Autumn 2019. There is still so much to enjoy throughout the resort with two excellent golf courses, a world-class spa and a host of indoor and outdoor sporting activities as well as the Marina. A choice of restaurants, including the Boat House and Claret Jug, offer a range of cuisine.

Rooms: 136 (9 family) (18 GF) ☏ **Facilities:** Spa STV WiFi ⌕ HL ⊛ ♨ 27 ⚑ Fishing ⛵ Gym Squash Motor boat Hairdresser Sea plane Falconry Archery Segways Rib boat Jet skis Xmas New Year **Conf:** Class 180 Board 80 Theatre 300 **Services:** Lift Night porter Air con **Parking:** 200 **Notes:** LB Civ Wed 200

BANCHORY
Aberdeenshire

Map 23 N069

Tor Na Coille Hotel & Restaurant
★★★★ 81% ◉◉ COUNTRY HOUSE HOTEL

tel: 01330 822242 **Inchmarlo Road AB31 4AB**
email: info@tornacoille.com **web:** www.tornacoille.com

This Victorian Hotel located in the village of Banchory, in Royal Deeside. Set in acres of wooded grounds, the magnificent granite building enjoys an elevated position offering panoramic views of the surrounding hillside. The individually styled en-suite bedrooms each have their own character and distinct charm, enhanced by the period furniture and unique shape of the room. Most enjoy views of the grounds and surrounding countryside. The rooms are equipped with modern amenities for the modern traveller. The lounge, with its large sofas and comfortable armchairs, is a great place to enjoy a drink or coffee and the restaurant has a relaxed atmosphere, in which to dine, and take in the views.

Rooms: 25 **D** fr £60 (including breakfast)* **Conf:** Class 60 Board 36 Theatre 120

BATHGATE
West Lothian

Map 21 NS96

Premier Inn Livingston (Bathgate)

Premier Inn

BUDGET HOTEL

tel: 0871 527 8630 (Calls cost 13p per minute plus your phone company's access charge) **Starlaw Road EH48 1LQ**
web: www.premierinn.com
dir: M8 junction 3A. At 1st roundabout 1st exit (Bathgate). Over bridge, at 2nd roundabout take 1st exit. Hotel 200 yards on left.

High quality, budget accommodation ideal for both families and business travellers. Spacious, en suite bedrooms feature free WiFi and tea and coffee making facilities, and in most hotels, Freeview TV is also available. The adjacent family restaurant features a wide and varied menu.

Rooms: 74

| **BLANTYRE** | **Map 20 NS65** |

South Lanarkshire

Crossbasket Castle

★★★★★ 86%  HOTEL

tel: 01698 829461 **Crossbasket Estate, Stoneymeadow Road G72 9UE**
email: info@crossbasketcastle.com **web:** www.crossbasketcastle.com
dir: *In High Blantyre close to East Kilbride and the M80/M74 motorways.*

This stunning, luxury hotel can trace its roots back to the early 15th century and the days of King Robert the Bruce. Many original castle features remain thoughout the building, but the surroundings are certainly more luxurious than previous tenants would have enjoyed. Tasteful design, flawless service and beautiful grounds combine to provide a wonderful experience for guests. Albert Roux and Michel Roux Jnr provide the inspiration for the menus in the elegant restaurant, the Baillie Room, with its gold-leafed ceiling.

Rooms: 9 S fr £270 **D** fr £300 (including breakfast) **Facilities:** FTV WiFi Fishing In room spa treatment Xmas New Year **Conf:** Class 150 Board 30 Theatre 350 **Services:** Lift Night porter **Parking:** 56 **Notes:** LB Civ Wed 300

| **CAIRNEYHILL** | **Map 21 NT08** |

Fife

HIGHLY RECOMMENDED

Forrester Park

★★★★ 83% HOTEL

tel: 01383 880505 & 882505 **Forrester Park Leisure, Pitdinnie Road KY12 8RF**
email: enquiries@forresterparkresort.com **web:** www.forresterparkresort.com
dir: *A994 off A985, left onto Pitdinnie Road, hotel on right approximately 0.5 mile up this road.*

Set in 350 acres of spectacular Fife countryside, Forrester Park is a visual and golfing delight. The hotel has a contemporary chic style which complements the original features of the house. The five bedrooms are stylishly decorated, using elegant fabrics, and all feature bespoke furniture. Luxurious extras include bath robes, Nespresso coffee machines and home-made petits fours and shortbread. Accomplished cooking, utilising much local produce, can be enjoyed in the stylish dining room. A visit to the cocktail bar is a must for its noteworthy range of enticing cocktails. Warm hospitality is assured throughout the hotel.

Rooms: 5 (5 GF) S fr £69 **D** fr £69 (including breakfast)* **Facilities:** FTV WiFi 18 Xmas **Conf:** Class 270 Board 50 Theatre 400 **Services:** Night porter **Parking:** 75 **Notes:** Civ Wed 200

| **CALLANDER** | **Map 20 NN60** |

Stirling

Roman Camp Country House Hotel

★★★★ 79% COUNTRY HOUSE HOTEL

tel: 01877 330003 **FK17 8BG**
email: mail@romancamphotel.co.uk **web:** www.romancamphotel.co.uk
dir: *North on A84, left at east end of High Street. 300 yards to hotel.*

Built in the 17th century and originally used as a shooting lodge, this charming country house has a rich history, and has been in the same ownership for nearly 30 years. 20 acres of gardens and grounds lead down to the River Teith, and the town centre and its attractions are only a short walk away. Each bedroom is individually and elegantly designed, and offers much pampering comfort. Food is a highlight of any stay and menus are dominated by high-quality Scottish produce that is sensitively treated by the talented kitchen team. Real fires warm the atmospheric public areas and service is friendly yet professional.

Rooms: 15 (4 family) (7 GF) **Facilities:** STV FTV WiFi Fishing Xmas New Year **Conf:** Class 50 Board 30 Theatre 150 **Parking:** 80 **Notes:** LB Civ Wed 150

| **CARNOUSTIE** | **Map 21 NO53** |

Angus

Carnoustie Golf Hotel & Spa

"bespoke"

★★★★ 80% HOTEL

tel: 01241 411999 **The Links DD7 7JE**
email: reservations.carnoustie@bespokehotels.com
web: www.bespokehotels.com/carnoustiegolfhotel
dir: *Follow A92 from Dundee or Arbroath. Take 'Upper Victoria' exit then follow signs to Carnoustie town centre and golf courses.*

Overlooking the world famous Carnoustie Golf Links which is a regular host of the British Open Golf Championship (including 2018), this popular hotel has now completed a full refurbishment. There is plenty to do here with golf, a spa and access to the beach – all available to guests. Bedrooms are comfortable and appealing. The popular bar is a great venue for telling tales of the day's golf, while the Calder's Bistro makes use of local, Scottish ingredients in an appealing menu.

Rooms: 96 (11 family) S fr £70 **D** fr £80 (including breakfast)* **Facilities:** Spa STV FTV WiFi Gym Sauna Steam room Spa bath Xmas New Year **Conf:** Class 150 Board 50 Theatre 350 **Services:** Lift Night porter **Parking:** 140 **Notes:** Civ Wed 120

C

CLYDEBANK
West Dunbartonshire
Map 20 NS47

Golden Jubilee Conference Hotel

★★★★ 76% ⊛ HOTEL

tel: 0141 951 6000 **Beardmore Street G81 4SA**
email: zico.iqbal@goldenjubilee.scot.nhs.uk **web:** www.goldenjubileehotel.com
dir: *M8 junction 19, follow signs for Clydeside Expressway to Glasgow road, then A814 (Dumbarton road), then follow Clydebank Business Park signs. Hotel on left.*

Attracting plenty of business and conference custom, this stylish modern hotel lies beside the River Clyde and shares an impressive site with a hospital (although the latter does not intrude). Spacious and imposing public areas include a stylish restaurant that provides innovative contemporary Scottish cooking, the Central Plaza Café, and The Bar lounge which offers a more extensive choice of lighter dishes. The leisure facilities include a 15-metre swimming pool, sauna and steam room. The hotel also has a keenly-adhered-to environmental policy.

Rooms: 168 (6 family) **S** fr £69 **D** fr £69* **Facilities:** FTV WiFi ↕ ☺ Gym Sauna Steam room Xmas New Year **Conf:** Class 84 Board 27 Theatre 240 **Services:** Lift Night porter Air con **Parking:** 300 **Notes:** Civ Wed 170

COMRIE
Perth & Kinross
Map 21 NN72

Royal Hotel

★★★ 77% ⊛ SMALL HOTEL

tel: 01764 679200 **Melville Square PH6 2DN**
email: reception@royalhotel.co.uk **web:** www.royalhotel.co.uk
dir: *A9 on A822 to Crieff, then B827 to Comrie. Hotel in main square on A85.*

The traditional facade gives little indication of the style and elegance to be found inside this long-established hotel located in the village centre. Public areas include a bar and library, a bright modern restaurant and a conservatory-style brasserie. The bedrooms are tastefully appointed and furnished with smart reproduction antiques.

Rooms: 13 (2 annexe) **Facilities:** STV WiFi Fishing Shooting arranged New Year **Conf:** Class 10 Board 20 Theatre 20 **Parking:** 22 **Notes:** Closed 25–26 December

---

CONNEL
Argyll & Bute
Map 20 NM93

Falls of Lora Hotel

THE INDEPENDENTS
HOTEL ASSOCIATION

★★★ 77% HOTEL

tel: 01631 710483 **Connel Ferry PA37 1PB**
email: enquiries@fallsoflora.com **web:** www.fallsoflora.com

(for full entry see Oban)

COVE
Argyll & Bute
Map 20 NS28

Knockderry House

★★★★ 79% ⊛⊛ COUNTRY HOUSE HOTEL

tel: 01436 842283 & 842813 **Shore Road G84 0NX**
email: info@knockderryhouse.co.uk **web:** www.knockderryhouse.co.uk
dir: *A82 to Lochlomondside, left onto A817 signed Garelochhead, through Glen Fruin to A814. Follow Coulport signs. At Coulport left at roundabout, 2 miles to hotel.*

Knockderry House is a stunning example of a mid 19th-century home and still boasts a host of stunning architectural features created by famed architect, William Leiper. Public areas are warm and welcoming, many with original stained-glass windows. Set in expansive grounds with beautiful views of Loch Long, the hotel features modern bedrooms and bathrooms. Hospitality is key to the hotel's success, and friendly staff deliver a high level of personalised service. Scotland's larder is well represented by the output from the kitchen.

Rooms: 15 ⸮ **S** fr £95 **D** fr £220* **Facilities:** FTV WiFi New Year **Conf:** Class 20 Board 24 Theatre 30 **Parking:** 30 **Notes:** LB Closed 11–26 December Civ Wed 48

CUMBERNAULD
North Lanarkshire
Map 21 NS77

The Westerwood Hotel & Golf Resort

QHOTELS
INSPIRED BY YOU

★★★★ 80% ⊛ HOTEL

tel: 01236 457171 **1 St Andrews Drive, Westerwood G68 0EW**
email: westerwood@qhotels.co.uk **web:** www.qhotels.co.uk
dir: *M80 junction 6, follow signs for hotel.*

This stylish, contemporary hotel enjoys an elevated position within 400 acres at the foot of the Camspie Hills. Accommodation is provided in spacious, bright bedrooms, many with super bathrooms, and day rooms include sumptuous lounges and an airy restaurant; extensive golf, fitness and conference facilities are available.

Rooms: 148 (16 family) (49 GF) ⸮ **S** fr £97 **D** fr £109 (including breakfast)* **Facilities:** Spa STV WiFi ↕ ☺ ♪ 18 ☺ Gym Beauty salon Relaxation room Sauna Steam room Rasul therapy Xmas New Year **Conf:** Class 120 Board 60 Theatre 400 **Services:** Lift Night porter **Parking:** 250 **Notes:** LB Civ Wed 350

Premier Inn Glasgow (Cumbernauld)

Premier Inn

BUDGET HOTEL

tel: 0871 527 8424 (Calls cost 13p per minute plus your phone company's access charge) **4 South Muirhead Road G67 1AX**
web: www.premierinn.com
dir: *From A80, A8011 follow Cumbernauld and town centre signs. Hotel opposite Asda and McDonalds.*

High quality, budget accommodation ideal for both families and business travellers. Spacious, en suite bedrooms feature free WiFi and tea and coffee making facilities, and in most hotels, Freeview TV is also available. The adjacent family restaurant features a wide and varied menu.

Rooms: 37

DALKEITH
Midlothian
Map 21 NT36

Premier Inn Edinburgh A7 (Dalkeith)

Premier Inn

BUDGET HOTEL

tel: 0871 527 9290 (Calls cost 13p per minute plus your phone company's access charge) **Melville Dykes Road EH18 1AN**
web: www.premierinn.com
dir: *Exit A720 at Sheriffhall roundabout onto A7 signed Galashiels/Harwick/Carlisle. At 2nd roundabout take 3rd exit into Melville Dykes Road (A768). Hotel on left.*

Rooms: 40

DRYMEN
Stirling   Map 20 NS48

Winnock Hotel

★★★ 73% HOTEL

tel: 01360 660245 **The Square G63 0BL**
email: info@winnockhotel.com **web:** www.winnockhotel.com
dir: *From south: M74 onto M8 junction 16b through Glasgow. Follow A809 to Aberfoyle.*

Occupying a prominent position overlooking the village green, this popular hotel offers well-equipped bedrooms of various sizes and styles. The public rooms include a bar, a lounge and an attractive formal dining room that serves dishes of good, locally sourced food.

Rooms: 73 (18 family) (19 GF) 🕯 **S** fr £50 **D** fr £59 (including breakfast)*
Facilities: FTV WiFi ⓑ Xmas New Year **Conf:** Class 60 Board 70 Theatre 140
Services: Night porter **Parking:** 60 **Notes:** Civ Wed 150

DUMBARTON
East Dunbartonshire   Map 20 NS37

Premier Inn Dumbarton/Loch Lomond

BUDGET HOTEL

tel: 0871 527 9274 (Calls cost 13p per minute plus your phone company's access charge) **Lomondgate Drive G82 2QU**
web: www.premierinn.com
dir: *From Glasgow follow A82 towards Crainlarich, right at Lomondgate roundabout onto A813, hotel on right. From north: A82 towards Glasgow, left at Lomondgate roundabout onto A813, hotel on right.*

High quality, budget accommodation ideal for both families and business travellers. Spacious, en suite bedrooms feature free WiFi and tea and coffee making facilities, and in most hotels, Freeview TV is also available. The adjacent family restaurant features a wide and varied menu.

Rooms: 114

DUMFRIES
Dumfries & Galloway   Map 21 NX97

Cairndale Hotel & Leisure Club

★★★ 78% HOTEL

tel: 01387 254111 **English Street DG1 2DF**
email: sales@cairndalehotel.co.uk **web:** www.cairndalehotel.co.uk
dir: *From south on M6 take A75 to Dumfries, left at 1st roundabout, cross rail bridge to lights, hotel 1st building on left.*

Within walking distance of the town centre, this hotel provides a wide range of amenities, including leisure facilities and an impressive conference and entertainment centre. Bedrooms range from stylish suites to cosy singles. There's a choice of eating options in the evening. The Reivers Restaurant is smartly modern with food to match.

Rooms: 91 (22 family) (5 GF) 🕯 **S** fr £59 **D** fr £69 (including breakfast)
Facilities: Spa STV WiFi ⓑ Gym Steam room Sauna Beauty treatment room ♫ Xmas New Year **Conf:** Class 150 Board 50 Theatre 300 **Services:** Lift Night porter **Parking:** 100 **Notes:** LB Civ Wed 300

Premier Inn Dumfries

BUDGET HOTEL

tel: 0871 527 8316 (Calls cost 13p per minute plus your phone company's access charge) **Annan Road, Collin DG1 3JX**
web: www.premierinn.com
dir: *At roundabout junction of Euroroute bypass (A75) and A780.*

High quality, budget accommodation ideal for both families and business travellers. Spacious, en suite bedrooms feature free WiFi and tea and coffee making facilities, and in most hotels, Freeview TV is also available. The adjacent family restaurant features a wide and varied menu.

Rooms: 102

DUNBLANE
Stirling   Map 21 NN70

Cromlix and Chez Roux

★★★★★ 86% ⓐ ⓐ ⓐ ☁ COUNTRY HOUSE HOTEL

tel: 01786 822125 **Kinbuck FK15 9JT**
email: enquiries@cromlix.com **web:** www.cromlix.com
dir: *M9 towards Stirling/Perth, bypassing Stirling and Dunblane (A9 towards Perth). Take exit signed Dunblane/Kinbuck on B8033. Turn right at junction for Kinbuck. Follow road through village, over the bridge. Entrance gates 100 yards on left.*

Owned by tennis star Sir Andy Murray, who was born in nearby Dunblane, this stunning hotel has been appointed to a luxurious standard. Expansive grounds are secluded and ideal for relaxing. Among the places of interest are a kitchen garden, a loch (stocked with trout; rods available) and a tennis court resplendent in Wimbledon colours. Bedrooms have been lovingly restored and include a number of unique suites. The hotel has its own chapel, a number of welcoming lounges and a billiards room. The modern, light dining space features an open kitchen where guests can observe some masterful cooking in action. Service is delivered to an impeccable standard.

Rooms: 15 🕯 **S** fr £180 **D** fr £235 (including breakfast)* **Facilities:** FTV WiFi ⓑ ⚘ Fishing Archery Falconry display Snooker Outdoor garden games In-room spa treatments Xmas New Year **Conf:** Class 26 Board 26 Theatre 60 **Services:** Night porter **Parking:** 51 **Notes:** Civ Wed 50

DUNDEE
Dundee   Map 21 NO43

Malmaison Dundee

★★★★ 80% ⓐ HOTEL

tel: 01382 339715 **44 Whitehall Crescent DD1 4AY**
web: www.malmaison.com/locations/dundee
dir: *A90, right onto riverfront, past airport and adjacent to train station.*

This iconic building, very close to the river, has been delightfully and lovingly restored – the public areas are stylish and plush. The main staircase is very notable for its beautiful ironwork, and the restaurant for its views. The contemporary bedrooms and suites are very well appointed, and the hotel provides a number of meeting rooms; there's also free WiFi. The cuisine in Chez Mal is a feature and a good range of menu options is on offer.

Rooms: 91 🕯 **S** fr £99 **D** fr £119* **Facilities:** STV FTV WiFi ⓑ Xmas New Year **Conf:** Class 120 Board 50 Theatre 170 **Services:** Lift Night porter Air con **Notes:** Civ Wed 150

DUNDEE *continued*

Premier Inn Dundee Centre

BUDGET HOTEL

tel: 0871 527 8320 (Calls cost 13p per minute plus your phone company's access charge) **Discovery Quay, Riverside Drive DD1 4XA**
web: www.premierinn.com
dir: *Follow signs for Discovery Quay, hotel on waterfront.*

High quality, budget accommodation ideal for both families and business travellers. Spacious, en suite bedrooms feature free WiFi and tea and coffee making facilities, and in most hotels, Freeview TV is also available. The adjacent family restaurant features a wide and varied menu.

Rooms: 40

Premier Inn Dundee East

BUDGET HOTEL

tel: 0871 527 8322 (Calls cost 13p per minute plus your phone company's access charge) **115-117 Lawers Drive, Panmurefield Village DD5 3UP**
web: www.premierinn.com
dir: *From north: A92 (Dundee and Arbroath). Hotel 1.5 miles after Sainsbury's. From south: A90. At end of dual carriageway follow Dundee to Arbroath signs.*

Rooms: 59

Premier Inn Dundee (Monifieth)

BUDGET HOTEL

tel: 0871 527 8318 (Calls cost 13p per minute plus your phone company's access charge) **Ethiebeaton Park, Arbroath Road DD5 4HB**
web: www.premierinn.com
dir: *From A90 (Kingsway Road) follow Carnoustie/Arbroath (A92) signs.*

Rooms: 40

Premier Inn Dundee North

BUDGET HOTEL

tel: 0871 527 8324 (Calls cost 13p per minute plus your phone company's access charge) **Camperdown Leisure Park, Dayton Drive DD2 3SQ**
web: www.premierinn.com
dir: *2 miles north of city centre on A90 at junction with A923, adjacent to cinema. At entrance to Camperdown Country Park.*

Rooms: 78

Premier Inn Dundee West

Premier Inn

BUDGET HOTEL

tel: 0871 527 8326 (Calls cost 13p per minute plus your phone company's access charge) **Kingsway West DD2 5JU**
web: www.premierinn.com
dir: *On A90 towards Aberdeen adjacent to Technology Park roundabout.*

Rooms: 87

King Malcolm Hotel

★★★ 75% HOTEL

tel: 01383 722611 **Queensferry Road KY11 8DS**
email: info@kingmalcolm-hotel-dunfermline.com **web:** www.peelhotels.co.uk
dir: *On A823, south of town.*

Located to the south of the town, this purpose-built hotel remains popular with business clientele and is convenient for access to both Edinburgh and Fife. Public rooms include a smart foyer lounge and a conservatory bar, as well as a restaurant. Bedrooms, although not large, are well laid out and well equipped.

Rooms: 48 (2 family) (24 GF) **Facilities:** STV WiFi 🎵 Xmas New Year **Conf:** Class 60 Board 50 Theatre 150 **Services:** Night porter **Parking:** 60 **Notes:** Civ Wed 120

Premier Inn Dunfermline

BUDGET HOTEL

tel: 0871 527 8328 (Calls cost 13p per minute plus your phone company's access charge) **4-12 Whimbrel Place, Fife Leisure Park KY11 8EX**
web: www.premierinn.com
dir: *M90 junction 3 (Forth Road Bridge exit) 1st left at lights signed Duloch Park. 1st left into Fife Leisure Park.*

High quality, budget accommodation ideal for both families and business travellers. Spacious, en suite bedrooms feature free WiFi and tea and coffee making facilities, and in most hotels, Freeview TV is also available. The adjacent family restaurant features a wide and varied menu.

Rooms: 78

Selborne Hotel

Leisureplex
HOLIDAY HOTELS

★★★ 72% HOTEL

tel: 01369 702761 **Clyde Street, West Bay PA23 7HU**
email: selborne.dunoon@alfatravel.co.uk **web:** www.leisureplex.co.uk
dir: *From Argyll Ferries pier. Past castle, left into Jane Street, right into Clyde Street. Ferry crossing to Dunoon via Gourock.*

This holiday hotel is situated overlooking the West Bay and provides unrestricted views of the Clyde estuary towards the Isles of Cumbrae. Tour groups are especially well catered for in this good-value establishment, which offers entertainment most nights. Bedrooms are comfortable and many have sea views.

Rooms: 98 (6 family) (13 GF) 🐾 **S** fr £37 **D** fr £56 (including breakfast)*
Facilities: FTV WiFi HL Pool table table tennis 🎵 Xmas New Year **Services:** Lift Night porter **Parking:** 30 **Notes:** Closed December to February (excluding Christmas/New Year) RS November, March

E

EAST KILBRIDE
South Lanarkshire   Map 20 NS65

Macdonald Crutherland House
★★★★ 74% HOTEL

 MACDONALD HOTELS & RESORTS

tel: 01355 577000 **Strathaven Road G75 0QZ**
email: crutherland@macdonald-hotels.co.uk
web: www.macdonaldhotels.co.uk/crutherland
dir: *Follow A726 signed Strathaven, straight over Torrance roundabout, hotel on left after 250 yards.*

This mansion is set in 37 acres of landscaped grounds two miles from the town centre. Behind its Georgian facade is a very relaxing hotel with elegant public areas plus extensive banqueting and leisure facilities. The bedrooms are spacious and comfortable. Staff offer good customer care, and enjoyable meals are served in the restaurant.

Rooms: 75 (16 family) (16 GF) **Facilities:** Spa STV WiFi ⓧ Gym Sauna Steam room Xmas New Year **Conf:** Class 100 Board 50 Theatre 500 **Services:** Lift Night porter **Parking:** 200 **Notes:** Civ Wed 300

Premier Inn Glasgow East Kilbride Central
Premier Inn

BUDGET HOTEL

tel: 0871 527 8450 (Calls cost 13p per minute plus your phone company's access charge) **Brunel Way, The Murray G75 0LD**
web: www.premierinn.com
dir: *M74 junction 5, follow East Kilbride A725 signs, then Paisley A726 signs, left at Murray roundabout, left into Brunel Way.*

High quality, budget accommodation ideal for both families and business travellers. Spacious, en suite bedrooms feature free WiFi and tea and coffee making facilities, and in most hotels, Freeview TV is also available. The adjacent family restaurant features a wide and varied menu.

Rooms: 58

Premier Inn Glasgow East Kilbride (Nerston Toll)
Premier Inn

BUDGET HOTEL

tel: 0871 527 8446 (Calls cost 13p per minute plus your phone company's access charge) **5 Lee's Burn Court, Nerston G74 3XB**
web: www.premierinn.com
dir: *M74 junction 5, follow East Kilbride/A725 signs. Into right lane, follow Glasgow/A749 signs. At lights left onto A749 signed East Kilbride Town Centre (A725). Take slip road to Lee's Burn Court.*

Rooms: 44

Premier Inn Glasgow East Kilbride (Peel Park)
Premier Inn

BUDGET HOTEL

tel: 0871 527 8448 (Calls cost 13p per minute plus your phone company's access charge) **Eaglesham Road G75 8LW**
web: www.premierinn.com
dir: *8 miles from M74 junction 5 on A726 at roundabout of B764.*

Rooms: 42

EDINBURGH
Edinburgh   Map 21 NT27

INSPECTOR'S CHOICE

The Balmoral
★★★★★ HOTEL

ROCCO FORTE HOTELS
RF

tel: 0131 556 2414 **1 Princes Street EH2 2EQ**
email: reservations.balmoral@roccofortehotels.com
web: www.roccofortehotels.com
dir: *Follow city centre signs. Hotel at east end of Princes Street, adjcent to Waverley Station.*

This elegant hotel enjoys a prestigious address at the top of Princes Street, with fine views over the city and the castle. Bedrooms and suites are stylishly furnished and all boast a thoughtful range of extras and impressive marble bathrooms. Hotel amenities include a Roman-style health spa, extensive function facilities, a choice of bars and two very different dining options – Hadrians is a bustling, informal brasserie, while Number One offers excellent Scottish and international fine dining.

Rooms: 188 (22 family) ⓢ **S** fr £180 **D** fr £180* **Facilities:** Spa STV WiFi ⓧ Gym Xmas New Year **Conf:** Class 180 Board 60 Theatre 350 **Services:** Lift Night porter Air con **Parking:** 100 **Notes:** Civ Wed 120

EDINBURGH *continued*

Prestonfield

★★★★★ @@ TOWN HOUSE HOTEL

tel: 0131 225 7800 **Priestfield Road EH16 5UT**
email: reservations@prestonfield.com **web:** www.prestonfield.com
dir: *A7 towards Cameron Toll. 200 metres beyond Royal Commonwealth Pool, into Priestfield Road.*

This centuries-old landmark has been lovingly restored and enhanced to provide deeply comfortable and dramatically furnished bedrooms. The building demands to be explored: from the tapestry lounge and the whisky room to the restaurant, where the walls are adorned with pictures of former owners. Facilities and services are up-to-the-minute, and carefully prepared meals are served in the award-winning Rhubarb restaurant.

Rooms: 23 (6 GF) ↝ **S** fr £335 **D** fr £335 (including breakfast)* **Facilities:** STV FTV WiFi ↝ ♨ 18 ☘ Xmas New Year **Conf:** Class 500 Board 40 Theatre 700 **Services:** Lift Night porter **Parking:** 250 **Notes:** Civ Wed 350

Waldorf Astoria Edinburgh - The Caledonian

★★★★★ 85% @@@ HOTEL

tel: 0131 222 8888 **Princes Street EH1 2AB**
email: guest_caledonian@waldorfastoria.com **web:** www.waldorfastoriaedinburgh.com
dir: *In city centre, at west end of Princes Street, adjacent to Rutland Street and Lothian Road.*

Set in the heart of Scotland's capital city, against the magnificent backdrop of Edinburgh Castle, this former Victorian railway hotel was built in 1903, and hasn't lost any of the charm and character that has made it famous. Spacious bedrooms and en suites offer comfort and luxury, and there is a choice of award-winning

restaurants and wonderful public areas. The Guerlain Spa is a popular destination for relaxation and rejuvenation. Many rooms enjoy breathtaking views of the castle.

Rooms: 241 (12 family) ↝ **S** fr £199 **D** fr £209 (including breakfast)* **Facilities:** Spa STV WiFi ↝ HL ⊛ Gym Sauna Steam room Xmas New Year **Conf:** Class 120 Board 80 Theatre 300 **Services:** Lift Night porter Air con **Parking:** 48 **Notes:** Civ Wed 300

Sheraton Grand Hotel & Spa

★★★★★ 84% @ HOTEL

tel: 0131 229 9131 **1 Festival Square EH3 9SR**
email: grandedinburgh@sheraton.com **web:** www.sheratonedinburgh.co.uk
dir: *In city centre. Phone for directions and parking details.*

This modern hotel boasts one of the best spas in Scotland – the external top-floor hydropool is definitely worth a look, while the thermal suite provides a unique venue for serious relaxation. The spacious bedrooms are available in a variety of styles, and the suites prove very popular. There is a wide range of dishes available in the One Square Bar & Restaurant which also offers 'Dining at The Pass'; The Kitchen Table is a private dining area where guests can meet the team of chefs.

Rooms: 269 ↝ **D** fr £185 (including breakfast)* **Facilities:** Spa STV FTV WiFi ↝ ↝ Gym Indoor/outdoor Hydropool Kinesis studio Thermal suite Fitness studio Beauty salon ♫ Xmas New Year **Conf:** Class 350 Board 120 Theatre 500 **Services:** Lift Night porter Air con **Parking:** 122 **Notes:** LB Civ Wed 485

Norton House Hotel & Spa

★★★★ @ ⚑ HOTEL

tel: 0131 333 1275 & 0845 072 7468 (Calls cost 5p per minute plus your phone company's access charge) **Ingliston EH28 8LX**
email: nortonhouse@handpicked.co.uk
web: www.handpickedhotels.co.uk/nortonhouse
dir: *Off A8, 5 miles west of city centre.*

This extended Victorian mansion, set in 55 acres of parkland, is peacefully situated just outside the city and is convenient for the airport. The original building dates from 1840, and was bought nearly 40 years later by John Usher of the Scottish brewing family. Today, both the contemporary bedrooms and the very spacious, traditional ones have an impressive range of accessories including large satellite TVs, DVD/CD players and free high-speed internet access. Executive rooms have more facilities, of course, including MP3 connection and 'television' TVs at the end of the baths. Public areas take in a choice of lounges as well as dining in the popular brasserie. There is a health club, and a spa which offers a long list of treatments.

Rooms: 83 (10 family) (20 GF) ↝ **S** fr £99 **D** fr £109 (including breakfast) **Facilities:** Spa STV WiFi ↝ HL ⊛ Gym Xmas New Year **Conf:** Class 100 Board 60 Theatre 300 **Services:** Lift Night porter **Parking:** 200 **Notes:** LB Civ Wed 140

Novotel Edinburgh Park

★★★★ 81% HOTEL

tel: 0131 446 5600 **15 Lochside Avenue EH12 9DJ**
email: h6515@accor.com **web:** www.novotel.com
dir: *Near Hermiston Gate shopping area, airport and Murrayfield.*

Located just off the city bypass and within minutes of the airport, this modern hotel offers bedrooms that are spacious and comfortable. The public areas include the open-plan lobby, a bar and a restaurant offering diverse and informal dishes. A swimming pool and small gym are also available to guests.

Rooms: 170 (130 family) **Facilities:** STV FTV WiFi HL Gym **Conf:** Class 60 Board 40 Theatre 150 **Services:** Lift Night porter Air con **Parking:** 96 **Notes:** Civ Wed 90

The Principal Edinburgh George Street

PRINCIPAL

★★★★ 81% HOTEL

tel: 0131 225 1251 **19-21 George Street EH2 2PB**
email: EdinburghReservationsGS@theprincipalhotel.com
web: www.phcompany.com/principal/edinburgh-george-street
dir: *In city centre.*

This long-established hotel enjoys a city centre location. The splendid public areas have many original features such as intricate plasterwork, a marble-floored foyer and chandeliers. The Printing Press offers menus that feature Scottish produce while Burr & Co is a relaxed coffee shop. The elegant, modern bedrooms come in a mix of sizes and styles; the upper ones having fine city views.

Rooms: 249 (20 family) (4 GF) **Facilities:** STV WiFi HL Xmas New Year **Conf:** Class 120 Board 50 Theatre 300 **Services:** Lift Night porter **Notes:** LB Civ Wed 300

Dalhousie Castle and Aqueous Spa

★★★★ 80% @ @ HOTEL

tel: 01875 820153 **Bonnyrigg EH19 3JB**
email: info@dalhousiecastle.co.uk **web:** www.dalhousiecastle.co.uk
dir: *A7 south from Edinburgh through Lasswade/Newtongrange, right at Shell Garage (B704), hotel 0.5 mile from junction.*

A popular wedding venue, this imposing medieval castle sits amid lawns and parkland and even has a falconry. Bedrooms offer a mix of styles and sizes, including richly decorated themed rooms named after various historical figures. The Dungeon restaurant provides an atmospheric setting for dinner, and the less formal Orangery serves food all day. The spa offers many relaxing and therapeutic treatments and hydro facilities.

Rooms: 35 (6 annexe) (3 family) **Facilities:** Spa FTV WiFi Fishing Falconry Clay pigeon shooting Archery Xmas New Year **Conf:** Class 60 Board 45 Theatre 120 **Services:** Night porter **Parking:** 110 **Notes:** Civ Wed 100

Hotel du Vin Edinburgh

★★★★ 80% @ TOWN HOUSE HOTEL

tel: 0131 247 4900 **11 Bristo Place EH1 1EZ**
email: reception.edinburgh@hotelduvin.com
web: www.hotelduvin.com/locations/edinburgh
dir: *M8 junction 1, A720 signed Kilmarnock/West Calder/Edinburgh West. Right at fork, follow A720 signs, merge onto A720. Take exit signed A703. At roundabout take A702/Biggar Road. 3.5 miles. Right into Lauriston Place which becomes Forrest Road. Right at Bedlam Theatre. Hotel on right.*

This hotel offers very stylish and comfortable accommodation; all bedrooms display the Hotel du Vin trademark facilities – air conditioning, free WiFi, plasma TVs, monsoon showers and Egyptian cotton linen to name but a few. Public areas include a whisky snug, and a mezzanine bar that overlooks the brasserie where

modern Scottish cuisine is served. For the wine connoisseur, there's La Roche tasting room where wines from around the world can be appreciated.

Rooms: 47 **Facilities:** STV FTV WiFi **Conf:** Class 10 Board 28 Theatre 30 **Services:** Lift Night porter Air con **Notes:** Civ Wed 28

The Principal Edinburgh Charlotte Square

PRINCIPAL

★★★★ 80% HOTEL

tel: 0131 240 5500 **38 Charlotte Square EH2 4HQ**
email: charlottesquarefrontoffice@principal-hayley.com
web: www.phcompany.com/principal/edinburgh-charlotte-square
dir: *On corner of Charlotte Square and George Street.*

This long-established hotel lies in the heart of the city overlooking Charlotte Square Gardens. Public areas are inviting and include relaxing lounges, a choice of bars (in the evening) and an inner concourse that looks onto a small lawned area. Smart bedrooms come in both classic and contemporary styles. Valet parking is available.

Rooms: 199 (6 family) **S** fr £120 **D** fr £135* **Facilities:** Spa FTV WiFi Gym Dance studio Sauna Steam room Xmas **Conf:** Class 180 Board 50 Theatre 340 **Services:** Lift Night porter Air con **Parking:** 20 **Notes:** Civ Wed 280

Novotel Edinburgh Centre

★★★★ 79% HOTEL

tel: 0131 656 3500 **Lauriston Place, Lady Lawson Street EH3 9DE**
email: H3271@accor.com **web:** www.novotel.com
dir: *From Edinburgh Castle right onto George IV Bridge from Royal Mile. Follow to junction, then right into Lauriston Place. Hotel 700 metres on right.*

This modern hotel is located in the centre of the city, close to Edinburgh Castle. Smart and stylish public areas include a cosmopolitan bar, brasserie-style restaurant and indoor leisure facilities. The air-conditioned bedrooms feature a comprehensive range of extras and the bathrooms have baths and separate shower cabinets.

Rooms: 180 (146 family) **S** fr £70 **D** fr £80 (including breakfast)* **Facilities:** STV WiFi HL Gym Sauna Steam room Xmas New Year **Conf:** Class 50 Board 32 Theatre 80 **Services:** Lift Night porter Air con **Parking:** 15 **Notes:** LB

Macdonald Holyrood Hotel

★★★★ 78% @ @ HOTEL

tel: 0131 550 4500 **Holyrood Road EH8 8AU**
email: general.holyrood@macdonald-hotels.co.uk
web: www.macdonaldhotels.co.uk/holyrood
dir: *Parallel to Royal Mile, near Holyrood Palace and Dynamic Earth.*

Situated just a short walk from Holyrood Palace, this impressive hotel is situated next to the Scottish Parliament building. Air-conditioned bedrooms are comfortably furnished, while the Club floor boasts a private lounge. Full business services complement the extensive conference suites.

Rooms: 156 (16 family) (13 GF) **S** fr £99 **D** fr £123* **Facilities:** Spa STV FTV WiFi Gym Sauna Steam room library Xmas New Year **Conf:** Class 100 Board 80 Theatre 200 **Services:** Lift Night porter Air con **Parking:** 38 **Notes:** LB Civ Wed 100

E

EDINBURGH *continued*

Malmaison Edinburgh

★★★★ 77% HOTEL

tel: 0131 468 5000 & 0844 693 0652 (Calls cost 5p per minute plus your phone company's access charge) **One Tower Place, Leith EH6 7BZ**
email: reception.edinburgh@malmaison.com
web: www.malmaison.com/locations/edinburgh
dir: *A900 from city centre towards Leith, at end of Leith Walk, through 3 sets of lights, left into Tower Street. Hotel on right at end of road.*

The trendy Port of Leith is home to this stylish Malmaison. Inside, bold contemporary designs create a striking effect. Bedrooms are comprehensively equipped with CD players, mini bars and loads of individual touches. Ask for one of the stunning superior rooms for a really memorable stay. The smart brasserie and a café bar are popular with the local clientele.

Rooms: 100 (18 family) 🐾 **Facilities:** STV FTV WiFi 🏊 Gym Xmas New Year
Conf: Class 32 Board 32 Theatre 80 **Services:** Lift Night porter **Parking:** 50
Notes: Civ Wed 70

Ten Hill Place Hotel

★★★★ 74% HOTEL

tel: 0131 662 2080 **10 Hill Place EH8 9DS**
email: reservations@tenhillplace.com **web:** www.tenhillplace.com
dir: *Into Hill Place, opposite Festival Theatre. Hotel at end.*

This centrally located luxury hotel near to the Festival Theatre is owned and operated by the Royal College of Surgeons, with all profits helping to train surgeons around the world. Stylish bedrooms and bathrooms are complemented by a range of welcoming and comfortable public areas including the popular 10 Wine Bar, an interesting wine-themed space, and the award-winning No.10 Restaurant. Limited parking is available on site.

Rooms: 129 (4 family) 🐾 D fr £195* **Facilities:** FTV WiFi 🏊 **Services:** Lift Night porter Air con **Parking:** 6 **Notes:** LB

Old Waverley Hotel

★★★ 78% HOTEL

tel: 0131 556 4648 **43 Princes Street EH2 2BY**
email: reservations@oldwaverley.co.uk **web:** www.oldwaverley.co.uk
dir: *In city centre, opposite Scott Monument, Waverley Station and Jenners.*

Occupying a commanding position opposite Sir Walter Scott's famous monument on Princes Street, this hotel lies right in the heart of the city, close to the station. The comfortable public rooms are all on first-floor level and along with front-facing bedrooms enjoy the fine views.

Rooms: 86 (5 family) **Facilities:** WiFi 🏊 Leisure facilities at sister hotel **Services:** Lift Night porter **Notes:** LB

Mercure Edinburgh City - Princes Street Hotel

★★★ 77% HOTEL

tel: 0131 226 8400 & 0844 815 9017 (Calls cost 7p per minute plus your phone company's access charge) **Princes Street EH2 2DG**
email: info@mercureedinburgh.co.uk **web:** www.mercureedinburgh.co.uk
dir: *Opposite Scott Monument and Waverley Station. At east end of Princes Street.*

With an enviable location in the heart of Princes Street, offering excellent views of the castle you really cannot be any more central. The front-facing bedrooms are the most spacious on offer; some benefit from having a balcony but all are well appointed. The large popular restaurant benefits from the wonderful views.

Rooms: 169 (9 family) **Facilities:** FTV WiFi 🏊 HL New Year **Services:** Lift Night porter

hub by Premier Inn Edinburgh City Centre (Rose Street)

BUDGET HOTEL

tel: 0333 321 3104 (Calls cost 13p per minute plus your phone company's access charge) **56-58 Rose Street EH2 2NN**
web: www.premierinn.com
dir: *Walking from Edinburgh Waverley Station, exit right onto Waverley Bridge and turn left onto Princes Street. Right onto Hanover Street then left onto Rose Street. Hotel on left.*

This modern hotel offers self-check-in kiosks, superfast free WiFi, and cleverly designed and compact bedrooms with all the entertainment and comfort you need: 40" flat-screen smart TV, temperature and lighting controlled by a special Premier Inn app, Hypnos bed, and monsoon shower. The Deli+Bar is open for grab-and-go breakfast boxes, pastries, grilled sandwiches, Costa Coffee, beer, wine and more.

Rooms: 145

Premier Inn Edinburgh A1 (Musselburgh)

Premier Inn

BUDGET HOTEL

tel: 0871 527 8358 (Calls cost 13p per minute plus your phone company's access charge) **Carberry Road, Inveresk EH21 8PT**
web: www.premierinn.com
dir: *From A1 follow Dalkeith (A6094) signs. At roundabout turn right, hotel 300 yards on right.*

High quality, budget accommodation ideal for both families and business travellers. Spacious, en suite bedrooms feature free WiFi and tea and coffee making facilities, and in most hotels, Freeview TV is also available. The adjacent family restaurant features a wide and varied menu.

Rooms: 82

Premier Inn Edinburgh Airport (Newbridge)

Premier Inn

BUDGET HOTEL

tel: 0871 527 9284 (Calls cost 13p per minute plus your phone company's access charge) **2A Kirkliston Road, Newbridge EH28 8SL**
web: www.premierinn.com
dir: *M9 junction 1, A89 signed Broxburn. At lights turn right, then 2nd right.*

Rooms: 119

Premier Inn Edinburgh Central Lauriston Place

Premier Inn

BUDGET HOTEL

tel: 0871 527 8366 (Calls cost 13p per minute plus your phone company's access charge) **82 Lauriston Place, Lady Lawson Street EH3 9DG**
web: www.premierinn.com
dir: *A8 onto A702 (Lothian Road). Left into Lauriston Place. Hotel on left.*

Rooms: 112

F

Premier Inn Edinburgh City Centre (Princes St)

BUDGET HOTEL

tel: 0871 527 9358 (Calls cost 13p per minute plus your phone company's access charge) **122-123 Princes Street EH2 4AD**
web: www.premierinn.com
dir: From Edinburgh bypass (A720) onto A702, take A700. (Note: Princes Street is not accessible by car; it is advisable to park in Castle Terrace Car Park EH1 2EW).

Rooms: 97

Premier Inn Edinburgh City Centre Royal Mile

BUDGET HOTEL

tel: 0871 527 9644 (Calls cost 13p per minute plus your phone company's access charge) **East Market Street EH8 8BG**
web: www.premierinn.com
dir: From Waverley train station right into Market Street, straight on into East Market Street, hotel in 0.4 mile.

Rooms: 127

Premier Inn Edinburgh City Centre (York Place)

BUDGET HOTEL

tel: 0871 527 9618 (Calls cost 13p per minute plus your phone company's access charge) **44 York Place EH1 3HU**
web: www.premierinn.com
dir: Phone for directions.

Rooms: 127

Premier Inn Edinburgh East

BUDGET HOTEL

tel: 0871 527 8370 (Calls cost 13p per minute plus your phone company's access charge) **228 Willowbrae Road EH8 7NG**
web: www.premierinn.com
dir: M8 junction 1, A720 south for 12 miles, then A1. At Asda roundabout turn left. In 2 miles, hotel on left before Esso garage.

Rooms: 50

Premier Inn Edinburgh Leith Waterfront

BUDGET HOTEL

tel: 0871 527 8360 (Calls cost 13p per minute plus your phone company's access charge) **51-53 Newhaven Place, Leith EH6 4TX**
web: www.premierinn.com
dir: From A1 follow coast road through Leith. Pass Ocean Terminal, straight ahead at mini-roundabout, 2nd exit signed Harry Ramsden's car park.

Rooms: 138

Premier Inn Edinburgh Park (The Gyle)

BUDGET HOTEL

tel: 0871 527 9336 (Calls cost 13p per minute plus your phone company's access charge) **Edinburgh Park (Airport), 1 Lochside Court EH12 9FX**
web: www.premierinn.com
dir: M8 junction 1, A720 (city bypass). At Gogar roundabout 3rd exit follow South Gyle/ station signs. Into right lane approaching Gyle roundabout, 3rd exit, follow Edinburgh Park train station signs into Lochside Crescent. Straight on at 2 roundabout, 400 yards. Hotel on left.

Rooms: 120

ELGIN
Moray — Map 23 NJ26

Premier Inn Elgin

BUDGET HOTEL

tel: 0871 527 8372 (Calls cost 13p per minute plus your phone company's access charge) **15 Linkwood Way IV30 1HY**
web: www.premierinn.com
dir: On A96, 1.5 miles east of city centre.

High quality, budget accommodation ideal for both families and business travellers. Spacious, en suite bedrooms feature free WiFi and tea and coffee making facilities, and in most hotels, Freeview TV is also available. The adjacent family restaurant features a wide and varied menu.

Rooms: 93

ERISKA
Argyll & Bute — Map 20 NM94

Isle of Eriska Hotel, Spa & Island

⭐

tel: 01631 720371 & 720800 **PA37 1SD**
email: office@eriska-hotel.co.uk **web:** www.eriska-hotel.co.uk
dir: From Glasgow take the A82 north to Tyndrum after the green wellyshop, first left for Oban A85. At Connel turn left and drive over Connel Bridge to Benderloch. Follow the brown sign on the left for Eriska.

Currently the rating for this establishment is not confirmed. This may be due to a change of ownership or because ot has only recently joined the AA rating scheme.

Rooms: 30 (14 annexe) (2 family) (7 GF) S fr £238.50 **D** fr £265.50 (including breakfast)* **Facilities:** Spa FTV WiFi 9 Gym Walking Cycling Clay pigeon shooting Badminton Xmas New Year **Conf:** Class 40 Board 50 Theatre 120 **Services:** Night porter **Parking:** 30 **Notes:** Closed January Civ Wed 280

FALKIRK
Falkirk — Map 21 NS88

Premier Inn Falkirk Central

BUDGET HOTEL

tel: 0871 527 8388 (Calls cost 13p per minute plus your phone company's access charge) **Main Street, Camelon FK1 4DS**
web: www.premierinn.com
dir: From Falkirk A803 signed Glasgow. At mini-roundabout right, continue on A803. At Rosebank roundabout 2nd exit signed Glasgow and Stirling.

Rooms: 31

FALKIRK *continued*

Premier Inn Falkirk (Larbert)

Premier Inn

BUDGET HOTEL

tel: 0871 527 8390 (Calls cost 13p per minute plus your phone company's access charge) **Glenbervie Business Park, Bellsdyke Road FK5 4EG**
web: www.premierinn.com
dir: *Just off A88. Approximately 1 mile from M876 junction 2.*

Rooms: 60

FINTRY	**Map 20 NS68**
Stirling	

Culcreuch Castle Hotel & Estate

★★★ 76% ◉◉ HOTEL

tel: 01360 860555 **Kippen Road G63 0LW**
email: info@culcreuch.com **web:** www.culcreuch.com
dir: *On B822, 17 miles west of Stirling.*

Peacefully located in 1,600 acres of parkland, this ancient castle dates back to 1296. Tastefully restored accommodation is in a mixture of individually themed castle rooms, some with four-poster beds, and more modern courtyard rooms which are suitable for families. Period-style public rooms include a bar, serving light meals, an elegant lounge and a wood-panelled dining room.

Rooms: 14 (4 annexe) (4 family) (4 GF) ✆ **S** fr £76 **D** fr £102 (including breakfast)*
Facilities: STV FTV WiFi ♨ New Year **Conf:** Class 70 Board 30 Theatre 140
Parking: 80 **Notes:** LB Closed 4–18 January, 25–26 December RS 19 January to mid March Civ Wed 110

FORT AUGUSTUS	**Map 23 NH30**
Highland	

The Inch

★★★ 76% ◉◉ SMALL HOTEL

tel: 01456 450900 **Inchnacardoch Bay PH32 4BL**
email: happy@inchhotel.com **web:** www.inchhotel.com
dir: *On A82. Turn right before entering Fort Augustus from Inverness.*

This 150-year-old former hunting lodge is set on the hillside looking over the south end of Loch Ness, making it a perfect base for exploring the Highlands. Guests can expect the finest hospitality here from staff that are always eager to please. The bedrooms are very individual in style; the Bridal Suite is a very well-appointed room with stunning views. The Yard Restaurant serves dishes based on the plentiful supply of local game and seafood.

Rooms: 17 (2 family) **Facilities:** FTV WiFi Fishing Xmas New Year **Conf:** Class 30 Board 26 Theatre 45 **Parking:** 30 **Notes:** Civ Wed 35

FORTINGALL	**Map 20 NN74**
Perth & Kinross	

Fortingall Hotel

★★★★ 76% ◉ SMALL HOTEL

tel: 01887 830367 **PH15 2NQ**
email: enquiries@fortingall.com **web:** www.fortingallhotel.com
dir: *B846 from Aberfeldy for 6 miles, left signed Fortingall for 3 miles. Hotel in village centre.*

Appointed to a very high standard, this hotel has plenty of charm. It lies at the foot of wooded hills in the heart of Glen Lyon. All the bedrooms are very well equipped and have an extensive range of thoughtful extras. The comfortable lounge, with its log fire, is ideal for pre-dinner drinks, and the small bar is full of character.

Rooms: 10 (1 family) **Facilities:** STV FTV WiFi ♨ Fishing ⚓ Deer stalking Grouse shoots Munro bagging Clay pigeon Guided walks Cycle hire ♫ Xmas New Year **Conf:** Board 20 Theatre 40 **Parking:** 20 **Notes:** LB Civ Wed 50

FORT WILLIAM	**Map 22 NN17**
Highland	

Inverlochy Castle Hotel

★★★★★ ◉◉◉ ≋ COUNTRY HOUSE HOTEL

RELAIS & CHÂTEAUX

tel: 01397 702177 **Torlundy PH33 6SN**
email: info@inverlochy.co.uk **web:** www.inverlochycastlehotel.com
dir: *Accessible from either A82 (Glasgow to Fort William road) or A9 (Edinburgh to Dalwhinnie road). Hotel 3 miles north of Fort William on A82, in Torlundy.*

With Ben Nevis as its backdrop, this imposing and gracious castle sits amidst extensive gardens and grounds overlooking its own loch. Lavishly appointed in classic country-house style, spacious bedrooms are extremely comfortable and boast laptops with internet access. The sumptuous main hall and lounge provide the perfect setting for afternoon tea or a pre-dinner cocktail, while imaginative modern British cuisine is served in one of three dining rooms. A snooker room and DVD library are also available.

Rooms: 17 (6 family) ✆ **Facilities:** STV FTV WiFi ⚐ ⚓ Fishing on loch Massage Riding Hunting Stalking Clay pigeon shooting Archery ♫ Xmas New Year **Conf:** Class 20 Board 20 Theatre 50 **Services:** Night porter **Parking:** 17 **Notes:** Civ Wed 80

Moorings Hotel

★★★★ 73% HOTEL

tel: 01397 772797 **Banavie PH33 7LY**
email: reservations@moorings-fortwilliam.co.uk **web:** www.moorings-fortwilliam.co.uk
dir: Take A830 north from Fort William, cross Caledonian Canal, 1st right signed Banavie.

Located on the Caledonian Canal next to a series of locks known as Neptune's Staircase and close to Thomas Telford's house, this hotel has a dedicated team offering friendly service. Accommodation comes in three distinct styles – Standard, Superior and Executive. The newer rooms with balconies are particularly appealing; many rooms offer canal and/or Ben Nevis views. Meals can be taken in the modern bistro, or alternatively, fine dining is offered in the more traditional dining room.

Rooms: 32 (1 family) (1 GF) **D** fr £100 (including breakfast) **Facilities:** FTV WiFi Gym New Year **Conf:** Class 60 Board 40 Theatre 140 **Services:** Night porter **Parking:** 60 **Notes:** Closed 24–26 December Civ Wed 120

Alexandra Hotel

★★★ 75% HOTEL

tel: 01397 702241 **The Parade PH33 6AZ**
email: salesalexandra@strathmorehotels.com **web:** www.strathmorehotels.com
dir: Off A82. Hotel opposite railway station.

This charming old hotel enjoys a prominent position in the town centre and is just a short walk from all the major attractions. Front-facing bedrooms have views over the town and the spectacular Nevis mountain range. There is a choice of restaurants, including a bistro serving meals until late, along with several stylish and very comfortable lounges.

Rooms: 93 (2 family) **S** fr £53.20 **D** fr £99.75 (including breakfast)*
Facilities: FTV WiFi Free use of nearby leisure club Xmas New Year **Conf:** Class 100 Board 40 Theatre 120 **Services:** Lift Night porter **Parking:** 50 **Notes:** LB

Croit Anna Hotel

★★★ 72% HOTEL

Leisureplex
HOLIDAY HOTELS

tel: 01397 702268 **Achintore Road, Drimarben PH33 6RR**
email: croitanna@leisureplex.co.uk **web:** www.leisureplex.co.uk
dir: From Glencoe on A82 into Fort William, hotel 1st on right.

Located on the edge of Loch Linnhe, just two miles out of town, this hotel offers spacious bedrooms, many with fine views over the loch. There is a choice of two comfortable lounges and a large airy restaurant. The hotel appeals to coach parties and independent travellers alike.

Rooms: 90 (5 family) (13 GF) **Facilities:** FTV WiFi Pool table Xmas New Year **Services:** Night porter **Parking:** 25 **Notes:** Closed December to January (excluding Christmas/New Year) RS November, February to March

Ben Nevis Hotel & Leisure Club

★★★ 71% HOTEL

tel: 01397 702331 **North Road PH33 6TG**
email: salesbennevis@strathmorehotels.com **web:** www.strathmorehotels.com
dir: Off A82.

This popular hotel is ideally situated on the outskirts of town. It provides comfortable, well-equipped bedrooms; many with views of the impressive Nevis mountains. The hotel's leisure centre is a firm favourite with guests at the hotel. Public areas include a spacious and welcoming bar with a great selection of whiskies.

Rooms: 119 (3 family) (30 GF) **Facilities:** WiFi Gym Xmas New Year **Conf:** Class 60 Board 40 Theatre 150 **Services:** Night porter **Parking:** 100 **Notes:** Civ Wed 60

Premier Inn Fort William

BUDGET HOTEL

Premier Inn

tel: 0871 527 8402 (Calls cost 13p per minute plus your phone company's access charge) **Loch Iall, An Aird PH33 6AN**
web: www.premierinn.com
dir: North end of Fort William Shopping Centre, just off A82 (ring road).

High quality, budget accommodation ideal for both families and business travellers. Spacious, en suite bedrooms feature free WiFi and tea and coffee making facilities, and in most hotels, Freeview TV is also available. The adjacent family restaurant features a wide and varied menu.

Rooms: 103

F

GALASHIELS
Scottish Borders   Map 21 NT43

Kingsknowes Hotel
★★★ 81% HOTEL

tel: 01896 758375 **Selkirk Road TD1 3HY**
email: enq@kingsknowes.co.uk **web:** www.kingsknowes.co.uk
dir: *33 miles south of Edinburgh on A7; 2 miles from Galashiels, 5 miles from Melrose.*

An imposing turreted mansion, this hotel lies in attractive gardens on the outskirts of town close to the River Tweed. It boasts elegant public areas and many spacious bedrooms, some with excellent views. There is a choice of bars, one with a popular menu to supplement the restaurant.

Rooms: 12 (2 family) S fr £89 D fr £110 (including breakfast)* **Facilities:** FTV WiFi HL **Conf:** Class 40 Board 30 Theatre 80 **Parking:** 65 **Notes:** LB Civ Wed 75

GATEHOUSE OF FLEET
Dumfries & Galloway   Map 20 NX55

Cally Palace Hotel
★★★★ 76% COUNTRY HOUSE HOTEL

tel: 01557 814341 **Cally Drive DG7 2DL**
email: info@callypalace.co.uk **web:** www.callypalace.co.uk
dir: *From M6 and A74, signed A75 Dumfries then Stranraer. At Gatehouse-of-Fleet right onto B727, left at Cally.*

A resort hotel with extensive leisure facilities, this grand 18th-century building is set in 500 acres of forest and parkland that incorporates its own golf course. Bedrooms are spacious and well equipped, while public rooms retain a quiet elegance. The short dinner menu focuses on freshly prepared dishes; a pianist plays most nights and for men, a jacket and tie is obligatory.

Rooms: 55 (7 family) (4 GF) S fr £98 D fr £136 (including breakfast & dinner)* **Facilities:** STV FTV WiFi 18 Fishing Gym Table tennis Practice fairway Snooker Pool Xmas New Year **Conf:** Class 40 Board 25 Theatre 40 **Services:** Lift Night porter **Parking:** 100 **Notes:** LB Closed January to early February Civ Wed 130

GLASGOW
Glasgow   Map 20 NS56

See also **Clydebank & Uplawmoor**

Blythswood Square
PRINCIPAL

★★★★★ 87% HOTEL

tel: 0141 248 8888 **11 Blythswood Square G2 4AD**
email: reserve@blythswoodsquare.com
web: www.phcompany.com/principal/glasgow-blythswood-square
dir: *Phone for directions.*

Built in 1821, and restored to its former glory, this was the headquarters of the Royal Scottish Automobile Club, which was the official start point for the 1955 Monte Carlo Rally. The bedrooms and bathrooms are sumptuous, and include suites and a penthouse. Afternoon tea and cocktails are served in the 35-metre, first-floor Salon Lounge, and the award-winning restaurant occupies the old RSAC's ballroom. The Spa includes a fantastic thermal suite.

Rooms: 113 (5 GF) S fr £105 D fr £105* **Facilities:** Spa STV FTV WiFi Gym Thermal experience Xmas New Year **Conf:** Class 80 Board 80 Theatre 130 **Services:** Lift Night porter Air con **Notes:** Civ Wed 80

ABode Glasgow
★★★★ 86% HOTEL

ABode HOTELS

tel: 0141 221 6789 **129 Bath Street G2 2SZ**
email: info@abodeglasgow.co.uk **web:** www.abodeglasgow.co.uk

Located a moment's walk from Glasgow's shopping centres and central transport links, this impressive building provides comfortable, luxury accommodation with a boutique hotel atmosphere. The air-conditioned bedrooms are stylish and tastefully appointed and have 32" TVs as standard; many have high ceilings that allude to the history of the property. The modern Brasserie Abode offers an interesting range of dishes all day, and a hearty traditional Scottish breakfast will set you up for the day ahead. There's an intimate, contemporary basement bar, Pie & Brew, offering a great range of craft beers and speciality home-made artisan pies.

Rooms: 59 **Facilities:** WiFi

Hotel du Vin at One Devonshire Gardens
★★★★ 80% TOWN HOUSE HOTEL

Hotel du Vin & Bistro

tel: 0141 339 2001 & 0844 736 4256 (Calls cost 5p per minute plus your phone company's access charge) **1 Devonshire Gardens G12 0UX**
email: info.odg@hotelduvin.com **web:** www.hotelduvin.com/locations/glasgow
dir: *M8 junction 17, follow signs for A82, in 1.5 miles left into Hyndland Road, 1st right, right at mini-roundabout, right at end.*

Situated in a tree-lined Victorian terrace this luxury 'boutique' hotel has stunning, individually designed bedrooms and suites that have the trademark Egyptian linen and seriously good showers. The oak-panelled Bistro offers a daily-changing menu of both classic and modern dishes with a Scottish influence. Naturally, wine is an important part of the equation here, and knowledgeable staff can guide guests around the impressive wine list.

Rooms: 49 (7 GF) S fr £127 D fr £140 (including breakfast)* **Facilities:** STV WiFi Gym Beauty treatment room Tennis and squash facilities at nearby club Xmas New Year **Conf:** Class 30 Board 30 Theatre 50 **Services:** Night porter **Notes:** Civ Wed 80

Malmaison Glasgow
★★★★ 78% HOTEL

Malmaison
hotels that dare to be different

tel: 0141 572 1000 & 0844 693 0653 (Calls cost 5p per minute plus your phone company's access charge) **278 West George Street G2 4LL**
email: reception.glasgow@malmaison.com **web:** www.malmaison.com/locations/glasgow
dir: *From south and east: M8 junction 18 Charing Cross. From west and north: M8 city centre.*

Built around a former church in the historic Charing Cross area, this hotel is a smart, contemporary establishment offering impressive levels of service and hospitality. Bedrooms are spacious and feature a host of modern facilities, such as CD players and mini bars. Dining is a treat here, with French brasserie-style cuisine, backed up by an excellent wine list, served in the original crypt.

Rooms: 72 (4 family) (19 GF) **Facilities:** STV WiFi New Year **Conf:** Class 20 Board 22 Theatre 56 **Services:** Lift Night porter **Notes:** Civ Wed 60

Golden Jubilee Conference Hotel

★★★★ 76% HOTEL

tel: 0141 951 6000 **Beardmore Street G81 4SA**
email: zico.iqbal@goldenjubilee.scot.nhs.uk **web:** www.goldenjubileehotel.com

(for full entry see Clydebank)

Hallmark Hotel Glasgow

★★★★ 75% HOTEL

tel: 0330 028 3407 **27 Washington Street G3 8AZ**
email: glasgow@hallmarkhotels.co.uk **web:** www.hallmarkhotels.co.uk
dir: M8 junction 19, follow signs for SECC and Broomielaw. Left at lights.

Centrally located, this modern hotel is a short drive from the airport and a short walk from the centre of the city. Bedrooms are generally spacious and boast a range of facilities, including high-speed internet access. Facilities include a brasserie restaurant and an impressive indoor leisure facility.

Rooms: 141 (16 family) **S** fr £80 **D** fr £90* **Facilities:** Spa STV FTV WiFi ⬙ ⓒ Gym **Conf:** Class 80 Board 70 Theatre 160 **Services:** Lift Night porter Air con **Parking:** 50 **Notes:** LB Civ Wed 150

The Principal Grand Central

PRINCIPAL

★★★★ 75% HOTEL

tel: 0141 240 3700 **99 Gordon Street G1 3SF**
email: grandcentralhotel@theprincipalhotel.com **web:** www.theprincipalhotel.com
dir: M8 junction 19 towards city centre, turn left at Hope Street. Hotel 200 metres on right.

This is the place where John Logie Baird transmitted the world's first long-distance television pictures in 1927, and this 'grand old lady' of the Glasgow hotel scene is appointed to a very good standard. The decor is a blend of contemporary, art deco and original Victorian styles. Bedrooms are well equipped and suit business travellers especially. There is Champagne Central, a glamorous bar, the Tempus Bar and Restaurant, and Deli Central (with direct access to the Central Station) which is an eat-in deli and a takeaway. Ample meeting facilities are available, and NCP car parks are nearby.

Rooms: 230 (15 family) ⬥ **S** fr £99 (including breakfast)* **Facilities:** FTV WiFi ⬙ New Year **Conf:** Class 336 Board 48 Theatre 400 **Services:** Lift Night porter **Notes:** Civ Wed 500

Holiday Inn Glasgow City Centre - Theatreland

★★★ 84% HOTEL

tel: 0141 352 8300 **161 West Nile Street G1 2RL**
email: reservations@higlasgow.com **web:** www.holidayinn.co.uk
dir: M8 junction 16, follow signs for Royal Concert Hall, hotel opposite.

Built on a corner site close to the Theatre Royal Concert Hall and the main shopping areas, this contemporary hotel features the popular La Bonne Auberge French restaurant, a bar area and conservatory. The bedrooms are well equipped and comfortable; suites are also available. The staff are friendly and attentive.

Rooms: 113 (20 family) (10 smoking) ⬥ **S** fr £80 **D** fr £80* **Facilities:** STV FTV WiFi ⬙ **Conf:** Class 60 Board 60 Theatre 100 **Services:** Lift Night porter Air con **Notes:** LB

Uplawmoor Hotel

THE CIRCLE

★★★ 79% SMALL HOTEL

tel: 01505 850565 **66 Neilston Road G78 4AF**
email: info@uplawmoor.co.uk **web:** www.uplawmoor.co.uk

(for full entry see Uplawmoor)

Novotel Glasgow Centre

NOVOTEL
HOTELS & RESORTS

★★★ 77% HOTEL

tel: 0141 222 2775 **181 Pitt Street G2 4DT**
email: H3136@accor.com **web:** www.novotel.com
dir: M8 junction 18 for Charing Cross. Follow to Sauchiehall Street. 3rd right.

Enjoying a convenient city centre location with only limited parking spaces, this hotel is ideal for both business and leisure travellers. Well-equipped bedrooms are brightly decorated and offer functional design. Modern public areas include a small fitness club and a lively bar serving a range of meals all day. The 'Virtual Concierge' system is available at reception – a great way to learn more about the city.

Rooms: 139 (139 family) **Facilities:** STV FTV WiFi Gym Sauna Steam room Xmas **Conf:** Class 20 Board 20 Theatre 40 **Services:** Lift Night porter Air con **Parking:** 19

Mercure Glasgow City Hotel

★★★ 75% HOTEL

tel: 0844 815 9103 (Calls cost 5p per minute plus your phone company's access charge) **201 Ingram Street G1 1DQ**
email: info@mercureglasgow.co.uk **web:** www.jupiterhotels.co.uk
dir: M8 junction 15, straight through 4 lights, left at 5th into Hanover Street, left into George Square, right into Frederick Street. Right at 2nd lights into Ingram Street.

This hotel enjoys a fantastic location in the heart of Glasgow with great access to shops, bars and restaurants. Bedrooms provide modern accommodation and a host of accessories including TVs and complimentary WiFi. Extensive conference facilities and the popular Bagio Café Bar mean you may not need to leave the hotel at all.

Rooms: 91 **Facilities:** New Year **Conf:** Class 40 Board 40 Theatre 80 **Services:** Lift Night porter **Parking:** 30 **Notes:** Civ Wed 80

Premier Inn Glasgow (Bearsden)

Premier Inn

BUDGET HOTEL

tel: 0871 527 8418 (Calls cost 13p per minute plus your phone company's access charge) **279 Milngavie Road G61 3DQ**
web: www.premierinn.com
dir: M8 junction 16, A81. Pass Asda on right. Hotel on left, behind The Burnbrae.

High quality, budget accommodation ideal for both families and business travellers. Spacious, en suite bedrooms feature free WiFi and tea and coffee making facilities, and in most hotels, Freeview TV is also available. The adjacent family restaurant features a wide and varied menu.

Rooms: 61

GLASGOW *continued*

Premier Inn Glasgow (Bellshill)

BUDGET HOTEL

tel: 0871 527 8421 (Calls cost 13p per minute plus your phone company's access charge) **New Edinburgh Road, Bellshill ML4 3PD**
web: www.premierinn.com
dir: *M74 junction 5, A725. Follow Bellshill A721 signs, bear left. At roundabout left, follow Tannochside sign. At next roundabout left into Bellziehill Road. Hotel on right.*

Rooms: 60

Premier Inn Glasgow Buchanan Galleries Hotel

BUDGET HOTEL

tel: 0871 527 9360 (Calls cost 13p per minute plus your phone company's access charge) **St Andrew House, 141 West Nile Street G1 2RN**
web: www.premierinn.com
dir: *Phone for directions.*

Rooms: 210

Premier Inn Glasgow (Cambuslang/M74 Jct 2A)

BUDGET HOTEL

tel: 0871 527 8422 (Calls cost 13p per minute plus your phone company's access charge) **Cambuslang Investment Park, Off London Road G32 8YX**
web: www.premierinn.com
dir: *At end of M74, turn right at roundabout. At 1st lights turn right, at 2nd lights straight ahead. Hotel on right.*

Rooms: 76

Premier Inn Glasgow City Centre Argyle St

BUDGET HOTEL

tel: 0871 527 8436 (Calls cost 13p per minute plus your phone company's access charge) & 0141 248 2355 **377 Argyle Street G2 8LL**
web: www.premierinn.com
dir: *From south: M8 junction 19, at pedestrian lights left into Argyle Street. Hotel 200 yards on right.*

Rooms: 124

Premier Inn Glasgow City Centre (Charing Cross)

BUDGET HOTEL

tel: 0871 527 8438 (Calls cost 13p per minute plus your phone company's access charge) **10 Elmbank Gardens G2 4PP**
web: www.premierinn.com
dir: *Phone for directions.*

Rooms: 278

Premier Inn Glasgow City Centre (George Square)

BUDGET HOTEL

tel: 0871 527 8440 (Calls cost 13p per minute plus your phone company's access charge) **187 George Street G1 1YU**
web: www.premierinn.com
dir: *M8 junction 15, into Stirling Road. Right into Cathedral Street. At 1st lights left into Montrose Street. Hotel after 1st lights.*

Rooms: 239

Premier Inn Glasgow City Centre South

BUDGET HOTEL

tel: 0871 527 8442 (Calls cost 13p per minute plus your phone company's access charge) **80 Ballater Street G5 0TW**
web: www.premierinn.com
dir: *M8 junction 21 follow East Kilbride signs, right onto A8 into Kingston Street. Right into South Portland Street, left into Norfolk Street, through Gorbals Street into Ballater Street.*

Rooms: 123

Premier Inn Glasgow East

BUDGET HOTEL

tel: 0871 527 8444 (Calls cost 13p per minute plus your phone company's access charge) **601 Hamilton Road, Uddington G71 7SA**
web: www.premierinn.com
dir: *At entrance to Glasgow Zoo, adjacent to junction 4 of M73 and M74.*

Rooms: 68

Premier Inn Glasgow Pacific Quay SECC

BUDGET HOTEL

tel: 0871 527 9340 (Calls cost 13p per minute plus your phone company's access charge) **Pacific Quay G51 1DZ**
web: www.premierinn.com
dir: *M8 junction 24, left into Helen Street, 2nd exit at roundabout, follow Glasgow Science Centre signs. Right into Govan Road. 1st exit at roundabout into Pacific Drive (pass Science Centre and BBC Scotland). Hotel on left.*

Rooms: 180

citizenM Glasgow

AA Advertised

tel: 020 3519 1111 **60 Renfrew Street G2 3BW**
email: supportgla@citizenm.com **web:** www.citizenm.com

Right in the heart of Glasgow, citizenM Glasgow is the height of urban, stylish, business-and-pleasure, boutique accommodation. From the '1 minute check in/out' promise to the new-media friendly meeting rooms and lobby, this is something different. The bedrooms are stylishly economical, making the most of limited space. They have super-sized beds, blackout blinds, free WiFi, ambient mood lighting, a rain shower and a wall-to-wall window above the bed. CanteenM serves breakfast, lunch and dinner, and offers a 24-hour bar.

Rooms: 198 **Facilities:** STV FTV WiFi

The Z Hotel Glasgow

AA Advertised

tel: 0141 212 4550 **36 North Frederick Street G1 2BS**
email: glasgow@thezhotels.com
dir: *0.1 mile from George Square.*

Stay in the heart of Glasgow for an out-of-town price, at Z Hotel Glasgow, a converted print works right next to George Square, with over 100 bedrooms arranged around a central lightwell over the ground and five upper floors. Each room has an en suite wet room, crisp bed linen, 40" TV with Sky channels, and complimentary WiFi.

Rooms: 104 (16 GF) ⭑ **Facilities:** STV FTV WiFi ⤵ **Services:** Lift Night porter Air con

GLASGOW AIRPORT
Renfrewshire   Map 20 NS46

Premier Inn Glasgow Airport

Premier Inn 🌙

BUDGET HOTEL

tel: 0871 527 8434 (Calls cost 13p per minute plus your phone company's access charge) **Whitecart Road, Glasgow Airport PA3 2TH**
web: www.premierinn.com
dir: *M8 junction 28, follow airport signs for Long Stay and Car Park 3 (Premier Inn signed). At 1st roundabout right into St Andrews Drive. At next roundabout right into Whitecart Road. Under motorway. Left at garage. Hotel on right.*

High quality, budget accommodation ideal for both families and business travellers. Spacious, en suite bedrooms feature free WiFi and tea and coffee making facilities, and in most hotels, Freeview TV is also available. The adjacent family restaurant features a wide and varied menu.

Rooms: 105

Premier Inn Glasgow (Paisley)

Premier Inn 🌙

BUDGET HOTEL

tel: 0871 527 8432 (Calls cost 13p per minute plus your phone company's access charge) **Phoenix Retail Park PA1 2BH**
web: www.premierinn.com
dir: *M8 junction 28a, A737 signed Irvine, take 1st exit signed Linwood, left at 1st roundabout to Phoenix Park.*

Rooms: 62

GLENEAGLES
See **Auchterarder**

GLENFINNAN
Highland   Map 22 NM98

The Prince's House

★★★ 82% ◉◉ SMALL HOTEL

tel: 01397 722246 **PH37 4LT**
email: princeshouse@glenfinnan.co.uk **web:** www.glenfinnan.co.uk
dir: *On A830, 0.5 mile on right past Glenfinnan Monument. 200 metres from railway station.*

This delightful hotel enjoys a well deserved reputation for fine food and excellent hospitality. The hotel has inspiring views and sits close to where 'Bonnie' Prince Charlie raised the Jacobite standard. Comfortably appointed bedrooms offer

pleasing decor. Excellent local game and seafood can be enjoyed in the restaurant and the bar.

Rooms: 9 ⭑ **S** fr £85 **D** fr £160 (including breakfast)* **Facilities:** STV FTV WiFi ⤵ New Year **Conf:** Class 20 Theatre 40 **Parking:** 18 **Notes:** LB Closed November, Christmas, January to February RS October, December and March

GLENROTHES
Fife   Map 21 NO20

Premier Inn Glenrothes

Premier Inn 🌙

BUDGET HOTEL

tel: 0871 527 8454 (Calls cost 13p per minute plus your phone company's access charge) **Beaufort Drive, Bankhead Roundabout KY7 4UJ**
web: www.premierinn.com
dir: *M90 junction 2a northbound, A92 to Glenrothes. At 2nd roundabout (Bankhead) take 3rd exit. Hotel on left.*

Rooms: 65

GRANGEMOUTH
Falkirk   Map 21 NS98

The Grange Manor

★★★★ 79% HOTEL

tel: 01324 474836 **Glensburgh FK3 8XJ**
email: info@grangemanor.co.uk **web:** www.grangemanor.co.uk
dir: *From east: M9 junction 6, hotel 200 metres to right. From west: M9 junction 5, A905 for 2 miles.*

Located south of town and close to the M9, this stylish hotel, popular with business and corporate clientele, benefits from hands-on family ownership. It offers spacious, high quality accommodation with superb bathrooms. Public areas include a comfortable foyer area, a lounge bar and a smart restaurant. Cook's Bar & Kitchen is adjacent to the main house in the converted stables. Staff throughout are very friendly.

Rooms: 36 (30 annexe) (6 family) (15 GF) **Facilities:** FTV WiFi Xmas New Year **Conf:** Class 68 Board 40 Theatre 120 **Services:** Lift Night porter **Parking:** 154 **Notes:** Civ Wed 120

GRANTOWN-ON-SPEY
Highland   Map 23 NJ02

Grant Arms Hotel

★★★ 84% HOTEL

tel: 01479 872526 **25-27 The Square PH26 3HF**
email: info@grantarmshotel.com **web:** www.grantarmshotel.com
dir: *Exit A9 north of Aviemore onto A95.*

Conveniently located in the centre of the town, this fine hotel is appointed to a high standard yet still retains the building's traditional character. The spacious bedrooms are stylishly presented and very well equipped. The restaurant is a popular venue for dinner, and lighter snacks can be enjoyed in the comfortable bar. Modern conference facilities are available and the hotel is very popular with birdwatchers and wildlife enthusiasts.

Rooms: 50 (7 family) ⭑ **Facilities:** STV FTV WiFi ⤵ Birdwatching and wildlife club 🎵 Xmas New Year **Conf:** Class 30 Board 16 Theatre 70 **Services:** Lift Night porter **Notes:** LB

G

GREENOCK
Inverclyde
Map 20 NS27

Premier Inn Greenock

Premier Inn

BUDGET HOTEL

tel: 0871 527 8476 (Calls cost 13p per minute plus your phone company's access charge) **The Point, 1-3 James Watt Way PA15 2AD**
web: www.premierinn.com
dir: *A8 to Greenock. At roundabout junction of East Hamilton Street and Main Street (McDonalds visable on right) take 3rd exit. Hotel on left.*

High quality, budget accommodation ideal for both families and business travellers. Spacious, en suite bedrooms feature free WiFi and tea and coffee making facilities, and in most hotels, Freeview TV is also available. The adjacent family restaurant features a wide and varied menu.

Rooms: 62

GRETNA GREEN SERVICE AREA (A74)
Dumfries & Galloway
Map 21 NY36

Days Inn Gretna Green - M74

WELCOMEBREAK

AA Advertised

tel: 01461 337566 **Welcome Break Service Area DG16 5HQ**
email: gretna.hotel@welcomebreak.co.uk **web:** www.welcomebreak.co.uk
dir: *Between junction 21 and 22 of A74(M), accessible from both northbound and southbound carriageways.*

This modern building offers accommodation in smart, spacious and well-equipped bedrooms suitable for families and business travellers, and all with en suite bathrooms. Continental breakfast is available and other refreshments may be taken at the nearby family restaurant.

Rooms: 64 (54 family) (64 GF) **Facilities:** FTV WiFi ↳ Xmas New Year **Parking:** 60

GRETNA (WITH GRETNA GREEN)
Dumfries & Galloway
Map 21 NY36

Smiths at Gretna Green

★★★★ 80% HOTEL

tel: 01461 337007 **Gretna Green DG16 5EA**
email: info@smithsgretnagreen.com **web:** www.smithsgretnagreen.com
dir: *From M74 junction 22 follow signs to Old Blacksmith's Shop. Hotel opposite.*

Located next to the World Famous Old Blacksmith's Shop Centre just off the motorway linking Scotland and England. The bedrooms offer a spacious environment, complete with TVs, DVD players and broadband. Family rooms feature a separate children's area with bunk beds, each with its own TV. Three suites and a penthouse apartment are also available. Open-plan contemporary day rooms lead to the brasserie restaurant; impressive conference and banqueting facilities are provided.

Rooms: 56 (6 annexe) (8 family) ☏ S fr £90 **D** fr £100 (including breakfast)*
Facilities: STV FTV WiFi ↳ HL Beauty treatment room New Year **Conf:** Class 100 Board 40 Theatre 250 **Services:** Lift Night porter Air con **Parking:** 115
Notes: Civ Wed 150

GULLANE
East Lothian
Map 21 NT48

Greywalls and Chez Roux

★★★★★ 83%  COUNTRY HOUSE HOTEL

tel: 01620 842144 **Muirfield EH31 2EG**
email: enquiries@greywalls.co.uk **web:** www.greywalls.co.uk
dir: *From Edinburgh follow A1, junction for North Berwick A198 then Gullane. Greywalls is at the end of village on left.*

Located in the magnificent East Lothian countryside, Greywalls is just half an hour's drive from Edinburgh, and is located beside the world-famous Muirfield golf course. The hotel offers easy access to some wonderful beaches and there are 10 golf courses within five miles. In the grounds are delightful gardens, and you may be lucky enough to see the beekeeper tending the hives. Inside, public areas are warm and welcoming with an array of seating areas and open fires adding to the charm. Bedrooms are well appointed in keeping with the style and character of the house. Award-winning food from the Chez Roux team is well worth staying in for, while the hearty breakfast will set you up for the day.

Rooms: 23 (6 annexe) (5 GF) ☏ **S** fr £93.50 **D** fr £269.50 (including breakfast)*
Facilities: FTV WiFi ↳ Holistic massage Walled gardens Golf retreats ♫ Xmas New Year **Conf:** Class 18 Board 18 Theatre 60 **Services:** Night porter **Parking:** 40
Notes: Civ Wed 120

INVERARAY
Argyll & Bute
Map 20 NN00

Loch Fyne Hotel & Spa

CRERAR

★★★★ 78%  HOTEL

tel: 01499 302980 **Shore Street PA32 8XT**
email: lochfyne@crerarhotels.com **web:** www.crerarhotels.com/loch-fyne-hotel-spa
dir: *From A83 Loch Lomond, through town centre on A80 to Lochgilphead. Hotel in 0.5 mile on the right, overlooking Loch Fyne.*

Loch Fyne Hotel & Spa is situated in a stunning location with uninterrupted views across the loch and the surrounding landscape; it is just a short drive from the shops and places of interest in Inveraray. Public areas include the Clansman Restaurant where excellent seafood can be enjoyed and a large lounge bar with comfy sofas. The bedrooms are modern and well equipped; some have views of the loch.

Rooms: 67 (9 family) (15 GF) ☏ S fr £175 **D** fr £195 (including breakfast)
Facilities: Spa FTV WiFi ↳ Sauna Steam room Xmas New Year **Conf:** Class 40 Board 25 Theatre 80 **Services:** Lift Night porter **Parking:** 60 **Notes:** LB Civ Wed 120

INVERGARRY	Map 22 NH30
Highland	

Glengarry Castle Hotel

★★★ 84% 🏅 COUNTRY HOUSE HOTEL

tel: 01809 501254 **PH35 4HW**
email: castle@glengarry.net **web:** www.glengarry.net
dir: On A82, 0.5 mile from A82/A87 junction.

This charming country house hotel is set in 50 acres of grounds on the shores of Loch Oich. The spacious day rooms include comfortable sitting rooms with lots to read and board games to play. The classical dining room boasts an innovative menu that showcases local Scottish produce. The smart bedrooms vary in size and style but all boast magnificent loch or woodland views. The grounds are well worth exploring, with a tennis court and paths along the loch to discover.

Rooms: 26 (2 family) 🐾 **Facilities:** FTV WiFi 🎣 Fishing **Parking:** 30 **Notes:** Closed mid November to mid March

INVERGORDON	Map 23 NH76
Highland	

Kincraig Castle Hotel

★★★★ 80% 🏅 COUNTRY HOUSE HOTEL

tel: 01349 852587 **IV18 0LF**
email: info@kincraig-castle-hotel.co.uk **web:** www.kincraig-castle-hotel.co.uk
dir: Off A9 past Alness towards Tain. Hotel on left 0.25 mile past Rosskeen Church.

This imposing castle is set in well-tended grounds in an elevated position with views over the Cromarty Firth. It offers smart, individually designed, well-equipped bedrooms with satellite TVs, and inviting public areas that retain original features. However, it is the friendly service and commitment to guest care that will leave a lasting impression.

Rooms: 15 (1 family) (1 GF) 🐾 **Facilities:** FTV WiFi ⌨ ⚓ 4 🏌 Xmas New Year **Conf:** Class 30 Board 40 Theatre 50 **Services:** Night porter **Parking:** 40 **Notes:** LB Civ Wed 70

INVERNESS	Map 23 NH64
Highland	

Rocpool Reserve and Chez Roux

★★★★★ 82% 🏅🏅 🍴 SMALL HOTEL

tel: 01463 240089 **14 Culduthel Road IV2 4AG**
email: info@rocpool.com **web:** www.rocpool.com
dir: A9 to Inverness, take exit for Raigmore Hospital then follow signs for city centre. Left at lights into Southside Road, right into Culduthel Road.

This luxury hotel enjoys a great location in a residential area close to the city centre. A high level of personal service is offered, and bedrooms provide comfort and quality. The stylish R Bar is the perfect location for a cocktail and their Chez Roux Restaurant (operated by Albert Roux) provides memorable food in a modern space. Some rooms have personal outdoor hot tubs.

Rooms: 11 (2 GF) 🐾 **S** fr £225 **D** fr £270 (including breakfast)* **Facilities:** FTV WiFi ⌨ **Conf:** Class 16 Board 18 Theatre 20 **Services:** Night porter Air con **Parking:** 14 **Notes:** Civ Wed 20

Loch Ness Country House Hotel

★★★★ 79% 🏅🏅 SMALL HOTEL

tel: 01463 230512 **Loch Ness Road IV3 8JN**
email: info@lochnesscountryhousehotel.co.uk **web:** www.lochnesscountryhousehotel.co.uk
dir: On A82, 1 mile from Inverness.

Built in the Georgian era, this fine house is perfectly situated in its own six acre private Highland estate. The hotel has luxurious bedrooms, four of which are in the garden suite cottages. The stylish restaurant serves the best local produce, and guests have a choice of cosy well-appointed lounges for after-dinner drinks. The terrace is ideal for relaxation and has splendid views over the landscaped gardens towards Inverness.

Rooms: 13 (2 annexe) (8 family) (3 GF) **Facilities:** FTV WiFi Xmas New Year **Conf:** Class 40 Board 40 Theatre 100 **Services:** Night porter **Parking:** 70 **Notes:** LB Civ Wed 150

The New Drumossie Hotel

★★★★ 78% 🏅🏅 HOTEL

MACDONALD
HOTELS & RESORTS

tel: 01463 236451 & 0870 194 2110 (Calls cost 13p per minute plus your phone company's access charge) **Old Perth Road IV2 5BE**
email: stay@drumossiehotel.co.uk **web:** www.drumossiehotel.co.uk
dir: From A9 follow signs for Culloden Battlefield, hotel on left after 1 mile.

Set in nine acres of landscaped, hillside grounds south of Inverness, this hotel has fine views of the Moray Firth towards Ben Wyvis. Art deco-style decoration together with a country-house atmosphere are found throughout. Service is friendly and attentive, the food imaginative and enjoyable, and the bedrooms spacious and well presented. The main function room is probably the largest in this area.

Rooms: 44 (10 family) (6 GF) 🐾 **Facilities:** STV FTV WiFi HL Fishing New Year **Conf:** Class 200 Board 40 Theatre 500 **Services:** Lift Night porter **Parking:** 200 **Notes:** Civ Wed 400

I

INVERNESS *continued*

Bunchrew House Hotel

★★★★ 76% @@ COUNTRY HOUSE HOTEL

tel: 01463 234917 **Bunchrew IV3 8TA**
email: welcome@bunchrewhousehotel.com **web:** www.bunchrewhousehotel.com
dir: *West on A862. Hotel 2 miles after canal on right.*

Overlooking Beauly Firth, this impressive mansion house dates from the 17th century and retains much original character. Individually styled bedrooms are spacious and tastefully furnished. A wood-panelled restaurant is the setting for artfully constructed dishes and there is a choice of comfortable lounges complete with real fires.

Rooms: 16 (4 family) (1 GF) S fr £95 **D** fr £95 (including breakfast) **Facilities:** FTV WiFi Fishing New Year **Conf:** Class 30 Board 30 Theatre 80 **Services:** Night porter **Parking:** 40 **Notes:** LB Civ Wed 92

Glenmoriston Town House Hotel

★★★★ 76% @ TOWN HOUSE HOTEL

tel: 01463 223777 **20 Ness Bank IV2 4SF**
email: reception@glenmoristontownhouse.com **web:** www.glenmoristontownhouse.com
dir: *On river opposite theatre.*

Bold contemporary designs blend seamlessly with the classical architecture of this stylish hotel which is situated on the banks of the River Ness. Delightful day rooms include a well-stocked piano bar with a fine selection of malt whiskies and an interesting cocktail menu. Contrast Brasserie features accomplished modern cooking based on the finest Scottish produce. When the weather allows, alfresco eating is possible with views over the River Ness. The sleek, modern, individually designed bedrooms have many facilities including free WiFi and DVD players.

Rooms: 30 (15 annexe) (1 family) (6 GF) S fr £60 **D** fr £70 (including breakfast)*
Facilities: STV FTV WiFi Xmas New Year **Conf:** Class 40 Board 60 Theatre 90 **Services:** Night porter **Parking:** 40 **Notes:** LB Civ Wed 70

Mercure Inverness Hotel

★★★★ 71% HOTEL

tel: 0844 815 9006 (Calls cost 7p per minute plus your phone company's access charge)
Church Street IV1 1DX
email: info@mercureinverness.co.uk **web:** www.mercureinverness.co.uk
dir: *From A9 junction A82 Kessock Bridge join A82 Inverness. At roundabout 2nd exit, next roundabout straight ahead, then at roundabout left onto B865. Right at lights continue past church, hotel on left.*

The Mercure Inverness Hotel is in an ideal location, with the bustling city centre to one side and the attractive River Ness on the other. Spacious public areas, an inviting gym area and comfortable bedrooms can all be found here. The Brasserie serves a wide-ranging selection of dishes. On-site parking and complimentary WiFi are also provided.

Rooms: 118 **Facilities:** FTV WiFi Gym 24 hour gym **Conf:** Class 130 Board 90 Theatre 200 **Services:** Lift Night porter **Parking:** 55 **Notes:** Civ Wed 200

Best Western Inverness Palace Hotel & Spa

★★★ 80% HOTEL

tel: 01463 223243 **8 Ness Walk IV3 5NG**
email: palace@miltonhotels.com **web:** www.invernesspalacehotel.co.uk
dir: *A82 Glenurquhart Road onto Ness Walk. Hotel 300 yards on right opposite Inverness Castle.*

Set on the north side of the River Ness close to the Eden Court theatre and a short walk from the town, this hotel has a contemporary look. The bedrooms are comfortable and modern, while public areas feature Matthew Algie freshly ground coffee and extensive leisure facilities. Dogs can be accommodated on request for a nightly fee – contact the hotel for further details.

Rooms: 109 (3 family) **Facilities:** Spa FTV WiFi Gym Beautician Sauna Steam room Xmas New Year **Conf:** Class 40 Board 30 Theatre 80 **Services:** Lift Night porter **Parking:** 18

Royal Highland Hotel

★★★ 77% HOTEL

tel: 01463 231926 **Station Square, Academy Street IV1 1LG**
email: info@royalhighlandhotel.co.uk **web:** www.royalhighlandhotel.co.uk
dir: *From A9 into town centre. Hotel next to rail station and Eastgate Retail Centre.*

Built in 1858 adjacent to the railway station, the Royal Highland Hotel has a typically grand Victorian foyer with comfortable seating. The contemporary ASH Brasserie and bar is a refreshing venue for both eating and drinking throughout the day. The generally spacious bedrooms are comfortably equipped especially for the business traveller. An art gallery showcases an impressive array of artwork.

Rooms: 86 (12 family) (2 GF) (10 smoking) **Facilities:** FTV WiFi Xmas New Year **Conf:** Class 80 Board 80 Theatre 200 **Services:** Lift Night porter **Parking:** 8 **Notes:** LB Civ Wed 200

Glen Mhor Hotel

★★★ 76% HOTEL

tel: 01463 234 308 **7-17 Ness Bank IV2 4SG**
email: manager@glen-mhor.com **web:** www.glen-mhor.com
dir: *Follow signs for city centre, Hotel underneath the castle on Ness Bank.*

This collection of Victorian townhouses and apartments is all stunningly located on the banks of the River Ness, in close proximity to central Inverness. The bedrooms cater for all leisure and business requirements – from single bedrooms for those on a modest budget to stunning suites with river views. Nicky Tam's Restaurant & Bar offers guests traditional Scottish meals with a twist. Spacious parking is available.

Rooms: 85 **S** fr £49 **D** fr £79* **Facilities:** WiFi New Year **Conf:** Class 50 Board 40 Theatre 80 **Notes:** Civ Wed 100

Premier Inn Inverness Centre (Milburn Rd)

Premier Inn

BUDGET HOTEL

tel: 0871 527 8544 (Calls cost 13p per minute plus your phone company's access charge) **Millburn Road IV2 3QX**
web: www.premierinn.com
dir: *From A9 and A96 junction (Raigmore Interchange, signed Airport/Aberdeen), take B865 towards town centre, hotel 100 yards after next roundabout.*

High quality, budget accommodation ideal for both families and business travellers. Spacious, en suite bedrooms feature free WiFi and tea and coffee making facilities, and in most hotels, Freeview TV is also available. The adjacent family restaurant features a wide and varied menu.

Rooms: 55

Premier Inn Inverness Centre (River Ness)

Premier Inn

BUDGET HOTEL

tel: 0871 527 9302 (Calls cost 13p per minute plus your phone company's access charge) **19-21 Huntly Street IV3 5PR**
web: www.premierinn.com
dir: *Exit A9 at Longman roundabout, 1st exit into Longman Road (A82) follow Inverness/Fort William signs. Straight on at 3 roundabouts. At Telford Street roundabout 1st exit into Wells Street. Right into Huntly Street. Hotel on right.*

Rooms: 99

Premier Inn Inverness East

Premier Inn

BUDGET HOTEL

tel: 0871 527 8546 (Calls cost 13p per minute plus your phone company's access charge) **Beechwood Business Park IV2 3BW**
web: www.premierinn.com
dir: *From A9 follow Raigmore Hospital, Police Headquarters and Inshes Retail Park signs.*

Rooms: 74

Premier Inn Inverness West

Premier Inn

BUDGET HOTEL

tel: 0871 527 9338 (Calls cost 13p per minute plus your phone company's access charge) **Glenurquhart Road IV3 5TD**
web: www.premierinn.com
dir: *From A9 exit at Kessock roundabout. At 4th roundabout 2nd exit into Kenneth Street. Right at lights into Glenurquhart Road, pass council offices, 1 mile, take A82 signed Fort William. Cross Caledonian Canal Bridge. Hotel on right.*

Rooms: 76

Find out more

about the AA Hotel of the Year for Scotland on page 17

INVERURIE	Map 23 NJ72
Aberdeenshire	

Macdonald Pittodrie House

 MACDONALD HOTELS & RESORTS

★★★★ 79% ◉◉ HOTEL

tel: 0121 643 9191 **Chapel of Garioch, Pitcaple AB51 5HS**
email: gm.pittodrie@macdonald-hotels.co.uk **web:** www.macdonald-hotels.com/pittodrie
dir: *From A96 towards Inverness, pass Inverurie under bridge with lights. Turn left and follow signs.*

Set in extensive grounds, this house dates from the 15th century and retains many historic features. Public rooms include a gracious drawing room, a restaurant and a cosy bar boasting an impressive selection of whiskies. The well-proportioned bedrooms are found in both the original house and in the extension that was designed to match the existing building.

Rooms: 27 (6 family) **Facilities:** STV FTV WiFi Clay pigeon shooting Quad biking Outdoor activities Xmas New Year **Conf:** Class 75 Board 50 Theatre 150 **Services:** Night porter **Parking:** 200 **Notes:** Civ Wed 120

IRVINE	Map 20 NS33
North Ayrshire	

Riverside Lodge Hotel

★★★★ 71% HOTEL

tel: 01294 279274 **46 Annick Road KA11 4LD**
email: frank.long@riversidelodgehotel.co.uk **web:** www.riversidelodgehotel.co.uk
dir: *From A78 at Warrix Interchange follow Irvine Central signs. At roundabout 2nd exit (town centre). At next roundabout right onto A71/Kilmarnock. Hotel 100 metres on left.*

Situated on the edge of Irvine with good transportation links (including Prestwick Airport just seven miles away), this is a well-presented hotel that has an extremely friendly team with good customer care awareness. The decor is contemporary throughout, and there is a brasserie-style restaurant, cocktail bar and spacious lounge.

Rooms: 128 (14 family) (64 GF) **Facilities:** STV FTV WiFi ⌖ Fishing Xmas New Year **Conf:** Class 140 Board 100 Theatre 280 **Services:** Night porter **Parking:** 180 **Notes:** Civ Wed 200

KELSO	Map 21 NT73
Scottish Borders	

Ednam House Hotel

★★★ 79% ◉ COUNTRY HOUSE HOTEL

tel: 01573 224168 **Bridge Street TD5 7HT**
email: contact@ednamhouse.com **web:** www.ednamhouse.com
dir: *Phone for directions.*

Ednam House was built in 1761 'with no expense spared' for a local with a rags-to-riches story. From the unassuming entrance in the town centre, guests will find that once inside the hotel there are majestic views of the Tweed from the public areas, restaurant and a good number of bedrooms. The hotel continues to undergo a rolling refurbishment programme which is revealing very good results. The public areas certainly have a wow factor with many of the original features still clearly evident. The team here provide warm Borders hospitality. There is a choice of menus in the bar lounge and river-view restaurant.

Rooms: 33 ⌖ **S** fr £69 **D** fr £120 (including breakfast)* **Facilities:** FTV WiFi ⌖ Xmas New Year **Conf:** Class 80 Board 70 Theatre 150 **Services:** Night porter **Parking:** 30 **Notes:** LB Civ Wed 140

K

KILCHRENAN
Argyll & Bute

Map 20 NN02

HIGHLY RECOMMENDED

Taychreggan Hotel

★★★ 87% ◉◉ COUNTRY HOUSE HOTEL

tel: 01866 833211 **PA35 1HQ**
email: info@taychregganhotel.co.uk **web:** www.taychregganhotel.co.uk
dir: *West from Crianlarich on A85 to Taynuilt, south for 7 miles on B845 (single track) to Kilchrenan.*

Surrounded by stunning Highland scenery, this stylish and superbly presented hotel, once a drover's cottage, enjoys an idyllic setting in 40 acres of wooded grounds on the shores of Loch Awe. The hotel has a smart bar with adjacent courtyard Orangerie and a choice of quiet lounges with deep, luxurious sofas. A well-earned reputation has been achieved by the kitchen for the skilfully prepared dinners that showcase the local and seasonal Scottish larder. Families, and also dogs and their owners, are welcome.

Rooms: 18 (1 family) **Facilities:** FTV WiFi Fishing Air rifle range Archery Clay pigeon shooting Falconry Mock deer stalk Xmas New Year **Conf:** Class 15 Board 20 **Parking:** 40 **Notes:** Closed 3 January to 9 February Civ Wed 70

KILLIECRANKIE
Perth & Kinross

Map 23 NN96

INSPECTOR'S CHOICE

Killiecrankie Hotel

★★★ ◉◉ SMALL HOTEL

tel: 01796 473220 **PH16 5LG**
email: enquiries@killiecrankiehotel.co.uk **web:** www.killiecrankiehotel.co.uk
dir: *Exit A9 at Killiecrankie onto B8079. Hotel 3 miles on right.*

Originally built in the 1840s, Killiecrankie sits in four acres of wooded grounds with beautifully landscaped gardens; it enjoys a tranquil location by the Pass of Killiecrankie and the River Garry. Public areas include a wood-panelled bar and a cosy sitting room with original artwork, and a blazing fire in colder months. All the bedrooms are individually decorated, well equipped and have wonderful countryside views.

Rooms: 10 (2 GF) **S** fr £160 **D** fr £280 (including breakfast & dinner)*
Facilities: FTV WiFi Xmas New Year **Parking:** 20 **Notes:** Closed 3 January to 22 March

KILMARNOCK
East Ayrshire

Map 20 NS43

The Fenwick Hotel

★★★ 80% HOTEL

tel: 01560 600478 **Fenwick KA3 6AU**
email: info@thefenwickhotel.co.uk **web:** www.thefenwickhotel.co.uk
dir: *M77 junction 8, B7061 towards Fenwick, follow hotel signs.*

The Fenwick Hotel benefits from a great location alongside the M77, with easy links to Ayr, Kilmarnock and Glasgow. The spacious bedrooms are thoughtfully equipped; complimentary WiFi is available throughout the hotel. The bright restaurant offers both formal and informal dining and there is an attractive lounge bar where you can relax and choose from the extensive cocktail list. The hotel also has extensive conference and function facilities.

Rooms: 29 (2 family) (9 GF) **S** fr £65 **D** fr £75 (including breakfast)*
Facilities: STV FTV WiFi Xmas New Year **Conf:** Class 280 Board 150 Theatre 280
Services: Lift Night porter **Parking:** 64 **Notes:** Civ Wed 275

Premier Inn Kilmarnock

Premier Inn

BUDGET HOTEL

tel: 0871 527 8566 (Calls cost 13p per minute plus your phone company's access charge) **Moorfield Roundabout, Annadale KA1 2RS**
web: www.premierinn.com
dir: *M74 junction 8 signed Kilmarnock (A71). From M77 onto A71 to Irvine. At next roundabout right onto B7064 signed Crosshouse Hospital. Hotel on right.*

High quality, budget accommodation ideal for both families and business travellers. Spacious, en suite bedrooms feature free WiFi and tea and coffee making facilities, and in most hotels, Freeview TV is also available. The adjacent family restaurant features a wide and varied menu.

Rooms: 64

KINCARDINE
Fife

Map 21 NS98

Premier Inn Falkirk North

Premier Inn

BUDGET HOTEL

tel: 0871 527 8394 (Calls cost 13p per minute plus your phone company's access charge) **Bowtrees Roundabout, Houghs of Airth FK2 8PJ**
web: www.premierinn.com
dir: *From north: M9 junction 7 (or from south: M876) towards Kincardine Bridge. On roundabout at end of slip road.*

Rooms: 66

KINCLAVEN
Perth & Kinross   Map 21 NO13

Ballathie House Hotel
★★★★ 79% ◉◉ COUNTRY HOUSE HOTEL

tel: 01250 883268 **PH1 4QN**
email: email@ballathiehousehotel.com **web:** www.ballathiehousehotel.com
dir: *From A9, 2 miles north of Perth, take B9099 through Stanley, follow signs. Or from A93 at Beech Hedge follow signs for hotel, 2.5 miles.*

Set in delightful grounds, this splendid Scottish mansion house combines classical grandeur with modern comfort. Bedrooms range from well-proportioned master rooms to modern standard rooms, and many boast antique furniture and art deco bathrooms. It might be worth requesting one of the Riverside Rooms, a purpose-built development right on the banks of the river, complete with balconies and terraces. The elegant restaurant has views over the River Tay.

Rooms: 41 (16 annexe) (2 family) (10 GF) ☔ **Facilities:** FTV WiFi Fishing ⛵ Xmas New Year **Conf:** Class 20 Board 30 Theatre 50 **Services:** Lift Night porter **Parking:** 50 **Notes:** Civ Wed 90

KIRKCALDY
Fife   Map 21 NT29

Dean Park Hotel
★★★ 77% HOTEL

tel: 01592 261635 **Chapel Level KY2 6QW**
email: reception@deanparkhotel.co.uk **web:** www.deanparkhotel.co.uk
dir: *Signed from A92 Kirkcaldy West junction.*

Popular with both business and leisure guests, this hotel has extensive conference and meeting facilities. The bedrooms are spacious, comfortable, well equipped and enjoy modern decor and up-to-date amenities. Public areas include the Dukes Bar, and Grill Room Restaurant which is well-known for its steaks.

Rooms: 33 (2 family) (5 GF) ☔ **Facilities:** STV FTV WiFi Xmas New Year **Conf:** Class 125 Board 54 Theatre 250 **Services:** Lift Night porter **Parking:** 250 **Notes:** LB Civ Wed 200

LANARK
South Lanarkshire   Map 21 NS84

Best Western Cartland Bridge Hotel
BW Best Western.
★★★ 75% COUNTRY HOUSE HOTEL

tel: 01555 664426 **Glasgow Road ML11 9UF**
email: sales@cartlandbridge.co.uk **web:** www.bw-cartlandbridgehotel.co.uk
dir: *A73 through Lanark towards Carluke. Hotel in 1.25 miles.*

Situated in wooded grounds on the edge of the town, this Grade I listed mansion continues to be popular with both business and leisure guests. Public areas feature wood panelling, a gallery staircase and a magnificent dining room. The well-equipped bedrooms vary in size. The hotel has an interesting history and even claims to have a ghost.

Rooms: 18 (4 family) ☔ **Facilities:** FTV WiFi Xmas New Year **Conf:** Class 180 Board 50 Theatre 250 **Services:** Night porter **Parking:** 120 **Notes:** Civ Wed 200

LIVINGSTON
West Lothian   Map 21 NT06

Mercure Livingston Hotel
★★★ 78% HOTEL

tel: 0844 815 9102 (Calls cost 5p per minute plus your phone company's access charge) **Almondview EH54 6QB**
email: info@mercurelivingston.co.uk **web:** www.mercurelivingston.co.uk
dir: *From M8 junction 3 take A899 towards Livingston, exit at Centre Interchange, left at next roundabout, hotel on left.*

This large, modern hotel is conveniently located in the town centre with easy access to the M8. Bedrooms offer good space and are comfortably appointed for both business and leisure guests. There is a large open-plan lobby and restaurant area; complimentary WiFi is available throughout, and there is also a small but well-appointed leisure club.

Rooms: 120 (17 family) (55 GF) **Facilities:** FTV WiFi ⌨ HL ⟲ Gym Sauna Steam room New Year **Conf:** Class 55 Board 60 Theatre 130 **Services:** Night porter **Parking:** 130 **Notes:** Civ Wed 120

Premier Inn Livingston M8 Jct 3
Premier Inn
BUDGET HOTEL

tel: 0871 527 8632 (Calls cost 13p per minute plus your phone company's access charge) **Deer Park Avenue, Deer Park EH54 8AD**
web: www.premierinn.com
dir: *At M8 junction 3. Hotel opposite roundabout.*

High quality, budget accommodation ideal for both families and business travellers. Spacious, en suite bedrooms feature free WiFi and tea and coffee making facilities, and in most hotels, Freeview TV is also available. The adjacent family restaurant features a wide and varied menu.

Rooms: 107

LOCHINVER
Highland   Map 22 NC02

Inver Lodge and Chez Roux

★★★★★ 83% ◉◉ HOTEL

tel: 01571 844496 **Iolaire Road IV27 4LU**
email: stay@inverlodge.com **web:** www.inverlodge.com
dir: *A837 to Lochinver, through village, left after village hall, follow private road for 0.5 mile.*

Genuine hospitality can be expected at this delightful, purpose-built hotel. Set high on the hillside above the village, the hotel and the grounds have stunning views over Loch Inver and the Western Isles. There is a choice of lounges, and the award-winning restaurant is under the direction of Albert Roux — his chefs make excellent use of the abundant local produce. The stylish bedrooms are spacious and come with an impressive range of accessories. Inver Lodge is a popular wedding venue. There's plenty of secure parking at the rear of the property.

Rooms: 21 (11 GF) ☔ **S** fr £190 **D** fr £290 (including breakfast)* **Facilities:** FTV WiFi ⌨ Fishing **Parking:** 21 **Notes:** LB Closed November to March

L

LOCKERBIE
Map 21 NY18
Dumfries & Galloway

Kings Arms Hotel

★★ 77% HOTEL

tel: 01576 202410 **High Street DG11 2JL**
email: reception@kingsarmshotel.co.uk **web:** www.kingsarmshotel.co.uk
dir: A74(M), 0.5 mile into town centre, hotel opposite town hall.

Dating from the 17th century, this former inn lies in the town centre. Now a family-run hotel, it provides attractive well-equipped bedrooms with WiFi access. At lunch, a menu ranging from snacks to full meals is served in both the cosy bars and the restaurant at dinner.

Rooms: 13 (2 family) ☎ **S** fr £60 **D** fr £90 (including breakfast)* **Facilities:** FTV WiFi Xmas New Year **Conf:** Class 40 Board 30 Theatre 80 **Parking:** 8

LUSS
Map 20 NS39
Argyll & Bute

The Lodge on Loch Lomond

★★★★ 79% ◉◉ HOTEL

tel: 01436 860201 **G83 8PA**
email: res@loch-lomond.co.uk **web:** www.loch-lomond.co.uk
dir: Off A82, follow sign for hotel.

This hotel is idyllically set on the shores of Loch Lomond. Public areas consist of an open-plan, split-level bar and fine dining restaurant overlooking the loch. The pine-finished bedrooms also enjoy these views and are comfortable, spacious and well equipped; some have saunas, and all have internet access. There is a stunning state-of-the-art leisure suite.

Rooms: 48 (19 annexe) (20 family) (15 GF) ☎ **S** fr £184 **D** fr £194 (including breakfast)* **Facilities:** FTV WiFi ⊗ Fishing Boating Kayaks Canoes Paddleboards Wake boarding Water skies Xmas New Year **Conf:** Class 120 Board 80 Theatre 200 **Services:** Night porter **Parking:** 120 **Notes:** LB Civ Wed 170

MELROSE
Map 21 NT53
Scottish Borders

HIGHLY RECOMMENDED

Burts Hotel

★★★ 81% ◉◉ HOTEL

tel: 01896 822285 **Market Square TD6 9PL**
email: enquiries@burtshotel.co.uk **web:** www.burtshotel.co.uk
dir: A6091, 2 miles from A68, 3 miles south of Earlston.

Recognised by its distinctive black-and-white facade and colourful window boxes, in the heart of a small market town, this hotel has been under the same family ownership for some 40 years. The genuine warmth of hospitality is notable. The smart bedrooms have been individually styled and include WiFi. Food is important at Burts, and the elegant restaurant is well complemented by the range of tasty meals in the bar.

Rooms: 20 ☎ **S** fr £78 **D** fr £145 (including breakfast)* **Facilities:** STV FTV WiFi Salmon fishing Shooting New Year **Conf:** Class 20 Board 20 Theatre 38 **Parking:** 40 **Notes:** Closed 24–26 December, 17–21 February Civ Wed 30

MILNGAVIE
Map 20 NS57
East Dunbartonshire

Premier Inn Glasgow (Milngavie)

BUDGET HOTEL

tel: 0871 527 8428 (Calls cost 13p per minute plus your phone company's access charge) **103 Main Street G62 6JQ**
web: www.premierinn.com
dir: M8 junction 16, follow Milngavie (A879) signs. Approximately 5 miles. Pass Murray Park Training Ground. Left at lights. Hotel on A81 adjacent to West Highland Gate Beefeater.

High quality, budget accommodation ideal for both families and business travellers. Spacious, en suite bedrooms feature free WiFi and tea and coffee making facilities, and in most hotels, Freeview TV is also available. The adjacent family restaurant features a wide and varied menu.

Rooms: 61

MOTHERWELL
Map 21 NS75
North Lanarkshire

Alona Hotel

★★★★ 74% HOTEL

tel: 01698 333888 **Strathclyde Country Park ML1 3RT**
email: gm@alonahotel.co.uk **web:** www.alonahotel.co.uk
dir: M74 junction 5, hotel approximately 250 yards on left.

Alona is a Celtic word meaning 'exquisitely beautiful'. This hotel is situated within the idyllic beauty of Strathclyde Country Park, with tranquil views over the picturesque loch and surrounding forests. There is a very contemporary feel, from the open-plan public areas to the spacious and well-appointed bedrooms. WiFi is available throughout. M&D's, Scotland's Family Theme Park, is just next door.

Rooms: 51 (24 family) (17 GF) ☎ **Facilities:** FTV WiFi ↻ ♫ Xmas New Year **Conf:** Class 100 Board 76 Theatre 400 **Services:** Lift Night porter Air con **Parking:** 100 **Notes:** Civ Wed 250

Premier Inn Glasgow (Motherwell)

BUDGET HOTEL

tel: 0871 527 8430 (Calls cost 13p per minute plus your phone company's access charge) **Edinburgh Road, Newhouse ML1 5SY**
web: www.premierinn.com
dir: From south: M74 junction 5, A725 towards Coatbridge. Take A8 towards Edinburgh, exit at junction 6, follow Lanark signs. Hotel 400 yards on right.

Rooms: 60

NAIRN
Highland   Map 23 NH85

Golf View Hotel & Spa
★★★★ 77% @ HOTEL

tel: 01667 452301 **Seabank Road IV12 4HD**
email: golfview@crerarhotels.com **web:** www.crerarhotels.com
dir: Exit A96 into Seabank Road, hotel at end on right.

This northern gem has wonderful sea views overlooking the Moray Firth and the Black Isle beyond. The championship golf course at Nairn is adjacent and guests can wander directly onto the long sandy beach. Guest rooms are of a high standard, and the public areas welcoming. The hotel also offers an outdoor hot tub, indoor swimming pool, spa bath, gym and Elemis Spa treatments.

Rooms: 42 (6 family) **S** fr £100 **D** fr £120 (including breakfast)* **Facilities:** Spa FTV WiFi ⊕ ⎯ Gym Sauna Steam room Outdoor hot tub Xmas New Year **Conf:** Class 40 Board 40 Theatre 100 **Services:** Lift Night porter **Parking:** 40 **Notes:** Civ Wed 100

NETHY BRIDGE
Highland   Map 23 NJ02

Nethybridge Hotel
★★★ 70% HOTEL

tel: 01479 821203 **PH25 3DP**
email: salesnethybridge@strathmorehotels.com **web:** www.strathmorehotels.com
dir: A9 onto A95, onto B970 to Nethy Bridge.

This popular tourist and coaching hotel enjoys a central location amidst the majestic Cairngorm Mountains. Bedrooms are stylishly furnished in bold tartans while traditionally styled day rooms include two bars and a popular snooker room. Staff are friendly and keen to please.

Rooms: 70 (3 family) (7 GF) ⋔ **Facilities:** FTV WiFi Snooker ♪ Xmas New Year **Conf:** Board 50 Theatre 150 **Services:** Lift Night porter **Parking:** 80 **Notes:** LB Civ Wed 150

NEWTON MEARNS
East Renfrewshire   Map 20 NS55

Premier Inn Glasgow Newton Mearns (M77 Jct4)
Premier Inn 🌙

BUDGET HOTEL

tel: 0871 527 9304 (Calls cost 13p per minute plus your phone company's access charge) **Greenlaw Crookfur Road G77 6NP**
web: www.premierinn.com
dir: From north exit M77 junction 4 towards Newton Mearns. At roundabout 1st left. Hotel on left.

High quality, budget accommodation ideal for both families and business travellers. Spacious, en suite bedrooms feature free WiFi and tea and coffee making facilities, and in most hotels, Freeview TV is also available. The adjacent family restaurant features a wide and varied menu.

Rooms: 60

NEWTON STEWART
Dumfries & Galloway   Map 20 NX46

The Bruce Hotel
★★★ 69% HOTEL

tel: 01671 402294 **88 Queen Street DG8 6JL**
email: mail@the-bruce-hotel.com **web:** www.the-bruce-hotel.com
dir: Exit A75 at Newton Stewart roundabout towards town. Hotel 800 metres on right.

Named after the Scottish patriot Robert the Bruce, this welcoming hotel is just a short distance from the A75. One of the well-appointed bedrooms features a four-poster bed, and popular family suites contain separate bedrooms for children. Public areas include a traditional lounge, a formal restaurant and a lounge bar, both offering a good choice of dishes.

Rooms: 20 (2 family) **Facilities:** FTV WiFi New Year **Conf:** Class 50 Board 14 Theatre 100 **Services:** Night porter **Parking:** 14

NORTH BERWICK
East Lothian   Map 21 NT58

Macdonald Marine Hotel & Spa
MACDONALD
HOTELS & RESORTS

★★★★ 81% @@ HOTEL

tel: 01620 897300 **Cromwell Road EH39 4LZ**
email: sales.marine@macdonald-hotels.co.uk **web:** www.macdonaldhotels.co.uk/marine
dir: From A198 turn into Hamilton Road at lights then 2nd right.

This imposing hotel commands stunning views across a golf course to the Firth of Forth. Stylish public areas provide a relaxing atmosphere; creative dishes are served in the restaurant and lighter bites in the lounge/bar. Bedrooms come in a variety of sizes and styles; all are well equipped and some are impressively large. The hotel boasts extensive leisure and conference facilities.

Rooms: 83 (7 family) (9 GF) ⋔ **Facilities:** Spa STV FTV WiFi ⌕ ⊕ ⁀ Gym Indoor and outdoor Hydropool Thermal areas Xmas New Year **Conf:** Class 120 Board 60 Theatre 300 **Services:** Lift Night porter **Parking:** 50 **Notes:** Civ Wed 150

N

OBAN
OBAN	Map 20 NM82
Argyll & Bute	

HIGHLY RECOMMENDED

Manor House Hotel

★★★ 86% ◉◉ HOTEL

tel: 01631 562087 **Gallanach Road PA34 4LS**
email: info@manorhouseoban.com **web:** www.manorhouseoban.com
dir: *Follow MacBrayne Ferries signs, pass ferry entrance for hotel on right.*

Handy for the ferry terminal and with views of the bay and harbour, this elegant Georgian residence was built in 1780 as the dower house for the family of the Duke of Argyll. Comfortable and attractive public rooms invite relaxation, while most of the well-equipped bedrooms are furnished with period pieces. Nelson's Bar has stunning views over the bay and fine dining is available in the restaurant. The hotel has its own mooring.

Rooms: 11 (1 GF) 🐾 **Facilities:** FTV WiFi Complimentary golf at Glencruitten Golf Club Complimentary use of Feel Good Fitness gym New Year **Parking:** 20
Notes: No children 12 years Closed 25–26 December Civ Wed 30

Follow us on twitter
@TheAA_Lifestyle

Falls of Lora Hotel

THE INDEPENDENTS
HOTEL ASSOCIATION

★★★ 77% HOTEL

tel: 01631 710483 **Connel Ferry PA37 1PB**
email: enquiries@fallsoflora.com **web:** www.fallsoflora.com
dir: *From Glasgow take A82, A85. Hotel 0.5 mile past Connel sign 5 miles before Oban.*

Personally run and welcoming, this long-established and thriving holiday hotel enjoys inspiring views over Loch Etive. The spacious ground floor takes in a comfortable, traditional lounge and a cocktail bar with over a hundred whiskies and an open log fire. Guests can eat in the popular, informal bistro, which is open all day. Bedrooms come in a variety of styles, ranging from the cosy standard rooms to high quality luxury rooms.

Rooms: 37 (2 family) (6 GF) 🐾 **S** fr £57 **D** fr £98 (including breakfast)*
Facilities: FTV WiFi ⌁ **Conf:** Class 20 Board 15 Theatre 45 **Parking:** 40
Notes: Closed mid December to January

Royal Hotel

★★★ 75% HOTEL

tel: 01631 563021 **Argyll Sqaure PA34 4BE**
email: salesroyaloban@strathmorehotels.com **web:** www.strathmorehotels.com
dir: *A82 from Glasgow towards Loch Lomond and Crianlarich then A85, past Loch Awe to Oban.*

Well situated in the heart of Oban, just minutes from the ferry terminal and with all the shops on its doorstep, this hotel really is central. The comfortable and well-presented bedrooms differ in size, and all public areas are smart. There is a first-floor restaurant overlooking the town square and a popular lounge bar on the ground floor where food and drink are served all day.

Rooms: 91 (3 family) 🐾 **Facilities:** FTV WiFi ⌁ ♫ Xmas New Year **Conf:** Class 60 Board 30 Theatre 140 **Services:** Lift Night porter **Parking:** 15 **Notes:** Civ Wed 100

OLDMELDRUM
Aberdeenshire

Map 23 NJ82

Meldrum House Country Hotel & Golf Course

★★★★ 83% ⊛⊛ COUNTRY HOUSE HOTEL

tel: 01651 872294 **AB51 0AE**
email: enquiries@meldrumhouse.com **web:** www.meldrumhouse.com
dir: 11 miles from Aberdeen on A947 – Aberdeen to Banff road.

Set in 350 acres of wooded parkland, this imposing baronial country mansion has a golf course as its centrepiece. Tastefully restored to highlight its original character, it provides a peaceful retreat. The bedrooms are massive, and like the public rooms, transport guests back to a bygone era, but at the same time provide stylish, modern amenities including smart bathrooms.

Rooms: 51 (13 annexe) (6 family) (14 GF) ⬩ **S** fr £145 **D** fr £145 (including breakfast) **Facilities:** FTV WiFi HL ⬩ 18 ⬩ Xmas New Year **Conf:** Class 200 Board 75 Theatre 200 **Services:** Lift Night porter **Parking:** 70 **Notes:** LB Civ Wed 150

ONICH
Highland

Map 22 NN06

Onich Hotel

★★★ 69% HOTEL

tel: 01855 821214 **PH33 6RY**
email: enquiries@onich-fortwilliam.co.uk **web:** www.onich-fortwilliam.co.uk
dir: Beside A82, 2 miles north of Ballachulish Bridge.

Genuine hospitality is part of the appeal of this hotel, which lies right beside Loch Linnhe with gardens extending to its shores. Nicely presented public areas include a choice of inviting lounges and contrasting bars, and views of the loch can be enjoyed from the attractive restaurant. Bedrooms, with pleasing colour schemes, are comfortably modern.

Rooms: 26 (6 family) ⬩ **Facilities:** STV FTV WiFi Games room ♫ New Year **Conf:** Board 40 Theatre 50 **Parking:** 50 **Notes:** LB Civ Wed 120

PEEBLES
Scottish Borders

Map 21 NT24

Macdonald Cardrona Hotel, Golf & Spa
MACDONALD HOTELS & RESORTS

★★★★ 77% HOTEL

tel: 01896 833600 **Cardrona EH45 8NE**
email: reception.cardrona@macdonald-hotels.co.uk
web: www.macdonald-hotels.co.uk/cardrona
dir: On A72 between Peebles and Innerleithen, 3 miles south of Peebles.

The rolling hills of the Scottish Borders are a stunning backdrop for this modern, purpose-built hotel. Spacious bedrooms are traditional in style, equipped with a range of extras, and most enjoy fantastic views of countryside. The hotel features impressive leisure facilities, including an 18-hole golf course, 18-metre indoor pool and state-of-the-art gym.

Rooms: 99 (19 family) (16 GF) ⬩ **S** fr £89 **D** fr £89 **Facilities:** Spa FTV WiFi ⬩ HL ⬩ ⬩ 18 Gym Sauna Steam room Xmas New Year **Conf:** Class 120 Board 90 Theatre 250 **Services:** Lift Night porter **Parking:** 200 **Notes:** LB Civ Wed 200

PERTH
Perth & Kinross

Map 21 NO12

Parklands Hotel

★★★★ 76% ⊛⊛ SMALL HOTEL

tel: 01738 622451 **2 St Leonards Bank PH2 8EB**
email: info@theparklandshotel.com **web:** www.theparklandshotel.com
dir: M90 junction 10, in 1 mile left at lights at end of park area, hotel on left.

Parklands Hotel is ideally located close to the centre of town, with open views over the South Inch. The enthusiastic proprietors continue to invest heavily in the business and the bedrooms have a smart contemporary feel. Public areas include a choice of restaurants, with a fine dining experience offered in 63@Parklands and more informal dining at the No.1 the Bank Bistro.

Rooms: 15 (3 family) (4 GF) ⬩ **S** fr £95 **D** fr £119 (including breakfast) **Facilities:** STV WiFi ⬩ **Conf:** Class 18 Board 20 Theatre 24 **Parking:** 30 **Notes:** LB Closed 26 December to 6 January Civ Wed 40

Murrayshall House Hotel & Golf Course

★★★★ 75% ⊛ HOTEL

tel: 01738 551171 **New Scone PH2 7PH**
email: info@murrayshall.co.uk **web:** www.murrayshall.co.uk
dir: From Perth take A94 Coupar Angus, 1 mile from Perth, right to Murrayshall just before New Scone.

This imposing country house is set in 350 acres of grounds, including two golf courses, one of which is of championship standard. Bedrooms come in two distinct styles: modern suites in a purpose-built building contrast with more classic rooms in the main building. The Clubhouse bar serves a range of meals all day, while more accomplished cooking can be enjoyed in the Old Masters Restaurant.

Rooms: 40 (14 annexe) (14 family) (5 GF) ⬩ **Facilities:** STV FTV WiFi HL ⬩ 36 Driving range New Year **Conf:** Class 60 Board 30 Theatre 150 **Services:** Night porter **Parking:** 120 **Notes:** Civ Wed 130

P

PERTH continued

Mercure Perth Hotel

★★★ 76% HOTEL

tel: 0844 815 9105 (Calls cost 5p per minute plus your phone company's access charge)
West Mill Street PH1 5QP
email: info@mercureperth.co.uk web: www.mercureperth.co.uk
dir: *A93/A989 to city centre, left into Caledonian Road, right at lights into Old High Street, hotel on left.*

This 15th-century former watermill has been converted into a modern hotel but still highlights the mill stream running through reception under a glass floor. Contemporary rooms include satellite TV and free WiFi. The hotel has extensive conference facilities, and a popular brasserie where tempting meals are served.

Rooms: 76 **S** fr £60 **D** fr £71* **Facilities:** FTV WiFi ≋ New Year **Conf:** Class 50 Board 40 Theatre 120 **Services:** Night porter **Parking:** 55 **Notes:** LB Civ Wed 120

Salutation Hotel

★★★ 75% HOTEL

tel: 01738 630066 **South Street PH2 8PH**
email: salessalutation@strathmorehotels.com web: www.strathmorehotels.com
dir: *At end of South Street on right before River Tay.*

Situated at the heart of Perth, the Salutation is reputed to be one of the oldest hotels in Scotland and has been welcoming guests through its doors since 1699. It offers traditional hospitality with all the modern comforts. Bedrooms vary in size and are thoughtfully equipped. An extensive menu is available in the Adam Restaurant, with its impressive barrel-vaulted ceiling and original features.

Rooms: 84 (5 family) ☞ **S** fr £35 **D** fr £70 (including breakfast)* **Facilities:** FTV WiFi ≋ HL ♫ Xmas New Year **Conf:** Class 180 Board 60 Theatre 300 **Services:** Lift Night porter **Notes:** LB Civ Wed 150

Best Western Queens Hotel

★★★ 73% HOTEL

tel: 01738 442222 **Leonard Street PH2 8HB**
email: enquiry@queensperth.co.uk web: www.queensperth.co.uk
dir: *From M90 follow to 2nd lights, turn left. Hotel on right, opposite railway station.*

This popular hotel benefits from a central location close to both the bus and rail stations. Bedrooms vary in size and style with top floor rooms offering extra space and excellent views of the town. Public rooms include a smart leisure centre and

versatile conference space. A range of meals is served in both the bar and restaurant.

Rooms: 50 (4 family) **S** fr £49 **D** fr £65* **Facilities:** FTV WiFi ⊛ Gym Steam room Sauna Xmas New Year **Conf:** Class 70 Board 50 Theatre 200 **Services:** Lift Night porter **Parking:** 50 **Notes:** LB Civ Wed 220

Premier Inn Perth City Centre

BUDGET HOTEL

Premier Inn 🌙

tel: 0871 527 9498 (Calls cost 13p per minute plus your phone company's access charge) **Mill Street PH1 5HZ**
web: www.premierinn.com
dir: *M90 junction 10, A912 (City Centre). At mini-roundabout into Edinburgh Road. Through 2 sets of lights. At T-junction right on to Marshall Place (A989). 1st exit at mini-roundabout into Tay Street. 2nd left into High Street, right into George Street. 1st left into Bridge Lane. Continue into Mill Street. Hotel on right.*

High quality, budget accommodation ideal for both families and business travellers. Spacious, en suite bedrooms feature free WiFi and tea and coffee making facilities, and in most hotels, Freeview TV is also available. The adjacent family restaurant features a wide and varied menu.

Rooms: 83

PETERHEAD	Map 23 NK14
Aberdeenshire	

Buchan Braes Hotel

★★★★ 77% ⊛ HOTEL

tel: 01779 871471 **Boddam AB42 3AR**
email: info@buchanbraes.co.uk web: www.buchanbraes.co.uk
dir: *From Aberdeen take A90, follow Peterhead signs. 1st right in Stirling signed Boddam. 50 metres, 1st right.*

This is a contemporary hotel located in Boddam that is an excellent base for exploring the attractions of this wonderful part of Scotland. There is an open-plan lounge for drinks and snacks and the Grill Room with an open kitchen that offers a weekly changing, seasonal menu of locally sourced produce. All the bedrooms, including three suites, have 32" TVs with satellite channels, king-sized beds and free WiFi.

Rooms: 47 (1 family) (26 GF) ☞ **S** fr £95 **D** fr £105 (including breakfast)* **Facilities:** FTV WiFi ≋ Xmas New Year **Conf:** Class 100 Board 130 Theatre 250 **Services:** Lift Night porter **Parking:** 80 **Notes:** Civ Wed 220

Palace Hotel

★★★ 75% HOTEL

tel: 01779 474821 **Prince Street AB42 1PL**
email: info@palacehotel.co.uk web: www.palacehotel.co.uk
dir: *A90 from Aberdeen, follow signs to Peterhead, on entering town turn into Prince Street, then right into main car park.*

This town centre hotel is popular with business travellers and for social events. Bedrooms come in two styles, with the executive rooms being particularly smart and spacious. Public areas include a themed bar, an informal diner reached via a spiral staircase, and a restaurant called The Front Room.

Rooms: 64 (1 family) (13 GF) ☞ **S** fr £65 **D** fr £75 (including breakfast)* **Facilities:** STV FTV WiFi ≋ Snooker and pool table ♫ New Year **Conf:** Class 100 Board 60 Theatre 250 **Services:** Lift Night porter **Parking:** 50 **Notes:** Civ Wed 250

PITLOCHRY
Perth & Kinross   Map 23 NN95

Fonab Castle Hotel & Spa

★★★★★ 84% HOTEL

tel: 01796 470140 **Foss Road PH16 5ND**
email: reservations@fonabcastlehotel.com **web:** www.fonabcastlehotel.com
dir: From A9 into Foss Road. Hotel 1st on left.

Sitting on the banks of Loch Faskally with stunning views, this elevated property was originally built as a home for the Sandeman family, the sherry and port merchants. Stylish bedrooms are situated in the main castle building and more modern annexe. Both The Brasserie and lounge offer panoramic views and provide a wide choice of quality produce cooked to a high standard. Impressive destination spa, pool and gym facilities are available on site.

Rooms: 42 (16 annexe) (2 family) (14 GF) ✆ **S** fr £185 **D** fr £195 (including breakfast)* **Facilities:** Spa FTV WiFi ♨ ⚒ Thermal and aromatherapy suite Steam room Nail salon Xmas New Year **Conf:** Class 100 Board 100 Theatre 150 **Services:** Lift Night porter **Parking:** 60 **Notes:** Civ Wed 140

Knockendarroch

★★★★ 80%  SMALL HOTEL

tel: 01796 473473 **Higher Oakfield PH16 5HT**
email: bookings@knockendarroch.co.uk **web:** www.knockendarroch.co.uk
dir: In town centre, just off A9.

This secluded hotel has outstanding views over the town and surrounding hills. The individually styled bedrooms are spacious and very well appointed – all have plasma TVs. The traditional, country-style public rooms have large sofas, welcoming open fires and an excellent whisky cabinet. Dinner is served every evening in the award-winning restaurant with only the best of Scottish produce being used. The staff are friendly and attentive.

Rooms: 12 (1 GF) ✆ **S** fr £165 **D** fr £195 (including breakfast & dinner)* **Facilities:** FTV WiFi ♨ **Parking:** 12 **Notes:** LB No children 10 years Closed December to January

East Haugh House Hotel

[U]

tel: 01796 473121 **East Haugh PH16 5TE**
email: info@easthaugh.co.uk **web:** www.easthaugh.co.uk

Currently the rating for this establishment is not confirmed. This may be due to a change of ownership or because ot has only recently joined the AA rating scheme.

Rooms: 14 **Notes:** Closed 18–28 December

POLMONT
Falkirk   Map 21 NS97

Macdonald Inchyra Hotel and Spa

★★★★ 76% HOTEL   MACDONALD HOTELS & RESORTS

tel: 01324 711911 **Grange Road FK2 0YB**
email: inchyra@macdonald-hotels.co.uk **web:** www.macdonaldhotels.co.uk
dir: 2 minutes from M9 junction 5.

Ideally placed for the M9 and Grangemouth terminal, this former manor house has been tastefully extended. The hotel provides comprehensive conference facilities and guests will find that The Scottish Steakhouse serves the highest quality produce in a contemporary style. The bedrooms are comfortable and most are

spacious. A visit to the hotel's luxurious spa and leisure facilities is highly recommended.

Rooms: 97 (6 annexe) (35 family) (32 GF) **Facilities:** Spa FTV WiFi ♨ ⚒ Gym Steam room Sauna Aromatherapy shower Ice fountain New Year **Conf:** Class 300 Board 80 Theatre 750 **Services:** Lift Night porter **Parking:** 500 **Notes:** Civ Wed 450

Premier Inn Falkirk East   Premier Inn

BUDGET HOTEL

tel: 0871 527 8392 (Calls cost 13p per minute plus your phone company's access charge) **Beancross Road FK2 0YS**
web: www.premierinn.com
dir: M9 junction 5, Polmont A9 signs. Hotel on left.

High quality, budget accommodation ideal for both families and business travellers. Spacious, en suite bedrooms feature free WiFi and tea and coffee making facilities, and in most hotels, Freeview TV is also available. The adjacent family restaurant features a wide and varied menu.

Rooms: 60

PORT APPIN
Argyll & Bute   Map 20 NM94

INSPECTOR'S CHOICE

Airds Hotel and Restaurant

★★★★  SMALL HOTEL   RELAIS & CHÂTEAUX

tel: 01631 730236 **PA38 4DF**
email: airds@airds-hotel.com **web:** www.airds-hotel.com
dir: From A828 Oban to Fort William road, turn at Appin signed Port Appin. Hotel 2.5 miles on left.

Airds shows how appearances can be deceiving, as its modest scale and appearance give little indication of what lies beyond the threshold. Once inside, you are in a luxurious environment where attention to detail and fine food are of paramount importance. The lounges are cosy and inviting, with log fires, welcoming sofas and service that is both top notch and friendly. A stay here is as much about the food as the stunning location, and the kitchen brigade makes full use of the wide range of superb quality produce that is on their doorstep. Both dinner and lunch include options for fish and meat eaters, with the added bonus of superb views across Loch Linnhe. Guests can also take lunch in the garden or conservatory, while families with young children can take dinner in the conservatory. The well-equipped bedrooms provide style and luxury, while many bathrooms are furnished in marble and have power showers.

Rooms: 11 (3 family) (2 GF) ✆ **S** fr £275 **D** fr £305 (including breakfast & dinner)* **Facilities:** STV FTV WiFi ♨ ⚓ In-room massage Xmas New Year **Conf:** Class 16 Board 16 Theatre 16 **Parking:** 20 **Notes:** LB Civ Wed 40

P

PORT APPIN *continued*

The Pierhouse Hotel

★★★ 81% ⊛ SMALL HOTEL

tel: 01631 730302 **PA38 4DE**
email: reservations@pierhousehotel.co.uk **web:** www.pierhousehotel.co.uk
dir: *A828 from Ballachulish to Oban. In Appin right at Port Appin and Lismore ferry sign. After 2.5 miles left after post office, hotel at end of road.*

Located on the shores of Loch Linnhe in Port Appin, this hotel offers a warm welcome and relaxing atmosphere with comfortable, contemporary styled bedrooms and wood-burning fires in the Ferry Bar and residents' snug lounge. With breathtaking views over the sea loch to the islands of Lismore and Mull, watch the sun set as you dine in the candlelit restaurant which serves freshly prepared, locally sourced seafood and game, simply cooked to create award-winning dishes.

Rooms: 12 (2 family) (6 GF) ♠ **Facilities:** FTV WiFi ♨ Aromatherapy massage Sauna Kayaking Walking Cycling New Year **Conf:** Class 20 Board 20 Theatre 20 **Parking:** 20 **Notes:** Closed 25–26 December Civ Wed 80

PORTAVADIE	Map 20 NR96
Argyll & Bute	

Portavadie Lodge Hotel and Marina Restaurant

★★★★ 76% ⊛⊛ HOTEL

tel: 01700 811075 **PA21 2DA**
email: info@portavadie.com **web:** www.portavadie.com
dir: *A82 along Loch Lomond to Tarbet, then A83 towards Inveraray and Campbeltown. At Cairndow, left on to A815, then at Strachur right on to A886, signed Glendaruel and Colintraive. Just after Glendaruel, right on to A8003 for Tighnabruaich then continue on A8000 towards Portavadie. At Millhouse follow signs to ferry and Portavadie Marina.*

Argyll's 'Secret Coast' provides the fantastic location for this spa resort which offers a variety of accommodation in addition to the Lodge Hotel. Rooms are spacious and contemporary. Dining options include a casual brasserie in the Lodge, the Spa Café and the flagship Marina Restaurant with its stunning views over Loch Fyne. Superb leisure facilities and a state-of-the-art spa are available to all guests.

Rooms: 16 (8 family) (10 GF) ♠ **S** fr £90 **D** fr £90 (including breakfast)*
Facilities: Spa FTV WiFi ⊛ ⌁ Gym Sauna Steam room Infinity pool Spa pools Xmas New Year **Services:** Night porter

---

RENFREW

See **Glasgow Airport**

RHU	Map 20 NS28
Argyll & Bute	

Rosslea Hall Hotel

★★★ 79% ⊛ HOTEL

tel: 01436 439955 **Ferry Road G84 8NF**
email: enquiries@rossleahallhotel.co.uk **web:** www.rossleahallhotel.co.uk
dir: *On A814, opposite church.*

Overlooking the Firth of the Clyde and close to Helensburgh, this imposing mansion is set in its own well tended gardens. The good sized bedrooms and bathrooms are well appointed to cater admirably for the modern traveller. The eating options include the Conservatory Restaurant, overlooking the grounds and the Clyde, which offers dishes cooked with imagination and flair. The hotel is a popular wedding venue.

Rooms: 30 (3 family) (2 GF) ♠ **S** fr £79 **D** fr £79 (including breakfast)*
Facilities: STV FTV WiFi Xmas New Year **Conf:** Class 60 Board 80 Theatre 150 **Services:** Night porter **Parking:** 30 **Notes:** Civ Wed 120

ST ANDREWS	Map 21 NO51
Fife	

Old Course Hotel, Golf Resort & Spa

★★★★★ ⊛⊛⊛ HOTEL

tel: 01334 474371 **KY16 9SP**
email: reservations@oldcoursehotel.co.uk **web:** www.oldcoursehotel.co.uk
dir: *M90 junction 8, A91 to St Andrews.*

The Old Course Hotel, Golf Resort & Spa sita alongside the famous par 4 17th, 'Road Hole', on the Old Course in St Andrews, known as the Home of Golf. The hotel has 144 luxurious rooms, including 35 stunning suites, and boasts five dining experiences, overseen by Executive Chef, Martin Hollis. The Road Hole Restaurant, with 3 Rosettes, overlooks the Old Course; family-friendly Sands with 1 Rosette; the popular Jigger Inn; the Duke's Clubhouse at the hotel's own championship course and also Hams Hame Pub & Grill, the closest '19th' to the Old Course's 18th green. Whether staying at this iconic hotel, out on the golf course, relaxing in the state-of-the-art Kohler Waters Spa or enjoying a meal, guests are assured a red-star experience.

Rooms: 144 (5 family) (3 GF) ♠ **Facilities:** Spa STV FTV WiFi ♨ HL ⊛ ⌁ 18 Gym Thermal suite ♫ Xmas New Year **Conf:** Class 250 Board 100 Theatre 300 **Services:** Lift Night porter Air con **Parking:** 125 **Notes:** Civ Wed 80

Fairmont St Andrews, Scotland

★★★★★ 87% ⊛ HOTEL

tel: 01334 837000 **KY16 8PN**
email: standrews.scotland@fairmont.com **web:** www.fairmont.com/standrews
dir: *Approximately 2 miles from St Andrews on A917 towards Crail.*

Sitting just a few miles from St Andrews, overlooking the rugged Fife coastline and the hotel's own championship golf courses, The Fairmont is situated on a 520-acre estate. Bedrooms and bathrooms are spacious and luxuriously appointed. The eating options are The Squire for brasserie-style food, La Cucina for Italian dishes, The St Andrews Bar and Grill in the clubhouse for steak and seafood, and The Atrium offering all-day menus. The hotel has an impressive spa and health club. Good standards of service are found throughout.

Rooms: 212 (212 family) (68 GF) ♠ **Facilities:** Spa STV FTV WiFi ♨ ⊛ ⌁ 36 Gym 106-seat cinema Nail salon Bike hire Dance studio Xmas New Year **Conf:** Class 300 Board 90 Theatre 550 **Services:** Lift Night porter Air con **Parking:** 150 **Notes:** Civ Wed 550

Rufflets Hotel

★★★★ ◉◉ COUNTRY HOUSE HOTEL

tel: 01334 472594 **Strathkinness Low Road KY16 9TX**
email: reservations@rufflets.co.uk **web:** www.rufflets.co.uk
dir: 1.5 miles west on B939.

Built in 1924 for a Dundee jute baron, this charming property is set in extensive gardens a few minutes' drive from the town centre. The stylish, spacious bedrooms are individually decorated, and include the Gilroy Suite, The Orchard Suite (which is separate from the main building), and Turret Rooms that have their own seating areas. Public rooms include a well-stocked bar, a choice of inviting lounges and the delightful Seasons Restaurant that serves imaginative, carefully prepared cuisine based on seasonal produce. Impressive conference and banqueting facilities are available in the adjacent Garden Suite. Families are very welcome, and the hotel is a popular wedding venue.

Rooms: 23 (4 annexe) (3 family) (4 GF) ✱ **S** fr £145 **D** fr £165 (including breakfast)* **Facilities:** FTV WiFi ⬇ 🛝 Children's outdoor games New Year **Conf:** Class 60 Board 60 Theatre 200 **Services:** Night porter **Parking:** 50 **Notes:** LB Civ Wed 130

Macdonald Rusacks Hotel

★★★★ 80% ◉◉◉ HOTEL

MACDONALD
HOTELS & RESORTS

tel: 01334 474321 **Pilmour Links KY16 9JQ**
email: general.rusacks@macdonald-hotels.co.uk **web:** www.macdonaldhotels.co.uk
dir: From A91 west, straight on at roundabout into St Andrews. Hotel 220 yards on left.

This long-established hotel enjoys an almost unrivalled location with superb views across the famous golf course. Bedrooms, though varying in size, are comfortably appointed and well equipped. Classically styled public rooms include an elegant reception lounge and a modern restaurant (Rocca, where the six-course taster menu comes recommended) and brasserie bar.

Rooms: 70 (1 annexe) (3 family) (7 GF) ✱ **Facilities:** STV FTV WiFi Xmas New Year **Conf:** Class 35 Board 20 Theatre 80 **Services:** Lift Night porter **Parking:** 21 **Notes:** Civ Wed 60

Hotel du Vin St Andrews

★★★★ 79% ◉ TOWN HOUSE HOTEL

Hotel du Vin & Bistro

tel: 01334 845313 **40 The Scores KY16 9AS**
email: reservations.standrews@hotelduvin.com
web: www.hotelduvin.com/locations/st-andrews
dir: M90 junction 3 north over Forth Road Bridge, A92. At roundabout take A914 then A91 signed St Andrews/Cupar.

Hotel du Vin St Andrews is stylish, modern and welcoming. There has been a hotel here for some years but today the Hotel du Vin group offer their own unique and popular brand of hospitality. Bedrooms are very well equipped; all have free WiFi, Nespresso coffee machines and Egyptian bed linen. The Bistro offers traditional French dishes while Ma Bells bar serves traditional pub food. The hotel overlooks golden beaches and is a mere two-minute walk from the world-famous Royal and Ancient Golf Club. Free parking is available just outside the hotel.

Rooms: 37 ✱ **D** fr £100 **Facilities:** STV FTV WiFi ⬇ HL Xmas New Year **Conf:** Class 60 Board 38 Theatre 150 **Services:** Lift Night porter **Parking:** 7 **Notes:** LB Civ Wed 110

Ardgowan Hotel

★★★ 84% ◉ HOTEL

tel: 01334 472970 **2 Playfair Terrace, North Street KY16 9HX**
email: info@ardgowanhotel.co.uk **web:** www.ardgowanhotel.co.uk
dir: A91 onto A917. Hotel 100 metres from roundabout on left.

The Ardgowan Hotel is ideally located just 200 yards from the Old Course Club House; the university, shops and beach are just a short walk from the hotel as well. This well-presented, family-run hotel was built in 1847 and offers well-appointed bedrooms and en suites. The award-winning restaurant uses the finest quality produce including great steaks alongside an array of seafood. Playfair's bar is lively, and enjoys good local trade.

Rooms: 36 (7 annexe) (4 family) (3 GF) ✱ **S** fr £80 **D** fr £103 (including breakfast) **Facilities:** FTV WiFi ⬇ **Services:** Night porter **Notes:** Closed 2/3 weeks over Christmas

S

ST ANDREWS *continued*

Best Western Scores Hotel

 Best Western.

★★★ 78% HOTEL

tel: 01334 472451 **76 The Scores KY16 9BB**
email: reception@scoreshotel.co.uk **web:** www.bw-scoreshotel.co.uk
dir: *M90 junction 2a, A92 east. Follow Glenrothes signs then St Andrews signs. Straight on at next 2 roundabouts, left into Golf Place, right into The Scores.*

Enjoying views over St Andrews Bay, this well-presented hotel is situated only a short pitch from the first tee of the famous Old Course. Bedrooms are impressively furnished and come in various sizes; many are quite spacious. Smart public areas include Champions Grill that offers food all day from breakfast to dinner; Scottish high teas are served here from 4.30–6.30pm. Alexander's Restaurant opens Thursday, Friday and Saturday evenings.

Rooms: 36 (1 family) **Facilities:** FTV WiFi ⓘ HL Xmas New Year **Conf:** Class 60 Board 40 Theatre 180 **Services:** Lift Night porter **Parking:** 12 **Notes:** Civ Wed 100

Russell Hotel

★★ 82% HOTEL

tel: 01334 473447 **26 The Scores KY16 9AS**
email: enquiries@russellhotelstandrews.co.uk **web:** www.russellhotelstandrews.co.uk
dir: *From A91 left at 2nd roundabout into Golf Place, right in 200 yards into The Scores, hotel in 300 yards on left.*

Lying on the east bay, this friendly, family-run Victorian terrace hotel provides well appointed bedrooms in varying sizes; some enjoy fine sea views. Cosy public areas include a popular bar and an intimate restaurant, both offering a good range of freshly prepared dishes. Situated in St Andrews, said to be 'The Home of Golf', this hotel offers a comprehensive range of golfing breaks, and is convenient for visits to the castle, cathedral and university.

Rooms: 10 (3 family) **Facilities:** WiFi ⓘ New Year **Services:** Night porter

Premier Inn St Andrews

Premier Inn 🌙

BUDGET HOTEL

tel: 0871 527 9428 (Calls cost 13p per minute plus your phone company's access charge) **Largo Road KY16 8NH**
web: www.premierinn.com
dir: *A91 to St Andrews. Follow signs for Kircaldy (A915). Straight on at 2 roundabouts to Largo Road. Hotel opposite VW car showroom.*

High quality, budget accommodation ideal for both families and business travellers. Spacious, en suite bedrooms feature free WiFi and tea and coffee making facilities, and in most hotels, Freeview TV is also available. The adjacent family restaurant features a wide and varied menu.

Rooms: 65

ST FILLANS Perth & Kinross	Map 20 NN62

The Four Seasons Hotel

★★★ 82% ◉◉ HOTEL

tel: 01764 685333 **Loch Earn PH6 2NF**
email: info@thefourseasonshotel.co.uk **web:** www.thefourseasonshotel.co.uk
dir: *On A85, towards west of village.*

Set on the edge of Loch Earn, this welcoming hotel and many of its bedrooms benefit from fine views. There is a choice of lounges, including a library, warmed by log fires during winter. Local produce is used to good effect in both the Meall Reamhar restaurant and the more informal Tarken Room.

Rooms: 18 (6 annexe) (7 family) **S** fr £84.50 **D** fr £99 (including breakfast)*
Facilities: FTV WiFi Fishing Xmas New Year **Conf:** Class 45 Board 38 Theatre 95
Parking: 40 **Notes:** LB Closed 2 January to 15 February RS November to December, 16 February to March Civ Wed 80

SOUTH QUEENSFERRY Edinburgh	Map 21 NT17

Premier Inn Edinburgh A1 (Newcraighall)

Premier Inn 🌙

BUDGET HOTEL

tel: 0871 527 8362 (Calls cost 13p per minute plus your phone company's access charge) **91 Newcraighall Road, Newcraighall EH21 8RX**
web: www.premierinn.com
dir: *At junction of A1 and A6095 towards Musselburgh.*

High quality, budget accommodation ideal for both families and business travellers. Spacious, en suite bedrooms feature free WiFi and tea and coffee making facilities, and in most hotels, Freeview TV is also available. The adjacent family restaurant features a wide and varied menu.

Rooms: 66

Premier Inn Edinburgh (South Queensferry)

Premier Inn 🌙

BUDGET HOTEL

tel: 0871 527 8364 (Calls cost 13p per minute plus your phone company's access charge) **Builyeon Road EH30 9YJ**
web: www.premierinn.com
dir: *M8 junction 2 follow M9 Stirling signs, exit at junction 1a take A8000 towards Forth Road Bridge, at 3rd roundabout 2nd exit into Builyeon Road. Note: do not go onto Forth Road Bridge.*

Rooms: 72

SPITTAL OF GLENSHEE Perth & Kinross	Map 21 NO17

Dalmunzie Castle Hotel

★★★ 76% ◉ COUNTRY HOUSE HOTEL

tel: 01250 885224 & 885225 **PH10 7QG**
email: reservations@dalmunzie.com **web:** www.dalmunzie.com
dir: *On A93 at Spittal of Glenshee, follow signs to hotel.*

This turreted mansion house sits in a secluded glen in the heart of a glorious 6,500-acre estate, yet is within easy reach of the Glenshee ski slopes. The Edwardian-style bedrooms, including spacious tower rooms and impressive four-poster rooms, are furnished with antique pieces. The drawing room enjoys

S

panoramic views over the lawns, and the restaurant serves the finest Scottish produce.

Rooms: 20 (2 family) **S** fr £115 **D** fr £130 (including breakfast)* **Facilities:** STV FTV WiFi ⌣ Fishing Xmas New Year **Conf:** Class 40 Board 40 Theatre 40 **Services:** Lift **Parking:** 14 **Notes:** LB Civ Wed 80

STEPPS
North Lanarkshire

Map 20 NS66

Premier Inn Glasgow Stepps (M80 Jct 3)

Premier Inn

BUDGET HOTEL

tel: 0871 527 8452 (Calls cost 13p per minute plus your phone company's access charge) **Crowwood Roundabout, Cumbernauld Road G33 6HN**
web: www.premierinn.com
dir: M8 junction 12, A80 (becomes dual carriageway) to Crowwood roundabout, 4th exit back onto A80, hotel 1st left. Or exit M80 at Crowwood roundabout, 3rd exit signed A80 West. Hotel 1st left.

High quality, budget accommodation ideal for both families and business travellers. Spacious, en suite bedrooms feature free WiFi and tea and coffee making facilities, and in most hotels, Freeview TV is also available. The adjacent family restaurant features a wide and varied menu.

Rooms: 80

STIRLING
Stirling

Map 21 NS79

The Stirling Highland Hotel

★★★★ 75% ◉ HOTEL

tel: 01786 272727 **Spittal Street FK8 1DU**
email: reservations@stirlinghighlandhotel.co.uk **web:** www.stirlinghighlandhotel.co.uk
dir: A84 into Stirling. Follow Stirling Castle signs to Albert Hall. Left, left again, follow Castle signs.

Enjoying a location close to the castle and historic town, this atmospheric hotel was previously a high school. Public rooms have been converted from the original classrooms and retain many interesting features. Bedrooms are more modern in style and comfortably equipped. Scholars Restaurant serves traditional and international dishes, and the Headmaster's Study is the ideal venue for enjoying a drink.

Rooms: 96 (4 family) (28 GF) ⌣ **S** fr £75 **D** fr £75* **Facilities:** Spa FTV WiFi ⌣ HL ⬇ Gym Squash Steam room Sauna Dance studio Beauty therapist New Year **Conf:** Class 60 Board 40 Theatre 120 **Services:** Lift Night porter **Parking:** 96 **Notes:** LB Civ Wed 100

Premier Inn Stirling City Centre

Premier Inn

BUDGET HOTEL

tel: 0871 527 9472 (Calls cost 13p per minute plus your phone company's access charge) **Forthside Way FK8 1QZ**
web: www.premierinn.com
dir: See website for directions.

High quality, budget accommodation ideal for both families and business travellers. Spacious, en suite bedrooms feature free WiFi and tea and coffee making facilities, and in most hotels, Freeview TV is also available. The adjacent family restaurant features a wide and varied menu.

Rooms: 60

Premier Inn Stirling South (M9 Jct 9)

Premier Inn

BUDGET HOTEL

tel: 0871 527 9038 (Calls cost 13p per minute plus your phone company's access charge) **Glasgow Road, Whins of Milton FK7 8EX**
web: www.premierinn.com
dir: On A872, 0.25 mile from M9/M80 junction 9.

Rooms: 82

STRANRAER
Dumfries & Galloway

Map 20 NX06

Corsewall Lighthouse Hotel

★★★ 76% HOTEL

tel: 01776 853220 **Corsewall Point, Kirkcolm DG9 0QG**
email: info@lighthousehotel.co.uk **web:** www.lighthousehotel.co.uk
dir: A718 from Stranraer to Kirkcolm (approximately 8 miles). Follow hotel signs for 4 miles.

Looking for something completely different? This is a unique hotel converted from buildings that adjoin a Grade A listed, 19th-century lighthouse set on a rocky coastline. Situated on the headland to the west of Loch Ryan, the lighthouse beam still functions to warn approaching ships. Bedrooms come in a variety of sizes, some reached by a spiral staircase, and like the public areas, are cosy and atmospheric. The cottage suites in the grounds offer greater space. The restaurant menus are based on Scottish produce such as venison and salmon.

Rooms: 11 (5 annexe) (4 family) (2 GF) (3 smoking) ⌣ **Facilities:** FTV WiFi Xmas New Year **Conf:** Theatre 20 **Parking:** 20 **Notes:** Civ Wed 28

STRONTIAN
Highland

Map 22 NM86

Kilcamb Lodge Hotel

★★★★ 78% ◉◉◉ COUNTRY HOUSE HOTEL

tel: 01967 402257 **PH36 4HY**
email: enquiries@kilcamblodge.co.uk **web:** www.kilcamblodge.co.uk
dir: Off A861, via Corran Ferry, in the village of Strontian.

This historic house on the shores of Loch Sunart was one of the first stone buildings in the area, and was used as military barracks around the time of the Jacobite uprising. It is situated on the beautiful and peaceful Ardamurchan Peninsula where otters, red squirrels and eagles can be spotted. The suites and bedrooms, with either loch or garden views, are stylishly decorated using designer fabrics and have TVs, DVD/CD players, bath robes, iced water and even guest umbrellas. Accomplished cooking, utilising much local produce, can be enjoyed in the stylish dining room. Warm hospitality is assured.

Rooms: 10 (2 family) ⌣ **Facilities:** FTV WiFi ⌣ Fishing Boating Hiking Bird/whale/ otter watching Stalking Clay pigeon shooting Xmas New Year **Conf:** Class 18 Board 18 Theatre 18 **Parking:** 20 **Notes:** Closed 2 January to 1 February RS November, February Civ Wed 120

S

TARBERT
Argyll & Bute

Map 20 NN30

Stonefield Castle Hotel

★★★★ 76% HOTEL

"bespoke" HOTELS

tel: 01880 820836 **PA29 6YJ**
email: reservations.stonefieldcastle@bespokehotels.com
web: www.bespokehotels.com/stonefieldcastle
dir: *From Glasgow take M8 towards Erskine Bridge onto A82, follow Loch Lomond signs. From Arrochar follow A83 signs through Inveraray and Lochgilphead, hotel on left 2 miles before Tarbert.*

This fine example of 19th-century Scottish baronial architecture sits proudly on the Kintyre peninsula overlooking Loch Fyne. The richly decorated public spaces convey a strong sense of the hotel's long history, and offer a choice of lounges and a billiards room. Bedrooms are split between those in the newer wing and more traditional rooms in the original house. Dinner is a highlight, rooted in the famed local seafood from the loch, with stunning views from the restaurant to match.

Rooms: 36 (20 annexe) (3 family) (11 GF) ✿ **Facilities:** FTV WiFi ♨ Fishing Xmas New Year **Conf:** Class 60 Board 60 Theatre 80 **Services:** Lift Night porter **Parking:** 50 **Notes:** Civ Wed 110

TARBOLTON
South Ayrshire

Map 20 NS42

The Black Bull Hotel

★★★ 78% HOTEL

tel: 01292 541909 **2b Montgomerie Street KA5 5PR**
email: kailyard@blackbulltarbolton.com web: www.blackbulltarbolton.com

It's worth a detour off the main road to visit this independent hotel set in the centre of historic Tarbolton, ideally situated for 'Burns Country' and the Royal Troon Golf course. The Black Bull offers six contemporary bedrooms. Diners are treated to the best local produce in creative dishes, with a roaring log-burner the centre piece of the Kailyard Restaurant.

Rooms: 6

TARLAND
Aberdeenshire

Map 23 NJ40

Douneside House

★★★★ 86% ❁❁❁ COUNTRY HOUSE HOTEL

tel: 013398 81230 **Tarland AB34 4UL**
email: manager@dounesidehouse.co.uk web: www.dounesidehouse.co.uk
dir: *Phone for directions.*

This country house has been developed to provide an impressive range of facilities, with extensive grounds, fishing, spa and leisure facilities as well as stunningly beautiful gardens. Bedrooms come in a range of sizes, all very well equipped and extremely comfortable. Public rooms reflect the interesting history of the estate, and blend contemporary style with refined comfort. Cuisine is a major feature; exciting and interesting dishes incorporate the best estate produce including ingredients from the splendid kitchen garden.

Rooms: 29 ✿ **S** fr £170 **D** fr £170* **Facilities:** FTV WiFi ♨ ⊛ ♒ Gym Xmas New Year **Conf:** Class 20 Board 20 Theatre 35 **Parking:** 30 **Notes:** Civ Wed 60

THORNHILL
Dumfries & Galloway

Map 21 NX89

The Buccleuch and Queensberry Arms Hotel

★★★ 80% ❁ HOTEL

tel: 01848 323101 **112 Drumlanrig Street DG3 5LU**
email: info@bqahotel.com web: www.bqahotel.com
dir: *On A76 in centre of Thornhill.*

This small, family-run hotel is located in the heart of the small town of Thornhill. The bedrooms are extremely well appointed and of a high quality. Public areas are warm and welcoming with an open log fire adding to the charm. Award-winning food is an important focus of the operation here and local produce features strongly on the menus.

Rooms: 13 (3 annexe) (3 family) (3 GF) ✿ **S** fr £65 **D** fr £75 (including breakfast)* **Facilities:** STV FTV WiFi Xmas New Year **Conf:** Class 40 Board 32 Theatre 80 **Services:** Night porter **Parking:** 3 **Notes:** LB

T

Red Stars
The AA Red Star rating denotes an Inspectors' Choice hotel. They stand out as the very best places to stay and appear in highlighted panels throughout the guide.

THURSO
Highland   Map 23 ND16

Forss House Hotel
★★★★ 77% ◉◉ SMALL HOTEL

tel: 01847 861201 **Forss KW14 7XY**
email: anne@forsshousehotel.co.uk **web:** www.forsshousehotel.co.uk
dir: *On A836 between Thurso and Reay.*

This delightful country house is set in its own 20 acres of woodland and was originally built in 1810. The hotel offers a choice of bedrooms from the traditional styled rooms in the main house to the more contemporary annexe rooms in the grounds. All rooms are very well equipped and well appointed. The beautiful River Forss runs through the grounds and is a firm favourite with fishermen.

Rooms: 14 (6 annexe) (1 family) (7 GF) ⟟ **S** fr £99 **D** fr £135 (including breakfast)*
Facilities: FTV WiFi ⟟ Fishing **Conf:** Class 12 Board 14 Theatre 20 **Parking:** 14
Notes: Closed 23 December to 3 January Civ Wed 26

TORRIDON
Highland   Map 22 NG95

The Torridon
★★★★★ 85% ◉◉◉ COUNTRY HOUSE HOTEL

tel: 01445 791242 **By Achnasheen, Wester Ross IV22 2EY**
email: info@thetorridon.com **web:** www.thetorridon.com
dir: *From A832 at Kinlochewe, A896 towards Torridon 1 mile, do not turn into village. Hotel on right.*

Delightfully set amid inspiring loch and mountain scenery, this elegant Victorian shooting lodge has been beautifully appointed to make the most of its many original features, and the 58 acres of surrounding parkland make it a perfect getaway destination. The attractive bedrooms are individually furnished and most enjoy stunning Highland views; expect to find Egyptian cotton sheets, duck down duvets, satellite TVs, iPod docks plus Victorian-style bathrooms; for complete privacy choose The Boathouse on the loch shore. Comfortable day rooms feature fine wood panelling and roaring fires in cooler months. The kitchen team creates menus based as much as possible on locally sourced ingredients; the hotel has its own herd of cattle. The whisky bar is aptly named, boasting over 300 malts and in-depth tasting notes. Outdoor activities include shooting, cycling and walking.

Rooms: 18 (2 GF) ⟟ **S** fr £265 **D** fr £265 (including breakfast)* **Facilities:** STV WiFi Fishing ⟟ Abseiling Archery Climbing Kayaking Mountain biking Clay pigeon shooting Xmas New Year **Conf:** Board 16 Theatre 42 **Services:** Lift **Parking:** 20
Notes: Closed 2 January to 9 February RS November to March Civ Wed 55

TROON
South Ayrshire   Map 20 NS33

Lochgreen House Hotel
★★★★ ◉◉◉ COUNTRY HOUSE HOTEL

tel: 01292 313343 **Monktonhill Road, Southwood KA10 7EN**
email: lochgreen@costley-hotels.co.uk **web:** www.costley-hotels.co.uk
dir: *From A77 follow Prestwick Airport signs. 0.5 mile before airport take B749 to Troon. Hotel 1 mile on left.*

Lochgreen House Hotel is on the west coast of Ayrshire, with commanding views across Royal Troon Golf Course to the Isle of Arran. Set in 30 acres of its own charming gardens and woodlands, with a spectacular coastal backdrop, this country house hotel offers facilities for spa breaks, golf getaways, and is the venue for balls, business meetings, conferences and weddings. Bedrooms have luxurious bathrooms, and are decorated with traditional furnishings in keeping with the character of the house. Beautifully decorated public rooms are filled with art and antiques. Lochgreen is within easy reach of many world-famous golf courses, as well as the M77 and Prestwick Airport. It is owned and managed by the Costley family and offers award-winning dining, overseen by Executive Head Chef Andrew Costley. Cookery and art demonstrations are on offer as well as tours to nearby Burns Cottage and Museum, and Culzean Castle.

Rooms: 32 (1 annexe) (23 family) (11 GF) ⟟ **S** fr £205 **D** fr £225 (including breakfast)* **Facilities:** Spa STV WiFi Beauty treatments Xmas New Year
Conf: Class 180 Board 50 Theatre 200 **Services:** Lift Night porter **Parking:** 50
Notes: LB Civ Wed 140

Piersland House
★★★★ 75% HOTEL

tel: 01292 314747 **15 Craigend Road KA10 6HD**
email: reservations@piersland.co.uk **web:** www.piersland.co.uk
dir: *Just off A77 on B749 opposite Royal Troon Golf Club.*

This delightful, historic hotel enjoys a prime location in its own grounds in the heart of the golfing centre that is Troon. Extensive public areas include conference and banqueting facilities and an elegant restaurant. The stylish bedrooms and suites are either within the main house or in lodge-style annexes.

Rooms: 37 (15 family) (22 GF) ⟟ **S** fr £95 **D** fr £105 (including breakfast)*
Facilities: STV FTV WiFi ⟟ Xmas New Year **Conf:** Class 50 Board 64 Theatre 100
Services: Night porter **Parking:** 100 **Notes:** LB Civ Wed 80

T

TURNBERRY
South Ayrshire   Map 20 NS20

INSPECTOR'S CHOICE

Trump Turnberry
★★★★★ ◉◉ HOTEL

tel: 01655 331000 **Maidens Road KA26 9LT**
email: turnberry@luxurycollection.com **web:** www.trumphotels.com/turnberry
dir: *From Glasgow take A77, M77 south towards Stranraer, 2 miles past Kirkoswald follow signs for A719 and Turnberry. Hotel 500 metres on right.*

Golf probably springs to mind when this hotel is mentioned, and with good reason. This famous establishment enjoys magnificent views over to Arran, Ailsa Craig and the Mull of Kintyre. Facilities include a world-renowned golf course, the excellent Turnberry Performance Golf Academy, a luxurious spa with pool, ESPA treatments and a techno fitness studio, as well as a host of outdoor pursuits for both adults and children. Some superbly modern rooms and more traditional, elegant bedrooms and suites are located in the main hotel, while adjacent villas provide more space. The public areas are stunning and include the Grand Tea Lounge and Bar, the Duel in the Sun restaurant and the 1906 restaurant.

Rooms: 192 (89 annexe) (2 family) (15 GF) ⌂ **S** fr £225 **D** fr £225 (including breakfast) **Facilities:** Spa STV FTV WiFi ↕ ⊛ ⅃ 45 Gym Leisure club Turnberry Adventures Turnberry Performance Academy Xmas New Year **Conf:** Class 130 Board 60 Theatre 700 **Services:** Lift Night porter **Parking:** 635 **Notes:** Civ Wed 300

Malin Court
★★★ 79% HOTEL

tel: 01655 331457 **KA26 9PB**
email: info@malincourt.co.uk **web:** www.malincourt.co.uk
dir: *A74 to Ayr then A719 to Turnberry and Maidens.*

Forming part of the Malin Court Residential and Nursing Home Complex, this friendly and comfortable hotel enjoys delightful views over the Firth of Clyde and Turnberry golf courses. Standard and executive rooms are available; all are well equipped. Public areas are plentiful, with the restaurant serving high teas, dinners and light lunches.

Rooms: 18 (9 family) ⌂ **S** fr £75 **D** fr £105 (including breakfast)* **Facilities:** STV WiFi New Year **Conf:** Class 60 Board 30 Theatre 200 **Services:** Lift Night porter **Parking:** 110 **Notes:** LB Closed 1–5 January RS October to March

UPHALL
West Lothian   Map 21 NT07

Macdonald Houstoun House
★★★★ 76% ◉◉ HOTEL   MACDONALD HOTELS & RESORTS

tel: 01506 853831 **EH52 6JS**
email: houstoun@macdonald-hotels.co.uk **web:** www.macdonaldhotels.co.uk
dir: *M8 junction 3 follow Broxburn signs, straight over roundabout, at mini-roundabout turn right towards Uphall, hotel 1 mile on right.*

This historic 17th-century tower house lies in beautifully landscaped grounds and gardens, and features a modern leisure club and spa, a choice of dining options, a vaulted cocktail bar and extensive conference and meeting facilities. Stylish bedrooms, some located around a courtyard, are comfortably furnished and well equipped.

Rooms: 73 (47 annexe) (12 family) (12 GF) ⌂ **Facilities:** Spa STV FTV WiFi ↕ ⊛ ⅃ Gym Health and beauty salon Xmas New Year **Conf:** Class 80 Board 80 Theatre 400 **Services:** Night porter **Parking:** 250 **Notes:** LB Civ Wed 200

UPLAWMOOR
East Renfrewshire   Map 20 NS45

Uplawmoor Hotel
★★★ 79% SMALL HOTEL   THE CIRCLE

tel: 01505 850565 **66 Neilston Road G78 4AF**
email: info@uplawmoor.co.uk **web:** www.uplawmoor.co.uk
dir: *M77 junction 2, A736 signed Barrhead and Irvine. Hotel 4 miles beyond Barrhead.*

Originally a coaching inn, this friendly hotel is set in a village off the Glasgow to Irvine road. The relaxed restaurant features imaginative dishes, while the popular lounge bar is a great setting for freshly prepared bar meals. The modern bedrooms are both comfortable and well equipped, and Uplawmoor Hotel prides itself on the level of hospitality it provides to guests.

Rooms: 14 (1 family) ⌂ **S** fr £60 **D** fr £74 **Facilities:** STV WiFi ↕ **Parking:** 40 **Notes:** LB Closed 26 December, 1 January

WICK
Highland   Map 23 ND35

Mackay's Hotel
★★★ 84% ◉ HOTEL

tel: 01955 602323 **Union Street KW1 5ED**
email: info@mackayshotel.co.uk **web:** www.mackayshotel.co.uk
dir: *Opposite Caithness General Hospital.*

This well-established hotel is situated just outside the town centre overlooking the River Wick and has an entrance onto the world's shortest street – Ebenezer Place. MacKay's provides well-equipped, attractive accommodation, suited to both the business and leisure guest. There is a stylish bistro offering food throughout the day and the main bar offers a wide selection of whiskies.

Rooms: 30 (1 family) ⌂ **Facilities:** FTV WiFi ↕ HL Complimentary use of local gym and pool **Conf:** Class 100 Board 60 Theatre 200 **Services:** Lift Night porter **Notes:** LB Civ Wed 200

Scottish Islands

ISLE OF HARRIS

TARBERT
Map 22 NB10

Hotel Hebrides

★★★★ 74% ⚘ HOTEL

tel: 01859 502364 **Pier Road HS3 3DG**
email: stay@hotel-hebrides.com **web:** www.hotel-hebrides.com
dir: *To Tarbert via ferry from Uig (Isle of Skye) or ferry from Ullapool to Stornaway, A859 to Tarbert; or by plane to Stornaway from Glasgow, Edinburgh or Inverness.*

Benefiting from an elevated position overlooking the town, this hotel is just a few minutes' walk from the centre. The small, hands-on team extend wonderful hospitality and customer care. The bedrooms are stylishly designed and include WiFi, high speed internet access and TVs; the deluxe rooms have iPod docking stations and some rooms have loch and harbour views. Award-winning food is served in the Pierhouse Restaurant. A complimentary bus service in the summer months is provided to the theatre.

Rooms: 21 (2 family) ☏ **Facilities:** FTV WiFi ☒ ♫ **Conf:** Class 35 Board 35 **Parking:** 10

ISLE OF ISLAY

PORT ASKAIG
Map 20 NR46

Port Askaig Hotel

★★ 65% SMALL HOTEL

tel: 01496 840245 **PA46 7RD**
email: hotel@portaskaig.co.uk **web:** www.portaskaig.co.uk
dir: *At ferry terminal.*

The building of this endearing family-run hotel dates back to the 18th century. The lounge provides fine views over the Sound of Islay to Jura, and there is a choice of bars that are popular with locals – the Snug Bar and the Old Malt Whisky Bar. There is also a beer garden. Traditional dinners and seafood fresh from the harbour are served in the bright 'Starboard' restaurant and a full range of bar snacks and meals is also on offer. The bedrooms are smart and comfortable, and free WiFi is available.

Rooms: 13 (2 annexe) (4 family) (11 GF) ☏ **Facilities:** WiFi **Parking:** 21 **Notes:** LB

SHETLAND

LERWICK
Map 24 HU44

Shetland Hotel

★★★ 79% HOTEL

tel: 01595 695515 **Holmsgarth Road ZE1 0PW**
email: reception@shetlandhotel.co.uk **web:** www.shetlandhotels.com
dir: *Opposite ferry terminal, on main road north from town centre.*

This purpose-built hotel is centrally opposite the main ferry terminal. Spacious and comfortable bedrooms are situated on three floors, and many look out over the harbour itself. The popular Waterfront Bar & Grill offers diverse, well-executed and enjoyable dishes. There is also the Beltramis Sports Bar on the ground floor.

Rooms: 64 (4 family) ☏ **S** fr £112 **D** fr £138 (including breakfast)* **Facilities:** FTV WiFi ☒ **Conf:** Class 75 Board 50 Theatre 300 **Services:** Lift Night porter **Parking:** 150 **Notes:** Closed 25–26 December, 1–2 January Civ Wed 200

SCALLOWAY
Map 24 HU33

Scalloway Hotel

★★★ 80% ⚘⚘ SMALL HOTEL

tel: 01595 880444 **Main Street ZE1 0TR**
email: info@scallowayhotel.com **web:** www.scallowayhotel.com
dir: *6 miles from main port of Lerwick on A970. Situated in Scalloway Main Street.*

Scalloway is the ancient capital of Shetland, and the Scalloway Hotel sits overlooking the waterfront. On offer is warm, friendly service and award-winning food using the best produce that the Shetland larder can provide. The bedrooms feature Shetland tweeds and sheepskin rugs and have very smart en suite bathrooms.

Rooms: 23 ☏ **Facilities:** FTV WiFi ☒ **Parking:** 10

ISLE OF SKYE

ARDVASAR
Map 22 NG60

Ardvasar Hotel

★★★ 82% SMALL HOTEL

tel: 01471 844223 **Sleat IV45 8RS**
email: bookings@ardvasarhotel.com **web:** www.ardvasarhotel.com
dir: *From ferry, 500 metres, left signed Ardvasar.*

The Ardvasar is situated on the waterfront, on the shores of sound of Sleat, only a ten-minute walk from the Armadale ferry terminal. The accommodation provided is comfortable, and most rooms have stunning views over the sound of Sleat to the mountains in the distance. The relaxed Bar/Restaurant offers a selection of fresh local produce including seafood. Ample car parking and relaxing terrace at the front.

Rooms: 10 (4 family) **S** fr £155 **D** fr £165 (including breakfast)* **Facilities:** FTV WiFi ☒ Fishing ♫ Xmas New Year **Conf:** Class 16 Board 16 **Parking:** 30

ISLEORNSAY
Map 22 NG71

Duisdale House Hotel

★★★★ 84% ⚘⚘ SMALL HOTEL

tel: 01471 833202 **Sleat IV43 8QW**
email: info@duisdale.com **web:** www.duisdale.com
dir: *7 miles south of Broadford on A851 towards Armadale. 7 miles north of Armadale ferry.*

This grand Victorian house stands in its own landscaped gardens overlooking the Sound of Sleat. The hotel has a contemporary and chic style which complements the original features of the house. Each bedroom is individually designed and the superior rooms have four-poster beds. The elegant lounge has sumptuous sofas, original artwork and blazing log fires in the colder months.

Rooms: 18 (1 family) (1 GF) ☏ **Facilities:** STV WiFi ☒ Private yacht Outdoor hydropool Golf and salmon fishing available at sister hotel (Skeabost House Hotel) Xmas New Year **Conf:** Board 28 Theatre 50 **Parking:** 30 **Notes:** LB Civ Wed 55

INSPECTOR'S CHOICE

Kinloch Lodge

★★★ ◎◎◎ ≋ COUNTRY HOUSE HOTEL

tel: 01471 833214 Sleat IV43 8QY
email: reservations@kinloch-lodge.co.uk web: www.kinloch-lodge.co.uk
dir: 6 miles south of Broadford on A851, 10 miles north of Armadale on A851.

Now a long established landmark on the Scottish hospitality scene, Lord and
Lady MacDonald's baronial hunting lodge has been refurbished and is now run
in a very hands-on fashion by their daughter, Isabella. Kinloch Lodge enjoys a
picture-postcard location surrounded by hills and a sea loch. Bedrooms and
bathrooms are well appointed and comfortable, while public areas boast
numerous open fires and relaxing seating areas. There is a cookery school run by
chef Marcello Tully, and also a shop that sells cookery books and produce. The
hotel employs a ghillie to oversee fishing, foraging and stalking.

Rooms: 19 (10 annexe) (3 GF) ⟑ S fr £150 D fr £400 (including breakfast)*
Facilities: Spa STV FTV WiFi Fishing Beauty treatment room Cookery classes
Foraging Stalking Wildlife adventures Xmas New Year Conf: Class 20 Board 20
Theatre 20 Parking: 40

HIGHLY RECOMMENDED

Toravaig House Hotel

★★★ 88% ◎◎ SMALL HOTEL

tel: 01471 820200 Knock Bay, Sleat IV44 8RE
email: info@toravaig.com web: www.toravaig.com
dir: From Skye Bridge, left at Broadford onto A851, hotel 11 miles on left. Or from ferry
at Armadale take A851, hotel 6 miles on right.

Set in two acres and enjoying panoramic views to the Knoydart Hills, this hotel is
a haven of peace, with stylish, well-equipped and beautifully decorated
bedrooms. There is an inviting lounge complete with deep sofas and an elegant
dining room where delicious meals are the order of the day. The hotel provides a
sea-going yacht for guests' exclusive use from April to September.

Toravaig House Hotel

Rooms: 9 ⟑ Facilities: STV WiFi ♨ Daily excursions (April to September) on hotel
yacht Xmas New Year Conf: Class 15 Board 15 Theatre 15 Parking: 15 Notes: LB
No children 5 years Civ Wed 25

Hotel Eilean Iarmain

★★★ 77% ◎ SMALL HOTEL
                                          THE CIRCLE

tel: 01471 833332 Sleat IV43 8QR
email: hotel@eileaniarmain.co.uk web: www.eileaniarmain.co.uk
dir: From Skye Bridge take A87 towards Broadford. Left onto A851 signed Armadale.
8 miles, left to hotel. Or from Armadale ferry take A851 signed Broadford. 7 miles to hotel.

A hotel of charm and character, this 19th-century former inn sits by the pier and
enjoys fine views across the sea loch. Bedrooms are individual and retain a
traditional style, and a stable block has been converted into four delightful suites.
Public rooms are cosy and inviting, and the restaurant offers award-winning menus
showcasing the island's best produce, especially seafood and game.

Rooms: 16 (10 annexe) (4 family) (3 GF) ⟑ S fr £70 D fr £80 (including breakfast)*
Facilities: FTV WiFi ♨ Fishing Shooting Art exhibitions Whisky tasting Tweed shop
Gift shop ♫ Xmas New Year Conf: Class 10 Board 14 Theatre 25 Parking: 20
Notes: Civ Wed 30

| PORTREE | Map 22 NG44 |

Bosville Hotel

★★★★ 76% ◎◎ HOTEL

tel: 01478 612846 9-11 Bosville Terrace IV51 9DG
email: reservations@bosvillehotel.co.uk web: www.bosvillehotel.co.uk
dir: Phone for directions.

This contemporary style hotel sits at the top of Portree town with views down to the
harbour and hills beyond. Comfortable rooms come well equipped with coffee
machines, bottled water and snug beds. Dulse & Brose offers the best quality local
produce in its relaxed dining room. A visit to the Merchants bar should not be
missed for its noteworthy range of local spirits and ales.

Rooms: 20 (1 annexe) (4 family) ⟑ Facilities: FTV WiFi Conf: Class 20 Board 20
Theatre 20 Services: Night porter Parking: 10

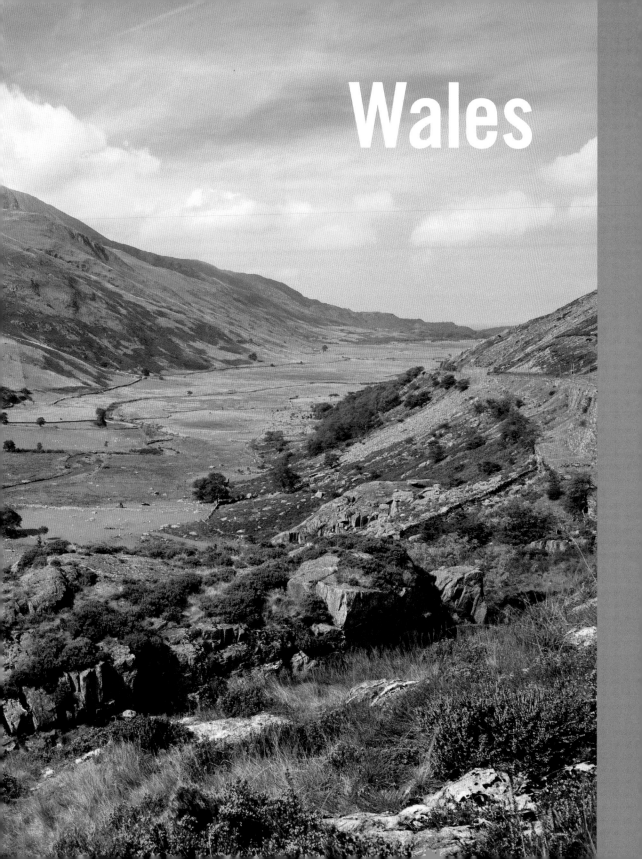

Wales

A

ABERDARE
Rhondda Cynon Taf

Map 9 SO00

Premier Inn Aberdare

Premier Inn

BUDGET HOTEL

tel: 0871 527 8002 (Calls cost 13p per minute plus your phone company's access charge) **Riverside Retail Park, Tirfounders Field CF44 0AH**
web: www.premierinn.com
dir: *M4 junction 32, A470 signed Merthyr Tydfil. In approximately 10 miles take A4059 signed Aberdare. Straight on at 1st roundabout, 3rd exit at next roundabout into Ffordd Tirwaun signed Riverside Retail Park, hotel in park.*

High quality, budget accommodation ideal for both families and business travellers. Spacious, en suite bedrooms feature free WiFi and tea and coffee making facilities, and in most hotels, Freeview TV is also available. The adjacent family restaurant features a wide and varied menu.

Rooms: 40

ABERDYFI
Gwynedd

Map 14 SN69

AA HOTEL OF THE YEAR FOR WALES 2018–19

Trefeddian Hotel

★★★ 82% HOTEL

tel: 01654 767213 **LL35 0SB**
email: info@trefwales.com **web:** www.trefwales.com

Perfectly summed up by the quote from the hotel literature as being "where the mountains meet the the sea". This family-run hotel is in a delightful location and provides many bedrooms that enjoy views over the golf course and sea. Traditional, welcoming hospitality and attentive service is assured, and many guests regularly return. In addition to walks along the beach, the hotel offers a heated indoor pool, treatment room, games room and a range of activities for the whole family. Dinner

is the highlight of a visit with a five-course, daily changing menu that uses carefully prepared local produce.

Trefeddian Hotel

Rooms: 59 (15 family) ⚫ **S** fr £83 **D** fr £166 (including breakfast & dinner)*
Facilities: WiFi HL 🕙 😊 Outdoor play area Beauty salon **Services:** Lift Night porter Air con **Parking:** 68 **Notes:** LB Closed mid December to mid January

ABERGAVENNY
Monmouthshire

HIGHLY RECOMMENDED

Angel Hotel

★★★★ 83% 🏵 HOTEL

tel: 01873 857121 **15 Cross Street NP7 5EN**
email: mail@angelabergavenny.com **web:** www.angelabergavenny.com
dir: *From A40 and A465 junction follow town centre signs, south of Abergavenny, past rail and bus stations.*

Once a coaching inn, this has long been a popular venue for both locals and visitors; the two traditional function rooms and the ballroom are in regular use.

In addition there is a comfortable lounge, a relaxed bar and a smart restaurant. In warmer weather there is a central courtyard that is ideal for alfresco eating. The bedrooms include a four-poster room and some that are suitable for families.

Angel Hotel

Rooms: 34 (4 annexe) (2 family) 🐾 **D** fr £99 (including breakfast)*
Facilities: FTV WiFi ⌂ 🎵 Xmas New Year **Conf:** Class 60 Board 60 Theatre 180
Services: Lift Night porter Air con **Parking:** 30 **Notes:** LB Closed 25 December Civ Wed 180

See advert on following page

Llansantffraed Court Hotel

★★★★ 77% ◉◉ COUNTRY HOUSE HOTEL

tel: 01873 840678 **Old Raglan Road, Llanvihangel Gobion NP7 9BA**
email: reception@llch.co.uk **web:** www.llch.co.uk
dir: *At A465 and A40 Abergavenny junction take B4598 signed Usk (do not join A40). Towards Raglan, hotel on left in 4.5 miles.*

In a commanding position and in its own extensive grounds, this very impressive, privately owned country house hotel has enviable views of the Brecon Beacons. Extensive public areas include a relaxing lounge and a spacious restaurant offering imaginative and enjoyable award-winning dishes. Bedrooms vary in size and reflect the individuality of the building; all are comfortably furnished and provide thoughtful extras. Extensive parking is available.

Rooms: 20 (1 family) 🐾 **Facilities:** STV FTV WiFi ⌂ Fishing 🎣 Clay pigeon shooting school Xmas New Year **Conf:** Class 120 Board 100 Theatre 220 **Services:** Lift Night porter **Parking:** 250 **Notes:** LB Civ Wed 200

Premier Inn Abergavenny

BUDGET HOTEL

tel: 0871 097 1089 (Calls cost 13p per minute plus your phone company's access charge) **Westgate, Llanfoist NP7 9LH**
web: www.premierinn.com
dir: *Follow A465 (signed Merthyr Tydfil). Take slip road left signed A4143 Abergavenney. Continue along this road where hotel is on left.*

High quality, budget accommodation ideal for both families and business travellers. Spacious, en suite bedrooms feature free WiFi and tea and coffee making facilities, and in most hotels, Freeview TV is also available. The adjacent family restaurant features a wide and varied menu.

Rooms: 61

ABERGELE — Conwy — Map 14 SH97

The Kinmel & Kinspa

★★★★ 77% ◉◉ HOTEL

tel: 01745 832014 **St George Road LL22 9AS**
email: reception@thekinmel.co.uk **web:** www.thekinmel.co.uk
dir: *A55 junction 24, hotel entrance on roundabout.*

In a rural location at the end of a long drive leading from the A55, parts of this notable, family-run hotel date from the 16th century. The hotel has a stunning Kinspa and leisure facility along with a range of smart, contemporary bedrooms. The stylish 1786 Brasserie serves modern British cuisine, while a Thai-inspired lighter option is available at Chiang Mai in the spa.

Rooms: 42 (8 family) (18 GF) 🐾 **S** fr £80 **D** fr £120 (including breakfast)*
Facilities: Spa FTV WiFi ⌂ 🕉 Gym Steam room Sauna Hydrotherapy pool Relaxation room Xmas New Year **Conf:** Class 100 Board 100 Theatre 250 **Services:** Lift Night porter **Parking:** 85 **Notes:** LB Civ Wed 150

ABERSOCH — Gwynedd — Map 14 SH32

Porth Tocyn Hotel

★★★ 81% ◉◉ COUNTRY HOUSE HOTEL

tel: 01758 713303 & 07789 994942 **Bwlchtocyn LL53 7BU**
email: bookings@porthtocynhotel.co.uk **web:** www.porthtocynhotel.co.uk
dir: *2.5 miles south of Abersoch follow Porth Tocyn signs after Sarnbach.*

Located above Abersoch with fine views across Cardigan bay, Porth Tocyn is set in its own attractive gardens. Several elegantly furnished sitting rooms are provided with space set aside for families. Bedrooms are comfortably appointed. Award-winning food is served in the restaurant with both a formal option and more relaxed menu offered.

Rooms: 17 (1 family) (3 GF) **S** fr £85 **D** fr £120 (including breakfast)* **Facilities:** FTV WiFi 🎾 🏊 Table tennis **Conf:** Class 15 **Parking:** 50 **Notes:** LB Closed November to week before Easter RS Low season

BALA — Gwynedd — Map 14 SH93

Palé Hall Hotel & Restaurant

★★★★★ ◉◉◉ COUNTRY HOUSE HOTEL

tel: 01678 530285 **Llandderfel LL23 7PS**
email: enquiries@palehall.co.uk **web:** www.palehall.co.uk
dir: *Phone for directions.*

Palé Hall was originally built in 1871 by industrialist Henry Robertson with the instruction that 'no expense should be spared'. The result was a grand Victorian mansion that has played host to many important figures including Churchill and Queen Victoria; the bath and bed used by Victoria are still in place today. Fully restored, this interesting house has a wealth of original features including a hydro-electric system powered by water from the nearby River Dee – it continues to provide electricity for the whole property. The comfortable bedrooms are individually decorated and furnished. Afternoon tea, in the sumptuous drawing room, is a must but make sure you leave room for dinner, a truly wonderful experience. In-room spa treatments are available to guests.

Rooms: 18 (6 family) (1 GF) 🐾 **S** fr £225 **D** fr £295 (including breakfast)*
Facilities: FTV WiFi ⌂ Fishing 🎣 In-room beauty treatment 🎵 Xmas New Year **Conf:** Board 12 Theatre 12 **Services:** Lift Night porter **Parking:** 50 **Notes:** Civ Wed 60

BANGOR
Gwynedd

Map 14 SH57

Premier Inn Bangor

BUDGET HOTEL

tel: 0871 527 8046 (Calls cost 13p per minute plus your phone company's access charge) **Parc Menai, Ffordd Y Parc LL57 4FA**
web: www.premierinn.com
dir: *A55 junction 9 (Holyhead, Ysbyty Gwynedd Hospital). Take 3rd exit off roundabout. Hotel next left.*

High quality, budget accommodation ideal for both families and business travellers. Spacious, en suite bedrooms feature free WiFi and tea and coffee making facilities, and in most hotels, Freeview TV is also available. The adjacent family restaurant features a wide and varied menu.

Rooms: 78

BEAUMARIS
Isle Of Anglesey

Map 14 SH67

Château Rhianfa

★★★★ 80% ֎ HOTEL

tel: 01248 880090 & 713656 **Beaumaris LL59 5NS**
email: hello@chateaurhianfa.com **web:** www.chateaurhianfa.com
dir: *Situated between Menai Bridge and Beaumaris.*

Built in the mid-19th century as a dower house in the style of a French château, Rhianfa has been carefully restored in recent years to create a luxurious venue. Mature grounds reach to the shore. Bedrooms are spacious with modern facilities. The bar and lounges are on an upper floor affording spectacular views of Snowdonia and the Menai Straits. A choice of bars is available including the 'Wine Cave', and dinner is a highlight of any stay.

Rooms: 23 (7 annexe) (4 GF) **Facilities:** FTV WiFi ⓢ Sauna Xmas New Year
Conf: Class 40 Theatre 50 **Services:** Lift Night porter **Parking:** 40
Notes: Civ Wed 100

The Bulkeley Hotel

★★★ 79% HOTEL

tel: 01248 810415 **Castle Street LL58 8AW**
email: reception@bulkeleyhotel.co.uk **web:** www.bulkeleyhotel.co.uk
dir: *A55 junction 8a to Beaumaris. Hotel in town centre.*

A Grade I listed hotel built in 1832, The Bulkeley is just 100 yards from the 13th-century Beaumaris Castle in the centre of town. Friendly staff create a relaxed atmosphere. Refreshments and meals are served throughout the day in a choice of bars, a coffee shop, the fine dining restaurant and bistro. The well-equipped

bedrooms and suites, some with four-posters, are generally spacious, and have pretty furnishings. Many of the rooms have fine panoramic views across the Menai Straits to the Snowdonian Mountains.

Rooms: 43 (3 family) **Facilities:** FTV WiFi Xmas New Year **Conf:** Class 40 Board 25 Theatre 160 **Services:** Lift Night porter **Parking:** 25 **Notes:** Civ Wed 100

HIGHLY RECOMMENDED

Bishopsgate House Hotel

★★ 85% ֎ SMALL HOTEL

tel: 01248 810302 **54 Castle Street LL58 8BB**
email: hazel@bishopsgatehotel.co.uk **web:** www.bishopsgatehotel.co.uk
dir: *From Menai Bridge onto A545 to Beaumaris. Hotel on left in main street.*

This immaculately maintained, privately-owned and personally-run small hotel dates back to 1760. It features fine examples of wood panelling and a Chinese Chippendale staircase. Thoughtfully furnished bedrooms are attractively decorated and two have four-poster beds. Quality cooking is served in the elegant restaurant and guests have a comfortable lounge and cosy bar to relax in.

Rooms: 9 **Facilities:** FTV WiFi ⓢ Xmas New Year **Parking:** 8

BETWS-Y-COED
Conwy

Map 14 SH75

Craig-y-Dderwen Riverside Hotel

★★★★ 77% ֎ COUNTRY HOUSE HOTEL

tel: 01690 710293 **LL24 0AS**
email: info@snowdoniahotel.com **web:** www.snowdoniahotel.com
dir: *A5 to Betws-y-Coed, cross Waterloo Bridge, take 1st left.*

This Victorian country-house hotel is set in well-maintained grounds alongside the River Conwy, at the end of a tree-lined drive. Views down the river can be enjoyed from the restaurant and deck. Many of the bedrooms have balconies, and the feature rooms include a four-poster bed and a hot tub. There are comfortable lounges and the atmosphere throughout is tranquil and relaxing.

Rooms: 18 (2 family) (1 GF) (1 smoking) **S** fr £110 **D** fr £130 (including breakfast)* **Facilities:** STV FTV WiFi ⓢ Fishing ⛳ Badminton Volleyball New Year
Conf: Class 50 Board 50 Theatre 100 **Services:** Night porter **Parking:** 50 **Notes:** LB Closed 23–26 December, 2 January to 1 February Civ Wed 100

Red Stars

The AA Red Star rating denotes an Inspectors' Choice hotel. They stand out as the very best places to stay and appear in highlighted panels throughout the guide.

B

BETWS-Y-COED *continued*

Royal Oak Hotel

★★★ 85% HOTEL

tel: 01690 710219 **Holyhead Road LL24 0AY**
email: reservations@royaloakhotel.net **web:** www.royaloakhotel.net
dir: *On A5 in town centre, adjacent to St Mary's Church.*

Centrally situated in the village, this elegant, privately owned hotel started life as a coaching inn and now provides very comfortable bedrooms with smart, modern en suite bathrooms. The extensive public areas retain much of their original charm and character. The choice of eating options includes the Grill Bistro, the Stables Bar which is much frequented by locals, and the more formal Llugwy Restaurant.

Rooms: 27 (1 family) **S** fr £85 **D** fr £115 (including breakfast)* **Facilities:** FTV WiFi New Year **Conf:** Class 40 Board 20 Theatre 80 **Services:** Night porter **Parking:** 90 **Notes:** Closed 25–26 December Civ Wed 60

See advert opposite

BODELWYDDAN Map 14 SJ07
Denbighshire

Bodelwyddan Castle Hotel

WARNERLEISUREHOTELS

★★★★ 76% HOTEL

tel: 01745 585088 **LL18 5YA**
email: claire.fletcher@bourne-leisure.co.uk **web:** www.warnerleisurehotels.co.uk
dir: *Exit A55 towards North Wales at junction 25, opposite Marble Church.*

This Grade II listed Victorian castle is situated on the north Wales coast within easy reach of Snowdonia and Cheshire. The famous Bodelwyddan marble church, set in the valley below, can be seen from the grounds and The National Portrait Gallery is also situated on site. The hotel is for adults only and offers a super range of leisure facilities plus numerous daily in-house and external activities such as archery, as well as nightly entertainment in the cabaret suite. Packages range from a minimum two-night, half-board stay.

Rooms: 233 (123 annexe) (114 GF) **Facilities:** Spa FTV WiFi HL Gym Archery Rifle shooting Dancing Xmas New Year **Services:** Lift Night porter **Parking:** 156 **Notes:** No children

BRIDGEND Map 9 SS97
Bridgend

Best Western Heronston Hotel & Spa

Best Western

★★★ 79% HOTEL

tel: 01656 668811 **Ewenny Road CF35 5AW**
email: reservations@bestwesternheronstonhotel.co.uk
web: www.bw-heronstonhotel.co.uk
dir: *M4 junction 35, follow signs for Porthcawl, at 5th roundabout left towards Ogmore-by-Sea B4265, hotel 200 yards on left.*

Situated within easy reach of the town centre and the M4, this large modern hotel offers spacious well-equipped accommodation, including ground-floor rooms. Public areas include an open-plan lounge/bar, attractive restaurant and a smart leisure and fitness club. The hotel also has a choice of function and conference rooms, and ample parking is available.

Rooms: 75 (3 family) (36 GF) **Facilities:** Spa STV FTV WiFi HL Gym Steam room Sauna New Year **Conf:** Class 80 Board 60 Theatre 250 **Services:** Lift Night porter **Parking:** 160 **Notes:** Civ Wed 200

Court Colman Manor

★★★ 70% COUNTRY HOUSE HOTEL

tel: 01656 720212 **Pen-y-Fai CF31 4NG**
email: experience@court-colman-manor.com **web:** www.court-colman-manor.com
dir: *M4 junction 36, A4063 towards Maesteg, after lights 1st exit to Bridgend, under motorway, next right, follow hotel signs.*

Dating back to the Tudor times, this fine mansion is set in its own peaceful grounds outside Bridgend, and is just a short distance from the M4. The spacious, comfortable bedrooms include 10 themed rooms inspired by exotic locations – India, Japan, Morocco etc. The food served in Bokhara Brasserie is imaginative, and Indian and Mediterranean dishes are included in the choices. Diners can watch their meals being prepared in the open-plan kitchen.

Rooms: 30 (6 family) **S** fr £70 **D** fr £100 (including breakfast)* **Facilities:** FTV WiFi HL Xmas New Year **Conf:** Class 60 Theatre 100 **Services:** Night porter **Parking:** 180 **Notes:** Civ Wed 150

Premier Inn Bridgend Central

Premier Inn

BUDGET HOTEL

tel: 0871 527 8146 (Calls cost 13p per minute plus your phone company's access charge) **The Derwen CF32 9ST**
web: www.premierinn.com
dir: *M4 junction 36, A4061 (signed Bridgend and Pen-y-Bont). Hotel at next roundabout.*

High quality, budget accommodation ideal for both families and business travellers. Spacious, en suite bedrooms feature free WiFi and tea and coffee making facilities, and in most hotels, Freeview TV is also available. The adjacent family restaurant features a wide and varied menu.

Rooms: 69

Premier Inn Bridgend M4 Jct 35

BUDGET HOTEL

tel: 0871 527 8144 (Calls cost 13p per minute plus your phone company's access charge) **Pantruthyn Farm, Pencoed CF35 5HY**
web: www.premierinn.com
dir: *At M4 junction 35, behind petrol station and McDonalds.*

Rooms: 60

BUILTH WELLS
Powys
Map 9 SO05

Caer Beris Manor

THE INDEPENDENTS
HOTEL ASSOCIATION

★★★ 78% COUNTRY HOUSE HOTEL

tel: 01982 552601 **Garth Road LD2 3NP**
email: caerberis@btconnect.com web: www.caerberis.com
dir: *From town centre follow A483/Llandovery signs. Hotel on the left. Keep in left hand lane but bear right, straight over mini-roundabout.*

Guests can expect a relaxing stay at this friendly and privately-owned boutique, country house hotel that has extensive and attractive landscaped grounds. Bedrooms are individually decorated and furnished to retain the atmosphere of a bygone era. The spacious and comfortable lounge, complete with log fire, and lounge bar continue this theme. Dining is available in the elegant 1896 Restaurant, complete with 16th-century panelling. Those aiming for total relaxation can also indulge in a wellbeing treatment including massages and facials.

Rooms: 23 (2 family) (3 GF) ♖ **S** fr £88 **D** fr £140 (including breakfast)
Facilities: STV WiFi ♿ Fishing Clay pigeon shooting Birdwatching Walking holidays Xmas New Year **Conf:** Class 80 Board 50 Theatre 100 **Services:** Night porter
Parking: 100 **Notes:** LB Closed 2–15 January Civ Wed 100

CAERNARFON
Gwynedd
Map 14 SH46

Premier Inn Caernarfon

BUDGET HOTEL

tel: 0871 527 8180 (Calls cost 13p per minute plus your phone company's access charge) **Victioria Dock, Balaclava Road LL55 1SQ**
web: www.premierinn.com
dir: *A55 junction 9, at roundabout 1st exit follow Caernarfon signs. In Caernarfon at roundabout (Morrisons on right) 1st exit, keep in right lane, at next roundabout 4th exit to mini-roundabout, hotel opposite.*

High quality, budget accommodation ideal for both families and business travellers. Spacious, en suite bedrooms feature free WiFi and tea and coffee making facilities, and in most hotels, Freeview TV is also available. The adjacent family restaurant features a wide and varied menu.

Rooms: 93

CAERPHILLY
Caerphilly
Map 9 ST18

Premier Inn Caerphilly (Corbetts Lane)

Premier Inn

BUDGET HOTEL

tel: 0871 527 8182 (Calls cost 13p per minute plus your phone company's access charge) **Corbetts Lane CF83 3HX**
web: www.premierinn.com
dir: *M4 junction 32, A470, 2nd left signed Caerphilly. At roundabout 4th exit, at next roundabout 2nd exit. Straight on at next roundabout and at Pwllypant Roundabout, hotel on left.*

High quality, budget accommodation ideal for both families and business travellers. Spacious, en suite bedrooms feature free WiFi and tea and coffee making facilities, and in most hotels, Freeview TV is also available. The adjacent family restaurant features a wide and varied menu.

Rooms: 62

C

CAERPHILLY *continued*

Premier Inn Caerphilly (Crossways)

Premier Inn

BUDGET HOTEL

tel: 0871 527 8184 (Calls cost 13p per minute plus your phone company's access charge) **Crossways Business Park, Pontypandy CF83 3NL**
web: www.premierinn.com
dir: *M4 junction 32, A470 towards Merthyr Tydfil (junction 4 take A458 towards Caerphilly). At Crossways Business Park (5th roundabout). Hotel on right at McDonald's roundabout.*

Rooms: 40

CARDIFF	Map 9 ST17
Cardiff	

The St David's Hotel

PRINCIPAL

★★★★★ 76% HOTEL

tel: 029 2045 4045 **Havannah Street CF10 5SD**
email: stdavids.reservations@thestdavidshotel.com
web: www.thestdavidshotel.com/partner/cardiff-st-davids-hotel-spa
dir: *M4 junction 33, A4232 for 9 miles, follow Cardiff Bay signs, then Techniquest signs, at top exit slip road, 1st left at roundabout, 1st right.*

This imposing, contemporary building sits in a prime position on Cardiff Bay and has a seven-storey atrium creating a dramatic impression. Leading from the atrium are the practically designed and comfortable bedrooms. The Admiral St David Restaurant, serving Australian and pan-Asian food, has views across the water to Penarth, and there is a quiet first-floor lounge for guests seeking peace and quiet. A well-equipped spa and extensive business areas complete the package.

Rooms: 142 ♥ **S** fr £99 **D** fr £99* **Facilities:** Spa FTV WiFi ♨ HL ⊙ Gym Fitness studio Hydrotherapy pool Aerobics studio ♫ **Conf:** Class 110 Board 76 Theatre 270 **Services:** Lift Night porter Air con **Parking:** 60 **Notes:** Civ Wed 270

Novotel Cardiff Central

NOVOTEL
HOTELS & RESORTS

★★★★ 77% HOTEL

tel: 029 2113 2800 & 2047 5000 **Schooner Way, Atlantic Wharf CF10 4RT**
email: h5982@accor.com **web:** www.novotel.com
dir: *M4 junction 29 onto A48(M), follow signs for city centre.*

Situated in the heart of the city's development area, this hotel is equally convenient for the city centre and Cardiff Bay. Bedrooms vary between standard rooms in the modern extension to executive rooms in the original wing. There is good seating space in public rooms, and the hotel has a popular leisure club. The Goods Shed Restaurant is an innovative dining concept.

Rooms: 138 (100 family) ♥ **Facilities:** FTV WiFi ♨ ⊙ Gym Sauna Steam room Xmas New Year **Conf:** Class 80 Board 50 Theatre 200 **Services:** Lift Night porter Air con **Parking:** 120 **Notes:** LB Civ Wed 200

Mercure Cardiff Holland House Hotel & Spa

Mercure
HOTELS

★★★★ 76% HOTEL

tel: 029 2043 5000 **24/26 Newport Road CF24 0DD**
email: h6622@accor.com **web:** www.mercure.com
dir: *M4 junction 33, A4232 to city centre, right at lights opposite prison, straight through next lights, hotel car park at end of lane opposite Magistrates Court.*

Conveniently located just a few minutes' walk from the city centre, this exciting hotel combines contemporary styling with a genuinely friendly welcome. Bedrooms, including five luxurious suites, are spacious and include many useful extras. A state-of-the-art leisure club and spa is available in addition to a large function room. An eclectic menu provides a varied range of freshly prepared, quality dishes.

Rooms: 165 (80 family) ♥ **S** fr £200 **D** fr £210* **Facilities:** Spa STV WiFi ⊙ Gym **Conf:** Class 250 Board 90 Theatre 700 **Services:** Lift Night porter Air con **Parking:** 90 **Notes:** Civ Wed 500

The Angel Hotel

★★★ 76% HOTEL

tel: 029 2064 9200 **Castle Street CF10 1SZ**
email: reservations@angelhotelcardiffcity.co.uk **web:** www.angelhotelcardiffcity.co.uk
dir: *Opposite Cardiff Castle.*

The Angel is a well-established hotel in the heart of the city, overlooking the famous castle and almost opposite the Millennium Stadium. All bedrooms offer air conditioning and are appointed to a good standard. Public areas include an impressive lobby, a modern restaurant and a selection of conference rooms. There is limited parking at the rear of the hotel.

Rooms: 102 (3 family) **S** fr £54 **D** fr £60* **Facilities:** FTV WiFi ♨ HL Xmas New Year **Conf:** Class 120 Board 50 Theatre 300 **Services:** Lift Night porter Air con **Parking:** 60 **Notes:** LB Civ Wed 200

Premier Inn Barry Island (Cardiff Airport)

Premier Inn

BUDGET HOTEL

tel: 0871 527 9370 (Calls cost 13p per minute plus your phone company's access charge) **Triangle Site, Fford Y Mileniwm CF62 5QN**
web: www.premierinn.com
dir: *M4 junction 33 A4232 signed A4050, pass through 8 roundabouts, left onto Trinity Street, right onto A4055 Broad Street. Left after 0.2 mile.*

High quality, budget accommodation ideal for both families and business travellers. Spacious, en suite bedrooms feature free WiFi and tea and coffee making facilities, and in most hotels, Freeview TV is also available. The adjacent family restaurant features a wide and varied menu.

Rooms: 80

Premier Inn Cardiff City Centre

Premier Inn

BUDGET HOTEL

tel: 0871 527 8196 (Calls cost 13p per minute plus your phone company's access charge) **Helmont House, 10 Churchill Way CF10 2HE**
web: www.premierinn.com
dir: *M4 junction 29 onto A48(M) towards Cardiff (East and South), 4.5 miles. Follow Cardiff (East), Docks and A4232 signs. Left at A4161 (Eastern Avenue North). At roundabout 2nd exit onto A4161 (Newport Road). 2 miles, left into Station Terrace. Right into Churchill Way.*

Rooms: 200

Premier Inn Cardiff City South

Premier Inn

BUDGET HOTEL

tel: 0871 527 8198 (Calls cost 13p per minute plus your phone company's access charge) **Keen Road CF24 5JT**
web: www.premierinn.com
dir: *Follow Cardiff Docks and Bay signs from A48(M), over flyover. At 5th roundabout, 3rd exit. Hotel 1st right, then 1st right again.*

Rooms: 97

C

Premier Inn Cardiff East

BUDGET HOTEL

tel: 0871 527 8200 (Calls cost 13p per minute plus your phone company's access charge) **Newport Road, Castleton CF3 2UQ**
web: www.premierinn.com
dir: *M4 junction 28, A48 signed Castleton. 3 miles, hotel on right.*

Rooms: 49

Premier Inn Cardiff North

BUDGET HOTEL

tel: 0871 527 8202 (Calls cost 13p per minute plus your phone company's access charge) **Pentwyn Road, Pentwyn CF23 7XH**
web: www.premierinn.com
dir: *Westbound: M4 junction 29, A48(M). (Eastbound: M4 junction 30, A4232 signs, A48(M) towards Cardiff). Follow Pentwyn signs, 3rd exit at roundabout. Hotel 200 yards on right.*

Rooms: 147

Premier Inn Cardiff (Roath)

BUDGET HOTEL

tel: 0871 527 8194 (Calls cost 13p per minute plus your phone company's access charge) **Ipswich Road, Roath CF23 9AQ**
web: www.premierinn.com
dir: *Westbound: M4 junction 29, A48(M). Eastbound: M4 junction 30 A48(M). Follow Cardiff (East) Docks and Cardiff Bay signs. Then follow brown signs for David Lloyd Tennis Centre. Into David Lloyd Leisure Club car park, follow hotel signs.*

Rooms: 75

Premier Inn Cardiff West

BUDGET HOTEL

tel: 0871 527 8204 (Calls cost 13p per minute plus your phone company's access charge) **Port Road, Nantisaf, Wenvoe CF5 6DD**
web: www.premierinn.com
dir: *M4 junction 33, south on A4232. Take 2nd exit (signed Airport), 3rd exit at Culverhouse Cross roundabout. Hotel 0.5 mile on Barry Road (A4050).*

Rooms: 59

CARMARTHEN
Carmarthenshire   Map 8 SN42

Ivy Bush Royal Hotel

★★★ 77% HOTEL

tel: 01267 235111 **Spilman Street SA31 1LG**
email: reception@ivybushroyal.co.uk **web:** www.ivybushroyal.co.uk
dir: *A48 to Carmarthen, over 1st roundabout, at 2nd roundabout right onto A4242. Straight over next 2 roundabouts. Left at lights. Hotel on right at top of hill.*

This hotel offers spacious, well-equipped bedrooms and bathrooms, a relaxing lounge with outdoor patio seating, and a comfortable restaurant serving a varied selection of carefully prepared meals. Weddings, meetings and conferences are all well catered for at this friendly, family-run establishment.

Rooms: 70 (4 family) **Facilities:** FTV WiFi Gym Xmas New Year **Conf:** Class 50 Board 40 Theatre 200 **Services:** Lift Night porter **Parking:** 83 **Notes:** LB Civ Wed 150

CONWY
Conwy   Map 14 SH77

Castle Hotel Conwy

★★★★ 79% TOWN HOUSE HOTEL

tel: 01492 582800 High Street LL32 8DB
email: castle@innmail.co.uk **web:** www.castlewales.co.uk
dir: *A55 junction 18, follow town centre signs, cross estuary (castle on left). Right then left at mini-roundabout onto one-way system. Right at Town Wall Gate, right into Berry Street then High Street.*

This family-run, 16th-century hotel is one of Conwy's most distinguished buildings and offers a relaxed and friendly atmosphere. Bedrooms are appointed to an impressive standard and include a stunning suite and a choice of individually-styled rooms. Downstairs there's a popular modern bar serving real ales, and the award-winning Dawsons restaurant. Healing Hands beauty and holistic therapy is an added bonus.

Rooms: 29 (2 family) **S** fr £115 **D** fr £125* **Facilities:** FTV WiFi Holistic therapy treatment room Xmas New Year **Services:** Night porter **Parking:** 34 **Notes:** LB

CRICCIETH
Gwynedd   Map 14 SH43

HIGHLY RECOMMENDED

Bron Eifion Country House Hotel

★★★★ 83% COUNTRY HOUSE HOTEL

tel: 01766 522385 LL52 0SA
email: enquiries@broneifion.co.uk **web:** www.broneifion.co.uk
dir: *A497 between Porthmadog and Pwllheli, 0.5 mile from Criccieth, on right towards Pwllheli.*

This delightful country house, built in 1883, is set in extensive grounds to the west of Criccieth, commanding impressive sea views. Now a privately-owned and personally-run hotel, it provides warm and very friendly hospitality. The interior styling highlights many retained period features. There is a choice of lounges and the very impressive central hall features a minstrels' gallery. The Gin List should not be missed — 50 varieties are served with a selection of accompaniments including pink grapefruit, blueberries and star anise.

Rooms: 18 (1 family) (1 GF) **S** fr £95 **D** fr £145 (including breakfast)*
Facilities: FTV WiFi **Conf:** Class 150 Board 60 Theatre 150 **Parking:** 50
Notes: LB Civ Wed 150

George IV Hotel

★★★ 75% HOTEL

Leisureplex
HOLIDAY HOTELS

tel: 01766 522168 **23-25 High Street LL52 0BS**
email: georgeiv.criccieth@alfatravel.co.uk **web:** www.leisureplex.co.uk
dir: *On A497 in town centre.*

This hotel stands back from the A497 in the town centre. The bedrooms, which in general are spacious, are attractively furnished and well equipped to meet the needs of both business guests and holidaymakers. George's Brasserie serves a menu based on locally sourced ingredients.

Rooms: 80 (5 family) **Facilities:** FTV WiFi Xmas New Year **Services:** Lift Night porter **Parking:** 16 **Notes:** Closed January RS November, February to March

CRICKHOWELL
Powys

Map 9 SO21

Manor Hotel

★★★ 77% <img_1> HOTEL

tel: 01873 810212 **Brecon Road NP8 1SE**
email: info@manorhotel.co.uk **web:** www.manorhotel.co.uk
dir: On A40, 0.5 mile from Crickhowell.

This impressive manor house, set in a stunning location, was the birthplace of Sir George Everest, after whom Mount Everest is named. The bedrooms and public areas are elegant, and there are extensive leisure facilities. The restaurant, with panoramic views, is the setting for exciting modern cooking.

Rooms: 22 (2 family) **S** fr £75 **D** fr £95 (including breakfast)* **Facilities:** STV FTV WiFi ♨ ⏱ Gym Xmas New Year **Conf:** Class 250 Board 150 Theatre 300 **Parking:** 200 **Notes:** LB Civ Wed 150

CWMBRAN
Torfaen

Map 9 ST29

The Parkway Hotel & Spa

★★★★ 80% <img_1> <img_1> HOTEL

tel: 01633 871199 **Cwmbran Drive NP44 3UW**
email: enquiries@theparkwayhotel.co.uk **web:** www.parkwayhotelandspa.com
dir: M4 junction 25a and 26, A4051 follow Cwmbran-Llantarnam Park signs. Right at roundabout, right for hotel.

This purpose-built hotel, in over seven acres of grounds, offers comfortable bedrooms and public areas that will suit a wide range of guests. The coffee shop is an informal eating option throughout the day, and there is fine dining in Ravellos Restaurant. The bedrooms, including suites, interconnecting family rooms and wheelchair access rooms, are stylishly appointed. Additional facilities include a spa, sports centre and conference and meeting rooms.

Rooms: 80 (4 family) (34 GF) ↾ **S** fr £80 **D** fr £90 (including breakfast)* **Facilities:** Spa FTV WiFi ♨ ⏱ 🏌 Gym Steam room Sauna Boules Table tennis Chess Badminton Snooker 🎵 Xmas New Year **Conf:** Class 240 Board 100 Theatre 500 **Services:** Lift Night porter **Parking:** 300 **Notes:** LB Civ Wed 500

Premier Inn Cwmbran

Premier Inn

BUDGET HOTEL

tel: 0871 57 8284 (Calls cost 13p per minute plus your phone company's access charge) **Avondale Road, Pontrhydyrun NP44 1DE**
web: www.premierinn.com
dir: M4 junction 26, A4501 signed Cwmbran, straight on at next 5 roundabouts. At 6th take Pontrhydyrun Road exit, left into Avondale Road.

High quality, budget accommodation ideal for both families and business travellers. Spacious, en suite bedrooms feature free WiFi and tea and coffee making facilities, and in most hotels, Freeview TV is also available. The adjacent family restaurant features a wide and varied menu.

Rooms: 41

DEGANWY
Conwy

Map 14 SH77

Quay Hotel & Spa

★★★★ 81% <img_1> HOTEL

tel: 01492 564100 **Deganwy Quay LL31 9DJ**
email: reservations@quayhotel.co.uk **web:** www.quayhotel.co.uk
dir: M56, A494, A55 junction 18, straight across 2 roundabouts. At lights bear left into The Quay. Hotel on right.

This luxury hotel occupies a stunning position beside the estuary on Deganwy's Quay. What was once an area for railway storage is now a property of modern architectural design. Spacious bedrooms, many with balconies and wonderful views, are decorated individually and boast a host of extras. Four penthouse suites command spectacular views. Extensive spa and leisure facilities and The Marina Restaurant complete the experience.

Rooms: 74 (15 family) (30 GF) ↾ **S** fr £120 **D** fr £120 (including breakfast)* **Facilities:** Spa WiFi HL ⏱ Gym Steam room Sauna Hydrotherapy pool 🎵 Xmas New Year **Conf:** Class 240 Board 90 Theatre 240 **Services:** Lift Night porter **Parking:** 96 **Notes:** LB Civ Wed 150

DOLGELLAU
Gwynedd

Map 14 SH71

HIGHLY RECOMMENDED

Penmaenuchaf Hall Hotel

★★★ 86% <img_1> COUNTRY HOUSE HOTEL

WELSH RAREBITS Hotels of Distinction

tel: 01341 422129 **Penmaenpool LL40 1YB**
email: relax@penhall.co.uk **web:** www.penhall.co.uk
dir: A470 onto A493 to Tywyn. Hotel approximately 1 mile on left.

Built in 1860, this impressive hall stands in 20 acres of formal gardens, grounds and woodland, and enjoys magnificent views across the River Mawddach. This comfortable and welcoming hotel has spacious day rooms and thoughtfully furnished bedrooms, some with private balconies. Fresh produce cooked in modern British style is served in an elegant conservatory restaurant, overlooking the countryside.

Rooms: 14 (2 family) ↾ **S** fr £125 **D** fr £185 (including breakfast) **Facilities:** STV FTV WiFi ♨ Fishing 🏌 Complimentary salmon and trout fishing Coracling In-room massage treatments Xmas New Year **Conf:** Class 30 Board 22 Theatre 50 **Parking:** 30 **Notes:** LB No children 6 years Civ Wed 65

EBBW VALE
Blaenau Gwent

Map 9 SO10

Premier Inn Ebbw Vale

BUDGET HOTEL

tel: 0871 527 8356 (Calls cost 13p per minute plus your phone company's access charge) **Victoria Business Park, Waunllwyd NP23 8AN**
web: www.premierinn.com
dir: M4 junction 28, A467 signed Risca, then Brynmawr. At roundabout at Brynithel 1st exit onto A4046, signed Ebbw Vale. At roundabout 3rd exit towards Waunllwyd. At roundabout 1st exit, next left. Hotel adjacent.

High quality, budget accommodation ideal for both families and business travellers. Spacious, en suite bedrooms feature free WiFi and tea and coffee making facilities, and in most hotels, Freeview TV is also available. The adjacent family restaurant features a wide and varied menu.

Rooms: 62

FISHGUARD
Pembrokeshire

Map 8 SM93

The Cartref Hotel

★★ 67% HOTEL

tel: 01348 872430 & 07813 305235 **15-19 High Street SA65 9AW**
email: cartrefhotel@btconnect.com **web:** www.cartrefhotel.co.uk
dir: On A40 in town centre.

Personally run by the proprietor, this friendly hotel offers convenient access to the town centre and ferry terminal. Bedrooms are well maintained and include some family rooms. There is also a cosy lounge bar and a welcoming restaurant that looks out onto the high street.

Rooms: 10 (2 family) ↟ **S** fr £50 **D** fr £75 (including breakfast)* **Facilities:** FTV WiFi **Services:** Night porter **Parking:** 4

HAVERFORDWEST
Pembrokeshire

Map 8 SM91

Premier Inn Haverfordwest North

BUDGET HOTEL

tel: 0871 527 9546 (Calls cost 13p per minute plus your phone company's access charge) **Glanafon Farm House, Fishguard Road SA62 4BP**
web: www.premierinn.com
dir: From east: A40 to Haverfordwest. At roundabout follow Fishguard (A40) signs. Straight on at next roundabout. At next roundabout (Withybush Roundabout) take 2nd exit to hotel.

High quality, budget accommodation ideal for both families and business travellers. Spacious, en suite bedrooms feature free WiFi and tea and coffee making facilities, and in most hotels, Freeview TV is also available. The adjacent family restaurant features a wide and varied menu.

Rooms: 60

HENSOL
Vale Of Glamorgan

Map 9 ST07

The Vale Resort

★★★★ 78% HOTEL

tel: 01443 667800 **Hensol Park CF72 8JY**
email: reservations@vale-hotel.com **web:** www.vale-hotel.com
dir: M4 junction 34 towards Pendoylan, hotel signed from junction.

A wealth of leisure facilities is offered at this large and modern, purpose-built complex, including two golf courses and a driving range plus an extensive health spa with a gym, swimming pool, squash courts, orthopaedic clinic and a range of treatments. Public areas are spacious and attractive, while bedrooms, many with balconies, are well appointed. Meeting and conference facilities are available. Guests can dine in the traditional Vale Grill, a brasserie-style restaurant serving quality fresh ingredients.

Rooms: 143 (114 annexe) (15 family) (35 GF) ↟ **S** fr £120 **D** fr £130 (including breakfast)* **Facilities:** Spa STV WiFi ⊕ 36 Fishing Gym Children's club Saturday morning and school holidays Xmas New Year **Conf:** Class 280 Board 60 Theatre 700 **Services:** Lift Night porter Air con **Parking:** 450 **Notes:** LB Civ Wed 700

KNIGHTON
Powys

Map 9 SO27

Milebrook House Hotel

★★★ 80% COUNTRY HOUSE HOTEL

tel: 01547 528632 **Milebrook LD7 1LT**
email: hotel@milebrookhouse.co.uk **web:** www.milebrookhouse.co.uk
dir: 2 miles east of Knighton, on A4113.

Set in three acres of grounds and gardens in the Teme Valley, this charming house dates back to 1760. Over the years, since its conversion into a hotel, it has acquired a well-deserved reputation for its warm hospitality, comfortable accommodation and the quality of its cuisine, which uses local produce and home-grown vegetables.

Rooms: 10 (1 family) (2 GF) **S** fr £94 **D** fr £152 (including breakfast)* **Facilities:** WiFi Table tennis Xmas New Year **Conf:** Class 30 **Parking:** 21 **Notes:** LB No children 8 years

LAMPETER
Ceredigion

Map 8 SN54

The Falcondale Hotel & Restaurant

★★★★ 78% COUNTRY HOUSE HOTEL

WELSH RAREBITS
Hotels of Distinction

tel: 01570 422910 **Falcondale Drive SA48 7RX**
email: info@thefalcondale.co.uk **web:** www.thefalcondale.co.uk
dir: 1 mile from Lampeter take A482 to Cardigan, turn right at petrol station, follow for 0.75 mile.

Built in the Italianate style, this charming Victorian property is set in extensive grounds and beautiful parkland. The individually-styled bedrooms are generally spacious, well equipped and tastefully decorated. Bars and lounges are similarly well appointed with additional facilities including a conservatory and terrace. The award-winning restaurant, with a relaxed and friendly atmosphere, offers menus based on the best seasonal, locally sourced produce.

Rooms: 17 (2 family) ↟ **S** fr £108 **D** fr £133 (including breakfast)* **Facilities:** FTV WiFi Xmas New Year **Conf:** Class 26 Board 26 Theatre 60 **Services:** Lift **Parking:** 60 **Notes:** LB Civ Wed 200

L

LAUGHARNE
Carmarthenshire
Map 8 SN31

The Corran Resort & Spa
★★★★ 74% 🏵🏵 HOTEL

tel: 01994 427417 **East Marsh SA33 4RS**
email: info@thecorran.com **web:** www.thecorran.com
dir: *From end of M4 onto A48, then A40 to St Clears. Take A4066 towards Pendine and Laugharne. Follow signs to hotel.*

Guests will enjoy the unique setting and surroundings of this unusual hotel located in the quiet marshlands of Carmarthenshire. Bedrooms, mostly located around a courtyard, are contemporary in style yet retain some of the original 16th-century farmhouse features. Dinner and breakfast, in the delightful, award-winning restaurant, utilise the best quality local produce; a sun terrace is available during warmer months. The spa has a pool, sauna, a gym and treatment rooms. Cookery courses are available at The Corran Academy with Jean-Christophe Novelli.

Rooms: 21 (16 annexe) (5 family) (15 GF) 🐾 **Facilities:** Spa STV FTV WiFi 🐾 ⛳ Gym Xmas New Year **Conf:** Class 120 Board 70 Theatre 150 **Services:** Night porter **Parking:** 90 **Notes:** Civ Wed 150

LLANBEDR
Gwynedd
Map 14 SH52

Ty Mawr Hotel
★★ 82% HOTEL

tel: 01341 241440 **LL45 2NH**
email: info@tymawrhotel.com **web:** www.tymawrhotel.com
dir: *From Barmouth A496 Harlech Road. In Llanbedr turn right after bridge, hotel 50 yards on left, follow brown tourist signs.*

Ty Mawr translates as 'Big House' and this particular house is located in the picturesque Snowdonia National Park. The attractive grounds, opposite the River Artro, provide a popular beer garden during fine weather. Family-run, with a relaxed, friendly atmosphere, the focus of the hotel is the rustically furnished bar offering a blackboard selection of food and real ales, and the restaurant where a more formal menu is available. Bedrooms are smart and brightly decorated.

Rooms: 10 (2 family) 🐾 **S** fr £59 **D** fr £89 (including breakfast)* **Facilities:** STV FTV WiFi 🐾 **Parking:** 15 **Notes:** Closed 24–26 December

LLANBERIS
Gwynedd
Map 14 SH56

The Royal Victoria Hotel Snowdonia
★★★ 76% HOTEL

tel: 01286 870253 **LL55 4TY**
email: enquiries@theroyalvictoria.co.uk **web:** www.theroyalvictoria.co.uk
dir: *On A4086 (Caernarfon to Llanberis road), directly opposite Snowdon Mountain Railway.*

This well-established hotel sits near the foot of Snowdon, between the Peris and Padarn lakes. Pretty gardens and grounds make an attractive setting for the many weddings held here. Bedrooms are well equipped. There are spacious lounges and bars, and a large dining room with a conservatory looking out over the lakes.

Rooms: 102 (5 family) 🐾 **S** fr £40 **D** fr £50 (including breakfast) **Facilities:** FTV WiFi 🎵 Xmas New Year **Conf:** Class 60 Board 50 Theatre 100 **Services:** Lift Night porter **Parking:** 140 **Notes:** LB Civ Wed 100

LLANDRINDOD WELLS
Powys
Map 9 SO06

Metropole Hotel & Spa
★★★★ 75% HOTEL

tel: 01597 823700 **Temple Street LD1 5DY**
email: info@metropole.co.uk **web:** www.metropole.co.uk
dir: *On A483 in town centre, car park at rear of hotel.*

The centre of this famous spa town is dominated by this large Victorian hotel, which has been personally run by the same family for well over 100 years. The lobby leads to Spencer's Bar and Brasserie and to the comfortable and elegantly styled lounge. Bedrooms vary in style, but all are spacious and well equipped. Facilities include an extensive range of modern conference and function rooms, as well as the impressive leisure centre. Extensive parking is provided to the rear of the hotel.

Rooms: 109 (11 family) 🐾 **S** fr £98 **D** fr £126 (including breakfast)* **Facilities:** Spa FTV WiFi 🐾 ⛳ Gym Beauty and holistic treatments Sauna Steam room Xmas New Year **Conf:** Class 200 Board 80 Theatre 300 **Services:** Lift Night porter **Parking:** 150 **Notes:** LB Civ Wed 300

LLANDUDNO
Conwy
Map 14 SH78

Bodysgallen Hall and Spa
★★★★ 🏵🏵🏵 COUNTRY HOUSE HOTEL

tel: 01492 584466 **LL30 1RS**
email: info@bodysgallen.com **web:** www.bodysgallen.com
dir: *A55 junction 19, A470 (The Royal Welsh Way) towards Llandudno. Hotel 2 miles on right.*

Situated in the idyllic surroundings of its own parkland and formal gardens, this 17th-century house is in an elevated position, with views towards Snowdonia and across to Conwy Castle. The lounges and dining room have fine antiques and great character. Accommodation is provided in the house, but also in delightfully converted cottages, together with a superb spa. Friendly and attentive service is discreetly offered, while the restaurant features fine local produce prepared with great skill.

Rooms: 31 (16 annexe) (4 family) (4 GF) 🐾 **S** fr £170 **D** fr £190 (including breakfast)* **Facilities:** Spa STV FTV WiFi 🐾 ⛳ Gym Spa treatments Steam room Relaxation room Sauna Xmas New Year **Conf:** Class 30 Board 22 Theatre 50 **Services:** Night porter **Parking:** 50 **Notes:** LB No children 6 years Civ Wed 50

Imperial Hotel

★★★★ 81% ◉◉ HOTEL

tel: 01492 877466 **The Promenade, Vaughan Street LL30 1AP**
email: reception@theimperial.co.uk **web:** www.theimperial.co.uk
dir: A470 to Llandudno.

The Imperial is a large and impressive hotel, situated on the promenade with lovely views out over the Blue Flag beaches to the bay, and within easy reach of the town centre and other amenities. Many of the bedrooms have sea views and there are also several suites available. The elegant Chantrey's Restaurant offers a fixed-price, monthly-changing menu that utilises local produce, and The Terrace is the place to relax and enjoy a leisurely lunch or a snack during the day.

Rooms: 98 (10 family) ☏ **S** fr £80 **D** fr £145 (including breakfast)* **Facilities:** FTV WiFi ☒ ☸ Gym Beauty therapist hairdressing ♫ Xmas New Year **Conf:** Class 50 Board 50 Theatre 120 **Services:** Lift Night porter **Parking:** 25 **Notes:** LB Civ Wed 120

Empire Hotel & Spa

★★★★ 81% HOTEL

tel: 01492 860555 **Church Walks LL30 2HE**
email: reservations@empirehotel.co.uk **web:** www.empirehotel.co.uk
dir: From Chester, A55 junction 19 for Llandudno. Follow signs to Promenade, turn right at war memorial and left at roundabout. Hotel 100 yards on right.

Family run for over 60 years, the Empire offers luxuriously appointed bedrooms with every modern facility. The 'Number 72' rooms in an adjacent house are particularly sumptuous. The indoor pool is overlooked by a lounge and café where snacks are served all day, and in summer an outdoor pool and roof garden are available. Watkins Restaurant offers an interesting fixed-price menu.

Rooms: 58 (8 annexe) (1 family) (2 GF) ☏ **S** fr £80 **D** fr £120 (including breakfast)* **Facilities:** Spa FTV WiFi ☒ HL ☸ ☈ Gym Sauna Steam room Fitness suite ♫ New Year **Services:** Lift Night porter Air con **Parking:** 57 **Notes:** LB Closed 16–28 December

St George's Hotel

★★★★ 80% ◉ HOTEL

tel: 01492 877544 **The Promenade LL30 2LG**
email: sales@stgeorgeswales.co.uk **web:** www.stgeorgeswales.co.uk
dir: A55, A470, follow to promenade, 0.25 mile, hotel on corner.

This large and impressive seafront property was the first hotel to be built in the town. Restored to its former glory, the accommodation is of very high quality and now include five rooftop rooms that have their own private balconies and amazing sea views. The many Victorian features at the hotel are evident in the splendid, ornate Wedgwood Room restaurant. The terrace restaurant and main lounges overlook the bay; hot and cold snacks are available all day.

Rooms: 81 (13 family) ☏ **S** fr £80 **D** fr £110 (including breakfast)* **Facilities:** STV FTV WiFi ☒ Xmas New Year **Conf:** Class 200 Board 45 Theatre 250 **Services:** Lift Night porter Air con **Parking:** 36 **Notes:** LB Civ Wed 200

L

Find out more about the AA Hotel of the Year for Wales on page 18

LLANDUDNO *continued*

include a choice of lounges, a games/snooker room and a ballroom where entertainment is provided every night. The hotel is a popular venue for coach tour parties.

Rooms: 120 (4 family) (9 GF) 🐾 **Facilities:** WiFi Table tennis Snooker 🎵 Xmas New Year **Services:** Lift Night porter **Parking:** 10 **Notes:** Closed January to mid February RS November to December (excluding Christmas), mid February to March

HIGHLY RECOMMENDED

Dunoon Hotel

★★★ 86% ◎◎ HOTEL

tel: 01492 860787 **Gloddaeth Street LL30 2DW**
email: reservations@dunoonhotel.co.uk **web:** www.dunoonhotel.co.uk
dir: *Exit Promenade at war memorial by pier into Gloddaeth Street. Hotel 200 yards on right.*

This impressive, privately-owned hotel is centrally located and offers a variety of well-equipped bedrooms. Elegant public areas include a tastefully appointed restaurant where technically accurate and nicely presented dishes are served together with a good choice of notable, reasonably priced wines. The caring and attentive service is also noteworthy.

Rooms: 48 (4 family) 🐾 **S** fr £73 **D** fr £126 (including breakfast)* **Facilities:** FTV WiFi 🎵 **Conf:** Board 12 Theatre 30 **Services:** Lift **Parking:** 24 **Notes:** LB Closed mid December to early March

Hydro Hotel

★★★ 69% HOTEL

Leisureplex
HOLIDAY HOTELS

tel: 01492 870101 **Neville Crescent LL30 1AT**
email: hydro.llandudno@alfatravel.co.uk **web:** www.leisureplex.co.uk
dir: *Follow signs for theatre to seafront, towards pier.*

This large hotel is situated on the promenade overlooking the sea, and offers good, value-for-money, modern accommodation. Public areas are quite extensive and

Cae Mor

[1]

tel: 01492 878101 & 077960 15613 **6 Penrhyn Crescent LL30 1BA**
email: sheymar@btconnect.com **web:** www.caemorhotel.co.uk
dir: *Exit A55 junction 19, follow A470/Llandudno/Town Centre signs. Straight on at 3 roundabouts, right at 4th. Into right lane, right at next roundabout, follow Promenade signs. Straight on at next roundabout, left at next roundabout onto Promenade. Adjacent to Venue Cymru.*

Currently the rating for this establishment is not confirmed. This may be due to a change of ownership or because ot has only recently joined the AA rating scheme.

Rooms: 23 (1 family) (2 GF) 🐾 **S** fr £70 **D** fr £98 (including breakfast)*
Facilities: FTV WiFi 🐾 Xmas **Conf:** Class 26 Board 24 Theatre 60 **Services:** Lift Night porter **Parking:** 26

Premier Inn Llandudno North (Little Orme)

Premier Inn 🌙

BUDGET HOTEL

tel: 0871 527 8636 (Calls cost 13p per minute plus your phone company's access charge) **Colwyn Road LL30 3AL**
web: www.premierinn.com
dir: *A55 junction 20 follow Rhos-on-Sea/Llandrillo-Yn-Rhos/B5115 signs. Onto B5115 (Brompton Avenue). Straight on at next 2 roundabouts. Hotel on left.*

High quality, budget accommodation ideal for both families and business travellers. Spacious, en suite bedrooms feature free WiFi and tea and coffee making facilities, and in most hotels, Freeview TV is also available. The adjacent family restaurant features a wide and varied menu.

Rooms: 19

LLANDUDNO JUNCTION
Conwy   Map 14 SH77

Premier Inn Llandudno (Glan-Conwy)

Premier Inn 🌙

BUDGET HOTEL

tel: 0871 527 8634 (Calls cost 13p per minute plus your phone company's access charge) **Afon Conwy LL28 5LB**
web: www.premierinn.com
dir: *A55 junction 19. Exit roundabout at A470 (Betws-y-Coed). Hotel immediately on left, opposite petrol station.*

High quality, budget accommodation ideal for both families and business travellers. Spacious, en suite bedrooms feature free WiFi and tea and coffee making facilities, and in most hotels, Freeview TV is also available. The adjacent family restaurant features a wide and varied menu.

Rooms: 69

LLANELLI
Carmarthenshire   Map 8 SN50

Best Western Diplomat Hotel and Spa

★★★ 79% HOTEL

tel: 01554 756156 **Felinfoel SA15 3PJ**
email: reservations@diplomat-hotel-wales.com **web:** www.diplomat-hotel-wales.com
dir: *M4 junction 48, A4138 then B4303, hotel 0.75 mile on right.*

This Victorian mansion, set in mature grounds, has been extended over the years to provide a comfortable and relaxing hotel. The well-appointed bedrooms are located in the main house and there is also a wing of equally comfortable modern rooms. Public areas include Trubshaw's Restaurant, a large function suite and a modern leisure centre.

Rooms: 50 (8 annexe) (2 family) (4 GF) ✿ **S** fr £110 **D** fr £120 (including breakfast) **Facilities:** Spa FTV WiFi ♨ 🎾 Gym Sauna Steam room Beauty treatments ♫ Xmas New Year **Conf:** Class 150 Board 100 Theatre 450 **Services:** Lift Night porter **Parking:** 250 **Notes:** LB Civ Wed 300

Ashburnham Hotel
★★★ 71% HOTEL

tel: 01554 834343 **Ashburnham Road, Pembrey SA16 0TH**
email: info@ashburnham-hotel.co.uk **web:** www.ashburnham-hotel.co.uk
dir: *M4 junction 48, A4138 to Llanelli, A484 west to Pembrey. Follow brown information signs.*

American aviatrix, Amelia Earhart stayed at this friendly hotel after finishing her historic trans-Atlantic flight in 1928. Public areas include the brasserie restaurant, and the conservatory lounge bar that serves an extensive range of bar meals. Bedrooms, varying from standard to superior, have modern furnishings and facilities. The hotel is licensed for civil ceremonies, and function and conference facilities are also available.

Rooms: 13 (2 family) **S** fr £60 **D** fr £75 (including breakfast)* **Facilities:** FTV WiFi ♨ **Conf:** Class 150 Board 80 Theatre 150 **Services:** Night porter **Parking:** 100 **Notes:** Civ Wed 130

Premier Inn Llanelli Central East

BUDGET HOTEL

tel: 0871 527 8638 (Calls cost 13p per minute plus your phone company's access charge) **Llandafen Road SA14 9BD**
web: www.premierinn.com
dir: *M4 junction 48, A4138, approximately 3 miles. Hotel on left.*

High quality, budget accommodation ideal for both families and business travellers. Spacious, en suite bedrooms feature free WiFi and tea and coffee making facilities, and in most hotels, Freeview TV is also available. The adjacent family restaurant features a wide and varied menu.

Rooms: 50

Premier Inn Llanelli Central West

BUDGET HOTEL

tel: 0871 527 9342 (Calls cost 13p per minute plus your phone company's access charge) **Sandpiper Road, Sandy Water Park SA15 4SG**
web: www.premierinn.com
dir: *M4 junction 48, A4138 towards Llanelli town centre. Then follow Carmarthen signs to Sandy Park roundabout. Hotel on left.*

Rooms: 28

LLANGAMMARCH WELLS
Powys   Map 9 SN94

The Lake Country House & Spa

★★★★ 80% COUNTRY HOUSE HOTEL

tel: 01591 620202 **LD4 4BS**
email: info@lakecountryhouse.co.uk **web:** www.lakecountryhouse.co.uk
dir: *West from Builth Wells on A483 to Garth (approximately 6 miles). Left for Llangammarch Wells, follow hotel signs.*

Expect good old-fashioned values and hospitality at this Victorian country house hotel. In fact, the service is so good that guests may believe they have their own butler. The establishment offers a 9-hole, par 3 golf course, 50 acres of wooded grounds and a spa with a hot tub that overlooks the lake. Bedrooms, some in an annexe, and some at ground-floor level, are individually styled and have many extra comforts. Traditional afternoon teas are served in the lounge, and modern Welsh cuisine is offered in the spacious and elegant restaurant.

Rooms: 31 (12 annexe) (8 GF) ✿ **Facilities:** Spa FTV WiFi ♨ ♿ 9 ♨ Fishing ⛳ Gym Archery Horse riding Mountain biking Quad biking Xmas New Year **Conf:** Class 30 Board 25 Theatre 80 **Services:** Night porter **Parking:** 70 **Notes:** LB No children 8 years Civ Wed 100

LLANRWST
Conwy   Map 14 SH86

Maenan Abbey
★★★ 80% COUNTRY HOUSE HOTEL

tel: 01492 660247 **Maenan LL26 0UL**
email: reservations@maenanabbey.co.uk **web:** www.maenanabbey.co.uk
dir: *A55/A470 (junction 19) in direction of Betws-y-Coed. Hotel 8 miles on right. From A5 turn onto A470 at Betws-y-Coed through Llanrwst. Hotel 2 miles on left.*

Maenan Abbey is a small and personally-run country house which is ideally located. Walkers can enjoy the National Park then retire to this quiet, well-equipped hotel. Bedrooms are individually designed with some large family rooms available. Cuisine is a highlight of any stay.

Rooms: 14 (3 family) (3 smoking) ✿ **Facilities:** FTV WiFi Fishing Guided mountain walks Xmas New Year **Conf:** Class 30 Board 30 Theatre 50 **Parking:** 60 **Notes:** Civ Wed 55

LLANTRISANT
Monmouthshire   Map 9 ST39

Premier Inn Llantrisant

BUDGET HOTEL

tel: 0871 527 8640 (Calls cost 13p per minute plus your phone company's access charge) **Gwaun Elai, Magden Park CF72 8LL**
web: www.premierinn.com
dir: *M4 junction 34, A4119 towards Llantrisant and Rhondda. At 1st roundabout take 2nd exit. At 2nd roundabout take 1st exit.*

Rooms: 51

L

LLANWDDYN
Powys
Map 15 SJ01

Lake Vyrnwy Hotel & Spa
★★★★ 76% COUNTRY HOUSE HOTEL

tel: 01691 870692 **Lake Vyrnwy SY10 0LY**
email: info@lakevyrnwyhotel.co.uk **web:** www.lakevyrnwy.com
dir: *On A4393, 200 yards past dam, turn sharp right into drive.*

This elegant Victorian country-house hotel lies in 26,000 acres of woodland above Lake Vyrnwy, and provides a wide range of bedrooms, most with superb views and many with four-poster beds and balconies. Extensive public rooms retain many period features, and informal dining is available in the popular Tower Tavern. Relaxing and rejuvenating treatments are a feature of the stylish health spa.

Rooms: 52 (12 family) **Facilities:** Spa STV FTV WiFi ⚡ 🏊 Fishing Gym Archery Birdwatching Canoeing Kayaking Clay shooting Sailing Fly fishing Cycling Xmas New Year **Conf:** Class 80 Board 60 Theatre 200 **Services:** Lift Night porter **Parking:** 70 **Notes:** LB Civ Wed 200

LLYSWEN
Powys
Map 9 S013

INSPECTOR'S CHOICE

Llangoed Hall
★★★★ ◉◉◉ COUNTRY HOUSE HOTEL

tel: 01874 754525 **LD3 0YP**
email: enquiries@llangoedhall.com **web:** www.llangoedhall.com
dir: *On A470 between Brecon and Builth Wells.*

Set against the stunning backdrop of the Black Mountains and the Wye Valley, this imposing country house is a haven of peace and quiet. The interior is no less impressive, with a noteworthy art collection complementing the many antiques in day rooms and bedrooms. Comfortable, spacious accommodation is matched by equally inviting lounges.

Llangoed Hall

Rooms: 23 **S** fr £150 **D** fr £175 (including breakfast)* **Facilities:** FTV WiFi ⚡ HL 🏊 Fishing Snooker table Outdoor chess Xmas New Year **Conf:** Class 30 Board 30 Theatre 80 **Services:** Night porter **Parking:** 50 **Notes:** Civ Wed 80

See advert opposite

MAESYCWMMER
Caerphilly
Map 9 ST19

Bryn Meadows Golf, Hotel & Spa
★★★★ 73% HOTEL

tel: 01495 225590 **CF82 7SN**
email: reservations@brynmeadows.co.uk **web:** www.brynmeadows.co.uk
dir: *M4 junction 28, A467 signed Brynmawr, 10 miles to Newbridge. Take A472 signed Ystrad Mynach. Hotel off Crown roundabout signed golf course.*

Surrounded by its own mature parkland and 18-hole golf course, this impressive hotel, golf, leisure and function complex provides a range of high quality, well-equipped bedrooms; several have their own balconies or patio areas. The attractive public areas include a pleasant restaurant which, like many of the bedrooms, enjoys striking views of the golf course and beyond. There are impressive function facilities and the hotel is a popular venue for weddings.

Rooms: 42 (4 family) (21 GF) **S** fr £140 **D** fr £155 (including breakfast)* **Facilities:** Spa FTV WiFi ⚡ 18 Gym Sauna Steam room Aromatherapy suite Hydro spa Rasul mud room Xmas New Year **Conf:** Class 300 Board 200 Theatre 600 **Services:** Night porter Air con **Parking:** 200 **Notes:** LB Civ Wed 600

MERTHYR TYDFIL
Merthyr Tydfil
Map 9 S000

Premier Inn Merthyr Tydfil
Premier Inn

BUDGET HOTEL

tel: 0871 527 8768 (Calls cost 13p per minute plus your phone company's access charge) **Pentrebach CF48 4BB**
web: www.premierinn.com
dir: *M4 junction 32, A470 to Merthyr Tydfil. At roundabout right to Pentrebach (A4060). At next roundabout 3rd exit signed Abergavenny (dual carriageway). Double back at next roundabout by Pentrebach Co-op onto A4060 towards Pentrebach. Left after layby, hotel adjacent to Pentrebach House.*

High quality, budget accommodation ideal for both families and business travellers. Spacious, en suite bedrooms feature free WiFi and tea and coffee making facilities, and in most hotels, Freeview TV is also available. The adjacent family restaurant features a wide and varied menu.

Rooms: 62

RELAIS &
CHATEAUX

Llangoed hall

Afternoon Tea | Dining | Accommodation

Llangoed Hall is a wonderfully elegant and historic country house hotel
situated in the beautiful Wye Valley in the heart of the Welsh countryside.
It offers the quintessential Edwardian country house experience.

Telephone 01874 754525

Events@llangoedhall.com | Twitter: @TheLlangoedHall

Llyswen, Brecon, Powys LD3 0YP

www.llangoedhall.com

M

MISKIN
Rhondda Cynon Taf

Map 9 ST08

Miskin Manor Hotel & Health Club

★★★★ 71% COUNTRY HOUSE HOTEL

tel: 01443 224204 **Pendoylan Road CF72 8ND**
email: amanda@miskin-manor.co.uk **web:** www.miskin-manor.co.uk
dir: *M4 junction 34, A4119, signed Llantrisant, hotel 300 yards on left.*

This historic manor house is peacefully located in 22-acre grounds yet is only minutes away from the M4. Bedrooms are furnished to a high standard and include some located in converted stables and cottages. The spacious public areas are comfortable and include a variety of function rooms. The relaxed atmosphere and lovely surroundings ensure that this hotel remains popular for weddings and for business functions. There is a separate, modern health and fitness centre which includes a gym, sauna, steam room and swimming pool.

Rooms: 42 (9 annexe) (4 family) (6 GF) ★ **S** fr £80 **D** fr £99 (including breakfast)*
Facilities: Spa FTV WiFi 🕸 ✈ Gym Sauna Steam room Dance studio Xmas New Year
Conf: Class 80 Board 65 Theatre 160 **Services:** Night porter **Parking:** 200
Notes: Civ Wed 200

MOLD
Flintshire

Map 15 SJ26

Beaufort Park Hotel

★★★ 78% HOTEL

tel: 01352 758646 **Alltami Road, New Brighton CH7 6RQ**
email: info@beaufortparkhotel.co.uk **web:** www.beaufortparkhotel.co.uk
dir: *A55, A494, through Alltami lights, over mini-roundabout by petrol station towards Mold, A5119. Hotel 100 yards on right.*

This large, modern hotel is conveniently located a short drive from the North Wales Expressway and offers various styles of spacious accommodation. There are

extensive public areas, and several meeting and function rooms are available. There is a wide choice of meals in the formal Orchard Restaurant and in the popular Arches Bar and Coffee Lounge.

Rooms: 106 (8 family) (32 GF) **S** fr £60 **D** fr £60 (including breakfast)*
Facilities: FTV WiFi Squash 🎵 Xmas New Year **Conf:** Class 120 Board 120 Theatre 250 **Services:** Night porter **Parking:** 200 **Notes:** LB Civ Wed 220

MONMOUTH
Monmouthshire

Map 10 SO51

Premier Inn Monmouth

Premier Inn 🌙

BUDGET HOTEL

tel: 0871 527 9636 (Calls cost 13p per minute plus your phone company's access charge) **NP25 5EZ**
web: www.premierinn.com
dir: *Phone for directions.*

High quality, budget accommodation ideal for both families and business travellers. Spacious, en suite bedrooms feature free WiFi and tea and coffee making facilities, and in most hotels, Freeview TV is also available. The adjacent family restaurant features a wide and varied menu.

Rooms: 60

NARBERTH
Pembrokeshire

Map 8 SN11

INSPECTOR'S CHOICE

Grove

★★★★ ◉◉◉ HOTEL

tel: 01834 860915 **Molleston SA67 8BX**
email: info@thegrove-narberth.co.uk **web:** www.thegrove-narberth.co.uk
dir: *A48 to Carmarthen, A40 to Haverfordwest. At A478 roundabout 1st exit to Narberth, through town towards Tenby. At bottom of hill right, 1 mile, hotel on right.*

The Grove is an elegant 17th-century country house set on a hillside in 26 acres of rolling countryside. The owners have lovingly restored the building with care, combining period features with excellent modern decor. There are bedrooms in the main house, and additional rooms in separate buildings; all are appointed with high levels of quality and comfort. Some bedrooms are on the ground floor, and most have fantastic views out over the Preseli Hills. There are two sumptuous lounge areas, one with an open fire and a small bar, and two separate restaurant options – fine dining in the Fernery and a dining alternative in the Artisan Rooms. Self-catering cottages are available.

Rooms: 26 (3 family) (7 GF) ★ **Facilities:** STV WiFi 🌙 In-room spa treatments boules Xmas New Year **Conf:** Class 30 Board 24 Theatre 60 **Services:** Night porter **Parking:** 34 **Notes:** LB Civ Wed

M

NEWPORT
Newport

Map 9 ST38

See also **Cwmbran**

The Celtic Manor Resort

★★★★★ 87% ◎ ◎ HOTEL

tel: 01633 413000 & 410262 **Coldra Woods NP18 1HQ**
email: bookings@celtic-manor.com **web:** www.celtic-manor.com
dir: *M4 junction 24, take B4237 towards Newport. Hotel 1st on right.*

This hotel is part of the outstanding Celtic Manor Resort. Here there are three challenging golf courses including the Twenty Ten Course specifically designed for the 2010 Ryder Cup; a huge convention centre; superb leisure clubs and two hotels. This hotel has excellent bedrooms, with suites and two Presidential suites, offering good space and comfort. Stylish, extensive public areas are set around a spectacular atrium lobby that features several eating options including The Epicure Experience. There is a choice of shops and boutiques as well.

Rooms: 334 (34 family) **Facilities:** Spa STV FTV WiFi ▷ ⊙ ⅃ 54 ⌂ Fishing Gym Golf academy Archery Laser combat Adventure golf Treetop ropes courses Laser clays ♫ Xmas New Year **Conf:** Class 600 Board 60 Theatre 1500 **Services:** Lift Night porter Air con **Parking:** 1300 **Notes:** Civ Wed 100

The Manor House

★★★★ 76% HOTEL

tel: 01633 413262 **The Celtic Manor Resort, Coldra Woods NP18 1HQ**
email: bookings@celtic-manor.com **web:** www.celtic-manor.com
dir: *M4 junction 24, B4237 towards Newport. Hotel 1st on right.*

Part of the Celtic Manor Resort complex, this 19th-century hotel offers country-house charm combined with modern comforts. Sitting in beautiful landscaped gardens, it has traditionally styled bedrooms, three with four-posters. An Asian inspired restaurant is located in this hotel with a further number of restaurants to be found at the main Celtic Manor Resort. Guests have access to all the hotel and leisure facilities at the resort; three challenging golf courses, a superb leisure complex and many other activities suitable for both adults and families.

Rooms: 65 (3 family) **Facilities:** Spa STV FTV WiFi ⊙ ⅃ 54 ⌂ Fishing Gym Golf academy Archery Laser combat Adventure golf Treetop ropes courses Laser clays ♫ Xmas New Year **Conf:** Class 80 Board 40 Theatre 200 **Services:** Lift Night porter Air con **Parking:** 1300 **Notes:** Civ Wed 180

Coldra Court Hotel

★★★★ 75% HOTEL

tel: 01633 413737 **Chepstow Road, Langstone NP18 2LX**
email: bookings@celtic-manor.com **web:** www.celtic-manor.com
dir: *Phone for directions.*

Although Coldra Court is part of the larger Celtic Manor resort, it retains its own identity and is located a short distance away. Free shuttle buses are provided for guests to move between the two. Now refurbished, bedrooms are spacious and offer high levels of comfort. The bustling Rib Smokehouse & Grill should not be missed. There is also a gym and swimming pool on site.

Rooms: 148 (41 family) (70 GF) **S** fr £58 **D** fr £58 (including breakfast)*
Facilities: FTV WiFi ▷ HL ⊙ Sauna Steam room New Year **Conf:** Class 150 Board 140 Theatre 300 **Parking:** 220 **Notes:** No children unless with adult Civ Wed

Premier Inn Newport City Centre (Wales)

BUDGET HOTEL

tel: 0871 527 9474 (Calls cost 13p per minute plus your phone company's access charge) **NP20 4GA**
web: www.premierinn.com
dir: *Phone for directions.*

High quality, budget accommodation ideal for both families and business travellers. Spacious, en suite bedrooms feature free WiFi and tea and coffee making facilities, and in most hotels, Freeview TV is also available. The adjacent family restaurant features a wide and varied menu.

Rooms: 61

Premier Inn Newport Wales (M4 Jct 24)

BUDGET HOTEL

tel: 0871 527 8814 (Calls cost 13p per minute plus your phone company's access charge) **Coldra Junction, Chepstow Rd NP18 2NX**
web: www.premierinn.com
dir: *M4 junction 24, A48 to Langstone, at next roundabout return towards junction 24. Hotel 50 metres on left.*

Rooms: 81

PEMBROKE
Pembrokeshire

Map 8 SM90

Lamphey Hall Hotel

★★★ 78% HOTEL

tel: 01646 672394 **Lamphey SA71 5NR**
web: www.lampheyhall.co.uk
dir: *From Carmarthen A40 to St Clears. Follow signs for A477, left at Milton.*

Set in a delightful village, this very friendly, privately owned and efficiently run hotel offers an ideal base from which to explore the surrounding countryside. Bedrooms are well equipped, comfortably furnished and include family rooms and ground floor rooms. Diners have a choice of three restaurant areas offering an extensive range of dishes. There is also a small lounge, a bar and attractive gardens.

Rooms: 10 (1 family) (2 GF) **S** fr £64.50 **D** fr £94.50 (including breakfast)*
Facilities: FTV WiFi New Year **Parking:** 32

Best Western Lamphey Court Hotel & Spa

 Best Western

★★★ 77% HOTEL

tel: 01646 672273 **Lamphey SA71 5NT**
email: info@lampheycourt.co.uk **web:** www.lampheycourt.co.uk
dir: *M4 then A477 to Pembroke. Left at Milton for Lamphey, hotel on right.*

This Georgian mansion, on an elevated site, is set in attractive countryside and is perfectly situated for exploring the stunning Pembrokeshire coast, the beaches and the Preseli Hills. Well-appointed bedrooms and family suites are situated in a converted coach house within the grounds. The elegant public areas include both formal and informal dining rooms that feature dishes inspired by local produce. Leisure facilities include a state-of-the-art spa with a swimming pool, gym, sauna, treatment rooms and much more.

Rooms: 38 (12 annexe) (7 family) (6 GF) **Facilities:** Spa FTV WiFi ⏳ 🕐 🏊 Gym Sauna Steam room Beauty therapy Xmas New Year **Conf:** Class 40 Board 30 Theatre 60 **Parking:** 50 **Notes:** Civ Wed 80

PENARTH
Vale Of Glamorgan

Map 9 ST17

Holm House Hotel

 WELSH RAREBITS Hotels of Distinction

★★★★ 79% HOTEL

tel: 029 2070 6029 **Marine Parade CF64 3BG**
email: reception@holmhousehotel.co.uk **web:** www.holmhousehotel.com
dir: *Phone for directions.*

A delightful hotel full of quality and comfort with excellent views over the Bristol Channel to the islands of Flatholm and Steepholm. Bedrooms include a number of suites and all are decorated and furnished to very high standards. The Welsh Room Restaurant looks out over the garden and the water and offers a range of well-prepared dishes using seasonal, quality produce. The relaxing garden and terrace is ideal in summer. Guests can also enjoy the spa with treatment rooms, a small gym and an elegant steam room.

Rooms: 12 (1 family) (2 GF) **Facilities:** Spa STV FTV WiFi ⏳ 🕐 Gym Steam room Xmas New Year **Conf:** Class 12 Board 12 Theatre 16 **Services:** Night porter Air con **Notes:** Civ Wed 70

PONTYPOOL
Torfaen

Map 9 SO20

Premier Inn Pontypool

 Premier Inn

BUDGET HOTEL

tel: 0871 527 8890 (Calls cost 13p per minute plus your phone company's access charge) **Tyr'felin, Lower Mill Field NP4 0RH**
web: www.premierinn.com
dir: *At junction of A4042 and A472.*

High quality, budget accommodation ideal for both families and business travellers. Spacious, en suite bedrooms feature free WiFi and tea and coffee making facilities, and in most hotels, Freeview TV is also available. The adjacent family restaurant features a wide and varied menu.

Rooms: 50

PONTYPRIDD
Rhondda Cynon Taf

Map 9 ST08

Llechwen Hall Hotel

★★★ 79% ⚜ COUNTRY HOUSE HOTEL

tel: 01443 742050 **Llanfabon CF37 4HP**
email: enquiries@llechwenhall.co.uk **web:** www.llechwen.co.uk
dir: *A470 north towards Merthyr Tydfil. At large roundabout take 3rd exit. At mini-roundabout take 3rd exit, hotel signed 0.5 mile on left.*

Set on top of a hill with a stunning approach, this country house has functioned in many roles in its 200-year-old history including time as a private school and a magistrates' court. The spacious, individually decorated bedrooms are well equipped; some are situated in the separate coach house nearby. There are ground-floor, twin, double and family bedrooms on offer. The Victorian-style public areas are attractively appointed, and the hotel is a popular venue for weddings.

Rooms: 20 (8 annexe) (6 family) (4 GF) **S** fr £50 **D** fr £60* **Facilities:** FTV WiFi ⏳ Xmas New Year **Conf:** Class 80 Board 40 Theatre 200 **Services:** Night porter **Parking:** 150 **Notes:** LB Civ Wed 90

P

PORTHCAWL
Bridgend

Map 9 SS87

Seabank Hotel

Leisureplex
HOLIDAY HOTELS

★★★ 70% HOTEL

tel: 01656 782261 **Esplanade CF36 3LU**
email: seabank@leisureplex.co.uk **web:** www.leisureplex.co.uk
dir: *M4 junction 37, A4229 to Porthcawl seafront.*

The Seabank Hotel stands in a prime location on the promenade of this seaside town, with panoramic views from most of the bedrooms. Porthcawl has several beaches and coastal walks; the world famous Royal Porthcawl golf course is within easy distance and the cities of Swansea and Cardiff are only a short drive away. The bedrooms are spacious. There is a large restaurant, a lounge bar and a choice of lounges with sea views. The hotel is a popular venue for coach tour parties, as well as weddings and conferences. There is ample parking around the hotel.

Rooms: 91 (3 family) (6 GF) ☎ **Facilities:** FTV WiFi ♫ Xmas New Year **Services:** Lift Night porter **Parking:** 100 **Notes:** Closed 2 January to 10 February

PORTHMADOG
Gwynedd

Map 14 SH53

Royal Sportsman Hotel

★★★ 76% HOTEL

tel: 01766 512015 **131 High Street LL49 9HB**
email: enquiries@royalsportsman.co.uk **web:** www.royalsportsman.co.uk/hotel
dir: *Opposite roundabout at junction of A487 and A497.*

This hotel has a very convenient location handy for the coast or for those wishing to visit the National Park or mountain railway. The hotel has a choice of dining options and food is notable here. Bedrooms are smartly appointed, and there is a spacious lounge. The staff are a friendly team and service is attentive. Covered parking is also available.

Rooms: 28 (7 family) (9 GF) ☎ **S** fr £55 **D** fr £80 (including breakfast)*
Facilities: STV FTV WiFi ♪ Xmas New Year **Conf:** Class 30 Board 30 Theatre 50
Services: Night porter **Parking:** 17 **Notes:** LB Civ Wed 60

PORTMEIRION
Gwynedd

Map 14 SH53

The Hotel Portmeirion

★★★★ 77% ◉◉ HOTEL

WELSH
RAREBITS
Hotels of
Distinction

tel: 01766 770000 **Minffordd LL48 6ET**
email: hotel@portmeirion.com **web:** www.portmeirion-village.com
dir: *2 miles west, Portmeirion village is south off A487.*

Saved from dereliction in the 1920s by Clough Williams-Ellis, the elegant Hotel Portmeirion enjoys one of the finest settings in Wales, located beneath the wooded slopes of the village, overlooking the sandy estuary towards Snowdonia. Many bedrooms have private sitting rooms and balconies with spectacular views. The staff, mostly Welsh-speaking, provide a good mix of warm hospitality and efficient service. Dinner and breakfast include the finest produce.

Rooms: 44 (30 annexe) (6 family) ☎ **D** fr £124 (including breakfast)* **Facilities:** Spa FTV WiFi ♪ ⚡ ♫ Xmas New Year **Conf:** Class 40 Board 30 Theatre 100
Services: Lift Night porter **Parking:** 44 **Notes:** LB Civ Wed 130

PORT TALBOT
Neath Port Talbot

Map 9 SS78

Premier Inn Port Talbot

Premier Inn

BUDGET HOTEL

tel: 0871 527 8896 (Calls cost 13p per minute plus your phone company's access charge) **Baglan Road, Baglan SA12 8ES**
web: www.premierinn.com
dir: *M4 junction 41 westbound. Hotel just off 4th exit at roundabout. M4 junction 42 eastbound, left towards Port Talbot. Take 2nd exit off 2nd roundabout.*

High quality, budget accommodation ideal for both families and business travellers. Spacious, en suite bedrooms feature free WiFi and tea and coffee making facilities, and in most hotels, Freeview TV is also available. The adjacent family restaurant features a wide and varied menu.

Rooms: 42

RHUDDLAN
Denbighshire

Map 15 SJ07

Premier Inn Rhuddlan

Premier Inn

BUDGET HOTEL

tel: 0871 527 8932 (Calls cost 13p per minute plus your phone company's access charge) **Castle View Retail Park, Marsh Road LL18 5UA**
web: www.premierinn.com
dir: *A55 junction 27, A525 signed Rhyl. At next roundabout 3rd exit into Station Road. Next left into Marsh Road. Hotel on left.*

High quality, budget accommodation ideal for both families and business travellers. Spacious, en suite bedrooms feature free WiFi and tea and coffee making facilities, and in most hotels, Freeview TV is also available. The adjacent family restaurant features a wide and varied menu.

Rooms: 44

RHYL
Denbighshire

Map 14 SJ08

Premier Inn Rhyl Seafront

Premier Inn

BUDGET HOTEL

R

tel: 0871 527 8000 (Calls cost 13p per minute plus your phone company's access charge) **21-26 West Parade LL18 1HE**
web: www.premierinn.com
dir: *Leave the A525 or B5119 onto A548 (Kimmel Street). Turn right onto Bodfor Street. Follow Bodfor Street into Queen Street. At the end of Queen Street, turn left onto West Parade.*

High quality, budget accommodation ideal for both families and business travellers. Spacious, en suite bedrooms feature free WiFi and tea and coffee making facilities, and in most hotels, Freeview TV is also available. The adjacent family restaurant features a wide and varied menu.

ROSSETT
Wrexham   Map 15 SJ35

Hallmark Hotel Chester Llyndir Hall
★★★ 81% HOTEL

tel: 0330 028 3417 **Llyndir Lane LL12 0AY**
email: llyndir@hallmarkhotels.co.uk **web:** www.hallmarkhotels.co.uk
dir: *5 miles south of Chester on B5445 follow Pulford signs.*

Located on the English/Welsh border within easy reach of Chester and Wrexham, this elegant manor house lies in several acres of mature grounds. The hotel is popular with both business and leisure guests, and facilities include conference rooms, an impressive leisure centre, a choice of comfortable lounges and a brasserie-style restaurant.

Rooms: 48 (3 family) (17 GF) **Facilities:** Spa FTV WiFi HL Gym Beauty salon Sauna Xmas New Year **Conf:** Class 60 Board 40 Theatre 120 **Services:** Night porter **Parking:** 80 **Notes:** LB Civ Wed 120

RUTHIN
Denbighshire   Map 15 SJ15

Ruthin Castle Hotel
★★★★ 79% HOTEL

tel: 01824 702664 **Castle Street LL15 2NU**
email: reservations@ruthincastle.co.uk **web:** www.ruthincastle.co.uk
dir: *From Manchester M56/A55/A494.*

Originally a medieval building, Ruthin Castle has been many things over the years and is now a luxurious hotel. Set in picturesque north Wales, it offers a variety of bedrooms, many of which have been patronised by royalty. In addition to dinner in the elegant Bertie's Restaurant (named after King Edward VII), guests can relax in the octagonal Library Bar. There are modern spa and leisure facilitates as well as extensive conference rooms on site.

Rooms: 55 (6 family) (13 GF) **S** fr £99 **D** fr £109 (including breakfast)*
Facilities: Spa FTV WiFi Gym Thermal suite Sauna Steam room Relaxation area Xmas New Year **Conf:** Class 80 Board 46 Theatre 180 **Services:** Lift Night porter Air con **Parking:** 80 **Notes:** Civ Wed 140

R

Find out more
about the AA's Hotel rating
scheme on pages 12–13

ST DAVIDS
Pembrokeshire   Map 8 SM72

HIGHLY RECOMMENDED

Twr Y Felin Hotel
★★★★ 86% HOTEL

tel: 01437 725555 & 725566 **Caerfai Road SA62 6QT**
email: stay@twryfelinhotel.com **web:** www.twryfelinhotel.com
dir: *Phone for directions.*

Located on the St Davids peninsula, Twr y Felin is a former windmill, which has been restored and extended to provide contemporary spaces with modern amenities. Bedrooms offer a deeply comfortable environment while embracing modern technology with plenty of attention to detail. The Tyddewi Suite is a unique space occupying the original windmill tower, which boasts spectacular 360-degree views of the coastline and beyond. You can be assured of a genuine and warm welcome from the dedicated team. Two Rosette Restaurant Blas (meaning 'Taste' in Welsh) offers award-winning cuisine, with a seasonal menu showcasing local suppliers and producers. The hotel also displays over 100 pieces of specially commissioned art inspired by the peninsula and Pembrokeshire, by well-known contemporary artists.

Rooms: 21 (8 GF) **S** fr £200 **D** fr £200 (including breakfast)* **Facilities:** STV FTV WiFi Xmas New Year **Conf:** Class 60 Board 42 Theatre 80 **Services:** Lift Night porter **Parking:** 27 **Notes:** No children 12 years Civ Wed 42

SARN PARK MOTORWAY SERVICE AREA (M4)
Bridgend
Map 9 SS98

Days Inn Bridgend Cardiff - M4

AA Advertised

tel: 01656 659218 **Sarn Park Services, M4 junction 36 CF32 9RW**
email: sarn.hotel@welcomebreak.co.uk **web:** www.welcomebreak.co.uk
dir: M4 junction 36.

This modern building offers accommodation in smart, spacious and well-equipped bedrooms, suitable for families and business travellers, and all with en suite bathrooms. Continental breakfast is available and other refreshments may be taken at the nearby family restaurant.

Rooms: 40 (15 family) (20 GF) (8 smoking) **Facilities:** FTV WiFi ⓘ **Services:** Night porter **Parking:** 40

SAUNDERSFOOT
Pembrokeshire
Map 8 SN10

HIGHLY RECOMMENDED

St Brides Spa Hotel

★★★★ 84% ⓦ HOTEL

tel: 01834 812304 **St Brides Hill SA69 9NH**
email: reservations@stbridesspahotel.com **web:** www.stbridesspahotel.com
dir: A478 onto B4310 to Saundersfoot. Hotel above harbour.

Set overlooking Carmarthen Bay, this contemporary hotel and spa takes prime position. Many of the stylish, modern bedrooms enjoy sea views and have balconies; there are also luxury apartments in the grounds. The hotel is open-plan and has excellent views of the bay from the split-level lounge areas. Fresh local seafood is a speciality in the modern airy restaurant, which has a terrace for alfresco dining when the weather allows. The destination spa enjoys some of the very best views from the double treatment room and spa pool.

Rooms: 46 (12 annexe) (6 family) (9 GF) ⓘ **S** fr £135 **D** fr £170 (including breakfast)* **Facilities:** Spa FTV WiFi ⓘ Gym Thermal suite Hydrotherapy pool Steam and herbal rooms Ice fountain Xmas New Year **Conf:** Class 40 Board 34 Theatre 100 **Services:** Lift Night porter **Parking:** 65 **Notes:** Civ Wed 90

SWANSEA
Swansea
Map 9 SS69

See also **Port Talbot**

The Dragon Hotel

★★★★ 73% HOTEL

tel: 01792 657100 **The Kingsway SA1 5LS**
email: enquiries@dragon-hotel.co.uk **web:** www.dragon-hotel.co.uk
dir: M4 junction 42, A483. Straight on at roundabout, onto A4067. At 5th lights into right lane, turn right. Into left lane signed The Dragon Hotel. Left at junction, into right lane. At 2nd lights turn left. Up hill, after 2nd lights, hotel visible ahead. With hotel on right take 1st right after Specsavers, car park 1st right.

The Dragon Hotel is located in the city centre and offers spacious modern accommodation with well-equipped, comfortable bedrooms. There is a bar and lounge facility on the first floor along with the Piano Restaurant serving dinner and breakfast. On the ground floor, the Dragons Brasserie provides a vibrant continental menu for both residents and non-residents. The health and fitness club offers an excellent choice of facilities and there is a good range of conference rooms.

Rooms: 106 (7 family) ⓘ **S** fr £79 **D** fr £89 **Facilities:** FTV WiFi ⓘ HL ⓘ Gym Treatment rooms Xmas New Year **Conf:** Class 120 Board 80 Theatre 230 **Services:** Lift Night porter Air con **Parking:** 52 **Notes:** Civ Wed 120

Mercure Swansea Hotel

★★★ 79% HOTEL

tel: 0844 815 9081 (Calls cost 5p per minute plus your phone company's access charge) **Phoenix Way SA7 9EG**
email: sales@mercureswansea.co.uk **web:** www.mercureswansea.co.uk
dir: M4 junction 44, A48 Llansamlet, left at 3rd lights, right at 1st mini-roundabout, left into Phoenix Way at 2nd roundabout. Hotel 800 metres on right.

Located in the business park area just outside of Swansea, this is a popular hotel with both business and leisure guests. A wide range of dishes is available throughout the day and evening from the relaxing lounge, or the well furnished restaurant. Bedrooms and bathrooms are located over two floors and include standard and executive options. Leisure facilities and a large car park are also provided.

Rooms: 119 (24 family) (55 GF) **Facilities:** FTV WiFi ⓘ ⓘ Gym Sauna Xmas New Year **Conf:** Class 80 Board 50 Theatre 180 **Services:** Night porter **Parking:** 180 **Notes:** Civ Wed 180

Premier Inn Swansea City Centre

Premier Inn ⓘ

BUDGET HOTEL

tel: 0871 527 9060 (Calls cost 13p per minute plus your phone company's access charge) **Salubrious Place, Wind Street SA1 1EE**
web: www.premierinn.com
dir: M4 junction 42, A483 towards the city centre. Pass Sainsburys on left, right into Salubrious Place, 2nd right, then 3rd exit at mini-roundabout.

High quality, budget accommodation ideal for both families and business travellers. Spacious, en suite bedrooms feature free WiFi and tea and coffee making facilities, and in most hotels, Freeview TV is also available. The adjacent family restaurant features a wide and varied menu.

Rooms: 116

S

SWANSEA *continued*

Premier Inn Swansea North

Premier Inn

BUDGET HOTEL

tel: 0871 527 9062 (Calls cost 13p per minute plus your phone company's access charge) **Upper Forest Way, Morriston SA6 8WB**
web: www.premierinn.com
dir: *M4 junction 45, A4067 towards Swansea. In 0.5 mile at 2nd exit left into Clase Road. Hotel 400 yards on left.*

Rooms: 63

Premier Inn Swansea Waterfront

Premier Inn

BUDGET HOTEL

tel: 0871 577 9212 (Calls cost 13p per minute plus your phone company's access charge) **The Waterfront Development, Langdon Road SA1 8PL**
web: www.premierinn.com
dir: *M4 junction 42, A483 towards Swansea/Abertawe (signed Fabian Way). Approximately 4.5 miles. At 2nd lights, left into SA1 Waterfront development. At roundabout take 2nd exit into Langdon Road. Hotel on left.*

Rooms: 132

TENBY
Pembrokeshire
Map 8 SN10

HIGHLY RECOMMENDED

Atlantic Hotel

★★★ 86% HOTEL

tel: 01834 842881 **The Esplanade SA70 7DU**
email: enquiries@atlantic-hotel.uk.com **web:** www.atlantic-hotel.uk.com
dir: *A478 into Tenby, follow town centre signs (keep town walls on left) right at Esplanade, hotel on right.*

This privately-owned and personally-run, friendly hotel has an enviable position looking out over South Beach towards Caldy Island. Bedrooms vary in size and style, but all are well equipped and tastefully appointed. The comfortable public areas include a choice of lounges and in fine weather, guests can also enjoy the cliff-top gardens. Relax in the salt-water swimming pool with jacuzzi, steam room and heated loungers.

Rooms: 43 (1 annexe) (11 family) (4 GF) S fr £88 D fr £125 (including breakfast) **Facilities:** FTV WiFi Steam room Spa bath **Services:** Lift Night porter **Parking:** 25 **Notes:** LB Closed December to beginning February

Penally Abbey Hotel

★★★ 81% SMALL HOTEL

tel: 01834 843033 **Penally SA70 7PY**
email: info@penally-abbey.com **web:** www.penally-abbey.com
dir: *Phone for directions.*

Perched on the hill overlooking Carmarthen Bay, near Tenby, Penally Abbey sits on a monastic site and was also once the home to the Irish whiskey distillers, Jameson. The 12th-century ruins of the original chapel can still be seen in the grounds today. The hotel has been fully restored by the owners and a warm welcome is assured from the friendly team. The distinct Gothic windows frame the sea views from many of the spacious bedrooms. A number of the Coach House rooms accept dogs. Local and seasonal produce are used by the kitchen for meals in the candlelit restaurant.

Rooms: 11 (4 annexe) (3 family) (2 GF) S fr £141 D fr £145 (including breakfast)* **Facilities:** FTV WiFi Xmas New Year **Conf:** Class 25 Board 25 Theatre 30 **Parking:** 12 **Notes:** Closed January Civ Wed 35

Cliffe Norton Hotel

★★★ 73% HOTEL

Leisureplex
HOLIDAY HOTELS

tel: 01834 842333 **10-13 The Norton SA70 8AA**
email: vladimir.jordan@leisureplex.co.uk **web:** www.thecliffenortonhotel.com
dir: *A40, roundabout to A477, roundabout to A478. Into Narberth Road, hotel on right.*

The Cliffe Norton Hotel is ideally located on the seafront in Tenby, with many rooms benefiting from sea views. Bedrooms are individually decorated, offering good quality, value-for-money accommodation. Entertainment is provided each evening after dinner. The restaurant offers good value home cooking and is open for both breakfast and dinner daily. A limited number of parking spaces is available. The hotel is a popular venue for coach tour parties.

Rooms: 50 (7 family) S fr £42 D fr £66 (including breakfast)* **Facilities:** FTV WiFi Xmas New Year **Services:** Lift Night porter **Parking:** 5 **Notes:** Closed 2 January to 18 February

Premier Inn Tenby Town Centre

Premier Inn

BUDGET HOTEL

tel: 0871 527 9514 (Calls cost 13p per minute plus your phone company's access charge) **White Lion Street SA70 7ET**
web: www.premierinn.com
dir: *A478 into Tenby. Left into Narbeth Road. On bay turn right into White Lion Street.*

High quality, budget accommodation ideal for both families and business travellers. Spacious, en suite bedrooms feature free WiFi and tea and coffee making facilities, and in most hotels, Freeview TV is also available. The adjacent family restaurant features a wide and varied menu.

Rooms: 61

S

TREARDDUR BAY
Isle Of Anglesey
Map 14 SH27

Trearddur Bay Hotel
★★★ 81% HOTEL

tel: 01407 860301 **LL65 2UN**
email: enquiries@trearddurbayhotel.co.uk **web:** www.trearddurbayhotel.co.uk
dir: *A55 junction 2, left, over 1st roundabout, left at 2nd roundabout, right after approximately 2 miles.*

A real seaside theme runs through this bright and welcoming hotel situated only 100 yards from a Blue Flag beach. Bedrooms include a large number of contemporary rooms; some with balconies and stunning views of the bay. Guests have a choice of dining in the more formal Bay Restaurant, or the Inn at The Bay which has an outdoor area for summer dining. Facilities include function rooms, an indoor swimming pool and children's play area.

Rooms: 47 (10 annexe) (6 family) (5 GF) **S** fr £65 **D** fr £80 (including breakfast)*
Facilities: FTV WiFi ⓓ ⓧ Xmas New Year **Conf:** Class 80 Board 60 Theatre 200
Services: Night porter **Parking:** 200 **Notes:** LB Civ Wed 140

USK
Monmouthshire
Map 9 SO30

The Three Salmons Hotel
★★★ 78% HOTEL

tel: 01291 672133 **Bridge Street NP15 1RY**
email: reception@threesalmons.co.uk **web:** www.threesalmons.co.uk
dir: *M4 junction 24, A449, 1st exit signed Usk. On entering town, hotel on main road.*

The Three Salmons Hotel is a 17th-century coaching inn located in the centre of a small market town with friendly, efficient staff that help create a welcoming atmosphere. The food in the contemporary restaurant is very popular. Bedrooms are comfortable and a good range of extras are provided. There is a large function suite ideal for weddings and parties. Parking is secure.

Rooms: 24 (14 annexe) (3 family) (7 GF) **Facilities:** FTV WiFi ⓓ **Conf:** Class 80 Board 40 Theatre 110 **Services:** Night porter **Parking:** 43 **Notes:** Civ Wed 100

WELSHPOOL
Powys
Map 15 SJ20

The Royal Oak Hotel
★★★ 81% HOTEL

tel: 01938 552217 **The Cross SY21 7DG**
email: royaloak@innmail.co.uk **web:** www.royaloakwelshpool.co.uk
dir: *By lights at junction of A483 and A458.*

Standing in the centre of Welshpool, The Royal Oak Hotel was once the manor house for the Earl of Powys, before being used as a coaching inn for travellers en route to the Welsh coast. A range of bedrooms styles offer high levels of comfort and are complemented by very good quality bathrooms, as well as Sky TV. A bustling coffee shop is located on the ground floor, with a number of interconnecting lounges ensuring there is always a quiet corner. The smart dining room offers a range of dishes to suit most tastes both at lunch and dinner. A small secure car park is a welcome additional feature.

Rooms: 25 (3 family) **Facilities:** WiFi Xmas New Year **Conf:** Class 60 Board 30 Theatre 100 **Services:** Night porter **Parking:** 19 **Notes:** Civ Wed 100

WOLF'S CASTLE
Pembrokeshire
Map 8 SM92

Wolfscastle Country Hotel
★★★ 81% COUNTRY HOUSE HOTEL

tel: 01437 741225 **SA62 5LZ**
email: enquiries@thewolfscastle.com **web:** www.wolfscastle.com
dir: *On A40 in village at top of hill. 6 miles north of Haverfordwest.*

This large stone house, a former vicarage, dates back to the mid-19th century and is now a friendly, privately-owned and personally-run hotel. It provides stylish, modern, well-maintained and well-equipped bedrooms. There is a pleasant bar and an attractive restaurant, which has a well deserved reputation for its food.

Rooms: 20 (2 family) **S** fr £75 **D** fr £100 (including breakfast)* **Facilities:** Spa STV FTV WiFi Treatment rooms New Year **Conf:** Class 100 Board 40 Theatre 150 **Parking:** 60 **Notes:** Closed 24–26 December Civ Wed 100

WREXHAM
Wrexham
Map 15 SJ35

Premier Inn Wrexham North (A483)
Premier Inn

BUDGET HOTEL

tel: 0871 527 9190 (Calls cost 13p per minute plus your phone company's access charge) **Chester Road, Gresford LL12 8PW**
web: www.premierinn.com
dir: *On B5445, just off A483 (dual carriageway) near Gresford.*

High quality, budget accommodation ideal for both families and business travellers. Spacious, en suite bedrooms feature free WiFi and tea and coffee making facilities, and in most hotels, Freeview TV is also available. The adjacent family restaurant features a wide and varied menu.

Rooms: 60

Premier Inn Wrexham Town Centre
Premier Inn

BUDGET HOTEL

tel: 0871 527 9458 (Calls cost 13p per minute plus your phone company's access charge) **Jacques Way LL11 2BY**
web: www.premierinn.com
dir: *A55 junction 38. At Wrexham Road Interchange, A483. At roundabout 2nd exit signed Wrexham. Exit at junction 5, at next roundabout take A541. Pass football ground, right at lights.*

Rooms: 83

W

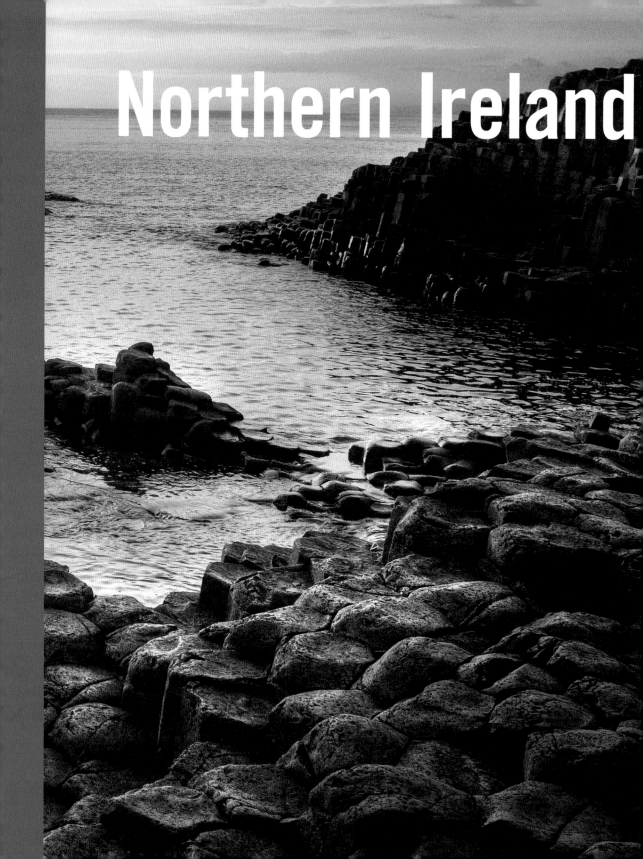

Northern Ireland

Additional information for Northern Ireland and the Republic of Ireland

Licensing Regulations

Northern Ireland: Public houses open Mon–Sat 11.30–23.00. Sun 12.30–22.00. Hotels can serve residents without restriction. Non-residents can be served 12.30–22.00 on Christmas Day. Children under 18 are not allowed in the bar area and may neither buy nor consume liquor in hotels.

Republic of Ireland: General licensing hours are Mon–Thu 10.30–23.30, Fri & Sat 10.30–00.30, Sun 12.30–23.00 (or 00.30 if the following day is a Bank Holiday). There is no service (except for hotel residents) on Christmas Day or Good Friday.

The Fire and Rescue Services (NI) Order 2006

This covers establishments accommodating more than six people, which must have a certificate from the Northern Ireland Fire Authority. Places accommodating fewer than six people need adequate exits. AA inspectors check emergency notices, fire fighting equipment and fire exits here.

The Republic of Ireland safety regulations are a matter for local authority regulations. For your own and others' safety, read the emergency notices and be sure you understand them.

Telephone numbers

Area codes for numbers in the Republic of Ireland apply only within the Republic. If dialling from outside check the telephone directory (from the UK the international dialling code is 00 353). Area codes for numbers in Britain and Northern Ireland cannot be used directly from the Republic.

For the latest information on the Republic of Ireland visit the AA Ireland's website: www.theAA.ie

---

NORTHERN IRELAND

AGHADOWEY
County Londonderry/Derry
Map 1 C6

Brown Trout Golf & Country Inn
★★★ 82% HOTEL

IRISH COUNTRY HOTELS

tel: 028 7086 8209 **209 Agivey Road BT51 4AD**
email: jane@browntroutinn.com **web:** www.browntroutinn.com
dir: *At junction of A54 and B66 on road to Coleraine.*

Set alongside the Agivey River and featuring its own 9-hole golf course, this welcoming inn offers a choice of spacious accommodation. Comfortably furnished bedrooms are situated around a courtyard area, while the cottage suites also have lounge areas. Home-cooked meals are served in the restaurant and lighter fare is available in the charming lounge bar which has entertainment at weekends.

Rooms: 15 (11 family) (15 GF) ⌂ **S** fr £70 **D** fr £90 (including breakfast)*
Facilities: STV FTV WiFi ⌂ ⚡ 9 Game fishing ♫ Xmas New Year **Conf:** Class 24 Board 28 Theatre 40 **Parking:** 80 **Notes:** Civ Wed 60

ARMAGH
County Armagh
Map 1 C5

The Charlemont Arms Hotel
★★★ 70% HOTEL

tel: 028 3752 2028 **57 - 65 English Street BT61 7LB**
email: info@charlemontarmshotel.com **web:** www.charlemontarmshotel.com
dir: *Phone for directions.*

The Charlemont Arms Hotel has thrived throughout the centuries, it was originally home to a Dr Atkinson, but by the 1760s it had became a hostelry known as The Caulfield Arms. In 176 3 it was renamed when the fourth Viscount Caulfield was created Earl of Charlemont. Now 30 en suite bedrooms as well as a larger foyer and reception area are on offer. Food is available throughout the day in the restaurant and wine bar known as Turners. Off-street parking and WiFi are readily available.

Rooms: 30 **S** fr £49 **D** fr £79 (including breakfast)* **Facilities:** WiFi ⌂ ♫ **Conf:** Class 100 Board 30 Theatre 80 **Services:** Lift Night porter **Parking:** 30 **Notes:** Civ Wed 100

BALLYMENA
County Antrim
Map 1 D5

HIGHLY RECOMMENDED

Galgorm Resort & Spa
★★★★ 89% ◉◉◉ HOTEL

tel: 028 2588 1001 **136 Fenaghy Road, Galgorm BT42 1EA**
email: reservations@galgorm.com **web:** www.galgorm.com
dir: *1 mile from Ballymena on A42, between Galgorm and Cullybackey.*

Standing in 163 acres of private woodland and sweeping lawns beside the River Maine, this 19th-century mansion offers spacious, comfortable bedrooms. The many eating and drinking options include a welcoming cocktail and gin bar and the elegant River Room Restaurant, as well as The Bar & Grill at Gillies, a lively and atmospheric locals' bar, and the family-friendly Fratelli Ristorante, Pizzeria & Bar. Also on the estate is an equestrian centre and a conference hall.

Rooms: 122 (17 family) (8 GF) ⌂ **S** fr £130 **D** fr £150 (including breakfast)*
Facilities: Spa FTV WiFi ⌂ ⚡ ⚡ 9 ⚓ Fishing Gym Clay pigeon shooting Archery Horseriding (all can be arranged off site) ♫ Xmas New Year **Conf:** Class 170 Board 30 Theatre 500 **Services:** Lift Night porter **Parking:** 400 **Notes:** LB Civ Wed 300

BELFAST
Belfast

Map 1 D5

INSPECTOR'S CHOICE

The Merchant Hotel
★★★★★ ◎ ◎ HOTEL

tel: 028 9023 4888 **16 Skipper Street BT1 2DZ**
email: info@themerchanthotel.com **web:** www.themerchanthotel.com
dir: *In city centre, 1st left after Albert Clock into Waring Street. 1st left into Skipper Street.*

The Merchant Hotel is a magnificent property situated in the historic Cathedral Quarter of the city centre. This Grade I listed building has been lovingly and sensitively restored to reveal its original architectural grandeur and interior opulence. All the bedrooms, including five suites, have air conditioning, high-speed internet access, TVs and luxury bathrooms. There are several eating options including the grand and beautifully decorated Great Room Restaurant.

Rooms: 62 (17 family) ⟨ **S** fr £150 **D** fr £180* **Facilities:** Spa FTV WiFi ⟨ Gym Steam room ♫ Xmas New Year **Conf:** Class 100 Board 60 Theatre 200 **Services:** Lift Night porter Air con **Parking:** 35 **Notes:** LB Civ Wed 130

Fitzwilliam Hotel Belfast
★★★★★ 84% ◎ HOTEL

tel: 028 9044 2080 **1-3 Victoria Street BT2 7BQ**
email: clanders@fitzwilliamhotelbelfast.com **web:** www.fitzwilliamhotelbelfast.com
dir: *See website for directions.*

The Fitzwilliam is perfectly placed for Belfast city centre, adjacent to the Grand Opera House and set amid a range of shops and restaurants. The modern contemporary style bedrooms are tastefully appointed and have a great range of facilities including air conditioning. The public areas feature a smart cocktail bar and guests can dine in the modern restaurant on the first floor – a range of bar food is also available.

Rooms: 130 **S** fr £130 **D** fr £150* **Facilities:** Small fitness suite **Conf:** Class 20 Board 20 Theatre 20

Radisson Blu Hotel Belfast
★★★★ 80% HOTEL

tel: 028 9043 4065 **3 Cromac Place BT7 2JB**
email: info.belfast@radissonblu.com **web:** www.radissonblu.co.uk/hotel-belfast
dir: *On corner of Ormeau Road and Cromac Street.*

This modern hotel is in the centre of the regenerated urban area close to the city centre. The bedrooms are stylishly presented, well equipped and all have air conditioning; there is a choice of business suites. Public areas include a spacious lounge bar and the Filini Restaurant, which serves good Italian and Sardinian cuisine. Ample secure parking and free WiFi (throughout the hotel) are available.

Rooms: 120 (11 family) **S** fr £89 **D** fr £99 (including breakfast)* **Facilities:** FTV WiFi ⟨ Xmas New Year **Conf:** Class 70 Board 50 Theatre 150 **Services:** Lift Night porter Air con **Parking:** 120 **Notes:** Civ Wed 90

Malmaison Belfast
★★★★ 79% HOTEL

tel: 0844 693 0650 (Calls cost 5p per minute plus your phone company's access charge) **34-38 Victoria Street BT1 3GH**
email: belfast@malmaison.com **web:** www.malmaison.com/locations/belfast
dir: *M1 along Westlink to Grosvenor Road. Follow city centre signs. Pass City Hall on right, left into Victoria Street. Hotel on right.*

Situated in a former seed warehouse, this luxurious, contemporary hotel is ideally located for the city centre. Comfortable bedrooms boast a host of modern facilities, while the deeply comfortable, stylish public areas include a popular bar lounge. The menu in the brasserie showcases local, seasonal ingredients. The warm hospitality is notable.

Rooms: 64 (8 family) **Facilities:** STV WiFi Gym **Conf:** Board 22 **Services:** Lift Night porter **Notes:** Civ Wed

Malone Lodge Hotel
★★★★ 76% HOTEL

tel: 028 9038 8000 **60 Eglantine Avenue BT9 6DY**
email: info@malonelodgehotel.com **web:** www.malonelodgehotelbelfast.com
dir: *At hospital roundabout exit towards Boucher Road, left at 1st roundabout, right at lights at top, then 1st left. Car park to rear of hotel.*

Situated in the leafy suburbs of the university area of south Belfast, this stylish hotel forms the centrepiece of an attractive row of Victorian terraced properties. The hotel offers a range of smart bedrooms and also apartments situated a very short walk away. The Knife and Fork restaurant offers relaxed and informal dining and Macklin's bar is just the place for a drink or two.

Rooms: 54 (7 family) **Facilities:** FTV WiFi ♫ **Conf:** Class 126 Board 48 Theatre 250 **Services:** Lift Night porter **Parking:** 70 **Notes:** Civ Wed 120

Premier Inn Belfast City Cathedral Quarter

BUDGET HOTEL

tel: 0871 527 8070 (Calls cost 13p per minute plus your phone company's access charge) **2-6 Waring Street BT1 1XY**
web: www.premierinn.com
dir: *M1 or M2 to Westlink to Grosvenor Road roundabout, signed city centre. Into Grosvenor Road. At 2nd lights left, take right lane, right (pass City Hall on right). At end of Chichester Street left into Victoria Street. Through next 2 lights, left into Waring Street. Hotel 300 yards on right.*

High quality, budget accommodation ideal for both families and business travellers. Spacious, en suite bedrooms feature free WiFi and tea and coffee making facilities, and in most hotels, Freeview TV is also available. The adjacent family restaurant features a wide and varied menu.

Rooms: 171

Premier Inn Belfast City Centre Alfred St

Premier Inn

BUDGET HOTEL

tel: 0871 527 8068 (Calls cost 13p per minute plus your phone company's access charge) **Alfred Street BT2 8ED**
web: www.premierinn.com
dir: *M1 or M2 to Westlink. Follow city centre signs. 1st right, 2nd left into Hope Street. At 2nd lights left into Bedford Street. At next lights right into Ormeau Avenue. Left into Alfred Street. Underground car park (chargeable) on left.*

Rooms: 148

Premier Inn Belfast Titanic Quarter

Premier Inn

BUDGET HOTEL

tel: 0871 527 9210 (Calls cost 13p per minute plus your phone company's access charge) **2A Queens Road BT3 9FB**
web: www.premierinn.com
dir: *From all major routes follow Odyssey Arena signs. From M3 junction 1 exit onto Queens Island, to lights. Hotel on left.*

Rooms: 122

Silver Stars

The AA Silver Star rating denotes a Hotel that we highly recommend. They have a superior level of quality within their star rating, high standards of hospitality, service and cleanliness.

BUSHMILLS
County Antrim — Map 1 D6

Bushmills Inn Hotel

★★★★ 82% HOTEL

tel: 028 2073 3000 **9 Dunluce Road BT57 8QG**
email: mail@bushmillsinn.com **web:** www.bushmillsinn.com
dir: *On A2 in village centre.*

Enjoying a prominent position in the heart of the village, this hotel offers a range of bedroom styles including spacious, creatively designed rooms that have the latest technology and a small dressing room. The charming public areas feature inglenook turf-burning fires, cosy snugs along with a very popular traditional bar. The restaurant has a well-deserved reputation for its food. The hotel is very popular with golfers; it is close to the Giants Causeway, Bushmills Distillery and the stunning scenery of the Antrim Coast.

Rooms: 41 (2 family) (20 GF) S fr £120 D fr £130 (including breakfast)*
Facilities: WiFi New Year **Conf:** Class 30 Board 18 Theatre 40 **Services:** Lift Night porter **Parking:** 70 **Notes:** LB Closed 25 December

CARRICKFERGUS
County Antrim — Map 1 D5

Premier Inn Carrickfergus

Premier Inn

BUDGET HOTEL

tel: 0871 527 8214 (Calls cost 13p per minute plus your phone company's access charge) **The Harbour, Alexandra Pier BT38 8BE**
web: www.premierinn.com
dir: *Exit at M2 junction 2, take M5 north onto A2 towards Carrickfergus. Follow Castle/Maritime Area signs. Right at roundabout adjacent to castle. Hotel straight ahead, adjacent to harbour.*

High quality, budget accommodation ideal for both families and business travellers. Spacious, en suite bedrooms feature free WiFi and tea and coffee making facilities, and in most hotels, Freeview TV is also available. The adjacent family restaurant features a wide and varied menu.

Rooms: 49

COLERAINE
County Londonderry/Derry — Map 1 C6

Premier Inn Coleraine

Premier Inn

BUDGET HOTEL

tel: 0871 527 8262 (Calls cost 13p per minute plus your phone company's access charge) **3 Riverside Park North, Castleroe Road BT51 3GE**
web: www.premierinn.com
dir: *A26 towards Coleraine. At roundabout left on A29 (ring road) signed Cookstown/Garragh. At roundabout A54 (Castleroe Road). Hotel on right.*

High quality, budget accommodation ideal for both families and business travellers. Spacious, en suite bedrooms feature free WiFi and tea and coffee making facilities, and in most hotels, Freeview TV is also available. The adjacent family restaurant features a wide and varied menu.

Rooms: 49

CRAWFORDSBURN
County Down

Map 1 D5

HIGHLY RECOMMENDED

The Old Inn
★★★★ 83% ⊛⊛ HOTEL

tel: 028 9185 3255 **15 Main Street BT19 1JH**
email: info@theoldinn.com **web:** www.theoldinn.com
dir: *A2 from Belfast, past Belfast City Airport and Transport Museum. 2 miles, left at lights onto B20. 1.2 miles to hotel.*

This delightful hotel enjoys a peaceful rural setting a short drive from Belfast. The property dates from 1614, and many of the day rooms are full of charm and character. Individually styled, comfortable bedrooms, some with feature beds, offer modern facilities. The popular bar and intimate restaurant have creative menus, and staff throughout are keen to please. The hotel has business facilities that make this the ideal place for a meeting or conference.

Rooms: 33 (1 annexe) (7 family) (5 GF) ⟁ **S** fr £90 **D** fr £90 (including breakfast)* **Facilities:** FTV WiFi ⌕ In-room spa/massage treatments ♫ Xmas New Year **Conf:** Class 120 Board 40 Theatre 150 **Services:** Lift Night porter **Parking:** 84 **Notes:** LB Civ Wed 100

DUNGANNON
County Tyrone

Map 1 C5

The Cohannon Inn
★★ 84% HOTEL

tel: 028 8772 4488 **212 Ballynakilly Road BT71 6HJ**
email: info@cohannon.com **web:** www.cohannon.com
dir: *400 yards from M1 junction 14.*

Handy for the M1 and the nearby towns of Dungannon and Portadown, this hotel offers well-maintained bedrooms, located behind the inn complex in a smart purpose-built wing. Public areas are smartly furnished and wide-ranging menus are served throughout the day.

Rooms: 42 (21 GF) ⟁ **S** fr £54.95 **D** fr £64.95* **Facilities:** FTV WiFi Hair and beauty salon New Year **Conf:** Class 100 Board 40 Theatre 140 **Services:** Night porter **Parking:** 160

ENNISKILLEN
County Fermanagh

Map 1 C5

Lough Erne Resort
★★★★★ 85% ⊛⊛⊛ HOTEL

tel: 028 6632 3230 **Belleek Road BT93 7ED**
email: info@lougherneresort.com **web:** www.lougherneresort.com
dir: *A46 from Enniskillen towards Donegal, hotel in 3 miles.*

This delightful resort enjoys a peaceful and idyllic setting and boasts championship golf courses, a wonderful Thai spa and a host of outdoor and leisure pursuits. Bedrooms and en suites are spacious, particularly well appointed and include a number of luxury suites. Day rooms are spacious, luxurious and include lounges, bars and restaurants with splendid views. Service is friendly and extremely attentive.

Rooms: 120 (61 annexe) **Facilities:** Spa STV WiFi ⊗ ♨ 18 Fishing Gym ♫ Xmas New Year **Conf:** Class 200 Board 80 Theatre 400 **Services:** Lift Night porter **Parking:** 240 **Notes:** Civ Wed 300

HIGHLY RECOMMENDED

Manor House Country Hotel
★★★★ 83% ⊛ COUNTRY HOUSE HOTEL

tel: 028 6862 2200 **Killadeas BT94 1NY**
email: info@manorhousecountryhotel.com
web: www.manorhousecountryhotel.com
dir: *On B82, 7 miles north of Enniskillen.*

This charming country house hotel enjoys a stunning location on the banks of Lower Lough Erne and is a short drive from the busy town of Enniskillen. Bedrooms are equipped to a very high standard with front-facing rooms having the fabulous lough views. There is a choice of restaurants, and afternoon tea is served in the comfortable lounge with its open fire. The hotel has first-class business, conference and leisure facilities including its own air-conditioned cruiser for tours and corporate events.

Rooms: 78 (12 family) (12 GF) ⟁ **S** fr £75 **D** fr £90 (including breakfast)* **Facilities:** FTV WiFi ⌕ ⊗ Gym Sauna Steam room ♫ Xmas New Year **Conf:** Class 120 Board 100 Theatre 400 **Services:** Lift Night porter **Parking:** 300 **Notes:** Civ Wed 300

Killyhevlin Lakeside Hotel & Lodges

★★★★ 82% HOTEL

 IRISH COUNTRY HOTELS

tel: 028 6632 3481 **BT74 6RW**
email: info@killyhevlin.com **web:** www.killyhevlin.com
dir: *2 miles south of Enniskillen, off A4.*

This modern, stylish hotel is situated on the shores of Lough Erne, south of the town. The well-equipped bedrooms are particularly spacious and enjoy fine views of the gardens and lake. The restaurant, informal bar and comfortable lounges all share the views. Staff are friendly and helpful. There are extensive leisure facilities and a spa.

Rooms: 71 (42 family) (22 GF) 🐾 **D** fr £150 (including breakfast & dinner)*
Facilities: Spa FTV WiFi ⬧ 🐟 Fishing Gym Aerobics studio Steam room Sauna Hydrotherapy area Relaxation room 🎵 New Year **Conf:** Class 160 Board 100 Theatre 500 **Services:** Lift Night porter **Parking:** 500 **Notes:** Closed 25 December RS 24 and 26 December Civ Wed 250

LIMAVADY   Map 1 C6
County Londonderry/Derry

Roe Park Resort

★★★★ 79% HOTEL

tel: 028 7772 2222 **BT49 9LB**
email: reservations@roeparkresort.com **web:** www.roeparkresort.com
dir: *On A2 (Londonderry to Limavady road), 1 mile from Limavady.*

This impressive, popular hotel is part of a modern golf resort. The spacious, contemporary bedrooms are well equipped and many have excellent views of the fairways and surrounding estate. Greens Restaurant provides a refreshing dining experience and the Coach House Brasserie offers a lighter menu. The leisure options are extensive.

Rooms: 118 (15 family) (37 GF) (5 smoking) 🐾 **Facilities:** Spa FTV WiFi HL 🐟 ♨ 18 Fishing Gym Driving range Indoor golf academy 🎵 Xmas New Year **Conf:** Class 190 Board 140 Theatre 450 **Services:** Lift Night porter **Parking:** 350 **Notes:** Civ Wed 300

LISBURN   Map 1 D5
County Antrim

Premier Inn Lisburn

 Premier Inn

BUDGET HOTEL

tel: 0871 527 8606 (Calls cost 13p per minute plus your phone company's access charge) **136-144 Hillsborough Road BT27 5QY**
web: www.premierinn.com
dir: *M1 onto A1 (Sprucefield Road). Left into Hillsborough Road. Approximately 1.5 miles, hotel on left.*

High quality, budget accommodation ideal for both families and business travellers. Spacious, en suite bedrooms feature free WiFi and tea and coffee making facilities, and in most hotels, Freeview TV is also available. The adjacent family restaurant features a wide and varied menu.

Rooms: 90

LONDONDERRY DERRY   Map 1 C5
County Londonderry/Derry

**AA HOTEL OF THE YEAR
FOR NORTHERN IRELAND 2018–19**

HIGHLY RECOMMENDED

Bishops Gate Hotel

★★★★ 83% 🏅 HOTEL

tel: 028 71140300 **24 Bishop Street, Derry BT48 6PP**
email: sales@bishopsgatehotelderry.com **web:** www.bishopsgatehotelderry.com
dir: *Phone for directions.*

Originally two private residential buildings, this property was remodelled by renowned architect Alfred A Forman to become home of the Northern Counties Club which saw many famous visitors. The hotel today has been lovingly restored to retain many original features and provide comfortable accommodation. Relax in the Wig Champagne bar or dining in Gown restaurant you will be well cared for. Parking is available and there is also a gym for residents.

Rooms: 31 (1 annexe) (3 family) (9 GF) 🐾 **S** fr £99 **D** fr £109 (including breakfast)* **Facilities:** FTV WiFi ⬧ HL Small fitness suite 🎵 New Year **Conf:** Class 40 Board 34 Theatre 90 **Services:** Lift Night porter **Parking:** 10 **Notes:** LB Closed 24–25 December Civ Wed 100

City Hotel

★★★★ 76% HOTEL

tel: 028 7136 5800 **Queens Quay BT48 7AS**
email: reservations@cityhotelderry.com **web:** www.cityhotelderry.com
dir: *Follow city centre signs. Hotel on waterfront.*

In a central position overlooking the River Foyle, this stylish, contemporary hotel will appeal to business and leisure guests alike. All bedrooms have excellent facilities including internet access; the executive rooms make particularly good working environments. Meeting and function facilities are extensive and there are good leisure options.

Rooms: 158 (16 family) 🐾 **S** fr £69 **D** fr £75 (including breakfast)* **Facilities:** FTV WiFi ⬧ 🐟 Gym Steam room 🎵 New Year **Conf:** Class 150 Board 80 Theatre 350 **Services:** Lift Night porter Air con **Parking:** 48 **Notes:** LB Closed 25 December Civ Wed 350

Premier Inn Derry / Londonderry

 Premier Inn

BUDGET HOTEL

tel: 0871 527 9414 (Calls cost 13p per minute plus your phone company's access charge) **Crescent Link BT47 6SA**
web: www.premierinn.com
dir: *Phone for directions.*

High quality, budget accommodation ideal for both families and business travellers. Spacious, en suite bedrooms feature free WiFi and tea and coffee making facilities, and in most hotels, Freeview TV is also available. The adjacent family restaurant features a wide and varied menu.

Rooms: 60

Ireland

REPUBLIC OF IRELAND

ARDMORE
County Waterford
Map 1 C2

Cliff House Hotel

★★★★ 90% HOTEL

tel: 024 87800
email: info@cliffhousehotel.ie **web:** www.cliffhousehotel.ie
dir: *From Dungarvan: N25, signed Cork. Left onto R673. From Youghal: N25 signed Waterford. Right onto R673 signed Ardmore. In Ardmore return right at Quinns food store, follow hotel signs.*

This unique property, virtually sculpted into the cliff face overlooking Ardmore Bay, is just a few minutes' walk from the village. Most of the individually designed bedroom suites and the public rooms enjoy the spectacular sea views, as do the stunning spa and leisure facilities. Rooms are very comfortable and artistically designed, in a palette of colours reflecting the natural setting. Dinner in the award-winning House Restaurant is a particular highlight – the menus feature imaginatively cooked, seasonal and local produce prepared with care and great flair. More casual fare is served in the bar, or on the terrace when weather permits. Some event spaces and valet parking are available.

Rooms: 39 (8 family) (7 GF) ☞ **D** fr €280 (including breakfast)* **Facilities:** Spa STV FTV WiFi ☼ ⊕ Fishing Gym Sauna Steam room Relaxation room Outdoor pursuits Outdoor seaweed baths New Year **Conf:** Class 30 Board 20 Theatre 50 **Services:** Lift Night porter Air con **Parking:** 52 **Notes:** LB Closed 24–26 December Civ Wed 60

BALLINA
County Mayo
Map 1 B4

Mount Falcon Estate

★★★★ 83% HOTEL

tel: 096 74472
email: info@mountfalcon.com **web:** www.mountfalcon.com
dir: *On N26, 6 miles from Foxford and 3 miles from Ballina. Hotel on left.*

Dating from 1876, this house has been lovingly restored to its former glory, and has a bedroom extension that is totally in-keeping with the original design. Relaxing lounges look out on the 100-acre estate, which has excellent salmon fishing on The Moy plus well-stocked trout lakes. Dinner is served in the original kitchen with choices from a varied and interesting menu; for lunch there is also the Boathole Bar. An air-conditioned gym is available.

Rooms: 32 (3 family) ☞ **Facilities:** Spa STV WiFi ☼ ⊕ Fishing Gym Sauna Steam room Driving range New Year **Conf:** Class 120 Board 80 Theatre 200 **Services:** Lift Night porter **Parking:** 260 **Notes:** LB Closed 24–27 December Civ Wed 200

Belleek Castle

★★★ 72% HOTEL

tel: 096 22400 **Belleek**
email: info@belleekcastle.eu **web:** www.belleekcastle.com
dir: *North of Ballina.*

This lovely manor house, formerly the ancestral home of the Earl of Arran, is set in wonderful parkland at the head of Belleek Wood on the River Moy estuary. The cosy public lounges are welcoming and are complemented by a series of banqueting suites that are decorated in a nautical theme. Bedroom accommodation varies in style; all rooms are comfortably appointed. Dinner in the Library Restaurant is the highlight of any visit; the food is all locally sourced, and the chef has a keen eye for seasonality. The hotel is a popular wedding venue. There is also a museum specialising in armoury and memorabilia from the Spanish Armada.

Rooms: 10 (2 family) ☞ **S** fr €75 **D** fr €220 (including breakfast)* **Facilities:** STV FTV WiFi ☼ Daily tours of Marshall Doran Museum Xmas **Conf:** Class 60 Board 30 Theatre 100 **Parking:** 200 **Notes:** LB Closed January to mid February Civ Wed 200

BALLINGEARY
County Cork
Map 1 B2

Gougane Barra Hotel

★★★ 78% HOTEL

tel: 026 47069 **Gougane Barra**
email: info@gouganebarrahotel.com **web:** www.gouganebarrahotel.com
dir: *On L4643. Exit R584 between N22 at Macroom and N71 at Bantry.*

This charming hotel, run by the Lucey family for over five generations, is in an idyllic location on the shores of Gougane Barra Lake, overlooking the tiny Oratory of St Finbarr, a popular venue for small weddings. The bedrooms vary in size, but they are all well decorated and very comfortable. Chef Katie Lucey prepares menus based on the best local and seasonal ingredients, some from artisan producers. The ground floor includes cosy lounge areas and a traditional bar, with a marquee theatre in the summer months for an innovative experience known as Theatre by the Lake.

Rooms: 25 (1 family) (8 GF) ☞ **S** fr €76 **D** fr €120 (including breakfast)* **Facilities:** WiFi Fishing Boating Cycling Hiking **Conf:** Class 12 Board 12 Theatre 22 **Parking:** 26 **Notes:** LB Closed 3 November to 24 March Civ Wed 60

BALLYFIN
County Laois
Map 1 C3

Ballyfin Demesne

★★★★★ HOTEL

tel: 057 8755866
email: info@ballyfin.com **web:** www.ballyfin.com
dir: *Phone for directions.*

Nestled in over 600 acres, this lavish Regency mansion has been painstakingly restored, yet all modern conveniences have been incorporated. With only 20 bedrooms, guests at Ballyfin have the feeling of visiting a friend's home; relaxation comes naturally when ensconced in any of the sumptuously decorated salons, library or the stunning Turner-designed conservatory. Hospitality is key here; a team of butlers is at hand to ensure guests are well cared for at all times. Cuisine is an important element of the Ballyfin experience, with daily-created menus on offer, together with suggested wine pairings – many featuring the Bordeaux estates of the Irish 'Wine Geese' who fled following the Battle of

Kinsale. Spa treatments are available, as are a number of country pursuits such as falconry, archery, fishing and clay shooting.

Ballyfin Demesne

Rooms: 20 (2 GF) 🐾 **Facilities:** Spa STV WiFi ⇗ 🐕 🏊 Fishing 🏌 Gym Clay pigeon Air rifle shooting Archery Falconry Horse riding Pony and carriage tour Boating on the lake Xmas New Year **Services:** Lift Night porter
Notes: No children 9 years Closed January Civ Wed 130

BALLYLICKEY
County Cork
Map 1 B2

Seaview House Hotel
★★★ ◉◉ HOTEL

tel: 027 50073 & 50462
email: info@seaviewhousehotel.com **web:** www.seaviewhousehotel.com
dir: *5 kilometres from Bantry, 11 kilometres from Glengarriff on N71.*

Colourful gardens and glimpses of Bantry Bay through the mature trees frame this delightful country house. Owner Kathleen O'Sullivan's team of staff are exceptionally pleasant, and there is a relaxed atmosphere in the cosy lounges. Guest comfort and good cuisine are top priorities. Bedrooms are spacious and individually styled, and some on the ground floor are appointed to suit less able guests.

Rooms: 25 (3 family) (5 GF) 🐾 **S** fr €100 **D** fr €140 (including breakfast)*
Facilities: STV FTV WiFi **Conf:** Class 30 Board 25 Theatre 25 **Parking:** 32 **Notes:** LB Closed mid November to mid March Civ Wed 75

BALLYLIFFIN
County Donegal
Map 1 C6

Ballyliffin Lodge & Spa
★★★★ 79% ◉ HOTEL

tel: 074 9378200 & 9378146 **Shore Road**
email: info@ballyliffinlodge.com **web:** www.ballyliffinlodge.com
dir: *From Derry take A2 towards Moville, exit for Carndonagh at Quigleys Point. Ballyliffin 10 kilometres.*

Located in the heart of the village, this property offers a range of very comfortable bedrooms and suites, many of which enjoy panoramic views of Malin Head and the famed Ballyliffin Golf Club. Dinner is served in the open-plan Jacks Bar & Restaurant, and less formal meals are served in the bar throughout the day. Guests are welcome to use the leisure facilities in the adjoining Crystal Rock Spa, where there is also a hairdressing salon. The hotel also caters well for weddings and family events.

Rooms: 40 (28 family) 🐾 **S** fr €83 **D** fr €114 (including breakfast)* **Facilities:** Spa STV WiFi ⇗ 🏌 Gym Hair salon Beauty salon Children's play areas 🎵 New Year **Conf:** Class 250 Board 125 Theatre 400 **Services:** Lift Night porter **Parking:** 80
Notes: LB Closed 24–25 December Civ Wed 150

BALLYVAUGHAN
County Clare
Map 1 B3

Gregans Castle
★★★ ◉◉◉ COUNTRY HOUSE HOTEL

tel: 065 7077005 **H91 CF60**
email: stay@gregans.ie **web:** www.gregans.ie
dir: *3.5 miles south of Ballyvaughan on N67.*

This hotel is a hidden gem in The Burren area, and the delightful restaurant and bedrooms enjoy splendid views towards Galway Bay. The Haden family, together with their welcoming staff, offer a high level of personal service. Bedrooms are individually decorated; superior rooms and suites are particularly comfortable; some are on the ground floor and have patio gardens. There are welcoming fires in the comfortable drawing room and the cosy cocktail bar where afternoon tea is served. Dinner is a highlight of any visit; the chef shows a real passion for food which is evident in his cooking of top quality local and organic produce. The area is rich in archaeological, geological and botanical interest, and cycling and walking tours can be organised. There is a beautiful garden to relax in.

Rooms: 21 (3 family) (7 GF) 🐾 **Facilities:** WiFi ⇗ 🏌 Reflexology and massage treatments Bikes and cycle tours Guided walks Sea kayaking **Conf:** Class 25 Board 14 Theatre 25 **Parking:** 25 **Notes:** Closed January to 12 February, 30 November to December Civ Wed 75

BARNA (BEARNA)
County Galway

Map 1 B3

The Twelve

★★★★ 80% @@ HOTEL

tel: 091 597000 **Barna Village**
email: enquire@thetwelvehotel.ie **web:** www.thetwelvehotel.ie
dir: *Take R336 from Galway. Hotel at crossroads in Barna.*

Located just ten minutes west of Galway city, this hotel looks as if it has been on the site for decades. However, once inside the decor is striking and contemporary. The bedrooms come in a number of different sizes, but all are furnished with taste and with guest comfort in mind. The Pins is a vibrant and popular bar and bistro where food is served throughout the day. West Restaurant opens during the evening, and features fine dining from a well-compiled menu of local and seasonal produce. Le Petit Spa offers treatments based on seaweed products.

Rooms: 47 (12 family) ☎ **S** fr €90 **D** fr €100 (including breakfast) **Facilities:** Spa STV FTV WiFi ☙ Beauty treatment room Children's cookery programme Art classes Wine classes ♫ Xmas New Year **Conf:** Class 70 Board 60 Theatre 80 **Services:** Lift Night porter Air con **Parking:** 140 **Notes:** LB Civ Wed 100

BLESSINGTON
County Wicklow

Map 1 D3

Tulfarris Hotel & Golf Resort

★★★★ 75% @ HOTEL

tel: 045 867600 **W91 EE95**
email: info@tulfarris.com **web:** www.tulfarrishotel.com
dir: *Phone or see website for directions.*

Set in 200 acres with views of the Blessington Lakes, the manor house dates from the 18th century and is a popular venue for sole-use wedding parties, with the events spaces in an adjoining building and terrace. There are a range of bedroom styles available. All-day lighter dining is offered in The Elk Bar, with evening dining in the Lime Tree Restaurant with its view toward the lakes. Plans are in place to create spa facilities during 2019.

Rooms: 74 **Facilities:** WiFi ☙ ⚓ 18 Beauty treatment rooms Archery Kayaking Bike rental Complimentary use of leisure facilities at sister hotel (Osprey Hotel) **Conf:** Class 220 Board 35 Theatre 350 **Services:** Lift **Notes:** Closed Civ Wed 250

CARRICKMACROSS
County Monaghan

Map 1 C4

Shirley Arms Hotel

★★★★ 78% @ HOTEL

tel: 042 9673100 **Main Street**
email: reception@shirleyarmshotel.ie **web:** www.shirleyarmshotel.ie
dir: *N2 to Derry, take Ardee Road to Carrickmacross.*

Set at the top of the town, this long established boutique hotel is an imposing 19th-century stone building with a contemporary interior. Bedrooms, in a purpose-built block to the rear, are spacious with clean, minimalist lines; there is also a comfortable suite in the original house overlooking the square. Food is an important element of the business here, with options available throughout the day in the bar and award-winning evening dining in the bistro. A night club is available for hire in the basement.

Rooms: 25 (2 family) ☎ **S** fr €95 **D** fr €130 (including breakfast)* **Facilities:** STV WiFi ☙ ♫ New Year **Conf:** Class 150 Board 200 Theatre 200 **Services:** Lift Night porter **Parking:** 80 **Notes:** LB Closed 24–26 December RS 14 April, Good Friday Civ Wed 150

CASHEL
County Galway

Map 1 A4

Cashel House Hotel

★★★ @@ COUNTRY HOUSE HOTEL

tel: 095 31001
email: sales@cashelhouse.ie **web:** www.cashelhouse.ie
dir: *South off N59, 1.5 kilometres west of Recess, well signed.*

Cashel House is a mid-19th century property, standing at the head of Cashel Bay in the heart of Connemara, set amidst secluded, award-winning gardens with woodland walks. Attentive service is delivered with the perfect balance of friendliness and professionalism from the McEvilly family and their staff. The comfortable lounges have turf fires and antique furnishings. The restaurant offers local produce such as the famous Connemara lamb, and fish from the nearby coast.

Rooms: 28 (4 family) (6 GF) ☎ **Facilities:** STV FTV WiFi Garden school Cookery classes Guided walks Xmas New Year **Parking:** 40 **Notes:** Closed 2 January to 1 March Civ Wed 120

CASTLETOWNBERE
County Cork

Map 1 A2

The Beara Coast Hotel

★★★★ 75% HOTEL

tel: 027 71446 **Cametringane**
email: reception@bearacoast.com **web:** www.bearacoast.com
dir: *Phone for directions.*

Located at the far end of the fishing port of Castletownbere, the cosy Beara Coast Hotel is welcoming and traditional. Bedrooms are warm and cosy in smart contemporary colourways. The character bar offers quality food throughout the day with more formal dining in The Coastal Restaurant in the evenings, where naturally, seafood is a feature. It's an unassuming looking property with a big heart with wonderfully warm and welcoming local staff.

Rooms: 16 (2 family) ☎ **S** fr €85 **D** fr €110 (including breakfast)* **Facilities:** STV FTV WiFi **Conf:** Class 100 Board 20 Theatre 300 **Services:** Lift Night porter **Parking:** 100 **Notes:** LB Closed 25–26 December Civ Wed 300

CAVAN
County Cavan

Map 1 C4

Farnham Estate Spa and Golf Resort
★★★★ 79% HOTEL

tel: 049 4377700 **Farnham Estate**
email: info.farnham@radissonblu.com **web:** www.farnhamestate.com
dir: *From Dublin take N3 to Cavan. From Cavan take Killeshandra road for 3 km.*

Situated on a 1,300 acre estate, this 16th-century Great House combines old-world grandeur with modern glamour. Interiors are light, airy and contemporary with a relaxing atmosphere. The spacious bedrooms and suites are in the newer building. Interesting dining options are available in the Botanica Restaurant and Wine Goose Cellar Bar. There are extensive banqueting facilities and the health spa offers a range of treatments.

Rooms: 158 (50 GF) **Facilities:** Spa STV WiFi ↓ ⊗ ⚲ ↥ 18 Fishing ↪ Gym In/outdoor infinity pool Mint thermal suite Relaxation rooms Walking trails ♫ Xmas New Year **Conf:** Class 150 Board 44 Theatre 380 **Services:** Lift Night porter **Parking:** 600 **Notes:** Civ Wed 150

Cavan Crystal Hotel
★★★★ 78% HOTEL

tel: 049 4360600 **Dublin Road**
email: info@cavancrystalhotel.com **web:** www.cavancrystalhotel.com
dir: *On outskirts of Cavan.*

Contemporary design using native timber and handcrafted brickwork together with crystal chandeliers make this a particularly distinctive hotel. Expect excellent hospitality from all the highly trained staff. Located on the southern edge of the town, the hotel also features a well-equipped health facility, plus beauty clinic and extensive banquet and conference facilities. Opus One is the award-winning restaurant for dinner, with all-day dining available in The Atrium Bar.

Rooms: 85 (2 family) (9 GF) **Facilities:** Spa WiFi ⊗ Gym Beauty and massage treatments Salon Sauna Steam room **Conf:** Class 300 Board 100 Theatre 500 **Services:** Lift Night porter **Parking:** 216 **Notes:** LB Closed 25–26 December Civ Wed 200

CLAREMORRIS
County Mayo

Map 1 B4

McWilliam Park Hotel
★★★★ 79% HOTEL

tel: 094 9378000
email: info@mcwilliamparkhotel.ie **web:** www.mcwilliampark.ie
dir: *Take Castlebar/Claremorris exit from N17, straight over roundabout. Hotel on right.*

McWilliam Park Hotel is situated on the outskirts of Claremorris just off the N17 between Galway and Sligo. It is approximately 20 minutes from the Knock Marian Shrine and Ireland West Airport Knock. There are comfortable lounges together with extensive conference, banqueting, leisure and health facilities. The spacious bedrooms are well appointed, with good communication technology. Food is served all day in Kavanagh's bar, and dinner is available each night in J.G's Restaurant which also serves a popular Sunday lunch. Traditional music, social dancing and other entertainment events are held on a regular basis in the McWilliam Suite.

Rooms: 103 (19 family) (15 GF) **Facilities:** Spa STV FTV WiFi ⊗ Gym ♫ Xmas New Year **Conf:** Class 250 Board 80 Theatre 600 **Services:** Lift Night porter **Parking:** 320 **Notes:** LB Civ Wed 200

CLONMEL
County Tipperary

Map 1 C2

Hotel Minella
★★★★ 80% HOTEL

tel: 052 6122388
email: frontdesk@hotelminella.ie **web:** www.hotelminella.ie
dir: *South of river in town.*

This family-run hotel is set in nine acres of well-tended gardens on the banks of the Suir River. The hotel originates from the 1860s, and the public areas include a cocktail bar and a range of lounges; some of the bedrooms are particularly spacious. The leisure centre in the grounds is noteworthy. Two-bedroom holiday homes are also available.

Rooms: 90 (8 family) (14 GF) (10 smoking) **Facilities:** FTV WiFi ↓ ⊗ ♨ Fishing ↪ Gym Beauty treatment room Sauna Steam room **Conf:** Class 300 Board 20 Theatre 500 **Services:** Lift Night porter **Parking:** 100 **Notes:** Closed 24–28 December

CONG
County Mayo

Map 1 B4

Ashford Castle
★★★★★ ֍֍ ⊜ COUNTRY HOUSE HOTEL

THE RED CARNATION HOTEL COLLECTION

tel: 094 9546003
email: ashford@ashfordcastle.com **web:** www.ashfordcastle.com
dir: *In Cross, left at church onto R345 signed Cong. Left at hotel sign, through castle gates.*

Dating from 1228, this magnificent castle is set in over 350 acres of rolling parklands, occupying a stunning position on the edge of Lough Corrib, and has now completed a multi-million refurbishment. Bedrooms and suites vary in style, but all benefit from a pleasing combination of character, charm and modern comforts. Dinner in the elegant George V Dining Room is a treat, with creative cookery of seasonal ingredients. Less formal dining is available in The Dungeon and other locations on the estate during peak periods. The hotel offers an extensive range of both indoor and outdoor leisure pursuits including falconry, golf, shooting, fishing, an equestrian centre and lake cruising. A spectacular spa and fitness facility in a striking bronze conservatory overlooks the lake.

Rooms: 83 (1 annexe) (5 family) (22 GF) **S** fr €295 **D** fr €315 (including breakfast) **Facilities:** Spa STV FTV WiFi ↓ ⊗ ↥ 9 ♨ Fishing Gym Archery Clay pigeon Falconry Horse riding Bike hire Lake cruises Water sports ♫ Xmas New Year **Conf:** Class 70 Board 32 Theatre 110 **Services:** Lift Night porter Air con **Parking:** 250 **Notes:** LB Civ Wed 160

REPUBLIC OF IRELAND

CONG continued

The Lodge at Ashford Castle

★★★★ 82% ⓐⓐ COUNTRY HOUSE HOTEL

tel: 094 9545400 **Ashford Estate**
email: reception@thelodgeac.com **web:** www.thelodgeac.com
dir: From N84 take first turn for Cong, go through Ashford main gates, first left.

This charming hotel, as the name suggests, is in the grounds of Ashford Castle; itself a large 5-star sister hotel. The original part of The Lodge is Victorian and was the estate manager's house back in the day. The first-floor restaurant (there is also a brasserie on the ground floor) offers stunning views over Lough Corrib as do some bedrooms; these are spacious, well equipped and suit leisure guests particularly well. The team are welcoming and friendly.

Rooms: 64 (54 annexe) (20 family) (20 GF) ⟁ **S** fr €130 **D** fr €150 (including breakfast)* **Facilities:** STV FTV WiFi ⓑ ⚓ 9 ⚓ Fishing Gym Beauty treatment room Falconry Archery Equestrian Boating Canoeing Kayaking ⎘ New Year **Conf:** Class 80 Board 80 Theatre 200 **Services:** Lift Night porter **Parking:** 80 **Notes:** LB Closed 24-25 December RS November to February Civ Wed 186

CORK	Map 1 B2
County Cork	

Hayfield Manor

★★★★★ 90% ⓐⓐ HOTEL

tel: 021 4845900 **Perrott Avenue, College Road**
email: enquiries@hayfieldmanor.ie **web:** www.hayfieldmanor.ie
dir: Phone for directions.

Dating originally from the early 1800s, Hayfield Manor is an oasis of comfort and calm set in two acres of mature gardens in the University quarter of the city. The bedrooms and suites come in a number of sizes, but the style is the same throughout; quality fabrics and furnishings married with the latest of the tech advances you would expect from a world class property. Lunch and dinner is served daily in Perrotts Garden Bistro, and on the terrace when weather permits. High end evening dining is in Orchids Restaurant. There's ample complimentary car parking in the grounds.

Rooms: 88 (5 family) (6 GF) ⟁ **S** fr €199 **D** fr €229 **Facilities:** Spa STV FTV WiFi ⓑ ⚓ Gym ⎘ Xmas New Year **Conf:** Class 60 Board 38 Theatre 120 **Services:** Lift Night porter Air con **Parking:** 112 **Notes:** LB Civ Wed 60

Maryborough Hotel & Spa

★★★★ 81% ⓐⓐ HOTEL

tel: 021 4365555 **Maryborough Hill, Douglas**
email: info@maryborough.ie **web:** www.maryborough.com
dir: From Jack Lynch Tunnel 2nd exit signed Douglas. Right at 1st roundabout, follow Rochestown signs to Fingerpost roundabout. Left, hotel on left.

Dating from 1715, this house was renovated and extended to become a fine hotel with beautifully landscaped grounds full of rare plant species. There are stylish suites in the main house, while the bedrooms in the wing are comfortably furnished, some with balconies or terraces. The bar and lounge are very popular for the range

of food served throughout the day; afternoon tea is a speciality. Bellini's Restaurant offers a mix of classic and contemporary dishes presented to a high standard. There are impressive spa, leisure and conference facilities, plus activities for children.

Rooms: 93 (6 family) ⟁ **S** fr €145 **D** fr €180 (including breakfast)* **Facilities:** Spa STV FTV WiFi ⓑ ⚓ Gym Sauna Steam room New Year **Conf:** Class 250 Board 60 Theatre 500 **Services:** Lift Night porter **Parking:** 300 **Notes:** LB Closed 24–26 December Civ Wed 250

The Kingsley

★★★★ 81% ⓐ HOTEL

tel: 021 4800500 **Victoria Cross**
email: info@thekingsley.ie **web:** www.thekingsley.ie
dir: N40 at Sarsfield junction follow N71 signs. At Wilton roundabout take 2nd exit (city centre). At lights turn left (signed Killarney). Hotel on right.

Set on the banks of the River Lee, a leisurely half hour stroll from the city centre, this is a wonderfully welcoming hotel that is sure to please. There are a number of accommodation options, some with river views. The Springboard Restaurant is a casual bistro-style operation at lunch and dinner, with breakfast being served in Fairbanks. The hotel offers extensive banqueting facilities, a health club and a spa. An ideal location for visitors to the university, ten minutes or so away. Both surface and underground parking is complimentary to guests.

Rooms: 131 (8 family) ⟁ **Facilities:** Spa FTV WiFi ⓑ ⚓ Gym ⎘ New Year **Conf:** Class 100 Board 60 Theatre 220 **Services:** Lift Night porter Air con **Parking:** 200 **Notes:** Closed 25 December RS 24 December Civ Wed 220

The Montenotte Hotel

★★★★ 78% HOTEL

tel: 021 4530050 **Middle Glanmire Road, Montenotte**
email: info@themontenottehotel.com **web:** www.themontenottehotel.com
dir: Phone for directions.

Perched on a steep hillside with southern views over the city, this former merchant prince's residence is now a plush, contemporary hotel. The public spaces are bright open areas that include Panorama Bistro & Terrace which makes the most of the views and overlooks the formal box garden. Other public areas are quite eclectic, with interesting combinations in decor styles; they include an in-house cinema, spa and leisure centre and event spaces. The spacious, smart, contemporary bedrooms are decorated in warm relaxing tones and are well equipped.

The Montenotte Hotel

Rooms: 145 (38 annexe) (11 family) ⌂ **S** fr €109 **D** fr €109* **Facilities:** Spa STV FTV WiFi ♨ ☺ Gym Hair salon Nail bar ♫ **Conf:** Class 60 Board 50 Theatre 200 **Services:** Lift Night porter **Parking:** 130 **Notes:** Closed 25 December RS 24 and 26 December

---

DELGANY
County Wicklow
Map 1 D3

Glenview Hotel

★★★★ 79% ◉◉ HOTEL

tel: 01 2873399 Glen o' the Downs
email: sales@glenviewhotel.com **web:** www.glenviewhotel.com
dir: *From Dublin city centre follow signs for N11, past Bray on N11 southbound, exit 9.*

This hotel is set in lovely terraced gardens overlooking the Glen o' the Downs. The comfortable bedrooms are spacious, and many enjoy the great views over the valley. The impressive public areas include a conservatory bar, lounge and choice of dining options including the first-floor Woodlands Restaurant where dinner is served. The hotel has an excellent range of leisure and conference facilities. A championship golf course and horse riding can be found nearby.

Rooms: 70 (11 family) (16 GF) ⌂ **S** fr €190 **D** fr €220 (including breakfast)* **Facilities:** Spa STV WiFi ☺ ⛱ Gym Aerobics studio Massage Beauty treatment rooms ♫ Xmas New Year **Conf:** Class 80 Board 80 Theatre 230 **Services:** Lift Night porter **Parking:** 200 **Notes:** Civ Wed 180

DINGLE (AN DAINGEAN)
County Kerry
Map 1 A2

Dingle Skellig Hotel & Peninsula Spa

★★★★ 80% ◉ HOTEL

tel: 066 9150200
email: reservations@dingleskellig.com **web:** www.dingleskellig.com
dir: *N86 to Dingle, hotel on harbour.*

This modern hotel, close to the town, overlooks Dingle Bay and has spectacular views from many of the comfortably furnished bedrooms and suites. Public areas offer a spacious bar and lounge and a bright, airy restaurant. There are extensive health and leisure facilities, and many family activities are organised in the Fungi Kids Club.

Rooms: 113 (10 family) (31 GF) ⌂ **Facilities:** Spa STV FTV WiFi ♨ ☺ Gym ♫ New Year **Conf:** Class 120 Board 100 Theatre 250 **Services:** Lift Night porter **Parking:** 110 **Notes:** Closed January RS November to December Civ Wed 250

DONEGAL
County Donegal
Map 1 B5

INSPECTOR'S CHOICE

Harvey's Point Hotel

★★★★ ◉◉ COUNTRY HOUSE HOTEL

tel: 074 9722208 Lough Eske
email: stay@harveyspoint.com **web:** www.harveyspoint.com
dir: *N56 from Donegal, then 1st right signed Lough Eske/Harvey's Point.*

Situated by the shores of Lough Eske, a short drive from Donegal, this family-run, welcoming hotel is an oasis of relaxation; comfort along with attentive guest care are the norm here. A wide range of particularly spacious suites and bedrooms is on offer, together with smaller Garden Suites in the courtyard annexe. The kitchen brigade maintains consistently high standards in The Lakeside Restaurant at dinner, with less formal dining in the atmospheric Harvey's Bar throughout the day; breakfast is also a highlight of a stay here. A very popular Sunday buffet lunch is served weekly, with dinner and cabaret entertainment on selected dates during the summer. Pet friendly accommodation is available.

Rooms: 64 (8 annexe) (17 family) (28 GF) ⌂ **S** fr €149 **D** fr €238 (including breakfast)* **Facilities:** STV FTV WiFi ♨ Beauty treatment rooms Walking tours ♫ Xmas New Year **Conf:** Class 200 Board 50 Theatre 200 **Services:** Lift Night porter **Parking:** 300 **Notes:** LB Civ Wed 250

Mill Park Hotel

★★★★ 76% HOTEL

tel: 074 9722880 The Mullins
email: info@millparkhotel.com **web:** www.millparkhotel.com
dir: *Phone for directions.*

Family-owned and operated, Mill Park Hotel is located within walking distance of the town and has a friendly and dedicated team who have a natural and warm approach. All the comfortable rooms and suites have been renovated to create stylish contemporary decor schemes. All-day dining is available in the Café Bar, a popular venue with the locals, with more formal evening dining in the first-floor Granary Restaurant that overlooks the main lobby. There is a spacious leisure centre available on a complimentary basis to resident guests, together with treatments and pampering in the Wellness Centre. The hotel has an excellent reputation for its banqueting and conference facilities.

Rooms: 110 (10 family) (43 GF) ⌂ **Facilities:** STV FTV WiFi ♨ ☺ Gym New Year **Conf:** Class 100 Board 30 Theatre 300 **Services:** Lift Night porter **Parking:** 200 **Notes:** Closed 24–26 December Civ Wed 350

DROGHEDA	Map 1 D4
County Louth	

Scholars Townhouse Hotel

★★★ 78% ◉◉ HOTEL

tel: 041 9835410 **King Street**
email: info@scholarshotel.com **web:** www.scholarshotel.com
dir: *From West Street, continue to St Laurence's Gate. Before gate, turn left, to top of hill. Hotel on left.*

Located a short stroll from Drogheda's centre, this family-owned and run boutique property was formerly a monastery built in the late 19th century; many architectural features have been retained. Space is rather compromised in the bedrooms as they were previously monks' cells, but they are en suite and have excellent beds and quality fabrics. All-day dining is available in the Gastrolounge where craft beers are a feature, and award-winning evening dining is offered in the restaurant; breakfasts are also noteworthy. The hotel is on an elevated site amid well-tended grounds and offers secure parking.

Rooms: 16 (1 family) **Facilities:** FTV WiFi ⇘ New Year **Conf:** Class 55 Board 18 Theatre 55 **Services:** Lift Night porter **Parking:** 30 **Notes:** Closed 25–26 December Civ Wed 70

DUBLIN	Map 1 D4
Dublin	

The Merrion Hotel

★★★★★ ◉◉◉◉ HOTEL

tel: 01 6030600 **21 Upper Merrion Street**
email: info@merrionhotel.com **web:** www.merrionhotel.com
dir: *At top of Upper Merrion Street on left, beyond Government buildings on right.*

This terrace of gracious Georgian buildings, said to be the birthplace of the Duke of Wellington, reflects many changes of use over the last 200 years. Bedrooms and suites are spacious, some in the original house, others in a modern wing overlooking the gardens; they all offer great comfort and a wide range of extra facilities. The lounges retain the charm and opulence of days gone by, while the Cellar bar area is a popular meeting point. Dining options include The Cellar Restaurant specialising in prime local ingredients and, for a very special occasion, the award-winning Restaurant Patrick Guilbaud is Dublin's finest. 'Art Tea' is an afternoon tea experience with a difference, where the delightful pastries are inspired by the hotel's vast art collection.

Rooms: 142 (21 GF) ⟁ **S** fr €555 **D** fr €575* **Facilities:** Spa STV FTV WiFi ⇘ ⊛ Gym Steam room Relaxation area ♫ Xmas New Year **Conf:** Class 25 Board 25 Theatre 60 **Services:** Lift Night porter Air con **Parking:** 60 **Notes:** LB Civ Wed 50

The Shelbourne Dublin, a Renaissance Hotel

★★★★★ ◉◉ HOTEL

RENAISSANCE.
HOTELS & RESORTS

tel: 01 6634500 **27 St Stephen's Green**
email: rhi.dubbr.reservations@renaissancehotels.com
web: www.theshelbourne.ie
dir: *M1 to city centre, along Parnell Street to O'Connell Street towards Trinity College, 3rd right into Kildare Street, hotel on left.*

This Dublin landmark exudes elegance and a real sense of history, having been established in 1824. The public areas are spacious and offer a range of dining and bar options. There is a selection of bedroom styles and suites available, many with commanding views over St Stephen's Green. No 27 is a popular bar and lounge for casual dining, while the Saddle Room is the main restaurant featuring a steak and seafood menu with a contemporary twist, and an enviable reputation for both its food and service. Afternoon tea is served in the elegant Lord Mayor's Lounge and is a real treat. An extensive leisure and fitness facility is also available, together with a range of meeting rooms, including The Constitution Room, where the Irish Constitution was drafted.

Rooms: 265 (2 smoking) ⟁ **S** fr €350 **D** fr €380* **Facilities:** Spa STV FTV WiFi ⇘ ⊛ Gym Relaxation room Thermal facilities Dance studio Hair salon Xmas New Year **Conf:** Class 252 Board 84 Theatre 450 **Services:** Lift Night porter Air con **Notes:** Civ Wed 350

The Westbury

★★★★★ 88% ◉◉ HOTEL

tel: 01 6791122 **Grafton Street**
email: westbury@doylecollection.com **web:** www.doylecollection.com
dir: *Adjacent to Grafton Street, half way between Trinity College and Stephen's Green.*

Located just off Grafton Street, Dublin's premier shopping district, this is an oasis of calm; guests are well cared for amid smart, contemporary surroundings. Spacious public areas include the relaxing Gallery Lounge where afternoon tea is popular with shoppers taking a break. Decor is smart, featuring interesting art pieces and sculptures. Balfes is the hotel's buzzing street-level brasserie bar, while Wilde is the first-floor restaurant with views of the bustling street below from the terrace. Bedrooms and suites come in a range of sizes, all are very comfortably appointed with large, deep beds and warm contemporary decor schemes. The Grafton Suite is an event space, augmented by a range of private dining and meeting rooms. Secure underground parking and a fitness suite are available to resident guests.

Rooms: 205 (9 family) ⟁ **S** fr €280 **D** fr €280* **Facilities:** STV FTV WiFi ⇘ Gym **Conf:** Class 90 Board 46 Theatre 200 **Services:** Lift Night porter Air con **Parking:** 100 **Notes:** Civ Wed 120

The Marker

★★★★★ 86%  HOTEL

tel: 01 6875100 **Grand Canal Square**
email: info@themarkerhoteldublin.com
web: www.themarkerhoteldublin.com
dir: M50 junction 1, 2nd exit North Wall Quay. Right into Commons Street, right into Mayor Street, right on Guild Street, over SB Bridge, left onto Quays. Right into Forbes Street, right into Hanover Quay.

The Marker makes its mark on the exciting Dublin Docklands architectural scene, with its chequerboard frontage. Very much to the fore in terms of contemporary design, all of the bedroom styles are bright and airy, some have dual aspect windows. The entire ground floor is open plan, under a spectacular abstract ceiling, and encompasses the buzzy Marker Bar and the brasserie. A roof-top bar and terrace specialising in cocktails operates in the summer and when the weather permits. Full spa and wellness facilities are available, together with valet parking.

Rooms: 187 ✆ **D** fr €229* **Facilities:** Spa STV FTV WiFi ⌨ ⓣ Gym Sauna Steam room New Year **Conf:** Class 180 Board 68 Theatre 250 **Services:** Lift Night porter Air con **Parking:** 13 **Notes:** LB Closed 25–26 December Civ Wed 250

Conrad Dublin

★★★★★ 83% HOTEL

tel: 01 6028900 **Earlsfort Terrace**
email: conrad_dublin@conradhotels.com **web:** www.conraddublin.com
dir: Phone for directions.

This fine property is located opposite The National Concert Hall, a 10-minute walk from the main shopping district of Grafton Street. It has very smart public areas, a choice of dining options and a range of accommodation choices. The decor scheme throughout is contemporary, in restful muted colourways. The Coburg is the all-day dining brasserie with a menu primarily based on local producers and suppliers. Lemuels is an elegant lounge, with a more casual atmosphere downstairs in Alfie Byrne's bar, featuring artisan and craft beers and bar food. A range of events spaces is available, together with a 24-hour fitness suite and valet parking.

Rooms: 192 (15 family) ✆ **S** fr €230 **D** fr €230* **Facilities:** STV FTV WiFi ⌨ HL Gym Xmas New Year **Conf:** Class 132 Board 22 Theatre 350 **Services:** Lift Night porter Air con **Parking:** 85 **Notes:** LB Civ Wed 240

Castleknock Hotel

FBD Hotels & Resorts

★★★★ 83% HOTEL

tel: 01 6406300 **Porterstown Road, Castleknock**
email: info@castleknockhotel.ie **web:** www.castleknockhotel.com
dir: M50 from airport. Exit at junction 6 signed Navan, Cavan and M3, onto N3, becomes M3. Exit at junction 3. At top of slip road 1st left signed Consilla R121. At T-junction left. 1 kilometre to hotel.

This modern hotel is set on a golf course only 15 minutes from Dublin. The bedrooms are very comfortable, with all the expected modern guest facilities. The spacious public rooms have an airy feel, and some rooms open onto a terrace that overlooks the golf course. The range of food and beverage outlets includes The Park Room, a steak house, a busy all-day brasserie, and The Lime Tree which is open in the evening. Excellent conference and banqueting facilities are available, together with a popular leisure centre.

Rooms: 190 (20 family) (9 GF) ✆ **S** fr €89 **D** fr €109 (including breakfast)* **Facilities:** Spa STV FTV WiFi ⌨ ⓣ ⌕ 18 Gym Sauna Steam room Children's pool ♫ New Year **Conf:** Class 200 Board 40 Theatre 400 **Services:** Lift Night porter **Parking:** 400 **Notes:** Closed 24–26 December Civ Wed 200

Radisson Blu St Helens Hotel

 Radisson BLU
HOTELS & RESORTS

★★★★ 82% HOTEL

tel: 01 2186000 **Stillorgan Road**
email: info.dublin@radissonblu.com **web:** www.radissonblu.ie/sthelenshotel-dublin
dir: On N11 (Stillorgan dual carriageway).

This carefully restored hotel is part of an early 18th-century estate just five kilometres south of the city and close to UCD. It offers over 150 well-appointed suites and bedrooms in a modern block to the side of the main building; many have garden views. The spectacular Orangerie and The Ballroom are popular venues for all-day dining, and for dinner, guests can choose the AA-Rosette awarded Italian restaurant, Talavera which is located in the original kitchens. Le Panto is a wonderfully decorated room, available for private dining. A fitness suite and beauty facilities are provided, together with extensive meeting and event spaces.

Rooms: 151 (22 family) (38 GF) ✆ **S** fr €150 **D** fr €200* **Facilities:** STV FTV WiFi ⌨ Gym Beauty salon ♫ Xmas New Year **Conf:** Class 150 Board 70 Theatre 350 **Services:** Lift Night porter Air con **Parking:** 220 **Notes:** LB Civ Wed 240

Clontarf Castle Hotel

★★★★ 81% HOTEL

tel: 01 8332321 **Castle Avenue, Clontarf**
email: jormston@clontarfcastle.ie **web:** www.clontarfcastle.ie
dir: M1 towards centre, left at Whitehall Church, left at T-junction, straight on at lights, right at next lights into Castle Avenue, hotel on right at roundabout.

Dating back to the 12th century, this castle retains many historic architectural features which have been combined with contemporary styling in the well-equipped bedrooms. Public areas offer relaxing lounges and galleries which display an eclectic collection of art work. Award-winning cuisine is served at dinner in Fahrenheit Restaurant, with interesting options in the gastropub-style Knights Bar throughout the day, and also a lunchtime offering in the Indigo Lounge. The Great Hall is a versatile venue for banqueting and conferences, and is very popular for family occasions.

Rooms: 111 (7 family) (11 GF) ✆ **Facilities:** STV WiFi ⌨ Gym Xmas New Year **Conf:** Class 250 Board 90 Theatre 600 **Services:** Lift Night porter Air con **Parking:** 134 **Notes:** LB Civ Wed 400

Crowne Plaza Hotel Dublin - Blanchardstown

CROWNE PLAZA
HOTELS & RESORTS

★★★★ 80% HOTEL

tel: 01 8977777 **The Blanchardstown Centre**
email: info@cpireland.crowneplaza.com **web:** www.cpireland.ie
dir: M50 junction 6 (Blanchardstown).

This landmark building is on the doorstep of a wide range of shops in Blanchardstown. Bedrooms are stylishly decorated with generously sized beds and well appointed en suites. The Sanctuary Bar serves an international range of informal dishes from lunchtime through to the evening, with Italian specialities (pasta dishes and pizzas) served in the evenings in Forchetta Restaurant. There is a floor of dedicated boardrooms and meeting facilities, together with banqueting rooms. Secure underground parking is complimentary to resident guests.

Rooms: 188 (60 family) ✆ **S** fr €90 **D** fr €90* **Facilities:** STV FTV WiFi ⌨ HL Gym Sauna ♫ New Year **Conf:** Class 300 Board 300 Theatre 500 **Services:** Lift Night porter Air con **Parking:** 250 **Notes:** Civ Wed 300

REPUBLIC OF IRELAND

DUBLIN *continued*

Ashling Hotel, Dublin

★★★★ 80% HOTEL

tel: 01 6772324 **Parkgate Street**
email: info@ashlinghotel.ie **web:** www.ashlinghotel.ie
dir: *Close to River Liffey, opposite Heuston Station.*

Situated on the banks of the River Liffey close to the city centre, railway station and law courts, this hotel is on the tram route and just a five-minute walk from Phoenix Park. The property is appointed to a high standard in a contemporary style. The bedrooms are comfortably furnished; the newer ones are more spacious. Food is available in the Iveagh Bar throughout the day and a popular carvery is served at lunchtime; Chesterfields Restaurant offers award-winning cuisine in the evenings. Staff are very friendly and service is attentive and professional. Meeting and events spaces are provided. Secure multi-storey parking is available at favourable rates.

Rooms: 225 (21 family) S fr €109 **D** fr €109* **Facilities:** FTV WiFi **Conf:** Class 110 Board 50 Theatre 200 **Services:** Lift Night porter **Parking:** 100 **Notes:** Closed 24–26 December

Talbot Hotel Stillorgan

★★★★ 80% HOTEL

tel: 01 2001800 **Stillorgan Road, Stillorgan**
email: info@talbotstillorgan.com **web:** www.talbothotelstillorgan.com
dir: *From N11 follow Wexford signs (pass RTE studios on left) through 5 sets of lights. Hotel on left.*

The Talbot Hotel Stillorgan is situated on the southern outskirts of the city, close to UCD, the shopping centre and The RTE Studios. Comfortable public areas include a spacious lobby, The Purple Sage Restaurant, and Brass, a brasserie/bar serving quality food throughout the day. Bedrooms and suites come in a range of styles and sizes, all well appointed and comfortable. There are extensive air-conditioned banqueting and conference facilities, and a compact gym. There is generous parking to the rear, and public transport by bus to the city centre is on hand.

Rooms: 150 (10 family) S fr €109 **D** fr €119* **Facilities:** STV WiFi Gym New Year **Conf:** Class 220 Board 130 Theatre 500 **Services:** Lift Night porter Air con **Parking:** 300 **Notes:** LB Closed 25 December RS 24 December Civ Wed 300

Radisson Blu Royal Hotel

★★★★ 79% HOTEL

tel: 01 8982900 **Golden Lane D08 VRR7**
email: info.royal.dublin@radissonblu.com
web: www.radissonblu.com/en/royalhotel-dublin
dir: *Phone for directions.*

Located within walking distance of the shopping district and theatres, this modern property is sure to please business and leisure visitors alike. Bedrooms come in a range of sizes, all in a contemporary decor scheme. All-day dining can be enjoyed in the bright and airy Sure Bar. Evening dining is on offer in V'nV Restaurant, an elegant dining space. Parking is onsite, with leisure facilities available at favourable rates at a nearby centre. A number of meeting and event spaces are also incorporated in this warm and welcoming hotel.

Rooms: 150 **Facilities:** WiFi Complimentary access to Iveagh Fitness Club **Conf:** Class 280 Board 50 Theatre 400 **Services:** Lift Air con **Parking:** 60 **Notes:** Civ Wed 50

Roganstown Hotel and Country Club

★★★★ 77% HOTEL

tel: 01 8433118 **Naul Road, Sword**
web: www.roganstown.com
dir: *Phone for directions.*

Developed from the original family home and farm some 10 years ago, Roganstown is now a quality hotel surrounded by parkland that includes a golf course and a well-equipped leisure centre and spa. Some bedrooms are in the original farmhouse, but most are in a separate, modern block around a well landscaped courtyard. The public areas include a cosy bar that doubles as the golf members' area and the busy O'Callaghan's Bar where food is served throughout the day. Evening fine dining takes place in the award-winning McLaughlin's Restaurant where the menu features carefully sourced, seasonal ingredients cooked with flair. A multi-use conference and events centre is located on the first floor.

Rooms: 52 (4 family) (20 GF) S fr €89 **D** fr €89* **Facilities:** Spa STV WiFi 18 Gym Aerobics studio **Conf:** Class 150 Board 128 Theatre 300 **Services:** Lift Night porter **Parking:** 370 **Notes:** LB Civ Wed 240

Red Cow Moran Hotel

★★★★ 76% HOTEL

tel: 01 4593650 **Red Cow Complex, Naas Road**
email: info@redcowmoranhotel.com **web:** www.redcowmoranhotel.com
dir: *At junction of M50 and N7 on city side of motorway.*

Located just off the M50 and N7, this hotel is 20 minutes from the airport, Heuston and Connolly train stations and close to the city centre via the Luas light rail system. The dedicated team of staff show a genuine willingness to create a memorable stay. Bedrooms are well equipped and comfortable, and the public areas and conference rooms are spacious. A seven-storey extension has increased the hotels capacity and ample free parking is available.

Rooms: 275 (152 annexe) (126 family) (5 smoking) S fr €80 **D** fr €80* **Facilities:** FTV WiFi Gym Xmas New Year **Conf:** Class 350 Board 200 Theatre 800 **Services:** Lift Night porter **Parking:** 350 **Notes:** Civ Wed 800

Cassidys Hotel

★★★ 78% HOTEL

tel: 01 8780555 **6–8 Cavendish Row, Upper O'Connell Street**
email: stay@cassidyshotel.com **web:** www.cassidyshotel.com
dir: *In city centre at north end of O'Connell Street.*

This long established family-run hotel is located at the northern end of O'Connell Street, in a terrace of red-brick Georgian townhouses, directly opposite the famed Gate Theatre. The warm and welcoming atmosphere created by the hospitable team in Groomes Bar and Bistro adds to the traditional atmosphere. An all-day menu is served, together with a pre-theatre offering. Bedrooms are individually styled and well appointed; many have air conditioning, with executive rooms in a modern block to the side. A residents' gym, conference facilities and limited parking are all available.

Rooms: 113 (26 annexe) (3 family) (12 GF) (30 smoking) **Facilities:** STV WiFi Gym **Conf:** Class 45 Board 45 Theatre 80 **Services:** Lift Night porter **Parking:** 8 **Notes:** Closed 24–26 December

Intercontinental Dublin

Tel: 01 6654000
email: sales@icdublin.com **web:** www.intercontinentaldublin.ie

Currently the rating for this establishment is not confirmed. This may be due to a change of ownership or because it has only recently joined the AA rating scheme.

Rooms: 197

DUBLIN AIRPORT   Map 1 D4
Dublin

Crowne Plaza Dublin Northwood

★★★★ 80% ◉ HOTEL

Tel: 01 8628888 **Northwood Park, Santry Demesne**
email: info@crowneplazadublin.ie **web:** www.cpdublin.crowneplaza.com
dir: M50 junction 4, left into Northwood Park, 1 km, hotel on left.

Located within minutes of Dublin Airport, and served by a complimentary shuttle service, this modern hotel is located in Northwood Park and benefits from an idyllic location overlooking 85 acres of mature woodland of the former Santry Demesne. Bedrooms come in a variety of styles, and each is comfortable and well appointed. Guests in the executive rooms have the use of a lounge facility where a light breakfast is served. The hotel offers a range of dining options, including full room service and a lobby café. There are extensive conference and event rooms at this property, together with a secure multi-storey car park. Guests also have use of a well-equipped gym.

Rooms: 204 (17 family) (5 smoking) **Facilities:** STV FTV WiFi HL Gym Xmas New Year **Conf:** Class 450 Board 100 Theatre 850 **Services:** Lift Night porter Air con **Parking:** 400 **Notes:** Civ Wed 300

DUNBOYNE   Map 1 D4
County Meath

Dunboyne Castle Hotel & Spa

★★★★ 79% ◉◉ HOTEL

Tel: 01 8013500 **A86 PW63**
email: info@dunboynecastlehotel.com **web:** www.dunboynecastlehotel.com
dir: In Dunboyne take R157 towards Maynooth. Hotel on left.

Located within walking distance of Dunboyne, this fine property is a successful combination of the traditional and contemporary. Set amid mature woodland and well-tended grounds, the original house is home to a number of meeting rooms, with the spacious bedrooms in a modern block to the side. All-day dining is offered in the Terrace Lounge, with evening meals and breakfast served in the Ivy Restaurant.

Dunboyne Castle Hotel & Spa

Rooms: 145 (37 GF) **S** fr €95 **D** fr €130 (including breakfast) **Facilities:** Spa STV WiFi Gym Xmas New Year **Conf:** Class 200 Board 80 Theatre 350 **Services:** Lift Night porter Air con **Parking:** 380 **Notes:** LB Civ Wed 250

See advert on following page

DUNDALK   Map 1 D4
County Louth

Ballymascanlon House Hotel

★★★★ 80% HOTEL

tel: 042 9358200
email: info@ballymascanlon.com **web:** www.ballymascanlon.com
dir: M1 junction 18 onto N52 signed Dundalk North/R173 at Carlingford. Exit at Faughart roundabout. 1st left at next roundabout. Hotel in approximately 1 km on left.

This Victorian mansion is set in 130 acres of woodland and landscaped gardens at the foot of the Cooley Mountains. The elegant house and the modern extension make this a very comfortable hotel that has really stylish bedrooms. Public areas include a spacious restaurant, lounge and bar, together with relaxing reading rooms that retain many original architectural features. There is a well-equipped leisure centre, and The Oak Room banqueting facility proves to be very popular for weddings and family occasions.

Rooms: 97 (11 family) (5 GF) **Facilities:** STV FTV WiFi 18 Gym Steam room Sauna Plunge pool Xmas New Year **Conf:** Class 220 Board 100 Theatre 400 **Services:** Lift Night porter **Parking:** 250 **Notes:** LB Civ Wed 300

REPUBLIC OF IRELAND

DUNFANAGHY
County Donegal   Map 1 C6

Arnolds Hotel
★★★ 78% ⊛ HOTEL

IRISH
COUNTRY
HOTELS

tel: 074 9136208
email: enquiries@arnoldshotel.com **web:** www.arnoldshotel.com
dir: *N56 from Letterkenny, hotel on left on entering village.*

This family-owned and run hotel, situated in a coastal village overlooking sandy beaches and beautiful scenery, is noted for its warm welcome and good food. The public areas and bedrooms are very comfortable; there is a traditional, cosy bar with turf fires and regular live music, a popular bistro that serves food throughout the day, and Seascapes Restaurant where local seafood features on the menu. The popular café opens daily with alfresco dining in the garden, weather permitting. There are stables attached to the hotel, with preferential terms for residents. Photographic and painting breaks are available, as is links-based golf.

Rooms: 30 (10 family) **Facilities:** FTV WiFi ♪ New Year **Conf:** Class 30 Board 20 Theatre 30 **Services:** Night porter **Parking:** 60 **Notes:** LB Closed Monday to Tuesday (November to March) Civ Wed 90

DUNGLOE
County Donegal   Map 1 B5

Waterfront Hotel Dungloe
★★★ 76% HOTEL

tel: 074 9522444 **Mill Road**
email: joseph@waterfronthoteldungloe.ie **web:** www.waterfronthoteldungloe.ie

Signposted in the Irish language as 'An Clochan Liath', Dungloe is the principal town of west Donegal. The Waterfront Hotel is a long established property on an elevated position at the end of the town. Eating options are the 106 Atlantic, the main restaurant, and a more casual bistro – both make the most of the views over Dungloe Bay. Menus feature all the family favourites and plenty of seafood options. Service is personable, with the typical Donegal warmth and hospitality to the fore. The cosy and comfortable bedrooms have a slightly maritime theme.

Rooms: 49 **Facilities:** WiFi

ENFIELD
County Meath

Map 1 C4

The Johnstown Estate

★★★★ 80% ◉ HOTEL

tel: 046 9540000 **A83 V070**
email: info@thejohnstownestate.com **web:** www.thejohnstownestate.com
dir: *Exit 9 off the M4. Between Johnstownbridge and Enfield.*

With its origins as a 1750s Georgian manor house, the estate, on over 120 acres is within easy reach of Dublin by motorway. The property has a strong reputation for its sporting facilities and is regularly used for training camps for visiting teams. The public areas have benefited from a recent refurbishment to a high quality standard, including Fire & Salt an airy brasserie style dining option with a buzzy

atmosphere. The Coach House offers a more casual menu, served throughout the day. The spacious event areas are in regular use for weddings and conferences.

The Johnstown Estate

Rooms: 126 **Facilities:** Spa STV WiFi ◊ 🔧 Gym Hair salon Sauna Steam room Relaxation room Fitness classes Sports training for football/rugby/GAA **Conf:** Class 400 Board 32 Theatre 750 **Notes:** Civ Wed 350

See advert below

ENNIS
County Clare

Map 1 B3

Temple Gate Hotel

★★★★ 78% ◉ HOTEL

tel: 065 6823300 **The Square**
email: info@templegatehotel.com **web:** www.templegatehotel.com
dir: *Exit N18 onto Tulla Road for 0.25 mile, hotel on left.*

This smart hotel is owned and run by the Madden family and is located in the centre of the town. It incorporates a 19th-century, Gothic-style Great Hall banqueting room. The public areas are well planned and include a comfortable library lounge, popular traditional pub, and Legends Restaurant. Bedrooms are attractive and well equipped, with some executive rooms and suites available.

Rooms: 70 (3 family) (11 GF) (20 smoking) **S** fr €99 **D** fr €109 (including breakfast)*
Facilities: STV FTV WiFi ◊ 🎵 New Year **Conf:** Class 100 Board 80 Theatre 250
Services: Lift Night porter **Parking:** 52 **Notes:** LB Closed 25–26 December
RS 24 December Civ Wed 200

ENNISKERRY
County Wicklow

Map 1 D3

Powerscourt Hotel Resort & Spa

★★★★★ 88% ◉◉ HOTEL

tel: 01 2748888 Powerscourt Estate
email: info@powerscourthotel.com web: www.powerscourthotel.com
dir: From Dublin take M50, M11, then N11, follow Enniskerry signs. In Enniskerry left up hill, hotel on right.

This very stylish hotel, built in the Palladian style, has a tranquil setting with stunning views over the gardens and woodlands to the Sugar Loaf Mountain. Being set in the heart of the renowned Powerscourt Estate makes for great walks and exploration. The bedrooms and suites are particularly spacious and well appointed. Impressive bathrooms have TVs, deep baths and walk-in showers. The luxuriously appointed public areas are airy and spacious with a variety of food options that includes the award-winning Sika Restaurant, Sugar Loaf Lounge and McGills Bar. The resort also has a stunning spa, two golf courses, and includes fly fishing and equestrian pursuits among its many leisure facilities. There are extensive conferencing and events spaces.

Rooms: 194 (39 GF) ♠ Facilities: Spa STV WiFi ▷ ⑤ ⟿ 36 Fishing Gym Cycling Mega chess Fitness classes Jogging trails ♫ Xmas New Year Conf: Class 240 Board 72 Theatre 500 Services: Lift Night porter Air con Parking: 384 Notes: Civ Wed 400

GALWAY
County Galway

Map 1 B3

The g Hotel & Spa

★★★★★ 87% ◉◉ HOTEL

tel: 091 865200 Wellpark, Dublin Road
email: info@theg.ie web: www.theghotel.ie
dir: Phone for directions.

Designed in association with the acclaimed milliner Philip Treacy who hails from the county, this hotel is the epitome of contemporary styling. The public areas include a series of eclectically furnished Signature Lounges, each with its own identity. The cutting-edge design is also apparent in the bedrooms and suites, which are very comfortable and appointed to a high standard. An interesting selection of menus is on offer at dinner each evening in gigi's, the atmospheric restaurant, and a very popular all-day menu is served in the lounges, including a range of traditional afternoon teas. The hotel has boardrooms, an events space, and an ESPA spa facility. Underground and valet parking is available.

Rooms: 101 (2 family) ♠ Facilities: Spa STV FTV WiFi HL Gym ♫ New Year Conf: Class 70 Board 70 Theatre 300 Services: Lift Night porter Air con Parking: 349 Notes: LB Closed 23–26 December Civ Wed 90

Glenlo Abbey Hotel

★★★★ 88% ◉◉ HOTEL

tel: 091 526666 & 519600 Kentfield, Bushypark
email: info@glenloabbey.ie web: www.glenloabbeyhotel.ie
dir: 2 miles from Galway city centre on N59 to Clifden.

The origins of Glenlo Abbey date from 1740 when the original house was built by the Ffrenchs, a wealthy merchant family. It is set on a spacious estate with wonderful views of Lough Corrib, yet only five kilometres from Galway on the road to Connemara. Great care has been taken over the years to retain the proportions and many original features of the public spaces. Most of the accommodation is in a wing to the rear; suites and bedrooms are finished to a very high level, with some offering lake or garden views. Guests have two restaurants to choose from – the elegant River Room Restaurant and The Pullman Restaurant, a unique dining

experience, created from two original carriages from Orient Express railway. Golf is available on the estate, which also features stand-alone banqueting facilities.

Rooms: 50 (13 family) (16 GF) ♠ S fr €179 D fr €199 (including breakfast)* Facilities: WiFi ▷ ⟿ 9 Fishing ⥺ 21 bay driving range Falconry 134-acre estate for walking/cycling ♫ Xmas New Year Conf: Class 100 Board 50 Theatre 180 Services: Lift Night porter Parking: 200 Notes: Civ Wed 150

Ardilaun Hotel & Leisure Club

★★★★ 81% ◉ HOTEL

tel: 091 521433 Taylor's Hill
email: info@theardilaunhotel.ie web: www.theardilaunhotel.ie
dir: M6 to Galway City West, then follow signs for N59 Clifden, then N6 towards Salthill.

This very smart country-house style hotel, appointed to a high standard, is located on the outskirts of the city near Salthill and has lovely landscaped gardens and ample parking. The bedrooms have been thoughtfully appointed and the deluxe rooms and suites are particularly spacious. Public areas include a selection of comfortable lounges, the Camilaun Restaurant which overlooks the garden, and extensive banqueting and leisure facilities. In the Ardilaun Bistro, the menu features artisanal seasonal ingredients in a contemporary and inventive style, with much of the produce coming from the walled garden.

Rooms: 123 (17 family) (8 GF) ♠ S fr €69 D fr €79 (including breakfast)* Facilities: Spa STV WiFi ▷ ⑤ Gym Beauty treatment and analysis rooms Beauty salon ♫ New Year Conf: Class 280 Board 100 Theatre 650 Services: Lift Night porter Parking: 286 Notes: LB Closed 23 December pm to 26 December Civ Wed 650

The Galmont Hotel & Spa

★★★★ 80% ◉ HOTEL

tel: 091 538300 Lough Atalia Road
email: reservations@thegalmont.com web: www.thegalmont.com
dir: Phone for directions.

This hotel is situated in a prime position on Lough Atalia's waterfront and overlooks Galway Bay. While parking is available, its location within minutes of both the train and bus stations makes this an ideal place for a car-free break. The striking interior design and levels of comfort are impressive in the bright and airy public areas. Bedrooms are well equipped and there is an executive floor where further privacy is guaranteed. Dining options include the very popular Marina Grill on the ground floor, offering a varied menu that is sure to please. A range of event spaces is available, with the capacity to accommodate nearly 1,000 delegates.

Rooms: 261 (5 family) Facilities: Spa STV FTV WiFi ▷ ⑤ Gym Sauna Steam room Salt spa Aerobics studios Xmas New Year Conf: Class 650 Board 25 Theatre 990 Services: Lift Night porter Air con Notes: LB Civ Wed

Park House Hotel & Restaurant

★★★★ 79% ◉ HOTEL

tel: 091 564924 Forster Street, Eyre Square
email: reservations@parkhousehotel.ie web: www.parkhousehotel.ie
dir: In city centre.

Situated just off Eyre Square, this well-established hotel offers comfortable facilities to suit business or leisure guests. Public areas and bedrooms are well appointed and attractively decorated in traditional schemes. The Park Restaurant has been a popular dining spot for the people of Galway for many years, and quality food is served throughout the day in Boss Doyle's bar. Some resident parking is available to the rear.

Rooms: 84 ♠ S fr €105 D fr €120 (including breakfast)* Facilities: STV FTV WiFi ▷ ♫ Services: Lift Night porter Air con Parking: 48 Notes: LB Closed 24–26 December

The Harbour Hotel

★★★★ 78% HOTEL

tel: 091 894800 **New Dock Road**
email: stay@harbour.ie **web:** www.harbour.ie
dir: *Phone for directions.*

Within a three-minute stroll of the bustling and vibrant Quay Street area of Galway, this hotel really is in the centre of things, yet easily accessed without driving through the city. Bedrooms come in a variety of sizes – all are modern and comfortable. The Harbour Bar, popular with locals and residents alike, offers interesting menus featuring home-made dishes, with seafood being a speciality. Limited secure parking at a reduced rate, and a fitness suite are also available.

Rooms: 96 (5 family) **S** fr €290 **D** fr €290 (including breakfast)* **Facilities:** STV FTV WiFi ♨ Fitness room ♫ Xmas New Year **Conf:** Class 60 Board 50 Theatre 150 **Services:** Night porter **Parking:** 70 **Notes:** LB Civ Wed 130

Hotel Meyrick

★★★★ 78% HOTEL

tel: 091 564041 **Eyre Square**
email: pfeeney@hotelmeyrick.ie **web:** www.hotelmeyrick.ie
dir: *Phone for directions.*

Dating from 1852, this grand old lady of the city has a commanding position overlooking Eyre Square, right in the centre of the city. Originally a railway hotel, it has witnessed many facets of Irish and international notoriety. The lobby and public areas retain much of its original grandeur, albeit presented with contemporary decor and modern comfort. Bedrooms and suites come in a number of sizes and styles. Gaslight is an buzzy all-day brasserie bar, with breakfast and dinner served in the No.15 Restaurant on the lower-ground floor.

Rooms: 97 (2 family) ♥ **S** fr €89 **D** fr €119 (including breakfast)* **Facilities:** Spa STV FTV WiFi ♨ Gym ♫ **Conf:** Class 120 Board 45 Theatre 250 **Services:** Lift Night porter **Parking:** 26 **Notes:** LB Closed 25 December Civ Wed 200

GLASLOUGH	Map 1 C5
County Monaghan	

The Lodge at Castle Leslie Estate

★★★★ 82% HOTEL

tel: 047 88100
email: info@castleleslie.com **web:** www.castleleslie.com
dir: *M1 junction 14, N2 to Monaghan, N12 to R185 to Glaslough.*

Set in 1,000 acres of rolling countryside dotted with mature woodland, The Lodge is the social hub of the Castle Leslie Estate which has been in the Leslie family since the 1660s. The comfortably furnished bedrooms are in the original hunting lodge and the converted stable block. Resident guests have two dining options – Snaffles

Restaurant and Conors Bar. There is a spa known as The Victorian Treatment Rooms, a world class equestrian centre and a private fishing lake. For those who enjoy country pursuits, this hotel is ideal for the many walks and interesting flora and fauna that the area has to offer.

Rooms: 29 (2 family) (10 GF) ♥ **D** fr €200 (including breakfast)* **Facilities:** Spa STV FTV WiFi ♨ Fishing Horse riding Kayaking Clay target Falconry Boating Hot air balloon rides **Conf:** Class 25 Board 24 Theatre 35 **Services:** Lift Night porter **Parking:** 100 **Notes:** LB Closed 24–27 December Civ Wed 40

GOREY	Map 1 D3
County Wexford	

Seafield Hotel & Spa Resort

★★★★ 81% HOTEL

tel: 053 942 4000 **Ballymoney**
email: reservations@seafieldhotel.com **web:** www.seafieldhotel.com
dir: *M11 exit 22.*

This contemporary hotel is part of a village style resort that includes an 18-hole championship golf course, courtyard family suites and the award-winning Oceo Spa. Set in 225 acres of parkland with mature trees, riverside walks and access onto Ballymoney Beach, the hotel offers stylish, spacious bedrooms and suites which have views of either the coastline or the golf course; some have balconies. There are two dining options – fine dining in the award-winning Greenroom Restaurant, and a more casual option in the Village Bar & Grill.

Rooms: 101 ♥ **S** fr €85 **D** fr €110 (including breakfast)* **Facilities:** Spa STV WiFi ♨ ⊙ Gym Playgrounds (x 2) ♫ New Year **Conf:** Class 220 Board 40 Theatre 300 **Services:** Lift Night porter **Parking:** 200 **Notes:** Civ Wed 280

Amber Springs Hotel

★★★★ 80% HOTEL

tel: 053 9484000 **Wexford Road**
email: info@ambersprings.ie **web:** www.amberspringshotel.ie
dir: *500 metres from Gorey by-pass at junction 23.*

This modern hotel, on the Wexford road, is within walking distance of the town. It enjoys a well-earned reputation for accommodating families with its dedicated facilities. Bedrooms are spacious and very comfortable, and guests have full use of the leisure facilities. All-day dining is offered in Brooks Bar & Grill, with an adult-only space at dinner in the award-winning Farm Steakhouse. Much of the produce is sourced from the proprietor's nearby farm that specialises in Angus beef. This is a popular wedding venue. Ample parking is available to the rear.

Rooms: 80 (34 family) (24 GF) ♥ **Facilities:** Spa STV WiFi ♨ ⊙ Gym Mini golf Petting farm Kids Train ♫ New Year **Conf:** Class 450 Board 30 Theatre 700 **Services:** Lift Night porter Air con **Parking:** 178 **Notes:** Closed 25–26 December Civ Wed 700

Follow us on twitter
@TheAA_Lifestyle

REPUBLIC OF IRELAND

GOREY *continued*

Ashdown Park Hotel

★★★★ 79% HOTEL

tel: 053 9480500 **The Coach Road**
email: info@ashdownparkhotel.com **web:** www.ashdownparkhotel.com
dir: *N11 junction 22, towards Gorey, 1st left (before railway bridge), hotel on left.*

Situated on an elevated position overlooking the town, this modern hotel has excellent health, leisure and banqueting facilities. There are comfortable lounge areas and two dining options – Ivy, a popular carvery bar, and The Rowan Tree, the first-floor fine dining restaurant that opens in the evenings. Bedrooms are available in a number of styles; all are spacious and well equipped. Close to a number of golf courses, this property is popular with golfers, and also with families as it is near the beaches.

Rooms: 79 (17 family) (22 GF) ✆ **S** fr €65 **D** fr €75 (including breakfast & dinner)
Facilities: Spa FTV WiFi ⇘ ⊛ Gym Leisure centre Massage rooms ♫ New Year
Conf: Class 315 Board 100 Theatre 600 **Services:** Lift Night porter **Parking:** 150
Notes: Closed 25 December Civ Wed 300

INSPECTOR'S CHOICE

Marlfield House Hotel

★★★ ◉◉ COUNTRY HOUSE HOTEL

tel: 053 9421124
email: info@marlfieldhouse.ie **web:** www.marlfieldhouse.com
dir: *N11 junction 23, follow signs for Courtown. At Courtown Road roundabout left for Gorey. Hotel 1 mile on left.*

This Regency-style building has been gracefully extended and developed into an excellent hotel. An atmosphere of elegance and luxury permeates every corner of the house, underpinned by truly friendly and professional service led by the Bowe family who are always in evidence. The bedrooms are decorated in keeping with the style of the house, with some really spacious rooms and suites on the ground floor. Dinner in the Conservatory Restaurant is always a highlight of a stay at Marlfield, with afternoon tea a speciality. Less formal all-day dining is available in The Duck which has a terrace.

Rooms: 21 (3 family) (9 GF) ✆ **Facilities:** STV FTV WiFi ⇘ ⊛ ⊛ Beauty treatment room **Conf:** Board 24 Theatre 60 **Parking:** 100 **Notes:** Closed 2 January to 15 February RS November to December, March to April Civ Wed 120

INSPECTOR'S CHOICE

Sheen Falls Lodge

★★★★★ ◉◉ COUNTRY HOUSE HOTEL

tel: 064 6641600
email: info@sheenfallslodge.ie **web:** www.sheenfallslodge.ie
dir: *From Kenmare take N71 to Glengarriff over suspension bridge, take 1st left.*

This former fishing lodge has been developed into a beautiful hotel with a friendly team of professional staff. The cascading Sheen Falls are floodlit at night, forming a romantic backdrop to top notch cuisine in The Falls restaurant. The Sun Lounge serves afternoon tea and light snacks throughout the day. The bedrooms are very comfortably appointed; many of the suites are particularly spacious. The leisure centre and beauty therapy facilities offer a number of exclusive treatments, and outdoor pursuits include walking, fishing, tennis, horse riding and clay pigeon shooting.

Rooms: 66 (14 family) (14 GF) ✆ **S** fr €160 **D** fr €190 (including breakfast)*
Facilities: Spa STV WiFi ⊛ ⊛ Fishing ⊛ Gym Table tennis Steam room Clay pigeon Shooting Cycling Vintage car rides Library ♫ Xmas New Year
Conf: Class 65 Board 50 Theatre 120 **Services:** Lift Night porter **Parking:** 76
Notes: LB Closed 30 November to 19 December, 2 January to 1 February RS 24–27 December Civ Wed 150

INSPECTOR'S CHOICE

Park Hotel Kenmare

★★★★ ◉◉ HOTEL

tel: 064 6641200
email: info@parkkenmare.com **web:** www.parkkenmare.com
dir: *On R569 beside golf course at top of town.*

This hotel is a luxurious house, situated on the famous Ring of Kerry, that has been welcoming guests for over 100 years. Warm hospitality and professional service come naturally to all the team, who endeavour to make guests feel pampered. All the suites and bedrooms are spacious and very well appointed, with either garden or sea views. The elegant restaurant serves very good food, much of it locally sourced, together with fine wines. Samas is the luxury treatment spa.

Park Hotel Kenmare

Rooms: 46 (3 family) 🏠 **Facilities:** Spa FTV WiFi 🕙 🏊 🏌 Gym 🎵 Xmas New Year **Conf:** Class 40 Board 28 Theatre 60 **Services:** Lift Night porter **Parking:** 60 **Notes:** Closed 10–22 December, 3 January to 16 February

---

KILKENNY
County Kilkenny   Map 1 C3

Lyrath Estate
★★★★ 86% ◉◉ HOTEL

tel: 056 7760088 **Paulstown Road R95 F685**
email: reservations@lyrath.com **web:** www.lyrath.com
dir: *M9 junction 8 signed Kilkenny. 1st exit at both 1st and 2nd roundabouts, hotel 1 kilometre.*

Located a short drive from Kilkenny and set in 170 acres of mature parkland and lakeland, this 17th-century house has been carefully restored and greatly expanded to become one of the country's largest convention centres, with myriad event spaces and public areas. The property is very popular for weddings, held in the main house which retains many original architectural features. Bedrooms are mainly in a separate block, all are well-appointed. The dining options include the elegant Yew Restaurant and Tupper's Bar for all-day dining. Guests have complimentary access to the health club and gym, with spa treatments; a thermal suite is available at a supplement.

Rooms: 139 (24 family) (31 GF) 🏠 **Facilities:** Spa FTV WiFi 🕙 Fishing Gym Private cinema Snooker room Outdoor Hydrotherapy pool 🎵 New Year **Conf:** Class 750 Board 75 Theatre 1500 **Services:** Lift Night porter Air con **Parking:** 420 **Notes:** Closed 20–27 December Civ Wed 120

KILLARNEY
County Kerry   Map 1 A2

Aghadoe Heights Hotel
★★★★★ 88% ◉◉ HOTEL

tel: 064 6631766
email: info@aghadoeheights.com **web:** www.aghadoeheights.com
dir: *From Killarney town centre take N22 towards Tralee. At Cleeney roundabout take 3rd exit, drive 800 metres, left onto L2019 and left at top of hill. Hotel 1 mile on right after church ruins.*

Located some 5km from Killarney Town, the views from Aghadoe Heights are nothing short of spectacular with views of the Lakes of Killarney below with the Kerry mountains as a backdrop. Most of the bedrooms and suites make the most of these views, some with the addition of balconies. All day dining is offered in the Heights Lounge, with award-winning evening dining in The Lake Room featuring seasonal and artisan produce cooked with flair and care. Breakfast is also a real treat. There is a range of spa treatments available, with a swimming pool and thermal suite for pure indulgence.

Rooms: 74 (9 family) (10 GF) 🏠 **S** fr €170 **D** fr €180 (including breakfast)* **Facilities:** Spa STV FTV WiFi 🕙 🏊 🏌 Gym Thermal suite Hair salon 🎵 New Year **Conf:** Class 70 Board 40 Theatre 120 **Services:** Lift Night porter Air con **Parking:** 84 **Notes:** LB Closed 23–26 December Civ Wed 195

The Brehon Killarney
★★★★ 81% ◉◉ HOTEL

tel: 064 6630700 **Muckross Road**
email: sinead.mccarthy@thebrehon.com **web:** www.thebrehon.com
dir: *1 mile from Killarney on N71.*

This is a spectacular hotel close to Killarney National Park and a 20-minute walk from the town. Public areas are particularly spacious with comfortable mezzanine lounge areas, and a bustling bar where a popular all-day menu is on offer. Danú is the bright and airy award-winning restaurant where breakfast and dinner are served from an interesting, well-compiled menu. The spacious bedrooms and suites are well equipped, many with great views towards the mountains. The hotel offers a specialist Thai spa experience and extensive conference facilities. Other leisure facilities are on offer at their nearby sister hotel.

Rooms: 125 (10 family) 🏠 **S** fr €125 **D** fr €145 (including breakfast)* **Facilities:** Spa STV FTV WiFi 🕙 HL 🕙 🏊 Gym 🎵 Xmas New Year **Conf:** Class 150 Board 50 Theatre 250 **Services:** Lift Night porter Air con **Parking:** 300 **Notes:** LB Civ Wed 220

The Lake Hotel
★★★★ 79% ◉◉ HOTEL

tel: 064 6631035 **Lake Shore, Muckross Road V93 RR59**
email: info@lakehotel.com **web:** www.lakehotel.com
dir: *N22 to Killarney. Hotel 2 km from town on Muckross Road.*

Enjoying a delightful location on the shores of Killarney's lake, this hotel is run by a second generation of the Huggard family, together with a dedicated and friendly team. There is a relaxed atmosphere, with log fires and stunning views from the lounges and restaurant. Guests could be lucky enough to see a herd of red deer wander by. The smartly furnished bedrooms have either lake or woodland views; some have balconies and four-poster beds. The spa offers good facilities, and there are cycle paths and lovely walks to enjoy.

Rooms: 131 (6 family) (23 GF) 🏠 **S** fr €79 **D** fr €99 (including breakfast)* **Facilities:** STV FTV WiFi 🕙 🏊 Fishing 🏌 Gym Beauty treatment room Sauna Steam room 🎵 **Services:** Lift Night porter **Parking:** 140 **Notes:** LB Closed December to January Civ Wed 60

KILLARNEY *continued*

Killarney Riverside Hotel

★★★★ 78% ◉ HOTEL

tel: 064 6639200 **Muckross Road V93 V260**
email: stay@riversidehotelkillarney.com **web:** www.riversidehotelkillarney.com
dir: *Phone for directions.*

Located just a five-minute walk from the town centre, this hotel is on the Muckross road, and ideal for the INEC events centre. Established two decades ago, it is a good base for exploring the town and the wider Kerry area. Bedrooms are comfortably decorated, with a choice of bed options available. All-day dining is in the River Bistro, with interesting menu options at dinner in the award-winning Bacchus Room. This is a quiet and relaxing hotel; Rejuvenate beauty and holistic treatment rooms are also available.

Rooms: 69 (2 family) (11 GF) **S** fr €64 **D** fr €80 (including breakfast)* **Facilities:** STV FTV WiFi ⌨ Rejuvenation suite Treatment room New Year **Services:** Lift Night porter **Parking:** 66 **Notes:** LB Closed 22–28 December

Cahernane House Hotel

★★★★ 76% ◉◉ HOTEL

tel: 064 6631895 **Muckross Road**
email: info@cahernane.com **web:** www.cahernane.com
dir: *From Killarney take N71. After 1 mile cross Flesk River Bridge, hotel on right.*

Situated on the edge of Killarney National Park, this boutique hotel dates from 1877 and is just a 10-minute walk from the town. Bedrooms, of which 12 are in the original house, are spacious and well appointed; some garden wing rooms feature terraces. There is an air of relaxation and peacefulness at Cahernane, where the public rooms retain the charm and many original features of the era. Log fires add to the atmosphere. Dinner in the award-winning Herbert Room is a real treat, featuring seasonal and local ingredients cooked with flair.

Rooms: 40 (8 family) (16 GF) 🛏 **S** fr €120 **D** fr €140 (including breakfast)* **Facilities:** FTV WiFi New Year **Conf:** Board 16 Theatre 50 **Services:** Lift Night porter **Parking:** 40 **Notes:** LB Closed January to February RS March Civ Wed 80

Castlerosse Hotel & Holiday Homes

★★★ 79% HOTEL

tel: 064 6631144 **Lakes of Killarney**
email: res@castlerosse.ie **web:** www.castlerosse.ie
dir: *From Killarney take R562 signed Killorglin and The Ring of Kerry. Hotel 2.5 km from town on left.*

This hotel is situated on 6,000 acres overlooking the Lakes of Killarney with the Magillycuddy Mountains as a backdrop. At times guests may be able to spot deer in Killarney National Park. Bedrooms and junior suites are well appointed and comfortable. There is live entertainment most nights in Mulligan's pub. Leisure facilities include a 9-hole parkland golf course, tennis courts, a leisure centre and treatment rooms.

Rooms: 120 (27 family) (116 GF) 🛏 **S** fr €80 **D** fr €100 (including breakfast)* **Facilities:** STV FTV WiFi ⌨ ⌖ ⌁ 9 ⌂ Gym Beauty treatment rooms Hairdresser Cycling Golf and Horse riding arranged 🎵 **Conf:** Class 100 Board 40 Theatre 200 **Services:** Lift Night porter **Parking:** 100 **Notes:** LB Closed November to March Civ Wed 80

The Killarney Park Hotel

[U]

tel: 064 663 5555 **Town Centre V93 CF30**
email: info@killarneyparkhotel.ie **web:** www.killarneyparkhotel.ie
dir: *On East Avenue, Town Centre, Killarney. From Killarney Bus and Rail Station. Veer left at Rail Station entrance and you will find the hotel on left just before Killarney Cinema.*

Currently the rating for this establishment is not confirmed. This may be due to a change of ownership or because ot has only recently joined the AA rating scheme.

Rooms: 67 **Facilities:** Spa WiFi ⌨ ⌖ Gym Steam room Adventure hub **Conf:** Theatre 120 **Services:** Air con **Notes:** Civ Wed 90

KILLINEY	Map 1 D3
Dublin	

Fitzpatrick Castle Hotel

★★★★ 81% ◉ HOTEL

tel: 01 2305400 & 2305558
email: reservations@fitzpatricks.com **web:** www.fitzpatrickcastle.com
dir: *From Dun Laoghaire port turn left, on coast road right at lights, left at next lights. Follow to Dalkey, right at Ivory Pub, immediate left, up hill, hotel at top.*

This family-owned and operated 18th-century castle is situated in lovely gardens with mature trees and spectacular views over Dublin Bay. The original castle rooms are appointed to a high standard and have four-poster beds, while the rooms in modern wings are spacious; some have balconies. There are comfortably furnished lounge, and extensive leisure and events spaces. The popular dining options are PJ's Restaurant, Mapas Restaurant, and The Library Bar where afternoon teas are served alongside informal meals. The original dungeon makes an atmospheric pre-dinner spot, or perhaps for a nightcap. Spacious parking plus a coach service to the airport are available.

Rooms: 113 (36 family) 🛏 **D** fr €140 **Facilities:** STV FTV WiFi ⌖ Gym Beauty/hairdressing salon Sauna Steam room Fitness centre 🎵 Xmas New Year **Conf:** Class 250 Board 80 Theatre 500 **Services:** Lift Night porter **Parking:** 300 **Notes:** LB Civ Wed 400

KILMESSAN	Map 1 C4
County Meath	

The Station House Hotel

★★★ 75% ◉ HOTEL

tel: 046 9025239
email: denise@stationhousehotel.ie **web:** www.stationhousehotel.ie

This family operated hotel retains much of the character of its former life as a railway station. This property is located in attractive gardens, right in the centre of The Boyne Valley, yet just a half hour from Dublin. The old signal box is now the quaint bridal suite, with most of the bedrooms in the converted goods buildings opposite. All-day dining is available in the Platform Lounge, with dinner in the Signal Restaurant, the former waiting rooms and booking office. The Station House has a well deserved reputation for hosting weddings and other family celebrations.

Rooms: 19

KILTIMAGH County Mayo	Map 1 B4

Park Hotel Kiltimagh

★★★ 77% HOTEL

IRISH COUNTRY HOTELS

tel: 094 9374922 **Swinford Road**
email: info@parkhotelmayo.com **web:** www.parkhotelmayo.com
dir: *N17 onto R322 or R323 (or N60 onto R320) to Kiltimagh.*

This smart hotel overlooks the Wetlands Wildlife Park and is within walking distance of Kiltimagh; it is just 15 minutes from Ireland West Knock Airport and Knock Marian Shrine. The spacious bedrooms are well appointed. Public areas are attractively decorated and include comfortable lounges, Café Bar, Park Restaurant and banqueting facilities. The Aroma Beauty Spa offers a range of treatments and there is also a fitness centre and steam room. A shuttle coach service operates to the airport, and for guests using the airport, parking can be arranged at the hotel.

Rooms: 46 (40 family) **Facilities:** WiFi ☼ New Year **Conf:** Class 120 Board 60 Theatre 450 **Services:** Lift Night porter **Parking:** 300 **Notes:** Closed 25 December RS 24 December Civ Wed 350

LAHINCH County Clare	Map 1 B3

Vaughan Lodge Hotel

★★★★ 81% HOTEL

tel: 065 7081111 **Ennistymon Road**
email: info@vaughanlodge.ie **web:** www.vaughanlodge.ie
dir: *From Ennis, take N85 to Ennistymon, then N67 west to Lahinch. Hotel in 50 km per hour zone on left.*

Located on the outskirts of Lahinch, where golf is a way of life, this modern townhouse, boutique property is operated and run by the Vaughans, a fourth generation local hotelier family. They are assisted by a small dedicated team of hospitable and engaging local people. Accommodation is spacious and well appointed. Dinner in VL, the bright and airy restaurant, is a highlight of a stay, featuring a modern approach to classic dishes, all based on high quality ingredients, many from the area. There are no conference or leisure facilities, here, just a relaxing environment to chill out and re-energise.

Rooms: 22 (6 GF) ⬤ **S** fr €130 **D** fr €190 (including breakfast)* **Facilities:** STV FTV WiFi ☼ **Services:** Lift Night porter **Parking:** 40 **Notes:** LB Closed November to March Civ Wed 50

LEIGHLINBRIDGE County Carlow	Map 1 C3

Lord Bagenal Inn

★★★★ 76% ⬤ HOTEL

tel: 059 9774000 **Main Street**
email: info@lordbagenal.com **web:** www.lordbagenal.com
dir: *Just off M9 junction 6 signed Leighlinbridge. From N9 in 1 km turn left onto R705, hotel 1 km on right.*

The family-run Lord Bagenal Inn enjoys an idyllic location on the banks of the River Barrow. Located just off the M9 in the picturesque village of Leighlinbridge, it is one hour from Dublin and Waterford airports. Bedrooms are comfortable and well equipped and the traditional bar is a cluster of cosy rooms with log fires. Fine dining is available in the restaurant.

Rooms: 39 (3 family) (3 GF) ⬤ **S** fr €80 **D** fr €105 (including breakfast)*
Facilities: STV FTV WiFi ☼ ♫ **Conf:** Class 80 Board 50 Theatre 450 **Services:** Lift Night porter **Parking:** 120 **Notes:** Closed 25–26 December Civ Wed 250

REPUBLIC OF IRELAND

Radisson Blu Hotel Letterkenny

★★★★ 78% 🌐 HOTEL

tel: 074 9194444 **Paddy Harte Road**
email: info.letterkenny@radissonblu.com **web:** www.radissonblu.com/hotel-letterkenny
dir: N14 into Letterkenny. At Polestar roundabout take 1st exit, to hotel.

Letterkenny is an ideal base for visiting the many peninsulas of County Donegal. Within walking distance of the town and the retail parks, this hotel offers a range of very comfortable rooms that have the facilities today's traveller expects. Guests can dine throughout the day in the popular Port Bar & Grill or, in the evening, enjoy seafood delights and other interesting dishes in Brasserie TriBeCa. Well-equipped meeting rooms are available, together with a large conference and banqueting hall. The leisure facilities are complimentary to residents.

Rooms: 114 (5 family) 🐾 S fr €64 **D** fr €69 (including breakfast)* **Facilities:** STV WiFi 🌊 🐵 Gym Sauna Steam room Olympic weights room Aqua classes Personal trainer Xmas New Year **Conf:** Class 270 Board 80 Theatre 600 **Services:** Lift Night porter **Parking:** 150 **Notes:** LB Civ Wed 200

Downings Bay Hotel

★★★ 77% HOTEL

tel: 074 9155586 & 9155770 **Downings**
email: info@downingsbayhotel.com **web:** www.downingsbayhotel.com
dir: 23 miles north of Letterkenny on R245. Hotel in village centre.

This long-established, friendly, family-run hotel is situated on Sheephaven Bay in the picturesque village of Downings. There is a cosy lobby lounge; J.C.'s a traditional-style bar where an extensive menu is available all day, and The Haven Restaurant which opens for dinner at peak times. The accommodation is spacious and all rooms are comfortable and well appointed. A popular location for families and within easy reach of a number of golf courses, this property hosts regular musical events, and there is a nightclub open at weekends. Guests have complimentary use of the local leisure centre, just a five-minute drive away.

Rooms: 40 (8 family) (4 smoking) 🐾 S fr €50 **D** fr €100 (including breakfast) **Facilities:** WiFi 🌊 🐵 Gym Sauna Steam room Indoor adventure play area 🎵 New Year **Conf:** Class 175 Board 50 Theatre 350 **Services:** Lift Night porter Air con **Parking:** 40 **Notes:** Closed 24–26 December RS November to March Civ Wed 120

Limerick Strand Hotel

★★★★ 80% 🌐 HOTEL

tel: 061 421800 **Ennis Road**
email: info@strandlimerick.ie **web:** www.strandlimerick.ie
dir: From Shannon/Galway follow N18 to Limerick. At Coonagh roundabout follow Ennis Road into city centre. Hotel on right on banks of river.

This hotel enjoys stunning views over the River Shannon, and all bedrooms are spacious and fitted to a high standard. The public areas make the most of the views, with meeting rooms on the penthouse level. All-day dining is available in the bar, with innovative evening meals served in the River Restaurant. Secure parking is available at a reduced rate for residents.

Rooms: 184 (13 family) 🐾 **Facilities:** STV FTV WiFi 🌊 🐵 Gym 🎵 Xmas New Year **Conf:** Class 400 Board 50 Theatre 600 **Services:** Lift Night porter Air con **Parking:** 200 **Notes:** Civ Wed 450

Radisson Blu Hotel & Spa Limerick

★★★★ 78% HOTEL

tel: 061 456200 **Ennis Road**
email: info.limerick@radissonblu.com **web:** www.radissonblu.com/en/hotel-limerick
dir: On N18 Ennis Road, close to Limerick city centre.

Situated between Limerick and Shannon International Airport, this smart hotel is set in 20 acres of parkland and has comfortable lounge areas and a choice of dining options; the contemporary Porters Restaurant offers fine dining, while more casual eating can be enjoyed in the Quench Bar. Bedrooms are comfortable, spacious and very well appointed. Guests have complimentary use of the Thermal Suite and outdoor Canadian hot tub in the Rain Spa. There are extensive leisure and corporate facilities, including seven meeting rooms with capacity up to 800 delegates.

Rooms: 154 (26 family) (43 GF) 🐾 S fr €89 **D** fr €89* **Facilities:** Spa STV FTV WiFi 🌊 🐵 🏊 Gym Hair salon Basketball court Fairy garden Walking trail Rain spa with treatment rooms, relaxation room, sauna and steam room 🎵 Xmas New Year **Conf:** Class 400 Board 100 Theatre 800 **Services:** Lift Night porter **Parking:** 220 **Notes:** LB Civ Wed 300

Sheedy's Country House Hotel

★★★ 78% 🌐🌐 HOTEL

tel: 065 7074026
email: info@sheedys.com **web:** www.sheedys.com
dir: 200 metres from The Square in town centre.

Dating in part from the 17th century and set in an unrivalled town centre location on the edge of The Burren, this house is full of character and has an intimate atmosphere. Family run by hosts Martina and John Sheedy, fine award-winning cuisine can be enjoyed in the contemporary restaurant, and the bedrooms are spacious and well appointed. Sheedy's makes an ideal base for touring, as it is close to Doolin, Lahinch Golf Course, and the Cliffs of Moher.

Rooms: 11 (1 family) (5 GF) 🐾 S fr €90 **D** fr €135 (including breakfast)* **Facilities:** STV FTV WiFi 🌊 **Parking:** 20 **Notes:** LB No children 12 years Closed mid October to April

Lucan Spa Hotel

★★★ 70% HOTEL

tel: 01 6280494
email: info@lucanspahotel.ie **web:** www.lucanspahotel.ie
dir: At N4 junction 4a, approximately 11 kilometres from city centre.

Set in its own grounds and 20 minutes from Dublin Airport, at the start of the M4, the main artery to the west of Ireland, the Lucan Spa is a lovely Georgian house with modern extensions. Originally built to accommodate guests taking the waters at the former spa, the building retains many of the architectural features of the period. Bedrooms vary in size but are well equipped. There are two dining options: dinner is served in Hanora D' Restaurant, and The Ballyneety Bar is for more casual dining. The event space has a good reputation for weddings and conference business.

Rooms: 71 (15 family) (9 GF) 🐾 S fr €55 **D** fr €75 (including breakfast) **Facilities:** STV FTV WiFi 🌊 Access to Lucan Golf Club opposite hotel **Conf:** Class 250 Board 80 Theatre 600 **Services:** Lift Night porter Air con **Parking:** 200 **Notes:** LB Closed 24–26 December Civ Wed 250

MACREDDIN
County Wicklow
Map 1 D3

BrookLodge & Macreddin Village
★★★★ 82% HOTEL

tel: 0402 36444 **Y14 A362**
email: info@brooklodge.com **web:** www.brooklodge.com
dir: N11 to Rathnew, R752 to Rathdrum, R753 to Aughrim, follow signs to Macreddin Village.

BrookLodge is a luxurious country house hotel in a village-style setting which includes an 18-hole golf course, a country pub, a café and food shop. There is a choice of dining options – the award-winning Strawberry Tree Restaurant specialising in organic and wild foods, and a more casual Italian restaurant specialising in southern Italian cuisine. Macreddin Village has 86 bedrooms, many of which feature four-poster or sleigh beds, as well as window seats from which you can admire the stunning views. There are also bedrooms in BrookHall, tailored for guests attending weddings and conferences. The Wells Spa offers extensive treatments and leisure facilities, and there are many mapped walks available, affording you the opportunity to enjoy the Wicklow countryside.

Rooms: 86 (32 annexe) (27 family) (4 GF) S fr €105 **D** fr €130 (including breakfast)* **Facilities:** Spa STV FTV WiFi Gym Archery Clay pigeon shooting Off road driving Cycling Walking New Year **Conf:** Class 100 Board 50 Theatre 250 **Services:** Lift Night porter Air con **Parking:** 200 **Notes:** Closed 24–25 December Civ Wed 150

MALLOW
County Cork
Map 1 B2

Springfort Hall Country House Hotel
★★★ 77% 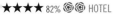 HOTEL

tel: 022 21278
email: stay@springfort-hall.com **web:** www.springfort-hall.com
dir: N20 onto R581 at Two Pot House, hotel 500 metres on right.

This 18th-century country manor is tucked away amid tranquil woodlands located just six kilometres from Mallow. There is an attractive oval dining room, a cosy drawing room and lounge bar where bistro-style food is served. The spacious bedrooms are comfortably furnished. There are extensive banqueting and conference facilities, and local amenities include championship golf courses, fishing on the Blackwater and Ballyhass Lakes, and horseracing at Cork.

Rooms: 49 (5 family) (17 GF) S fr €79 **D** fr €120 (including breakfast) **Facilities:** STV FTV WiFi **Conf:** Class 180 Board 50 Theatre 360 **Services:** Night porter **Parking:** 200 **Notes:** Closed 23–26 December Civ Wed 300

MAYNOOTH
County Kildare
Map 1 D4

Carton House Hotel Golf & Spa
★★★★ 79% HOTEL

tel: 01 5052000
email: sales@cartonhouse.com **web:** www.cartonhouse.com
dir: From Dublin Airport follow M50, N4 then M4 towards Sligo. At junction 6 take R449 to Leixlip. Continue to R148. Located 4 miles outside Maynooth.

Carton House dates from 1739 and many of features of that period are reflected in the careful renovation of the fine public rooms and event spaces. While some suites of the hotel are in the original house, most of the bedrooms are in a modern block to the side. All are spacious and comfortable, appointed to a high standard. There are a number of dining options on the estate, including The Coach House in the golf club and The Linden Tree for more formal evening dining. Set in over 1,000 acres, there are plenty of walks and cycle paths to be enjoyed. The property is surrounded by two golf courses and has a strong reputation for its many sport training facilities and spa treatment rooms.

Rooms: 165 (12 family) (46 GF) **Facilities:** Spa STV WiFi 36 Fishing Gym Sauna Steam room Xmas New Year **Conf:** Class 280 Board 90 Theatre 500 **Services:** Lift Night porter **Parking:** 500 **Notes:** Civ Wed 280

MOHILL
County Leitrim
Map 1 C4

Lough Rynn Castle Estate & Gardens
★★★★ 80% HOTEL

tel: 071 9632700 **Lough Rynn**
email: creidy@hanlycastle.com **web:** www.loughrynn.ie
dir: Phone for directions.

This sympathetically restored Victorian manor is renowned for the hospitality of its dedicated team. Many of the public rooms retain their original style and grandeur, yet are warm and relaxing, with real fires. Bedrooms come in a range of styles, some in the main house and others in converted out-buildings and the former estate manager's house. The Baronial Hall is a popular location for casual all-day dining, while more formal meals are served in the Sandstone Restaurant where great care is lavished on the prime ingredients, some of which come from the hotel's walled garden. Plans are in place to develop the property further, with additional rooms and treatment facilities.

Rooms: 44 (16 annexe) (3 family) (12 GF) S fr €99 **D** fr €125 (including breakfast) **Facilities:** STV FTV WiFi Fishing Xmas New Year **Conf:** Class 300 Board 50 Theatre 500 **Services:** Night porter Air con **Parking:** 150 **Notes:** Civ Wed

---

MOVILLE Map 1 C6
County Donegal

Redcastle Hotel, Golf & Spa Resort

★★★★ 79% ⊛⊛ HOTEL

tel: 074 9385555 **Inishowen Peninsula**
email: info@redcastlehotel.com web: www.redcastlehotel.com
dir: *On R238 between Derry and Greencastle.*

Perched beside the sea in mature parkland just outside Redcastle, this hotel has an enviable position on the Inishowen Peninsula with great views over Lough Foyle. It offers spacious, well-equipped bedrooms; some on the ground floor and some with balconies. The public areas include a range of relaxing lounges with an atmospheric bar where food is served throughout the day, and a large terrace for relaxing when the weather permits. The Edge Restaurant is right on the water's edge, and offers a well-thought-out menu with interesting options. There is a conference centre and an extensive leisure club offering spa treatments. The hotel has its own private 9-hole golf course, with sea fishing available from the shore.

Rooms: 93 (17 family) (16 GF) ☞ **S** fr €65 **D** fr €86 (including breakfast)*
Facilities: Spa STV FTV WiFi ☒ ⊛ ⅃ 9 Fishing ⅃ Gym Sauna Steam room
Experience shower ♫ Xmas New Year **Conf:** Class 150 Board 50 Theatre 350
Services: Lift Night porter **Parking:** 232 **Notes:** LB Civ Wed 250

MULRANNY Map 1 A4
County Mayo

Mulranny Park Hotel

★★★★ 79% ⊛⊛ HOTEL

tel: 098 36000
email: info@mulrannyparkhotel.ie web: www.mulrannyparkhotel.ie
dir: *R311 from Castlebar to Newport onto N59. Hotel on right.*

Set on an elevated site, this property has commanding views over Clew Bay. Originally a railway hotel dating from the late 1800s, it has a range of smart public rooms that retain many of the period features. Bedrooms vary in size but are comfortable and decorated in a contemporary style. Dinner in the Nephin Restaurant is a highlight of any stay, with casual dining available throughout the day in the Waterfront Bar and Bistro. A programme of activities is offered weekly for resident guests, in addition to a well-appointed leisure club.

Rooms: 60 (25 family) ☞ **S** fr €45 **D** fr €70 (including breakfast)* **Facilities:** WiFi ☒ ⊛ Gym Steam room Health and beauty Hairdressing Cycling Beach access ♫ New Year **Conf:** Class 140 Board 50 Theatre 400 **Services:** Lift Night porter **Parking:** 200 **Notes:** LB Closed 4–21 January, 1–25 December Civ Wed 250

NAVAN Map 1 C4
County Meath

Bellinter House

★★★★ 75% ⊛⊛ COUNTRY HOUSE HOTEL

tel: 046 9030900
web: www.bellinterhouse.com
dir: *N3 towards Navan, left at Tara Na Ri pub, travel 5 minutes, hotel on right.*

Set in rolling parkland, this Palladian-style Georgian house dates from 1749 and retains much of the scale and architectural features of the period. The decor however is very contemporary in the public areas where comfort and relaxation is key. Bedrooms are mainly set around two courtyards and feature a minimalist approach to decoration, with lots of timber and white surfaces. Dinner in Eden Restaurant in the vaulted basement is a delight, with more casual fare served in

the bar throughout the day. Spa treatments are available in The Bathhouse, with weddings and other events held in the Refectory.

Rooms: 34 (5 family) (12 GF) **Facilities:** Spa STV FTV WiFi Fishing Steam room Sauna **Conf:** Class 30 Board 24 Theatre 50 **Services:** Lift Night porter **Parking:** 80 **Notes:** Civ Wed 200

NEWMARKET-ON-FERGUS Map 1 B3
County Clare

Dromoland Castle Hotel

★★★★★ ⊛⊛ HOTEL

tel: 061 368144
email: sales@dromoland.ie web: www.dromoland.ie
dir: *N18 to Ennis/Galway from Shannon for 8km to 'Dromoland Interchange' signed Quin exit 11. Take slip road left, 4th exit at 1st roundabout, 2nd exit at 2nd roundabout. Hotel 500 metres on left.*

Dromoland Castle, dating from the early 18th century, stands on a 375-acre estate and offers extensive indoor leisure activities and outdoor pursuits. The professional team are wholly committed to caring for guests, in a warm and informal manner. The thoughtfully equipped bedrooms and suites vary in style, but they all provide excellent levels of comfort. The magnificent public rooms, warmed by log fires, are no less impressive. The hotel has several dining options; the elegant fine-dining Earl of Thomond Restaurant, where award-winning cuisine is available together with the less formal Fig Tree in the golf clubhouse, and The Gallery, which offers a menu suitable for all day dining.

Rooms: 97 (20 family) ☞ **S** fr €252 **D** fr €252 (including breakfast)*
Facilities: Spa STV WiFi ☒ ⊛ ⅃ 18 ☺ Fishing Gym Archery Clay shooting Mountain bikes Falconry Pony and trap Golf academy ♫ Xmas New Year **Conf:** Class 220 Board 80 Theatre 450 **Services:** Lift Night porter **Parking:** 120 **Notes:** LB Civ Wed 70

NEWTOWNMOUNTKENNEDY Map 1 D3
County Wicklow

Druids Glen Hotel & Golf Resort

★★★★★ 85% ⊛⊛ HOTEL

tel: 01 2870800
email: reservations@druidsglenresort.com web: www.druidsglenresort.com
dir: *N11 southbound, off at Newtownmountkennedy. Follow signs for hotel.*

This hotel, situated between the Wicklow Mountains and the coast, has two fabulous golf courses and a range of smart indoor leisure facilities and treatment rooms. Bedrooms have been equipped to the highest standard and service is delivered in a most professional manner, and always with a smile. Guests may choose to dine in the Gardens Room and Bar or the more formal Hugo's Restaurant.

Rooms: 145 (79 family) (40 GF) 🐾 **S** fr €155 **D** fr €165 (including breakfast)*
Facilities: Spa STV WiFi 🐾 📷 ♨ 36 Gym Sauna Steam room Indoor playroom Outdoor playground Giant games 🎵 Xmas New Year **Conf:** Class 160 Board 50 Theatre 400
Services: Lift Night porter Air con **Parking:** 400 **Notes:** Civ Wed 220

Parkview Hotel

★★★ 70% HOTEL

tel: 01 2015600 **Main Street**
email: info@parkviewhotel.ie **web:** www.parkviewhotel.ie

Located in the heart of the village of Newtownmountkennedy, 35 kilometres south of Dublin, this modern hotel offers a range of bedroom styles, all are very comfortably appointed. The Park Lounge is the main bar which enjoys a solid reputation for casual dining. Synnott's Restaurant opens for dinner at peak periods and for private use. The Park Room is a popular wedding venue, catering for events up to 250 guests. Secure parking is available to the rear.

Rooms: 60 (4 family) **Facilities:** STV FTV WiFi Xmas **Conf:** Class 250 Theatre 500
Services: Lift Night porter **Parking:** 60 **Notes:** Civ Wed 300

ORANMORE
County Galway
Map 1 B3

The Coach House Hotel

★★★ 68% 🌐 HOTEL

tel: 091 788367 & 483693 **Main Street**
email: info@coachhousehotel.ie **web:** www.coachhousehotel.ie
dir: In the village centre next to petrol station.

A renovated former coach house in the centre of the Oranmore, this property is probably better known locally as Basilico Restaurant and Bar, a well-established Italian restaurant, with great authenticity to its menu and cooking. Bedrooms are warm and comfortable. There's limited parking but plenty is available around the town. This is an ideal base for touring The Burren and the city of Galway.

Rooms: 16 (2 family) 🐾 **Facilities:** WiFi HL New Year **Services:** Lift Night porter
Parking: 14 **Notes:** Closed 24–25 December

PORTMARNOCK
Dublin
Map 1 D4

Portmarnock Hotel and Golf Links

★★★★ 81% 🌐🌐 HOTEL

tel: 01 8460611
email: info@portmarnock.com **web:** www.portmarnock.com
dir: Phone for directions.

With its origins as the summer residence for the Jameson family of Irish Whiskey fame, the Portmarnock Hotel has been updated to offer well-appointed bedrooms and suites. They are serious about their food here, with a number of outlets that are sure to please. The headline act is The 1780, a contemporary dining space overlooking the gardens through picture windows. There are a number of event spaces and meeting rooms, but the property is best known for its championship golf links that surrounds the hotel.

Rooms: 131 (43 GF) 🐾 **S** fr €159 **D** fr €199 (including breakfast)* **Facilities:** Spa STV FTV WiFi ♨ ♨ 18 Gym 🎵 Xmas New Year **Conf:** Class 120 Theatre 300
Services: Lift Night porter **Notes:** LB Civ Wed 130

RATHNEW
County Wicklow
Map 1 D3

Tinakilly Country House

★★★★ 78% 🌐🌐 HOTEL

tel: 0404 69274
email: info@tinakilly.ie **web:** www.tinakilly.ie
dir: Follow N11/M11 to Rathnew, then R750 towards Wicklow. Entrance to hotel approximately 500 metres from village on left.

Located south of the village, there is an elegant oak-lined avenue leading to Tinakilly House, a Victorian mansion steeped in history. It was built in 1884 for Captain Robert Halpin, Master Mariner and Commander of Brunel's SS *Great Eastern* who laid the telegraphic cable joining Europe to America. There are lovely garden views from the lounges that have open log fires. Some of the comfortable bedrooms and suites enjoy views over the Irish Sea and the bird sanctuary at Broadlough Coastal Lagoon. Furnishings throughout reflect the Victorian period yet provide all modern comforts. Fine dining is available in the Brunel Restaurant, and snacks and afternoon tea are served in the drawing room, or in pods on the lawn when weather permits.

Rooms: 51 (15 family) (14 GF) 🐾 **Facilities:** STV WiFi 🐾 🎵 New Year **Conf:** Class 70 Board 35 Theatre 90 **Services:** Lift Night porter **Parking:** 60 **Notes:** Closed 24–26 December Civ Wed 100

Hunter's Hotel

★★★ 78% 🌐 HOTEL

tel: 0404 40106
email: reception@hunters.ie **web:** www.hunters.ie
dir: 1.5 kilometres from village of Rathnew. From Dublin, N11/M11 exit 15, turn left at bridge in Ashford, follow signs to hotel.

One of Ireland's oldest coaching inns, this charming country house was built in 1720 and is full of character and atmosphere. The comfortable bedrooms have wonderful views over prize-winning gardens that border the River Vartry. The restaurant has a good reputation for carefully prepared dishes which make the best use of high quality local produce, including fruit and vegetables from the hotel's own garden.

Rooms: 16 (2 family) (2 GF) **S** fr €75 **D** fr €150 (including breakfast)* **Facilities:** WiFi **Conf:** Class 40 Board 16 Theatre 40 **Parking:** 50 **Notes:** LB Closed 24–26 December Civ Wed 40

RECESS (SRAITH SALACH)
County Galway
Map 1 A4

Ballynahinch Castle Hotel

★★★★ 81% 🌐🌐 COUNTRY HOUSE HOTEL

tel: 095 31006
email: info@ballynahinch-castle.com **web:** www.ballynahinchcastle.com
dir: Phone for directions.

Located on a 450-acre wooded estate in the heart of Connemara, Ballynahinch Castle is a warm and welcoming country house that is sure to impress. The management and staff are knowledgeable and very hospitable. Bedroom suites are in a traditional country-house style, many have river views. The hotel has a number of relaxing lounges, some with real log fires, and the atmospheric Fisherman's Pub & Ranji Room offering high-end food throughout the day. Dinner in the Owenmore Restaurant is the highlight of a stay; menus reflect both the seasons and what is best from local producers.

Rooms: 48 (8 family) (6 GF) 🐾 **S** fr €200 **D** fr €220 (including breakfast) **Facilities:** STV FTV WiFi 🐾 Fishing Walking trails Clay shooting Fly fishing Hiking Cycling and boat trips 🎵 Xmas New Year **Conf:** Class 20 Board 16 Theatre 20
Services: Lift Night porter **Parking:** 60 **Notes:** LB Civ Wed 60

REPUBLIC OF IRELAND

RECESS (SRAITH SALACH) *continued*

INSPECTOR'S CHOICE

Lough Inagh Lodge Hotel

★★★ COUNTRY HOUSE HOTEL

tel: 095 34706 **Inagh Valley**
email: inagh@iol.ie **web:** www.loughinaghlodgehotel.ie
dir: *From Recess take R344 towards Kylemore.*

Dating from 1880, this former fishing lodge is akin to a family home, where guests are encouraged to relax and enjoy the peace. Overlooking Lough Inagh, and situated amid the mountains of Connemara, it is in an ideal location for those who enjoy walking and fishing. Bedrooms are individually decorated, some with spacious seating areas, and each is dedicated to an Irish literary figure. There are two cosy lounges where welcoming turf fires are often lit. Informal dining from a bar menu is available during the day. Dinner is a highlight of a visit to the lodge; the menus feature locally sourced produce cooked with care – seafood is a speciality.

Rooms: 13 (1 family) (4 GF) **Facilities:** WiFi Fly fishing Cycling **Conf:** Class 20 Board 20 Theatre 20 **Services:** Air con **Parking:** 16 **Notes:** Closed mid December to mid March Civ Wed 50

ROSCOMMON
County Roscommon

Map 1 B4

Kilronan Castle Estate & Spa

★★★★ 80% HOTEL

tel: 071 9618000 **Ballyfarnon**
email: enquiries@kilronancastle.ie **web:** www.kilronancastle.ie
dir: *M4 to N4, R299, R207 (Droim ar Snámh/Drumsna/Droim). Onto R280, left onto R284 (Keadue Road).*

Located on the shores of Lough Meelagh in almost 50 acres of rolling park and woodland, this restored Gothic revival castle dates from the early 19th century. Great care has been taken in its restoration, with many of the fine bedrooms and suites housed in the adjoining, sympathetically-built modern block. The Drawing Room is a cosy lounge serving food throughout the day. The highlight is dinner in the Douglas Hyde Restaurant, where the friendly professional team go to great lengths to offer fine food in elegant surroundings. The impressive spa has a wide range of treatments on offer. There is also a leisure centre together with a wonderful events centre accessed by a tunnel from the main building.

Rooms: 85 (9 family) **Facilities:** Spa FTV WiFi Gym Xmas New Year **Conf:** Class 360 Board 60 Theatre 500 **Services:** Lift Night porter Air con **Parking:** 300 **Notes:** Civ Wed 200

ROSSCARBERY
County Cork

Map 1 B2

Celtic Ross Hotel

★★★ 81% HOTEL

tel: 023 88 48722
email: info@celticross.com **web:** www.celticrosshotel.com
dir: *N71 from Cork, through Bandon towards Clonakilty. Follow signs for Skibbereen.*

This hotel is situated on the edge of Rosscarbery overlooking the bay. The public areas are relaxing places, with a variety of lounges, a library, and the Warren Suite which enjoys panoramic views as far as Galley Head. Food is available in the Kingfisher Bar & Bistro, and on the Kingfisher Terrace in the summer months. Afternoon tea is a speciality here and can be booked in advance. The spacious bedrooms are comfortable and well appointed, many have wonderful sea views. There are extensive leisure and banqueting facilities plus music and dancing events on a regular basis. This hotel enjoys a strong reputation in the region for wedding celebrations and other family occasions.

Rooms: 66 (5 family) **S** fr €55 **D** fr €70 (including breakfast)* **Facilities:** Spa FTV WiFi Gym New Year **Conf:** Class 200 Board 60 Theatre 300 **Services:** Lift Night porter **Parking:** 250 **Notes:** LB Closed 24–26 December Civ Wed 250

ROSSLARE
County Wexford

Map 1 D2

INSPECTOR'S CHOICE

Kelly's Resort Hotel & Spa

★★★★ HOTEL

tel: 053 9132114
email: info@kellys.ie **web:** www.kellys.ie
dir: *N25 onto Rosslare/Wexford road, signed Rosslare Strand.*

The Kelly family have been offering hospitality here since 1895, where together with a dedicated team, they provide very professional and friendly service. The resort overlooks the sandy beach and is within minutes of the ferry port at Rosslare. Bedrooms are thoughtfully equipped and comfortably furnished. The extensive leisure facilities include a smart spa, swimming pools, a crèche, young adults' programme and spacious well-tended gardens. Both the eating options, La Marine Bistro and Beaches restaurant, have been awarded AA Rosettes for the quality of their cuisine.

Rooms: 118 (15 family) (20 GF) **Facilities:** Spa STV FTV WiFi Gym Bowls Badminton Crazy golf Table tennis Snooker Billiards Sauna Steam room Fitness classes Hair salon **Conf:** Class 30 Board 20 Theatre 30 **Services:** Lift Night porter **Parking:** 150 **Notes:** LB Closed early December to late February

SAGGART — Map 1 D3
Dublin

Citywest Hotel
★★★★ 77% HOTEL

tel: 01 4010500
email: info@citywesthotel.com web: www.citywesthotel.com
dir: Phone for directions.

Set among some 240 acres along the N7, Citywest Hotel is Ireland's largest hotel. Even so, the personal touch has not been lost and the helpful team ensure that guests are well cared for. There's a range of spacious rooms, many now refurbished to a high standard. Dining options include The Woodlock Brasserie which opens three times a day, with more casual, all-day dining in Swifts Bars & Hotel Lounge. There's also pan-Asian cuisine on offer in the Lemongrass Restaurant. Meeting and event spaces can cater for anything for up to 4,000 delegates. The well-equipped leisure facilities are available to resident guests.

Rooms: 764 (98 family) (128 GF) ☏ S fr €99 D fr €99 Facilities: FTV WiFi ⓣ ⓣ 18 Gym Hair and beauty salon ♫ Conf: Class 1050 Board 100 Theatre 2100 Services: Lift Night porter Parking: 2000 Notes: LB Closed 25–26 December Civ Wed 250

SHANNON — Map 1 B3
County Clare

Shannon Springs Hotel
★★★ 73% HOTEL

tel: 016 364047 Ballycasey V14A336
email: info@shannonspringshotel.com web: www.shannonspringshotel.com

Ideally located for Shannon International Airport, the bedrooms are comfortably appointed and very quiet given the location. Food is a major element of the business enjoyed, with locals and guests alike mingling in the buzzy atmosphere of the Old Lodge Gastro Pub. Leisure facilities are available nearby at favourable rates. There's plenty of car parking space.

Rooms: 54 Facilities: WiFi

SALTHILL
See Galway

SKIBBEREEN — Map 1 B1
County Cork

West Cork Hotel
★★★ 77% HOTEL

tel: 028 21277 Ilen Street
email: info@westcorkhotel.com web: www.westcorkhotel.com
dir: In Skibbereen, N71 into Bridge Street, with The Corner Bar on left to right into Ilen Street, hotel on right. From Cork Road, N71 to Schull, left at next roundabout towards town centre, hotel on left.

This charming hotel was built in 1902 and is family owned and run. It is located in the centre of town beside the River Ilen, where guests can enjoy an outdoor drink while sitting on the historic old West Cork railway bridge. There is a cosy lounge with log fire, and furnishings and decor successfully mix the best of old and new. Food is available throughout the day in the Railway Bar and in the evening in Kennedy's Restaurant. Bedrooms vary in size and are comfortably furnished, some with riverside views. There are extensive banqueting facilities and ample parking at the rear of the hotel.

Rooms: 49 (8 family) ☏ S fr €65 D fr €89 (including breakfast)* Facilities: FTV WiFi ⓣ Use of facilities at Skibbereen Sports Centre New Year Conf: Class 20 Board 24 Theatre 250 Services: Lift Night porter Parking: 100 Notes: LB Closed 24–28 December Civ Wed 300

Liss Ard Estate & Country House
Ⓤ

tel: 028 40000 Castletownsend Road, Russagh P81 NP44
email: reservations@lissard.com web: www.lissardestate.com
dir: Phone for directions.

Currently the rating for this establishment is not confirmed. This may be due to a change of ownership or because ot has only recently joined the AA rating scheme.

Rooms: 25 Notes: Civ Wed 120

SLANE — Map 1 D4
County Meath

Conyngham Arms Hotel
★★★ 74% HOTEL

tel: 041 984444 Main Street
email: info@conynghamarms.ie web: www.conynghamarms.ie
dir: Exit 10 for Navan from M1. Through village, hotel on the left of Main Street.

This 17th-century coaching inn has been beautifully appointed to high standards, and is situated in the centre of the village, close to Slane Castle, the World Heritage Site of Newgrange and many other historical sites. The bedrooms vary in size due to the age of the house and are very smartly decorated with guest comfort in mind. Food is bistro-style featuring the best local produce, and breads and confectionary are made in their own bakery, served throughout the day in the cosy bar with its open log fire. Private off-street parking is available.

Rooms: 15 ☏ S fr €59 D fr €79 (including breakfast)* Facilities: FTV WiFi ⓣ Conf: Class 100 Board 50 Theatre 200 Services: Night porter Parking: 20 Notes: LB Civ Wed 200

SLIGO — Map 1 B5
County Sligo

Radisson Blu Hotel & Spa Sligo
★★★★ 79% HOTEL

tel: 071 9140008 Rosses Point Road, Ballincar
email: info.sligo@radissonblu.com web: www.radissonblu.com/en/hotel-sligo
dir: From N4 into Sligo to main bridge. Take R291 on left. Hotel 1.5 miles on right.

Located four kilometres north of the town overlooking Sligo Bay, this contemporary hotel offers standard and business class bedrooms which are all appointed with up-to-date facilities. The Benwiskin bar offers tasty casual dining throughout the day, and for more formal dining in the evening there's Classiebawn Restaurant, featuring local ingredients cooked with international flair. Residents are welcome to use the Healthstyles leisure club during their stay, and relaxing treatment facilities are also available in the Solas Spa. A range of 11 rooms is provided for meetings and events.

Rooms: 132 (25 family) (32 GF) ☏ S fr €92 D fr €102 (including breakfast)* Facilities: Spa STV WiFi ⓣ ⓣ Gym Steam room Thermal suite Sauna ♫ Xmas New Year Conf: Class 400 Board 40 Theatre 740 Services: Lift Night porter Air con Parking: 320 Notes: Civ Wed 500

REPUBLIC OF IRELAND

SLIGO *continued*

Sligo Park Hotel & Leisure Club

★★★★ 79% ⊛ HOTEL

tel: 071 9190400 **Pearse Road F91 Y762**
email: sligo@leehotels.com **web:** www.sligopark.com
dir: *N4 to Sligo take exit S2 Sligo South Carrowroe/R287. Follow signs for Sligo. Hotel 1 mile on right.*

Set in seven acres of parkland on the southern outskirts of the town, this hotel is well located for visiting the many attractions of the northwest and Yeats' Country. Bedrooms come in a range of styles, but all are spacious and appointed to a high standard. There are two dining options, the award-winning Hazelwood Restaurant for dinner, and the Rathanna Bar for carvery lunches and all-day dining. Guests have full use of the leisure facilities.

Rooms: 136 (10 family) (52 GF) ⸙ **S** fr €59 **D** fr €69* **Facilities:** WiFi ⸖ ⊛ ⸑ Gym Holistic treatment suite Plunge pool Steam room ♫ Xmas New Year **Conf:** Class 290 Board 80 Theatre 520 **Services:** Lift Night porter **Parking:** 200 **Notes:** LB Civ Wed 520

The Glasshouse

★★★★ 79% HOTEL

tel: 071 9194300 **Swan Point**
email: info@theglasshouse.ie **web:** www.theglasshouse.ie
dir: *From N4 right at 2nd junction. Left at Post Office into Wine Street. Hotel on right.*

This landmark building in the centre of town makes a bold statement with its cutting-edge design and contemporary decor. Bright cheerful colours are used throughout the hotel; the bedrooms have excellent facilities including LCD TVs, workspace and internet access. There is a buzzing café bar serving food throughout the day, with a board walk for alfresco riverside dining. More formal evening dining takes place in The Kitchen restaurant. Secure underground parking is available together with a fitness suite.

Rooms: 116 ⸙ **Facilities:** STV FTV WiFi ⸖ Gym ♫ New Year **Conf:** Class 100 Board 60 Theatre 120 **Services:** Lift Night porter Air con **Parking:** 250 **Notes:** Closed 25–26 December RS 24 December Civ Wed 120

STRAFFAN	Map 1 C4
County Kildare	

The K Club

★★★★★ ⊛⊛ COUNTRY HOUSE HOTEL

tel: 01 6017200
email: sales@kclub.ie **web:** www.kclub.ie
dir: *From Dublin take N4, exit for R406, hotel on right in Straffan.*

The K Club is set in 550 acres of rolling woodland, and there are two magnificent championship golf courses and a spa facility to complement the truly luxurious hotel at the centrepiece of the resort. Public areas, suites and bedrooms are opulently furnished, and many have views of the formal gardens that lead down to the banks of the River Liffey. Additional rooms and family suites are a feature of the Liffey Wing. Dining options include the elegant River Room, with more informal dining options offered in Legends in the Arnold Palmer Golf Clubhouse,

and in The K Thai Restaurant in The Smurfit Clubhouse. The K Club was home to the 2016 Irish Open, and the Ryder Cup in 2006.

The K Club

Rooms: 134 (30 family) (18 GF) ⸙ **S** fr €199 **D** fr €199 (including breakfast)* **Facilities:** Spa STV FTV WiFi ⸖ ⊛ ⸻ 36 ⸑ Fishing ⸜ Gym Beauty salon Fishing tuition Clay pigeon shooting Horse riding Falconry ♫ Xmas New Year **Conf:** Class 180 Board 160 Theatre 460 **Services:** Lift Night porter **Parking:** 200 **Notes:** Civ Wed 250

Barberstown Castle

★★★★ 78% HOTEL

tel: 01 6288157
email: info@barberstowncastle.ie **web:** www.barberstowncastle.ie
dir: *R406, follow signs for Barberstown.*

With parts dating from the 13th century, this castle hotel provides the very best in standards of comfort. The inviting public areas range from the original keep which houses one of the restaurant areas, to the warmth of the drawing room and its cocktail bar. Bedrooms, some in a purpose-built wing, are elegantly appointed with relaxing seating areas. The airy Tea Room serves light meals throughout the day. The Castle is a popular venue for weddings and other family celebrations.

Rooms: 55 (2 family) (21 GF) ⸙ **S** fr €145 **D** fr €180 (including breakfast)* **Facilities:** STV WiFi ⸖ ♫ New Year **Conf:** Class 100 Board 72 Theatre 200 **Services:** Lift Night porter **Parking:** 200 **Notes:** LB Closed 24–26 December, January to February Civ Wed 280

THOMASTOWN	Map 1 C3
County Kilkenny	

The Manor House at Mount Juliet Estate

★★★★ ⊛⊛⊛ COUNTRY HOUSE HOTEL

tel: 056 7773000
email: info@mountjuliet.ie **web:** www.mountjuliet.ie
dir: *M7 from Dublin, M9 towards Waterford, exit at junction 9 (Stoneyford) for hotel.*

The Mount Juliet Estate is set in 1,500 acres of parkland with a Jack Nicklaus-designed golf course and an equestrian centre. The elegant and spacious public areas of the house retain many original architectural features including ornate plasterwork and Adam fireplaces. Bedrooms and suites are elegant and comfortably appointed to a high standard, with more compact rooms available in the Clubhouse annexe, less than a five-minute walk away. Award-winning fine dining is on offer in the ornate Lady Helen Restaurant overlooking the river; with brasserie-style cuisine in Kendal's located in the golf clubhouse. The President's Bar is the location for all-day dining and the opportunity for alfresco dining when the weather permits. The hotel has an excellent spa and health club, with other country pursuits and activities also available.

The Manor House at Mount Juliet Estate

Rooms: 46 (14 annexe) (6 family) (7 GF) **Facilities:** Spa STV WiFi ⊗ ⅃ 18 ⚲ Fishing ⚓ Gym Archery Cycling Equestrian Estate tours Xmas New Year **Conf:** Class 40 Board 20 Theatre 75 **Services:** Night porter **Parking:** 200 **Notes:** LB Civ Wed 100

THURLES
County Tipperary   Map 1 C3

Horse & Jockey Hotel
★★★★ 79% HOTEL

tel: 0504 44192 **Horse & Jockey**
email: info@horseandjockeyhotel.com **web:** www.horseandjockeyhotel.com
dir: *800 metres from M8 junction 6.*

Located just off the motorway, this hotel offers smart and well-appointed bedrooms which are very comfortable. Dining options are the Enclosure Bar with a varied menu, and for more formal dining in the evening there is Silks Restaurant. There is also a well-equipped leisure centre with spa treatments and an equestrian-themed gift shop. The conference facilities include ten self-contained meeting rooms and a tiered auditorium seating 200 delegates.

Rooms: 67 (4 family) (15 GF) **S** fr €90 **D** fr €140 (including breakfast)*
Facilities: Spa STV FTV WiFi ⊗ Gym Sauna Steam room Hydrotherapy area ♫
Conf: Class 24 Board 25 Theatre 200 **Services:** Lift Night porter **Parking:** 450
Notes: Closed 25 December RS 24 December

TRALEE
County Kerry   Map 1 A2

Ballyseede Castle
★★★ HOTEL

tel: 066 7125799
email: info@ballyseedecastle.com **web:** www.ballyseedecastle.com
dir: *On N21 just after junction of N21/N22.*

Located within minutes of Tralee, Ballyseede Castle is steeped in history dating back to 1590 and has been fought over, lived in and lovingly restored to a high standard which still pays homage to its ancient grandeur. The spacious bedrooms are elegantly decorated; some have four-poster beds and antique furnishings. There are gracious reception rooms with original ornamental cornices and marble fireplaces, a carved oak library, a cosy bar and a splendid banqueting hall. The castle stands in its own grounds at the end of a winding drive through formal gardens and natural woodland. All-day dining is available

in the atmospheric Pappy's Bar, with more formal evening dining in the award-winning O'Connell Room. The Castle is popular for hosting wedding celebrations and other family events.

Ballyseede Castle

Rooms: 48 (4 family) (10 GF) **Facilities:** STV FTV WiFi Fishing **Services:** Night porter **Parking:** 180 **Notes:** Closed January to 3 March Civ Wed 220

TULLOW
County Carlow   Map 1 D3

Mount Wolseley Hotel, Spa & Golf Resort
★★★★ 80% HOTEL

tel: 059 9180100
email: info@mountwolseley.ie **web:** www.mountwolseley.ie
dir: *N7 from Dublin. In Naas, take N9 towards Carlow. In Castledermot left for Tullow.*

Beautifully situated in the tranquil countryside of County Carlow, just one hour from Dublin City, the Mount Wolseley is a great location for a leisure break. With its own 18-hole championship golf course, and featuring the Wolseley Spa and Leisure Club, the hotel offers luxury accommodation matched with an elegant, chic interior, ultra modern amenities and impeccable service. The hotel offers a number of dining options including the Aaron lounge, Fredrick's Restaurant, and The Library.

Rooms: 143 (10 family) (5 smoking) **Facilities:** Spa STV FTV WiFi HL ⊗ ⅃ 18 ⚲ Gym Childrens play areas Games room ♫ New Year **Conf:** Class 288 Board 70 Theatre 750 **Services:** Lift Night porter Air con **Parking:** 160 **Notes:** Closed 25–26 December Civ Wed 450

WATERFORD
County Waterford   Map 1 C2

Waterford Castle Hotel and Golf Club
★★★★ 80% COUNTRY HOUSE HOTEL

tel: 051 878203 **The Island, Ballinakill**
email: info@waterfordcastleresort.com **web:** www.waterfordcastleresort.com
dir: *From city centre continue onto Dunmore Road for 2 kilometres. At hospital, take exit for Dunmore Road. Left at 3rd set of lights. Free ferry available to hotel.*

This enchanting and picturesque castle dates back to Norman times and is located on a 320-acre island just a five-minute journey from the mainland by chain-link ferry. Bedrooms vary in style and size, but all are individually decorated and offer high standards of comfort. Dinner is served in the oak-panelled Munster Room, with breakfast taken in the conservatory. The 18-hole golf course is set in beautiful parkland where deer can be seen.

Rooms: 19 (3 family) (4 GF) **S** fr €265 **D** fr €295 (including breakfast)*
Facilities: STV FTV WiFi ⅃ 18 ⚲ ⚓ Clay shooting Falconry **Conf:** Board 12
Services: Lift Night porter **Parking:** 50 **Notes:** Closed 25 December and January RS November to December Civ Wed 120

WATERFORD *continued*

Faithlegg House Hotel & Golf Resort

FBD Hotels & Resorts

★★★★ 79% ◉◉ HOTEL

tel: 051 382000 **Faithlegg**
email: reservations@fhh.ie **web:** www.faithlegg.com
dir: *From Waterford follow Dunmore East Road then Cheekpoint Road.*

This hotel is surrounded by a parkland championship golf course and overlooks the estuary of the River Suir. The house has 14 original bedrooms, and the others in a more contemporary style are in an adjacent modern block. There is a range of comfortable lounges together with comprehensive meeting facilities. The leisure and treatment rooms are the perfect way to work off the food offered in the Roseville Restaurant. Lighter options are served throughout the day in the Piano Bar and in the golf clubhouse.

Rooms: 82 (6 family) (30 GF) ☎ **Facilities:** Spa FTV WiFi ◷ ⅃ 18 ⚐ Gym Sauna Steam room New Year **Conf:** Class 90 Board 44 Theatre 180 **Services:** Lift Night porter **Parking:** 100 **Notes:** LB Closed 20–27 December Civ Wed 220

Granville Hotel

★★★★ 77% ◉ HOTEL

tel: 051 305555 **The Quay**
email: stay@granvillehotel.ie **web:** www.granvillehotel.ie
dir: *N25 to waterfront, hotel opposite clock tower.*

Centrally located on the quayside, this long established hotel was originally a coaching house. It is appointed to a very high standard, and retains much of its original character. The bedrooms come in a choice of standard or executive grades; all are well equipped and very comfortable. The Meagher Bar offers food throughout the day, and is a popular lunch venue with shoppers and the business community of Waterford. The Bianconi is an elegant restaurant where evening dinner is served. Friendliness and hospitality are hallmarks of a stay here.

Rooms: 100 (5 family) (10 smoking) ☎ **S** fr €90 **D** fr €120 (including breakfast)* **Facilities:** STV ⅃ New Year **Conf:** Class 150 Board 30 Theatre 200 **Services:** Lift Night porter **Parking:** 300 **Notes:** Closed 25–26 December Civ Wed 200

Dooley's Hotel

★★★ 78% HOTEL

tel: 051 873531 **30 The Quay**
email: hotel@dooleys-hotel.ie **web:** www.dooleys-hotel.ie
dir: *Adjacent to N25, on the Quay on R680.*

This hotel has been operating since the 19th century and is approaching its seventh decade in the hospitable hands of the Darrer family with the help of their friendly team. It is situated on the quay overlooking the River Suir at the bus station, within walking distance of the railway station. An interesting dinner menu is offered in the New Ship Restaurant, and casual dining is available in the Dry Dock Bar. Bedrooms are attractively decorated in keeping with the age of the property and offer a good standard of comfort. There is a public car park opposite the hotel.

Rooms: 110 (13 family) ☎ **Facilities:** STV WiFi ◈ ⅃ New Year **Conf:** Class 150 Board 100 Theatre 240 **Services:** Lift Night porter **Notes:** LB Closed 25–27 December RS 24 December

---

WESTPORT	**Map 1 B4**
County Mayo	

Knockranny House Hotel

★★★★ 84% ◉◉ HOTEL

tel: 098 28600
email: info@khh.ie **web:** www.knockrannyhousehotel.ie
dir: *On N5 Westport-Castlebar Road.*

Perched high up overlooking Westport, with Clew Bay and Croagh Patrick in the distance, this fine family-run property is set in landscaped grounds. The reception rooms take full advantage of the stunning views, and include The Brehon, a lounge where food is served throughout the day, and La Fougère, the award-winning restaurant that is a real treat. The comfortable furnishings create an inviting and relaxing atmosphere throughout the lounges, bar and restaurant. Bedrooms are very well appointed and come in a number of styles, with the newer ones being particularly spacious. Guests have complimentary use of extensive leisure facilities, with wellbeing treatments on offer in Spa Salveo. There are extensive banqueting and conference facilities.

Rooms: 97 (4 family) (18 GF) ☎ **Facilities:** Spa STV FTV WiFi ◈ HL Gym Vitality pool (over 18s only) Thermal suites ⅃ New Year **Conf:** Class 350 Board 40 Theatre 600 **Services:** Lift Night porter **Parking:** 150 **Notes:** Closed 24–26 December Civ Wed 250

Hotel Westport Leisure, Spa & Conference

★★★★ 81% ◉ HOTEL

tel: 098 25122 **Newport Road**
email: reservations@hotelwestport.ie **web:** www.hotelwestport.ie
dir: *N5 to Westport. Right at end of Castlebar Street, 1st right before bridge, right at lights, left before church. Follow to end of street.*

Located in seven acres of woodlands and just a short riverside walk from the town, this hotel offers spacious public areas, including The Islands restaurant and the all-day Maple Bar. Bedrooms come in a range of styles and are comfortable and well appointed. Both leisure and business guests are well catered for by the enthusiastic and friendly team who go to great lengths to ensure residents enjoy their stay. This hotel is a popular choice with special interest groups and also families, who enjoy the leisure facilities, and in summer time, the children's club.

Rooms: 129 (67 family) (42 GF) (12 smoking) ☎ **S** fr €59 **D** fr €78 (including breakfast) **Facilities:** Spa STV WiFi ◈ HL ◷ Gym Children's pool Lounger pool Steam room Sauna Fitness suite ⅃ Xmas New Year **Conf:** Class 150 Board 60 Theatre 500 **Services:** Lift Night porter **Parking:** 220 **Notes:** LB Civ Wed 350

Mill Times Hotel Westport

★★★ 73% HOTEL

tel: 098 29200 **Mill Street**
email: info@milltimeshotel.ie **web:** www.milltimeshotel.ie
dir: *N59 signed town centre, in Bridge Street keep in left lane, into Mill Street, hotel on left.*

This family-run hotel is situated in the centre of Westport, close to the shops and many pubs of this bustling town. It is ideal for visiting north Mayo with its many beaches and golf courses, or as a base for climbing the pilgrimage mountain of Croagh Patrick. Bedrooms are traditional in style and public areas are comfortable. Uncle Sam's café bar is a lively venue with entertainment at weekends. Temptations Restaurant offers good value meals during the evening, and is the venue for a hearty breakfast. Underground parking is provided.

Rooms: 34 (6 family) **Facilities:** WiFi ⅃ New Year **Conf:** Class 100 Board 60 Theatre 180 **Services:** Lift Night porter Air con **Parking:** 25 **Notes:** Closed 24–25 December Civ Wed 200

Gibraltar

GIBRALTAR
Gibraltar

Sunborn Yacht Hotel

★★★★★ 82% ◉◉ HOTEL

tel: 00 350 200 161000 **Ocean Village GX11 1AA**
email: info@sunborngibraltar.com **web:** www.sunbornhotels.com/gibraltar
dir: *Ocean Village Marina.*

This floating hotel is situated in the Ocean Village Marina; the yacht has 189 individually designed bedrooms with up-to-date technology to control the lighting, heating, curtains and TVs; most of the rooms have views over the marina and some rooms have large terraces. The Yacht has a range of spacious public areas that include a choice of dining options, lounges, bars, a casino, a spa and leisure facilities.

Rooms: 189 (1 family) (19 GF) ☏ **S** fr £209 **D** fr £217* **Facilities:** Spa STV FTV WiFi ⟡ ⟲ Gym ♫ Xmas New Year **Conf:** Class 200 Board 80 Theatre 360 **Services:** Lift Air con **Parking:** 12 **Notes:** LB Civ Wed 80

Caleta Hotel

★★★★ 80% ◉◉ HOTEL

tel: 00 350 200 76501 **Sir Herbert Miles Road, GX11 1AA**
email: reservations@caletahotel.gi **web:** www.caletahotel.com
dir: *Enter Gibraltar via Spanish border and cross runway. At 1st roundabout turn left, hotel in 2 km.*

For travellers arriving in Gibraltar by plane, the Caleta is an eye-catching coastal landmark that can be spotted from the air if arriving from the east. This imposing and stylish hotel sits on a cliff top and all sea-facing rooms enjoy panoramic views across the straights to Morocco. Bedrooms vary in size and style; some have spacious balconies, TVs and mini bars. Several dining venues are available, but Nunos provides an award-winning, fine dining Italian experience. The staff are friendly and service is professional.

Rooms: 161 (89 annexe) (13 family) (80 smoking) **Facilities:** Spa STV FTV WiFi ⟡ ⟲ Gym Health and beauty club Xmas New Year **Conf:** Class 172 Board 85 Theatre 216 **Services:** Lift Night porter Air con **Parking:** 32 **Notes:** Civ Wed 300

O'Callaghan Eliott Hotel

★★★★ 80% HOTEL

tel: 00 350 200 70500 **2 Governor's Parade GX11 1AA**
email: eliott@ocallaghanhotels.com **web:** www.ocallaghanhotels.com
dir: *Phone for directions.*

Located in the heart of the old town, this hotel provides a convenient central base for exploring the duty-free shopping district and other key attractions on foot. The bedrooms are stylish, spacious and well equipped. The roof-top restaurant provides stunning bay views, while guests can also take a swim in the roof-top pool.

Rooms: 130 ☏ **S** fr £148 **D** fr £163 (including breakfast)* **Facilities:** STV WiFi ⟡ ⟲ Gym ♫ Xmas New Year **Services:** Lift Night porter Air con **Parking:** 17 **Notes:** LB Civ Wed 50

The Rock Hotel

★★★★ 79% ◉ HOTEL

tel: 00 350 200 73000 **Europa Road GX11 1AA**
email: reservations@rockhotel.gi **web:** www.rockhotelgibraltar.com
dir: *From airport follow tourist board signs. Hotel on left half way up Europa Road.*

Enjoying a prime elevated location directly below the Rock, this long-established art deco styled hotel has been the destination of celebrities and royalty since it was built in 1932. The bedrooms are spacious and well equipped, and many boast stunning coastal views that stretch across the Mediterranean to Morocco. The staff are friendly and service is delivered with flair and enthusiasm. Creative dinners and hearty breakfasts can be enjoyed in the stylish restaurant.

Rooms: 94 ☏ **S** fr £125 **D** fr £135* **Facilities:** STV WiFi ⟲ Xmas New Year **Conf:** Class 120 Board 30 Theatre 150 **Services:** Lift Night porter Air con **Parking:** 40 **Notes:** LB Civ Wed 200

AA WALKING GUIDES

The 50 Best Walks of 2–10 Miles by Region and City

- Easy-to-follow directions with clear waypointed maps
- Colour-coded routes – pick from easy strolls through to more challenging walks
- Fascinating background reading for every walk
- Advice for dog owners
- Great for a full day out with recommended sights and attractions plus places to eat and drink

AA
50 Walks in
BRECON BEACONS
& SOUTH WALES
50 Walks of 2-10 Miles

AA
50 Walks in
HAMPSHIRE &
THE ISLE OF WIGHT
50 Walks of 2-10 Miles

AA
50 Walks in
THE LAKE DISTRICT
50 Walks of 2-10 Miles

AA
50 Walks in
BERKSHIRE &
BUCKINGHAMSHIRE
50 Walks of 2-10 Miles

AA
50 Walks in
KENT
50 Walks of 2-10 Miles

AA
50 Walks in
DERBYSHIRE
50 Walks of 2-10 Miles

AA
50 Walks in
SOMERSET
50 Walks of 2-10 Miles

AA
50 Walks in
THE COTSWOLDS
50 Walks of 2-10 Miles

AA
50 Walks in
DURHAM &
NORTHUMBERLAND
50 Walks of 2-10 Miles

AA
50 Walks in
CORNWALL
50 Walks of 2-10 Miles

AA
50 Walks in
NORFOLK
50 Walks of 2-10 Miles

AA
50 Walks in
SUSSEX &
SOUTH DOWNS
50 Walks of 2-10 Miles

AA
50 Walks in
OXFORDSHIRE
50 Walks of 2-10 Miles

AA
50 Walks in
THE PEAK DISTRICT
50 Walks of 2-10 Miles

AA
50 Walks in
WARWICKSHIRE &
WEST MIDLANDS
50 Walks of 2-10 Miles

AA
50 Walks in
DORSET
50 Walks of 2-10 Miles

AA
50 Walks in
THE YORKSHIRE
DALES
50 Walks of 2-10 Miles

AA
50 Walks in
SNOWDONIA &
NORTH WALES
50 Walks of 2-10 Miles

Dine & Stay
Restaurants with Rooms

Make the most of your evening at a top-notch restaurant, by staying over in one of our recommended 'restaurants with rooms'. Most of these venues have been awarded AA Rosettes for their food, and all offer overnight accommodation. This category of establishment is assessed under the AA's Guest Accommodation scheme.

They all have AA star ratings, but these are Guest Accommodation scheme ratings, details of which can be found opposite, on our website at **www.theaa.com/bed-and-breakfasts** or in the *AA B&B Guide*.

What is a 'Restaurant with Rooms'?

A 'restaurant with rooms' is best described as a destination restaurant offering overnight accommodation, with dining being the main business, and open to non-residents. The restaurant should offer a high standard of food and restaurant service at least five nights a week. A liquor licence is necessary and there is a maximum of 12 bedrooms.

Guest Accommodation Stars

AA Stars classify guest accommodation at five levels of quality, from one at the simplest, to five offering the highest quality. In order to achieve a one-Star rating an establishment must meet certain minimum entry requirements. For example:

- A cooked breakfast or substantial continental option is provided
- The proprietor and/or staff are available for your arrival, departure and at all meal times
- Once registered, guests have access to the establishment at all times unless previously notified
- All areas of operation meet minimum quality requirements for cleanliness, maintenance and hospitality as well as facilities and the delivery of services
- A dining room or similar eating area is available unless meals are served in bedrooms

Left: San Pietro Restaurant Rooms (see page 548)

To obtain a higher Star rating, an establishment must provide increased quality standards across all areas, with particular emphasis in four key areas:

- Cleanliness and housekeeping
- Hospitality and service
- Quality and condition of bedrooms, bathrooms and public rooms
- Food quality

There are also particular requirements in order for an establishment to achieve three, four or five Stars, for example:

Three Stars and above

- access to both sides of all beds for double occupancy
- bathrooms/shower rooms cannot be used by the proprietor
- there is a washbasin in every guest bedroom (either in the bedrooms or the en suite/private facility)

Four Stars

- half of bedrooms must be en suite or have private facilities

Five Stars

- all bedrooms must be en suite or have private facilities

Establishments applying for AA recognition are visited by one of the AA's qualified accommodation inspectors as a mystery guest. Inspections are a thorough test of the accommodation, food, and hospitality. The inspector completes a full report, resulting in a recommendation for the appropriate Star rating. After this first visit, the establishment will receive a regular visit to check that standards are maintained. If it changes hands, the new owners must re-apply for classification, as standards can change. Guests can expect to find the following minimum standards at all levels:

- Pleasant and helpful welcome and service, and sound standards of housekeeping and maintenance
- Comfortable accommodation equipped to modern standards
- Bedding and towels changed for each new guest, and at least weekly if the room is taken for a long stay

- Adequate storage, heating, lighting and comfortable seating
- A sufficient hot water supply at reasonable times
- A full cooked breakfast (If this is not provided, the fact must be advertised and a substantial continental breakfast must be offered)

When an AA inspector has visited a property, and evaluated all the aspects of the accommodation for comfort, facilities, attention to detail and presentation, you can be confident the Star rating will help you make the right choice.

★ **Gold Star Award**

AA Gold Stars are awarded to the very best Guest Accommodation within the three, four, or five Star ratings.

★ **Silver Star Award**

Guest Accommodation with Silver Stars offer a superior level of quality within their Star rating, high standards of hospitality, service and cleanliness.

Symbols & abbreviations

As well as the symbols used in the rest of the guide, Restaurants with Rooms may use some of the following:

🍽	A very special dinner, with an emphasis on freshly prepared local ingredients
TVL	Lounge with television
Lounge	Lounge without television
TV4B	Television in four bedrooms
tea/coffee	Tea and coffee-making facilities
🔒	Secure storage
pri fac	Private facilities (not all rooms will be en suite; some may have private bathrooms. These will not be shared with any other guests, or the proprietor.)

ARLINGHAM
Gloucestershire   Map 4 SO71

The Old Passage Inn
★★★★ ⓖⓖ ⓔ RESTAURANT WITH ROOMS

tel: 01452 740547 **Passage Road GL2 7JR**
email: oldpassage@btconnect.com **web:** www.theoldpassage.com
dir: A38 onto B4071 through Frampton on Severn. 4 miles to Arlingham, through village to river.

Delightfully located on the very edge of the River Severn, this relaxing restaurant with rooms combines high quality food with an air of tranquillity. Bedrooms and bathrooms are decorated in a modern style, and have a collection of welcome extras including a well-stocked mini-bar. The menu offers a wide range of seafood and shellfish dishes including crab, oysters and lobsters from Cornwall, kept alive in seawater tanks. An outdoor terrace is available in warmer months. No children under 10 at dinner please.

Rooms: 2 en suite **S** fr £80 **D** fr £120* **Facilities:** FTV DVD Lounge tea/coffee Dinner available WiFi ⓐ **Extras:** Mini-bar – chargeable **Parking:** 30 **Notes:** Closed 25–26 December RS January to February closed for dinner Tuesday and Wednesday

ARUNDEL
West Sussex   Map 6 TQ00

The Town House
★★★★ ⓖⓖ RESTAURANT WITH ROOMS

tel: 01903 883847 **65 High Street BN18 9AJ**
email: enquiries@thetownhouse.co.uk **web:** www.thetownhouse.co.uk
dir: A27 to Arundel, into High Street, establishment on left at top of hill.

This is an elegant, Grade II listed Regency building overlooking Arundel Castle, just a short walk from the shops and centre of the town. Bedrooms and public areas retain the building's unspoilt character. The ceiling in the dining room is particularly spectacular and originated in Florence in the 16th century. The excellent food has been awarded two AA Rosettes.

Rooms: 5 en suite (1 fmly) **S** fr £75 **D** fr £110* **Facilities:** FTV iPod docking station tea/coffee Dinner available WiFi ⓐ **Extras:** Speciality toiletries **Notes:** Closed 2 weeks Easter, 2 weeks October RS Sunday to Monday restaurant closed

ASENBY
North Yorkshire   Map 19 SE37

Crab Manor
★★★★★ ⓖⓖ RESTAURANT WITH ROOMS

tel: 01845 577286 **Dishforth Road YO7 3QL**
web: www.crabandlobster.co.uk
dir: A1(M) junction 49, on outskirts of village.

This stunning 18th-century, Grade II listed Georgian manor is located in the heart of the North Yorkshire Dales. Each bedroom is themed around the world's most famous hotels and has high-quality furnishings, beautiful wallpapers and thoughtful extras. Scandinavian log cabins are also available in the grounds – each has its own terrace with hot tub. There is a comfortable lounge bar where guests can relax in the manor before enjoying dinner next door in the Crab & Lobster Restaurant which specialises in fresh local seafood. The attractive landscape gardens are noteworthy too.

Rooms: 8 en suite 12 annexe en suite (3 fmly) **Facilities:** FTV iPod docking station Lounge tea/coffee Dinner available Direct dial WiFi Sauna ⓐ **Conf:** Max 16 Board 16 **Parking:** 90 **Notes:** Civ wed 105

AUSTWICK
North Yorkshire   Map 18 SD76

The Traddock
★★★★★ ⓖⓖ ⓔ RESTAURANT WITH ROOMS

tel: 015242 51224 **Settle LA2 8BY**
email: info@thetraddock.co.uk **web:** www.thetraddock.co.uk
dir: From Skipton take A65 towards Kendal, 3 miles after Settle turn right signed Austwick, cross hump back bridge, 100 yards on left.

Situated within the Yorkshire Dales National Park and a peaceful village environment, this fine Georgian country house with well-tended gardens offers a haven of calm and good hospitality. There are two comfortable lounges with real fires and fine furnishings, as well as a cosy bar and an elegant dining room serving fine cuisine. Bedrooms are individually styled with many homely touches.

Rooms: 12 en suite (2 fmly) (1 GF) **Facilities:** FTV DVD Lounge tea/coffee Dinner available Direct dial WiFi ⓐ **Extras:** Speciality toiletries, fruit, home-made biscuits, bottled water – complimentary **Conf:** Max 24 Thtr 24 Class 16 Board 16 **Parking:** 20 **Notes:** LB

AXBRIDGE
Somerset   Map 4 ST45

The Oak House
★★★★★ ⓖⓖ ⓔ RESTAURANT WITH ROOMS

tel: 01934 732444 **The Square BS26 2AP**
email: info@theoakhousesomerset.com **web:** www.theoakhousesomerset.com
dir: M5 junction 22, A38 north, turn right towards Axbridge and Cheddar.

This impressive restaurant with rooms is located in the middle of the village and provides a relaxed, high quality experience, whether guests are coming to enjoy the restaurant or to stay in one of the nine bedrooms above. Hospitality and service are delivered in an efficient and helpful manner by a young and enthusiastic team. The kitchen has a serious approach and delivers delightful dishes full of flavour, utilising the best quality produce.

Rooms: 9 en suite (2 fmly) **Facilities:** FTV DVD Lounge tea/coffee Dinner available WiFi **Notes:** Closed 2–5 January RS Sunday evening and Monday evening restaurant closed

BAINBRIDGE
North Yorkshire   Map 18 SD99

INSPECTOR'S CHOICE

Yorebridge House
★★★★★ ⓖⓖⓖ ⓔ RESTAURANT WITH ROOMS

tel: 01969 652060 **DL8 3EE**
email: enquiries@yorebridgehouse.co.uk **web:** www.yorebridgehouse.co.uk
dir: A648 to Bainbridge. Yorebridge House north of centre on right before river.

Yorebridge House is situated by the river on the edge of Bainbridge, in the heart of the North Yorkshire Dales. In the Victorian era this was a schoolmaster's house and school; the building now offers luxury boutique-style accommodation. Each bedroom is individually designed with high-quality furnishings and thoughtful extras. All rooms have stunning views of the Dales and some have their own terrace with hot tub. There is a comfortable lounge bar where guests can relax before enjoying an excellent, three AA Rosette award-winning dinner in the attractive and elegant dining room.

Rooms: 7 en suite 4 annexe en suite (11 fmly) (5 GF) **Facilities:** STV FTV DVD iPod docking station Lounge tea/coffee Dinner available Direct dial WiFi ⓐ Fishing **Extras:** Speciality toiletries **Conf:** Max 70 Thtr 70 Class 60 Board 30 **Parking:** 30 **Notes:** LB Civ wed 100

BARNET
Greater London
Map 6 TQ29

Savoro Restaurant with Rooms
★★★★ ◉ RESTAURANT WITH ROOMS

tel: 020 8449 9888 **206 High Street EN5 5SZ**
email: savoro@savoro.co.uk web: www.savoro.co.uk
dir: *M25 junction 23, A1000. Establishment in crescent behind Hadley Green Jaguar Garage.*

Set back from the main high street, the traditional frontage of this establishment belies the stylishly contemporary bedrooms within. Several have modern four-poster beds, and all have well designed bathrooms. The award-winning restaurant is an additional bonus, serving food that is freshly prepared in-house – from the breads to the ice creams.

Rooms: 11 rms (9 en suite) (2 pri facs) (2 fmly) (3 GF) **Facilities:** FTV tea/coffee Dinner available WiFi **Extras:** Bottled water – complimentary **Conf:** Max 20 Class 20 Board 20 **Parking:** 9 **Notes:** LB

BARTLOW
Cambridgeshire
Map 12 TL54

The Three Hills
★★★★★ ◉◉ RESTAURANT WITH ROOMS

tel: 01223 890500 **Dean Road CB21 4PW**
email: info@thethreehills.co.uk web: www.thethreehills.co.uk
dir: *From A11 onto A1307 signed Haverhill. Pass Linton, turn right signed Bartlow. At crossroads, turn right, pub on left.*

This 17th-century, Grade II listed building in the heart of Bartlow has undergone a major refurbishment to create a delightful, modern restaurant with rooms with landscaped gardens leading down to the river. The stylish, contemporary bedrooms, in various sizes, have character and come with Egyptian cotton bed linen, soft lighting, a bath and/or power shower and luxury toiletries. The award-winning food served in the orangery is based on quality local produce and the dishes are created with skill and flair. Eating outside on the patio is possible in warm weather.

Rooms: 2 en suite 4 annexe en suite (2 GF) **D** fr £100* **Facilities:** FTV TVL tea/coffee Dinner available WiFi **Extras:** Speciality toiletries, Nespresso coffee machine **Parking:** 25

BARTON-ON-SEA
Hampshire
Map 5 SZ29

Pebble Beach
★★★★★ ◉ ◉ RESTAURANT WITH ROOMS

tel: 01425 627777 **Marine Drive BH25 7DZ**
email: mail@pebblebeach-uk.com web: www.pebblebeach-uk.com
dir: *A35 from Southampton onto A337 to New Milton, left into Barton Court Avenue to clifftop.*

Situated on the clifftop, the restaurant at Pebble Beach boasts stunning views towards The Needles. Bedrooms and bathrooms (situated above the restaurant) are well equipped and provide a range of accessories. A freshly cooked breakfast is served in the main restaurant or outside on the wonderful terrace. Next door, Petit Pebbles delicatessen is well worth a visit.

Rooms: 4 rms (3 en suite) (1 pri facs) **S** fr £69.95 **D** fr £69.95* **Facilities:** FTV tea/coffee Dinner available Direct dial WiFi **Extras:** Speciality toiletries **Conf:** Max 16 Thtr 16 Class 16 Board 16 **Parking:** 20 **Notes:** RS 25 December and 1 January dinner not available

BISHOP'S CASTLE
Shropshire
Map 15 SO38

The Coach House
★★★★★ ◉◉ ◉ RESTAURANT WITH ROOMS

tel: 01588 650846 & 07930 694516 **Norbury SY9 5DX**
email: info@coachhousenorbury.com web: www.coachhousenorbury.com
dir: *3 miles northeast of Bishop's Castle. Exit A488/A489 into Norbury.*

Located in an Area of Outstanding Natural Beauty, this quaint, fully refurbished property in the centre of a pretty Shropshire village has been welcoming travellers since the 1700s. A warm welcome is assured by the current owners. Bedrooms offer comfortable accommodation and are located either in the main building or the attached coach house annexe which is dog friendly. Cosy lounges with log-burning fires are an ideal place to enjoy a locally-produced beer or one of the quality wines on offer. Award-winning dinners and breakfasts offer innovative menus showcasing the best local produce.

Rooms: 4 rms (3 en suite) (1 pri facs) 3 annexe en suite (1 fmly) (1 GF) **Facilities:** FTV DVD Lounge tea/coffee Dinner available WiFi ◉ **Extras:** Speciality toiletries, home-made biscuits **Conf:** Max 18 Thtr 18 Class 18 Board 18 **Parking:** 8 **Notes:** LB No children 5 years Closed 2–31 January

BOROUGHBRIDGE
North Yorkshire
Map 19 SE36

The Crown Inn
★★★★★ ◉◉ ◉ RESTAURANT WITH ROOMS

tel: 01423 322300 **Roecliffe YO51 9LY**
email: info@crowninnroecliffe.co.uk web: www.crowninnroecliffe.co.uk
dir: *A1(M) junction 48, follow signs for Boroughbridge. At roundabout exit towards Roecliffe.*

The Crown is a 16th-century coaching inn providing an excellent combination of traditional charm and modern comforts. Service is friendly and professional and food is a highlight of any stay. The kitchen team uses the finest Yorkshire produce from the best local suppliers to create a weekly-changing seasonal menu. Bedrooms are attractively furnished with stylish en suite bathrooms.

Rooms: 4 en suite (1 fmly) **S** fr £85 **D** fr £85* **Facilities:** FTV DVD tea/coffee Dinner available WiFi ◉ **Extras:** Home-made chocolates and biscuits **Conf:** Max 100 Thtr 100 Class 60 Board 30 **Parking:** 40 **Notes:** Civ wed 120

BRAITHWAITE
Cumbria
Map 18 NY22

The Cottage in the Wood
★★★★ ◉ RESTAURANT WITH ROOMS

tel: 017687 78409 & 07730 312193 **Whinlatter Pass CA12 5TW**
email: relax@thecottageinthewood.co.uk web: www.thecottageinthewood.co.uk
dir: *M6 junction 40, A66 west. After Keswick exit for Braithwaite via Whinlatter Pass (B5292), establishment at top of pass.*

This charming property sits on wooded hills with striking views of Skiddaw, and is conveniently placed for Keswick. The owners provide excellent hospitality in a relaxed manner. The award-winning food, freshly prepared and locally sourced, is served in the bright and welcoming conservatory restaurant with its stunning views. The comfortable bedrooms are well appointed and have many useful extras.

Rooms: 9 en suite **Facilities:** FTV Lounge tea/coffee Dinner available Direct dial WiFi ◉ **Parking:** 15 **Notes:** LB No children 10 years Closed January RS Monday closed

BRILL
Buckinghamshire
Map 11 SP61

The Pointer
★★★★★ ⑥⑥ 🍴 RESTAURANT WITH ROOMS

tel: 01844 238339 **27 Church Street HP18 9RT**
email: info@thepointerbrill.co.uk **web:** www.thepointerbrill.co.uk
dir: *M40 junction 9, onto A41 signed Aylesbury. Right signed Brill, on left next to church.*

The Pointer is a stylish country pub and restaurant with rooms in the picturesque village of Brill near Aylesbury. Part of the business is a working organic farm and kitchen garden as well as an adjacent butcher's shop for pedigree meats. Inside, there are heavy low beams entwined with bare twigs and exposed, roughcast stone walls. In the restaurant, guests are treated to a range of crowd-pleasing dishes all served in a relaxed and informal setting. The four modern bedrooms, located just over the road, are spacious and attractively presented; all have coffee machines and extremely comfortable beds. The bathrooms are equipped to the same high standard and include luxurious towels and luxury toiletries.

Rooms: 4 en suite **D** fr £140* **Facilities:** FTV tea/coffee Dinner available WiFi **Extras:** Home-made biscuits, Nespresso machine, still and sparking water, fresh milk, speciality toiletries **Parking:** 3 **Notes:** Closed 1st week of January

BRISTOL
Bristol
Map 4 ST57

Berwick Lodge
★★★★★ ⑥⑥⑥ RESTAURANT WITH ROOMS

tel: 0117 958 1590 **Berwick Drive, Henbury BS10 7TD**
email: info@berwicklodge.co.uk **web:** www.berwicklodge.co.uk
dir: *M5 junction 17, A4018 (Westbury-on-Trym). At 2nd roundabout 1st left (Westbury-on-Trym). At next roundabout double back on dual carriageway (signed M5 (M4)). Left after brown Clifton RFC sign. At crossroads straight on, follow Berwick Lodge signs.*

This delightful property was built in the late 1890s as a private manor house and is surrounded by rose and woodland gardens. It provides very high standards of quality and comfort throughout, with luxurious bedrooms and bathrooms offered in a range of shapes and sizes. Fine dining can be experienced in the opulent restaurant where both dinner and breakfast will be sure to delight even the most discerning guests.

Rooms: 12 en suite 2 annexe en suite (2 fmly) **S** fr £85 **D** fr £125* **Facilities:** STV FTV DVD Lounge tea/coffee Dinner available Direct dial Lift WiFi ⛳ Beauty therapy treatments **Extras:** Robes, fruit **Conf:** Max 100 Thtr 100 Class 60 Board 30 **Parking:** 100 **Notes:** LB Civ wed 100

BROADWAY
Worcestershire
Map 10 SP03

Russell's
★★★★★ ⑥⑥ 🍴 RESTAURANT WITH ROOMS

tel: 01386 853555 **20 High Street WR12 7DT**
email: info@russellsofbroadway.co.uk **web:** www.russellsofbroadway.co.uk
dir: *Opposite village green.*

Situated in the centre of picturesque Broadway, this restaurant with rooms makes a great base for exploring local attractions. The superbly appointed bedrooms, each with its own character, have air conditioning and a wide range of extras. The cuisine is a real draw here with skilful use made of freshly-prepared, local produce.

Rooms: 4 en suite 3 annexe en suite (4 fmly) (2 GF) **Facilities:** FTV DVD tea/coffee Dinner available Direct dial WiFi **Extras:** Honesty bar **Conf:** Max 12 Board 12 **Parking:** 7

BURNSALL
North Yorkshire
Map 19 SE06

The Devonshire Fell
★★★★ ⑥ RESTAURANT WITH ROOMS

tel: 01756 729000 & 718111 **BD23 6BT**
email: manager@devonshirefell.co.uk **web:** www.devonshirefell.co.uk
dir: *From roundabout on A59 at Bolton Abbey take B6160 to Burnsall. 6 miles.*

Located on the edge of the attractive village of Burnsall, The Devonshire Fell is colourful, contemporary and quirky. Originally a gentleman's club, it enjoys what may be one of the finest locations in the country. A brasserie-style menu is served in the light and airy conservatory restaurant, which has original modern artwork and views of the Fells and Dales. Intimate and friendly, The Devonshire Fell is a superb choice for those looking to escape from it all. Expect quality throughout, home comforts and a friendly, warm welcome.

Rooms: 16 en suite (2 fmly) **Facilities:** STV FTV DVD tea/coffee Dinner available Direct dial WiFi 🎣 Fishing 🛁 Free use of spa facilities at sister hotel **Conf:** Max 50 Thtr 50 Class 30 Board 24 **Parking:** 40 **Notes:** LB Civ wed 80

BURY ST EDMUNDS
Suffolk
Map 13 TL86

The Northgate
★★★★★ RESTAURANT WITH ROOMS

tel: 01284 339604 **13–14 Northgate Street IP33 1HP**
email: info@thenorthgate.com **web:** www.thenorthgate.com
dir: *A14 junction 43 onto A1101 towards town centre. 1st exit at roundabout into Northgate Street.*

This historic house is situated a short stroll from the town centre and the Abbey with its beautiful grounds. The individually styled bedrooms are tastefully appointed and equipped with modern facilities (TVs and Nespresso coffee machines). The smartly presented public areas include a contemporary cocktail bar, conservatory, open-plan restaurant and a separate chef's table in the heart of the kitchen; there is a heated outside terrace for alfresco dining too.

Rooms: 9 en suite (1 fmly) **S** fr £115 **D** fr £120* **Facilities:** FTV tea/coffee Dinner available WiFi **Extras:** Nespresso coffee machine **Conf:** Max 25 Thtr 15 Class 18 Board 25 **Parking:** 10

CAMBER
East Sussex
Map 7 TQ91

The Gallivant
★★★★ ⑥⑥ 🍴 RESTAURANT WITH ROOMS

tel: 01797 225057 **New Lydd Road TN31 7RB**
email: enquiries@thegallivant.co.uk **web:** www.thegallivant.co.uk
dir: *Phone for directions.*

The Gallivant is located right on the edge of Camber Sands, just a short drive from the historic town of Rye. The inn offers modern, well-equipped, coastal-themed accommodation with light, airy decor and reconditioned driftwood furniture. There's a bar and an award-winning restaurant that opens out onto a secluded decking area serving food daily. The large function suite is open all year round and is perfect for parties or weddings. The sand dunes and beach are just across the road in front of the inn.

Rooms: 16 en suite 4 annexe en suite (4 fmly) (20 GF) **Facilities:** FTV DVD Lounge tea/coffee Dinner available Direct dial WiFi ⛳ 🛁 **Extras:** Speciality toiletries **Conf:** Max 120 Thtr 120 Class 60 Board 40 **Parking:** 25 **Notes:** Civ wed 150

CANTERBURY
Kent
Map 7 TR15

The Corner House

★★★★ RESTAURANT WITH ROOMS

tel: 01227 780793 & 01843 823000 **1 Dover Street CT1 3HD**
email: matt@cornerhouserestaurants.co.uk **web:** www.cornerhouserestaurants.co.uk
dir: Phone for directions.

Located right in the city centre, The Corner House offers three stylishly decorated bedrooms. They are very spacious and appointed to a high standard yet still showcase some of the building's original features. Lunch, dinner and breakfast are available in the restaurant, though dinner is not available on a Monday when the restaurant is closed.

Rooms: 3 en suite **Facilities:** FTV DVD tea/coffee Dinner available WiFi
🔒 **Extras:** Fridge **Conf:** Max 20 Class 20 Board 10

CARTMEL
Cumbria
Map 18 SD37

INSPECTOR'S CHOICE

L'Enclume

★★★★★ ⦿⦿⦿⦿⦿ RESTAURANT WITH ROOMS

tel: 015395 36362 **Cavendish St LA11 6PZ**
email: info@lenclume.co.uk **web:** www.lenclume.co.uk
dir: From A590 turn left for Cartmel before Newby Bridge.

L'Enclume is a delightful 13th-century property in the heart of a lovely village, and offers incredible 21st-century cooking that draws foodies from far and wide. Once the village forge (l'enclume is French for 'the anvil') it's now the location for some of Britain's best food, and Simon Rogan's imaginative and adventurous cooking may be sampled in the stylish restaurant. Individually designed, modern, en suite rooms of varying sizes and styles are in the main property and dotted about the village only a few moments' walk from the restaurant.

Rooms: 5 en suite 11 annexe en suite (3 fmly) (2 GF) **Facilities:** STV DVD iPod docking station tea/coffee Dinner available Direct dial WiFi **Extras:** Mini-bar, speciality toiletries **Parking:** 3

CASTLE CARY
Somerset
Map 4 ST63

The Pilgrims

★★★★ ⦿⦿ RESTAURANT WITH ROOMS

tel: 01963 240600 **Lovington BA7 7PT**
email: jools@thepilgrimsatlovington.co.uk **web:** www.thepilgrimsatlovington.co.uk
dir: On B3153, 1.5 miles east of lights on A37 at Lydford.

The Pilgrims describes itself as 'the pub that thinks it's a restaurant', which is pretty accurate. With a real emphasis on fresh, local and carefully prepared produce, both dinner and breakfast are the focus of any stay here. In addition, the resident family proprietors provide a friendly and relaxed atmosphere. Comfortable and well-equipped bedrooms are available in the adjacent converted cider barn.

Rooms: 5 annexe en suite (5 GF) **Facilities:** FTV Lounge tea/coffee Dinner available WiFi **Extras:** Speciality toiletries **Parking:** 5 **Notes:** LB No children 14 years RS Sunday lunch to Tuesday lunch Restaurant and bar closed to non-residents

CAVENDISH
Suffolk
Map 13 TL84

The George

★★★★ ⦿⦿ 🍽 RESTAURANT WITH ROOMS

tel: 01787 280248 **The Green CO10 8BA**
email: thegeorgecavendish@gmail.com **web:** www.thecavendishgeorge.co.uk
dir: A1092 into Cavendish, The George next to village green.

The George is situated in the heart of the pretty village of Cavendish and has stylish bedrooms which have retained many of their original features, as well as being comfortable and spacious. The front-facing rooms overlook the village. The award-winning restaurant is very well appointed and dinner should not be missed. Guests are guaranteed to receive a warm welcome, attentive friendly service and great food.

Rooms: 4 en suite (1 fmly) **S** fr £60 **D** fr £85* **Facilities:** FTV DVD tea/coffee Dinner available WiFi 🔒 **Extras:** Speciality toiletries, mineral water, sweets **Notes:** Closed 25 December and 1 January

CHIEVELEY
Berkshire
Map 5 SU47

Crab & Boar

★★★★ ⦿⦿ 🍽 RESTAURANT WITH ROOMS

tel: 01635 247550 **Wantage Road RG20 8UE**
email: info@crabandboar.com **web:** www.crabandboar.com
dir: 1.5 miles west of Chieveley on B4494.

Part of The Epicurean Collection pub and inn group, the Crab & Boar has been appointed to a very high standard and bedrooms include a full range of modern amenities. Some ground-floor rooms have a small, private patio area complete with a luxury hot tub. The warm and cosy restaurant offers an extensive and award-winning range of dishes, using the best suppliers in the south. In summer, eating outside on the patio area, with its sweeping countryside views, is a delight.

Rooms: 9 en suite 5 annexe en suite (8 GF) **Facilities:** FTV tea/coffee Dinner available Direct dial WiFi Hot tub suites **Extras:** Home-made biscuits **Conf:** Max 14 Thtr 14 Class 14 Board 14 **Parking:** 80 **Notes:** LB

CHILGROVE
West Sussex
Map 5 SU81

The White Horse

★★★★★ ⦿ RESTAURANT WITH ROOMS

tel: 01243 519444 **High Street PO18 9HX**
email: info@thewhitehorse.co.uk **web:** www.thewhitehorse.co.uk
dir: From Chichester take A286 north, turn left onto B2141 to village.

Part of The Epicurean Collection, this spacious property offers stylish and relaxed surroundings on the edge of the South Downs. The bar and dining areas have an opulent feel, with lots of quirky touches and interesting features. Guests are welcome to enjoy a pint and relax, or choose dishes from the appealing and wide-ranging menus. The emphasis is on local produce and food is a highlight. Bedrooms offer an attractive blend of traditional and contemporary features, with wooden beams, sheepskin rugs and king-size beds. Most open out onto the private courtyard and feature either copper baths or large rain showers; a couple even have hot tubs.

Rooms: 15 en suite **Facilities:** FTV Lounge tea/coffee Dinner available Direct dial WiFi Fishing **Conf:** Max 20 **Notes:** LB

CHIPPING CAMPDEN
Gloucestershire
Map 10 SP13

The Kings

★★★★ ◎◎◎ ⬚ RESTAURANT WITH ROOMS

tel: 01386 840256 & 841056 **The Square, High Street GL55 6AW**
email: info@kingscampden.co.uk **web:** www.kingscampden.co.uk
dir: In centre of town square.

Located in the centre of this delightful Cotswold town, The Kings effortlessly blends a relaxed and friendly welcome with efficient service. Bedrooms and bathrooms come in a range of shapes and sizes and all are appointed to a high level of quality and comfort. Dining options, whether in the main Jackrabbit Restaurant or the comfortable bar area, serve a tempting menu to suit all tastes, from light salads and pasta, to meat and fish dishes.

Rooms: 13 en suite 5 annexe en suite (3 fmly) (3 GF) **Facilities:** FTV tea/coffee Dinner available Direct dial WiFi **Parking:** 14 **Notes:** LB Civ wed 60

CLITHEROE
Lancashire
Map 18 SD74

The Assheton Arms

★★★★★ ◎ RESTAURANT WITH ROOMS

tel: 01200 441227 **Downham BB7 4BJ**
email: info@asshetonarms.com **web:** www.seafoodpubcompany.com
dir: A59 to Chatburn, then follow Downham signs.

This historic Grade II listed building is located in the conservation village of Downham, with stunning views of Pendle Hill. The inn is owned by the Seafood Pub Company which means you can expect outstanding seafood. The smart bedrooms are spacious with a combination of traditional and contemporary decor; some rooms are dog-friendly. The team here are young, friendly and guarantee a warm welcome.

Rooms: 1 en suite 11 annexe en suite (4 fmly) (6 GF) **S** fr £70 **D** fr £80* **Facilities:** FTV Lounge tea/coffee Dinner available WiFi ⬚ ⬚ **Extras:** Mineral water, fresh milk **Conf:** Max 20 **Parking:** 18

COWAN BRIDGE
Lancashire
Map 18 SD67

INSPECTOR'S CHOICE

Hipping Hall

★★★★★ ◎◎◎ ⬚ RESTAURANT WITH ROOMS

tel: 015242 71187 **LA6 2JJ**
email: info@hippinghall.com **web:** www.hippinghall.com
dir: M6 junction 36, A65 through Kirkby Lonsdale towards Skipton. On right after Cowan Bridge.

Close to the market town of Kirkby Lonsdale, Hipping Hall offers spacious bedrooms, designed using soft shades with sumptuous textures and fabrics; the bathrooms use natural stone, slate and limestone to great effect. There are also three spacious cottage suites that create a real hideaway experience. The sitting room, with large, comfortable sofas has a traditional feel. The three AA Rosette-worthy restaurant is a 15th-century hall with tapestries and a minstrels' gallery that is as impressive as it is intimate.

Rooms: 7 en suite 8 annexe en suite (7 GF) **Facilities:** FTV Lounge Dinner available Direct dial WiFi ⬚ **Extras:** Speciality toiletries, fruit **Conf:** Max 12 Board 12 **Parking:** 30 **Notes:** No children 12 years Civ wed 42

CRAYKE
North Yorkshire
Map 19 SE57

The Durham Ox

★★★★★ ◪ RESTAURANT WITH ROOMS

tel: 01347 821506 **Westway YO61 4TE**
email: enquiries@thedurhamox.com **web:** www.thedurhamox.com
dir: A19 to Easingwold. Through market place to Crayke, 1st left up hill.

The Durham Ox is some 300 years old. The owners pride themselves on offering a friendly and efficient service, plus traditional pub food using only the best local ingredients. The pub has a breathtaking outlook over the Vale of York on three sides, and a charming view up the hill to the medieval church on the other. Accommodation is in converted farm cottages and a studio suite in the main building. Crayke is in the heart of 'Herriot Country' and about a 30 minute drive from York city centre.

Rooms: 1 en suite 5 annexe en suite (1 fmly) (3 GF) **Facilities:** FTV DVD iPod docking station tea/coffee Dinner available WiFi ⬚ Shooting, fishing, riding by arrangement **Extras:** Speciality toiletries, honesty bar **Conf:** Max 80 Thtr 80 Class 60 Board 30 **Parking:** 35 **Notes:** LB

DEVIZES
Wiltshire
Map 4 SU06

The Peppermill

★★★★★★ ◎◎ RESTAURANT WITH ROOMS

tel: 01380 710407 **40 Saint John's Street SN10 1BL**
email: philip@peppermilldevizes.co.uk **web:** www.peppermilldevizes.co.uk
dir: In market place, town centre.

Situated in the heart of Devizes, The Peppermill offers seven bedrooms located above the restaurant which is one of the oldest buildings in the town. The en suite bath/shower rooms have underfloor heating, limestone floors and heated mirrors. Hypnos Royal Lansdowne beds, three of which split into twins if needed, have goose-down bedding and Egyptian cotton linen to ensure a good night's sleep. The restaurant serves breakfast, lunch and dinner daily.

Rooms: 7 en suite **D** fr £115* **Facilities:** FTV iPod docking station TVL tea/coffee Dinner available WiFi ⬚ ⬚ **Extras:** Robes **Notes:** LB

DOVER
Kent
Map 7 TR34

The Marquis at Alkham

★★★★★ ◎◎ RESTAURANT WITH ROOMS

tel: 01304 873410 & 822945 **Alkham Valley Road, Alkham CT15 7DF**
email: info@themarquisatalkham.co.uk **web:** www.themarquisatalkham.co.uk
dir: A256 from Dover, at roundabout 1st exit into London Road, left into Alkham Road, Alkham Valley Road. Establishment 1.5 miles after sharp bend.

Located between Dover and Folkestone, this contemporary restaurant with rooms offers luxury accommodation with modern features – TVs, WiFi, monsoon showers and bathrobes, to mention a few. All the stylish bedrooms are individually designed and have fantastic views of the Kent Downs. The award-winning restaurant, open for lunch, afternoon tea and dinner, specialises in modern British cuisine with a strong emphasis on locally sourced ingredients. Both continental and a choice of cooked breakfasts are offered.

Rooms: 10 en suite (3 fmly) (1 GF) **Facilities:** FTV DVD Lounge tea/coffee Dinner available Direct dial WiFi **Extras:** Speciality toiletries **Conf:** Max 20 Thtr 20 Class 20 Board 16 **Parking:** 22 **Notes:** LB Civ wed 55

EDGEHILL
Warwickshire   Map 11 SP34

Castle at Edgehill

★★★★ ◉ RESTAURANT WITH ROOMS

tel: 01295 670255 **Main Street OX15 6DJ**
email: enquiries@castleatedgehill.co.uk **web:** www.castleatedgehill.co.uk
dir: *Phone for directions.*

Built in 1742 to mark the centenary of the Battle of Edgehill (when Charles I raised his standard at the start of the Civil War), this striking castellated property has a unique history. Many original features have can still be seen – the wood-panelling in the restaurant and exposed stone walls and arches really add to the charm of the building. The Tower bedrooms (Rupert and Kings) boast four-poster beds and panoramic views; there is also a room suitable for families and one on the ground floor – all are stylish. Dinner in the AA Rosette award-winning restaurant should not be missed, and breakfast features the best local produce.

Rooms: 2 en suite 2 annexe en suite (1 fmly) (1 GF) **Facilities:** FTV tea/coffee Dinner available WiFi **Conf:** Max 30 Thtr 24 Class 30 Board 18 **Parking:** 22

EMSWORTH
Hampshire   Map 5 SU70

INSPECTOR'S CHOICE

36 on the Quay

★★★★ ◉◉◉ RESTAURANT WITH ROOMS

tel: 01243 375592 & 372257 **47 South Street PO10 7EG**
email: info@36onthequay.co.uk **web:** www.36onthequay.co.uk
dir: *Last building on right in South Street, which runs from square in centre of Emsworth.*

Occupying a prime position with far-reaching views over the estuary, this 16th-century house is the scene for accomplished and exciting cuisine. The elegant restaurant occupies centre stage with peaceful pastel shades, local art and crisp napery together with glimpses of the bustling harbour outside. The contemporary bedrooms offer style, comfort and thoughtful extras.

Rooms: 4 en suite **Facilities:** FTV iPod docking station tea/coffee Dinner available WiFi **Parking:** 6 **Notes:** LB Closed 3 weeks January, 1 week late May

ERMINGTON
Devon   Map 3 SX65

Plantation House

★★★★★ ◉◉ ≋ RESTAURANT WITH ROOMS

tel: 01548 831100 & 830741 **Totnes Road PL21 9NS**
email: info@plantationhousehotel.co.uk **web:** www.plantationhousehotel.co.uk
dir: *Phone for directions.*

Peacefully situated in the picturesque South Hams, this former rectory provides an intimate and relaxing base from which to explore the area. Quality, comfort and individuality are hallmarks throughout, with bedrooms offering impressive standards and a host of thoughtful extras. The stylish bathrooms come equipped with fluffy towels, robes and underfloor heating. A drink beside the crackling log fire is the ideal prelude to dinner, where skill and passion underpin menus focusing on wonderful local produce. Breakfast is equally enjoyable, with superb eggs provided by the resident hens.

Rooms: 8 en suite **S** fr £65 **D** fr £110 **Facilities:** FTV DVD iPod docking station Lounge tea/coffee Dinner available Direct dial WiFi ☻ ♨ Fishing Riding Massage and therapies **Extras:** Speciality toiletries, fruit, home-made cakes and biscuits, robes, mineral water, fresh milk **Conf:** Max 16 **Parking:** 30 **Notes:** LB

EXETER
Devon   Map 3 SX99

Chi Restaurant & Bar with Accommodation

★★★★ ◕ RESTAURANT WITH ROOMS

tel: 01626 890213 **Fore Street, Kenton EX6 8LD**
email: enquiries@chi-restaurant.co.uk **web:** www.chi-restaurant.co.uk
dir: *5 miles south of Exeter. M5 junction 30, A379 towards Dawlish, in village centre.*

This former pub has been spectacularly transformed into a chic and contemporary bar, allied with a stylish Chinese restaurant. Dishes are beautifully presented with an emphasis on quality produce and authenticity, resulting in a memorable dining experience. Bedrooms are well equipped and all provide good levels of space and comfort, along with modern bathrooms.

Rooms: 5 en suite (1 fmly) **S** fr £55 **D** fr £70 (room only)* **Facilities:** FTV DVD Lounge tea/coffee Dinner available WiFi ♨ **Parking:** 26 **Notes:** Closed Sunday to Monday

FAVERSHAM
Kent   Map 7 TR06

Faversham Creek & Red Sails Restaurant

★★★★ ◉◉ RESTAURANT WITH ROOMS

tel: 01795 533535 & 534689 **Conduit Street ME13 7BH**
email: office@favershamcreekhotel.co.uk **web:** www.favershamcreekhotel.co.uk
dir: *M2 junction 6 onto A251. At T-junction left then right into The Mall. Pass railway station, continue on B2041. Left into Quay Lane.*

Located in the heart of Faversham and adjacent to the creek, this restaurant with rooms offers modern accommodation with its own individual style, and rooms named after characters from the Faversham area. Bedrooms are well equipped and ideal for both business and leisure guests alike. There is a courtyard terrace where guests can enjoy lunch or pre-dinner drinks before dining in the award-winning Red Sails Restaurant. Parking is available on site.

Rooms: 6 en suite (4 fmly) **S** fr £75 **D** fr £85* **Facilities:** STV FTV Lounge tea/coffee Dinner available Direct dial WiFi ☼ ♨ **Parking:** 4

FIVEHEAD
Somerset   Map 3 ST32

Langford Fivehead

★★★★★ ◉◉ ≋ RESTAURANT WITH ROOMS

tel: 01460 282020 **Lower Swell TA3 6PH**
email: rebecca@thelangford.co.uk **web:** www.langfordfivehead.co.uk
dir: *Phone for directions.*

Documents indicate that there has been a house on this site since 1255 and the current property retains a significant proportion of a 15th-century hall house. In keeping with the grand character found throughout the building, guests can be assured of the most pleasant of welcomes and helpful, relaxing hospitality and service. Bedrooms come in a range of shapes and styles, but all are decorated and equipped to very high standards (although deliberately, there are no TVs in the bedrooms). The restaurant is a delight of home-grown and local produce, providing delicious dishes at both dinner and breakfast.

Rooms: 6 en suite **Facilities:** Dinner available **Notes:** Closed 25 July to 7 August, 2–15 January

RESTAURANTS WITH ROOMS

| **FLAX BOURTON** | Map 4 ST56 |

Somerset

Backwell House

★★★★★ ◎◎ RESTAURANT WITH ROOMS

tel: 0117 325 1110 **Farleigh Road BS48 3QA**
email: guy@backwellhouse.co.uk **web:** www.backwellhouse.co.uk
dir: *Phone for directions.*

Located in a peaceful countryside setting with delightful views, this stylish property is surprisingly only a 10-minute drive from Bristol's city centre. The luxurious bedrooms and bathrooms come in a range of shapes and sizes but all include very comfortable beds plus some welcome extras. Breakfast includes a range of high quality hot and cold dishes while dinner is available on Wednesday to Saturday evenings and has an emphasis on local, seasonal and organic produce – much is provided by Backwell House's own garden.

Rooms: 9 en suite **Facilities:** Dinner available **Notes:** Closed 24–27 December

| **FOLKESTONE** | Map 7 TR23 |

Kent

Rocksalt Rooms

★★★★ ◎◎ RESTAURANT WITH ROOMS

tel: 01303 212070 **2 Back Street CT19 6NN**
email: info@rocksaltfolkestone.co.uk **web:** www.rocksaltfolkestone.co.uk
dir: *M20 junction 13 follow signs to harbour (A259). At harbour left onto Fish Market.*

Overlooking the busy harbour, often crowded with small leisure boats, and with wonderful sea views, Rocksalt Rooms enjoys a great location in Folkestone. Bedrooms are stylish, well-appointed with original antique beds and equipped with a host of thoughtful little extras. Continental breakfasts are delivered promptly to the guests' rooms each morning, and dinner is served in the award-winning restaurant, also blessed with panoramic views.

Rooms: 4 en suite (1 fmly) **Facilities:** FTV iPod docking station tea/coffee Dinner available WiFi **Extras:** Nespresso machine, fruit, speciality toiletries

| **GLOUCESTER** | Map 10 SO81 |

Gloucestershire

The Wharf House Restaurant with Rooms

★★★★ ◎ RESTAURANT WITH ROOMS

tel: 01452 332900 **Over GL2 8DB**
email: enquiries@thewharfhouse.co.uk **web:** www.thewharfhouse.co.uk
dir: *From A40 between Gloucester and Highnam exit at lights for Over. Establishment signed.*

The Wharf House was built to replace the old lock cottage and it's located at the very edge of the river; it has pleasant views and an outdoor terrace. The bedrooms and bathrooms have been appointed to a high standard, and there are plenty of guest extras. Seasonal, local produce can be enjoyed both at breakfast and dinner in the delightful AA Rosette-awarded restaurant. Dogs are allowed in the ground-floor room and on the terrace, and there is 20-minute rapid car charger and a slow charger. The Wharf House is owned and run by the Herefordshire & Gloucestershire Canal Trust – all profits go towards the promotion and restoration of the canal.

Rooms: 7 en suite (1 fmly) (1 GF) **Facilities:** STV FTV DVD Lounge tea/coffee Dinner available WiFi Fishing 🛁 **Extras:** Speciality toiletries – complimentary; Mini-bar – chargeable **Parking:** 37 **Notes:** Closed 22 December to 8 January RS Sunday to Monday check in before 6pm/restaurant closed evening

| **GORING** | Map 5 SU68 |

Oxfordshire

The Miller of Mansfield

★★★★ ◎◎ RESTAURANT WITH ROOMS

tel: 01491 872829 & 07702 853413 **High Street RG8 9AW**
email: reservations@millerofmansfield.com **web:** www.millerofmansfield.com
dir: *M4 junction 12, south on A4 towards Newbury. 3rd roundabout onto A340 to Pangbourne. A329 to Streatley, right at lights onto B4009 into Goring.*

The frontage of this former coaching inn hides sumptuous rooms furnished in a distinctive and individual style. The two AA Rosette restaurant serves appealing dishes using locally sourced ingredients, and there is a comfortable bar, which serves real ales, fine wines and afternoon tea; a bar menu provides quick bites to eat.

Rooms: 13 en suite (2 fmly) **S** fr £79 **D** fr £99* **Facilities:** FTV Lounge tea/coffee Dinner available WiFi 🛁 Boat hire and beauty therapies can be arranged **Extras:** Speciality toiletries, home-made biscuits **Conf:** Max 12 Board 12 **Parking:** 2 **Notes:** LB Closed 27–28 December

| **GRASSINGTON** | Map 19 SE06 |

North Yorkshire

Grassington House

★★★★★ ◎◎ 🍽 RESTAURANT WITH ROOMS

tel: 01756 752406 **5 The Square BD23 5AQ**
email: bookings@grassingtonhouse.co.uk **web:** www.grassingtonhouse.co.uk
dir: *A59 into Grassington, in town square opposite post office.*

Located in the square of the popular village of Grassington, this beautifully converted Georgian house is personally run by owners John and Sue. Delicious food, individually designed bedrooms and warm hospitality ensure an enjoyable stay. There is a stylish lounge bar looking out to the square and the restaurant is split between two rooms; here guests will find the emphasis is on fresh, local ingredients and attentive, friendly service.

Rooms: 9 en suite (2 fmly) **S** fr £117.50 **D** fr £135* **Facilities:** STV FTV tea/coffee Dinner available Direct dial WiFi 🛁 **Extras:** Speciality toiletries **Parking:** 25 **Notes:** LB Closed 25 December Civ wed 44

| **GREAT TOTHAM** | Map 7 TL81 |

Essex

The Bull & Willow Room at Great Totham

★★★★ ◎◎ RESTAURANT WITH ROOMS

tel: 01621 893385 & 894020 **2 Maldon Road CM9 8NH**
email: reservations@thebullatgreattotham.co.uk **web:** www.thebullatgreattotham.co.uk
dir: *Exit A12 at Witham junction to Great Totham.*

A 16th-century, former coaching inn located in the village of Great Totham, The Bull is a very stylish restaurant with rooms that offers en suite bedrooms with satellite TVs with Freeview; WiFi is available throughout. Guests can enjoy dinner in the gastro-pub or in the two AA Rosette award-winning fine dining restaurant, The Willow Room.

Rooms: 4 annexe en suite (2 GF) **S** fr £80 **D** fr £90* **Facilities:** STV FTV TVL tea/coffee Dinner available WiFi 🛁 **Conf:** Max 75 Thtr 40 Class 40 Board 16 **Parking:** 80 **Notes:** LB

HAWORTH
West Yorkshire   Map 19 SE03

The Old Registry Restaurant and Rooms

★★★★ 🍽 RESTAURANT WITH ROOMS

tel: 01535 646503 **2–6 Main Street BD22 8DA**
email: enquiries@theoldregistryhaworth.co.uk **web:** www.theoldregistryhaworth.co.uk
dir: *Phone for directions.*

A warm welcome is guaranteed at this owner-run establishment in a great location in the West Yorkshire village of Haworth. All rooms, some with four-poster beds, are individually designed and have modern accessories such as complimentary WiFi and TVs. Dinners can be enjoyed in the restaurant, and hearty, cooked breakfasts are provided each morning. On-site parking is not provided but permits are given to guests for a local car park which is a short walk away.

Rooms: 8 en suite **S** fr £65 **D** fr £80* **Facilities:** STV FTV DVD Dinner available WiFi

HETTON
North Yorkshire   Map 18 SD95

The Angel Inn

★★★★★ 🏵🏵 🍽 RESTAURANT WITH ROOMS

tel: 01756 730263 **BD23 6LT**
email: info@angelhetton.co.uk **web:** www.angelhetton.co.uk
dir: *B6265 from Skipton towards Grassington. At Rylstone turn left by pond, follow signs to Hetton.*

This roadside inn, easily recognised by the creeper on the walls and the green canopies, is steeped in history – parts of the building go back more than 500 years. The Angel's restaurant and bar are in the main building, and the food is a highlight of any stay; the kitchen uses excellent ingredients to produce skilfully prepared and carefully presented dishes. The large, stylish bedrooms are across the road in a converted barn which has great views of the Dales. There is private parking and the inn has its own wine cave.

Rooms: 9 en suite (3 GF) **Facilities:** FTV tea/coffee Dinner available Direct dial WiFi 🍷 Wine tasting cave **Conf:** Max 16 Board 14 **Parking:** 40 **Notes:** LB Closed 25 December and 1 week January Civ wed 40

HIGHCLERE
Hampshire   Map 5 SU45

The Yew Tree

★★★★ 🏵🏵 RESTAURANT WITH ROOMS

tel: 01635 253360 **Hollington Cross RG20 9SE**
email: info@theyewtree.co.uk **web:** www.theyewtree.co.uk
dir: *1 mile south of Highclere village.*

Part of The Epicurean Collection, this attractive 17th-century country inn has comfortable bedrooms decorated with William Morris print wallpaper and traditional features have been retained which creates a cosy atmosphere. Great British cooking can be enjoyed in the attractively-decorated restaurant, where good use is made of high-quality produce and fresh ingredients. The garden, with its own bar and dining areas, is a real bonus.

Rooms: 6 en suite 2 annexe en suite (2 GF) **S** fr £110 **D** fr £110* **Facilities:** FTV Lounge tea/coffee Dinner available WiFi 🍷 **Extras:** Speciality toiletries **Parking:** 35

HOLT
Norfolk   Map 13 TG03

The Lawns

★★★★ 🏵 RESTAURANT WITH ROOMS

tel: 01263 713390 **26 Station Road NR25 6BS**
email: info@lawnshotelholt.co.uk **web:** www.lawnshotelholt.co.uk
dir: *A148 (Cromer road). 0.25 mile from Holt roundabout, turn left, 400 yards along Station Road, on left.*

The Lawns is a superb Georgian house situated in the centre of this delightful north Norfolk market town. The open-plan public areas include a large wine bar, a conservatory and a smart restaurant. The spacious bedrooms are tastefully appointed with co-ordinated soft furnishings and have many thoughtful touches.

Rooms: 8 en suite 2 annexe en suite (2 GF) **S** fr £95 **D** fr £105* **Facilities:** FTV DVD TVL tea/coffee Dinner available WiFi **Extras:** Speciality toiletries **Conf:** Max 20 Thtr 20 Class 12 **Parking:** 18

HORNCASTLE
Lincolnshire   Map 17 TF26

Magpies Restaurant with Rooms

★★★★★ 🏵🏵 RESTAURANT WITH ROOMS

tel: 01507 527004 **71–73 East Street LN9 6AA**
email: info@magpiesrestaurant.co.uk **web:** www.magpiesrestaurant.co.uk
dir: *A158 into Horncastle, continue at lights. On left opposite Trinity Centre.*

This quaint and charming property is situated in the popular market town of Horncastle. The spacious en suite accommodation features three individually appointed rooms; all provide TVs, complimentary WiFi, home-made biscuits, mini-bar and luxurious bathrooms. There is a cosy lounge area with a wood-burning stove which is perfect for chilly winter evenings. The two AA Rosette award-winning restaurant provides a good choice of imaginative dishes at both lunch and dinner, and afternoon tea is also served. On-street parking is available nearby.

Rooms: 3 en suite **S** fr £70 **D** fr £110* **Facilities:** FTV iPod docking station Lounge tea/coffee Dinner available WiFi **Extras:** Bottled water, home-made biscuits and jam, mini-bar **Notes:** No children Closed 26–30 December and 1–7 January RS Monday to Tuesday closed

HUDDERSFIELD
West Yorkshire   Map 16 SE11

315 Bar and Restaurant

★★★★★ 🏵🏵 RESTAURANT WITH ROOMS

tel: 01484 602613 **315 Wakefield Road, Lepton HD8 0LX**
email: info@315barandrestaurant.co.uk **web:** www.315barandrestaurant.co.uk
dir: *M1 junction 38, A637 towards Huddersfield. At roundabout take A642 towards Huddersfield. Establishment on right in Lepton.*

In a wonderful setting, 315 Bar and Restaurant benefits from countryside views from the well-appointed dining room and conservatory areas. The interior is modern, with open fires that add character and ambiance, while the chef's table gives a real insight into the working of the two AA Rosette, award-winning kitchen. Bedrooms are modern, and most have feature bathrooms; some have air conditioning. Staff are friendly and attentive, and there are excellent parking facilities. There is a fantastic spa facility; treatments and use of the facilities is at an extra charge.

Rooms: 10 en suite 8 annexe en suite (3 fmly) (8 GF) **S** fr £85 **D** fr £95*
Facilities: FTV DVD tea/coffee Dinner available Lift WiFi Sauna **Conf:** Max 150 Thtr 100 Class 75 Board 60 **Parking:** 97 **Notes:** Civ wed 120

HUNSTANTON
Norfolk   Map 12 TF64

INSPECTOR'S CHOICE

The Neptune Restaurant with Rooms

★★★★★ ◉◉◉ RESTAURANT WITH ROOMS

tel: 01485 532122 **85 Old Hunstanton Road, Old Hunstanton PE36 6HZ**
email: reservations@theneptune.co.uk **web:** www.theneptune.co.uk
dir: On A149, past Hunstanton, 200 metres on left after post office.

This charming 18th-century coaching inn, now a restaurant with rooms, is ideally situated for touring the Norfolk coastline. The smartly appointed bedrooms are brightly finished with co-ordinated fabrics and hand-made New England furniture. Public rooms feature white clapboard walls, polished dark wood floors, fresh flowers and Lloyd Loom furniture. Obviously, the food is very much a draw here – the carefully prepared, award-winning cuisine uses excellent local produce such as oysters and mussels from Thornham and quinces grown on a neighbouring farm.

Rooms: 5 en suite **S** fr £160 **D** fr £280* **Facilities:** FTV tea/coffee Dinner available Direct dial WiFi ⓼ **Parking:** 6 **Notes:** No children 10 years Closed 1 week November, 3 weeks January, 1 week May RS October to April closed Monday

HURLEY
Berkshire   Map 5 SU88

Hurley House

★★★★★ ◉◉◉ ⓼ RESTAURANT WITH ROOMS

tel: 01628 568500 **Henley Road SL6 5LH**
email: hello@hurleyhouse.co.uk **web:** www.hurleyhouse.co.uk
dir: Phone for directions.

Hurley House is a beautiful restaurant with rooms located in a quiet village. The 10 stunning bedrooms vary in size, but all have air conditioning, underfloor heating, a mini-bar, coffee machine and extremely comfortable king-size beds. The bathrooms are equipped to the same high standard and have luxurious towels and high-quality toiletries. A wood-burning stove, flagstone floors and plenty of comfortable seating of different styles help create a relaxing atmosphere. There is a popular, character bar with a snug and private dining areas. In the restaurant, the menu showcases the finest local produce in modern British dishes. Snacks are also available in the bar and outside areas which are covered and heated. Expect fine ales, beer, spirits and an excellent wine list. WiFi is available throughout, plus there is a treatment room and plenty of convenient parking.

Rooms: 10 en suite **Facilities:** Dinner available WiFi

KINGHAM
Oxfordshire   Map 10 SP22

The Wild Rabbit

★★★★★ ◉◉◉ ⓼ RESTAURANT WITH ROOMS

tel: 01608 658389 **Church Street OX7 6YA**
email: theteam@thewildrabbit.co.uk **web:** www.thewildrabbit.co.uk
dir: Phone for directions.

Situated in the idyllic Cotswold village of Kingham, this Grade II listed Georgian building has been lovingly restored to create a thoroughly modern restaurant with rooms. The very stylish bedrooms, in muted colours, feature exposed brick walls and old beams, and include smart TVs, DAB radios, iPod docks, free WiFi, and luxury toiletries in the stunning en suites. The public spaces are equally noteworthy with a large bar, open-plan restaurant-kitchen and an outside dining area. The food is

exceptional, with many French influences evident in the cooking. Service is informal yet professional and very friendly. Ample parking is provided.

Rooms: 11 en suite 1 annexe en suite (1 fmly) (4 GF) **Facilities:** FTV DVD iPod docking station Lounge tea/coffee Dinner available WiFi ⓼ Spa, cookery and floristry classes available at Daylesford Organic Farm **Extras:** Mini-bar – chargeable **Conf:** Max 20 Thtr 20 Board 20 **Parking:** 15

KIRKBY LONSDALE
Cumbria   Map 18 SD67

The Sun Inn

★★★★★ ◉◉ ⓼ RESTAURANT WITH ROOMS

tel: 015242 71965 **6 Market Street LA6 2AU**
email: email@sun-inn.info **web:** www.sun-inn.info
dir: From A65 follow signs to town centre. Inn on main street.

The Sun is a 17th-century inn situated in the destination market town of Kirkby Lonsdale and overlooks St Mary's Church. The atmospheric bar features stone walls, wooden beams and log fires with real ales available. Delicious meals are served in the bar or in the relaxed and modern restaurant. Traditional and modern styles are blended together in the beautifully appointed bedrooms with excellent en suites.

Rooms: 11 en suite (1 fmly) **S** fr £99.50 **D** fr £117* **Facilities:** FTV tea/coffee Dinner available Direct dial WiFi ⓼ ⓲ **Extras:** Bath robes, speciality toiletries **Notes:** LB

Plato's

★★★★★ ⓼ ⓰ RESTAURANT WITH ROOMS

tel: 015242 74180 **2 Mill Brow LA6 2AT**
email: hello@platoskirkby.co.uk **web:** www.platoskirkbylonsdale.co.uk
dir: M6 junction 36, A65 Kirkby Lonsdale, after 5 miles at roundabout take 1st exit, onto one-way system.

Tucked away in the heart of this popular market town, Plato's is steeped in history. The bedrooms have a wealth of thoughtful extras and personal touches. Imaginative food is available in the elegant restaurant with its open-plan kitchen or downstairs in the vaulted cellar. The lounge bar has a more relaxed vibe with open fires and soft seating. A warm welcome and professional service is always assured.

Rooms: 8 en suite **S** fr £70 **D** fr £87* **Facilities:** FTV DVD iPod docking station TVL tea/coffee Dinner available WiFi ⓲ **Notes:** LB

KNARESBOROUGH
North Yorkshire   Map 19 SE35

General Tarleton Inn

★★★★★ ◉◉ RESTAURANT WITH ROOMS

tel: 01423 340284 **Boroughbridge Road, Ferrensby HG5 0PZ**
email: gti@generaltarleton.co.uk **web:** www.generaltarleton.co.uk
dir: A1(M) junction 48 at Boroughbridge, take A6055 to Knaresborough. 4 miles on right.

This 18th-century coaching inn is both beautiful and stylish. Though the physical aspects are impressive, the emphasis here is on food with high-quality, skilfully prepared dishes served in the smart bar-brasserie and in the Orangery. There is also a richly furnished cocktail lounge with a galleried private dining room above it. Bedrooms are very comfortable and business guests are also well catered for.

Rooms: 13 en suite (7 GF) **S** fr £75 **D** fr £129* **Facilities:** FTV Lounge tea/coffee Dinner available Direct dial WiFi ⓼ **Extras:** Speciality toiletries, home-made biscuits **Conf:** Max 40 Thtr 40 Class 35 Board 20 **Parking:** 40 **Notes:** LB Closed 24–26 December, 1 January

LACOCK
Wiltshire   Map 4 ST96

Sign of the Angel
★★★★ ◉◉ RESTAURANT WITH ROOMS

tel: 01249 730230 **6 Church Street SN15 2LB**
email: info@signoftheangel.co.uk **web:** www.signoftheangel.co.uk
dir: *M4 junction 17 onto A350 signed Poole. After 8 mile, left signed Lacock. Left into Church Street.*

This delightful 15th-century inn is located in the heart of the National Trust village of Lacock. Packed full of character, rooms vary in size according to the quirks of the building, but all offer very comfortable beds, quality bedding and a welcoming ambience. Guests are welcome to use the cosy bar and outdoor seating in the garden, while the dining room offers top quality British food, carefully sourced from local suppliers. Neither dinner nor breakfast should be missed here.

Rooms: 5 en suite (2 fmly) **S** fr £70 **D** fr £110* **Facilities:** Lounge tea/coffee Dinner available WiFi ⚓ **Extras:** Fudge, home-made cookies **Conf:** Max 16 Board 16
Notes: RS Sunday evening and Monday closed

LEINTWARDINE
Herefordshire   Map 9 SO47

The Lion
★★★★★ ◉ 🍸 RESTAURANT WITH ROOMS

tel: 01547 540203 & 540747 **High Street SY7 0JZ**
email: enquiries@thelionleintwardine.co.uk **web:** www.thelionleintwardine.co.uk
dir: *Beside bridge on A4113 (Ludlow to Knighton road) in Leintwardine.*

This quiet country restaurant with rooms in the picturesque village of Leintwardine, set beside the River Teme, is just a short distance from Ludlow and Craven Arms. The interior is stylish and all the contemporary bedrooms are en suite. Eating is taken seriously here and the modern, imaginative food uses the freshest local ingredients. The well-stocked bar offers a selection of real ales and lagers, and there is a separate drinkers' bar too. The Lion is particularly popular with families as the garden has a secure children's play area, and in warmer months guests can eat alfresco. The friendly staff help to make a visit memorable.

Rooms: 8 en suite (1 fmly) **Facilities:** FTV Lounge tea/coffee Dinner available WiFi Fishing ⚓ **Extras:** Home-made shortbread – complimentary **Conf:** Max 25 Class 25 Board 25 **Parking:** 25 **Notes:** Closed 25 December

LINCOLN
Lincolnshire   Map 17 SK97

The Old Bakery
★★★★ ◉◉ RESTAURANT WITH ROOMS

tel: 01522 576057 & 07772 667606 **26–28 Burton Road LN1 3LB**
email: enquiries@theold-bakery.co.uk **web:** www.theold-bakery.co.uk
dir: *Exit A46 at Lincoln North follow signs for cathedral. 3rd exit at 1st roundabout, 1st exit at next roundabout.*

Situated close to the castle at the top of the town, this converted bakery offers well-equipped bedrooms and a delightful dining operation. The cooking has gained two AA Rosettes, and uses much local produce. Expect good friendly service from the dedicated staff.

Rooms: 3 rms (2 en suite) (1 pri facs) (1 fmly) **Facilities:** FTV tea/coffee Dinner available WiFi ⚓ **Extras:** Bottled water, home-made cookies – complimentary **Notes:** Closed 25–26 December, 1–16 January, 1–12 August RS Sunday to Monday closed

LONDON E1

The Culpeper
★★★★ ◉ RESTAURANT WITH ROOMS PLAN 3 J3

tel: 020 7247 5371 **40 Commercial Street E1 6LP**
email: bookings@theculpeper.com **web:** www.theculpeper.com
dir: *From Aldgate East tube station left into Commercial Street, The Culpeper on right.*

Located on Commercial Street and just a stone's throw from Spitalfields Market and Brick Lane, The Culpeper offers comfortably appointed en suite bedrooms. All showcase stripped-back decor and original features yet still include modern furnishings and fixtures. There is a busy pub on the ground floor, a roof-top terrace and conservatory which serves barbecue tapas, and a main restaurant on the second floor which is open for breakfast, lunch and dinner. This is a real gem in the heart of East London, ideal for leisure and business guests alike.

Rooms: 5 en suite **D** fr £120* **Facilities:** FTV tea/coffee Dinner available WiFi **Extras:** Home-made cookies **Notes:** Closed 24–30 December

LONG MELFORD
Suffolk   Map 13 TL84

AA RESTAURANT WITH ROOMS OF THE YEAR 2018–19

INSPECTOR'S CHOICE

Long Melford Swan
★★★★★ ◉◉ RESTAURANT WITH ROOMS

tel: 01787 464545 **Hall Street CO10 9JQ**
email: info@longmelfordswan.co.uk **web:** www.longmelfordswan.co.uk
dir: *From A134 into Long Melford, on main road through village.*

Located in the very heart of Long Melford, the Swan offers home-made refreshments on arrival, bedrooms with stylish decor and modern fixtures, feature bathrooms and a turn-down service. All the bedrooms are located just next door in Melford House, adjacent to the main bar and restaurant. This family-run business offers an excellent restaurant with attentive service and a large alfresco dining area in the walled garden. Lunch and dinner are served daily, and a range of cooked and continental dishes are offered for breakfast in the restaurant.

Rooms: 3 en suite 4 annexe en suite (1 fmly) (2 GF) **Facilities:** FTV DVD iPod docking station tea/coffee Dinner available Direct dial WiFi ⚓ Spa treatments by arrangement **Extras:** Speciality toiletries, fruit **Notes:** LB

LUDLOW
Shropshire

Map 10 SO57

INSPECTOR'S CHOICE

Old Downton Lodge

★★★★★★ ◉◉◉ ⬚ RESTAURANT WITH ROOMS

tel: 01568 771826 & 07977 475881 **Downton on the Rock SY8 2HU**
email: bookings@olddowntonlodge.com **web:** www.olddowntonlodge.com
dir: *From Ludlow onto A49 towards Shrewsbury, 1st left onto A4113. After 1.9 miles turn left signed Downton, 3 miles on single track road. Turn right, signed.*

Peacefully situated, Old Downton Lodge is within easy reach of Ludlow's many attractions and has good parking, pleasant grounds, and is ideal for walks and country pursuits. Originally a farmhouse, this high-end establishment has bags of character and style. Bedrooms are spacious and very well appointed with comfortable beds and luxurious bathrooms. There is an honesty bar and excellent wine list. Breakfast should not be missed, and the three AA Rosette-worthy dinner is a highlight; offered every Tuesday to Saturday evening, the imaginative five- or seven-course tasting menus use local, seasonal and foraged produce.

Rooms: 10 en suite (5 GF) **S** fr £145 **D** fr £145* **Facilities:** FTV DVD Lounge tea/coffee Dinner available Direct dial WiFi **Extras:** Speciality toiletries, home-made biscuits **Conf:** Max 40 Thtr 40 Class 40 Board 40 **Parking:** 20 **Notes:** LB No children 13 years Closed 24–26 December Civ wed 60

The Clive Bar & Restaurant with Rooms

★★★★★ ◉ ⬚ RESTAURANT WITH ROOMS

tel: 01584 856565 & 856665 **Bromfield SY8 2JR**
email: info@theclive.co.uk **web:** www.theclive.co.uk
dir: *2 miles north of Ludlow on A49 in Bromfield.*

The Clive is just two miles from the busy town of Ludlow and is a convenient base for guests visiting the local attractions or for those on business. Based at the Ludlow Food Centre, good use is made of food made on site or from the company farms, ensuring local, seasonal produce at every meal. The bedrooms, located in an annexe, are spacious and very well equipped; one is suitable for families and many are on the ground-floor level. Meals are available in the well-known Clive Restaurant or in the bar areas. The property also has a small meeting room.

Rooms: 14 annexe en suite (1 fmly) (10 GF) **Facilities:** FTV tea/coffee Dinner available Direct dial WiFi ⬚ **Extras:** Mini-bar with local produce **Conf:** Max 40 Thtr 40 Class 40 Board 24 **Parking:** 80 **Notes:** LB Closed 25–26 December

The Cliffe at Dinham

★★★★ ◉◉ ⬚ RESTAURANT WITH ROOMS

tel: 01584 872063 & 876975 **Halton Lane, Dinham SY8 2JE**
email: info@thecliffeatdinham.co.uk **web:** www.thecliffeatdinham.co.uk
dir: *Phone for directions.*

This former gentleman's residence is a short stroll from the River Teme, with magnificent views of Ludlow Castle and just a short walk from the vibrant centre of Ludlow. The Cliffe is a successful blend of the Victorian features and more contemporary style. The bedrooms are comfortable and well equipped. Relaxed dining and modern British dishes are offered in the attractive dining room, and there is a pleasant terraced area overlooking the gardens.

Rooms: 11 en suite 2 annexe en suite (3 fmly) (2 GF) **S** fr £65 **D** fr £80*
Facilities: FTV tea/coffee Dinner available Direct dial WiFi ⬚ **Parking:** 30 **Notes:** LB Closed 26 December and 1–15 January

Dinham Hall

★★★★ RESTAURANT WITH ROOMS

tel: 01584 876464 **By The Castle SY8 1EJ**
email: info@dinhamhall.com **web:** www.dinhamhall.com
dir: *In town centre, opposite castle.*

Built in 1792, this lovely house stands in attractive gardens immediately opposite Ludlow Castle, and it has a well-deserved reputation for warm hospitality. The well-equipped bedrooms include two in a converted cottage, and some rooms have four-poster beds. The comfortable public rooms are elegantly appointed. Dishes served in the brasserie-style restaurant are based on good, seasonal produce.

Rooms: 11 en suite 2 annexe en suite (2 fmly) (2 GF) **S** fr £99 **D** fr £119*
Facilities: Lounge tea/coffee Dinner available WiFi **Parking:** 13
Notes: No children 7 years

LYMINGTON
Hampshire

Map 5 SZ39

INSPECTOR'S CHOICE

The Elderflower Restaurant

★★★★ ◉◉◉ RESTAURANT WITH ROOMS

tel: 01590 676908 **4–5 Quay Street SO41 3AS**
email: reservations@elderflowerrestaurant.co.uk **web:** www.elderflowerrestaurant.co.uk
dir: *Phone for directions.*

Situated on the cobbled streets in the heart of Lymington, just moments from the quay and a short drive into the New Forest National Park. Owned and run by a husband and wife team, The Elderflower is the realisation of a lifelong dream. Bedrooms and bathrooms are well appointed and situated above the restaurant. Cuisine is a real treat, with the team preparing modern British food with French influences using only the very best of locally sourced, sustainable produce. Parking is available nearby in the town's many car parks.

Rooms: 2 en suite **Facilities:** FTV tea/coffee Dinner available WiFi
Notes: No children 12 years (weekend only) Closed 26 December

MARKET RASEN
Lincolnshire

Map 17 TF18

The Advocate Arms

★★★★★ ◉◉ RESTAURANT WITH ROOMS

tel: 01673 842364 **2 Queen Street LN8 3EH**
email: info@advocatearms.co.uk **web:** www.advocatearms.co.uk
dir: *In town centre.*

Appointed to a high standard, this 18th-century property is located in the heart of Market Rasen and combines historic character with contemporary design. The operation centres around the stylish restaurant where service is friendly yet professional and the food is a highlight. The attractive bedrooms are very well equipped and feature luxury bathrooms.

Rooms: 10 en suite (2 fmly) **Facilities:** FTV tea/coffee Dinner available WiFi ⬚ ⬚ **Conf:** Max 22 Thtr 18 Class 22 Board 18 **Parking:** 6

MEDMENHAM
Buckinghamshire   Map 5 SU88

The Dog and Badger

★★★★★ ◉ RESTAURANT WITH ROOMS

tel: 01491 579944 **Henley Road SL7 2HE**
email: thedogandbadger@oakmaninns.co.uk **web:** www.thedogandbadger.com
dir: *Phone for directions.*

The Dog and Badger is a beautifully restored restaurant with rooms located in the quiet village of Medmenham. The six stunning bedrooms are located in a separate cottage; all are spacious and highly comfortable with smart TVs, air conditioning, mini-bars and coffee machines provided as standard. The bathrooms are just as smart with soft fluffy towels and luxury toiletries. There is a popular feature bar which serves a great range of wines, spirits, beers and cocktails and throughout the property there's contemporary art which blends with original features such as exposed brick, wooden beams and decorative floor tiles. In the informal restaurant, guests are treated to a range of crowd-pleasing dishes. WiFi is available throughout plus there's outside seating and plenty of parking space.

Rooms: 6 en suite **Facilities:** Dinner available

MELBOURN
Cambridgeshire   Map 12 TL34

Sheene Mill

★★★★ ◉◉ RESTAURANT WITH ROOMS

tel: 01763 261393 **39 Station Road SG8 6DX**
email: reservations@sheenemill.com **web:** www.sheenemill.com
dir: *M11 junction 10 onto A505 towards Royston. Right to Melbourn, pass church on right, on left before old bridge.*

This 16th-century watermill is ideally situated just off the A10, a short drive from both Cambridge and Royston. The bedrooms are individually decorated and well equipped; some rooms overlook the mill pond and terrace. Public rooms include a comfortable lounge, a bar, conservatory and a delightful restaurant overlooking the pond.

Rooms: 10 en suite (4 fmly) **Facilities:** FTV Lounge tea/coffee Dinner available WiFi ⅃ Sauna ⅂ **Extras:** Speciality toiletries – complimentary **Conf:** Max 180 Thtr 120 Class 120 Board 60 **Parking:** 60 **Notes:** Civ wed 120

MIDDLETON TYAS
North Yorkshire   Map 19 NZ20

INSPECTOR'S CHOICE

The Coach House

★★★★★ ◉◉◉ RESTAURANT WITH ROOMS

tel: 01325 377977 **Middleton Lodge DL10 6NJ**
email: info@middletonlodge.co.uk **web:** www.middletonlodge.co.uk
dir: *Phone for directions.*

In a picturesque setting, this former coach house, on a 200-acre estate, is surrounded by tall trees and winding footpaths. There is variety of luxury bedrooms – garden rooms with private terraces, hayloft rooms looking down on the courtyard and the spacious Tack Room suite. Traditional features such as exposed beams and high ceilings are coupled with a wide range of modern accessories such as TV, Nespresso machines and complimentary WiFi. The kitchen takes a modern approach, using seasonal, regional produce for an interesting range of dishes served in both the The Forge Restaurant and Coach House Restaurant. Beauty treatments are offered, and weddings and private functions are held in the main house, Middleton Lodge.

Rooms: 16 en suite 29 annexe en suite (10 fmly) (10 GF) **S** fr £125 **D** fr £150*
Facilities: STV FTV DVD Lounge tea/coffee Dinner available Direct dial WiFi ⅃ ⅃ ⅃ ⅂ **Extras:** Snacks, juice – complimentary **Parking:** 70 **Notes:** LB Civ wed 120

NAILSWORTH
Gloucestershire   Map 4 ST89

Wild Garlic Restaurant and Rooms

★★★★ ◉◉ ⅃ RESTAURANT WITH ROOMS

tel: 01453 832615 **3 Cossack Square GL6 0DB**
email: info@wild-garlic.co.uk **web:** www.wild-garlic.co.uk
dir: *M4 junction 18, A46 towards Stroud. Enter Nailsworth, left at roundabout, immediately left. Establishment opposite Britannia pub.*

Situated in a quiet corner of charming Nailsworth, this restaurant with rooms offers a delightful combination of welcoming, relaxed hospitality and serious cuisine. The spacious and well-equipped bedrooms are situated above the award-winning restaurant. The small and friendly team of staff ensure guests are very well looked after throughout their stay.

Rooms: 5 en suite (2 fmly) **Facilities:** STV FTV DVD tea/coffee Dinner available WiFi ⅃ Fishing Riding Shooting Hot air ballooning **Extras:** Speciality toiletries, spring water – complimentary; mini-bar – chargeable **Conf:** Max 6 Thtr 6 Class 6 Board 6

RESTAURANTS WITH ROOMS

NEWQUAY
Cornwall & Isles of Scilly   Map 2 SW86

Lewinnick Lodge

★★★★ RESTAURANT WITH ROOMS

tel: 01637 878117 **Pentire Headland TR7 1QD**
email: thelodge@hospitalitycornwall.com **web:** www.lewinnicklodge.co.uk
dir: From A392, at roundabout exit into Pentire Road then Pentire Avenue. Turn right to Lewinnick Lodge.

Set above the cliffs of Pentire Headland, looking out across the mighty Atlantic, guests are guaranteed amazing coastal views here at Lewinnick Lodge. The bedrooms were designed by Guy Bostock and are modern, spacious, and offer many thoughtful extras; some have open-plan bathrooms. Modern British food (with an emphasis on fresh fish) is served all day.

Rooms: 17 en suite (1 fmly) **S** fr £116 **D** fr £155 (room only)* **Facilities:** FTV Lounge tea/coffee Dinner available Direct dial Lift WiFi Surf board store **Extras:** Speciality toiletries, robes, bottled water – complimentary **Parking:** 50

NORWICH
Norfolk   Map 13 TG20

Brasteds

★★★★★ ◉◉ RESTAURANT WITH ROOMS

tel: 01508 491112 **Manor Farm Barns, Fox Road NR14 7PZ**
email: enquiries@brasteds.co.uk **web:** www.brasteds.co.uk
dir: A11 onto A47 towards Great Yarmouth, then A146. 0.5 mile, right into Fox Road, 0.5 mile on left.

Brasteds is a lovely detached property set in 20 acres of mature, landscaped parkland on the outskirts of Norwich. The tastefully appointed bedrooms have beautiful soft furnishings and fabrics along with comfortable seating and many thoughtful touches. Public rooms include a cosy snug with plush sofas, and a smart dining room where breakfast is served. Dinner is available in Brasteds Restaurant, which can be found in an adjacent building.

Rooms: 6 en suite (1 fmly) (3 GF) **Facilities:** FTV DVD iPod docking station TVL tea/coffee Dinner available Direct dial WiFi **Extras:** Mini-bar **Conf:** Max 120 Thtr 120 Class 100 Board 40 **Parking:** 50 **Notes:** LB Civ wed 160

The Old Rectory

★★★★★ ◉◉ RESTAURANT WITH ROOMS

tel: 01603 700772 **103 Yarmouth Road, Thorpe St Andrew NR7 0HF**
email: enquiries@oldrectorynorwich.com **web:** www.oldrectorynorwich.com
dir: From A47 southern bypass onto A1042 towards Norwich north and east. Left at slip road onto A1042. Follow signs to "All routes" and Thorpe St Andrew, at mini roundabout left onto A1242. Straight on at lights, entrance on right.

This delightful Grade II listed Georgian property is ideally located in a peaceful area overlooking the River Yare, just a few minutes' drive from the city centre. Spacious bedrooms are individually designed with carefully chosen soft fabrics, plush furniture and many thoughtful touches; many of the rooms overlook the swimming pool and landscaped gardens. Accomplished cooking is offered via an interesting daily-changing menu, which features skilfully prepared local produce.

Rooms: 5 en suite 3 annexe en suite **Facilities:** FTV iPod docking station Lounge tea/coffee Dinner available Direct dial WiFi ↝ Extras: Robes, speciality toiletries **Conf:** Max 14 Thtr 14 Class 10 Board 14 **Parking:** 12 **Notes:** LB Closed 22 December to 3 January RS Sunday to Monday no dinner served

Stower Grange

★★★★ ◉ RESTAURANT WITH ROOMS

tel: 01603 860210 **40 School Road, Drayton NR8 6EF**
email: enquiries@stowergrange.co.uk **web:** www.stowergrange.co.uk
dir: Norwich ring road north to Asda supermarket. Take A1067 (Fakenham Road) at Drayton, right at lights into School Road. Stower Grange 150 yards on right.

Expect a warm welcome at this 17th-century, ivy-clad property situated in a peaceful residential area close to the city centre and airport. The individually decorated bedrooms are generally quite spacious; each is tastefully furnished and equipped with many thoughtful touches. Public rooms include a smart open-plan lounge bar and an elegant restaurant.

Rooms: (1 fmly) **Facilities:** ↝ **Notes:** Civ wed 100

NOTTINGHAM
Nottinghamshire   Map 11 SK53

Restaurant Sat Bains with Rooms

★★★★★ ◉◉◉◉◉ RESTAURANT WITH ROOMS

tel: 0115 986 6566 **Lenton Lane, Trentside NG7 2SA**
email: info@restaurantsatbains.net **web:** www.restaurantsatbains.com
dir: M1 junction 24, A453 Nottingham south. Over River Trent into central lane to roundabout. Left, left again towards river. Establishment on left after bend.

This charming restaurant with rooms, a stylish conversion of Victorian farm buildings, is situated on the river and close to the industrial area of Nottingham. The bedrooms create a warm atmosphere by using quality soft furnishings together with antique and period furniture; suites and four-poster rooms are available. Public areas are chic and cosy, and the delightful restaurant complements the truly outstanding, world-famous cuisine.

Rooms: 7 en suite **Facilities:** STV tea/coffee Dinner available **Parking:** 22 **Notes:** No children 8 years Closed 1st week January and 2 weeks mid August

OLDSTEAD
North Yorkshire   Map 19 SE57

The Black Swan at Oldstead

★★★★★ ◉◉◉◉ RESTAURANT WITH ROOMS

tel: 01347 868387 **YO61 4BL**
email: reception@blackswanoldstead.co.uk **web:** www.blackswanoldstead.co.uk
dir: Exit A19, 3 miles south Thirsk for Coxwold, left in Coxwold, left at Byland Abbey for Oldstead.

The Black Swan, run by the Banks family, is set amidst the stunning scenery of the North York Moors National Park, and parts of the building date back to the 16th century. The well-appointed, very comfortable and stylish bedrooms provide the perfect luxury getaway; some are on the ground floor overlooking the kitchen garden, others are in the Georgian House and feature both baths and wet-room showers. These lovely bedrooms, welcoming open fires and a traditional bar all combine with the outstanding, award-winning food of Tommy Banks to make this a 'real little gem' of a property.

Rooms: 4 en suite 5 annexe en suite (6 GF) **S** fr £350 **D** fr £350* **Facilities:** FTV tea/coffee Dinner available WiFi **Extras:** Home-made biscuits, speciality toiletries **Parking:** 20 **Notes:** No children 18 years

ORFORD
Suffolk Map 13 TM45

The Crown & Castle
★★★★★ ◎◎ RESTAURANT WITH ROOMS

tel: 01394 450205 **IP12 2LJ**
email: info@crownandcastle.co.uk **web:** www.crownandcastle.co.uk
dir: Turn right from B1084 on entering village, towards castle.

The Crown & Castle is a delightful property situated adjacent to the Norman castle keep. Contemporary bedrooms are spilt between the main house and the garden wing; the latter are more spacious and have patios with access to the garden. The restaurant has an informal atmosphere with polished tables and local artwork, and a menu that features quality, locally sourced produce.

Rooms: 7 en suite 14 annexe en suite (2 fmly) (13 GF) **D** fr £140* **Facilities:** FTV DVD tea/coffee Dinner available Direct dial WiFi ⅃ **Extras:** Speciality toiletries, fresh milk **Parking:** 17 **Notes:** LB No children 8 years

ORMSKIRK
Lancashire Map 15 SD40

INSPECTOR'S CHOICE

Moor Hall Restaurant with Rooms
★★★★★ ◎◎◎◎◎ ⌂ RESTAURANT WITH ROOMS

tel: 01695 572511 **Prescot Road, Aughton L39 6RT**
email: enquiry@moorhall.com **web:** www.moorhall.com
dir: From M58 junction 1, take first exit at roundabout then first left. Continue for 1.7 miles. Moor Hall is signed on right.

Located within west Lancashire in five-acre gardens with stunning views over a beautiful lake, said to be the remains of a medieval moat. This Grade II listed house has been transformed with care and attention to detail into a true destination restaurant with rooms. Bedrooms are stunning, with many showcasing original features paired with exciting modern styling. Mark Birchall is at the helm here and has created a refined dining experience in relaxed surroundings. Local provenance is at the forefront of this modern British cuisine; produce grown on the five-acre Moor Hall site or by local suppliers is used whenever possible. The Barn offers a more casual dining experience with the same strong ethos. Throughout the establishment, the knowledgeable and friendly team are passionate about what they do. Please note, children under 12 are welcome at lunch only.

Rooms: 5 en suite 2 annexe en suite (2 fmly) (2 GF) **S** fr £195 **D** fr £195*
Facilities: FTV Lounge tea/coffee Dinner available WiFi **Extras:** Fruit, snacks, mini-bar **Parking:** 40 **Notes:** Closed 3 January for 2 weeks and 31 July for 2 weeks

OSMOTHERLEY
North Yorkshire Map 19 SE49

The Cleveland Tontine
★★★★★ ◎◎ ⌂ RESTAURANT WITH ROOMS

tel: 01609 882671 **Staddlebridge DL6 3JB**
email: enquiries@provenanceinns.com **web:** www.theclevelandtontine.co.uk
dir: Just off A172 junction on A19 northbound.

This iconic destination restaurant with rooms is a stunning place. Contemporary public areas sit alongside a traditional restaurant with open fires, tiled flooring and great food. Afternoon tea can be taken in the conservatory overlooking the gardens. Bedrooms are individually designed, with modern furniture and feature bathrooms. The service is friendly and relaxed, there is ample parking and major road links are close by.

Rooms: 7 en suite (4 fmly) **Facilities:** FTV Lounge tea/coffee Dinner available Direct dial WiFi **Extras:** Speciality toiletries **Conf:** Max 70 Thtr 56 Class 28 Board 38 **Parking:** 60 **Notes:** Civ wed 56

OSWESTRY
Shropshire Map 15 SJ22

Sebastians
★★★★★ ◎◎ ⌂ RESTAURANT WITH ROOMS

tel: 01691 655444 **45 Willow Street SY11 1AQ**
email: info@sebastians-hotel.com **web:** www.sebastians-hotel.com
dir: From town centre, take turn signed Selattyn into Willow Street. 400 yards from junction on left opposite Willow Street Gallery.

Sebastians is an intrinsic part of the leisure scene in Oswestry and has built up a loyal local following. The meals feature French influences, with a monthly-changing, three-course menu with complimentary appetiser and sorbet before main courses. Bedrooms are set around a pretty terrace courtyard and provide very comfortable accommodation with all the comforts of home.

Rooms: 2 en suite 4 annexe en suite (2 fmly) (2 GF) **S** fr £75 **D** fr £85 (room only)*
Facilities: iPod docking station Lounge tea/coffee Dinner available WiFi
Extras: Speciality toiletries, fruit, sweets – complimentary **Parking:** 6
Notes: Closed Christmas/New Year and bank holidays

PADSTOW
Cornwall & Isles of Scilly Map 2 SW97

INSPECTOR'S CHOICE

Padstow Townhouse
★★★★★ ◎◎◎◎ ⌂ RESTAURANT WITH ROOMS

tel: 01841 550950 **16/18 High Street PL28 8BB**
email: stay@padstowtownhouse.co.uk **web:** www.paul-ainsworth.co.uk
dir: Phone for directions.

This cosy 18th-century townhouse offers six individually styled suites, providing all home comforts as well as some extra little luxuries. Each room has its own 40" curved TV complete with Apple TV, as well as free WiFi. Breakfast is served in Rojano's in the Square (one AA Rosette), and guests are welcome to dine there or at the four AA-Rosette restaurant, Paul Ainsworth at No.6 restaurant.

Rooms: 6 en suite **Facilities:** Dinner available WiFi **Extras:** Speciality toiletries

RESTAURANTS WITH ROOMS

PADSTOW *continued*

INSPECTOR'S CHOICE

The Seafood Restaurant

★★★★★ ◉◉◉ ⑧ RESTAURANT WITH ROOMS

tel: 01841 532700 **Riverside PL28 8BY**
email: reservations@rickstein.com **web:** www.rickstein.com
dir: *Into town centre, down hill (Station Road), follow signs to harbour car park, opposite car park.*

Food lovers continue to beat a well-trodden path to this famous restaurant. Situated on the edge of the harbour, just a stone's throw from the shops, The Seafood Restaurant offers chic and comfortable bedrooms that boast numerous thoughtful extras; some have views of the estuary and a couple have private balconies with stunning sea views. Service is relaxed and friendly; booking is essential for both the accommodation and a table in the restaurant.

Rooms: 16 en suite 6 annexe en suite (12 fmly) (3 GF) **S** fr £165 **D** fr £165*
Facilities: FTV DVD tea/coffee Dinner available Direct dial Lift WiFi ⊛ Cookery School **Extras:** Speciality toiletries, robes, mini-bar **Notes:** LB Closed 24–26 December RS 24 December limited restaurant service times

St Petroc's Bistro

★★★★★ ◉ RESTAURANT WITH ROOMS

tel: 01841 532700 **4 New Street PL28 8EA**
email: reservations@rickstein.com **web:** www.rickstein.com
dir: *A39 onto A389, follow signs to Padstow town centre.*

One of the oldest buildings in town, this charming establishment is just up the hill from the picturesque harbour. Style, comfort and individuality are all great strengths here, particularly so in the impressively equipped bedrooms. Breakfast, lunch and dinner all reflect a serious approach to cuisine, and the popular restaurant has a relaxed, bistro style. Comfortable lounges, a reading room and lovely gardens complete the picture.

Rooms: 10 en suite (2 fmly) **S** fr £165 **D** fr £165* **Facilities:** FTV Lounge tea/coffee Dinner available Direct dial WiFi **Extras:** Speciality toiletries – complimentary; mini-bar, snack basket – chargeable **Notes:** LB Closed 24–26 December

| **PEWSEY** | Map 5 SU15 |
| Wiltshire | |

INSPECTOR'S CHOICE

Troutbeck Guest House at the Red Lion Freehouse

★★★★★ ◉◉◉ ⑧ RESTAURANT WITH ROOMS

tel: 01980 671124 **East Chisenbury SN9 6AQ**
email: enquiries@redlionfreehouse.com **web:** www.redlionfreehouse.com
dir: *A345 to Upavon, left at T-junction, right signed East Chisenbury.*

Troutbeck Guest House at the Red Lion Freehouse offers an interesting blend of sumptuous accommodation and food, yet it retains the informality and laidback atmosphere of a traditional pub. Each of the five rooms have been individually appointed and offers plenty of in-room amenities coupled with beautiful views of the surrounding countryside. The cooking is confident, and a particular flair is brought to the dishes based on seasonal, local ingredients. The pub rears its own pigs and keeps rescue hens. Tucked behind the property is a tranquil tree-shaded beer garden.

Rooms: 5 en suite (1 fmly) (5 GF) **Facilities:** FTV tea/coffee Dinner available WiFi ⌁ Fishing **Extras:** Speciality toiletries, snacks, robes – complimentary; mini-bar – chargeable **Conf:** Max 16 **Parking:** 5 **Notes:** LB

| **POOLEY BRIDGE** | Map 18 NY42 |
| Cumbria | |

1863 Bar Bistro Rooms

★★★★ ◉ RESTAURANT WITH ROOMS

tel: 017684 86334 **High Street CA10 2NH**
email: info@1863ullswater.co.uk **web:** www.1863ullswater.co.uk
dir: *M6 junction 40 onto A66 towards Keswick. At roundabout take 2nd exit onto A592. Continue for 4 miles, at junction turn left onto B5320 signed Pooley Bridge. Continue to village, opposite St Paul's church.*

1863 Bar Bistro Rooms is located in the idyllic village of Pooley Bridge on the edge of the majestic Ullswater. Built in 1863, as its names suggests, it was once the village blacksmiths and then the post office before becoming an accommodation provider. All bedrooms are well appointed and comfortable with many modern extras including TVs, DVD players, WiFi and bathrobes provided as standard. A rolling refurbishment programme has introduced two new stylish suites, which like the other rooms, feature colourful Designer Guild wallpapers. The award-winning dishes use the best produce that the Cumbrian larder can offer and are served in relaxed surroundings.

Rooms: 7 en suite **Facilities:** FTV Lounge Dinner available WiFi
Notes: No children 10 years Closed 24–26 December, 2–13 January

| **PORTHLEVEN** | Map 2 SW62 |
| Cornwall & Isles of Scilly | |

Kota Restaurant with Rooms

★★★★ ◉◉◉ RESTAURANT WITH ROOMS

tel: 01326 562407 **Harbour Head TR13 9JA**
email: kota@btconnect.com **web:** www.kotarestaurant.co.uk
dir: *B3304 from Helston into Porthleven. Kota on harbour opposite slipway.*

Overlooking the water, this 300-year-old building is the home of Kota Restaurant ('kota' being the Maori word for 'shellfish'). The bedrooms are approached from a granite stairway to the side of the building. The family room is spacious and has the benefit of harbour views, while the smaller, double room is at the rear of the property. The enthusiastic young owners ensure guests enjoy their stay here, and a meal in the award-winning restaurant is a must. Food and drink is also served in the Kota Kai Bar & Kitchen. Breakfast features the best local produce.

Rooms: 2 annexe en suite (1 fmly) **S** fr £70 **D** fr £85* **Facilities:** FTV DVD tea/coffee Dinner available WiFi ⌁ ⊛ **Extras:** Fridge **Parking:** 1 **Notes:** Closed January to 10 February

| **QUARNDON** | Map 10 SK34 |
| Derbyshire | |

Kedleston Country House

★★★★ ◉ RESTAURANT WITH ROOMS

tel: 01332 477222 **Kedleston Road, Kedleston DE22 5JD**
email: kedlestonreception@derbybrewing.co.uk **web:** www.thekedleston.co.uk
dir: *From Derby on Kedleston Road towards Allestree. Turn left (staying on Kedleston Road), on right before golf club.*

Located on the outskirts of Derby and close to the Peak District, this Robert Adams designed Georgian property has been lovingly and tastefully restored to create five boutique bedrooms, along with a bar and snug, modern country restaurant and orangery. Service is friendly and attentive and you are assured of a warm welcome.

Rooms: 5 en suite (1 fmly) **S** fr £150 **D** fr £150* **Facilities:** Lounge tea/coffee Dinner available WiFi ⌣ **Extras:** Speciality toiletries **Conf:** Max 80 Thtr 70 Class 80 Board 40 **Notes:** LB Civ wed 70

RAVENGLASS
Cumbria   Map 18 SD09

The Inn at Ravenglass
★★★★ ⚬ RESTAURANT WITH ROOMS

tel: 01229 717230 **Main Street CA18 1SQ**
email: gm@penningtonhotels.com **web:** www.theinnatravenglass.co.uk
dir: *Phone for directions.*

The Inn at Ravenglass enjoys picture-postcard views and is ideally located overlooking the estuary where the three rivers merge before entering the Irish Sea. This 17th-century inn not only offers great real ales but also good quality food in the upstairs, panoramic à la carte restaurant; in the downstairs pub guests will find more relaxed, comfort food. The inn shares some facilities with its sister hotel located a couple of doors away – this is where breakfast is served. The spacious, well-appointed bedroom has views of the estuary and village and has its own private entrance.

Rooms: 1 en suite **Facilities:** Dinner available

READING
Berkshire   Map 5 SU77

The French Horn
★★★★ ⚬⚬ RESTAURANT WITH ROOMS

tel: 0118 969 2204 **Sonning RG4 6TN**
email: info@thefrenchhorn.co.uk **web:** www.thefrenchhorn.co.uk
dir: *From A4 into Sonning, follow B478 through village over bridge, on right, car park on left.*

This long-established Thames-side establishment has a lovely village setting and retains the traditions of classic hospitality. The restaurant is a particular attraction and has been awarded two AA Rosettes. Bedrooms, including four cottage suites, are spacious and comfortable; many offer stunning views over the river. A private boardroom is available for corporate guests.

Rooms: 12 en suite 8 annexe en suite (4 GF) **Facilities:** FTV iPod docking station Lounge tea/coffee Dinner available Direct dial WiFi ⚓ Fishing **Extras:** Speciality toiletries, safe, mineral water **Conf:** Max 14 Board 14 **Parking:** 43 **Notes:** Closed 1–2 January RS 25 December evening closed for dinner

RETFORD
Nottinghamshire   Map 17 SK78

Blacksmiths
★★★★★ ⚬ RESTAURANT WITH ROOMS

tel: 01777 818171 **Town Street, Clayworth DN22 9AD**
email: enquiries@blacksmithsclayworth.com **web:** www.blacksmithsclayworth.com
dir: *From A631, 2.4 miles to Clayworth.*

Blacksmiths is a modern restaurant with annexed accommodation, situated in the quiet village of Clayworth, which is a short drive from Retford. Meals in the restaurant are one of the many highlights of a stay here – the hearty breakfasts can be delivered as room service. Bedrooms have been finished to an excellent standard and include many gadgets and accessories such as climate control, large wide-screen TVs, WiFi, fluffy bathrobes and luxurious toiletries. A warm welcome is guaranteed at this owner-run establishment.

Rooms: 4 en suite (2 fmly) (2 GF) **S** fr £108 **D** fr £120 **Facilities:** FTV iPod docking station tea/coffee Dinner available WiFi **Conf:** Max 120 Thtr 70 Class 20 Board 20 **Parking:** 31 **Notes:** Civ wed 70

ROSS-ON-WYE
Herefordshire   Map 10 SO52

Wilton Court Restaurant with Rooms
★★★★★ ⚬⚬ ⚬ RESTAURANT WITH ROOMS

tel: 01989 562569 **Wilton Lane HR9 6AQ**
email: info@wiltoncourthotel.com **web:** www.wiltoncourthotel.com
dir: *M50 junction 4, A40 towards Monmouth at 3rd roundabout left signed Ross-on-Wye, 1st right, on right.*

Dating back to the 16th century, Wilton Court has great charm and a wealth of character. It stands on the banks of the River Wye, just a short walk from the town centre, and a genuinely relaxed, friendly and unhurried atmosphere is created by hosts Roger and Helen Wynn and their reliable team. The bedrooms are tastefully furnished and well equipped, while public areas include a comfortable lounge, traditional bar and pleasant restaurant with a conservatory extension overlooking the garden. High standard food, using fresh, locally sourced ingredients, is offered.

Rooms: 11 en suite (1 fmly) (1 GF) **S** fr £100 **D** fr £135* **Facilities:** FTV DVD Lounge tea/coffee Dinner available Direct dial WiFi ⚓ ⚓ Fishing **Extras:** Kimonos, bottled water **Parking:** 20 **Notes:** LB Closed 3–15 January

ROWDE
Wiltshire   Map 4 ST96

The George & Dragon
★★★★ ⚬⚬ RESTAURANT WITH ROOMS

tel: 01380 723053 **High Street SN10 2PN**
email: gm@thegeorgeanddragonrowde.co.uk **web:** www.thegeorgeanddragonrowde.co.uk
dir: *1.5 mile from Devizes on A350 towards Chippenham.*

The George & Dragon dates back to the 14th century when it was a meeting house. Exposed beams, wooden floors, antique rugs and open fires create a warm atmosphere in the bar and restaurant. Bedrooms and bathrooms are very well decorated and equipped with some welcome extras. Dining in the bar or restaurant should not be missed, as local produce and fresh fish deliveries from Cornwall are offered on the daily-changing blackboard menu.

Rooms: 3 rms (2 en suite) (1 pri facs) (1 fmly) **S** fr £75 **D** fr £75* **Facilities:** FTV DVD Lounge TVL tea/coffee Dinner available WiFi **Extras:** Mini-bar, snacks, robes – complimentary **Parking:** 14

Follow us on twitter
@TheAA_Lifestyle

SCUNTHORPE
Lincolnshire

Map 17 SE81

San Pietro Restaurant Rooms

★★★★ ◉◉ RESTAURANT WITH ROOMS

tel: 01724 277774 **11 High Street East DN15 6UH**
email: info@sanpietro.uk.com **web:** www.sanpietro.uk.com
dir: *3 miles from M180, follow signs for Scunthorpe town centre and railway station, left into Brigg Road/Station Road. Near windmill.*

This family-run restaurant with rooms was purpose-built and offers comfortable, modern and stylish accommodation. Bedrooms and bathrooms provide a range of additional extras such as smart TVs, mini bars, home-made cakes and complimentary WiFi. Meals are served in the annexed Ristorante. Dinner menus reveal the chef's Italian heritage, and guests have plenty of choice including a chef's tasting menu as well as a full à la carte. Continental breakfasts are included but guests can upgrade to a hearty, cooked breakfast.

Rooms: 14 en suite (5 GF) **Facilities:** STV FTV iPod docking station tea/coffee Dinner available Direct dial Lift WiFi ⚐ ⚐ Cooking masterclasses **Extras:** Speciality toiletries, home-made cake, mini-bar, complimentary mineral water **Conf:** Max 100 Thtr 100 Class 50 Board 24 **Parking:** 25 **Notes:** Closed 1–7 January, Bank holiday Monday RS 8–10 January at 6pm, Sunday pm restaurant closed Civ wed 100

SHAFTESBURY
Dorset

Map 4 ST82

La Fleur de Lys Restaurant with Rooms

★★★★ ◉◉ RESTAURANT WITH ROOMS

tel: 01747 853717 **Bleke Street SP7 8AW**
email: info@lafleurdelys.co.uk **web:** www.lafleurdelys.co.uk
dir: *From junction of A30 and A350, 0.25 mile towards town centre.*

Located just a few minutes' walk from the famous Gold Hill, this light and airy restaurant with rooms combines efficient service with a relaxed and friendly atmosphere. Bedrooms, which are suitable for both business and leisure guests, vary in size but all are well equipped, comfortable and tastefully furnished. A relaxing guest lounge and courtyard are available for afternoon tea or pre-dinner drinks. The excellent food has been awarded two AA Rosettes.

Rooms: 8 en suite (2 fmly) (1 GF) **S** fr £85 **D** fr £100* **Facilities:** FTV Lounge tea/coffee Dinner available Direct dial WiFi ⚐ **Extras:** Home-made biscuits, fresh milk – complimentary **Conf:** Max 12 Board 10 **Parking:** 10 **Notes:** LB RS 1–21 January restaurant closed

SHREWSBURY
Shropshire

Map 15 SJ41

Darwin's Kitchen

★★★★ ⬗ RESTAURANT WITH ROOMS

tel: 01743 358870 & 761220 **15 Saint Mary's Street SY1 1EQ**
email: hello@darwinskitchen.co.uk **web:** www.darwinskitchen.co.uk
dir: *Follow one-way system around town, opposite St Mary's church.*

Situated in the heart of the town, this establishment offers four individually designed bedrooms, including a suite, that are very comfortable and have spacious and contemporary bathrooms. Food, based on locally sourced ingredients, is the focal point of the operation and can be enjoyed in the smart restaurant or conservatory area. Continental breakfasts are delivered to the bedrooms, or if a cooked breakfast is required then they are served at Darwin's Townhouse or The

Loopy Shrew (both in the same company) a couple of minutes' walk away. Secure parking is available in a nearby public car park.

Rooms: 4 en suite (1 fmly) **Facilities:** FTV tea/coffee Dinner available WiFi **Extras:** Speciality toiletries, robes, chef's complimentary treats **Notes:** LB Closed 25–26 December and 1 January RS Christmas and New Year

SIDLESHAM
West Sussex

Map 5 SZ89

The Crab & Lobster

★★★★★ ◉◉ ⬗ RESTAURANT WITH ROOMS

tel: 01243 641233 **Mill Lane PO20 7NB**
email: enquiries@crab-lobster.co.uk **web:** www.crab-lobster.co.uk
dir: *A27 onto B2145 signed Selsey. 1st left after garage at Sidlesham into Rookery Lane to Crab & Lobster.*

Hidden away on the south coast near Pagham Harbour and only a short drive from Chichester, is this stylish restaurant with rooms. Bedrooms are superbly appointed and bathrooms are a feature, with luxury toiletries and powerful 'raindrop' showers. Guests can enjoy lunch or dinner in the smart restaurant, where the menu offers a range of locally-caught, fresh fish together with other regionally-sourced, seasonal produce.

Rooms: 4 en suite **S** fr £90 **D** fr £185* **Facilities:** FTV DVD iPod docking station tea/coffee Dinner available WiFi **Extras:** Speciality toiletries, fresh milk **Parking:** 12

SIDMOUTH
Devon

Map 3 SY18

The Salty Monk

★★★★★ ◉◉ ⬗ RESTAURANT WITH ROOMS

tel: 01395 513174 **Church Street, Sidford EX10 9QP**
email: info@saltymonk.com **web:** www.saltymonk.co.uk
dir: *On A3052 opposite church in Sidford village.*

Set in the village of Sidford, this attractive property dates from the 16th century. There's plenty of style and appeal here and each bedroom has a unique identity. Bathrooms are equally adorned with multi-jet showers, spa baths and cosseting robes and towels. The output from the kitchen is impressive with excellent local produce very much in evidence, served in the elegant surroundings of the restaurant. A mini-spa facility is available.

Rooms: 5 en suite 2 annexe en suite (4 GF) **S** fr £85 **D** fr £135* **Facilities:** FTV Lounge tea/coffee Dinner available WiFi Sauna Gym ⚐ Outdoor hot tub, massage therapists **Extras:** Speciality toiletries, robes, bottled water, snacks, magazines – complimentary **Parking:** 20 **Notes:** LB Closed 1 week November and January

SOLIHULL
West Midlands   Map 10 SP17

INSPECTOR'S CHOICE

Hampton Manor

★★★★★ ◉◉◉◉ ⚲ RESTAURANT WITH ROOMS

tel: 01675 446080 **Shadowbrook Lane, Hampton-in-Arden B92 0EN**
email: info@hamptonmanor.com **web:** www.hamptonmanor.com
dir: M42 junction 6 follow signs for A45 (Birmingham). At 1st roundabout, 1st exit onto B4438 (Catherine de Barnes Lane). Left into Shadowbrook Lane.

Beautiful Hampton Manor is set in 45 acres of mature woodland, only minutes from Birmingham's major transport links and the NEC. The manor offers luxurious accommodation with a contemporary and sophisticated style while still maintaining many original features. The bedrooms are beautifully and uniquely designed and boast sumptuous beds. Outstanding fine dining can be enjoyed at Peel's restaurant, which is a fabulous venue for innovative cooking, and will prove the highlight of any stay.

Rooms: 15 en suite (3 fmly) (1 GF) **S** fr £175 **D** fr £190* **Facilities:** FTV DVD iPod docking station Lounge tea/coffee Dinner available Direct dial WiFi Beauty treatments **Extras:** Bottled water, home-made cookies, fresh fruit **Conf:** Max 120 Thtr 120 Class 60 Board 35 **Parking:** 30 **Notes:** LB No children 12 years Civ wed 120

SOUTHAMPTON
Hampshire   Map 5 SU41

Ennio's Restaurant & Boutique Rooms

★★★★★ ⚲ ⬡ RESTAURANT WITH ROOMS

tel: 023 8022 1159 & 07748 966113 **Town Quay Road SO14 3AS**
email: info@ennios.co.uk **web:** www.ennios.co.uk
dir: Opposite Red Funnel Ferry terminal.

This fine property, lovingly converted from a former Victorian warehouse, offers luxurious accommodation on Southampton's waterfront. All bedrooms are en suite and are furnished to a very high standard, including mini-bars and over-sized showers. Downstairs, the popular Ennio's Restaurant and bar is the ideal setting in which to dine, offering an authentic Italian atmosphere and a wonderful selection of dishes. There is limited parking to the rear of the building.

Rooms: 10 en suite **Facilities:** FTV iPod docking station Lounge tea/coffee Dinner available WiFi **Extras:** Speciality toiletries, mini-bar, trouser press **Parking:** 6 **Notes:** LB Closed 24–26 December

SOUTH FERRIBY
Lincolnshire   Map 17 SE92

The Hope and Anchor Pub

★★★★★ ◉◉ RESTAURANT WITH ROOMS

tel: 01652 635334 **Sluice Road DN18 6JQ**
email: info@thehopeandanchorpub.co.uk **web:** www.thehopeandanchorpub.co.uk
dir: Phone for directions.

This pub dates back to the 19th century and is perfectly situated in the town of South Ferriby with stunning views of the Humber Bridge. The bedrooms are modern and furnished to a high standard with exceptionally comfortable beds plus amenities such as Nespresso machines, TVs and complimentary WiFi. Dinner in the award-winning restaurant will surely be a highlight of any stay as are the hearty breakfasts. The staff are friendly and welcoming and a relaxed atmosphere is guaranteed. Complimentary on-site parking is provided.

Rooms: 5 en suite **Facilities:** iPod docking station Lounge Dinner available WiFi **Extras:** Nespresso machine, speciality toiletries **Notes:** RS Sunday to Monday closed

SOUTHWOLD
Suffolk   Map 13 TM57

Sutherland House

★★★★★ ◉◉ RESTAURANT WITH ROOMS

tel: 01502 724544 **56 High Street IP18 6DN**
email: enquiries@sutherlandhouse.co.uk **web:** www.sutherlandhouse.co.uk
dir: A1095 into Southwold, on High Street on left after Victoria Street.

Situated in the heart of the bustling town centre, this delightful 16th-century house has a wealth of character – oak beams, exposed brickwork, open fireplaces and two superb ornate plasterwork ceilings. The stylish bedrooms are tastefully decorated using co-ordinated fabrics and include many thoughtful touches. Public rooms feature a large open-plan contemporary restaurant, which has been awarded two AA Rosettes. There's a modern British menu created with care, and the food miles are listed alongside each dish.

Rooms: 5 en suite (1 fmly) **D** fr £100* **Facilities:** FTV DVD tea/coffee Dinner available WiFi **Notes:** No children 10 years RS Monday restaurant closed

STAMFORD
Lincolnshire   Map 11 TF00

Candlesticks

★★★ RESTAURANT WITH ROOMS

tel: 01780 764033 **1 Church Lane PE9 2JU**
email: info@candlestickshotel.co.uk **web:** www.candlestickshotel.co.uk
dir: B1081 into Stamford. Left onto A43. Right into Worthorpe Road, right into Church Lane.

Candlesticks is a 17th-century property situated in a quiet lane in the oldest part of Stamford, just a short walk from the centre of town. The bedrooms are pleasantly decorated and equipped with a good range of useful extras. Public rooms include Candlesticks restaurant and a cosy bar.

Rooms: 8 en suite **Facilities:** STV FTV Lounge tea/coffee Dinner available Direct dial WiFi ⚲ **Parking:** 8 **Notes:** LB RS Monday no restaurant or bar service

STOCKBRIDGE
Hampshire   Map 5 SU33

The Greyhound on the Test

★★★★ ◉◉ ⚲ RESTAURANT WITH ROOMS

tel: 01264 810833 **31 High Street SO20 6EY**
email: info@thegreyhoundonthetest.co.uk **web:** www.thegreyhoundonthetest.co.uk
dir: 9 miles northwest of Winchester, 8 miles south of Andover. Off A303.

The River Test, famous worldwide for its fishing, flows at the back of this restaurant with rooms. The luxury bedrooms are generally spacious, beautifully styled and come with a host of extras (one is on the ground-floor); most of the modern bathrooms have walk-in showers. The inn holds two AA Rosettes for its modern cuisine that's based on local ingredients; the food is a real draw. There is also ample parking and well-kept grounds.

Rooms: 10 en suite (1 GF) **Facilities:** FTV DVD Lounge tea/coffee Dinner available WiFi ⚲ Fishing Riding **Extras:** Speciality toiletries – complimentary; honesty bar **Conf:** Max 12 Board 12 **Parking:** 28 **Notes:** Closed 24–25 December

STOW-ON-THE-WOLD
Gloucestershire

Map 10 SP12

Old Stocks Inn

★★★★★ ◉ ≋ RESTAURANT WITH ROOMS

tel: 01451 830666 **The Square GL54 1AP**
email: info@oldstocksinn.com **web:** www.oldstocksinn.com
dir: *From A429 turn into Market Square, located opposite Town Hall.*

Old Stocks Inn has been lovingly restored and offers a mix of modern facilities and 17th-century charm. Stylish bedrooms are well designed and make good use of space; there are some unique features in the 'Amazing Great Rooms'. Cuisine is very much at the heart of the operation with a café, restaurant and bar making up the impressive ground floor. Not only are the breakfasts award-winning, but so is the food served at lunch and dinner.

Rooms: 13 en suite 3 annexe en suite (4 fmly) (3 GF) **Facilities:** FTV iPod docking station Lounge tea/coffee Dinner available Direct dial WiFi ⬠ **Extras:** Mini-bar, Nespresso machine **Conf:** Max 16 Thtr 10 Board 16 **Parking:** 10 **Notes:** Closed 25 December RS 24 December no accommodation

SUDBURY
Suffolk

Map 13 TL84

The Case Restaurant with Rooms

★★★★ ◉ RESTAURANT WITH ROOMS

tel: 01787 210483 **Further Street, Assington CO10 5LD**
email: restaurant@thecaserestaurantwithrooms.co.uk
web: www.thecaserestaurantwithrooms.co.uk
dir: *Exit A12 at Colchester onto A134 to Sudbury. 7 miles, establishment on left.*

The Case Restaurant with Rooms offers dining in comfortable surroundings, along with luxurious accommodation in bedrooms that all enjoy independent access. Some bathrooms come complete with a corner jacuzzi, while internet access comes as standard. In the restaurant, local produce is used in all dishes and bread and delicious desserts are made fresh every day.

Rooms: 7 en suite (2 fmly) (7 GF) **S** fr £59 **D** fr £79* **Facilities:** FTV Lounge tea/coffee Dinner available WiFi **Extras:** Speciality toiletries – complimentary; snacks – chargeable **Parking:** 25 **Notes:** LB

TOLLARD ROYAL
Wiltshire

Map 4 ST91

King John Inn

★★★★ ◉◉ RESTAURANT WITH ROOMS

tel: 01725 516207 **SP5 5PS**
email: info@kingjohninn.co.uk **web:** www.kingjohninn.co.uk
dir: *From A354 or A350 onto B3081.*

Part of The Epicurean Collection, the King John Inn is a traditional country inn located in a country village. It has a Victorian-style garden pavilion serving seasonal dishes such as chargrilled lobster and pigeon salad. Along with the five bedrooms in the main building, there are three more in The Dove Cottage – all have feature bathrooms. Excellent hospitality and customer care together with good food and wine are real highlights here. Ample parking is provided.

Rooms: 5 en suite 3 annexe en suite (2 GF) **Facilities:** FTV Lounge tea/coffee Dinner available Direct dial WiFi ⚓ **Parking:** 18 **Notes:** LB RS 25 December restaurant closed for dinner

TORQUAY
Devon

Map 3 SX96

Orestone Manor

★★★★ ◉◉ ≋ RESTAURANT WITH ROOMS

tel: 01803 328098 **Rockhouse Lane, Maidencombe TQ1 4SX**
email: info@orestonemanor.com **web:** www.orestonemanor.com
dir: *North of Torquay on A379, on sharp bend in village of Maidencombe.*

Set in a fabulous location overlooking the bay, Orestone Manor has a long history of providing fine food and very comfortable accommodation, coupled with friendly, attentive service. Log fires burn in cooler months, and there is a conservatory, a bar and a sitting room for guests to enjoy. AA Rosettes have been awarded for the uncomplicated modern cuisine which is based on quality local produce.

Rooms: 11 en suite 3 annexe en suite (6 fmly) (3 GF) **S** fr £95 **D** fr £110*
Facilities: STV FTV iPod docking station Lounge tea/coffee Dinner available Direct dial WiFi ⬠ **Extras:** Speciality toiletries, robes, bottled water **Conf:** Max 90 Thtr 45 Class 60 Board 30 **Parking:** 38 **Notes:** LB Closed 3–29 January

ULVERSTON
Cumbria

Map 18 SD27

Virginia House

★★★ ◉◉ RESTAURANT WITH ROOMS

tel: 01229 584844 & 07495 128499 **24 Queen Street LA12 7AF**
email: hello@virginiahouseulverston.co.uk **web:** www.virginiahouseulverston.co.uk
dir: *M6 junction 36 onto A590 towards Barrow-in-Furness. In Ulverston take 3rd exit at Tank Square roundabout and follow one-way system. 1st exit at mini-roundabout into King Street, then Queen Street. 200 metres on right.*

A warm, personal welcome is guaranteed at this family-run property where the restaurant is at the heart of the operation. The award-winning meals, based on very good quality local produce, are served in modern and comfortable surroundings. The gin parlour has a selection of over 100 gins to choose from. The bedrooms are comfortable and well appointed, and complimentary WiFi is available throughout. There is no parking on-site, but there is provision within a short walking distance.

Rooms: 8 en suite **S** fr £59 **D** fr £89* **Facilities:** FTV iPod docking station tea/coffee Dinner available WiFi ⬠ **Extras:** Speciality toiletries, home-made biscuits **Conf:** Max 30 Thtr 30 Class 11 Board 16 **Notes:** No children 18 years

UPPINGHAM
Rutland

Map 11 SP89

The Lake Isle

★★★★ ◉◉ ≋ RESTAURANT WITH ROOMS

tel: 01572 822951 **16 High Street East LE15 9PZ**
email: info@lakeisle.co.uk **web:** www.lakeisle.co.uk
dir: *From A47, turn left at 2nd lights, 100 yards on right.*

This attractive townhouse centres around a delightful restaurant and small elegant bar. There is also an inviting first-floor guest lounge, and the bedrooms are extremely well appointed and thoughtfully equipped; spacious split-level cottage suites situated in a quiet courtyard are also available. The imaginative cooking and an extremely impressive wine list are highlights here.

Rooms: 9 en suite 3 annexe rms (3 pri facs) (1 fmly) (1 GF) **S** fr £70 **D** fr £90*
Facilities: FTV Lounge tea/coffee Dinner available Direct dial WiFi ⬠ **Extras:** Home-made biscuits – complimentary **Conf:** Max 16 Board 16 **Parking:** 7
Notes: Closed 1 January and bank holidays RS Sunday evening and Monday lunch closed

WADDESDON
Buckinghamshire
Map 11 SP71

The Five Arrows

★★★★ ◉◉ ≈ RESTAURANT WITH ROOMS

tel: 01296 651727 High Street HP18 0JE
email: reservations@thefivearrows.co.uk web: www.waddesdon.org.uk/fivearrows
dir: On A41 in Waddesdon. Into Baker Street for car park.

This Grade II listed building with its elaborate Elizabethan-style chimney stacks stands at the gates of Waddesdon Manor and was named after the Rothschild family emblem. The individually styled, en suite bedrooms are comfortable and well appointed. Friendly staff are on hand to offer a warm welcome. Alfresco dining is possible in the warmer months.

Rooms: 8 en suite 8 annexe en suite (2 fmly) (3 GF) Facilities: FTV tea/coffee Dinner available WiFi ✆ Conf: Max 20 Thtr 20 Class 20 Board 20 Parking: 40
Notes: Civ wed 60

WANTAGE
Oxfordshire
Map 5 SU38

La Fontana Restaurant with Accommodation

★★★★ ➾ RESTAURANT WITH ROOMS

tel: 01235 868287 & 07836 730048 Oxford Road, East Hanney OX12 0HP
email: anna@la-fontana.co.uk web: www.la-fontana.co.uk
dir: A338 from Wantage towards Oxford. Restaurant on right in East Hanney.

Guests are guaranteed a warm welcome at this family-run Italian restaurant located on the outskirts of the busy town of Wantage. The stylish bedrooms are individually designed, well equipped and very comfortable. Dinner should not be missed – the menu features a wide range of regional Italian specialities.

Rooms: 12 en suite 3 annexe en suite (1 fmly) (4 GF) S fr £67.50 D fr £87.50*
Facilities: FTV Lounge tea/coffee Dinner available Direct dial WiFi Parking: 30
Notes: Civ wed 120

WEST WITTON
North Yorkshire
Map 19 SE08

The Wensleydale Heifer

★★★★★ ◉ ≈ RESTAURANT WITH ROOMS

tel: 01969 622322 Main Street DL8 4LS
email: info@wensleydaleheifer.co.uk web: www.wensleydaleheifer.co.uk
dir: A1 to Leeming Bar junction, A684 towards Bedale for approximately 10 miles to Leyburn, then towards Hawes 3.5 miles to West Witton.

Describing itself as 'boutique style', this 17th-century former coaching inn is very much of the 21st century. The bedrooms, with Egyptian cotton linen and Molton Brown toiletries as standard, are each designed with an interesting theme – for example, Malt Whisky, Night at the Movies, James Bond and Shooters, and for chocolate lovers, there's a bedroom where you can eat as much chocolate as you like! The food is very much the focus here in both the informal fish bar and the contemporary restaurant. The kitchen prides itself on sourcing the freshest fish and locally reared meats.

Rooms: 9 en suite 4 annexe en suite (2 fmly) (2 GF) S fr £80 D fr £120*
Facilities: FTV DVD Lounge tea/coffee Dinner available Direct dial WiFi
Extras: Speciality toiletries, fruit, snacks Parking: 30 Notes: LB

WHITBY
North Yorkshire
Map 19 NZ81

Estbek House

★★★★ ◉◉ ≈ RESTAURANT WITH ROOMS

tel: 01947 893424 East Row, Sandsend YO21 3SU
email: info@estbekhouse.co.uk web: www.estbekhouse.co.uk
dir: From Whitby take A174. In Sandsend, left into East Row.

The speciality seafood restaurant on the first floor is the focus of this listed building in a small coastal village north-west of Whitby. The seasonal menu is based on fresh, local ingredients, and is overseen by Tim the chef, who has guided his team to two AA Rosettes. There is also a small bar and breakfast room, and four individually appointed bedrooms offering high levels of comfort.

Rooms: 4 rms (3 en suite) (1 pri facs) Facilities: tea/coffee Dinner available WiFi
Parking: 6 Notes: LB No children 14 years

WILMINGTON
East Sussex
Map 6 TQ50

Crossways

★★★★ ◉◉ RESTAURANT WITH ROOMS

tel: 01323 482455 Lewes Road BN26 5SG
email: stay@crosswayshotel.co.uk web: www.crosswayshotel.co.uk
dir: On A27 between Lewes and Polegate, 2 miles east of Alfriston roundabout.

Proprietors David Stott and Clive James have been welcoming guests to this elegant restaurant with rooms for nearly 30 years. Crossways sits amid stunning gardens and attractively tended grounds. The well-presented bedrooms are tastefully decorated and provide an abundance of thoughtful amenities including free WiFi. Guest comfort is paramount and the warm hospitality ensures guests often return.

Rooms: 7 en suite S fr £85 D fr £150* Facilities: FTV tea/coffee Dinner available Direct dial WiFi ✆ Extras: Speciality toiletries, mini-bar, fresh milk Parking: 30
Notes: LB No children 12 years Closed 24 December to 23 January

WIMBORNE MINSTER
Dorset
Map 5 SZ09

Les Bouviers Restaurant with Rooms

★★★★★ ◉◉ RESTAURANT WITH ROOMS

tel: 01202 889555 Arrowsmith Road, Canford Magna BH21 3BD
email: info@lesbouviers.co.uk web: www.lesbouviers.co.uk
dir: A31 onto A349. Left in 0.6 mile. In approximately 1 mile right into Arrowsmith Road. Establishment approximately 100 yards on right.

Les Bouviers is an excellent restaurant with rooms in a great location, set in five and a half acres of grounds. Food is obviously a highlight of any stay here, as is the friendly, attentive service. Chef patron Leonard James Coward and his team turn out impressive cooking, which has been recognised with two AA Rosettes. The bedrooms are extremely well equipped, and the beds are supremely comfortable. Cream teas can be taken on the terrace.

Rooms: 6 en suite (4 fmly) S fr £70 D fr £80* Facilities: FTV DVD Lounge tea/coffee Dinner available Direct dial WiFi All bathrooms have steam showers or air baths
Extras: Robes, slippers, mineral water Conf: Max 120 Thtr 100 Class 100 Board 100
Parking: 50 Notes: LB RS Sunday evening restricted opening and restaurant closed Civ wed 120

WINCHCOMBE
Gloucestershire

Map 10 SP02

Wesley House

★★★★ ◉◉ ⌒ RESTAURANT WITH ROOMS

tel: 01242 602366 **High Street GL54 5LJ**
email: enquiries@wesleyhouse.co.uk **web:** www.wesleyhouse.co.uk
dir: *In town centre.*

This 15th-century, half-timbered property is named after John Wesley, founder of the Methodist Church, who stayed here while preaching in the town. Bedrooms are small and full of character. In the rear dining room, where the food has been awarded two AA Rosettes, a unique lighting system changes colour to suit the mood required, and also highlights the various floral displays created by a world-renowned flower arranger. A glass atrium covers the outside terrace.

Rooms: 5 en suite **S** fr £75 **D** fr £95* **Facilities:** FTV Lounge tea/coffee Dinner available WiFi ⚓ **Notes:** RS Sunday evening to Monday restaurant closed Civ wed 60

WINGHAM
Kent

Map 7 TR25

The Dog at Wingham

★★★★ ◉ RESTAURANT WITH ROOMS

tel: 01227 720339 **Canterbury Road CT3 1BB**
email: marc@thedog.co.uk **web:** www.thedog.co.uk
dir: *On A257, in village of Wingham.*

Located in the village of Wingham, The Dog has undergone a complete make-over – the public areas retain plenty of original character along with stylish new furnishings. Bedrooms and en suite shower rooms are also of high quality throughout with modern designer-decor, Hypnos beds and WiFi. Breakfast, lunch and dinner are served downstairs in the airy, wood-panelled restaurant; the award-winning menus are based on seasonal British ingredients.

Rooms: 8 en suite (1 fmly) (1 GF) **S** fr £60 **D** fr £90* **Facilities:** Lounge tea/coffee Dinner available WiFi ⚓ **Parking:** 13 **Notes:** LB Civ wed 60

WINTERINGHAM
Lincolnshire

Map 17 SE92

INSPECTOR'S CHOICE

Winteringham Fields

★★★★★ ◉◉◉◉ RESTAURANT WITH ROOMS

tel: 01724 733096 **1 Silver Street DN15 9ND**
email: reception@winteringhamfields.co.uk **web:** www.winteringhamfields.co.uk
dir: *In village centre at crossroads.*

This highly regarded restaurant with rooms, located deep in the countryside in Winteringham village, is six miles west of the Humber Bridge. Public rooms and bedrooms, some of which are housed in renovated barns and cottages, are delightfully luxurious. There is an abundance of charm, and period features are combined with rich furnishings and fabrics. The award-winning food is a highlight of any stay and guests can expect highly skilled dishes, excellent quality and stunning presentation.

Rooms: 4 en suite 11 annexe en suite (6 fmly) (3 GF) **Facilities:** iPod docking station tea/coffee Dinner available Direct dial WiFi ⚓ **Conf:** Max 50 Thtr 50 Class 50 Board 50 **Parking:** 14 **Notes:** LB Closed 25 December for 2 weeks, last week October, 2 weeks August Civ wed 60

WYE
Kent

Map 7 TR04

Wife of Bath

★★★★ ◉◉ RESTAURANT WITH ROOMS

tel: 01233 812232 **4 Upper Bridge Street TN25 5AF**
email: info@thewifeofbath.com **web:** www.thewifeofbath.com
dir: *M20 junction 10, A2070 signed Kennington. At roundabout right onto A28 (Canterbury Road). Right at crossroads into Harville Road signed Wye. At T-junction (station opposite) right into Bridge Road, becomes Churchfield Way. Right into Church Street. At T-junction left, Wife of Bath on right.*

Located in the heart of this picturesque village of Wye, the Wife of Bath offers stylish en suite bedrooms that are very comfortably appointed and still show original features including exposed oak beams. All have Egyptian cotton bedding, TVs, free WiFi, Nespresso machines and complimentary toiletries. The restaurant is open daily for breakfast, lunch and dinner. Menus are influenced by northern Spanish cuisine to create vibrant, award-winning dishes.

Rooms: 3 en suite 3 annexe en suite (3 GF) **S** fr £105 **D** fr £105* **Facilities:** FTV tea/coffee Dinner available WiFi **Extras:** Fruit, snacks, robes **Parking:** 10

YAXLEY
Suffolk

Map 13 TM17

The Auberge

★★★★★ ◉◉ ⌒ RESTAURANT WITH ROOMS

tel: 01379 783604 **Ipswich Road IP23 8BZ**
email: aubmail@the-auberge.co.uk **web:** www.the-auberge.co.uk
dir: *On A140 between Norwich and Ipswich at crossroads with B1117.*

A warm welcome awaits at The Auberge, a charming 15th-century property, which was once a rural pub but is now a smart restaurant with rooms. The restaurant has gained two AA Rosettes for the good use of fresh, quality produce in well-crafted dishes. The public areas have a wealth of character, such as exposed brickwork and beams, and the grounds are particularly well kept and attractive. The spacious bedrooms are tastefully appointed and have many thoughtful touches; one bedroom has a four-poster.

Rooms: 11 annexe en suite (2 fmly) (6 GF) **Facilities:** FTV tea/coffee Dinner available Direct dial WiFi ⚓ **Conf:** Max 30 Thtr 30 Class 20 Board 12 **Parking:** 40 **Notes:** LB

YEOVIL
Somerset

Map 4 ST51

INSPECTOR'S CHOICE

Little Barwick House

★★★★★ ◉◉◉ ⌒ RESTAURANT WITH ROOMS

tel: 01935 423902 **Barwick BA22 9TD**
email: info@littlebarwick.co.uk **web:** www.littlebarwickhouse.co.uk
dir: *From Yeovil A37 towards Dorchester, left at 1st roundabout, 1st left, 0.25 mile on left.*

Situated in a quiet hamlet in three and half acres of gardens and grounds, this listed Georgian dower house is an ideal retreat for those seeking peaceful surroundings and good food. Just one of the highlights of a stay here is a meal in the restaurant, where good use is made of local ingredients. Each of the bedrooms has its own character, and a range of thoughtful extras such as fresh flowers, bottled water and magazines is provided.

Rooms: 6 en suite **Facilities:** FTV iPod docking station tea/coffee Dinner available Direct dial WiFi ⚓ **Parking:** 30 **Notes:** LB No children 5 years RS Sunday evening and Monday closed

SCOTLAND

ABERFELDY
Perth & Kinross
Map 23 NN84

Errichel House

★★★★ ◉◉ 🛏 RESTAURANT WITH ROOMS

tel: 01887 829562 & 07921 507458 Errichel Farm, Crieff Road PH15 2EL
email: paulnewman@errichel.co.uk web: www.errichel.co.uk
dir: 2 miles from Aberfeldy on Crieff Road (A826).

The accommodation on this family-run working farm occupies a stunning location in an elevated location above Aberfeldy, with breathtaking views of the Perthshire hills. The beautiful grounds, with a duck pond, are home to an array of wildlife. Bedrooms and public areas are luxuriously presented and deeply comfortable. A stay here is not complete without sampling the food on offer at the restaurant 'Thyme at Errichel' or taking home some of the many home-made delicacies from their 'Thyme to Eat' shop. In fact, all the lamb, beef and pork sold here comes from the farm itself.

Rooms: 4 en suite (1 fmly) D fr £129* Facilities: FTV iPod docking station Lounge tea/coffee Dinner available WiFi 🐾 Conf: Max 40 Thtr 40 Class 16 Board 20 Parking: 12 Notes: LB Closed 23–26 December RS 12 January to 1 March restaurant open Thursday to Friday and Saturday evening Civ wed 120

ABERLADY
East Lothian
Map 21 NT47

Ducks Inn

★★★★ ◉◉ RESTAURANT WITH ROOMS

tel: 01875 870682 Main Street EH32 0RE
email: info@ducks.co.uk web: www.ducks.co.uk
dir: A1 (Bankton junction) take 1st exit to North Berwick. At next roundabout 3rd exit onto A198 signed Longniddry, left towards Aberlady. At T-junction, facing river, right to Aberlady.

The name of this restaurant with rooms is referenced around the building – Ducks Restaurant for award-winning cuisine, Donald's Bistro and the Ducklings informal coffee shop. The warm and welcoming public areas include a great bar, full of collected objets d'art, offering real ales, a range of malt whiskies and Cuban cigars kept in a large humidor. The comfortable bedrooms are well appointed and have stylish en suites. The team are informal and friendly, taking the time to chat to their guests.

Rooms: 23 en suite (1 fmly) (6 GF) S fr £85 D fr £110* Facilities: STV FTV Lounge TVL tea/coffee Dinner available Direct dial WiFi 🐾 Conf: Max 100 Thtr 100 Class 60 Board 30 Parking: 15

ACHARACLE
Highland
Map 22 NM66

Mingarry Park

★★★★ ◉◉ RESTAURANT WITH ROOMS

tel: 01967 431202 & 07791 115467 Mingarry PH36 4JX
email: info@mingarryparkhouse.co.uk web: www.mingarryparkhouse.co.uk
dir: From Fort William at roundabout take A82 (Inverness road). At Lochy Bridge junction left onto A830 (Mallaig Road). 26 miles to Lochailort. Left onto A861 (Acharacle/Salen Road). 16 miles to Mingarry. Mingarry Park 1st on left, pass village hall, follow signs.

Set in breathtaking scenery, Mingarry Park offers individually designed, contemporary bedrooms; each has great views across the deer park and surrounding countryside. Some rooms have balconies and decked areas for

relaxation. Diners are treated to the best local produce in creative dishes, with a roaring log-burner as the centrepiece of the restaurant. Afternoon tea is served every other Sunday.

Rooms: 6 en suite (3 GF) Facilities: FTV iPod docking station tea/coffee Dinner available WiFi 🐾 Notes: Closed February to March

ANSTRUTHER
Fife
Map 21 NO50

The Waterfront

★★★★ 🍽 RESTAURANT WITH ROOMS

tel: 01333 312200 18–20 Shore Street KY10 3EA
email: info@anstruther-waterfront.co.uk web: www.anstruther-waterfront.co.uk
dir: Off A917, opposite marina.

Situated overlooking the harbour, The Waterfront offers spacious, stylish, contemporary accommodation, with bedrooms located in lovingly restored buildings in a courtyard behind the restaurant. There is a comfortable lounge with a smartly fitted kitchen and dining room, and laundry facilities are available in the granary. Dinner and breakfast are served in the attractive restaurant that offers a comprehensive menu featuring the best local produce.

Rooms: 10 en suite (3 fmly) (2 GF) Facilities: FTV DVD Lounge tea/coffee Dinner available WiFi 🐾 Extras: Mineral water Notes: LB

COLBOST
Isle of Skye
Map 22 NG24

INSPECTOR'S CHOICE

The Three Chimneys & The House Over-By

★★★★★ ◉◉◉ 🛏 RESTAURANT WITH ROOMS

tel: 01470 511258 IV55 8ZT
email: eatandstay@threechimneys.co.uk web: www.threechimneys.co.uk
dir: 4 miles west of Dunvegan village on B884 signed Glendale.

A visit to this delightful property will make a trip to Skye even more memorable. The stunning food is the result of a deft approach using quality local ingredients. Breakfast is an impressive array of local fish, meats and cheeses, served with fresh home baking and home-made preserves. The stylish lounge-breakfast area has the real wow factor. Bedrooms, in the House Over-By, are creative and thoughtfully equipped – all have spacious en suites, wonderful views across Loch Dunvegan and direct access to the garden which leads down to the sea. Five of the six rooms are split level; the other is on one level and has a walk-in shower.

Rooms: (1 family) (6 GF) Facilities: FTV WiFi Bookings can be made for leisure activities Conf: Class 12 Board 12 Theatre 12 Notes: Closed 10 December to 19 January

EDDLESTON
Scottish Borders
Map 21 NT24

The Horseshoe Restaurant with Rooms

★★★★ ⚜ RESTAURANT WITH ROOMS

tel: 01721 730225 **Edinburgh Road EH45 8QP**
email: reservations@horseshoeinn.co.uk **web:** www.horseshoeinn.co.uk
dir: *A703, 5 miles north of Peebles.*

The Horseshoe is five miles north of Peebles and only 18 miles south of Edinburgh. Originally a blacksmith's shop, it has a very good reputation for its delightful atmosphere and excellent cuisine. There are eight luxuriously appointed and individually designed bedrooms. Please note: children are welcome, but dinner is not served to under fives except in the private dining room.

Rooms: 8 en suite (1 fmly) (6 GF) **Facilities:** FTV Lounge tea/coffee Dinner available Direct dial WiFi **Extras:** Speciality toiletries, fruit, mineral water – complimentary **Parking:** 20 **Notes:** LB Closed 25 December, 1st 2 weeks January and 2 weeks July RS Monday and Tuesday closed

EDINBURGH
Map 21 NT27

21212

★★★★★ ⚜⚜⚜⚜ RESTAURANT WITH ROOMS

tel: 0131 523 1030 **3 Royal Terrace EH7 5AB**
email: reservations@21212restaurant.co.uk **web:** www.21212restaurant.co.uk
dir: *Calton Hill, city centre.*

A real jewel in Edinburgh's crown, this establishment takes its name from the number of choices at each course on the five-course dinner menu. Located on the prestigious Royal Terrace, this light and airy, renovated Georgian townhouse stretches over four floors. The four individually-designed bedrooms epitomise luxury living and the bathrooms certainly have the wow factor. At the heart of this restaurant with rooms is the creative and impressive four AA Rosette award-winning cooking of Paul Kitching. Service throughout is friendly and very attentive.

Rooms: 4 en suite **S** fr £150 **D** fr £150 **Facilities:** STV FTV iPod docking station Lounge Dinner available WiFi **Extras:** Speciality toiletries, mineral water, sloe gin **Notes:** No children 5 years Closed 1 week January, 1 week Autumn RS Sunday to Monday restaurant closed

The Witchery by the Castle

★★★★★ ⚜ RESTAURANT WITH ROOMS

tel: 0131 225 5613 **Castlehill, The Royal Mile EH1 2NF**
email: mail@thewitchery.com **web:** www.thewitchery.com
dir: *Top of Royal Mile at gates of Edinburgh Castle.*

Originally built in 1595, The Witchery by the Castle is situated in a historic building at the gates of Edinburgh Castle. The two luxurious and theatrically decorated suites, known as the Inner Sanctum and the Old Rectory, are located above the restaurant and are reached via a winding stone staircase. Filled with antiques, opulently draped beds, large roll-top baths and a plethora of memorabilia, this ancient and exciting establishment is often described as one of the country's most romantic destinations.

Rooms: 4 en suite 5 annexe en suite (1 GF) **Facilities:** STV FTV DVD tea/coffee Dinner available Direct dial WiFi **Extras:** Bottled water – complimentary **Notes:** No children 12 years Closed 25–26 December

FORRES
Moray
Map 23 NJ0

Cluny Bank

★★★★ ⚜ RESTAURANT WITH ROOMS

tel: 01309 674304 **69 St Leonards Road IV36 1DW**
email: info@clunybankhotel.co.uk **web:** www.clunybankhotel.co.uk

Historic, listed Cluny Bank occupies a quiet location within walking distance of the centre of Forres, and is an ideal base for exploring the north-east of Scotland. Family-run, the building retains many original architectural features. Public areas include the Altyre Bar with a wide range of whiskies, and Franklin's Restaurant where a real taste of Moray can be experienced. Room service, complimentary WiFi and memorable breakfasts are also provided for guests.

Rooms: 6 en suite 1 annexe en suite (2 GF) **S** fr £85 **D** fr £122.50* **Facilities:** FTV iPod docking station Lounge tea/coffee Dinner available Direct dial WiFi **Parking:** 7 **Notes:** LB

INVERKEILOR
Angus
Map 23 NO64

Gordon's

★★★★★ ⚜⚜⚜ RESTAURANT WITH ROOMS

tel: 01241 830364 **Main Road DD11 5RN**
email: gordonsrest@aol.com **web:** www.gordonsrestaurant.co.uk
dir: *Exit A92 between Arbroath and Montrose into Inverkeilor.*

It's worth a detour off the main road to this family-run restaurant with rooms set in the centre of the village. The food in the restaurant has been awarded three AA Rosettes, and the excellent breakfasts are equally memorable. A huge fire dominates the restaurant on cooler evenings. Individually designed rooms all come with contemporary Wenge furniture, oversized headboards, chandeliers, decorative cornicing and designer wallpaper. The showcase Thistle Suite is in purple, stone and lavender and has an en suite bathroom with roll-top bath and monsoon shower.

Rooms: 4 en suite 1 annexe en suite (1 GF) **S** fr £110 **D** fr £110* **Facilities:** tea/coffee Dinner available WiFi ⚜ **Extras:** Speciality toiletries – complimentary **Parking:** 6 **Notes:** No children 12 years Closed January

KINGUSSIE
Highland   Map 23 NH70

INSPECTOR'S CHOICE

The Cross
★★★★ ◉◉◉ ⬥ RESTAURANT WITH ROOMS

tel: 01540 661166 **Tweed Mill Brae, Ardbroilach Road PH21 1LB**
email: relax@thecross.co.uk **web:** www.thecross.co.uk
dir: *From lights in Kingussie centre take Ardbroilach Road, 300 yards left into Tweed Mill Brae.*

Built as a water-powered tweed mill in the late 19th century, The Cross is situated in the picturesque Cairngorms National Park and surrounded by four acres of riverside grounds that teem with an abundance of wildlife, including red squirrels. Comfortable lounges and a selection of well-appointed bedrooms are offered, and award-winning dinners are served by an open fire in the stone-walled and wood-beamed restaurant.

Rooms: 8 en suite **S** fr £90 **D** fr £100* **Facilities:** FTV DVD Lounge tea/coffee Dinner available Direct dial WiFi Riding ⬥ **Extras:** Bottled water, speciality toiletries **Conf:** Max 20 Thtr 20 Class 20 Board 20 **Parking:** 20 **Notes:** LB Closed January and Christmas

LOCHGOILHEAD
Argyll & Bute   Map 20 NN10

The Lodge on Loch Goil
★★★★★ ◉◉ ⬥ RESTAURANT WITH ROOMS

tel: 01301 703193 **Loch Goil PA24 8AE**
email: dining@thelodge-scotland.com **web:** www.thelodge-scotland.com
dir: *Phone for directions.*

Very accessible from nearby main routes (and by boat), though tucked away near the head of a sea loch, this peaceful retreat is now a restaurant with rooms. The lodge is superbly appointed, and its restoration has been a labour of love for the current owners. In addition to the seven luxury rooms in the main house, there's the summerhouse right on the loch's edge from where guests can also relax and enjoy the spectacular scenery. Food is taken seriously here, with imaginative, award-winning cuisine served at dinner plus superb breakfasts each morning. Hospitality is generously given, ensuring the warmest of Scottish welcomes.

Rooms: 7 en suite **S** fr £225 **D** fr £250* **Facilities:** Dinner available

NEWPORT-ON-TAY
Fife   Map 21 NO42

The Newport Restaurant
★★★★ ◉◉ RESTAURANT WITH ROOMS

tel: 01382 541449 **1 High Street DD6 8AB**
email: info@thenewportrestaurant.co.uk **web:** www.thenewportrestaurant.co.uk
dir: *Phone for directions.*

Jamie Scott's restaurant with rooms is situated on the shore in Newport looking out over the Tay to Dundee. The style here is modern with a nod to the local maritime and fishing history. The modern restaurant is set over two floors, both enjoying panoramic views. The four bedrooms are spacious and well equipped with comfortable beds and added luxuries.

Rooms: 4 en suite (2 fmly) **Facilities:** FTV iPod docking station Dinner available WiFi **Parking:** 10 **Notes:** Closed 24 December to 9 January

PEAT INN
Fife   Map 21 NO40

INSPECTOR'S CHOICE

The Peat Inn
★★★★★ ◉◉◉ RESTAURANT WITH ROOMS

tel: 01334 840206 **KY15 5LH**
email: stay@thepeatinn.co.uk **web:** www.thepeatinn.co.uk
dir: *At junction of B940 and B941, 5 miles southwest of St Andrews.*

This 300-year-old former coaching inn enjoys a rural location and is close to St Andrews. The Peat Inn is spacious, very well appointed, and offers rooms that all have lounge areas. The inn is steeped in history and for years has proved a real haven for food lovers – the three dining areas create a romantic setting, and chef/owner Geoffrey Smeddle produces excellent, award-winning dishes (please note, no children under 7 years at dinner). Expect welcoming open fires and a relaxed ambiance. An extensive continental breakfast selection is served to guests in their bedrooms each morning.

Rooms: 8 annexe en suite (3 fmly) (8 GF) **S** fr £205 **D** fr £225* **Facilities:** FTV Lounge tea/coffee Dinner available Direct dial WiFi ⬥ **Extras:** Speciality toiletries, home-made brownies, fruit, sherry – complimentary **Parking:** 24 **Notes:** LB Closed 25–26 December, 2 weeks January RS Sunday to Monday closed

PORTPATRICK
Dumfries & Galloway   Map 20 NW95

INSPECTOR'S CHOICE

Knockinaam Lodge
★★★★★ ◉◉◉ RESTAURANT WITH ROOMS

tel: 01776 810471 **DG9 9AD**
email: reservations@knockinaamlodge.com **web:** www.knockinaamlodge.com
dir: *From A77 or A75 follow signs to Portpatrick. Through Lochans. After 2 miles left at signs for lodge.*

Any tour of Dumfries & Galloway wouldn't be complete without a stay at this haven of tranquillity and relaxation. Knockinaam Lodge is an extended Victorian house set in an idyllic cove with its own pebble beach (ideal for a private swim in the summer) and sheltered by majestic cliffs and woodlands. Surrounded by 30 acres of delightful grounds, the lodge was the location for a meeting between Churchill and General Eisenhower in World War II. Today, a warm welcome is assured from the proprietors and their committed team, and much emphasis is placed on providing a sophisticated but intimate home-from-home experience. There are just 10 suites – each individually designed and all with TVs with DVD players, luxury toiletries and complimentary bottled water. The cooking is a real treat and showcases prime Scottish produce on the daily-changing, four-course set menus; guests can always discuss the choices in advance if they wish.

Rooms: 10 en suite (1 fmly) **Facilities:** Dinner available ⬥ Fishing Shooting, walking, sea fishing, clay pigeon shooting **Notes:** Civ wed 40

SANQUHAR
Dumfries & Galloway

Map 21 NS70

Blackaddie House

★★★★ @@@ RESTAURANT WITH ROOMS

tel: 01659 50270 **Blackaddie Road DG4 6JJ**
email: ian@blackaddiehotel.co.uk **web:** www.blackaddiehotel.co.uk
dir: *300 yards from A76 on north side of Sanquhar.*

Overlooking the River Nith, in two acres of secluded gardens, this family-run country house offers friendly and attentive hands-on service. The bedrooms and suites, including family accommodation, are all well presented and comfortable, with many useful extras provided as standard. The award-winning food, served in the restaurant, with its lovely garden views, is based on prime Scottish ingredients.

Rooms: 6 en suite 1 annexe en suite (1 GF) **Facilities:** FTV DVD Lounge tea/coffee Dinner available Direct dial WiFi ⚓ Chef for a Day experience **Extras:** Speciality toiletries, mineral water, home-made shortbread, home-made scottish tablet, robes, slippers **Conf:** Max 16 Thtr 16 Class 16 Board 12 **Parking:** 20 **Notes:** LB Civ wed 25

SPEAN BRIDGE
Highland

Map 22 NN28

Smiddy House

★★★★★ @@ RESTAURANT WITH ROOMS

tel: 01397 712335 **Roy Bridge Road PH34 4EU**
email: enquiry@smiddyhouse.com **web:** www.smiddyhouse.com
dir: *In village centre, A82 onto A86.*

Set in the Great Glen which stretches from Fort William to Inverness, this was once the village smithy and is now a very friendly restaurant with rooms. The attractive bedrooms, named after places in Scotland, are comfortably furnished and well equipped. A relaxing garden room is available for guests' use. Delicious evening meals are served in the award-winning Russell's restaurant.

Rooms: 4 en suite 1 annexe en suite (1 GF) **D** fr £120* **Facilities:** FTV Lounge tea/coffee Dinner available WiFi **Extras:** Speciality toiletries – complimentary **Parking:** 15 **Notes:** No children 12 years Closed Monday RS November to March limited opening

STRUAN
Isle of Skye

Map 22 NG33

INSPECTOR'S CHOICE

Ullinish Country Lodge

★★★★★ @@@ RESTAURANT WITH ROOMS

tel: 01470 572214 **IV56 8FD**
email: ullinish@theisleofskye.co.uk **web:** www.theisleofskye.co.uk
dir: *From Skye bridge take A87 north, then left onto A863. Lodge signed after Struan on left.*

Set in some of Scotland's most dramatic landscape, with views of the Black Cuillin and MacLeod's Tables, this lodge has lochs on three sides. Samuel Johnson and James Boswell stayed here in 1773 and were impressed with the hospitality even then – hosts, Brian and Pam hope to extend the same welcome to their guests today. As you would expect, all bedrooms have amazing views; each room has a half-tester bed and some of the en suites have roll-top baths. Modern, award-winning Scottish dishes are created with skill and precision and served in the candlelit dining room. Free WiFi is available.

Rooms: 6 en suite **S** fr £125 **D** fr £190* **Facilities:** FTV Lounge tea/coffee Dinner available WiFi **Extras:** Sherry, sweets, mineral water – complimentary **Parking:** 8 **Notes:** LB No children 16 years Closed 24 December to January

TOBERMORY
Isle of Mull

Map 22 NM55

Highland Cottage

★★★★★ @@ RESTAURANT WITH ROOMS

tel: 01688 302030 **24 Breadalbane Street PA75 6PD**
email: davidandjo@highlandcottage.co.uk **web:** www.highlandcottage.co.uk
dir: *From A848 at Craignure/Fishnish ferry terminal, pass Tobermory signs, straight on at mini roundabout, across narrow bridge, turn right. On right opposite fire station.*

Providing the highest level of natural and unassuming hospitality, this delightful little gem lies high above the island's capital. Don't be fooled by its side street location, a stunning view over the bay is just a few metres away. 'A country house in town', it is an Aladdin's Cave of collectables and treasures, as well as masses of books and magazines. There are two inviting lounges, one with an honesty bar. The cosy dining room offers memorable dinners and splendid breakfasts. Bedrooms are individual in design; some have four-posters and all are comprehensively equipped including TVs and music centres.

Rooms: 6 en suite (1 GF) **D** fr £145* **Facilities:** FTV Lounge tea/coffee Dinner available Direct dial WiFi ⚓ **Extras:** Speciality toiletries, fruit, phone/tablet charger **Notes:** No children 10 years Closed November to March

WALKERBURN
Scottish Borders

Map 21 NT33

Windlestraw

★★★★★ @@ RESTAURANT WITH ROOMS

tel: 01896 870636 **Galashiels Road EH43 6AA**
email: stay@windlestraw.co.uk **web:** www.windlestraw.co.uk
dir: *East of Innerleithen on A72. On left, just before leaving the village.*

The present owners are breathing fresh life into this beautiful Edwardian manor situated in two-acre grounds in the rolling hills. It's in a peaceful location yet Edinburgh is easily accessible. The house was built in 1906 for the wife of a Scottish cashmere mill owner and many detailed architectural features remain. The smart, spacious bedrooms come with Egyptian cotton bed linen, TVs and WiFi. Expect a warm welcome and relaxed atmosphere together with superb Scottish cooking at breakfast and in the evening (please note, no children under 11 years at dinner).

Rooms: 6 en suite **S** fr £175 **D** fr £200* **Facilities:** FTV Lounge tea/coffee Dinner available Direct dial WiFi ⚓ **Extras:** Speciality toiletries **Parking:** 10 **Notes:** LB Closed 20 December to 10 February Civ wed 25

WALES

ABERGELE
Conwy

Map 14 SH97

The Kinmel Arms

★★★★★ ◉◉ RESTAURANT WITH ROOMS

tel: 01745 832207 **The Village, St George LL22 9BP**
email: info@thekinmelarms.co.uk **web:** www.thekinmelarms.co.uk
dir: *From A55 junction 24a to St George. East on A55, junction 24. 1st left to Rhuddlan, 1st right into St George. 2nd right.*

This converted 17th-century coaching inn stands close to the church in the village of St George. The restaurant specialises in skilfully prepared produce from Wales and north-west England. Friendly, helpful staff will ensure you have a relaxing stay. The four attractive suites are kitted out with small kitchenettes where continental breakfasts are placed each day to enjoy at your leisure. Each suite is individually designed in a natural style with luxurious bathrooms to match.

Rooms: 4 en suite (2 GF) **S** fr £115 **D** fr £135 **Facilities:** STV Lounge tea/coffee Dinner available ⚸ ♨ **Extras:** Speciality toiletries, fruit, snacks, bottled water – complimentary **Conf:** Max 12 Board 12 **Parking:** 50 **Notes:** LB No children 16 years Closed 25 December and 1 January RS Monday closed (excluding bank holidays)

BRECON
Powys

Map 9 SO02

Peterstone Court

★★★★★ ◉ ⌂ RESTAURANT WITH ROOMS

tel: 01874 665387 **Llanhamlach LD3 7YB**
email: info@peterstone-court.com **web:** www.peterstone-court.com
dir: *3 miles from Brecon on A40 towards Abergavenny.*

Situated on the edge of the Brecon Beacons, this establishment affords stunning views overlooking the River Usk. The atmosphere is friendly and informal, with no unnecessary fuss. No two bedrooms are alike, but all share comparable levels of comfort, quality and elegance. Public areas reflect similar standards, eclectically styled with a blend of the contemporary and the traditional. Quality produce is cooked with care in a range of enjoyable dishes.

Rooms: 8 en suite 4 annexe en suite (2 fmly) **Facilities:** FTV DVD iPod docking station Lounge tea/coffee Dinner available Direct dial WiFi ⚸ Fishing Riding Sauna Gym ♨ Pool open mid April to 1 October, spa facilities **Conf:** Max 100 Thtr 100 Class 100 Board 60 **Parking:** 60 **Notes:** LB Civ wed

EGLWYS FACH
Ceredigion

Map 14 SN69

Ynyshir

★★★★★ ◉◉◉◉ RESTAURANT WITH ROOMS

tel: 01654 781209 **SY20 8TA**
email: info@ynyshir.co.uk **web:** www.ynyshir.co.uk
dir: *Exit A487, 5.5 miles south of Machynlleth, signed from main road.*

Set in beautifully landscaped grounds and surrounded by the RSPB Ynys-hir Nature Reserve, Ynyshir is a haven of calm. The house was once owned by Queen Victoria and is surrounded by mountain scenery. Lavishly styled bedrooms, each individually themed around a great painter, provide high standards of luxury and comfort. The lounge and bar, adorned with an abundance of fresh flowers, have different moods. The dining room offers highly accomplished cooking using the best, locally sourced ingredients including herbs, soft fruit and vegetables from the hotel's own kitchen garden, and wild foods gathered nearby. This restaurant with rooms makes an idyllic location for weddings.

Rooms: 7 en suite 3 annexe en suite (4 GF) **S** fr £130 **D** fr £150* **Facilities:** FTV DVD Lounge tea/coffee Dinner available Direct dial WiFi ♨ RSPB Bird Reserve **Extras:** Speciality toiletries, bottled water **Parking:** 15 **Notes:** Closed 6 weeks in year, Sunday, Monday and Tuesday Civ wed 40

HAVERFORDWEST
Pembrokeshire

Map 8 SM91

Slebech Park Estate

★★★★★ ◉◉ ⌂ RESTAURANT WITH ROOMS

tel: 01437 752000 & 752002 **SA62 4AX**
email: enquiries@slebech.co.uk **web:** www.slebech.co.uk
dir: *East of Haverfordwest on A40, take exit signed Picton Castle.*

A delightful and peaceful retreat located on the shores of Dau Gleddau Estuary – one of Europe's largest natural harbours. The estate covers 650 acres, with an array of walks leading from the door through meadows and woodlands and by the river. Guests are ensured a warm welcome and excellent service throughout their stay. Bedrooms come in a range of shapes and sizes – all have quality fittings, organic toiletries and deeply-comfortable beds with Egyptian cotton sheets. Both the award-winning dinner and breakfast are served in a separate restaurant – the range of carefully prepared dishes makes good use of top quality, local produce; lunch and afternoon tea are also available. Dogs are welcome here too.

Rooms: 19 en suite (5 fmly) (7 GF) **S** fr £75 **D** fr £85* **Facilities:** STV FTV Lounge tea/coffee Dinner available Direct dial WiFi ⚸ ⚸ ⚸ Fishing ♨ Shooting **Extras:** Speciality toiletries, home-made cakes **Conf:** Max 200 Thtr 200 Class 180 Board 160 **Parking:** 60 **Notes:** LB Civ wed 120

LLANDUDNO	Map 14 SH78
Conwy	

The Lilly Restaurant with Rooms

★★★★ ◉ ≘ RESTAURANT WITH ROOMS

tel: 01492 876513 **West Parade, West Shore LL30 2BD**
email: thelilly@live.co.uk **web:** www.thelilly.co.uk
dir: *Phone for detailed directions.*

Located on the seafront on the West Shore with views over the Great Orme, this establishment has good facilities and bedrooms that offer high standards of comfort. Children are very welcome here, and a relaxed atmosphere is found in Madhatter's Brasserie which takes its name from Lewis Carroll's *Alice in Wonderland* – part of the book may have been written while the author was staying on the West Shore. The Lilly also has a fine-dining restaurant.

Rooms: 5 en suite **Facilities:** FTV iPod docking station Lounge tea/coffee Dinner available Direct dial WiFi **Extras:** Speciality toiletries **Conf:** Max 35 Thtr 25 Board 20 **Notes:** LB

LLANSTEFFAN	Map 8 SN31
Carmarthenshire	

Mansion House Llansteffan

★★★★ ◉◉ RESTAURANT WITH ROOMS

tel: 01267 241515 & 07768 194539 **Pantyrathro SA33 5AJ**
email: info@mansionhousellansteffan.co.uk **web:** www.mansionhousellansteffan.co.uk
dir: *From Carmarthen on B4312 towards Llansteffan, follow brown signs.*

Mansion House has been lovingly restored by the current owners, and is set in five acres of grounds with enviable views over the Towy Estuary and Carmarthen Bay. While bedrooms differ in size and style, all are well-equipped and complemented by smart bathrooms. With a wealth of quality produce right on the doorstep it's not surprising that the head chef focuses on using seasonal, local and home-grown produce on the constantly changing, interesting menu. Pre-dinner drinks can be taken in the bar, where there is an excellent range of gins.

Rooms: 8 en suite (1 fmly) (2 GF) **S** fr £110 **D** fr £120* **Facilities:** FTV Lounge tea/coffee Dinner available Direct dial WiFi ⅃ ⌘ **Extras:** Speciality toiletries, robes, home-made cookies **Conf:** Max 200 Thtr 150 Class 80 Board 40 **Parking:** 50 **Notes:** LB Civ wed 120

LLANWRTYD WELLS	Map 9 SN84
Powys	

Lasswade Country House

★★★★ ◉◉ RESTAURANT WITH ROOMS

tel: 01591 610515 **Station Road LD5 4RW**
email: info@lasswadehotel.co.uk **web:** www.lasswadehotel.co.uk
dir: *Exit A483 into Irfon Terrace, right into Station Road, 350 yards on right.*

This friendly establishment on the edge of the town has impressive views over the countryside. Bedrooms are comfortably furnished and well equipped, while the public areas consist of a tastefully decorated lounge, an elegant restaurant with a bar, and an airy conservatory which looks towards the neighbouring hills. The kitchen makes good use of fresh, local produce to provide an enjoyable, award-winning dining experience.

Rooms: 8 en suite (1 fmly) **D** fr £90* **Facilities:** FTV Lounge TVL tea/coffee Dinner available WiFi ⌘ **Conf:** Max 20 Thtr 20 Class 20 Board 20 **Parking:** 6 **Notes:** LB Closed Christmas and New Year

Carlton Riverside

★★★★ ◉◉ RESTAURANT WITH ROOMS

tel: 01591 610248 **Irfon Crescent LD5 4SP**
email: carltonriverside@hotmail.co.uk **web:** www.carltonriverside.co.uk
dir: *Phone for directions.*

Located riverside as the name suggests, this pleasant restaurant with rooms offers friendly and personal hospitality and service in a relaxed and comfortable setting. Bedrooms come in a range of shapes and sizes but are all comfortably furnished. The real highlight here however is the food; carefully sourced, mainly local and seasonal produce is expertly combined under the guidance of talented head chef Luke Roberts. An interesting wine list accompanies the menu, with an especially good selection by the half bottle.

Rooms: 4 en suite **S** fr £50 **D** fr £75* **Facilities:** FTV Lounge tea/coffee Dinner available WiFi **Notes:** LB Closed 15–30 December

MANORBIER	Map 8 SS09
Pembrokeshire	

Castlemead

★★★★ ≘ RESTAURANT WITH ROOMS

tel: 01834 871358 **SA70 7TA**
email: castlemeadhotel@aol.com **web:** www.castlemeadhotel.com
dir: *A4139 towards Pembroke, B4585 into village, follow signs to beach and castle, establishment on left.*

Benefiting from a superb location with spectacular views of the bay, the Norman church and Manorbier Castle, this family-run business is friendly and welcoming. Bedrooms, including some in a converted former coach house at ground floor level, are generally quite spacious and have modern facilities. There is a sea-view residents' lounge, a cosy bar and a restaurant accessed by stairs which is also open to non-residents. There are extensive gardens to the rear of the property.

Rooms: 5 en suite 3 annexe en suite (2 fmly) (3 GF) **S** fr £75 **D** fr £110 **Facilities:** FTV Lounge tea/coffee Dinner available Direct dial WiFi ⌘ **Parking:** 20 **Notes:** Closed January to February RS November maybe bed and breakfast only

NEWPORT	Map 8 SN03
Pembrokeshire	

Llys Meddyg

★★★★ ◉◉ ≘ RESTAURANT WITH ROOMS

tel: 01239 820008 **East Street SA42 0SY**
email: info@llysmeddyg.com **web:** www.llysmeddyg.com
dir: *On A487 in centre of town.*

Llys Meddyg is a Georgian townhouse offering a blend of old and new, with elegant furnishings, deep sofas and a welcoming fire. The owners of the property employed local craftsmen to create a lovely interior that has an eclectic style. The focus of the quality restaurant menu is on fresh, seasonal, locally sourced ingredients. The spacious bedrooms are comfortable and contemporary in design; the bathrooms vary in style.

Rooms: 5 en suite 3 annexe en suite (3 fmly) (1 GF) **S** fr £70 **D** fr £100* **Facilities:** FTV iPod docking station Lounge tea/coffee Dinner available WiFi Riding ⌘ **Extras:** Speciality toiletries – complimentary; mini-bar – chargeable **Conf:** Max 20 Class 20 Board 20 **Parking:** 8 **Notes:** LB Civ wed 90

PENARTH
Map 9 ST17
Vale of Glamorgan

INSPECTOR'S CHOICE

Restaurant James Sommerin

★★★★★ ◎◎◎◎ RESTAURANT WITH ROOMS

tel: 029 2070 6559 **The Esplanade CF64 3AU**
email: info@jamessommerinrestaurant.co.uk
web: www.jamessommerinrestaurant.co.uk
dir: Phone for directions.

Restaurant James Sommerin stands proudly by the pier in Penarth with unrivalled views across the bay and is just a short distance from the centre of Cardiff. The cuisine is outstanding and exciting, with three different tasting menus offered in addition to the à la carte – all showcase the passion for food from this innovative chef and his team. It's a great idea to stay in one of individually styled, elegant bedrooms after taking full advantage of the interesting and extensive wine list. This is truly a family business – the friendly front-of-house team are under the watchful eye of Louise Sommerin and, James and Louise's oldest daughter can be seen assisting in the kitchen too.

Rooms: 9 en suite **S** fr £130 **D** fr £150* **Facilities:** FTV tea/coffee Dinner available Lift WiFi **Extras:** Bottled water, fresh milk, slippers **Conf:** Max 60 **Notes:** LB Closed 25–26 December, 1 January RS Monday closed

ROCKFIELD
Map 9 SO41
Monmouthshire

The Stonemill & Steppes Farm Cottages

★★★★ ◎◎ RESTAURANT WITH ROOMS

tel: 01600 775424 **NP25 5SW**
email: bookings@thestonemill.co.uk **web:** www.steppesfarmcottages.co.uk
dir: A48 to Monmouth, take B4233 to Rockfield. 2.6 miles.

Located in a small hamlet just west of Monmouth, close to the Forest of Dean and the Wye Valley, this restaurant with rooms offers six very well-appointed cottages. The comfortable rooms (available for self-catering or on a B&B basis) have been lovingly restored to retain many original features. In a separate, converted 16th-century barn is the award-winning Stonemill Restaurant with its oak beams, vaulted ceilings and an old cider press. A breakfast hamper is delivered to each cottage. This establishment's location proves handy for golfers wishing to play on the many courses in the area.

Rooms: 6 en suite (6 fmly) (6 GF) **S** fr £80 **D** fr £160* **Facilities:** FTV DVD TVL tea/coffee Dinner available WiFi ⚓ Free golf **Conf:** Max 60 Thtr 60 Class 56 Board 40 **Parking:** 53 **Notes:** LB Civ wed 120

SOLVA
Map 8 SM82
Pembrokeshire

Crug Glas Country House

★★★★★ ◎◎ RESTAURANT WITH ROOMS

tel: 01348 831302 **Abereiddy SA62 6XX**
email: janet@crug-glas.co.uk **web:** www.crug-glas.co.uk
dir: From Solva to St Davids on A487. From St Davids take A487 towards Fishguard. 1st left after Carnhedryn, house signed.

This house, on a dairy, beef and cereal farm of approximately 600 acres, is situated about a mile from the coast on the St Davids Peninsula. Comfort, relaxation and flawless attention to detail are provided by the charming host, Janet Evans. Each

spacious bedroom has the hallmark of assured design plus a luxury bathroom with both bath and shower; one suite on the top floor has great views. In addition there are two suites in separate buildings.

Rooms: 7 en suite (1 fmly) (2 GF) **S** fr £110 **D** fr £150 **Facilities:** FTV Lounge tea/coffee Dinner available WiFi ⚓ **Extras:** Speciality toiletries **Conf:** Max 200 Thtr 200 Class 200 Board 200 **Parking:** 10 **Notes:** Closed 22–29 December Civ wed 220

TAL-Y-CAFN
Map 14 SH77
Conwy

Bodnant Welsh Food Centre

★★★★★ ☕ RESTAURANT WITH ROOMS

tel: 01492 651100 & 651102 **Furnace Farm LL28 5RP**
email: reception@bodnant-welshfood.co.uk **web:** www.bodnant-welshfood.co.uk
dir: A55 junction 19, follow signs for A470, 4 miles towards Tal-y-Cafn.

Overlooking the River Conwy and neighbouring Bodnant Gardens, this 18th-century farm has been fully restored and is now the home to Bodnant Welsh Food Centre. It is ideally placed to explore the North Wales coastline, Snowdonia and the nearby surf park. The Hayloft Restaurant serves interesting lunches and dinners, including a seven-course tasting menu. A range of bedroom types and sizes is offered plus a guest lounge and kitchen. The buildings include a tea room, farm shop and a wine merchant with a focus on Welsh products. There is a cookery school on site, and small conferences and weddings can be catered for here.

Rooms: 6 en suite (1 GF) **Facilities:** FTV Lounge TVL tea/coffee Dinner available Lift WiFi **Conf:** Max 80 Thtr 80 Class 18 Board 22 **Parking:** 80 **Notes:** LB Closed 25–26 December Civ wed 80

USK
Map 9 SO30
Monmouthshire

Newbridge on Usk

★★★★★ ◎◎ ☕ RESTAURANT WITH ROOMS

tel: 01633 451000 & 410262 **Tredunnock NP15 1LY**
email: bookings@celtic-manor.com **web:** www.celtic-manor.com
dir: M4 junction 24, signed Newport, onto B4236. At Ship Inn turn right, over mini roundabout onto Llangybi/Usk road. Turn right opposite Cwrt Bleddyn Hotel, signed Tredunnock, through village and down hill.

This cosy country inn is tucked away in a beautiful village setting alongside the River Usk. The well-equipped bedrooms, in a separate building, provide comfort and a good range of extras. Guests can eat at rustic tables around the bar or in the upstairs dining room where award-winning, seasonal food is served; there is also a small private dining room. Breakfast is one of the highlights of a stay, with quality local ingredients offered in abundance.

Rooms: 6 en suite (2 fmly) (4 GF) **Facilities:** STV FTV DVD tea/coffee Dinner available Direct dial WiFi 🐾 ♨ Fishing Sauna Gym Facilities available at Celtic Manor Resort **Extras:** Speciality toiletries – complimentary **Conf:** Max 14 Thtr 14 Class 14 Board 14 **Parking:** 60 **Notes:** LB Civ wed 80

WHITEBROOK
Monmouthshire

Map 4 SO50

INSPECTOR'S CHOICE

The Whitebrook

★★★★★ ◉◉◉◉ ⚬ RESTAURANT WITH ROOMS

tel: 01600 860254 **NP25 4TX**
email: info@thewhitebrook.co.uk web: www.thewhitebrook.co.uk
dir: *4 miles from Monmouth on B4293, left at sign to Whitebrook, 2 miles on unclassified road, on right.*

Peacefully located and surrounded by woods and rivers, this delightful restaurant with rooms offers a tranquil escape. The bedrooms are located above the main restaurant and come in a range of shapes and sizes – all are very comfortably decorated and furnished. The outstanding, four AA Rosette award-winning food makes great use of the finest local produce and the relaxing surroundings and friendly service provide a memorable dining experience.

Rooms: 8 en suite **S** fr £187 **D** fr £265* **Facilities:** FTV Lounge tea/coffee Dinner available Direct dial WiFi **Extras:** Speciality toiletries, Welsh cakes **Parking:** 20 **Notes:** No children 12 years Closed 2–15 January

WREXHAM
Wrexham

Map 15 SJ35

The Lemon Tree

★★★ ⚬ RESTAURANT WITH ROOMS

tel: 01978 261211 **29 Rhosddu Road LL11 2LP**
email: info@thelemontree.org.uk web: www.thelemontree.org.uk
dir: *A483 junction 5 follow signs for town centre, pass university and football stadium. Keep left, left at 1st roundabout.*

A modern and stylish restaurant setting awaits within this unassuming Gothic, Grade II listed building in the heart of Wrexham. The owners have a relaxed approach and offer locally sourced, modern British cuisine in the evenings. Straightforward and good-value bedrooms, in a range of sizes, are smartly appointed and comfortable.

Rooms: 12 en suite **Facilities:** FTV TVL tea/coffee Dinner available WiFi **Conf:** Max 40 Thtr 40 Class 20 Board 20 **Parking:** 15 **Notes:** LB

NORTHERN IRELAND

MAGHERA
County Londonderry Derry

Map 1 C5

Ardtara Country House

★★★★ ◉◉ RESTAURANT WITH ROOMS

tel: 028 7964 4490 **8 Gorteade Road BT46 5SA**
email: info@ardtara.com web: www.ardtara.com
dir: *Take M2, M22, A6 towards Derry. 7 miles past Castledawson roundabout take A29 through Maghera. Continue on A29 towards Coleraine for 3 miles. Right onto B75 for 1 mile. Ardtara located on left.*

Set in its own extensive gardens, Ardtara Country House enjoys a secluded location just a short drive from the beautiful north Antrim coast and the famous Giant's Causeway. This fine 19th-century house offers guests spacious bedrooms with views over the landscaped gardens. There is a comfortable lounge, a cosy bar and many original features have been sympathetically restored. The award-winning restaurant offers the best fresh seasonal produce and the hearty breakfasts served in the conservatory are not to be missed. The city of Derry is a short drive away as is the challenging Royal Portrush golf course.

Rooms: 9 en suite (1 GF) **Facilities:** Lounge tea/coffee Dinner available Direct dial WiFi ⚓ Fishing Riding ♨ **Extras:** Robes, slippers **Conf:** Max 50 **Parking:** 100 **Notes:** LB Civ wed 65

REPUBLIC OF IRELAND

BALTIMORE
County Cork

Map 1 B1

Rolfs Country House

★★★ ◉ RESTAURANT WITH ROOMS

tel: 028 20289 **Baltimore Hill**
email: info@rolfscountryhouse.com web: www.rolfscountryhouse.com
dir: *Before village turn sharp left up hill. House signed.*

Situated on a hill above the fishing village of Baltimore, these 400-year-old stone buildings have been successfully converted by the Haffner family. There are 10 traditionally furnished en suite bedrooms in an annexe, a cosy bar with an open fire and a rustic restaurant set on two levels. Dinner is served nightly during the high season and at weekends in the winter; the menu features quality meats, artisan cheeses and fish landed at the busy pier. This is a lovely place to stay and the hosts are very friendly.

Rooms: 10 annexe en suite (4 GF) **Facilities:** FTV Lounge tea/coffee Dinner available WiFi **Parking:** 60 **Notes:** LB Closed 20–26 December

DONEGAL   Map 1 B5
County Donegal

The Red Door Country House

★★★★ ◉ RESTAURANT WITH ROOMS

tel: 074 9360289 **Fahan, Inishowen**
email: info@thereddoor.ie **web:** www.thereddoor.ie
dir: *In Fahan village, church on right, The Red Door signed on left.*

Situated amidst mature trees and landscaped gardens, this warm and welcoming restaurant with rooms stands proudly on the shore of Lough Swilly, in the historic village of Fahan just south of Buncrana. Dating from 1789, the original features of the house are cleverly combined with contemporary styling. Bedrooms are cosy and comfortable, each individually decorated and en suite. The house has a fine reputation in the region for the quality of its evening meals and alfresco lunches. Breakfast is also a highlight and is designed to be lingered over.

Rooms: 4 en suite **Facilities:** FTV Lounge tea/coffee Dinner available WiFi ♿
Conf: Max 100 Thtr 100 Board 100 **Parking:** 40 **Notes:** RS Monday to Tuesday closed Civ wed 160

DUBLIN   Map 1 D4
Dublin

Cliff Townhouse

★★★★★ ◉◉ RESTAURANT WITH ROOMS

tel: 01 6383939 **22 St Stephens Green D02 HW54**
email: vbracken@clifftownhouse.ie **web:** www.clifftownhouse.ie
dir: *Phone for directions.*

This fine Georgian property is located on one of the quieter areas of St Stephens Green, very much at the heart of the government district with both the Concert Hall and Grafton Street shopping district within walking distance. The bedrooms, some with park views, are comfortably appointed with really cosy, top-quality beds and bedding. The public spaces include an award-winning restaurant where seafood is a speciality. There is also an atmospheric bar in the basement serving authentic Spanish tapas.

Rooms: 9 en suite (3 fmly) **Facilities:** STV FTV iPod docking station Dinner available Direct dial Lift WiFi **Extras:** Speciality toiletries **Conf:** Max 50 Thtr 50 Class 25 Board 20 **Notes:** LB Closed 25–27 December

DURRUS   Map 1 A2
County Cork

Blairscove House & Restaurant

★★★★★ ◉◉ RESTAURANT WITH ROOMS

tel: 027 61127
email: mail@blairscove.ie **web:** www.blairscove.ie
dir: *From Durrus on R591 towards Crookhaven, 2.4 km, blue gate on right.*

Blairscove comprises four elegant suites located in the courtyard of a Georgian country house outside the pretty village of Durrus near Bantry; each room is individually decorated in a contemporary style and has stunning views over Dunmanus Bay and the mountains. The restaurant is renowned for its wide range of hors d'oeuvres and its open wood-fire grill. The piano-playing and candlelight add to a unique dining experience.

Rooms: 4 annexe en suite (1 fmly) **Facilities:** FTV DVD tea/coffee Dinner available Direct dial WiFi ♿ **Extras:** Speciality toiletries, sherry – complimentary; wine – chargeable **Parking:** 30 **Notes:** Closed November to mid March Civ wed 35

GALWAY   Map 1 B3
County Galway

Screebe House

★★★★★ ◉◉ RESTAURANT WITH ROOMS

tel: 091 574110 **Rosmuc**
email: booking@screebe.com **web:** www.screebe.com
dir: *Phone for directions.*

This house was a hunting and fishing lodge in the 19th century and is situated right on the edge of Camus Bay – it cannot get any closer to the Atlantic. Each of the spacious bedrooms is designed with relaxation and comfort in mind – unusually, there are no TVs in the rooms. The public rooms retain their original charm, most have real fires in the cooler months. Dinner is a particular highlight; the daily-changing, seven-course set menu is driven by the season and the market. Breakfast is also noteworthy for its range and quality. An ideal base for country pursuits, with an adjacent pool and sauna for the less sporty.

Rooms: 10 rms (8 en suite) (2 pri facs) (2 GF) **Facilities:** Lounge TVL Dinner available Direct dial WiFi ♿ Fishing Sauna Gym **Conf:** Max 20 Thtr 20 Class 20 Board 20 **Parking:** 10 **Notes:** No children 16 years Closed 30 November to 10 February RS Monday to Tuesday closed

KINSALE   Map 1 B2
County Cork

The White House

★★★★ ◉ RESTAURANT WITH ROOMS

tel: 021 4772125 **Pearse Street, The Glen**
email: info@whitehouse-kinsale.ie **web:** www.whitehouse-kinsale.ie
dir: *In town centre.*

Centrally located among the narrow, twisting streets of the charming maritime town of Kinsale, this restaurant with rooms dates from 1850. It is a welcoming hostelry with smart, comfortably appointed, contemporary bedrooms. The atmospheric bar and bistro are open for lunch and dinner, with Restaurant d'Antibes also open during the evenings. The varied menu features local fish and beef. The courtyard at the rear makes a perfect setting in summer and there is regular entertainment in the bar.

Rooms: 10 en suite (2 fmly) **S** fr €70 **D** fr €120* **Facilities:** STV tea/coffee Dinner available Direct dial WiFi **Notes:** LB Closed 24–25 December

WEXFORD   Map 1 D3
County Wexford

Aldridge Lodge Restaurant and Guest Accommodation

★★★★ ◉◉ RESTAURANT WITH ROOMS

tel: 051 389116 **Duncannon**
email: info@aldridgelodge.com **web:** www.aldridgelodge.com
dir: *Phone for directions.*

Just a 45-minute drive from Rosslare, Aldridge Lodge is an ideal first night stop following a ferry crossing. It makes a great base for exploring the many attractions and activities of the Hook Peninsula. Hosts Joanne and Billy, who is also the chef, take a keen interest in their guests and it's no wonder so many return – weekend reservations are essential. While each of the three guest rooms is warm and cosy, what brings most visitors here is the food; Billy has a strong reputation for his use of local, seasonal ingredients. The breakfast experience is noteworthy too – quality dishes cooked with skill and care and enjoyed in a relaxed environment.

Rooms: 3 en suite **S** fr €60 **D** fr €100* **Facilities:** FTV tea/coffee Dinner available WiFi ♿ **Parking:** 20 **Notes:** No children Closed 1st week January, 1st week May RS Monday to Wednesday closed Civ wed 30

RESTAURANTS WITH ROOMS

COUNTY MAPS

England
1. Bedfordshire
2. Berkshire
3. Bristol
4. Buckinghamshire
5. Cambridgeshire
6. Greater Manchester
7. Herefordshire
8. Hertfordshire
9. Leicestershire
10. Northamptonshire
11. Nottinghamshire
12. Rutland
13. Staffordshire
14. Warwickshire
15. West Midlands
16. Worcestershire

Scotland
17. City of Glasgow
18. Clackmannanshire
19. East Ayrshire
20. East Dunbartonshire
21. East Renfrewshire
22. Perth & Kinross
23. Renfrewshire
24. South Lanarkshire
25. West Dunbartonshire

Wales
26. Blaenau Gwent
27. Bridgend
28. Caerphilly
29. Denbighshire
30. Flintshire
31. Merthyr Tydfil
32. Monmouthshire
33. Neath Port Talbot
34. Newport
35. Rhondda Cynon Taf
36. Torfaen
37. Vale of Glamorgan
38. Wrexham

Na h-Eileanan
an Iar

Highland

Moray

City of
Aberdeen

Aberdeenshire

SCOTLAND

Angus

Perth &
Kinross

City of
Dundee

Argyll
& Bute

Stirling

Fife

East
Lothian

North
Ayrshire

19

24

Scottish
Borders

South
Ayrshire

Dumfries &
Galloway

Northumberland

Tyne & Wear

Durham

Cumbria

Isle of
Man

North
Yorkshire

Lancashire

West
Yorkshire

East Riding
of Yorkshire

Isle of
Anglesey

Merseyside

6

South
Yorkshire

Lincolnshire

Conwy

30

Cheshire

Derbyshire

29

38

11

Gwynedd

ENGLAND

13

Shropshire

9

12

Norfolk

15

14

10

5

Ceredigion

WALES

Powys

16

1

Suffolk

7

Pembrokeshire

Carmarthenshire

Gloucestershire

4

8

Essex

Swansea

3

Oxfordshire

Greater
London

31 26 32

2

Cardiff

33

35 28 36

Wiltshire

Surrey

Kent

27

34

Somerset

Hampshire

West
Sussex

East
Sussex

37

Devon

Dorset

Isle of
Wight

Cornwall

Isles of
Scilly

Guernsey

Jersey

Orkney Islands

Shetland Islands

Argyll
& Bute

Stirling

18

22

Fife

25

20

Falkirk

Inverclyde

23

17

North
Lanarkshire

West
Lothian

City of
Edinburgh

North
Ayrshire

21

Midlothian

19

South Lanarkshire

Scottish
Borders

0	20	40	60	80	100 miles
0 20 40	60	80 100	120	140	160 kilometres

KEY TO ATLAS

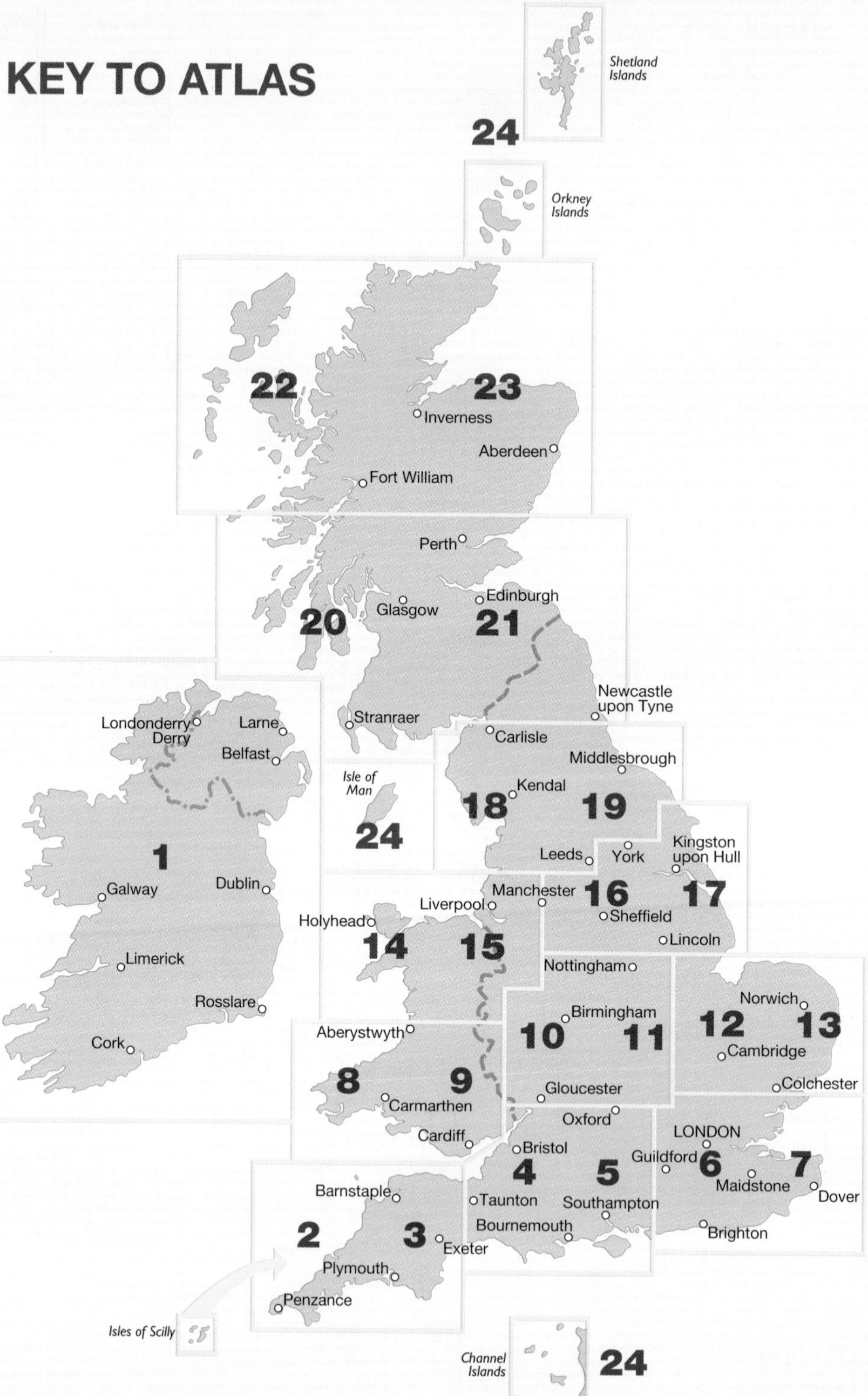

24 Shetland Islands

Orkney Islands

22

23
○ Inverness
Aberdeen ○
○ Fort William

Perth ○

○ Edinburgh
Glasgow ○
20 **21**

○ Stranraer

Newcastle upon Tyne

Londonderry ○ Larne ○
Derry
Belfast ○

○ Carlisle
Middlesbrough ○

Isle of Man
24 ○ Kendal
18 **19**

1
Galway ○ Dublin ○
Leeds ○ York ○
Kingston upon Hull

Holyhead ○
Liverpool ○ Manchester ○
16
Sheffield ○
17
Lincoln ○

Limerick ○
14 **15**

Rosslare ○
Nottingham ○

Cork ○
Birmingham ○
Norwich ○
12 **13**
Aberystwyth ○
10 **11**
Cambridge ○

8 **9**
Gloucester ○
Colchester ○
Carmarthen ○
Oxford ○
LONDON
Cardiff ○
Bristol ○
Guildford ○ **6**
4 **5** Maidstone ○ **7**
Barnstaple ○
Taunton ○ Southampton ○ Dover ○
Bournemouth ○
2 **3** Exeter ○ Brighton ○
Plymouth ○
Penzance ○

Isles of Scilly

Channel Islands **24**

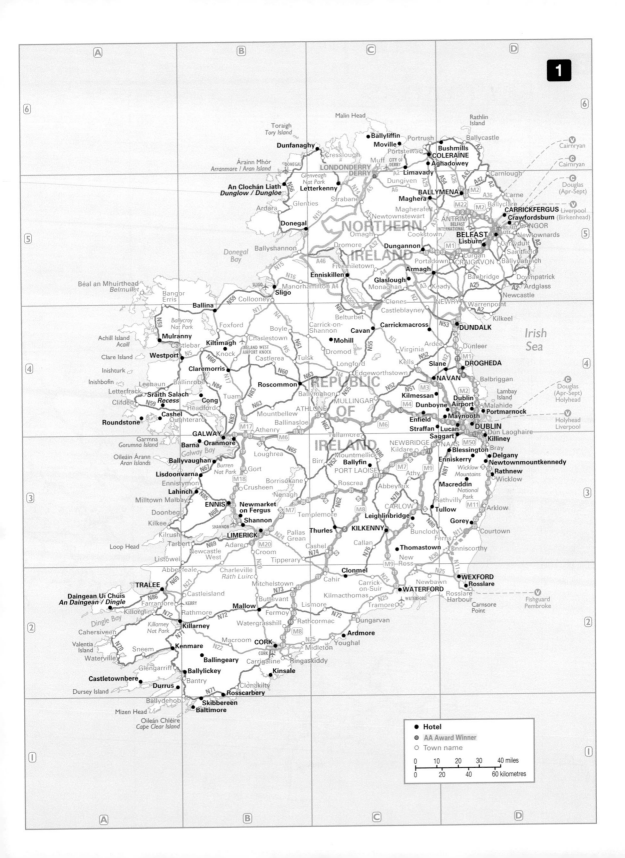

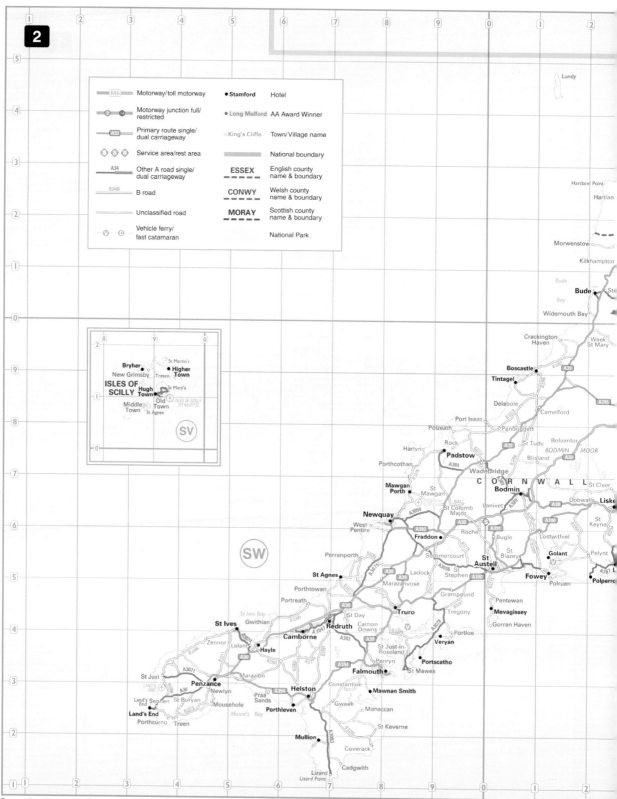

═══ M6 ═══ Motorway/toll motorway	● **Stamford** Hotel
Motorway junction full/restricted	● **Long Melford** AA Award Winner
A33 Primary route single/dual carriageway	○ King's Cliffe Town/Village name
◇ ◇ ◇ Service area/rest area	National boundary
A34 Other A road single/dual carriageway	**ESSEX** English county name & boundary
B3400 B road	**CONWY** Welsh county name & boundary
Unclassified road	**MORAY** Scottish county name & boundary
Ⓥ Ⓒ Vehicle ferry/fast catamaran	National Park

ISLES OF SCILLY

Bryher · New Grimsby · Tresco · St Martin's · **Higher Town**
Hugh Town · St Mary's · Old Town · *ISLES OF SCILLY (ST MARY'S)*
Middle Town · St Agnes

SV

SW

CORNWALL

Lundy

Hartland Point
Hartlan

Morwenstow
Kilkhampton
Bude
Bude Stra
Bay
Widemouth Bay

Crackington Haven
Week St Mary
Boscastle A39
Tintagel
Delabole · Camelford A395
Port Isaac · Pendoggett
Polzeath · Bolventor
Rock · St Tudy · BODMIN MOOR
Harlyn · **Padstow** · Blisland A30
Porthcothan · A389 · Wadebridge
Mawgan Porth · St Mawgan · **Bodmin** · St Cleer
Newquay · St Columb Major · Lanivet A38 · Dobwalls · **Liske**
West Pentire · St Keyne
Perranporth · Roche · Bugle · Lostwithiel · St
Fraddon · Summercourt · St Blazey · **Golant** · Pelynt
Ladock · St Stephen · **St Austell** · **Fowey** · **Polperro**
St Agnes · Marazanvose · Grampound · Polruan
Porthtowan · Pentewan · **Mevagissey**
Portreath · St Day · Tregony · Gorran Haven
St Ives Bay · Carnon Downs · **Truro** · Portloe
St Ives · Gwithian · **Redruth** · **Veryan**
Zennor · Lelant · **Camborne** · St Just-in-Roseland · **Portscatho**
Hayle · Penryn · St Mawes
St Just · Marazion · **Falmouth**
Penzance · Newlyn · **Helston** · Constantine · **Mawnan Smith**
Land's End · Sennen · St Buryan · Mousehole · Prae Sands · Gweek · Manaccan
Land's End · Porthcurno · Treen · **Porthleven** · St Keverne
Mount's Bay · **Mullion** · Coverack
Lizard · Cadgwith
Lizard Point

For continuation pages refer to numbered arrows

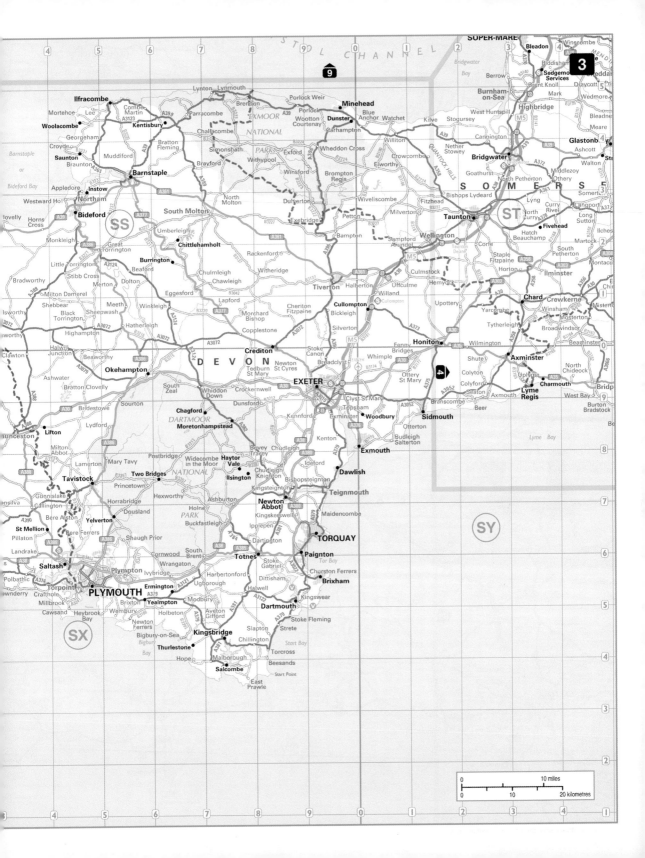

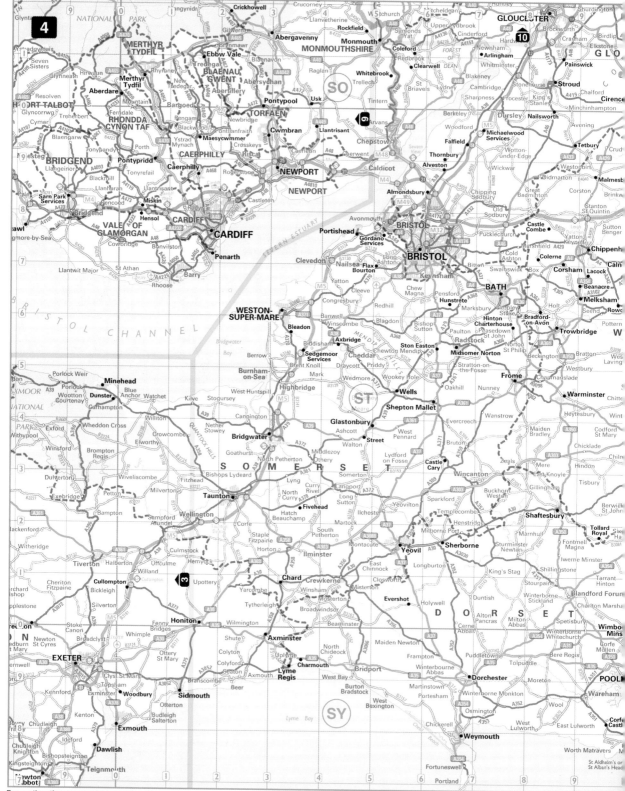

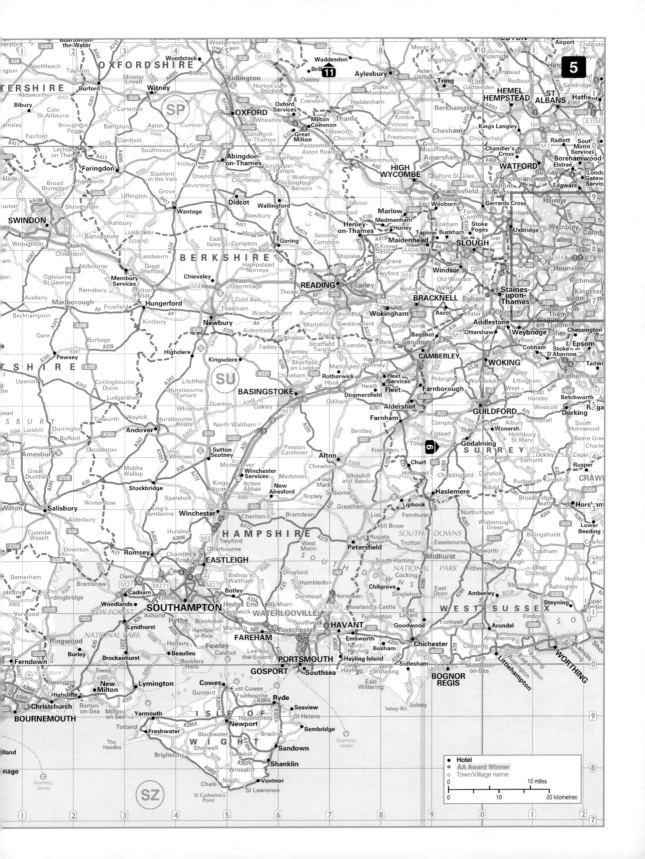

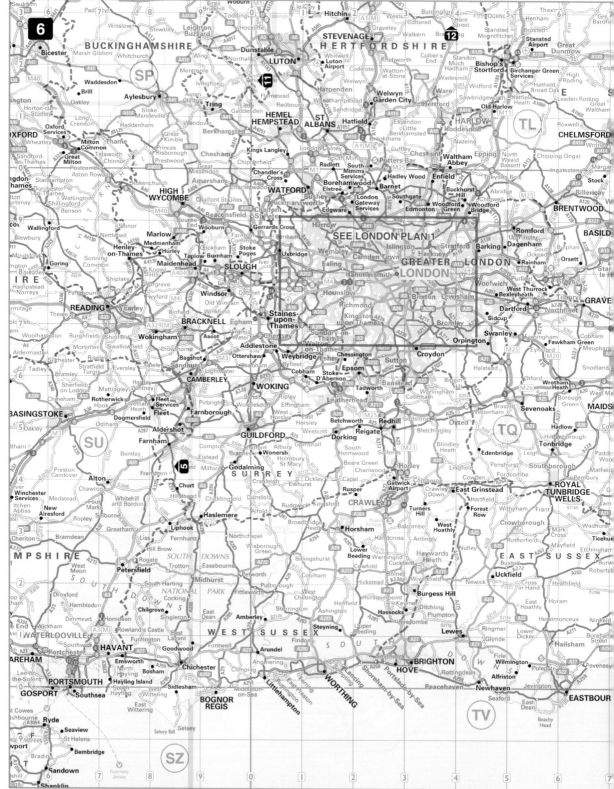

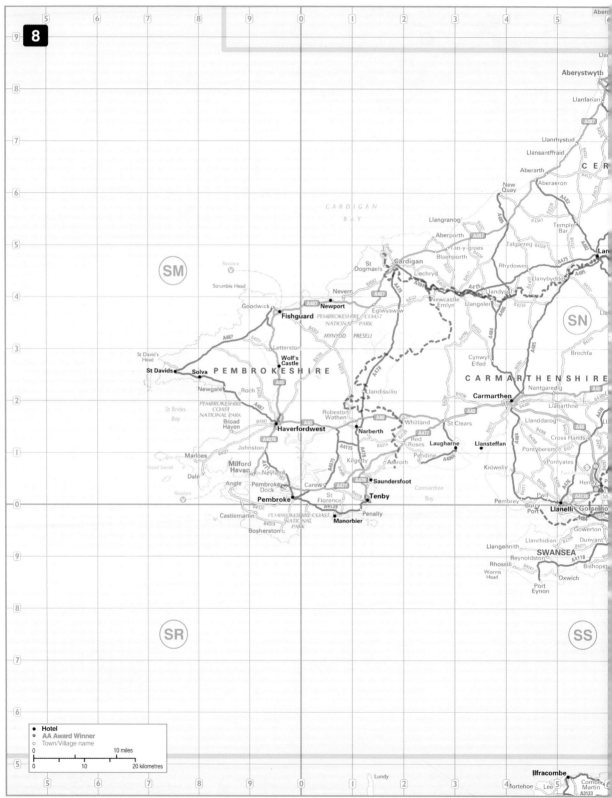

Aber

Aberystwyth

Llanfarian

Llanrhystud

Llansantffraid

Aberarth

C E R

New
Quay

Aberaeron

CARDIGAN
BAY

Llangranog

Lan

Aberporth

Tan-y-groes

Talgarreg

Temple
Bar

SM

Rassiare

Strumble Head

St
Dogmaels

Cardigan

Blaenporth

Rhydowen

Llanybydder

Llechryd

Llandysul

Nevern

Newcastle
Emlyn

Llangeler

SN

Goodwick

Newport

Eglwyswrw

Fishguard

PEMBROKESHIRE COAST
NATIONAL PARK

Brechfa

Letterston

MYNYDD   PRESELI

St David's
Head

Wolf's
Castle

Cynwyl
Elfed

C A R M A R T H E N S H I R E

St Davids

Solva

P E M B R O K E S H I R E

A40

Llandissilio

Nantgaredig

A40

Newgale

Roch

Carmarthen

Llanarthne

St Brides
Bay

PEMBROKESHIRE
COAST
NATIONAL PARK

Robeston
Wathen

Whitland

St Clears

Llanddarog

Cross Hands

Broad
Haven

Haverforwest

Narberth

Red
Roses

Laugharne

Llansteffan

Pontyberem

Pontyates

Johnston

Kilgetty

Amroth

Pendine

Kidwelly

Marloes

Milford
Haven

Neyland

Broad Sound

Dale

Angle

Pembroke
Dock

Carew

St
Florence

Saundersfoot

Carmarthen
Bay

Pembrey

Burry
Port

Llanelli

Gorseino

Rassiare

Pembroke

Tenby

Pembrey

Castlemartin

PEMBROKESHIRE COAST
NATIONAL PARK

Manorbier

Penally

Gowerton

Bosherston

Llanrhidian

Dunvant

SWANSEA

Llangennith

Reynoldston

SR

Rhossili

Worms
Head

Oxwich

Bishopst

SS

Port
Eynon

● Hotel
◉ AA Award Winner
○ Town/Village name

0   10 miles

0   10   20 kilometres

Lundy

Ilfracombe

Mortehoe

Lee

Combe
Martin
A3123

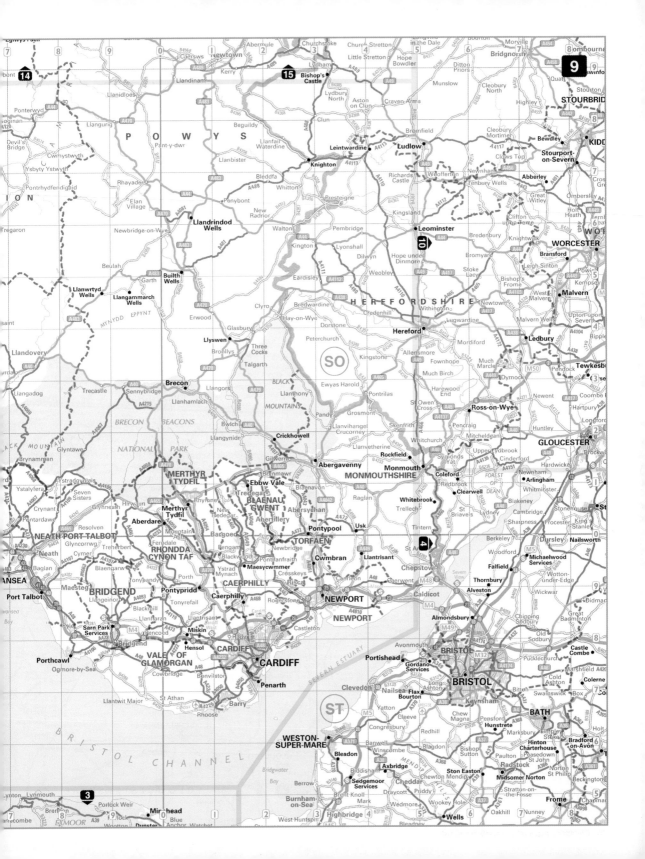

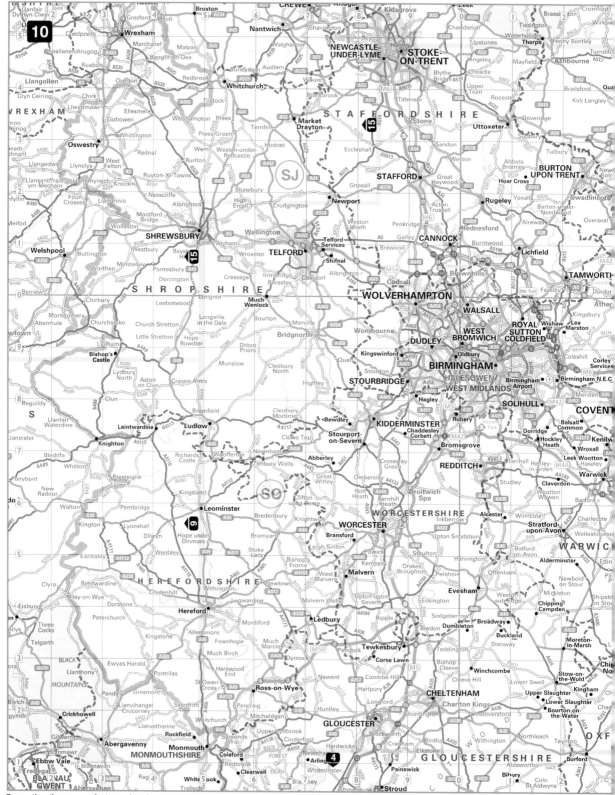

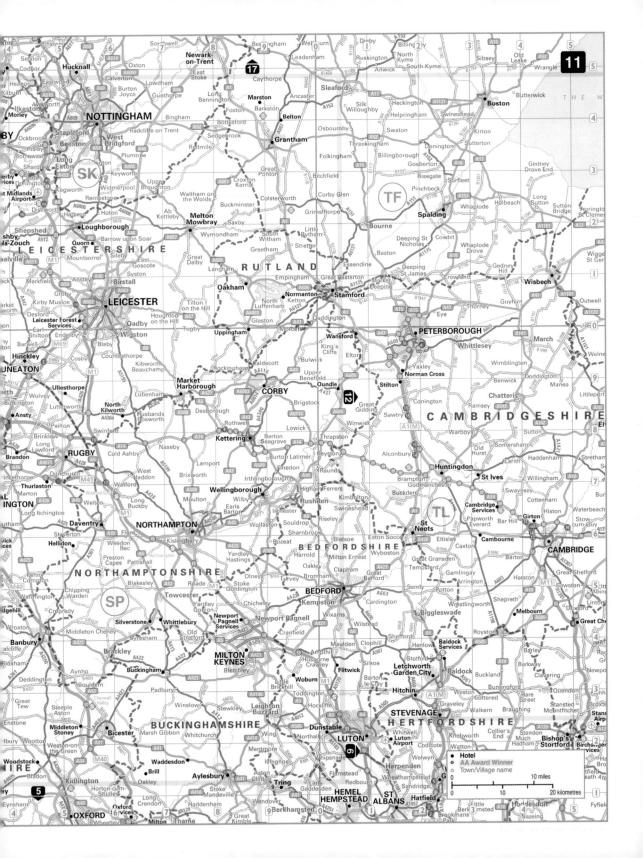

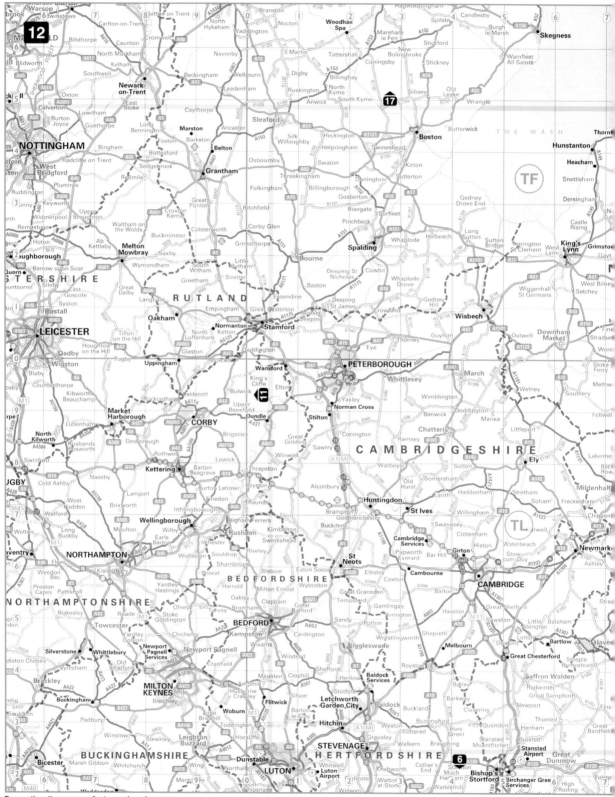

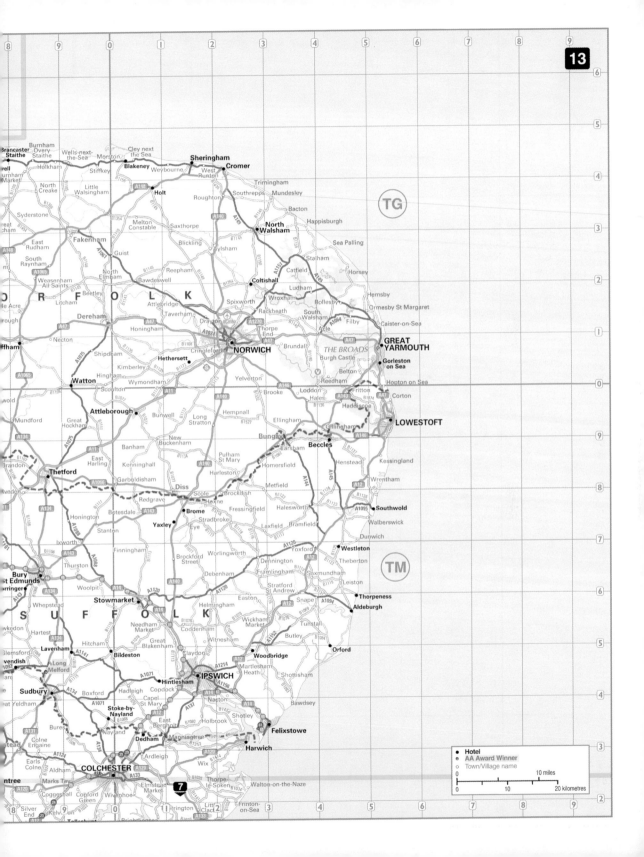

IRISH SEA

Dublin

Dublin

Cemaes
Amlwch

ISLE OF
ANGLESEY
Llanerchymedd

Holyhead
Llanfachraeth
Benllech
Red
Wharf Bay
Llangoed
Llandudno
Deganwy
Rhôs-
on-Sea
Colwyn Bay

Trearddur Bay
Llandudno Junction
Conwy
Llanddulas
Abe

Holy
Island
Pentraeth
Penmaenmawr
Llansanffraid
Glan Conwy
Bodelwyd

Rhosneigr
Llangefni
Menai
Bridge
Beaumaris
Llanfairfechan
Betws-yn-Rhos

Bangor
Llanfairpwll
Tal-y-Cafn

Aberffraw
Llanfair
P-G
Llanllechid
Tal-y-Bont
Llanfair
Talhaiarn
Llansa

Y Felinheli
Bethesda
Llangernyw

Newborough
Caernarfon
Llanrug
Trefriw

Bontnewydd
Llanberis
Llanrwst
Bylchau

Caernarfon
Bay
Llandwrog
Llanwnda
Capel Curig
CONWY

Clynnog-fawr
Penygroes
Rhyd-Ddu
Betws-y-Coed

SH
Dolwyddelan
Penmachno
Pentrefoelas
Cerrigydrudion

Llanaelhaearn
Beddgelert
Blaenau Ffestiniog
Y

Morfa Nefyn
Nefyn
Prenteg
Maentwrog
Ffestiniog

Bodfuan
Llanystumdwy
Tremadog
Penrhyndeudraeth
Llane

PENINSULA
Porthmadog
Portmeirion
Bala

Sarn
Criccieth
Borth-y-Gest
Talsarnau
SNOWDONIA

LLYN
Pwllheli
Trawsfynydd
NATIONAL
Llanuwchllyn

Aberdaron
Y Rhiw
Llanbedrog
Harlech
GWYNEDD
PARK

Abersoch
Llanbedr

Bardsey
Island
Dyffryn Ardudwy
Ganllwyd

Tal-y-bont
Dolgellau
Dinas-Mawddwy

Barmouth
Mallwyd
Llang

Fairbourne

Llwyngwril
Corris

Cemmaes
Road
Llanbrynmair

Bryncrug
Machynlleth

Tywyn
Pennal
Carno

SN
Aberdyfi
Eglwys Fach

Borth
Tal-y-bont

9

Llandre
Llanidloes

Aberystwyth
Capel
Bangor
Ponterwyd

● Hotel
● AA Award Winner
○ Town/Village name

0 _____ 10 miles
0 ____ 10 ____ 20 kilometres

9 0 1 2 3 4 5 6 7 8 9

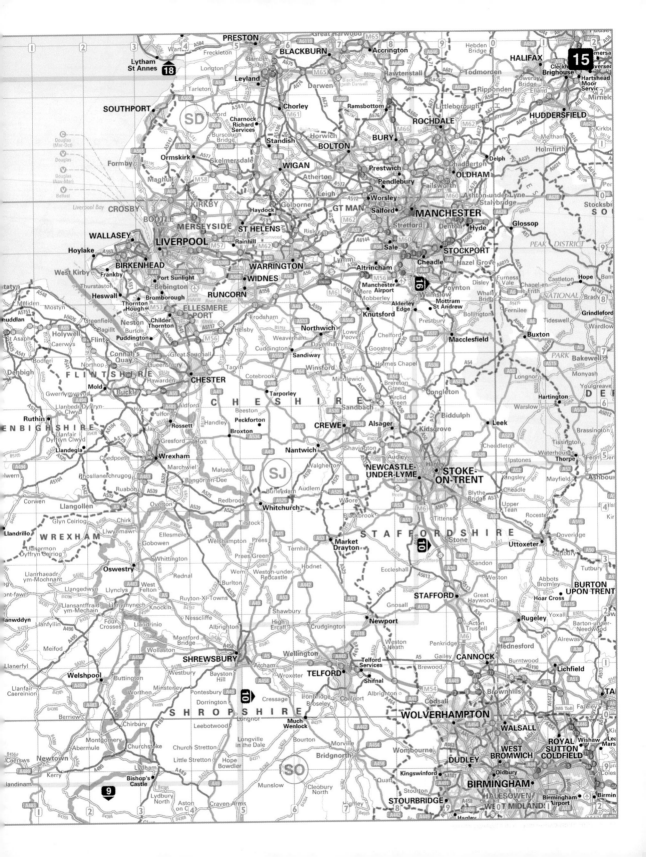

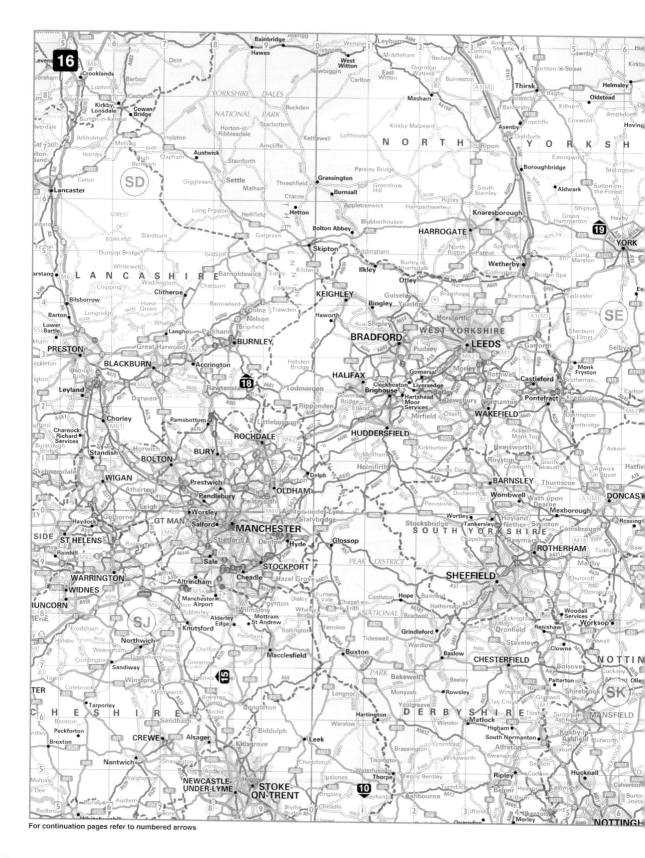

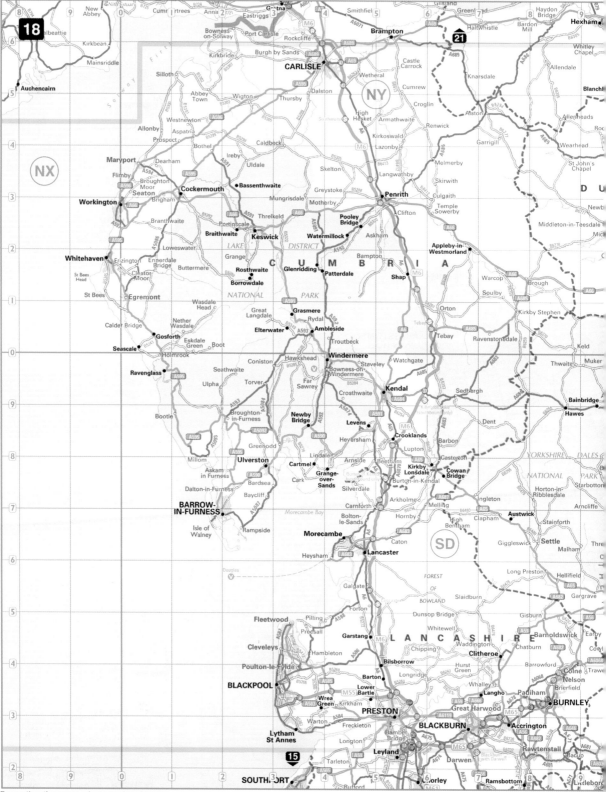

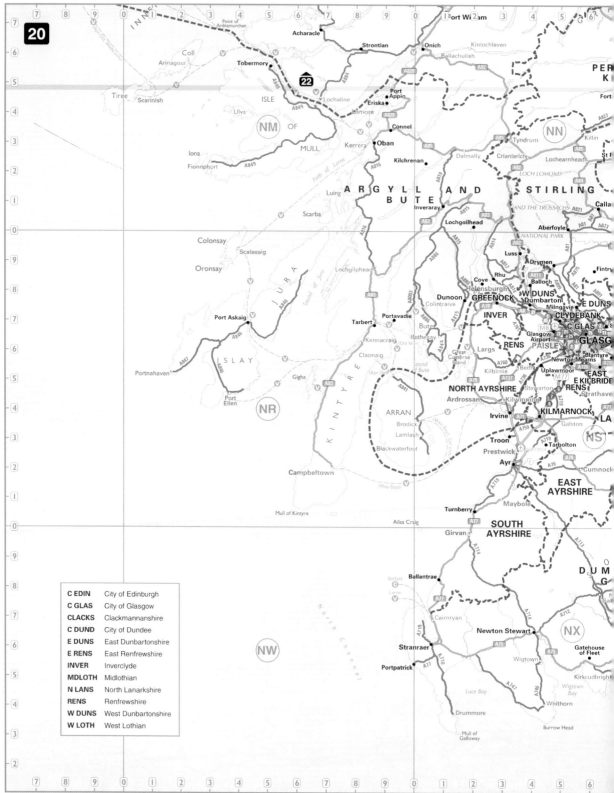

22

PERTH & KINROSS

Fort William
Kinlochleven
Ballachulish
Acharacle
Strontian
Onich
Tobermory
Coll
Arinagour
Point of Ardnamurchan
Tiree
Scarinish
Lochaline
Port Appin
Eriska
ISLE
OF
MULL
Lismore
Connel
Oban
Kerrera
Tyndrum
Killin
Iona
Fionnphort
Ulva
Kilchrenan
Dalmally
Crianlarich
Lochearnhead
St F
Luing
Scarba
ARGYLL AND BUTE
Inveraray
Dalmally
LOCH LOMOND
Fort
NM
NN
Colonsay
Scalasaig
Oronsay
Lochgilphead
Lochgoilhead
STIRLING
AND THE TROSSACHS
NATIONAL PARK
Aberfoyle
Calla
Luss
Drymen
Fintr
Cove
Rhu
Balloch
Helensburgh
Dunoon
Colintraive
W DUNS
Dumbarton
Milngavie
E DUNS
CLYDEBANK
C GLAS
PAISLEY
GLASG
Port Askaig
Portnahaven
ISLAY
Port Ellen
NR
Tarbert
Portavadie
Bute
Rothesay
Kennacraig
Claonaig
Gigha
Largs
Great Cumbrae Island
Kilbirnie
Beith
Uplawmoor
EAST
E KILBRIDE
E RENS
Strathave
GREENOCK
INVER
RENS
Glasgow Airport
Newton Mearns
Blantyre
NORTH AYRSHIRE
Ardrossan
Irvine
KILMARNOCK
Galston
LA
NS
Stevarton
Kilwinning
Strathave
ARRAN
Brodick
Lamlash
Blackwaterfoot
Troon
Prestwick
Ayr
Tarbolton
EAST AYRSHIRE
Cumnock
Campbeltown
Turnberry
Maybole
SOUTH AYRSHIRE
Girvan
Mull of Kintyre
Ailsa Craig
North Channel
NW
Ballantrae
Belfast
Larne
Cairnryan
Stranraer
Portpatrick
Newton Stewart
NX
Gatehouse of Fleet
Wigtown
Kirkcudbright
DUM
G
Luce Bay
Wigtown Bay
Whithorn
Drummore
Burrow Head
Mull of Galloway

C EDIN	City of Edinburgh
C GLAS	City of Glasgow
CLACKS	Clackmannanshire
C DUND	City of Dundee
E DUNS	East Dunbartonshire
E RENS	East Renfrewshire
INVER	Inverclyde
MDLOTH	Midlothian
N LANS	North Lanarkshire
RENS	Renfrewshire
W DUNS	West Dunbartonshire
W LOTH	West Lothian

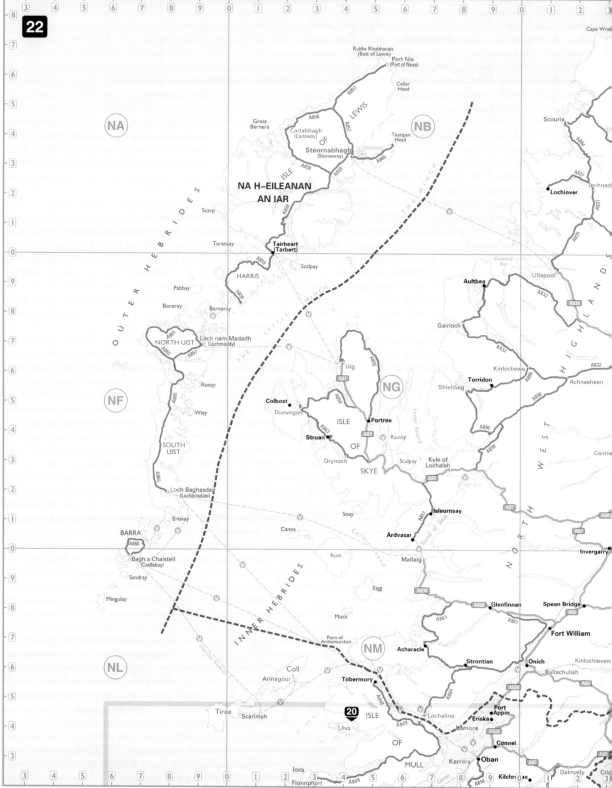

NA

NB

Cape Wrath

Scourie

Lochinver

Inchnad

Rubha Rhobhanais
(Butt of Lewis)
Port Nis
(Port of Ness)

Cellar
Head

LEWIS

A857

A858

Great
Bernera

Carlabhagh
(Carloway)

OF

A858

Steornabhagh
(Stornoway)

A859

A857

Tiumpan
Head

STORNOWAY

A866

**NA H–EILEANAN
AN IAR**

ISLE

A859

Scarp

OUTER

HEBRIDES

Taransay

Tairbeart
(Tarbert)

A859

Scalpay

HARRIS

THE MINCH

Pabbay

A859

Boreray

Berneray

NORTH UIST

A865

Loch nam Madadh
(Lochmaddy)

A867

THE LITTLE MINCH

NF

Ronay

A865

Wiay

SOUTH
UIST

A865

Loch Baghasdail
(Lochboisdale)

A865

Eriskay

BARRA

A888

Bagh a Chaisteil
(Castlebay)

Sandray

Mingulay

NL

Coll

Arinagour

Tiree

Scarinish

Ulva

20

ISLE

OF

MULL

Iona

Fionnphort

A849

Canna

Rum

Eigg

Muck

Point of
Ardnamurchan

INNER HEBRIDES

Tobermory

A848

Lochaline

A849

Kerrera

Gruinard
Bay

Ullapool

Aultbea

A832

Gairloch

A832

Kinlochewe

Torridon

Shieldaig

A896

Uig

A865

A87

NG

Colbost

Dunvegan

ISLE

A863

Portree

Raasay

Struan

A87

OF

Drynoch

SKYE

Scalpay

Kyle of
Lochalsh

Inner Sound

A896

A890

Achnasheen

HIGHLAND

NORTH WEST

A890

A832

A835

Cannie

Soay

Cuillin Sound

Isleornsay

A851

Ardvasar

Sound of Sleat

Mallaig

Invergarry

A87

A87

A830

Glenfinnan

A830

Spean Bridge

A82

A861

Fort William

NM

Acharacle

A861

Strontian

Onich

Kinlochleven

Ballachulish

A828

Port
Appin

Eriska

Lismore

Kilmore

A82

A828

Connel

Oban

A85

Dalmally

Kilchrenan

A816

A85

Isle
Canna

Shieldaig

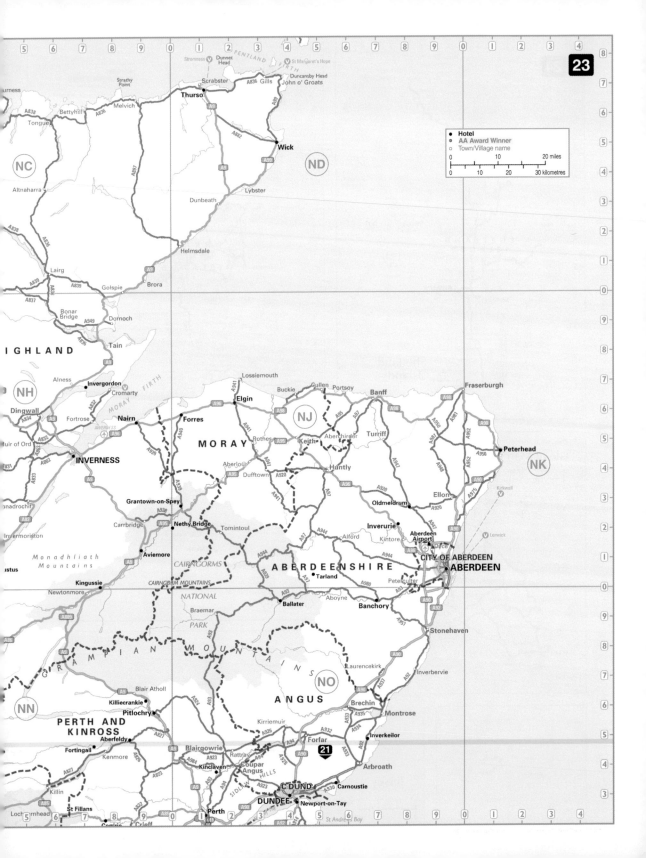

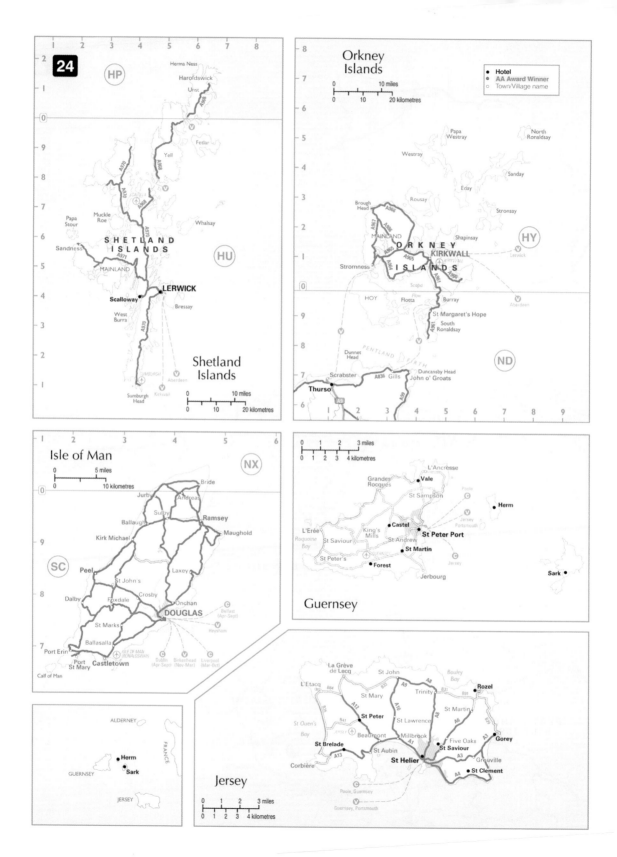

Readers' Report Form

Please send this form to:–
Editor, The Hotel Guide,
Lifestyle Guides,
AA Media,
Fanum House,
Basingstoke RG21 4EA

e-mail: lifestyleguides@theAA.com

Please use this form to recommend any hotel where you have stayed, whether it is included in the guide or not currently listed. You can also help us to improve the guide by completing the short questionnaire on the reverse.

Please note that the AA does not undertake to arbitrate between you and the hotel management, or to obtain compensation or engage in protracted correspondence.

Date

Your name (BLOCK CAPITALS)

Your address (BLOCK CAPITALS)

Post code

E-mail address

Name of hotel

Location

Comments

(please attach a separate sheet if necessary)

Please tick here ☐ if you DO NOT wish to receive details of AA offers or products

PTO

Readers' Report Form *continued*

Have you bought this guide before? ☐ YES ☐ NO

Do you regularly use any other, accommodation, restaurant, pub or food guides? ☐ YES ☐ NO
If YES, which ones?

Why did you buy this guide? (tick all that apply)

Holiday ☐   Short break ☐   Business travel ☐   Special occasion ☐
Overnight stop ☐   Find a venue for an event e.g. conference ☐
Other (please state)

How often do you stay in hotels? (tick one choice)

More than once a month ☐   Once a month ☐   Once in 2-3 months ☐
Once in six months ☐   Once a year ☐   Less than once a year ☐
Other (please state)

Please answer these questions to help us make improvements to the guide:

Which of these factors are the most important when choosing a hotel? (tick all that apply)

Price ☐   Location ☐   Awards/ratings ☐   Service ☐
Decor/surroundings ☐   Previous experience ☐ Recommendation ☐
Other (please state)

Do you use the location atlas? ☐ YES ☐ NO

What elements of the guide do you find most useful when choosing somewhere to stay? (tick all that apply)

Description ☐   Photo ☐   Advertisement ☐   Star rating ☐

Is there any other information you would like to see added to this guide?

Readers' Report Form

Please send this form to:–
Editor, The Hotel Guide,
Lifestyle Guides,
AA Media,
Fanum House,
Basingstoke RG21 4EA

e-mail: lifestyleguides@theAA.com

Please use this form to recommend any hotel where you have stayed, whether it is included in the guide or not currently listed. You can also help us to improve the guide by completing the short questionnaire on the reverse.

Please note that the AA does not undertake to arbitrate between you and the hotel management, or to obtain compensation or engage in protracted correspondence.

Date

Your name (BLOCK CAPITALS)

Your address (BLOCK CAPITALS)

Post code

E-mail address

Name of hotel

Location

Comments

(please attach a separate sheet if necessary)

Please tick here ☐ if you DO NOT wish to receive details of AA offers or products

PTO

Readers' Report Form *continued*

Have you bought this guide before? ☐ YES ☐ NO

Do you regularly use any other, accommodation, restaurant, pub or food guides? ☐ YES ☐ NO
If YES, which ones?

Why did you buy this guide? (tick all that apply)
Holiday ☐   Short break ☐   Business travel ☐   Special occasion ☐
Overnight stop ☐   Find a venue for an event e.g. conference ☐
Other (please state)

How often do you stay in hotels? (tick one choice)
More than once a month ☐   Once a month ☐   Once in 2-3 months ☐
Once in six months ☐   Once a year ☐   Less than once a year ☐
Other (please state)

Please answer these questions to help us make improvements to the guide:
Which of these factors are the most important when choosing a hotel? (tick all that apply)
Price ☐   Location ☐   Awards/ratings ☐   Service ☐
Decor/surroundings ☐   Previous experience ☐   Recommendation ☐
Other (please state)

Do you use the location atlas? ☐ YES ☐ NO

What elements of the guide do you find most useful when choosing somewhere to stay? (tick all that apply)
Description ☐   Photo ☐   Advertisement ☐   Star rating ☐

Is there any other information you would like to see added to this guide?